Lecture Notes in Computer Science   16412

Founding Editors

Gerhard Goos
Juris Hartmanis

Editorial Board Members

Elisa Bertino, *Purdue University, West Lafayette, IN, USA*
Wen Gao, *Peking University, Beijing, China*
Bernhard Steffen, *TU Dortmund University, Dortmund, Germany*
Moti Yung, *Columbia University, New York, NY, USA*

The series Lecture Notes in Computer Science (LNCS), including its subseries Lecture Notes in Artificial Intelligence (LNAI) and Lecture Notes in Bioinformatics (LNBI), has established itself as a medium for the publication of new developments in computer science and information technology research, teaching, and education.

LNCS enjoys close cooperation with the computer science R & D community, the series counts many renowned academics among its volume editors and paper authors, and collaborates with prestigious societies. Its mission is to serve this international community by providing an invaluable service, mainly focused on the publication of conference and workshop proceedings and postproceedings. LNCS commenced publication in 1973.

Jakub Lokoč · Ladislav Peška · Jan Zahálka ·
Stevan Rudinac · Marc Kastner · Jingjing Chen ·
Min-Chun Hu · Jiaxin Wu · Ujjwal Sharma
Editors

MultiMedia Modeling

32nd International Conference on Multimedia Modeling, MMM 2026
Prague, Czech Republic, January 29–31, 2026
Proceedings, Part I

 Springer

Editors
Jakub Lokoč
Charles University
Prague, Czech Republic

Jan Zahálka
Czech Technical University in Prague
Prague, Czech Republic

Marc Kastner
Hiroshima City University
Hiroshima, Japan

Min-Chun Hu
National Tsing Hua University
Hsinchu, Taiwan

Ujjwal Sharma
University of Amsterdam
Amsterdam, The Netherlands

Ladislav Peška
Charles University
Prague, Czech Republic

Stevan Rudinac
University of Amsterdam
Amsterdam, The Netherlands

Jingjing Chen
Fudan University
Shanghai, China

Jiaxin Wu
Shenzhen University
Shenzhen, China

ISSN 0302-9743   ISSN 1611-3349 (electronic)
Lecture Notes in Computer Science
ISBN 978-981-95-6949-6   ISBN 978-981-95-6950-2 (eBook)
https://doi.org/10.1007/978-981-95-6950-2

Preface

These four proceedings volumes contain the papers presented at the 32nd International Conference on Multimedia Modeling (MMM 2026), held in Prague, Czech Republic, from January 29 to 31, 2026. Traditionally, MMM brings together experts from various fields related to multimedia modeling and machine learning models dealing with multimedia data. The conference venue in Prague provided a unique combination of medieval experience with modern city attractions. All these aspects offered great opportunities for researchers and industry practitioners to meet, present new ideas, share original research results, and discuss practical experiences. As in previous years, the topics included exciting challenges in multimedia content analysis, multimedia signal processing and communications, multimedia applications and services, as well as the ethical, legal, and societal aspects of multimedia. Part of the conference consisted of special sessions focusing on specific cutting-edge areas. MMM also featured a practical demonstration session that enabled interactive experiences with scientific applications. The Video Browser Showdown (VBS) competition was another unique aspect of MMM, a live demonstration event where teams competed in various challenging video retrieval tasks using advanced video search tools. The program further included three inspiring keynote talks by Jiri Matas from the Czech Technical University, Marcel Worring from the University of Amsterdam, and Giuseppe Amato from CNR-ISTI.

This year, MMM 2026 received a total of 251 valid regular paper submissions. Of these, 137 high-quality papers were accepted following a rigorous double-blind peer-review process. Each submission was evaluated by at least three program committee members or reviewers. In addition, 8 demonstration papers and 12 VBS systems were selected for presentation at the conference. The program also included 11 special session papers, each addressing one of the following topics:

- Human-Centric Multimodal Behavior Analysis
- Modelling Robustness and Security for Multimedia AI (MARS)
- Multi-Object Multi-Sensor Tracking (MOMST)

Behind the success of a conference is always a huge amount of work by the people who participated in all phases of the organization. Therefore, we would like to express our sincere thanks to the members of the organizing committee, special session, demonstration and VBS organizers, the steering and technical program committee members, reviewers, keynote speakers, authors, and Springer for making MMM 2026 a great event.

December 2025

Jakub Lokoč
Ladislav Peška
Jan Zahálka
Stevan Rudinac
Marc Kastner
Jingjing Chen
Min-Chun Hu
Jiaxin Wu
Ujjwal Sharma

Organization

General Chairs

Jakub Lokoč	Charles University, Czech Republic
Ladislav Peška	Charles University, Czech Republic

Program Committee Chairs

Jingjing Chen	Fudan University, China
Min-Chun Hu	National Tsing Hua University, Taiwan
Marc Kastner	Hiroshima City University, Japan
Stevan Rudinac	University of Amsterdam, The Netherlands
Jan Zahálka	Czech Technical University in Prague, Czech Republic

Special Session Chairs

Rahel Arnold	University of Basel, Switzerland
Werner Bailer	Joanneum Research, Austria
Luca Rossetto	Dublin City University, Ireland

Demonstration Chairs

Kai Uwe Barthel	HTW Berlin, Germany
Lucia Vadicamo	CNR-ISTI, Italy

Video Browser Showdown Chairs

Werner Bailer	Joanneum Research, Austria
Cathal Gurrin	Dublin City University, Ireland
Jakub Lokoč	Charles University, Czech Republic
Klaus Schöffmann	Klagenfurt University, Austria

Publicity Chairs

Cathal Gurrin	Dublin City University, Ireland
Richang Hong	Hefei University of Technology, China

Proceedings Chairs

Ujjwal Sharma	University of Amsterdam, The Netherlands
Jiaxin Wu	Shenzhen University, China

Steering Committee

Kiyoharu Aizawa	University of Tokyo, Japan
Phoebe Chen	La Trobe University, Australia
Wen-Huang Cheng	National Taiwan University, Taiwan
Tat-Seng Chua	National University of Singapore, Singapore
Peng Cui	Tsinghua University, China
Cathal Gurrin	Dublin City University, Ireland
Richang Hong	Hefei University of Technology, China
Benoit Huet	Median Technologies Inc., France
Björn Þór Jónsson	Reykjavik University, Iceland
Guo-Jun Qi	University of Central Florida, USA
Klaus Schöffmann	Klagenfurt University, Austria

Special Session Organizers

Human-Centric Multimodal Behavior Analysis

Yu-Gang Jiang	Fudan University, China
Hong Liu	Xiamen University, China
Wenjing Li	Hefei University of Technology, China
Nan Pu	University of Trento, Italy
Zhun Zhong	Hefei University of Technology, China

Modelling Robustness and Security for Multimedia AI (MARS)

Nandor Knust	UIT Arctic University of Norway, Norway
Michael A. Riegler	Simula Research Laboratory, Norway

Multi-object Multi-sensor Tracking (MOMST)

Mario Döller	University of Applied Sciences Kufstein, Austria
Ruben Tous	Universitat Politècnica de Catalunya, Spain

Program Committee

Avinash Anand	Singapore Institute of Technology, Singapore
Rahel Arnold	University of Basel, Switzerland
Qian Cao	Renmin University of China, China
Wei-Ta Chu	National Cheng Kung University, Taiwan
Keisuke Doman	Chukyo University, Japan
Zhicheng Du	Tsinghua University, China
Peter Eisert	Humboldt Universität zu Berlin, Germany
Alex Falcon	University of Udine, Italy
Gylfi Þór Guðmundsson	Reykjavik University, Iceland
Jaime Roblero	Dublin City University, Ireland
Shintami Hidayati	Institut Teknologi Sepuluh Nopember, Indonesia
Jian Hou	Dongguan University of Technology, China
Bastian Jäckl	University of Konstanz, Germany
Naye Ji	Communication University of Zhejiang, China
Vijay John	Lawrence Technological University, USA
Björn Þór Jónsson	Reykjavik University, Iceland
Klaus Jung	HTW Berlin, Germany
Yasutomo Kawanishi	RIKEN, Japan
Chutisant Kerdvibulvech	National Institute of Development Administration, Thailand
Tran Khoa	National Institute of Information and Communications Technology, Japan
Takahiro Komamizu	Nagoya University, Japan
Yongqiang Kong	Beijing Polytechnic College, China
Satoshi Kosugi	Tokyo Institute of Technology, Japan
Haruya Kyutoku	Aichi University of Technology, Japan
Bao Le Hoang	Dublin City University, Ireland
Mario Leopold	Klagenfurt University, Austria
Feng Li	Anhui University of Finance and Economics, China
Chih-Wei Lin	Fujian Agriculture and Forestry University, China
Yu Liu	Tongji University, China
Vasileios Mezaris	Centre for Research and Technology Hellas, Greece

Atsuyuki Miyai	University of Tokyo, Japan
Hisashi Miyamori	Kyoto Sangyo University, Japan
Eisei Nakahara	Nihon University, Japan
Takayuki Nakatsuka	National Institute of Advanced Industrial Science and Technology, Japan
Thu Nguyen	SimulaMet, Norway
Thang-Long Nguyen-Ho	Dublin City University, Ireland
Naoko Nitta	Kansai University, Japan
Tse-Yu Pan	National Taiwan University of Science and Technology, Taiwan
Nick Pantelidis	CERTH, Greece
Maria Pegia	Centre for Research & Technology Hellas, Greece
Halvorsen Pål	SimulaMet, Norway
Na Qi	Beijing University of Technology, China
Joseph Robinson	Meta, USA
Albert Ali Salah	Utrecht University, Netherlands
Shin'ichi Satoh	National Institute of Informatics, Japan
Konstantin Schall	vviinn, Germany
Udo Schlegel	LMU München, Germany
Francesca Scotti	CNR-ISTI, Italy
Palaiahnakote Shivakumara	University of Salford, UK
Thitirat Siriborvornratanakul	National Institute of Development Administration, Thailand
Ivana Sixtova	Charles University, Czech Republic
Shih-Wei Sun	Taipei National University of the Arts, Taiwan
Cheng-Kang Tan	National Cheng Kung University, Taiwan
Marion Taschwer	Klagenfurt University, Austria
Masahiro Toyoura	University of Yamanashi, Japan
Quang-Linh Tran	Dublin City University, Ireland
Kosetsu Tsukuda	National Institute of Advanced Industrial Science and Technology, Japan
Huy Quang Ung	KDDI Research, Inc., Japan
Stefanos Vrochidis	Centre for Research and Technology Hellas, Greece
Haodian Wang	CHN Energy Digital Intelligence Technology Development (Beijing) Co., Ltd., China
Ling Xiao	Hokkaido University, Japan
Yoko Yamakata	University of Tokyo, Japan
Toshihiko Yamasaki	University of Tokyo, Japan
Yuan Zeng	Shenzhen Technology University, China
Fan Zhang	Communication University of Zhejiang, China
Pengcheng Zhao	Nanjing Audit University, China

Additional Reviewers

Ali Abdari
Abir Baâzaoui
Yannan Bai
Werner Bailer
Amit Banerjee
Walid Barhoumi
Tianyu Cai
Changxin Chen
Feiyu Chen
Hongyou Chen
Lucy Chen
Zhiting Chen
Ziyu Chen
Doru Constantin
Yan Deng
Zhixuan Deng
Thomas Derrien
Haizhou Du
Qing Duan
Shijie Fan
Ziyang Fan
Xiaojing Feng
Cheng Fu
Tian Gao
Ziyuan Gao
Hajer Ghodhbani
Chao Gong
Timothy Greer
Yuanyuan Guan
Lili Guo
YuNong Guo
Hongze Han
Shijie Hao
Xu Hao
Haoran Hu
Yuka Hashizume
Steven Hicks
Luong Ho
Jiayi Hu
Min-Chun Hu
Weiyi Hu
Yizheng Hu
Yunteng Hu

Yunming Hui
Adam Jakobsen
Caiyan Jia
Heng Jia
Meng kun Jia
Dongming Jiang
Xuerong Jiang
Pengkun Jiao
Xin Jin
Zhe Jin
Marc A. Kastner
Seon Ho Kim
Onanong Kongmeesub
Haishan Lai
Hoang Bao Le
Lehan Zhang
Hai Li
Hao Li
Hongyang Li
Jiafeng Li
Jiashuo Li
Jiayi Li
Junhao Li
Leixin Li
Li Li
Qingfeng Li
Qingguan Li
Yiqian Li
Yizhi Li
Yuxuan Li
Fang Liang
Lanbin Liang
Peirou Liang
Yun Liao
Hailan Lin
Yuzhen Lin
Anqi Liu
Chengji Liu
Dongqin Liu
Guoshan Liu
Guozhen Liu
Jing Liu
Na Liu

Nana Liu
Wenlong Liu
Yanfei Liu
Yuming Liu
Jakub Lokoč
Nengbo Lu
Weihai Lu
Na Lyu
Zhiyong Ma
Zhiyang Mai
Fuyou Mao
Iván Martín-Fernández
Lyu Meiyi
Xiangwu Meng
Zixiang Meng
Ryota Mibayashi
Nicolas Müller
Phuong-Anh Nguyen
Thanh Binh Nguyen
Thu Nguyen
Trong-Thuan Nguyen
Trung Thanh Nguyen
Wenlong Niu
Stefanie Onsori-Wechtitsc
Yangjun Ou
Hongting Pan
Bo Peng
Ladislav Peška
Itthisak Phueaksri
Wenzhi Ping
Mengyu Qiao
Wanxiang Qin
Weibin Qiu
Ruichao Ren
Xuena Ren
Loris Sauter
Ujjwal Sharma
Yutong Shen
Qifeng Shi
Tong Shi
Mantek Singh
Yingying Song
Florian Spiess
Dimitrios Stefanopoulos
Jianmei Su

Zijin Su
Hao Sun
Zhicong Sun
Junliang Tan
Zhenjun Tang
Adane Tarekegn
Shangzhi Teng
Vajira Thambawita
Hao Tian
Allie Tran
Quoc Khanh Tran
Teng Tu
Kazuya Ueki
Haihui Wan
Chaoyue Wang
Dongsheng Wang
Haoyang Wang
Jiwei Wang
Lin Wang
Quan Wang
Shibin Wang
Shuai Wang
Yongxiang Wang
Yue Wang
Zhangyi Wang
Wentong Wang
Kento Watanabe
Jobin Idiculla Wattasseril
Guangcun Wei
Lijing Wei
Xinyue Wei
Jie Wen
Junchao Wen
Bo Wu
Chunzhuang Wu
Jiaxin Wu
Xinlan Wu
Wen Xie
Zhihua Xie
Zhonghao Xie
Jiahang Xin
Jian Xing
Feifei Xu
Hang Xu
Man Xu

Contents

Regular Papers

Regular Papers

Multi-granular Feature Selection Fusion Method for Multimodal Named Entity Recognition

Guohui Ding, Tengyu Fan[✉], and Chufei Wang

School of Computer Science, Shenyang Aerospace University, Liaoning, China
dingguohui@sau.edu.cn, {fantengyu,wangchufei}@stu.sau.edu.cn

Abstract. Multimodal Named Entity Recognition (MNER) aims to enhance entity recognition accuracy by incorporating visual information to complement textual data. Existing approaches have made notable progress by introducing multi-granular visual features to strengthen cross-modal semantic alignment. However, they generally lack effective filtering of feature relevance, which often leads to the inclusion of excessive irrel-evant features and a consequent decline in model performance. To address this limitation, we propose a Multi-granular Feature Selection Fusion (MGFS) method that progressively filters and integrates visual features through three stages: overview inspection, detailed inspection, and feature decision. MGFS combines cross-modal attention, adaptive gating mechanisms, and a dynamic feature selection network guided by uncertainty estimation to effectively filter out irrelevant visual information. Experimental results on two public datasets fully validate the effectiveness and superiority of our proposed method. Specifically, MGFS not only outperforms conventional multimodal approaches but also surpasses recent multimodal frameworks integrated with large language models (LLMs), achieving superior overall performance.

Keywords: Multimodal Named Entity Recognition · Multi-Granular Visual Features · Uncertainty Evaluation

1 Introduction

In recent years, with the rapid development of social media platforms such as Twitter and Facebook, user-generated content has increasingly exhibited characteristics of short text, high unstructuredness, and multimodality. These features have posed unprecedented challenges to traditional Natural Language Processing (NLP) tasks [1–3]. Against this backdrop, MNER has gradually emerged as a research hotspot. MNER aims to identify entities with specific semantic categories from inputs that contain both text and images, extending the traditional Named Entity Recognition (NER) task. For example, as shown in Fig. 1(a), by incorporating the image, the entities "Alex" and "American Univ of Sharjah" in the sentence can be recognized as PER and ORG, respectively–where PER (person), ORG (organization), LOC (location), and MISC (miscellaneous) are the common entity categories in MNER. This task enhances cross-modal semantic

© The Author(s), under exclusive license to Springer Nature Singapore Pte Ltd. 2026
J. Lokoč et al. (Eds.): MMM 2026, LNCS 16412, pp. 3–16, 2026.
https://doi.org/10.1007/978-981-95-6950-2_1

4   G. Ding et al.

understanding by fusing textual and visual information, thereby improving the accuracy of named entity recognition [4–8]. Compared to text-only NER methods, multimodal approaches significantly enhance the model's ability to disambiguate polysemous expressions and improve the precision of entity boundary identification by introducing contextual cues from images [9].

(a)   (b)   (c)

(a) Alex[PER] and I spent a delightful morning at the American Univ of Sharjah[ORG].
(b) LeBron James[PER] has returned to the Cleveland Cavaliers[ORG].
(c) Good night Costa Rica[LOC].

Fig. 1. Information requirements of different texts for images

Compared to text, image information typically contains richer semantic content. To further enhance the role of visual information in MNER, an increasing number of studies have begun to incorporate multi-granular visual features [10–12]. For instance, Zhang et al. [12] were the first to integrate both global images and segmented object-level images for named entity recognition; building upon this, Liu et al. [11] further introduced spatial location information of images to improve the modeling of multi-granular visual cues. In general, the core idea of multi-granular visual modeling is to exploit semantic information at different levels of granularity–such as global, regional, and object-level–to support more precise recognition of different types of entities. As shown in Fig. 1(a), recognizing the background entity "American Univ of Sharjah" may rely on broader regional-level visual features, while identifying the person entity "Alex" depends more on object-level features. By introducing multi-granular visual representations, existing methods have effectively enhanced the model's understanding of visual semantics, thereby improving the accuracy and robustness of the MNER task.

However, since different textual contexts often require different levels of visual granularity, multi-granular visual features may introduce irrelevant visual information. Irrelevant visual information refers to image content that does not contribute to named entity recognition. If not properly filtered, such information can negatively affect model performance. Existing methods, however, typically lack the capability to explicitly filter out these features. For example, as illustrated in Fig. 1(b), object-level features extracted using object detection tools–such as players and team logos–can effectively guide the recognition of PER and ORG entities. However, the inclusion of unrelated blurred background regions may introduce semantic noise, interfering with the model's understanding of visual content and ultimately leading to incorrect predictions. Similarly, in Fig. 1(c), the ocean scene dominates the image, and regional-level features are crucial for correctly identifying the LOC label "Costa Rica." When irrelevant object-level features–such as detected portraits–are reintroduced, they may disrupt the initial region-based judgment and result in misclassification. Therefore, a key challenge in MNER lies in effectively filtering multi-granular visual features to remove irrelevant information, thereby enabling the precise extraction of salient visual cues aligned with the textual context.

To address the above issues, we draw inspiration from human cognitive behavior when interpreting multimodal content: humans typically undergo a process that progresses from coarse to fine, from perception to understanding–first forming an initial impression through a quick overview of the entire image-text input, and then focusing on local details to obtain more precise information before making a final decision. Motivated by this observation, we propose a Multi-granular Feature Selection Fusion method for multimodal named entity recognition, which divides the feature modeling process into three stages: overview inspection, detailed inspection, and feature decision. The overview and detailed inspection stages simulate the acquisition of information from global to local, aiming to filter out key information from multi-granular visual and textual features that is helpful for entity recognition. The feature decision stage mimics the human decision-making process after information integration, further selecting and fusing the effective features obtained in the previous stages to support the final entity classification. Through this staged modeling approach, MGFS can more efficiently focus on critical information within multi-granular inputs, thereby improving recognition accuracy and robustness.

Specifically, during the overview inspection stage, to effectively aggregate key information from regional image features relevant to the text, the cross-modal feature aggregation module computes the matching degree between global image and textual features to dynamically adjust the weights of regional features. These adjusted features are then aligned with the corresponding textual representations via a cross-modal attention mechanism, enhancing regional-level cross-modal interactions. To avoid ineffective fusion, a cross-modal adaptive gated fusion module introduces a soft gating mechanism that dynamically modulates the fusion strength, while concatenating global image features as weak semantic signals to better highlight key regional features. In the detailed inspection stage, object regions are extracted using a detector, and segmented regions are encoded through a ResNet backbone to generate multi-scale object-level pyramid features. These features supplement fine-grained semantics and complete object information, addressing the semantic discontinuity introduced by rigid region partitioning. Through these two inspection stages, the model simulates a coarse-to-fine, perception-to-understanding process of visual-textual reasoning, effectively reducing irrelevant noise and providing comprehensive, detailed data support for subsequent analysis. In the feature decision stage, to further eliminate irrelevant information, we design a dynamic multi-granular feature selection module based Bayesian linear layers, which estimates feature uncertainty to filter out uninformative components. The selected features are then concatenated and fused with the complete textual semantics within a Transformer layer, enabling guided integration. This strategy enhances the model's ability to distinguish relevant features while preserving semantic completeness, thereby improving both accuracy and robustness in the MNER task. Our contributions are as follows:

1. This study proposes a multi-granular feature selection and fusion strategy inspired by human cognition, which divides the information modeling process in the MNER task into three stages, enabling dynamic selection and efficient utilization of multi-granular features to enhance the accuracy and robustness of entity recognition.
2. We design a dynamic multi-granular feature selection network that incorporates Bayesian sampling to quantify model prediction confidence, and employs reverse-weight control to select and infer multi-granular features. This approach reduces the inclusion of irrelevant features, mitigates the risk of overfitting, and improves the model's ability to handle cross-modal data diversity during feature fusion.
3. Experiments conducted on two popular datasets, Twitter-15 and Twitter-17, demonstrate that the proposed method outperforms the baselines on both datasets, validating the effectiveness of MGFS.

2   Related Work

2.1   Multimodal Named Entity Recognition

Multimodal Named Entity Recognition (MNER) has significantly advanced entity recognition by integrating textual and visual information, particularly enhancing semantic disambiguation. Early methods primarily exploited global visual features to support textual understanding [5,6,13], yet they lacked fine-grained semantic alignment. Later studies focused on localized and multi-scale visual cues. Wu et al. [7] employed dense co-attention using object labels; Wang et al. [8] integrated external knowledge to strengthen entitylabel associations; and Chen et al. [14] refined visual hierarchies through pyramid-based structures.

Despite these advancements, most existing approaches insufficiently filter irrelevant visual information, leading to semantic noise and performance degradation. Recent LLM-enhanced multimodal frameworks improve contextual reasoning but still lack mechanisms for selective fusion across granularities.

To address these limitations, our proposed Multi-granular Feature Selection Fusion (MGFS) method introduces a progressive feature selection strategy combining cross-modal attention, adaptive gating, and uncertainty-guided fusion. Unlike prior models, MGFS emphasizes effective relevance filtering and fine-grained semantic integration, achieving robust and interpretable multimodal entity recognition.

3 Methodology

Building upon previous research, we formulate the MNER task as a sequence labeling problem [13]. The overall framework of our model is shown in Fig. 2.

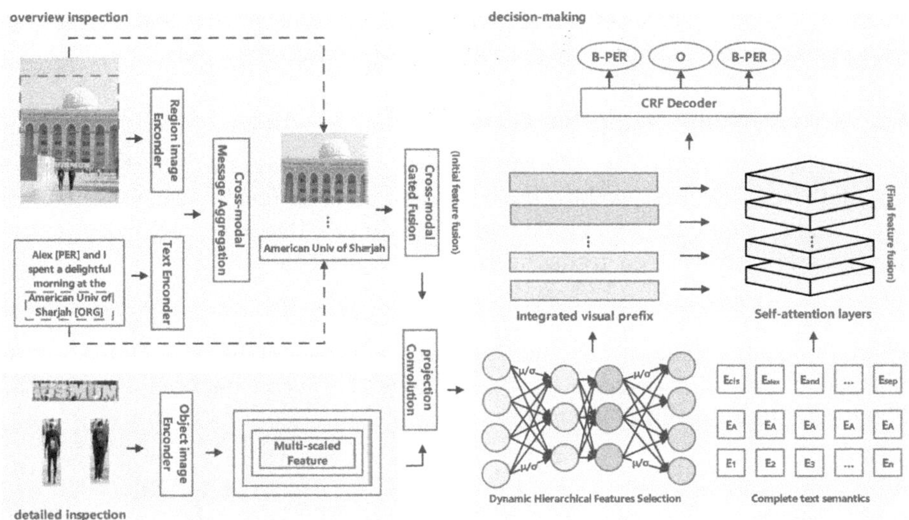

Fig. 2. The overall architecture of our MGFS

3.1 Cross-Modal Feature Aggregation Module

In the overview inspection stage, we utilize a BERT encoder [17] to map the input sequence $X = (x_1, \ldots, x_n)$ into contextual representations $T = (t_{\mathrm{cls}}, t_1, \ldots, t_n)$. The global semantic token t_{cls} is further projected into a global text feature T_g via a fully connected layer with Tanh activation.For the visual modality, we adopt a ResNet [18] backbone (without the classification layer) to extract regional features $V^r = (V_1^r, \ldots, V_{49}^r)$ and global visual feature V_g via 7×7 average pooling. Regional features are projected to match the dimensionality of textual features.

To emphasize informative regions, we compute a dynamic control weight $M_r \in [-1, 1]$ based on the correlation between T_g and V_g:

$$C_r = \tanh(T_g W_{TI} V_g) \tag{1}$$

$$M_r = \tanh(W_T T_g + W_I V_g C_r) \tag{2}$$

The refined region features V_i' are subsequently computed as follows:

$$V_i' = W_N([M_r V_g, V_i^r]) \tag{3}$$

where $W_{TI}, W_T, W_I \in \mathbb{R}^{d \times d}$ and $W_N \in \mathbb{R}^{2d \times d}$ are learnable parameters.

Next, We compute an affinity matrix $A \in \mathbb{R}^{R \times N}$ between V' and T, apply softmax normalization, and use the result to aggregate textual features:

$$T_{\text{att}} = softmax(\frac{A}{\sqrt{d_h}})T \tag{4}$$

where $T_{\text{att}} \in \mathbb{R}^{R \times d}$ denotes the aggregated region-specific text features aligned with visual regions, enabling region-level cross-modal interaction.

3.2   Cross-Modal Adaptive Gated Fusion Module

To enhance fusion quality and ensure that textual features effectively guide regional visual features, we introduce a cross-modal adaptive gating mechanism. Let v_i and t_i denote the i-th visual region feature and its aligned attended textual feature, respectively. The gating vector is computed by:

$$\mathbf{g}_i = \sigma(v_i \odot t_i), \quad i = 1, \ldots, R \tag{5}$$

where $\odot$ denotes element-wise multiplication and $\sigma(\cdot)$ is the sigmoid activation. The set of gates $G_v = [g_1, \ldots, g_R]$ modulates the fusion between V' and T_{att}. The gated fusion result is defined as:

$$V_{\text{fus}} = \mathcal{F}_v \left(G_v \odot (V' \oplus T_{\text{att}}) \right) + V' \tag{6}$$

$$\tilde{V}_{\text{fus}} = [V_g; V_{\text{fus}}] \tag{7}$$

where $\oplus$ denotes element-wise addition, and $\mathcal{F}_v$ is a learnable transformation composed of a linear layer followed by non-linear activation. The final output $\tilde{V}_{\text{fus}} \in \mathbb{R}^{(R+1) \times d}$ represents the region-level visual features enriched with contextual semantic guidance (Fig. 3).

3.3   Multi-granular Visual Composition Module

To enrich visual semantics, we extract m salient object regions using a visual grounding toolkit [19] during the detailed inspection stage. These objects are encoded using a pretrained ResNet backbone to generate a set of multi-scale feature maps $F = \{F_1, F_2, \ldots, F_c\}$. Each feature map is transformed via pooling and 1×1 convolution to produce object-level features O_i. To align dimensions with the Transformer encoder, we flatten the fused regional representation $\tilde{V}_{\text{fus}}$ and split it into c equal parts:

$$\text{Flatten}(\tilde{V}_{\text{fus}}) \rightarrow [X_1; X_2; \ldots; X_c] \tag{8}$$

$$R_i = W_M X_i, \quad i = 1, \ldots, c \tag{9}$$

Each $X_i \in \mathbb{R}^{\frac{(R+1)d}{4}}$ is linearly projected by $W_M \in \mathbb{R}^{\frac{(R+1)d}{4} \times 5d}$.

Finally, we concatenate the object-level features O_i with the projected fused regional features R_i to form integrated multi-granular representations:

$$P_i = \text{Concat}(R_i, O_i), \quad i = 1, \ldots, c \tag{10}$$

The resulting P_i captures both fine-grained object details and regional context, providing diverse visual cues for downstream reasoning.

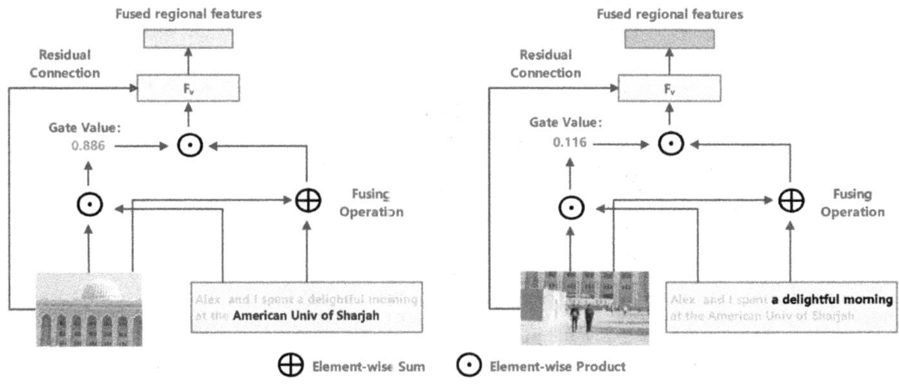

Fig. 3. Illustration of the fusion between regional features and attended textual features via cross-modal gating

3.4 Dynamic Multi-granular Feature Selection Module

To refine visual feature composition and eliminate irrelevant information, we introduce a dynamic multi-granular feature selection network. At each Transformer layer l, the integrated features P_i are passed through global average pooling to produce compact descriptors:

$$P_{\text{agg}} = \frac{1}{h_i w_i} \sum_{j=1}^{h_i} \sum_{k=1}^{w_i} P_i[j,k] \tag{11}$$

The averaged features are fed into a Bayesian-regulated MLP layer W_{Bayesian}, which estimates uncertainty-aware logits:

$$\beta^{(l)} = f\left(W_{\text{Bayesian}}\left(\frac{1}{c}\sum_{i=1}^{c} P_{\text{agg},i}\right)\right) \tag{12}$$

where $f(\cdot)$ is the LeakyReLU activation. Applying the softmax function yields the feature importance distribution:

$$s^{(l)} = \text{Softmax}(\beta^{(l)}) \tag{13}$$

Using $s^{(l)}$, we compute a weighted aggregation to obtain contextual visual features $P_{\text{allocated}}^{(l)}$, and concatenate across levels to form the final multi-granular representation:

$$\tilde{P}_{\text{allocated}}^{(l)} = [P_{\text{allocated}}^{(l,R)}; P_{\text{allocated}}^{(l,o_1)}; \dots; P_{\text{allocated}}^{(l,o_m)}] \tag{14}$$

These fused visual features are prepended to the textual input X_T, resulting in a unified input $X_{TV} = [\tilde{P}_{\text{allocated}}^{(l)}; X_T]$. In the multi-head self-attention mechanism, the projections are computed as:

$$Q'_h = X_{TV}W_h^Q, \quad K'_h = X_{TV}W_h^K, \quad V'_h = X_{TV}W_h^V \tag{15}$$

3.5 Classifier

After fusing textual and visual modalities, we obtain the final hidden representation from BERT, denoted as:

$$H^L = U(X, \tilde{P}^{(l)}_{\text{allocated}}) \tag{16}$$

where $U(\cdot)$ denotes the integration of multi-granular visual features into the BERT encoder.

To perform named entity recognition, we employ a Conditional Random Field (CRF) decoder. Given a label sequence $Y = (y_1, \ldots, y_n)$ under the BIO tagging scheme, the CRF defines the conditional probability as:

$$p(Y|H^L) = \frac{\prod_{i=1}^{n} S_i(y_{i-1}, y_i, H^L)}{\sum_{Y'} \prod_{i=1}^{n} S_i(y'_{i-1}, y'_i, H^L)} \tag{17}$$

The NER loss is given by:

$$\mathcal{L}_{\text{NER}} = -\sum_{i=1}^{M} \log(p(Y^{(i)}|H^{(i)})) \tag{18}$$

We adopt a reparameterized variational inference framework to model uncertainty within the Bayesian linear layers. KL divergence is used to regularize the learned variational posteriors $q(W_i)$ and $q(b_i)$ with respect to their priors $p(W_i)$ and $p(b_i)$:

$$\mathcal{L}_{\text{KL}} = \frac{1}{N} \sum_{i=1}^{12} [D_{\text{KL}}(q_{W_i} \| p_{W_i}) + D_{\text{KL}}(q_{b_i} \| p_{b_i})] \tag{19}$$

The total loss function combines CRF prediction loss with uncertainty-based regularization:

$$\mathcal{L}_{\text{total}} = \mathcal{L}_{\text{NER}} + \beta_t \mathcal{L}_{\text{KL}} \tag{20}$$

where β_t is a step-wise annealing coefficient controlling KL strength during training.

4 Experiments

4.1 Comparative Experiment

To evaluate the performance of MGFS, we conduct experiments on two widely used multimodal public datasets: TWITTER-2015 [6] and TWITTER-2017 [5]. Following the evaluation protocol established in prior work [21], we adopt Precision, Recall, and F1 Score as the primary performance metrics. As shown in Table 1, we compare our method against a comprehensive set of state-of-the-art multimodal models, including AdaCAN-CNN-BiLSTM-CRF (ACBC) [6], GVATTHBiLSTM-CRF (GHC) [13], GVATT-BERT-CRF [21], AdaCANBERT-CRF [21], MT-BERT-CRF [21], ATTR-MMKG-MNER [23], OCSGA [7], ObjectAGBAN [10], HGMAF [16], GPT4 [16], Visual ChatGPT [16], MGCMT [24],

Table 1. Experimental Results on the TWITTER-2015 and TWITTER-2017 Dataset. The results for RpBERT are from Zhao et al. [22], while the rest of the results are from original paper data.

Methods	TWITTER-2015							TWITTER-2017						
	Single Type(F1)				Overall			Single Type(F1)				Overall		
	PER	LOC	ORG	MISC	Pre	Rec	F1	PER	LOC	ORG	MISC	Pre	Rec	F1
ACBC	81.98	78.95	53.37	34.02	72.75	68.74	70.69	89.63	77.46	79.24	62.77	84.16	80.24	82.15
GHC	82.66	77.21	55.06	35.25	73.96	67.90	70.80	89.34	78.53	79.12	62.21	83.41	80.38	81.87
GAVTT-BERT-CRF	84.43	80.87	59.02	38.14	69.15	74.46	71.70	89.34	78.53	79.12	62.21	83.41	80.38	81.87
AdaCAN-BERT-CRF	85.28	80.64	59.39	38.88	69.87	74.59	72.15	90.20	82.97	82.67	64.83	85.13	83.20	84.10
MT-BERT-CRF	85.30	81.21	61.10	37.97	70.84	74.80	72.58	91.47	82.05	81.84	65.80	84.60	84.16	84.42
OCSGA	84.68	79.95	56.64	39.47	74.41	71.21	72.92	–	–	–	–	–	–	–
Object-AGBAN	84.75	79.41	58.31	40.72	74.13	72.39	73.25	–	–	–	–	–	–	–
ATTR-MMKG-MNER	84.28	79.42	58.97	41.47	74.78	71.82	73.27	–	–	–	–	–	–	–
RpBERT	85.18	81.19	58.68	37.88	71.15	74.30	72.69	89.05	84.03	82.60	63.67	82.85	84.38	83.61
UMT	85.24	81.58	63.03	39.45	71.67	75.23	73.41	91.56	84.73	82.24	70.10	85.28	85.34	85.31
UMGF	84.26	**83.17**	62.45	42.42	74.49	75.21	74.85	91.92	85.22	83.13	69.83	86.54	84.50	85.51
MAF	84.67	81.18	63.35	41.82	71.86	75.10	73.42	91.51	85.80	85.10	68.79	86.13	86.38	86.25
GPT4	–	–	–	–	–	–	57.98	–	–	–	–	–	–	66.61
Visual ChatGPT	–	–	–	–	–	–	41.45	–	–	–	–	–	–	47.24
MGCMT	–	–	–	–	73.57	75.59	74.57	–	–	–	–	86.03	86.16	86.09
HVPNet	–	–	–	–	73.87	76.82	75.32	–	–	–	–	85.84	87.93	86.87
HGMAF	–	–	–	–	75.46	77.13	76.29	–	–	–	–	86.69	86.36	87.66
R-GCN	86.36	82.08	60.78	41.56	73.95	76.18	75.00	92.86	86.10	84.05	72.38	86.72	87.57	87.11
MRC-MNER	85.71	81.97	61.12	40.20	**78.10**	71.45	74.63	92.64	86.47	83.16	72.66	**88.78**	85.00	86.85
SMVAE	85.82	81.56	63.20	43.67	71.40	75.76	75.07	91.96	81.89	84.13	**74.07**	85.77	86.97	86.37
MENR-QG(Oracle)	85.68	81.42	63.62	41.53	77.76	72.31	74.94	93.17	86.02	84.64	71.83	88.57	85.96	87.25
DebiasCL	85.97	81.84	**64.02**	43.38	74.45	76.13	75.28	93.46	84.15	84.42	67.88	87.59	86.11	86.84
MGFS	**87.12**	82.82	63.89	**45.93**	75.32	**77.43**	**76.32**	**93.97**	**87.39**	**86.19**	68.71	87.57	**88.23**	**87.89**

UMT [21], RpBERT [25], UMGF [12], MAF [15], HVPNeT [14], R-GCN [22], MRC-MNER [26], SMVAE [27], MNER-QG (Oracle) [28], DebiasCL [29].

Through an in-depth analysis and comprehensive evaluation of the experimental results, we draw the following conclusions:

1. Compared to early multimodal approaches, models incorporating CRF decoders such as AdaCAN-BERT-CRF and GVATT-BERT-CRF consistently outperform those without CRF, highlighting its effectiveness in sequence modeling. Among recent methods, results show that incorporating fine-grained object-level visual guidance (e.g., OCSGA vs. UMGF) and assessing cross-modal alignment while suppressing visual noise (e.g., UMT vs. MAF) are both crucial. Our method surpasses UMT and UMGF, demonstrating the advantage of multi-granular visual integration in enhancing MNER performance.

2. Compared with recent models such as DebiasCL and SMVAE, our method achieves better performance. We attribute this to the fact that these approaches do not explicitly address the impact of irrelevant visual information. This further demonstrates that our model effectively reduces erro-

neous sensitivity to non-informative visual content. In addition, compared with models that directly leverage or are assisted by large language models (LLMs), such as HGMAF, GPT-4, and Visual ChatGPT, our method also delivers superior results. These findings suggest that the application of LLMs in the MNER domain still requires further advancement and exploration.

4.2   Ablation Study

To evaluate the effectiveness of each component in MGFS, we conduct a series of ablation studies, as summarized in Table 2, where "w/o" denotes the removal of specific modules. The results reveal several key findings:

Table 2. Ablation Study

Methods	TWITTER-2015							TWITTER-2017						
	Single Type(F1)				Overall			Single Type(F1)				Overall		
	PER	LOC	ORG	MISC	Pre	Rec	F1	PER	LOC	ORG	MISC	Pre	Rec	F1
MGFS	87.12	82.82	63.89	45.93	75.23	77.43	**76.32**	93.97	87.39	86.19	68.71	87.57	88.23	**87.89**
w/o CMFA	86.39	82.35	61.99	43.44	74.52	75.63	<u>75.08</u>	93.00	86.44	85.14	68.59	86.32	87.79	<u>87.05</u>
w/o CAGF	83.87	82.05	62.40	39.21	73.38	75.86	74.60	92.79	86.04	83.98	68.85	85.77	87.42	86.58
w/o MGVC	86.68	82.18	61.89	41.03	74.15	76.02	75.07	93.30	86.91	84.90	66.02	86.44	87.27	86.85
w/o DMFS	85.99	82.08	62.01	43.13	74.35	74.89	74.62	92.63	84.03	84.03	68.87	85.50	87.27	86.37

Removing the Cross-Modal Feature Aggregation (CMFA) module leads to a significant performance drop, confirming the essential role of modality alignment in utilizing visual context. Excluding the Cross-Modal Adaptive Gated Fusion (CAGF) module results in a notable decline in accuracy, underscoring its effectiveness in suppressing noise. The removal of object features from the Multi-Granular Visual Composition (MGVC) module degrades performance, indicating that fine-grained object-level cues are crucial for comprehensive semantic understanding. Finally, replacing the Bayesian linear layers in the Dynamic Multi-Granular Feature Selection (DMFS) module with standard linear layers causes the most substantial degradation, highlighting the importance of uncertainty-aware filtering in refining multi-granular features.

Overall, these results validate the necessity and complementarity of each component in enhancing the robustness and precision of MNER.

4.3   Case Study

To better understand the effectiveness of our method in handling multi-level information, we selected a set of representative test samples to compare the predictions of MGFS with other methods. The prediction results and their details are illustrated in Fig. 4.

(a)   (b)   (c)

(a) Stephen Colbert [PER][1] appeared on the cover of TIME [ORG][2].
(b) Hello Istanbul [LOC][1]! A great turnout for the launch of Apple Watch [MISC][2] in Turkey [LOC][3] today.
(c) Manarola [LOC][1], Italy [LOC][2]. Photo by Lars Kehrel [PER][3].

UMT:	1-[PER] 2-[None]	1-[LOC] 2-[None] 3-[LOC]	1-[PER] 2-[LOC] 3-[PER]
UMGF:	1-[PER] 2-[ORG]	1-[LOC] 2-[None] 3-[LOC]	1-[LOC] 2-[LOC] 3-[None]
HVPNet:	1-[PER] 2-[LOC]	1-[LOC] 2-[ORG] 3-[LOC]	1-[LOC] 2-[LOC] 3-[PER]
MGFS:	1-[PER] 2-[ORG]	1-[LOC] 2-[MISC] 3-[LOC]	1-[LOC] 2-[LOC] 3-[PER]

Fig. 4. Case study

In Fig. 4(a), UMT fails to detect "time" as an ORG, likely due to the absence of object-level visual guidance. HVPNet incorrectly classifies "time" as LOC, which may result from the lack of alignment between textual and visual features, leading to ineffective use of image information. In Fig. 4(b), both UMT and UMGF fail to identify "Apple Watch" as a MISC entity, while HVPNet detects the entity but incorrectly classified. In contrast, MGFS correctly recognizes "Apple Watch," possibly because its two-stage multimodal fusion enables deeper semantic understanding compared to the other methods. In Fig. 4(c), UMGF fails to identify "Lars Kehrel" as a PER, despite the absence of any human object in the image, suggesting that visual features may have interfered with the textual semantics. In comparison, both HVPNet and MGFS make accurate predictions, indicating that the gating mechanism in these models may effectively filter out irrelevant visual signals and preserve meaningful semantic cues.

4.4 Hyperparameter Analysis

Hyperparameter tuning is critical for model performance. We employ a reparameterized variational inference framework, approximating posterior distributions via Monte Carlo sampling. During training, Bayesian linear layers utilize stochastic variational inference (SVI) to optimize variational parameters, sampling weights N times per forward pass to balance gradient bias and computational efficiency. For inference, deterministic prediction is executed using posterior means. Empirical results demonstrate: increasing sampling count N from 1 to 30 consistently enhances performance, yet with diminishing marginal returns and significant computational overhead beyond this range. We therefore

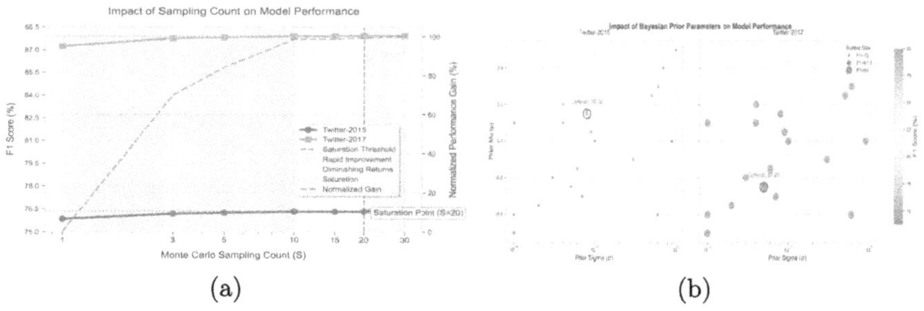

Fig. 5. Hyperparameter analysis

fix $N = 20$ in subsequent experiments. Next, with the sampling number fixed at $N = 20$, we conduct a series of experiments to analyze the impact of two key prior-related hyperparameters (Fig. 5).

(1) Prior Mean (priorμ): Uniformly sampled within the range of $[-0.5, 0.5]$ to evaluate the impact of positive/negative bias on feature selection.
(2) Prior Standard Deviation (priorσ): Sampled on a logarithmic scale within $[0.01, 1.0]$ to control the strength of regularization.

Experiments show that on the Twitter-2015 dataset, the model achieves the highest F1 score of 76.32% when prior$\sigma \in [0.08, 0.1]$, indicating that moderate regularization helps improve generalization. On the Twitter-2017 dataset, the best F1 score of 87.89% is obtained when prior$\mu = -0.5$ and prior$\sigma = 0.01$, suggesting that negative bias can enhance the robustness of sparse feature selection.

Moreover, sensitivity analysis reveals that when prior$\sigma \leq 0.05$ or ≥ 0.5, the average F1 score drops by $1.7\% \pm 0.3\%$, further validating the importance of aligning the regularization strength with the underlying data distribution.

5   Conclusion

This paper presents a multi-granular feature selection and fusion framework for MNER. Our method captures both coarse-grained context and fine-grained visual details through a multi-stage structure. A Bayesian-based dynamic feature Layer further enhances robustness by filtering irrelevant information across multi-granular feature. Experiments on benchmark datasets confirm the superiority of our approach over existing methods, and ablation studies verify the complementary effectiveness of each component. Future work will explore advanced cross-modal interaction paradigms, including the integration of external knowledge bases and vision-language foundation models, to further improve model generalizability.

References

1. Olshannikova, E., Olsson, T., Huhtamäki, J., Kärkkäinen, H.: Conceptualizing big social data. J. Big Data **4**, 1–19 (2017)
2. Batrinca, B., Treleaven, P.C.: Social media analytics: a survey of techniques, tools and platforms. AI Soc. **30**, 89–116 (2015)
3. Comito, C., Caroprese, L., Zumpano, E.: Multimodal fake news detection on social media: a survey of deep learning techniques. Soc. Netw. Anal. Min. **13**(1), 101 (2023)
4. Qian, S., Jin, W., Chen, Y., Ma, J., Qiao, Y., Lu, J.: A survey on multimodal named entity recognition. In: International Conference on Intelligent Computing, pp. 609–622. Springer (2023)
5. Moon, S., Neves, L., Carvalho, V.: Multimodal named entity recognition for short social media posts. arXiv preprint arXiv:1802.07862 (2018)
6. Zhang, Q., Fu, J., Liu, X., Huang, X.: Adaptive co-attention network for named entity recognition in tweets. In: Proceedings of the AAAI Conference on Artificial Intelligence, vol. 32 (2018)
7. Wu, Z., Zheng, C., Cai, Y., Chen, J., Leung, H.F., Li, Q.: Multimodal representation with embedded visual guiding objects for named entity recognition in social media posts. In: Proceedings of the 28th ACM International Conference on Multimedia, pp. 1038–1046 (2020)
8. Wang, X., et al.: CAT-MNER: multimodal named entity recognition with knowledge-refined cross-modal attention. In: 2022 IEEE International Conference on Multimedia and Expo (ICME), pp. 1–6. IEEE (2022)
9. Cheng, M., Xiong, S., Li, F., Liang, P., Gao, J.: Multi-task learning for Chinese clinical named entity recognition with external knowledge. BMC Med. Inform. Decis. Mak. **21**, 1–11 (2021)
10. Zheng, C., Wu, Z., Wang, T., Cai, Y., Li, Q.: Object-aware multimodal named entity recognition in social media posts with adversarial learning. IEEE Trans. Multimedia **23**, 2520–2532 (2020)
11. Liu, P., et al.: Hierarchical aligned multimodal learning for NER on tweet posts. In: Proceedings of the AAAI Conference on Artificial Intelligence, vol. 38, pp. 18680–18688 (2024)
12. Zhang, D., Wei, S., Li, S., Wu, H. Zhu, Q., Zhou, G.: Multi-modal graph fusion for named entity recognition with targeted visual guidance. In: Proceedings of the AAAI Conference on Artificial Intelligence, vol. 35, pp. 14347–14355 (2021)
13. Lu, D., Neves, L., Carvalho, V., Zhang, N., Ji, H.: Visual attention model for name tagging in multimodal social media. In: Proceedings of the 56th Annual Meeting of the Association for Computational Linguistics (Volume 1: Long Papers), pp. 1990–1999 (2018)
14. Chen, X., et al.: Good visual guidance makes a better extractor: hierarchical visual prefix for multimodal entity and relation extraction. arXiv preprint arXiv:2205.03521 (2022)
15. Xu, B., Huang, S., Sha, C., Wang, H.: MAF: a general matching and alignment framework for multimodal named entity recognition. In: Proceedings of the Fifteenth ACM International Conference on Web Search and Data Mining, pp. 1215–1223 (2022)
16. He, X., Li, S., Zhang, Y., Li, B., Xu, S., Zhou, Y.: The more quality information the better: hierarchical generation of multi-evidence alignment and fusion model for multimodal entity and relation extraction. Inf. Process. Manag. **62**(1), 103875 (2025)

17. Devlin, J., Chang, M.W., Lee, K., Toutanova, K.: Bert: pre-training of deep bidirectional transformers for language understanding. In: Proceedings of the 2019 Conference of the North American Chapter of the Association for Computational Linguistics: Human Language Technologies, Volume 1 (Long and Short Papers), pp. 4171–4186 (2019)
18. He, K., Zhang, X., Ren, S., Sun, J.: Deep residual learning for image recognition. In: Proceedings of the IEEE Conference on Computer Vision and Pattern Recognition, pp. 770–778 (2016)
19. Yang, Z., Gong, B., Wang, L., Huang, W., Yu, D., Luo, J.: A fast and accurate one-stage approach to visual grounding. In: Proceedings of the IEEE/CVF International Conference on Computer Vision, pp. 4683–4693 (2019)
20. Vaswani, A., et al.: Attention is all you need. In: Advances in Neural Information Processing Systems, vol. 30 (2017)
21. Yu, J., Jiang, J., Yang, L., Xia, R.: Improving multimodal named entity recognition via entity span detection with unified multimodal transformer. Association for Computational Linguistics (2020)
22. Zhao, F., Li, C., Wu, Z., Xing, S., Dai, X.: Learning from different text-image pairs: a relation-enhanced graph convolutional network for multimodal NER. In: Proceedings of the 30th ACM International Conference on Multimedia, pp. 3983–3992 (2022)
23. Chen, D., Li, Z., Gu, B., Chen, Z.: Multimodal named entity recognition with image attributes and image knowledge. In: Jensen, C.S., et al. (eds.) DASFAA 2021. LNCS, vol. 12682, pp. 186–201. Springer, Cham (2021). https://doi.org/10.1007/978-3-030-73197-7_12
24. Liu, P., et al.: Multi-granularity cross-modal representation learning for named entity recognition on social media. Inf. Process. Manag. **61**(1), 103546 (2024)
25. Sun, L., Wang, J., Zhang, K., Su, Y., Weng, F.: Rpbert: a text-image relation propagation-based BERT model for multimodal NER. In: Proceedings of the AAAI Conference on Artificial Intelligence, vol. 35, pp. 13860–13868 (2021)
26. Jia, M., et al.: MNER-QG: an end-to-end MRC framework for multimodal named entity recognition with query grounding. In: Proceedings of the AAAI Conference on Artificial Intelligence, vol. 37, pp. 8032–8040 (2023)
27. Zhou, B., et al.: A span-based multimodal variational autoencoder for semi-supervised multimodal named entity recognition. In: Proceedings of the 2022 Conference on Empirical Methods in Natural Language Processing, pp. 6293–6302 (2022)
28. Jia, M., et al.: Query prior matters: a MRC framework for multimodal named entity recognition. In: Proceedings of the 30th ACM International Conference on Multimedia, pp. 3549–3558 (2022)
29. Zhang, X., Yuan, J., Li, L., Liu, J.: Reducing the bias of visual objects in multimodal named entity recognition. In: Proceedings of the Sixteenth ACM International Conference on Web Search and Data Mining, pp. 958–966 (2023)

DS-HGCN: A Dual-Stream Hypergraph Convolutional Network for Predicting Student Engagement via Social Contagion

Ziyang Fan[1], Li Tao[1(✉)] [iD], Yi Wang[1] [iD], Jingwei Qu[1] [iD], Ying Wang[1] [iD], and Fei Jiang[2] [iD]

[1] Southwest University, Chongqing 400715, China
`tli@swu.edu.cn`
[2] Chongqing Academy of Science and Technology, Chongqing, China

Abstract. Student engagement is a critical factor influencing academic success and learning outcomes. Accurately predicting student engagement is essential for optimizing teaching strategies and providing personalized interventions. However, most approaches focus on single-dimensional feature analysis and assessing engagement based on individual student factors. In this work, we propose a dual-stream multi-feature fusion model based on hypergraph convolutional networks (DS-HGCN), incorporating **social contagion** of student engagement. DS-HGCN enables accurate prediction of student engagement states by modeling multi-dimensional features and their propagation mechanisms between students. The framework constructs a hypergraph structure to encode engagement contagion among students and captures the emotional and behavioral differences and commonalities by multi-frequency signals. Furthermore, we introduce a hypergraph attention mechanism to dynamically weigh the influence of each student, accounting for individual differences in the propagation process. Extensive experiments on a public benchmark dataset demonstrate that our proposed method achieves superior performance and significantly outperforms existing state-of-the-art approaches.

Keywords: Student Engagement · Hypergraph Convolutional Network · Social Contagion · Multi-feature Fusion · Hypergraph Attention

1 Introduction

Student engagement is a critical factor influencing academic success and learning outcomes [16]. It is a multi-dimensional construct encompassing behavioral, emotional, and cognitive aspects, which collectively provide a holistic perspective on a student's participation in the learning process [10]. In modern digital classrooms, accurately predicting student engagement is essential for enhancing teaching strategies and providing personalized interventions (Fig. 1).

© The Author(s), under exclusive license to Springer Nature Singapore Pte Ltd. 2026
J. Lokoč et al. (Eds.): MMM 2026, LNCS 16412, pp. 17–31, 2026.
https://doi.org/10.1007/978-981-95-6950-2_2

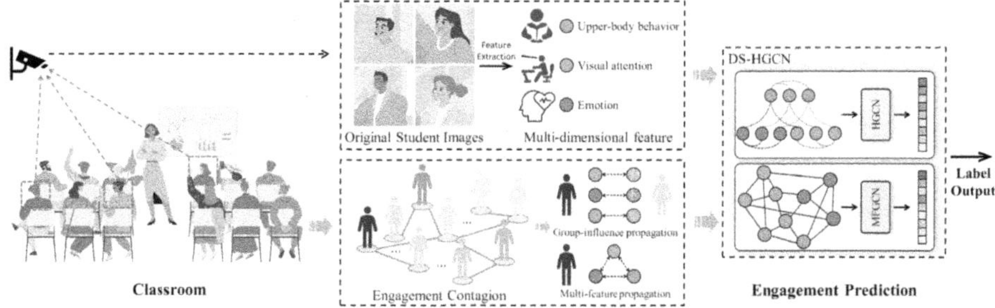

Fig. 1. This figure presents the schematic illustration of classroom student engagement prediction. The DS-HGCN leverages the multi-dimensional features and the engagement contagion of students to infer their engagement status.

Given the complexity of engagement, research has progressed from subjective methods like surveys and observations [2,23,28] to data-driven techniques that use machine learning to analyze diverse data sources, including facial expressions, body language, and physiological signals [2]. However, these approaches often focus on individual students or unimodal features, providing only a partial understanding. This overlooks the well-documented phenomenon of **engagement contagion**, where emotions and behaviors spread within a group, significantly influencing individual learning and motivation [14,19]. This leaves a significant research gap, as current models lack the capability to explicitly model the group-level, high-order dependencies inherent in classroom engagement contagion.

To bridge this gap, we introduce the **Dual-Stream Hypergraph Convolutional Network (DS-HGCN)**, a framework designed specifically to model social contagion for engagement prediction. Our approach leverages a hypergraph to capture the complex, many-to-many relationships within a student group. It operates via two parallel components: a multivariate propagation module to model how engagement spreads among students, and a multi-frequency propagation module to capture the fine-grained distinctions in individual behaviors. To account for varying levels of influence, we further integrate a hypergraph attention mechanism that dynamically assigns weights to these interactions. Our extensive experiments on the RoomReader dataset validate the superiority of our approach. DS-HGCN achieves state-of-the-art accuracy of 94.02% in binary and 81.37% in ternary classification, outperforming prior methods by 2.5% and 5.95%, respectively. In summary, the main contributions of this work are as follows:

- We introduce the concept of engagement contagion into a predictive model, using a hypergraph to capture the complex, group-level influences among students in a classroom.
- We propose a dual-stream architecture, DS-HGCN, that synergistically models both high-order social dependencies and fine-grained feature details.

- We design a hypergraph attention mechanism that dynamically learns the individual differences in engagement propagation.

2   Related Work

2.1   Student Engagement Analysis

Student engagement analysis is a pivotal research area in educational data mining. Traditional engagement analysis has relied on subjective methods like surveys and direct observation, which lack real-time applicability [2,23,28]. Consequently, modern approaches leverage machine learning to analyze visible behaviors like attention [11,13,15,22], but their common reliance on a single data modality fails to capture the multifaceted nature of engagement.

To overcome the limitations of unimodal methods, recent research has explored multimodal data fusion. For instance, researchers have combined visual and temporal data (e.g., CNNs and GRUs) to capture emotional dynamics [8], integrated various biosignals from wearables to gauge physiological states [25], and utilized eye-gaze with other signals in VR environments [1]. Others have analyzed engagement through combined behavioral, emotional, and cognitive lenses [29]. More recently, graph-based models have been proposed to fuse textual, audio, and visual data, offering new perspectives on multimodal analysis [17]. Building on this foundation, our work not only incorporates features related to emotional and behavioral engagement but also models the intricate dependencies between them using a novel graph-based architecture.

2.2   Graph Neural Networks

Graph Neural Networks (GNNs) have proven effective for modeling relational data across diverse domains. In educational contexts, they have been applied to classify student behavioral patterns [21] and to evaluate engagement by fusing multimodal data sources [17].

Standard GNNs are limited to pairwise relationships, whereas classroom interactions are often group-based. Hypergraph Neural Networks (HGNNs) [9] are better suited for these high-order relationships, with advancements including dynamic construction [12] and attention mechanisms [3]. However, a key research gap persists: existing methods overlook **engagement contagion**. Our work is the first to use a hypergraph to explicitly model this group-level peer influence, addressing a critical limitation in prior research.

3   Method

The complete pipeline of the proposed DS-HGCN is illustrated in Fig. 2, which consists of four components. To begin with, the Multi-feature Encoder is designed to extract students' multi-dimensional features (Sect. 3.1). Subsequently, the

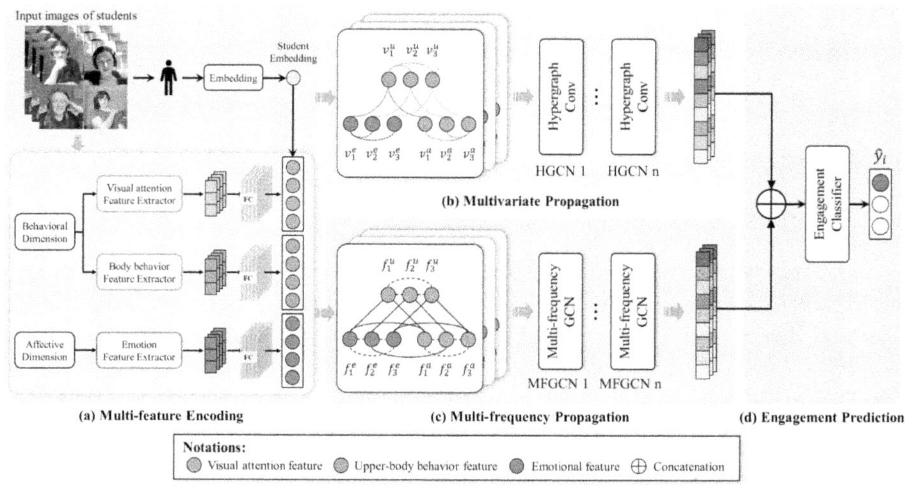

Fig. 2. The pipeline of the proposed DS-HGCN.

Multivariate Propagation module models the contagion of engagement among students (Sect. 3.2). In parallel, the Multi-frequency Propagation module captures multi-frequency information from the extracted features (Sect. 3.3). At the final stage, the Engagement Classifier predicts engagement levels based on the fused representations (Sect. 3.4).

3.1   Multi-feature Encoder

Student engagement consists of behavioral, affective, and cognitive engagement. The multi-feature encoder processes groups of images $\{x_1, x_2, \ldots, x_N\}$, each capturing N students in a classroom at a single moment. For each student S_i, the encoder extracts features corresponding to the affective and behavioral dimensions of engagement, which are the primary focus of this vision-based study.

Specifically, we extract three unimodal representations. For emotional features (x_i^e), we use a pre-trained DDAMFN++ [32] model, omitting its final classification layer. For visual attentional features (x_i^a), we follow prior work [17,24] and use OpenFace [4] to obtain gaze direction, head pose, and facial action units. For upper-body behavior features (x_i^u), we employ HRNet [18] to extract human skeleton movements.

These representations are then projected into a unified D_h-dimensional space using three separate multilayer perceptrons (MLPs):

$$c_i^t = W_t x_i^t + b_i^t, \quad t \in \{e, a, u\} \tag{1}$$

where $c_i^t \in \mathbb{R}^{D_h}$. To account for individual differences, we introduce a student-specific embedding $\hat{s}_i$, which is added to each feature representation. The embedding is computed from a one-hot identifier s_i:

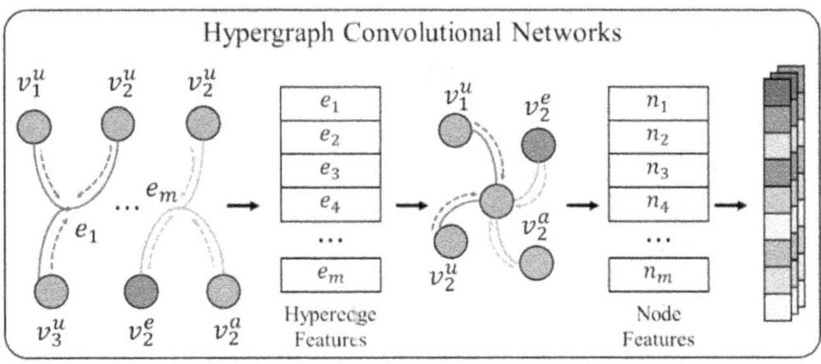

Fig. 3. The illustration of the hyperedge convolution layer, which can perform node-edge-node transform, better refining the features using the hypergraph structure.

$$\hat{s}_i = W_s * s_i, \tag{2}$$

where $\hat{s}_i \in \mathbb{R}^{D_h}$ and W_s is a trainable weight matrix. The final encoded representation for each feature is thus:

$$\hat{c}_i^t = c_i^t + \hat{s}_i, \quad t \in \{e, a, u\}. \tag{3}$$

3.2 Multivariate Propagation

To model engagement contagion, we employ a multivariate propagation module on a hypergraph $\mathcal{H}$. This structure captures heterogeneous feature influences within each student and enables information fusion across different students and dimensions.

Hypergraph Construction. For a classroom of N students, we construct a hypergraph $\mathcal{H} = (\mathcal{V}_{\mathcal{H}}, \mathcal{E}_{\mathcal{H}})$. Its structure is defined by nodes, hyperedges, and an incidence matrix.

Nodes. The node set $\mathcal{V}_{\mathcal{H}}$ contains $3N$ nodes, where each student S_i is represented by a triplet of nodes $\{v_i^e, v_i^a, v_i^u\}$, corresponding to their emotional, attentional, and upper-body behavior features. The initial representation for each node is the corresponding encoded feature $\{\hat{c}_i^e, \hat{c}_i^a, \hat{c}_i^u\}$ derived from Eq. 3.

Hyperedges. To capture both internal feature interactions and external group influences, we define two types of hyperedges in $\mathcal{E}_{\mathcal{H}}$:

- **Multi-dimensional Hyperedges**: To model the dependencies among a single student's affective and behavioral features, a hyperedge connects the three feature nodes $\{v_i^e, v_i^a, v_i^u\}$ for each student S_i.
- **Group Influence Hyperedges**: To model social contagion, for each feature type $t \in \{e, a, u\}$, a hyperedge connects all corresponding nodes $\{v_1^t, \ldots, v_N^t\}$ across all students.

This design, comprising $e \in \mathcal{E}_{\mathcal{H}}(|\mathcal{E}_{\mathcal{H}}| = 3 + N)$ hyperedges, allows the model to capture high-order correlations beyond simple pairwise interactions.

Incidence Matrix. The hypergraph's topology is encoded in an incidence matrix $\mathbf{H} \in \mathbb{R}^{|\mathcal{V}_{\mathcal{H}}| \times |\mathcal{E}_{\mathcal{H}}|}$, where each entry indicates if a node belongs to a hyperedge.

$$H_{ve} = \begin{cases} 1, & \text{if node } v \in \text{hyperedge } e \\ 0, & \text{otherwise} \end{cases} \tag{4}$$

This binary matrix serves as a foundation, which will be dynamically weighted by our attention mechanism in **Hypergraph Attention**.

Hypergraph Convolution. Information propagation across the hypergraph is achieved via a hypergraph convolution operation, which updates node representations by aggregating information from connected nodes through shared hyperedges. We formulate the hypergraph convolution layer as follows:

$$\mathbf{Q}^{(l+1)} = \sigma(\mathbf{D}_{\mathcal{H}}^{-1}\mathbf{H}\mathbf{W}_e\mathbf{B}^{-1}\mathbf{H}^T\mathbf{Q}^{(l)}\mathbf{P}^{(l)}) \tag{5}$$

where $\mathbf{Q}^{(l)} \in \mathbb{R}^{|\mathcal{V}_{\mathcal{H}}| \times D_h}$ is the matrix of node features at layer l, and σ is a non-linear activation function. $\mathbf{D}_{\mathcal{H}}$ and $\mathbf{B}$ are the diagonal degree matrices for the vertices and hyperedges, respectively. $\mathbf{W}_e$ is a diagonal matrix containing learnable weights for each hyperedge, and $\mathbf{P}^{(l)}$ is the trainable weight matrix for the linear transformation at layer l.

This operation is fully differentiable, allowing the model to be trained end-to-end via gradient descent. As illustrated in Fig. 3, the module performs a node-edge-node transformation, effectively refining feature representations based on the high-order relationships encoded in the hypergraph. After L layers of propagation, we obtain the final multivariate representations from the last layer's output $v^x_{i,(L)}$:

$$\overline{v^e_i} = v^e_{i,(L)}, \overline{v^a_i} = v^a_{i,(L)}, \overline{v^u_i} = v^u_{i,(L)} \tag{6}$$

Hypergraph Attention. To overcome the static nature of the binary incidence matrix $\mathbf{H}$, which limits the model's ability to adapt to varying interaction strengths, we introduce a hypergraph attention mechanism. Inspired by [3], this mechanism dynamically learns the importance of each node v within a hyperedge e by computing an attention score $\gamma_e(v)$.

$$\gamma_{e_j}(v_i) = \frac{\exp(\sigma(\text{sim}(v_i\mathbf{P}, e_j\mathbf{P})))}{\sum_{k \in \mathcal{N}_v} \exp(\sigma(\text{sim}(v_i\mathbf{P}, e_k\mathbf{P})))} \tag{7}$$

where $\sigma(\cdot)$ is a non-linear activation function and $\mathcal{N}_v$ denotes the neighborhood set of node v_i. The similarity function, $\text{sim}(\cdot)$, is defined as a learnable projection:

$$\text{sim}(v_i, e_j) = a^T[v_i][e_j] \tag{8}$$

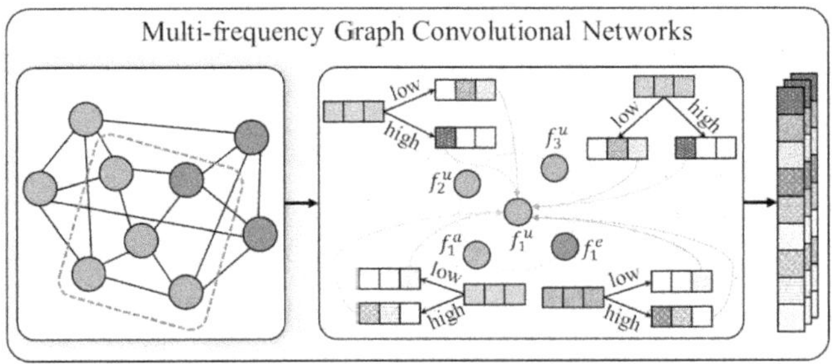

Fig. 4. The illustration of the MFGCN is presented. It aggregates low-frequency and high-frequency signals from neighboring nodes.

where $[\cdot][\cdot]$ denotes concatenation and $\mathbf{a}$ is a trainable weight vector. In this manner, the initial association matrix of the hypergraph is enriched. We represent the attention scores as edge-dependent node weights $\gamma_e(v)$, forming a dynamic weighted association matrix:

$$H_{ve} = \begin{cases} \gamma_e(v), & \text{if node } v \in \text{hyperedge } e \\ 0, & \text{otherwise} \end{cases} \tag{9}$$

By making $\mathbf{H}$ in Eq. 5 dependent on these learnable attention scores, the model can dynamically modulate information flow, effectively capturing the subtle and changing dependencies among student features and group influences during propagation.

3.3   Multi-frequency Propagation

While the multivariate module's aggregation acts as a low-pass filter to capture smoothed dependencies, it risks losing high-frequency details. These details are not noise but often encode critical feature distinctions vital for prediction. To preserve these signals, we introduce a parallel multi-frequency propagation module, inspired by MFGCN [5], designed to integrate both low- and high-frequency information from student features (Fig. 4).

Graph Construction. We construct an undirected graph $\mathcal{G} = (\mathcal{V}_{\mathcal{G}}, \mathcal{E}_{\mathcal{G}})$ that operates in parallel with the hypergraph $\mathcal{H}$. The node set $\mathcal{V}_{\mathcal{G}}$ is identical to $\mathcal{V}_{\mathcal{H}}$, with each node f_i^t ($t \in \{e, a, u\}$) initialized using the encoded representations $\{\hat{c}_i^e, \hat{c}_i^a, \hat{c}_i^u\}$.

Unlike the hypergraph, which uses hyperedges for group dependencies, $\mathcal{G}$ is built on pairwise connectivity to facilitate direct frequency-aware propagation. An edge is created between any two nodes that are connected in the hypergraph structure. This means each node f_i^t is connected to: (1) all nodes $\{f_j^t | j \neq i\}$ representing the same feature from other students, and (2) the other two feature nodes $\{f_i^z | z \neq t\}$ from the same student. The structure is represented by an adjacency matrix $\mathbf{A} \in \mathbb{R}^{|\mathcal{V}_\mathcal{G}| \times |\mathcal{V}_\mathcal{G}|}$, from which we derive the normalized graph Laplacian:

$$\mathbf{L} = \mathbf{I} - \mathbf{D}_\mathcal{G}^{-1/2} \mathbf{A} \mathbf{D}_\mathcal{G}^{-1/2} \tag{10}$$

where $\mathbf{D}_\mathcal{G}$ is the diagonal degree matrix of $\mathcal{G}$ and $\mathbf{I}$ is the identity matrix. This Laplacian matrix is fundamental for defining our frequency-based filters.

Multi-frequency Graph Convolution. To explicitly capture signals across the frequency spectrum, we employ two distinct graph filters: a low-pass filter $\mathcal{F}_l$ and a high-pass filter $\mathcal{F}_h$. Following the design in [5], these are defined based on the graph structure:

$$\begin{aligned}
\mathcal{F}_l &= \mathbf{I} + \mathbf{D}_\mathcal{G}^{-1/2} \mathbf{A} \mathbf{D}_\mathcal{G}^{-1/2} = 2\mathbf{I} - \mathbf{L} \\
\mathcal{F}_h &= \mathbf{I} - \mathbf{D}_\mathcal{G}^{-1/2} \mathbf{A} \mathbf{D}_\mathcal{G}^{-1/2} = \mathbf{L}
\end{aligned} \tag{11}$$

The low-pass filter $\mathcal{F}_l$ averages features from neighbors, promoting smoothness, while the high-pass filter $\mathcal{F}_h$, being the graph Laplacian itself, amplifies the differences between a node and its neighbors, capturing high-frequency distinctions.

We then integrate these filters into a unified propagation layer where the model learns to adaptively combine the low- and high-frequency components. The feature update rule for layer k, which takes the feature matrix $\mathbf{F}^{(k)}$ as input, is:

$$\mathbf{F}^{(k+1)} = \sigma\left((\mathcal{F}_l \mathbf{F}^{(k)}) \mathbf{W}_l^{(k)} + (\mathcal{F}_h \mathbf{F}^{(k)}) \mathbf{W}_h^{(k)} \right) \tag{12}$$

Here, $\mathbf{F}^{(k)}$ is the matrix of node features $f_{i,(k)}^t$ at layer k. $\mathbf{W}_l^{(k)}$ and $\mathbf{W}_h^{(k)}$ are learnable weight matrices that adaptively balance the influence of low- and high-frequency signals, and σ is a non-linear activation function.

By stacking K such layers, the module iteratively propagates and refines the multi-frequency information. After K layers of message passing, the final frequency-aware engagement representations are obtained as:

$$\overline{f_i^e} = f_{i,(K)}^e, \overline{f_i^a} = f_{i,(K)}^a, \overline{f_i^u} = f_{i,(K)}^u \tag{13}$$

3.4   Engagement Prediction

After obtaining representations from both the multivariate and multi-frequency modules, the final step is to predict the engagement state for each student, categorized into one of C predefined classes. To achieve this, we first form a comprehensive representation μ_i for each student S_i by concatenating the outputs from both propagation streams:

$$\mu_i = \overline{v_i^e} \oplus \overline{f_i^e} \oplus \overline{v_i^a} \oplus \overline{f_i^a} \oplus \overline{v_i^u} \oplus \overline{f_i^u} \tag{14}$$

where μ_i serves as a comprehensive feature representation, capturing engagement contagion and multi-frequency interactions relevant to engagement prediction.

The engagement classification is then performed by passing μ_i through a transformation layer followed by a softmax function:

$$\mathcal{P}_i = \mathrm{softmax}(W_4 \cdot \mathrm{ReLU}(\mu_i) + b_4),$$
$$\hat{y}_i = \arg\max_{\tau}(\mathcal{P}_i[\tau]), \tag{15}$$

where W_4 is a trainable weight matrix, $\mathcal{P}_i \in \mathbb{R}^C$ represents the probability distribution over engagement categories, and $\hat{y}_i$ is the predicted engagement label for student S_i.

The model is trained end-to-end by minimizing the standard categorical cross-entropy loss, averaged over all student samples in the training set $\mathcal{D}$, with L2 regularization to prevent overfitting. The loss function is defined as:

$$\mathcal{L} = -\frac{1}{|\mathcal{D}|} \sum_{i \in \mathcal{D}} \log \mathcal{P}_i[y_i] + \lambda \|\theta\|_2^2 \tag{16}$$

where y_i is the ground-truth label for student S_i, $\mathcal{P}_i[y_i]$ is the model's predicted probability for that true class, θ represents all trainable parameters of the model, and λ is the hyperparameter controlling the strength of the L2 regularization.

4 Experimental Results

In this section, we conduct a series of comprehensive experiments to rigorously evaluate the effectiveness and robustness of our proposed DS-HGCN. We first detail the experimental setup in Sect. 4.1. We then demonstrate the superiority of our model by comparing it against state-of-the-art methods in Sect. 4.2. To validate our design choices, we present in-depth ablation studies in Sect. 4.3 to analyze the contribution of each core component. Finally, we provide further analysis on hyperparameter sensitivity and data efficiency in Sect. 4.4 to offer a holistic assessment of the model.

4.1 Experimental Setup

Data Preparation. We evaluate our method on the RoomReader dataset [24], a benchmark for student engagement analysis. Following data filtering and frame extraction, we address the dataset's significant class imbalance as noted in prior work [17]. Following established protocols [17,26], we formulate two tasks from the continuous annotations: a **binary** task ('Engaged' vs. 'Disengaged') and a **ternary** task ('low' vs. 'medium' vs. 'high' engagement), resulting in a final evaluation set of 1,252 unique classroom snapshots.

Implementation Details. Our model is implemented in PyTorch and trained on a single NVIDIA 3090 GPU. We use the Adam optimizer with an initial learning rate of 1×10^{-5}. A dropout rate of 0.5 is applied to the network to mitigate overfitting. To address the remaining class imbalance, we incorporate class weights into the cross-entropy loss function during training. The number of hypergraph convolution layers (L) and graph convolution layers (K) were set to 3 and 3, respectively. Model performance is evaluated using Accuracy, F_1-score, and Area Under the Curve (AUC).

4.2   Baseline Comparisons

To validate the effectiveness of our proposed DS-HGCN, we conducted comprehensive comparisons against several representative and state-of-the-art engagement prediction models. For a fair evaluation, We reimplemented these baselines using the RoomReader dataset, adhering to the specified data formats. The baselines include:

- **Single-Feature Models:** This category benchmarks conventional, non-graph-based approaches that model engagement from a single feature. Key examples include: **TCCT-NET** [30], which analyzes behavioral signals via a two-stream fusion network; **EnsModel** [27], which uses a deep network to predict engagement from facial behaviors; **ConvLSTM** [7], which processes video frames with an integrated convolutional regression model; **ED-MTT** [6], which improves accuracy through a multi-task training framework; and **EG-NET** [20], which applies a standard CNN for facial expression analysis.
- **Multi-Feature Model:** To demonstrate the benefit of incorporating multiple features, we compared **Bootstrap** [31], a method that combines both head and body features, representing a step beyond single-feature analysis.
- **Graph-based Model (SOTA):** Finally, to position our work against the direct state-of-the-art, we benchmark against **Haar-MGL** [17]. This model employs a multimodal graph learning framework to fuse text, audio, and image data, providing the most relevant and powerful point of comparison for graph-based engagement prediction.

Table 1 presents the quantitative results, averaged over five independent trials with an 80%/20% training/testing split. As shown, DS-HGCN significantly outperforms all baselines across both binary and ternary classification tasks. The comparison reveals two key insights. First, multi-feature methods consistently surpass single-feature models, confirming the value of a holistic behavioral analysis. Second, DS-HGCN establishes a new state-of-the-art, outperforming the strong graph-based Haar-MGL. This superiority highlights the unique advantage of our dual-stream hypergraph network in explicitly modeling higher-order social contagion–a critical dynamic overlooked by previous approaches.

4.3   Ablation Study

Our ablation study (Table 2) validates the contribution of each component in DS-HGCN. Removing the multivariate propagation stream (Variant 1) causes

Table 1. Comparison with previous state-of-the-art methods on the RoomReader dataset. Entries marked with $\circ$ are taken from paper [17], whereas those with $\dagger$ come from our re-implementation using open-source codes.

Methods	Binary Classification Acc.(%)	Ternary Classification Acc.(%)	Feature Dimension Type
TCCT-NET[30]	73.99 ± 1.43	60.48 ± 1.18	Single
EnsModel[27]	75.30 ± 3.50	69.53 ± 3.54	Single
ConvLSTM[7]	76.50 ± 1.85	74.53 ± 1.50	Single
EG-NET[20]	77.38 ± 1.27	72.76 ± 2.24	Single
ED-MTT[6]	73.80 ± 3.35	71.20 ± 1.35	Single
Bootstrap[31]	82.42 ± 2.15	75.42 ± 2.43	Multiple
Haar-MGL[17]	90.18 ± 1.34	-	Multiple
DS-HGCN(Ours)	**94.02 ± 0.49**	**81.37 ± 0.34**	Multiple

Table 2. Ablation studies of DS-HGCN. We compare our method with a collection of variants described in Sect. 4.3

Candidates	Binary Classification Task			Ternary Classification Task		
	Acc. (%)	F_1	AUC	Acc. (%)	F_1	AUC
DS-HGCN(full)	**94.02**	**0.939**	**0.893**	**81.37**	**0.816**	**0.921**
1 w/o multivariate info.	89.84	0.891	0.845	75.70	0.755	0.885
2 w/o multi-frequency info.	92.13	0.917	0.857	77.29	0.776	0.904
3 w/o visual attention features.	84.50	0.832	0.805	68.45	0.685	0.843
4 w/o body behavior features.	86.37	0.859	0.823	73.37	0.742	0.862
5 w/o emotion features.	81.56	0.803	0.784	62.77	0.631	0.784
6 w/o Hypergraph Attention.	92.73	0.925	0.872	79.23	0.793	0.867

the most significant accuracy drop (4.18%/5.67% in binary/ternary tasks), confirming that modeling social contagion via hypergraphs is the primary driver of our model's success. The multi-frequency stream (Variant 2) is also crucial, as its absence markedly degrades performance. An analysis of input features (Variants 3–5) reveals that emotional cues are indispensable, with their removal causing the sharpest performance decline (12.46% in binary accuracy). Finally, disabling hypergraph attention (Variant 6) impairs performance, validating our dynamic weighting scheme. These results affirm that each design choice is integral to our model's state-of-the-art performance.

4.4 Further Analysis

Discussions on Graph Layers. We analyzed the impact of model depth by varying the number of hypergraph (L) and graph (K) layers from 1 to 6. As illustrated in Fig. 5, performance peaks at $L = 3$ and $K = 3$ for both classification tasks. This suggests a depth of 3 is optimal for capturing engagement contagion without causing over-smoothing, as deeper models yield negligible gains.

Impact of Training Data Scale. To assess data efficiency, we trained our model on subsets of the training data, ranging from 20% to 80%. Figure 6 shows that DS-HGCN consistently outperforms baselines, even in low-data regimes. Notably, its smaller and more stable standard deviation across all data scales confirms its superior robustness and generalization capability.

Analysis of Computational Complexity. We evaluated the overhead of our hypergraph attention (HA) mechanism. Table 3 shows that the full DS-HGCN model introduces only a marginal increase in parameters (3.076M to 3.079M) and a slight rise in training time compared to a version without attention. Crucially, the inference time remains highly efficient (8.52 ms/batch), making our approach practical for applications like generating periodic engagement reports.

Table 3. Comparison of computational costs and efficiency.

Model	Parameters (M)	Training Time (s/epoch)	Inference Time (ms/batch)
DS-HGCN (w/o HA)	3.076	3.69	7.31
DS-HGCN (full)	3.079	4.39	8.52

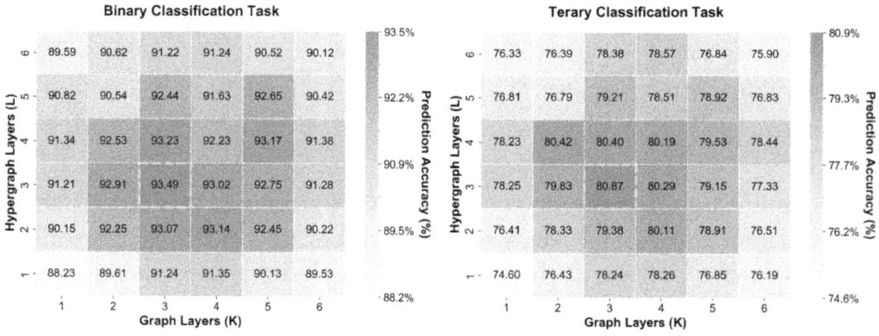

Fig. 5. Heatmaps illustrating the performance on binary and ternary classification tasks with varying numbers of hypergraph layers (L) and graph layers (K).

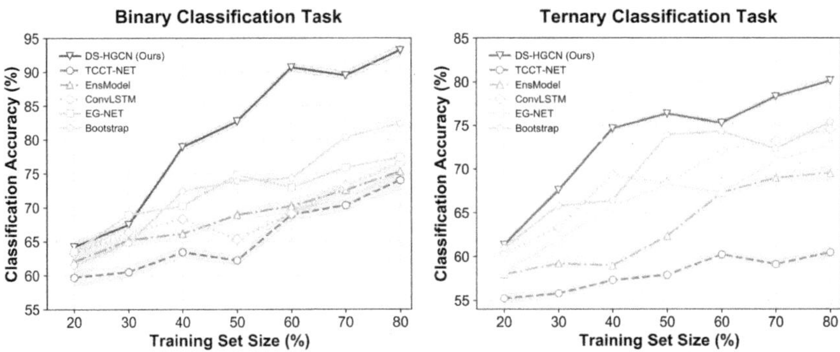

Fig. 6. Comparing models' performance under varying training data proportions for both classification tasks. Shaded area indicates standard deviation.

5   Conclusion

In this paper, we introduced DS-HGCN, a dual-stream hypergraph convolutional network that models social contagion to predict student engagement. Our approach employs parallel hypergraph and graph convolutional networks to explore high-order and complex relationships among various student features and fully leverage the correlations and dependencies of features across different frequency information. Extensive experiments on the RoomReader dataset demonstrate the superiority of our method, achieving 94.02% accuracy in binary and 81.37% in ternary classification. While our image-based approach is effective, future work could enhance it by incorporating other modalities like audio and text or exploring proxies for cognitive engagement. Ultimately, DS-HGCN highlights the importance of social context in learning analytics and provides a powerful tool for automated engagement monitoring.

References

1. Asish, S.M., Kulshreshth, A.K., Borst, C.W.: Detecting distracted students in educational VR environments using machine learning on eye gaze data. Comput. Graph. **109**, 75–87 (2022)
2. Azevedo, R.: Defining and measuring engagement and learning in science: conceptual, theoretical, methodological, and analytical issues. Educ. Psychol. **50**(1), 84–94 (2015)
3. Bai, S., Zhang, F., Torr, P.H.: Hypergraph convolution and hypergraph attention. Pattern Recogn. **110**, 107637 (2021)
4. Baltrušaitis, T., Robinson, P., Morency, L.P.: OpenFace: an open source facial behavior analysis toolkit. In: 2016 IEEE Winter Conference on Applications of Computer Vision (WACV), pp. 1–10. IEEE (2016)
5. Bo, D., Wang, X., Shi, C., Shen, H.: Beyond low-frequency information in graph convolutional networks. In: Proceedings of the AAAI Conference on Artificial Intelligence, vol. 35, pp. 3950–3957 (2021)

6. Copur, O., Nakıp, M., Scardapane, S., Slowack, J.: Engagement detection with multi-task training in e-learning environments. In: International Conference on Image Analysis and Processing, pp. 411–422. Springer (2022)
7. Del Duchetto, F., Baxter, P., Hanheide, M.: Are you still with me? Continuous engagement assessment from a robot's point of view. Front. Robot. AI **7**, 116 (2020)
8. Ding, L.: Online teaching emotion analysis based on GRU and nonlinear transformer algorithm. PeerJ Comput. Sci. **9**, e1696 (2023)
9. Feng, Y., You, H., Zhang, Z., Ji, R., Gao, Y.: Hypergraph neural networks. In: Proceedings of the AAAI Conference on Artificial Intelligence, vol. 33, pp. 3558–3565 (2019)
10. Fredricks, J.A., Blumenfeld, P.C., Paris, A.H.: School engagement: potential of the concept, state of the evidence. Rev. Educ. Res. **74**(1), 59–109 (2004)
11. Gupta, S., Kumar, P., Tekchandani, R.K.: Facial emotion recognition based real-time learner engagement detection system in online learning context using deep learning models. Multimedia Tools Appl. **82**(8), 11365–11394 (2023)
12. Jiang, J., Wei, Y., Feng, Y., Cao, J., Gao, Y.: Dynamic hypergraph neural networks. In: Proceedings of the International Joint Conference on Artificial Intelligence (IJCAI), pp. 2635–2641 (2019)
13. Khenkar, S., Jarraya, S.K.: Engagement detection based on analyzing micro body gestures using 3D CNN. Comput. Mater. Continua **70**(2) (2022)
14. King, R.B., Mendoza, N.B.: The social contagion of students' social goals and its influence on engagement in school. Learn. Individ. Differ. **88**, 102004 (2021)
15. Kodithuwakku, J., Arachchi, D.D., Rajasekera, J.: An emotion and attention recognition system to classify the level of engagement to a video conversation by participants in real time using machine learning models and utilizing a neural accelerator chip. Algorithms **15**(5), 150 (2022)
16. Kuh, G.D.: Assessing what really matters to student learning inside the national survey of student engagement. Change Mag. High. Learn. **33**(3), 10–17 (2001)
17. Li, M., Zhuang, X., Bai, L., Ding, W.: Multimodal graph learning based on 3D Haar semi-tight framelet for student engagement prediction. Inf. Fusion **105**, 102224 (2024)
18. Lu, B., Sun, Y., Yang, Z., Song, R., Jiang, H., Liu, Y.: HRNet: 3D object detection network for point cloud with hierarchical refinement. Pattern Recogn. **149**, 110254 (2024)
19. Mendoza, N.B., King, R.B.: The social contagion of student engagement in school. Sch. Psychol. Int. **41**(5), 454–474 (2020)
20. Mohamad Nezami, O., Dras, M., Hamey, L., Richards, D., Wan, S., Paris, C.: Automatic recognition of student engagement using deep learning and facial expression. In: Brefeld, U., Fromont, E., Hotho, A., Knobbe, A., Maathuis, M., Robardet, C. (eds.) ECML PKDD 2019. LNCS (LNAI), vol. 11908, pp. 273–289. Springer, Cham (2020). https://doi.org/10.1007/978-3-030-46133-1_17
21. Mubarak, A.A., Cao, H., Hezam, I.M., Hao, F.: Modeling students' performance using graph convolutional networks. Complex Intell. Syst. **8**(3), 2183–2201 (2022)
22. Ngoc Anh, B., et al.: A computer-vision based application for student behavior monitoring in classroom. Appl. Sci. **9**(22), 4729 (2019)
23. Pekrun, R., Goetz, T., Frenzel, A.C., Barchfeld, P., Perry, R.P.: Measuring emotions in students' learning and performance: the achievement emotions questionnaire (AEQ). Contemp. Educ. Psychol. **36**(1), 36–48 (2011)

24. Reverdy, J., Russell, S.O., Duquenne, L., Garaialde, D., Cowan, B.R., Harte, N.: RoomReader: a multimodal corpus of online multiparty conversational interactions. In: Proceedings of the Thirteenth Language Resources and Evaluation Conference, pp. 2517–2527 (2022)
25. Södergård, C., Laakko, T.: Inferring students' self-assessed concentration levels in daily life using biosignal data from wearables. IEEE Access **11**, 30308–30323 (2023)
26. Sümer, Ö., Goldberg, P., D'Mello, S., Gerjets, P., Trautwein, U., Kasneci, E.: Multimodal engagement analysis from facial videos in the classroom. IEEE Trans. Affect. Comput. **14**(2), 1012–1027 (2021)
27. Thong Huynh, V., Kim, S.H., Lee, G.S., Yang, H.J.: Engagement intensity prediction withfacial behavior features. In: 2019 International Conference on Multimodal Interaction, pp. 567–571 (2019)
28. Vallerand, R.J., Pelletier, L.G., Blais, M.R., Briere, N.M., Senecal, C., Vallieres, E.F.: The academic motivation scale: a measure of intrinsic, extrinsic, and amotivation in education. Educ. Psychol. Measur. **52**(4), 1003–1017 (1992)
29. Vanneste, P., et al.: Computer vision and human behaviour, emotion and cognition detection: a use case on student engagement. Mathematics **9**(3), 287 (2021)
30. Vedernikov, A., Kumar, P., Chen, H., Seppänen, T., Li, X.: TCCT-Net: two-stream network architecture for fast and efficient engagement estimation via behavioral feature signals. In: Proceedings of the IEEE/CVF Conference on Computer Vision and Pattern Recognition, pp. 4723–4732 (2024)
31. Wang, K., Yang, J., Guo, D., Zhang, K., Peng, X., Qiao, Y.: Bootstrap model ensemble and rank loss for engagement intensity regression. In: 2019 International Conference on Multimodal Interaction, pp. 551–556 (2019)
32. Zhang, S., Zhang, Y., Zhang, Y., Wang, Y., Song, Z.: A dual-direction attention mixed feature network for facial expression recognition. Electronics **12**(17), 3595 (2023)

Dissecting Deepfake Artifacts
via Multimodal Explanations

Yannan Bai[1,2], Danding Wang[1(✉)], Sheng Tang[1,2], Juan Cao[1,2],
and Jintao Li[1]

[1] Institute of Computing Technology, Chinese Academy of Sciences, Beijing, China
`{baiyannan21b,wangdanding,ts,caojuan,jtli}@ict.ac.cn`
[2] University of Chinese Academy of Sciences, Beijing, China

Abstract. The rapid advancement of AIGC technologies has enabled the widespread creation of realistic deepfake images, posing significant challenges for laypeople to recognize fake images. In high-stakes scenarios such as media forensics, convincing and interpretable explanations of deepfake detectors are crucial for human decision-making. However, existing methods primarily provide binary real-or-fake predictions, and their visual explanations–such as CAM saliency maps or forgery localization–are typically coarse-grained and fail to indicate which artifacts should be inspected. Recent multimodal large language model (MLLM)-based efforts have explored textual explanations, yet the difficulty of grounding descriptions in images and the risk of contradictory outputs undermine their reliability. To address these challenges, we present FakeArti, a new dataset containing 1,414 high-quality deepfake images with detailed artifact-level explanations and 4,170 pixel-level artifact masks, establishing a benchmark for deepfake explanation evaluation. Furthermore, we propose Attentive Deepfake Artifact Dissection (ADAD), an interpretable detection framework that generates visual grounding of artifacts and textual explanations, offering explicit cues on what artifacts appear and where they are located. ADAD disentangles forgery artifacts from semantic content and enhances multimodal alignment, thereby bridging the gap between model decisions and human reasoning. Extensive experiments demonstrate that ADAD not only achieves state-of-the-art performance in explanation generation and deepfake detection but also exhibits superior generalization ability. This work highlights how incorporating human-perceptible visual artifacts into deepfake detection facilitates more trustworthy and human-centered deepfake forensics.

Keywords: Deepfake Detection · Multimedia Forensics · Explainable Artificial Intelligence · Vision-Language Models

1 Introduction

The prevalence of deepfake tools and applications has significantly lowered the threshold for generating deepfakes. People can easily create unlimited deepfake

J. Lokoč et al. (Eds.): MMM 2026, LNCS 16412, pp. 32–45, 2026.
https://doi.org/10.1007/978-981-95-6950-2_3

videos and images through a 'one-click' operation, which may spread misinformation and lead to potential societal issues. It is challenging for laypeople to distinguish realistic deepfakes from tremendous media content [1,2]. Advanced deepfake detection methods have been proposed to combat the emergent deepfake generation techniques.

Despite the state-of-the-art performance of deepfake detectors, there remains a critical demand for convincing and reliable explanations, particularly in high-stakes domains such as media forensics and economic security. Interpretable deepfake detection models can help laypeople understand the reasoning process and build trust in the model's predictions. Consequently, there is a growing interest in developing interpretable deepfake detection methods that can provide human-understandable explanations and better AI support.

Earlier studies have leveraged forgery traces, such as blending boundary [3], eye blinking [4], and gaze tracking [5], to detect deepfake images. However, these approaches focus on specific forgery cues that evolving deepfake techniques can easily circumvent. In addition, the binary real-or-fake classification offers no insight into the model's reasoning process. Classic Explainable Artificial Intelligence (XAI) methods have been applied to generate visual explanations of the deepfake detector's decision (Fig. 1a). Nevertheless, human studies indicate that the widely-used explanation methods, such as highlighting salient regions with Class Activation Mapping (CAM), do not improve human accuracy [6]. XAI-based visualizations are often coarse-grained, lack clear guidance on what artifacts may exist, and sometimes highlight irrelevant background areas.

Recently, MLLMs achieve remarkable performance across visual tasks, including deepfake detection, as demonstrated by prompt-engineering experiments [7] and comprehensive benchmarks [8]. Reformulating deepfake detection as a Visual Question Answering (VQA) task allows detailed textual explanations [9,10]. Nonetheless, grounding text phrases to corresponding image regions remains challenging, and lengthy or contradictory descriptions can obscure key information, reducing the interpretability and reliability of the model's explanations (Fig. 1b).

To address these challenges, we first introduce FakeArti, a novel dataset comprising 1,414 high-quality deepfake images with detailed artifact-level explanations and 4,170 manually annotated pixel-level artifact masks. Building upon this dataset, we design an evaluation framework for deepfake explanation, comprehensively assessing the explanations from two perspectives: artifact type and manipulated facial regions. We propose Attentive Deepfake Artifact Dissection (ADAD), an interpretable deepfake detection method that disentangles forgery artifacts from semantic content and enhances the modality consistency. ADAD provides multimodal explanations that integrate visual grounding and textual guidance, offering laypeople explicit instructions on what artifacts to attend to and where they appear.

We summarize our contributions as follows:

- We introduce FakeArti, a challenging dataset for interpretable deepfake detection with pixel-level artifacts annotations and detailed explanations of diverse

deepfake images, effectively addressing the lack of explanation evaluation within deepfake detection.
- We propose ADAD, a deepfake detection method with visual grounding of various artifacts and explanation generation, bridging the gap between model decision and human reasoning.
- We enhance the image-text alignment of our multimodal deepfake explanation, and extensive experiments demonstrate that ADAD not only achieves state-of-the-art performance in explanation generation and deepfake detection, exhibiting superior generalization ability.

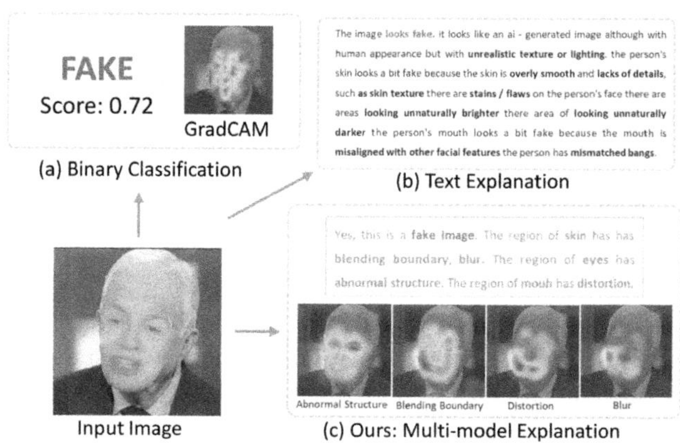

Fig. 1. (a) represents conventional deepfake detectors, which output a binary decision with a probability score and visualization of GradCAM. (b) represents LLM-based detectors, which output textual explanations. (c) In this work, we present an interpretable deepfake detector that generates visual grounding of artifacts and textual explanations.

2   Related Works

2.1   Interpretable Deepfake Detection

Deep learning has achieved certain results in the field of forged image detection. Advanced forgery detectors can achieve an accuracy of 86.3% at identifying AI-generated images, while under the same scene setting [11], the recognition accuracy of humans is only 61.3%. After relevant training and guidance in forgery detection, humans can better identify forged images. Experiments in [12] show that given the types and locations of artifacts that exist in deepfake images, the recognition accuracy of humans increases from 59% to 64%; and the short-term (10-min) training course designed by [13] can improve the accuracy of volunteers in identifying deepfake images by about 30%, while the recognition accuracy of real images decreases by 9%.

In contrast, the superior deepfake detection model cannot help users identify deepfake images. Thus, interpretable deepfake detection models are required to provide better guidance with explanations in either a visual or a textual format. Although Grad-CAM exhibits excellent interpretability in indoor scene and landscape recognition [14], it fails to improve human performance in deepfake detection tasks [15]. The visual explanation is generated through Explainable Artificial Intelligence (XAI) methods, such as Grad CAM [16], SHAP [17], and relevancy map [18]. A quantitative assessment framework [19] proves that LIME scores the best among Grad CAM−+, RISE, SHAP, LIME and SOBOL. However, the visualization of LIME only provides coarse segments of relevant or manipulated regions without further explanations. The popular visualization method of using CAM to highlight the model's salient regions does not help human's determination in the deepfake detection task [6].

Recent works explore the textual explanation of face forgery by leveraging the capabilities of Large Language Models (LLMs). VLFFD [9] proposes a novel annotation process to generate text descriptions for deepfake images and then jointly fine-tunes the multimodal model through these image-text pairs. A DD-VQA (Deepfake Detection VQA) dataset [10] is constructed to train a BLIP model to reason based on common sense knowledge and generate textual explanations to describe the authenticity of images. MFCLIP [20] mines comprehensive and fine-grained forgery traces via hierarchical text prompts.

2.2 Multimodal Large Language Models

Recently, multimodal large language models (MLLMs) such as GPT-4o and other open-source MLLMs like LLaVA [21] and MiniGPT4 [22] have demonstrated their significant multimodal understanding and analysis capabilities. Some preliminary work [8] explores their capabilities in deepfake detection through well-designed prompt engineering.

Benchmarks [23,24] are designed to evaluate the fine-grained forgery detection capabilities of multiple multimodal large language models in binary classification, multiple-choice questions, and open VQA. Fakeshield [25] and SIDA [26] fine-tunes the MLLM based on the constructed dataset and applies it to the fields of deepfake detection and tampering localization, respectively, providing user-friendly and interpretable results. M2F2-Det [27] uses customized forgery cue learning to migrate the CLIP model to the field of deepfake detection and integrates LLMs to provide detailed textual explanations of its detection decisions. Existing forgery detection explanation methods based on large models only evaluate the performance of forgery detection without explanations of their reasoning and judgment. The evaluation of textual explanations is often based on qualitative result presentation and machine translation evaluation indicators (such as BLEU and ROUGE) and lacks an evaluation of the accuracy of fine-grained visual artifact recognition. At the same time, most methods focus mainly on textual explanation generation and have not explored the fine-grained visual localization of artifacts.

3   Methodology

To deliver clear and concise guidance on where and what to focus on in deepfake images, we design a multi-modal explanation in the format of region and artifact, as shown in Fig. 1. Text explanation consists of facial regions and recognized visual artifacts, where *artifact* stands for the spotted visual artifact (such as blur, blending boundary, and distortion) in deepfake images, and *region* indicates the located facial areas of artifacts. The Artifact Highlighting module provides a set of images with artifacts highlighted as visual explanations.

Figure 2 demonstrates the internal workflow of the proposed method. We dissect the deepfake artifacts from the extracted features in the Attentive Artifacts Dissection module, allowing image embeddings related to artifacts and semantic information to be decoupled. Then we leverage MLLM's capability to incorporate alignment between image and text. Given the language instruction of forgery detection and a list of possible artifacts, text descriptions of manipulated regions and their corresponding artifact types are generated. Artifact Highlighting indicates the locations of spotted artifacts in the image through the interaction between text and image in the attention block.

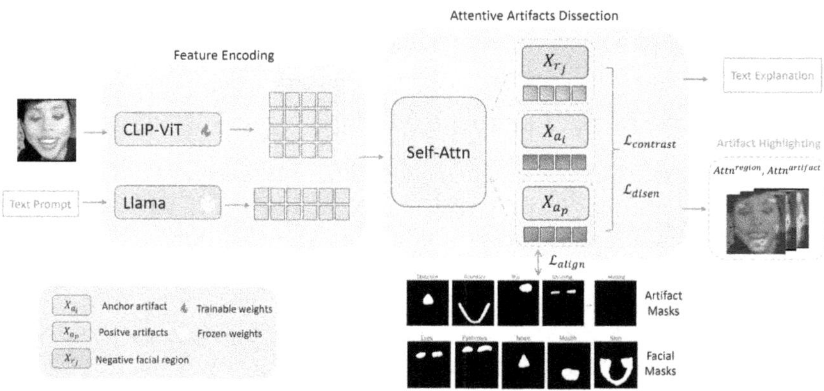

Fig. 2. The workflow of our proposed method.

3.1   FakeArti Dataset Collection

Existing deepfake datasets contain binary labels (real or fake) or sentence annotations, lacking the discrimination of various artifacts. Thus, we categorize six common artifacts (blur, blending boundary, color inconsistency, distortion, abnormal structure, and abnormal skin texture) and construct our FakeArti dataset with annotations of artifact labels and masks.

The annotated images are collected from FaceForensics++ [28], DeeperForensics [29], DFDC [30] and ForgeryNet [31]. We extract one frame from the selected videos and crop the human face from the frame.

We recruited 77 participants via the Prolific platform and implemented a two-stage human annotation process to construct the FakeArti dataset. Participants were aged 1858 years (mean = 28.3), with a balanced gender distribution (41 females, 36 males) and diverse nationalities from 20 countries, including the United Kingdom, United States, Canada, and China. Before annotation, all participants were briefed on the study's purpose–detecting perceptible artifacts in AI-generated images–and were fairly compensated in accordance with Prolific standards. In the first stage, participants were presented with individual images and asked to judge their authenticity (real vs. AI-generated). For images judged as fake, they are required to select the visible artifacts. To ensure reliability, images for which more than half of the participants disagreed with the ground-truth labels were excluded from the next stage. In the second stage, participants were shown only the filtered subset and asked to precisely localize the designated artifact regions using an interactive brush-based labeling tool.

Before the main task, each participant completed a pilot tutorial covering six artifact categories with corresponding visual examples, as shown in Fig. 3. Participants proceeded only after completing a qualification test and demonstrating understanding of expert-provided reference labels. During annotation, redundant labeling was employed, where each image was annotated by three independent participants. Disagreements were resolved by majority voting, and all final annotations were manually reviewed for quality control.

The final FakeArti dataset contains 1,414 images and 4,170 artifact masks. The artifacts include blur, blending boundary, color inconsistency, distortion, abnormal structure, and abnormal skin texture.

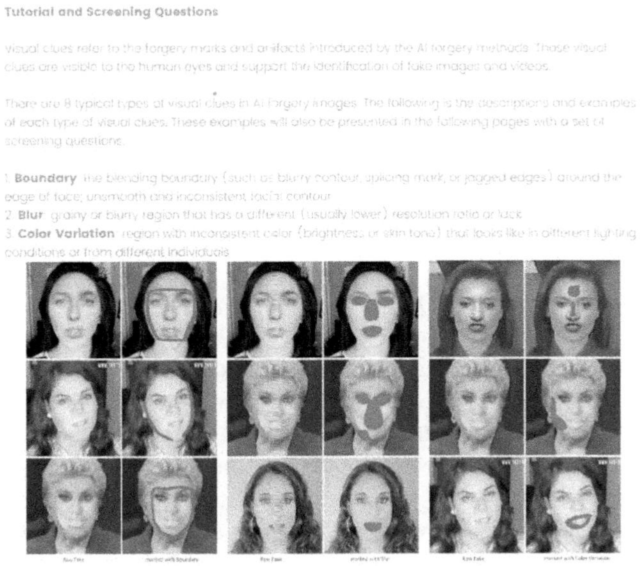

Fig. 3. Pilot tutorial for the artifact annotation.

3.2   Attentive Artifacts Dissection

Both real and fake images contain content information that can establish the identity, which makes the distinct artifacts critical for deepfake detection [32]. To this end, we propose an Artifacts Dissection module that leverages MLLM's knowledge to disentangle deepfake artifacts from content information.

To preserve the discriminative power of artifact-related features, the Artifact Dissection module is designed to pull together the embedding of different artifacts and pull away the semantic features of content information. Based on the popular InfoNCE loss [33], our artifact-dissection contrastive loss can be written as follows:

$$\mathcal{L}_{contrast} = -\sum_i log\frac{exp(X_{a_i}, X_{ap})}{exp(X_{a_i}, X_{ap}) + \sum_j exp(X_{a_i}, X_{r_j})}, \tag{1}$$

where X_{a_i} is the image embedding related to the ith artifact, X_{ap} is all the other artifacts, and X_{r_j} is the image embedding related to the jth content information.

The Artifact Dissection module contrasts the self-inconsistency within the image. We segment the artifact embedding X_a from the image embedding X in line with the artifact masks $\mathcal{M}_a$ and the content embedding X_r in line with the face segmentation masks $\mathcal{M}_r$. The artifact masks are the hand-annotated labels from the FakeArti dataset, while the face segmentation masks are automatically generated by a BiseNet [34] face parser.

For real image features X_r, since all patches belong to authentic images and there is no artifact, we expect the attentive image embeddings to be homogeneous. Thus, we obtain the contrastive loss for real ones from its self-similarity calculation.

3.3   Artifact Alignment and Highlighting

To strengthen the faithfulness of textual explanation to the deepfake image and provide precise localization of artifacts, we propose a Text-and-Image Alignment loss to align text tokens with their associated image embeddings and enhance the modality consistency.

The visual embeddings' dependency on the text tokens can be calculated from the attention scores as follows:

$$Attention(Q, K, V) = softmax(\frac{QK^T}{\sqrt{d_k}})V, \tag{2}$$

where the query vector Q is obtained from the text tokens, the key vector K from the image embeddings, and the value vector V reflects the relative contribution of each image patch. Given such a dependency relationship between text and image tokens, we can highlight the spotted artifacts on the attention map, thus providing instructions on what to focus on to discriminate the deepfake images.

Based on the relevancy between text tokens and visual embeddings, we can locate the corresponding image patches of recognized artifacts. A Binary Cross-Entropy Loss is applied to align the attention map $\mathcal{A}$ of these image patches with the annotated artifact mask $\mathcal{M}$, which is defined as below:

$$\mathcal{L}_{align} = -(\mathcal{M}log\mathcal{A} + (1 - \mathcal{M})log(1 - \mathcal{A})), \tag{3}$$

To further refine the dissected artifacts and improve the fine-grained detection performance, we design an artifact disentanglement loss to constrain the distance between different artifacts. Let $\{X_{a_i}\}_{i=1}^{K}$ be the set of explanation heatmaps for K types of deepfake artifacts as defined in Sect. 3.2, and $D(\cdot,\cdot)$ calculates the distance.

$$\mathcal{L}_{disen} = -\sum_{i}^{K}\sum_{k,k\neq i}^{K} D(X_{a_i}, X_{a_k}), \tag{4}$$

During training, the overall loss function is defined as:

$$\mathcal{L} = \mathcal{L}_{contrast} + \lambda_1\mathcal{L}_{disen} + \lambda_2\mathcal{L}_{align}, \tag{5}$$

where λ_1 and λ_2 are hyperparameters that control the weights of the different loss components.

4 Experiments

Dataset: We evaluate our method on both general deepfake detection (real and fake) and fine-grained detection (artifacts and manipulated facial regions) tasks. For general detection, we conduct experiments on four challenging datasets: DD-VQA [10], FakeArti, Celeb-DF [30], and DFDC [30]. For fine-grained detection, we evaluate on DD-VQA, FakeArti, and SeqDeepFake [35].

DD-VQA dataset includes 1,223 question-answer pairs of 242 images, which follows the FaceForensics++ [28] train/test splits. The question-answer pairs contain manually annotated text descriptions of different facial regions to discern their authenticity, including skin, eyes, nose, mouth, and eyebrows.

FakeArti, our newly constructed dataset, contains 1414 images and 4170 artifact masks. The training set complements the DD-VQA dataset with human-annotated artifact masks. The testing set is collected from the test split of FF++, DeeperForensics [29], DFDC, and ForgeryNet [31]. Details can be found in Sect. 3.1.

SeqDeepFake dataset consists of 85K sequentially manipulated face images generated using two different facial manipulation methods. The subset of facial component manipulation is utilized for testing.

Implementation. ADAD is implemented using PyTorch and trained on the DD-VQA dataset with our newly annotated artifact masks, which is a subset of the FF++ dataset. We use Llava-1.5-13B as our backbone and all experiments were conducted using four NVIDIA A100 GPUs with 40GB of memory. We use an Adam optimizer with a learning rate that decays from 2×10^{-4} to 1×10^{-7}.

Metrics: Accuracy and AUC (Area Under Curve) are the most common metrics in the deepfake detection task. However, as AUC is calculated based on multiple thresholds and the VQA task provides text answers of binary decisions, it has minimal value in our task. Considering the imbalance of the deepfake dataset, we use **Accuracy** and **F1-score** as indicators of the deepfake binary and fine-grained classification performance.

State-of-the-Art Comparison: For the comparison of fine-grained detection performance, we compared our approach with two sets of methods: 1) the classic backbones of deepfake detectors, ResNet [36] and Xception [37], retrained as multi-label classifiers to recognize artifacts and manipulated facial regions. 2) MLLM-based interpretable deepfake detection methods, DDVQA-BLIP [10] and M2F2-Det [27], which provide fine-grained text explanations of different facial areas, despite their weakness in recognizing artifacts. ADAD is also evaluated against state-of-the-art(SOTA) methods (such as UIA-ViT [38], SBI [39], and CADDM [40]) for deepfake detection under the same testing scheme.

4.1   Fine-Grained Explanation Performance

Besides the real-or-fake binary classification, the text explanation generated by our method provides instructions on spotted artifacts and their locations. As shown in Table 1, our method achieves comparable in-dataset performance in recognizing different manipulated facial regions while retaining better generalization in cross-dataset detection of the FakeArti and SeqDeepFake datasets.

Table 1. Explanation performance in recognizing manipulated facial regions. The **best results** are highlighted in bold font, while the second-best results are underlined.

Dataset	Method	Eyes		Nose		Mouth		Eyebrows		Skin	
		Acc	F1	Acc	F1	Acc	F1	Acc	F1	Acc	F1
Intra-dataset Testing											
DDVQA	ResNet [36]	0.6755	0.7525	0.6016	0.4846	0.6069	0.6863	0.6069	0.6575	0.7124	0.8022
	Xception [37]	0.657	0.739	0.5884	0.4765	0.6227	0.7052	0.6121	0.6636	0.7071	0.8014
	DDVQA-BLIP [10]	**0.7045**	**0.7986**	0.5303	0.6213	**0.6755**	**0.7718**	0.6332	0.7311	**0.7731**	**0.8532**
	M2F2-Det [27]	0.4063	0.0816	0.5805	0.0914	0.4512	0.0877	0.4723	0.0291	0.504	0.4919
	ADAD(Ours)	0.6992	0.7816	**0.6517**	**0.7528**	0.6649	0.7475	**0.6807**	**0.7796**	0.7414	0.8212
Cross-dataset Testing											
FakeArti	ResNet [36]	0.5648	0.6392	0.5205	0.3762	0.5577	0.6451	0.5537	0.5843	0.4929	0.5743
	Xception [37]	0.5411	0.6481	0.5348	0.4764	0.5916	0.7017	0.5387	0.6148	0.4684	0.5749
	DDVQA-BLIP [10]	0.575	0.6786	0.5221	0.6286	0.6011	0.7113	0.5608	0.6576	0.5039	**0.5824**
	M2F2-Det [27]	0.4826	0.1208	0.5071	0.1896	0.4147	0.1083	0.4826	0.0521	**0.6106**	0.4417
	ADAD(Ours)	**0.5956**	**0.6941**	**0.5695**	**0.6566**	**0.628**	**0.7285**	**0.5861**	**0.6584**	0.5182	0.5674
SeqDeepFake components	ResNet [36]	0.6513	0.7300	0.5448	0.2735	0.5449	0.5587	0.5485	0.4709	-	-
	Xception [37]	0.6702	0.7454	0.5282	0.2954	0.5894	0.6102	0.5607	0.4937	-	-
	DDVQA-BLIP [10]	0.3294	0.2346	0.458	0.5242	0.3969	0.4316	0.4434	0.5158	-	-
	M2F2-Det [27]	0.1913	0.0493	0.4944	0.0985	0.378	0.0471	0.4703	0.0711	-	-
	ADAD(Ours)	**0.8444**	**0.9095**	**0.6217**	**0.7188**	**0.686**	**0.7928**	**0.6073**	**0.7126**	-	-

Table 2 demonstrates that our method achieves the best or second-best performance in recognizing different types of artifacts. Although ResNet and Xception outperform our method in the artifact recognition of blur, blending boundary, and color inconsistency, their extremely low F1-score reflects the significant bias in the detection results and indicates that visual artifacts are not being accurately identified. Our method makes a trade-off between Accuracy and F1-Score so that it can handle real-world scenarios and demonstrates better generalization in cross-dataset detection. Our method also allows for flexible interactions with users, enabling the overall analysis of visual artifacts and a single query of a specific facial area to be handled. In comparison, the SOTA method fails in the former format of artifact analysis query. Moreover, the answers to different questions for the same image in the SOTA method appear to be inconsistent or even contradictory, which will greatly undermine the trustworthiness of the model's explanations.

Table 2. Explanation performance in recognizing visual artifacts. The shaded area denotes the invalid performance due to highly uneven detection results on an imbalanced dataset (F1-score < 0.2).

Dataset	Method	Blur		Boundary		Color		Distortion		Structure		Texture	
		Acc	F1	Acc	F1	Acc	F1	Acc	F1	Acc	F1	Acc	F1
						Intra-dataset Testing							
DDVQA	ResNet[36]	**0.7579**	0.0463	<u>0.7018</u>	0.0813	**0.6148**	0.6422	0.6042	<u>0.5399</u>	0.7071	0.7963	0.6807	0.7669
	Xception[37]	<u>0.7553</u>	0.0311	**0.723**	0.0541	0.5858	0.6253	<u>0.5831</u>	0.5062	0.7098	0.8043	0.6464	0.7452
	DDVQA-BLIP [10]	0.5383	0.3346	0.6781	<u>0.2738</u>	0.6042	**0.7047**	0.5435	0.5387	**0.752**	**0.8418**	**0.715**	**0.8125**
	M2F2-Det [27]	0.686	<u>0.4251</u>	0.6016	0.3463	0.5646	0.5015	0.6174	0.484	0.5383	0.5407	0.5224	0.4958
	ADAD(Ours)	0.6069	**0.4335**	0.6253	0.3039	**0.6201**	<u>0.6975</u>	**0.6385**	**0.5566**	<u>0.7309</u>	<u>0.8104</u>	<u>0.7098</u>	<u>0.7901</u>
						Cross-dataset Testing							
FakeArti	ResNet[36]	0.4889	0.1542	<u>0.8096</u>	0.0141	<u>0.5671</u>	0.2857	**0.6051**	0.2106	**0.4068**	0.3221	<u>0.4392</u>	0.312
	Xception[37]	0.4858	0.1094	**0.8199**	0.0156	0.4709	0.3074	0.5364	0.2246	0.3318	0.3752	0.3522	0.3152
	DDVQA-BLIP [10]	0.4992	<u>0.4645</u>	0.7156	0.1667	0.4194	**0.46**	0.4818	<u>0.3915</u>	0.3752	**0.4119**	0.3744	**0.4107**
	M2F2-Det [27]	<u>0.5134</u>	0.4369	0.613	0.2643	**0.5703**	0.3539	<u>0.5995</u>	0.381	<u>0.6035</u>	0.3412	**0.5877**	0.2965
	ADAD(Ours)	**0.5687**	**0.5991**	0.6959	0.2062	0.4123	<u>0.4473</u>	0.5719	**0.4295**	0.3973	<u>0.3959</u>	0.3815	<u>0.3907</u>

Table 3. Comparison of intra-dataset and cross-dataset deepfake detection performance with existing deepfake detection methods. * uses the model from the original paper, ** uses the reproduced model following the same training scheme.

Method	Venue	Intra-dataset				Cross-dataset					
		DDVQA		FakeArti		Celeb–DF		DFDC			
		Acc ↑	F1 ↑	Acc ↑	F1 ↑	Acc ↑	F1 ↑	Acc ↑	F1 ↑		
Xception** [37]	CVPR17	0.7889	0.8738	<u>0.8667</u>	<u>0.9236</u>	0.5467	0.6733	0.5527	0.6509		
UIA-ViT*[38]	ECCV22	0.7546	0.8208	0.6303	0.756	<u>0.6638</u>	0.7284	0.5963	0.528		
SBI*[39]	CVPR22	0.6042	0.6622	0.5679	0.6996	**0.779**	**0.8339**	0.5943	0.397		
CADDM*[40]	CVPR23	<u>0.8417</u>	0.8909	0.6232	0.7499	0.6041	0.6157	<u>0.6044</u>	0.4546		
DDVQA-BLIP** [10]	ECCV24	**0.8628**	**0.9172**	0.7852	0.8781	0.6411	0.7648	0.6026	<u>0.6524</u>		
M2F2-Det* [27]	CVPR25	0.7704	0.8703	0.4471	0.5798	0.6475	0.7822	0.5065	0.6652		
ADAD(Ours)	-	0.8285	<u>0.9051</u>	**0.8784**	**0.9331**	0.6506	<u>0.7853</u>	**0.657**	**0.7034**		

4.2   General Detection Performance

In this section, we assess the deepfake detection performance with the state-of-the-art methods using frame-level Accuracy rate (Acc) and F1-score (F1) metrics, as shown in Table 3.

Our method is trained on the DD-VQA dataset, which collects images extracted from videos in the FF++ dataset without data augmentation. Using a much smaller subset for training, our method achieves comparable results on intra-dataset detection performance. Furthermore, our method exhibits a notable improvement in cross-dataset detection performance, especially on challenging datasets, such as DFDC and FakeArti. The FakeArti dataset contains a collection of diversified forgery types, such as DeeperForensics [29], DFDC [30] and ForgeryNet [31]. The cross-dataset performance demonstrates the generalization of our method and validates the effectiveness of universal visual artifacts.

4.3   Visualization of Artifact Highlighting

The proposed Artifact Dissection Module disentangles artifacts from content information, enabling the visualization of the model's attention saliency for different artifacts. Figure 4 demonstrates the visual explanations from the Artifact Highlighting module and textual explanations. The saliency map highlights the recognized fine-grained visual artifacts, and the corresponding artifact type is marked on top of the image. Text explanations are displayed on the right side, which is in a structured format of artifacts and its located facial regions.

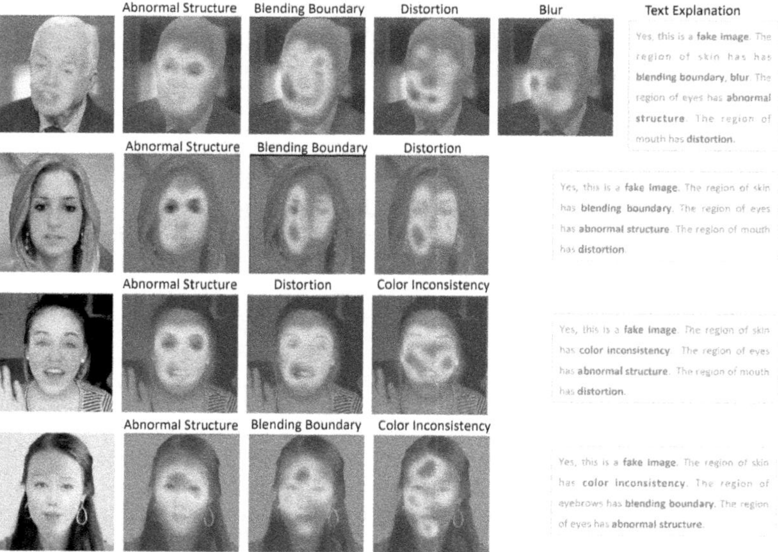

Fig. 4. Visualization of our multimodal explanations

Highlighting visual artifacts and providing text explanations provides clear guidance on where and what to focus on in deepfake images, making the deepfake detector more convincing and understandable. It also helps laypeople to recognize deepfakes quickly and improve their accuracy.

5 Conclusion

In this paper, we present a novel dataset for interpretable deepfake detection with detailed explanations of visual artifacts and a proposed ADAD method that grounds visual artifacts and generates multimodal deepfake explanations. We establish an evaluation framework for deepfake explanations that assesses the explanation performance based on the hit accuracy of forgery traces and forged areas. This work presents a feasible approach to enhance laypeople's ability to recognize deepfake images by providing human-understandable and trustworthy multimodal explanations. Compared with the current state-of-the-art model, our method shows promising performance on both binary classification and fine-grained artifact detection, especially in cross-dataset settings.

In the future, we aim to enhance detection in complex scenarios by extending to AI-generated images with human-understandable artifacts, offering more explainable and reliable solutions for forgery detection.

Acknowledgement. This study was supported by the Innovation Funding of Institute of Computing Technology, Chinese Academy of Sciences under Grant No. E561160 and No. E561090.

References

1. Groh, M., Epstein, Z., Firestone, C., Picard, R.: Deepfake detection by human crowds, machines, and machine-informed crowds. Proc. Natl. Acad. Sci. **119**(1), e2110013119 (2022)
2. Hashmi, A., Shahzad, S.A., Lin, C.W., Tsao, Y., Wang, H.M.: Unmasking illusions: understanding human perception of audiovisual deepfakes, arXiv preprint arXiv:2405.04097 (2024)
3. Li, L., et al.: Face X-ray for more general face forgery detection. In: Proceedings of the IEEE/CVF Conference on Computer Vision and Pattern Recognition, pp. 5001–5010 (2020)
4. Li, Y., Chang, M.-C., Lyu, S.: In ictu oculi: exposing AI created fake videos by detecting eye blinking. In: 2018 IEEE International Workshop on Information Forensics and Security (WIFS), pp. 1–7. IEEE (2018)
5. Demir, I., Ciftci, U.A.: Where do deep fakes look? Synthetic face detection via gaze tracking. In: ACM Symposium on Eye Tracking Research and Applications, pp. 1–11 (2021)
6. Boyd, A., Tinsley, P., Bowyer, K., Czajka, A.: The value of AI guidance in human examination of synthetically-generated faces. In: Proceedings of the AAAI Conference on Artificial Intelligence, vol. 37, no. 5, pp. 5930–5938 (2023)

7. Jia, S., et al.: Can chatgpt detect deepfakes? A study of using multimodal large language models for media forensics. In: Proceedings of the IEEE/CVF Conference on Computer Vision and Pattern Recognition, pp. 4324–4333 (2024)

8. Yan, Z., Zhang, Y., Yuan, X., Lyu, S., Wu, B.: Deepfakebench: a comprehensive benchmark of deepfake detection. In: Proceedings of the 37th International Conference on Neural Information Processing Systems, pp. 4534–4565 (2023)

9. Sun, K., et al.: Towards general visual-linguistic face forgery detection. In: Proceedings of the Computer Vision and Pattern Recognition Conference, pp. 19576–19586 (2025)

10. Zhang, Y., Colman, B., Guo, X., Shahriyari, A., Bharaj, G.: Common sense reasoning for deepfake detection. In: European Conference on Computer Vision, pp. 399–415. Springer (2024)

11. Lu, Z., et al.: Seeing is not always believing: benchmarking human and model perception of AI-generated images. In: Advances in Neural Information Processing Systems, vol. 36, pp. 25435–25447 (2023)

12. Bray, S.D., Johnson, S.D., Kleinberg, B.: Testing human ability to detect 'deepfake' images of human faces. J. Cybersecur. **9**, tyad011 (2023)

13. Tahir, R., et al.: Seeing is believing: exploring perceptual differences in DeepFake videos. In: Proceedings of the 2021 CHI Conference on Human Factors in Computing Systems, Yokohama Japan, pp. 1–16. ACM (2021)

14. Müller, R., Thoß, M., Ullrich, J., Seitz, S., Knoll, C.: Interpretability is in the eye of the beholder: human versus artificial classification of image segments generated by humans versus XAI. Int. J. Hum.-Comput. Interact. **41**(4), 2371–2393 (2025)

15. Boyd, A., Tinsley, P., Bowyer, K., Czajka, A.: The value of AI guidance in human examination of synthetically-generated faces. In: Proceedings of the AAAI Conference on Artificial Intelligence, vol. 37, pp. 5930–5938 (2023)

16. Selvaraju, R.R., Cogswell, M., Das, A., Vedantam, R., Parikh, D., Batra, D.: Gradcam: visual explanations from deep networks via gradient-based localization. In: Proceedings of the IEEE International Conference on Computer Vision, pp. 618–626 (2017)

17. Ghorbani, A., Zou, J.Y.: Neuron shapley: discovering the responsible neurons. Adv. Neural. Inf. Process. Syst. **33**, 5922–5932 (2020)

18. Chefer, H., Gur, S., Wolf, L.: Transformer interpretability beyond attention visualization. In: Proceedings of the IEEE/CVF Conference on Computer Vision and Pattern Recognition, pp. 782–791 (2021)

19. Tsigos, K., Apostolidis, E., Baxevanakis, S., Papadopoulos, S., Mezaris, V.: Towards quantitative evaluation of explainable AI methods for deepfake detection. In: Proceedings of the 3rd ACM International Workshop on Multimedia AI Against Disinformation, pp. 37–45 (2024)

20. Zhang, Y., Wang, T., Yu, Z., Gao, Z., Shen, L., Chen, S.: MFCLIP: multi-modal fine-grained clip for generalizable diffusion face forgery detection. IEEE Trans. Inf. Forensics Secur. (2025)

21. Liu, H., Li, C., Wu, Q., Lee, Y.J.: Visual instruction tuning. In: Advances in Neural Information Processing Systems, vol. 36 (2024)

22. Zhu, D., Chen, J., Shen, X., Li, X., Elhoseiny, M.: Minigpt-4: enhancing vision-language understanding with advanced large language models. In: ICLR (2024)

23. Foteinopoulou, N.M., Ghorbel, E., Aouada, D.: A hitchhiker's guide to fine-grained face forgery detection using common sense reasoning. Adv. Neural. Inf. Process. Syst. **37**, 2943–2976 (2024)

24. Wang, J., et al.: Forensics-bench: a comprehensive forgery detection benchmark suite for large vision language models. In: Proceedings of the Computer Vision and Pattern Recognition Conference, pp. 4233–4245 (2025)
25. Xu, Z., Zhang, X., Li, R., Tang, Z., Huang, Q., Zhang, J.: Fakeshield: explainable image forgery detection and localization via multi-modal large language models. In: International Conference on Learning Representations (2025)
26. Huang, Z., et al.: Sida: social media image deepfake detection, localization and explanation with large multimodal model. In: Proceedings of the Computer Vision and Pattern Recognition Conference, pp. 28831–28841 (2025)
27. Guo, X., Song, X., Zhang, Y., Liu, X., Liu, X.: Rethinking vision-language model in face forensics: multi-modal interpretable forged face detector. In: Proceedings of the Computer Vision and Pattern Recognition Conference, pp. 105–116 (2025)
28. Rossler, A., Cozzolino, D., Verdoliva, L., Riess, C., Thies, J., Nießner, M.: Faceforensics++: learning to detect manipulated facial images. In: Proceedings of the IEEE/CVF International Conference on Computer Vision, pp. 1–11 (2019)
29. Jiang, L., Li, R., Wu, W., Qian, C., Loy, C.C.: Deeperforensics-1.0: a large-scale dataset for real-world face forgery detection. In: Proceedings of the IEEE/CVF Conference on Computer Vision and Pattern Recognition, pp. 2889–2898 (2020)
30. Dolhansky, B., et al.: The deepfake detection challenge (DFDC) dataset, arXiv preprint arXiv:2006.07397 (2020)
31. He, Y., et al.: Forgerynet: a versatile benchmark for comprehensive forgery analysis. In: Proceedings of the IEEE/CVF Conference on Computer Vision and Pattern Recognition, pp. 4360–4369 (2021)
32. Liang, J., Shi, H., Deng, W.: Exploring disentangled content information for face forgery detection. In: European Conference on Computer Vision, pp. 128–145. Springer (2022)
33. Oord, A.V.D., Li, Y., Vinyals, O.: Representation learning with contrastive predictive coding, arXiv preprint arXiv:1807.03748 (2018)
34. Yu, C., Wang, J., Peng, C., Gao, C., Yu, G., Sang, N.: Bisenet: bilateral segmentation network for real-time semantic segmentation. In: Proceedings of the European Conference on Computer Vision (ECCV), pp. 325–341 (2018)
35. Shao, R., Wu, T., Liu, Z.: Detecting and recovering sequential deepfake manipulation. In: European Conference on Computer Vision (ECCV) (2022)
36. Targ, S., Almeida, D., Lyman, K.: Resnet in resnet: generalizing residual architectures, arXiv preprint arXiv:1603.08029 (2016)
37. Chollet, F.: Xception: deep learning with depthwise separable convolutions. In: Proceedings of the IEEE Conference on Computer Vision and Pattern Recognition, pp. 1251–1258 (2017)
38. Zhuang, W., et al.: UIA-ViT: Unsupervised inconsistency-aware method based on vision transformer for face forgery detection. In: European Conference on Computer Vision, pp. 391–407. Springer (2022)
39. Shiohara, K., Yamasaki, T.: Detecting deepfakes with self-blended images. In: Proceedings of the IEEE/CVF Conference on Computer Vision and Pattern Recognition, pp. 18720–18729 (2022)
40. Dong, S., Wang, J., Ji, R., Liang, J., Fan, H., Ge, Z.: Implicit identity leakage: the stumbling block to improving deepfake detection generalization. In: Proceedings of the IEEE/CVF Conference on Computer Vision and Pattern Recognition, pp. 3994–4004 (2023)

Graph Contrastive Learning with Popularity and Neighborhood Awareness for Long-Tail Item Recommendation

Yuma Dose and Takahiro Hara[✉]

The University of Osaka, Suita, Osaka, Japan
{douse.yuma,hara}@ist.osaka-u.ac.jp

Abstract. Long-tail recommendation has emerged as a promising solution to mitigate the popularity bias inherent in graph-based recommender systems. Recently, contrastive learning-based models have shown their effectiveness in this field. However, typical data augmentation strategies relying on random edge dropout or noise injection are often ill-suited to the sparsity and imbalance inherent in long-tail data. In this paper, we propose two contrastive learning strategies, combined in the framework GCLLT, that are specifically designed for long-tail recommendation. The popularity-aware contrastive learning strategy enhances tail-item connectivity by linking tail nodes to nearby head nodes in the embedding space and pruning less informative edges from head items. This results in cleaner and more informative graph views for tail items. In neighborhood-aware contrastive learning, head and tail items are clustered separately, and each tail item is assigned the centroid of its nearest head cluster as a prototype, enabling semantic supervision without relying on structural augmentation. Finally, these contrastive learnings are applied to tail items, allowing their representations to be refined without being dominated by head items during optimization. Experimental results on real-world datasets demonstrate that GCLLT outperforms baseline models, achieving up to 10.25% improvement in Recall@20.

Keywords: Recommender system · Collaborative filtering · Long-tail recommendation · Contrastive learning

1 Introduction

Recommender systems have become essential tools for mitigating information overload [1]. They help users to discover potentially relevant items across various domains such as e-commerce [2], online news [3], and multimedia content [4]. The core idea of recommender systems is to learn low-dimensional latent embeddings for users and items by leveraging their observed interactions [5]. With the recent

---

Our code is available at https://anonymous.4open.science/r/GCLLT-7F76.

© The Author(s), under exclusive license to Springer Nature Singapore Pte Ltd. 2026
J. Lokoč et al. (Eds.): MMM 2026, LNCS 16412, pp. 46–59, 2026.
https://doi.org/10.1007/978-981-95-6950-2_4

success of graph neural networks (GNN) [6,7], several graph-based collaborative filtering (CF) models have emerged [8–10]. Typically, these models construct a user-item interaction graph where edges denote user behaviors (e.g., purchases, clicks, or views). Subsequently, GNN is employed on the graph to learn user and item embeddings by iteratively aggregating feature information from their respective local neighborhoods.

Although these CF models have been extensively studied, prevalent recommendation models such as matrix factorization (MF) [12] and LightGCN [10] often struggle with popularity bias, particularly on long-tail datasets where user interactions are concentrated on a small subset of popular items. This bias leads to several issues, including the over-recommendation of popular items, reduced recommendation diversity [11], and a tendency for models to favor popular items irrespective of true user preferences [13,14]. These challenges are notably exacerbated in graph-based models, where multi-hop aggregation can further intensify the influence of popular items, diminishing recommendation diversity and fairness. To counteract these challenges, some studies have increasingly focused on long-tail item recommendation, which emphasizes improving recommendations for less popular items [15–17]. Recently, contrastive learning (CL) has demonstrated notable effectiveness in recommender systems and has been introduced to long-tail item recommendation [18]. Despite the effectiveness of CL, its data augmentation strategy is typically based on general-purpose noise injection, which is not specifically tailored to long-tail scenarios. This specific limitation consequently highlights the need for further refinement in capturing the fine-grained characteristics of tail items and enhancing recommendation accuracy for them.

In this study, we explore contrastive learning strategies specifically designed for long-tail recommendation. Because of the inherently sparse interactions of long-tail items, common augmentation techniques such as random edge dropout or noise injection can substantially distort their representations, potentially degrading recommendation performance. Additionally, the contrastive loss is dominated by head items, so gradients are mostly driven by these popular nodes. As a result, tail items contribute little to optimization, thus further skewing the model toward already well-represented head items. To address these issues, we highlight the importance of two key aspects:(1) tail-focused data augmentation techniques that account for the intrinsic sparsity of tail items and their susceptibility to noisy signals; and (2) a contrastive learning mechanism tailored for tail items to prevent domination by head items. Based on the above idea, we propose a novel **Graph Contrastive Learning** framework for **Long-Tail** recommendation (**GCLLT**). GCLLT employs two contrastive learning strategies specifically designed for long-tail recommendation. First, inspired by [19], we design a popularity-aware contrastive learning. To enhance the connectivity of tail items, GCLLT introduces item-to-item edge addition based on node degree. Specifically, new edges are added from tail items to embedding-wise similar head items, allowing the tail items to receive informative messages through graph propagation. In addition, we design a degree-aware edge dropping mechanism that preserves the more important edges for tail items while removing the less informative edges from head items. This leads to richer and more informative embeddings for tail items. Secondly, to further enhance supervision signals for tail items, we develop a neighborhood-aware contrastive learning approach that relies not on graph augmentation but on semantic neighbors. *Semantic head neighbors* refers to items that are similar to tail items in the representation space, though they may lack direct connections in the original graph. To extract semantic neighbors, GCLLT performs clustering separately for head and tail items. For each tail item, the centroid of the most similar head item cluster is selected as its prototype, representing a group of semantically related head items in the embedding space. These prototypes are then used as positive samples in a prototypical contrastive learning objective, where each node (either a user or an item) is aligned with its corresponding prototype. Finally, these contrastive learnings are applied to tail items, allowing their representations to be refined without being dominated by head items during optimization. We adopt state-of-the-art LAGCL as our base model and integrate the above two contrastive learning techniques to improve the long-tail recommendation performance further. Experiments on real-world datasets demonstrate that GCLLT achieves a 10.25% improvement in Recall@20 over the state-of-the-art baseline on the Yelp dataset.

In a nutshell, the contributions of this paper are summarized as follows:

- We propose two novel contrastive learning strategies for long-tail item recommendation: *popularity-aware contrastive learning* and *neighborhood-aware contrastive learning*. Based on tail item connectivity and semantic neighbors, GCLLT provides informative supervision signals in long-tail scenarios.
- These contrastive learning techniques specifically applied to tail items, enabling their representations to be effectively refined without being dominated by head items during optimization.
- Experimental results show that GCLLT significantly outperforms the baseline methods, especially in long-tail item recommendation. This result confirms the effectiveness of our two novel contrastive learning strategies.

2   Preliminaries

2.1   Graph-Based Recommendation

Graph-based recommendation models utilize a user-item interaction graph whose edges represent users' preferences. An interaction graph is a bipartite graph with a set of users U and a set of items I as nodes. Edges $\mathcal{E}$ are the observed interactions between U and I. Formally, the interaction graph $\mathcal{G}$ is defined as $\mathcal{G} = (\mathcal{V}, \mathcal{E})$, where the node set $\mathcal{V} = U \cup I$. The core idea of graph-based recommendation models is to employ a neighborhood aggregation approach on $\mathcal{G}$. The representation of each node is updated by aggregating the representations of its neighboring nodes.

LightGCN Brief. LightGCN [10] is a simple, effective, and widely used collaborative filtering model. After obtaining the initial representations $r_u^{(0)}$, $r_i^{(0)}$, it leverages a linear GNN to update representations by iteratively aggregating representations of neighbor nodes in the interaction graph. The representations in each GNN layer are denoted as

$$r_u^{(l+1)} = \sum_{i \in N_u} \frac{1}{\sqrt{|N_u||N_i|}} r_i^{(l)}, \quad r_i^{(l+1)} = \sum_{u \in N_i} \frac{1}{\sqrt{|N_u||N_i|}} r_u^{(l)}, \tag{1}$$

where $r_u^{(l)}$ and $r_i^{(l)}$ are the respective representations of user u and item i at the l-th layer. N_u is the set of interacted items of user u, and N_i is the set of interacted users of item i. The final representations are obtained by combining the representations of all layers, formulated as

$$r_u = \sum_{l=0}^{L} \frac{1}{k+1} r_u^{(l)} , \quad r_i = \sum_{l=0}^{L} \frac{1}{k+1} r_i^{(l)}, \tag{2}$$

where L denotes the number of layers. Then LightGCN utilizes a simple and efficient inner product to predict the preference score $\hat{y}_{ui}$ between user u and item i, based on their final representations. Formally, $\hat{y}_{ui} = r_u^{\top} \cdot r_i$.

2.2   Problem Definition

Traditional top-K recommendation models focus on identifying the K most relevant items for each user and maximizing the average recommendation performance. However, the long-tail distribution implies that many items have little feedback, resulting in poor recommendations for these tail items. Our goal is to improve the recommendations for tail items, while concurrently maintaining or enhancing overall performance levels.

3   Methodology

In this paper, we propose a Graph Contrastive Learning framework for Long-Tail recommendation, named GCLLT. Figure 1 provides an overview of GCLLT. GCLLT employs two contrastive learning strategies specifically designed for long-tail recommendation. These data augmentation strategies are illustrated in Fig. 2, and their details are discussed in the following sections.

3.1   Popularity-Aware Contrastive Learning

For popularity-aware contrastive learning, we construct an augmented graph $\mathcal{G}'$ by performing node-degree-aware data augmentation on the original graph $\mathcal{G}$. This data augmentation is exemplified in Fig. 2(a).

Edge Drop. We adopt a novel strategy called *adaptive heterogeneous edge dropping*, which drops more edges for head items and fewer for tail items [19]. Instead

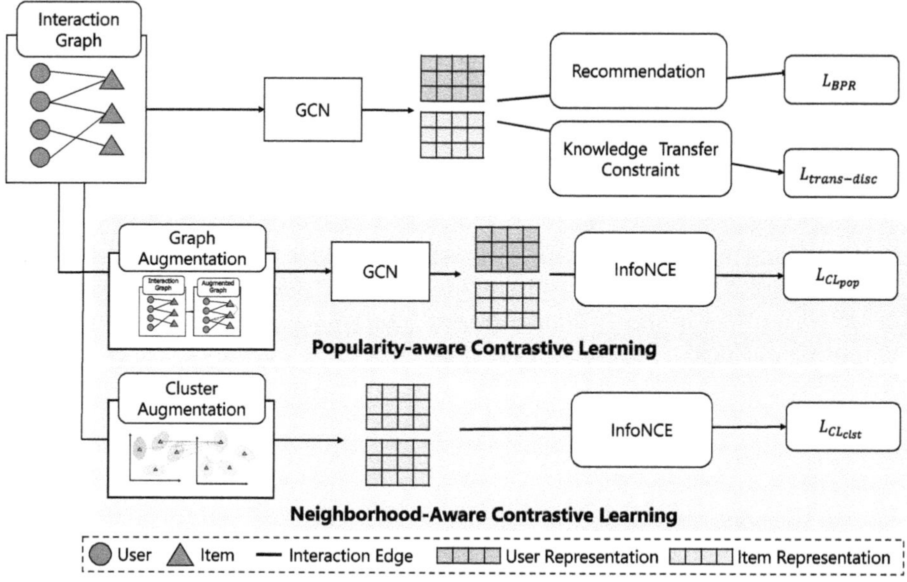

Fig. 1. The overall architecture of GCLLT.

of relying on traditional metrics such as node degree, we adopt a *long-tail coefficient* l_i for each item i to quantify how strongly it belongs to the tail of the popularity distribution. It is defined as:

$$l_i = \min\left(\log(\deg(i) + 1)^{-1}, \; l_c\right), \tag{3}$$

where $\deg(i)$ is the degree of item i and l_c is a threshold. A higher value of l_i indicates that the item has received fewer user interactions. We compute the probability p_{ui} of dropping the edge between user u and item i as:

$$p_{ui} = \max\left(\frac{l_{\max} - l_i}{l_{\max} - l_{\min}} \cdot p_e, \; p_c\right), \tag{4}$$

where $l_{\max}$ and $l_{\min}$ are the maximum and minimum long-tail coefficients among all items, respectively. Here, p_e is a hyperparameter controlling the overall dropping rate, and $p_c < 1$ is a lower bound to avoid over-dropping.

Edge Add. To enhance the connectivity of tail items, we establish new item-to-item edges by identifying semantically similar head items based on their embedding representations. Given the embeddings of tail items $\mathbf{E}_t \in \mathbf{R}^{n_t \times d}$ and head items $\mathbf{E}_h \in \mathbf{R}^{n_h \times d}$, we compute a similarity matrix $S \in \mathbf{R}^{n_t \times n_h}$ by using cosine similarity. Each entry S_{ij} represents the similarity between the i-th tail item and the j-th head item and is calculated as the cosine of the angle between their embedding vectors. For each tail item, we first apply partial sorting to extract the indices of the top-k head items with the highest similarity scores. Then, we further sort these k candidates in descending order of similarity to obtain a ranked list of the most relevant head items. These selected top-k head items are subsequently used to construct new edges that link each tail item to semantically similar head items, thereby improving message propagation in the graph.

By adding these edges to, or cropping them from, the original interaction graph, we construct an augmented graph $\mathcal{G}'$ that facilitates more effective representation learning for tail items.

Finally, the InfoNCE loss [28, 40] is calculated using representations acquired from $\mathcal{G}$ and $\mathcal{G}'$ and based on Eq. (1) and (2). Loss for popularity-aware contrastive learning is defined as

$$\mathcal{L}_{CL_{pop}} = \sum_{u \in U} -\log \frac{\exp(s(\boldsymbol{r}_u, \boldsymbol{r}'_u)/\tau)}{\sum_{v \in U} \exp(s(\boldsymbol{r}_u, \boldsymbol{r}'_v)/\tau)} + \sum_{i \in I} -\log \frac{\exp(s(\boldsymbol{r}_i, \boldsymbol{r}'_i)/\tau)}{\sum_{j \in I} \exp(s(\boldsymbol{r}_i, \boldsymbol{r}'_j)/\tau)},$$

$$(5)$$

where $\boldsymbol{r}$ is the representations acquired from $\mathcal{G}$, and $\boldsymbol{r}'$ is the representations acquired from $\mathcal{G}'$. The symbol $s(.)$ is a function that measures the similarity between the two representations, and τ is a temperature hyperparameter. By minimizing $\mathcal{L}_{CL_{pop}}$, GCLLT maximizes the consistency between the representations of the same nodes ($i.e., \{(\boldsymbol{r}_u, \boldsymbol{r}'_u) | u \in U\}$) and minimizes the consistency between the representations of the different nodes ($i.e., \{(\boldsymbol{r}_u, \boldsymbol{r}'_v) | u, v \in U, u \neq v\}$).

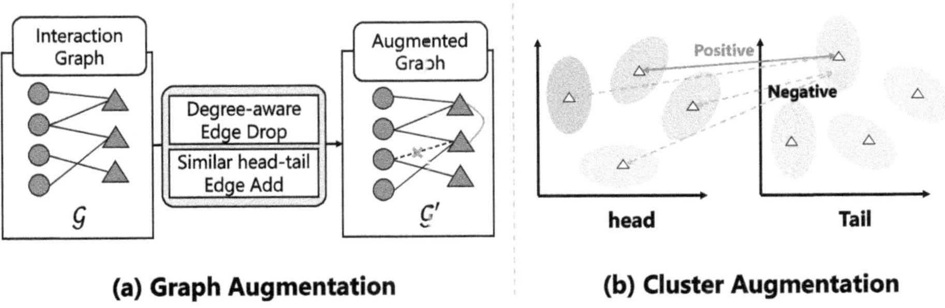

Fig. 2. Illustration of two data augmentation strategies: (a) Popularity-aware and (b) Neighborhood-aware Contrastive Learning.

3.2   Neighborhood-Aware Contrastive Learning

In neighborhood-aware contrastive learning, we extract semantic head item neighbors for each tail item by performing clustering in the embedding space. Inspired by previous works [41], we can identify the semantic neighbors by learning the latent prototype for each user and item. As illustrated Fig. 2(b), we perform clustering separately for head and tail items via the k-means algorithm. For each tail item cluster centroid $\mathbf{c}_i^{tail}$, we identify the most semantically similar head item cluster centroid $\mathbf{c}_i^{head}$ based on their distance in the embedding space, and treat $\mathbf{c}_i^{head}$ as a semantic neighbor of $\mathbf{c}_i^{tail}$. Subsequently, we perform contrastive learning where $\mathbf{c}_i^{head}$ serves as a positive sample, and the negative samples are defined as the remaining cluster centroids (*i.e.*, $\mathbf{c}_t \in \mathcal{C}_j^{tail} | j \neq i$).

We define the neighborhood-aware contrastive learning loss as

$$\mathcal{L}_{CL_{clst}} = \sum_{i \in \mathcal{I}_{tail}} -\log \frac{\exp(\mathbf{e}_i \cdot \mathbf{c}_i^{head}/\tau)}{\sum_{\mathbf{c}^{tail} \in \mathcal{C}} \exp(\mathbf{e}_i \cdot \mathbf{c}_j^{tail}/\tau)}, \tag{6}$$

where $\mathbf{e}_i$ is the embedding of tail item $i \in \mathcal{I}_{tail}$ and $\mathbf{c}_j$ is its corresponding head item prototype (semantic neighbor). This loss is computed and optimized exclusively for tail items, enabling their representations to be refined without being dominated by head items.

3.3 Model Optimization

GCLLT is trained through multi-task training that incorporates popularity-aware contrastive learning and neighborhood-aware learning for the recommendation task.

In the recommendation task, the model is optimized by minimizing the Bayesian personalized ranking (BPR) loss [39], which uses the predicted preference scores of users for items and the actual preference scores. The BPR loss is defined as

$$\mathcal{L}_{BPR} = \sum_{u \in U} \sum_{i \in N_u} \sum_{j \in I, j \notin N_u} -\log \sigma(\hat{y}_{ui} - \hat{y}_{uj}), \tag{7}$$

where $\sigma(\cdot)$ represents the sigmoid function. GCLLT calculates $\hat{y}_{ui}$ using a simple and efficient inner product based on the representations $\boldsymbol{r}$, obtained by applying the graph convolution with LightGCN [10] to the interaction graph $\mathcal{G}$. In training with BPR loss, the model is trained so that the preference scores for pairs of users and items with interactions are relatively higher than those without interactions. In addition, the loss $\mathcal{L}_{trans-disc}$ for knowledge transfer and generative adversarial learning is computed based on the training protocol of LAGCL [18].

For popularity-aware contrastive learning and neighborhood-aware contrastive learning, GCLLT is optimized by using Eq. (5) and (6).

GCLLT is trained by minimizing the overall loss by integrating the above losses. The overall loss is defined as

$$\mathcal{L} = \mathcal{L}_{BPR} + \mathcal{L}_{trans-disc} + \lambda_1 \mathcal{L}_{CL_{pop}} + \lambda_2 \mathcal{L}_{CL_{clst}} + \lambda_3 ||\Theta||_2^2, \tag{8}$$

where λ_1 adjusts the influence of the popularity-aware contrastive learning and λ_2 regulates the impact of the neighborhood-aware contrastive learning. λ_3 is a hyperparameter that controls the strength of L_2 regularization, and Θ represents all trainable model parameters.

4   Experiments

4.1   Experimental Settings

Datasets. We conduct experiments on two public benchmark datasets: Yelp[1] and Gowalla [10]. The basic statistics of these datasets are summarized in Table 1. The Gowalla dataset originates from a social networking platform where users share their locations through check-ins. The Yelp dataset consist of 5-point ratings provided for restaurants. The datasets are partitioned into training, validation, and test sets in a 7:1:2 ratio, consistent with prevailing recommendation research practices [18].

Table 1. Statistics of the datasets.

Dataset	# Users	# Items	# Interactions	Density
Yelp2018	5,215	4 742	38,746	0.00135
Gowalla	14,648	20,489	418,797	0.00136

Baseline. In our experiments, we compare our GCLLT with the following baseline models:

- **LightGCN** [10]: It proposes to simplify the burdensome NGCF [9] framework by removing the non-linear projection and embedding transformation during message passing.
- **SGL** [21]: It adopts self-supervised learning to enhance recommendation. We adopt SGL-ED as the instantiation of SGL.
- **SimGCL** [23]: It develops a graph augmentation-free CL method to improve the recommendation performance. It constructs the contrastive pairs by simply perturbing the learned node representations.
- **NCL** [22]: It designs structure-aware contrastive learning that pulls the representations of a node (a user or item) and the representative embedding for its k-hop structural neighbors.
- **LAGCL** [18]: A long-tail recommendation model incorporating contrastive learning, in which noise is injected into embeddings for data augmentation.

Evaluation. By following the settings of [18], we employ two widely adopted evaluation metrics for recommender systems, i.e., Recall@K, and NDCG@K (K = 10, 20, 40). Recall measures the proportion of ground-truth positive items successfully retrieved within the top-K recommendations. NDCG (Normalized Discounted Cumulative Gain) assesses the ranking quality by considering both the relevance of the items and their positions in the list.

---

[1] https://www.yelp.com/dataset.

Hyperparameter Settings. To ensure a fair evaluation, all models are trained with the Adam optimizer [20]. The size of the embedding is set to 64, and the batch size to 2048. We set $tail\_k\_threshold = 10$ to divide head and tail items. The parameter for ℓ_2 regularization is set to 10^{-4}. The regularization weights, λ_1 and λ_2, are tuned from the ranges $\{5\times10^{-4}, 1\times10^{-3}, 5\times10^{-3}, 1\times10^{-2}, 5\times10^{-2}\}$ and $\{5 \times 10^{-7}, 1 \times 10^{-6}, 5 \times 10^{-5}, 1 \times 10^{-2}, 5 \times 10^{-2}\}$, respectively.

Table 2. Performance comparison of *Recall* and *NDCG* on Gowalla.

Model	Overall				Tail			
	R@10	N@10	R@20	N@20	R@10	N@10	R@20	N@20
LightGCN [10]	0.1557	0.1408	0.2114	0.1502	0.0124	0.0064	0.0249	0.0100
SGL [21]	0.1612	0.1443	0.2137	0.1532	0.0133	0.0068	0.0231	0.0094
SimGCL [23]	0.1652	0.1489	0.2221	0.1579	0.0145	0.0078	0.0262	0.0107
NCL [22]	0.1575	0.1414	0.2195	0.1562	0.0164	0.0088	0.0342	0.0141
LAGCL [18]	0.1653	0.1516	0.2375	0.1718	0.0177	**0.0099**	0.0360	0.0154
GCLLT	**0.1682**	**0.1537**	**0.2391**	**0.1731**	**0.0184**	0.0098	**0.0376**	**0.0157**
Improv.(%)	+1.754	+1.385	+0.674	+0.757	+3.955	-1.010	+4.444	+1.948

Table 3. Performance comparison of *Recall* and *NDCG* on Yelp.

Model	Overall				Tail			
	R@20	N@20	R@40	N@40	R@20	N@20	R@40	N@40
LightGCN [10]	0.1756	0.0888	0.2629	0.1109	0.0069	0.0023	0.0103	0.0031
SGL [21]	0.1815	0.0932	0.2568	0.1110	0.0070	0.0021	0.0122	0.0033
SimGCL [23]	0.1747	0.0907	0.2580	0.1122	0.0074	0.0024	0.0124	0.0036
NCL [22]	0.1763	0.0914	0.2661	0.1142	0.0073	0.0022	0.0120	0.0033
LAGCL [18]	0.1887	0.0980	0.2763	0.1206	0.0078	0.0025	0.0141	0.0039
GCLLT	**0.1895**	**0.0988**	**0.2774**	**0.1215**	**0.0086**	**0.0026**	**0.0150**	**0.0040**
Improv.(%)	+0.424	+0.816	+0.398	+0.746	+10.256	+4.000	+6.383	+2.564

4.2 Performance Comparisons

Tables 2 and 3 show the overall performance comparison between GCLLT and baseline models. We have the following observations:

- Among the baseline models, LAGCL achieves higher accuracy on both overall and tail item evaluations. We attribute this improvement to the effectiveness of the adversarial learning and knowledge transfer mechanisms incorporated in LAGCL, which enhance the model's ability to learn from the biased data distribution.

– When we compare GCLLT with all baselines, we observe that it consistently achieves the best performance in most cases. This validates the effectiveness of the two contrastive learning strategies we designed, each targeting a different challenge in long-tail recommendation. We believe that this result indicates that our graph contrastive learning improves representation learning by capturing structural information from both head and tail items. In addition, the cluster-based contrastive learning further enhances tail item representations by utilizing their semantic neighbors, resulting in significant improvement in recommendation accuracy. Furthermore, when comparing the overall and tail results, we observe that the performance improvement is more pronounced for tail items, with a maximum gain of 10.25%. This demonstrates that the proposed two contrastive learning strategies are particularly effective for tail items, validating their intended design for enhancing long-tail item recommendation.

– Finally, when we compare the performance improvements across datasets, we observe that the improvement is more significant on the Yelp dataset. We attribute this to the inherent characteristics of the datasets. As Yelp is based on review data, it likely contains fewer noisy or incorrect interactions compared to Gowalla, which is based on location check-in data. As a result, the data augmentation strategies relying on embedding cosine similarity and clustering are more effective on Yelp, leading to greater performance improvement.

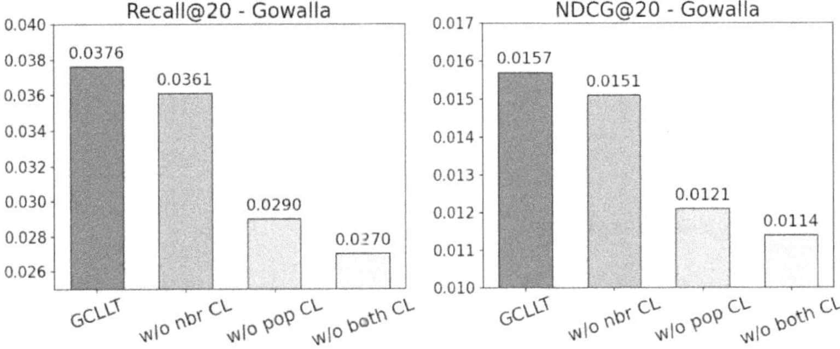

Fig. 3. Ablation study on key components of GCLLT in the Gowalla dataset.

4.3   Ablation Study

To exploit the effectiveness of each component of the proposed GCLLT, we conduct an ablation study on the Gowalla dataset. Figure 3 shows the results for the tail items of Recall and NDCG when each element is removed from GCLLT.

This result indicates that removing any component degrades performance, with the ablation of popularity-aware contrastive learning (pop CL) having the most significant impact. The removal of pop CL substantially decreases tail item Recall@20 and NDCG@20, highlighting its crucial role in enhancing their representations by using interaction graph structural information. While pop CL alone provides notable improvements, integrating neighborhood-aware contrastive learning (nbr CL), designed for tail items, yields further performance gains. This suggests that nbr CL effectively captures the semantic relations among tail items and complements pop CL by refining these specific representations. Collectively, pop CL and nbr CL synergistically improve the overall recommendation performance. These findings confirm that all proposed components are instrumental in addressing long-tail item recommendations.

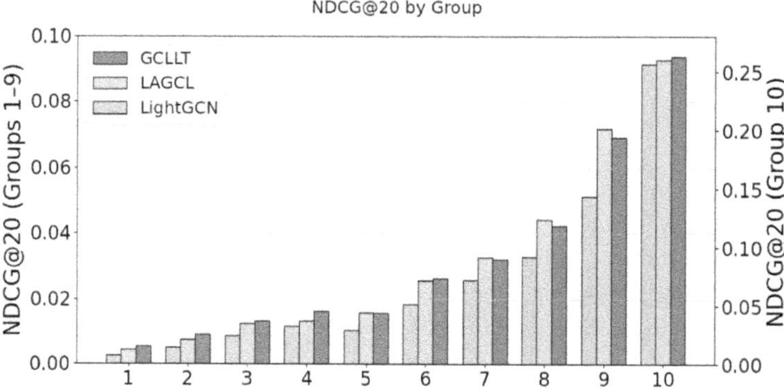

Fig. 4. Performance comparison of different item groups in the Gowalla dataset. Due to differences in the value ranges, the y-axis for Group 10 is placed on the right side of the plot.

4.4   Item Degree Analysis

To determine whether GCLLT can provide additional performance improvements for tail nodes, we divide each user into 10 groups of equal size based on their node degree in the user-item bipartite graph, as shown in Fig. 4. Items in smaller group IDs have lower popularity and fewer interactions from users.

As shown in the figure, GCLLT consistently outperforms LightGCN across all item groups, demonstrating its robustness and general effectiveness. In particular, it achieves especially significant improvements for groups with fewer interactions. Notably, it surpasses LAGCL by up to +22.22% in group 1, where items are most sparse. These results confirm that our contrastive learning strategies are effective in addressing the challenges of long-tail item recommendation.

5 Related Work

5.1 Long-Tail Recommendation

Long-tail recommendation has received increasing attention in recent years due to its relevance in mitigating popularity bias in collaborative filtering models. [36–38]. To address this issue, prior works have explored various strategies: Huang et al. [33] introduced a reweighting approach for sample selection, Grozin et al. [34] employed clustering based on association rules, and Yin et al. [35] utilized item similarity graphs with random walks to model preference relations.

More recently, researchers have explored more sophisticated techniques for addressing the long-tail recommendation problem. GALORE [19] introduces a graph-based augmentation method for long-tail item recommendation and provides empirical evidence for its effectiveness in addressing the challenges of long-tail scenarios. MGL [11] enhances long-tail recommendation by utilizing item side information to learn an auxiliary item graph via meta-learning, thereby mitigating negative transfer. LAGCL [18] introduced a contrastive learning-based model for long-tail recommendation. However, its noise-based data augmentation is not optimized for long-tail contexts, leaving room for performance improvements.

5.2 Contrastive Learning for Recommendation

As a widely adopted self-supervised learning paradigm, contrastive learning attempts to learn invariant embedding representations through data augmentation. It generates contrastive views through data augmentation and maximizes mutual information to ensure consistency among views [28,29]. Contrastive learning has demonstrated effective performance across a diverse range of domains, including visual data representation [30], natural language processing [31], and so on [32]. These approaches study task-specific data augmentation methods.

Recently, contrastive learning has been actively explored in the context of recommender systems [21–24,27]. SGL [21] applies structural graph augmentations to construct contrasting views, whereas SimGCL [23] introduces a simpler alternative based on feature perturbation. NCL [22] generates views by leveraging k-hop neighbors, and recent approaches further extend contrastive learning using VAE and SVD-based techniques [25,26]. While contrastive learning has been investigated for various tasks in recommender systems, its application to long-tail recommendation remains limited [18].

6 Conclusion

In this paper, we proposed GCLLT, a novel framework that introduces two contrastive learning strategies for long-tail recommendation: popularity-aware and neighborhood-aware contrastive learning. The popularity-aware contrastive learning strategy enhances tail-item connectivity by linking tail nodes to nearby head nodes in the embedding space and pruning less informative edges from head items. This results in cleaner and more informative graph views for tail items. In neighborhood-aware contrastive learning, head and tail items are clustered separately. Each tail item is assigned the centroid of its nearest head cluster as a prototype, enabling semantic supervision without relying on structural augmentation. By applying these strategies specifically to tail items, GCLLT mitigates the dominance of head items during optimization and improves the quality of tail item representations. Experimental results on real-world datasets show that GCLLT consistently outperforms baseline models, validating its effectiveness.

References

1. Wu, S., et al.: Graph neural networks in recommender systems: a survey. ACM Comput. Surv. **55**(5), 1–37 (2022)
2. Greenstein-Messica, A., Rokach, L.: Personal price aware multi-seller recommender system: evidence from eBay. Knowl.-Based Syst. **150**, 14–26 (2018)
3. Wu, C., et al.: Neural news recommendation with multi-head self-attention. In: EMNLP-IJCNLP (2019)
4. Yi, X., et al.: Sampling-bias-corrected neural modeling for large corpus item recommendations. In: RecSys (2019)
5. Dong, X., et al.: A hybrid collaborative filtering model with deep structure for recommender systems. In: AAAI, vol. 31, no. 1 (2017)
6. Kipf, T.N., Max, W.: Semi-supervised classification with graph convolutional networks. arXiv preprint arXiv:1609.02907 (2016)
7. Hamilton, W., Ying, Z., Leskovec, J.: Inductive representation learning on large graphs. In: NIPS 30 (2017)
8. van den Berg, R., Kipf, T.N., Welling, M.: Graph convolutional matrix completion. arXiv preprint arXiv:1706.02263 (2017)
9. Wang, X., et al.: Neural graph collaborative filtering. In: SIGIR (2019)
10. He, X., et al.: Lightgcn: simplifying and powering graph convolution network for recommendation. In: SIGIR (2020)
11. Wei, C., et al.: Meta graph learning for long-tail recommendation. In: SIGKDD (2023)
12. Koren, Y., Bell, R., Volinsky, C.: Matrix factorization techniques for recommender systems. Computer **42**(8), 30–37 (2009)
13. Abdollahpouri, H., Burke, R., Mobasher, B.: Controlling popularity bias in learning-to-rank recommendation. In: RecSys (2017)
14. Ma, J., et al.: Off-policy learning in two-stage recommender systems. In: WWW (2020)
15. Liu, S., Zheng, Y.: Long-tail session-based recommendation. In: RecSys (2020)
16. Qin, J.: A survey of long-tail item recommendation methods. Wirel. Commun. Mob. Comput. **2021**(1), 7536316 (2021)
17. Lee, G., Kim, K., Shin, K.: Post-training embedding enhancement for long-tail recommendation. In: CIKM (2024)
18. Zhao, Q., et al.: Long-tail augmented graph contrastive learning for recommendation. In: ECML PKDD (2023)
19. Luo, S., et al.: Improving long-tail item recommendation with graph augmentation. In: CIKM (2023)
20. Kingma, D.P.: Adam: a method for stochastic optimization. arXiv preprint arXiv:1412.6980 (2014)

21. Wu, J., et al.: Self-supervised graph learning for recommendation. In: SIGIR (2021)
22. Lin, Z., et al.: Improving graph collaborative filtering with neighborhood-enriched contrastive learning. In: WWW (2022)
23. Yu, J., et al.: Are graph augmentations necessary? Simple graph contrastive learning for recommendation. In: SIGIR (2022)
24. Xia, L., et al.: Hypergraph contrastive collaborative filtering. In: SIGIR (2022)
25. Yang, Y., et al.: Generative-contrastive graph learning for recommendation. In: SIGIR (2023)
26. Cai, X., et al.: LightGCL: simple yet effective graph contrastive learning for recommendation. In: ICLR (2023)
27. Ren, X., et al.: SSLRec: a self-supervised learning framework for recommendation. In: WSDM (2024)
28. van den Oord, A., Li, Y., Vinyals, O.: Representation learning with contrastive predictive coding. arXiv preprint arXiv:1807.03748 (2018)
29. Wei, W., et al.: Contrastive meta learning with behavior multiplicity for recommendation. In: WSDM (2022)
30. Chen, T., et al.: A simple framework for contrastive learning of visual representations. In: ICML (2020)
31. Stojanovski, D., et al.: ContraCAT: contrastive coreference analytical templates for machine translation. In: COLING (2020)
32. Qiu, J., et al.: GCC: graph contrastive coding for graph neural network pre-training. In: SIGKDD (2020)
33. Huang, J., et al.: Correcting sample selection bias by unlabeled data. In: Advances in Neural Information Processing Systems 19 (2006)
34. Grozin, V., Levina, A.: Similar Product Clustering for Long-Tail Cross-Sell Recommendations. AIST (Supplement) (2017)
35. Yin, H., et al.: Challenging the long tail recommendation. arXiv preprint arXiv:1205.6700 (2012)
36. Zhang, Y., et al.: A model of two tales: dual transfer learning framework for improved long-tail item recommendation. In: WWW (2021)
37. Gong, Z., et al.: Full index deep retrieval: end-to-end user and item structures for cold-start and long-tail item recommendation. In: RecSys (2023)
38. Hu, Y., et al.: Memory bank augmented long-tail sequential recommendation. In: CIKM (2022)
39. Rendle, S., et al.: BPR: Bayesian personalized ranking from implicit feedback. arXiv preprint arXiv:1205.2618 (2012)
40. Gutmann, M., Hyvärinen, A.: Noise-contrastive estimation: a new estimation principle for unnormalized statistical models. In: AISTATS (2010)
41. Lin, S., et al.: Prototypical graph contrastive learning. IEEE Trans. Neural Netw. Learn. Syst. **35**(2), 2747–2758 (2022)

MAGNet: Multi-level Attention For Guided Thermal Infrared Image Super-Resolution

Zhoutong Xu and Zhangye Wang$^{(\boxtimes)}$

State Key Lab of CAD&CG, College of Computer Science and Technology,
Zhejiang University, Hangzhou 310058, China
22321093@zju.edu.cn, zywang@cad.zju.edu.cn

Abstract. Thermal infrared (TIR) images play a crucial role in applications such as object detection and autonomous driving. However, unlike high-resolution visible light cameras, which are now widely available, capturing high-resolution TIR images typically requires costly specialized equipment. In this paper, we propose MAGNet, a novel model designed to synthesize high-resolution TIR images from low-resolution TIR images and high-resolution visible light images. Our approach first employs a CNN to extract multi-scale features from both input images. These features are then fused using a Swin Transformer, producing a series of hierarchical feature maps. Finally, a sequence of convolutional and upsampling layers decodes these hierarchical representations into a high-resolution TIR image. Unlike other methods, MAGNet combines multi-level CNN and Swin Transformer for image fusion and reconstruction, which improves the SR results, especially in complicated scenarios. We evaluate MAGNet on the VGTSR dataset, where it outperforms state-of-the-art methods. Furthermore, its symmetric architecture allows for potential extension to cross-modal image fusion, real-time thermal enhancement, and unaligned SR tasks.

Keywords: Guided super-resolution · Thermal image super-resolution · Multimodal · Image fusion

1 Introduction

Thermal infrared (TIR) imaging plays an important role in a wide range of applications such as automation [1], surveillance [2], and secure-inspection [3], due to its ability to capture heat radiation and operate under challenging lighting conditions. However, acquiring high-resolution TIR images remains a significant challenge, as thermal sensors are often expensive and limited in spatial resolution [4]. In contrast, visible light cameras are inexpensive and capable of capturing rich structural and textural details at high resolutions. This complementary nature of RGB and TIR modalities has motivated a growing interest in

J. Lokoč et al. (Eds.): MMM 2026, LNCS 16412, pp. 60–73, 2026.
https://doi.org/10.1007/978-981-95-6950-2_5

cross-modal super-resolution, where high-resolution (HR) RGB images are used to guide the enhancement of low-resolution (LR) TIR inputs [5].

Despite recent progress in deep learning-based single image super-resolution methods [6–8], effectively bridging the modality gap between TIR and RGB images remains challenging. The two modalities differ not only in appearance and texture but also in semantic representation, which makes simple feature concatenation or fusion insufficient for accurate reconstruction. Moreover, capturing fine-grained cross-modal correspondences while preserving modality-specific characteristics requires careful network design.

To address these challenges, we propose MAGNet, a novel Multi-level Attention-Guided Network that leverages hierarchical Swin Transformer [9,10] blocks for cross-modal feature fusion and reconstruction. Our model adopts a U-shaped encoder-decoder architecture [11] with multiple Cross-Modal Fusion Modules (CMFM), each composed of bidirectional Swin Cross-Attention and Self-Attention blocks. These modules progressively integrate thermal and visible information across scales while maintaining modality-specific processing paths. In addition, we introduce structural modifications such as improved layer normalization placement and a residual output strategy to further enhance training stability and reconstruction quality.

The experiments conducted on the VGTSR [12] dataset demonstrate that MAGNet consistently outperforms existing state-of-the-art methods in both quantitative metrics and perceptual fidelity. Our contributions can be summarized as follows:

- We design a multi-scale cross-modal fusion network that integrates Transformer-based attention mechanisms for effective TIR super-resolution guided by RGB images.
- We adopt a U-Net-like architecture to capture long-range dependencies while reducing the number of Transformer layers to improve training efficiency and memory usage.
- We introduce a novel training strategy using cropped full-image, which increase the training efficiency and data diversity.

2   Related Work

In this section, we review the works aiming at synthesizing high-resolution TIR images. This includes single image super-resolution(SISR) methods, modality conversion(MC) methods, and guided super-resolution(GSR) methods.

2.1   Single Image Super-Resolution

Single image super-resolution has been extensively studied in the field of low-level vision [4], converting LR images to HR images. Classical methods based on deep learning such as SRCNN [13], VDSR [6], and EDSR [8] apply convolutional neural networks to learn a mapping from low-resolution to high-resolution images. With the growing popularity of generative adversarial networks (GANs) [14], several GAN-based SISR approaches have been proposed, such as SPSR [15]. These methods focus on enhancing perceptual quality and high-frequency texture reconstruction by introducing adversarial and perceptual losses. More recently, transformer-based [16] methods like SwinIR [7] and diffusion-based methods like ResShift [17] have shown strong performance in recovering global and local structures. While effective in general-purpose SISR tasks, these methods typically do not consider the modality-specific characteristics of thermal images, limiting their performance in TIR scenarios.

2.2   Modality Conversion

Modality conversion (MC) methods focus on learning mappings between visible and thermal domains. This includes GAN-based methods, such as [18,19], which utilize GANs to generate synthetic TIR images from visible inputs. Recently, diffusion-based methods have also been explored for modality conversion [20], offering improved generation quality and semantic fidelity by modeling the image distribution in a probabilistic framework. However, although modality conversion methods can learn the statistical correspondence between the two modalities, some features in the thermal domain have no direct counterpart in the visible domain due to fundamental physical differences. As a result, these methods are inherently limited in their ability to fully reconstruct the thermal image.

2.3   Guided Super-Resolution

Guided super-resolution (GSR) methods aim to enhance a low-resolution target image by exploiting high-resolution information from a guidance image in another modality. In the thermal domain, methods like MGNet [12], UGSR [5] and CENet [21] have demonstrated the effectiveness of using visible images to guide thermal SR. Our work builds on this line of research by introducing a multi-level Swin Transformer-based fusion mechanism that allows bidirectional cross-modal interaction while preserving hierarchical structure.

3   Methodology

3.1   Overall Architecture

We propose MAGNet, a novel encoder-decoder network designed for visible-guided thermal infrared super-resolution. The overall architecture follows a U-Net-like [11] structure, consisting of multiple downsampling and upsampling stages. Given a low-resolution thermal infrared image (LR-TIR) and a high-resolution visible image (HR-RGB), the network aims to reconstruct a super-resolved thermal infrared image (SR-TIR). The overall structure is shown in Fig. 1, where each Cross-Modal Fusion Module (CMFM) includes several Swin

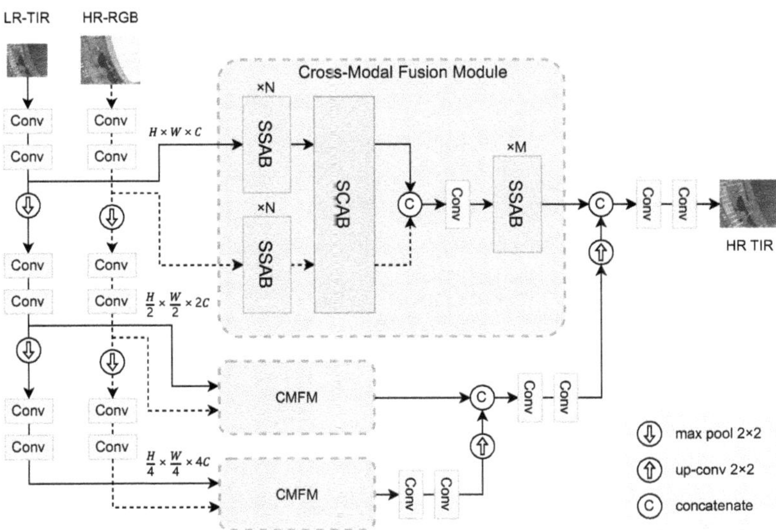

Fig. 1. Overall architecture of the proposed MAGNet. The model follows a U-shaped encoder-decoder structure with three hierarchical Cross-Modal Fusion Modules (CMFM). Each CMFM consists of multiple Swin Self-Attention Blocks (SSABs) and a Swin Cross-Attention Block (SCAB).

Self-Attention Blocks (SSAB) and a Swin Cross-Attention Block (SCAB), as detailed in Fig. 2.

In the encoder stage, we employ two parallel convolutional neural network (CNN) branches to extract local features from the TIR and RGB images, respectively. Each branch produces multi-scale feature maps with 64, 128, and 256 channels, capturing hierarchical texture and structural information.

These multi-level features are then fed into a Cross-Modal Fusion Module(CMFM) based on Swin Transformer [9,10]. A sequence of Swin Self-Attention modules is utilized to extract deep features. After that, we introduce a Swin Cross-Attention mechanism to enable effective interaction between thermal and visible features, followed by other Swin Self-Attention layers to refine and reconstruct the fused representation. Residual connections are applied throughout the Transformer blocks to stabilize training and enhance feature learning.

In the decoder stage, a series of upsampling and convolutional layers are used to progressively restore the spatial resolution of the feature maps. At each scale, the upsampled features are concatenated with the corresponding feature maps from the cross-modal fusion module. This is followed by convolutional refinement to enhance structural details and visual quality. Finally, the output of the last convolutional layer is passed through a tanh activation function, and the result is added to the original low-resolution thermal image via a residual connection to produce the final high-resolution output.

3.2   Cross-Modal Fusion Module

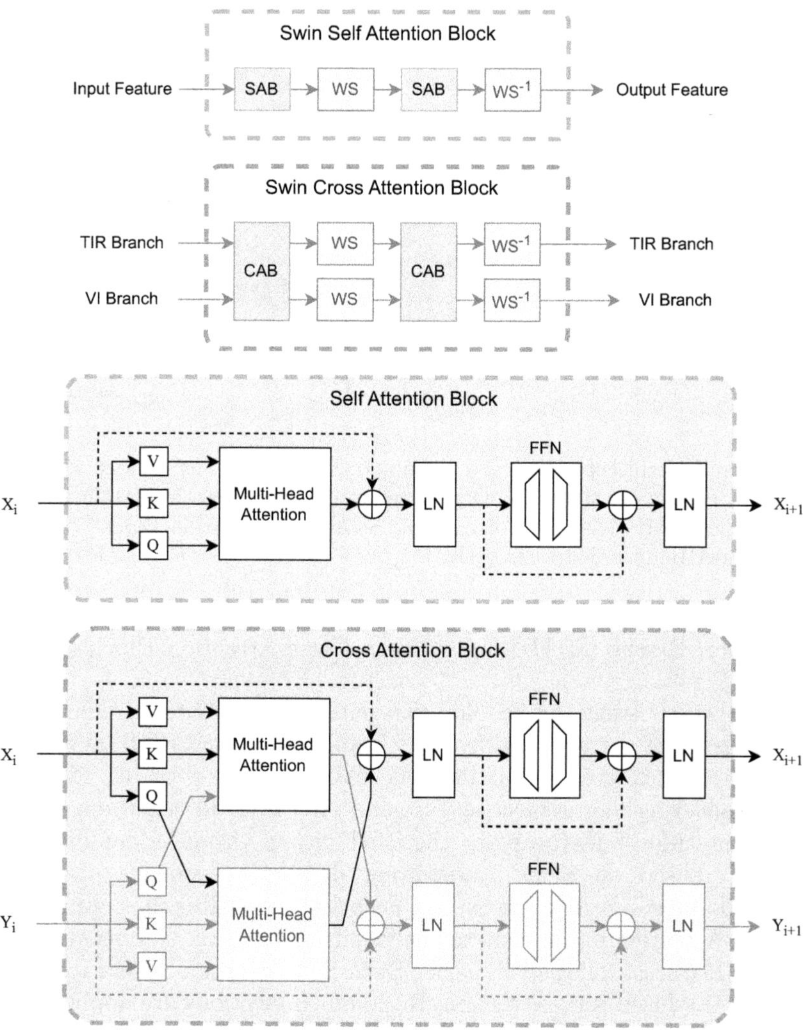

Fig. 2. Architecture of Swin Self Attention Block(SSAB) and Swin Cross Attention Block(SCAB). The Feed Forward Network(FFN) contains two linear layers with a scale factor of 2.

Inspired by SwinFusion [22], we design our Cross-Modal Fusion Module(CMFM) to deeply fuse the features from two modalities, shown in Fig. 1. In CMFM, the feature maps from the two modalities are first processed by N Swin Self-Attention Blocks (SSABs) for deep feature extraction. Then, a Swin Cross-Attention Block (SCAB) is used to perform feature fusion. Finally, the fused features are further refined and reconstructed through M additional SSABs. N and M are set to 3 and 4 in our implementation, respectively. The structure of SSAB and SCAB is shown in Fig. 2.

Each SSAB consists of two Self-Attention Blocks (SABs), with a window shift applied before the second SAB to enable cross-window interaction, where the entire feature map is shifted by half the window size to enable cross-window interaction across adjacent regions. The structure of the SCAB is similar, also including two attention blocks (CABs) with an intermediate window shift.

Inside SAB, local Self-Attention [16] is applied within non-overlapping windows to model intra-image spatial dependencies, shown as follows: Given an input feature map $X \in \mathbb{R}^{N \times d}$, where N is the number of pixels within a window and d is the feature dimension, the query, key, and value matrices are computed through linear transformations with learnable weight matrices $W_Q, W_K, W_V \in \mathbb{R}^{d \times d}$:

$$Q_X = XW_Q, \quad K_X = XW_K, \quad V_X = XW_V \tag{1}$$

The self-attention mechanism is then computed as:

$$Attention(Q, K, V) = softmax(QK^T/\sqrt{d_k} + B)V \tag{2}$$

where $B \in \mathbb{R}^{N \times N}$ is the learnable relative positional bias matrix. The whole process of Self-Attention Block (SAB) can be computed as follows:

$$\begin{aligned} SAB(X) &= LN(FFN(X') + X') \\ X' &= LN(Attention(Q_X, K_X, V_X) + X) \end{aligned} \tag{3}$$

where LN denotes Layer Normalization and FFN is the Feed-Forward Network that further refines the features. Residual connections are applied following the original Swin Transformer architecture. The output of SAB is identical to the input feature map, which can be fed to the next layer.

In CAB, we compute bidirectional cross-attention between corresponding windows of the two modalities. In the first direction, thermal features serve as queries, and visible features as keys and values–updating the TIR representation with fine-grained visual cues. Simultaneously, in the second direction, visible features serve as queries, and thermal features as keys and values–injecting thermal context into the visible branch. The updated features are then added back to their respective branches via residual connections, enabling each modality to be enhanced by the other while preserving their structural independence for further processing. The whole process of Cross-Attention Block(CAB) can be computed as follows:

$$\begin{aligned} CAB(X, Y) &= LN(FFN(X') + X') \\ X' &= LN(Attention(Q_X, K_Y, V_Y) + X) \end{aligned} \tag{4}$$

$$\{X_{i+1}, Y_{i+1}\} = \{CAB(X_i, Y_i), CAB(Y_i, X_i)\} \tag{5}$$

Here, X and Y denote feature maps from different modalities. The attention result is then added to the original X through a residual connection, and the combined output is passed through a Layer Normalization (LN) layer. This residual-normalized representation preserves the original modality structure while incorporating cross-modal information from the other modality.

After each branch has incorporated complementary information through SCAB, the updated feature maps from both modalities are concatenated along the channel dimension. The fused feature map is then fed into a series of SSAB, similar to those used in the earlier stages, to reconstruct and refine the fused multi-modal representations. This process allows the network to exploit cross-modal context while maintaining a unified, high-level semantic understanding of the image.

We introduce two major enhancements to SwinFusion [22]. The first key modification involves restructuring the interplay between Self-Attention and Cross-Attention layers. We strategically reduce the number of Cross-Attention layers to just two, leading to a substantial decrease in VRAM requirements for model training. Within our multi-scale framework, this modification proves more effective for feature fusion than the alternating attention design in SwinFusion.

Secondly, we modify the position of the Layer Normalization layers after the residual connection to ensure consistent feature distribution during propagation. The main branch of features is normalized after each attention and Feed-Forward layer. Comparing with SwinFusion [22], this adjustment leads to a more stable gradient in the training phase, especially for deeper networks.

3.3   Loss Function

To enhance the pixel accuracy, structural consistency, and edge sharpness of the generated images, we design a composite loss function that combines three complementary components: mean squared error (MSE) loss, structural similarity (SSIM) loss, and image gradient loss. The final loss is a weighted sum of these three terms:

MSE Loss This pixel-wise loss measures the direct difference between the generated super-resolved TIR image and the ground truth high-resolution TIR image. It effectively encourages overall luminance and pixel-level accuracy.

SSIM Loss To improve the structural integrity of the reconstructed image, we introduce the SSIM loss, which evaluates local structural similarity in terms of luminance, contrast, and texture. This term promotes better perceptual quality.

Gradient Loss To preserve edge sharpness and fine details, we compute the gradient loss by measuring the difference in image gradients between the generated and ground truth images along both horizontal and vertical directions. This guides the network to restore sharper boundaries and contours.

The final loss function is formulated as:

$$\mathcal{L}_{total} = \lambda_1 \cdot \mathcal{L}_{MSE} + \lambda_2 \cdot \mathcal{L}_{SSIM} + \lambda_3 \cdot \mathcal{L}_{grad} \tag{6}$$

In our experiments, the weights are set to $\lambda_1 = 1.0$, $\lambda_2 = 0.1$, and $\lambda_3 = 0.1$.

4   Experiments

4.1   Experimental Setup

We conduct our experiments on the VGTSR dataset [12], which contains 1025 image pairs. Each group includes six images: a high-resolution thermal infrared (TIR) image, a high-resolution visible image, two versions of 4× downsampled TIR images (one using Gaussian blur and one using bicubic interpolation), and two versions of 8× downsampled TIR images (blurred and interpolated). The resolution of the high-resolution images is 640×512. Following the protocol of previous works, we split the dataset into 800 groups for training and 225 for validation and testing.

In our proposed MAGNet, the number of feature extraction SSABs(N), the number of feature reconstruction SSABs(M), and the size of the window are set to 3, 4, and 8×8, respectively. The initial learning rate is set to 1×10^{-4}, and training is conducted for 300 epochs. As we train the model on full-resolution images rather than small patches, the batch size is set to 2, making our setup more efficient in terms of memory usage and training iterations. Comparing with patch-based input, full-resolution images contain the correlation between adjacent patches, which can be captured by the swin transformer modules.

Compared to other pure Transformer-based methods, our approach first transforms images into multi-resolution feature maps through convolutional neural networks. This enables us to achieve better performance with fewer Transformer layers while reducing memory consumption during training, allowing us to train the model on a single RTX 4080 GPU with only 16GB of memory.

4.2   Data Augmentation

To improve the generalization of our model, we introduce a structured random cropping strategy during training. Given that the minimum effective spatial unit in our network is 64×64 pixels, we crop each 640×512 image to a fixed resolution of 576×448. Specifically, 64 pixels are removed in total from the width and height, and the removed regions are randomly distributed to either the left or right side (for width) and top or bottom (for height). This allows the model to observe different spatial contexts while maintaining alignment with the network's architecture. This approach not only ensures compatibility with the network but also enhances robustness to image boundary variations. A comparison between our cropping strategy and the traditional random patch-based training method is shown in Fig. 3. The effectiveness of this cropping scheme is further verified in our ablation study.

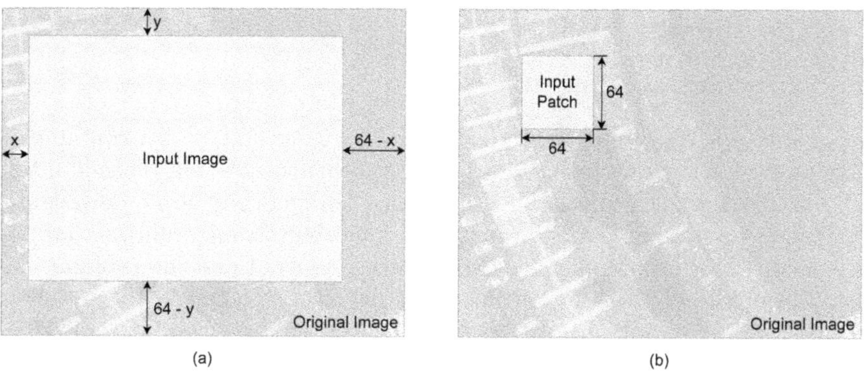

Fig. 3. Comparision between random cropping(a) and random patch-based method(b).

4.3   Evaluation

Table 1. Quantitative comparison with state-of-the-art methods for ×4 SR on the VGTSR dataset under bicubic (BI) and blur-downscale (BD) degradation models.

Method	Year	S/G	BI		BD	
			PSNR	SSIM	PSNR	SSIM
Bicubic		Single	26.65	0.7792	25.67	0.7551
SAN [23]	2019	Single	30.54	0.8916	30.44	0.8909
HAN [24]	2020	Single	30.61	0.8928	30.52	0.8933
SwinIR [7]	2021	Single	30.72	0.8943	30.71	0.8969
Restormer [25]	2022	Guided	30.71	0.8933	30.70	0.8962
MultiNet [26]	2017	Guided	30.31	0.8872	30.21	0.8449
PAG-SR [27]	2020	Guided	30.74	0.8951	30.74	0.8970
UGSR [5]	2021	Guided	30.29	0.8872	30.21	0.8875
MGNet [12]	2023	Guided	31.16	0.9033	31.08	0.9039
CENet [21]	2024	Guided	31.24	0.9035	31.22	0.9072
MagNet(Ours)		Guided	**33.25**	**0.9219**	**33.15**	**0.9196**

To validate the performance of MAGNet, we compare it with several state-of-the-art Guided Super-Resolution(GSR) methods, including CENet [21], MGNet [12], and UGSR [5]. We also compare our model with some other Single-Image Super-Resolution(SISR) methods. These methods represent the current mainstream approaches for cross-modal image fusion and thermal infrared super-resolution.

We use two common evaluation metrics: peak signal-to-noise ratio (PSNR) and structural similarity index measure (SSIM). Higher PSNR and SSIM values are better. As shown in Table 1 and Table 2, under both 4× and 8× super-resolution settings, and for both bicubic interpolation (BI) and blur degradation

Table 2. Quantitative comparison with state-of-the-art methods for ×8 SR on the VGTSR dataset under bicubic (BI) and blur-downscale (BD) degradation models.

Method	Year	S/G	BI		BD	
			PSNR	SSIM	PSNR	SSIM
Bicubic		Single	22.69	0.5951	22.48	0.6122
SAN [23]	2019	Single	25.11	0.6952	24.43	0.7147
HAN [24]	2020	Single	25.15	0.7094	24.46	0.7109
SwinIR [7]	2021	Single	25.28	0.7240	24.70	0.7286
Restormer [25]	2022	Guided	25.08	0.7174	24.46	0.7152
MultiNet [26]	2017	Guided	25.10	0.7186	24.49	0.7186
PAG-SR [27]	2020	Guided	25.28	0.7253	24.78	0.7331
UGSR [5]	2021	Guided	25.04	0.7160	24.43	0.7164
MGNet [12]	2023	Guided	25.86	0.7492	25.39	0.7566
CENet [21]	2024	Guided	26.03	0.7602	25.56	0.7658
MagNet(Ours)		Guided	**28.42**	**0.8246**	**28.03**	**0.8236**

(BD) downsampling methods, our model achieves significantly higher PSNR and SSIM scores than all existing methods.

In addition to achieving superior quantitative results, our method also demonstrates visually favorable perceptual quality. As illustrated in Fig. 4, the proposed approach preserves finer structural details and recovers more high-frequency textures compared to existing methods. For instance, in the third and sixth rows, competing approaches yield over-smoothed results, failing to reconstruct the building's distinct contours. In contrast, MAGNet restores these fine details by leveraging structural information from the RGB image, underscoring the effectiveness of our cross-modal fusion strategy.

4.4   Ablation Study

Table 3. Ablation study: Effect of SSAB in feature extraction and reconstruction.

Method	PSNR	SSIM
$N = 1, M = 4$	27.06	0.7708
$N = 2, M = 4$	27.94	0.8070
$N = 3, M = 2$	27.73	0.7948
$N = 3, M = 3$	28.04	0.8117
$N = 3, M = 4$	**28.42**	**0.8246**

To better understand the effectiveness of different components in our proposed MAGNet, we conduct a series of ablation studies. Specifically, we investigate the impact of the feature extraction layers, the reconstruction layers, the number of

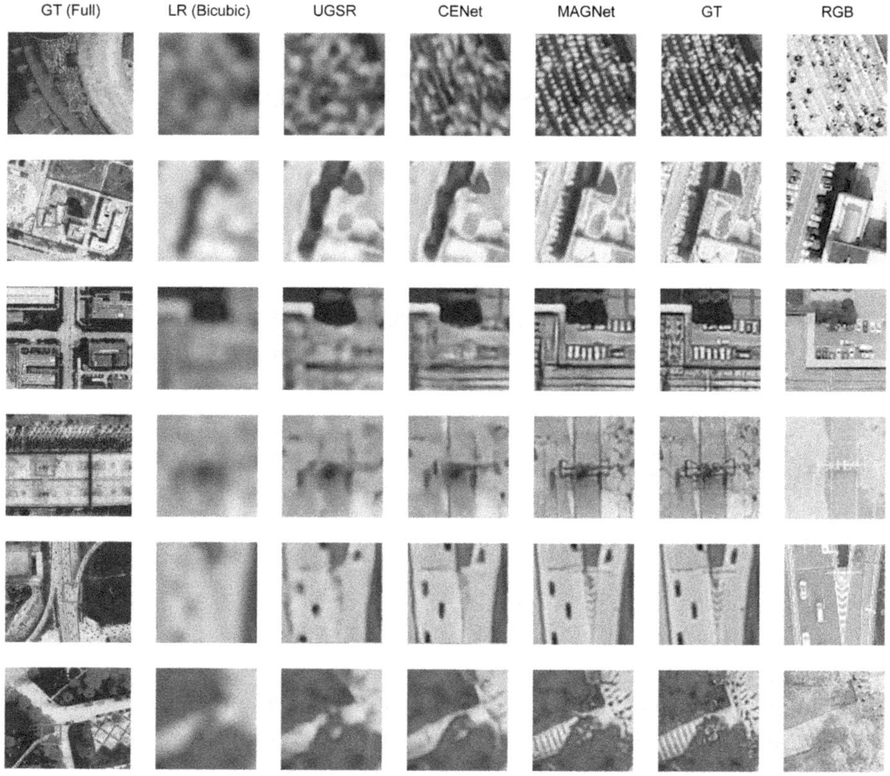

Fig. 4. Visual comparison of 8× super-resolution results, alongside the low-resolution input, RGB guidance, and ground truth.

downsampling stages, the position of layer normalization, and the use of data augmentation during training. For each ablation setting, we modify only the targeted component while keeping the rest of the network unchanged, ensuring a fair and isolated evaluation. In the ablation study, we train all models using bicubic degradation and setting the super-resolution scale to 8.

We first explore the effect of varying the number of Swin Self-Attention Blocks (SSAB) used in the feature extraction (N) and reconstruction (M) stages. As shown in Table 3, increasing N and M leads to steady improvements.

Next, we analyze the impact of the number of downsampling stages in the encoder. As shown in Table 4, increasing downsampling stages to 3 significantly improves both PSNR and SSIM compared to a single-stage setup, indicating the benefit of deeper hierarchical feature extraction and multi-scale fusion. We also examine the role of data augmentation and main branch normalization. The results are shown in Table 5.

Table 4. Ablation study: Effect of the number of downsampling stages in the U-shape encoder-decoder structure.

Method	PSNR	SSIM
downsampling stages $= 1$	27.08	0.7713
downsampling stages $= 2$	28.00	0.8102
downsampling stages $= 3$	**28.42**	**0.8246**

Table 5. Ablation study: Effect of data augmentation and main branch Layer Normalization(LN).

Method	PSNR	SSIM
w/o data augmentation	28.17	0.8102
w/o main branch LN	27.65	0.7941
MAGNet	**28.42**	**0.8246**

5 Conclusion

In this paper, we proposed MAGNet, a novel multi-level cross-modal fusion network designed for RGB-guided thermal infrared image super-resolution. Our method integrates a hierarchical CNN-based feature extraction structure with Swin Transformer-based self-attention and cross-attention modules, enabling effective cross-modal information exchange and deep feature reconstruction. We further introduced several architectural refinements, such as a redesigned attention fusion module and improved normalization placement, which contribute to training stability and performance. The experiments on the VGTSR dataset demonstrate that MAGNet outperforms existing state-of-the-art methods in both objective metrics and visual quality. Ablation studies validate the contributions of each component and highlight the benefits of multi-scale fusion, deep reconstruction, and data augmentation. In future work, we plan to extend MAGNet to real-time thermal enhancement, unaligned multi-modal super-resolution, and video-based cross-modal restoration.

References

1. Borges, P.V.K., Vidas, S.: Practical infrared visual odometry. IEEE Trans. Intell. Transp. Syst. **17**, 2205–2213 (2016)
2. Wong, W.K., Lim, H.L., Loo, C.K. Lim, W.S.: Home alone faint detection surveillance system using thermal camera. In: 2010 Second International Conference on Computer Research and Development, pp. 747–751 (2010)
3. Shao, Z., Tao Liang, Y., Tian, F., Song, S., Deng, R.: Constructing 3D land surface temperature model of local coal fires using UAV thermal images. IEEE Trans. Geosci. Remote Sens. **60**, 1–9 (2022)
4. Huang, Y., Miyazaki, T., Liu, X.F., Omachi, S.: Infrared image super-resolution: systematic review, and future trends. arXiv abs/2212.12322 (2022)

5. Gupta, H., Mitra, K.: Toward unaligned guided thermal super-resolution. IEEE Trans. Image Process. **31**, 433–445 (2021)
6. Kim, J., Lee, J.K., Lee, K.M.: Accurate image super-resolution using very deep convolutional networks. In: 2016 IEEE Conference on Computer Vision and Pattern Recognition (CVPR), pp. 1646–1654 (2015)
7. Liang, J., Cao, J., Sun, G., Zhang, K., Van Gool, L., Timofte, R.: Swinir: image restoration using swin transformer. In: Proceedings of the IEEE/CVF International Conference on Computer Vision, pp. 1833–1844 (2021)
8. Lim, B., Son, S., Kim, H., Nah, S., Lee, K.M.: Enhanced deep residual networks for single image super-resolution. In: 2017 IEEE Conference on Computer Vision and Pattern Recognition Workshops (CVPRW), pp. 1132–1140 (2017)
9. Liu, Z., et al.: Swin transformer: hierarchical vision transformer using shifted windows. In: Proceedings of the IEEE/CVF International Conference on Computer Vision, pp. 10012–10022 (2021)
10. Liu, Z., et al.: Swin transformer v2: Scaling up capacity and resolution. In: Proceedings of the IEEE/CVF Conference on Computer Vision and Pattern Recognition, pp. 12009–12019 (2022)
11. Ronneberger, O., Fischer, P., Brox, T.: U-net: convolutional networks for biomedical image segmentation. arXiv abs/1505.04597 (2015)
12. Zhao, Z., Zhang, Y., Li, C., Xiao, Y., Tang, J.: Thermal UAV image super-resolution guided by multiple visible cues. IEEE Trans. Geosci. Remote Sens. **61**, 1–14 (2023)
13. Dong, C., Loy, C.C., He, K., Tang, X.: Image super-resolution using deep convolutional networks. IEEE Trans. Pattern Anal. Mach. Intell. **38**, 295–307 (2014)
14. Goodfellow, I., et al.: Generative adversarial networks. Commun. ACM **63**(11), 139–144 (2020)
15. Ma, C., Rao, Y., Cheng, Y., Chen, C., Lu, J., Zhou, J.: Structure-preserving super resolution with gradient guidance. In: Proceedings of the IEEE/CVF Conference on Computer Vision and Pattern Recognition, pp. 7769–7778 (2020)
16. Vaswani, A., et al.: Attention is all you need. In: Neural Information Processing Systems (2017)
17. Yue, Z., Wang, J., Loy, C.C.: Efficient diffusion model for image restoration by residual shifting. IEEE Trans. Pattern Anal. Mach. Intell. **47**, 116–130 (2024)
18. Zhu, J.Y., Park, T., Isola, P., Efros, A.A.: Unpaired image-to-image translation using cycle-consistent adversarial networks. In: 2017 IEEE International Conference on Computer Vision (ICCV), pp. 2242–2251 (2017)
19. Özkanoğlu, M.A., Ozer, S.: InfraGAN: a GAN architecture to transfer visible images to infrared domain. Pattern Recogn. Lett. **155**, 69–76 (2022)
20. Mao, F., et al.: PID: physics-informed diffusion model for infrared image generation. arXiv abs/2407.09299 (2024)
21. Zhao, Z., Wang, C., Li, C., Zhang, Y., Tang, J.: Modality conversion meets super-resolution: a collaborative framework for high-resolution thermal UAV image generation. IEEE Trans. Geosci. Remote Sens. **62**, 1–14 (2024)
22. Ma, J., Tang, L., Fan, F., Huang, J., Mei, X., Ma, Y.: Swinfusion: Cross-domain long-range learning for general image fusion via swin transformer. IEEE/CAA J. Automatica Sinica **9**(7), 1200–1217 (2022)
23. Dai, T., Cai, J., Zhang, Y., Xia, S.T., Zhang, L.: Second-order attention network for single image super-resolution. In: 2019 IEEE/CVF Conference on Computer Vision and Pattern Recognition (CVPR), pp. 11057–11066 (2019). https://doi.org/10.1109/CVPR.2019.01132

24. Niu, B., et al.: Single image super-resolution via a holistic attention network. In: Vedaldi, A., Bischof, H., Brox, T., Frahm, J.-M. (eds.) ECCV 2020. LNCS, vol. 12357, pp. 191–207. Springer, Cham (2020). https://doi.org/10.1007/978-3-030-58610-2_12
25. Zamir, S.W., Arora, A., Khan, S., Hayat, M., Khan, F.S., Yang, M.H.: Restormer: efficient transformer for high-resolution image restoration. In: CVPR (2022)
26. Han, T.Y., Kim, Y.J., Song, B.C.: Convolutional neural network-based infrared image super resolution under low light environment. In: 2017 25th European Signal Processing Conference (EUSIPCO), pp. 803–807 (2017). https://doi.org/10.23919/EUSIPCO.2017.8081318
27. Gupta, H., Mitra, K.: Pyramidal edge-maps and attention based guided thermal super-resolution. In: Bartoli, A., Fusiello, A. (eds.) ECCV 2020. LNCS, vol. 12537, pp. 698–715. Springer, Cham (2020). https://doi.org/10.1007/978-3-030-67070-2_42

MMDocBench: Benchmarking Large Vision-Language Models for Fine-Grained Visual Document Understanding and Grounding

Fengbin Zhu[1,2]([✉]) [iD], Ziyang Liu[2] [iD], NG Xiang Yao[2] [iD], Haohui Wu[2] [iD],
Wenjie Wang[3] [iD], Fuli Feng[3] [iD], Chao Wang[2] [iD], Huanbo Luan[2] [iD],
and Tat-Seng Chua[1] [iD]

[1] National University of Singapore, Singapore, Singapore
[2] 6Estates Pte Ltd, Singapore, Singapore
`zhfengbin@gmail.com`
[3] University of Science and Technology of China, Hefei, China

Abstract. Large Vision-Language Models (LVLMs) have achieved remarkable performance in many vision-language tasks, yet their capabilities in fine-grained visual understanding remain insufficiently evaluated. Existing benchmarks either contain limited fine-grained evaluation tasks and/or samples or are confined to object-level assessments in natural images. To holistically assess LVLMs' fine-grained visual understanding capabilities, we propose using document images with multi-granularity and multi-modal information to supplement natural images. In this light, we construct MMDocBench, a benchmark with various OCR-free document understanding tasks for the evaluation of fine-grained visual perception, reasoning and grounding abilities. MMDocBench defines 15 main tasks with $4,338$ QA pairs and $11,353$ supporting regions, covering various document images such as research papers, receipts, financial reports, Wikipedia tables, charts, and infographics. Based on MMDocBench, we conduct extensive experiments using 17 open-source and 5 proprietary advanced LVLMs, assessing their strengths and weaknesses across different tasks and document image types. The official website is https://mmdocbench.github.io/.

Keywords: Vision-Language Models · Visual Document Understanding

1 Introduction

Large Vision-Language Models (LVLMs) have attained remarkable performance across various vision-language tasks [32]. However, current LVLMs, e.g. GPT-4V [17] and LLaVA [9], struggle with understanding fine-grained visual details in images. For instance, many LVLMs perform poorly in visual grounding of image

© The Author(s), under exclusive license to Springer Nature Singapore Pte Ltd. 2026
J. Lokoč et al. (Eds.): MMM 2026, LNCS 16412, pp. 74–88, 2026.
https://doi.org/10.1007/978-981-95-6950-2_6

- We highlight the gap in existing benchmarks for evaluating LVLMs' fine-grained visual understanding capabilities. Besides, we propose leveraging document images with multi-granularity and multi-type information to complement natural images in assessing the fine-grained visual perception and reasoning abilities of LVLMs.
- We construct MMDocBench, a comprehensive benchmark for tracking LVLMs' progress in fine-grained visual document understanding. MMDocBench defines 15 main tasks and 48 sub-tasks over a wide range of document types, involving 2,400 document images, 4,338 QA pairs, and 11,353 supporting regions for a holistic evaluation.
- We conduct extensive experiments with 22 representative LVLMs on MMDocBench. We report the major strengths and weaknesses of LVLMs in different tasks and document types and provide valuable insights, facilitating the advancements of LVLMs in future.

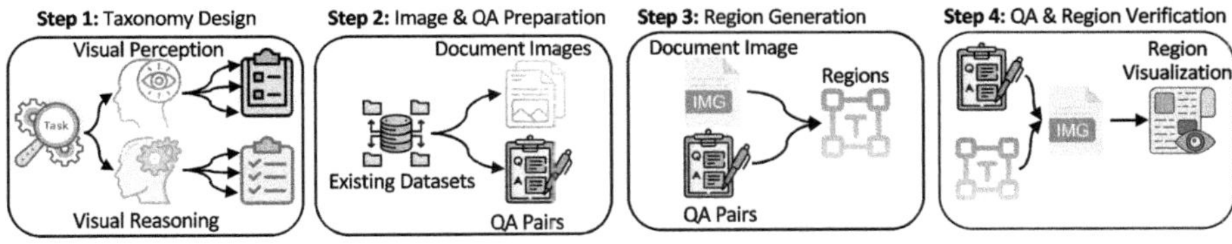

Fig. 2. An illustration of the benchmark construction pipeline for MMDocBench.

2 Proposed MMDocBench

2.1 Problem Definition

On MMDocBench, LVLMs are expected to output the precise answer to a natural language query given a document image while highlighting supporting regions within the image contributing to inferring the answer. Formally, given a document image d possibly containing text, table, chart, and/or figure, for a question q, a Large Vision-Language Model $\mathcal{M}$ is required to produce a response including the answer a and corresponding regions R as supporting evidence:

$$\mathcal{M}(d, q) = (a, R). \tag{1}$$

Each region in R is a bounding box that is represented by the coordinates of its top-left and bottom-right corners in the format of $[x_1, y_1, x_2, y_2]$.

2.2 Construction Pipeline

The pipeline for constructing our MMDocBench is illustrated in Fig. 2.
Step 1: Taxonomy Design. Targeting at a comprehensive evaluation of LVLMs' fine-grained visual understanding capabilities, we design the taxonomy of MMDocBench following two principles.

Table 1. Taxonomy and statistics of MMDocBench.

Main Task	Sub Task	Document Image Type	#Image	#QA	#Region
Fine-Grained Visual Perception					
Text Recognition	TextOCR [24]	Scene-Text Images	100	100	100
	BookOCR [16]	Book Covers	100	100	438
Table Recognition	FinTabNet [38]	Financial Reports	100	100	1,864
	PubTables-1M [25]	Scientific Papers	100	100	3,520
Text Localization	Text2Bbox ([22] etc.)	Industry Doc.	100	100	100
	Bbox2Text ([22] etc.)	Industry Doc.	100	100	100
Table Cell Localization	FinTabNet [38]	Financial Reports	100	100	100
	PubTables-1M [25]	Scientific Papers	100	100	100
Key Information Extraction	SROIE [5]	Receipts	100	303	303
	WildReceipt [26]	Receipts	100	512	512
	CORD [18]	Receipts	100	372	372
Doc Forgery Detection	T-SROIE [37]	Receipts	100	100	286
	DocTamper [21]	Cross-Domain Doc.	100	100	129
Document QA	DocVQA [14]	Industry Doc.	100	262	262
	WTQ [19]	Wikipedia Tables	100	351	351
	TAT-DQA [41]	Financial Reports	100	214	214
Chart QA	ChartQA [12]	Cross-Domain Charts	100	104	104
	CharXiv [30]	Scientific Charts	100	149	149
Infographic QA	InfographicVQA [13]	Infographics	100	281	281
Fine-Grained Visual Reasoning					
Arithmetic Reasoning	DUDE [28]	General Doc.	13	15	34
	WTQ [19]	Wikipedia Tables	54	55	159
	TAT-DQA [41]	Financial Table-Text Doc.	98	217	453
	CharXiv [30]	Scientific Charts	23	23	67
	InfographicVQA [13]	Infographics	34	53	90
Logical Reasoning	DUDE [28]	General Doc.	10	11	20
	WTQ [19]	Wikipedia Tables	11	11	41
	TAT-DQA [41]	Financial Table-Text Doc.	1	1	2
	CharXiv [30]	Scientific Charts	7	7	12
	InfographicVQA [13]	Infographics	2	2	3
Spatial Reasoning	DUDE [28]	General Doc.	38	41	43
	WTQ [19]	Wikipedia Tables	4	4	8
	CharXiv [30]	Scientific Charts	7	7	12
	InfographicVQA [13]	Infographics	17	23	54
Comparison	DUDE [28]	Cross-Domain Doc.	3	3	6
	WTQ [19]	Wikipedia Tables	33	34	74
	TAT-DQA [41]	Financial Table-Text Doc.	10	10	30
	CharXiv [30]	Scientific Charts	16	16	44
	InfographicVQA [13]	Infographics	13	15	44
Sorting	DUDE [28]	General Doc.	3	3	6
	WTQ [19]	Wikipedia Tables	6	12	23
	TAT-DQA [41]	Financial Table-Text Doc.	7	7	14
	CharXiv [30]	Scientific Charts	15	15	29
	InfographicVQA [13]	Infographics	20	29	57
Counting	DUDE [28]	General Doc.	51	55	244
	WTQ [19]	Wikipedia Tables	15	15	76
	TAT-DQA [41]	Financial Table-Text Doc.	14	14	26
	CharXiv [30]	Scientific Charts	38	40	149
	InfographicVQA [13]	Infographics	44	52	248

- **Fine-grained Discrimination**: The MMDocBench must provide tasks that can adeptly evaluate LVLMs' visual comprehension capabilities with sufficient discriminability of fine-grained details in the image, rather than treating the image as a whole.
- **Diversity**: The MMDocBench must encompass a broad range of tasks in terms of required capabilities (e.g., perception, reasoning), content granularity

(e.g., characters, words, tables), and document types (e.g., scientific papers, financial reports, receipts).

To address the challenges in MMDocBench, two capabilities are at the core for LVLMs, i.e. fine-grained visual perception and fine-grained visual reasoning [10]. To investigate both capabilities, we design 15 tasks in MMDocBench. Specifically, we encompass nine tasks for fine-grained visual perception: Text Recognition, Table Recognition, Text Localization, Table Cell Localization, Key Information Extraction, Document Forgery Detection, Document Question Answering, Chart Question Answering, and Infographic Question Answering; for fine-grained visual reasoning, we include six tasks: Arithmetic Reasoning, Logical Reasoning, Spatial Reasoning, Comparison, Sorting and Counting. Further, we include one or multiple sub-tasks per task to cover more diverse document image types, e.g. research papers, book covers, financial reports, scene-text images, receipts, Wikipedia tables, charts, infographics, and other industry documents, leading to totally 48 sub-tasks in MMDocBench. See a summary in Table 1.

Table 2. Comparison with other benchmarks for evaluating LVLMs.

Benchmark	Image Type	Visual Grounding	Grounding Level	Total # of Regions	Average # Regions per Image	# Images	# QA Pairs
MMVet	Mix	✗	N/A	N/A	N/A	200	218
MME	Mix	✗	N/A	N/A	N/A	1,187	2,374
MMBench	Mix	✗	N/A	N/A	N/A	3,217	3,217
TextVQA	Document Image	✗	N/A	N/A	N/A	28,408	45,336
DocVQA	Document Image	✗	N/A	N/A	N/A	12,767	50,000
OCRBench	Document Image	✗	N/A	N/A	N/A	1,000	1,000
MMLongBench-Doc	Document Image	✗	N/A	N/A	N/A	6,412	1,082
GVT-Bench	Natural Image	✗	N/A	N/A	N/A	12,823	40,000
Ref-COCO	Natural Image	✓	Object	50,000	2.5	19,994	142,209
Visual7W	Natural Image	✓	Object	561,459	12	47,300	327,939
MMDocBench	Document Image	✓	Element	11,353	4.7	2,400	4,338

Step 2: Document Image & QA Pair Preparation. As shown in Table 1, we create BookOCR, Bbox2Text, and Text2Bbox by ourselves and use original task settings for other sub-tasks. In particular, we build BookOCR, a text recognition dataset, based on selected document images (i.e., book covers) from OCR-VQA [16]. After collecting document images, we use a pre-defined template for text recognition as the question and automatically identify all the OCR content from the image as the ground-truth answer. We build Text2Bbox and Bbox2Text with the same document images, which are selected from DocILE [22], RVL-CDIP [4], DocBank [7], PubLayNet [40] and PubTabNet [39] to cover more diverse document types. The former task requires an LVLM to find the region in the document image given a piece of textual content, while the latter needs the model to identify corresponding text in the document image based on a specified bounding box. For the three sub-tasks, our annotators (6 undergraduate or graduate students majored in computer science) manually create one QA pair for each selected document image.

For other sub-tasks, our annotators manually analyze and select appropriate document images with annotated input-output pairs from the source dataset.

Then, the input-output pairs are transformed into QA pairs following pre-defined templates. Note that all document images and QA pairs are selected from the test set of the source dataset except CORD [18], DUDE [28] and CharXiv [30]. CORD has an insufficient number of high-quality document images in its test set, so we select some from its validation set. DUDE and CharXiv have not yet released their test sets, and thus we utilize their validation sets instead. For each sub-task, we at most select 100 document images.

Note that for preparing sub-tasks of fine-grained visual reasoning, we purposely select five existing datasets to ensure MMDocBench to cover a great diversity of document image types, including DUDE [28] containing general documents from various industries, WTQ [19] containing table-based documents from Wikipedia, TAT-DQA [41] containing table-text documents from financial reports, ChartXiv [30] containing chart-based documents from scientific papers, and InfographicVQA [13] containing infographic-based documents.

Step 3: Region Generation. We generate ground truth regions for each QA pair in MMDocBench to facilitate evaluation. Similar to [1,31], we normalize the coordinates representing the bounding box to the range [0, 1000] w.r.t. the image dimensions. For the tasks regarding fine-grained visual perception, we set the answer's location on the image as the region to be annotated, while for those regarding fine-grained visual reasoning, we annotate the locations of all supporting evidences used to infer the final answer. Specifically, we first obtain the OCR results using Google OCR service for each document image in MMDocBench. For fine-grained visual perception tasks, we automatically identify the corresponding value and its bounding box in the OCR result based on the answer. If only one value matches, we use the region of this value as the correct one; otherwise, our annotators manually review and select the appropriate region for the answer. For fine-grained visual reasoning tasks, we search for the regions for each supporting evidence if the source dataset already provides the annotation of supporting evidence, like TAT-DQA [41]; for the rest, our annotators manually check supporting evidence and annotate the appropriate region for each one.

Step 4: QA & Region Verification. To ensure high quality of MMDocBench, we further verify the collected data. First, we develop a program to automatically highlight the answer or supporting evidence with its corresponding regions on the document image. Then, different annotators review the rendered document image in three rounds to ensure that the answer and supporting regions to the question are correct.

2.3   Comparison with Other Benchmarks

We provide a comparison of our MMDocBench with existing benchmarks to stress its merits, as shown in Table 2. It can be observed that most existing LVLM benchmarks are inadequate for assessing the visual LVLMs' grounding capabilities. While some benchmarks like Visual7W [42], RefCOCO [35], support visual grounding evaluation, they focus primarily on *object-level* grounding within natural images. This limits their applicability to document images containing diverse *semantic elements* such as tables, charts, and text. Moreover, these benchmarks involve fewer tasks compared to our MMDocBench, restricting their utility for comprehensively assessing LVLMs' visual grounding capabilities.

2.4   Statistics and Analysis

Since the semantic content (e.g., textual words) in MMDocBench plays a vital role. To assess this, We analyzed the information density by measuring the number of characters, words, and the area occupied by content in each image. The results in Table Table 3 indicate that over 50% of the document images in MMDocBench contain more than 160 words while occupying only 15% of the area. This high information density demands that LVLMs possess strong fine-grained visual grounding and understanding capabilities to accurately locate and interpret the relevant information required to answer questions.

Furthermore, we analyze the position distribution and area distribution of the annotated supporting regions for each QA pair in our MMDocBench. To compute the position distribution, given a region $[x_1, y_1, x_2, y_2]$, we first calculate the center point by $(\frac{x_1+x_2}{2}, \frac{y_1+y_2}{2})$. Then, we plot all the center points on an image with a dimension of 1000×1000. As shown in Fig. 3, all points are scattered across the entire image, indicating no clear positional bias for supporting regions in MMDocBench. We also analyze the area distribution of all regions to examine their granularity. We first calculate the area of each region and then apply a logarithmic transformation with a base of 10 on the computed area value. As shown in Fig. 4, the granularity of regions shows a diversity and the majority of the region areas fall between $1,000$ and $10,000$, corresponding to regions sized between 10×100 and 100×100. These analyses well highlight the high quality of our MMDocBench, which is crucial for accurately assessing the capabilities of LVLMs in fine-grained visual grounding and understanding.

Table 3. Analysis of information density in document images.

Statistic	Min	Max	Median	Mean
Number of Chars per Image	5	21,670	411	849
Number of Words per Image	1	4,581	163	163
Percentage of Areas with Content	6%	91%	15%	16%

3   Experiments

3.1   Experimental Setup

Evaluated LVLMs. We conduct experiments with 17 open-source LVLMs and 5 proprietary LVLMs on the MMDocBench. These models show a noticeable diversity in respective parameter sizes, visual encoders, and language models.

Instruction Design. For each main task in MMDocBench, we manually design an instruction template to guide the LVLM to output the answer and supporting regions in JSON format, e.g., {"answer":"{answer}", "bbox":["{bbox1}", "{bbox2}"]}. **Evaluation Metrics.** For each question, we use *Exact Match (EM)* and *F1-score* to evaluate the predicted answer, and *Intersection over Union (IOU)* and *IOU@0.5* to assess the predicted region(s).

Table 4. Overall performance of different LVLMs on MMDocBench. Best results are marked in bold; second-best are underlined in the category (open-source or close-source). Metric values below 1% are marked with '-'.

Model	Size	Fine-Grained Visual Perception				Fine-Grained Visual Reasoning				Overall			
		EM	F1	IOU	IOU@0.5	EM	F1	IOU	IOU@0.5	EM	F1	IOU	IOU@0.5
Close-Source LVLMs													
Claude-3.5-Sonnet	-	61.13	63.87	1.95	-	78.14	78.70	1.10	-	69.64	71.28	1.52	-
Gemini-1.5-Pro	-	64.31	66.49	15.51	10.91	**82.09**	**82.50**	4.18	**2.04**	**73.20**	**74.50**	9.85	6.47
GPT-4o	-	**65.91**	**67.78**	3.21	-	78.08	78.63	1.68	-	71.99	73.20	2.45	-
GPT-4V	-	57.82	60.82	2.49	-	66.04	66.59	1.04	-	61.93	63.70	1.76	-
Qwen-VL-Max	-	63.55	67.27	**18.63**	**17.16**	77.43	77.80	**4.27**	1.61	70.49	72.53	**11.45**	**9.38**
Open-Source LVLMs													
InternVL2-Llama3-76B	76B	58.13	61.03	2.30	-	75.12	75.92	-	-	66.62	68.48	1.54	-
Qwen2.5-VL-72B-Instruct	73B	**72.74**	**74.75**	**41.59**	**48.70**	**82.73**	**83.28**	**28.54**	**28.51**	**77.73**	**79.02**	**35.07**	**38.61**
LLaVA-OV-Chat-72B	73B	53.33	57.89	2.28	-	71.03	72.45	-	-	62.18	65.17	1.58	-
Yi-VL-34B	35B	6.66	10.48	-	-	14.50	15.44	-	-	10.58	12.96	-	-
LLaVA-V1.6-34B	34B	29.44	35.00	2.41	-	32.67	34.13	-	-	31.06	34.56	1.46	-
DeepSeek-VL2	27B	52.12	56.51	3.40	-	67.51	68.62	-	-	59.82	62.57	2.03	-
CogVLM2-Chat-19B	19B	26.42	30.16	-	-	23.30	24.22	-	-	24.86	27.19	-	-
TextMonkey	9B	32.31	36.52	19.28	20.57	15.23	16.12	-	-	23.77	26.32	9.89	10.37
mPLUG-DocOwl1.5-Omni	8B	10.84	15.26	1.13	-	19.84	20.55	-	-	15.34	17.91	-	-
mPLUG-Owl3	8B	15.88	19.84	-	-	16.46	17.63	-	-	16.17	18.74	-	-
Qwen2-VL-7B-Instruct	8B	53.53	56.49	13.97	13.05	38.01	39.55	2.40	1.17	45.77	48.02	8.19	7.11
Qwen2.5-VL-7B-Instruct	8B	65.04	67.62	27.40	29.44	66.55	67.45	10.41	9.33	65.79	67.53	18.91	19.38
InternVL2-8B	8B	45.62	49.75	2.00	-	40.82	42.69	-	-	43.22	46.22	1.27	-
Janus-Pro-7B	8B	20.06	25.10	-	-	25.28	26.79	-	-	22.67	25.94	-	-
MiniCPM-Llama3-V2.5	8B	37.50	42.91	5.64	3.52	30.72	32.27	1.29	-	34.11	37.59	3.47	1.86
MiniCPM-V2.6	8B	49.75	55.28	4.70	2.63	52.89	54.39	-	-	51.32	54.84	2.74	1.36
Ferret	7B	4.20	7.15	4.33	4.01	-	-	-	-	4.20	7.15	4.33	4.01

3.2 Main Results

We conduct a comprehensive comparison of different LVLMs with our proposed MMDocBench, and show the results in Table 4. We make below key findings: 1) Among all LVLMs, Qwen2.5-VL-72B-Instruct significantly outperforms all other LVLMs in both answer prediction and region prediction. Specifically, Qwen2.5-VL-72B-Instruct achieves 77.73% in EM and 79.02% in F1 for answer prediction, and 38.61% in IOU and 35.07% in IOU@0.5 for region prediction. The second-best open-source model for region prediction is Qwen2.5-VL-7B-Instruct, which achieves 18.91% and 19.38% in IOU and IOUR@0.5. The superior performance in region prediction can be attributed to the Qwen2.5-VL family's improved visual grounding abilities, which are developed during pre-training using an extensive dataset that includes both bounding box and point annotations. 2) Among all close-source LVLMs, the best model for answer prediction is Gemini-1.5-Pro, which achieves 73.20% in EM and 74.50% in F1, but only 9.85% in IOU for region prediction. Another close-source model, Qwen-VL-Max, which has comparable answer prediction performance (i.e.,70.49%) to Gemini-1.5-Pro, is the best-performing model for region prediction, with an IOU score of 11.45% only. This could be explained by these close-source models using insufficient samples with visual grounding requirements when training, leading to a lack of visual grounding capability. This reveals the significant challenges of region prediction in MMDocBench for close-source LVLMs, which demand strong visual grounding capabilities from LVLMs. 3) LVLMs trained on document images with text-grounding requirements, such as Qwen2-VL-7B-Instruct, and TextMonkey, show improvements in region prediction, while those trained with object-level grounding over natural images, like Ferret, exhibit no such improvements. This highlights the necessity of establishing a benchmark that supports visual grounding at various and finer granularities on document images, such as our MMDocBench.

Answer Prediction. We make below key findings. 1) Qwen2.5-VL-72B-Instruct consistently beats all other models on both fine-grained visual perception and fine-grained visual reasoning tasks in all evaluation metrics, demonstrating its superior effectiveness. 2) Larger models, like GPT-4o, Qwen-VL-Max, InternVL2-Llama3-76B, and LlaVA-OV-Chat-72B tend to perform better on fine-grained visual reasoning tasks than fine-grained visual perception tasks, while smaller models, conversely. excel in fine-grained visual perception tasks over reasoning tasks, possibly because reasoning capabilities improve significantly as the model size increases.

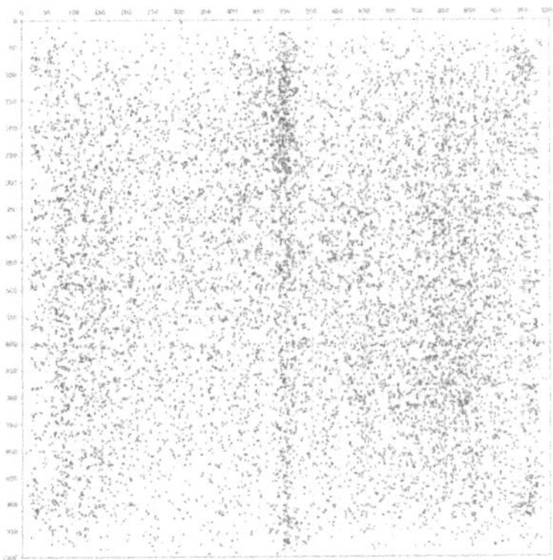

Fig. 3. Regions' position distribution

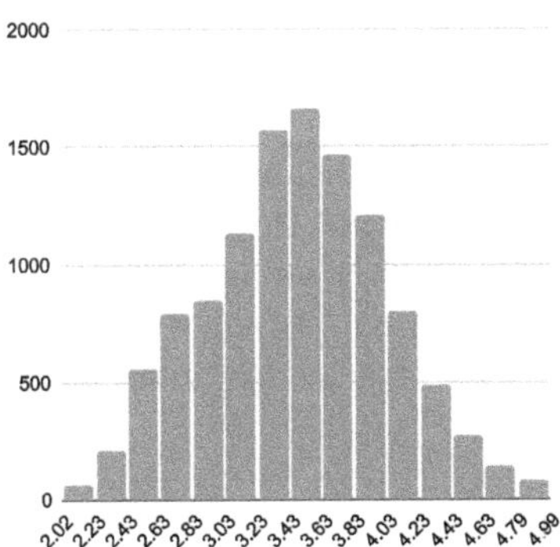

Fig. 4. Regions' area distribution.

Region Prediction. We make below key findings. 1) All LVLMs face challenges in predicting supporting regions for fine-grained visual reasoning tasks. The performance of most LVLMs on fine-grained visual reasoning tasks is notably worse than that on fine-grained visual perception tasks. Qwen2.5-VL-72B-Instruct, the best model for region prediction on fine-grained visual reasoning tasks, earns only 28.54% in IOU, indicating the remarkable challenges of this task. 2) Qwen2.5-VL-72B-Instruct achieves the best results on both fine-grained visual perception and fine-grained visual reasoning tasks with 41.59% and 28.54% in IOU and IOU@0.5. 3) TextMonkey achieves comparable region prediction performance to Qwen2.5-VL-7B-Instruct on fine-grained visual perception tasks, but it cannot provide supporting regions for visual reasoning tasks One possible reason is that TextMonkey only involves perception-related samples and instructions for training its grounding ability, resulting in its inability to ground the supporting evidence for reasoning tasks.

3.3   Analysis on Different Tasks

We compare the performance of various LVLMs across tasks and present the results in Fig. 5 and Fig. 6. We make below key findings. 1) As shown in Fig. 5, Qwen2.5-VL-72B-Instruct outperforms other LVLMs on most tasks. However, GPT-4o achieves the highest F1 score (20.5%) on the Document Forgery Detection task, surpassing all other LVLMs. This low score highlights the inherent difficulty of the task. 2) As shown in Fig. 6, all LVLMs struggle with the prediction of supporting regions on almost all the tasks, except for Text Recognition, where the best model, Qwen2.5-VL-72B-Instruct, achieves around 83.8% in IOU and 96.3% in IOU@0.5. Qwen2.5-VL-72B-Instruct delivers the best results in region prediction across most tasks, except for Forgery Detection and Table Localization, where Gemini-1.5-Pro ranks first. 3) Among all the tasks, Document Forgery Detection, a fine-grained visual perception task, is the most challenging for all LVLMs, with the best result being only around 20.0% in EM for answer prediction and 5.0% in IOU for region prediction; As illustrated in Fig. 1, this task requires the model to identify the inconsistent word(s) against other words within the image. In addition, the answer prediction performance of all LVLMs on Text Localization and Table Cell Localization is poor, underscoring the challenges posed by both tasks.

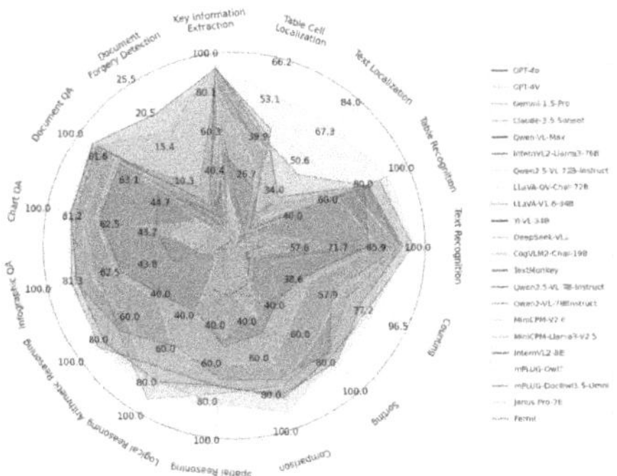 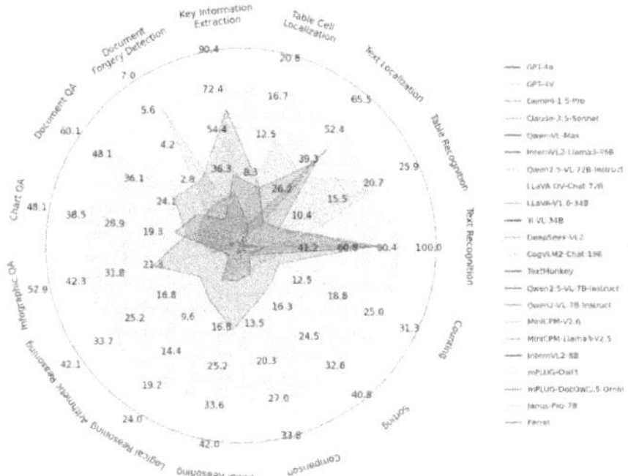

Fig. 5. Performance comparison in F1.

Fig. 6. Performance comparison in IOU.

4 Related Work

4.1 Benchmarks for Evaluating LVLMs

Lots of multimodal benchmarks have been built to holistically assess LVLMs' integrated capabilities, like recognition, knowledge, math, reasoning and safety [3,11,33,36]. These benchmarks include some samples that can be used to evaluate LVLMs' fine-grained visual understanding capability, but they are either limited in the number of tasks and/or samples or difficult to separate these samples from others. Moreover, their evaluations rely solely on natural language output without supporting region prediction involved, which is a crucial measure for achieving fine-grained visual understanding in LVLMs [20]. Current available benchmarks [10,35,42], especially for evaluating fine-graded visual understanding, are centered on *object-level* recognition and interpretation within natural images, offering limited information granularity. MMDocBench is the first comprehensive benchmark aiming to evaluate LVLMs' fine-grained visual understanding capability with various OCR-free document understanding tasks.

4.2 Visual Grounding in LVLMs

Visual Grounding (VG), i.e. localizing the relevant object or region to a given natural language description in the visual input [2], has been applied in LVLMs to facilitate generating more informative and comprehensive responses, benefiting various downstream applications [8,15,35]. Existing grounded LVLMs can be classified into 1) region-level (i.e., bounding box) grounding based [31] and 2) pixel-level grounding based LVLMs [34]. However, their training and evaluation sorely rely on *object-level* tasks involving natural images, overlooking the various granularities in document images. Here we build MMDocBench that requires LVLMs to perform region-level grounding following typical settings in most document understanding tasks [5,24].

5   Conclusion

We introduce MMDocBench to comprehensively evaluate LVLMs' fine-grained visual perception and reasoning capabilities via various OCR-free document understanding tasks. With MMDocBench, we evaluate 22 open-source and proprietary LVLMs, analyzing their performance in fine-grained visual document image understanding. We observe that MMDocBench presents significant challenges to current LVLMs, especially for region prediction. We believe MMDocBench can enable a thorough and multi-faceted evaluation of fine-grained visual document understanding and grounding capabilities of LVLMs, facilitating LVLMs' future advancement.

References

1. Chen, W., et al.: Guicourse: From general vision language models to versatile gui agents. arXiv preprint arXiv:2406.11317 (2024)
2. Deng, C., Wu, Q., Wu, Q., Hu, F., Lyu, F., Tan, M.: Visual grounding via accumulated attention. In: Proceedings of the IEEE Conference on Computer Vision and Pattern Recognition, pp. 7746–7755 (2018)
3. Fu, C., et al.: Mme: a comprehensive evaluation benchmark for multimodal large language models (2024). https://arxiv.org/abs/2306.13394
4. Harley, A.W., Ufkes, A., Derpanis, K.G.: Evaluation of deep convolutional nets for document image classification and retrieval. In: 2015 13th International Conference on Document Analysis and Recognition (ICDAR), pp. 991–995. IEEE (2015)
5. Huang, Z., Chen, K., He, J., Bai, X., Karatzas, D., Lu, S., Jawahar, C.V.: Icdar2019 competition on scanned receipt ocr and information extraction. In: 2019 International Conference on Document Analysis and Recognition (ICDAR), pp. 1516–1520 (2019)
6. Kim, G., et al.: Ocr-free document understanding transformer. In: European Conference on Computer Vision, pp. 498–517. Springer (2022)
7. Li, M., Xu, Y., Cui, L., Huang, S., Wei, F., Li, Z., Zhou, M.: Docbank: a benchmark dataset for document layout analysis. arXiv preprint arXiv:2006.01038 (2020)
8. Lin, T.Y., Maire, M., Belongie, S., Hays, J., Perona, P., Ramanan, D., Dollár, P., Zitnick, C.L.: Microsoft coco: Common objects in context. In: Computer Vision–ECCV 2014: 13th European Conference, Zurich, Switzerland, September 6-12, 2014, Proceedings, Part V 13, pp. 740–755. Springer (2014)
9. Liu, H., Li, C., Wu, Q., Lee, Y.J.: Visual instruction tuning. In: Advances in Neural Information Processing Systems, pp. 34892–34916. Curran Associates, Inc. (2023)
10. Liu, Y., et al.: Mmbench: Is your multi-modal model an all-around player? arXiv preprint arXiv:2307.06281 (2023)
11. Ma, Y., et al.: Mmlongbench-doc: Benchmarking long-context document understanding with visualizations. arXiv preprint arXiv:2407.01523 (2024)
12. Masry, A., Do, X.L., Tan, J.Q., Joty, S., Hoque, E.: ChartQA: A benchmark for question answering about charts with visual and logical reasoning. In: Muresan, S., Nakov, P., Villavicencio, A. (eds.) Findings of the Association for Computational Linguistics, pp. 2263–2279. Association for Computational Linguistics (2022)
13. Mathew, M., Bagal, V., Tito, R., Karatzas, D., Valveny, E., Jawahar, C.: Infographicvqa. In: Proceedings of the IEEE/CVF Winter Conference on Applications of Computer Vision, pp. 1697–1706 (2022)

14. Mathew, M., Karatzas, D., Jawahar, C.: Docvqa: A dataset for vqa on document images. In: Proceedings of the IEEE/CVF Winter Conference on Applications of Computer Vision, pp. 2200–2209 (2021)
15. Minaee, S., Boykov, Y., Porikli, F., Plaza, A., Kehtarnavaz, N., Terzopoulos, D.: Image segmentation using deep learning: a survey. IEEE Trans. Pattern Anal. Mach. Intell. **44**(7), 3523–3542 (2022)
16. Mishra, A., Shekhar, S., Singh, A.K., Chakraborty, A.: Ocr-vqa: Visual question answering by reading text in images. In: 2019 International Conference on Document Analysis and Recognition (ICDAR), pp. 947–952. IEEE (2019)
17. OpenAI: Gpt-4v(ision) system card (2023)
18. Park, S., Shin, S., Lee, B., Lee, J., Surh, J., Seo, M., Lee, H.: Cord: a consolidated receipt dataset for post-ocr parsing. In: Workshop on Document Intelligence at NeurIPS 2019 (2019)
19. Pasupat, P., Liang, P.: Compositional semantic parsing on semi-structured tables. In: Zong, C., Strube, M. (eds.) Proceedings of the 53rd Annual Meeting of the Association for Computational Linguistics and the 7th International Joint Conference on Natural Language Processing (Volume 1: Long Papers), pp. 1470–1480. Association for Computational Linguistics (2015)
20. Peng, Z., et al.: Grounding multimodal large language models to the world. In: The Twelfth International Conference on Learning Representations (2024)
21. Qu, C., Liu, C., Liu, Y., Chen, X., Peng, D., Guo, F., Jin, L.: Towards robust tampered text detection in document image: New dataset and new solution. In: Proceedings of the IEEE/CVF Conference on Computer Vision and Pattern Recognition, pp. 5937–5946 (2023)
22. Šimsa, Š., et al.: Docile benchmark for document information localization and extraction. In: International Conference on Document Analysis and Recognition, pp. 147–166. Springer (2023)
23. Singh, A., et al.: Towards vqa models that can read. In: Proceedings of the IEEE/CVF Conference on Computer Vision and Pattern Recognition, pp. 8317–8326 (2019)
24. Singh, A., Pang, G., Toh, M., Huang, J., Galuba, W., Hassner, T.: Textocr: towards large-scale end-to-end reasoning for arbitrary-shaped scene text. In: Proceedings of the IEEE/CVF Conference on Computer Vision and Pattern Recognition, pp. 8802–8812 (2021)
25. Smock, B., Pesala, R., Abraham, R.: Pubtables-1m: Towards comprehensive table extraction from unstructured documents. In: Proceedings of the IEEE/CVF Conference on Computer Vision and Pattern Recognition, pp. 4634–4642 (2022)
26. Sun, H., Kuang, Z., Yue, X., Lin, C., Zhang, W.: Spatial dual-modality graph reasoning for key information extraction. arXiv preprint arXiv:2103.14470 (2021)
27. Tong, S., Liu, Z., Zhai, Y., Ma, Y., LeCun, Y., Xie, S.: Eyes wide shut? exploring the visual shortcomings of multimodal llms. In: Proceedings of the IEEE/CVF Conference on Computer Vision and Pattern Recognition, pp. 9568–9578 (2024)
28. Van Landeghem, J., et al.: Document understanding dataset and evaluation (dude). In: Proceedings of the IEEE/CVF International Conference on Computer Vision, pp. 19528–19540 (2023)
29. Wang, G., Ge, Y., Ding, X., Kankanhalli, M., Shan, Y.: What makes for good visual tokenizers for large language models? arXiv preprint arXiv:2305.12223 (2023)
30. Wang, Z., et al.: Charxiv: charting gaps in realistic chart understanding in multimodal llms. arXiv preprint arXiv:2406.18521 (2024)

31. Xuan, S., Guo, Q., Yang, M., Zhang, S.: Pink: unveiling the power of referential comprehension for multi-modal llms. In: Proceedings of the IEEE/CVF Conference on Computer Vision and Pattern Recognition, pp. 13838–13848 (2024)
32. Yin, S., Fu, C., Zhao, S., Li, K., Sun, X., Xu, T., Chen, E.: A survey on multimodal large language models (2024). https://arxiv.org/abs/2306.13549
33. Ying, K., et al.: Mmt-bench: a comprehensive multimodal benchmark for evaluating large vision-language models towards multitask agi. arXiv preprint arXiv:2404.16006 (2024)
34. You, H., et al.: Ferret: refer and ground anything anywhere at any granularity. In: The Twelfth International Conference on Learning Representations (2024)
35. Yu, L., Poirson, P., Yang, S., Berg, A.C., Berg, T.L.: Modeling context in referring expressions. In: Computer Vision–ECCV 2016: 14th European Conference, Proceedings, Part II 14, pp. 69–85. Springer (2016)
36. Yu, W., Yang, Z., Li, L., Wang, J., Lin, K., Liu, Z., Wang, X., Wang, L.: Mm-vet: Evaluating large multimodal models for integrated capabilities. arXiv preprint arXiv:2308.02490 (2023)
37. Yuxin, W., Boqiang, Z., Hongtao, X., Yongdong, Z.: Tampered text detection via rgb and frequency relationship modeling. Chinese Journal of Network and Information Security, p. 29 (2022)
38. Zheng, X., Burdick, D., Popa, L., Zhong, P., Wang, N.X.R.: Global table extractor (gte): A framework for joint table identification and cell structure recognition using visual context. Winter Conference for Applications in Computer Vision (WACV) (2021)
39. Zhong, X., ShafieiBavani, E., Jimeno Yepes, A.: Image-based table recognition: data, model, and evaluation. In: European Conference on Computer Vision, pp. 564–580. Springer (2020)
40. Zhong, X., Tang, J., Yepes, A.J.: Publaynet: largest dataset ever for document layout analysis. In: 2019 International Conference on Document Analysis and Recognition (ICDAR), pp. 1015–1022. IEEE (2019)
41. Zhu, F., Lei, W., Feng, F., Wang, C., Zhang, H., Chua, T.S.: Towards complex document understanding by discrete reasoning. In: Proceedings of the 30th ACM International Conference on Multimedia, pp. 4857–4866 (2022)
42. Zhu, Y., Groth, O., Bernstein, M., Fei-Fei, L.: Visual7w: Grounded question answering in images. In: Proceedings of the IEEE Conference on Computer Vision and Pattern Recognition, pp. 4995–5004 (2016)

WavGateMamba: A Frequency-Enhanced and Gated Mamba Model for Multimodal Depression Detection

Haiyang Ye, Dengshi Li[(✉)], Wei Li, Yulin Wu, Yu Fang, and YuXin Li

Jianghan University, Wuhan, China
{y0h1y8,fyz,lyx251226006026}@stu.jhun.edu.cn,
{reallds,wuyulin}@jhun.edu.cn, liweifire@126.com

Abstract. Automated depression detection from audio-visual cues faces a key challenge: subtle behavioral indicators are often masked by dominant low-frequency signals. To address this, we propose WavGateMamba, a novel architecture integrating wavelet analysis with state space models. Our method employs Discrete Wavelet Transform (DWT) to decompose inputs into multi-scale frequency components, a gating mechanism for dynamic feature recalibration, and Mamba blocks with shared state-space matrices for cross-modal modeling. Extensive experiments show our approach significantly outperforms existing methods, achieving consistent improvements of 3–4% on key evaluation metrics including Accuracy, Precision, Recall, and F1-Score. This work presents an effective paradigm for incorporating frequency-domain inductive bias into behavioral analysis, enabling better capture of subtle depressive cues.

Keywords: Depression Detection · Mamba · Wavelet Transform · Gated Mechanism

1 Introduction

Depression, a leading global cause of disability, demands efficient diagnostic methods [1]. Automated audio-visual behavior analysis offers promising avenues by capturing subtle cues like facial microexpressions and vocal patterns. However, these discriminative signals—often high-frequency and low-energy—are frequently overwhelmed by dominant low-frequency information, limiting detection performance [2].

Recent advances in state space models, particularly Mamba architectures, demonstrate strong capabilities in long-sequence processing with linear complexity [3]. While DepMamba provides a robust baseline for multimodal depression detection [4], its data-driven approach lacks inductive bias for critical frequency components, hindering subtle feature perception.

To address this, we integrate wavelet transform principles—explicitly decomposing signals into multi-frequency components—with adaptive gating mechanisms. This combination provides strong spectral priors while enabling dynamic

J. Lokoč et al. (Eds.): MMM 2026, LNCS 16412, pp. 89–102, 2026.
https://doi.org/10.1007/978-981-95-6950-2_7

feature selection. Our proposed WavGateMamba architecture processes audio and visual inputs through parallel pipelines featuring: (1) discrete wavelet decomposition for frequency-aware feature extraction, (2) gated recalibration of frequency components, and (3) cross-modal Mamba blocks with shared state-transition matrices for efficient long-range dependency modeling.

The main contributions are:

1. WavGateMamba architecture integrating wavelet priors and gating with state space models
2. Gated dual-branch SSM with shared state-transition matrices enabling multi-scale fusion
3. Consistent 3–4% improvements across metrics on D-Vlog and LMVD datasets
4. Empirical validation through eigenvalue analysis demonstrating the stability of the shared state-space and its alignment with behavioral dynamics.

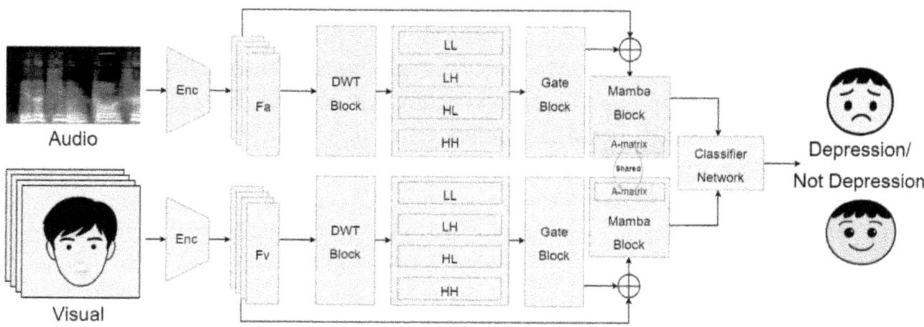

Fig. 1. The proposed WavGateMamba framework for multimodal depression detection employs dual-branch ViT encoders [5] to extract high-level features from audio (Mel-spectrograms) and video (frame sequences). These features are decomposed via Discrete Wavelet Transform (DWT) into frequency sub-bands, emphasizing discriminative high-frequency cues. A gating mechanism dynamically fuses components before Mamba-based sequence modeling with shared state-transition matrices (A-matrix) captures long-range dependencies and cross-modal interactions. Final fusion yields the depression classification output.

2 Related Work

Audio-Visual Depression Detection. Audio-visual depression detection has evolved through multiple paradigms. Early methods used handcrafted features like LBP, HOG, and MFCC with shallow classifiers [4,6,7], but were limited in expressiveness and temporal modeling. Deep learning brought significant improvements: CNN/RNN models enhanced feature learning but struggled with long-term dependencies [8]; Transformers improved context modeling but suffered quadratic complexity [9]; State Space models (e.g., Mamba) recently emerged with linear complexity and efficient long-sequence processing. Dep-Mamba [4] applied Mamba to depression detection using hierarchical fusion, but lacks explicit frequency-domain modeling—motivating our approach.

Visual State-Space Models. State-space models (SSMs) have advanced long-sequence modeling. Foundational S4 introduced structured state spaces, enhanced by Mamba with data-dependent selection. Vision adaptations like VMamba [10] and Vision Mamba [11] extended SSMs to 2D data, improving visual task efficiency. While promising for behavioral signal processing, they remain limited in frequency-aware reasoning—a gap our work addresses.

Frequency-Domain Methods. Frequency-domain techniques provide powerful signal analysis priors. In low-level vision, wavelet and Fourier transforms are widely used for denoising and dehazing [12,13]. In medical imaging [14], wavelets have been applied but remain underexplored for behavioral analysis. Our work is the first to integrate wavelet decomposition with SSMs for depression detection, bridging signal processing and semantic understanding.

2.1   Gating Mechanism

Gating mechanisms enable dynamic feature selection in architectures like LSTMs [15] and GLUs [16], proving effective for multimodal fusion [17] through adaptive modality weighting. While Mamba [18] incorporates data-dependent gating via its selection process, we extend this by applying gating to wavelet-decomposed frequency components, enabling dynamic frequency-band selection for improved depression cue extraction.

3   Proposed Method

3.1   Overall Architecture

Figure 1 illustrates the overall framework of our proposed WavGateMamba. The model is designed to process audio and visual inputs through two symmetric yet interactive branches, explicitly leveraging frequency-domain priors for effective depression detection.

Given an input sample, the audio stream and visual stream are first processed by their respective modality-specific encoders to extract high-level feature representations, denoted as $\mathbf{F}_a \in \mathbb{R}^{T \times D}$ and $\mathbf{F}_v \in \mathbb{R}^{T \times D}$, where T represents the sequence length and D is the feature dimension.

Instead of directly feeding these features into subsequent networks, we explicitly decompose them into frequency-aware components to isolate subtle depressive cues. Both $\mathbf{F}_a$ and $\mathbf{F}_v$ are passed through a Wavelet Decomposition Module, which utilizes a two-dimensional Discrete Wavelet Transform (DWT) to break down the features into four sub-bands: **LL**, **LH**, **HL**, and **HH**. These sub-bands capture multi-scale information ranging from low-frequency approximations to high-frequency details.

The decomposed features are then fed into a Gated Dual-branch State Space Model (SSM). This core component consists of three key parts:

Gating Network. A Gating Network that dynamically generates modulation weights for each frequency sub-band, performing adaptive feature recalibration.

Wavelet Decomposition (DWT). The Discrete Wavelet Transform module decomposes the input features into multi-scale frequency components, facilitating the extraction of depression-related cues across different frequency bands.

Parallel Mamba Blocks. Parallel Mamba Blocks process the gated features. The state-transition matrices (**A**-matrices) of the Mamba blocks across the two modalities are shared, enabling efficient cross-modal interaction and correlation learning within a common state-space.

The outputs from the dual-branch SSM are then fused through a concatenation operation followed by a linear projection layer, yielding a unified representation. This representation is finally fed into a classifier network to produce the final depression recognition result.

The entire model is trained end-to-end with a combined loss function $\mathcal{L}_{\text{total}}$ that optimizes both the depression classification task and other potential auxiliary objectives.

3.2   Wavelet Decomposition Module

To explicitly inject frequency-domain inductive bias and facilitate the isolation of subtle depressive cues, we introduce a Wavelet Decomposition Module as a core component of our architecture. The detailed process is illustrated in Fig. 2.

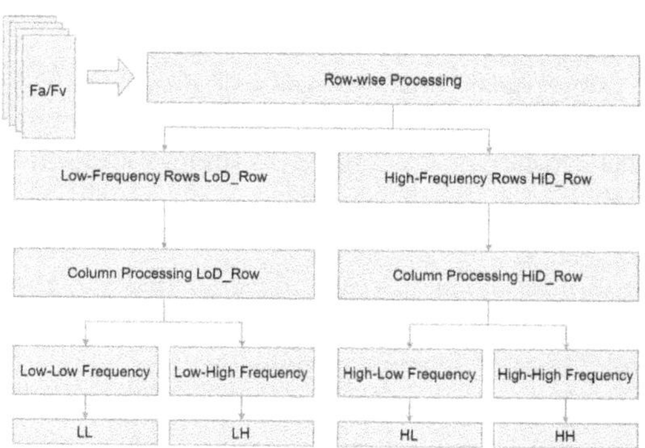

Fig. 2. Illustration of the 2D Discrete Wavelet Transform (DWT) process applied to a feature map. The input is decomposed along its rows and columns using low-pass (L) and high-pass (H) filters, resulting in four distinct frequency sub-bands: LL, LH, HL, and HH.

The input to this module is the high-level feature representation of a modality, i.e., $\mathbf{F}_a$ (audio) or $\mathbf{F}_v$ (visual), which can be viewed as a 2D feature map where one dimension corresponds to the temporal sequence length T and the other to the feature dimension D. Rather than treating this feature map as a monolithic entity, we process it with a two-dimensional Discrete Wavelet Transform (DWT) to decompose it into four distinct frequency sub-bands.

As shown in Fig. 2, the DWT operation employs a set of low-pass (h) and high-pass (g) filters to analyze the input feature map $\mathbf{F}$ along both its spatial (or temporal) and feature dimensions. This decomposition is implemented efficiently using a convolutional approach with stride 2, which also serves to downsample the representation, reducing computational burden.

The process yields a multi-scale representation comprising four sub-bands:

- **LL (Low-Low)**: The approximation coefficient, obtained by applying the low-pass filter in both dimensions. This sub-band captures the smooth, low-frequency components of the feature map, representing the global contour and primary structural information.
- **LH (Low-High)**: The vertical detail coefficient, obtained by applying a low-pass filter horizontally and a high-pass filter vertically. It captures high-frequency variations along the feature dimension, which often correspond to fine-grained textual details.
- **HL (High-Low)**: The horizontal detail coefficient, obtained by applying a high-pass filter horizontally and a low-pass filter vertically. It captures high-frequency variations along the temporal sequence, which can indicate rapid, transient changes.
- **HH (High-High)**: The diagonal detail coefficient, obtained by applying the high-pass filter in both dimensions. It captures the highest frequency information, often representing noise or the finest details and corners.

Formally, for an input feature map $\mathbf{F}$, the decomposition can be expressed as:

$$\{\mathbf{LL}, \mathbf{LH}, \mathbf{HL}, \mathbf{HH}\} = \mathrm{DWT}(\mathbf{F}) \tag{1}$$

Each resulting sub-band has a size of $\mathbb{R}^{\frac{T}{2} \times \frac{D}{2} \times C}$, where C is the number of channels.

The key advantage of this explicit decomposition is that it provides a powerful prior for the model. It forces the separation of information by frequency, ensuring that subsequent modules can independently process and recalibrate both the dominant low-frequency signals and the often-overlooked yet critical high-frequency components where subtle depressive behaviors may reside. The output of this module is the set of these four sub-band tensors $\{\mathbf{LL}, \mathbf{LH}, \mathbf{HL}, \mathbf{HH}\}$, which are then passed to the gating mechanism for adaptive recalibration.

3.3   Gated Feature Recalibration Module

Following the wavelet decomposition, the derived frequency sub-bands contain information of varying importance for the depression detection task. To dynamically highlight the most discriminative features and suppress less useful ones,

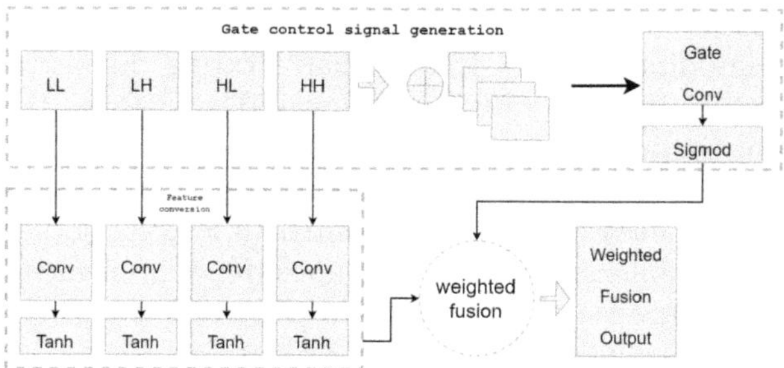

Fig. 3. Architecture of the Gated Feature Recalibration Module. The module consists of two main processes: (1) Gate control signal generation that produces adaptive weights for each frequency sub-band, and (2) Feature conversion and weighted fusion that applies the weights to recalibrate the sub-bands.

we introduce a Gated Feature Recalibration Module, the details of which are depicted in Fig. 3.

The input to this module is the tuple of four sub-bands $\{\mathbf{LL}, \mathbf{LH}, \mathbf{HL}, \mathbf{HH}\}$ for a given modality. Instead of treating these sub-bands equally, we employ a lightweight gating network that learns to adaptively recalibrate each sub-band through a self-gating mechanism, inspired by squeeze-and-excitation networks but applied in the frequency domain.

The gating process consists of three main components, as shown in Fig. 3:

Gate Control Signal Generation. First, we generate a set of modulation weights for the four sub-bands. Each sub-band is passed through a global average pooling layer to squeeze global spatial-temporal information into a channel-wise descriptor, producing a vector $\mathbf{z} \in \mathbb{R}^C$. This descriptor is then fed into a multi-layer perceptron (MLP) with a sigmoid activation function in its output layer. The MLP acts as an excitation network, learning to output a set of four scalar weights $\{\alpha_{\mathrm{LL}}, \alpha_{\mathrm{LH}}, \alpha_{\mathrm{HL}}, \alpha_{\mathrm{HH}}\}$, each between 0 and 1, representing the estimated importance of its corresponding frequency sub-band for the current input sample.

Feature Conversion. Before applying the weights, each sub-band undergoes feature transformation through convolutional layers followed by hyperbolic tangent (Tanh) activation functions. This process enhances the representational capacity of the features and prepares them for the subsequent weighted fusion. The transformation can be expressed as:

$$\mathbf{X}_{\mathrm{transformed}} = \tanh(\mathrm{Conv}(\mathbf{X})) \tag{2}$$

where $\mathbf{X}$ represents any of the four sub-bands $\{\mathbf{LL}, \mathbf{LH}, \mathbf{HL}, \mathbf{HH}\}$.

Weighted Fusion. The generated weights are then used to perform a channel-wise multiplication (modulation) of their corresponding transformed sub-band tensors. Formally, the output of the gating module for each sub-band is computed as:

$$\mathbf{LL}' = \alpha_{\mathrm{LL}} \cdot \mathbf{LL}_{\mathrm{transformed}} \tag{3}$$

$$\mathbf{LH}' = \alpha_{\mathrm{LH}} \cdot \mathbf{LH}_{\mathrm{transformed}} \tag{4}$$

$$\mathbf{HL}' = \alpha_{\mathrm{HL}} \cdot \mathbf{HL}_{\mathrm{transformed}} \tag{5}$$

$$\mathbf{HH}' = \alpha_{\mathrm{HH}} \cdot \mathbf{HH}_{\mathrm{transformed}} \tag{6}$$

This element-wise multiplication adaptively amplifies features from informative sub-bands and attenuates features from less relevant ones.

The key advantage of this design is its input-dependent adaptability. For instance, if the model learns that high-frequency details ($\mathbf{LH}$, $\mathbf{HL}$, $\mathbf{HH}$) in the visual modality are crucial for identifying a specific micro-expression related to depression, the gating network can learn to assign higher weights to these sub-bands. Conversely, for samples where low-frequency structural information ($\mathbf{LL}$) is more stable and reliable, the gate can shift its focus accordingly.

The output of this module is the set of spatially and temporally recalibrated sub-bands $\mathbf{LL}'$, $\mathbf{LH}'$, $\mathbf{HL}'$, $\mathbf{HH}'$, which are then ready for subsequent processing by the dual-branch Mamba blocks to model long-range dependencies within and across these refined frequency-specific features.

3.4   Cross-Modal Interaction via Shared State Space

The recalibrated frequency-aware features from both audio and visual branches, $\{\mathbf{LL}', \mathbf{LH}', \mathbf{HL}', \mathbf{HH}'\}_a$ and $\{\mathbf{LL}', \mathbf{LH}', \mathbf{HL}', \mathbf{HH}'\}_v$, are then processed by their respective modality-specific Mamba blocks to model long-range temporal dependencies. The key innovation in this stage, as illustrated in Fig. 4, is our shared state-transition matrix ($\mathbf{A}$-matrix) mechanism, which enables efficient and implicit cross-modal interaction without direct feature fusion.

As depicted in Fig. 4, the audio and visual Mamba blocks are structured as parallel branches. However, unlike traditional dual-stream architectures where parameters are entirely independent, we enforce that the state-transition matrices $\mathbf{A}$ in both blocks are shared and identical. This design is grounded in the hypothesis that the underlying temporal dynamics governing the evolution of depressive states, while expressed through different modalities (audio and visual), may follow a common or highly correlated latent pattern.

State Space Model Formulation. The continuous state space model underlying the Mamba architecture is defined by the following equations:

$$\mathbf{h}'(t) = \mathbf{A}\mathbf{h}(t) + \mathbf{B}\mathbf{x}(t) \tag{7}$$

$$\mathbf{y}(t) = \mathbf{C}\mathbf{h}(t) + \mathbf{D}\mathbf{x}(t) \tag{8}$$

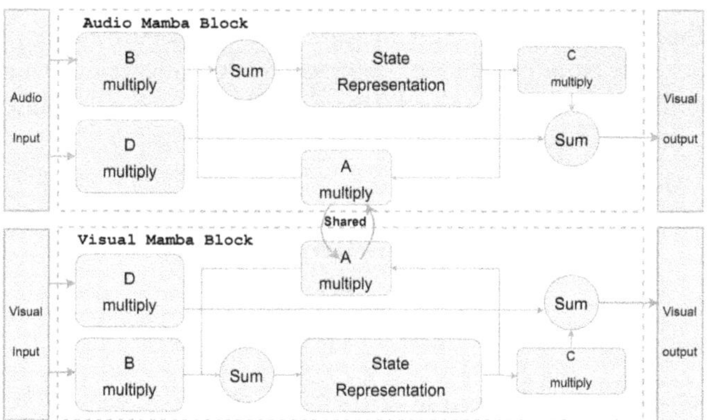

Fig. 4. Architecture of the cross-modal interaction mechanism through shared state space. The audio and visual branches share the same state-transition matrix $\mathbf{A}$, enabling implicit cross-modal interaction while maintaining modality-specific processing through separate selective parameters ($\mathbf{B}$, $\mathbf{C}$, Δ).

where $\mathbf{h}(t)$ is the hidden state at time t, $\mathbf{x}(t)$ is the input signal, $\mathbf{y}(t)$ is the output signal, $\mathbf{A}$ is the state-transition matrix, $\mathbf{B}$ is the input matrix, $\mathbf{C}$ is the output matrix, and $\mathbf{D}$ is the skip connection matrix.

For discrete-time implementation, the model is discretized using the zero-order hold (ZOH) method:

$$\overline{\mathbf{A}} = \exp(\Delta\mathbf{A}) \tag{9}$$

$$\overline{\mathbf{B}} = (\Delta\mathbf{A})^{-1}(\exp(\Delta\mathbf{A}) - \mathbf{I}) \cdot \Delta\mathbf{B} \tag{10}$$

where Δ is the time step parameter, and the discrete recurrence becomes:

$$\mathbf{h}_t = \overline{\mathbf{A}}\mathbf{h}_{t-1} + \overline{\mathbf{B}}\mathbf{x}_t \tag{11}$$

$$\mathbf{y}_t = \mathbf{C}\mathbf{h}_t + \mathbf{D}\mathbf{x}_t \tag{12}$$

Shared State-Transition Mechanism. The shared $\mathbf{A}$-matrix acts as a common dynamical system that governs how both audio and visual features evolve through time. During the selective scanning process:

- The audio features are processed by the audio-specific Mamba block, which utilizes its own selective parameters (Δ_a, $\mathbf{B}_a$, $\mathbf{C}_a$) but uses the shared $\mathbf{A}$-matrix for state transition.
- Simultaneously, the visual features are processed by the visual-specific Mamba block with its own selective parameters (Δ_v, $\mathbf{B}_v$, $\mathbf{C}_v$), also utilizing the same shared $\mathbf{A}$-matrix.

This mechanism allows the two modalities to interact and co-influence each other implicitly through the gradients during backpropagation. The shared $\mathbf{A}$-matrix becomes a conduit for cross-modal knowledge transfer, learning a unified representation of temporal dynamics that is beneficial for both modalities.

It forces the model to discover a common ground in the state-space that can effectively represent the progression of behavioral cues relevant to depression, regardless of their source.

Feature Fusion and Classification. The output of this stage is two refined feature sequences: $\mathbf{O}_a$ from the audio Mamba block and $\mathbf{O}_v$ from the visual Mamba block. These outputs have been enriched by both intra-modal long-context modeling and implicit cross-modal interaction facilitated by the shared state-space.

For the final fusion and classification, we employ a multi-level fusion strategy:

$$\mathbf{O} = \mathrm{Concat}\left(\mathrm{GAP}(\mathbf{O}_a), \mathrm{GAP}(\mathbf{O}_v), \mathrm{GAP}(\mathbf{O}_a \odot \mathbf{O}_v), \mathrm{GAP}(\mathbf{O}_a + \mathbf{O}_v)\right) \tag{13}$$

where $\mathrm{GAP}(\cdot)$ denotes global average pooling, $\odot$ represents element-wise multiplication, and Concat is the concatenation operation. This combined representation $\mathbf{O}$ captures both modality-specific and cross-modal interactive information.

The fused representation is then passed through a linear classifier layer with softmax activation to produce the final prediction:

$$\hat{y} = \mathrm{softmax}(\mathbf{W}\mathbf{O} + \mathbf{b}) \tag{14}$$

where $\mathbf{W}$ and $\mathbf{b}$ are the weight matrix and bias vector of the classification layer, respectively.

3.5   Loss Function

To train the entire WavGateMamba framework in an end-to-end manner while ensuring robust feature learning, we employ a composite loss function $\mathcal{L}_{\text{total}}$ that strategically combines a primary task-oriented loss with auxiliary regularization terms. This multi-objective optimization scheme encourages the model to not only excel at depression classification but also to learn discriminative and generalizable feature representations.

The overall loss function is defined as the weighted combination of two principal components:

$$\mathcal{L}_{\text{total}} = \mathcal{L}_{\text{cls}} + \lambda \cdot \mathcal{L}_{\text{aux}} \tag{15}$$

where $\lambda \in \mathbb{R}^+$ is a tunable hyperparameter that balances the contribution of the auxiliary regularization term.

Cross-Entropy Classification Loss. As the primary objective for depression detection, we employ the standard cross-entropy loss, which quantifies the discrepancy between the predicted probability distribution and the ground-truth labels. For a batch of N samples, this loss is formulated as:

$$\mathcal{L}_{\text{cls}} = -\frac{1}{N} \sum_{i=1}^{N} \sum_{c=1}^{C} y_{i,c} \cdot \log(\hat{y}_{i,c}) \tag{16}$$

where C represents the number of classes, $y_{i,c} \in \{0,1\}$ denotes the ground-truth label (employing one-hot encoding) for the i-th sample belonging to class c, and $\hat{y}_{i,c} \in [0,1]$ represents the corresponding predicted probability generated by the classifier network.

Auxiliary Feature Reconstruction Loss. To ensure that the frequency decomposition and subsequent non-linear transformations preserve semantically meaningful information from the original inputs, we introduce an auxiliary feature reconstruction loss. This loss function encourages the refined feature representations produced by our framework to remain discriminative while maintaining fidelity to the original feature space. Specifically, we minimize the Mean Squared Error (MSE) between the fused feature representation $\mathbf{O}$ (obtained after the cross-modal Mamba blocks) and a projected version of the original encoded features $\mathbf{F}$:

$$\mathcal{L}_{\text{aux}} = \frac{1}{N} \sum_{i=1}^{N} \|\text{MLP}_{\text{proj}}(\mathbf{O}_i) - \text{MLP}_{\text{proj}}(\mathbf{F}_i)\|_2^2 \tag{17}$$

Here, $\text{MLP}_{\text{proj}}(\cdot)$ denotes a small multi-layer perceptron that projects both feature vectors into a common latent subspace where the Euclidean distance is computed. This constraint serves as an effective regularizer that prevents the model from deviating excessively from the original feature manifold, thereby enhancing the generalization capability and stability of the learned representations.

The complete set of model parameters Θ is optimized by minimizing the combined loss $\mathcal{L}_{\text{total}}$ over the training dataset $\mathcal{D}$ using gradient-based optimization methods (e.g., AdamW):

$$\Theta^* = \arg\min_{\Theta} \mathbb{E}_{(\mathbf{X},y)\sim\mathcal{D}} [\mathcal{L}_{\text{total}}] \tag{18}$$

The incorporation of $\mathcal{L}_{\text{aux}}$ provides additional learning signals that facilitate more stable training dynamics and promote the learning of robust feature representations, ultimately complementing the primary classification objective and contributing to improved model performance.

4   Experiments

4.1   Datasets

We evaluate WavGateMamba on two multimodal depression detection benchmarks: D-Vlog [24] (1,045 clips, 325 subjects) and LMVD [30] (2,832 samples, 708 subjects). Both provide pre-extracted features: facial landmarks for visual and LLDs/VGGish for audio modalities. Standard splits are used (D-Vlog: 7:1:2, LMVD: 8:1:1).

Table 1. Performance comparison on D-Vlog and LMVD datasets. Best results in bold.

Methods	D-Vlog					LMVD				
	Acc	Prec	Rec	F1	Avg	Acc	Prec	Rec	F1	Avg
KNN [19]	60.38	61.41	85.64	71.47	69.72	56.83	57.43	50.92	53.92	54.77
Bi-LSTM [20]	64.47	67.68	75.34	71.10	69.65	66.85	65.81	70.33	67.83	67.71
TBN [21]	63.21	69.99	65.31	67.16	66.42	67.94	67.06	70.33	68.56	68.47
STFT [22]	61.79	64.67	77.51	69.77	68.44	67.76	69.20	64.01	66.23	66.80
TFN [23]	67.14	72.38	70.19	71.23	70.23	63.93	64.08	62.64	63.34	63.50
DepTrans [24]	62.89	64.43	84.82	72.54	71.17	61.93	60.36	72.16	65.08	64.88
MIL [25]	66.51	67.27	67.77	66.64	67.05	65.00	68.55	66.37	65.64	65.92
CAIINET [26]	67.00	66.56	66.98	66.55	66.52	65.12	65.56	65.98	65.55	65.52
Depressformer [27]	65.05	61.32	58.14	59.11	60.34	63.00	58.04	57.98	58.87	58.92
XGBoost [28]	71.45	71.38	84.00	77.18	75.50	68.11	71.32	82.12	76.00	74.10
TAMFN [29]	67.45	68.08	82.93	74.75	73.30	70.49	71.15	68.86	69.84	70.09
DepMamba [4]	68.87	68.19	86.99	76.44	75.12	72.13	70.18	76.56	73.20	73.02
WavGateMamba	**71.77**	67.19	**88.33**	**80.24**	**78.12**	**75.13**	**73.18**	76.19	**76.20**	**76.02**

4.2 Implementation Details

Implemented in PyTorch, we train on RTX 4090 GPUs using AdamW ($lr = 1e-4$, batch $= 16$). Key configurations: hidden dim $= 256$, Haar wavelet, Mamba state dim $= 16$, 2-layer gating MLP with ReLU, and $\lambda = 0.1$ for auxiliary loss.

4.3 Comparisons with State-of-the-Art Methods

Table 1 compares our method with existing approaches. WavGateMamba achieves competitive performance, outperforming DepMamba in 6 of 9 metrics. While our model shows significant gains in Recall and F1-score, it exhibits slightly lower Precision on D-Vlog dataset. We attribute this to enhanced sensitivity to subtle depressive cues from wavelet decomposition and gating. This trade-off is clinically desirable in screening scenarios, where minimizing false negatives (high Recall) is prioritized over false positives, ensuring potential cases are referred for expert assessment.

4.4 Ablation Studies

Table 2 shows ablation results on D-Vlog. The full model achieves best performance, demonstrating the value of each component.

To validate the effectiveness of the shared state-transition matrix, we conducted an eigenvalue analysis of the learned **A** matrix and compared it with matrices from ablated models trained with independent **A** for each modality. The eigenvalue spectrum of the shared $\mathbf{A}$ exhibited a stable, tightly-clustered distribution within the left half-plane, characteristic of a damped dynamical system well-suited for modeling behavioral time series. In contrast, the independently learned matrices showed dispersed and less stable eigenvalue patterns. This analysis confirms that the shared $\mathbf{A}$ matrix learns a unified and stable dynamical representation, justifying its role in facilitating cross-modal interaction.

Table 2. Ablation studies on the D-Vlog dataset.

Model Variants	Accuracy	Precision	Recall	F1	Avg
baseline [4]	68.87	68.19	86.99	76.44	75.12
wo Wavelet	69.20	67.63	87.02	78.80	76.41
wo Gating	69.92	67.21	87.11	77.44	75.76
wo Shared A	68.49	65.92	86.48	76.09	74.75
Full Model	**71.77**	67.19	**88.33**	**80.24**	**78.12**

5   Conclusion

This paper proposes WavGateMamba, a novel architecture that integrates wavelet decomposition and gating mechanisms into the Mamba framework for multimodal depression detection. Our method addresses the challenge of discriminative subtle cues being overwhelmed by low-frequency information through frequency-domain inductive bias and adaptive feature recalibration. Extensive experiments demonstrate that WavGateMamba achieves state-of-the-art performance, significantly outperforming existing approaches. While focusing on audio and visual modalities, future work will incorporate textual modalities (e.g., speech transcripts) to capture linguistic cues like sentiment and topic coherence, enabling a more comprehensive multimodal framework for depression analysis.

Acknowledgements. This work was supported by the National Natural Science Foundation of China-Guangxi Joint Fund Key Project (U22A2035), the New Engineering Practice Base Construction Project of Hubei Provincial Department of Education (XGK04029), the Wuhan Municipal Education Bureau Project (2025KCJ05), and the Hubei Higher Education Society Project (2024XD198).

References

1. Malhi, G.S., Mann, J.J.: Depression. Lancet (London, England) 392(10161), 2299–2312 (2018)
2. Wang, H.G., et al.: Sad-time: a spatiotemporal-fused network for depression detection with automated multi-scale depth-wise and time-interval-related common feature extractor (2024)

3. Gu, A., Dao, T.: MAMBA: linear-time sequence modeling with selective state spaces. ArXiv, abs/2312.00752 (2023)
4. Ye, J., Zhang, J., Shan, H.: Progressive fusion mamba for multimodal depression detection, Depmamba (2024)
5. Oorloff, T., et al.: Audio-visual feature fusion for video deepfake detection. IEEE AVFF (2024)
6. Fan, H., et al.: Transformer-based multimodal feature enhancement networks for multimodal depression detection integrating video, audio and remote photoplethysmograph signals. Inf. Fus., 104 (2024)
7. Zhang, L., Zhang, S., Zhang, X., Zhao, Y.: A multimodal artificial intelligence model for depression severity detection based on audio and video signals. Electronics 14(7), 2079-9292 (2025)
8. Ramalakshmi, N.R., Kumar, M.G., Raghavi, S.: Automated depression detection using CNN and transformer-based pre-trained language models. In: International Conference on Computer, Communication, and Signal Processing (2025). https://doi.org/10.1007/978-3-031-73617-9_4
9. Zhao, J., Jin, Q.: A two-stage depression recognition model based on improved YOLOv5 and spatial-temporal CNN-transformer network. In: 2024 IEEE Cyber Science and Technology Congress (CyberSciTech)
10. Chen, Q., Li, J., Fang, X.: Dual triple attention guided CNN-VMamba for medical image segmentation. Multimedia Syst. 30, 275 (2024). https://doi.org/10.1007/s00530-024-01498-3
11. Bi, H., Yu, G., He, Y., Liu, W., Zheng, Z.: VM-BHINet: vision mamba bimanual hand interaction network for 3D interacting hand mesh recovery from a single RGB image (2025)
12. Intriago, A., Paspatis, A., Liberati, F., Konstantinou, C.: Admittance identification of grid-forming inverters using time and frequency-domain techniques (2025)
13. Kortiš, J., Maliar, L., Daniel, Ľ.: Estimation of natural frequencies of the laboratory truss structure with output only subspace and frequency-domain techniques. In: MATEC Web of Conferences (2020)
14. Grandhe, P., Sreenivasa Reddy He, E.: A novel method for content based 3D medical image retrieval system using dual tree m-band wavelets transform and multiclass support vector machine. J. Adv. Res. Dyn. Control Syst. (2020)
15. Chalasani, T., Smolic, A.: Egocentric hand gesture recognition on untrimmed videos using state activation gate LSTMS (2022). https://doi.org/10.1007/978-3-031-37660-3_25
16. Tajima, Y., Inoue, N., Sekikawa, Y., Sato, I. and Yokota, R.: Masked gated linear unit (2025)
17. Wu, J., et al.: DuagNet: an unrestricted multimodal speech recognition framework using dual adaptive gating fusion. Appl. Intell. (2024)
18. Kwak, D., Jang, Y., Kim, S., Chung, J.S.: EDNet: a distortion-agnostic speech enhancement framework with gating mamba mechanism and phase shift-invariant training (2025)
19. Pampouchidou, A., et al.: Facial geometry and speech analysis for depression detection. In: Proceedings of the Annual International Conference of the IEEE Engineering in Medicine and Biology Society (EMBC), pp. 1433–1436 (2017)
20. Yin, S., Liang, C., Ding, H., Wang, S.: A multi-modal hierarchical recurrent neural network for depression detection. In: Ringeval, F., Schuller, B.W., Valstar, M.F., Cummins, N., Cowie, R., Pantic, M. (eds.) Proceedings of the International Audio/Visual Emotion Challenge and Workshop (AVEC), pp. 65–71 (2019)

21. Kazakos, E., Nagrani, A., Zisserman, A., Damen, D.: EPIC-fusion: audio-visual temporal binding for egocentric action recognition. In: Proceedings of the IEEE/CVF International Conference on Computer Vision (ICCV), pp. 5491–5500 (2019)
22. Tao, Y., Yang, M., Yushan, W., Lee, K., Kline, A.S., Bin, H.: Depressive semantic awareness from vlog facial and vocal streams via spatio-temporal transformer. Digit. Commun. Netw. **10**(3), 577–585 (2024)
23. Zadeh, A., Chen, M., Poria, S., Cambria, E., Morency, L.P.: Tensor fusion network for multimodal sentiment analysis. In: Palmer, M., Hwa, R., Riedel, S. (eds.) Proceedings of the Conference on Empirical Methods in Natural Language Processing (EMNLP), pp. 1103–1114 (2017)
24. Yoon, J., Kang, C., Kim, S., Han, J.: D-Vlog: multimodal Vlog dataset for depression detection. In: Proceedings of the AAAI Conference on Artificial Intelligence, pp. 12226–12234 (2022)
25. Shangguan, Z., Li, X., Dong, Y., Yuan, X.: Automatic depression detection using attention-based deep multiple instance learning. In: International Conference on Heterogeneous Networking for Quality, Reliability, Security and Robustness, pp. 40–51. Springer (2023). https://doi.org/10.1007/978-3-031-65126-7_4
26. Zhou, L., Liu, Z., Yuan, X., Shangguan, Z., Li, Y., Hu, B.: CAIINet: neural network based on contextual attention and information interaction mechanism for depression detection. Digit. Sig. Process. **137**, 103986 (2023)
27. He, L., et al.: DepressFormer: leveraging video SWIN transformer and fine-grained local features for depression scale estimation. Biomed. Signal Process. Control **96**, 106490 (2024)
28. Kowalewski, M., Stroinski, M., Kwarciak, K., Laptiev, V., Hemmerling, D.: End-to-end multimodal system for depression detection from online recordings. In: 45th Annual International Conference of the IEEE Engineering in Medicine & Biology Society (EMBC), pp. 1–4. IEEE (2023)
29. Zhou, L., Liu, Z., Shangguan, Z., Yuan, X., Li, Y., Bin, H.: TAMFN: Time-aware Attention Multimodal Fusion Network for depression detection. IEEE Trans. Neural Syst. Rehabil. Eng. **31**, 669–679 (2022)
30. He, L., et al.: LMVD: a large-scale multimodal vlog dataset for depression detection in the wild. Inf. Fus. **126**, 103632 (2024)

A Case Study on Large Visual-Language Model Attention Explainability After Adaptation Using Persuasion Strategies in Advertisements

Iván Martín-Fernández[1(✉)] , Mihai Gabriel Constantin[2] ,
Bogdan Ionescu[2] , Sergio Esteban-Romero[1] ,
Fernando Fernández-Martínez[1] , and Manuel Gil-Martín[1]

[1] Grupo de Tecnología del Habla y Aprendizaje Automático (THAU), Information
Processing and Telecommunications Center, E.T.S.I. de Telecomunicación,
Universidad Politécnica de Madrid, Madrid, Spain
`ivan.martinf@upm.es`
[2] AI Multimedia Lab, National University of Science and Technology Politehnica
Bucharest, Bucharest, Romania

Abstract. Large Vision-Language Models (LVLMs) demonstrate
impressive capabilities across multimodal tasks, yet their inner workings remain poorly understood, particularly in subjective domains that
involve human perception. In this paper, we examine how attention patterns in LVLMs shift with task-specific adaptation, using the task of
detecting persuasion strategies in advertisements as a case study. This
task attempts to model 16 different techniques used to influence behavior
or decision-making in marketing. In particular, we leverage PaliGemma
to classify persuasion strategies by applying a score-based logit post-
processing approach. Under this setting, we compare zero-shot performance with fine-tuning of the linear projector that maps image features
to the language embedding space, achieving 19.6% and 66.0% accuracy,
respectively, on the test set of the Persuasion Strategies in Advertisements corpus. We perform an exhaustive model interpretability analysis to understand how this lightweight adaptation method influences
downstream performance, showing that fine-tuning sharpens attention
to image regions and reduces noise. Fine-tuning makes image token representations more task-specific, evidenced by distinct attention patterns
across persuasion strategies. These findings motivate deeper exploration
into LVLM interpretability.

Keywords: Large Vision-Language Models · Persuasion Strategies ·
Model Interpretability · Multimodal Learning · Subjective Perception

1 Introduction

Large Vision-Language Models (LVLMs) have emerged as powerful tools for
bridging visual and linguistic modalities, offering insight into complex perceptual tasks that mirror human cognitive processes. Researchers can investigate the

J. Lokoč et al. (Eds.): MMM 2026, LNCS 16412, pp. 103–116, 2026.
https://doi.org/10.1007/978-981-95-6950-2_8

inner workings of LVLMs as a proxy for the human brain, gaining insight both about how machines and people think. In this work, we examine how LVLMs solve a perceptual task via supervised adaptation. Specifically, we investigate the result of efficiently adapting the PaliGemma model [2] by keeping both the image encoder and the text decoder frozen and adapting the weights of the linear projector that connects both modalities. We do this in the context of identifying persuasion strategies in advertisements, a 16-class multi-label problem that involves principles like reciprocation, authority, scarcity, and emotional content [6,14] to motivate consumers to purchase a product or service. The strong connections between this problem and the areas of human behavior and subjective perception, which have posed significant challenges to traditional computational models, motivate our study. Advances in persuasion strategy analysis can foster more ethical media generation and consumption.

The aim of this research is to advance the understanding of how LVLMs analyze visual inputs and perform intricate cognitive functions that result in the ability to predict human reactions to multimedia, using persuasion strategy detection as a case study. In particular, our main contributions are listed below:

1. We apply logit-based post-processing to the base PaliGemma LVLM for persuasion strategy detection in advertisements. Following this, to examine the resulting shifts in attention we fine-tune the image-to-text linear projector and produce a task-adapted PaliGemma checkpoint.
2. We conduct a post-hoc analysis of attention patterns in both the zero-shot and fine-tuned models, yielding the following key insights:
   (a) Fine-tuning the image-to-text projector shifts the attention in the Language Model (LM) away from image tokens and toward the special BOS token.
   (b) Attention to image representations becomes more spatially localized after fine-tuning.
   (c) While both the zero-shot and fine-tuned models attend similarly to objects, the fine-tuned model exhibits more dispersed attention across its various heads.
   (d) With the fine-tuned projector, different regions of the LM are activated more distinctly for each persuasion strategy, whereas the zero-shot model shows more uniform activation across strategies.

The rest of this document is structured as follows. Section 2 reviews related work in the fields of computational modeling of persuasion and LVLMs. Section 3 details the proposed methods for adapting LVLMs to the task of persuasion strategy detection. The experimental setup and evaluation metrics are presented in Sect. 4. The results of zero-shot and fine-tuned systems are provided in Sect. 5 and the attention pattern analysis is described in Sect. 6. Finally, conclusions and directions for future work are discussed in Sect. 7.

2   Related Work

Building on psychology and neurobiology foundations, computational methods have sought to quantify and predict persuasive communication using Machine Learning (ML) and natural language processing techniques.

2.1   Computational Prediction of Persuasion Strategies

Advanced ML methods have tackled persuasion prediction in text by modeling semantics, sentiment, and argumentation [5,7,18,21]. However, understanding persuasion strategies in ads, particularly visual ones, remained underexplored until the emergence of annotated corpora and advances in neural reasoning. Hussain et al. [11] curated the Pitts Image and Video Ads Dataset, which was annotated using free-form text responses to a questionnaire and subsequently post-processed into categorical class labels. Kumar et al. [13] annotated an image-only subset of this corpus in terms of persuasion strategies following a novel ontology and proposed a predictive model that combines OCR features, captions, object detections, and symbol embeddings using an attention-based fusion model. Using a similar ontology, Bhattacharyya et al. [3] generated a novel annotated video corpus, which includes enriched captions generated by a Large Language Model (LLM) from meta-data such as comments, likes, and scene descriptions. New corpora in persuasion strategy detection enable research into model design, validation, and generalization.

2.2   Large Vision-Language Models and Applications

LLMs have revolutionized Artificial Intelligence, excelling in tasks such as machine translation, document interpretation, and code synthesis by leveraging large scale pre-training. Moreover, LVLMs built from a pre-trained LLM and an image encoder enable the benefit of these potent capabilities in computer vision-related scenarios. The process of coupling the image and text modules often involves training a projector that translates the output hidden states into the input latent vector space of the LLM, using a multistage adaptation process with extensive multimodal data [2,19].

Recent studies have proposed different adaptation strategies to enable LVLMs to act as classifiers or regressors in downstream tasks, a challenge far from being solved. Some approaches adapt LVLMs by training a task-specific linear projector and performing classification using appended Multi-Layer Perceptron heads or softmax over raw logits [1,8,9]. Others use pretrained LVLMs as feature extractors or apply lightweight low-rank adaptations [8,16]. Although prior work has explored the application of LVLMs in multimodal and perceptual tasks, their adaptation to highly subjective domains, such as the detection of persuasion strategies, remains underexplored.

2.3 Explaining Attention Patterns in LVLMs

Recent work has begun to illuminate how LVLMs integrate visual information through attention. Kaduri et al. [12] show that, when prompted to describe an image, the LM selectively attends to image regions containing salient or descriptive objects. While textual tokens often serve as high-level global descriptors, fine-grained visual details are retrieved via attention to image tokens in the middle layers of the model. Neo et al. [17] find that, in deeper transformer layers, visual token representations become semantically aligned with textual concepts and are essential for accurate object recognition and localization. Complementarily, Bi et al. [4] identify that LVLMs dedicate specific attention heads to visual processing, indicating a degree of structural specialization for cross-modal fusion. However, these studies are limited to analyzing pre-trained models and largely focus on objective tasks such as captioning or object recognition. The effects of fine-tuning on attention patterns, especially in subjective reasoning tasks like persuasion strategy detection, remain underexplored, a gap our work addresses.

3 Method

We describe a lightweight PaliGemma-based LVLM for persuasion strategy detection, which serves as the basis for analyzing attention shifts induced by fine-tuning. Subsection 3.1 outlines the architecture, while Subsects. 3.2 and 3.3 detail the logit preprocessing and fine-tuning procedures.

3.1 Model Architecture

An overview of the architecture used in our experiments is shown in Fig. 1. The starting point is a checkpoint[1] of PaliGemma [2], a relatively small but competent and versatile LVLM, that has been fine-tuned on a diverse set of academic downstream tasks. It consists of a SigLIP image encoder [22] based on a ViT architecture for visual token generation, a linear projector that aligns these tokens with the text embedding space, and a Gemma-2B LM [20] that serves as the core autoregressive decoder.

The model receives an image and textual prompt as input. The image is divided into a grid of 32×32, resulting in $1,024$ patches, which are processed by the image encoder. This encoder outputs 1,024 feature vectors, each with 1,024 dimensions. These intermediate representations are then projected using a linear layer to the dimension of the LM output as visual tokens of 2,048 dimensions, which match its internal structure. The projected visual tokens are then concatenated with the textual prompt tokens and fed into the, which generates new output tokens conditioned on both modalities.

The simultaneous pre-training of the image encoder and textual decoder on extensive and diverse data results in a model that is able to understand intricate

---

[1] https://huggingface.co/google/paligemma-3b-mix-448.

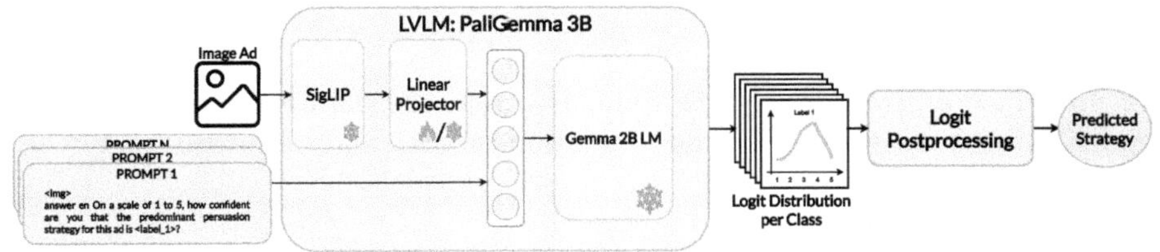

Fig. 1. LVLM-based architecture for persuasion strategy classification. Snowflakes indicate modules with frozen weights, whilst the flame icon denotes the component which is updated during training.

relationships between the vision and language modalities. This enables effective zero-shot prompting and fine-tuning without heavy computational demands. Additionally, the use of a single linear projection layer between modalities offers a clear and interpretable interface for analysing how vision and language features interact within the shared embedding space. Our goal is to understand model behavior when adapted to a specific task–persuasion strategy classification–that lies outside the distribution of the pre-training data.

3.2   Zero Shot Prediction

We adapt the LVLM for multi-label classification by running 16 forward passes, each prompting the model to rate confidence (1–5) that a specific persuasion strategy applies. We extract logits for tokens 1–5, apply softmax, and aggregate the resulting class scores. The prompt used to query the model is shown below:

```
answer en On a scale of 1 to 5, how confident are you that
    the predominant persuasion strategy for this ad is
    <label> ?
```

Listing 1.1. List of the prompts used for inference. The "answer en" tags are task specifiers for the model [2].

3.3   Fine-tuning

Based on recent works that explore efficient adaptation of similar models to downstream tasks [1,8,10,15], we opt for adapting only the linear layer that translates the visual feature vectors extracted from the image encoder into tokens that are processed by the LLM decoder (that is, the Linear Projector). With 2.34M trainable parameters (0.08% of the total for the whole LVLM), this relatively non-invasive method leverages the knowledge of the frozen image encoder and text decoder while learning a more adequate image representation for the problem at hand.

4   Experimental Setup

We introduce an overview of the data used and the details of the experiment implementation together with the evaluation metrics and hardware used.

4.1   Datasets

In this study, the Persuasion Strategies in Advertisements dataset is used for experimentation [13]. The dataset consists of 3,000 annotated images, split into 2,750 training and 250 testing samples, extracted from the Pitts Ads corpus of 64,832 advertisements [11]. Each image is labeled with up to three persuasion strategies based on definitions and examples provided to the annotators, ensuring consistency across annotations. As a result, the dataset is annotated with 16 different strategies: *Active, Amazed, Authority, Cheerful, Concreteness, Creative, Eager, Emotion, Fashionable, Feminine, Reciprocity, Social Identity, Social Impact, Trustworthiness, Unclear* and *Others*. Each sample may contain between 1 and 3 labels that depict the most predominant strategies in that ad. Persuasion strategies were derived from theoretical and empirical studies in the literature on marketing, social psychology, and ML.

4.2   Training and Evaluation Details

We train on the 2,750 samples from the train and validation splits and report results on the 250-sample test set. We train for 5 epochs using 4 RTX A5000 GPUs (batch size 4, with gradient accumulation). Optimization uses cosine LR scheduling (base 1e−3, 10K warm-up steps). The experiments were conducted using Hugging Face Transformers and PyTorch. **Accuracy@1** and **accuracy@3** were used as evaluation metrics following the baseline protocol [13], measuring the ability of the model to correctly identify the ground-truth persuasion strategy either as its top prediction (accuracy@1) or among its top three predictions (accuracy@3).

In order to train the model using the logit post-processing technique, the ground-truth labels must also be adapted to this formulation. Specifically, we train the model to predict the confidence score for each of the 16 persuasion strategies, assigning a score of 5 to strategies present in a given sample and 1 to those that are absent. Therefore, the model receives 16 image-prompt pairs per advertisement, each corresponding to one candidate strategy, and generates a single vocabulary token per input. During inference, logit postprocessing is applied to align the outputs of the model with the evaluation framework. This results in an ordered list of labels based on how confident the model is in each strategy being present in the ad, which is used for **accuracy@1** and **accuracy@3** evaluation following the protocol detailed in the baseline article.

5   Performance Evaluation

Table 1. Results for the image persuasion strategy on the test set of the corpus.

Model	Acc@1 (%)	Acc@3 (%)
Baseline [13]	59.2 ± 6.09	$\mathbf{84.8 \pm 4.45}$
Zero-Shot	19.6 ± 4.92	45.6 ± 6.17
Fine-tuned Linear Projector	$\mathbf{66.0 \pm 5.87}$	84.4 ± 4.50

We present a quantitative analysis of the performance of the model on the persuasion strategy detection task as a starting point for the subsequent interpretability study. Table 1 shows the accuracy of our evaluated systems. The results from Kumar et al. [13] serve as an external baseline for system performance. The zero-shot model achieves 19.6% top-1 accuracy, underperforming the approach from Kumar et al. [13]. This highlights the limitations of LVLMs in performing classification tasks out-of-the-box. Moreover, the PaliGemma researchers recommend fine-tuning the model to a specific use case for best results.

Fine-tuning the 2.34M-parameter linear projector boosts prediction accuracy from 19.6% to 66.0%, which is now comparable to the baseline [13], which extracts several features, combines them using a learnable cross-attention module, and trains a Transformer decoder to learn the final strategies. This suggests that, although the LLM is not able to follow precise instructions regarding an out-of-distribution task without adaptation, there is an implicitly encoded knowledge about the task that can be unlocked just by adapting the representation used for feeding visual information. The smaller gain in top-3 accuracy reflects sharper confidence toward the dominant label rather than broader predictions. In the next section, we explore how the frozen Gemma model understands image-related tokens after projector fine-tuning, in contrast to the zero-shot counterpart.

6   Attention Pattern Analysis

We analyze how fine-tuning the linear projection layer alters how the LM interprets visual tokens by examining attention over image regions. For each of the 250 test image–prompt pairs, we extract attention tensors from all 18 layers and 8 heads of the Gemma model, yielding arrays of shape $(18, 8, SL)$ that capture how generated tokens attend to every element in the sequence, with emphasis on the relative weighting of image tokens.

6.1   Attention over Image, Text and BOS tokens

We analyze the attention patterns across layers and heads, comparing how the model attends to text tokens versus image tokens. For each prompted label, we compute the average attention scores over language, visual and Beggining of Sentence (BOS) tokens across the 250 test samples. The mean attention plot per

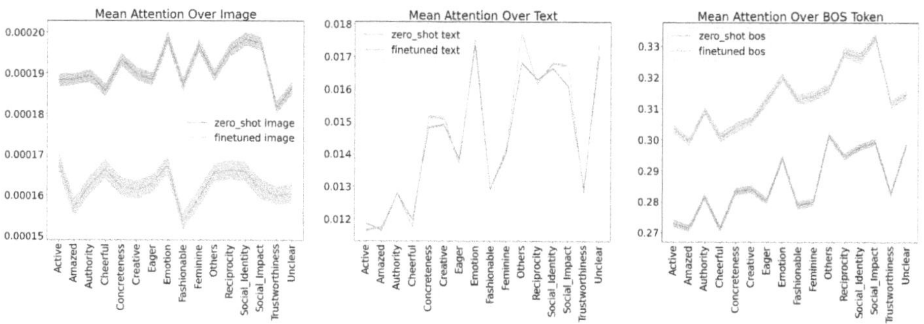

Fig. 2. Mean LLM attention per label over the sequence tokens, separated by image (left), text (center) and BOS (right), with 95% confidence intervals.

label, separated by token type, is shown in Fig. 2. Our results show that both models pay constant attention to text tokens on labels. However, the fine-tuned projector causes the LLM to shift its attention away from image tokens and toward the BOS token. This seems counter-intuitive, since image tokens carry the semantic content about the task and should be key in decoding the persuasion strategy information it contains. However, it remains unknown whether there is any relevant information encoded in the BOS token as a byproduct of the original self-supervised LVLM pre-training. We focus on analyzing the attention patterns on the image tokens and leave a further study of the BOS token for future work. In the subsequent analysis, we discard the attention scores over text and BOS tokens and keep the attention over the $1,024$ image tokens, reshaping the $(18, 8, 1024)$ tensor into (18×8) attention maps of (32×32) patches that can be overlayed on the pre-processed image.

6.2 Unsupervised Analysis of Image Token Attention Distribution

We analyze activation levels in the attention maps, comparing activation values in the zero-shot model versus the fine-tuned model. We start by normalizing

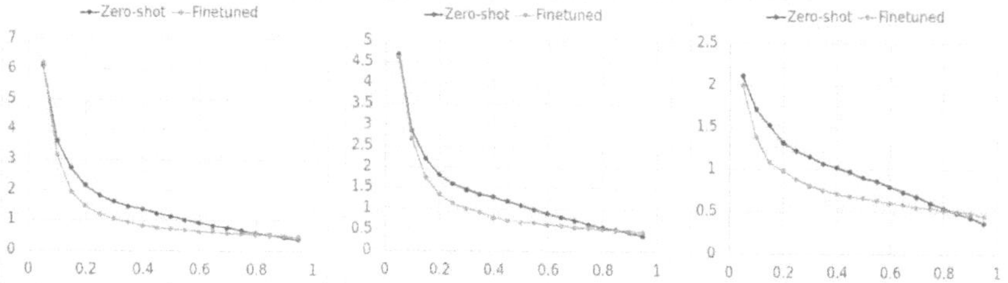

(a) Values above a certain threshold

(b) Clusters obtained using a certain threshold

(c) Cluster sizes obtained using a certain threshold

Fig. 3. Normalized values in the top most activated attention map for the zero-shot and fine-tuned models, obtained by applying threshold values in increments of 0.1, and averaging across all samples in the testing set.

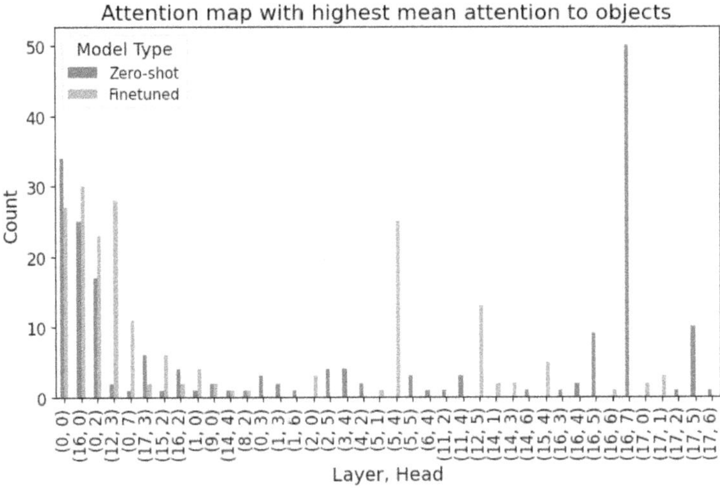

Fig. 4. Attention maps with highest mean per-patch attention to objects.

the values in the attention maps. Given the set of (18×8) attention maps for a single sample for the predicted label, $\mathcal{M} = \{M_1, ..., M_{144}\}$, we compute the global maximum value across these maps, and use the maximum to normalize all the values in $\mathcal{M}$. Computing the sum across each of the 144 maps gives us the most activated map, i.e., the map with the highest sum. We perform an analysis of the values recorded in the most activated map, comparing the zero-shot and the fine-tuned models, and computing the following indicators: (i) number of values above certain thresholds in M_i, (ii) clusters of values above a certain threshold, where clusters are defined as adjacent values above the threshold in the bidimensional (32×32) representation of the attention map, (iii) size of the largest cluster. This analysis is shown in Fig. 3. All three methods of analysis seem to indicate that a higher number of values between 0 and 0.8 can be found in the attention maps for the zero-shot method, thus creating a higher number of clusters and clusters of larger sizes for those values. However, for values above 0.85 the reverse seems to happen, and a higher number of values, clusters, and cluster sizes appear for the fine-tuned model. This would seem to indicate that the fine-tuned approach focuses more and is less affected by noisy values that may surround the important and defining characteristics of the images. Although not presented in Fig. 3 due to the lack of space, the same trend can be observed for the second and third most activated maps.

6.3   Image Token Attention Distribution to Objects

Our experiments indicate that the fine-tuned model assigns lower overall attention to visual tokens compared to the zero-shot model but concentrates more on specific regions. We explore links between these regions and semantic cues by using an object detector[2] to classify the image patches as either "object" or "background" based on the presence of bounding boxes. Then, for each attention tensor, we compute the mean attention over object patches across all layers and heads, the mean attention over background patches and the ratio between them.

Firstly, in Fig. 4 a bar plot for the (32×32) attention maps that are the most focused on the object patches are shown. The results show that the zero-shot model mainly designates the $(16, 7)$ map for object processing, whilst for the fine-tuned model there is no such clear tendency. This might be related to the strong pretraining of the PaliGemma LVLM generating specialist regions inside the neural networks devoted to different subtasks that help solve the downstream problem. However, by transforming the image token subspace, these dependencies are broken, and the attention inside the LM is no longer clearly distributed across information sources.

We compare the distribution of the ratios between objects and background for each sample in Fig. 5. Though distributions differ, mean and median values show no significant difference. This suggests that both models are equally focused on objects when processing the image, and that the differences observed in Subsect. 6.2 are not explained by the model being more focused on the semantic information carried out by the objects in the image. This invites further work to correlate attended image regions with task-relevant features.

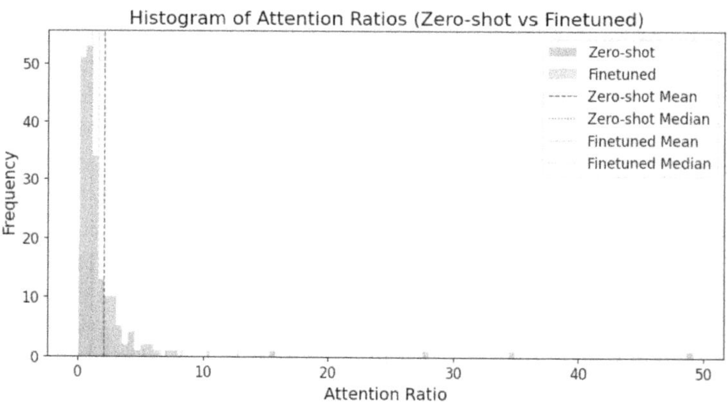

Fig. 5. Histogram of the ratio between mean attention over objects and background for both zero-shot and fine-tuned models.

6.4 Image Token Attention Distribution over Labels

We hypothesize that supervised adaptation refines the high-dimensional image representations generated by the projector, making them more task-specific and

---

[2] https://huggingface.co/facebook/detr-resnet-50.

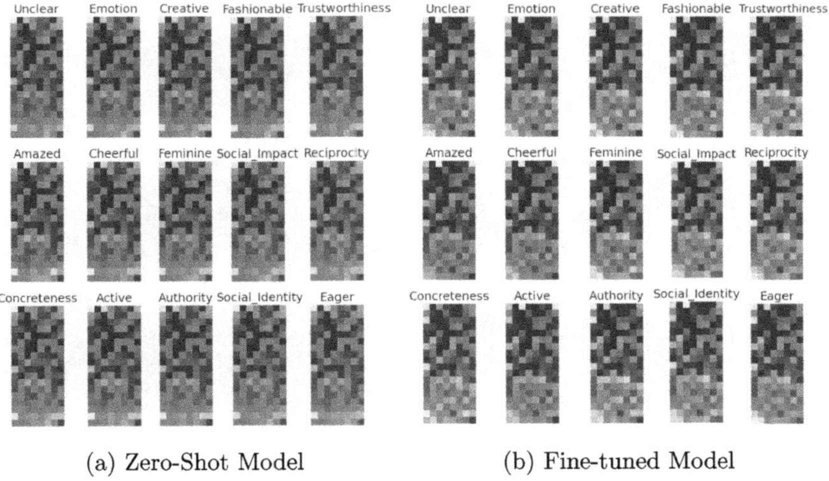

(a) Zero-Shot Model   (b) Fine-tuned Model

Fig. 6. Mean attention map per label for the zero-shot and fine-tuned models. "Others" is not included due to space limitations.

separable rather than capturing general image features. To test this hypothesis, we calculate the mean attention over image tokens across all Transformer layers and heads for each persuasion strategy p:

$$\overline{a_{l,h,p}} = \sum_{i=1}^{1024} \sum_{s=1}^{250} \frac{a_{l,h,p,i,s}}{\max_{s \in \mathcal{S}} a_{l,h,p,i,s}},$$

where $a_{l,h,p,i,s}$ represents the attention score in head h of layer l to token i in sample s when asked about the persuasion strategy p, normalized by the maximum value in all samples. This calculation results in $|\mathcal{P}|$ matrices of shape (l, h), where $|\mathcal{P}|$ is the number of unique strategy labels in $\mathcal{P}$. These matrices provide a detailed representation of the mean attention patterns in the model for each label, allowing us to investigate whether specific regions of the model exhibit greater activation for certain strategies.

Figure 6 shows the mean attention matrices for each label, calculated for both models. The zero-shot model displays less variation in attention across strategies, with image tokens consistently activating the same model regions at similar intensities. In contrast, the fine-tuned model exhibits more variation, where similar regions are activated, but their intensity changes depending on the label. To confirm this observation, we performed a paired t-test on all pairs of strategy-specific attention distributions, represented as $\mathcal{A} = \{\{a_{l,h,p,i,s}\} \ \forall p \in \mathcal{P}\}$. The resulting significance matrix is shown in Fig. 7. The reduced p-values for the fine-tuned model indicate that its attention distributions are more distinct across labels, supporting our hypothesis that fine-tuning the projector creates task-specific visual representations that better distinguish between classes.

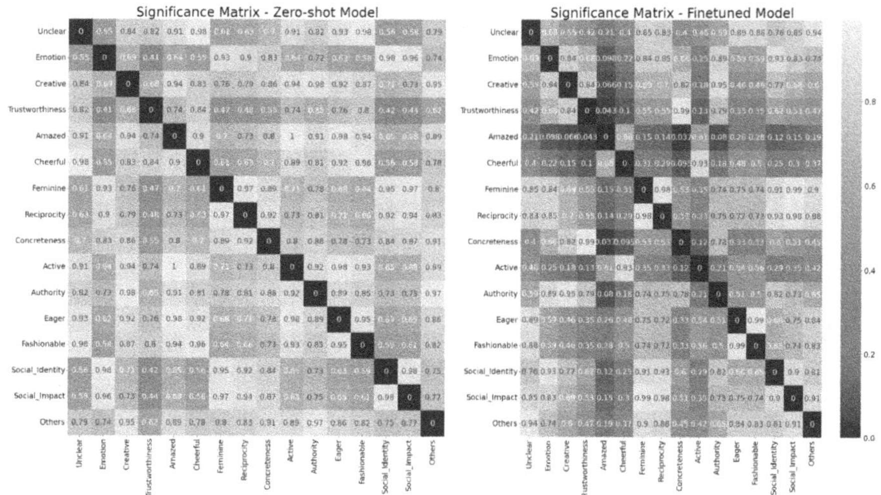

Fig. 7. Significance of label-wise paired t-test p-values: the fine-tuned model varies its attention patterns across labels more than the zero shot model.

7   Conclusions and Future Work

This work examines how adapting Large Vision-Language Models (LVLMs) to subjective perception tasks influences their attention mechanisms. By efficiently fine-tuning the linear projector, we achieve competitive performance, demonstrating that LVLMs can be specialized for downstream applications without full retraining. The analysis reveals that adaptation sharpens attention to specific image regions and modifies visual token representations. Future work will investigate how these representations align with semantic cues and task-relevant features, and whether the observed attention behavior generalizes to other datasets and tasks. This study provides a foundation for understanding how LVLMs transfer their general capabilities to real-world subjective perception problems.

Acknowledgments. I. M.-F.'s research was supported by the Universidad Politécnica de Madrid (Programa Propio I+D+i). This work was funded by Project ASTOUND (101071191—HORIZON-EIC-2021-PATHFINDERCHALLENGES-01) of the European Commission, by the Spanish Ministry of Science and Innovation through the projects GOMINOLA (PID2020-118112RB-C22) and TRUSTBOOST (PID2023-150584OB-C21) , funded by MCIN/AEI/10.13039/501100011033 and by the European Union "NextGenerationEU/PRTR", and by UEFISCDI projects RoNLP, grant PN-IV-P6-6.3-SOL-2024-2-0238, and DeteRel grant PN-IV-P6-6.3-SOL-2024-0060. This work is supported under UEFISCDI projects RoNLP, grant PN-IV-P6-6.3-SOL-2024-2-0238, and DeteRel grant PN-IV-P6-6.3-SOL-2024-0060.

Disclosure of Interests. The authors have no competing interests to declare that are relevant to the content of this article.

References

1. Bellver, J., et al.: Multimodal audio-language model for speech emotion recognition. In: The Speaker and Language Recognition Workshop, Odyssey 2024, pp. 288–295 (2024). https://doi.org/10.21437/odyssey.2024-41
2. Beyer, L., et al.: PaliGemma: a versatile 3B VLM for transfer. arXiv preprint arXiv:2407.07726 (2024)
3. Bhattacharyya, A., Singla, Y.K., Krishnamurthy, B., Shah, R.R., Chen, C.: A video is worth 4096 tokens: Verbalize videos to understand them in zero shot. In: Bouamor, H., Pino, J., Bali, K. (eds.) Proceedings of the 2023 Conference on Empirical Methods in Natural Language Processing, December 2023, pp. 9822–9839. Association for Computational Linguistics, Singapore (2023). https://doi.org/10.18653/v1/2023.emnlp-main.608, https://aclanthology.org/2023.emnlp-main.608
4. Bi, J., et al.: Unveiling visual perception in language models: an attention head analysis approach. In: Proceedings of the Computer Vision and Pattern Recognition Conference (CVPR), pp. 4135–4144 (June 2025)
5. Braca, A., Dondio, P.: Persuasive communication systems: a machine learning approach to predict the effect of linguistic styles and persuasion techniques. J. Syst. Inf. Technol. **25**(2), 160–191 (2023). https://doi.org/10.1108/JSIT-07-2022-0166
6. Cialdini, R.B.: The science of Persuasion. Sci. Am. Mind **14**(1), 70–77 (2004). http://www.jstor.org/stable/24939368
7. Da San Martino, G., Barrón-Cedeño, A., Nakov, P., Glass, M.: Fine-grained analysis of propaganda in news articles. In: Proceedings of the 2019 Conference on Empirical Methods in Natural Language Processing and the 9th International Joint Conference on Natural Language Processing, pp. 5636–5646 (2019). https://doi.org/10.18653/v1/D19-1565
8. Esteban-Romero, S., et al.: THAU-UPM at EmoSpeech-IberLEF2024: efficient adaptation of mono-modal and multi-modal large language models for automatic speech emotion recognition. In: Proceedings of the Iberian Languages Evaluation Forum, IberLEF 2024, co-located with the 40th Conference of the Spanish Society for Natural Language Processing, SEPLN 2024. CEUR-WS. org. Conference of the Spanish Society for Natural Language Processing (SEPLN 2024), CEUR-WS. org (2024)
9. Esteban-Romero, S., et al.: LLM-driven multimodal fusion for human perception analysis. In: Proceedings of the 5th on Multimodal Sentiment Analysis Challenge and Workshop: Social Perception and Humor, MuSe'24, pp. 45–51. Association for Computing Machinery, New York, NY, USA (2024). https://doi.org/10.1145/3689062.3689084
10. Han, J., et al.: ImageBind-LLM: multi-modality instruction tuning (2023). https://arxiv.org/abs/2309.03905
11. Hussain, Z., et al.: Automatic understanding of image and video advertisements. In: Proceedings of the IEEE Conference on Computer Vision and Pattern Recognition, pp. 1705–1715 (2017)
12. Kaduri, O., Bagon, S., Dekel, T.: What's in the image? A deep-dive into the vision of vision language models. In: Proceedings of the Computer Vision and Pattern Recognition Conference (CVPR), June 2025, pp. 14549–14558 (2025)
13. Kumar, Y., et al.: Persuasion strategies in advertisements. In: Proceedings of the AAAI Conference on Artificial Intelligence, vol. 37, pp. 57–66 (2023)
14. Lau-Gesk, L., Meyers-Levy, J.: Emotional persuasion: when the valence versus the resource demands of emotions influence consumers' attitudes. J. Consum. Res. **36**(4), 585–599 (2009). https://doi.org/10.1086/605297

15. Li, J., Li, D., Savarese, S., Hoi, S.: BLIP-2: bootstrapping language-image pre-training with frozen image encoders and large language models. In: Krause, A., Brunskill, E., Cho, K., Engelhardt, B., Sabato, S., Scarlett, J. (eds.) Proceedings of the 40th International Conference on Machine Learning, 23–29 July 2023, vol. 202, pp. 19730–19742. Proceedings of Machine Learning Research. PMLR (2023). https://proceedings.mlr.press/v202/li23q.html
16. Martín-Fernández, I., Esteban-Romero, S., Bellver-Soler, J., Fernández-Martínez, F., Gil-Martín, M.: Larger encoders, smaller regressors: exploring label dimensionality reduction and multimodal large language models as feature extractors for predicting social perception. In: Proceedings of the 5th on Multimodal Sentiment Analysis Challenge and Workshop: Social Perception and Humor, MuSe'24, pp. 20–27. Association for Computing Machinery, New York, NY, USA (2024). https://doi.org/10.1145/3689062.3689083
17. Neo, C., Ong, L., Torr, P., Geva, M., Krueger, D., Barez, F.: Towards interpreting visual information processing in vision-language models. In: The Thirteenth International Conference on Learning Representations (2025). https://openreview.net/forum?id=chanJGoa7f
18. Pryzant, R., Shen, K., Jurafsky, D., Wagner, S.: Deconfounded lexicon induction for interpretable social science. In: Proceedings of the 2018 Conference of the North American Chapter of the Association for Computational Linguistics: Human Language Technologies, Volume 1 (Long Papers), pp. 1615–1625 (2018)
19. Steiner, A., et al.: PaliGemma 2: a family of versatile VLMs for transfer. arXiv preprint arXiv:2412.03555 (2024)
20. Team, G., et al.: Gemma: open models based on Gemini research and technology. arXiv preprint arXiv:2403.08295 (2024)
21. Vorakitphan, V., Cabrio, E., Villata, S.: "don't discuss": investigating semantic and argumentative features for supervised propagandist message detection and classification. In: Recent Advances in Natural Language Processing, RANLP 2021 (2021)
22. Zhai, X., Mustafa, B., Kolesnikov, A., Beyer, L.: Sigmoid loss for language image pre-training. In: International Conference on Computer Vision (ICCV) (2023)

FIGROTD: A Friendly-to-Handle Dataset for Image Guided Retrieval with Optional Text

Hoang-Bao Le[1,2](✉), Allie Tran[1,2], Binh T. Nguyen[1,2], Liting Zhou[1,2], and Cathal Gurrin[1,2]

[1] ADAPT Centre, School of Computing, Dublin City University, Dublin, Ireland
`bao.le2@mail.dcu.ie {allie.tran,liting.zhou,cathal.gurrin}@dcu.ie`
[2] Ho Chi Minh University of Science, Vietnam National University, Ho Chi Minh City, Vietnam

Abstract. Image-Guided Retrieval with Optional Text (IGROT) unifies visual retrieval (without text) and composed retrieval (with text). Despite its relevance in applications like Google Image and Bing, progress has been limited by the lack of an accessible benchmark and methods that balance performance across subtasks. Large-scale datasets such as MagicLens are comprehensive but computationally prohibitive, while existing models often favor either visual or compositional queries. We introduce **FIGROTD**, a lightweight yet high-quality IGROT dataset with 16,474 training triplets and 1,262 test triplets across CIR, SBIR, and CST-BIR. To reduce redundancy, we propose the **Variance Guided Feature Mask (VaGFeM)**, which selectively enhances discriminative dimensions based on variance statistics. We further adopt a dual-loss design (InfoNCE + Triplet) to improve compositional reasoning. Trained on FIGROTD, VaGFeM achieves competitive results on nine benchmarks, reaching 34.8 mAP@10 on CIRCO and 75.7 mAP@200 on Sketchy, outperforming stronger baselines despite fewer triplets. Our dataset and code are available at here.

1 Introduction

Given a reference image with or without a textual description, **Image-Guided Retrieval with Optional Text (IGROT)** aims to retrieve one or more images from a collection that are visually similar to the input image and semantically aligned with the caption if it exists. This paradigm is widely used in real-world search engines such as Google Image[1], Google Lens[2], and Bing[3]. By allowing queries to be expressed visually or visually + textually, IGROT provides users with more flexible search options, especially in scenarios where they lack precise textual descriptions. Moreover, beyond images, IGROT can serve as a stepping

---

[1] https://images.google.com/.
[2] https://lens.google/.
[3] https://www.bing.com/.

J. Lokoč et al. (Eds.): MMM 2026, LNCS 16412, pp. 117–132, 2026.
https://doi.org/10.1007/978-981-95-6950-2_9

stone toward retrieval in more complex domains such as video [6,20], which require spatio-temporal reasoning and human-centric understanding.

In general, IGROT can be divided into two main settings: **without text** and **with text**. *Without text*, IGROT reduces to classical **Visual Retrieval** [3], where the system must return images visually consistent with the input. With the emergence of Vision-Language Models (VLMs) such as CLIP [19] and BLIP [10], this task has become more robust, as these models provide joint embeddings that capture image semantics and their alignment with language. *With text*, IGROT covers cases where users wish to apply modifications to a reference image via natural language. Two representative tasks are **Composed Image Retrieval (CIR)** [22], where the reference is an image plus a relative text modification, and **Composite Sketch+Text Based Image Retrieval (CSTBIR)** [5], where a sketch is refined with text to query a photo. These extensions have become increasingly important as VLMs reshape how humans interact with visual search systems.

Despite progress, two major challenges hinder further research in IGROT. First, the lack of an accessible, unified benchmark. Existing datasets are separated by subtask, making cross-task study difficult. Large-scale datasets such as MagicLens [28] contain tens of millions of triplets, offering diversity but at the cost of accessibility, as their size demands enormous computational and annotation resources. This limits participation, especially from students and researchers with modest resources. Second, through our experiments, we observe the necessity of a **shared embedding space** between query and target features. Without it, retrieval consistency degrades. To address this, we introduce a dual-loss design combining InfoNCE and Triplet loss. The latter provides complementary supervision by discouraging trivial matches to the reference image alone, thus improving compositional reasoning.

To tackle these issues, we propose **FIGROTD**, a *Friendly IGROT Dataset* containing 16,474 training triplets and 1,262 test triplets. FIGROTD is designed to be lightweight yet high-quality, making it practical for both resource-limited researchers and students. Alongside the dataset, we present a simple but effective baseline, the **Variance Guided Feature Mask (VaGFeM)**, which introduces a variance-based masking strategy to emphasise discriminative dimensions in fused representations. Our method achieves competitive performance against state-of-the-art approaches on nine diverse benchmarks, including FashionIQ [24], CIRR [15], CIRCO [1], PatternCom [18], Sketchy [13], TUBerlin [27], QuickDraw [4], PKU [17] and the test set of FIGROTD.

In summary, the main contributions of this paper are:

- We introduce **FIGROTD**, a high-quality and resource-friendly dataset for IGROT tasks, enabling fair comparison and easier experimentation across CIR, SBIR, and CSTBIR.
- We propose the **Variance Guided Feature Mask (VaGFeM)**, a lightweight yet effective module that selectively emphasizes informative dimensions, yielding competitive results on six public benchmarks.

– We design a dual-loss training objective that combines InfoNCE with Triplet loss, demonstrating its benefits in CIR and analyzing its trade-offs in SBIR.

2   Related Works

Composed Image Retrieval (CIR), SBIR, and CSTBIR. Composed Image Retrieval (CIR) has been extensively studied, where the goal is to retrieve a target image given a reference image and a textual modification. Early methods such as TIRG [22] and ComposeAE focused on simple feature concatenation or gating mechanisms. More recent methods, including TransAgg [14], PVLF [23], and CoLLM [7], exploit transformers or large-scale language models to better align visual and textual cues. Despite strong results, these approaches often require millions of triplets for training, making them computationally expensive and annotation-heavy.

Sketch-Based Image Retrieval (SBIR) has a longer history, focusing on aligning sketches with natural images. Works such as ZSE-SBIR [12], DCDL [11], and CAT [21] design cross-modal encoders to handle modality gaps between sketches and real images. However, SBIR queries are purely visual and often emphasize structural cues rather than compositional semantics, making it challenging to incorporate fine-grained text modifications.

Compositional Sketch-Text-Based Image Retrieval (CSTBIR), introduced recently in [5], extends this paradigm by allowing users to query with a sketch plus textual description. This setting addresses real-world cases where users cannot name an object precisely but can visualize it through a sketch. CSTBIR unifies the strengths of CIR and SBIR, but research in this area remains limited due to the lack of accessible datasets and efficient training strategies.

Datasets for Retrieval. The dataset landscape for multimodal retrieval is diverse, differing widely in scale and accessibility. In CIR, LaSCo [8] introduced 360k compositional triplets, while TransAgg [14] provided 32k curated pairs. MTCIR [7] scaled this trend significantly with 3.4M synthetic triplets. MagicLens [28] further expanded the scale by generating over 36M triplets using web images and large language model captions. Although such large-scale resources are valuable, they are often impractical for researchers and students due to massive storage and computational costs.

In SBIR, classical datasets such as Sketchy [13], TU-Berlin [27], and Quick-Draw [4] have been widely used. While they provide strong baselines, their limited compositional supervision makes them less effective for tasks that require fine-grained reasoning.

Motivation for IGROT and Our Contribution. From these shortcomings, our work introduces FIGROTD under the IGROT benchmark, which provides a unified yet accessible dataset across CIR, SBIR, and CSTBIR. Unlike large-scale datasets that emphasize quantity, FIGROTD focuses on quality, efficiency, and usability, offering a friendly-to-handle resource for both researchers and students with limited computational resources. Furthermore, our proposed method, Variance-Guided Feature Mask (VaGFeM), demonstrates that competitive performance can be achieved with only 10k triplets, highlighting the importance of efficient representation learning over raw dataset scale.

3   Dataset Construction

To construct FIGROTD, we integrate data from multiple sources covering CIR, SBIR, and CSTBIR subtasks in a lightweight but diverse way. For the CIR branch, we start from a subset of the LAION dataset[4], also used in LAION_combined [14], where we employ CLIP (ViT-L) [19] to compute similarity scores and retain only pairs above a threshold of 0.9 [1], ensuring reliable image–text alignment. For SBIR, we rely on the TU-Berlin dataset [27], selecting 140 object categories with 10,979 sketches. Each sketch is randomly paired with one of several transfer prompts such as "a real image of this sketch", "an image illustrating this sketch", or "a real image that is similar to this sketch", which provides diverse textual queries for sketch–image matching. For CSTBIR, we employ LLaVA-v1.6-Mistral-7B to automatically generate single-sentence captions describing each image, serving as the compositional component in training triplets.

To construct the test set, we adopt a semi-automatic pipeline in which candidate modification texts are generated using LLaVA-NeXT-Interleave [9], trained on the INOVA Challenge 2025 dataset[5] [2], and subsequently refined by *annotators* who select queries that consistently satisfy both the target image group and the intended textual modification. Table 1 reports the statistics of FIGROTD: the training set contains 16,474 triplets across three subtasks with an average text length of 15.09 words, while the test set contains 1,262 triplets with shorter queries for CIR and CSTBIR (8–10 words on average). Finally, to provide a unified retrieval index, we merge the ground truths of SBIR and CSTBIR with the CIRCO index set [1], resulting in a large-scale gallery of 126,026 images, which supports consistent evaluation across all IGROT subtasks.

---

[4] https://laion.ai/blog/laion-coco/.
[5] https://inovachallenge.github.io/ICME2025/.

Table 1. Statistics of three benchmarks in FIGROTD. We report the average text length for each class in the train and test splits. For the SBIR test set, transfer queries are randomly sampled from the list in Sect. 3.

Class	Train		Test	
	# Triplets	Text Length	# Triplets	Text Length
CIR	5,495	18.57	250	8.32
SBIR	5,099	17.66	770	–
SBTIR	5,880	8.36	242	9.87
TOTAL	16,474	15.09	1,262	–

4   Methodology

Motivation. Retrieval tasks such as CIR, SBIR, and SBTIR demand embeddings that are both discriminative and robust across modalities. However, conventional fusion methods often introduce redundant or noisy dimensions, while existing losses may bias retrieval towards reference images without fully capturing fine-grained modifications. To address these issues, we design the **Variance Guided Feature Mask (VaGFeM)** to selectively enhance informative features, and introduce a **triplet loss** that explicitly penalizes over-reliance on reference images. Together, these components strengthen compositional understanding while maintaining shared embedding consistency across tasks.

4.1   Variance Guided Feature Mask (VaGFeM)

To reduce redundancy and emphasise discriminative cues in joint visual-textual embeddings, we introduce the **Variance Guided Feature Mask (VaGFeM)** module in Fig. 1a. The pipeline consists of two stages: (1) constructing a union representation from image and text features, and (2) refining it using a variance-based mask.

United Feature Construction. Given a batch of images and corresponding texts, the image encoder produces embeddings $\mathbf{V} \in \mathbb{R}^{B \times D}$, and the text encoder produces embeddings $\mathbf{T} \in \mathbb{R}^{B \times D}$. Both embeddings are concatenated and passed through a lightweight transformer to capture cross-modal interactions:

$$\mathbf{H} = \mathrm{Transformer}\big([\mathbf{V}; \mathbf{T}]\big) \in \mathbb{R}^{B \times 2 \times D}. \tag{1}$$

We split $\mathbf{H}$ into modality-specific hidden states, $\mathbf{H}_V, \mathbf{H}_T \in \mathbb{R}^{B \times D}$, and obtain a scalar fusion weight through a linear projection:

$$\boldsymbol{\omega} = \mathrm{Linear}\big([\mathbf{H}_V; \mathbf{H}_T]\big) \in \mathbb{R}^{B \times 1}. \tag{2}$$

The united feature is constructed as a convex combination of image and text embeddings:

$$\mathbf{U} = \boldsymbol{\omega} \cdot \mathbf{V} + (1 - \boldsymbol{\omega}) \cdot \mathbf{T}, \quad \mathbf{U} \in \mathbb{R}^{B \times D}, \tag{3}$$

followed by ℓ_2 normalization to stabilise training.

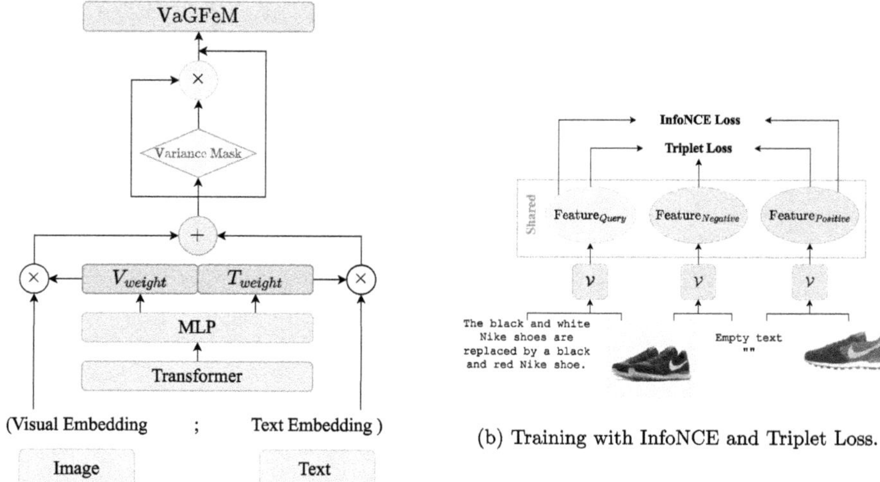

(a) Variance Guided Feature Mask (VaGFeM).

(b) Training with InfoNCE and Triplet Loss.

Fig. 1. Illustration of our proposed methodology. (a) VaGFeM enhances query features by applying variance-guided masking on fused embeddings. (b) Training employs both InfoNCE loss and triplet loss to improve compositional discrimination in a shared embedding space.

Variance Masking. To suppress uninformative dimensions, we compute the variance across the batch for each embedding dimension:

$$\sigma_d^2 = \mathrm{Var}(\mathbf{U}_{:,d}), \quad d = 1, \ldots, D. \tag{4}$$

We select the top-k dimensions with the highest variance and define a binary mask $\mathbf{M} \in \{0,1\}^{B \times D}$:

$$\mathbf{M}_{:,d} = \begin{cases} 1, & \text{if } d \in \mathrm{Top}\text{-}k(\sigma^2), \\ 0, & \text{otherwise.} \end{cases} \tag{5}$$

The mask scales the embedding by its learned channel-wise activation:

$$\boldsymbol{\alpha} = \sigma(\mathbf{U}), \quad \boldsymbol{\alpha} \in \mathbb{R}^{B \times D}, \tag{6}$$

$$\mathbf{U}' = \boldsymbol{\alpha} \odot \mathbf{M} \odot \mathbf{U} + \mathbf{U}, \tag{7}$$

where $\odot$ denotes element-wise multiplication.

Final Representation. The fused representation is finally normalised:

$$\mathcal{V} = \frac{\mathbf{U}'}{\|\mathbf{U}'\|_2}, \quad \mathcal{V} \in \mathbb{R}^{B \times D}. \tag{8}$$

This variance-guided masking ensures that only the most informative (high-variance) dimensions contribute significantly to the final query embedding $\mathcal{V}$, while redundancy is suppressed. The residual connection $(+U)$ guarantees that original information is preserved, making the representation both discriminative and robust.

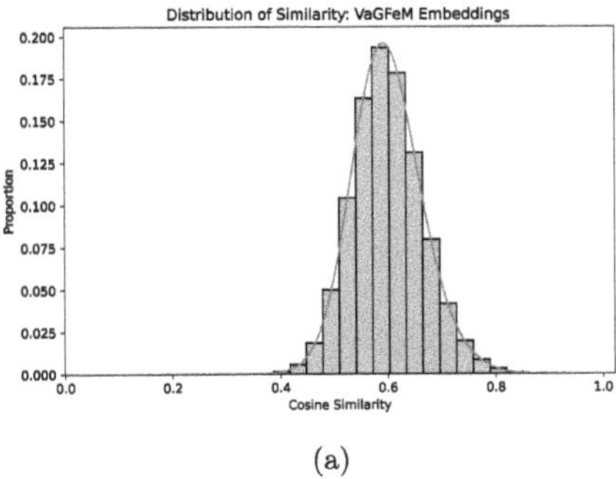
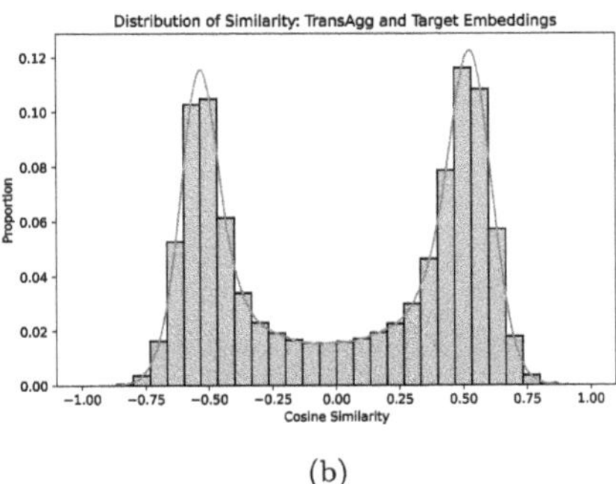

(a)   (b)

Fig. 2. Comparison of cosine similarity distributions, highlighting the superior alignment of our proposed VaGFeM method (left) in Fig. 2a which produces a single, high-similarity peak, against the bimodal distribution (Fig. 2b) of the baseline TransAgg [14] model (right).

Based on the similarity distributions, VaGFeM demonstrates significantly superior alignment compared to the TransAgg [14] and Target embeddings from Vision Language Model (BLIP [10] in this paper). The TransAgg distribution is bimodal, indicating that while it learns to separate positive from negative pairs, it fails to bring the positive pairs into tight alignment, with their similarity peaking at a modest +0.5. In stark contrast, the VaGFeM distribution is sharply unimodal and centered at a much higher similarity score of approximately +0.6. This indicates that VaGFeM consistently maps corresponding query and target embeddings to nearly the same point in the feature space. This strong alignment is crucial for retrieval tasks, as it creates a clear and reliable margin between the correct match and all other candidates, directly translating to higher precision and top-k accuracy.

4.2 Loss Design with Triplet Loss

Our training framework adopts a dual-loss objective as illustrated in Fig. 1b. The first component is the **InfoNCE loss**, which encourages alignment between a query representation (reference image plus modification text) and its corresponding target image, while contrasting against all other negatives in the batch:

$$\mathcal{L}_{\text{InfoNCE}}(x, y) = \frac{-1}{B} \sum_{i=1}^{B} \log \frac{\exp(\mathcal{S}(x_i, y_i)/\tau)}{\sum_{j=1}^{B} \exp(\mathcal{S}(x_i, y_j)/\tau)},$$

where $\mathcal{S}$ denotes similarity and τ is the temperature.

To further strengthen compositional reasoning, we introduce a **triplet loss** where the unmodified reference image (paired with an empty text prompt) is explicitly used as a hard negative. This design compels the query representation q_i to be closer to its modified target p_i than to the original reference n_i, thereby discouraging trivial matches and emphasizing semantic changes such as color, attribute, or style modifications:

$$\mathcal{L}_{\text{Triplet}}(x, y) = \frac{1}{B} \sum_{i=1}^{B} \max\left(0, \|q_i - p_i\|^2 - \|q_i - n_i\|^2 + \alpha\right), \qquad (9)$$

where α is the margin.

The final training objective combines both components:

$$\mathcal{L}_{\text{final}} = \mathcal{L}_{\text{InfoNCE}} + \lambda \mathcal{L}_{\text{Triplet}}. \qquad (10)$$

This dual-loss formulation has distinct benefits and trade-offs. On CIR benchmarks, the triplet loss substantially boosts performance by sharpening sensitivity to subtle modifications, preventing the model from over-relying on the reference alone. On the other hand, in SBIR settings, where sketches often share structural similarity with their paired references, treating the reference as a hard negative can weaken alignment, leading to slight drops in performance. Overall, the triplet loss complements InfoNCE by enhancing compositional discrimination, though it introduces a trade-off between CIR gains and SBIR robustness (Details in Table 2 and Fig. 3a).

5   Experiments

In this section, we conducted experiments and compared the results in two different ways. Firstly, we compare the model performance with other baselines. Secondly, to present the efficient of the proposed loss function, we show itself results with and without $\mathcal{L}_{\text{Triplet}}(\cdot, \cdot)$. Moreover, we also show the impact of data in the ascending order of data amount.

5.1   Dataset

We select several benchmark datasets in Composed Image Retrieval: 1) **FashionIQ**: The FashionIQ dataset [24] contains 2,005 triplets covering three fashion categories (Dress, Shirt, and Toptee) and 5,179 images in the image pool. 2) **CIRR**: The CIRR dataset [15] comprises 4,148 image-caption input pairs targeting 2,316 images. 3) **CIRCO**: The CIRCO dataset [1] includes 800 queries and a 123,403-image target collection. 4) **PatternCom**: The PatternCom dataset [18] has 21,571 queries across 6 attributes in Remote Sensing domain and 30,400 images in the target collection. In Sketch-Based Image Retrieval domain: 1)

Sketchy: The Sketchy dataset [25] has 12,694 queries including 21 classes from ImageNet-1k and 12,694 target images. 2) **TUBerlin**: The TUBerlin dataset [27] with 2,400 sketches across 30 categories and 27,989 index images. 3) **Quick-Draw**: The QuickDraw dataset [4] consists of 92,291 queries of 30 classes and a collection of 54,146 images. 4) **PKU-Sketch-ReID** [17] contains 200 sketch images and 400 identification photos (2 photos for each sketch).

5.2   Experiment Setting

Our framework is implemented with Pytorch. We follow the TransAgg setups [14] and use the transformer-based 2 layer fusion module with 8 heads and GELU activation. For visual and text encoders, we utilise BLIP with ViT-B [10] as it gains the best performance in TransAgg's experiments. In the UNION architecture, we use a 2-layer transformer architecture similar to the T5 Transformer [19] with 2 layers, 8 attention heads for BLIP with each head having 64 dimensions. In the loss function, we set $\tau = 0.01$ similar to TransAgg [14] settings. For a fair comparison, all experiments use 224×224 images to ensure, and additionally, we only choose the results used the aforementioned pre-trained models. We keep top-20% of dimension D in Eq. 5. In the triplet loss 9 and final loss function 10, we set $\alpha = 0.3$ and $\lambda = 0.2$.

The model is optimised with AdamW [16] optimiser with a weight decay of $1e^{-2}$. All experiments are conducted with 2 epochs using learning rate $1e^{-4}$ and a batch size of 32 on one NVIDIA A100 80 GB. For the generated captions in LlavaSCo, we adapt the vision language model LLaVA-v1.6-Mistral-7B[6]. The checkpoint of LLaVA-NeXT-Interleave[7] was trained on the given data in INOVA Challenge 2025[8].

5.3   Experimental Results and Discussion

Main Result. We compare our methodology with TransAgg [14] but trained on our dataset FIGROTD and evaluated on its testset. We report mean Average Precision (mAP) for each class (CIR, SBIR, CSTBIR). Besides, in CIR and CST-BIR task, we add Recall at K (R@K) following the metrics used in FashionIQ and in SBIR task, we report Precision at K (P@K) as in other datasets.

The results in Table 2 show that our Variance-Guided Feature Mask (VaGFeM) achieves the best overall performance on FIGROTD. Compared to TransAgg, which excels mainly on CIR (33.83 mAP@100, 47.57 R@10), VaGFeM delivers more balanced results with strong gains in SBIR (**51.38 mAP, 54.55 P@10**) and CSTBIR (**5.96 mAP@100, 11.26 R@10**), leading to the highest average score of **29.63 mAP@100**. Incorporating triplet loss improves SBIR further (e.g., 54.89/58.34 for TransAgg$_{Triplet}$) but significantly reduces CIR (5.09 vs. 33.83), indicating that false negatives from reference-as-negative sampling harm

---

[6] https://huggingface.co/llava-hf/llava-v1.6-mistral-7b-hf.

[7] https://huggingface.co/lmms-lab/llava-next-interleave-qwen-7b.

[8] https://inovachallenge.github.io/ICME2025/.

Table 2. Comparison of our method against existing frameworks on three tasks of FIGROTD. Red numbers indicate the best results, Blue ones indicate the second best.

Method	CIR		SBIR		CSTBIR		mAP@100$_{Average}$
	mAP@100	R@10	mAP	P@10	mAP@100	R@10	
TransAgg$_{Original}$	3.49	5.85	0.03	0.00	0.82	1.45	1.45
TransAgg	33.83	47.57	43.88	46.16	4.25	9.30	27.32
TransAgg$_{Triplet}$	5.09	8.86	54.89	58.34	4.82	7.78	21.60
VaGFeM	31.52	47.17	51.38	54.55	5.96	11.26	29.63
VaGFeM$_{Triplet}$	19.47	29.26	46.33	49.68	4.34	9.71	23.38

compositional reasoning. Overall, VaGFeM provides the most robust trade-off across CIR, SBIR, and CSTBIR. It can be explained that in the Triplet Loss Function 9, the negative image is not the input sketch so it makes the model understand the negative sample wrongly.

Comparison with Other Baselines. In the zero-shot CIR benchmarks, we compare VaGFeM with strong baselines including TransAgg [14], CoLLM [7], and PVLF [23], all of which use BLIPbase as the backbone. As shown in Table 3, VaGFeM trained with only **10K triplets** achieves competitive or superior results across benchmarks. On CIRCO, VaGFeM reaches **34.8** mAP@10 and **39.0** mAP@50, outperforming both TransAgg (32.2/36.2) and TransAgg$_{FIGROTD}$, which relies on more data (**16K triplets**) but achieves only 19.7/23.1. Similarly, on PatternCom, VaGFeM improves to 25.9 mAP compared to 18.7 from TransAgg$_{FIGROTD}$.

While CoLLM attains stronger results on FashionIQ and CIRR by leveraging millions of triplets (e.g., 34.6/56.0 on FashionIQ and 78.6/94.2 on CIRR), VaGFeM remains highly competitive with two orders of magnitude fewer annotations. This highlights the effectiveness of variance-guided feature masking for efficient learning. Finally, although FIGROTD contains 16K triplets, our experiments show that performance already peaks with 10K, underscoring the robustness and data efficiency of VaGFeM under limited supervision.

We compare VaGFeM to strong ZS-SBIR baselines—DCDL [11], CAT [21], IVT [26], ZSE-SBIR [12], MagicLens [28]—and to TransAgg trained on **FIGROTD**, all evaluated in Table 4. Despite using only 16k pairs with a BLIP$_{base}$ backbone, VaGFeM and its triplet variant are highly competitive against methods trained with far more data (e.g., 57k/236k for DCDL/CAT and 36.7M pairs for MagicLens). On Sketchy, VaGFeM$_{Triplet}$ attains the best mAP@200 = 75.7, while plain VaGFeM is second (74.0); DCDL has the top P@200 = 76.9, but requires orders of magnitude more supervision. On TU-Berlin, VaGFeM sets the new best with mAP = 64.1 and P@100 = 74.7, surpassing DCDL (63.4/74.1) and MagicLens (62.9/73.1). On QuickDraw, our models are competitive (23.2–24.8 mAP; 34.3–34.4 P@200) but trail the best mAP of DCDL (33.6) and the best P@200 of CAT (38.8), reflecting the larger domain gap of doodle-style sketches. Finally,

Table 3. Comparison of our method against baseline on four benchmarks of ZS-CIR task. Although FIGROTD contains 16K triplets, we notice that the results reach the peak at the 10K triplet amount. While we reproduce the results of TransAgg on CIRCO and PatternCom, the others are from the original papers. Red and Blue numbers indicate the best and second-best results.

Method	#Triplets	FashionIQ (R)		CIRR (R)		CIRCO (mAP)		PatternCom (mAP)	
		@10	@50	@10	@50	@10	@50	@200	@all
PVLF [23]	32K	35.7	56.9	82.4	95.4	-	-	-	-
CoLLM [7]	3.4M	34.6	56.0	78.6	94.2	20.4	23.1	-	-
TransAgg [14]	32K	34.4	55.1	77.9	93.4	32.2	36.2	37.4	26.6
TransAgg$_{\mathrm{FIGROTD}}$	16K	25.4	45.2	71.6	91.9	19.7	23.1	19.6	18.7
VaGFeM	10K	27.3	47.7	76.9	93.3	33.3	37.4	20.9	19.0
VaGFeM$_{\mathrm{Triplet}}$	10K	28.7	48.8	77.1	92.8	34.8	39.0	34.1	25.9

on PKU-Sketch, our approach leads the board with rank-1 = 28.5 and strong mAP (25.2–25.9), clearly outperforming TransAgg$_{\mathrm{FIGROTD}}$ (20.0/20.2). Overall, VaGFeM demonstrates robust generalisation across diverse sketch domains, and the triplet variant further boosts Sketchy and PKU-Sketch, while incurring only minor trade-offs on TU-Berlin/QuickDraw—highlighting an effective accuracy–data-efficiency balance.

Table 4. Comparison of our method against existing frameworks on four benchmarks of ZS-SBIR task. Except ours, the others are trained on their own training sets. Red and Blue numbers indicate the best and second-best results.

Method	Backbone	# Pairs	Sketchy		TU-Berlin		QuickDraw		PKU-Sketch	
			mAP@200	P@200	mAP	P@100	mAP	P@200	rank-1	mAP
DCDL [11]	CLIP-B	57K/15K/236K	72.6	76.9	63.4	74.1	33.6	29.6	-	-
CAT [21]	CLIP-B	57K/15K/236K	71.3	72.5	63.1	72.2	20.2	38.8	-	-
IVT [26]	ViT-B	57K/15K/236K	61.5	69.4	55.7	62.9	32.4	16.2	-	-
ZSE-SBIR [12]	ViT-L	57K/15K/236K	52.5	62.4	54.2	65.7	14.5	21.6	-	-
MagicLens [28]	CLIP-L	36.7M	68.2	75.8	62.9	73.1	15.1	20.4	-	-
TransAgg$_{\mathrm{FIGROTD}}$	BLIP-B	16K	73.4	70.9	63.1	73.4	24.9	34.8	20.0	20.2
VaGFeM	BLIP-B	16K	74.0	71.9	64.1	74.7	24.8	34.4	28.0	25.9
VaGFeM$_{\mathrm{Triplet}}$	BLIP-B	16K	75.7	72.9	62.4	73.3	23.2	34.3	28.5	25.2

Impact of Triplet Loss. Figure 3a compares the baseline InfoNCE objective with the combined InfoNCE + Triplet formulation. On the CIR benchmarks (FashionIQ, CIRR, CIRCO, and PatternCom), incorporating triplet loss consistently improves retrieval accuracy. For example, FashionIQ rises from 26.35 to **29.26** R@10, CIRCO increases from 32.42 to **33.97** mAP@10, and PatternCom improves substantially from 19.65 to **25.0** mAP. These gains highlight the effectiveness of triplet loss in encouraging fine-grained compositional reasoning, as the negative sample (reference image with empty text) prevents the model from overly relying on the reference alone.

In contrast, the SBIR datasets show mixed results. While Sketchy remains stable (74.86 → 75.03), TU-Berlin and QuickDraw experience small drops (62.04 → 60.79 and 24.07 → 22.53, respectively), and PKU-Sketch decreases from 24.5 to 22.76. This reflects the fact that sketches rely heavily on coarse visual cues; penalizing the reference as a negative can weaken robustness when queries lack textual modifications.

Finally, on FIGROTD—which integrates CIR, SBIR, and CSTBIR—the overall performance decreases from 27.61 to 21.55 mAP@100 when adding triplet loss. This suggests that while triplet loss is beneficial for CIR tasks requiring subtle compositional discrimination, it introduces a trade-off by harming generalisation in sketch-based scenarios where visual-only queries dominate. In summary, triplet loss sharpens compositional understanding in CIR but comes at the cost of reduced flexibility in SBIR, highlighting the challenge of designing a unified loss across multimodal retrieval tasks.

Impact of Training Data Size. Figure 3b presents the performance of VaGFeM across eight benchmarks when trained with different amounts of data. Overall, the results indicate that the model reaches its peak effectiveness at around **10K triplets**, beyond which additional data offers diminishing or even negative returns. For instance, on CIRR, performance improves steadily from 75.3 at 1K to **77.1** at 10K, but drops slightly to 76.3 at 16K. Similarly, CIRCO achieves its highest score of **34.8 mAP@10** at 10K, but decreases to 31.8 at 16K. On PatternCom, performance rises from 19.3 (1K) to **25.9** (10K) before falling back to 24.5 at 16K. SBIR benchmarks such as Sketchy and TU-Berlin

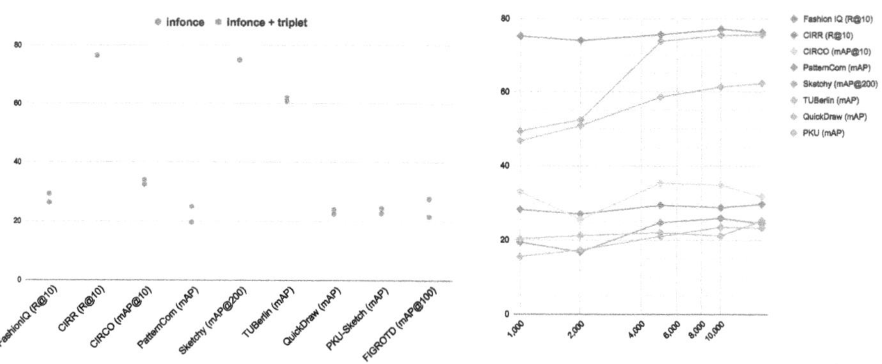

(a) Effect of Loss Function on Retrieval Performance   (b) Effect of Training Data Size on Retrieval Performance

Fig. 3. Comparison of model performance across different loss functions and training data sizes on nine benchmarks. (a) Impact of loss type (infonce vs. infonce+triplet). (b) Effect of varying training data size (1K, 2K, 5K, 10K, all).

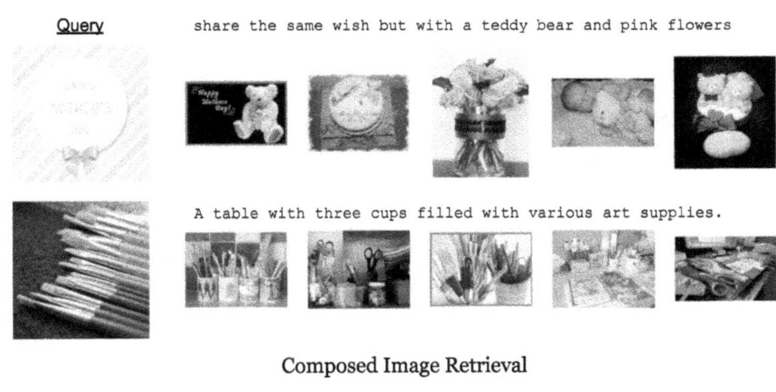

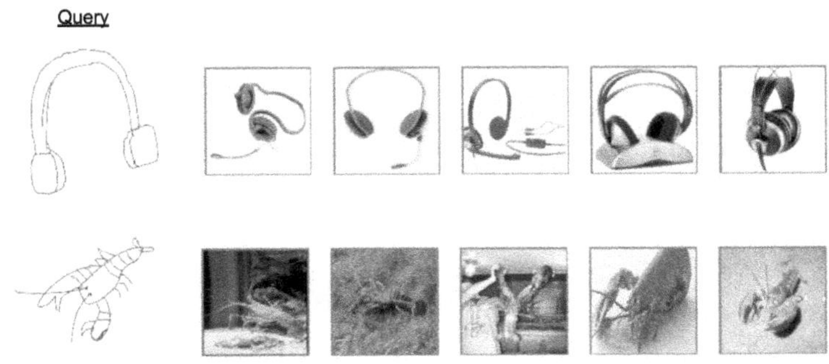

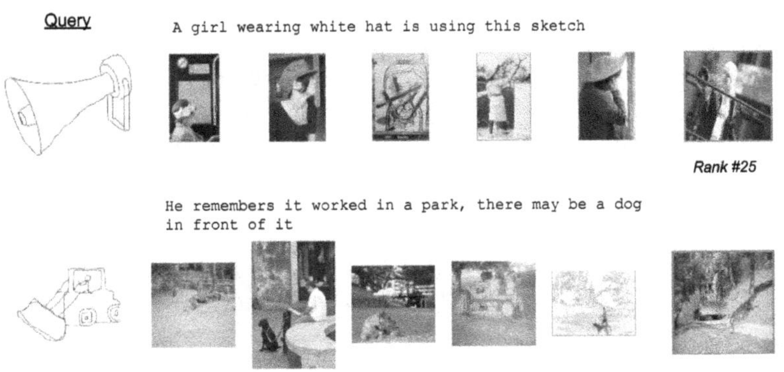

Fig. 4. Qualitative retrieval examples on the three FIGROTD tasks. VaGFeM achieves strong results on CIR and SBIR, but shows limited effectiveness on CSTBIR, where fine-grained compositional reasoning is required. (Color figure online)

also plateau after 10K, with Sketchy peaking at **75.5 mAP@200** and TU-Berlin at **61.4 mAP**.

We attribute this behavior to two factors. First, *variance-guided masking* already provides strong regularisation by suppressing redundant dimensions, making the model less dependent on very large training sets. Once the key discriminative features are learned (around 10K triplets), additional noisy or weakly aligned pairs can introduce redundancy and harm generalisation. Second, tasks such as CIRCO and PatternCom are more sensitive to data imbalance, where increasing training size may emphasise easier negatives rather than truly informative contrasts, thus diluting the benefit of harder compositional reasoning.

These results highlight that VaGFeM is not only competitive but also **data-efficient**, achieving strong generalisation with an order of magnitude fewer samples than competing methods. Training beyond 10K triplets brings limited benefit and can even slightly hurt performance, underscoring the robustness of variance-guided fusion under constrained data regimes.

Qualitative Results. In Fig. 4, we demonstrate qualitative retrieval examples on three tasks of FIGROTD test set (two for each class). We present the top-5 retrieved images, with the correct target(s) outlined in red. We hypothesise that the lack of supervised annotation can lead to the synthetic biases, and we leave the analysis of this phenomenon in the future.

6   Conclusion

In this paper, we introduce FIGROTD - a friendly-to-handle Image Guided Retrieval with Optional Text that is built in a good quality for researchers to conduct experiments, apply new ideas and exploit new insights on it. We introduce VaGFeM - a simple architecture despite owning the smaller parameters, still gains competitive results. Moreover, we also perform that with additional loss function - Triplet Margin, the performance of model increases in Composed Image Retrieval Task while slightly decreases in Sketch Based Image Retrieval problem. We hope that these insights can be helpful for researchers to develop new experiments and solve the problem in the category imbalance of FIGROTD as same as improve the quality of its test set.

Acknowledgment. This publication has emanated from research supported in part by research grants from Science Foundation Ireland (SFI) under grant numbers SFI/13/RC/2106_P2 and 18/CRT/6223, and co-funded by the European Regional Development Fund.

References

1. Agnolucci, L., Baldrati, A., Bertini, M., Del Bimbo, A.: iSEARLE: improving textual inversion for zero-shot composed image retrieval. arXiv preprint arXiv:2405.02951 (2024)

2. Cuong, D.V., Le, H.B., Nguyen, A.P.N., Zhou, L., Gurrin, C.: Quizzard@INOVA challenge 2025 – track a: Plug-and-play technique in interleaved multi-image model (2025). https://arxiv.org/abs/2506.11737

3. Datta, R., Joshi, D., Li, J., Wang, J.Z.: Image retrieval: ideas, influences, and trends of the new age. ACM Comput. Surv. (CSUR) **40**(2), 1–60 (2008)

4. Dey, S., Riba, P., Dutta, A., Llados, J., Song, Y.Z.: Doodle to search: practical zero-shot sketch-based image retrieval. In: Proceedings of the IEEE/CVF Conference on Computer Vision and Pattern Recognition, pp. 2179–2188 (2019)

5. Gatti, P., Parikh, K.G., Paul, D.P., Gupta, M., Mishra, A.: Composite sketch+text queries for retrieving objects with elusive names and complex interactions. In: AAAI (2024)

6. Hummel, T., Karthik, S., Georgescu, M.I., Akata, Z.: EgoCVR: an egocentric benchmark for fine-grained composed video retrieval. In: Leonardis, A., Ricci, E., Roth, S., Russakovsky, O., Sattler, T., Varol, G. (eds.) Computer Vision, ECCV 2024. LNCS, vol. 15095, pp. 1–17. Springer, Cham (2025). https://doi.org/10.1007/978-3-031-72913-3_1

7. Huynh, C., et al.: CoLLM: a large language model for composed image retrieval. arXiv preprint arXiv:2503.19910 (2025)

8. Levy, M., Ben-Ari, R., Darshan, N., Lischinski, D.: Data roaming and quality assessment for composed image retrieval. Proc. AAAI Conf. Artif. Intell. **38**(4), 2991–2999 (2024). https://doi.org/10.1609/aaai.v38i4.28081, https://ojs.aaai.org/index.php/AAAI/article/view/28081

9. Li, F., et al.: LLaVA-next-interleave: tackling multi-image, video, and 3d in large multimodal models. arXiv preprint arXiv:2407.07895 (2024)

10. Li, J., Li, D., Xiong, C., Hoi, S.: BLIP: bootstrapping language-image pre-training for unified vision-language understanding and generation. In: ICML (2022)

11. Li, Q., Wang, S., Zhang, W., Bai, S., Nie, W., Liu, A.: DCDL: dual causal disentangled learning for zero-shot sketch-based image retrieval. IEEE Trans. Multimedia (2025)

12. Lin, F., Li, M., Li, D., Hospedales, T., Song, Y.Z., Qi, Y.: Zero-shot everything sketch-based image retrieval, and in explainable style. In: Proceedings of the IEEE/CVF Conference on Computer Vision and Pattern Recognition, pp. 23349–23358 (2023)

13. Liu, L., Shen, F., Shen, Y., Liu, X., Shao, L.: Deep sketch hashing: Fast free-hand sketch-based image retrieval. In: Proceedings of the IEEE Conference on Computer Vision and Pattern Recognition, pp. 2862–2871 (2017)

14. Liu, Y., Yao, J., Zhang, Y., Wang, Y., Xie, W.: Zero-shot composed text-image retrieval. arXiv preprint arXiv:2306.07272 (2023)

15. Liu, Z., Rodriguez-Opazo, C., Teney, D., Gould, S.: Image retrieval on real-life images with pre-trained vision-and-language models. In: Proceedings of the IEEE/CVF International Conference on Computer Vision (ICCV), October 2021, pp. 2125–2134 ()

16. Loshchilov, I., Hutter, F.: Decoupled weight decay regularization. arXiv preprint arXiv:1711.05101 (2017)

17. Pang, L., Wang, Y., Song, Y.Z., Huang, T., Tian, Y.: Cross-domain adversarial feature learning for sketch re-identification. In: Proceedings of the 26th ACM international conference on Multimedia, pp. 609–617 (2018)

18. Psomas, B., et al.: Composed image retrieval for remote sensing. In: 2024 IEEE International Geoscience and Remote Sensing Symposium, IGARSS 2024 (2024)

19. Radford, A., et al.: Learning transferable visual models from natural language supervision. In: International Conference on Machine Learning, pp. 8748–8763. PMLR (2021)
20. Rossetto, L., et al.: The CASTLE 2024 dataset: advancing the art of multimodal understanding. arXiv preprint arXiv:2503.17116 (2025)
21. Sain, A., Bhunia, A.K., Chowdhury, P.N., Koley, S., Xiang, T., Song, Y.Z.: Clip for all things zero-shot sketch-based image retrieval, fine-grained or not. In: Proceedings of the IEEE/CVF Conference on Computer Vision and Pattern Recognition, pp. 2765–2775 (2023)
22. Vo, N., et al.: Composing text and image for image retrieval - an empirical odyssey. In: Proceedings of the IEEE/CVF Conference on Computer Vision and Pattern Recognition (CVPR), June 2019 (2019)
23. Wang, P., Chen, Z., Zhao, Z., Su, F.: Prompting vision-language fusion for zero-shot composed image retrieval. In: The 16th Asian Conference on Machine Learning (Conference Track) (2025)
24. Wu, H., et al.: The fashion IQ dataset: retrieving images by combining side information and relative natural language feedback. In: CVPR (2021)
25. Yelamarthi, S.K., Reddy, S.K., Mishra, A., Mittal, A.: A zero-shot framework for sketch based image retrieval. In: Ferrari, V., Hebert, M., Sminchisescu, C., Weiss, Y. (eds.) ECCV 2018. LNCS, vol. 11208, pp. 316–333. Springer, Cham (2018). https://doi.org/10.1007/978-3-030-01225-0_19
26. Zhang, H., Cheng, D., Kou, Q., Asad, M., Jiang, H.: Indicative vision transformer for end-to-end zero-shot sketch-based image retrieval. Adv. Eng. Inform. **60**, 102398 (2024)
27. Zhang, H., Liu, S., Zhang, C., Ren, W., Wang, R., Cao, X.: SketchNet: sketch classification with web images. In: Proceedings of the IEEE Conference on Computer Vision and Pattern Recognition, pp. 1105–1113 (2016)
28. Zhang, K., et al.: MagicLens: self-supervised image retrieval with open-ended instructions. In: The Forty-First International Conference on Machine Learning (ICML), pp. 59403–59420 (2024)

Co-teaching for Unsupervised Domain Expansion

Hailan Lin, Qijie Wei, Kaibin Tian, Ruixiang Zhao,
and Xirong Li[✉]

Renmin University of China, Beijing, China
`xirong@ruc.edu.cn`
`https://github.com/ruc-aimc-lab/co-teaching`

Abstract. Unsupervised Domain Adaptation (UDA) essentially trades a model's performance on a source domain for improving its performance on a target domain. To overcome this, Unsupervised Domain Expansion (UDE) has been introduced, which adapts the model to the target domain while preserving its performance in the source domain. In both UDA and UDE, a model tailored to a given domain is assumed to well handle samples from the given domain. We question the assumption by reporting the existence of *cross-domain visual ambiguity*: Due to the unclear boundary between the two domains, samples from one domain can be visually close to the other domain. Such sorts of samples are typically in the minority in their host domain, so they tend to be overlooked by the domain-specific model, but can be better handled by a model from the other domain. We exploit this finding by proposing *Co-Teaching* (CT), which is instantiated with knowledge distillation based CT (kdCT) plus mixup based CT (miCT). Specifically, kdCT leverages a dual-teacher architecture to enhance the student network's ability to handle cross-domain ambiguity. Meanwhile, miCT further enhances the generalization ability of the student. Extensive experiments on image classification and driving-scene segmentation show the viability of CT for UDE.

Keywords: Unsupervised domain expansion · Knowledge distillation

1 Introduction

Unsupervised Domain Adaptation (UDA), aiming to adapt a model trained on a *labeled* source domain for an *unlabeled* target domain with no need of relabeling any data, is crucial for real-world applications. With novel UDA methods continuously developed [13,42], we witness an ever-growing performance on the target domain, as manifested on public datasets such as Office-Home [30] for image classification and ACDC [24] for driving scene segmentation. However, it has been documented recently that UDA in fact trades the model's classification performance on the source domain for improving its performance on the target

J. Lokoč et al. (Eds.): MMM 2026, LNCS 16412, pp. 133–146, 2026.
https://doi.org/10.1007/978-981-95-6950-2_10

domain [32,36]. Such a finding is disturbing, as it suggests that one may have to deploy simultaneously two models to support both domains. Even putting the doubled deployment cost aside, how to swiftly switch between the models is nontrivial, as from which domain a test sample comes is unknown. Source-domain performance degeneration puts the real-world use of UDA into question.

To remedy the issue, GSFDA [36] resorts to continual learning to preserve a model's ability on the source domain while being adapted to the target domain. Since the method assumes zero availability of the source-domain samples, it has little chance to recover once degeneration occurs. Indeed, our evaluation shows that GSFDA also suffers source-domain performance loss.

To explicitly quantify the issue, a variant of UDA termed Unsupervised Domain Expansion (UDE) has been developed [32]. UDE has the same starting point as UDA, *i.e.* a set of *labeled* training samples from the source domain and a set of *unlabeled* training samples from the target domain. The key difference is that UDE explicitly reports the source-domain performance and consequently the performance on an expanded domain covering the source and target domains. The KDDE method for UDE assumes that a model tailored to a given domain can well handle samples from the given domain [32]. Accordingly, KDDE runs in two steps, where two domain-specific models are first trained for the source and target domains, respectively. It then performs knowledge distillation, where the dark knowledge of the source-specific (target-specific) teacher is transferred to a student model via source-domain (target-domain) samples exclusively.

We question the assumption of KDDE by reporting the existence of cross-domain visual ambiguity, see Fig. 1. We consider a test image in domain A *cross-domain ambiguous* if the image is wrongly predicted by a model well-trained on domain A, yet correctly classified by a model targeted at a different domain B. Table 1 shows the percentage of such ambiguous images on Office-Home. These (minority) samples tend to be overlooked by domain-specific models.

Table 1. Percentage of ambiguous test images on domain A.

Dataset: Office-Home		*Domain A*			
		Art	Clipart	Product	Real
Domain B	Art	–	3.9	2.4	3.9
	Clipart	5.0	–	1.9	4.1
	Product	6.0	4.0	–	3.9
	Real	7.5	4.6	2.6	–

In order to tackle such ambiguity, we propose Co-Teaching (CT) for UDE. The proposed method comprises knowledge distillation based CT (kdCT) and mixup based CT (miCT), see Fig. 2. Specifically, kdCT transfers knowledge from a leader-teacher network and an assistant-teacher network to a student network for cross-domain ambiguity, while miCT further enhances the generalization ability

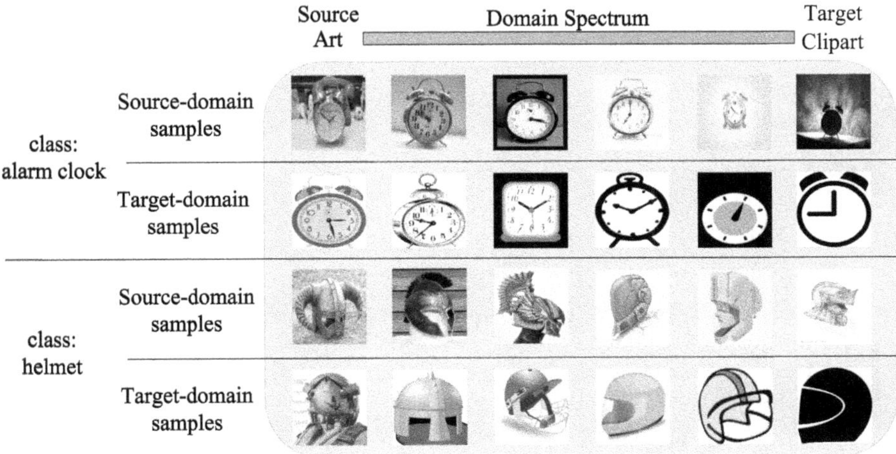

Fig. 1. Cross-domain visual ambiguity. Samples from a target domain (*Clipart*) can be visually realistic as samples from a source domain (*Art*), and vice versa.

of the student. Extensive experiments on multi-class image classification and driving scene segmentation verify the effectiveness of CT.

2   Related Work

Progress on UDA. The major line of research on UDA is to learn domain-invariant feature representations, either by domain discrepancy reduction [3, 12,29] or by adversarial training [2,7,15]. More recently, the mixup technique, originally developed for supervised deep learning [40], has been actively leveraged for learning domain-invariant features [19,34]. FixBi, for instance, uses fixed ratio-based mixup to train a source-biased classifier and a target-biased classifier [19], enforcing consistency on domain-mixed samples. More recent studies exploit pretrained vision-language models [5,13].

There is also an increasing interest in extending image-level UDA to the pixel level for cross-domain semantic image segmentation. AdaSegNet [28] and Advent [31] use adversarial training at the output space, while pixel-level adaptation is performed in DCAN [33] and Cycada [11]. FDA [37] uses self-predicted labels for self-supervised training.

Our proposed CT conceptually differs from the above works as it essentially performs meta learning on top of a specific UDA method. Moreover, in contrast to the prior art which cares only the target-domain performance, CT aims for a broader scope covering both the source and target domains. While there are efforts on preventing the source-domain performance deterioration [17,22,36], our experiment indicates that the deterioration remains.

Progress on UDE. CT is inline with KDDE [32], as both aim for training a model that suits the expanded domain by knowledge distillation (KD). In

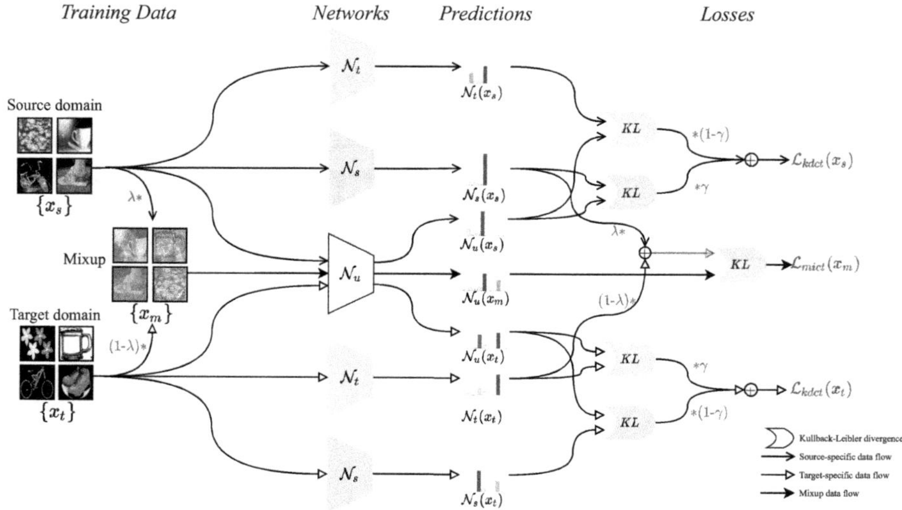

Fig. 2. Proposed CT method. Given labeled data $\{(x_s, y_s)\}$ from a source domain and unlabeled data $\{x_t\}$ from a target domain, CT obtains a *domain-expanded* network $\mathcal{N}_u$ by two-stage training. In the first stage, two *domain-specific* teacher networks $\mathcal{N}_s$ and $\mathcal{N}_t$ are obtained, where $\mathcal{N}_s$ for the source domain is trained on $\{(x_s, y_s)\}$ by standard supervised learning, whilst $\mathcal{N}_t$ for the target domain is trained on $\{(x_s, y_s)\}$ and $\{x_t\}$ by an existing UDA method. In the second stage, $\mathcal{N}_s$ and $\mathcal{N}_t$ co-teach $\mathcal{N}_u$ via **knowledge distillation based CT** (kdCT) that minimizes $L_{kdct}(\{x_s\}) + L_{kdct}(\{x_t\})$, and **mixup based CT** (miCT), minimizing $L_{mict}(\{x_m\})$ for mixup instances $\{x_m\}$. Once trained, only $\mathcal{N}_u$ is needed for inference.

KDDE, however, knowledge from the source-domain teacher is only transferred via source samples, and similarly for the target domain. Consequently, KDDE lacks the ability to leverage the teacher network derived from one domain in handling cross-domain ambiguity for the other domain. While multi-teacher KD has been used in multi-source UDA by training domain-adapted teachers through target and multiple source domain pairings [14,16], this tactic is inapplicable to the single-source scenario as considered in this work.

Co-teaching. The term co-teaching has been used in other contexts which conceptually and technically differ from ours. For supervised learning, Decoupling [18] and Co-Teach [8] aim for label denoising within a single domain. Decoupling simultaneously trains two models h_1 and h_2, updating them with samples having $h_1(x) \neq h_2(x)$ in a given mini-batch. Co-Teach alternately uses samples correctly classified by one model to train the other model. Since both methods are fully supervised, they are inapplicable for UDA / UDE. CGCT [23] proposes a co-teaching strategy using a dual-head classifier to provide pseudo labels for unlabeled target-domain samples. CT is a *model-agnostic* meta learner, so any UDA method including CGCT can in principle be used as its UDA module.

3   Method

3.1   Problem Formalization

We use x to indicate a specific sample. For a manually labeled sample, we use y to indicate its label, which can be a one-hot vector or a multi-dimensional binary mask. Let $\mathcal{N}$ be a deep neural network, which outputs $\mathcal{N}(x)$ that well matches the (unknown) label of a novel sample. Following [32], we formalize the UDE task as follows. Given a set of n_s *labeled* samples $\{(x_s, y_s)\}$ randomly sampled from a source domain D_s and a set of n_t *unlabeled* samples $\{x_t\}$ randomly sampled from a target domain D_t, the goal is to train $\mathcal{N}$ that works for an expanded domain covering both D_s and D_t which named as D_{s+t}.

The previous approach to UDE is KDDE [32]. At a high level, KDDE works in two stages. In the first stage, two domain-specific teacher networks $\mathcal{N}_s$ and $\mathcal{N}_t$ are trained, where $\mathcal{N}_s$ for D_s is learned from the labeled set $\{(x_s, y_s)\}$ by standard supervised learning, while $\mathcal{N}_t$ for D_t is trained on $\{(x_s, y_s)\}$ and $\{x_t\}$ by an off-the-shelf UDA method. In the second stage, knowledge distillation (KD) is performed to inject the dark knowledge of the teacher networks into a student network $\mathcal{N}_u$, which will be eventually used for inference. Depending on the domain identity of a training sample, KDDE uses the two teachers, *i.e.* $\mathcal{N}_s$ to deal with samples from D_s and $\mathcal{N}_t$ for samples from D_t, see Eq. (1).

$$\begin{cases} \mathcal{N}_s \leftarrow \text{supervised-learning}(\{(x_s, y_s)\}) \\ \mathcal{N}_t \leftarrow \text{UDA}(\{(x_s, y_s)\}, \{x_t\}) \\ \mathcal{N}_u \leftarrow \begin{cases} \text{KD}(\mathcal{N}_s, \{x\}), & x \in D_s \\ \text{KD}(\mathcal{N}_t, \{x\}), & x \in D_t \end{cases} \end{cases} \tag{1}$$

The two-stage property of KDDE ensures flexibility in choosing UDA methods for implementing $\mathcal{N}_t$. We inherit this property and introduce a novel Co-Teaching (CT) method into the second stage.

3.2   Framework

CT consists of knowledge distillation based CT (kdCT) and mixup based CT (miCT). As Fig. 2 shows, kdCT allows the student network to simultaneously learn the two teacher networks' dark knowledge about every training sample. Meanwhile, miCT improves the generalization ability of the student by using the mixup technique in a cross-domain manner. As the two implementations of CT are orthogonal to each other, they can be used either alone or jointly.

Knowledge Distillation Based Co-teaching. We depart from a standard KD process with one student network $\mathcal{N}_u$ and one teacher network, either $\mathcal{N}_s$ or $\mathcal{N}_t$. Let us consider $\mathcal{N}_s$ for instance. Given a set of samples $\{x\}$, KD from $\mathcal{N}_s$ to $\mathcal{N}_u$ is achieved by minimizing the Kullback-Leibler (KL) divergence between $\mathcal{N}_s(\{x\})$ and $\mathcal{N}_u(\{x\})$, denoted as $KL(\mathcal{N}_s(\{x\}), \mathcal{N}_u(\{x\}))$. Similarly, we have the loss of KD from $\mathcal{N}_t$ to $\mathcal{N}_u$ as $KL(\mathcal{N}_t(\{x\}), \mathcal{N}_u(\{x\}))$. For multi-teacher KD, simply averaging losses is suboptimal since teachers specialize in distinct domains.

Therefore, we shall not treat them equally. For training samples from D_s, we expect that $\mathcal{N}_s$ leads the teaching process, while the $\mathcal{N}_t$ acts as an assistant, and vice versa. This is implemented via a parameter γ that weighs the importance of each teacher in the kdCT process:

$$L_{kdct}(\{x\}) = \begin{cases} \gamma \cdot KL(\mathcal{N}_s, \mathcal{N}_u) + (1 - \gamma) \cdot KL(\mathcal{N}_t, \mathcal{N}_u) & x \in D_s \\ \gamma \cdot KL(\mathcal{N}_t, \mathcal{N}_u) + (1 - \gamma) \cdot KL(\mathcal{N}_s, \mathcal{N}_u) & x \in D_t \end{cases} \tag{2}$$

Given Eq. (2), KDDE can now be viewed as a special case of kdCT with $\gamma = 1$. kdCT extends the loss of KDDE to exploit multiple teachers in a biased manner, which improves kdCT in making correct decisions on samples of domain ambiguity. We define the overall loss L_{kdct} as the sum of two domain-specific losses $L_{kdct}(\{x_s\})$ and $L_{kdct}(\{x_t\})$ by Eq. (2).

We assign γ larger than 0.5 to emphasize the leading-teacher network, *i.e.* $\mathcal{N}_s$ for samples from D_s and $\mathcal{N}_t$ for samples from D_t. To enhance robustness against noise, we introduce randomness by sampling γ per mini-batch from $Beta(\alpha, \beta)$, whose shape parameters enable diversified probability distributions [6,10].

Mixup Based Co-teaching. The mixup technique [40], synthesizing a new training sample by a convex combination of two real samples, is shown to be effective for improving image classification networks. We thus re-purpose this technique to generate new domain-expanded samples denoted by $\{x_m\}$. In particular, x_m is obtained by blending x_s randomly chosen from D_s with x_t randomly chosen from D_t.

Our mixup based CT (miCT) is implemented by transferring the two-teacher knowledge via mixed samples to the student network. The teachers' joint knowledge w.r.t. x_m is reflected by combined prediction denoted as $\hat{y}_m$. Given $\lambda \sim Beta(1, 1)$ as a mixup rate, the loss of miCT L_{mict} is computed as

$$\begin{cases} x_m & = \lambda \cdot x_s + (1 - \lambda) \cdot x_t \\ \hat{y}_m & = \lambda \cdot \mathcal{N}_s(\{x_s\}) + (1 - \lambda) \cdot \mathcal{N}_t(\{x_t\}) \\ L_{mict} & = KL(\hat{y}_m, \mathcal{N}_u(\{x_m\})) \end{cases} \tag{3}$$

Both L_{kdct} and L_{mict} are KL-divergence based losses for knowledge distillation. So they can be directly summed up and minimized together for the joint use of kdCT and miCT.

4 Experiments

We evaluate CT for multi-class image classification and driving scene segmentation. We use ResNet-50 [9] as the student network for image classification, and DeepLabv2 [1] for semantic segmentation, unless otherwise stated. It is worth pointing out that UDE as an emerging topic is less studied. So for a fair and comprehensive evaluation, we organize the baselines into the following three groups: methods targeted at UDE, methods targeted at UDA, and methods technically related. All experiments are run with PyTorch on two NVIDIA Tesla P40 cards.

4.1   Task 1. Multi-class Image Classification

Experimental Setup. We adopt the popular Office-Home dataset [30], which contains 15,588 images of 65 object classes common in office and home scenes with four different domains, *i.e.* artistic images (A), clip art (C), product images (P), and real-world images (R). We adopt the data split of [32]: images per domain have been divided randomly into training and testing subsets[1]. Pairing the individual domains leads to 12 UDE tasks in total.

Baseline Methods. We include as a baseline ResNet-50 trained by standard supervised learning on D_s. As mentioned above, we compare with existing methods from the following three groups:
- Method for UDE: KDDE [32].
- Methods for UDA: DDC [29], DANN [7], DAAN [39], CDAN [15], SRD [26], PDA [17], GSFDA [36], CGCT [23], FixBi [19], SDAT [21] and ELS [41].
- Method technically related: MultiT [38].

Since each method is trained on the same data to yield a distinct ResNet-50 model for inference, our setup allows for a fair, head-to-head comparison.

In order to study whether CT also works with a transformer-based UDA method, we try CDTrans [35]. Different from the baselines mentioned above, CDTrans uses DeiT-Base [27] as its backbone. We simply use the same training protocol (optimizer, initial learning rate, learning rate adjustment strategy, *etc.*) as used for CNN.

Performance Metric. We report accuracy (%), *i.e.* the percentage of test images correctly classified.

Results. Table 2 shows the performance of the varied methods on the source (D_s), target (D_t) and expanded (D_{s+t}) domains, respectively. The UDA methods consistently show performance degeneration on D_s, including GSFDA (from 82.43 to 79.90) which aims for maintaining the source-domain performance. For the UDA setting wherein only the target-domain performance matters, CT compares favorably against the best UDA baseline (ELS). As for UDE, CT is again the best. The lower performance of MultiT than KDDE and CT confirms our hypothesis that the two teacher networks shall not be treated equally in the knowledge distillation process. As shown in the last three rows of Table 2, CT also works with the Transformer-based UDA method (CDTrans).

On Addressing the Cross-Domain Ambiguity. A fine-grained analysis is shown in Table 3. We can mostly attribute the success of CT to its superior performance on the inconsistent group, which confirms the effectiveness of CT's compensation mechanism. As Fig. 3 shows, the activated regions produced by the proposed method are more precise than the others. Both quantitative and qualitative results justify the efficacy of CT.

Influence of kdCT and miCT. As Table 4 shows, kdCT is better than miCT when used alone. The lower performance of miCT is because we train on mixup

---

[1] https://github.com/li-xirong/ude.

Table 2. Multi-class image classification. Methods per group are sorted in terms of their expanded-domain performance. Top performers within each group are highlighted with bold font.

Method	Source D_s	Target D_t	Expanded D_{s+t}
ResNet-50 as $\mathcal{N}_s$	82.43	57.84	70.13
Choice of $\mathcal{N}_t$:			
CDAN [15]	80.36	61.57	70.96
DANN [7]	81.36	60.65	71.01
CGCT [23]	79.70	61.44	70.57
FixBi [19]	77.10	64.31	70.71
DDC [29]	82.35	60.51	71.43
DAAN [39]	**82.38**	60.84	71.62
SRDC [26]	78.68	65.30	71.99
GSFDA [36]	79.90	66.53	73.22
SDAT [21]	81.48	68.42	74.95
ELS [41]	81.74	**68.51**	**75.13**
DDC as $\mathcal{N}_t$:			
PDA [17]	76.90	54.01	65.46
KDDE [32]	82.74	62.19	72.47
CT	**82.92**	**63.06**	**72.99**
CDAN as $\mathcal{N}_t$:			
PDA	78.44	57.65	68.04
KDDE	81.03	62.96	72.00
CT	**82.17**	**64.55**	**73.36**
SRDC as $\mathcal{N}_t$:			
MultiT [38]	82.23	61.66	71.94
KDDE	81.54	67.20	74.37
CT	**82.32**	**67.45**	**74.89**
CT (FixBi as $\mathcal{N}_t$)	80.88	65.46	73.17
CT (SDAT as $\mathcal{N}_t$)	81.87	**68.86**	75.37
CT (ELS as $\mathcal{N}_t$)	**82.10**	68.82	**75.46**
DeiT-Base [27] as $\mathcal{N}_s$	**88.31**	72.38	80.35
CDTrans [35] as $\mathcal{N}_t$	85.37	78.78	82.07
CT	88.04	**79.19**	**83.62**

samples exclusively, without using original samples. The joint use of kdCT and miCT is recommended for image classification.

Effect of γ. Table 5 shows the performance of kdCT given γ specified in varied manners. We observe that using the fixed value 0.909, which is the expectation

Table 3. Fine-grained analysis. Each test set is divided into two disjoint subsets, *i.e.* consistent and inconsistent, where each sample x in the consistent set has $\mathcal{N}_s(x) == \mathcal{N}_t(x)$, while each sample in the inconsistent set has $\mathcal{N}_s(x) \neq \mathcal{N}_t(x)$. The classification accuracy score is calculated per subset. The gain of CT against KDDE and MultiT is mostly attributed to the method's better performance on the inconsistent group.

Task R→P	D_s $=$	$\neq$	D_t $=$	$\neq$	D_{s+t} $=$	$\neq$
$\mathcal{N}_s$	90.00	42.75	87.54	21.88	88.80	30.20
$\mathcal{N}_t$	90.00	30.07	87.54	48.31	88.80	41.04
KDDE	88.96	42.39	87.32	51.20	88.16	47.69
MultiT	88.96	44.57	86.61	41.59	87.81	42.77
CT	89.53	47.46	87.54	52.88	88.56	50.72

Task A→C	D_s $=$	$\neq$	D_t $=$	$\neq$	D_{s+t} $=$	$\neq$
$\mathcal{N}_s$	85.19	43.30	66.50	16.13	74.41	22.90
$\mathcal{N}_t$	85.19	18.30	66.50	27.61	74.41	25.31
KDDE	81.90	36.14	65.13	29.99	72.26	31.52
MultiT	83.87	40.19	65.45	27.51	73.25	30.67
CT	82.98	43.30	66.75	32.78	73.62	35.40

Table 4. Ablation Study

kdCT	miCT	D_s	D_t	D_{s+t}
DDC as $\mathcal{N}_t$				
✓		82.85	62.42	72.63
	✓	80.32	61.90	71.11
✓	✓	**82.92**	**63.06**	**72.99**
SRDC as $\mathcal{N}_t$				
✓		**82.52**	67.19	74.86
	✓	77.46	63.85	70.65
✓	✓	82.32	**67.45**	**74.89**

value of $Beta(10, 1)$, results in lower performance, justifying the benefit of using γ in a stochastic manner.

4.2   Task 2. Driving Scene Segmentation

Experimental Setup. We follow [24], using Cityscapes [4] as D_s and ACDC [24] as D_t. Both datasets have pixel-level ground truth. Different from Cityscapes consisting of normal lighttime driving scenes, ACDC has four adverse conditions, see Fig. 4. We adopt their official data splits, *i.e.* 2,975 training and 500 test images in Cityscapes and 1,600 training and 406 test images in ACDC. Previous

Table 5. Effect of γ on kdCT.

	D_s	D_t	D_{s+t}
(α, β) of the beta distribution			
10, 1	82.85	62.42	72.63
5, 1	82.84	62.02	72.43
1, 1	82.86	61.54	72.20
1, 5	82.78	60.61	71.70
1, 10	82.65	60.61	71.63
Fixed			
0.5	82.75	61.41	72.08
0.909	82.81	61.67	72.24
1	82.74	62.19	72.47

work on semantic image segmentation [20] reports that the mixup technique has an adverse effect, which is also observed in our preliminary experiment on driving scene segmentation. We therefore use kdCT for this task.

Baselines. We again compare with KDDE [32]. Following [24], we choose DeepLabv2 [1] as $\mathcal{N}_s$. As for $\mathcal{N}_t$, we adopt AdaSegNet [28] and FDA [37].

Performance Metric. We report Intersection over Union (IoU) per class, and mean IoU (mIoU) as the overall performance.

Results. As Table 6 shows, the source-domain performance of AdaSegNet and FDA decreases, confirming the necessity of UDE for semantic segmentation. Using either AdaSegNet or FDA as its UDA module, CT restores the source-domain performance. In the adverse conditions, CT reduces misclassification of sky into buildings, see Fig. 4. Pixel-level classification accuracy is given in Table 7. The higher accuracy of CT on the pixels with inconsistent $\mathcal{N}_s$ and $\mathcal{N}_t$ predictions shows its effectiveness in tackling the cross-domain ambiguity.

Table 6. Driving scene segmentation.

Method	D_s	D_t	D_{s+t}
DeepLabv2 as $\mathcal{N}_s$	**63.34**	30.25	49.29
AdaSegNet [28]	61.69	38.20	52.22
FDA [37]	60.93	41.11	53.33
AdaSegNet as $\mathcal{N}_t$:			
KDDE	61.98	39.47	53.55
CT	62.72	40.88	54.27
FDA as $\mathcal{N}_t$:			
KDDE	62.09	41.83	54.38
CT	62.18	**42.77**	**55.14**

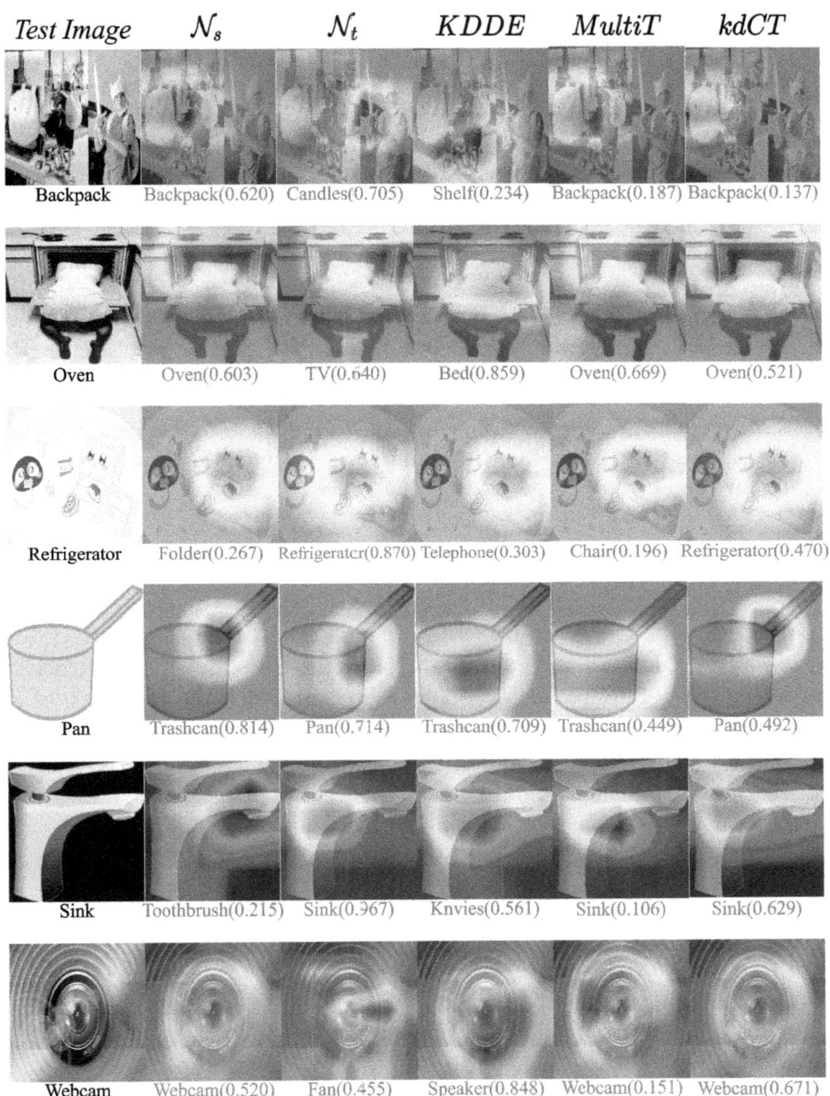

Fig. 3. Grad-CAM [25] visualization. The top three rows are from a source domain (*Art*), while the bottom three rows are from a target domain (*Clipart*). Texts under heatmaps are predicted labels with scores.

Table 7. Pixel-level classification accuracy

Method	D_s		D_t		D_{s+t}	
	=	≠	=	≠	=	≠
DeepLabv2	95.99	3.06	86.31	9.92	92.20	5.74
FDA	95.99	2.55	86.31	21.30	92.20	9.89
CT	95.29	3.49	86.66	26.13	91.91	12.35

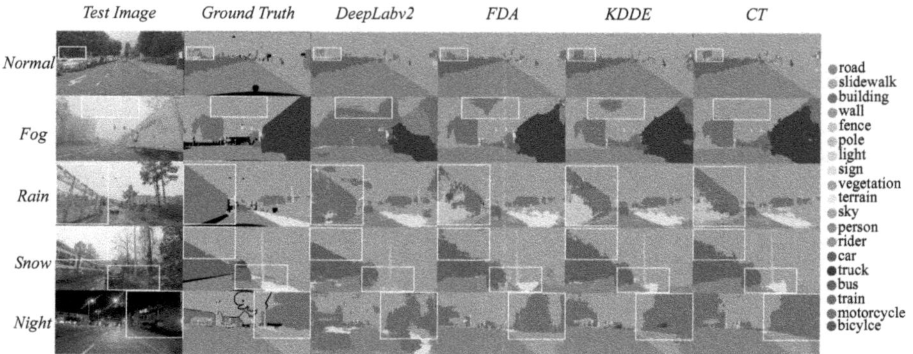

Fig. 4. Qualitative results of driving scene segmentation. The first row is from D_s (normal condition), while the other rows are from D_t (adverse conditions in the nighttime, fog, snow and rain). Important difference between the results is marked out by white bounding boxes. Best viewed digitally.

5   Conclusions

This paper develops Co-Teaching (CT), a new method for unsupervised domain expansion (UDE). Extensive experiments on multi-class image classification and driving scene support our conclusions as follows. Due to the existence of cross-domain ambiguity, a domain-specific model is not universally applicable to handle samples from its targeted domain. CT, with its ability to resolve such ambiguity, provides a unified framework to improve a model's performance on the target domain, and meanwhile maintains mostly its performance on the source domain. For its simplicity and effectiveness, CT is a new baseline for UDE.

Acknowledgments. This research was supported by National Natural Science Foundation of China (62576348, 62172420) and Beijing Natural Science Foundation (L254039).

References

1. Chen, L.C., Papandreou, G., Kokkinos, I., Murphy, K., Yuille, A.L.: DeepLab: semantic image segmentation with deep convolutional nets, atrous convolution, and fully connected CRFs. IEEE Trans. Pattern Anal. Mach. Intell. **40**(4), 834–848 (2017)
2. Chen, W., Hu, H.: Generative attention adversarial classification network for unsupervised domain adaptation. Pattern Recogn. **107**, 107440 (2020)
3. Chen, Y., Yang, C., Zhang, Y.: Deep domain similarity adaptation networks for across domain classification. Pattern Recogn. Lett. **112**, 270–276 (2018)
4. Cordts, M., et al.: The cityscapes dataset for semantic urban scene understanding. In: CVPR (2016)
5. Du, Z., Li, X., Li, F., Lu, K., Zhu, L., Li, J.: Domain-agnostic mutual prompting for unsupervised domain adaptation. In: CVPR (2024)

6. Fawzi, A., Moosavi-Dezfooli, S.M., Frossard, P.: Robustness of classifiers: From adversarial to random noise. In: NeurIPS (2016)
7. Ganin, Y., Ustinova, E., Ajakan, H., Germain, P., Larochelle, H., Laviolette, F., March, M., Lempitsky, V.: Domain-adversarial training of neural networks. J. Mach. Learn. Res. **17**(59), 1–35 (2016)
8. Han, B., et al.: Co-teaching: robust training of deep neural networks with extremely noisy labels. In: NeurIPS (2018)
9. He, K., Zhang, X., Ren, S., Sun, J.: Deep residual learning for image recognition. In: CVPR (2016)
10. He, Z., Rakin, A.S., Fan, D.: Parametric noise injection: trainable randomness to improve deep neural network robustness against adversarial attack. In: CVPR (2019)
11. Hoffman, J., et al.: CyCADA: cycle-consistent adversarial domain adaptation. In: ICML (2018)
12. Kang, G., Jiang, L., Yang, Y., Hauptmann, A.G.: Contrastive adaptation network for unsupervised domain adaptation. In: CVPR (2019)
13. Li, X., Li, Y., Du, Z., Li, F., Lu, K., Li, J.: Split to merge: unifying separated modalities for unsupervised domain adaptation. In: CVPR (2024)
14. Liu, Y.H., Ren, C.X.: A two-way alignment approach for unsupervised multi-source domain adaptation. Pattern Recogn. **124**, 108430 (2022)
15. Long, M., Cao, Z., Wang, J., Jordan, M.I.: Conditional adversarial domain adaptation. In: NeurIPS (2018)
16. Luo, Z., Zhang, X., Lu, S., Yi, S.: Domain consistency regularization for unsupervised multi-source domain adaptive classification. Pattern Recogn. **132**, 108955 (2022)
17. Lv, F., et al.: Pareto domain adaptation. In: NeurIPS (2021)
18. Malach, E., Shalev-Shwartz, S.: Decoupling "when to update" from "how to update". In: NeurIPS (2017)
19. Na, J., Jung, H., Chang, H.J., Hwang, W.: Fixbi: bridging domain spaces for unsupervised domain adaptation. In: CVPR (2021)
20. Panfilov, E., Tiulpin, A., Klein, S., Nieminen, M.T., Saarakkala, S.: Improving robustness of deep learning based knee MRI segmentation: Mixup and adversarial domain adaptation. In: ICCV Workshop (2019)
21. Rangwani, H., Aithal, S.K., Mishra, M., Jain, A., Radhakrishnan, V.B.: A closer look at smoothness in domain adversarial training. In: ICML (2022)
22. Rostami, M.: Lifelong domain adaptation via consolidated internal distribution. In: NeurIPS (2021)
23. Roy, S., Krivosheev, E., Zhong, Z., Sebe, N., Ricci, E.: Curriculum graph co-teaching for multi-target domain adaptation. In: CVPR (2021)
24. Sakaridis, C., Dai, D., Van Gool, L.: ACDC: the adverse conditions dataset with correspondences for semantic driving scene understanding. In: ICCV (2021)
25. Selvaraju, R.R., Cogswell, M., Das, A., Vedantam, R., Parikh, D., Batra, D.: Grad-CAM: visual explanations from deep networks via gradient-based localization. In: ICCV (2017)
26. Tang, H., Chen, K., Jia, K.: Unsupervised domain adaptation via structurally regularized deep clustering. In: CVPR (2020)
27. Touvron, H., Cord, M., Douze, M., Massa, F., Sablayrolles, A., Jégou, H.: Training data-efficient image transformers & distillation through attention. In: ICML (2021)
28. Tsai, Y.H., Hung, W.C., Schulter, S., Sohn, K., Yang, M.H., Chandraker, M.: Learning to adapt structured output space for semantic segmentation. In: CVPR (2018)

29. Tzeng, E., Hoffman, J., Zhang, N., Saenko, K., Darrell, T.: Deep domain confusion: maximizing for domain invariance. ArXiv arXiv:1412.3474 (2014)
30. Venkateswara, H., Eusebio, J., Chakraborty, S., Panchanathan, S.: Deep hashing network for unsupervised domain adaptation. In: CVPR (2017)
31. Vu, T.H., Jain, H., Bucher, M., Cord, M., Perez, P.: ADVENT: adversarial entropy minimization for domain adaptation in semantic segmentation. In: CVPR (2019)
32. Wang, J., Tian, K., Ding, D., Yang, G., Li, X.: Unsupervised domain expansion for visual categorization. ACM Trans. Multimed. Comput. Commun. Appl. **17**(4), 1–24 (2021)
33. Wu, Z., et al.: Dcan: dual channel-wise alignment networks for unsupervised scene adaptation. In: ECCV (2018)
34. Xu, M., Zhang, J., Ni, B., Li, T., Wang, C., Tian, Q., Zhang, W.: Adversarial domain adaptation with domain mixup. In: AAAI (2020)
35. Xu, T., Chen, W., Wang, P., Wang, F., Li, H., Jin, R.: CDTrans: cross-domain transformer for unsupervised domain adaptation. In: ICLR (2022)
36. Yang, S., Wang, Y., van de Weijer, J., Herranz, L., Jui, S.: Generalized source-free domain adaptation. In: ICCV (2021)
37. Yang, Y., Soatto, S.: FDA: fourier domain adaptation for semantic segmentation. In: CVPR (2020)
38. You, S., Xu, C., Xu, C., Tao, D.: Learning from multiple teacher networks. In: KDD (2017)
39. Yu, C., Wang, J., Chen, Y., Huang, M.: Transfer learning with dynamic adversarial adaptation network. In: ICDM (2019)
40. Zhang, H., Cisse, M., Dauphin, Y.N., Lopez-Paz, D.: mixup: beyond empirical risk minimization. In: ICLR (2018)
41. Zhang, Y., Liang, J., Zhang, Z., Wang, L., Jin, R., Tan, T., et al.: Free lunch for domain adversarial training: Environment label smoothing. In: ICLR (2023)
42. Zhang, Y., Bin, M., Zhang, Y., Wang, Z., Han, Z., Liang, C.: Link-based contrastive learning for one-shot unsupervised domain adaptation. In: CVPR (2025)

Taming Image-Based Vision-Language Pre-training Model with Bootstrapped Auxiliary Tasks for Video Captioning

Ziyu Chen[1,2,3] and Hanli Wang[1,2,3]($\boxtimes$)

[1] College of Electronic and Information Engineering, Tongji University, Shanghai, China
`{ziyuchen1997,hanliwang}@tongji.edu.cn`
[2] School of Computer Science and Technology, Tongji University, Shanghai, China
[3] Key Laboratory of Embedded System and Service Computing, Ministry of Education, Tongji University, Shanghai, China

Abstract. Current video captioning rely on pre-training on massive video-text data to align spatictemporal and linguistic information, often ignoring fine-grained object interactions and temporal ordering because of high data costs. To address these issues in a resource-friendly way, a novel framework **BAT-VLP** is proposed, which adapts image-based Vision-Language Pre-training (**VLP**) models for video captioning by introducing three **B**ootstrapped **A**uxiliary **T**asks into fine-tuning, without modification on network structure or extra video-text data. The three tasks are separately: 1) Temporal-Ordering Question Answering for perceiving orders between events, 2) Multi-Frame Multiple-Object Tracking for capturing fine-grained object interactions, and 3) Information-Decomposed Conversation for mining dynamic and static words and then composing them. To be compatible with image-based VLP models' input, image-grid format is further proposed to represent video frames, and various spatiotemporal resolutions can be flexibly obtained for generalization. All data for the BAT are automatically constructed from existing video captioning datasets, by taking advantage of the VLP model itself, Part-of-Speech Tagger and designed programs. Experiments show that BAT-VLP achieves state-of-the-art performance, and extensive ablation studies validate the effectiveness of the BAT and image-grid format.

Keywords: Video Captioning · Bootstrapped Auxiliary Tasks · Vision-Language Pre-training Model · Temporal Ordering · Object Interaction

1 Introduction

The advent of the Internet and the era of big data have given rise to an unprecedented volume of multimedia content, making the analysis and understanding of

This work was supported in part by National Natural Science Foundation of China under Grant 62371343 and Fundamental Research Funds for the Central Universities (No. 2024-1-ZD-02).

such content a cornerstone of artificial intelligence. Among the diverse research in the multimedia domain, video captioning has emerged as a classic yet enduringly active topic, with applications such as assistive technologies for the visually impaired and video retrieval in large-scale content repositories. However, the inherent complexity of video data, *e.g.*, high redundancy and high dimension, poses significant challenges for this task. Improving the accuracy of generated captions, covering objects, actions and states, is essential for advancing the effectiveness of related applications.

Early approaches to video captioning have no pre-training stage for cross-modal alignment, which mainly focus on designing network architectures [23] or tailored loss functions [4] to fit multimodal data, with the majority of model parameters trained from scratch. Visual feature extractors and textual feature extractors are often independently pre-trained on large-scale datasets. Augmentation modules are introduced [21] to enhance visual representations. Furthermore, considering that videos are inherently sequential data, temporal modeling is incorporated [5] to capture temporal dynamics. In addition, research also explores feature fusion and object interaction [30].

With the growth of computational capacity and the demand for generalizability, recent research has increasingly built video captioning models upon Vision–Language Pre-training (VLP) models, which demonstrate superior capabilities on feature extraction and fusion [13,19]. In this new paradigm, the primary challenge has shifted to efficiently adapting VLP models to video captioning as a downstream task. Image-based VLP models fit on paired image-text data, so they often require fine-tuning extra temporal modeling modules to capture temporal dynamics [19] for video data. These methods are constrained by the lightweight design of temporal modeling modules, the relatively small scale of video captioning datasets and the coarse granularity of annotations, leading to suboptimal temporal dynamics. In comparison, video-based VLP models are initially designed to capture temporal dynamics in video-text data and therefore can be directly adapted to video captioning without architectural modification [7,13,15,18]; however, they typically rely on more costly paired video–text data, which is more difficult to collect and annotate.

The preceding analysis raises the following challenge: Keep adaptation flexible and resource-friendly for learning temporal dynamics while capturing fine-grained object interactions. Motivated by this, we propose a novel framework **BAT-VLP** that adapts image-based **VLP** models for video captioning by incorporating three additional **B**ootstrapped **A**uxiliary **T**asks into fine-tuning phase, without any architectural modification or any extra video-text data. Besides, to ensure compatibility with input of image-based VLP models and enhance generalization, we introduce a novel input format that arranges a collection of video frames into a grid image, where frame size and frame number can be flexibly adjusted to obtain rich spatiotemporal resolutions.

Specifically, three Bootstrapped Auxiliary Tasks (BAT) are newly introduced: Temporal-Ordering Question Answering (TOQA), Multi-Frame Multi-Object Tracking (MFMOT), and Information-Decomposed Conversation (IDC).

The TOQA task aims to perceive temporal ordering of events, which is crucial for understanding actions that depend on sequential or time-sensitive dynamics. The MFMOT task focuses on fine-grained spatiotemporal interactions at the object level. The IDC task encourages to integrate static and dynamic information during caption generation. These bootstrapped auxiliary tasks are interleaved with video captioning during fine-tuning, and all formatted data and annotations are automatically constructed from existing video captioning datasets without any manual efforts. For TOQA, we design program to divide video frames into two groups, which are then shuffled and annotated accordingly to indicate temporal ordering. For MFMOT, we leverage the detection capability of image-based VLP models to localize objects frame by frame, and then convert bounding box to coordinates in the sense of image-grid format. For IDC, we employ a Part-of-Speech (PoS) tagger tool [29] to identify static information (nouns and adjectives) and dynamic information (verbs) in captions, which are subsequently reformulated to conversational annotations. Conversations are designed to sequentially elicit static information, dynamic information, and finally compose a complete caption through a question–answer process. To conclude, the contributions of this work are listed as follows:

- We propose a framework BAT-VLP that adapts image-based VLP models for video captioning by incorporating three bootstrapped auxiliary tasks into fine-tuning stage, without any modification on network or extra video-text data. Image-grid formatted input is proposed for compatibility.
- Three bootstrapped auxiliary tasks are introduced as TOQA, MFMOT and IDC, separately aimed at perceiving temporal ordering, fine-grained object interactions and composing static and dynamic information into complete caption.
- We propose to leverage image-based VLP models, PoS tagger tool and designed program to automatically construct data, format and annotate for auxiliary tasks.
- The proposed BAT-VLP framework demonstrates State-of-the-art performance compared to existing video captioning methods that does not rely on extra video-text data.

2   Related Work

2.1   Video Captioning Without Pre-training for Cross-Modal Alignment

Pioneering works like Venugopalan et al. [23] initiate the field of video captioning by leveraging RNNs to generate sentences from video features extracted by CNNs. Subsequently, attention-based mechanisms [5] are introduced to capture spatiotemporal information. CNN-based visual feature extractors are often pretrained on datasets, and textual encoders such as BERT [3] formed the core of these methods. Several methods introduce enhancements for fine-grained modeling. For example, Li et al. [10] design hierarchical modular networks to capture multi-level semantic structures, while Zhang et al. [30] model object interactions via an Object Relational Graph and leveraging external language models through Teacher-Recommended Learning. Efforts to strengthen temporal reasoning appears through attention mechanisms that adapt over time [5]. Others explored auxiliary tasks [4] or dynamic representations [21] to mitigate information loss in temporal modeling. While these approaches advanced the field, their dependence on learning multimodal alignments from scratch posed generalizability and scalability challenges, especially in low-resource settings.

2.2 Vision-Language Pre-training Models for Video Captioning

With the success of vision-language pre-training models, recent video captioning approaches have shifted toward leveraging large-scale image-text or video-text corpora to learn cross-modal representations prior to task-specific fine-tuning. Image-based VLP models are pre-trained on massive image-text datasets, offering strong feature representations but lack temporal modeling capabilities. To address this, VL-Adapter [19] incorporate lightweight temporal adapters or spatiotemporal feature aggregators. However, such adaptations often face limitations due to coarse video annotations and insufficient temporal granularity in the fine-tuning data. In contrast, video-based VLP models are pre-trained directly on video-text data and thus inherently capture temporal dynamics. Notable examples include UniVL [15,20], which unifies vision and language encoding through joint pre-training on video-text data; VLAB [7], which blends features across modalities with attention-based fusion; and SwinBERT [13], which applies sparse transformers for scalable video understanding. These methods demonstrate superior performance but depend heavily on costly large-scale video-text datasets, which are labor-intensive to collect and annotate. Generative pre-training for video captioning has also gained traction. For example, end-to-end generative pre-training frameworks [18] have shown that leveraging generative objectives during pre-training leads to richer cross-modal representations.

3 Methodology

In the following, we begin by briefly introducing image-based VLP models in Sect. 3.1. Then, we formally introduce image-grid formatted input in Sect. 3.2. At last, each of the three bootstrapped auxiliary tasks will be presented sequentially in Sect. 3.3, 3.4 and 3.5, focusing on their definitions and data automatic construction from original video captioning dataset without any extra video-text data. The overview of framework BAT-VLP is shown in Fig. 1.

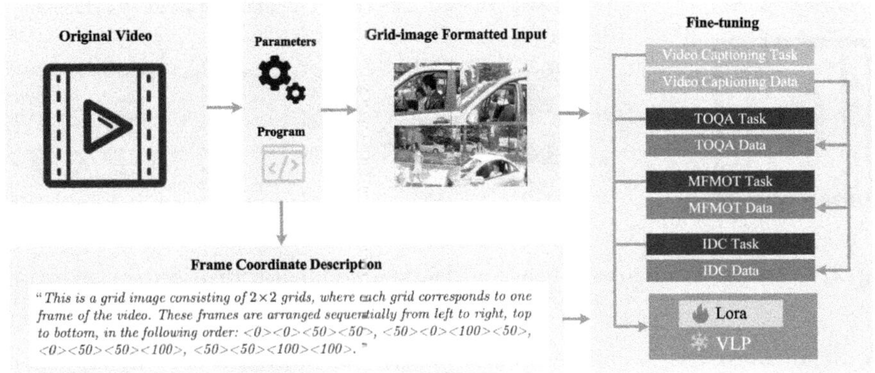

Fig. 1. Overview of the proposed BAT-VLP framework.

3.1 Image-Based Vision-Language Pre-training Models

Image-based VLP models generally take as input a single image (denoted as $\mathcal{I}$) and a prompt (denoted as $\mathcal{P}$) as shown in Eq. 1. A prompt is generally composed of two parts, one (denoted as $\mathcal{T}_{\text{inst}}$) stands for instruction that is model specific and the other (denoted as $\mathcal{T}_{\text{in}}$) is natural language related to visual contents.

$$\mathcal{P} = [\mathcal{T}_{\text{inst}}; \mathcal{T}_{\text{in}}], \tag{1}$$

$$\mathcal{T}_{\text{out}} = \text{VLP}(\mathcal{I}, \mathcal{P}), \tag{2}$$

where $[;]$ means concatenation and $\mathcal{T}_{\text{out}}$ means output by image-based VLP models. The model can be trained or finetuned with ground truth text $\mathcal{T}_{\text{out}}^{\text{gt}}$.

Specifically, we choose MiniGPT-v2 as the image-based VLP model for the proposed framework BAT-VLP. MiniGPT-v2 incorporates coordinate representations into the natural language $\mathcal{T}_{\text{in}}$, thereby endowing the model with the capability of object detection and referential grounding. For example, if a cat is located at position (x_1, y_1, x_2, y_2) in the image, the corresponding description for the image could be "*There is a cat at* $<x_1><y_1><x_2><y_2>$.", where (x_1, y_1) and (x_2, y_2) separately represent the top-left and the bottom-right coordinate. All coordinates are converted to integers between 0 and 100 as pre-defined in MiniGPT-v2, where 0 denotes the min and 100 denotes the max.

3.2 Image-Grid Formatted Input

In image-based VLP models, the input image I has fixed size $H_{\text{I}} \times W_{\text{I}}$ to facilitate stable training and inference, where H_{I} and W_{I} denotes the height and width. To represent a video in a compatible and efficient way, we propose to format a series of video frames to a grid image as shown in Fig. 2. This design guarantees a seamless shift to video-text data without any modification on network architecture. In detail, suppose a video is of size $T_{\text{V}} \times H_{\text{V}} \times W_{\text{V}}$, where T_{V}, H_{V} and

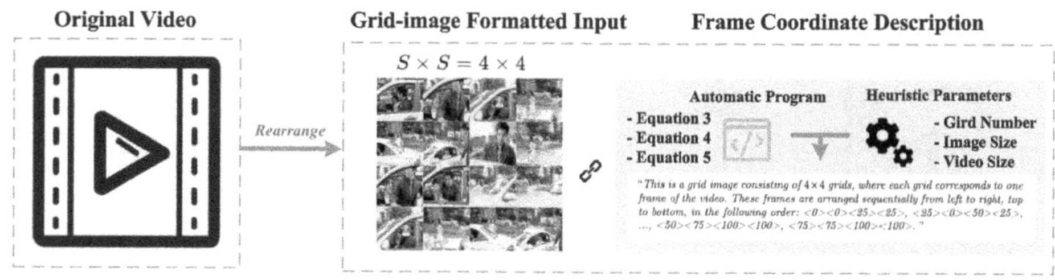

Fig. 2. Details and examples of image-grid formatted input with grid size equal to 4×4.

W_V denotes the frame number, frame height and frame width, and suppose the video is arranged into $S \times S$ grids. This means that video frames need resizing and resizing ratio r_H and r_W can be calculated as the following Eq. 3 and 4. Also, sampling $S \times S$ frames from total T_V frames is needed.

$$r_H = \frac{H_I}{H_V \times S}, \quad r_W = \frac{W_I}{W_V \times S}. \tag{3}$$

To better represent videos, the BAT-VLP explicitly tag the coordinates of each frame in the prompt, enabling image-based VLP models to shift their visual understanding from a single-image perspective to a multi-frame one. The coordinates of a frame located at $(i, j)^{\text{th}}$ grid in a grid image can be calculated as below:

$$x_1^{i,j} = \text{Round}(100 \times j/S), \quad y_1^{i,j} = \text{Round}(100 \times i/S), \tag{4}$$

$$x_2^{i,j} = x_1^{i,j} + W_I/S, \quad y_2^{i,j} = y_1^{i,j} + H_I/S, \tag{5}$$

where $(x_1^{i,j}, y_1^{i,j})$ and $(x_2^{i,j}, y_2^{i,j})$ separately represent the top-left and the bottom-right coordinate, and Round denotes the rounding function that converts a decimal number to the nearest integer.

Based on the input format and coordinate representation described above, we can generate task-agnostic and generic language $\mathcal{T}_{\text{gene}}$ to describe a video as the following example:

"This is a grid image consisting of $<S> \times <S>$ grids, where each grid corresponds to one frame of the video. These frames are arranged sequentially from left to right and top to bottom, in the following order: $<x_1^{1,1}><y_1^{1,1}><x_2^{1,1}><y_2^{1,1}>, x_1^{1,2}><y_1^{1,2}><x_2^{1,2}><y_2^{1,2}>, ..., <x_1^{2,1}><y_1^{2,1}><x_2^{2,1}><y_2^{2,1}>, ..., <x_1^{s,s}><y_1^{s,s}><x_2^{s,s}><y_2^{s,s}>."

With this coordinate representation, we further decompose input text $\mathcal{T}_{\text{in}}$ into generic language $\mathcal{T}_{\text{gene}}$ and task-specific language $\mathcal{T}_{\text{task}}$, as shown below as a complement to Eq. 1:

$$\mathcal{T}_{\text{in}} = [\mathcal{T}_{\text{gene}}; \mathcal{T}_{\text{task}}]. \tag{6}$$

3.3   Temporal-Ordering Question Answering

The TOQA task aims to capture the temporal ordering relationships between events or actions, a capability crucial for understanding time-sensitive dynamics.

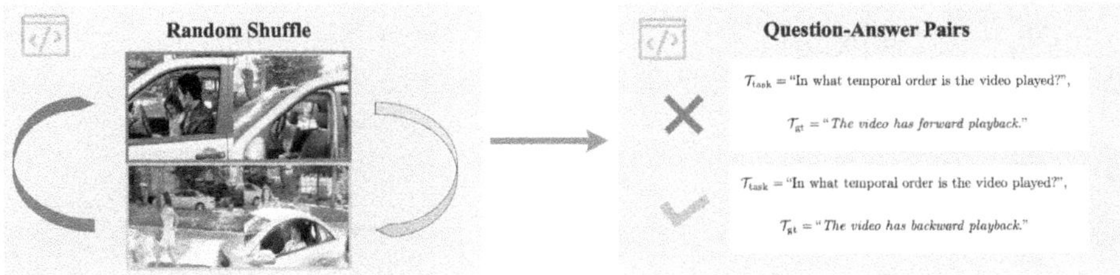

Fig. 3. Illustration of TOQA task and data construction.

The task is formulated as a question–answering problem in which the model is trained to determine the temporal ordering between two groups of video frames as shown in Fig. 3. Specifically, $S \times S$ frames of a video are divided into two groups $\mathcal{G}_1 = (f_1, f_2, ..., f_{\frac{s^2}{2}})$ and $\mathcal{G}_2 = (f_{\frac{s^2}{2}}, f_{\frac{s^2}{2}+1}, ..., f_{s^2})$, where f_* denotes video frames. When $\mathcal{G}_1$ is placed in the upper region of the image grid and $\mathcal{G}_2$ is placed in the lower region, this corresponds to a forward playback of the video when the frames are scanned according to the sequential order in the natural language description $\mathcal{T}_{gene}$, indicating that $\mathcal{G}_1$ occurs before $\mathcal{G}_2$. Conversely, placing $\mathcal{G}_1$ in the lower region implies a reversed playback, where $\mathcal{G}_1$ follows $\mathcal{G}_2$. These two types of placement are explicitly marked as "forward" and "backward" in the natural language description, and the placement is randomly determined by automatic program. The following formulation exhibits how to construct task-specific input $\mathcal{T}_{task}$ and ground truth $\mathcal{T}_{gt}$:

$$\mathcal{T}_{task} = \text{"In what temporal order is the video played?"}, \tag{7}$$

$$\mathcal{T}_{gt} = \begin{cases} \text{"}\textit{The video has forward playback.}\text{"}, & \text{if } \mathcal{G}_1 \text{ is on upper half region,} \\ \text{"}\textit{The video has backward playback.}\text{"}, & \text{if } \mathcal{G}_1 \text{ is on lower half region.} \end{cases} \tag{8}$$

3.4   Multi-frame Multi-object Tracking

The MFMOT task aims to capture fine-grained interactions at object level, which encourages more accurate captions. The task is formulated as a coordinate-centric caption generation problem in which the model is trained to detect all related objects in a grid image. To finetune on this task, per-frame annotations and coordinate conversion are required as shown in Fig. 4. In fact, image-based VLP models can detect objects in a single image by prompting with special instructions, which can be leveraged to obtain per-frame annotations automatically. This process can be formulated as following equations (similar to Eq. 2):

$$\mathcal{T}_k = \text{VLP}(f_k, \mathcal{P}_{obj}), k = 1, 2, ..., S^2, \tag{9}$$

where f_k denotes a video frame, $\mathcal{T}_k$ denotes corresponding output containing detection results and $\mathcal{P}_{obj}$ is specially designed prompts with "[$detection$]" token to instruct the VLP models to perform object detection based on the ground truth of video caption $\mathcal{T}_{\text{gt}}^{\text{cap}}$. To extract numeric coordinates from $\mathcal{T}_k$ for further conversion, a regular expression matching program is leveraged.

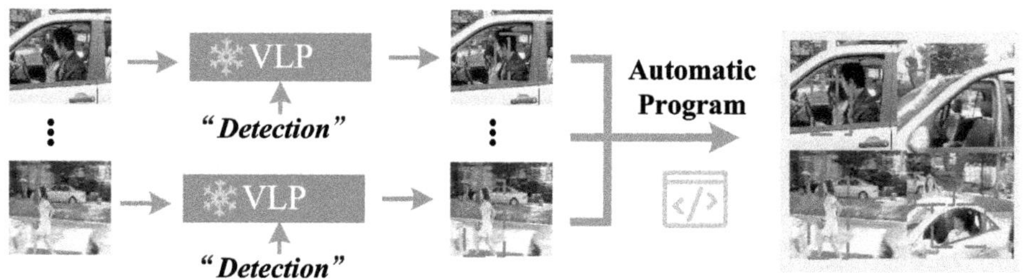

Fig. 4. Illustration of MFMOT task and data construction.

Next, it is necessary to determine how to convert coordinates from a single image to those on the grid image. Suppose the coordinates of an object C detected in frame f_k are given as $(x_{1,C}, y_{1,C}, x_{2,C}, y_{2,C})$. First, the grid index (i, j) of this frame can be calculated using the following equation:

$$i = \left\lfloor \frac{k}{S} \right\rfloor, \quad j = k \bmod S. \tag{10}$$

Then, according to Eqs. 4 and 5, the top-left position of this frame on the grid image is obtained as $x_1^{i,j}, y_1^{i,j}$. Finally, the coordinates of object C on the grid image are converted to $(x_1^{i,j} + x_{1,C} * r_{\text{W}}, y_1^{i,j} + y_{1,C} * r_{\text{H}}, x_1^{i,j} + x_{2,C} * r_{\text{W}}, y_1^{i,j} + y_{2,C} * r_{\text{H}})$, where r_{W} and r_{H} are resizing ratio in Eq. 3. After get all objects' coordinates in the grid image, they are organized as task-specific text $\mathcal{T}_{\text{task}}$ for MFMOT.

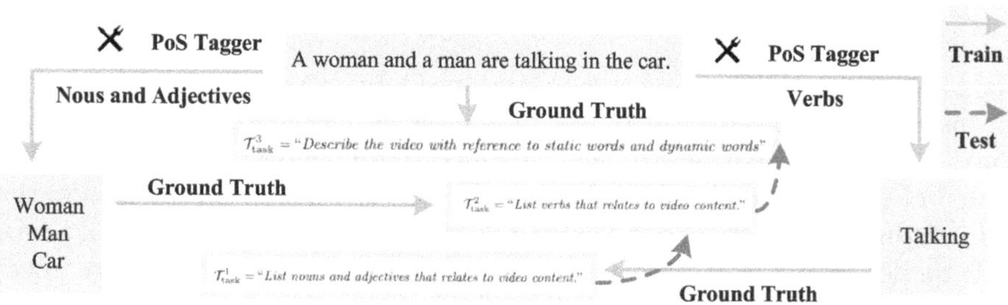

Fig. 5. Illustration of IDC task and data construction.

3.5 Information-Decomposed Conversation

The IDC task aims to progressively extract static and dynamic information with precision, and subsequently integrate them into a complete caption. The task is formulated as a dialogue problem as shown in Fig. 5, in which the model is trained to elicit the necessary information in multiple steps and eventually synthesize a coherent caption. To construct necessary annotation for dialogue, the PoS tagger tool is first used to get static and dynamic words from ground truth caption $\mathcal{T}_{\mathrm{gt}}^{\mathrm{cap}}$ as follows:

$$\mathcal{W}_{\mathrm{static}} = \mathrm{PoSTagger}(\mathcal{T}_{\mathrm{gt}}^{\mathrm{cap}}, (\text{``ADJ''}, \text{``NOUN''})), \tag{11}$$

$$\mathcal{W}_{\mathrm{dynamic}} = \mathrm{PoSTagger}(\mathcal{T}_{\mathrm{gt}}^{\mathrm{cap}}, (\text{``VERB''})), \tag{12}$$

where $\mathcal{W}_{\mathrm{static}}$ denotes extracted static words including adjectives and nouns by PoS tagger tool, and $\mathcal{W}_{\mathrm{dynamic}}$ denotes extracted dynamic words including verbs by PoS tagger tool.

Building upon these tagged words, we design the inputs and ground truth annotations necessary for a three-turn dialogue. The first turn targets the extraction of static information, with input $\mathcal{T}_{\mathrm{task}}^{1}$ and corresponding ground truth $\mathcal{T}_{\mathrm{gt}}^{1}$, and the second turn focuses on extracting dynamic information, with input $\mathcal{T}_{\mathrm{task}}^{2}$ and corresponding ground truth $\mathcal{T}_{\mathrm{gt}}^{2}$, as formulated in the below equations:

$$\mathcal{T}_{\mathrm{task}}^{1} = \text{``\textit{List nouns and adjectives that relates to videocontent.}''}, \tag{13}$$

$$\mathcal{T}_{\mathrm{task}}^{2} = \text{``\textit{List verbs that relates to video content.}''}, \tag{14}$$

$$\mathcal{T}_{\mathrm{gt}}^{1} = \mathcal{W}_{\mathrm{static}}, \mathcal{T}_{\mathrm{gt}}^{2} = \mathcal{W}_{\mathrm{dynamic}}. \tag{15}$$

The third turn aims at composing both static and dynamic information into a complete caption, with input $\mathcal{T}_{\mathrm{task}}^{3}$ and corresponding ground truth $\mathcal{T}_{\mathrm{gt}}^{3}$ formulated as below equation:

$$\mathcal{T}_{\mathrm{task}}^{3} = \text{``\textit{Describe the video with reference to static words and dynamic words.}''}, \tag{16}$$

$$\mathcal{T}_{\mathrm{gt}}^{3} = \mathcal{T}_{\mathrm{gt}}^{\mathrm{cap}}. \tag{17}$$

4 Experiments and Analysis

4.1 Experimental Settings

We adopt MiniGPT-v2 as the baseline VLP model, where LoRA is applied during fine-tuning while keeping all other parameters frozen. The learning rate is set as low as 1e-6 with a batch size of 2, and training is conducted on 8 L40 GPUs. We adopt AdamW optimizer with a weight decay of 0.05 and a linear warmup strategy for the first 5% of steps. During training, input sequences are truncated or padded to a maximum length of 2048 tokens. The fine-tuning is run for 15 epochs on the bootstrapped auxiliary task dataset, and checkpoints are evaluated periodically on validation sets to prevent overfitting. Following common practice, the vision encoder remains frozen throughout the training process, while only the projection layers and LoRA parameters in the language model are updated.

4.2 Datasets

Microsoft Research Video Description (MSVD) dataset [2] is one of the earliest and most influential. It consists of approximately 2,000 short video clips collected from YouTube, each annotated with around 40 human-generated captions. Despite its relatively small size, MSVD provides diverse sentence-level descriptions and remains a standard benchmark for evaluating generalization ability and linguistic richness in video captioning models.

Microsoft Research Video-to-Text (MSR-VTT) dataset [27] expands the scale to 10,000 video clips, covering 20 broad categories such as sports, music, and news. Each video is paired with 20 different captions, leading to a total of 200,000 sentence annotations. Its large scale and wide domain coverage make MSR-VTT one of the most widely used datasets for both training and evaluation, particularly for measuring robustness across diverse video scenarios.

VATEX dataset [25] further advances video captioning benchmarks by introducing a large-scale, multilingual design. It contains 41,250 open-domain videos, each annotated with 10 captions in English and 10 in Chinese, making it one of the few bilingual resources in the field. VATEX not only enables the study of cross-lingual video captioning, but also facilitates research on multilingual alignment, cultural diversity, and language transfer in multimodal understanding.

4.3 Evaluation Metrics

Video captioning performance is commonly evaluated using automatic metrics such as BLEU [17], METEOR [1], ROUGE [12], and CIDEr [22]. BLEU measures n-gram precision with a brevity penalty, while METEOR improves semantic matching through stemming and synonyms with a balanced consideration of precision and recall. ROUGE, originally proposed for summarization, emphasizes recall by capturing n-gram and sequence overlaps. CIDEr is specifically designed for captioning tasks, computing consensus with TF-IDF weighted n-grams, and has been shown to correlate strongly with human judgment. Together, these metrics provide complementary perspectives, forming the standard toolkit for benchmarking video captioning systems.

4.4 Main Results

We conduct a comprehensive comparison between the proposed BAT-VLP and existing state-of-the-art methods. As shown in Table 1, under the setting without using any additional video-text data, our method achieves superior performance, with particularly notable improvements on the CIDEr metric across three benchmark datasets, surpassing the previous best by +3.1/+13.8/+4.4 on MSVD/MSRVTT/VATEX. For the more challenging METEOR metric, BAT-VLP also leads other approaches by a non-negligible margin, surpassing the previous best by +1.2/+2.2/+1.4 on MSVD/MSRVTT/VATEX. Compared with

Table 1. Comparison with other video captioning methods. Among methods that do not rely on extra video-text data, the best performance is indicated in **boldface**, while the second-best performance is <u>underlined</u>.

Method	MSR-VTT				MSVD				VATEX			
	B@4	M	R	C	B@4	M	R	C	B@4	M	R	C
Methods require extra video-text data												
SwinBERT [13]	41.9	29.9	62.1	53.8	58.4	41.3	77.5	120.6	38.7	26.2	53.2	73.0
CLIP4Caption [20]	46.1	30.7	63.7	57.7	-	-	-	-	-	-	-	-
MV-GPT [18]	48.9	38.7	64.0	60.0	-	-	-	-	-	-	-	-
GiT [24]	53.8	32.9	67.7	73.9	79.5	51.1	87.3	180.2	41.6	28.1	55.4	91.5
VLAB$_L$ [7]	54.3	32.7	67.9	72.5	78.7	50.3	86.9	174.1	-	-	-	
VLAB$_G$ [7]	54.6	33.4	68.3	74.9	79.3	51.2	87.9	179.8	-	-	-	
mPLUG-2 [26]	57.8	34.9	70.1	80.0	70.5	48.4	85.3	165.8	-	-	-	-
Methods require no extra video-text data												
ORG-TRL [30]	43.6	28.8	62.1	50.9	54.3	36.4	73.9	95.2	-	-	-	-
UniVL [15]	42.2	28.8	61.2	49.9	-	-	-	-	-	-	-	-
HSRA [5]	46.9	30.9	64.8	55.3	62.2	39.2	78.4	110.1	-	-	-	-
Track4Cap [16]	44.6	30.5	63.6	57.7	62.1	42.5	79.8	127.2	-	-	-	-
MM-Diff-Net [8]	44.7	27.8	61.9	46.9	-	-	-	-	37.0	24.3	52.4	58.9
MICap [6]	48.0	29.4	63.7	52.1	-	-	-	-	30.5	23.6	43.5	40.0
IcoCap [11]	47.0	<u>31.1</u>	64.9	60.2	59.1	39.5	76.5	110.3	<u>37.4</u>	<u>25.7</u>	<u>53.1</u>	<u>67.8</u>
QAVidCap [14]	<u>48.5</u>	30.9	64.8	62.2	-	-	-	-	-	-	-	-
HiTeA [28]	**49.2**	30.7	<u>65.0</u>	65.1	**71.0**	<u>45.3</u>	<u>81.4</u>	146.9	-	-	-	-
CaptionT5 [9]	-	-	-	<u>66.1</u>	-	-	-	-	-	-	-	67.5
BAT-VLP (ours)	**49.2**	**32.3**	**65.8**	**69.2**	<u>70.9</u>	**47.5**	**84.7**	**160.7**	**40.8**	**27.1**	**55.8**	**72.2**

Table 2. Ablation study on three bootstrapped auxiliary tasks. The best performance is indicated in **boldface**, while the second-best performance is <u>underlined</u>

No.	TOQA	MFMOT	IDC	MSR-VTT				MSVD				VATEX			
				B@4	M	R	C	B@4	M	R	C	B@4	M	R	C
1				46.7	30.1	58.8	66.7	65.5	44.3	81.8	140.6	38.7	26.7	54.2	70.6
2	✔			46.9	30.1	58.9	66.6	65.5	44.7	82.1	143.6	39.0	26.7	54.3	71.0
3		✔		46.8	30.4	58.8	67.1	66.0	44.3	81.8	145.6	38.5	26.9	54.5	70.7
4			✔	47.9	31.5	62.3	68.1	68.2	45.3	83.1	145.3	39.7	26.9	54.8	71.1
5	✔	✔		47.2	30.9	59.9	68.1	67.2	45.0	82.6	147.6	38.3	26.6	54.8	70.8
6	✔		✔	48.8	<u>31.6</u>	<u>64.3</u>	68.7	69.6	<u>46.5</u>	83.9	153.3	40.1	**27.3**	**56.1**	<u>72.1</u>
7		✔	✔	<u>49.1</u>	31.3	**65.8**	68.6	<u>70.3</u>	46.2	**85.0**	<u>155.5</u>	<u>40.6</u>	26.9	55.2	72.0
8	✔	✔	✔	**49.2**	**32.3**	**65.8**	**69.2**	**70.9**	**47.5**	<u>84.7</u>	**160.7**	**40.8**	<u>27.1</u>	<u>55.8</u>	**72.2**

Table 3. Ablation study on grid number ($S \times S$). The best performance is indicated in **boldface**, while the second-best performance is underlined

No.	grid number $S \times S$	MSR-VTT				MSVD				VATEX			
		B@4	M	R	C	B@4	M	R	C	B@4	M	R	C
1	$\{1 \times 1\}$	45.9	30.2	57.8	66.3	65.4	42.0	78.8	139.9	37.1	26.7	53.2	69.9
2	$\{4 \times 4\}$	47.8	31.1	61.9	68.5	67.7	45.4	82.0	141.3	38.8	27.0	53.7	71.0
3	$\{16 \times 16\}$	48.5	<u>31.8</u>	63.1	68.1	68.1	45.3	**84.7**	152.6	39.1	26.9	54.7	70.7
4	$\{1 \times 1, 4 \times 4\}$	47.7	31.3	62.0	68.0	67.7	45.4	83.0	139.3	38.7	27.0	53.6	70.9
5	$\{4 \times 4, 16 \times 16\}$	**49.2**	**32.3**	**65.8**	**69.2**	<u>70.9</u>	**47.5**	**84.7**	**160.7**	**40.8**	<u>27.1</u>	**55.8**	<u>72.2</u>
6	$\{1 \times 1, 4 \times 4, 16 \times 16\}$	<u>49.0</u>	<u>31.8</u>	**65.8**	**69.2**	**71.1**	**47.5**	<u>84.5</u>	<u>157.3</u>	**40.6**	**27.2**	**55.8**	**72.3**

methods trained or fine-tuned on extra video-text data, our BAT-VLP still demonstrates competitive results, surpassing approximately half of them.

In further analyzing the advantages of our approach, we observe that although Track4Cap and QAVideCap incorporate additional tasks during fine-tuning, their performance remains significantly weaker than ours. This highlights the effectiveness of the proposed bootstrapped auxiliary tasks and automatically constructed training data. Moreover, methods such as UniVL, CaptionT5, and HiTeA also benefit from cross-modal pre-training, yet their inferior results compared to ours reveal that BAT-VLP is able to utilize prior aligned vision–language semantics more effectively.

4.5   Ablation Study

We conduct a comprehensive ablation study on the proposed method. First, we examine the effect of removing each of the three bootstrapped auxiliary tasks individually. From the comparison of No.1, 2, 3, and 4 in Table 2, it can be observed that No.4 clearly outperforms the others, indicating that the IDC task contributes most significantly to performance improvement. A similar trend can be seen in the comparison of No.5, 6, and 7. We conjecture that this is because the IDC task simplifies the video captioning process by sequentially learning static and dynamic information, making the training easier while also better leveraging the temporal information learned from TOQA and the object interaction cues captured by MFMOT. Besides, the last turn of conversation in IDC task contains captioning generation, which can be another reason for its boosting performance.

We also conduct an ablation study on the number of grids to validate the effectiveness of using rich spatiotemporal resolutions. As shown in Table 3, No.5 and No.6 achieve the best performance, indicating that the grid configurations of 4×4 and 16×16 play a crucial role in boosting performance. Further comparing No.2 and No.3 reveals that either 4×4 or 16×16 alone brings only limited improvements. This further demonstrates that combining different spatiotemporal resolutions can better facilitate training and lead to stronger performance.

Besides, this observation indicate that it is necessary to employ image-grid format in adaptation of image-based VLP models for video captioning.

5   Conclusion

In summary, we propose BAT-VLP, a novel framework that adapts image-based VLP models for video captioning in a resource-friendly manner. By introducing three bootstrapped auxiliary tasks—Temporal-Ordering Question Answering, Multi-Frame Multi-Object Tracking, and Information-Decomposed Conversation, BAT-VLP effectively captures temporal dynamics and fine-grained object interactions without architectural modifications or additional video-text data. The image-grid input design further enhances generalization by supporting flexible spatiotemporal resolutions. Extensive experiments and ablation studies demonstrate that BAT-VLP achieves state-of-the-art performance while validating the importance of auxiliary tasks and image-grid formatted input in modeling temporal ordering and fine-grained object interactions for video captioning.

References

1. Banerjee, S., Lavie, A.: Meteor: an automatic metric for MT evaluation with improved correlation with human judgments. In: Proceedings of the ACL Workshop on Intrinsic and Extrinsic Evaluation Measures for Machine Translation and/or Summarization, pp. 65–72 (2005)
2. Chen, D.L., Dolan, W.B.: Collecting highly parallel data for paraphrase evaluation. In: Proceedings of the 49th Annual Meeting of the Association for Computational Linguistics: Human Language Technologies, pp. 190–200 (2011)
3. Devlin, J., Chang, M.W., Lee, K., Toutanova, K.: Bert: pre-training of deep bidirectional transformers for language understanding. In: Proceedings of the 2019 Conference of the North American Chapter of the Association for Computational Linguistics: Human Language Technologies, Volume 1 (Long and Short Papers), pp. 4171–4186 (2019)
4. Gao, L., Lei, Y., Zeng, P., Song, J., Wang, M., Shen, H.T.: Hierarchical representation network with auxiliary tasks for video captioning and video question answering. IEEE Trans. Image Process. **31**, 202–215 (2021)
5. Han, T., Xu, Y., Yu, J., Yu, Z., Zhao, S.: Action-driven semantic representation and aggregation for video captioning. IEEE Trans. Circ. Syst. Video Technol. (2024)
6. Hanna-Asaad, A., Aspandi, D., Zaharia, T.: Multi-modal interpretable automatic video captioning. arXiv preprint arXiv:2411.06872 (2024)
7. He, X., et al.: Vlab: enhancing video language pre-training by feature adapting and blending. IEEE Trans. Multimedia (2024)
8. Kainulainen, J., Guo, Z., Laaksonen, J.: Diffusion-based multimodal video captioning. In: Proceedings of the Asian Conference on Computer Vision, pp. 2820–2837 (2024)
9. Kim, B., Hwang, D., Cho, S., Jang, Y., Lee, H., Lee, M.: Show think and tell: thought-augmented fine-tuning of large language models for video captioning. In: Proceedings of the IEEE/CVF Conference on Computer Vision and Pattern Recognition, pp. 1808–1817 (2024)

10. Li, G., et al.: Learning hierarchical modular networks for video captioning. IEEE Trans. Pattern Anal. Mach. Intell. **46**(2), 1049–1064 (2023)
11. Liang, Y., Zhu, L., Wang, X., Yang, Y.: Icocap: improving video captioning by compounding images. IEEE Trans. Multimedia **26**, 4389–4400 (2023)
12. Lin, C.Y.: Rouge: a package for automatic evaluation of summaries. In: Text Summarization Branches Out: Proceedings of the ACL-04 Workshop, pp. 74–81 (2004)
13. Lin, K., et al.: Swinbert: end-to-end transformers with sparse attention for video captioning. In: Proceedings of the IEEE/CVF Conference on Computer Vision and Pattern Recognition, pp. 17949–17958 (2022)
14. Liu, H., Wan, X.: Qavidcap: enhancing video captioning through question answering techniques. In: Proceedings of the 2024 International Conference on Multimedia Retrieval, pp. 155–164 (2024)
15. Luo, H., et al.: Univl: a unified video and language pre-training model for multimodal understanding and generation. arXiv preprint arXiv:2002.06353 (2020)
16. Luo, H., Cai, X., Shark, L.K.: Frame-by-frame multi-object tracking-guided video captioning. IEEE Trans. Circ. Syst. Video Technol. (2025)
17. Papineni, K., Roukos, S., Ward, T., Zhu, W.J.: Bleu: a method for automatic evaluation of machine translation. In: Proceedings of the 40th Annual Meeting of the Association for Computational Linguistics, pp. 311–318 (2002)
18. Seo, P.H., Nagrani, A., Arnab, A., Schmid, C.: End-to-end generative pretraining for multimodal video captioning. In: Proceedings of the IEEE/CVF Conference on Computer Vision and Pattern Recognition, pp. 17959–17968 (2022)
19. Sung, Y.L., Cho, J., Bansal, M.: VL-adapter: parameter-efficient transfer learning for vision-and-language tasks. In: Proceedings of the IEEE/CVF Conference on Computer Vision and Pattern Recognition, pp. 5227–5237 (2022)
20. Tang, M., Wang, Z., Liu, Z., Rao, F., Li, D., Li, X.: Clip4caption: clip for video caption. In: Proceedings of the 29th ACM International Conference on Multimedia, pp. 4858–4862 (2021)
21. Tu, Y., Zhou, C., Guo, J., Gao, S., Yu, Z.: Enhancing the alignment between target words and corresponding frames for video captioning. Pattern Recogn. **111**, 107702 (2021)
22. Vedantam, R., Lawrence Zitnick, C., Parikh, D.: Cider: consensus-based image description evaluation. In: Proceedings of the IEEE Conference on Computer Vision and Pattern Recognition (CVPR), pp. 4566–4575 (2015)
23. Venugopalan, S., Xu, H., Donahue, J., Rohrbach, M., Mooney, R., Saenko, K.: Translating videos to natural language using deep recurrent neural networks. In: Conference of the North American Chapter of the Association for Computational Linguistics: Human Language Technologies, NAACL HLT 2015, pp. 1494–1504 (2015)
24. Wang, J., et al.: Git: a generative image-to-text transformer for vision and language. Trans. Mach. Learn. Res.
25. Wang, X., Wu, J., Chen, J., Li, L., Wang, Y.F., Wang, W.Y.: Vatex: a large-scale, high-quality multilingual dataset for video-and-language research. In: Proceedings of the IEEE/CVF International Conference on Computer Vision, pp. 4581–4591 (2019)
26. Xu, H., et al.: mplug-2: a modularized multi-modal foundation model across text, image and video. In: International Conference on Machine Learning, pp. 38728–38748 (2023)
27. Xu, J., Mei, T., Yao, T., Rui, Y.: MSR-VTT: a large video description dataset for bridging video and language. In: Proceedings of the IEEE Conference on Computer Vision and Pattern Recognition (CVPR), pp. 5288–5296 (2016)

28. Ye, Q., et al.: Hitea: hierarchical temporal-aware video-language pre-training. In: Proceedings of the IEEE/CVF International Conference on Computer Vision, pp. 15405–15416 (2023)
29. Yogish, D., Manjunath, T., Hegadi, R.S.: Review on natural language processing trends and techniques using NLTK. In: International Conference on Recent Trends in Image Processing and Pattern Recognition, pp. 589–606 (2018)
30. Zhang, Z., et al.: Object relational graph with teacher-recommended learning for video captioning. In: Proceedings of the IEEE/CVF Conference on Computer Vision and Pattern Recognition, pp. 13278–13288 (2020)

Benchmarking SmolVLM for Parking Occupancy Detection

Jobin Idiculla Wattasseril[(✉)] [iD], Willy Scheibel [iD], and Jürgen Döllner [iD]

Hasso Plattner Institute, Digital Engineering Faculty, University of Potsdam,
Potsdam, Germany
{jobin.wattasseril,willy.scheibel}@hpi.uni-potsdam.de,
doellner@uni-potsdam.de

Abstract. Parking occupancy detection plays a critical role in optimizing urban spaces by enabling dynamic resource allocation and reducing traffic congestion. While prior approaches relying on lightweight architectures offer fast inference, their task-specific designs necessitate architectural modifications for new applications, limiting adaptability. Multimodal Large Language Models (MLLMs) have emerged as versatile alternatives, with efficient variants now deployable on edge devices. This paper presents the first benchmark of an existing efficient MLLM, SmolVLM, for the task of parking occupancy detection. We systematically evaluate the model's feasibility in a zero-shot setting, along with parameter-efficient fine-tuned variants across different model sizes and user/system prompt configurations, and further assess its ability for cross-dataset generalization. Experiments on two benchmark datasets, PKLot and CNRPark+EXT, demonstrate that our approach exhibits strong in-domain and cross-dataset performance, and either compete with or surpass prior task-specific architectures, despite training on significantly lesser data (91% reduction for PKLot; 40% reduction for CNR-Park+EXT). Source code for replicating our experiments is available at: https://osf.io/kdhe5?view_only=72e17f288d2f471eb4deb464d177a50c

1 Introduction

The integration of artificial intelligence into video processing pipelines has revolutionized smart surveillance systems, enabling data-driven decision-making for urban space optimization. By automating the analysis of visual data, AI-based systems enhance resource allocation, improve traffic management, and support sustainable city planning. A critical challenge in this domain is parking occupancy detection, the task of identifying whether individual parking spaces are occupied, directly affecting urban mobility, congestion reduction, and user convenience. Traditional solutions leveraging CNNs or ViTs (Vision Transformers), are performant but face limitations in adaptability and contextual reasoning.

Recent advancements in Large Language Models (LLMs), particularly Multimodal LLMs (MLLMs), have expanded the horizons of AI applications. These models, capable of processing and correlating diverse data modalities (e.g., text,

J. Lokoč et al. (Eds.): MMM 2026, LNCS 16412, pp. 162–174, 2026.
https://doi.org/10.1007/978-981-95-6950-2_12

images, and sensor inputs), offer unprecedented flexibility in understanding complex real-world scenarios, with applications in domains such as document understanding [23] and video comprehension [13]. A growing focus has emerged on developing efficient MLLMs, which balance performance with computational efficiency, making them viable for edge processing in resource-constrained environments. Such models are potentially suited for real-time tasks where low-latency inference and deployment on edge devices (e.g., cameras, IoT systems) are critical.

In investigating efficient MLLMs for parking occupancy detection, the core motivation lies not only in computational efficiency but in architectural versatility. Traditional vision models, while effective for single tasks like parking occupancy detection, require task-specific architectural modifications and retraining for adaptation to new settings. MLLMs, by contrast, leverage their instruction-tuning capability to unify diverse tasks under a single framework. By training on task-specific instruction datasets, the same MLLM can dynamically adapt to perform classification, spatio-temporal reasoning, or multimodal queries without structural overhauls. This shift from rigid, task-bound models to a flexible, generalizable architecture reduces deployment complexity and opens pathways for multifunctional systems that combine perception, reasoning, and contextual analysis—a critical advantage for scalable smart parking solutions.

This paper takes the first step in the aforementioned direction by investigating the feasibility of using efficient MLLMs for the task of parking occupancy detection. The contributions of this paper are:

1. We present the first benchmark evaluation of efficient MLLMs for the task of parking occupancy detection, establishing baseline performance metrics for the community.
2. We introduce instruction-tuning versions of two existing benchmark datasets on parking occupancy detection, reformatting raw visual data along with class labels into multimodal question/answer pairs, and use them to create and evaluate fine-tuned model variants.
3. We provide a comprehensive analysis of performance factors, including zero-shot baselines, trade-offs between model size and performance, evaluations of the fine-tuned variants across diverse prompt configurations, cross-dataset evaluation, and comparison with prior non-MLLM architectures.

Our work bridges the gap between multimodal AI research and practical urban optimization challenges, offering insights into the deployment of efficient, adaptable multimodal models for smart city applications.

2   Related Work

Parking Occupancy Detection. Early approaches for parking occupancy detection relied on traditional machine learning methods like SVMs with handcrafted features and texture-based descriptors [20]. The advent of deep learning shifted focus to approaches employing CNNs. Amato et al. developed lightweight CNN models for decentralized parking detection, introducing the CNRPark dataset [3], and an extension, the CNRPark-EXT dataset [2], to address viewpoint and weather variations. Màrmol et al. [18] proposed QuickSpot, a motion detection and tracking pipeline for real-time vacancy detection. Nyambal et al. [19] demonstrated high accuracy using LeNet and AlexNet architectures, validated on the PKLot dataset [1]. Edge computing and real-time optimization became prominent with Bura et al. [4], who integrated deep learning with edge devices for scalable parking systems. Cai et al. [5] enhanced video-based systems using deep CNNs and tracking filters to improve accuracy under occlusions. Farley et al. [7] proposed a system for real-time parking occupancy detection for IP camera-based systems, and evaluated their approach using multiple architectures. Goumiri et al. [8] introduced a minimalistic single-layer CNN, outperforming deeper models in speed and accuracy. Kročka et al. [11] extended models via transfer learning to address night-time and snowy conditions.

Recent advancements include comprehensive frameworks such as those by Ludwisiak et al. [15], which integrate segmentation, occupancy detection, and violation monitoring while achieving high precision in real-world deployments. Martynova et al. [17] benchmarked vision transformers against CNNs, proposing an EfficientNet-based pipeline that outperformed existing methods across multiple datasets.

Efficient Multimodal LLMs. MLLMs represent a rapidly evolving field, with efficient variants being particularly nascent. While there is no strict consensus on model size for efficient MLLMs, most such works prioritize architectures under 4B parameters to balance performance and computational cost. Chu et al. [6] introduced MobileVLM and its successor, emphasizing mobile-friendly designs like lightweight language models and efficient cross-modality projectors. Yao et al. [22] pushed deployment boundaries with MiniCPM-V, achieving GPT-4V-level performance on mobile devices. Jin et al. [10] gives a comprehensive survey of the topic.

Recent breakthroughs focus on MLLMs with sub-1B parameters, challenging the trade-off between size and capability. Zhu et al. introduced 1B-parameter variants [24] of the InternVL MLLM series, achieving state-of-the-art results through test-time scaling and Chain-of-Thought reasoning. Li et al. [12] proposed LLaVA-OneVision with a 500M-parameter variant, emphasizing task transfer across images and videos. Marafioti et al. [16] redefined efficiency for multimodal tasks with SmolVLM (256M, 500M parameters), the MLLM used in this paper, whose 256M-parameter variant became the smallest general-purpose MLLM at the time of writing, leveraging aggressive tokenization and optimized training.

3   Research Objectives

Parking occupancy detection is formalized as an image classification problem: given an image I of a parking lot and a set of regions $R = \{r_1, r_2, \ldots, r_n\}$, where each $r_i \subseteq I$ represents a distinct parking space, the task is to classify every region r_i into one of two classes: $\{Empty, Occupied\}$. Here, *Empty* denotes a vacant parking space devoid of vehicles, while *Occupied* indicates the presence of a vehicle. Formally, the goal is to learn a mapping function $f : R \rightarrow \{Empty, Occupied\}$ that generalizes across diverse environmental and structural conditions. The task is complicated by several factors: (i) low image resolution of parking space regions, which limits the visibility of fine-grained vehicle details; (ii) partial or full obstructions from objects such as trees, lampposts, or shadows, which occlude the view of parking spaces; and (iii) environmental variability due to weather conditions or lighting changes, which alter the visual appearance of parking spaces.

This study benchmarks multiple variants of an efficient MLLM architecture, SmolVLM [16], based on model size and prompt guidance configurations, for the task of parking occupancy detection, using two established benchmark datasets: PKLot [1] and CNRPark+EXT [2]. Our objectives are twofold: (i) Evaluate performance factors influencing the MLLM in this task; and (ii) Assess cross-dataset generalization by testing models trained on one dataset against the other.

Specifically, we perform experiments to address the following research questions, within the framework of parking occupancy detection:

(RQ1) Zero-Shot performance: Can SmolVLM be used as a Zero-Shot parking space occupancy classifier?

(RQ2) Prompt guidance: Does explicit guidance through user and system prompts enhance SmolVLM's performance?

(RQ3) Model size: Does increasing the number of parameters in SmolVLM correlate with improved performance?

(RQ4) Cross-dataset generalization: Does SmolVLM trained on one dataset generalize well to an unseen dataset?

4   Experiments

4.1   Datasets

We benchmark our approach on two widely used datasets for parking occupancy detection:

PKLot. Introduced by Almeida et al. [1], the PKLot dataset comprises 12,417 surveillance camera images of parking lots, with 695,899 segmented parking space patch images.

CNRPark+EXT. Developed by Amato et al. [2], the CNRPark+EXT dataset expands on the original CNRPark dataset [3] by adding 144,965 patches from 9 cameras, totaling 157,549 parking space patch images.

Both datasets comprise patch-level annotations specifying the occupancy status ($\{Empty, Occupied\}$) of individual parking spaces, as well as weather condition labels $\{Sunny, Cloudy, Rainy\}$. The CNRPark+EXT dataset incorporates more challenging instances characterized by partial occlusions, inclusions, and adverse lighting conditions such as shadows, presenting greater complexity for analysis. We partition both datasets into training, testing, and validation splits using a 6:3:1 ratio, stratified by weather label annotations, and use these splits for all our experiments.

4.2   Model Variants

We consider the existing instruction fine-tuned version of SmolVLM (i.e., subjected to visual instruction tuning [14] to follow instruction prompts), with two size variants: a 256 million-parameter model (*256M*) and a 500 million-parameter model (*500M*). The *256M* variant represents the smallest publicly available MLLM at the time of writing, while the *500M* variant provides a mid-scale counterpart within the same architectural family. SmolVLM was selected for this study due to its dual advantages of minimal computational footprint and architectural consistency across parameter scales. The inclusion of both *256M* and *500M* variants enables a direct comparison of performance relative to model size, while controlling for differences in architecture, training methodology, and modality alignment. This design ensures that observed performance variations can be attributed primarily to model scale, rather than confounding architectural factors.

4.3   Prompt Configurations

In LLMs, system prompts configure the model's behavior and role, while user prompts define task-specific instructions provided by the user. Both have been shown to be critical for steering model outputs, particularly in vision-language tasks where precise contextual alignment is essential [16].

We conduct an ablation study to assess the impact of prompt guidance by evaluating four configurations: *(i) base*, which uses minimal system and user prompts without contextual or expert cues; *(ii) with-expert-guidance (weg)*, which modifies the base system prompt by casting the model as a domain expert in parking occupancy detection to prime specialized reasoning; *(iii) with-context-guidance (wcg)*, which augments the base user prompt by prepending image context text to anchor the task in the visual domain; and *(iv) with-expert-guidance-and-with-context-guidance (wcg+weg)*, which combines both expert and context guidance. This combined configuration examines synergies between domain expertise and contextual grounding. The exact prompt formulations used can be found in Fig. 1.

4.4   Parameter-Efficient Fine-Tuning (PEFT)

While Zero-Shot inference provides initial insights into the model's capabilities, adapting MLLMs to downstream tasks often requires fine-tuning. However, conventional full-parameter tuning is often computationally prohibitive for LLMs. To address this, Parameter-Efficient Fine-Tuning (PEFT) techniques were proposed [21], which update only a small subset of parameters while preserving the pretrained model's generalizability. Specifically, we focus on visual instruction tuning [14], a paradigm that aligns vision-language representations through task-specific instructions, and adopt LoRA (Low-Rank Adaptation) [9] based PEFT to achieve training efficiency. LoRA introduces low-rank matrices to approximate

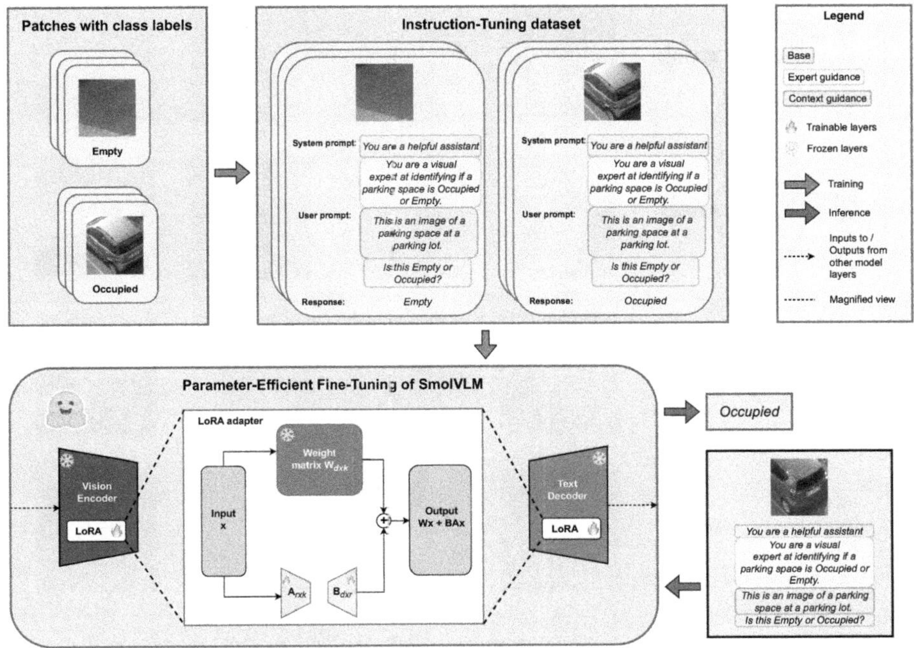

Fig. 1. Overview of our approach. First, instruction-tuning versions of the datasets are created from patch-level parking space annotations, using multiple prompt configurations. These versions of the datasets are then used for LoRA fine-tuning of the SmolVLM vision encoder and text decoder layers (we omit the full architecture for brevity). Finally, all variants across prompt configurations and model size are evaluated on two benchmark datasets.

weight updates, drastically reducing trainable parameters without compromising performance.

For parameter-efficient adaptation, we introduce visual instruction-tuning versions of the datasets, incorporating the prompt configurations described in the previous subsection, and train LoRA adapters to generate predictions $p \in \{Empty, Occupied\}$, as follows:

Let $\mathbf{W} \in \mathbb{R}^{d \times k}$ denote a pretrained weight matrix. The LoRA decomposition is then given by:

$$\Delta\mathbf{W} = \mathbf{BA}, \tag{1}$$

where $\mathbf{A} \in \mathbb{R}^{r \times k}$, $\mathbf{B} \in \mathbb{R}^{d \times r}$, and $r \ll \min(d, k)$. The adapted forward pass becomes:

$$\mathbf{h} = \mathbf{Wx} + \Delta\mathbf{Wx} = \mathbf{Wx} + \mathbf{BAx}, \tag{2}$$

We implement this adaptation within the attention layers of the vision encoder as well as the attention and linear projection layers of the text decoder within the SmolVLM architecture, enabling task-specific adjustments while retaining pretrained knowledge. Figure 1 shows the overall pipeline of our approach.

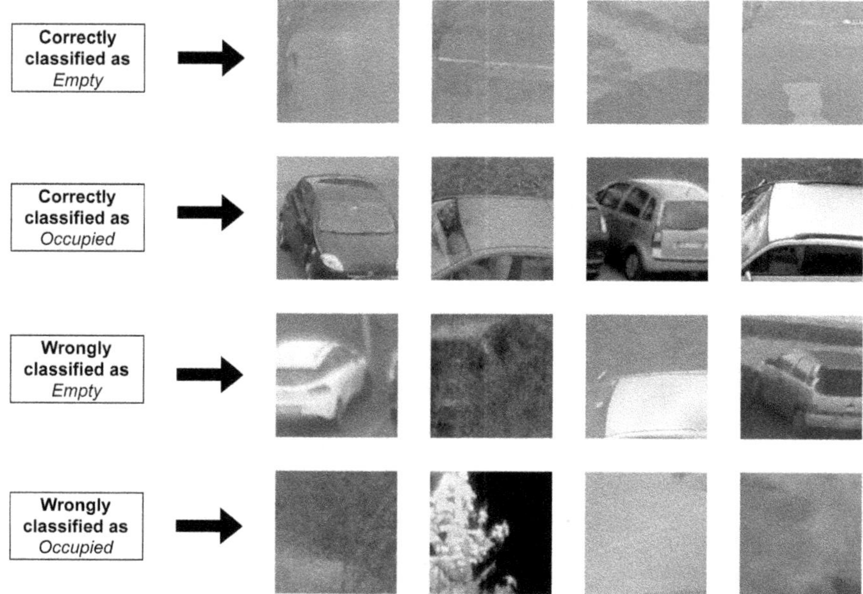

Fig. 2. Qualitative inference examples of our trained models on test splits.

4.5   Evaluation Methodology

Baseline Evaluations. We consider two baselines to evaluate our approach: *(i)* *Random baseline*: Predictions are randomly assigned as *Empty* or *Occupied*; and (ii) *Zero-Shot (ZS) baselines*: we evaluate SmolVLM across both datasets and model size variants, using the *base* prompt configurations outlined in Sect. 4.3. During experimentation, we observed frequent generation of invalid responses that deviated from the required class labels ({*Empty, Occupied*}). These non-compliant outputs are treated as incorrect predictions in our Zero-Shot evaluation.

We develop LoRA fine-tuned variants of SmolVLM as described in Sect. 4.4, across all combinations of datasets (PKLot, CNRPark+EXT), model size variants, and prompt configurations. Each variant is compared against both baselines, as well as with prior non-MLLM based architectures. Following standard practice in parking occupancy detection, we adopt the F_1-score as our primary evaluation metric. Due to computational resource constraints, we employed only a subset of the training data: for the evaluation of different prompt configurations, we use 10% of the PKLot and 50% of the CNRPark+EXT train splits. Further, we vary the training data volume and assess its impact on model performance using the *base* prompt configuration, reporting our best scores in Table 4 and Table 3.

Cross-Dataset Generalization Evaluation. We also conduct cross-dataset evaluation, i.e. (i) train on PKLot and test on CNRPark+EXT (denoted as *PKLot* →

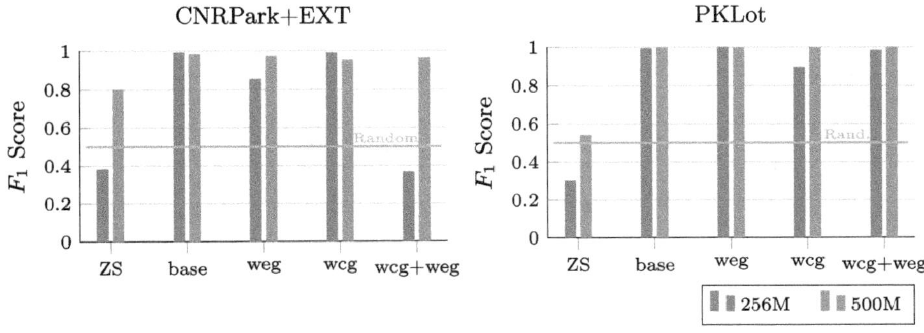

Fig. 3. Comparison of different prompt configurations with baselines.

CNRPark+EXT); and (ii) train on CNRPark+EXT and test on PKLot (denoted as *CNRPark+EXT → PKLot*). This measures domain adaptation capabilities across distinct parking lot topologies and camera setups.

5   Discussion

Figure 3 Tables 1, 2, 3, 4 and convey the main results of our experiments. Figure 2 shows qualitative inference examples of our trained models.

Zero-Shot (ZS) Performance. As shown in Fig. 3, the *Zero-Shot baseline* performance of the MLLM is consistently poor across both datasets and model sizes. For the *256M* variant, accuracy falls below that of the *Random baseline*, indicating no meaningful signal in the model's predictions. The *500M* model exhibits marginal improvement over the *Random baseline* on PKLot, while achieving notably higher, yet uncompetitive performance, on CNRPark+EXT. These results suggest limited Zero-Shot generalization capabilities, with neither size variant demonstrating practical utility without further adaptation. This outcome indicates that **SmolVLM is not suitable for Zero-Shot classification** in this domain, answering Sect. 3 (RQ1) in the negative. The likely cause is the domain mismatch: parking lot imagery differs substantially from the natural image distributions on which the MLLM was pre-trained. Consequently, instruction-tuning is required to assess the true potential of the MLLM for this task.

Ablation Study on Prompt Configurations. As illustrated in Tables 1 and 2 and Fig. 3, results indicate that prompt configurations incorporating expert or context guidance generally fail to enhance performance, with notable deterioration observed in the *256M* variant. For this size variant, *weg* yields a marginal improvement (+0.6%) exclusively on the PKLot dataset, while all other configurations degrade performance across both datasets. Notably, *wcg+weg* causes a significant performance decline for the CNRPark+EXT dataset (−62.4%),

Table 1. Ablations on prompt configurations for the *256M* size variant. Green cells indicate best performing configuration on F_1-score.

Expert guidance	Context guidance	Dataset	
		PKLot	CNRPark+EXT
✗	✗	0.992	0.99
✓	✗	0.998	0.853
✗	✓	0.895	0.988
✓	✓	0.983	0.366

Table 2. Ablations on prompt configurations for the *500M* size variant. Green cells indicate best performing configuration on F_1-score.

Expert guidance	Context guidance	Dataset	
		PKLot	CNRPark+EXT
✗	✗	0.998	0.982
✓	✗	0.998	0.971
✗	✓	0.998	0.951
✓	✓	0.997	0.961

potentially attributable to the model's limited capacity. Surprisingly, this phenomenon was not observed for the PKLot dataset. This discrepancy could stem from inherent differences in dataset complexity. PKLot, for instance, contains fewer occlusions and may represent a simpler classification task compared to CNRPark+EXT. However, the exact reasons for this contrast warrant further investigation. In contrast, the *500M* variant exhibits stagnation in the *base* configuration (lacking both expert and context guidance), for both datasets (Table 2). This suggests that larger models may inherently capture task-relevant patterns without external guidance, rendering additional prompting superfluous. These findings collectively address Sect. 3 (RQ2): **explicit guidance through prompts does not enhance SmolVLM's performance on the evaluated datasets.** The limited utility of prompt engineering here may stem from either insufficient model scale (for smaller variants) or inherent task-specific saturation in larger models, underscoring the need for scale-aware prompt design strategies in future work.

Impact of Model Size. Our analysis indicates that increasing model size yields only marginal gains in in-domain performance (i.e., train/test splits belonging to same dataset) for this specific task configuration (see Table 1 and 2). For instance, on the CNRPark-EXT dataset, the larger variant even shows a slight degradation in performance (-0.8%), suggesting a potential performance plateau. This may reflect a saturation point on the benchmark datasets, where additional parameters offer diminishing returns, possibly due to overfitting or redundancy rather than improved representational capacity. These findings suggest that the *256M* model strikes a strong balance between efficiency and accuracy for the evaluated benchmarks, making it a practical choice in resource-constrained settings. In the context of Sect. 3 (RQ3), we conclude that **scaling up SmolVLM's parameters does not strongly correlate with improved in-domain task performance**, emphasizing instead the importance of prompt design and instruction tuning.

Cross-Dataset Generalization Performance. In line with the in-domain results, our cross-dataset evaluation using *base* prompt configuration reveals that larger

Table 3. Cross-dataset evaluation of our approach using *base* prompt configuration on F_1-score.

	Model Variant	
Setting	256M	500M
PKLot → CNRPark+EXT	0.964	0.93
CNRPark+EXT → PKLot	0.97	0.968

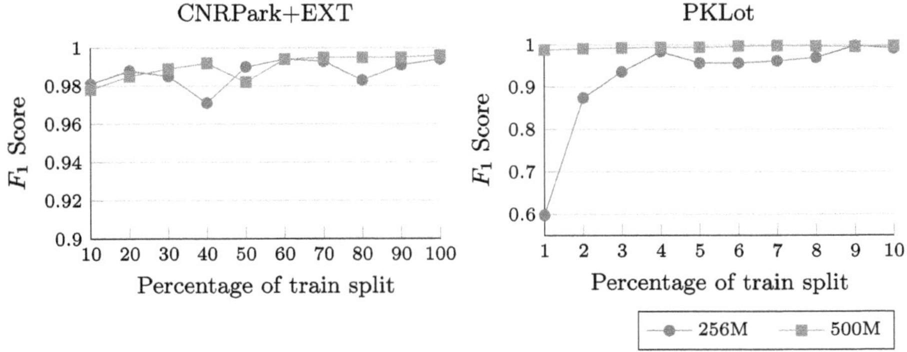

Fig. 4. Assessment of model performance by varying training data volume.

models do not necessarily exhibit improved generalization. As shown in Table 3, all models perform well, with the *500M* variant performing worse than the *256M* variant in both settings (-3.4% on *PKLot* → *CNRPark+EXT*; -0.2% on *CNRPark+EXT* → *PKLot*). This suggests that while size may not significantly impact performance on familiar data, it also does not guarantee better transfer to unseen data. This answers Sect. 3 (RQ4) affirmatively, **demonstrating robust cross-dataset generalization**. However, to extend these findings to real-world deployment, further testing across more varied and challenging datasets is warranted.

Impact of Training Data Volume. Figure 4 illustrates the relationship between the percentage of training data used and the resulting F_1 score across both the PKLot and CNRPark+EXT datasets. Notably, the scales differ between the two: due to computational constraints, the training data for PKLot was varied from 1% to 10% in 1% increments, while for CNRPark+EXT, it ranged from 10% to 100% in 10% increments. Despite the limited data ranges, all models achieve competitive performance with significantly reduced data volumes. On PKLot, the F_1 score peaks at 0.998 using just 9% and 7% of the training data for the *256M* and *500M* variants, respectively. The *500M* variant, in particular, maintains strong performance even at just 1% of the data, whereas the *256M* variant shows markedly lower performance in the 1%–3% range. On CNRPark+EXT, both variants already exceed an F_1 score of 0.97 with just 10% of the training data, with only marginal improvements thereafter. The *256M* variant peaks at

Table 4. Comparison of our approach using *base* prompt configuration with prior architectures on F_1-score, as reported in [17]. For each listed architecture, the best performing variant is chosen. Percentage gains and losses are denoted by ↑ green and ↓ red, respectively. Best performing architecture in each category is highlighted in **bold**.

Category	Architecture	Dataset	
		PKLot	CNRPark+EXT
Transformer-based	ViT	**0.997**	**0.919**
	DeiT	0.993	0.890
	PiT	0.982	0.908
CNN-based	AlexNet	**0.999**	0.956
	CFEN	0.997	0.848
	VGG	**0.999**	0.963
	ResNet50	0.993	0.938
	MobileNet	**0.999**	0.966
	CarNet	0.998	0.933
	EfficientNet	**0.999**	**0.968**
MLLM-based	SmolVLM-256M (Ours)	**0.998** ↓0.1%	0.994 ↑2.6%
	SmolVLM-500M (Ours)	**0.998** ↓0.1%	**0.996** ↑2.8%

an F_1 score of 0.994 using 60% of the data, while the *500M* variant reaches its peak at 100%, though the gain over 60% is a mere 0.1%. These results collectively demonstrate that **despite using as little as 9% of PKLot and 60% of CNRPark+EXT training data, fine-tuned variants of SmolVLM achieve competitive or superior performance.**

Comparison with Prior Architectures. We also compare our approach against prior CNN and ViT based architectures, as reported by Martynova et al. [17]. Results across model size and dataset are summarized in Table 4. On the PKLot dataset, performance appears saturated, with prior architectures achieving up to 99.9% accuracy. Our approach is a close second, reaching just 0.1% below the best-reported result. In contrast, for the more challenging CNRPark+EXT dataset, our method outperforms previous architectures, with gains of +2.6% and +2.8% on the previously best-reported score, for the *256M* and *500M* variants, respectively. While these earlier CNN and ViT based models retain an advantage in inference and model complexity, our MLLM-based approach offers notable benefits in task adaptability and data efficiency.

6 Conclusions

This work introduces the first benchmark evaluation of efficient MLLMs for parking occupancy detection, offering baseline metrics and instruction-tuned datasets to drive progress in this domain. Our findings reveal that Zero-Shot SmolVLM performance is inadequate for this task, but fine-tuned variants trained on only fractions of available data achieve competitive or superior results to prior approaches. Interestingly, model scaling and prompt engineering offer limited gains, while cross-dataset generalization remains strong. Future work will investigate performance under more stringent data constraints and evaluate on less saturated benchmarks. Our findings advocate for broader adoption of efficient MLLMs in edge-computing applications for smart urban management.

Acknowledgments. This project is supported by the Federal Ministry for Economic Affairs and Climate Action (BMWK) on the basis of a decision by the German Budenstag (FK 16KN113522 SPUR-OPT), and by the Research School on "Service-Oriented Systems Engineering" of Hasso Plattner Institute, Potsdam, Germany.

References

1. de Almeida, P.R.L., Oliveira, L.S., Britto, A.S., Silva, E.J., Koerich, A.L.: PKLot – a robust dataset for parking lot classification. Expert Syst. Appl. **42**(11), 4937–4949 (2015). https://doi.org/10.1016/j.eswa.2015.02.009
2. Amato, G., Carrara, F., Falchi, F., Gennaro, C., Meghini, C., Vairo, C.: Deep learning for decentralized parking lot occupancy detection. Expert Syst. Appl. **72**, 327–334 (2017). https://doi.org/10.1016/j.eswa.2016.10.055
3. Amato, G., Carrara, F., Falchi, F., Gennaro, C., Vairo, C.: Car parking occupancy detection using smart camera networks and deep learning. In: 2016 IEEE Symposium on Computers and Communication (ISCC), pp. 1212–1217 (2016). https://doi.org/10.1109/ISCC.2016.7543901
4. Bura, H., Lin, N., Kumar, N., Malekar, S., Nagaraj, S., Liu, K.: An edge based smart parking solution using camera networks and deep learning. In: 2018 IEEE International Conference on Cognitive Computing (ICCC), pp. 17–24 (2018). https://doi.org/10.1109/ICCC.2018.00010
5. Cai, B.Y., Alvarez, R., Sit, M., Duarte, F., Ratti, C.: Deep learning-based video system for accurate and real-time parking measurement. IEEE Internet Things J. **6**(5), 7693–7701 (2019). https://doi.org/10.1109/JIOT.2019.2902887
6. Chu, X., et al.: MobileVLM : A Fast, Strong and Open Vision Language Assistant for Mobile Devices (2023). https://doi.org/10.48550/arXiv.2312.16886, http://arxiv.org/abs/2312.16886, arXiv:2312.16886 [cs]
7. Farley, A., Ham, H., Hendra: Real time IP camera parking occupancy detection using deep learning. Procedia Comput. Sci. **179**, 606–614 (2021). https://doi.org/10.1016/j.procs.2021.01.046
8. Goumiri, S., Benboudjema, D., Pieczynski, W.: One convolutional layer model for parking occupancy detection. In: 2021 IEEE International Smart Cities Conference (ISC2), pp. 1–5 (2021). https://doi.org/10.1109/ISC253183.2021.9562946, iSSN: 2687-8860
9. Hu, E.J., et al.: Lora: low-rank adaptation of large language models. In: The Tenth International Conference on Learning Representations (ICLR). OpenReview.net (2022). https://openreview.net/forum?id=nZeVKeeFYf9
10. Jin, Y., et al.: Efficient multimodal large language models: a survey. arXiv preprint arXiv:2405.10739 (2024)

11. Kročka, M., Dakić, P., Vranić, V.: Extending parking occupancy detection model for night lighting and snowy weather conditions. In: 2022 IEEE Zooming Innovation in Consumer Technologies Conference (ZINC), pp. 203–208 (2022). https://doi.org/10.1109/ZINC55034.2022.9840556

12. Li, B., et al.: LLaVA-OneVision: Easy Visual Task Transfer (2024). https://doi.org/10.48550/arXiv.2408.03326, http://arxiv.org/abs/2408.03326, arXiv:2408.03326 [cs]

13. Li, Y., Wang, C., Jia, J.: LLaMA-VID: an image is worth 2 tokens in large language models. In: Computer Vision – ECCV 2024, pp. 323–340. Springer (2025). https://doi.org/10.1007/978-3-031-72952-2_19

14. Liu, H., Li, C., Wu, Q., Lee, Y.J.: Visual instruction tuning. In: Advances in Neural Information Processing Systems 36: Annual Conference on Neural Information Processing Systems 2023 (NeurIPS) (2023). http://papers.nips.cc/paper_files/paper/2023/hash/6dcf277ea32ce3288914faf369fe6de0-Abstract-Conference.html

15. Ludwisiak, T., Mazur-Milecka, M.: Automated parking management for urban efficiency: a comprehensive approach. In: 2024 16th International Conference on Human System Interaction (HSI), pp. 1–4 (2024). https://doi.org/10.1109/HSI61632.2024.10613584, iSSN: 2158-2254

16. Marafioti, A., et al.: SmolVLM: redefining small and efficient multimodal models (2025). https://doi.org/10.48550/arXiv.2504.05299, http://arxiv.org/abs/2504.05299, arXiv:2504.05299 [cs]

17. Martynova, A., et al.: Revising deep learning methods in parking lot occupancy detection (2024). https://doi.org/10.48550/arXiv.2306.04288, http://arxiv.org/abs/2306.04288, arXiv:2306.04288 [cs]

18. Màrmol, E., Sevillano, X.: QuickSpot: a video analytics solution for on-street vacant parking spot detection. Multimedia Tools Appl. **75**(24), 17711–17743 (2016). https://doi.org/10.1007/s11042-016-3773-8

19. Nyambal, J., Klein, R.: Automated parking space detection using convolutional neural networks. In: 2017 Pattern Recognition Association of South Africa and Robotics and Mechatronics (PRASA-RobMech), pp. 1–6 (2017). https://doi.org/10.1109/RoboMech.2017.8261114

20. Tschentscher, M., Koch, C., König, M., Salmen, J., Schlipsing, M.: Scalable real-time parking lot classification: an evaluation of image features and supervised learning algorithms. In: 2015 International Joint Conference on Neural Networks (IJCNN), pp. 1–8 (2015). https://doi.org/10.1109/IJCNN.2015.7280319, iSSN: 2161-4407

21. Xu, L., Xie, H., Qin, S.J., Tao, X., Wang, F.L.: Parameter-efficient fine-tuning methods for pretrained language models: a critical review and assessment. CoRR abs/2312.12148 (2023). https://doi.org/10.48550/ARXIV.2312.12148

22. Yao, Y., et al.: MiniCPM-V: A GPT-4V Level MLLM on Your Phone (2024). https://doi.org/10.48550/arXiv.2408.01800, http://arxiv.org/abs/2408.01800, arXiv:2408.01800 [cs]

23. Yu, Y.Q., Liao, M., Wu, J., Liao, Y., Zheng, X., Zeng, W.: TextHawk: Exploring Efficient Fine-Grained Perception of Multimodal Large Language Models (2024). https://doi.org/10.48550/arXiv.2404.09204, http://arxiv.org/abs/2404.09204, arXiv:2404.09204 [cs]

24. Zhu, J., et al.: InternVL3: Exploring Advanced Training and Test-Time Recipes for Open-Source Multimodal Models (2025). https://doi.org/10.48550/arXiv.2504.10479, http://arxiv.org/abs/2504.10479, arXiv:2504.10479 [cs]

SAP-DQR: Joining Spatial-Adaptive Pyramid and Adaptive Query Reorganization for Speed-Accuracy Instance Segmentation

Jiahao Zou[1], Congxuan Zhang[1,2]($\boxtimes$), Liyue Ge[1], Chao He[1], Jiawen Yang[2], Zhen Chen[1,2], and Ke Lu[3]

[1] Key Laboratory of Image Processing and Pattern Recognition, Nanchang Hangkong University, Nanchang, China
`zcxdsg@163.com`

[2] School of Instrument Science and Optoelectronic Engineering, Nanchang Hangkong University, Nanchang, China

[3] School of Engineering Science, University of Chinese Academy of Sciences, Beijing, China

Abstract. Instance segmentation plays a vital role in practical applications, including autonomous driving and robotic vision. Among deep learning methods, query-based approaches have recently attracted significant attention due to their effectiveness in building end-to-end pipelines that eliminate complex post-processing steps. However, existing methods often fail to strike an optimal balance between accuracy and real-time performance. To address this challenge, we propose SAP-DQR, a framework integrating Spatial-Adaptive Pyramid features and Adaptive Query Reorganization to optimize the speed-accuracy trade-off. First, we design a Spatial-Adaptive Pyramid Feature Network (SAP-FPN) that integrates Asymmetric and Separable Multi-scale Pooling (ASMP) and Spatial-Channel Grouped Fusion (SCG). This design significantly accelerates and improves the efficiency of multi-scale feature processing. Additionally, we introduce a novel lightweight Global Semantic-guided Multi-stage Adaptive Query Reorganization (GSMR) mechanism that effectively provides finer-grained, higher-quality adaptive queries for various decoder stages. Our method is the first ResNet-50-based approach to surpass 40 AP on COCO while achieving real-time inference ($\geq$30 FPS), delivering an optimal speed-accuracy trade-off for latency-sensitive applications like autonomous driving. It significantly outperforms current mainstream methods, setting a new state-of-the-art for real-time instance segmentation with optimized speed-accuracy trade-off.

Keywords: Instance segmentation · real time · speed-accuracy trade-off

J. Lokoč et al. (Eds.): MMM 2026, LNCS 16412, pp. 175–188, 2026.
https://doi.org/10.1007/978-981-95-6950-2_13

1 Introduction

Instance segmentation, as a fundamental task in computer vision, plays a critical role in real-time applications that demand a precise balance between speed and accuracy, such as autonomous driving and robotic perception. Early mainstream approaches—such as Mask R-CNN [11,16] and its variants—rely on a two-stage detect-then-segment paradigm, where multiple region proposals are first generated, followed by instance segmentation within each bounding box. Although this approach is conceptually straightforward, the repetitive generation of region proposals leads to significant computational redundancy, which severely limits efficiency for real-time processing.

Aiming to address this bottleneck, researchers have proposed single-stage methods based on Fully Convolutional Networks (FCNs), such as SOLO [26] and SOLOv2 [27]. These methods directly predict instance masks on feature maps through encoder-decoder architectures, eliminating the need for explicit region proposals. The simplified pipeline facilitates competitive inference speeds, making these methods suitable for real-time scenarios. However, inherent limitations arise from the pixel-wise dense prediction framework, and these approaches still rely on manually designed post-processing steps—such as Non-Maximum Suppression (NMS)—to eliminate overlapping predictions. This dependence restricts the ability to optimize model accuracy and speed simultaneously.

With the goal of realizing end-to-end solutions without complex post-processing, Transformer-based architectures [1,2,31] have recently garnered increasing attention. Transformers have achieved remarkable success across various computer vision tasks. For instance, instance segmentation models leveraging this architecture (e.g., Mask2Former [3]) have substantially improved segmentation accuracy by utilizing attention mechanisms and learnable queries. Nevertheless, the deep and multi-level designs characteristic of these models impose significant computational costs, which result in increased inference latency and limit their suitability for real-time applications.

Efforts to reconcile accuracy and efficiency have motivated the development of real-time instance segmentation methods. FastInst [10], for example, enhances inference speed through dynamic query generation, dual-path collaborative optimization, and ground-truth mask guidance. Despite these advantages, FastInst still faces two main limitations: (1) its PPM-FPN structure relies on element-wise summation for feature fusion, providing only basic spatial alignment and lacking strong cross-scale semantic correlation necessary for effective multi-level contextual information integration; (2) queries in the decoder layers are progressively refined from initial learnable queries along a single path, resulting in an over-reliance on iterative attention-based refinement. This single-path evolution limits the adaptability of query representations to the diverse needs of different decoder stages, where earlier stages benefit from global semantic guidance while later stages emphasize capturing local details. These constraints hinder FastInst's ability to obtain rich contextual information and restrict query representation flexibility during multi-stage decoding.

Addressing the challenges inherent in real-time query-based instance segmentation and balancing speed with accuracy, this paper introduces the SAP-DQR framework. Our key contributions are as follows:

(1) We propose the Spatially Adaptive Pyramid Feature Network (SAP-FPN), which effectively models long-range spatial dependencies and broadens the contextual receptive field through Asymmetric Separable Multi-scale Pooling (ASMP). Additionally, SAP-FPN employs Spatial-Channel Grouped Fusion (SCG) to dynamically modulate cross-scale features.
(2) We develop the Global Semantic-Guided Multi-stage Adaptive Query Reorganization (GSMR), which combines learnable query groups with layer-aware weighting and incorporates a progressive reorganization mechanism to reduce reliance on extensive iterative updates.
(3) Extensive experiments validate the effectiveness and efficiency of our framework. On benchmarks like MS COCO 2017 [18] and Cityscapes [7], SAP-DQR demonstrates an optimal speed-accuracy balance. **Remarkably, it sets a new state-of-the-art as the first ResNet-50-based real-time method ($\geq$30 FPS) to surpass 40 AP on COCO.** The speed-accuracy trade-off on the COCO test-dev dataset is illustrated in Fig. 1, where SAP-DQR clearly surpasses state-of-the-art methods, further validating the effectiveness of our approach.

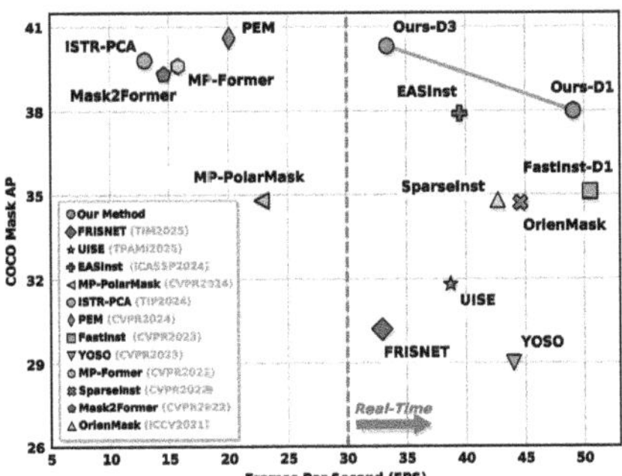

Fig. 1. Speed-Accuracy trade-off on COCO test-dev.

2   Related Work

Instance segmentation has rapidly evolved over recent years, driven by diverse methodologies that can be generally grouped into three principal categories. These categories reflect different paradigms in balancing accuracy, speed, and computational efficiency, each with its unique strengths and limitations.

Region-based methods adhere to the detect-then-segment paradigm, first generating object proposals and then predicting masks for each proposal. Representative works include Mask R-CNN [11], which innovatively introduced RoIAlign for improved accuracy; PANet [24], which enhanced multi-scale feature integration; and Mask Scoring R-CNN [16], which further optimized mask quality assessment. However, their reliance on explicit region proposal generation and per-region processing leads to significant computational redundancy, severely limiting inference speed and hindering real-time applications.

Instance activation-based methods abandon explicit region proposal generation, instead directly activating instance mask prediction by locating key pixels. Representative works include SOLO [26,27], which decouples instance segmentation into location classification and mask generation, though its grid-based mechanism can cause overlaps in dense object scenes; CondInst [23], which employs conditional convolution for dynamic mask generation; and SparseInst [5], which uses a sparse activation strategy. While proposal-free, these pixel-level or sparse predictions often require post-processing like Non-Maximum Suppression (NMS) to remove redundancies, remaining a performance bottleneck.

Query-based methods represent instances as sparse embedded queries and train them end-to-end via set prediction, thereby completely eliminating NMS post-processing. Representative works include Mask2Former [3,4], featuring a mask attention decoder that unifies prediction tasks, and SOLQ [8], which employs dense query embeddings. While generally achieving excellent performance, their complex decoder structures often limit inference speed. Recent methods like FastInst [10] have made significant strides in real-time performance through various optimizations. However, limitations in its internal feature aggregation efficiency and adaptive query optimization hinder the full exploitation of the model's accuracy potential. This paper aims to address these core issues to achieve an efficient balance between accuracy and speed.

3   Method

3.1   Overall Architecture

As shown in Fig. 2, the overall model architecture comprises a Backbone, a Pixel Decoder, and a Transformer Decoder. Feature maps $\{S_3, S_4, S_5\}$ from the last three Backbone stages are fed into the Pixel Decoder. This Pixel Decoder is implemented by our proposed Spatially Adaptive Pyramid Feature Network (SAP-FPN), which outputs enhanced multi-scale feature maps $\{E_3, E_4, E_5\}$ by aggregating contextual information from the Backbone's multi-scale features $\{S_3, S_4, S_5\}$. Subsequently, the Global Semantic-Guided Multi-stage Adaptive Query Reorganization (GSMR) module uses feature map E_4 to extract global semantic information and generates stage-specific adaptive queries Q_{re}^l for each decoding stage l ($l = 1, 2, \ldots, L - 1$). Then, each stage's adaptive query Q_{re}^l is recombined with the output query Q^l from the previous decoding stage to form the stage-specific reconstructed query Q_{red}^l. Finally, the Transformer Decoder processes the interactively updated pixel features from E_3 and the current stage's reconstructed query Q^l_{red}, producing the prediction results.

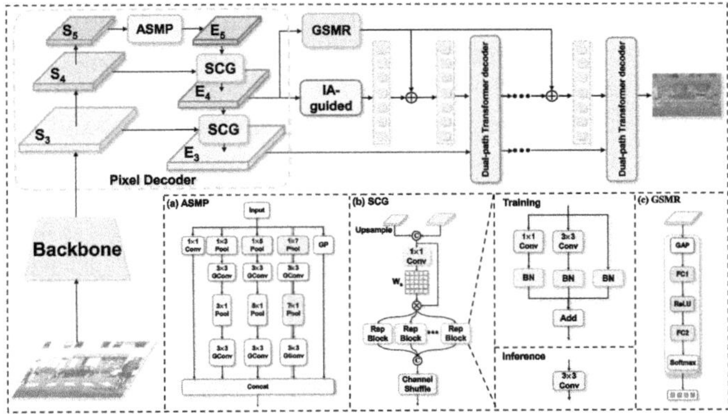

Fig. 2. Model Overview. SAP-DQR consists of three components: backbone, pixel decoder and Transformer decoder.

3.2 Spatial-Adaptive Pyramid Feature Network

The pixel decoder plays a critical role in extracting multi-scale features for precise segmentation. To significantly enhance feature representation capabilities while maintaining high efficiency, thereby optimizing the speed-accuracy trade-off for instance segmentation, we propose the Spatial-Adaptive Pyramid Feature Network (SAP-FPN). This network is designed to overcome the inherent limitations of existing pixel decoders (such as FastInst's PPM-FPN) in balancing large receptive fields with computational efficiency and fully integrating cross-scale semantic information to improve accuracy. Its core lies in two innovations that enable efficient yet precise multi-scale feature extraction, thereby substantially accelerating the entire inference process and boosting segmentation performance. First, we design the ASMP module, which uses asymmetric kernels combined with a global pooling branch to capture cross-scale contextual relationships, significantly reducing computational burden while effectively expanding contextual awareness. Second, we develop the SCG module, which synergistically enhances feature interaction via feature modulation guided by spatial attention weights and grouped reparameterized convolution, thereby markedly improving feature fusion effectiveness while maintaining efficient inference.

Asymmetric and Separable Multi-scale Pooling. The Pyramid Pooling Module (PPM) [5] typically constructs global scene representations using multi-scale square pooling. However, enlarging square pooling kernels to capture large-scale spatial context greatly increases computational complexity, challenging real-time performance. To address this efficiency bottleneck of traditional square pooling, especially given the S_5 feature map's rich semantics and smallest resolution, this paper proposes the Asymmetric and Separable Multi-scale Pooling (ASMP) module, inspired by separable convolution [12]. Applied specifically to the top-level S_5 feature map, ASMP is designed to achieve an optimal speed-accuracy balance by employing asymmetric pooling kernels and lightweight, separable operations to build efficient long-range horizontal and vertical correlations. This design significantly reduces computational overhead for multi-scale feature processing, accelerating inference, while effectively expanding spatial context and enriching feature representation for enhanced accuracy in capturing intricate details. ASMP comprises three asymmetric pooling layers of different sizes and a global average pooling layer. After pooling, Grouped Convolution (GConv) is introduced for further lightweight feature processing. Concurrently, a 1×1 grouped convolution compresses the S_5 feature map channels to preserve crucial texture information for precise segmentation. Finally, the processed multi-scale feature maps are concatenated, yielding a computationally efficient and semantically rich representation, underpinning our speed-accuracy optimized instance segmentation approach.

Spatial-Channel Grouped Fusion. As shown in Fig. 2(b), the SCG module adopts three core design principles to efficiently fuse cross-layer features and address cross-scale semantic correlation, optimizing model speed-accuracy. First, it employs a spatial focusing mechanism: a 1×1 convolution followed by Sigmoid generates a spatial attention map, enhancing feature responses in key regions for improved accuracy. Second, a grouped reparameterization strategy divides feature maps into n (default $n = 4$) channel groups for parallel processing. Each group utilizes a RepVGG-style structure, combining 3×3 and 1×1 convolutions during training which reparameterize into a single convolutional layer for faster inference while maintaining feature diversity. Finally, a channel reorganization mechanism introduces a shuffle operation to enhance inter-group channel information interaction. This synergistic design effectively improves cross-scale semantic feature modeling and accuracy, concurrently ensuring computational efficiency, embodying our speed-accuracy optimized approach.

3.3 Global Semantic-Guided Multi-stage Adaptive Query Reorganization

Object queries play a pivotal role in Transformer architectures, fundamentally influencing both segmentation accuracy and the overall efficiency of instance segmentation models. Taking the classic DETR model [1] as an example, object queries are initialized as a set of learnable parameter vectors $Q^0 \in \mathbb{R}^{N \times C}$, which iteratively evolve through a series of decoder layers during decoding (as illustrated in Fig. 3(a)). However, this layer-by-layer evolution design, relying on a single initial query Q^0, presents significant limitations: it mainly depends on Self-Attention and Cross-Attention mechanisms to progressively refine the input queries Q^l based on the initial vector Q^0. This effectively means the query evolution in each decoder layer follows a fixed, single evolutionary path. Notably, different decoder layers typically perform distinct tasks—for example, earlier layers focus on identifying object semantic categories and coarse location, while later layers emphasize fine-grained bounding box refinement. Consequently, query representations require differentiated feature granularity and semantic focus across layers to achieve optimal segmentation performance. However, within this single-path evolution paradigm, relying solely on progressively refining initial queries may lack the flexibility and capacity to sufficiently adapt query representations to these varying demands as decoding depth increases, thereby limiting the potential for a truly speed-accuracy optimized solution in query-based segmentation.

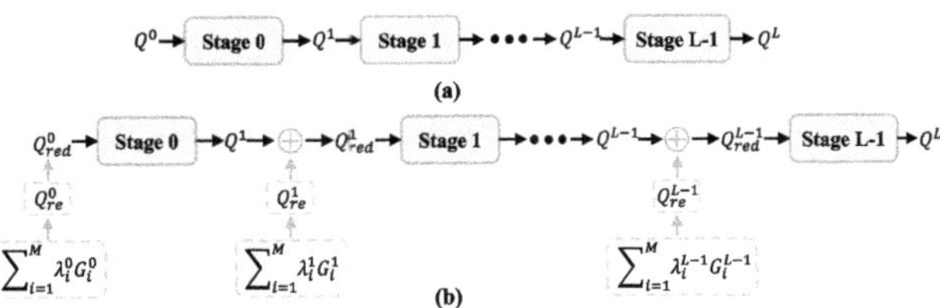

Fig. 3. Different query update methods.(a) Typical method. (b) GSMR.

To overcome the aforementioned limitations, as shown in Fig. 2(c), we propose the GSMR method. This network first applies Global Average Pooling (GAP) to the feature maps output by the encoder. Subsequently, a two-stage Fully Connected (FC) layer with ReLU activations performs a non-linear transformation to generate a high-dimensional vector F, as shown in Eq. (1):

$$F = \mathrm{ReLU}\left(W_2^\top \mathrm{ReLU}\left(W_1^\top \mathrm{GAP}(E_4)\right)\right) \tag{1}$$

Then, F is partitioned into k group vectors $F^l \in \mathbb{R}^M$ for $l = 0, \ldots, L - 1$. A temperature-scaled Softmax function (temperature $\tau = 30$) is applied to each group F^l to generate the stage-aware weight vector λ^l:

$$\lambda_i^l = \frac{\exp(F_i^l/\tau)}{\sum_{j=1}^M \exp(F_j^l/\tau)}, \quad l = 0, \ldots, L - 1; \quad i = 1, \ldots, M \tag{2}$$

Concurrently, as shown in Fig. 3(b), we construct k multi-layer learnable query groups $G^l = \{G_i^l\}_{i=1}^M$ for $l = 0, \ldots, L - 1$. At the start of decoding stage l, the initial object query for slot i is generated by the linear combination:

$$Q_{\mathrm{re}}^l = \sum_{i=1}^M \lambda_i^l G_i^l, \quad l = 0, \ldots, L - 1; \quad i = 1, \ldots, M \tag{3}$$

These initial stage queries are then fused with the output queries from the previous decoder stage through a progressive reorganization mechanism:

$$Q_{\mathrm{red}}^l = Q^l + Q_{\mathrm{re}}^l, \quad l = 0, \ldots, L - 1 \tag{4}$$

4 Experiments

This section evaluates the performance and inference speed of the proposed method on the COCO 2017 [18] and Cityscapes [7] datasets. We compare it with several existing state-of-the-art methods; unless otherwise specified, comparison data are taken from results reported in their original papers. Furthermore, we analyze the effectiveness of each key design through detailed ablation studies.

4.1 Dataset and Evaluation Metrics

COCO 2017 [18] is an instance segmentation dataset comprising approximately 123k images, covering 80 categories. Among these, 118k images are used for training, 5k for validation, and 20k for testing. Cityscapes [7] features 19 distinct categories found in urban environments, further subdivided into 8 stuff and 11 thing categories. We choose Average Precision (AP) and Frames Per Second (FPS) as evaluation metrics. Based on the Intersection-over-Union (IoU) ratio and object size, AP is further broken down into AP^{50}, AP^{75}, AP^{S}, AP^{M}, and AP^{L}.

4.2 Implementation Details

Our implementation is based on Detectron2 [28] and trained with the AdamW optimizer [20], using an initial learning rate of 1×10^{-4} and weight decay of 0.05. A step learning rate decay reduces the rate by a factor of 0.1 at 90% and 95% of the total 50 training epochs (batch size 16). The backbone network (ImageNet pretrained) uses an initial learning rate of 0.1. For data augmentation, we adopt scale jittering and random cropping from FastInst [10], scaling input images so the shorter side lies within [416, 640] pixels while limiting the longer side to 864 pixels. Loss weights λ_{cls}, λ_{ce}, and λ_{dice} are set to 2.0, 5.0, and 5.0, respectively, with λ_{clsq} and λ_{loc} set to 20.0 and 1000.0. Performance is evaluated by Average Precision (AP) and Frames Per Second (FPS), measured on an NVIDIA A100 GPU over the entire validation set with batch size 1. Unless otherwise specified, all tests and benchmarks use an input short side resolution of 640 pixels.

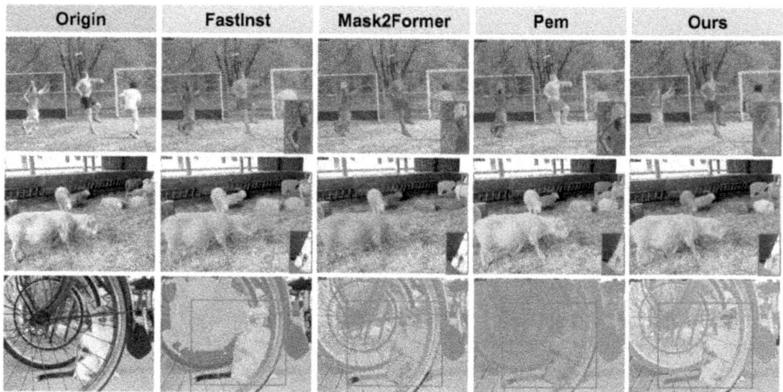

Fig. 4. Comparison of segmentation results on the COCO dataset.

Table 1. Instance Segmentation on COCO test-dev. We mark the best performance in **bold** and the second-best underlined. † denotes a light version of the Mask2Former series models that under consistent decoder layer counts. Ours-Dα represents our models with α Transformer decoder layers.

	Method	Backbone	FPS	AP	AP^{50}	AP^{75}	AP^S	AP^M	AP^L
Real-Time Models	OrienMask [9]	Darknet-53	42.7	34.8	56.7	36.4	16.0	38.2	47.8
	SparseInst [6]	R50	44.6	34.7	55.3	36.6	14.3	36.2	50.7
	FastInst-D1 [10]	R50	**50.5**	35.1	56.8	36.4	16.0	38.2	53.9
	YOSO [14]	R50	44.0	29.0	47.0	29.9	6.4	29.5	55.4
	EASInst [29]	Searched	39.5	37.9	57.7	39.7	15.9	39.5	56.8
	MP-PolarMask [25]	R101	22.8	34.8	57.8	35.9	15.4	37.2	51.1
	FRISNET [30]	R-101-FBiFPN	32.94	30.2	49.1	31.5	10	31.6	48.4
	UISE [13]	R50	38.7	31.8	51.2	33.0	10.0	33.4	**58.0**
	Ours-D1	R50	49.1	**38.0**	**59.3**	**39.9**	**17.5**	**41.3**	56.8
Accuracy Models	Mask2Former † [3]	R50	14.6	39.3	60.4	42.0	18.8	42.6	60.0
	MP-Former † [31]	R50	15.8	39.6	60.6	43.2	18.6	42.8	60.6
	ISTR-PCA [15]	R50	13.0	39.8	-	-	**23.2**	42.1	51.1
	PEM † [2]	R50	20.1	**40.6**	**62.2**	**43.6**	20.5	**44.0**	**60.9**
	Ours-D3	R50	**33.4**	40.3	62.1	42.9	19.7	43.6	60.4

4.3   Main Result

Instance Segmentation on COCO2017. As shown in Table 1, we systematically evaluate the performance of our proposed method against existing state-of-the-art solutions on the COCO dataset. Unless otherwise specified, all comparative data are obtained from results published in relevant papers or their official open-source code under standard settings. To explore the model's potential in the speed-accuracy trade-off, we test configurations with varying numbers of Transformer decoder layers, demonstrating that our method meets real-time requirements and achieves a better balance between accuracy and speed. For a fair comparison among real-time algorithms, we reproduce FastInst's performance using its official code and configuration under the same A100 experimental environment to obtain accurate comparative data. Under the ResNet-50 backbone, our D1 model achieves higher segmentation accuracy (AP) while maintaining comparable inference speed (FPS) to FastInst-D1. Meanwhile, it significantly outperforms UISE in both accuracy (AP) and speed (FPS). These results fully demonstrate that our model surpasses most existing real-time instance segmentation methods in terms of both performance and speed. Comparing our D3 model with Mask2Former series models under the same ResNet-50 backbone and consistent decoder layer counts (aligned with our D3 configuration), results show that our D3 model exhibits a significant advantage in inference speed (FPS) while maintaining comparable segmentation accuracy. Furthermore, for qualitative analysis, as shown in Fig. 4, we provide visualizations of FastInst, Mask2Former, PEM, and our method on the COCO dataset. It can be observed that our model demonstrates excellent performance. Notably, although PEM may have higher overall accuracy, our method outperforms it in occluded scenes. This proves that our method can effectively guarantee real-time performance ($\geq$30 FPS) while meeting the accuracy requirements of practical applications, demonstrating excellent engineering practicality. Importantly, experiments show that, based on the ResNet-50 backbone, our method achieves high segmentation accuracy (AP > 40) while maintaining a smooth real-time rate ($\geq$30 FPS). To our knowledge, this is currently the only publicly available method achieving such a comprehensive performance balance in real-time instance segmentation, setting a new SOTA record in this field.

Table 2. Performance comparison on Cityscapes test set. We mark the best performance in **bold** and the second-best underlined.

Method	Backbone	FPS	AP	AP^{50}
CenterPoly [22]	HG104	22.2	15.5	39.5
CenterPolV2 [19]	HG104	22.3	16.6	39.5
DeepSnake [21]	HG104	2.2	<u>31.7</u>	<u>58.4</u>
FastInst-D1 [10]	R50	**31.2**	30.1	54.7
YOSO [14]	R50	11.1	26.8	48.7
UISE [13]	R50	11.1	27.3	49.6
Ours-D1	R50	<u>30.5</u>	**32.6**	**59.4**

Instance Segmentation on Cityscapes. Experiments on the Cityscapes dataset (Table 2) demonstrate a breakthrough in real-time instance segmentation: our ResNet-50-based SAP-DQR-D1 model achieves the highest segmentation accuracy among current methods while maintaining a real-time speed of 30.5 FPS. This result indicates that the model successfully overcomes the accuracy bottleneck under strict real-time constraints. Furthermore, our model exceeds UISE and YOSO in both accuracy and speed. In summary, in dynamic urban scenarios such as Cityscapes, our method effectively balances the two critical practical demands of high-precision segmentation and efficient real-time inference.

Table 3. Effect of GSMR and SAP

	FPS	AP	AP^{50}	AP^{75}	AP^S	AP^M	AP^L
baseline	**34.7**	38.1	59.6	39.8	17.5	40.7	58.8
b+GSMR	34.3	39.2	61.0	41.3	18.6	41.9	59.4
b+SAP-FPN	34.0	40.1	61.2	42.4	19.0	43.3	59.9
all	33.4	**40.4**	**62.3**	**42.9**	**19.8**	**43.5**	**60.3**

4.4 Ablation Studies

This section presents ablation studies conducted on the COCO val2017 dataset. First, we validate the effectiveness of key components (see Table 3): adding GSMR alone improves AP by 1.1 over the baseline; adding SAP-FPN alone increases AP by 2.0; when both modules are combined, AP further improves to 40.4, while inference speed decreases by only 1.3 FPS. These results demonstrate the effectiveness and complementarity of the two module designs, laying the foundation for in-depth analysis of each module's internal design and impact. Based on this, we perform: (1) detailed ablation experiments on internal components of GSMR and SAP-FPN to analyze contributions of different sub-structures; (2) comparative experiments with similar modules to verify the designn's superiority.

Table 4. Ablation Study on SAP-FPN

	FPS	AP	AP^{50}	AP^{75}	AP^S	AP^M	AP^L
baseline	**34.7**	37.9	59.0	39.5	16.0	40.7	60.1
b+SCG	34.3	39.5	60.8	41.5	18.2	42.1	61.0
b+ASMP	34.5	38.7	59.8	40.5	17.1	41.1	60.5
all	34.0	**40.1**	**61.2**	**42.4**	**19.0**	**43.3**	**61.6**

SAP-FPN. Integrating Spatial Context Guidance (SCG) and Asymmetric Separable Multi-scale Pooling (ASMP), SAP-FPN demonstrates significant synergistic enhancement effects in ablation studies (Table 4). The complete architecture with both components achieves 40.1 AP, improving by 0.6 and 1.4 AP compared to the variants with individual submodules, and increasing by 2.2 AP over the baseline PPM-FPN. Notably, the small-object AP_s reaches 19.0. This validates the complementarity and synergy of the two components in optimizing multi-scale features. Further comparative experiments with similar modules (Table 5) demonstrate that SAP-FPN achieves state-of-the-art instance segmentation accuracy while maintaining high frame rates, establishing its advantage in accuracy-efficiency balance.

Table 5. Comparison of Pixel Decoders

	FPS	FLOPs	AP	AP^S	AP^M	AP^L
FPN [17]	**35.7**	**75.4G**	37.4	15.5	40.3	59.4
Transformer-Encoder [1]	29.5	78.5G	38.9	17.3	41.6	61.4
MSDeformAttn [32]	21.2	114.7G	40.0	17.5	**43.5**	**62.2**
PPM-FPN [6]	34.7	75.5G	37.9	16.0	40.7	60.1
SAP-FPN	33.4	75.9G	**40.4**	**19.8**	**43.5**	60.3

Table 6. Impact of Number of Groups (M)

M	FPS	AP	AP^{S}	AP^{M}	AP^{L}
2	**33.5**	39.9	18.0	41.7	59.8
4	**33.5**	40.1	18.1	**43.6**	**60.3**
6	33.4	**40.4**	**19.8**	43.5	**60.3**
8	33.2	40.0	18.2	42.4	60.1

Table 7. Comparison of Query Generation Methods

	FPS	FLOPs	AP	AP^{S}	AP^{M}	AP^{L}
zero [1]	**36.1**	**74.3G**	37.2	15.4	40.3	58.6
learnable [3]	**36.1**	**74.3G**	37.5	15.0	40.6	59.0
IA-guided [10]	35.5	75.5G	37.9	16.0	40.7	60.1
GSMR	33.4	75.7G	**40.4**	**19.8**	**43.5**	**60.3**

GSMR. The intra-group ablation study investigates the impact of parameter m, which controls the number of adaptive query groups; all variants use the same training strategy. Results show that $m = 6$ yields the best performance (Table 6). Comparative experiments with similar modules further verify the superiority of GSMR. As shown in Table 7, under a configuration with three decoding layers, GSMR achieves 40.4 AP, significantly outperforming zero-initialized query-based methods [1] and learned query-based methods [3]. Meanwhile, compared with the best-performing IA-guided method among the baselines, GSMR improves AP by 2.3 while only reducing inference speed by 1.3 FPS, demonstrating a better accuracy-efficiency balance.

5 Conclusion

This study presented SAP-DQR, a novel framework designed to achieve an optimal speed-accuracy balance in real-time instance segmentation. Through its efficient Spatial-Adaptive Pyramid Feature Network (SAP-FPN) and lightweight Global Semantic-guided Multi-stage Adaptive Query Reorganization (GSMR) modules, SAP-DQR rigorously optimizes multi-scale feature extraction and query generation. This unique approach establishes a new state-of-the-art (SOTA) for real-time instance segmentation, becoming the first ResNet-50-based solution to achieve real-time 40 AP on COCO, alongside excellent results on Cityscapes. Ultimately, SAP-DQR offers a robust and practical solution by uniquely optimizing speed and accuracy for real-time applications.

Acknowledgments. This work was supported in part by the National Natu-ral Science Foundation of China (62222206, U2441241, 62272209, and 62401243), the Natural Science Foundation Youth FundProgram of Jiangxi Province (20242BAB212003), the Jiangxi Province Natural Science Foundation (20242BAB20048, 20252BAC240010), and the Innovation Fund Designated for Graduate Students of Jiangxi Province (YC2024-S621).

References

1. Carion, N., Massa, F., Synnaeve, G., Usunier, N., Kirillov, A., Zagoruyko, S.: End-to-end object detection with transformers. In: European Conference on Computer Vision, pp. 213–229. Springer (2020)
2. Cavagnero, N., et al.: PEM: prototype-based efficient maskformer for image segmentation. In: Proceedings of the IEEE/CVF Conference on Computer Vision and Pattern Recognition, pp. 15804–15813 (2024)
3. Cheng, B., Misra, I., Schwing, A.G., Kirillov, A., Girdhar, R.: Masked-attention mask transformer for universal image segmentation. In: Proceedings of the IEEE/CVF Conference on Computer Vision and Pattern Recognition, pp. 1290–1299 (2022)
4. Cheng, B., Schwing, A., Kirillov, A.: Per-pixel classification is not all you need for semantic segmentation. In: Neural Information Processing Systems (2021)
5. Cheng, T., et al.: Sparse instance activation for real-time instance segmentation (2022)
6. Cheng, T., et al.: Sparse instance activation for real-time instance segmentation. In: Proceedings of the IEEE/CVF Conference on Computer Vision and Pattern Recognition, pp. 4433–4442 (2022)
7. Cordts, M., et al.: The cityscapes dataset for semantic urban scene understanding. arXiv Computer Vision and Pattern Recognition (2016)
8. Dong, B., Zeng, F., Wang, T., Zhang, X., Wei, Y.: Solq: segmenting objects by learning queries. arXiv Computer Vision and Pattern Recognition (2021)
9. Du, W., Xiang, Z., Chen, S., Qiao, C., Chen, Y., Bai, T.: Real-time instance segmentation with discriminative orientation maps. In: Proceedings of the IEEE/CVF International Conference on Computer Vision, pp. 7314–7323 (2021)
10. He, J., Li, P., Geng, Y., Xie, X.: Fastinst: a simple query-based model for real-time instance segmentation. In: Proceedings of the IEEE/CVF Conference on Computer Vision and Pattern Recognition, pp. 23663–23672 (2023)
11. He, K., Gkioxari, G., Dollár, P., Girshick, R.: Mask R-CNN. In: Proceedings of the IEEE International Conference on Computer Vision, pp. 2961–2969 (2017)
12. Howard, A.G., et al.: Mobilenets: efficient convolutional neural networks for mobile vision applications. arXiv preprint arXiv:1704.04861 (2017)
13. Hu, J., Cao, L., Jin, X., Zhang, S., Ji, R.: Universal image segmentation with efficiency. IEEE Trans. Pattern Anal. Mach. Intell. (2025)
14. Hu, J., Huang, L., Ren, T., Zhang, S., Ji, R., Cao, L.: You only segment once: towards real-time panoptic segmentation. In: Proceedings of the IEEE/CVF Conference on Computer Vision and Pattern Recognition, pp. 17819–17829 (2023)
15. Hu, J., Lu, Y., Zhang, S., Cao, L.: ISTR: mask-embedding-based instance segmentation transformer. IEEE Trans. Image Process. **33**, 2895–2907 (2024)
16. Huang, Z., Huang, L., Gong, Y., Huang, C., Wang, X.: Mask scoring R-CNN. In: Proceedings of the IEEE/CVF Conference on Computer Vision and Pattern Recognition, pp. 6409–6418 (2019)
17. Lin, T.Y., Dollar, P., Girshick, R., He, K., Hariharan, B., Belongie, S.: Feature pyramid networks for object detection. In: 2017 IEEE Conference on Computer Vision and Pattern Recognition (CVPR) (2017). https://doi.org/10.1109/cvpr.2017.106
18. Lin, T.Y., et al.: Microsoft coco: common objects in context. In: European Conference on Computer Vision, pp. 740–755. Springer (2014)
19. Jodogne-del Litto, K., Bilodeau, G.A.: Real-time instance segmentation with polygons using an intersection-over-union loss. In: 2023 20th Conference on Robots and Vision (CRV), pp. 153–160. IEEE (2023)

20. Loshchilov, I., Hutter, F.: Decoupled weight decay regularization. Learning, Learning (2017)
21. Peng, S., Jiang, W., Pi, H., Li, X., Bao, H., Zhou, X.: Deep snake for real-time instance segmentation. In: 2020 IEEE/CVF Conference on Computer Vision and Pattern Recognition (CVPR) (2020). https://doi.org/10.1109/cvpr42600.2020.00856
22. Perreault, H., Bilodeau, G.A., Saunier, N., Héritier, M.: Centerpoly: real-time instance segmentation using bounding polygons. In: Proceedings of the IEEE/CVF International Conference on Computer Vision, pp. 2982–2991 (2021)
23. Tian, Z., Zhang, B., Chen, H., Shen, C.: Instance and panoptic segmentation using conditional convolutions. IEEE Trans. Pattern Anal. Mach. Intell. **45**(1), 669–680 (2022)
24. Wang, K., Liew, J.H., Zou, Y., Zhou, D., Feng, J.: Panet: few-shot image semantic segmentation with prototype alignment. In: Proceedings of the IEEE/CVF International Conference on Computer Vision, pp. 9197–9206 (2019)
25. Wang, K.L., Chou, P.H., Chou, Y.C., Liu, C.J., Lin, C.K., Tseng, Y.C.: Mppolarmask: a faster and finer instance segmentation for concave images. In: Proceedings of the IEEE/CVF Conference on Computer Vision and Pattern Recognition, pp. 3705–3714 (2024)
26. Wang, X., Kong, T., Shen, C., Jiang, Y., Li, L.: Solo: segmenting objects by locations. In: European Conference on Computer Vision, pp. 649–665. Springer (2020)
27. Wang, X., Zhang, R., Kong, T., Li, L., Shen, C.: Solov2: dynamic and fast instance segmentation. Adv. Neural. Inf. Process. Syst. **33**, 17721–17732 (2020)
28. Wu, Y., Kirillov, A., Massa, F., Lo, W.Y., Girshick, R.: Detectron2 (2019)
29. Xia, R., et al.: Efficient architecture search for real-time instance segmentation. In: ICASSP 2024-2024 IEEE International Conference on Acoustics, Speech and Signal Processing (ICASSP), pp. 3310–3314. IEEE (2024)
30. Xie, Y., Shang, J., Deng, R., Tang, X., Yang, W.: Frisnet: a fast real-time instance segmentation network fusing frequency domain and multi-level features. IEEE Trans. Instrum. Measur. (2025)
31. Zhang, H., et al.: Mp-former: mask-piloted transformer for image segmentation. In: Proceedings of the IEEE/CVF Conference on Computer Vision and Pattern Recognition, pp. 18074–18083 (2023)
32. Zhu, X., Su, W., Lu, L., Li, B., Wang, X., Dai, J.: Deformable DETR: deformable transformers for end-to-end object detection. arXiv Computer Vision and Pattern Recognition (2020)

Towards Effective Long-Video Event Prediction via Multi-level Event Semantics Mining

Bo Peng, YuanJie Lyu, PengGang Qin, and Tong Xu[✉]

University of Science and Technology of China, Hefei, China
tongxu@ustc.edu.cn

Abstract. Accurately predicting future events is fundamental to content understanding and decision-making across various domains. While prior research has primarily focused on text or short-video scenarios, long-video event prediction—characterized by vast multimodal context and more complex narratives—remains underexplored. Meanwhile, although recent Long-Video Language Models (LVLMs), built on Large Language Models (LLMs) and Vision–Language Models (VLMs), have shown promise in long-video question answering and summarization, they struggle to generalize to event prediction, as they can neither precisely extract event-related details nor perform fine-grained analysis of event development. To address this gap, we propose VISTA, a multi-level event semantics mining framework for long-video event prediction. Initially, VISTA applies a character-centric visual prompt to precise extract event-related visual details, enhancing detail-level semantics; subsequently, it employs a knowledge-enhanced iterative retrieval strategy, guiding the LLM to progressively construct logically coherent event chains, thereby improving event-level narratives; ultimately, VISTA adopts a human-like propose-then-retrieve strategy to generate diverse future-oriented proposals and integrate multi-level clues, producing robust and accurate predictions. Extensive experiments on real-world datasets validate the effectiveness of VISTA for long-video event prediction.

Keywords: Long Video Event Prediction · Long Video Understanding · Event Prediction

1 Introduction

Future event prediction (FEP) aims to forecast the future trend of events based on historical information, thus providing strong support for content understanding and decision-making. Traditional FEP researches focus on the textual descriptions of historical events [11,16,21] or short videos that typically span only a few seconds [14,15]. However, with the development of multimedia technologies, more and more events are presented in long videos like movies and TV

J. Lokoč et al. (Eds.): MMM 2026, LNCS 16412, pp. 189–203, 2026.
https://doi.org/10.1007/978-981-95-6950-2_14

series. The complexity of long videos—characterized by vast multimodal contexts and intricate event narratives—poses significant challenges that existing FEP methods fail to address.

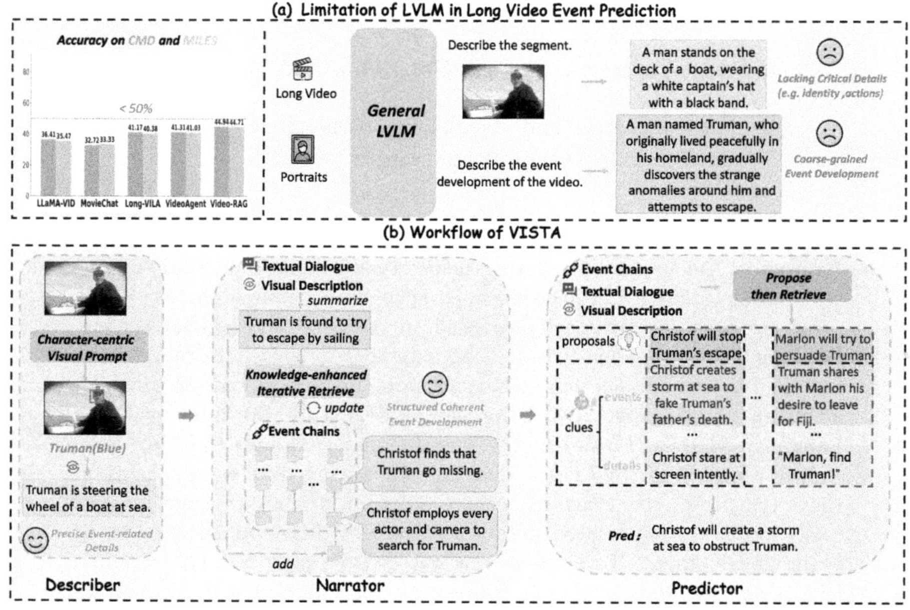

Fig. 1. Illustration of the limitation of general LVLMs on long-video event prediction, and the overall workflow of VISTA.

Fortunately, the recent emergence of Large Language Models (LLMs) and Vision-Language Models (VLMs) has demonstrated strong capabilities in content understanding and reasoning, shedding light on the effective analysis of long-video content. Building on these advances, multiple Long-Video Language Models (LVLMs) [8,17,19,28] have been developed, showing promising performance on long-video question answering and summarization tasks. However, as illustrated in Fig. 1(a), their poor performance on long-video event prediction suggests that effectively leveraging LLMs and VLMs for this task is far from trivial, primarily due to the following critical issues:

- **Semantic limitation of visual details.** Current VLMs focus more on low-level visual elements [12] (e.g. objects, costumes) than on high-level event-related cues (e.g. character identity and actions). This bias introduces interference from irrelevant details and omits crucial event-related information, thereby undermining the detail-level event semantics of long videos.
- **Coarse-grained reflection of event development.** Although LVLMs can summarize long videos, such summaries are highly conclusive, while lacking fine-grained analysis of event development. The resulting obscured event

development logic and key events omission lead to substantial event-level semantic loss, and further affect future-oriented event reasoning.

To address these challenges, we propose VISTA, a multi-level event semantics mining framework for long-video event prediction. VISTA progressively distills detail- and event-level semantics and integrates multi-level cues to enable robust and reliable prediction. As shown in Fig. 1(b), it consists of three modules:

Initially, the **Describer** apply *character-centric visual prompts*, constructed through fine-grained in-frame feature matching, to raw video frames, to focus the VLM on character identities and actions, which serve as the foundational visual semantics of events.

Subsequently, the **Narrator** integrates these visual details with transcribed dialogues into textual event descriptions and applies a *knowledge-enhanced iterative retrieval* strategy, where a commonsense expert aligns causal relations between historical and current events, to progressively integrate them into structured event chains. Each chain forms a logically coherent sequence of events, enabling fine-grained and coherent event-level narrative.

Ultimately, the **Predictor** employs a *propose-then-retrieve* strategy to extend and integrate the multi-level event semantics established above. Inspired by human cognition, this strategy mirrors how people first generate multiple hypotheses from past event trajectories and then retrieve pertinent cues to refine the most plausible one. Concretely, the **Predictor** extends each event chain to produce diverse, future-oriented proposals and, via multi-granular feature matching, retrieves clues at both the detail- and event-levels for each proposal. The combination of coarse-grained proposals with fine-grained, multi-level clues enables the LLM to deliver reliable, robust event predictions.

The technical contributions of this paper are as follows:

- To the best of our knowledge, we are among the first ones who elaborate on predicting future events based on long videos.
- We propose VISTA, a multi-level event semantics framework that: (i) extracts precise event-related visual details, (ii) constructs fine-grained and coherent event chains, and (iii) adopts a human-like propose-then-retrieve strategy to fully leverage multi-level event semantics for reliable prediction.
- Extensive experiments on real-world datasets demonstrate the superiority of VISTA, while ablation studies validate the effectiveness of each module.

2   Related Work

Future Event Prediction. Early studies on future event prediction primarily focused on well-structured events such as texts from ontology and news articles [11,16,21]. They generally adopted graph neural networks to model structured events and formulated future event prediction as a link prediction task on graph networks. With the development of multimedia technologies, research has been extended to short videos. [15] first introduced the video event prediction task and propose a transformer-based method to integrate multimodal clues

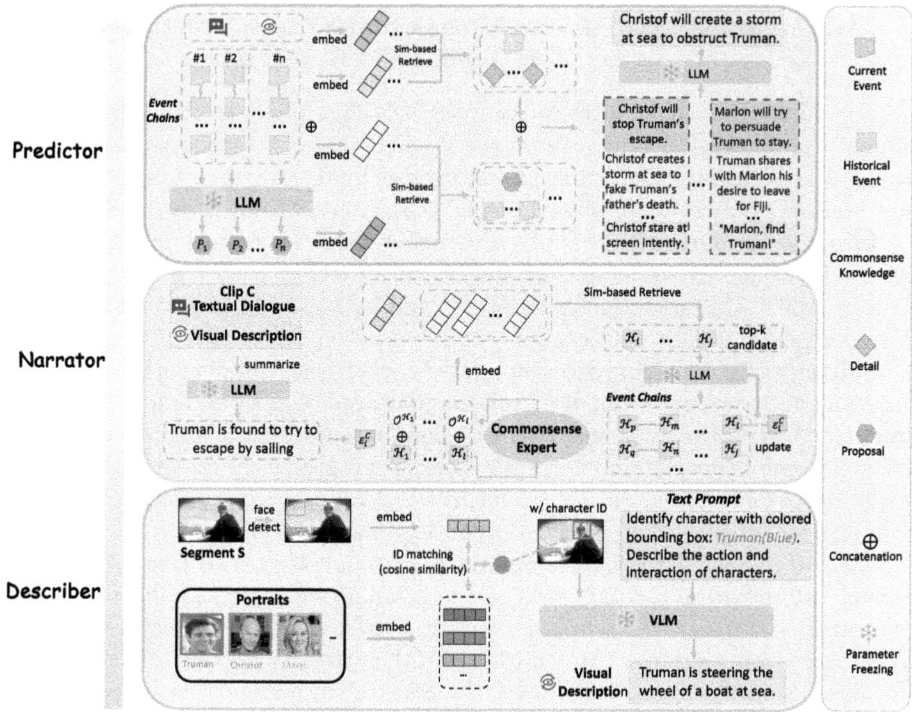

Fig. 2. Illustration of our VISTA framework: Describer featured by *character-centric visual prompt* for more precise event-related visual detail extraction, Narrator featured by *knowledge-enhanced iterative retrieval* to generate coherent event chains, and Predictor featured by *propose-then-retrieve* strategy to effectively utilize detail- and event-level cues for more precise prediction.

from video content. [14] advanced the field by integrating an object-centric cross-modal reasoning chains into VLMs. While these methods are effective for local event reasoning within short videos, they cannot handle the vast multimodal information of long videos, while lacking sufficient reasoning ability to analyze long-horizon event development.

Long-Video-Language Models. The strong understanding and reasoning capabilities of Large Language Models (LLMs) and Vision-Language Models (VLMs) have driven significant advances in multimodal research. Building on them, various general Long-Video Language Models (LVLMs) have emerged and shown effectiveness in long video understanding. Structurally, these models fall into two categories: end-to-end models [5,17,19,28,29] and agent-based models [1,7,19,32]. End-to-end models aim to manage the vast multimodal context of long videos through efficient token-level representation or memory mechanisms. Agent-based models, in contrast, leverage LLMs as central agents in combination with VLMs for visual perception, enabling interactive extraction and aggregation of key information. Although effective for long-video question answering and summarization, we find they fail to effectively capture and reason over event development in long videos. In this work, we address this gap by enhancing multi-level event semantic mining and predictive analysis based on LLMs and VLMs.

3   Methodology

We now introduce VISTA, a multi-level event semantics framework for long-video event prediction. Figure 2 illustrate the key modules of VISTA.

3.1   Problem Formulation

We formally define the long-video event prediction task as follows:

- **Input**: A raw long video V spanning tens of minutes along with portraits of relevant characters $\{P_i\}_{i=1}^{K}$.
- **Output**: A textual description of predicted future event $\hat{\mathcal{E}}$.

3.2   Multimodal Preprocessing

Given the raw long video V, we begin by utilizing WhisperX [2], a widely used ASR tool, to transcribe the audio of the long video into textual dialogue T, which serve as valuable clues for event understanding and reasoning.

Next, we used PySceneDetect, an established scene detection tool, to identify scene variations. The original video V is then divided into shorter video segments $\{S_i\}_{i=1}^{N}$ based on the detected scene boundaries. Considering that overly short segments could lead to insufficient context, we further concatenate consecutive segments into video clips $\{C_i\}_{i=1}^{M}$ in chronological order, ensuring each clip spans no less than 3 min.

3.3   Describer: Character-Centric Visual Prompt

Prior works [26] have proven that visual prompts can effectively highlight key visual elements to facilitate more precise visual clue extraction of VLMs. Motivated by this, we propose character-centric visual prompts to focus VLM on character identity and actions—fundamental semantics of events.

Given a video segment S, we first employ InsightFace [24], an off-the-shelf face detection model, to detect facial regions frame-by-frame in the form of bounding boxes. We then utilize CLIP [22] to extract facial embeddings from these bounding boxes as $\{f_i\}_{i=1}^{N}$. Similarly, each character portrait P_i is processed by CLIP, forming a set of portrait embeddings $\{p_i\}_{i=1}^{K}$. Subsequently, we compute the cosine similarities between the two sets of embeddings and identify the best-matching portrait face for each face bounding box. Formally,

$$bbox_j = \arg \max_{i \in \{1,...,K\}} \left(\frac{p_i \cdot f_j}{|p_i||f_j|} \right) \tag{1}$$

We overlay each bounding boxes with colors corresponding to its best-matching characters, where each character is pre-assigned a unique color. The video frames with colored bounding boxes are then fed into the VLM, accompanied by a text prompt that explicitly specifies the color-to-character mappin, (e.g. *Truman(Blue)*). This visual-text collaborative prompt emphasizes character identity and action to VLM, thereby enhancing accurate event-related visual details:

$$vd = \mathcal{VLM}(S; \{bbox_j\}_{j=1}^{N}) \tag{2}$$

3.4   Narrator: Knowledge-Enhanced Iterative Retrieve

Leveraging the powerful summarization capabilities of LLMs, we can reliably summarize the transcribed dialogues D_C and visual descriptions vd_C within the temporal domain of each video clip C, yielding chronologically ordered event descriptions $\{\mathcal{E}_j^C\}_{j=1}^{l}$, where $\mathcal{E}_j^C$ corresponds to the j-th event occuring in C:

$$\{\mathcal{E}_j^C\}_{j=1}^{l} = \mathcal{LLM}(D_C, vd_C) \tag{3}$$

However, as illustrated in the Fig. 3, temporally sequential events in long video narratives often lack logical coherence, potentially hampering subsequent reasoning and prediction. To address this, we further integrate events into structured event chains—each reflecting clear causality—using a knowledge-enhanced iterative retrieval strategy, to produce logically coherent event-level narratives.

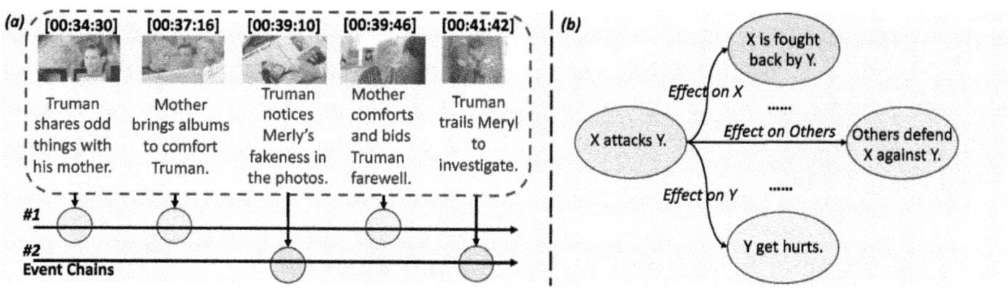

Fig. 3. Illustration of event chains and commonsense expert.

This strategy processes events iteratively in chronological order. In each iteration, the event being processed is treated as the current event $\mathcal{E}$, and all preceding events are considered historical events $\{\mathcal{H}_i\}_{i=1}^{h}$. To strengthen the correlation between causally related events for more accurate identification, we introduce an off-shelf LLM fine-tuned with a large-scale commonsense knowledge graph as a commonsense expert f_{CE} to generate comprehensive potential causal outcomes $\{\mathcal{O}_j^{\mathcal{H}_i}\}_{j=1}^{o}$ of each $\mathcal{H}_i$, as shown in Fig. 3. These causal commonsense insights have been shown by previous research [20] to effectively highlight the semantic similarity between causally related events. Thus, we embed the concatenated pairs of each historical event with its causal outcomes, as well as the current event $\mathcal{E}$, using an embedding model f_t. The embedding of the current event $\mathbf{e}^{\mathcal{E}}$ is set as the pivot, and the cosine similarity between it and each historical event embedding $\mathbf{e}_j^{\mathcal{H}_i}$ is calculated accordingly:

$$\mathrm{sim}(\mathbf{e}_j^{\mathcal{H}_i}, \mathbf{e}^{\mathcal{E}}) = \frac{\mathbf{e}_j^{\mathcal{H}_i} \cdot \mathbf{e}^{\mathcal{E}}}{\|\mathbf{e}_j^{\mathcal{H}_i}\|\|\mathbf{e}^{\mathcal{E}}\|}, \quad \mathbf{e}_j^{\mathcal{H}_i} = f_t(\mathcal{H}_i \oplus \mathcal{O}_j^{\mathcal{H}_i}), \quad \mathbf{e}^{\mathcal{E}} = f_t(\mathcal{E}) \qquad (4)$$

Based on the similarity scores, we select the top- top-k historical events as the final candidates, as a higher similarity indicates a greater potential for causality. Top-$k(A, f)$ denotes selecting the top k elements from the set A, ranked in descending order of their f values:

$$\mathcal{H}_c = \mathrm{Top}\text{-}k\left(\bigcup_{i=1}^{l}\{(\mathcal{H}_i, \mathcal{O}_j^{\mathcal{H}_i}) \mid j = 1, 2, \ldots\}, \mathrm{sim}(\mathbf{e}_j^{\mathcal{H}_i}, \mathbf{e}^{\mathcal{E}})\right) \qquad (5)$$

The event chain each candidate locates, along with the causal guidance and the current event, are fed into the LLM. The refined context and explicit causal guidance enable the LLM to effectively determine the event chain to which the current event should be added. Starting from the first event of the initial clip, the event chain is iteratively updated until the final one, ultimately forming a complete set of event chains that cover the entire video content.

3.5 Predictor: Propose-then-Retrieve

The details extracted by the Describer, along with the structured and coherent event chains constructed by the Narrator, establish a solid semantic foundation for event prediction. To fully leverage these multi-level clues, we design a propose-then-retrieve strategy that emulates the human cognition.

We begin by generating a diverse set of future proposals to capture a broad range of future potentials. Intuitively, each event chain EC can be viewed as a branch of the storyline, inherently capable of extending into the future. Inspired by this, we feed each event chain into the LLM to generate multiple predictive proposals $\{\mathcal{P}_k\}_{k=1}^{p}$ that extend the storyline:

$$\{\mathcal{P}_k\}_{k=1}^{p} = \mathcal{LLM}(EC) \qquad (6)$$

Subsequently, we retrieve relevant clues from multi-level historical information for each proposal $\mathcal{P}_k$. These clues help highlight and refine the most probable proposal into precise prediction. Specifically, we first reuse the embeddings of each event-outcome pairs $\mathbf{e}_j^{\mathcal{H}_i}$ to compute cosine similarity with each proposal embedding $\mathbf{e}^{\mathcal{P}_k}$, with a threshold τ_e for filtering, to get event-level clues $\mathcal{C}_{\mathcal{P}_k}^{\mathcal{E}}$:

$$\mathcal{C}_{\mathcal{P}_k}^{\mathcal{E}} = \{\mathcal{H}_i \mid \mathrm{sim}(\mathbf{e}_j^{\mathcal{H}_i}, \mathbf{e}^{\mathcal{P}_k}) > \tau_e, \forall i \in [1, |\mathcal{H}|], j \in [1, |\mathcal{O}^{\mathcal{H}_i}|]\} \qquad (7)$$

For more fine-grained detail-level clues, we further filter the detail-level clues within the temporal scope of each event-level clue. Considering that there is no causal semantic gap between events and their associated details, we directly compute the cosine similarity between the raw embedding of each event and all details it contains, with a threshold τ_d for filtering, to get details-level clues $\mathcal{C}^{\mathcal{D}}_{\mathcal{P}_k}$.

Finally, we combine each proposal $\mathcal{P}_k$ with corresponding multi-granularity clues $\mathcal{C}^{\mathcal{E}}_{\mathcal{P}_k}$ and $\mathcal{C}^{\mathcal{D}}_{\mathcal{P}_k}$, and feed them into an LLM to determine and refine the most probable proposal, based on its retrieved clues, into the final prediction $\hat{\mathcal{E}}$:

$$\hat{\mathcal{E}} = \mathcal{LLM}(\{(\mathcal{P}_k, \mathcal{C}^{\mathcal{E}}_{\mathcal{P}_k}, \mathcal{C}^{\mathcal{D}}_{\mathcal{P}_k})\}_{k=1}^{p}) \tag{8}$$

4   Experiment

4.1   Experimental Settings

Dataset Description. We adopt the following two evaluation datasets for long-video event prediction: (1) **CMD**: Adapted from the Condensed Movies (CMD) test set [3]. Original CMD collects abundant movies with timestamped textual event description annotations, each event presenting a key stage of the storyline. By segmenting the original movies according to the timestamp, we construct event-video pairs as evaluation samples. To prevent data leakage, following [9], we feed anonymized movie synopses to every LLMs/VLMs used in our experiments to predict future events; any correctly identified movies are excluded. This results in 4,987 samples with an average duration of 48.6 min. (2) **MILES**: Contains 624 event-video pairs with an average duration of 78.5 min from 80 TV series released after January 2025, ensuring no overlap with the pretraining data of any models in the experiments. Annotation follows a two-stage process: two annotators select key events from each TV series, and two additional annotators independently review these selections to minimize bias and ensure quality. For both datasets, we include IMDb character portraits as prior knowledge.

Evaluation Metrics. To comprehensively assess the performance of different models, we conducted both generative and multiple-choice evaluations. For the generative evaluation, we use widely adopted metrics in generation tasks: ROUGE-L(R) [18], METEOR(M) [4], and CIDEr(C) [31], along with Sentence-BERT (SB) [23]. For the multiple-choice evaluation, we use accuracy (Acc).

Compared Methods. We selected various state-of-the-art general LVLMs for comprehensive comparison. As introduced in Sect. 2, they are grouped into two types: *end-to-end models*, including MovieChat [28], Llama-VID [17], Movie-LLM [29], LongVILA [5], Video-CCAM [8], LongLLaVA [33], Video-XL [27] and *agent-based models*, including VideoAgent (F) [7], VideoAgent (W) [32], Goldfish [1], Video-RAG [19]. For more comprehensive evaluation, we additionally fine-tune several end-to-end models on the CMD validation set, which contains 3,348 samples from 358 movies. Moreover, we include two state-of-the-art short video prediction methods—VLEP [15] and OC-2-Reasoning [14]—as baselines. Since these methods cannot process long video inputs, we feed them only the last 10 s of each video. Notably, VLEP lacks generative capability and is therefore evaluated solely under the multiple-choice setting.

Implementation Details. Our VISTA implementation adopts LLaMA-3.1-8B-Instruct [10] as the default LLM and Qwen2.5-VL-7B-Instruct as the default VLM, with all-MiniLM-L6-v2 [23] used as the embedding model across all components. The commonsense expert is implemented as a Flan-T5 [6] model fine-tuned on ATOMIC [25], following [20]. For the multiple-choice evaluation, GPT-4.1 is employed to generate three distractor options from the original event descriptions. The default LLM then selects the option most consistent with VISTA's generated prediction as its answer. To prevent data leakage, all dialogue text and character names are anonymized throughout the evaluation. Relevant prompts of VISTA can be found in https://anonymous.4open.science/r/VISTA-6BBF.

4.2   Performance Comparison

Table 1. Comparison of different methods on CMD and MILES datasets.

	CMD					MILES				
	R	M	C	SB	Acc(%)	R	M	C	SB	Acc(%)
MovieChat	12.34	13.52	11.81	34.61	32.72	12.12	13.83	11.62	35.13	33.33
Movie-LLM	12.89	14.43	12.71	35.61	33.23	13.92	16.12	13.35	39.57	37.50
LLaMA-VID	12.54	14.57	12.75	36.36	36.14	12.75	14.51	12.21	35.85	35.47
LongVILA	14.72	18.23	15.31	42.61	41.17	14.41	17.71	15.01	42.32	40.38
Video-CCAM	13.61	16.54	14.64	41.42	39.56	13.12	16.23	14.41	40.24	38.46
LongLLaVA	13.25	16.71	14.34	39.72	39.32	13.44	16.41	14.79	39.71	38.61
Video-XL	13.21	15.54	13.34	38.14	37.24	12.63	15.23	12.97	38.01	36.24
MovieChat (ft)	13.34	14.32	12.83	35.87	35.43	12.67	14.53	12.41	35.18	34.78
LLaMA-VID (ft)	12.91	14.83	13.32	37.64	37.02	12.87	14.35	12.48	36.85	35.10
LongVILA (ft)	15.72	17.79	16.67	42.23	42.94	15.84	18.03	16.31	41.32	42.21
Video-CCAM (ft)	16.23	18.54	16.64	41.42	42.31	15.72	18.51	16.21	40.24	41.03
Video-CCAM (ft)	16.23	18.54	16.64	41.42	42.31	15.72	18.51	16.21	40.24	41.03
VideoAgent (F)	16.72	20.02	17.21	44.91	42.73	16.41	19.77	17.42	44.15	43.24
VideoAgent (W)	15.49	18.24	16.64	42.42	41.31	15.67	18.12	16.35	42.31	41.03
Goldfish	17.34	20.03	16.67	43.91	43.41	15.47	19.31	16.51	43.57	41.72
Video-RAG	17.78	22.06	18.33	46.06	44.94	17.78	21.71	18.13	45.62	44.71
VLEP	-	-	-	-	23.88	-	-	-	-	25.16
OC-2-Reasoning	7.12	6.24	5.45	30.18	25.64	7.16	8.14	6.93	32.14	27.88
VISTA (Ours)	**25.92**	**33.12**	**24.94**	**63.14**	**62.43**	**25.73**	**32.52**	**25.34**	**63.42**	**62.81**

Table 1 shows the performance comparison between VISTA and existing methods on the CMD and MILES, from which we can draw the following conclusions:

- VISTA significantly outperforms all the other methods across both datasets, achieving absolute improvements of at least 8.14%, 11.06%, 6.61%, 17.08%, and 17.49% across every metric in CMD, and at least 7.95%, 10.81%, 7.21%, 17.80%, and 18.10% in MILES. The great performance exhibited by VISTA demonstrates its remarkable effectiveness for long video event prediction.

- On both CMD (movie-based) and MILES (TV-series-based), VISTA achieves stable performance with accuracy exceeding 60%. This demonstrates its strong generality across different long-video genre, from movies featured by compact storytelling to TV series featured by loosely structured plots.

- End-to-end LVLMs perform poorly, and further task-specific fine-tuning only brings marginal performance gains, indicating that their end-to-end architectures fail to effectively extract and exploit event semantics for prediction.

- Agent-based LVLMs generally outperform end-to-end models, benefiting from LLM-based retrieval and reasoning modules that improve fine-grained content analysis. However, their mediocre absolute performance suggests that such mechanisms remain insufficient to comprehensively capture and leverage multi-level event semantics.

- Short video event prediction methods fail almost completely, with their accuracy approaching random prediction (25%). They can neither handle the excessive multimodal information in long videos, nor predict high-level future events simply based on low-level reasoning of local details.

4.3   Ablation Study

Effect of Multi-level Semantics. We compare VISTA with the following two variants to examine the role of detail- and event-level semantics plays in long-video event prediction, as shown in Table 2: (1) *w/o VD*: Without the visual details (VD), we only take textual dialogues as detail-level information, which leads to catastrophic performance loss, highlighting the indispensable event-related semantics visual details contain for long-video event prediction. (2) *w/o EC*: Without the event chains (EC) as event-level narratives, we simply arrange the events in chronological order as input to the predictor. Event chains contribute to improved overall performance, indicating that event chains provide more logically coherent event-level semantics, facilitating further reasoning and prediction. Together, these findings confirm that both detail-level and event-level semantics are essential for the success of VISTA in long-video event prediction.

Effect of Specialized Components. We compare VISTA with the following three variants to examine the effectiveness of the key components in VISTA, as shown in Table 2: (1) *w/o CVP*: Without the character-centric visual prompt (CVP), the character portraits and raw video frames are directly feed into the VLM to generate visual descriptions. The marked performance degradation demonstrates the effectiveness of CVP in focusing the VLM on event-related visual details. (2) *w/o KIR*: Without the knowledge-enhanced iterative retrieval (KIR) strategy, all events are directly feed into the LLM to generate event chains.

Table 2. Ablation on multi-level semantics and components.

	R	M	C	SB	Acc
VISTA	25.7	32.5	25.3	63.4	62.8
w/o VD	12.8	13.5	11.7	33.3	32.9
w/o EC	20.1	23.7	18.2	49.1	49.2
w/o CVP	23.7	28.5	22.4	56.2	55.6
w/o KIR	20.4	24.0	18.5	51.3	51.9
w/o PtR	19.8	25.5	19.7	54.0	52.9

Table 3. Ablation on backbone LLM.

	R	M	C	SB	Acc
Llama3-8B	25.7	32.5	25.3	63.4	62.8
Qwen2.5-7B	24.9	32.6	25.7	61.4	62.3
Mistral-7B	24.3	31.9	24.1	60.7	61.1
Gemma3-4B	24.2	31.2	23.6	60.3	59.9
GPT-4o	28.2	34.1	27.4	65.2	66.5
GPT-4.1	**28.9**	**35.1**	**28.6**	**67.2**	**67.9**

The noticeable performance degradation reflects the pivotal role KIR plays in enhancing LLM's casual analysis and reasoning over events. (3) *w/o PtR*: Without the propose-then-retrieve (PtR) strategy, the LLM is asked to directly make prediction according to the input details and event chains. The evident performance drop indicates that PtR substantially enhances future-oriented analysis and clues integration during the prediction process. Together, these results confirm that CVP, KIR, and PtR are indispensable components, jointly ensuring the robustness and effectiveness of VISTA in long-video event prediction.

Effect of Backbone LLM. To further analyze the generality of VISTA across different LLMs, we replace the default LLM in VISTA with the following: Qwen-2.5-7B-instruct, Mistral-7B-instruct-v0.2 [13], Gemma3-4B [30], GPT-4o, and GPT-4.1. As shown in Table 3, the two commercial LLMs, GPT-4o and GPT-4.1, exhibit the best performance. Among the four smaller-scale open-source LLMs, LLaMA-3.1-8B-instruct (our default LLM) performs best overall, while the other three deliver competitive results. Generally, it is evident that our VISTA demonstrates strong compatibility and scalability with various LLMs, proving generally effective for the widely-used LLMs.

Effect of Hyperparameters. As illustrated in Fig. 4, we analyze the impact of three hyperparameters on VISTA's performance: the candidate count k in knowledge-enhanced iterative retrieval, and the similarity thresholds τ_e and τ_d in propose-then-retrieve. As these hyperparameters increase, VISTA's performance curves exhibit similar rise–then–fall trends, peaking at $k = 3$, $\tau_e = 0.6$, and $\tau_d = 0.75$. This is intuitively reasonable, as they all control the trade-off between diversity and interference in the retrieval process: higher k or lower τ introduces more noise, while smaller k or higher τ risks discarding valuable clues—both leading to degraded performance. Moreover, VISTA's performance remains relatively stable across hyperparameter variations, with accuracy consistently above 50%, demonstrating the robustness of the framework.

4.4   Case Study

As shown in Fig. 5, we present visualization results to qualitatively analyze VISTA and its internal components.

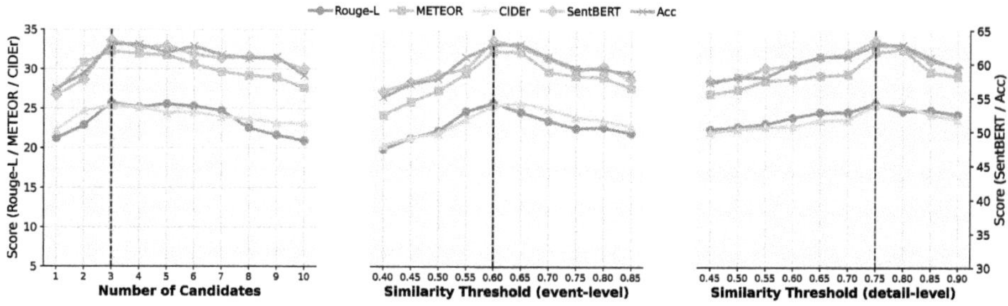

Fig. 4. Ablation on three key hyperparamters of VISTA.

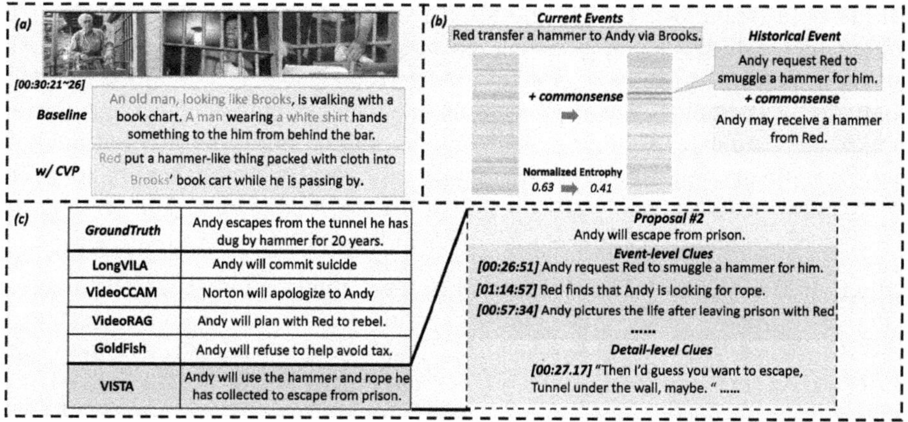

Fig. 5. Visualization of a long-video event prediction case.

Part (a) shows the VLM output with and without the character-centric visual prompt(CVP). With CVP, the model accurately identifies the characters *Red* and *Brooks* and concisely describes their actions. In contrast, the baseline not only fails to accurately identify their identities but also includes trivial event-irrelevant details such as *white shirt*.

Part(b) shows heatmaps of semantic similarity between embeddings of historical and current events, where darker red indicates higher similarity. We compute the normlized entrophy(NE) to judge the distribution evenness, where lower NE represents more uneven distribution. It is evident that the distribution of post-commonsense heatmap become more uneven after incorporating commonsense, with the similarity between the two causally-related events - *"Andy request Red to smuggle a hammer for him"* and current event - significantly increased. This proves the effectiveness of commonsense expert to facilitate more accurate causal reasoning during event chain construction.

Part(c) shows the predictions of various methods on a sample from *The Shawshank Redemption*. We find that all general LVLMs' predictions deviate significantly from the ground truth, whereas VISTA not only aligns with the ground truth but also contains concrete details (*using the hammer and rope*), showing its superiority in long video event prediction. We further extract VISTA's intermediate results and find that during the propose-then-retrieve, VISTA first generates a proposal *"Andy will escape from prison"*, and then collects key clues such as Andy's prior acquisition of tools (*hammer* and *rope*), as well as Red's suspicion when Andy requested the hammer. These clues makes VISTA prioritizes this proposal and further refine it with collected clues into the final prediction. This both demonstrates the effectiveness of the propose-then-retrieve strategy and highlights the explainability of our VISTA framework.

5 Conclusion

In this paper, we propose VISTA, a multi-level event semantics mining framework for long-video event prediction. VISTA first extracts precise event-related visual details by the character-centric visual prompt, then progressively constructs structured and coherent event chains through a knowledge-enhanced iterative retrieval strategy to capture event evolution. Finally, it adopts a human-like propose-then-retrieve strategy, which generates diverse predictive proposals from event chains and refines them by retrieving detail- and event-level clues from historical information, ultimately producing accurate and explainable predictions. Extensive experiments on real-world datasets demonstrate the superiority of VISTA, while ablation and qualitative studies further validate the robustness and effectiveness of its internal design.

Acknowledgements. This work was supported by the grants from National Natural Science Foundation of China (No. 62222213, 62072423).

References

1. Ataallah, K., et al.: Goldfish: vision-language understanding of arbitrarily long videos. arXiv preprint arXiv:2407.12679 (2024)
2. Bain, M., Huh, J., Han, T., Zisserman, A.: Whisperx: time-accurate speech transcription of long-form audio. arXiv preprint arXiv:2303.00747 (2023)
3. Bain, M., Nagrani, A., Brown, A., Zisserman, A.: Condensed movies: story based retrieval with contextual embeddings. In: Proceedings of the Asian Conference on Computer Vision (2020)
4. Banerjee, S., Lavie, A.: Meteor: an automatic metric for MT evaluation with improved correlation with human judgments. In: Proceedings of the ACL Workshop on Intrinsic and Extrinsic Evaluation Measures for Machine Translation and/or Summarization, pp. 65–72 (2005)
5. Chen, Y., et al.: Longvila: scaling long-context visual language models for long videos. arXiv preprint arXiv:2408.10188 (2024)
6. Chung, H.W., et al.: Scaling instruction-finetuned language models. J. Mach. Learn. Res. **25**(70), 1–53 (2024)

7. Fan, Y., et al.: Videoagent: a memory-augmented multimodal agent for video understanding. In: European Conference on Computer Vision, pp. 75–92. Springer (2025)

8. Fei, J., Li, D., Deng, Z., Wang, Z., Liu, G., Wang, H.: Video-ccam: enhancing video-language understanding with causal cross-attention masks for short and long videos. arXiv preprint arXiv:2408.14023 (2024)

9. Ghermi, R., Wang, X., Kalogeiton, V., Laptev, I.: Short film dataset (SFD): a benchmark for story-level video understanding. arXiv preprint arXiv:2406.10221 (2024)

10. Grattafiori, A., et al.: The llama 3 herd of models. arXiv e-prints pp. arXiv–2407 (2024)

11. Halawi, D., Zhang, F., Yueh-Han, C., Steinhardt, J.: Approaching human-level forecasting with language models. arXiv preprint arXiv:2402.18563 (2024)

12. He, Y., Lin, Y., Wu, J., Zhang, H., Zhang, Y., Le, R.: Storyteller: improving long video description through global audio-visual character identification. arXiv preprint arXiv:2411.07076 (2024)

13. Jiang, F.: Identifying and mitigating vulnerabilities in LLM-integrated applications. Master's thesis, University of Washington (2024)

14. Lai, C., Wang, H., Ge, W., Xue, X.: Object-centric cross-modal knowledge reasoning for future event prediction in videos. IEEE Trans. Circ. Syst. Video Technol. (2024)

15. Lei, J., Yu, L., Berg, T.L., Bansal, M.: What is more likely to happen next? Video-and-language future event prediction. arXiv preprint arXiv:2010.07999 (2020)

16. Li, M., et al.: The future is not one-dimensional: complex event schema induction by graph modeling for event prediction. arXiv preprint arXiv:2104.06344 (2021)

17. Li, Y., Wang, C., Jia, J.: Llama-vid: an image is worth 2 tokens in large language models. In: European Conference on Computer Vision, pp. 323–340. Springer (2025)

18. Lin, C.Y.: Rouge: a package for automatic evaluation of summaries. In: Text Summarization Branches Out, pp. 74–81 (2004)

19. Luo, Y., et al.: Video-rag: visually-aligned retrieval-augmented long video comprehension. arXiv preprint arXiv:2411.13093 (2024)

20. Lyu, Y., Xu, T., Niu, Z., Peng, B., Ke, J., Chen, E.: Generating event-oriented attribution for movies via two-stage prefix-enhanced multimodal LLM. arXiv preprint arXiv:2409.09362 (2024)

21. Ma, Y., Ye, C., Wu, Z., Wang, X., Cao, Y., Chua, T.S.: Context-aware event forecasting via graph disentanglement. In: Proceedings of the 29th ACM SIGKDD Conference on Knowledge Discovery and Data Mining, pp. 1643–1652 (2023)

22. Radford, A., et al.: Learning transferable visual models from natural language supervision. In: International Conference on Machine Learning, pp. 8748–8763. PmLR (2021)

23. Reimers, N.: Sentence-bert: sentence embeddings using siamese bert-networks. arXiv preprint arXiv:1908.10084 (2019)

24. Ren, X., Lattas, A., Gecer, B., Deng, J., Ma, C., Yang, X.: Facial geometric detail recovery via implicit representation. In: 2023 IEEE 17th International Conference on Automatic Face and Gesture Recognition (FG) (2023)

25. Sap, M., et al.: Atomic: an atlas of machine commonsense for if-then reasoning. In: Proceedings of the AAAI Conference on Artificial Intelligence, vol. 33, pp. 3027–3035 (2019)

26. Shtedritski, A., Rupprecht, C., Vedaldi, A.: What does clip know about a red circle? visual prompt engineering for VLMs. In: Proceedings of the IEEE/CVF International Conference on Computer Vision, pp. 11987–11997 (2023)
27. Shu, Y., et al.: Video-xl: extra-long vision language model for hour-scale video understanding. In: Proceedings of the Computer Vision and Pattern Recognition Conference, pp. 26160–26169 (2025)
28. Song, E., et al.: Moviechat: from dense token to sparse memory for long video understanding. In: Proceedings of the IEEE/CVF Conference on Computer Vision and Pattern Recognition, pp. 18221–18232 (2024)
29. Song, Z., et al.: Moviellm: enhancing long video understanding with AI-generated movies. arXiv preprint arXiv:2403.01422 (2024)
30. Kamath, A., et al.: Gemma 3 technical report. arXiv preprint arXiv:2503.19786 (2025)
31. Vedantam, R., Lawrence Zitnick, C., Parikh, D.: Cider: consensus-based image description evaluation. In: Proceedings of the IEEE Conference on Computer Vision and Pattern Recognition, pp. 4566–4575 (2015)
32. Wang, X., Zhang, Y., Zohar, O., Yeung-Levy, S.: Videoagent: long-form video understanding with large language model as agent. In: European Conference on Computer Vision, pp. 58–76. Springer (2025)
33. Wang, X., Song, D., Chen, S., Zhang, C., Wang, B.: Longllava: scaling multimodal LLMs to 1000 images efficiently via a hybrid architecture. arXiv preprint arXiv:2409.02889 (2024)

Comparative Robustness of CNNs, ViTs, and MLLMs Under Image Corruption

Xinkuan Qiu[1,2,4] and Yongbin Zhou[1,3(✉)]

[1] Institute of Information Engineering, Chinese Academy of Sciences, Beijing, China
`qiuxinkuan@iie.ac.cn`
[2] School of Cyber Security, University of Chinese Academy of Sciences, Beijing, China
[3] School of Cyber Science and Engineering, Nanjing University of Science and Technology, Nanjing, China
`zhouyongbin@njust.edu.cn`
[4] State Key Laboratory of Cyberspace Security Defense, Beijing, China

Abstract. Robustness to image corruption is essential for the safe and reliable deployment of deep learning systems in safety-critical applications. While prior work has extensively investigated the corruption robustness of Convolutional Neural Networks (CNNs) and Vision Transformers (ViTs), the robustness of Multimodal Large Language Models (MLLMs) remains underexplored—particularly in direct comparison with vision-only architectures. To bridge this gap, we propose UniCorrupt-Bench, the first unified benchmark designed to systematically evaluate and compare the corruption robustness of CNNs, ViTs, and MLLMs under consistent settings. We conduct a comprehensive evaluation of nine representative models across a diverse range of common corruption types. Our analysis reveals that MLLMs generally exhibit superior robustness compared to traditional vision models, although they show slightly reduced resilience to noise and color distortions relative to ViTs. We observe that geometric transformations and color shifts have limited impact on performance, whereas compression artifacts and blurring present persistent challenges across all architectures. Notably, the robustness advantage of MLLMs appears to stem primarily from their capacity to extract higher-quality visual representations, rather than from the language components that distinguish them from vision-only models. These findings offer novel cross-architecture insights and emphasize the importance of robust feature extraction in multimodal systems. The full benchmark, appendix, and codes are publicly available at https://github.com/EdyQiu/UniCorrupt-Bench.

Keywords: computer vision · image corruption · model robustness

1 Introduction

Deep learning models have achieved impressive performance across a wide range of computer vision tasks, including image classification, object detection, and

© The Author(s), under exclusive license to Springer Nature Singapore Pte Ltd. 2026
J. Lokoč et al. (Eds.): MMM 2026, LNCS 16412, pp. 204–218, 2026.
https://doi.org/10.1007/978-981-95-6950-2_15

visual question answering [1, 11, 19]. However, in real-world scenarios, images are often subject to degradations such as noise, blur, compression artifacts, occlusions, and adverse weather conditions [12, 43, 51]. These corruptions significantly degrade input quality and raise concerns about the reliability and safety of deploying such models in safety-critical environments.

Initial studies on robustness to image corruption primarily focused on Convolutional Neural Networks (CNNs) [5, 10, 22, 30, 37, 40]. With the rise of Vision Transformers (ViTs), the research community has shifted toward comparative analyses between CNNs and ViTs, examining their respective vulnerabilities and strengths under corruptions [2, 28, 31, 34, 45, 49, 52]. More recently, Multimodal Large Language Models (MLLMs) have demonstrated strong capabilities in vision-language tasks by jointly modeling visual and textual information [32, 44, 47]. Despite their success, little is known about how MLLMs perform under corrupted visual conditions, and no systematic comparison has been made against traditional vision-only models such as CNNs and ViTs.

One major obstacle to such comparisons lies in the incompatibility of existing benchmarks. Most robustness benchmarks are tailored either for vision-only models or for vision-language models, each operating with fundamentally different input-output modalities. Specifically, CNNs and ViTs take an image as input and output a class label, while MLLMs require both an image and a textual prompt as input and generate free-form textual outputs. These differences hinder direct, fair comparisons across model families.

To address this gap, we propose **UniCorrupt-Bench**—a unified evaluation framework that enables standardized and architecture-agnostic assessment of model robustness under image corruption. Our benchmark contains 80,000 samples spanning 32 fine-grained corruption types, which are further grouped into six broad categories. UniCorrupt-Bench allows for consistent evaluation across CNNs, ViTs, and MLLMs. Although we focus on image classification as the canonical evaluation task, the framework itself is readily extensible to other modalities and tasks.

This study aims to answer the following research questions:

– How does the corruption robustness of MLLMs compare to that of CNNs and ViTs?
– Which types of corruption most significantly affect each model family?
– What architectural or functional factors contribute to the observed robustness of MLLMs?

To the best of our knowledge, this work presents the first benchmark that supports robust, cross-architecture evaluation of CNNs, ViTs, and MLLMs under corrupted conditions. It also delivers the first large-scale, systematic comparison of these three model families in a unified setting. We believe our findings provide critical insights into the design of more robust vision and vision-language models, and we hope UniCorrupt-Bench will serve as a foundation for future research on multimodal robustness.

2 Related Work

Table 1. Comparison of existing image corruption robustness benchmarks and the proposed UniCorrupt-Bench. UniCorrupt-Bench is the first to support standardized and direct evaluation of CNNs, ViTs, and MLLMs within a unified framework.

Vision Benchmark	Architecture	Evaluation Tasks	# Corruptions
CIFAR10-C [14]	CNNs, ViTs	Classification	15
ImageNet-C [14]	CNNs, ViTs	Classification	15
RB-CTA [20]	CNNs, ViTs	Classification	15
Pascal-C [29]	CNNs, ViTs	Detection	15
Cityscapes-C [24]	CNNs, ViTs	Detection	15
COCO-C [24]	CNNs, ViTs	Detection	16
Kamann2020 [18]	CNNs, ViTs	Segmentation	19
Dalva2024 [7]	CNNs, ViTs	Segmentation	16
V-L Benchmark	Architecture	Evaluation Tasks	# Corruptions
MSRVTT-P [38]	MLLMs	Text-to-video retrieval	18
MMC-Bench [50]	MLLMs	Image captioning	29
R-Bench [21]	MLLMs	Multiple choice, VQA and captioning	33
VRB-VQA [16]	MLLMs	VQA	14
MMRobustness [36]	MLLMs	Visual entailment, image captioning, visual reasoning, image-text retrieval and text-to-image generation	17
VCR-Bench [39]	CNNs, ViTs, CLIP	Classification	14
UniCorrupt-Bench	CNNs, ViTs, MLLMs	Classification	32

Benchmarks on Image Corruption Robustness. The study of visual robustness under image corruption gained momentum with the introduction of the ImageNet-C benchmark [14], which applied 15 artificial distortions to the ImageNet dataset to assess classification performance under corrupted inputs. Building on this foundation, subsequent efforts extended corruption-based evaluations to other tasks, including object detection [11] and image segmentation [27], giving rise to a family of standardized robustness benchmarks [7,18,24,29]. With the rapid emergence of MLLMs, new benchmarks have been proposed to evaluate robustness in multimodal settings, such as MSRVTT-P [38], MMC-Bench [50], R-Bench [21], MMRobustness [36] and VRB-VQA [16], which extend robustness analysis to a broader range of multimodal capabilities. In terms of cross-architecture evaluation, concurrent efforts VCR-Bench [39] further broaden the architectural scope by including CNNs, ViTs, and CLIP models. A comparative summary of existing image corruption robustness benchmarks is presented in Table 1.

Model Behavior Under Image Corruption. Initial studies on corruption robustness primarily examined CNNs in classification tasks. A widely held view is that CNNs exhibit a texture bias, and shifting toward a shape bias can improve

Table 2. Hierarchical organization of image corruptions in UniCorrupt-Bench.

Coarse Corruptions	Fine Corruptions
Color Channel	Brightness, Contrast, Saturation, Invert, Gamma Contrast, Channel Shuffle
Geometric Transform	Scale x, Scale y, Scale xy, Shear x, Shear y, Rotate
Blur	Defocus, Glass, Zoom, Motion, and Gaussian Blur
Compression	Average and Max Pooling, Pixelate, JPEG Compression
Weather Condition	Snow, Frost, Fog, Rain, Snowflake, Spatter
Noise	Impulse, Shot, Speckle, Gaussian, and Poisson Noise

robustness [10,40]. However, complementary findings suggest that texture features may remain more stable under certain corruptions [22,37]. Beyond shape-texture analysis, frequency-domain studies highlight the role of phase and low-frequency components in maintaining robustness [5,30].The robustness of ViTs has been increasingly explored since their introduction, with several studies attributing their advantages over CNNs to self-attention mechanisms [28,52], flexible receptive fields [31], a stronger focus on structural cues [49], and benefits from large-scale pretraining [2]. Conversely, other works argue that CNNs can match or even exceed ViT robustness when equipped with similar training regimes or architectural enhancements [34,45].

Despite these advances, two critical gaps remain: (1) the robustness of MLLMs under image corruption is still underexplored, particularly in comparison to CNNs and ViTs; and (2) there is a lack of unified benchmarks that support fair, cross-architecture evaluations across both vision-only and vision-language models. These limitations motivate our work and the development UniCorrupt-Bench, which aims to address both issues.

3   UniCorrupt-Bench

To enable systematic and fair comparisons of CNNs, ViTs, and MLLMs under image corruption, we propose UniCorrupt-Bench—a unified benchmark comprising 80,000 image–answer pairs across 32 fine-grained and 6 coarse-grained corruption types. UniCorrupt-Bench is designed to support comprehensive robustness evaluation while addressing the specific input–output requirements of diverse model architectures. Below, we outline the key design components.

Task Selection. Although CNNs, ViTs, and MLLMs support a range of tasks including image classification, object detection, and segmentation, we focus on image classification in this initial study. Classification is widely regarded as the most standard and well-established task for evaluating robustness to image corruption in the computer vision community.

Data Selection. We adopt the ImageNet test set as our source of clean images, given its ubiquity in benchmarking classification performance. Specifically, we

Fig. 1. Illustration of the input format used in UniCorrupt-Bench for evaluating MLLMs: prompt and corrupted images.

select 10 representative subcategories from ImageNet, since the reduced label space helps mitigate instruction-following failures in MLLMs, which can arise with large candidate lists. Subcategories are chosen to ensure semantic diversity (e.g., a balance of animals and man-made objects), following the hierarchical structure of ImageNet [3]. The dataset size is constrained to accommodate the relatively slow inference speeds of MLLMs.

Corruption Type Selection. Following the increasing diversity in recent robustness benchmarks, we select 32 fine-grained corruption types based on the `imgaug` library [17], and organize them into 6 coarse-grained categories. This hierarchical structure, illustrated in Table 2, enables both detailed and aggregated robustness analysis. Each corruption type is applied at five severity levels, following the design principles of ImageNet-C [14]. For corruptions with fixed-range parameters, we discretize the range into five intervals. For open-range parameters, the maximum severity corresponds to the highest value at which the image remains human-recognizable, with lower levels scaled accordingly. Representative examples of all 32 corruption types are provided in Appendix A. The code used to generate the corruptions is adapted from the `imgaug` library [17] and is included in the GitHub repository.

Input Generation. All models receive corrupted images as input, while MLLMs additionally require corresponding textual prompts. We generate 80,000 corrupted images by applying 32 fine-grained corruption types, each at five severity levels, to the clean ImageNet subset of 500 images. Each corrupted image is paired with a standardized classification prompt for MLLMs, as illustrated in Fig. 1. To mitigate position-based bias in MLLM responses, the order of candidate options is randomly shuffled for each inference.

Output Standardization. CNNs and ViTs are pretrained on ImageNet-1K, with outputs spanning a 1,000-class label space. To constrain predictions to the 10 selected categories, we zero out the logits corresponding to all other classes. For MLLMs, we expect the output as a free-form text response containing one of the 10 category names. To handle variations in phrasing (e.g., punctuation, casing, or introductory phrases), we implement template-based post-processing that allows for minor formatting inconsistencies.

4   Evaluating Model Robustness Under Image Corruption

This section presents a comparative analysis of the corruption robustness of nine models from three architectural families (CNNs, ViTs, and MLLMs) under a wide range of image corruption scenarios.

Experimental Settings. We evaluate three state-of-the-art MLLMs selected from recent vision-language benchmarks [23,25,48]: LLaVA [23], Honeybee [4], and TransCore-M [33]. All MLLMs are tested using their official configurations to ensure consistency and fairness. For comparison, we include three widely used CNNs: ResNet50 [13], VGG16 [41], and MobileNetV3 [15], and three Vision Transformers: ViT [8], Swin Transformer [42], and DeiT [26]. Pretrained weights for all models are obtained from the MMPretrain library [6]. Further implementation details, including model configurations and computing environments, are provided in Appendix B.

Evaluation Metrics. We adopt two primary evaluation metrics: accuracy (**Acc**) and accuracy ratio (**AR**). **Acc** measures the model's raw performance on corrupted images, offering insight into practical utility. **AR** quantifies robustness by normalizing performance relative to clean inputs, thereby isolating sensitivity to corruption. Formally, Acc and AR under corruption type c are defined as:

$$\text{Acc}_c = \text{Eval}(M(I_{\text{corrupt}_c}), \text{gt}), \text{Acc Ratio}_c = \frac{\text{Eval}(M(I_{\text{corrupt}_c}), \text{gt})}{\text{Eval}(M(I_{\text{clean}}), \text{gt})} \times 100\%. \quad (1)$$

where I_{corrupt_c} denotes corrupted inputs, gt the ground truth labels, and M the model being evaluated.

4.1   Overall Robustness

As shown in Table 3, all models perform well on clean images, with accuracies around 96%. However, their robustness to corruption varies significantly. CNNs suffer the greatest degradation, with an average accuracy drop of 20.2% and up to 34.3% at the highest severity. MLLMs exhibit the smallest decline—averaging only 5.5%, with a maximum drop of 12.7%. ViTs lie in between, with an average decrease of 8.5% and a worst-case drop of 16.7%. These results confirm that despite recent progress, image corruption remains a key challenge—though MLLMs show promising robustness.

Figure 2 further illustrates model sensitivity across severity levels. CNNs show the steepest decline, reflecting high vulnerability. MLLMs maintain the flattest curves, indicating better resilience, with ViTs again in the middle.

4.2   Robustness to Different Corruptions

To examine robustness across corruption types, we evaluate accuracy ratios at severity level 5 across six coarse-grained corruption categories. Results are visualized in Fig. 3 as a radar chart.

Table 3. Accuracy of CNNs, ViTs, and MLLMs on clean and corrupted images.

Model	Acc_{clean}	Acc_c Avg	Acc_c S5
ResNet	96.8	79.9	65.9
VGG	94.2	71.2	56.7
MobileNet	95.2	74.5	60.7
VIT	98.2	90.3	82.7
DeiT	97.4	88.8	81.0
Swin	93.0	84.0	74.7
LLaVA	96.8	90.5	82.6
Honeybee	95.8	90.8	84.0
TransCoreM	97.0	91.6	84.9
CNN avg	95.4	75.2	61.1
ViT avg	96.2	87.7	79.5
MLLM avg	96.5	91.0	83.8

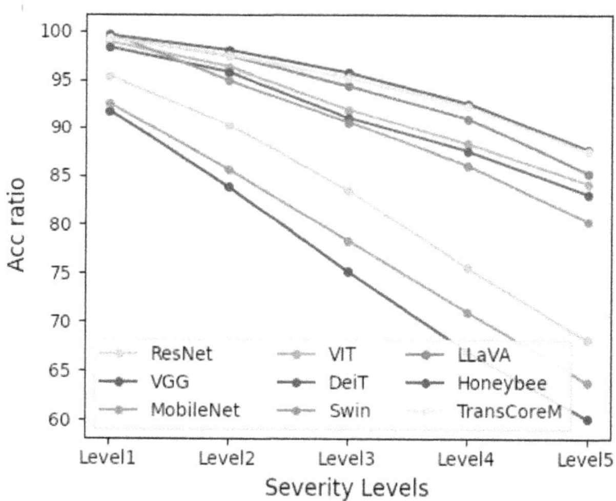

Fig. 2. Accuracy ratio of CNNs (blue), ViTs (green), and MLLMs (red) across five levels of corruption severity. (Color figure online)

Architecture-Wise Analysis: Models within each family exhibit similar degradation patterns, suggesting that vulnerability is closely tied to architectural design. MLLMs consistently outperform CNNs across all corruption types. Compared to ViTs, MLLMs are more robust to weather, blur, and compression, particularly excelling under compression. However, MLLMs show slightly greater vulnerability to noise and color perturbations than ViTs, challenging the common belief that MLLMs are uniformly superior in robustness.

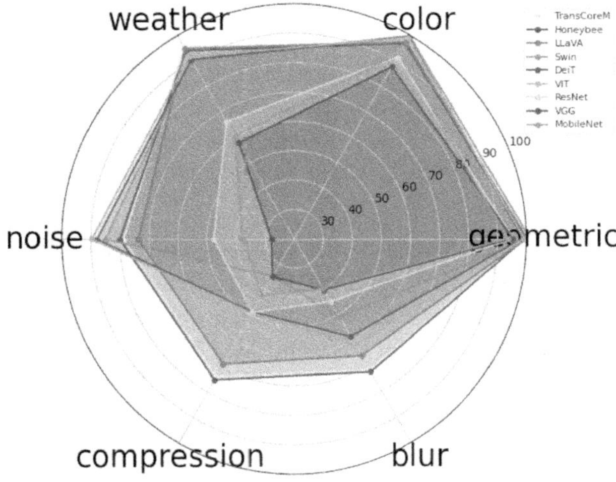

Fig. 3. Accuracy ratio of CNNs (blue), ViTs (green), and MLLMs (red) across six coarse-level corruption types at severity level 5. (Color figure online)

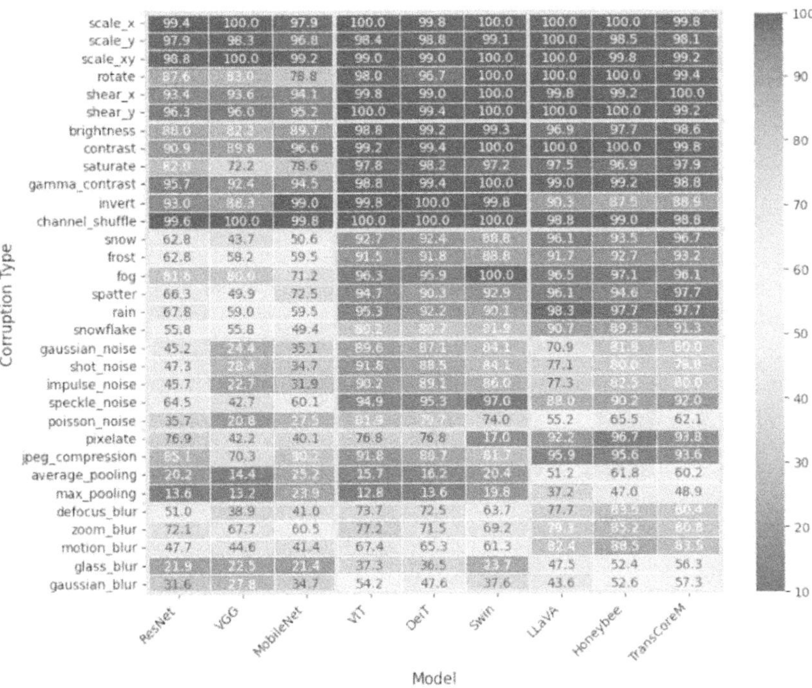

Fig. 4. Heatmap of accuracy ratios for all models across 32 fine-grained corruptions.

Figure 4 presents a heatmap of accuracy ratios across all 32 fine-grained corruptions. Yellow lines delineate model families and corruption categories.

Warmer colors denote higher accuracy ratios, with distinct and coherent patterns observed across models and coarse-grained corruption types.

These findings highlight specific corruption types that exert minimal influence across all model architectures, as well as those that lead to substantial performance degradation. The latter category warrants particular consideration in model development—especially when such corruptions are prevalent in real-world deployment scenarios.

Corruption-Wise Analysis: Geometric transformations and color perturbations exert minimal influence, with ViTs and MLLMs showing less than 1% degradation. In contrast, noise and weather effects cause substantial performance drops in CNNs and moderate impacts on ViTs and MLLMs. Compression and blur corruptions are universally challenging, with MLLMs retaining only 70% of their clean accuracy under these conditions.

5   Understanding the Robustness of MLLMs

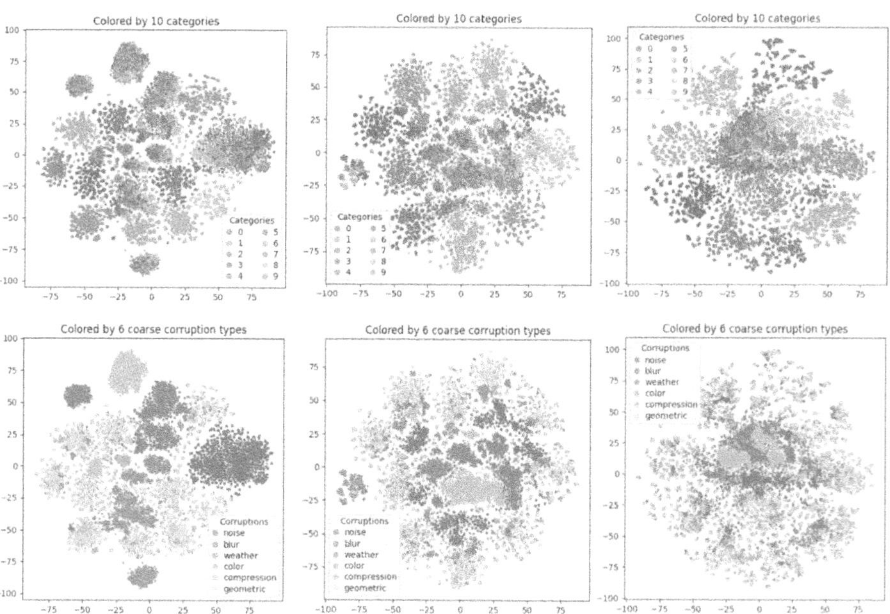

Fig. 5. t-SNE visualizations of features extracted by ResNet (left column), ViT (mid column), and LLaVA (right column) under severe corruption.

As shown in Sect. 4, MLLMs consistently demonstrate greater robustness to image corruption compared to ViTs and CNNs. To investigate the underlying causes of this advantage, we analyze the inference pipeline of MLLMs.

In typical MLLM architectures, the input image is first encoded by a visual encoder into a sequence of image tokens. Simultaneously, the textual prompt is tokenized into language tokens. These two token streams are concatenated and processed by a language model to enable joint visual–textual reasoning. Based on this architecture, we hypothesize two potential contributors to MLLMs' robustness, which are examined in the following subsections:

1. The visual encoder may generate more robust features under corruption than standard vision models (CNNs/ViTs).
2. The integration of language information may enhance robustness via high-level reasoning or contextual priors.

5.1 Impact of Image Feature Quality

Qualitative Analysis. To evaluate the quality of visual feature representations under corruption scenarios, we employ t-distributed Stochastic Neighbor Embedding (t-SNE) to project high-dimensional features into a two-dimensional space. This method preserves local neighborhood relationships, allowing for an intuitive assessment of feature separability and clustering structure. Figure 5 visualizes features extracted from three representative models—ResNet (left), ViT (middle), and LLaVA (right). The upper row is color-coded by semantic category, while the lower row is color-coded by corruption type.

In the top-row plots, all three model families exhibit a clear decline in class separability under heavy corruption. The previously well-defined clusters collapse into large mixed-color regions, indicating that features from different categories become highly entangled. This phenomenon suggests that severe corruption disrupts semantic discrimination, making it difficult for models to preserve meaningful inter-class boundaries in the feature space.

The bottom-row plots provide a complementary perspective. When features are colored by corruption type, large contiguous areas of uniform color overlap substantially with the mixed regions observed above. This alignment implies that corrupted samples are grouped primarily by distortion type rather than semantic class, revealing that corruption induces the encoding of distortion-specific artifacts instead of semantic information.

Among the three models, the MLLM (LLaVA) demonstrates the strongest robustness in its feature space. Its clusters remain relatively compact and well-separated by category while showing minimal corruption-dominated grouping. This indicates that MLLMs are more capable of resisting corruption-induced feature collapse and of maintaining semantic consistency under perturbations. Notably, the most severe degradation is consistently observed under compression (yellow clusters) and blur (green clusters), echoing the quantitative trends reported in Fig. 4. These qualitative results reinforce the strong correlation between feature quality and model robustness: models that retain compact, semantically organized representations exhibit higher corruption resilience.

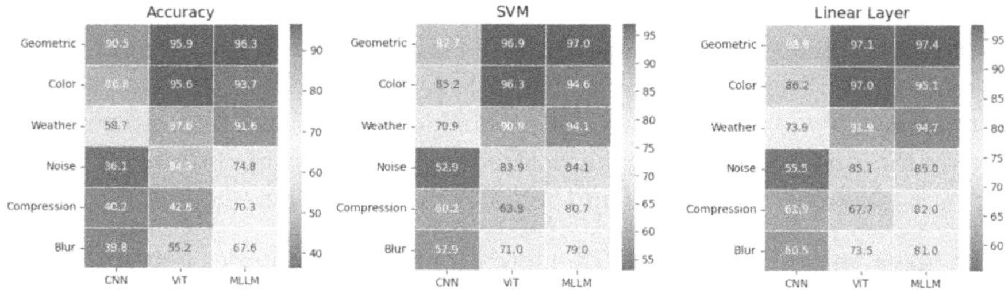

Fig. 6. Heatmaps of model accuracy (left), SVM classification accuracy (middle), and linear classifier accuracy (right) across corruption types and model architectures.

Quantitative Analysis. To complement visual observations, we quantitatively evaluate feature quality by measuring feature utility, whether the features contain sufficient information to support downstream tasks. We follow Zhang et al. [51] and train lightweight classifiers (SVM and linear layers) on the extracted features for each corruption type. Classifiers are trained on 80% of the data and evaluated on the remaining 20%.

As shown in Fig. 6, MLLMs consistently achieve higher classification accuracy across corruption types. Furthermore, the heatmaps for classifier accuracy closely resemble those from the model robustness analysis, underscoring a strong correlation between feature quality and corruption resilience. These results confirm that MLLMs' superior robustness primarily stems from their ability to extract higher-quality visual features, even in the presence of severe corruption.

5.2 Impact of Language Integration

One distinctive feature of MLLMs is their ability to process natural language, which may offer potential robustness advantages under degraded visual conditions. Drawing inspiration from prior work in zero-shot learning [9,35,46], domain adaptation [12,36,43,49], and shape-biased modeling [10,40,49], we evaluate three types of auxiliary prompts to assess whether explicit textual cues can enhance performance under corruption: (1) category descriptions, (2) corruption Descriptions, and (3) shape-biased instructions. Detailed motivations and examples for each prompt type are listed in Appendix C.

Contrary to expectations, all three types of auxiliary prompts resulted in reduced accuracy across corruption types (Table 4). These findings indicate that the robustness of MLLMs is unlikely to originate from language integration, and may even be negatively affected by redundant or distracting textual input. This further supports our core conclusion: the primary driver of robustness in MLLMs lies in the quality of visual representations, rather than in the use of natural language reasoning or linguistic context.

Table 4. Impact of additional textual inputs on MLLM accuracy under corruption.

Model	None	Category	Corruption	Shape-biased
LLaVA	90.5	72.9	69.0	81.6
Honeybee	90.8	68.3	86.5	87.3
TransCoreM	91.6	88.7	83.0	88.7

6 Discussion and Limitations

Building on the empirical findings presented in Sects. 4 and 5, this section revisits the three key research questions outlined in the beginning of this paper, providing a comprehensive discussion of model behavior under image corruption.

(1) How does the corruption robustness of MLLMs compare to that of CNNs and ViTs? Our results confirm that image corruption remains a major challenge across all architectures. While CNNs are the most vulnerable—experiencing sharp accuracy degradation—ViTs show moderate resilience, and MLLMs consistently outperform both. On average, MLLMs demonstrate stronger robustness across corruption types and severity levels. However, fine-grained analysis reveals exceptions: MLLMs underperform ViTs under specific perturbations, particularly noise and color distortions, suggesting that their robustness is not universally superior.

(2) Which types of corruption most significantly affect each model family? Geometric transformations and color perturbations have limited impact on all three model families, especially for ViTs and MLLMs. In contrast, weather effects and noise severely degrade CNN performance, while moderately affecting ViTs and MLLMs. Compression and blurring are consistently harmful across all models, representing critical weaknesses even for state-of-the-art MLLMs. These corruption types are especially relevant for real-world applications, such as low-bandwidth transmission or adverse environmental conditions.

(3) What architectural or functional factors contribute to the observed robustness of MLLMs? Through both qualitative visualizations and quantitative metrics, we identify the quality of visual features as the primary driver of robustness. MLLMs extract significantly more discriminative and corruption invariant features than CNNs and ViTs. Conversely, the integration of task-relevant textual information or the use of language-based reasoning appears to have limited effect under corruption. In some cases, adding external prompts even reduces performance, suggesting that visual encoders—not language components—play the dominant role in MLLMs' corruption resilience.

Limitations and Future Work. This study has two main limitations. First, our current analysis focuses on image classification, which, while foundational, represents only one aspect of model robustness. Extending UniCorrupt-Bench to a broader set of tasks, including object detection, semantic segmentation, and multimodal reasoning such as visual question answering and image captioning, constitutes an important next step. These extensions will help determine whether the cross-architecture robustness patterns observed in this study can generalize beyond the classification setting. Second, although visual feature quality has been identified as a key determinant of robustness, the specific factors underlying this property, including the diversity of pretraining data, architectural inductive biases, and multimodal fusion mechanisms, remain to be disentangled. Future work will investigate these aspects in a more systematic manner and incorporate statistical significance analysis across multiple runs to establish stronger empirical confidence in the observed trends.

7   Conclusion

This paper introduces UniCorrupt-Bench, a unified benchmark designed to evaluate the corruption robustness of CNNs, ViTs, and MLLMs under a standardized classification framework. Empirical results reveal that MLLMs consistently outperform vision-only models across a broad range of corruption types, though all architectures remain sensitive to blur and compression. Further analysis attributes the robustness of MLLMs primarily to their ability to extract high-quality visual features under corruption, rather than to language integration or reasoning components. These findings identify visual feature robustness as a critical bottleneck and suggest that strengthening visual encoders is a promising avenue for enhancing the real-world reliability of multimodal systems.

Acknowledgements. This work is partially supported by the National Key R&D Program of China (No. 2022YFB3103800) and the National Natural Science Foundation of China (No. U2336205).

References

1. Antol, S., Agrawal, A., Lu, J., et al.: VQA: visual question answering. In: ICCV (2015)
2. Bhojanapalli, S., Chakrabarti, A., Glasner, D., et al.: Understanding robustness of transformers for image classification. In: ICCV (2021)
3. Bostock, M.: Imagenet hierarchy (2018). https://observablehq.com/@mbostock/imagenet-hierarchy
4. Cha, J., Kang, W., Mun, J., Roh, B.: Honeybee: locality-enhanced projector for multimodal LLM. In: CVPR (2024)
5. Chen, G., Peng, P., Ma, L., et al.: Amplitude-phase recombination: rethinking robustness of convolutional neural networks in frequency domain. In: ICCV (2021)
6. Contributors, M.: Openmmlab's pre-training toolbox and benchmark (2023). https://github.com/openmmlab/mmpretrain
7. Dalva, Y., Pehlivan, H., Altındiş, S.F., Dundar, A.: Benchmarking the robustness of instance segmentation models. TNNLS (2024)
8. Dosovitskiy, A., Beyer, L., Kolesnikov, A., et al.: An image is worth 16×16 words: transformers for image recognition at scale. In: ICLR (2021)
9. Elhoseiny, M., Saleh, B., Elgammal, A.: Write a classifier: zero-shot learning using purely textual descriptions. In: ICCV (2013)

10. Geirhos, R., Rubisch, P., Michaelis, C., et al.: Imagenet-trained CNNs are biased towards texture. In: ICLR (2018)
11. Girshick, R., Donahue, J., Darrell, T., Malik, J.: Region-based convolutional networks for accurate object detection and segmentation. TPAMI (2015)
12. Han, Z., Zhou, G., He, R., et al.: How well does GPT-4V (ision) adapt to distribution shifts? A preliminary investigation. In: ICLR Workshop (2024)
13. He, K., Zhang, X., Ren, S., Sun, J.: Deep residual learning for image recognition. In: CVPR (2016)
14. Hendrycks, D., Dietterich, T.: Benchmarking neural network robustness to common corruptions and perturbations. In: ICLR (2019)
15. Howard, A., Sandler, M., Chu, G., et al.: Searching for mobilenetv3. In: ICCV (2019)
16. Ishmam, M.F., Tashdeed, I., Saadat, T.A., Ashmafee, M.H., Kamal, A.R.M., Hossain, M.A.: Visual robustness benchmark for visual question answering (VQA). In: WACV (2025)
17. Jung, A.B., Wada, K., Crall, J., et al.: imgaug (2020). https://github.com/aleju/imgaug
18. Kamann, C., Rother, C.: Benchmarking the robustness of semantic segmentation models with respect to common corruptions. In: IJCV (2021)
19. Krizhevsky, A., Sutskever, I., Hinton, G.E.: Imagenet classification with deep convolutional neural networks. In: NeurIPS (2012)
20. Kumar, V., Shukla, S., Agarwal, A.: Robustness benchmarking of convolutional and transformer architectures for image classification. Big Data (2025)
21. Li, C., Zhang, J., Zhang, Z., et al.: R-bench: are your large multimodal model robust to real-world corruptions? arXiv preprint arXiv:2410.05474 (2024)
22. Li, Y., Yu, Q., Tan, M., et al.: Shape-texture debiased neural network training. In: ICLR (2020)
23. Liu, H., Li, C., Wu, Q., Lee, Y.J.: Visual instruction tuning. In: NeurIPS (2024)
24. Liu, J., Wang, Z., Ma, L., et al.: Benchmarking object detection robustness against real-world corruptions. In: IJCV (2024)
25. Liu, Y., Duan, H., Zhang, Y., et al.: Mmbench: is your multi-modal model an all-around player? In: ECCV (2025)
26. Liu, Z., Lin, Y., Cao, Y., et al.: Swin transformer: hierarchical vision transformer using shifted windows. In: ICCV (2021)
27. Long, J., Shelhamer, E., Darrell, T.: Fully convolutional networks for semantic segmentation. In: CVPR (2015)
28. Mao, X., Qi, G., Chen, Y., et al.: Towards robust vision transformer. In: CVPR (2022)
29. Michaelis, C., Mitzkus, B., Geirhos, R., et al.: Benchmarking robustness in object detection: autonomous driving when winter is coming. arXiv preprint arXiv:1907.07484 (2019)
30. Mukai, K., Kumano, S., Yamasaki, T.: Improving robustness to out-of-distribution data by frequency-based augmentation. In: ICIP (2022)
31. Naseer, M.M., Ranasinghe, K., Khan, S.H., et al.: Intriguing properties of vision transformers. In: NeurIPS (2021)
32. OpenAI, Achiam, J., Adler, S., et al.: GPT-4 technical report (2024). https://arxiv.org/abs/2303.08774
33. PCI-research: Transcorem (2023). https://github.com/PCIResearch/TransCore-M
34. Pinto, F., Torr, P., Dokania, P.K.: Are vision transformers always more robust than convolutional neural networks? In: NeurIPS Workshop (2021)

35. Pourpanah, F., Abdar, M., Luo, Y., et al.: A review of generalized zero-shot learning methods. TPAMI (2022)
36. Qiu, J., Zhu, Y., Shi, X., et al.: Benchmarking robustness of multimodal image-text models under distribution shift. DMLR (2023)
37. Qiu, X., Kan, M., Zhou, Y., Bi, Y., Shan, S.: Shape-biased CNNs are not always superior in out-of-distribution robustness. WACV (2024)
38. Schiappa, M., Vyas, S., Palangi, H., et al.: Robustness analysis of video-language models against visual and language perturbations. In: NeurIPS (2022)
39. Shen, H., Hu, B.C., Czarnecki, K., Marsso, L., Chechik, M.: Assessing visually-continuous corruption robustness of neural networks relative to human performance. In: WACV (2025)
40. Shi, B., Zhang, D., Dai, Q., et al.: Informative dropout for robust representation learning: a shape-bias perspective. In: ICML (2020)
41. Simonyan, K., Zisserman, A.: Very deep convolutional networks for large-scale image recognition. arXiv preprint arXiv:1409.1556 (2014)
42. Touvron, H., Cord, M., Douze, M., et al.: Training data-efficient image transformers & distillation through attention. In: ICML (2021)
43. Verma, A.A., Saeidi, A., Hegde, S., et al.: Evaluating multimodal large language models across distribution shifts and augmentations. In: CVPR Workshop (2024)
44. Wang, J., Jiang, H., Liu, Y., et al.: A comprehensive review of multimodal large language models: performance and challenges across different tasks. arXiv preprint arXiv:2408.01319 (2024)
45. Wang, Z., Bai, Y., Zhou, Y., Xie, C.: Can CNNs be more robust than transformers? In: ICLR (2022)
46. Xu, W., Xian, Y., Wang, J., et al.: Attribute prototype network for zero-shot learning. In: NeurIPS (2020)
47. Yin, S., Fu, C., Zhao, S., et al.: A survey on multimodal large language models. National Science Review (2024)
48. Yin, Z., Wang, J., Cao, J., et al.: Lamm: language-assisted multi-modal instruction-tuning dataset, framework, and benchmark. In: NeurIPS (2024)
49. Zhang, C., Zhang, M., Zhang, S., et al.: Delving deep into the generalization of vision transformers under distribution shifts. In: CVPR (2022)
50. Zhang, J., Pang, T., Du, C., et al.: Benchmarking large multimodal models against common corruptions. arXiv preprint arXiv:2401.11943 (2024)
51. Zhang, X., Li, J., Chu, W., et al.: On the out-of-distribution generalization of multimodal large language models. arXiv preprint arXiv:2402.06599 (2024)
52. Zhou, D., Yu, Z., Xie, E., et al.: Understanding the robustness in vision transformers. In: ICML (2022)

Stereo3D-NeRF: Generating 3D Visualizations with Paired Stereoscopic Views

Yongxiang Wang[1], Gang Zhou[1]([✉]), Wei Liu[2], and Yang Zhou[2]

[1] Xinjiang University, Urumqi, China
gangzhou_xju@126.com
[2] Yangtze Delta Region Institute, Tsinghua University, Jiaxing, China

Abstract. The integration of Novel View Synthesis (NVS) and 3D display technology opens unprecedented opportunities for 3D visualization across diverse fields. However, generating high-quality 3D content in complex, detail-intensive scenarios remains challenging due to high production costs and insufficient stereoscopic detail rendering in existing methods. In response, we propose a new rendering framework (Stereo3D-NeRF) that leverages pairwise left-right eye inputs and implicitly introduces disparity, enabling the network to capture richer spatial depth and structure without explicit disparity maps. By exploiting natural viewpoint differences for pixel-level matching, Stereo3D-NeRF significantly improves the reconstruction of fine textures and sharp edges, resulting in more immersive and realistic 3D content. Experimental results show that this strategy greatly improves the reconstruction quality of complex model surfaces and textures, while demonstrating outstanding fidelity in a range of 3D visualization tasks, laying a solid foundation for broader adoption of novel view synthesis.

Keywords: Neural Radiance Fields · Binocular Rendering ·
Multi-View Consistency

1 Introduction

In recent years, Novel View Synthesis (NVS) has become a key research focus in both computer graphics and computer vision, aiming to synthesize arbitrary new viewpoints of a scene from a limited set of observed perspectives. This technology shows great promise for a wide range of 3D applications, including virtual reality (VR), augmented reality (AR), and 3D film and video production.

To achieve stereoscopic vision in 3D display, it is generally necessary to provide slightly different viewing information for the left and right eyes. Currently, traditional 3D content generation methods such as depth image-based rendering (DIBR) [5] often rely on converting depth maps or employing high-cost 3D modeling. Such approaches not only risk creating holes and discontinuities if depth estimation is inaccurate, but also involve complicated workflows that

J. Lokoč et al. (Eds.): MMM 2026, LNCS 16412, pp. 219–232, 2026.
https://doi.org/10.1007/978-981-95-6950-2_16

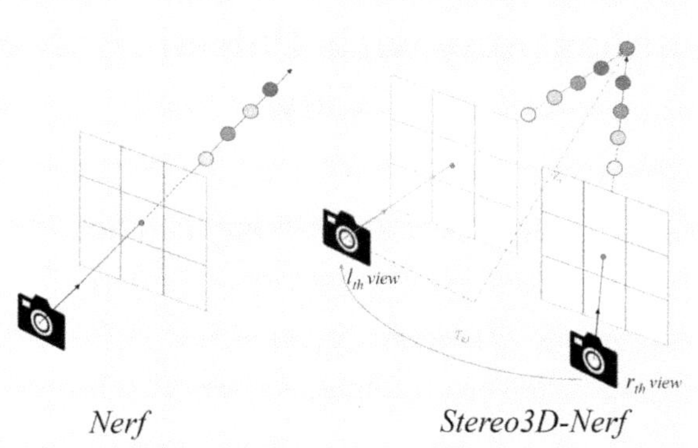

Fig. 1. Single-Ray vs. Stereo-Ray Sampling.

struggle to balance high quality and efficiency. Furthermore, while structured light or LiDAR-based 3D reconstruction excels in geometric precision, it is frequently limited in terms of rich multi-view data and production flexibility [11,29]. Directly using a stereo camera requires meticulous conditions—such as baseline distance, lighting, and camera synchronization—thereby reducing the scalability of data acquisition [9]. In response to these challenges, a significant body of novel view synthesis (NVS) research has emerged in recent years within the deep learning community [8]. Among these methods, Neural Radiance Fields (NeRF) [22] utilize a multi-layer perceptron (MLP) to implicitly model the color and density of a scene, enabling high-quality, continuous novel-view rendering from only a small set of multi-view images and associated camera parameters.

However, directly applying novel view synthesis techniques to complex objects (e.g., highly detailed human organ structures) still faces significant challenges. As shown in Fig. 1, a single-view NeRF training approach cannot fully exploit stereoscopic information. Binocular vision, by simulating the way human eyes observe the world, can obtain accurate depth information, but most existing models are monocular, often leading to insufficient depth perception and clarity when reconstructing objects with complex geometry and textures.

To address this, we propose a virtual binocular dataset construction method tailored to complex objects. By feeding paired left- and right-eye images into the NeRF training process, we implicitly incorporate matched pixel rays without explicitly computing a disparity map. Through the subtle differences in ray directions between the two viewpoints, our approach provides additional three-dimensional structural cues for the model. Under this design, the model automatically captures, exploits, and integrates these implicit stereoscopic signals during training, thereby more accurately restoring complex object shapes and enhancing both consistency and realism in the final render. The main contributions of this study are as follows:

- We constructed a high-fidelity virtual binocular dataset. In contrast to widely used datasets such as NeRF-Synthetic, which primarily consist of rigid and geometrically simple objects, our dataset incorporates anatomically accurate organ models featuring complex structures and rich textures. This dataset offers abundant stereo training samples for novel view synthesis models and establishes a solid foundation for subsequent research in stereoscopic matching and related tasks.
- Without relying on explicit disparity maps, we introduce a binocular training approach that integrates a multi-view consistency construction module with a depth-consistency loss. This guides the model to learn scene depth and geometric structures.
- Compared to NeRF methods trained with monocular data, this approach shows significantly improved performance in complex and demanding scenarios, producing 3D content with greater immersion. It thereby offers a new solution for high-fidelity visualization tasks where structural accuracy and image quality are critical.

2 Related Work

2.1 Novel View Synthesis

Novel View Synthesis (NVS) aims to generate high-quality target-view images from a limited set of input perspectives. Due to its potential applications in computer vision and graphics—such as Virtual Reality (VR), Augmented Reality (AR), and 3D displays—NVS has become a major research focus. Recent developments in NVS have largely revolved around two major approaches: geometric modeling and deep learning. Early NVS methods often relied on geometric modeling techniques such as optical triangulation and multi-view geometry [12]. Representative work includes viewpoint interpolation based on multi-view stereo matching [3] and volumetric rendering [15]. These methods typically require precise geometric calibration and dense input data, restricting their performance in sparse-data scenarios. Subsequently, in order to reduce the complexity of geometric modeling, image interpolation and light field techniques have been widely explored. Light field cameras capture 4D light field data and employ disparity-based interpolation to synthesize target viewpoints [23]. However, light field methods usually demand dense sampling and involve high computational costs. In recent years, deep learning–based disparity-guided interpolation [5] has demonstrated robust performance in sparse sampling scenarios. For instance, Hou et al. [13] introduced a joint optimization of disparity estimation and image synthesis that significantly improves non-Lambertian viewpoint generation; Zhou et al. [32] proposed a multi-layer disparity fusion strategy that further refines edge transitions in synthesized images. Advancements in geometric modeling and deep learning have spurred significant progress in NVS, although key research challenges remain in boosting synthesis quality under sparse data conditions and reducing computational overhead.

2.2   Neural Radiance Fields

Neural Radiance Fields (NeRF) is a seminal work in novel view synthesis. Its introduction greatly propelled the field of NVS, providing a foundational approach for many subsequent methods. For instance, FastNeRF [10] and PlenOctrees [30] aim to accelerate NeRF's training and inference through spatial partitioning and voxel-based subdivision. Mip-NeRF [2] incorporates a multiscale anti-aliasing mechanism to enhance high-frequency detail synthesis. In dynamic scenarios, Dynamic-NeRF [16] and Nerfies [24] leverage temporal modeling and pose adaptation for high-quality scene generation. Furthermore, Depth-supervised NeRF [4] and NeuralRGBD [1] add depth supervision to strengthen geometric consistency and depth information. Deepview [7] offers dense modeling of complex geometry for significantly improved synthesis quality. More recently, hybrid approaches that integrate geometric priors such as point clouds or depth maps [20] continue to enhance reconstruction capabilities under sparse-view conditions. NeRF's original framework laid the groundwork for novel view synthesis; subsequent research focusing on efficiency, dynamic scenes, and geometry consistency has further expanded its applications.

2.3   3D Content Generation

Producing binocular images is central to creating 3D content, with the goal of generating stereo-consistent image pairs to achieve stereoscopic perception. Traditional solutions rely on geometric modeling and multi-view geometry [9], coupling stereo cameras and structured light systems [31] to generate left and right images, followed by disparity computation to reconstruct 3D content. Recently, deep learning–based approaches have seen remarkable progress: for example, NeRF implicitly renders high-quality stereo image pairs, and StereoGAN [18] applies geometric constraints to further improve view consistency. In addition, depth-based image rendering (Depth Image-Based Rendering, DIBR) leverages depth guidance from a single viewpoint to produce the target viewpoint, reducing the complexity of synchronized multi-camera capture. Meanwhile, depth estimation [25] and optical flow guidance [27] have made notable strides in refining stereo consistency and detail accuracy in left and right eye views. Collectively, these techniques are widely employed in VR, AR, and 3D video, providing a robust foundation for high-quality 3D content generation (Fig. 2).

3   Method

3.1   Model Overview

Based on the original NeRF framework, our model refines the input design and incorporates cooperative inputs from both the left and right eye channels, thereby enhancing the modeling of implicit disparity information and enabling high-quality stereo image synthesis even in the absence of explicit disparity or depth data.

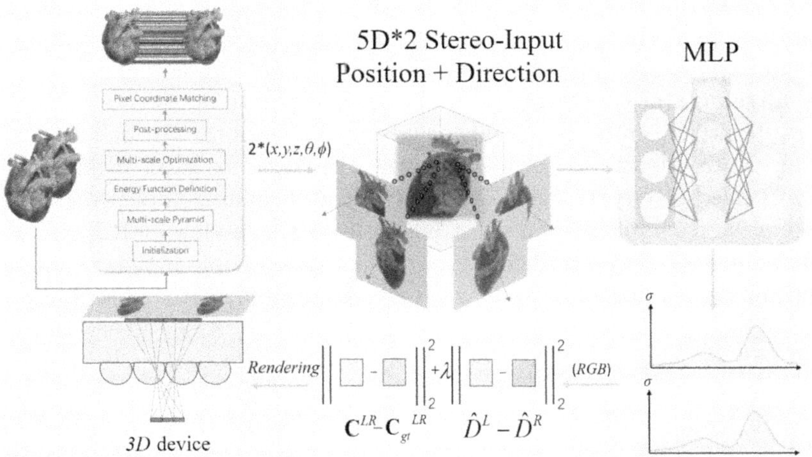

Fig. 2. The left and right views respectively generate rays, and a multi-layer perceptron (MLP) is employed to estimate the color and density at each sampled point. A volumetric rendering strategy with hierarchical sampling implicitly captures the stereoscopic differences between the two sets of rays, progressively reconstructing more accurate 3D structures and depth. Beyond basic reconstruction losses, a depth consistency constraint is imposed to encourage a unified spatial interpretation of the two ray sets.

At the input stage, we employ a dual-channel structure. For the left and right images, we separately construct corresponding rays (directions) and normalized coordinates, then feed both sets of data into the model simultaneously. Unlike the original single-view NeRF, which samples and renders based on monocular image, our training phase can utilize multi-view rays from both channels. This not only enriches the network with more extensive image data but also allows the model to naturally learn the implicit stereoscopic features arising from the differences between the left and right viewpoints. As the network jointly optimizes these paired rays, geometric discrepancies between the two eyes become implicitly constrained in the radiance field, providing a solid basis for subsequent disparity matching and stereoscopic rendering.

Whereas many existing methods rely on explicit disparity or depth maps, our approach instead models left and right rays jointly via a multi-view consistency construction module and performs implicit matching during radiance field rendering. Concretely, as the rays undergo hierarchical sampling, the model simultaneously considers the color and density distributions for samples on both the left and right channels. To render the final pixel color from sampled points, we adopt NeRF's volumetric rendering formulation. The pixel color is computed as:

$$C(r) = \sum_{i=1}^{N} T_i \cdot \alpha_i \cdot \mathbf{c}_i, \quad T_i = \exp\left(-\sum_{j=1}^{i-1} \sigma_j \Delta t_j\right), \quad \alpha_i = 1 - \exp(-\sigma_i \Delta t_i) \quad (1)$$

where $\mathbf{c}_i$ and σ_i denote the color and density at the i-th sample, and Δt_i is the distance between adjacent samples along the ray. This formulation enables joint learning of appearance and geometry in a fully differentiable manner.

By aligning and comparing adjacent sample points or feature vectors, the network iteratively enforces spatial consistency between the left and right views, reducing depth information loss. This avoids the need for explicit disparity calculation while better preserving depth details in visually complex regions (e.g., object edges or complex textures). Compared to single-view NeRF, this binocular matching strategy significantly mitigates stereoscopic artifacts and depth discontinuities, leading to a smoother, more accurate disparity distribution.

3.2 Dataset Construction

To construct a high-fidelity binocular dataset tailored for structurally intricate scenes, we imported finely modeled 3D object assets into Blender and implemented a multi-view stereoscopic rendering pipeline. Given the geometric complexity and morphological diversity of various objects, we designed a customized camera trajectory strategy to ensure comprehensive coverage of both external and internal structures. Specifically, we adopted a circular camera trajectory to capture external object surfaces from multiple viewpoints, ensuring uniform coverage—crucial for stable model training and accurate 3D reconstruction. To simulate human binocular vision, we enabled Blender's stereoscopic rendering mode and set the baseline distance between the left and right cameras to 65 mm, corresponding to the average human interpupillary distance. This configuration preserves natural depth perception and geometric consistency across stereo image pairs. Each camera pose generates a pair of left and right images, resulting in a well-structured binocular dataset suitable for NeRF-based novel view synthesis and depth-aware rendering. The final dataset comprises 5,200 high-resolution images (2,600 stereo pairs) across 13 complex scenes, covering a diverse range of targets with complex geometry and fine-grained textures. Compared to the widely used NeRF-Synthetic dataset—which primarily consists of rigid and geometrically simple objects—our dataset is specifically designed for tasks involving complex structure and fine-grained texture modeling. It offers a diverse and realistic benchmark for downstream applications such as novel view synthesis, stereo matching, and depth estimation, thereby supporting the development of more generalizable and high-fidelity 3D modeling techniques.

3.3 Multi-view Consistency Construction Module

In a binocular rendering scenario, simply providing simultaneous left and right views can make it difficult for Stereo3D-NeRF to learn implicit disparity information. The key challenge is how to ensure geometric consistency between the two eye views while incorporating disparity cues implicitly. To address this, we introduce a Multi-View Consistency Construction Module, which uses DIS optical flow [14] to achieve dense matching, thereby establishing pixel-level correspondences between left and right images. Firstly, to ensure stereoscopic consistency,

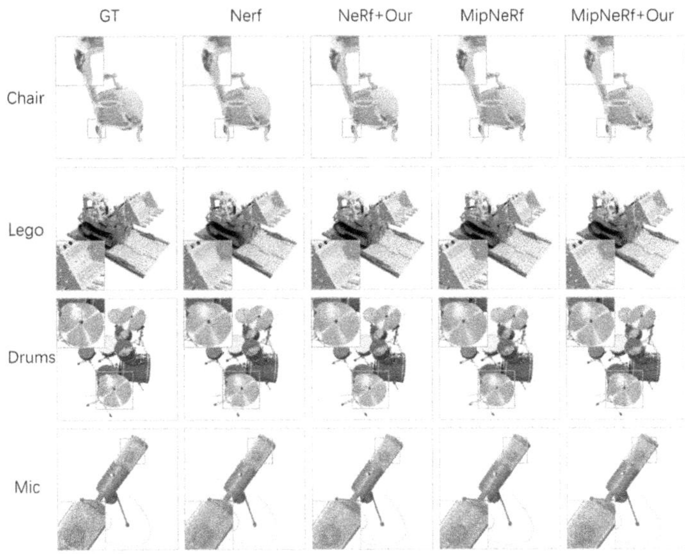

Fig. 3. Qualitative Comparison of Our Stereo3D-NeRF Approach on Nerf-Synthetic. From left to right: NeRF, NeRF+Our, MipNeRF, and MipNeRF+Our. Our binocular approach enhances anatomical detail, smooths surface textures.

we transform the baseline distance between cameras to the world coordinate system to obtain the right-eye pose. Using these poses, the module matches pixels between left and right images, determining ray directions and spatial relationships. To establish pixel correspondences, we use the DIS optical flow algorithm to compute dense mappings from the left to the right image. For each pixel x in the left view, its corresponding location in the right view is computed as:

$$x_R = x + \mathbf{f}(x), \quad \text{where } \mathbf{f}(x) \in \mathbb{R}^2 \text{ is the DIS optical flow} \tag{2}$$

These pixel-level correspondences define a matching set used in the consistency module:

$$\mathcal{M}_{\text{stereo}} = \{(x, x + \mathbf{f}(x)) \mid x \in \Omega_L\} \tag{3}$$

This mapping is later used to impose depth and color consistency constraints across stereo views.

Integrated into the rendering pipeline, this enhances depth learning and scene understanding, improving 3D reconstruction and producing more realistic stereoscopic outputs without explicit disparity maps.

3.4 Loss Function

Under the binocular training strategy, the goal is to simultaneously reconstruct both left- and right-eye images while leveraging their implicit geometric

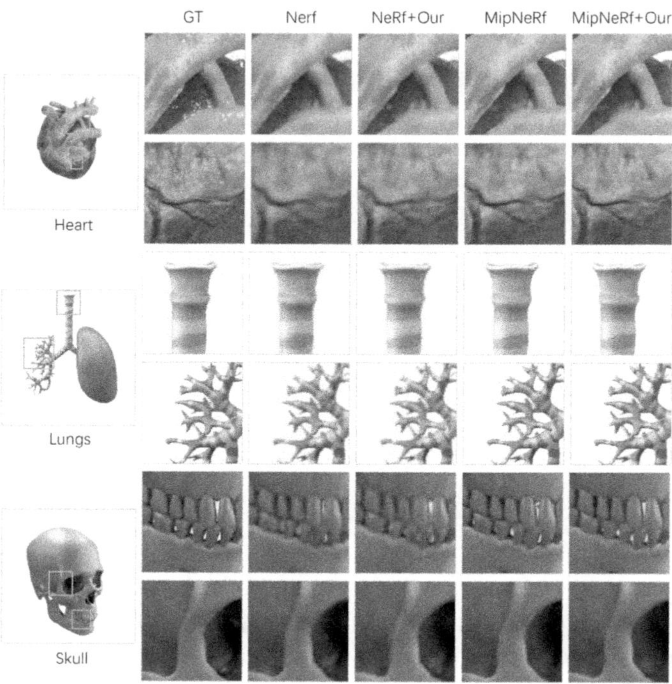

Fig. 4. Qualitative Comparison of Our Stereo3D-NeRF Approach on Blender-Medical Datasets.

constraints to strengthen the model's understanding of scene depth and stereoscopic structures. Concretely, we begin by sampling rays emitted from the camera according to the volumetric rendering equation, then synthesize the corresponding pixel colors and define a reconstruction error to measure the difference between synthesized and real images. Consistent with the original NeRF, each ray is rendered to produce a synthesized pixel color $\mathbf{C}(\mathbf{r})$, which is compared against its corresponding true color $\mathbf{C}_{\mathrm{gt}}$. Since each pixel in the left-right image pair has a known correspondence, we can write an identical form of reconstruction loss for both the left and right views (Fig. 4):

$$L_{\mathrm{recon}} = \sum_{\mathbf{x}\in\mathrm{Left}} \left\| \mathbf{C}^L(\mathbf{r}) - \mathbf{C}^L_{\mathrm{gt}}(\mathbf{x}) \right\|^2 + \sum_{\mathbf{x}^R\in\mathrm{Right}} \left\| \mathbf{C}^R(\mathbf{r}) - \mathbf{C}^R_{\mathrm{gt}}(\mathbf{x}^R) \right\|^2 \quad (4)$$

This term enforces consistency between the model's predicted colors and the actual observations for both eye views. As the model jointly optimizes reconstruction for two viewpoints, it naturally seeks a 3D structure that explains the binocular differences. While the reconstruction loss alone can capture some degree of stereo information, we introduce an additional depth-consistency constraint for high-quality or texture-intensive scenarios. By aligning the estimated depth distributions $\hat{D}^L, \hat{D}^R$ during training, the model encourages a unified geometric interpretation for the left and right rays:

$$L_{\text{stereo}} = \sum_{\mathbf{x} \in \Omega_L} \left\| \hat{D}^L(\mathbf{x}) - \Psi\left(\hat{D}^R(\mathbf{x}^R)\right)\right\| \tag{5}$$

where $\Psi(\cdot)$ denotes the warping operator based on stereo correspondence.

$$L_{\text{total}} = L_{\text{recon}} + \lambda L_{\text{stereo}} \tag{6}$$

where $\lambda = 0.2$ is a weighting factor that balances reconstruction fidelity against stereo consistency.

In practice, this loss design enables Stereo3D-NeRF not only to reconstruct the appearance of both binocular views but also to substantially utilize and preserve the 3D structural information present in the left and right perspectives. As a result, the final rendered output is more realistic, stable, and exhibits enhanced stereoscopic detail.

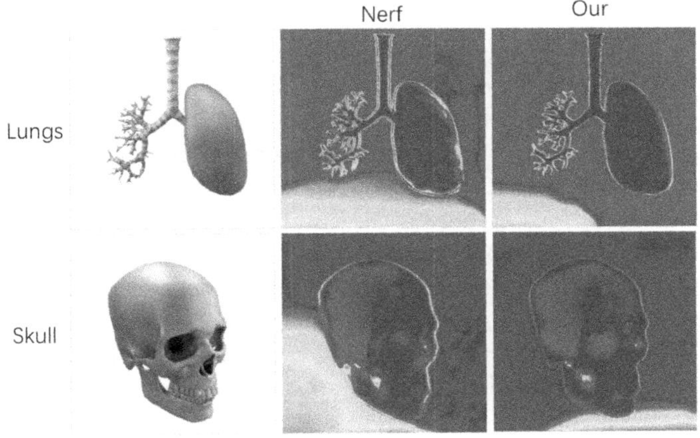

Fig. 5. Disparity heatmap comparison generated from stereo image pairs rendered by NeRF and Stereo3D-NeRF.

4 Experiments and Results

4.1 Metrics and Datasets

To objectively evaluate the performance of our proposed method, we conduct experiments on both the official NeRF-Synthetic dataset [22] and our custom Blender-Medical dataset. We employ PSNR, SSIM, and LPIPS as quantitative indicators to assess image reconstruction quality, and additionally use EPE and D1 metrics to evaluate stereo consistency and disparity estimation accuracy. The official dataset consists of eight different objects, and we strictly follow the original NeRF's training and evaluation protocols to ensure comparability and fairness. Our custom dataset encompasses 13 types of anatomically detailed objects and is organized in a similar manner.

Table 1. Comparison of PSNR, SSIM, and LPIPS on the official NeRF-Synthetic (Chair, Lego, Drums, Mic) and Blender-Medical datasets.

Method	NeRF-Synthetic			Blender-Medical		
	PSNR↑	SSIM↑	LPIPS↓	PSNR↑	SSIM↑	LPIPS↓
SNR [26]	22.26	0.846	0.169	-	-	-
NV [19]	25.92	0.905	0.136	30.45	0.915	0.157
LLFF [21]	24.88	0.911	0.114	-	-	-
NSVF [17]	31.23	0.963	0.036	34.97	0.961	0.058
NeRF [22]	30.70	0.960	0.049	34.80	0.968	0.051
NeRF+Our	<u>31.92</u>	<u>0.967</u>	<u>0.043</u>	<u>35.97</u>	<u>0.973</u>	<u>0.048</u>
MipNeRF [2]	33.48	0.973	**0.027**	37.49	0.978	0.036
Mip+Our	**33.99**	**0.975**	0.029	**37.93**	**0.978**	**0.033**

4.2   Implementation Details

During our experiments, we endeavored to maintain the same training strategy and hyperparameter settings as the original NeRF [22], ensuring fair and reproducible comparisons. We preserve the total number of training iterations at 100,000. Considering that our binocular strategy introduces twice the amount of data in each iteration, we halved the number of rays per batch from 1,024 to 512, keeping the GPU memory usage and computational overhead comparable to the monocular case. Other key parameters—such as learning rate, optimizer, and the number of coarse and fine samples (64 and 128, respectively)—remain consistent with the original NeRF, minimizing confounding factors and highlighting the actual contribution of the binocular strategy.

4.3   Experimental Results and Analysis

As shown in Fig. 3, our method achieves notable gains over both the original NeRF [22] and MipNeRf [2] in terms of visual appearance and quantitative metrics on the Nerf-synthetic dataset (e.g., Chair, Lego, Drums, Mic). Table 1 reveals that compared to the original NeRF, integrating our binocular strategy ("Nerf+Our") increases PSNR and SSIM by approximately 1.2 and 0.007, respectively, while reducing LPIPS by around 0.006. This indicates a marked improvement in both color fidelity and structural detail, particularly benefiting high-frequency areas. Moreover, combining our binocular strategy with MipNeRF yields a modestly smaller increase in PSNR and SSIM (about 0.5 and 0.002), yet maintains a low LPIPS value, suggesting robust multi-scale adaptability and enhanced perceptual quality overall.

The advantage is even more pronounced on our custom Blender-Medical dataset. As the Table 1 shows, relative to the baseline NeRF and MipNeRF, the binocular training approach further elevates PSNR (up to 35.97 and 37.93) and SSIM (up to 0.973 and 0.978). Meanwhile, the overall reduction in LPIPS

Table 2. EPE and D1 comparison of NeRF and Stereo3D-NeRF under three stereo matching methods.

Model	Stereo Matching	EPE↓	D1↓ (%)
NeRF [22]	DIS Optical Flow [14]	4.38	7.52
NeRF+Our		**3.72**	**6.10**
NeRF [22]	RAFT [28]	3.74	7.02
NeRF+Our		**2.92**	**5.87**
NeRF [22]	MC-Stereo [6]	3.34	6.14
NeRF+Our		**2.13**	**4.77**

Table 3. Quantitative evaluation on the NeRF-Synthetic and Blender-Medical datasets comparing the baseline NeRF, "Stereo Input," and "Ours".

Method	NeRF-Synthetic			Blender-Medical		
	PSNR↑	SSIM↑	LPIPS↓	PSNR↑	SSIM↑	LPIPS↓
NeRF [22]	30.70	0.960	0.049	34.80	0.968	0.051
Stereo	31.24	0.960	0.045	35.19	0.970	0.051
Ours	**31.92**	**0.967**	**0.043**	**35.97**	**0.973**	**0.048**

demonstrates that the model better conforms to human visual perception when reconstructing fine textures and intricate geometries. Beyond these measurable improvements, qualitative comparisons indicate our model excels at reproducing smoother texture transitions and preserving edge details on organ surfaces, outperforming existing methods in high-fidelity rendering tasks involving complex scenes.

To evaluate the stereo consistency of our model, we employ MC-Stereo to estimate disparity maps from the rendered left and right eye images and visualize the results as heatmaps to assess structural restoration. As shown in Fig. 5, the disparity maps generated by NeRF exhibit blurry edges and unclear structural boundaries, whereas those from Stereo3D-NeRF demonstrate sharper contours and more accurate geometry, indicating improved spatial consistency. Furthermore, we apply three mainstream stereo matching algorithms—DIS Optical Flow, RAFT, and MC-Stereo—to quantitatively evaluate the stereo consistency of the rendered image pairs from NeRF and Stereo3D-NeRF Table 2. Across all methods, Stereo3D-NeRF consistently outperforms the baseline. In the MC-Stereo setting, for example, the EPE is reduced from 3.34 to 2.13, and the D1 error rate drops from 6.14 to 4.77. Similar trends are observed with DIS and RAFT, confirming that our approach enhances geometric alignment and depth consistency across stereo views. These results demonstrate the superior stereo perception and spatial fidelity achieved by our method.

4.4   Ablation Study

To validate the independent contributions and synergistic effects of dual-channel input and the multi-view consistency construction module, we progressively add these two modules to the NeRF baseline and perform comparative tests.

In Table 3, "Stereo Input" shows a moderate improvement over baseline NeRF on both the NeRF-Synthetic and Blender-Medical datasets. For example, on NeRF-Synthetic, PSNR increases from 30.70 to 31.24, and LPIPS decreases from 0.049 to 0.045. We surmise that this benefit mainly comes from the implicit stereo constraints introduced by the dual-channel input (left and right images), which effectively bolster the reconstruction of texture and appearance. When further incorporating the multi-view consistency construction module ("Ours"), the model's PSNR and SSIM achieve more substantial gains on both datasets, reaching the highest performance observed (e.g., PSNR rising again to 31.92 and SSIM from 0.960 to 0.967), indicating stronger geometric understanding and more accurate depth estimation. The same pattern holds for the Blender-Medical dataset, where PSNR and SSIM climb to 35.97 and 0.973, respectively, distinctly enhancing the perceived quality of intricate organ structures. Overall, these results affirm that the combined effect of dual-channel input and multi-view consistency more fully exploits stereoscopic information, yielding more precise and smoother 3D reconstructions.

5   Conclusion

In this paper, we propose a binocular NeRF architecture tailored for complex and structurally challenging scenarios, which effectively enhances the model's capability to learn 3D depth and stereo structures without explicit disparity supervision. The core of our approach lies in integrating a multi-view consistency module and a depth consistency loss. The multi-view consistency module ensures pixel-level geometric alignment by explicitly providing ray direction vectors while simultaneously enforcing stronger stereo constraints in volumetric rendering. Meanwhile, the depth consistency loss encourages left and right views to maintain coherence in depth interpretation, significantly improving reconstruction accuracy and sharpness in complex geometric regions. In future work, we aim to leverage more advanced models to further enhance real-time performance, enabling efficient reconstruction while facilitating rapid modeling, thereby broadening the applicability of our approach to diverse high-fidelity 3D visualization tasks.

Acknowledgments. This work was supported by the National Natural Science Foundation of China (No.62166040), the Tianshan Talent Training Project, and the Technology Innovation Team Program (2023TSYCTD0012).

References

1. Azinović, D., Martin-Brualla, R., Goldman, D.B., Nießner, M., Thies, J.: Neural RGB-D surface reconstruction. In: Proceedings of the IEEE/CVF Conference on Computer Vision and Pattern Recognition, pp. 6290–6301 (2022)
2. Barron, J.T., Mildenhall, B., Tancik, M., Hedman, P., Martin-Brualla, R., Srinivasan, P.P.: Mip-nerf: a multiscale representation for anti-aliasing neural radiance fields. In: Proceedings of the IEEE/CVF International Conference on Computer Vision, pp. 5855–5864 (2021)
3. Chen, S.E., Williams, L.: View interpolation for image synthesis. In: Seminal Graphics Papers: Pushing the Boundaries, vol. 2, pp. 423–432 (2023)
4. Deng, K., Liu, A., Zhu, J.Y., Ramanan, D.: Depth-supervised nerf: fewer views and faster training for free. In: Proceedings of the IEEE/CVF Conference on Computer Vision and Pattern Recognition, pp. 12882–12891 (2022)
5. Fehn, C.: Depth-image-based rendering (dibr), compression, and transmission for a new approach on 3d-tv. In: Stereoscopic Displays and Virtual Reality Systems XI, vol. 5291, pp. 93–104. SPIE (2004)
6. Feng, M., Cheng, J., Jia, H., Liu, L., Xu, G., Yang, X.: Mc-stereo: multi-peak lookup and cascade search range for stereo matching. In: 2024 International Conference on 3D Vision (3DV), pp. 344–353. IEEE (2024)
7. Flynn, J., et al.: Deepview: high-quality view synthesis by learned gradient descent. In: Conference on Computer Vision and Pattern Recognition (CVPR), vol. 3 (2019)
8. Flynn, J., Neulander, I., Philbin, J., Snavely, N.: Deepstereo: learning to predict new views from the world's imagery. In: Proceedings of the IEEE Conference on Computer Vision and Pattern Recognition, pp. 5515–5524 (2016)
9. Furukawa, Y., Ponce, J.: Accurate, dense, and robust multiview stereopsis. IEEE Trans. Pattern Anal. Mach. Intell. **32**(8), 1362–1376 (2009)
10. Garbin, S.J., Kowalski, M., Johnson, M., Shotton, J., Valentin, J.: Fastnerf: high-fidelity neural rendering at 200fps. In: Proceedings of the IEEE/CVF International Conference on Computer Vision, pp. 14346–14355 (2021)
11. Gupta, M., Yin, Q., Nayar, S.K.: Structured light in sunlight. In: Proceedings of the IEEE International Conference on Computer Vision, pp. 545–552 (2013)
12. Hartley, R.: Multiple View Geometry in Computer Vision, vol. 665. Cambridge University Press (2003)
13. Hou, Y., Kannala, J., Solin, A.: Multi-view stereo by temporal nonparametric fusion. In: Proceedings of the IEEE/CVF International Conference on Computer Vision, pp. 2651–2660 (2019)
14. Kroeger, T., Timofte, R., Dai, D., Van Gool, L.: Fast optical flow using dense inverse search. In: Leibe, B., Matas, J., Sebe, N., Welling, M. (eds.) ECCV 2016. LNCS, vol. 9908, pp. 471–488. Springer, Cham (2016). https://doi.org/10.1007/978-3-319-46493-0_29
15. Levoy, M., Hanrahan, P.: Light field rendering. In: Seminal Graphics Papers: Pushing the Boundaries, vol. 2, pp. 441–452 (2023)
16. Li, Z., Niklaus, S., Snavely, N., Wang, O.: Neural scene flow fields for space-time view synthesis of dynamic scenes. In: Proceedings of the IEEE/CVF Conference on Computer Vision and Pattern Recognition, pp. 6498–6508 (2021)
17. Liu, L., Gu, J., Zaw Lin, K., Chua, T.S., Theobalt, C.: Neural sparse voxel fields. Adv. Neural. Inf. Process. Syst. **33**, 15651–15663 (2020)
18. Liu, R., Yang, C., Sun, W., Wang, X., Li, H.: Stereogan: bridging synthetic-to-real domain gap by joint optimization of domain translation and stereo matching.

In: Proceedings of the IEEE/CVF Conference on Computer Vision and Pattern Recognition, pp. 12757–12766 (2020)

19. Lombardi, S., Simon, T., Saragih, J., Schwartz, G., Lehrmann, A., Sheikh, Y.: Neural volumes: learning dynamic renderable volumes from images. arXiv preprint arXiv:1906.07751 (2019)

20. Martin-Brualla, R., Radwan, N., Sajjadi, M.S., Barron, J.T., Dosovitskiy, A., Duckworth, D.: Nerf in the wild: neural radiance fields for unconstrained photo collections. In: Proceedings of the IEEE/CVF Conference on Computer Vision and Pattern Recognition, pp. 7210–7219 (2021)

21. Mildenhall, B., et al.: Local light field fusion: practical view synthesis with prescriptive sampling guidelines. ACM Trans. Graph. (ToG) **38**(4), 1–14 (2019)

22. Mildenhall, B., Srinivasan, P.P., Tancik, M., Barron, J.T., Ramamoorthi, R., Ng, R.: Nerf: representing scenes as neural radiance fields for view synthesis. Commun. ACM **65**(1), 99–106 (2021)

23. Ng, R., Levoy, M., Brédif, M., Duval, G., Horowitz, M., Hanrahan, P.: Light field photography with a hand-held plenoptic camera. Ph.D. thesis, Stanford university (2005)

24. Park, K., et al.: Nerfies: deformable neural radiance fields. In: Proceedings of the IEEE/CVF International Conference on Computer Vision, pp. 5865–5874 (2021)

25. Ranftl, R., Bochkovskiy, A., Koltun, V.: Vision transformers for dense prediction. In: Proceedings of the IEEE/CVF International Conference on Computer Vision, pp. 12179–12188 (2021)

26. Sitzmann, V., Zollhöfer, M., Wetzstein, G.: Scene representation networks: continuous 3D-structure-aware neural scene representations. In: Advances in Neural Information Processing Systems, vol. 32 (2019)

27. Sun, D., Yang, X., Liu, M.Y., Kautz, J.: Pwc-net: CNNs for optical flow using pyramid, warping, and cost volume. In: Proceedings of the IEEE Conference on Computer Vision and Pattern Recognition, pp. 8934–8943 (2018)

28. Teed, Z., Deng, J.: RAFT: recurrent all-pairs field transforms for optical flow. In: Vedaldi, A., Bischof, H., Brox, T., Frahm, J.-M. (eds.) ECCV 2020. LNCS, vol. 12347, pp. 402–419. Springer, Cham (2020). https://doi.org/10.1007/978-3-030-58536-5_24

29. Wang, R., Peethambaran, J., Chen, D.: Lidar point clouds to 3-D urban models: a review. IEEE J. Sel. Top. Appl. Earth Obs. Remote Sens. **11**(2), 606–627 (2018)

30. Yu, A., Li, R., Tancik, M., Li, H., Ng, R., Kanazawa, A.: Plenoctrees for real-time rendering of neural radiance fields. In: Proceedings of the IEEE/CVF International Conference on Computer Vision, pp. 5752–5761 (2021)

31. Zhang, S., Huang, P.S.: High-resolution, real-time three-dimensional shape measurement. Opt. Eng. **45**(12), 123601 (2006)

32. Zhou, T., Tucker, R., Flynn, J., Fyffe, G., Snavely, N.: Stereo magnification: learning view synthesis using multiplane images. arXiv preprint arXiv:1805.09817 (2018)

MS-MRFNet: A Multi-scale and Multi-receptive Field Network for UAV Aerial Object Detection

Hao Li and Zhenchao Cui[✉]

Hebei University, Baoding 071002, China
`cuizhenchao@hbu.edu.cn`

Abstract. Small object detection is a critical and challenging task in UAV applications due to limited pixel information and feature degradation in deep neural networks. To address these issues, this paper proposes a novel object detector, the Multi-Scale and Multi-Receptive Field Network (MS-MRFNet). A Multi-Scale Weighted Feature Pyramid Network (MSWFPN) is designed to enhance feature fusion across scales by adaptively weighting semantic and spatial features. Additionally, a Multi-Channel Feature Aggregation (MCFA) module is developed to aggregate features at the same level, employing reparameterization trick to retain critical information. Finally, Wise-IoU (WIoU) is adopted as the bounding box regression loss, balancing gradient gains from samples of varying quality across scales and feature groups, thereby accelerating model convergence. Experimental results on the VisDrone 2019, TinyPerson, and NWPU VHR-10 datasets demonstrate mAP50 improvements of 8.6%, 8.4%, and 1.7%, respectively, along with reduced parameter usage. Ablation experiments further validate the effectiveness and applicability of the proposed method in UAV-based small object detection scenarios.

Keywords: Multi-Scale · Feature Aggregation · UAV · Small Object Detection

1 Introduction

In recent years, advancements in unmanned aerial vehicle (UAV) technology have enabled the extensive use of camera-equipped UAVs in diverse areas such as traffic [16], agriculture, public safety, and military operations [1]. These diverse applications have heightened the demand for robust object detection algorithms in UAVs. Achieving both high accuracy and real-time performance remains a key challenge in UAV image recognition.

Deep learning-based object detection technology has rapidly advanced and is frequently applied across various visual domains [20], providing substantial improvements in UAV object detection. In deep learning-based object detection, one-stage and two-stage architectures are the primary approaches, each employing distinct strategies and characteristics for handling detection tasks.

J. Lokoč et al. (Eds.): MMM 2026, LNCS 16412, pp. 233–246, 2026.
https://doi.org/10.1007/978-981-95-6950-2_17

Despite the significant advancements made by these models, general-purpose object detection models often perform poorly in detecting small objects. Therefore, applying these general object detection models to UAV-based small object detection presents several challenges. The main issues include the following: (1) Small objects occupy fewer pixels, leading to fewer features being extracted. Small object features are often lost during the feature extraction process. (2) The size of small objects may vary across different images, and the scale of objects in UAV images can change. Current object detection algorithms often use anchor box settings biased toward larger objects, causing small objects to be frequently overlooked or misclassified. (3) The backgrounds in images containing small objects often vary significantly, with some backgrounds having textures and colors similar to the objects, making complete object detection challenging. In densely populated areas with small objects, the repeated appearance of similar objects often results in missed detections.

In response to these challenges, several researchers have explored various approaches. RepVGG [4] employs reparameterization trick, combining identity connections, 1×1 branches, and 3×3 branches as parallel components during training. During inference, these branches are consolidated into a single 3×3 convolution. This structure enables the model to learn richer features and accelerate inference. Building on RepVGG, Kang et al. [7] proposed the RCS module. This module processes features in groups and utilizes channel shuffling to enhance information flow between them. Tong et al. [21] developed Wise-IoU, introducing a new gradient gain allocation strategy. This strategy mitigates harmful gradients from extreme samples, accelerating model convergence and enhancing generalization. However, these methods have not fully addressed the challenges posed by UAV-based small object detection. Building on these studies, we propose a novel Multi-Scale and Multi-Receptive Field Network (MS-MRF Network). To address the challenge of small objects occupying fewer pixels and losing essential features, we design the Multi-Scale Weighted Feature Pyramid Network (MSWFPN), which improves feature integration across different scales. For objects with varying sizes, we incorporate a Multi-Channel Feature Aggregation (MCFA) module that processes features through several channels, enabling the network to capture both intricate details and broader object structures. Finally, a WIoU loss function tackles the challenge of densely packed small objects by dynamically refining focus during training. The main contributions of our work are as follows:

(1) The MSWFPN is designed to enhance the integration of high- and low-dimensional features by enriching high-dimensional data with complementary low-dimensional information. This strengthens the model's ability to perceive object coordinates and size accurately.
(2) The MCFA module is proposed to process features through different channels, generating diverse receptive fields. This allows the network to effectively capture both intricate details and broader context.

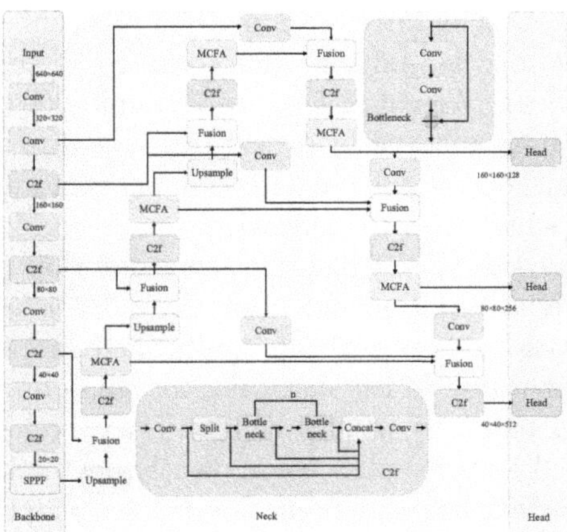

Fig. 1. Overview of the proposed MS-MRFNet. The Fusion operation refers to concatenating different parts based on adaptive weights.

(3) The WIoU loss function is introduced to dynamically adjust the focus during training, aiming to improve detection accuracy, particularly for densely packed small objects.

2   Method

The proposed MS-MRFNet, illustrated in Fig. 1, consists of three key enhancements: the MSWFPN, the MCFA module, and the WIoU loss function.

2.1   The Multi-scale Weighted Feature Pyramid Network

Most current neural networks employ a bottom-up structure for feature extraction, generating feature layers at different resolutions for the neck. Lower feature layers offer higher resolution and contain more detailed information, which is advantageous for object localization, whereas higher feature layers have a larger receptive field and provide richer semantic information, which is useful for object classification. As network depth increases during feature extraction, some features are inevitably lost. To mitigate this, mainstream object detection algorithms perform feature fusion after feature extraction, leveraging the multi-scale capabilities of the model to minimize feature loss due to network depth.

PAFPN, as a variant of FPN, introduces an additional bottom-up pathway in addition to FPN's original top-down structure. This addition enhances the model's multi-scale capabilities and strengthens the contextual and spatial features extracted by the backbone network. Therefore, YOLOv8 uses PAFPN as its neck. However, during the feature fusion across multiple scales in PAFPN, detailed information from the lower layers can be diminished, negatively impacting the localization of small objects and subsequently affecting small object detection. As a result, this feature fusion method presents challenges in the field of small object detection. To enhance the accuracy of small object detection, we propose a Multi-Scale Weighted Feature Pyramid Network (MSWFPN), as illustrated in Fig. 2. This module fuses features across multiple scales, reduces computational cost without sacrificing detection performance, and retains crucial details necessary for small object localization.

First, in the proposed MSWFPN, the low-resolution detection layer P5 is removed, and the high-resolution detection layer P2 is added. Removing P5 helps reduce computational cost without significantly sacrificing detection accuracy. This adjustment is due to the fact that, for small objects occupying fewer pixels, downsampling to P5 frequently results in a 1×1 feature map, leading to insufficient retained features and, consequently, lower detection accuracy. In contrast, adding P2, which has undergone fewer downsampling steps, enables the network to retain more detailed information, thereby enhancing its suitability for small object detection.

Secondly, a newly added connection links the backbone layer directly to the output feature layers in the neck. High-level feature maps, after multiple convolutions, have a larger receptive field and rich semantic information. However, their resolution is low, making them suitable for object classification. In contrast, low-level feature maps possess high resolution and abundant detailed information, making them particularly ideal for object localization. Moreover, the features within the backbone layer have not yet undergone multi-scale feature fusion, thereby preserving more details. The newly added path incorporates detailed information from the lower layers of the backbone into the semantic information of the output features. This fusion improves the accuracy of small object detection.

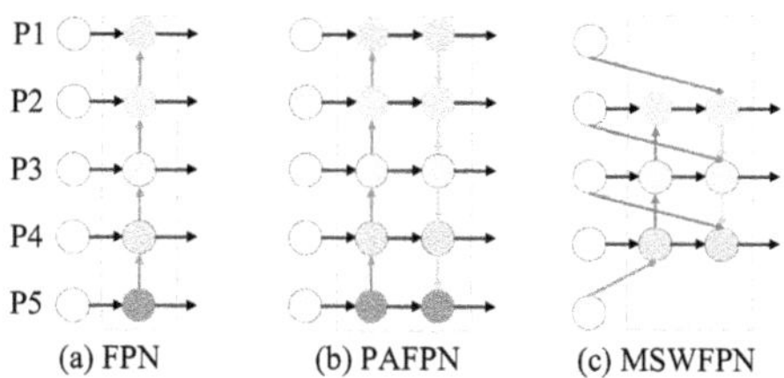

Fig. 2. Popular neck frameworks and the proposed MSWFPN.

Finally, different weights are assigned to the various feature layers during feature fusion. In PAFPN, Concat is used to merge different feature layers, which fuses features of varying resolutions without considering their relative importance, potentially reducing the effectiveness of the final fused feature. Therefore, the importance of different feature layers in feature fusion varies. The method of adding weights is as follows:

$$O = \sum_i \frac{w_i}{\epsilon + \Sigma_j w_j} \cdot I_i \tag{1}$$

where w_i represents the weight of the input features from the i-th layer, while $\epsilon = 0.0001$ is used to prevent the denominator from being zero, which could lead to instability during training, a ReLU function ensures $w_i \geq 0$. I_i represents each input feature layer, and O is the output value. This equation normalizes each weight value to the [0,1] range to improve efficiency.

2.2   The Multi-channel Feature Aggregation Module

Although MSWFPN fuses features across different scales, small objects in UAV images often suffer from challenges like overlap, occlusion, and background confusion, which cannot be fully addressed by cross-layer fusion alone. The MCFA module focuses on fusing features within the same layer to retain crucial details and improve small object detection. This subsection describes the structure and function of the MCFA module.

Small objects in UAV images are susceptible to issues such as overlap, occlusion, and background confusion. To address these issues, we propose a Multi-Channel Feature Aggregation (MCFA) module, as shown in Fig. 3. It divides the features into multiple channels, applies different operations to obtain distinct feature maps, and enhances the receptive field of each channel. Finally, the different parts are concatenated. By leveraging information from multiple receptive fields, the model refines object boundaries, enabling it to effectively distinguish objects from the background and neighboring objects. Specifically, the input features of the MCFA module are first processed through RepVGG to retain feature effectiveness and then divided into four parts. The first two parts are forwarded without any further processing, while the latter two are passed through the RCS module. Half of the channels are assigned larger receptive fields to enhance overall recognition accuracy, while the other half retain smaller receptive fields to provide the necessary information for detecting small objects. Dividing the feature maps into parts, compared to traditional residual structures, allows for richer gradient information, leading to better training outcomes. Additionally, it reduces redundant gradient information without increasing detection time. Finally, the four parts are concatenated, followed by channel shuffling, and then passed through the RepVGG module before being output. After incorporating the MCFA module following the C2f module in the neck, a multi-branch structure is employed to extract diverse features. These features undergo different operations before being fused together. Channel shuffling is applied to further enhance the information flow between different groups within the same feature layer, thereby improving the model's capability for small object detection.

2.3   The Loss Function

Multi-scale feature fusion and feature aggregation within the same scale have been previously discussed. This subsection focuses on balancing samples of varying quality across different layers and groups within the same layer. This approach aims to optimize the training process and accelerate model convergence.

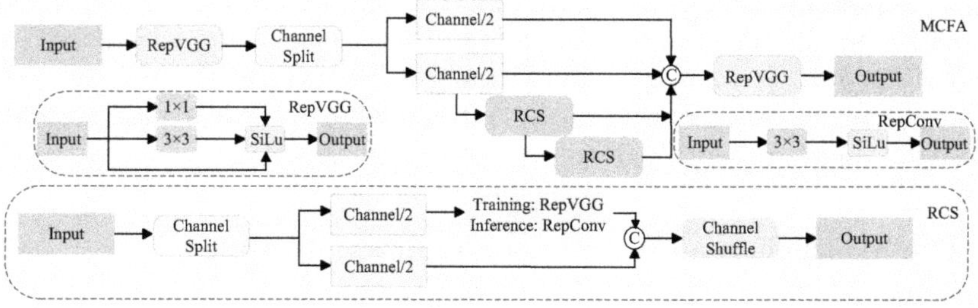

Fig. 3. The structure of the MCFA module. Rectangles denote feature maps, and rounded rectangles represent operations.

In deep learning-based object detection tasks, Intersection over Union (IoU) is widely employed as a metric to evaluate the overlap between the predicted and ground truth bounding boxes. The bounding box loss function uses IoU to penalize the difference between the predicted and ground truth bounding boxes. This penalization helps achieve accurate object localization. When the predicted bounding box and the ground truth bounding box do not overlap, IoU equals 0, making it impossible to compute gradients. To address this issue, YOLOv8 adopts Complete IoU (CIoU), which considers both the geometric distance and the aspect ratio between the predicted and ground truth bounding boxes. However, CIoU does not account for the varying impact of samples of different quality on training, which can result in slow model convergence. These limitations make CIoU insufficient for effectively handling the unique characteristics of small object detection in UAV imagery, which often involves dense, cluttered scenes. To enable the model to balance the learning of objects with different qualities from various scales and groups within the same scale during training, we introduce Wise-IoU (WIoU). We replace CIoU with WIoU to optimize small object detection better. WIoU introduces a dynamic, non-monotonic focusing mechanism for bounding box regression. By dynamically adjusting gradient gains, this mechanism mitigates the adverse impact of extreme samples, whether they result in excessively large or very small gradients. This adjustment enables the bounding box regression to focus on medium-quality anchor boxes, thereby enhancing localization accuracy, accelerating model convergence, and optimizing small object bounding box prediction. The calculation formula for WIoU is given as follows:

$$L_{\mathrm{WIoU}} = \frac{\beta}{\delta\alpha^{\beta-\delta}} \cdot e^{\left(\frac{(x-x_{gt})^2+(y-y_{gt})^2}{w_{gt}^2+h_{gt}^2}\right)} \tag{2}$$

$$\beta = \frac{L_{\mathrm{IoU}}^*}{\overline{L_{\mathrm{IoU}}}} \tag{3}$$

In Eq. (2), x and y represent the coordinates of the predicted bounding box center, x_{gt} and y_{gt} represent the coordinates of the ground truth bounding box center, and w_{gt} and h_{gt} represent the width and height of the minimum enclosing rectangle that covers both the predicted and ground truth bounding boxes. The parameter β represents the degree of outlierness, while α and δ are hyperparameters used to assign different gradients to anchor boxes of varying quality. The symbol $*$ denotes the separation operation, and $\overline{L}_{IoU}$ represents the moving average of all anchor points within a batch.

3   Experiments

We evaluate the proposed MS-MRFNet using three public datasets: VisDrone2019 [5], TinyPerson [23], and NWPU VHR-10 [9]. First, we introduce these datasets and describe the experimental setup. Then, we compare our method with existing state-of-the-art approaches. We also perform a series of ablation studies on the VisDrone2019 dataset to assess the contribution of each module. Finally, we present visualizations of the experimental results.

3.1   Datasets and Implementation Details

The VisDrone2019 dataset, collected by the AISKYEYE team, includes 8,629 drone images with 2.6 million annotated objects across ten categories. Covering diverse conditions, it serves as a robust testbed for small object detection. We evaluated our model on this dataset and conducted ablation experiments to validate each module.

The TinyPerson dataset, proposed by the University of Chinese Academy of Sciences, includes 1,610 drone images with 72,651 annotated small objects, averaging 18 pixels, posing challenges for detection.

The NWPU VHR-10 dataset, collected by Northwestern Polytechnical University, comprises 800 images (500×500 to 1100×1100 pixels) with 3,651 targets across ten classes. Captured under varied conditions, it is ideal for aerial object detection evaluation.

Experiments were conducted on Ubuntu 20.04 with a GeForce RTX 4090 using Python 3.8, CUDA 11.8, and PyTorch 2.0.0. Momentum (0.9) and weight decay (5×10^{-3}) were applied to enhance convergence and reduce overfitting. Input images were resized to 640×640, and all models were trained from scratch for fair comparison.

3.2   Comparison Experiments

To demonstrate the effectiveness of the proposed MS-MRFNet in detecting small objects within UAV imagery, a series of comparative experiments were performed on the VisDrone2019 dataset. The comparison includes both classic one-stage and two-stage object detection models, along with several state-of-the-art approaches specifically designed for small object detection. The comparison experiment results are shown in Table 1. According to Table 1, our proposed model achieved 45.9% mAP50 and 27.9% mAP50:95, representing improvements of 8.6% and 5.8% over the baseline, respectively. Our model outperforms the latest YOLO models, including YOLOv9s and YOLOv10s, in terms of detection accuracy, demonstrating its capability to handle complex UAV scenes more effectively. In comparison with the second-best model, MC-YOLOv5 [2], our approach attains comparable mAP50 performance with fewer than 25% of the parameters and further improves mAP50-95 by 1.3%. Compared to the enhanced model SOD-YOLO [8], which is also based on YOLOv8s, our model achieved an increase of 0.8% in mAP50 and 1.3% in mAP50:95. The results demonstrate that our model exhibits superior detection performance, effectively detecting small objects in noisy backgrounds within UAV images, making UAV detection more feasible.

Table 1. Detection performance (%) of different algorithms on Visdrone2019 validation dataset.

Models	mAP50	mAP50:95	Params (M)	GFLOPs
SSD [14]	23.9	13.1	24.5	87.9
RetinaNet [10]	27.3	15.5	19.8	93.7
Faster-RCNN [18]	33.2	17.0	41.2	207.1
ATSS [24]	31.7	18.6	10.3	57.0
Swin Transformer [15]	35.6	20.6	34.2	44.5
DTSSNet [3]	39.9	24.2	10.1	50.4
YOLOv5s	35.4	20.5	9.1	23.8
YOLOv8s	37.3	22.1	11.1	28.5
TPH-YOLO [6]	39.3	23.6	51.5	138.1
YOLOv9s	41.2	24.6	13.7	60.4
LV-YOLOv5 [22]	41.7	25.6	36.6	38.8
RT-DETR [26]	42.2	25.3	32.7	85.1
EdgeYOLO [12]	45.4	26.9	41.2	-
SOD-YOLO [8]	45.1	26.6	11.5	-
MC-YOLOv5 [2]	**45.9**	26.6	38.2	69.7
YOLOv8x	44.1	27.2	68.1	257.4
YOLOv10s	31.9	18.2	**7.2**	**21.6**
Ours	**45.9**	**27.9**	9.5	62.7

Additionally, we compared our model with other algorithms on the TinyPerson dataset, with the results shown in Table 2. According to Table 2, the proposed model improves mAP50 and mAP50:95 by 8.4% and 2.8%, respectively, over the original YOLOv8s, with significant improvements in both precision and recall. Compared to PS-YOLO [17], our model improves mAP50 by 6.3% and mAP50:95 by 1.7%. The TinyPerson dataset consists of objects with significantly smaller pixel sizes compared to other datasets. Thus, the experimental results on TinyPerson strongly emphasize the robustness and effectiveness of our proposed model in detecting small-scale objects.

Finally, we evaluated the proposed algorithm on the NWPU VHR-10 dataset based on mAP50, mAP50:95, and the number of parameters. The results are shown in Table 3. Our algorithm achieved a mAP50 of 85.6%, surpassing the latest algorithms in the YOLO series. Compared to the baseline, the mAP50 increased by 1.7%, indicating that our algorithm has stronger detection performance. At the same time, a decrease of 0.8% in mAP50:95 suggests that the proposed algorithm's generalization ability could be further enhanced, particularly under stricter IoU threshold conditions.

Table 2. Detection performance (%) of different algorithms on TinyPerson validation dataset.

Method	mAP50	mAP50:95	P	R	Params(M)
YOLOv3	18.8	7.0	37.4	18.6	12.1
YOLOv5s	17.8	6.4	37.2	18.2	**7.2**
YOLOv6s	16.3	5.8	33.6	17.5	16.3
YOLOv8s	15.6	5.2	35.6	18.0	11.2
YOLOv10s	17.2	6.0	34.9	19.6	8.0
PS-YOLO [17]	17.7	6.4	33.1	18.7	19.4
Ours	**24.0**	**8.0**	**38.0**	**26.9**	9.7

P denotes the Precision, while R denotes the Recall.

Table 3. Detection performance (%) of different algorithms on NWPU VHR-10 dataset.

Method	mAP50	mAP50:95	P	R	Params(M)
YOLOv3	81.8	47.3	87.3	76.5	12.1
YOLOv6s	84.5	52.4	88.4	80.6	16.3
YOLOv8s	83.9	52.1	87.9	**81.0**	11.2
YOLOv9s	85.0	**53.1**	**91.0**	80.1	9.0
YOLOv10s	78.2	49.1	76.1	73.9	**8.0**
Ours	**85.6**	51.3	89.3	78.8	9.5

3.3 Ablation Experiments

The comparative experiments in Sect. 3.2 highlight the enhanced performance achieved by the proposed model. In Sect. 3.3, we conducted ablation experiments to further analyze the contributions of each architectural component—MSWFPN, MCFA, and WIoU—towards enhancing detection accuracy, especially in challenging scenarios involving small objects. To investigate the impact of different neck structures, we conducted experiments on the VisDrone2019 dataset, comparing the proposed MSWFPN with PAFPN [13], BiFPN [19], and FPN. To achieve optimized multi-scale object detection, each network structure is equipped with a Modified Prediction Head(MPH) consisting of three detection heads: P2, P3, and P4. The experimental results are shown in Table 4. Table 4 indicates that with MSWFPN, we achieved a 2.3% improvement in mAP50 and a 1.5% improvement in mAP50:95 at a computational cost of only 4.8 GFLOPs while also reducing the parameter count to 77% compared to the base model. Compared to FPN, which has a similar parameter count, MSWFPN improves mAP50 by 2.9% and mAP50:95 by 2%. In comparison with BiFPN, which has a similar computational complexity (GFLOPs), MSWFPN achieves a 20% reduction in parameter count while enhancing mAP50 by 2.1% and mAP50:95 by 1.7%.

As shown in Table 5, an ablation study was conducted on the VisDrone dataset to evaluate the impact of the hyperparameters α and β in the WIoU loss function. Three configurations were tested: $\alpha = 1.4/1.6/1.9$ and $\beta = 5/4/3$. The results indicate that increasing α and decreasing β gradually improve overall detection performance. Specifically, the configuration $\alpha = 1.9$ and $\beta = 3$ achieved the best results, with improvements of 0.8% in mAP50, 0.9% in Precision, and 1.0% in Recall. Therefore, this setting is adopted as the default configuration in the subsequent experiments.

To further evaluate the detection performance of the proposed model and verify the contribution of each improvement, we conducted ablation experiments on the VisDrone2019 dataset. The experiments were evaluated in terms of metrics, including mAP50, the number of parameters, and inference time. The experimental results are shown in Table 6. At the same time, the ablation experiments for each category are shown in Table 7. The results indicate that each enhancement method improves detection accuracy for different categories to varying degrees. Introducing the MSWFPN module into the network's neck effectively aggregates features from different layers, fully integrating and utilizing low-level detailed information and high-level semantic information. This results in a significant 2.3% increase in mAP50. This improvement enhances the accuracy across all categories, with the largest gains observed in the pedestrian and van categories, achieving an improvement of 4.2% and 3%, respectively. Next, we applied WIoU to the network, which focuses on samples of moderate quality to optimize the prediction of small object bounding boxes. While accelerating inference speed, this improvement achieved a 0.3% increase in mAP50 at the cost of adding 0.7 M parameters. This enhancement significantly improved detection performance for the tricycle and bus categories. Additionally, integrating the MCFA module after the C2f module in the neck raised the mAP50 to 45.9%, representing an improvement of 8.6% over the baseline. Significant improvements in detection accuracy were observed for the people, truck, and motor categories, demonstrating the effectiveness of this module. According to Table 6, compared to the base model, our model substantially enhanced detection performance while also achieving a 15% reduction in the number of parameters. Precision increased from 49.3% to 54.5%, recall improved from 36.8% to 44%, mAP50 rose from 37.3% to 45.9%, and mAP50:95 increased from 22.1% to 27.9%. The final experimental results demonstrate that each of the three enhancements markedly boosts the model's capacity for small object detection.

Table 4. Comparison of different feature pyramid structures on VisDrone2019.

Models	mAP50	mAP50:95	Params(M)	GFLOPs
PAFPN	42.4	25.7	9.9	36.1
FPN	41.8	25.2	**6.6**	**30.0**
BiFPN	42.6	25.5	9.7	37.5
MSWFPN(Ours)	**44.7**	**27.2**	7.7	40.9

Table 5. Performance (%) comparison under different WIoU hyperparameter settings

Hyperparameter	mAP50	mAP50:95	P	R
CIoU	42.4	25.7	53.2	40.4
Focal-EIoU [25]	42.1	25.1	50.6	40.7
Powerful-IoU [11]	42.7	25.7	53.5	40.7
WIoU($\alpha = 1.4\ \beta = 5$)	43.0	26.0	54.1	41.3
WIoU($\alpha = 1.6\ \beta = 4$)	42.9	26.0	53.8	41.1
WIoU($\alpha = 1.9\ \beta = 3$)	**43.2**	**26.1**	**54.1**	**41.4**

3.4   Visualization

To provide visual evidence of the model's enhanced detection capabilities, particularly in challenging conditions such as low visibility and crowded scenes, we present visualizations of our results in Fig. 4. Figure 4(a) shows that MS-MRFNet improves its capability to detect small objects at long distances. Figure 4(b) demonstrates that the improved model performs better under low-light conditions. Figure 4(c) demonstrates the superior performance of the MS-MRFNet in densely populated areas. Figure 4(d) demonstrates the robustness of MS-MRFNet under occlusion conditions.

Table 6. Detection results following the adoption of different improvement strategies, presented as percentages

Baseline	MPH	MSWFPN	WIoU	MCFA	P	R	mAP50	mAP50:95	DT(ms)	Params(M)
✓					49.3	36.8	37.3	22.1	**1.9**	11.2
✓	✓				53.2	40.4	42.4	25.7	**1.9**	9.9
✓	✓	✓			54.1	42.2	44.7	27.2	2.6	**7.1**
✓	✓	✓	✓		54.1	43.4	45.0	27.0	2.1	7.7
✓	✓	✓	✓	✓	**54.5**	**44.0**	**45.9**	**27.9**	3.6	9.5

MPH for the modified prediction head, and DT for the Detection Time.

Table 7. The comparison between the results of ten categories after subsequent operations on the VisDrone2019 dataset, with percentages presented.

Models	PED	PEO	BC	CAR	VAN	TRUNK	TR	AW	BUS	MO
Baseline	39.2	30.6	11.5	78.3	43.4	34.4	25.3	14.9	54.1	41.4
Baseline + MPH	49.3	40.2	15.1	82.9	47.6	36.2	28.4	16.6	58.7	49.5
Baseline + MPH + MSWFPN	53.5	42.8	16.7	84.9	50.6	38.3	30.3	18.8	59.2	52.3
Baseline + MPH + MSWFPN + WIoU	54.2	42.9	17.0	84.9	50.5	37.5	30.9	17.9	**61.6**	52.4
Baseline + MPH + MSWFPN + WIoU + MCFA	**54.8**	**44.8**	**18.4**	**85.7**	**51.2**	**40.4**	**31.8**	**20.5**	57.8	**54.4**

PED for pedestrian, PEO for person, BC for bicycle, TR for tricycle, AW for awning-tricycle, and MO for motor.

Fig. 4. Visualization of different algorithms on the VisDrone2019 validation set.

4   Conclusion

This paper proposes MS-MRFNet, a novel small object detector, aimed at tackling the challenges of feature extraction from small objects and information loss across deep neural networks. Our approach integrates three key innovations: the Multi-Scale Weighted Feature Pyramid Network (MSWFPN) to retain lower-layer details for better localization, the Multi-Channel Feature Aggregation module (MCFA) for effective intra-level feature aggregation to reduce information loss, and the enhanced Wise-IoU (WIoU) loss function to optimize localization and accelerate convergence by reducing the influence of extreme gradient gains. We evaluated the proposed model on three public datasets—VisDrone2019, TinyPerson, and NWPU VHR-10. The results reveal substantial enhancements in detection accuracy, particularly for small and distant objects, achieving higher mAP values compared to baseline models. Although our model achieved notable gains in detection accuracy, these improvements come with the trade-off of increased computational requirements. Moreover, the performance under stricter IoU thresholds indicates that the model's robustness can still be further enhanced. Moving forward, we aim to maintain high detection accuracy while significantly reducing computational costs for deployment on mobile platforms like drones.

References

1. Bo, W., Liu, J., Fan, X., Tjahjadi, T., Ye, Q., Fu, L.: Basnet: burned area segmentation network for real-time detection of damage maps in remote sensing images. IEEE Trans. Geosci. Remote Sens. **60**, 1–13 (2022)
2. Chen, H., et al.: Mc-yolov5: a multi-class small object detection algorithm. Biomimetics **8**(4), 342 (2023)
3. Chen, L., Liu, C., Li, W., Xu, Q., Deng, H.: Dtssnet: dynamic training sample selection network for UAV object detection. IEEE Trans. Geosci. Remote Sens. (2024)
4. Ding, X., Zhang, X., Ma, N., Han, J., Ding, G., Sun, J.: Repvgg: making VGG-style convnets great again. In: Proceedings of the IEEE/CVF Conference on Computer Vision and Pattern Recognition, pp. 13733–13742 (2021)
5. Du, D., et al.: Visdrone-det2019: the vision meets drone object detection in image challenge results. In: 2019 IEEE/CVF International Conference on Computer Vision Workshop (ICCVW), pp. 213–226 (2019). https://doi.org/10.1109/ICCVW.2019.00030
6. Jiang, S., Wang, Y., Zhang, J., Zheng, J.: Full-field deformation measurement of structural nodes based on panoramic camera and deep learning-based tracking method. Comput. Ind. **146**, 103840 (2023)
7. Kang, M., Ting, C.M., Ting, F.F., Phan, R.C.W.: RCS-yolo: a fast and high-accuracy object detector for brain tumor detection. In: International Conference on Medical Image Computing and Computer-Assisted Intervention, pp. 600–610. Springer, Cham (2023)
8. Khalili, B., Smyth, A.W.: Sod-yolov8–enhancing yolov8 for small object detection in traffic scenes. arXiv preprint arXiv:2408.04786 (2024)
9. Li, K., Wan, G., Cheng, G., Meng, L., Han, J.: Object detection in optical remote sensing images: a survey and a new benchmark. ISPRS J. Photogramm. Remote. Sens. **159**, 296–307 (2020)
10. Lin, T.: Focal loss for dense object detection. arXiv preprint arXiv:1708.02002 (2017)
11. Liu, C., Wang, K., Li, Q., Zhao, F., Zhao, K., Ma, H.: Powerful-IoU: more straightforward and faster bounding box regression loss with a nonmonotonic focusing mechanism. Neural Netw. **170**, 276–284 (2024)

12. Liu, S., Zha, J., Sun, J., Li, Z., Wang, G.: Edgeyolo: an edge-real-time object detector. In: 2023 42nd Chinese Control Conference (CCC), pp. 7507–7512. IEEE (2023)

13. Liu, S., Qi, L., Qin, H., Shi, J., Jia, J.: Path aggregation network for instance segmentation. In: Proceedings of the IEEE Conference on Computer Vision and Pattern Recognition, pp. 8759–8768 (2018)

14. Liu, W., et al.: SSD: single shot multibox detector. In: Leibe, B., Matas, J., Sebe, N., Welling, M. (eds.) ECCV 2016. LNCS, vol. 9905, pp. 21–37. Springer, Cham (2016). https://doi.org/10.1007/978-3-319-46448-0_2

15. Liu, Z., et al.: Swin transformer: hierarchical vision transformer using shifted windows. In: Proceedings of the IEEE/CVF International Conference on Computer Vision, pp. 10012–10022 (2021)

16. Ma, X., Wei, W., Dong, J., Zheng, B., Ma, J.: Rtod-yolo: traffic object detection in UAV images based on visual attention and re-parameterization. In: 2023 International Joint Conference on Neural Networks (IJCNN), pp. 1–8 (2023). https://doi.org/10.1109/IJCNN54540.2023.10191514

17. Peng, S., Fan, X., Tian, S., Yu, L.: Ps-yolo: a small object detector based on efficient convolution and multi-scale feature fusion. Multimedia Syst. **30**(5), 1–16 (2024)

18. Ren, S., He, K., Girshick, R., Sun, J.: Faster R-CNN: towards real-time object detection with region proposal networks. IEEE Trans. Pattern Anal. Mach. Intell. **39**(6), 1137–1149 (2016)

19. Tan, M., Pang, R., Le, Q.V.: Efficientdet: scalable and efficient object detection. In: Proceedings of the IEEE/CVF Conference on Computer Vision and Pattern Recognition, pp. 10781–10790 (2020)

20. Tang, G., Ni, J., Zhao, Y., Gu, Y., Cao, W.: A survey of object detection for UAVs based on deep learning. Remote Sens. **16**(1), 149 (2023)

21. Tong, Z., Chen, Y., Xu, Z., Yu, R.: Wise-IoU: bounding box regression loss with dynamic focusing mechanism. arXiv preprint arXiv:2301.10051 (2023)

22. Wang, J., Liu, W., Zhang, W., Liu, B.: Lv-yolov5: a light-weight object detector of VIT on drone-captured scenarios. In: 2022 16th IEEE International Conference on Signal Processing (ICSP), vol. 1, pp. 178–183. IEEE (2022)

23. Yu, X., Gong, Y., Jiang, N., Ye, Q., Han, Z.: Scale match for tiny person detection. In: Proceedings of the IEEE/CVF Winter Conference on Applications of Computer Vision, pp. 1257–1265 (2020)

24. Zhang, S., Chi, C., Yao, Y., Lei, Z., Li, S.Z.: Bridging the gap between anchor-based and anchor-free detection via adaptive training sample selection. In: Proceedings of the IEEE/CVF Conference on Computer Vision and Pattern Recognition, pp. 9759–9768 (2020)

25. Zhang, Y.F., Ren, W., Zhang, Z., Jia, Z., Wang, L., Tan, T.: Focal and efficient IoU loss for accurate bounding box regression. Neurocomputing **506**, 146–157 (2022)

26. Zhao, Y., et al.: Detrs beat yolos on real-time object detection. In: Proceedings of the IEEE/CVF Conference on Computer Vision and Pattern Recognition, pp. 16965–16974 (2024)

HDBC: A Heterogeneous Dual-Branch Convolutional Network for Audio Splicing Detection

Xiaojing Feng, Zhenhua Tan[✉], Ziwei Cheng, and Jiayuan Luo

Software College, Northeastern University, Shenyang 110819, China
`tanzh@mail.neu.edu.cn`

Abstract. Audio splicing is a typical form of audio forgery that enables arbitrary tampering of original audio content, disrupting both time-domain continuity and frequency-domain structure. However, most existing methods focus exclusively on frequency-domain information and seldom exploit splicing cues embedded in the time domain, thereby failing to comprehensively capture the cues present in both domains and overlooking their intrinsic correlation and complementarity. To address this limitation, this paper proposes a heterogeneous dual-branch convolutional network, named HDBC. Specifically, we employ a multi-scale convolutional module to fuse dynamic frequency-domain features: log spectrograms and Constant-Q Transform (CQT) spectrograms, thereby constructing a complementary time-frequency representation. Subsequently, dual-branch heterogeneous modeling is performed separately on the time domain and frequency domain. Their outputs are fused by an adaptive weighting mechanism for final classification. Additionally, a discrepancy-sensitive consistency loss is introduced to guide the dual-branch module in minimizing prediction discrepancies between the time and frequency domains. Experiments show HDBC achieves 93.85% accuracy on a TIMIT splicing dataset and 99.84% accuracy on ASV2015_EVA_S10 dataset, outperforming comparative methods and demonstrating its effectiveness. Noise robustness analysis further confirms its stable performance in complex environments.

Keywords: Audio splicing detection · Time-domain dependency · Frequency-domain dependency

1 Introduction

With the proliferation of audio editing tools, audio splicing has become a prevalent forgery method [25], which alters audio content by merging segments from different recordings of the same speaker [18]. It is increasingly exploited to spread misinformation and fabricate evidence, posing a serious threat to information security and judicial fairness. Thus, effective audio splicing detection methods are urgently needed.

© The Author(s), under exclusive license to Springer Nature Singapore Pte Ltd. 2026
J. Lokoč et al. (Eds.): MMM 2026, LNCS 16412, pp. 247–260, 2026.
https://doi.org/10.1007/978-981-95-6950-2_18

Existing splicing detection approaches mainly fall into three categories. Methods based on Electrical Network Frequency (ENF) [7,9,11,15,24,29] identify splicing by ENF signals from audio, which enable detection even in short segments. However, not all recordings contain ENF, and the signal is highly susceptible to noise [5]. To address these limitations, some scholars have proposed methods based on background noise [13,16,22,28]. These methods are robust to noise and independent of ENF, but their performance degrades in quiet conditions and after post-processing like noise reduction or compression. Methods based on frequency-domain features [6,18,26,27] detect splicing by analyzing the frequency information of audio signals. They have lower requirements for recording devices and environments, making them more widely applicable. However, their performance is highly dependent on feature selection and often lacks generalization and robustness.

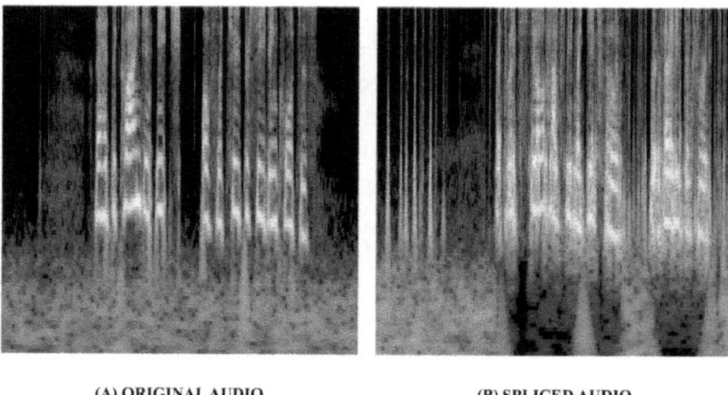

Fig. 1. Comparison of Constant-Q Transform (CQT) spectrograms for original and spliced audio. The horizontal axis denotes time (s), while the vertical axis indicates frequency (Hz) on a logarithmic scale. The spliced audio reveals (1) temporal discontinuities (abrupt energy transitions between frames) and (2) spectral anomalies (broken harmonic structures and localized energy outliers). These traces of audio splicing indicate that splicing affects both time and frequency domains.

Motivation. In recent years, methods based on audio frequency-domain features have shown promising results. Audio splicing disrupts both the temporal continuity and the spectral structures of the audio signals (as shown in Fig. 1). However, most existing audio splicing detection methods either focus solely on static frequency-domain features, such as MFCCs [1], which retain only coarse spectral representations and lose fine-grained temporal structures, or employ a unified modeling approach to analyze dynamic frequency-domain features that encompass both temporal and spectral information. Nevertheless, these methods often fail to fully exploit the splicing cues embedded in both domains and overlook the inherent correlation and complementarity between temporal and spectral information. This limits their ability to capture the complex cues introduced by splicing operations.

Solution and Contribution. Therefore, this paper proposes a novel audio splicing detection model, named HDBC, which leverages the complementarity of time-frequency features via a heterogeneous dual-branch architecture and consistency optimization. The HDBC integrates dynamic frequency features: log spectrograms and CQT spectrograms to capture time-frequency information simultaneously, achieving collaborative learning of time-frequency details. Ultimately, HDBC completes classification by adaptively fusing dual-branch features and is optimized using a combination of Binary Cross-Entropy (BCE) loss and the Discrepancy-Sensitive Consistency (DSC) loss proposed in this paper. The main contributions of this paper are as follows:

- We employ log spectrograms and CQT spectrograms as complementary time–frequency features to enhance perceptual representation.
- A heterogeneous dual-branch modeling module captures temporal continuity and spectral structure anomalies, respectively, improving sensitivity to splicing cues.
- We propose a discrepancy-sensitive consistency loss to enforce consistency between time-domain and frequency-domain predictions, which measures and minimizes the prediction differences between the two branches.
- The experimental results demonstrate the effectiveness and noise robustness of the HDBC method across various metrics.

2   Related Work

Audio Splicing Detection Based on ENF. The ENF is the ac grid's transmission frequency, which fluctuates slightly around a nominal value with high stability [10]. Traditional methods extract ENF signals from audio and compare them with ENF databases to verify authenticity. Liu et al. [11] highlighted the importance of accurate ENF estimation and reliable references. Karantaidis et al. [7] used superpixel segmentation for tampering detection via correlation analysis. Due to the limited accessibility of ENF databases, reference-free methods emerged. Reis et al. [15] used ESPRIT-Hilbert estimation and SVMs based on ENF kurtosis. Zhao et al. [29] applied LSTM-Inception networks to spectral-kurtosis features. Zeng et al. [24] built a UBM-based end-to-end detection framework using deep networks. Li et al. [9] detect tampered audio via ICZT-enhanced ENF extraction and a dual-sampling isolation forest. Although ENF-based audio splicing detection performs well, it depends on grid-powered recordings and is sensitive to environmental noise [29], limiting its robustness and practicality.

Audio Splicing Detection Based on Background Noise. This approach avoids reliance on ENF signals by analyzing changes in ambient noise characteristics. Zhao et al. [28] used vocal tract impulse responses and noise magnitudes as environmental signatures, identifying splicing via normalized cross-correlation. Meng et al. [13] used audio kurtosis to locate syllables and compared background noise variance to detect audio tampering. Yan et al. [22]

estimated noise, extracted Mel-frequency features, and applied change point detection. Su et al. [16] proposed a method using multistage filterbank spectral sketches (MFBSS) and decision fusion. This approach has minimal requirements for recording devices, but is susceptible to post-processing operations (e.g., noise addition, filtering) [14], and noise-speech separation errors reduce robustness.

Audio Splicing Detection Based on Frequency-Domain Features. This approach captures anomalies in the frequency space, leveraging intrinsic audio characteristics for broad applicability. Jadhav et al. [6] were the first to apply Convolutional Neural Networks (CNNs) to audio splicing detection based on spectrogram representations. Zhang et al. [27] introduced an encoder-decoder model using LFCCs and MFCCs with an FCN to produce splicing masks. Zhang et al. [26] combined singularity features and LFCCs with Lightweight Convolutional Neural Network (LCNN) for audio splicing detection. Ustubioglu et al. [18] used cochleagrams with EfficientNet-B4 [17] and ArCapsNet to achieve detection of audio splicing. Additionally, CQT has proven effective in speaker verification tasks due to its multi-resolution frequency analysis capability [23]. These methods have attracted extensive attention and have achieved certain progress. However, audio splicing affects both time and frequency domains. This paper extracts complementary time–frequency information and models them separately to facilitate detection. Previous methods' feature selection and unified modeling fail to fully exploit splicing cues, limiting their performance.

3   Methods

We propose a heterogeneous dual-branch convolutional network based on two-channel time-frequency features: log spectrograms and CQT spectrograms, which achieves audio splicing detection through time-frequency separation modeling and dynamic fusion. In this section, we detail three components of HDBC: feature preprocessing, heterogeneous dual-branch modeling, adaptive decision and joint optimization. The overall architecture of HDBC is shown in Fig. 2.

3.1   Feature Preprocessing

The HDBC uses log spectrograms and CQT spectrograms as inputs. Log spectrograms retain full-band energy and high-frequency details, while CQT spectrograms with adaptive filters capture spectral structure anomalies and non-stationary patterns. Their complementarity boosts model robustness. Extracted features have shape (B, C, F, T), denoting batch size, channels, frequency bins, and time frames, respectively.

To exploit the complementarity of log spectrograms and CQT spectrograms, these two features are preprocessed and fused. Adaptive pooling aligns their dimensions, followed by two-channel concatenation. Channel normalization mitigates magnitude differences. A multiscale convolutional block (using 3×3 kernels with dilation rates 1 and 2) further integrates these features via standard and dilated convolutions to capture both local details and long-range dependencies, yielding the final time-frequency base features.

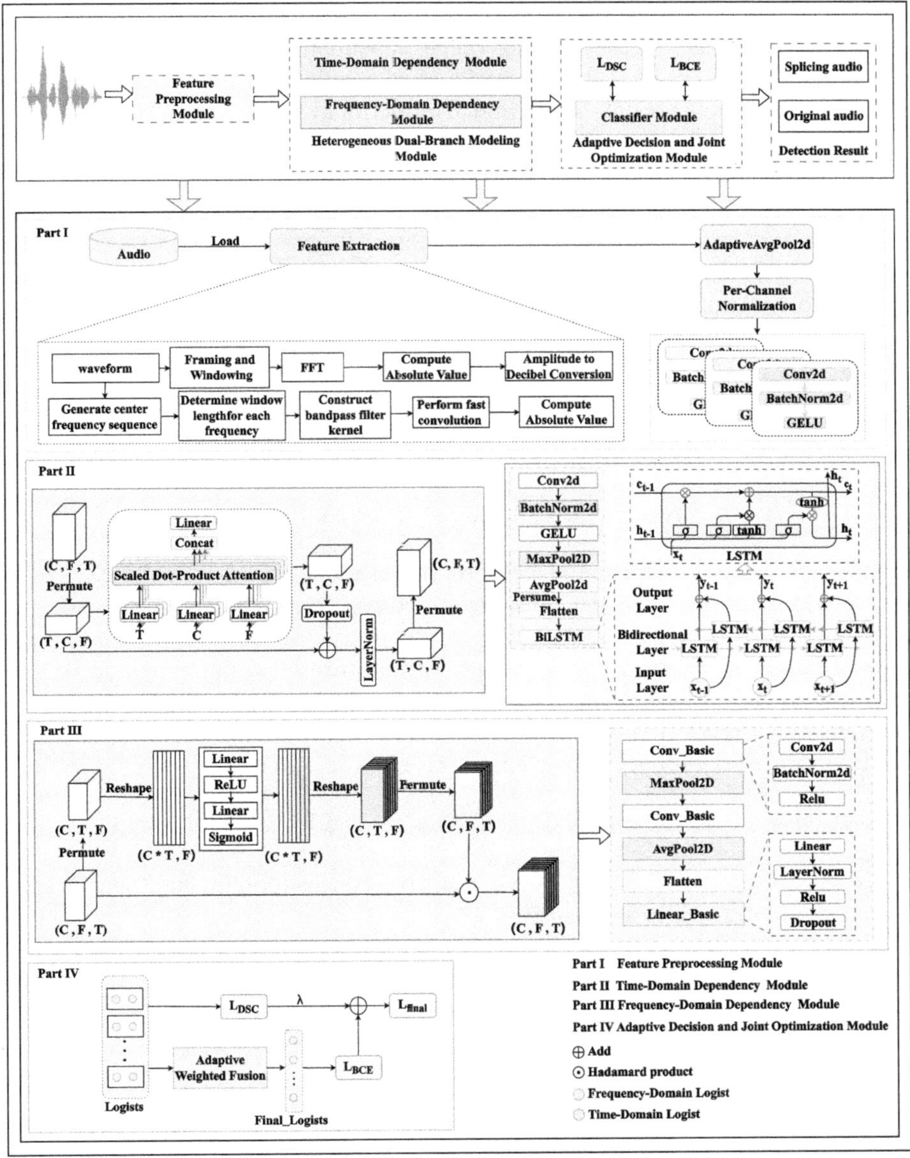

Fig. 2. An overall architecture of HDBC. The audio signal is processed by the feature preprocessing module, then passed through the heterogeneous dual-branch modeling module, and finally classified by the adaptive decision and joint optimization module.

3.2   Heterogeneous Dual-Branch Modeling

This paper designs a heterogeneous dual-branch modeling module that enhances and differentiates joint time-frequency base features from temporal and spectral perspectives to capture audio splicing cues.

Time-Domain Dependency Module. Audio splicing breaks the continuity between frames. To model long-range dependencies, temporal Multi-Head Self-Attention (MHSA) [19] with residual normalization captures global context. Then, convolution, pooling, and Bidirectional Long Short-Term Memory (BiLSTM) [2] extract time-frame features in the time domain.

Time-Domain Feature Enhancement. The input features are enhanced using MHSA along the time-frame dimension. Given input tensor $X \in \mathbb{R}^{B \times C \times F \times T}$, it is reshaped for temporal modeling as $H \in \mathbb{R}^{T \times (BC) \times F}$. Then, the MHSA is applied to capture global dependencies:

$$H' = \text{MHSA}(H) = \text{Concat}(head_1, \ldots, head_4)W^O \tag{1}$$

where $head_i$ denotes the attention output of the i-th head and W^O is the projection matrix. Residual connections and layer normalization stabilize the model:

$$H_{out} = \text{LayerNorm}\left(H + \text{Dropout}\left(H'\right)\right) \tag{2}$$

Finally, the output is reshaped back to the original size, $Y \in \mathbb{R}^{B \times C \times F \times T}$, to ensure compatibility with the subsequent processing pipeline.

Time-Domain Discriminative Modeling. To capture local patterns and contextual dependencies, the enhanced feature Y is further processed with convolution, pooling, and BiLSTM. First, convolution and max pooling are used to reduce the temporal and channel dimensions:

$$Z = \text{MaxPool2D}\left(\text{Conv2D}(Y)\right) \in \mathbb{R}^{B \times C' \times F \times T'} \tag{3}$$

where $C' = C/4$ and $T' = T/4$. Next, adaptive average pooling and permutation flatten the features into sequences:

$$S = \text{Flatten}(\text{Permute}(\text{AdaptiveAvgPool2}D(Z))) \in R^{B \times T' \times C'} \tag{4}$$

Then, BiLSTM models bidirectional temporal dependencies:

$$H_{lstm} = \text{BiLSTM}(S) \in \text{R}^{B \times T' \times 128} \tag{5}$$

Finally, the final time-step representation is extracted as $H_{time} \in \mathbb{R}^{B \times 128}$ for further processing.

Frequency-Domain Dependency Module. To better capture frequency-domain characteristics, Squeeze-and-Excitation (SE) [4] attention weights frequency features. Then, convolution, pooling, and fully connected layers capture local spectral details. This produces high-level frequency representations for classification.

Frequency-Domain Feature Enhancement. Given input $X \in \mathbb{R}^{B \times C \times F \times T}$, frequency features are compressed and passed through a fully connected network for channel dependency modeling:

$$S_{se} = \mathrm{SE}(X) = \mathrm{Sigmoid}\left(W_2 \,\mathrm{ReLU}\left(W_1 \,\mathrm{Reshape}(X)\right)\right) \in \mathrm{R}^{(BCT) \times F} \qquad (6)$$

where weight $W_1 \in \mathbb{R}^{F \times (F/4)}$, $W_2 \in \mathbb{R}^{(F/4) \times F}$. The attention output S_{se} is reshaped and permuted to its original dimensions, then element-wise multiplied with the input for adaptive enhancement. Finally, Dropout2D is applied for regularization, yielding the final output Y_{out}.

Frequency-Domain Discriminative Modeling. The SE-enhanced features Y_{out} are further processed for capturing local spectral pattern details and temporal correlations. First, apply 2D convolution along the frequency dimension:

$$Z = \mathrm{Conv}\,2\mathrm{D}\,(Y_{out}) \in \mathrm{R}^{B \times C/4 \times F \times T} \qquad (7)$$

Next, max pooling is used to downsample the frequency resolution. This is followed by an additional convolution layer for higher-order frequency feature extraction, and adaptive average pooling is used to generate a fixed-size representation. The resulting tensor is then flattened into a vector representation, denoted as $S_{flat} \in \mathbb{R}^{B \times (CF/4)}$. Finally, the flattened feature is passed through a layer normalization, ReLU activation, dropout, and a fully connected layer to obtain the final frequency-domain discriminative representation:

$$H_{freq} = \mathrm{Dropout}\left(\mathrm{ReLU}\left(\mathrm{LayerNorm}\left(W_S S_{flat} + b\right)\right)\right) \qquad (8)$$

where W_S is the weight of S_{flat}.

3.3   Adaptive Decision and Joint Optimization

This module adaptively fuses dual-branch outputs to improve classification robustness. It combines DSC loss and BCE loss as a joint optimization objective to enhance prediction consistency. In this paper, our classifier module is implemented as a sequential block consisting of a linear layer followed by a sigmoid activation.

Adaptive Decision. Time-domain prediction p_t and frequency-domain prediction p_f are fused using a learnable weight ω_1:

$$p = \sigma(\omega_1) \cdot p_f + (1 - \sigma(\omega_1)) \cdot p_t \qquad (9)$$

where $\sigma(\cdot)$ is the sigmoid function. Additionally, the main classification objective is optimized using BCE loss, calculated between the final prediction p and the ground-truth label $y \in \{0, 1\}$:

$$\mathrm{L_{BCE}} = -[y \cdot \log(\mathrm{p}) + (1 - y)\log(1 - p)] \qquad (10)$$

Discrepancy-Sensitive Consistency Loss. To enforce consistency between time-domain and frequency-domain predictions, a discrepancy-sensitive consistency loss is introduced. It measures and minimizes prediction differences between the two branches.

First, compute the absolute discrepancy:

$$D = |p_f - p_t| \tag{11}$$

Normalize by the max value to reduce scale effects:

$$\tilde{D} = \frac{D}{\max(D) + \epsilon} \tag{12}$$

where $\epsilon = 10^{-6}$. A discrepancy sensitivity coefficient τ is introduced to adjust the sensitivity of the normalized discrepancy. A sigmoid function is used to generate weights that dynamically modulate the loss focus, enabling the model to concentrate on hard samples and prevent easy samples from dominating the training:

$$\omega_2 = \sigma\left(\frac{\tilde{D}}{\tau}\right) \tag{13}$$

where $\sigma(\cdot)$ is the sigmoid function. After extensive experiments, τ is set to 0.2. Finally, the DSC loss is defined as:

$$L_{DSC} = E\left[\omega_2 \cdot (p_f - p_t)^2\right] \tag{14}$$

Joint Optimization. The BCE loss supervises the final fused prediction, while the DSC loss enforces agreement between time-domain and frequency-domain outputs. Their weighted combination ensures consistency between time-frequency predictions and improves the overall accuracy. Finally, the overall joint optimization objective of the model is defined as:

$$L = L_{BCE} + \lambda L_{DSC} \tag{15}$$

where the balancing coefficient λ is set to 0.4, validated experimentally.

4   Experiments

4.1   Datasets and Preprocessing

This study selects the subset of the ASVspoof2015 [21] public dataset and a self-constructed splicing dataset based on TIMIT [8] as the experimental datasets.

ASVspoof2015 is the first benchmark dataset designed for research on speech spoofing and detection. Its evaluation set contains both genuine speech and fake speech generated using ten different spoofing algorithms, labeled S1 through S10. Among them, S10 generates spoofed audio using a splicing-based synthesis algorithm [30]. In this study, we selected 9,404 genuine audio samples and 18,400

S10 spoofed audio samples from the evaluation set to construct a spliced speech dataset named ASV2015_EVA_S10.

TIMIT is a speech recognition dataset consisting of 6,300 audio samples, each lasting approximately 2 to 6 s. In this study, 4,952 original audio samples were randomly retained, while the remaining samples were randomly segmented into clips of 1 to 3 s in length. Then, two segments from different utterances of the same speaker were selected and concatenated to ensure that the total duration of each spliced audio falls within 2 to 6 s. A total of 4,146 spliced audio samples were generated. A spliced version of the TIMIT dataset was successfully constructed.

To simulate noise interference encountered in real-world environments, Gaussian white noise with varying Signal-To-Noise Ratios (SNRs) of 5 dB, 10 dB, 15 dB, and 20 dB was added to the TIMIT splicing dataset, thereby creating several versions of TIMIT-noise-corrupted datasets. Additionally, this study used the Python library named Librosa [12] to extract MFCCs, log spectrograms, and CQT spectrograms from the above data, which were subsequently saved as .pt files.

4.2 Experimental Setup

Baselines. This study compares HDBC with the CNN-based method of Jadhav et al. [6], the ASLNet approach of Zhang et al. [27], and two widely used backbones, ResNet18 [3] and LCNN [20]. ResNet18, a classic residual network, is widely used in tampering detection; LCNN has demonstrated strong performance in tasks such as speech spoofing detection and speaker recognition, and has emerged as a key baseline for audio tampering detection in recent years.

Training Details and Metrics. For fair comparison, all models are trained for 80 epochs using the same feature extraction process to obtain log spectrograms and CQT spectrograms as input features. Log spectrograms use an FFT window of 512 and a hop length of 160; CQT spectrograms use a hop length of 160; MFCC takes the first 13 coefficients. For ASLNet, we use a threshold of 0.5. These experiments were performed on an NVIDIA GeForce RTX 2060 SUPER GPU with 8 GB of dedicated memory. In this paper, we adopt the accuracy, precision, recall, and Fscore as the evaluation metrics.

4.3 Comparison Experiments

To demonstrate the effectiveness of our approach, we conducted comparison experiments on the TIMIT and ASV2015_EVA_S10 datasets. The experimental results are shown in Table 1.

According to these results, HDBC achieves the best overall performance on the TIMIT dataset, with 93.85% accuracy and 92.95% Fscore. Compared to the best baseline (ResNet18: 92.37% accuracy, 91.36% Fscore), it improves by 1.48% and 1.59%, respectively, showing better detection of spliced audio. Notably, it attains the highest precision and recall, reflecting a good balance

Table 1. Comparison of our method with baselines and the best results are highlighted in bold.

Dataset	Method	Accuracy (%)	Precision (%)	Recall (%)	Fscore (%)
TIMIT	ResNet18 [3]	92.37	92.57	90.18	91.36
	LCNN [20]	92.31	92.56	90.06	91.29
	CNN [6]	91.54	93.77	86.87	90.19
	ASLNet [27]	87.42	86.35	85.40	85.87
	HDBC	**93.85**	**95.47**	**90.55**	**92.95**
ASV2015_EVA_S10	ResNet18 [3]	98.85	99.41	98.81	99.11
	LCNN [20]	99.50	99.69	99.53	99.61
	CNN [6]	99.19	99.31	99.44	99.38
	ASLNet [27]	98.85	99.89	98.33	99.10
	HDBC	**99.84**	**99.97**	**99.78**	**99.87**

between false positives and negatives. On the ASV2015_EVA_S10 dataset, HDBC also outperforms all baselines, reaching 99.84% accuracy, 99.97% precision, 99.78% recall, and 99.87% Fscore. The promising results verify the effectiveness of HDBC.

The performance gap between datasets suggests our TIMIT splicing data poses greater challenges for detection, potentially due to subtler cues. Despite this, HDBC consistently achieves solid results, confirming its robustness and generalization.

4.4   Ablation Study

To verify the importance of the three key components in HDBC, ablation experiments were conducted on the TIMIT splicing dataset, comparing four configurations: (1)time-domain branch with BCE loss, (2)frequency-domain branch with BCE loss, (3)dual-branch with BCE loss, and (4)dual-branch with BCE loss and DSC loss. The results are shown in Table 2.

Results (Table 2) show that the time-domain model achieved 92.48% accuracy and 91.30% Fscore. The frequency-domain model achieved 92.81% accuracy and 91.42% Fscore. The dual-branch architecture enhanced overall performance (93.36% accuracy, 92.26% Fscore), confirming the effectiveness of jointly modeling time and frequency information for capturing diverse splicing cues. HDBC, which combines a dual-branch architecture with BCE loss and DSC loss, achieves the best performance (93.85% accuracy, 90.55% recall, 92.95% Fscore), showing that DSC loss helps the model focus on branch prediction discrepancies and improves robustness.

In addition, as shown in Fig. 3, t-SNE visualization illustrates that time-domain features yield better intra-class compactness (as shown in subfigure (c) of Fig. 3), while frequency-domain features enhance inter-class separability (as shown in subfigure (d) of Fig. 3) across training epochs. This further supports the effectiveness of the dual-branch time-frequency modeling (as shown in subfigure (e) of Fig. 3).

Table 2. Ablation study of three key components in HDBC and the best results are highlighted in bold.

Model	Accuracy (%)	Precision (%)	Recall (%)	Fscore (%)
Time-domain + BCE loss	92.48	94.61	88.22	91.30
Frequency-domain + BCE loss	92.81	**98.03**	85.64	91.42
Dual-branch + BCE loss	93.36	96.39	88.47	92.26
Dual-branch + BCE loss + DSC loss	**93.85**	95.47	**90.55**	**92.95**

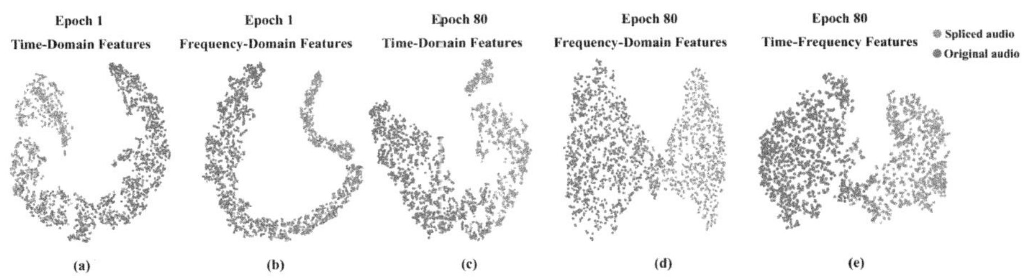

Fig. 3. Spatial distribution visualization of deep features from the time-domain and frequency-domain branches on the TIMIT dataset.

4.5 Feature Effectiveness Analysis

To assess the impact of different features and their combinations, we experiment with log spectrograms, CQT spectrograms, and MFCCs. The results are shown in Table 3. The results show that using only the log spectrograms achieves 93.36% accuracy and 92.39% Fscore, slightly lower than the combination of log spectrograms and MFCCs (93.47% accuracy, 92.49% Fscore). Combining log spectrograms and CQT spectrograms further improves accuracy to 93.85% and Fscore to 92.95%, representing gains of 0.49% and 0.56% over log spectrograms alone, and 0.38% and 0.46% over the combination of log spectrograms and MFCCs. This pair also attains the highest precision (95.47%) with balanced recall (90.55%). Adding MFCCs increases recall to 91.17% but lowers accuracy to 93.47% and precision to 94.05%, slightly reducing Fscore to 92.59%. These results suggest that effective feature fusion requires balancing complementarity and redundancy, with log spectrograms and CQT spectrograms providing the best overall performance.

Table 3. Feature effectiveness analysis on the TIMIT dataset and the best results are highlighted in bold.

Feature			Accuracy (%)	Precision (%)	Recall (%)	Fscore (%)
log spec	CQT spec	MFCCs				
✓	×	×	93.36	94.72	90.18	92.39
✓	×	✓	93.47	95.19	89.94	92.49
✓	✓	✓	93.47	94.05	**91.17**	92.59
✓	✓	×	**93.85**	**95.47**	90.55	**92.95**

* The feature combination used in HDBC is log spectrograms and CQT spectrograms.

Table 4. Experimental results for verifying robustness on noisy datasets.

Dataset	Accuracy (%)	Precision (%)	Recall (%)	Fscore (%)
Clean data	93.85	95.47	90.55	92.95
with Gaussian white noise 20dB	91.82	93.82	87.48	90.54
with Gaussian white noise 15dB	91.76	93.01	88.22	90.55
with Gaussian white noise 10dB	91.32	92.50	87.73	90.05
with Gaussian white noise 5dB	90.01	91.26	85.89	88.50

4.6 Robustness to Noise

To evaluate the robustness of HDBC, we conduct experiments on four TIMIT-noise-corrupted datasets with SNRs of 20 dB, 15 dB, 10 dB, and 5dB, to simulate scenarios with light, moderate, and extreme noise levels. The experimental results are shown in Table 4, indicating that HDBC exhibits strong robustness under various noise conditions. Compared with the clean dataset (accuracy: 93.85%, Fscore: 92.95%), the model maintains high performance on noisy data: at 20 dB and 15 dB, the accuracy remains above 91.70%, and Fscore above 90.50%. Even under more severe noise (10 dB and 5 dB), accuracy only drops by 2.53% and 3.84%. These results validate the noise robustness of HDBC and its effectiveness in noisy environments.

5   Conclusions

This study proposes a novel audio splicing detection model, HDBC, which performs splicing detection by separately modeling the time and frequency domains, followed by dynamic fusion. Specifically, HDBC employs a dual-branch architecture that integrates log-spectrograms and CQT spectrograms to capture complementary cues from time and frequency domains. The time-domain branch combines the MHSA mechanism with BiLSTM to capture sequential dependencies, while the frequency-domain branch incorporates frequency-sensitive SE attention to model spectral anomalies. Through an adaptive weighting mechanism, the model dynamically fuses features from both branches, and a discrepancy-sensitive consistency loss is designed to optimize the model with a binary cross-entropy loss jointly. The experimental results demonstrate the effectiveness of HDBC for the audio splicing detection task. This work establishes a key technical foundation for protecting minors among cyberspace, which will be further strengthened by future benchmarking against a broader range of challenges, including variability from multiple languages, recording devices and codecs.

Acknowledgments. This work is supported by the National Key Research and Development Program of China under Grant No. 2023YFC3306201.

References

1. Abdul, Z.K., Al-Talabani, A.K.: Mel frequency cepstral coefficient and its applications: a review. IEEE Access **10**, 122136–122158 (2022)
2. Graves, A., Schmidhuber, J.: Framewise phoneme classification with bidirectional lstm and other neural network architectures. Neural Netw. **18**(5–6), 602–610 (2005)
3. He, K., Zhang, X., Ren, S., Sun, J.: Deep residual learning for image recognition. In: Proceedings of the IEEE Conference on Computer Vision and Pattern Recognition, pp. 770–778 (2016)
4. Hu, J., Shen, L., Sun, G.: Squeeze-and-excitation networks. In: Proceedings of the IEEE Conference on Computer Vision and Pattern Recognition, pp. 7132–7141 (2018)
5. Hua, G., Zhang, H.: Enf signal enhancement in audio recordings. IEEE Trans. Inf. Forensics Secur. **15**, 1868–1878 (2019)
6. Jadhav, S., Patole, R., Rege, P.: Audio splicing detection using convolutional neural network. In: 2019 10th International Conference on Computing, Communication and Networking Technologies (ICCCNT), pp. 1–5. IEEE (2019)
7. Karantaidis, G., Kotropoulos, C.: An automated approach for electric network frequency estimation in static and non-static digital video recordings. J. Imaging **7**(10), 202 (2021)
8. Lamel, L.F., Kassel, R.H., Seneff, S.: Speech database development: Design and analysis of the acoustic-phonetic corpus. In: Proc. SIOA 1989, pp. Vol-2 (1989)
9. Li, B., Duan, J., Qiu, W., Yin, H., Yao, W.: A tampering detection framework for digital audio signals under low-snr conditions. IEEE Sensors J. (2025)
10. Li, Y., Lu, T., Peng, S., He, C., Zhao, K., Yang, G., Chen, Y.: Detection of electric network frequency in audio using multi-hcnet. Sensors **25**(12), 3697 (2025)
11. Liu, Y., Yuan, Z., Markham, P.N., Conners, R.W., Liu, Y.: Wide-area frequency as a criterion for digital audio recording authentication. In: 2011 IEEE Power and Energy Society General Meeting, pp. 1–7. IEEE (2011)
12. McFee, B., Raffel, C., Liang, D., Ellis, D.P., McVicar, M., Battenberg, E., Nieto, O.: librosa: audio and music signal analysis in python. SciPy **2015**, 18–24 (2015)
13. Meng, X., Li, C., Tian, L.: Detecting audio splicing forgery algorithm based on local noise level estimation. In: 2018 5th International Conference on Systems and Informatics (ICSAI), pp. 861–865. IEEE (2018)
14. Nasr, M.A., El-Shafai, W., Abdel-Salam, N., El-Rabaie, E.S.M., El-Fishawy, A.S., El-Samie, F.E.A.: A comprehensive survey of audio forgery detection: challenges and novel trends. J. Electr. Syst. Inf. Technol. **12**(1), 1–42 (2025)

15. Reis, P.M.G.I., da Costa, J.P.C.L., Miranda, R.K., Del Galdo, G.: Esprit-hilbert-based audio tampering detection with svm classifier for forensic analysis via electrical network frequency. IEEE Trans. Inf. Forensics Secur. **12**(4), 853–864 (2016)
16. Su, Z., Fang, Z., Lian, C., Zhang, G., Li, M.: Audio splicing detection and localization using multistage filterbank spectral sketches and decision fusion. Multimedia Syst. **30**(2), 92 (2024)
17. Tan, M., Le, Q.: Efficientnet: Rethinking model scaling for convolutional neural networks. In: International Conference on Machine Learning, pp. 6105–6114. PMLR (2019)
18. Ustubioglu, B., Dincer, S., Ustubioglu, A., Ulutas, G.: Arcapsnet for audio splicing forgery detection. In: 2024 47th International Conference on Telecommunications and Signal Processing (TSP), pp. 298–301. IEEE (2024)
19. Vaswani, A., Shazeer, N., Parmar, N., Uszkoreit, J., Jones, L., Gomez, A.N., Kaiser, Ł., Polosukhin, I.: Attention is all you need. Advances in neural information processing systems **30** (2017)
20. Wu, X., He, R., Sun, Z., Tan, T.: A light cnn for deep face representation with noisy labels. IEEE Trans. Inf. Forensics Secur. **13**(11), 2884–2896 (2018)
21. Wu, Z., Kinnunen, T., Evans, N., Yamagishi, J., Hanilçi, C., Sahidullah, M., Sizov, A.: Asvspoof 2015: the first automatic speaker verification spoofing and countermeasures challenge. In: INTERSPEECH 2015, Automatic Speaker Verification Spoofing and Countermeasures Challenge, colocated with INTERSPEECH 2015, pp. 2037–2041. ISCA (2015)
22. Yan, D., Dong, M., Gao, J.: Exposing speech transsplicing forgery with noise level inconsistency. Secur. Commun. Networks **2021**(1), 6659371 (2021)
23. Yang, M., Zheng, K., Wang, X., Sun, Y., Chen, Z.: Comparative analysis of asv spoofing countermeasures: Evaluating res2net-based approaches. IEEE Signal Process. Lett. **30**, 1272–1276 (2023)
24. Zeng, C., Kong, S., Wang, Z., Feng, S., Zhao, N., Wang, J.: Deletion and insertion tampering detection for speech authentication based on fluctuating super vector of electrical network frequency. Speech Commun. **158**, 103046 (2024)
25. Zeng, C., Kong, S., Wang, Z., Li, K., Zhao, Y., Wan, X., Chen, Y.: Digital audio tampering detection based on spatio-temporal representation learning of electrical network frequency. Multimed. Tools Appl. **83**(36), 83917–83939 (2024)
26. Zhang, K., Liang, S., Nie, S., He, S., Pan, J., Zhang, X., Ma, H., Yi, J.: A robust deep audio splicing detection method via singularity detection feature. In: ICASSP 2022-2022 IEEE International Conference on Acoustics, Speech and Signal Processing (ICASSP), pp. 2919–2923. IEEE (2022)
27. Zhang, Z., Zhao, X., Yi, X.: Aslnet: an encoder-decoder architecture for audio splicing detection and localization. Secur. Commun. Networks **2022**(1), 8241298 (2022)
28. Zhao, H., Chen, Y., Wang, R., Malik, H.: Audio splicing detection and localization using environmental signature. Multimed. Tools Appl. **76**, 13897–13927 (2017)
29. Zhao, J., Lu, B., Huang, L., Huang, M., Huang, J.: Digital audio tampering detection using enf feature and lst-minception net. In: AIIPCC 2022; The Third International Conference on Artificial Intelligence, Information Processing and Cloud Computing, pp. 1–4. VDE (2022)
30. Zheng, r., Meng, f., wang, z.: Research on audio anti-spoofing detection and defense technology. Police Technology (01), 17–22 (2023)

AdSum: Two-Stream Audio-Visual Summarization for Automated Video Advertisement Clipping

Wen Xie[1(✉)] ⬤, Yanjun Zhu[1], Gijs Overgoor[2], Yakov Bart[1], Agata Lapedriza Garcia[1], and Sarah Ostadabbas[1]

[1] Northeastern University, Boston, MA 02115, USA
{we.xie,ya.zhu,y.bart,a.lapedriza,s.ostadabbas}@northeastern.edu
[2] Southern Methodist University, Dallas, TX 75205, USA
govergoor@mail.smu.edu

Abstract. Advertisers commonly need multiple versions of the same advertisement (ad) at varying durations for a single campaign. The traditional approach involves manually selecting and re-editing shots from longer video ads to create shorter versions, which is labor-intensive and time-consuming. In this paper, we introduce a framework for automated video ad clipping using video summarization techniques. We are the first to frame video clipping as a shot selection problem, tailored specifically for advertising. Unlike existing general video summarization methods that primarily focus on visual content, our approach emphasizes the critical role of audio in advertising. To achieve this, we develop a two-stream audio-visual fusion model that predicts the importance of video frames, where importance is defined as the likelihood of a frame being selected in the firm-produced short ad. To address the lack of ad-specific datasets, we present AdSum204, a novel dataset comprising 102 pairs of 30-second and 15-second ads from real advertising campaigns. Extensive experiments demonstrate that our model outperforms state-of-the-art methods across various metrics, including Average Precision, Area Under Curve, Spearman, and Kendall. The dataset and code are available (https://github.com/ostadabbas/AdSum204).

Keywords: Ad clipping · Video summarization · Visual-audio learning

1 Introduction

As content production and consumption continue to grow, our attention spans are diminishing. This trend compels content creators to adapt long-form videos into shorter versions efficiently. This need is particularly evident in the advertising industry. For instance, social platforms often require shorter ads (e.g., 15 s), while TV ads typically span 30 s (see examples in Fig. 1). Advertisers currently address these needs through a costly, labor-intensive, and time-consuming process of manually selecting video shots. To mitigate these challenges, industry leaders call for solutions [21].

J. Lokoč et al. (Eds.): MMM 2026, LNCS 16412, pp. 261–275, 2026.
https://doi.org/10.1007/978-981-95-6950-2_19

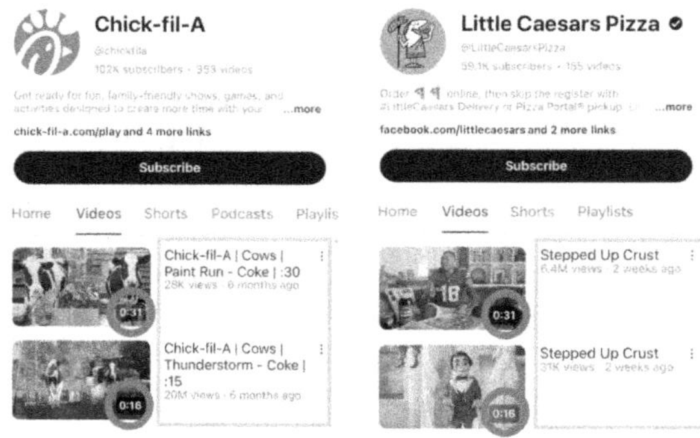

Fig. 1. Video ads with various durations in the same campaign. The screenshots include two examples of long (i.e., 31-second) and short (i.e., 16-second) video ads from brands' YouTube channels. Red circles (orange squares) highlight the ad durations (titles). (Color figure online)

Video summarization is promising to automate the process. However, summarization for ad clipping has several challenges. First, video summarization is inherently domain-specific, limiting the applicability of existing methods in the advertising context [16]. For instance, in sports, summarization creates highlights, capturing the most exciting moments (typically characterized by abrupt motion changes). In contrast, advertising requires summarized videos to maintain a coherent storyline that effectively promotes the products or services. This distinction suggests the need for a summarization approach specifically tailored to advertising, a gap that has yet to be addressed in the literature. Second, existing video summarization datasets [2,8,9,23] are not well-suited for advertising applications. Most datasets feature videos that are several minutes long, whereas video ads typically last less than a minute. Additionally, the content of these datasets differs significantly from ad content, making it difficult for algorithms to learn relevant representations of advertising. Therefore, developing a specialized dataset is essential to support video ad summarization. Third, most existing summarization techniques primarily focus on the visual information [19]. In advertising, however, the accompanying audio plays an equally critical role. Audio conveys essential information such as product name, benefits, and calls-to-actions, complementing the visual content [29]. Therefore, an effective summarization model capable of integrating both visual and audio modalities offers significant potential [11].

We first introduce a video summarization task specifically designed for ad clipping in advertising. Due to the prevalence of 15-second and 30-second ads in advertising and the preference from media users [26], we regard 30-second ads as long ads and 15-second ads as short ads in this study. Our objective is to produce 15-second ads from their 30-second counterparts by leveraging both long and short versions used within the same marketing campaigns. We define the task as a shot selection problem driven by practical needs: given all the shots in a 30-second ad, the goal is to select a subset of shots to create a 15-second ad. Figure 2 illustrates one 30- and 15-second ad pair. Due to the availability of 15-second ads, we can address the task using supervised learning methods. To this end, we present AdSum204, a novel dataset comprising 102 pairs of 30-second and 15-second video ads from real advertising campaigns. Each pair is annotated with precise shot boundaries to enable effective training and the evaluation of machine learning (ML) models.

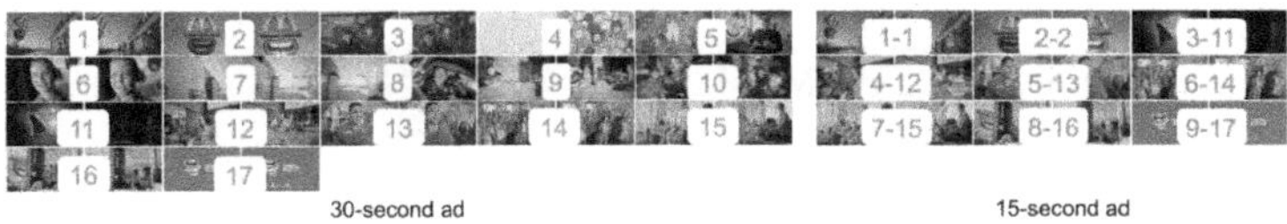

Fig. 2. Shot selection. The figure illustrates a pair of 30-second and 15-second ads from a McDonald's ad campaign. The 30-second ad (left) contains 17 shots. The 15-second ad (right) contains 9 shots from the 30-second ad, as indicated by the matching (e.g., shot 1 - shot 1). We show the first and last frames of each shot for better presentation.

To benchmark the task, we propose a two-stream audio-visual fusion model to predict frame importance for constructing short video ads, where the audio and video are temporally synchronized. In the visual stream, we use 3D convolutional neural networks (CNN) for clip-level feature embedding. Compared to 2D CNN for frame-level features [1], we combine a 3D CNN and an attention module [22] to capture spatial and temporal relationships. A linear classifier then predicts the importance score of each frame. In the audio stream, we adopt a similar pipeline but use Wav2Vec2 (Wave-to-Vector 2) to extract clip-level features [4]. We investigate both early fusion (e.g., feature fusion) and late fusion (e.g., importance score fusion) techniques to enhance overall performance.

In sum, our contributions are three-fold. First, we introduce a novel audio-visual summarization task, specifically for advertising. Second, we present Ad-Sum204, a first-ever dataset dedicated to ad summarization. Third, we propose a two-stream audio-visual fusion model that achieves state-of-the-art performance compared to [1, 22] on AdSum204. This work provides a robust framework for ad clipping, aligning with current trends in content consumption and advertising while addressing the urgent need of research in this domain.

2   Related Work

2.1   Video Summarization Applications and Datasets

Existing literature has applied video summarization techniques to diverse applications with unique objective. In surveillance, researchers aim to extract events or activities from cameras to enhance security [6]. In sports, they capture player actions across multiple cameras for highlights [11, 19]. The film industry uses key-frame extraction to summarize characters and scenes for trailers [14]. News clips condense anchors, interviews, and debates for quick overviews, and personal videos extract meaningful moments for easy sharing [8].

Table 1. Video summarization: applications and datasets.

Application	Dataset	Size	Duration (minutes)
Surveillance	OLCB [7]	17	5–15
	BL-7F [18]	19	7.1
General	VSUMM [5]	50	1–4
	SumMe [8]	25	1–6
	MED [20]	160	1–5
	TVSum [23]	50	2–10
	RAD [27]	200	2–3
Advertising	**AdSum204 (ours)**	204	0–1

Table 1 compares existing video summarization datasets and applications to ours. Notably, no existing datasets apply to advertising because their video durations are much longer than those of video ads, and the video content differs significantly. Moreover, the ground truth in those datasets is created by human annotators, suffering from subjectivity [17]. In contrast, the ground truth (i.e., short video ads) in our dataset comes directly from advertisers. We reasonably assume that these short ads represent the best firms' attempt to replicate the effectiveness of the longer video ads by selecting the most relevant shots. Thus, our goal is to automate the selection of these crucial shots.

This paper is the first to introduce ad clipping as a novel application of video summarization. Instead of picking out highlights, motions, or events, video ads require a cohesive storyline, demanding a new summarization methodology.

2.2   Video Summarization Techniques

Video summarization aims to produce a concise and informative summary of long videos by either selecting key frames (storyboard) or shots (video skim) [16]. While static summaries struggle to maintain coherence with the original narrative, dynamic summaries composed of different shots can better preserve the storyline, which is desired in this study.

Summarization models typically predict an importance score for each frame and select the most important ones to create the summary. Techniques like convolutional neural networks, recurrent neural networks, long short-term memory networks, and reinforcement learning have been widely used to extract features and capture temporal dependencies between frames [16]. Attention mechanisms, such as self-attention, further enhance these models by focusing on salient frames, improving summarization quality [10]. Meanwhile, researchers have been considering the tradeoff between summary diversity and representativeness [13] or the relation between temporal and spatial information [30]. For instance, [1] incorporates a context-awareness module to consider the global video context, resulting in more coherent and contextually relevant summaries. Recently, [22] proposes to use CNN to learn spatial and temporal cues simultaneously, which shows competitive performance. Our approach adopts a similar attention strategy due to the importance of temporal contiguity in video ads.

3   Problem Formulation and Dataset

3.1   Problem Formulation

Given a sequence of shots in a 30-second ad, our goal is to select a combination of shots that are used to create a 15-second ad. We formulated the task as follows:

$$S^* = F(\text{shot}_1, \text{shot}_2, \ldots, \text{shot}_m), \tag{1}$$

where F is the summarization model that selects the optimal subset of shots S^* from the 30-second ad. This task can be fulfilled by supervised ML as we have both 30- and 15-second ads provided by companies.

3.2   AdSum204 Dataset

We introduce **AdSum204**, a video summarization dataset specifically for advertising; it contains 102 pairs of video ads, with each pair consisting of a 15-second and a 30-second ad used within the same marketing campaign by companies, collected from YouTube.

First, we select the brand names of the top 50 fast-food chains ranked by sales according to QSR Magazine [15], as well as the names of the top 10 most popular soft drink brands in the USA [25]. We focus on these two sectors to demonstrate the crucial needs of ad summarization tools, as the market is projected to grow from \$6.2 trillion in 2024 to \$9.8 trillion by 2032 globally, and firms in the food and beverage market invest heavily in advertising [12]. We manually gather their YouTube handles and channel IDs. Second, we utilize the YouTube Data API to collect the playlists and videos from each brand and sort the results by video name and duration. These steps enable us to quickly identify potential ad pairs. For instance, the two video ads in the left panel of Fig. 1 from Chick-fil-A form an ad pair. In total, we gathered 135 30 s-15 s ad pair candidates, of which 127 pairs are English speaking.

The main challenge of making a qualified dataset is the ground-truth annotation of shot selections. For each pair, it is necessary to find which video shots are selected from a 30 s ad to make the 15 s ad. To this end, we present our two-step approach: (1) shot boundary detection and (2) shot matching. We first apply the shot boundary detection model, TransNetV2 [24], to each pair. TransNetV2 predicts the probability of each video frame being a shot boundary. We experiment with probability thresholds 0.1, 0.3, and 0.5 to ensure accuracy. These automated steps significantly improving annotation efficiency.

Next, we compare the shot-level similarity between the 15-second and 30-second ads. To do this, we extract SIFT (scale-invariant feature transform) features from the first, middle, and last frames of each shot. SIFT is well-suited for this task because it detects and describes local keypoints in images that are robust to changes in scale, rotation, and illumination. By comparing the keypoints and their descriptors between two frames, we can quantify their visual similarity. The average similarity score across these frames is used to match each shot in the 15-second ad with the shot in the 30-second ad that has the largest similarity score. Following this process, we manually review the shot mapping to ensure 100% annotation accuracy[1]. Out of 135 candidate ad pairs, 33 are removed due to missing shots in the 30-second ad. This leaves us with a total of 102 valid ad pairs.

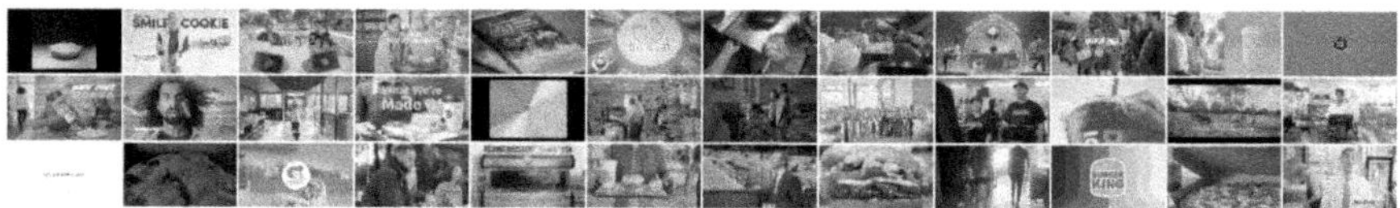

Fig. 3. An overview of videos in our dataset. We sample frames from 36 (3x12) videos.

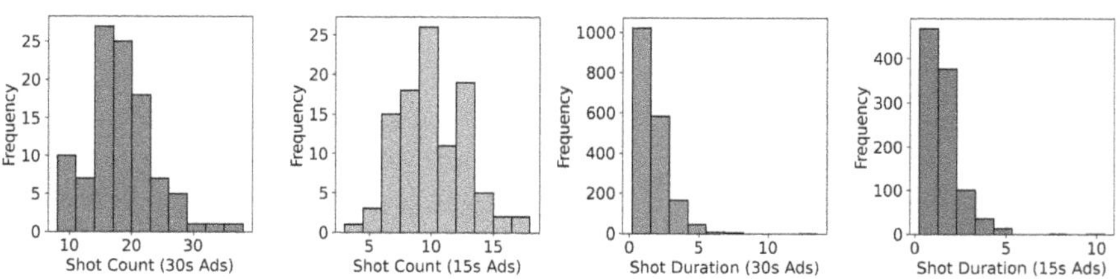

Fig. 4. Shot count and duration histogram. 30-second (15-second) ads contain 18 (10) shots on average; the average shot duration is 1.67 (1.53) seconds, respectively.

We illustrate the video ads in Fig. 3 using 36 frames, with each frame sampled from a different video. Among the 102 ad pairs, 74 have a frame rate of 23.98 frames per second (FPS), 18 have 25 FPS, 9 have 29.97 FPS, and one pair has 30 FPS. We standardize all 30-second videos to 23.98 FPS so that each second

---

[1] Note that this process is used solely to assist in identifying the ground truth, which already exists in our case, i.e., the 15-second ads. This differs from other datasets, where ground truth summaries are generated by human annotators.

contains the same number of frames across all videos. Figure 4 shows the basic statistics. The 30-second ads have an average shot count of 18, with a minimum of 8 and a maximum of 38 shots. In contrast, the 15-second ads have an average shot count of 8, with a minimum of 3 and a maximum of 18 shots. The average shot duration is 1.67 s in the 30-second ads and 1.52 s in the 15-second ads. The shot durations range from 0.19 to 13.56 s in the 30-second ads, and from 0.23 to 10.44 s in the 15-second ads.

To facilitate future research, we will release the following: unique ad pair identifier, YouTube video IDs, shot boundaries for each ad, and shot mapping from 30-second ads to 15-second ads. We divide the dataset into five folds based on the pair ID for cross-validation, ensuring that each fold is used as a testing set once while the remaining four folds serve as the training set, similar to existing datasets [e.g., 23].

4   Methodology

We first show the pipeline of our ad clipping framework. Then, we introduce the proposed two-stream audio-visual ad summarization (AdSum) model.

4.1   Ad Clipping Pipeline

Figure 5 shows our ad clipping pipeline, consisting of three steps: (1) shot generation, (2) frame importance prediction, and (3) shot selection. We briefly discuss Step 1 and 3 below and present Step 2 in details in the next subsection, which is the core of the pipeline. In Step 1, we first applied TransNetV2 for shot boundary detection, followed by manual validation to ensure accuracy. In step 3, we first average the importance scores of frames within each shot to determine the shot's overall importance. We then rank the shots based on these importance scores and compute the duration of each shot based on the number of frames and FPS. Starting from the top-ranked shots, we select each shot until the cumulative duration reaches or exceeds the threshold.

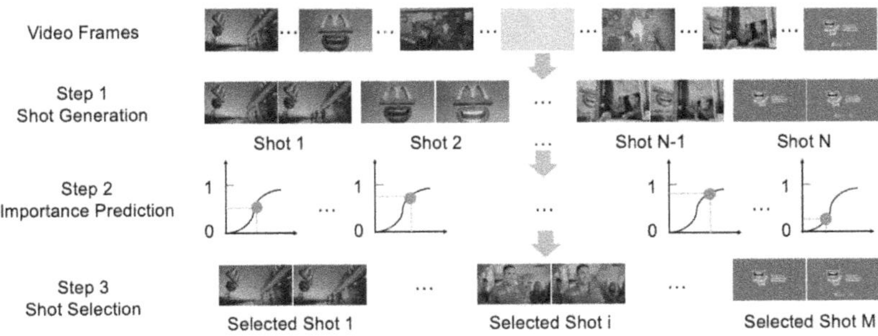

Fig. 5. Ad clipping pipeline. Our methodology includes three steps: (1) shot generation, (2) frame importance prediction, and (3) shot selection to make a short video ad.

4.2   AdSum Architecture

Predicting frame importance is the crucial step in ad clipping. Figure 6 illustrates our ad summarization model (AdSum hereafter) with two streams, i.e., the visual stream (AdSum-V) and the audio stream (AdSum-A). Given an input video, AdSum predicts the importance score of each frame by fusing the two streams.

Visual Stream (AdSum-V). In the visual stream, we start with feature embeddings. Existing studies utilize pre-trained 2DCNNs, such as GoogleNet [22], to extract frame-level features. For each video frame, 2DCNNs output a single-dimensional vector of length D. However, frame-level feature embeddings ignore contextual and temporal information across frames within shots. Additionally, frame-level features may fail to capture the nuances of transitions between shots, where frames could appear visually similar. To address the challenge, we apply 3DCNN for clip-level feature embedding. 3DCNN takes as input a sequence of frames (i.e., a clip) rather than a simple frame. The selection of frames to make each clip is crucial. As we aim to select the most important shots, ideal clips are those that can reflect the uniqueness of each shot. We split a video into T clips, where frames in each clip are from the same shot. For each clip, 3DCNN generates a D-dimensional embedding; for a single video, we can obtain a (T x D) feature map. Since video shots and clips may have limited frames, we use the pre-trained video Swin Transformer (Swin3D) [13] as the 3DCNN, which generates 1024-dimensional features, without specifying a fixed temporal length as input, which is typically required in other models [28].

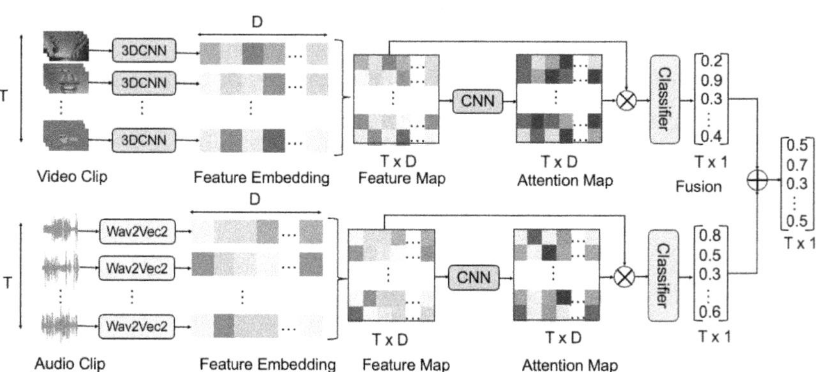

Fig. 6. Two-stream audio-video fusion model. In the visual stream, we use 3DCNN to extract segment-level feature map for a video. Then, we use CNN for attention [22], followed by a classifier to predict the importance score. The audio stream has a similar procedure except that we use Wac2Vec2 [3] for audio segment feature embedding. We show the late fusion (importance score fusion) in the figure. In contrast, the early fusion combines the visual and audio feature maps. Note that each input audio clip is temporally synchronized with the video clip.

Next, we regard the feature map as an image and apply a CNN to generate an attention map as [22] shows that such a method can improve the performance while largely improving the efficiency. CNN-based attention maps can capture spatial and temporal relations simultaneously because one dimension of the feature map is spatial while another is temporal. We deploy GoogleNet for producing the attention map and Hadamard product to merge the feature map and attention map together. Finally, a linear classifier with a sigmoid layer is used to predict the importance score of each clip, similar to [22].

Audio Stream (AdSum-A). Overall, the audio stream has a similar pipeline to the visual stream except for the implementation of the feature embedding. With a video and its clips used in the visual stream, we accordingly obtain the audio clip of each video clip. As such, each audio clip contains information that reflects the corresponding visual part. Put it another way, each input audio clip is temporally synchronized with the video clip. For each audio clip, we use the Wav2Vec2 technique to embed the raw auditory signal into D-dimensional vectors. Specifically, we deploy the pre-trained Wav2Vec2-BERT [4] for the embedding of the audio clip, generating a 1024-dimensional vector for each audio clip. Then, we stack the embeddings together to construct a feature map with size (T X D) for the audio. The following process includes applying CNN for attention and predicting the importance scores similar to the visual stream.

Two-Stream Fusion. Both visual and auditory signals play a critical role in video advertisements, contributing to the effective promotion of products or services. To better understand how advertisers create short ads, we employ two fusion techniques. Figure 6 shows the late fusion, where the final importance score vector is computed as follows:

$$I = \alpha \times I_{\text{visual}} + (1 - \alpha) \times I_{\text{audio}}. \tag{2}$$

where α is a coefficient to balance the weights of the two streams. In addition, we also explore an early fusion strategy. We combine the visual and audio feature maps as follows:

$$FM = \beta \times FM_{\text{visual}} + (1 - \beta) \times FM_{\text{audio}}, \tag{3}$$

where FM represents the feature map and β is a coefficient to balance the two streams. Using these fused features, we train the model to predict the final importance scores.

Loss Function. The mean squared error (MSE) loss is commonly used in summarization models [22]. However, in our dataset, the ground truth is binary, with values of 0 or 1 indicating whether each frame is selected. Therefore, we employ binary cross-entropy loss (BCE), defined as:

$$L = -\frac{1}{T} \sum_{i=1}^{T} \left[S_g^{(i)} \log(S_p^{(i)}) + (1 - S_g^{(i)}) \log(1 - S_p^{(i)}) \right], \tag{4}$$

where $S_p^{(i)}$ is the predicted score for the i-th frame, $S_g^{(i)}$ is the ground truth label, and T is the total number of frames.

5   Experiments

5.1   Settings

Training Strategies. Similar to prior work on the TVSum [23] and SumMe [8] datasets, we employ a five-fold cross-validation approach. The dataset is divided into five distinct subsets, and in each iteration, one subset is used for testing while the remaining four subsets are used for training. This process is repeated five times. We thus report the average evaluation performance across all splits. During training, we use the Adam optimizer. We set the number of epochs to 50, with a batch size of 1, and a learning rate of 0.001. We set the fusion parameters α and β in (2) and (3) as 0.5.

Clip-level Feature Embedding. Videos in our dataset have an FPS of 23.98. To align with the convention of 2 FPS used in prior studies [30], we sample every 12th frame in each video as the focal frame. For the clip-level feature, we use half-window sizes (HWS) 3 and 5. Specifically, we group the left and right 3 or 5 frames into a single clip for each sampled frame. As a comparison to 3DCNN embedding, we obtain feature embedding from GoogleNet (as used in [22]) for each frame in a clip, followed by an average pooling.

Evaluation Metrics. Recent studies use correlation metrics [22,28]. We use four metrics for a comprehensive assessment: AP and the area under the ROC curve (AUROC), Spearman (σ), and Kendall (τ) correlation. Specifically, based on the selected shots and ground truth shots for each video ad, we calculate the number of true positives, false positives, and false negatives. Accordingly, we compute the Precision, Recall, and F1 score.

Table 2. Model performance. ^{T} (^{S}) represents pre-trained models on TVSum (SumMe). Our two fusion models are based on a HWS of 3. The best performances are highlighted in bold.

Model	AP	AUROC	σ	τ
CA-SUM^T [1]	0.659	0.504	0.006	0.005
CA-SUM^S [1]	0.649	0.468	−0.025	−0.020
CSTA^T [22]	0.651	0.477	−0.038	−0.032
CSTA^S [22]	0.622	0.432	−0.107	−0.088
CSTA [22]	0.773	0.646	0.241	0.199
CSTA + BCE Loss	0.777	0.647	0.242	0.199
AdSum (early fusion)	**0.783**	**0.665**	**0.273**	**0.224**
AdSum (late fusion)	0.764	0.649	0.245	0.201

5.2   Results

In this subsection, we first show the quantitative performance of our AdSum model and then explore the qualitative results of the two streams.

Quantitative Results. To benchmark our model, we compare it against two recent methods: the unsupervised learning model CA-SUM [1] and the supervised learning model CSTA [22]. For both CA-SUM and CSTA, we follow the original implementation, downsampling each video to 2fps and using the pool5 layer of GoogleNet to extract frame-level features. Then, we use the pre-trained weights on TVSum and SumMe to predict the frame importance scores and select shots to make 15-second ads accordingly. We report the average performance on all videos.

We conduct several ablation studies by training CSTA on our AdSum204 dataset with different settings: (1) use the original MSE loss, (2) use BCE loss, (3) use 3 and 5 half window size (HWS) to enrich the feature map. We also compare the performance of the visual stream (AdSum-V) vs. the audio stream (AdSum-A). We report the five-fold cross-validation results on the testing datasets.

Table 3. Ablation study results on loss function, window size, and comparisons of the visual and audio stream. The best performances are highlighted in bold.

Ablation Item	Model	AP	AUROC	σ	τ
Loss Function	CSTA [22]	0.773	0.646	0.241	0.199
	CSTA + BCE Loss	**0.777**	**0.647**	**0.242**	0.199
Window Size	CSTA (3HWS) + BCE	**0.781**	**0.652**	**0.251**	**0.207**
	CSTA (5HWS) + BCE	0.779	0.650	0.247	0.204
Stream	**AdSum-V** (3HWS)	0.775	0.654	0.256	0.210
	AdSum-A (3HWS)	**0.780**	**0.664**	**0.270**	**0.224**
Fusion	**AdSum** (early fusion)	**0.783**	**0.665**	**0.273**	**0.224**

Table 2 presents the evaluation results. As expected, the pre-trained models, including both CA-SUM and CSTA, do not perform well on video ads since they were not trained on video ads. Training CSTA on our dataset improves the performance. However, our proposed two-stream model with an early fusion strategy achieves the best performance across all four metrics. In contrast, the late fusion variant does not yield performance gains.

In the early fusion approach, we combine the visual and audio feature maps before applying attention, whereas in the late fusion approach, we fuse the final predicted importance scores. The results highlight the advantage of integrating visual and audio embeddings prior to attention: applying attention at this stage more effectively captures the interplay between modalities, thereby improving overall performance.

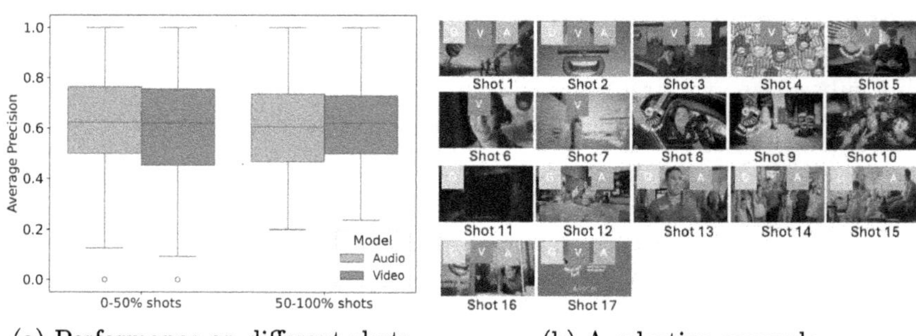

(a) Performance on different shots   (b) A selection example

Fig. 7. Performance comparison between audio and visual stream. The audio stream performs better than the visual stream in selecting certain shots (e.g., ending shots).

Table 3 documents the results of our ablation studies. First, replacing the mean squared error loss used in [22] with binary cross-entropy (BCE) loss leads to improved performance in terms of AP, AUROC, and σ. Second, incorporating features from surrounding frames further enhances model performance. Notably, using a half window size of 3 consistently outperforms a window size of 5 across all four metrics. These findings underscore the effectiveness of our proposed 3D-CNN clip-level feature embedding in capturing temporal information.

In comparing the two single-modality streams, the audio stream (AdSum-A) outperforms the visual stream (AdSum-V) across all four metrics, i.e., AP, AUROC, σ, and τ. Recall that the input audio and visual clips are temporally synchronized. This result underscores the critical role of audio in video ad summarization. This contrasts with other domains, such as sports video summarization, where visual features alone often suffice to capture key content like motion. In advertising, however, audio carries essential information, such as product details, contact information, and promotional messages, making it a vital contributor to effective summarization.

To provide further evidence of the advantages of both models, especially the audio information, we analyze the performance of AdSum_A and AdSum_V by splitting shots in each video into two parts: 0–50% and 50–100%. The AP score boxplots in Panel (a) of Fig. 7 illustrate that, overall, AdSum_A demonstrates better performance in the first half (0–50%), whereas AdSum-V performs better in selecting shots from the latter half of the video (50–100%). This result may align well with the structural characteristic of video ads: the beginning often emphasizes engaging elements, such as attention-grabbing questions through audio, while the latter half focuses more on product visualization via visuals. Moreover, the ad narrative could play a crucial role in maintaining the coherence of selected shots, addressing the unique challenge in advertising.

Qualitative Results. We further demonstrate the importance of audio in ad summarization through one example of a McDonald's ad ("video 7") titled "*McHappy Day 2023*". Figure 7, Panel (b) shows the shot selection results by the proposed models. The 30-second ad narrative is "*It's more than just a day. **From now until Saturday, November 18**, it's the McHappiest time of the year. So give a helping hand. One more. Would you like silly socks with that? Yep. Pull up your silly socks and **give \$2 back with every Big Mac. Who ordered the Big Macs? I did! To help families with seriously ill or injured children. Have a good day.**"* The bold text indicates the narrative in the 15-second ad. Audio delivers contextual information, such as specific dates and actionable instructions. In Panel (b) of Fig. 7, the audio model indeed performs better in selecting the ending shots, potentially guided by the ending narratives. This example highlights the critical role of audio in maintaining the storyline's integrity and effectiveness.

5.3 Limitations and Future Work

We discuss limitations related to both the dataset and the modeling approach below to help guide future research directions. First, although the size of our AdSum204 dataset is larger or comparable to the existing public dataset for video summarization, it is worth scaling up the dataset further by incorporating more video pairs and covering a broader range of industries. Nonetheless, this does not diminish the contribution of our work, i.e., a novel application with particular significance in the food and beverage industry, given its substantial market size. Second, while our proposed two-stream model already outperforms benchmarks, it still has room for improvement. For example, while we fuse visual and audio features, future work could explore integrating cross-attention mechanisms to enable deeper interaction across modalities. Third, while 30-second and 15-second ads dominate TV and most social media advertising, future work can apply our framework to generate ad versions of various durations without sacrificing generalizability.

6   Conclusion

Automated video ad clipping from long video ads into shorter versions is crucial for advertisers aiming to adapt content effectively across diverse formats while minimizing costs. To address this need, we introduce a novel ad clipping task and develop a dedicated dataset AdSum204, which consists of 204 video ads with temporally synchronized visual and audio information. Our proposed two-stream audio-visual fusion model demonstrates the effectiveness of integrating visual and audio modalities for predicting the importance of video frames. Our findings highlight the superiority of 3D CNNs for feature embedding, surpassing traditional 2D CNN-based approaches [e.g., 22]. Moreover, the early fusion strategy, which integrates both visual and audio cues, achieves the best performance. Furthermore, early fusion strategies that combine both visual and audio cues deliver the best performance, emphasizing the importance of audio in video ad clipping.

References

1. Apostolidis, E., Balaouras, G., Mezaris, V., Patras, I.: Summarizing videos using concentrated attention and considering the uniqueness and diversity of the video frames. In: Proceedings of the 2022 International Conference on Multimedia Retrieval, pp. 407–415 (2022)
2. Argaw, D.M., et al.: Scaling up video summarization pretraining with large language models. In: Proceedings of the IEEE/CVF Conference on Computer Vision and Pattern Recognition, pp. 8332–8341 (2024)
3. Baevski, A., Zhou, Y., Mohamed, A., Auli, M.: Wav2vec 2.0: a framework for self-supervised learning of speech representations. Adv. Neural Inf. Process. Syst. **33**, 12449–12460 (2020)
4. Barrault, L., et al.: Seamless: multilingual expressive and streaming speech translation. arXiv Preprint ArXiv:2312.05187 (2023)
5. De Avila, S.E.F., Lopes, A.P.B., da Luz Jr, A., de Albuquerque Araújo, A.: Vsumm: a mechanism designed to produce static video summaries and a novel evaluation method. Pattern Recognit. Lett. **32**(1), 56–68 (2011)
6. Fang, Z., et al.: Abnormal event detection in crowded scenes based on deep learning. Multimedia Tools Appl. **75**(22), 14617–14639 (2016). https://doi.org/10.1007/s11042-016-3316-3
7. Fu, Y., Guo, Y., Zhu, Y., Liu, F., Song, C., Zhou, Z.H.: Multi-view video summarization. IEEE Trans. Multimedia **12**(7), 717–729 (2010)
8. Gygli, M., Grabner, H., Riemenschneider, H., Van Gool, L.: Creating summaries from user videos. In: Fleet, D., Pajdla, T., Schiele, B., Tuytelaars, T. (eds.) ECCV 2014. LNCS, vol. 8695, pp. 505–520. Springer, Cham (2014). https://doi.org/10.1007/978-3-319-10584-0_33
9. Ji, Z., Ma, Y., Pang, Y., Li, X.: Query-aware sparse coding for web multi-video summarization. Inf. Sci. **478**, 152–166 (2019)
10. Ji, Z., Xiong, K., Pang, Y., Li, X.: Video summarization with attention-based encoder-decoder networks. IEEE Trans. Circuits Syst. Video Technol. **30**(6), 1709–1717 (2019)
11. Khan, A.A., Shao, J., Ali, W., Tumrani, S.: Content-aware summarization of broadcast sports videos: an audio-visual feature extraction approach. Neural Process. Lett. **52**(3), 1945–1968 (2020)
12. LeverX: Top 2025 challenges in food & beverage industry (2025). https://leverx.com/newsroom/plm-for-the-food-industry
13. Liu, T., Meng, Q., Huang, J.J., Vlontzos, A., Rueckert, D., Kainz, B.: Video summarization through reinforcement learning with a 3D spatio-temporal u-net. IEEE Trans. Image Process. **31**, 1573–1586 (2022)
14. Liu, X., Shi, S.W., Teixeira, T., Wedel, M.: Video content marketing: the making of clips. J. Mark. **82**(4), 86–101 (2018)
15. Magazine, Q.: The top 50 fast-food chains in America (2023). https://www.qsrmagazine.com/operations/fast-food/ranked-the-top-50-fast-food-chains-in-america/
16. Meena, P., Kumar, H., Yadav, S.K.: A review on video summarization techniques. Eng. Appl. Artif. Intell. **118**, 105667 (2023)
17. Otani, M., Nakashima, Y., Rahtu, E., Heikkila, J.: Rethinking the evaluation of video summaries. In: Proceedings of the IEEE/CVF Conference on Computer Vision and Pattern Recognition, pp. 7596–7604 (2019)

18. Ou, S.H., Lee, C.H., Somayazulu, V.S., Chen, Y.K., Chien, S.Y.: On-line multi-view video summarization for wireless video sensor network. IEEE J. Sel. Top. Signal Process. **9**(1), 165–179 (2014)

19. Tejero-de Pablos, A., Nakashima, Y., Sato, T., Yokoya, N., Linna, M., Rahtu, E.: Summarization of user-generated sports video by using deep action recognition features. IEEE Trans. Multimedia **20**(8), 2000–2011 (2018)

20. Potapov, D., Douze, M., Harchaoui, Z., Schmid, C.: Category-specific video summarization. In: Fleet, D., Pajdla, T., Schiele, B., Tuytelaars, T. (eds.) ECCV 2014. LNCS, vol. 8694, pp. 540–555. Springer, Cham (2014). https://doi.org/10.1007/978-3-319-10599-4_35

21. Reduct.Video: Video summarizer for marketing professionals - 17 use cases (2023). https://reduct.video/blog/summarizer-for-marketing

22. Son, J., Park, J., Kim, K.: CSTA: CNN-based spatiotemporal attention for video summarization. In: Proceedings of the IEEE/CVF Conference on Computer Vision and Pattern Recognition, pp. 18847–18856 (2024)

23. Song, Y., Vallmitjana, J., Stent, A., Jaimes, A.: Tvsum: summarizing web videos using titles. In: Proceedings of the IEEE Conference on Computer Vision and Pattern Recognition, pp. 5179–5187 (2015)

24. Souček, T., Lokoč, J.: Transnet v2: an effective deep network architecture for fast shot transition detection. arXiv Preprint ArXiv:2008.04838 (2020)

25. Statista: Leading soft drink brands ranked by brand awareness in the united states in 2023 (2024). https://www.statista.com/statistics/1346276/most-well-known-soft-drink-brands-in-the-united-states/

26. TVision Insights: Study: Online and on tv, consumers prefer longer ads to shorter ones (2023). https://www.tvisioninsights.com/resources/study-online-and-on-tv-consumers-prefer-longer-ads-to-shorter-ones

27. Vasudevan, A.B., Gygli, M., Volokitin, A., Van Gool, L.: Query-adaptive video summarization via quality-aware relevance estimation. In: Proceedings of the 25th ACM International Conference on Multimedia, pp. 582–590 (2017)

28. Xie, S., Sun, C., Huang, J., Tu, Z., Murphy, K.: Rethinking spatiotemporal feature learning: speed-accuracy trade-offs in video classification. In: Proceedings of the European Conference on Computer Vision (ECCV), pp. 305–321 (2018)

29. Xie, W., Luan, L., Zhu, Y., Bart, Y., Ostadabbas, S.: Multimodal drivers of attention interruption to baby product video ads. In: International Conference on Pattern Recognition, pp. 303–318. Springer (2024)

30. Zhang, K., Chao, W.-L., Sha, F., Grauman, K.: Video summarization with long short-term memory. In: Leibe, B., Matas, J., Sebe, N., Welling, M. (eds.) ECCV 2016. LNCS, vol. 9911, pp. 766–782. Springer, Cham (2016). https://doi.org/10.1007/978-3-319-46478-7_47

A Case Study of a Transparent and Controllable Music Recommender System with Multi-relational Layers

Kosetsu Tsukuda[✉], Keisuke Ishida, Takumi Takahashi, Masahiro Hamasaki, and Masataka Goto

National Institute of Advanced Industrial Science and Technology (AIST), Tsukuba, Japan
k.tsukuda@aist.go.jp

Abstract. In recommending songs to users, various types of relationships can be considered, such as songs liked by users with similar preferences or songs that are acoustically similar to those the target user already likes. Providing explanations for recommendations based on such relationships improves transparency and trust, but users currently have no control over which relationships are emphasized. To solve this problem, we extend an existing recommendation method based on a graph convolutional network (GCN) by representing each relationship as a separate graph layer with adjustable weights. By applying this method, we implemented a song recommender system with three types of relationships (user preference similarity, acoustic similarity, and creator commonality) on a music web service called "Kiite." On the service, four types of recommendation results are displayed, depending on which relationships are emphasized and to what degree. The recommender system offers both transparency and controllability in that users can freely switch between the four recommendation result types. An analysis of over two years of usage logs demonstrates the effectiveness of combining transparency and controllability in music recommendation.

Keywords: Music recommendation · Graph convolutional network · Web service · User interaction · User behavior analysis

1 Introduction

With the rise of music-streaming and video-sharing services, users now have access to a vast number of songs. Because it is challenging for users to find songs that match their preferences, many music services incorporate recommender systems to estimate and suggest songs that users might like. Such systems often rely on multiple types of relationships, such as "similarity in song preferences between users" and "similarity in acoustic features between songs" [2,13]. Recent research also focuses on improving recommendation accuracy by leveraging multiple relationships [28,36].

Beyond accuracy, transparency is also critical in recommender systems [6, 7,29], as it builds user trust [7,21,29] and encourages continued use. A common way to enhance transparency is to provide explanations [4,38]. In music

J. Lokoč et al. (Eds.): MMM 2026, LNCS 16412, pp. 276–291, 2026.
https://doi.org/10.1007/978-981-95-6950-2_20

recommendation, one such approach is to show the relationship used in a recommendation, such as "Users with similar tastes to yours like this song" or "This song is acoustically similar to songs you like."

Although presentation of the reasons for recommendations improves transparency, the relationship used to explain each recommended song is determined by the recommender system. Therefore, if a user sees that most recommended songs come with the explanation "Users with similar tastes to yours like this song," for example, but the user instead wants to see more results based on "This song is acoustically similar to songs you like," that intent cannot be captured in current recommendation systems. The incorporation of controllability, allowing users to choose which relationship to emphasize, could enhance users' interactions and help them discover songs more efficiently, while maintaining transparency.

To address this issue, we propose a recommender system that offers both transparency and controllability. We extend a method based on a graph convolutional network (GCN) [11,35] to handle multiple relationships and emphasize specific ones. Our method introduces a layered structure where each layer represents a different relationship via a graph of vectorized nodes for users, songs, and creators. By assigning weights to each layer and optimizing the node vectors accordingly, the system generates recommendation results that reflect the intended emphasis.

In addition, for a case study, we implemented this method in a music web service called "Kiite"[1] which supports three relationships: "user preference similarity," "acoustic similarity," and "creator commonality." Kiite displays four recommendation result types: three emphasizing a specific relationship, and one combining the relationships equally. Users can freely switch between these types while listening to songs and giving feedback. We analyzed over two years of usage logs from Kiite to examine how users interacted with these recommendation types. Our analysis showed that users who explored more types engaged more actively, and that about 40% of users discovered preferred songs via multiple recommendation types. These findings demonstrate the value of adding controllability to recommender systems.

2   Related Work

In recommender systems, the display of reasons for recommendations to users helps them efficiently find items [23,34], improves system transparency [15,21], and builds trust [5,21,23]. Accordingly, various explanation methods and interfaces have been proposed [4,38]. One approach to explain recommendations is to present estimated user preferences [1,10,34]. For example, Balog et al. [1] generated textual explanations based on tags assigned to movies and presented them alongside recommendations.

---

[1] https://kiite.jp.

Another approach is to provide explanations for each recommended item [5, 12,15,21,23,32], such as evaluations from similar users [12] or feature similarities with respect to previously liked items [5]. Some methods present multiple explanations based on different relationships [19,20,31]. Kouki et al. [20] used up to seven relationships (e.g., user similarity, metadata similarity, popularity) and offered corresponding explanations. As user preferences for explanation types vary [20,32], the presentation of multiple explanation types can better meet individual needs. However, existing systems typically do not allow users to request more recommendations based on a specific relationship that they prefer.

To address this issue, some studies introduced controllability via slider-based interfaces [3,25,30]. For instance, Bostandjiev et al. [3] allowed users to adjust sliders to control the weights of three relationships. The system then combined results accordingly and presented a unified list. Other studies adopted similar techniques [25,30]. Although sliders offer fine control, users tend to use them more when searching for known items and less when exploring new ones [30].

Our study aims to support new song discovery by presenting recommendations based on multiple relationships. Following prior insights [30], we avoid sliders and instead let users switch between recommendation results that each emphasize a different relationship. This design lowers the user effort and improves the usability relative to slider-based interfaces. When incorporating controllability into a recommender system that considers multiple relationships, prior work has commonly used separate recommendation methods for each relationship [3,25,30]. Alternatively, there have been simple approaches where users choose whether to incorporate meta-information linked to song content into the recommendation results, and filtering is then performed accordingly [14,24,27]. In contrast to those approaches, we leverage the high recommendation accuracy of GCN-based methods [36] and generate recommendations within a unified framework. Moreover, most prior systems offering controllability were evaluated in small, short-term user studies [3,14,24,25,27,30]. In contrast, we implemented our system in a public web service and analyzed logs from 3,264 users over more than two years. This large-scale, long-term analysis highlights how users interact with a recommender system that supports both transparency and controllability.

3   Song Recommendation Method Based on Layered Graph Structure

This section describes our recommendation method that considers various relationships and generates recommendation results with an emphasis on a specific relationship.

3.1   Graph Construction on Layers (Fig. 1(a))

In our method, various relationships considered in recommendation are represented by graphs. A separate graph is constructed for each relationship and treated as a "layer," which enables the generation of recommendation results

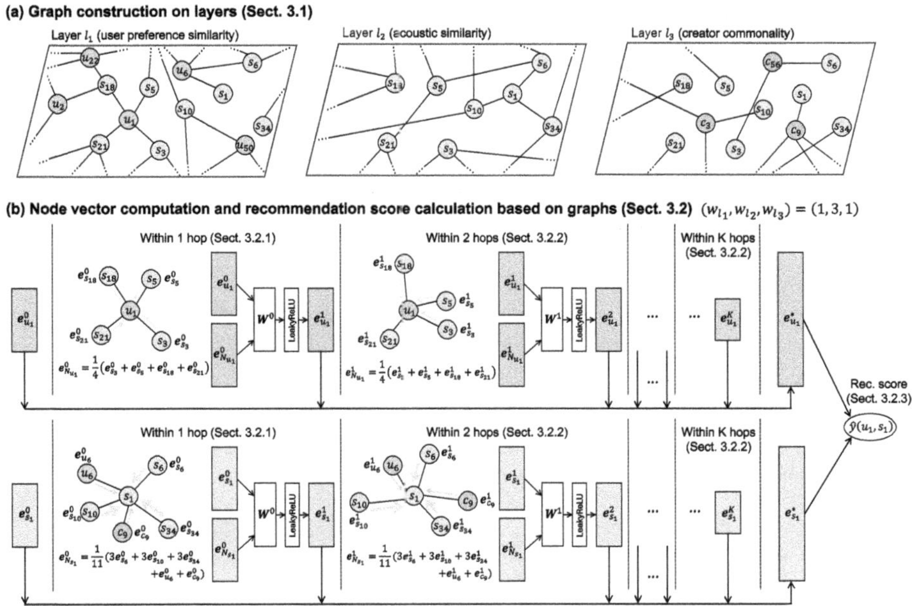

Fig. 1. Method overview.

emphasizing a specific layer. Let L denote the set of layers, and let $G_l = (V_l, E_l)$ denote the graph on a layer $l \in L$, where G_l is an undirected graph, and V_l and E_l represent the sets of nodes and edges in G_l, respectively. For example, for a layer l_1 corresponding to the relationship "user preference similarity," the graph G_{l_1} has nodes $V_{l_1} = U \cup S$ (where U and S are the sets of all users and all songs, respectively), and the edges E_{l_1} are defined between each user $u \in U$ and each song $s \in S$ that the user likes. Here, $\{u, s\}$ denotes an edge between user u and song s.

The set of nodes included in a graph may differ across layers. In addition to the above relationship, suppose we also consider the relationship "acoustic similarity." In this case, the graph on the corresponding layer l_2 is defined as G_{l_2} with $V_{l_2} = S$, and E_{l_2} contains edges between each song $s \in S$ and its similar songs $s' \in S$. Similarly, for the relationship "creator commonality," the graph on the corresponding layer l_3 is defined as G_{l_3} with $V_{l_3} = C \cup S$ (where C is the set of all creators), and E_{l_3} contains edges between each creator $c \in C$ and each song $s \in S$ created by c.[2]

3.2   Graph-Based Vector Calculation for Nodes (Fig. 1(b))

In our method, each node on a graph is represented by a d-dimensional vector $e^0 \in \mathbb{R}^d$, following GCN-based recommendation approaches [36]. A single node

---

[2] For the rest of this section, we use these three relationships and their corresponding layers (l_1, l_2, l_3) as examples.

that appears in multiple layers is represented by the same vector. For example, a song s that appears in all three layers (l_1, l_2, and l_3) is represented by the same vector $\boldsymbol{e}_s^0$. By using the message-passing architecture [9,37], the value of each node vector is updated according to its neighbors within K-hops in the graph. Below, we first describe how to compute vectors based on 1-hop neighbors; then, we generalize this to k-hops ($1 \le k \le K$). Finally, we explain how to compute recommendation scores using the resulting node vectors.

Vector Calculation Based on 1-Hop Neighbors To calculate the vector values of nodes, we assign a weight $w_l \in \mathbb{R}^+$ to each layer $l \in L$. Larger weights are assigned to layers corresponding to relationships that the recommendation should emphasize. Let $N_n^l = \{(t, w_l) \mid \{n, t\} \in E_l\}$ be the set of pairs of neighbor node $t \in V_l$ and weight w_l for node $n \in V_l$ in graph G_l. The union of these sets over all layers is denoted as $N_n = \bigcup_{l \in L} N_n^l$. Then, the vector $\boldsymbol{e}_{N_n}^0$ based on the 1-hop neighbors of node n is computed as follows:

$$\boldsymbol{e}_{N_n}^0 = \sum_{(t, w_l) \in N_n} \pi(n, t, w_l) \boldsymbol{e}_t^0, \quad \text{where} \quad \pi(n, t, w_l) = \frac{w_l}{\sum_{(t', w_l') \in N_n} w_l'}. \tag{1}$$

This equation computes the weighted sum of neighbor vectors, where nodes in layers with higher weights have a greater impact on the value of $\boldsymbol{e}_{N_n}^0$. While existing GCN-based methods use attention mechanisms to automatically learn the importance of each relationship [35], our method enables manual specification of relationship importance to produce recommendation results focused on a specific relationship. Finally, the updated vector $\boldsymbol{e}_n^1$ for node n (according to its 1-hop neighbors, including itself) is computed as:

$$\boldsymbol{e}_n^1 = \text{LeakyReLU}\left(\boldsymbol{W}^0 \left(\boldsymbol{e}_n^0 + \boldsymbol{e}_{N_n}^0\right)\right). \tag{2}$$

In GCNs, this is a common aggregation method for integrating two vectors (in this case, $\boldsymbol{e}_n^0$ and $\boldsymbol{e}_{N_n}^0$) [18]. Here, $\boldsymbol{W}^0 \in \mathbb{R}^{d' \times d}$ is a trainable parameter matrix (with d' typically equal to d or $\frac{d}{2}$), and LeakyReLU [22] introduces nonlinearity.

Vector Calculation Based on k-Hop Neighbors. To compute the vector for node n according to its 2-hop neighbors, we first calculate $\boldsymbol{e}_{N_n}^1$ similarly to $\boldsymbol{e}_{N_n}^0$:

$$\boldsymbol{e}_{N_n}^1 = \sum_{(t, w_l) \in N_n} \pi(n, t, w_l) \boldsymbol{e}_t^1. \tag{3}$$

As $\boldsymbol{e}_t^1$ incorporates the 1-hop neighbors of t, $\boldsymbol{e}_{N_n}^1$ captures the 2-hop neighbors of n. The vector $\boldsymbol{e}_n^2$ for node n is then computed as

$$\boldsymbol{e}_n^2 = \text{LeakyReLU}\left(\boldsymbol{W}^1 \left(\boldsymbol{e}_n^1 + \boldsymbol{e}_{N_n}^1\right)\right). \tag{4}$$

By generalizing this process, we obtain the vector for node n according to its k-hop neighbors:

$$\boldsymbol{e}_n^k = \text{LeakyReLU}\left(\boldsymbol{W}^{k-1} \left(\boldsymbol{e}_n^{k-1} + \boldsymbol{e}_{N_n}^{k-1}\right)\right). \tag{5}$$

Recommendation Score Calculation (Fig. 1(b))

To compute the recommendation score $\hat{y}(u, s)$ for a user u and song s, we first aggregate the vectors for u and s up to K hops across all layers:

$$e_u^* = e_u^0 || \cdots || e_u^K. \tag{6}$$

$$e_s^* = e_s^0 || \cdots || e_s^K. \tag{7}$$

Here, $||$ denotes vector concatenation, which is a commonly used aggregation method in GCNs for incorporating multi-hop information [37].

The recommendation score $\hat{y}(u, s)$ is then computed as the vectors' inner product:

$$\hat{y}(u, s) = e_u^{*\top} e_s^*. \tag{8}$$

3.3   Parameter Learning

For parameter optimization, we adopt the Bayesian Personalized Ranking (BPR) [26]. In BPR, the training data D is defined as follows:

$$D = \{(u, s, s') \mid u \in U \wedge s \in S_u^+ \wedge s' \in S \setminus S_u^+\}, \tag{9}$$

where S_u^+ is the set of songs liked by user u, and the tuple (u, s, s') indicates that u prefers song s over song s'. The loss function based on D is given as

$$L = \sum_{(u,s,s')\in D} -\ln \sigma(\hat{y}(u, s) - \hat{y}(u, s')) + \lambda\|\boldsymbol{\Theta}\|_2^2, \tag{10}$$

where σ denotes the sigmoid function, λ is a hyperparameter, and $\boldsymbol{\Theta} = \{\boldsymbol{E}, \boldsymbol{W}^0, \cdots, \boldsymbol{W}^{K-1}\}$ represents all the model parameters. Note that $\boldsymbol{E}$ is a matrix containinig the initial vectors of all nodes in the layers. For example, in the case of the relationships described in Sect. 3.1, we have:

$$\boldsymbol{E} = \left[e_{u_1}^0, \cdots, e_{u_{|U|}}^0, e_{s_1}^0, \cdots, e_{s_{|S|}}^0, e_{c_1}^0, \cdots, e_{c_{|C|}}^0\right]. \tag{11}$$

4   Application to Music Web Service

By applying our recommendation method, we implemented a recommender system with transparency and controllability on the music web service Kiite. This section first provides an overview of Kiite and then describe how we applied our method to Kiite's data to train the recommendation model. We then explain the recommender system that we implemented using the trained model. While we describe the system with a screenshot of the desktop version of Kiite, there is also a mobile interface allowing users to perform the same operations.

4.1   Overview of Kiite

Song data on Kiite are routinely collected from Nico Nico Douga[3], which is one of the most popular video sharing services in Japan. On Nico Nico Douga, it is quite common for both amateur and professional musicians to upload songs created with singing voice synthesizer software called VOCALOID [16]. As of August 2025, more than 550,000 songs are available on Kiite. Because songs on Nico Nico Douga are published as music videos, songs on Kiite are played using an embedded video player provided by Nico Nico Douga. On Kiite, a registered user can set her own icon image, add songs to her list of favorite songs, create playlists, and listen to other users' playlists.

4.2   Training of Recommendation Model

On Kiite, users can listen to songs through a variety of features. We considered songs that users added to their favorites lists or playlists to be the songs that matched their preferences (i.e., S_u^+ in Sect. 3.3). For the recommendation task, we used the three relationships introduced as examples in Sect. 3.1. In the graph for layer l_1, corresponding to the relationship "user preference similarity," edges were created between a user node $u \in U$ and each song node in S_u^+. In the graph for layer l_2, corresponding to "acoustic similarity," we computed similarity scores using acoustic features [33] obtained as audio embeddings through self-supervised learning, and created edges between each song $s \in S$ and its top 5 most similar songs. Lastly, in the graph for layer l_3, corresponding to "creator commonality," edges were created between each creator node $c \in C$ and each song node $s \in S$ that c created, according to Kiite's metadata.

In addition to a balanced setting of $(w_{l_1}, w_{l_2}, w_{l_3}) = (1, 1, 1)$, we trained three other recommendation models, each emphasizing one relationship: $(w_{l_1}, w_{l_2}, w_{l_3}) = (100, 1, 1)$, $(1, 100, 1)$, and $(1, 1, 100)$. Thus, a total of four recommendation models were trained. All models shared the same training data, hyperparameters (except for the layer weights), and training process. Regarding the hyperparameters, following Wang et al. [35], the dimension d of the node vector e^0 was 64, the maximum hop number K was 3, and the parameter matrices W^0, W^1, and W^2 were matrices in $\mathbb{R}^{64 \times 64}$, $\mathbb{R}^{32 \times 64}$, and $\mathbb{R}^{16 \times 32}$, respectively. As a result, both e_u^* in Eq. (6) and e_s^* in Eq. (7) were 176-dimensional vectors $(64 + 64 + 32 + 16)$. We used the mini-batch Adam optimizer [17] for parameter training.

4.3   Recommender System

On Kiite, we use the term "recommendation engine" instead of "recommender system" so that users can more easily understand the concept. In this paper, we use both terms interchangeably. Figure 2 shows the recommendation engine's interface, which incorporates the four recommendation models. For clarity, Kiite

---

[3] https://www.nicovideo.jp.

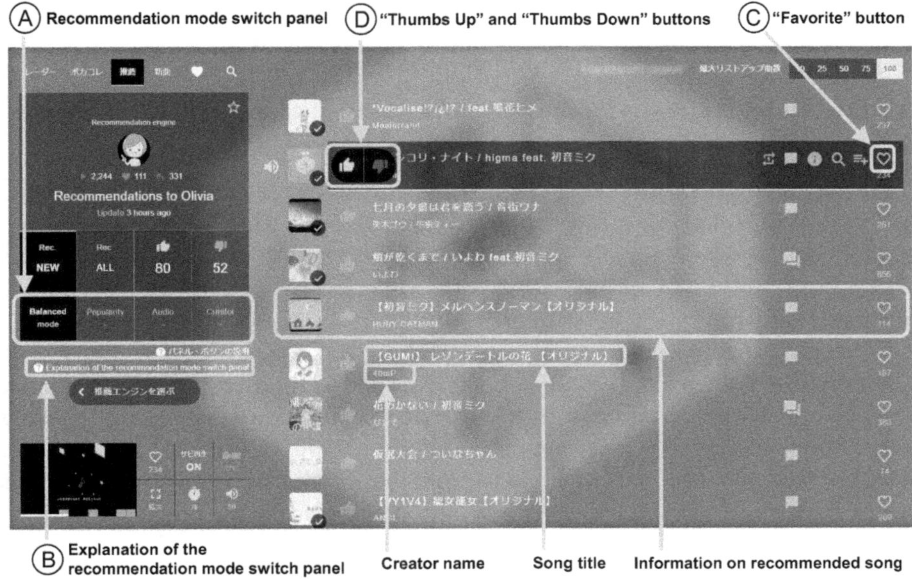

Fig. 2. Interface of the recommendation engine (partially translated into English).

refers to these models as "recommendation modes." To help users distinguish them easily, it uses the following labels:

Balanced Mode: The balanced mode $((w_{l_1}, w_{l_2}, w_{l_3}) = (1, 1, 1))$.

Popularity Mode: The mode emphasizing "user preference similarity" $((w_{l_1}, w_{l_2}, w_{l_3}) = (100, 1, 1))$.

Audio Mode: The mode emphasizing "acoustic similarity" $((w_{l_1}, w_{l_2}, w_{l_3}) = (1, 100, 1))$.

Creator Mode: The mode emphasizing "creator commonality" $((w_{l_1}, w_{l_2}, w_{l_3}) = (1, 1, 100))$.

It is possible to add more layers, such as a layer using tags associated with songs, but previous studies suggest it is preferable to provide around four explanations [20]. Thus, Kiite has only these four recommendation modes.

When a user accesses the recommendation system for the first time, it displays results from the Balanced Mode. The "recommendation mode switch panel" (Fig. 2 Ⓐ) displays toggle buttons for the four modes. When a user selects one, the recommendation results from that mode are shown. Clicking on "Explanation of the recommendation mode switch panel" (Ⓑ) brings up a popup with explanations of each mode, to help users intuitively understand the differences between the modes and to enhance the system's transparency. The popup's descriptions for each mode are as follows:

Balanced Mode: Considers the following three factors in a balanced manner.

Popularity Mode: Emphasizes the popularity of songs on Kiite.

Audio Mode: Emphasizes similarity in the musical characteristics of songs.

Creator Mode: Emphasizes the creators of songs.

Users can compare results across modes or switch to a preferred mode and listen to songs, thus achieving controllability. When users revisit the recommendation engine page, it automatically shows results from the last selected mode, which allows users to easily continue using their preferred mode without switching it manually each time.

The recommendation results include up to 100 songs. Clicking on a song thumbnail or title plays the song. Users can add a song to their favorites list with the "Favorite" button (ⓒ). They can also provide feedback by clicking either the "Thumbs Up" (relevant) or "Thumbs Down" (irrelevant) button (ⓓ), with the feedback used later for model updates. Users can listen to entire songs or opt for a more efficient experience by automatically playing only choruses, via chorus detection technology [8].

Kiite updates all four recommendation models once a day according to user interactions. Among the songs with such interactions, those added to favorites lists or marked "Thumbs Up," are treated as positive examples, while those marked "Thumbs Down" are treated as negative examples. Each positive song is added to S_u^+ for user u, and new edges are created between u and those songs in the graph for layer l_1. These newly added edges are then incorporated in vector calculations (e.g., Eq. (1)). Similarly, negative examples are used in the BPR loss calculation (Eq. (10)). Typically, in BPR, songs s' are randomly sampled from $S \setminus S_u^+$, but Kiite samples some s' from the user's negative examples with a certain probability. This helps the model learn parameters more effectively.

When updating the model, the system does not retrain the parameters from scratch; instead, the previous day's parameters are updated incrementally. If there are newly registered users, newly created songs, or first-time creators, their vectors must also be initialized. To efficiently determine the vector values for such new data, rather than initializing them randomly, we use the following strategy: for a new song s, the initial vector is set to the average vector of the top 10 songs most similar to s in terms of acoustic features; for a new user u, the initial vector is set to the average vector of the songs included in S_u^+; and for a new creator c, the initial vector is set to the average vector of the songs created by c.

5   Analysis

For a case study, we released the recommender system described in Sect. 4 on Kiite on November 22, 2022. In this section, we analyze the resulting user interactions with the system, which offers both transparency and controllability. For this purpose, we used over two years of user activity logs collected between November 22, 2022, and December 24, 2024[4]. We focused on 3,264 individual users (i.e., 3,264 recommendation engines) who played at least one song in the recommender system during the analysis period.

Table 1. Number of users who used m different recommendation modes.

$m = 1$	$m = 2$	$m = 3$	$m = 4$
1,503 (46.05%)	533 (16.33%)	404 (12.38%)	824 (25.24%)

5.1   Switching Between Recommendation Modes

Table 1 gives the distribution of the number of recommendation modes used. First, 46.05% users used a single mode ($m = 1$), which indicates that those users never switched modes and only used the default Balanced Mode. As the system automatically creates recommendation engines for all users, it is likely that those users were not very interested in receiving recommendations, stopped using the recommendation engine after briefly exploring it, or simply did not notice they could change the recommendation mode. Nevertheless, among the 3,264 users, 1,761 (53.95%) switched at least once from the initial Balanced Mode. In addition, among those who used two or more modes, the number of users who accessed all four recommendation modes ($m = 4$) was the highest. This was likely because once users started using the recommendation modes, they recognized the usefulness and became interested in exploring and comparing all four.

Next, we analyzed how the number of recommendation modes used (m) affected the frequency of interactions with the recommended songs. The analyzed interaction types were: "Song Plays," "Added to Favorites," "Thumbs Up", and "Thumbs Down." Table 2 lists the results. For example, the cell under "Song Plays" and $m = 2$ shows "51.96 (144.23)," meaning that among the 533 users who used two modes, the average number of song plays was 51.96, with a standard deviation of 144.23.

The results show that, for all interaction types, the average frequency of interaction increased with the number of recommendation modes used. This suggests that users who used more recommendation modes tended to engage more actively

---

[4] According to Kiite's terms of service, user activity logs may be used for academic research purposes.

Table 2. Average frequency (standard deviation in parentheses) of user interactions by the number of recommendation modes used (m).

Interaction Type	$m = 1$	$m = 2$	$m = 3$	$m = 4$
Song Plays	29.78 (90.55)	51.96 (144.23)	96.64 (262.5)	263.55 (1010.40)
Added to Favorites	3.46 (13.43)	10.26 (39.95)	13.85 (53.40)	37.00 (145.03)
Thumbs Up	7.75 (32.15)	13.07 (37.53)	21.04 (72.42)	62.47 (244.01)
Thumbs Down	7.14 (40.90)	9.87 (52.33)	27.95 (221.34)	91.41 (661.26)

with the system and discovered more songs matching their preferences (i.e., songs added to their favorites). These findings suggest that Kiite could encourage users who only use one mode to try other modes, possibly by displaying a message on the interface. This is an interesting topic for further research: if such messages successfully increased interaction, it would provide evidence of a causal link between controllability in recommendation explanations and increased user engagement.

5.2   Interaction Within Recommendation Modes

In this section, we analyze the distribution of interactions within each recommendation mode to assess whether offering multiple switchable modes adds value. To focus on engaged users, we limited our analysis to 1,228 users who had at least 10 total interactions across three types: "Added to Favorites," "Thumbs Up," and "Thumbs Down."

We first counted the number of users who performed each interaction type at least once per recommendation mode, as well as the total frequency of those interactions. The results are summarized in Table 3. For all interaction types, the numbers of users followed this order: Balanced > Audio > Popularity > Creator.

Next, we analyzed which recommendation mode was most frequently used per interaction type for each user. For instance, if a user played 22 songs in Balanced Mode, 39 in Popularity Mode, 24 in Audio Mode, and 16 in Creator Mode, the most used mode for "Song Plays" would be Popularity Mode for this user. To ensure that the modes were used meaningfully, we only included users who accessed their most-used mode at least three times during a given interaction. The results are given in Table 4. We can see that Balanced Mode was the most preferred across all interaction types, followed by Audio Mode, Popularity Mode, and Creator Mode. Although Popularity and Creator Modes were used less frequently, there were still users who preferred them, thus validating the importance of offering multiple selectable modes.

Finally, to assess whether users actually used multiple modes, we identified the number of modes used at least three times for each interaction. For example, if a user played one song in Balanced Mode, two in Popularity Mode, nine in Audio Mode, and five in Creator Mode, we would regard two modes (i.e., Audio

Table 3. Number of users with at least one interaction per mode (total interactions in parentheses).

Interaction Type	Balanced	Popularity	Audio	Creator
Song Plays	1,180 (138,891)	601 (53,019)	750 (90,888)	442 (21,084)
Added to Favorites	935 (20,739)	389 (7,814)	548 (13,621)	233 (2,765)
Thumbs Up	970 (39,477)	430 (15,704)	612 (18,067)	293 (4,197)
Thumbs Down	638 (41,560)	244 (17,885)	377 (35,813)	174 (7,165)

Table 4. Number of users who used each recommendation mode the most for each interaction type.

Interaction Type	Balanced	Popularity	Audio	Creator
Song Plays	799	127	300	37
Added to Favorites	621	125	217	24
Thumbs Up	698	118	265	31
Thumbs Down	398	55	151	20

and Creator) as being actively used for "Song Plays" by this user. The results are listed in Table 5. For every type of interaction, almost 40% or more of users who performed the interaction at least three times in any recommendation mode actively used two or more recommendation modes. Combined with the results in Table 4, which show that the most preferred recommendation mode varied from user to user, these findings indicate that users switched between modes depending on the context. Therefore, it is insufficient to allow users to access only their most-preferred mode. These results highlight the importance of pro-

Table 5. Number of users who actively used k recommendation modes for each interaction type.

Interaction Type	k				Proportion of users with $k \geq 2$
	1	2	3	4	
Song Plays	579	279	155	237	53.68%
Added to Favorites	586	216	96	73	39.65%
Thumbs Up	613	227	116	135	43.81%
Thumbs Down	367	108	46	93	40.23%

viding controllability by enabling users to freely switch between recommendation modes.

6   Conclusion

This paper addressed the development of a recommender system that incorporates both transparency and controllability. Our main contributions can be summarized as follows:

- By extending the existing GCN-based recommendation method, we realized a method that considers various relationships in recommendation and enables the generation of recommendation results emphasizing specific relationships.
- By applying our method, we implemented a recommender system with four switchable recommendation modes and we released it on the music web service Kiite in a publicly accessible form as a case study.
- We analyzed over two years of usage logs from the Kiite recommender system and demonstrated the value of incorporating controllability by allowing users to freely switch between recommendation results based on different recommendation reasons.

Although the layer weight of 100 mentioned in Sect. 4.2 was determined experimentally so that the recommendation results would differ across modes without degrading the recommendation accuracy, the effect on user behavior of using other weight values remains unexplored. Also, in Sect. 5.1, we showed a correlation between the number of different recommendation modes used and the frequency of user interactions with recommended songs, but a causal relationship was not established. While these issues are beyond this paper's scope, we believe they can be examined through A/B testing, and we thus identify them as important topics for future work. Although the current study has limitations regarding these aspects, the academic value of our research remains high, as we have successfully implemented a practical recommender system with transparency and controllability, and we have demonstrated its effectiveness through long-term usage log analysis.

Finally, although Kiite focuses on VOCALOID songs, the included genres are highly diverse, suggesting that our proposed system is effective across a wide range of songs. Furthermore, because our recommendation method can generate recommendations for any data that can be represented as a graph, the same approach can be applied beyond VOCALOID music. We hope that such recommender systems with transparency and controllability will be developed and widely adopted across various music domains.

Acknowledgement. We thank Crypton Future Media, INC. for developing Kiite with us and Nico Nico Douga for initially tacitly (later explicitly) encouraging us to work on this research. We also would like to extend our appreciation to users of Kiite and Nico Nico Douga, creators of VOCALOID songs, and all people who have created, supported, and enjoyed the VOCALOID culture.

This work was supported in part by JST CREST Grant Number JPMJCR20D4 and JSPS KAKENHI Grant Number JP25H01174.

References

1. Balog, K., Radlinski, F., Arakelyan, S.: Transparent, scrutable and explainable user models for personalized recommendation. In: Proceedings of SIGIR '19, pp. 265–274 (2019)
2. Bontempelli, T., Chapus, B., Rigaud, F., Morlon, M., Lorant, M., Salha-Galvan, G.: Flow Moods: recommending music by Moods on Deezer. In: Proceedings of RecSys '22, pp. 452–455 (2022)
3. Bostandjiev, S., O'Donovan, J., Höllerer, T.: TasteWeights: a visual interactive hybrid recommender system. In: Proceedings of RecSys '12, pp. 35–42 (2012)
4. Chatti, M.A., Guesmi, M., Muslim, A.: Visualization for recommendation explainability: a survey and new perspectives. ACM Trans. Interact. Intell. Syst. **14**(3), 1–40 (2024)
5. Dominguez, V., Messina, P., Donoso-Guzmán, I., Parra, D.: The effect of explanations and algorithmic accuracy on visual recommender systems of artistic images. In: Proceedings of IUI '19, pp. 408–416 (2019)
6. Gajdusek, P., Peska, L.: SpotifyGraph: visualisation of user's preferences in music. In: Proceedings of MMM '21, pp. 379–384 (2021)
7. Gedikli, F., Jannach, D., Ge, M.: How should I explain? A comparison of different explanation types for recommender systems. Int. J. Hum Comput Stud. **72**(4), 367–382 (2014)
8. Goto, M.: A chorus section detection method for musical audio signals and its application to a music listening station. IEEE Trans. Audio Speech Lang. Process. **14**(5), 1783–1794 (2006)
9. Hamilton, W.L., Ying, R., Leskovec, J.: Inductive representation learning on large graphs. In: Proceedings of NIPS '17, pp. 1025–1035 (2017)
10. He, X., Chen, T., Kan, M.Y., Chen, X.: TriRank: review-aware explainable recommendation by modeling aspects. In: Proceedings of CIKM '15, pp. 1661–1670 (2015)
11. He, X., Deng, K., Wang, X., Li, Y., Zhang, Y., Wang, M.: LightGCN: simplifying and powering graph convolution network for recommendation. In: Proceedings of SIGIR '20, pp. 639–648 (2020)
12. Herlocker, J.L., Konstan, J.A., Riedl, J.: Explaining collaborative filtering recommendations. In: Proceedings of CSCW '00, pp. 241–250 (2000)
13. Jacobson, K., Murali, V., Newett, E., Whitman, B., Yon, R.: Music personalization at Spotify. In: Proceedings of RecSys '16, p. 373 (2016)
14. Jin, Y., Htun, N.N., Tintarev, N., Verbert, K.: ContextPlay: evaluating user control for context-aware music recommendation. In: Proceedings of UMAP '19, pp. 294–302 (2019)
15. Jin, Y., Seipp, K., Duval, E., Verbert, K.: Go with the flow: effects of transparency and user control on targeted advertising using flow charts. In: Proceedings of AVI '16, pp. 68–75 (2016)
16. Kenmochi, H., Ohshita, H.: VOCALOID - commercial singing synthesizer based on sample concatenation. In: Proceedings of INTERSPEECH '07, pp. 4009–4010 (2007)

17. Kingma, D.P., Ba, J.: Adam: a method for stochastic optimization. In: Proceedings of ICLR '15, pp. 1–13 (2015)
18. Kipf, T.N., Welling, M.: Semi-supervised classification with graph convolutional networks. In: Proceedings of ICLR '17, pp. 1–14 (2017)
19. Kouki, P., Fakhraei, S., Foulds, J., Eirinaki, M., Getoor, L.: HyPER: a flexible and extensible probabilistic framework for hybrid recommender systems. In: Proceedings of RecSys '15, pp. 99–106 (2015)
20. Kouki, P., Schaffer, J., Pujara, J., O'Donovan, J., Getoor, L.: Personalized explanations for hybrid recommender systems. In: Proceedings of IUI '19, pp. 379–390 (2019)
21. Ma, B., Lu, M., Taniguchi, Y., Konomi, S.: CourseQ: the impact of visual and interactive course recommendation in university environments. Res. Pract. Technol. Enhanc. Learn. **16**(18), 1–24 (2021)
22. Maas, A.L., Hannun, A.Y., Ng, A.Y.: Rectifier nonlinearities improve neural network acoustic models. In: Proceedings of ICML '13, pp. 1–6 (2013)
23. Millecamp, M., Htun, N.N., Conati, C., Verbert, K.: To explain or not to explain: The effects of personal characteristics when explaining music recommendations. In: Proceedings of IUI '19, pp. 397–407 (2019)
24. Millecamp, M., Htun, N.N., Jin, Y., Verbert, K.: Controlling Spotify recommendations: effects of personal characteristics on music recommender user interfaces. In: Proceedings of UMAP '18, pp. 101–109 (2018)
25. Parra, D., Brusilovsky, P., Trattner, C.: See what you want to see: Visual user-driven approach for hybrid recommendation. In: Proceedings of IUI '14, pp. 235–240 (2014)
26. Rendle, S., Freudenthaler, C., Gantner, Z., Schmidt-Thieme, L.: BPR: Bayesian personalized ranking from implicit feedback. In: Proceedings of UAI '09, pp. 452–461 (2009)
27. Saito, Y., Itoh, T.: MusiCube: A visual music recommendation system featuring interactive evolutionary computing. In: Proceedings of VINCI '11, pp. 1–6 (2011)
28. Schedl, M.: Deep learning in music recommendation systems. Front. Appl. Math. Statist. **5**, 1–9 (2019)
29. Sinha, R., Swearingen, K.: The role of transparency in recommender systems. In: Proceedings of CHI EA '02, pp. 830–831 (2002)
30. Tsai, C.H., Brusilovsky, P.: Providing control and transparency in a social recommender system for academic conferences. In: Proceedings of UMAP '17, pp. 313–317 (2017)
31. Tsukuda, K., Goto, M.: DualDiv: diversifying items and explanation styles in explainable hybrid recommendation. In: Proceedings of RecSys '19, pp. 398–402 (2019)
32. Tsukuda, K., Goto, M.: Explainable recommendation for repeat consumption. In: Proceedings of RecSys '20, pp. 462–467 (2020)
33. Tsukuda, K., Takahashi, T., Ishida, K., Hamasaki, M., Goto, M.: Kiite world: socializing map-based music exploration through playlist sharing and synchronized listening. In: Proceedings of MMM '25, pp. 197–211 (2025)
34. Vig, J., Sen, S., Riedl, J.: Tagsplanations: explaining recommendations using tags. In: Proceedings of IUI '09, pp. 47–56 (2009)
35. Wang, X., He, X., Cao, Y., Liu, M., Chua, T.S.: KGAT: knowledge graph attention network for recommendation. In: Proceedings of KDD '19, pp. 950–958 (2019)
36. Wu, S., Sun, F., Zhang, W., Xie, X., Cui, B.: Graph neural networks in recommender systems: a survey. ACM Comput. Surv. **55**(5), 1–37 (2022)

37. Xu, K., Li, C., Tian, Y., Sonobe, T., Kawarabayashi, K., Jegelka, S.: Representation learning on graphs with jumping knowledge networks. In: Proceedings of ICML '18, pp. 5453–5462 (2018)
38. Zhang, Y., Chen, X.: Explainable recommendation: a survey and new perspectives. Found. Trends Inf. Retr. **14**(1), 1–101 (2020)

RIDA: Detection of Adversarial Examples Through Image Adaptive Local Reconstruction

Xiaoyu Wang and Jing Liu$^{(\boxtimes)}$

Inner Mongolia University, Hohhot 010021, China
`liujing@imu.edu.cn`

Abstract. Deep neural networks (DNNs) are vulnerable to adversarial attacks, which inject subtle perturbations into input data, leading to misclassifications. Detecting adversarial examples before classification can effectively mitigate the risk of misclassification. However, existing detection methods typically employ global reconstruction with a single strategy, which not only disrupts clean regions but also fails to adapt to varying image complexity, often overprocessing simple areas while underprocessing complex ones, ultimately reducing detection accuracy. To address these issues, we propose a novel detection approach using image-adaptive local reconstruction (RIDA). Instead of applying uniform global reconstruction, RIDA selectively reconstructs classification-relevant regions and dynamically adjusts the reconstruction strategy based on local complexity: smooth regions are denoised with lightweight filtering, while structurally complex areas undergo refined restoration using deep residual modeling. This targeted reconstruction enhances the difference between pre- and post-reconstruction predictions, which are concatenated and classified by a lightweight SVM to detect adversarial examples. Experimental results on CIFAR-10 and ImageNet demonstrate that RIDA significantly improves adversarial example detection accuracy over baseline methods across diverse attack types.

Keywords: Adversarial examples Detection · Image Adaptive Local Reconstruction · Adversarial Robustness

1 Introduction

With the rapid development of AI, deep neural networks (DNNs) demonstrate outstanding performance in fields such as financial security [1], autonomous driving [2], and medical diagnostics [3]. However, the fundamental visual task underlying these systems, image classification, faces severe challenges from adversarial attacks. These attacks mislead DNNs through subtle perturbations [4], posing serious security risks. Therefore, detecting such adversarial examples before classification is crucial to ensuring the robustness and reliability of AI systems.

Among adversarial detection methods, comparing classification inconsistencies before and after reconstruction is an effective strategy for identifying adversarial examples. Existing reconstruction-based detection methods often rely on

© The Author(s), under exclusive license to Springer Nature Singapore Pte Ltd. 2026
J. Lokoč et al. (Eds.): MMM 2026, LNCS 16412, pp. 292–305, 2026.
https://doi.org/10.1007/978-981-95-6950-2_21

globally applying a fixed reconstruction strategy to the entire image [5], regardless of the spatial distribution of adversarial perturbations or the local structural complexity. However, research shows that adversarial perturbations often concentrate on key regions critical to classification [4,6]. Such uniform global processing introduces two critical limitations. First, benign, unperturbed regions are often unnecessarily altered, disrupting important semantic content. Second, applying a single reconstruction strategy uniformly across the image fails to accommodate differences in regional complexity, leading to over-processing in simple areas and under-processing in complex areas—both of which degrade detection accuracy. Therefore, adopting a more adaptive reconstruction method is essential to address these challenges.

To address the limitations of uniform global reconstruction, we propose RIDA, a detection framework based on region-aware, structure-adaptive local reconstruction. RIDA selectively reconstructs regions critical to classification and adjusts the reconstruction strategy according to the structural complexity of each region, estimated via local entropy. Low-complexity regions are restored with lightweight filtering to gently suppress perturbations, whereas high-complexity regions undergo structural refinement with deep residual modeling to recover essential semantic structures. By performing structure-adaptive reconstruction only on classification-critical regions, RIDA suppresses perturbations while preserving clean content, thereby amplifying the prediction divergence between benign and adversarial inputs. This divergence is captured by concatenating the model's outputs before and after reconstruction, which are then classified by a lightweight SVM to detect adversarial examples.

The main contributions of this paper are as follows:

- Incorporating region-focused reconstruction into adversarial detection: We confine reconstruction to classification-critical regions instead of applying it uniformly to the entire image, thereby suppressing perturbations where they are most likely to occur while minimizing unnecessary alterations to clean areas.
- Entropy-aware local adaptive reconstruction strategy: We propose an entropy-aware mechanism that adapts the reconstruction method to regional structural complexity: simple regions are processed with lightweight filtering to preserve clean information, while complex regions undergo structural refinement to remove perturbations more thoroughly, thus maximizing the predictive disparity between benign and adversarial inputs.

2   Related Work

2.1   Adversarial Attacks

Adversarial attacks craft small perturbations η added to clean inputs x to fool machine learning models without perceptible changes to humans. Formally, given a model $f(\cdot)$ with true label y, adversarial examples satisfy:

$$\tilde{x} = x + \eta, \quad \text{with } f(x) = y, \quad f(\tilde{x}) \neq y, \quad \text{and } \|\eta\|_\infty < \epsilon, \tag{1}$$

where ϵ bounds the perturbation magnitude. Such perturbations expose vulnerabilities in deep models and motivate robust defense mechanisms.

2.2 Existing Defense

Defending against adversarial attacks is more challenging than generating them. Existing defense strategies generally fall into three categories: robustness enhancement, data preprocessing, and detection-based defenses [7].

Robustness enhancement methods aim to improve model resistance through adversarial training or network distillation [8]. While effective against known attacks, these approaches are computationally intensive and less generalizable to adaptive attacks [9]. Preprocessing-based defenses attempt to mitigate adversarial perturbations via transformations such as JPEG compression [10,11], total variation minimization [12], and random cropping [13]. However, such operations may degrade clean sample accuracy due to information loss.

Detection defenses focus on identifying adversarial inputs without modifying the model structure. These methods typically leverage auxiliary classifiers, statistical analysis, or prediction consistency checking [7]. Auxiliary classifiers detect adversarial inputs but risk overfitting and reducing clean accuracy [14]. Statistical analysis identifies perturbations by comparing input distributions, but often relies on strong assumptions [15,16]. Prediction consistency methods evaluate output stability under input transformations. For instance, Feature Squeezing (FS) [17] applies input quantization and smoothing to reveal inconsistencies, SFAD [18] reconstructs perturbed intermediate features via autoencoders to detect deviations, and Argos [19] generates semantically consistent alternative views to check prediction agreement. However, such methods often suffer from sensitivity to adaptive attacks, high computational cost, or dependence on generation quality. Global reconstruction-based methods using autoencoders [20] or GANs [21] aim to neutralize perturbations but may unnecessarily alter benign regions, diluting localized adversarial signals.

To address these challenges, we propose RIDA, which leverages entropy-guided adaptive local reconstruction to selectively restore critical regions, thus enhancing detection performance while preserving clean semantics.

3   Method

The proposed RIDA framework (Fig. 1) comprises three main phases. First, it identifies image regions that are most influential to the classifier's decision, ensuring reconstruction is applied only where adversarial perturbations are most likely to affect predictions. Second, it adaptively reconstructs the selected regions according to their structural complexity, using lightweight denoising for simple regions and structural refinement for complex ones. Finally, it detects adversarial inputs by concatenating the classifier's output vectors before and after reconstruction into a joint representation, which is then classified to distinguish clean and adversarial examples.

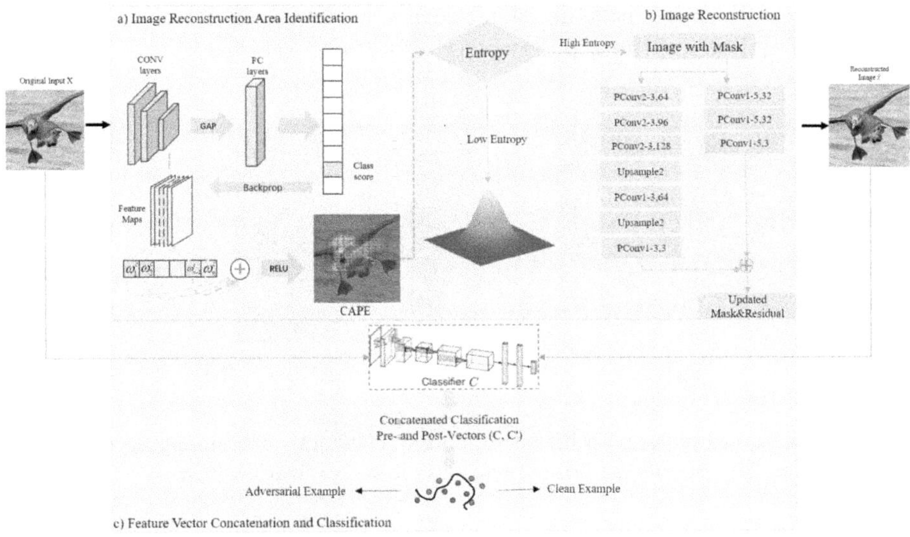

Fig. 1. Overall Framework Diagram of the RIDA Method.

3.1 Determine the Image Reconstruction Region

Adversarial perturbations often achieve misclassification by selectively altering regions most critical to a model's decision [22]. This observation motivates RIDA to avoid reconstructing the entire image and instead concentrate processing on the truly classification-critical areas. To achieve this, we draw inspiration from the Class Activation Probability Estimation (CAPE) technique [23], which provides a practical means of quantifying the contribution of each spatial location to the final prediction.

Our innovation lies in extending this idea into a targeted reconstruction framework. Rather than merely visualizing important regions, we explicitly define a reconstruction target set that captures locations whose contribution to at least one class is positive:

$$\mathcal{R} = (i, j) \mid \exists c \in C, \hat{P}ijc > 0 \tag{2}$$

Here, $\hat{P}ijc$ denotes the absolute contribution score at spatial position (i, j) for class c, derived from an attribution mechanism such as CAPE. This formalization ensures that reconstruction is applied precisely where perturbations most significantly distort the model's attention, while leaving unaffected regions untouched to preserve clean content.

Figure 2 illustrates this effect. In clean images (Fig. 2a), high-contribution regions align with semantically meaningful content, whereas adversarial perturbations (Fig. 2b) can create spurious high-contribution areas while suppressing genuine discriminative features. By isolating $\mathcal{R}$, RIDA focuses its reconstruction effort on restoring the most decision-relevant evidence, effectively suppressing adversarial artifacts without unnecessary alterations elsewhere.

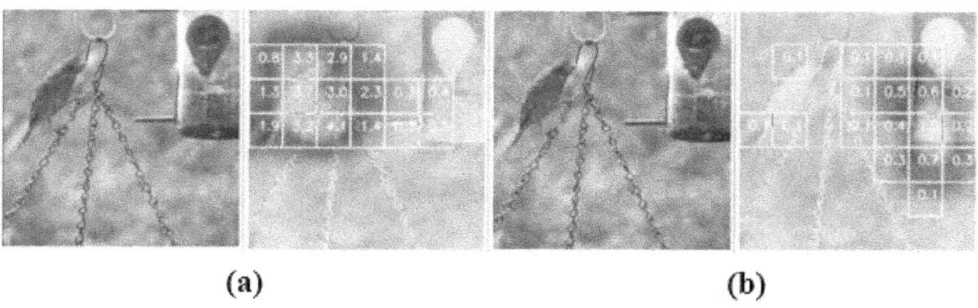

(a)   **(b)**

Fig. 2. (a) Clean example with its corresponding class activation mapping; (b) Adversarial counterpart generated from (a) with its altered activation map.

3.2 Adaptive Local Image Reconstruction Strategy

To suppress adversarial perturbations while preserving semantic content, we restrict reconstruction to class-discriminative regions with non-zero contribution scores, as identified in Sect. 3.1. However, applying the same reconstruction strategy to all selected regions may still be suboptimal. Aggressive restoration in structurally simple areas may distort clean content, while insufficient processing in structurally rich areas can leave adversarial perturbations intact. To resolve this trade-off, RIDA adopts an entropy-aware adaptive reconstruction policy that selects an appropriate restoration mode for each targeted region.

For each selected reconstruction region $\mathcal{R}$, we compute its Shannon entropy:

$$H(\mathcal{R}) = -\sum_{b=1}^{B} p_b \log p_b \tag{3}$$

where p_b is the normalized frequency of pixels in the b-th intensity bin, and B is the number of bins. Each region is converted to grayscale and normalized before histogram construction; in our experiments $B = 64$ is used to balance resolution and statistical stability. Higher entropy indicates greater structural complexity [24].

Based on $H(\mathcal{R})$, we adopt two processing modes within a unified adaptive policy: For low-entropy regions, we apply Gaussian smoothing [25] to suppress high-frequency perturbations while preserving dominant structures. This lightweight approach effectively maintains semantic integrity and prevents perturbations caused by overfitting simple patterns. For high-entropy regions where smoothing is inadequate, we adopt a refinement network $\mathcal{F}_{FRRN}$ [26] that operates at full image resolution. In our setting, it is used not as a general inpainting tool but as a targeted perturbation remover: one branch maintains spatial details, while the other focuses on correcting residual noise within the masked region. This design enables recovery of complex patterns where simple smoothing is insufficient.

The adaptive local reconstruction workflow operates as follows. We first employ the CAPE method to locate adversarially perturbed regions and produce a binary mask M, where $M(i,j) = 1$ denotes regions requiring reconstruction (i.e., $\hat{P}_{ijc} > 0$, derived from the CAPE-generated attention map). To restore the identified regions, we adopt an entropy-guided strategy that selects an appropriate reconstruction method based on the local structural complexity. Specifically, for each masked region $\mathcal{R}$, we compute its entropy $H(\mathcal{R})$, and apply:

$$I_{recon} = M \odot \left\{ \begin{array}{ll} \mathcal{G}_\sigma(I_{orig}) & \text{if } H(\mathcal{R}) < \theta \\ \mathcal{F}_{FRRN}(I_{orig}) & \text{if } H(\mathcal{R}) \geq \theta \end{array} \right\} + (1 - M) \odot I_{orig} \qquad (4)$$

Here, $\mathcal{G}_\sigma$ denotes a Gaussian smoothing operator, and $\mathcal{F}_{FRRN}$ represents the progressive refinement function implemented by the FRRN. The threshold θ is empirically determined (see Sect. 4.4).

3.3 Fusion and Classification of Feature Vectors

To capture prediction shifts caused by reconstruction, we extract the logit vectors of the original and reconstructed images, $f(I_{org}), f(I_{recon}) \in \mathbb{R}^C$, where C is the number of classes. These are concatenated to form:

$$v_{concat} = \text{concat}(f(I_{org}), f(I_{recon})) \in \mathbb{R}^{2C} \qquad (5)$$

Clean inputs yield stable predictions, whereas adversarial ones often exhibit larger changes, making v_{concat} discriminative for detection. An SVM with RBF kernel is trained on v_{concat} to separate clean from adversarial samples, with C and γ tuned via grid search.

4   Experimental Setup and Analysis of Results

We evaluate RIDA on adversarial example detection, following the standard protocol [27] of testing only on clean samples correctly classified by the backbone model.

4.1   Experimental Setup

Datasets and Target Networks: Experiments are conducted on CIFAR-10 [28] and a 100-class subset of ImageNet [29]. CIFAR-10 contains 60,000 32×32 RGB images from 10 categories, with ResNet-18 [30] as the backbone classifier. For ImageNet, we randomly select 100 classes due to computational constraints, resize images to 224×224, and adopt ResNet-50 [28].

Adversarial Attack Methods: We evaluate under six white-box attack methods with L_∞ perturbation bound $\epsilon = 8/255$ unless otherwise specified: FGSM

[31], BIM [32] (10 steps, step size 2/255), PGD [33] (40 steps, step size 2/255, random start), DeepFool [34] (L_2, 50 iterations, candidates $= 10$, overshoot $= 0.02$), CW [35] (L_2, targeted, 1000 iterations, confidence $= 5$), and AutoAttack [36] (100 steps, default ensemble setting). These cover both fast gradient and optimization-based attacks.

Baseline Models: We compare RIDA with four representative detectors: LID [15], PASA [16], FS [17], SFAD [18], and Argos [19] (details in Sect. 2.2).

Evaluation Indicators: Detection performance is evaluated using Accuracy, False Positive Rate (FPR), Recall, and F1-score, following standard definitions.

4.2   Overall Performance

We first evaluate the detection performance of the proposed method under various adversarial attacks on CIFAR-10 and ImageNet. Table 1 reports the top-1 accuracy (ACC), false positive rate (FPR), F1 score, and recall for different attack methods. The results show that our approach maintains high detection accuracy across all attacks, including strong iterative attacks such as PGD and AutoAttack. Notably, on CIFAR-10, our method achieves 100% ACC against PGD with zero false positives, and consistently yields F1 scores above 0.84 even for more subtle perturbations such as DeepFool. On ImageNet, the method remains robust, achieving over 90% ACC for AutoAttack and nearly perfect detection for PGD, CW, and DeepFool.

Table 1. Overall detection performance of RIDA on CIFAR-10 and ImageNet under different attacks.

Dataset	Attack	ACC (%)	FPR (%)	F1	Recall (%)
CIFAR-10	FGSM	88.30	7.67	0.92	90.33
	BIM	97.50	2.50	0.98	97.50
	PGD	100.00	0.00	1.000	100.00
	CW	97.35	4.49	0.98	99.00
	DeepFool	83.42	17.20	0.84	84.00
	AutoAttack	86.60	9.00	0.89	87.10
ImageNet	FGSM	86.25	15.00	0.86	87.50
	BIM	94.50	3.33	0.94	92.33
	PGD	99.30	0.00	0.99	98.61
	CW	98.62	1.37	0.99	98.62
	DeepFool	99.33	0.67	0.99	99.33
	AutoAttack	90.25	7.67	0.92	91.80

In addition to the quantitative evaluation, we further provide a qualitative comparison to visually illustrate the effectiveness of our approach. Figure 3 visualizes class activation maps (CAMs) for clean, adversarial, and reconstructed samples. Adversarial perturbations shift attention away from key semantic regions, while our adaptive local reconstruction effectively restores focus to the areas highlighted in clean inputs. These visual observations align with the numerical findings, confirming the method's ability to suppress adversarial noise while preserving essential semantics.

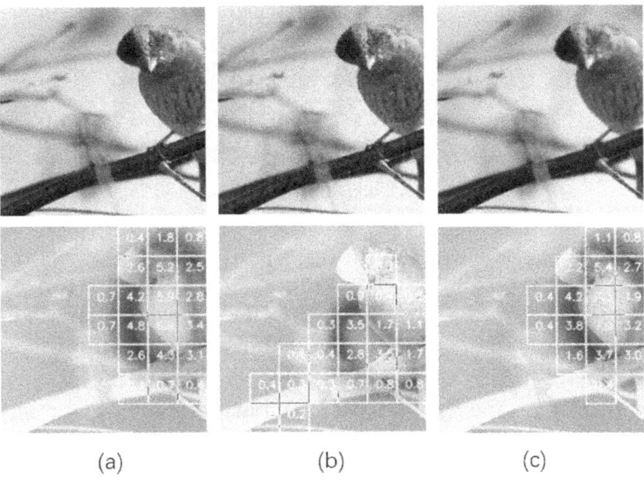

(a)   (b)   (c)

Fig. 3. Visual comparison of clean, adversarial, and reconstructed examples along with their class activation maps.

4.3   Smoothing Method Selection and Validation

To identify an effective smoothing technique for reconstructing low-entropy regions, we compare three commonly used image filtering techniques—Gaussian, median, and mean filtering—on the CIFAR-10 and ImageNet datasets. We evaluate each method's ability to disrupt adversarial influence while preserving clean image classification accuracy. Disruption is measured by the KL divergence between classifier outputs before and after smoothing, and fidelity by the top-1 accuracy on clean samples. All smoothing operations use a 3×3 kernel. For Gaussian filtering, a standard deviation of 1 is adopted.

The results are summarized in Table 2. In this table, Clean KL and Adv KL denote the KL divergence between classifier outputs before and after smoothing, computed on clean and adversarial examples, respectively. Accuracy refers to the top-1 classification accuracy on clean samples after smoothing. To quantify the relative effect on adversarial versus clean examples, we define:

$$\text{KL Ratio} = \frac{\text{Adv KL} - \text{Clean KL}}{\text{Clean KL}} \tag{6}$$

A higher KL Ratio indicates stronger disruption of adversarial perturbations with minimal impact on clean examples, representing a favorable trade-off between robustness and fidelity.

Table 2. KL divergence and clean accuracy of different smoothing methods.

Dataset	Method	Clean KL	Adv KL	KL Ratio	Acc (%)
CIFAR-10	Gaussian	0.000043	0.030709	**714.200**	**100.00**
	Median	3.156860	0.737852	0.765	36.93
	Mean	0.191813	0.260199	0.356	91.06
ImageNet	Gaussian	0.142252	0.023825	**0.833**	**93.02**
	Median	0.100774	0.019174	0.809	92.71
	Mean	431.687324	78.719345	0.817	6.55

From the results, Gaussian filtering achieves the highest KL Ratio with negligible accuracy loss (100% on CIFAR-10, 93.02% on ImageNet). Median and mean filters degrade accuracy substantially, especially median filtering on CIFAR-10 (36.93%) and mean filtering on ImageNet (6.55%). These results justify selecting Gaussian smoothing as the default filter for low-entropy regions in our adaptive reconstruction framework.

4.4   Entropy Threshold Selection for Adaptive Reconstruction

To select optimal entropy thresholds for distinguishing low- and high-entropy regions in our adaptive reconstruction framework, we evaluated detection F1-score across thresholds from 5% to 95% at 5% increments.

On CIFAR-10 (Fig. 4a), F1-score peaks at the 50% threshold, indicating a balanced trade-off between smoothing simple regions and applying complex reconstruction to detailed areas. Lower or higher thresholds degrade performance, likely due to over-smoothing or insufficient reconstruction in critical regions. On ImageNet (Fig. 4b), the F1-score attains maximum at the 75% threshold, with a relatively stable performance trend across thresholds. The higher optimal threshold reflects the greater complexity of ImageNet images, necessitating more detailed reconstruction.

Based on these results, we set the entropy threshold to 50% for CIFAR-10 and 75% for ImageNet in subsequent experiments.

4.5   Ablation Experiment

We conduct ablation experiments focusing on two critical aspects: (1) the effectiveness of the semantic-driven CAPE region selection compared with random selection under controlled reconstruction area, and (2) the benefit of the proposed adaptive reconstruction strategy over single-method reconstructions. We maintain the total number of reconstructed pixels consistent across all variants

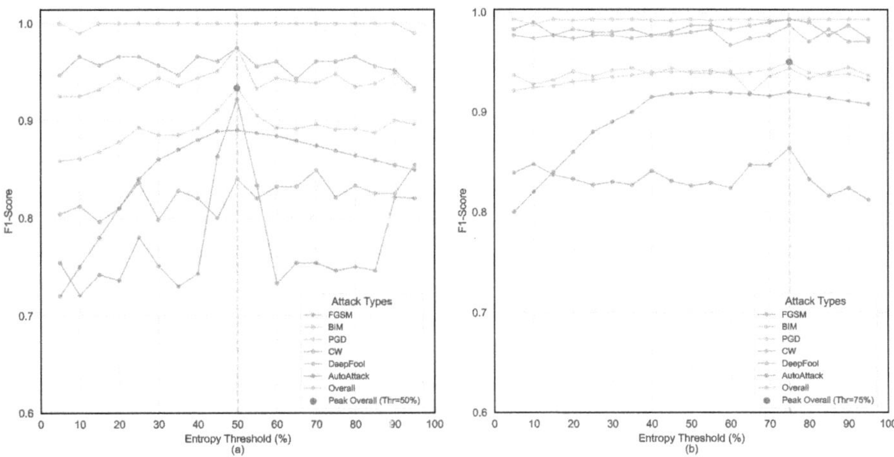

Fig. 4. F1-score versus entropy threshold for adaptive reconstruction on CIFAR-10 (a) and ImageNet (b). Entropy thresholds vary from 5% to 95%. The red dot marks the threshold with the highest average detection performance across five attack types. (Color figure online)

to ensure fair comparison and isolate the impact of selection strategy and reconstruction method. The variants are defined as follows:

Full RIDA: Adaptive reconstruction applied on CAPE-selected regions, dynamically combining FRRN and Gaussian smoothing. **RandMask**: Reconstruction applied on randomly selected regions with area equal to the CAPE selection, using the same adaptive reconstruction strategy as Full RIDA. **FRRN Only**: FRRN reconstruction applied solely on CAPE regions. **Gaussian Only**: Gaussian smoothing applied solely on CAPE regions.

These variants are evaluated on CIFAR-10 and ImageNet datasets against multiple adversarial attacks, including FGSM, BIM, PGD, CW, DeepFool, and AutoAttack. The key performance metrics are classification accuracy under attack.

Table 3. Classification accuracy (%) of different reconstruction variants under various attacks. The reconstruction area is fixed for fair comparison.

Dataset	Model variant	FGSM	BIM	PGD	CW	DeepFool	AutoAttack
CIFAR-10	Full RIDA	88.30	97.50	100.00	97.35	83.42	86.60
	RandMask	62.30	68.20	71.50	67.80	58.40	55.33
	FRRN Only	85.40	85.40	98.97	93.33	78.97	80.05
	Gaussian Only	85.56	94.87	99.18	92.84	77.69	79.12
ImageNet	Full RIDA	86.25	94.50	99.30	98.62	99.33	90.25
	RandMask	54.10	49.80	52.30	50.90	48.20	48.70
	FRRN Only	83.45	78.57	99.44	97.33	97.89	76.10
	Gaussian Only	80.92	39.40	99.01	98.48	97.60	73.44

As shown in Table 3, the *RandMask* baseline exhibits substantially degraded performance compared to all CAPE-based methods, confirming that random region reconstruction disrupts critical semantic structures, thereby impairing defense effectiveness. This validates the importance of semantic-aware region selection. Within CAPE-selected regions, *Full RIDA* consistently outperforms both *FRRN Only* and *Gaussian Only* across nearly all attacks and datasets. This demonstrates that the adaptive fusion of FRRN and Gaussian smoothing leverages their complementary strengths, improving robustness and generalization to diverse perturbations. The single-method variants lag behind due to their limited adaptability to varying local complexities.

Overall, this ablation study supports the design rationale of our framework: semantic-guided local region selection combined with adaptive reconstruction yields superior adversarial robustness, beyond what is achievable with random selection or single reconstruction methods.

4.6   Comparison with Baseline Methods

As shown in Table 4, RIDA achieves the highest overall detection accuracy on both CIFAR-10 (92.20%) and ImageNet (94.71%). It consistently outperforms baselines under most attacks, notably excelling on stronger attacks such as BIM, PGD, and CW, demonstrating superior robustness and adaptability. While some baselines show competitive performance on specific attacks (e.g., SFAD on FGSM, Argos on CW, PASA on AutoAttack), their accuracy fluctuates significantly across different perturbations. In contrast, RIDA maintains stable and high detection rates across all attacks and datasets, thanks to its adaptive local reconstruction that effectively suppresses adversarial noise while preserving semantic features.

Table 4. Comparison of adversarial detection accuracy (%) between RIDA and baseline methods on CIFAR-10 and ImageNet datasets.

Dataset	Method	FGSM	BIM	PGD	CW	DeepFool	AutoAttack	Overall
CIFAR-10	FS	84.64	83.87	78.64	98.27	90.35	70.12	84.32
	LID	87.87	75.50	88.19	80.00	81.50	71.45	80.75
	SFAD	**89.81**	86.00	66.72	99.02	89.80	64.38	82.62
	Argos	72.65	65.37	99.62	**99.89**	**92.73**	68.90	83.19
	PASA	87.81	75.32	97.99	82.20	83.41	**97.01**	87.29
	RIDA (Ours)	88.30	**97.50**	**100.00**	97.35	83.42	86.60	**92.20**
ImageNet	FS	50.67	64.56	78.57	91.51	81.10	52.33	69.79
	LID	82.00	68.28	70.00	79.00	83.00	60.15	73.74
	SFAD	67.31	85.09	89.92	80.03	90.00	58.42	78.46
	Argos	**89.48**	84.72	84.43	79.32	83.31	61.08	80.39
	PASA	65.62	93.41	97.25	94.32	96.41	90.00	89.50
	RIDA (Ours)	86.25	**94.50**	**99.30**	**98.62**	**99.33**	90.25	**94.71**

5   Conclusion

In this paper, we propose RIDA, a novel adversarial detection framework that identifies adversarial examples through classification inconsistencies before and after adaptive local reconstruction. By selecting key regions and adjusting reconstruction strategies based on local entropy, RIDA suppresses perturbations while preserving semantic content. Fused classification outputs enhance separation between clean and adversarial inputs. Experimental results on CIFAR-10 and a subset of ImageNet confirm the effectiveness of RIDA in improving detection performance.

Future work will explore lightweight reconstruction backbones and more adaptive parameterization strategies to reduce latency and enhance generalization to unseen domains and larger-scale datasets.

Acknowledgments. This work was supported in part by the Inner Mongolia Key R&D and Achievement Transformation Project (No. 2025YFDZ0029), the Natural Science Foundation of China (No. 62462047), the Natural Science Foundation of Inner Mongolia of China (No. 2023ZD18), and the Engineering Research Center of Ecological Big Data, Ministry of Education.

References

1. Zou, J., et al.: Stock Market Prediction via Deep Learning Techniques: A Survey. arXiv preprint arXiv:2212.12717 (2023)
2. Buddareddygari, P., Zhang, Ren, Y.: Targeted attack on deep RL-based autonomous driving with learned visual patterns. In: 2022 International Conference on Robotics and Automation (ICRA), pp. 10571–10577. IEEE, Philadelphia, USA (2022)
3. Ma, X., et al.: Understanding adversarial attacks on deep learning based medical image analysis systems. Pattern Recognit. **110**, 107332 (2021)
4. Szegedy, C., Zaremba, W., Sutskever, I., Bruna, J., Erhan, D., Goodfellow, I., Fergus, R.: Intriguing properties of neural networks. arXiv preprint arXiv:1312.6199 (2014)
5. Li, X., Li, F.: Adversarial examples detection in deep networks with convolutional filter statistics. In: Proceedings of the IEEE International Conference on Computer Vision (ICCV), pp. 5764–5772 (2017)
6. Papernot, N., McDaniel, P., Jha, S., Fredrikson, M., Celik, Z.B., Swami, A.: The limitations of deep learning in adversarial settings. In: 2016 IEEE European Symposium on Security and Privacy (EuroS&P), pp. 372–387. IEEE (2016)
7. Xu, H., et al.: Adversarial attacks and defenses in images, graphs and text: a review. Int. J. Autom. Comput. **17**, 151–178 (2020)
8. Zhou, S., Liu, C., Ye, D., Zhu, T., Zhou, W., Yu, P.S.: Adversarial attacks and defenses in deep learning: from a perspective of cybersecurity. ACM Comput. Surv. **55**(8), 1–39 (2022)
9. Zhou, S., Liu, C., Ye, D., Zhu, T., Zhou, W., Yu, P.S.: Adversarial attacks and defenses in deep learning: from a perspective of cybersecurity. ACM Comput. Surv. **55**(8), 1–39 (2022)

10. Agarwal, A., Singh, R., Vatsa, M., Ratha, N.: Image transformation-based defense against adversarial perturbation on deep learning models. IEEE Trans. Dependable Secure Comput. **18**(5), 2106–2121 (2020)

11. Dziugaite, G.K., Ghahramani, Z., Roy, D.M.: A study of the effect of JPG compression on adversarial images. arXiv preprint arXiv:1608.00853 (2016)

12. Rudin, L.I., Osher, S., Fatemi, E.: Nonlinear total variation based noise removal algorithms. Phys. D Nonlinear Phenom. **60**(1–4), 259–268 (1992)

13. Zhang, C., Gao, P.: Countering adversarial examples: Combining input transformation and noisy training. In: Proceedings of IEEE/CVF International Conference on Computer Vision (ICCV), pp. 102–111 (2021)

14. Grosse, K., Manoharan, P., Papernot, N., Backes, M., McDaniel, P.: On the (statistical) detection of adversarial examples. arXiv preprint arXiv:1702.06280 (2017)

15. Ma, X., Li, B., Wang, Y., Erfani, S.M., et al.: Characterizing adversarial subspaces using local intrinsic dimensionality. arXiv preprint arXiv:1801.02613 (2018)

16. Bhusal, D., et al.: PASA: attack agnostic unsupervised adversarial detection using prediction & attribution sensitivity analysis. In: 2024 IEEE 9th European Symposium on Security and Privacy (EuroS&P). IEEE (2024)

17. Xu, W., Evans, D., Qi, Y.: Feature squeezing: Detecting adversarial examples in deep neural networks. arXiv preprint arXiv:1704.01155 (2017)

18. Aldahdooh, A., Hamidouche, W., Déforges, O.: Revisiting model's uncertainty and confidences for adversarial example detection. Appl. Intell. **53**(1), 509–531 (2023)

19. Kiani, S., Awan, S., Lan, C., Li, F., Luo, B.: Two souls in an adversarial image: towards universal adversarial example detection using multi-view inconsistency. In: Proceedings of the 37th Annual Computer Security Applications Conference (ACSAC), pp. 31–44 (2021)

20. Li, X., Li, F.: Adversarial examples detection in deep networks with convolutional filter statistics. In: Proceedings of the IEEE International Conference on Computer Vision (ICCV), pp. 5764–5772 (2017)

21. Liu, S., Shao, M., Liu, X.: GAN-based classifier protection against adversarial attacks. J. Intell. Fuzzy Syst. **39**(5), 7085–7095 (2020)

22. Schwinn, L., Raab, R., Nguyen, A.: Exploring misclassifications of robust neural networks to enhance adversarial attacks. Appl. Intell. **53**(17), 19843–19859 (2023)

23. Chowdhury, T.F., et al.: CAPE: CAM as a probabilistic ensemble for enhanced DNN interpretation. In: Proceedings of IEEE/CVF Conference on Computer Vision and Pattern Recognition, pp. 11072–11081 (2024)

24. Ben-Naim, A.: Entropy and information theory: uses and misuses. Entropy **21**(12), 1170 (2019)

25. Garg, B., Sharma, G.K.: A quality-aware energy-scalable Gaussian smoothing filter for image processing applications. Microprocess. Microsyst. **45**, 1–9 (2016)

26. Guo, Z., Chen, Z., Yu, T., Chen, J., Liu, S.: Progressive image inpainting with full-resolution residual network. In: Proceedings of the 27th ACM International Conference on Multimedia (MM), pp. 2496–2504 (2019)

27. Prakash, A., Moran, N., Garber, S., DiLillo, A., Storer, J.: Deflecting adversarial attacks with pixel deflection. In: Proceedings of the IEEE Conference on Computer Vision and Pattern Recognition (CVPR), pp. 8571–8580 (2018)

28. Krizhevsky, A., Hinton, G.: Learning multiple layers of features from tiny images. Technical Report, University of Toronto (2009)

29. Deng, J., Dong, W., Socher, R., Li, L.J., Li, K., Fei-Fei, L.: ImageNet: a large-scale hierarchical image database. In: Proceedings of IEEE Conference on Computer Vision and Pattern Recognition (CVPR), pp. 248–255. IEEE (2009)

30. He, K., Zhang, X., Ren, S., Sun, J.: Deep residual learning for image recognition. In: Proceedings of IEEE Conference on Computer Vision and Pattern Recognition (CVPR), pp. 770–778 (2016)
31. Goodfellow, I.J., Shlens, J., Szegedy, C.: Explaining and harnessing adversarial examples. arXiv preprint arXiv:1412.6572 (2014)
32. Kurakin, A., Goodfellow, I., Bengio, S.: Adversarial machine learning at scale. arXiv preprint arXiv:1611.01236 (2016)
33. Madry, A., Makelov, A., Schmidt, L., Tsipras, D., Vladu, A.: Towards deep learning models resistant to adversarial attacks. arXiv preprint arXiv:1706.06083 (2017)
34. Moosavi-Dezfooli, S.M., Fawzi, A., Frossard, P.: DeepFool: a simple and accurate method to fool deep neural networks. In: Proceedings of IEEE Conference on Computer Vision and Pattern Recognition (CVPR), pp. 2574–2582 (2016)
35. Carlini, N., Wagner, D.: Towards evaluating the robustness of neural networks. In: Proceedings of IEEE Symposium on Security and Privacy (SP), pp. 39–57. IEEE (2017)
36. Croce, F., Hein, M.: Reliable evaluation of adversarial robustness with an ensemble of diverse parameter-free attacks. In: International Conference on Machine Learning, pp. 2206–2216. PMLR (2020)

AIT3D-DSR: An Adjustable Integration Targeted 3D Adversarial Attack Based on Differentiable Structured Rendering

Yunong Guo and Jing Liu[✉][iD]

College of Computer Science, Inner Mongolia University, Hohhot, China
`liujing@imu.edu.cn`

Abstract. Deep Neural Networks (DNNs) exhibit notable susceptibility to adversarial attacks, which introduces substantial risks in safety-sensitive applications like self-driving vehicles and face identification. Unlike traditional targeted 2D attacks, targeted 3D adversarial attacks are more practical in real-world scenarios due to their effectiveness from multiple viewpoints. However, the transferability of adversarial examples generated by existing targeted 3D adversarial attack methods across different architectural models remains relatively limited. These methods inadequately capture the gradient differences among surrogate models, lack structured perturbation optimization, and fail to incorporate multi-view robustness constraints, thereby hindering the generalization of adversarial examples to unknown models and diverse physical conditions. To address these issues, we propose AIT3D-DSR, a novel method combining model integration with differentiable structured rendering. AIT3D-DSR employs a dynamic multi-model gradient integration strategy to align decision boundaries and incorporates block-level geometry-texture joint perturbations with physics-aware noise injection and randomized viewpoint transformations, thereby enhancing multi-view robustness. Comprehensive experiments show that AIT3D-DSR enhances the attack success rate by 27% compared to the best baseline, with an average success rate of 86.80%. It also demonstrates superior adversarial naturalness, as evidenced by a high SSIM value of 0.9002, a PSNR value of 30.59 dB, and a low LPIPS score of 0.0819. These results highlight AIT3D-DSR's effectiveness in improving transferability while maintaining visual naturalness.

Keywords: Transferability · Adversarial examples · Robustness · 3D perturbation · Model integration

1 Introduction

Deep neural networks (DNNs) have transformed computer vision tasks, achieving state-of-the-art performance across applications from autonomous driving to medical imaging. However, their susceptibility to adversarial perturbations, which are carefully designed subtle inputs aimed at deceiving models, presents a significant security concern. Among adversarial threats, transferable targeted

© The Author(s), under exclusive license to Springer Nature Singapore Pte Ltd. 2026
J. Lokoč et al. (Eds.): MMM 2026, LNCS 16412, pp. 306–320, 2026.
https://doi.org/10.1007/978-981-95-6950-2_22

attacks present a particularly severe risk, as they systematically manipulate model outputs to induce specific misclassifications. Compared to traditional targeted 2D attacks, targeted 3D adversarial attacks demonstrate greater applicability in real-world scenarios due to their effectiveness from multiple viewpoints. This vulnerability is particularly concerning given the increasing reliance on 3D perception systems in real-world applications, where robustness against adversarial attacks is essential.

Recent studies in 3D adversarial attacks primarily focus on texture modifications (e.g., AdvTurtle [1]) and hybrid geometry-texture perturbations (e.g., MeshAdv [28]) to ensure multi-view effectiveness. However, existing methods face fundamental limitations. First, they exhibit an inherent trade-off between cross-model transferability and targeted attack capability. For instance, while DTA [20] achieves physical transferability, it neglects targeted manipulation, whereas Adv-Turtle [1] supports label-specific attacks but fails to generalize across models. Second, adversarial naturalness remains a persistent challenge. Most existing methods introduce perceptible artifacts (e.g., MeshAdv [28]), thereby compromising their imperceptibility, while only a few approaches, such as FCA [25], partially mitigate this issue. These limitations arise from two key interconnected issues: the insufficient representation of gradient variations across surrogate models, which leads to overfitting, as well as the lack of structured approaches for optimizing perturbations under the constraints of real-world perspectives and noise.

To address these challenges, we propose AIT3D-DSR, an Adjustable Integration Targeted 3D adversarial attack based on Differentiable Structured Rendering. Our method pioneers a novel combination of model integration and physics-aware differentiable rendering. By designing a dynamic multi-model gradient integration strategy, AIT3D-DSR adaptively harmonizes decision boundary discrepancies across diverse architectures, thereby substantially enhancing the cross-model transferability of adversarial examples. To ensure robustness against the challenges posed by real-world perspectives and noise, we introduce structured 3D perturbations via block-level geometry-texture joint optimization. In this process, localized adjustments are constrained by perceptual similarity metrics and further enhanced through physics-aware noise injection and randomized viewpoint transformations. Extensive experiments on 11 CNN/ViT models demonstrate AIT3D-DSR's superiority. It achieves an average attack success rate of 86.80%, surpassing state-of-the-art baselines by 27.21%, while preserving high visual naturalness, as evidenced by the following metrics: SSIM of 0.9002, PSNR of 30.59 dB, and LPIPS of 0.0819. These results underscore AIT3D-DSR's ability to bridge the gap between adversarial effectiveness and imperceptibility, setting a new benchmark for practical targeted 3D adversarial attacks.

2 Related Works

2.1 Transferable Targeted Adversarial Attack

Transferable targeted adversarial attacks, which are designed to manipulate models into generating specific predictions such as predefined target labels, have been thoroughly studied in the context of 2D domains. Recent studies propose various methodologies to enhance transferability: Li *et al..* [11] mitigate gradient instability by employing self-adaptive magnitudes and distance metric learning, while Zhao *et al..* [32] show that attacks based on logit loss are capable of achieving comparable performance to resource-intensive methods with minimal computational cost. Advanced techniques such as class distribution alignment [26] and hierarchical generative networks [29] further highlight the potential of structured feature learning and generative models in synthesizing adversarial examples. Additionally, Inkawhich *et al..* [9] utilize auxiliary networks to model layer-wise feature distributions, and Gao *et al..* [4] leverage translation-invariant high-order statistics to measure feature similarity. Efforts to align global and local distributions [15] or diversify inputs through differentiable 3D rendering [2] also contribute to improving targeted transferability. However, existing approaches predominantly rely on partial feature or label information, failing to comprehensively capture the semantics of target classes, thereby limiting their effectiveness. Notably, while 2D attacks are well-documented, the extension of transferable targeted attacks to 3D scenarios remains largely unexplored, highlighting a critical gap in adversarial robustness research.

2.2   3D Adversarial Attack

The development of 3D adversarial attacks has primarily centered on texture manipulation and hybrid geometry-texture perturbations. Building upon the foundational work by Athalye *et al..* [1], which validated the existence of 3D adversarial examples, texture-based methods have emerged as a dominant approach. These techniques can be classified into two main categories: direct modification of vertex colors in high-dimensional mesh spaces, which often results in overfitting [16], and texture map optimization combined with physical rendering, which enhances transferability but remains limited to non-targeted attacks [20]. Hybrid approaches such as MeshAdv [28] aim to integrate geometry and texture perturbations, yet struggle to achieve both targeted objectives and cross-model transferability. A persistent challenge lies in balancing three critical requirements: cross-model transferability, targeted attack capability, and adversarial naturalness. For instance, while methods like DTA [20] and ACTIVE [21] demonstrate transferable physical attacks, they do not support targeted label manipulation. Conversely, techniques including AdvTurtle [1] and MeshAdv [28] enable label-specific attacks but exhibit limited transferability across models. Moreover, adversarial naturalness remains largely unresolved, as most methods [16, 28] introduce perceptible artifacts despite partial improvements by FCA [25] and ACTIVE [21]. Existing approaches also heavily depend on precise 3D mesh priors for attack generation, significantly constraining their applicability in real-world scenarios where complete 3D models are often unavailable. While existing 3D attacks focus on non-targeted scenarios, the combination of transferability and targeted manipulation remains unexplored. This gap motivates our work to propose a unified framework for transferable targeted 3D attacks through 3D mesh optimization and multi-model gradient integration.

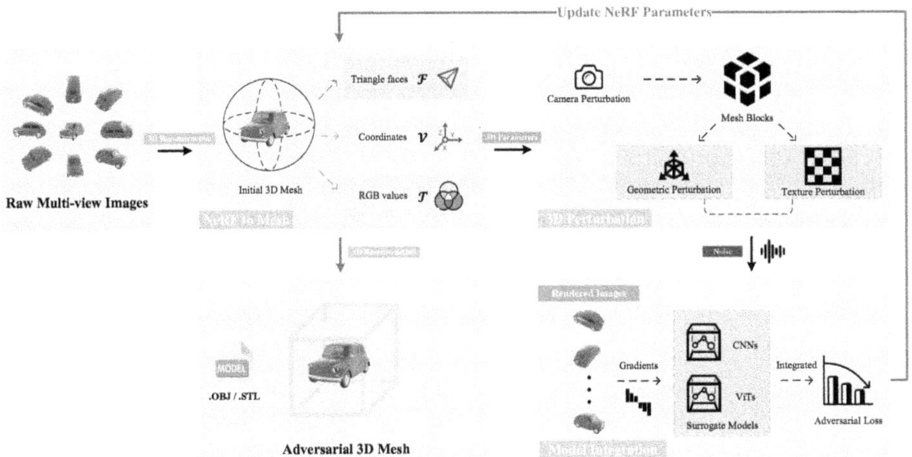

Fig. 1. The overall flowchart of the proposed AIT3D-DSR.

3   Design of AIT3D-DSR

The overall flowchart of our method is illustrated in Fig. 1. Our framework takes the original multi-view image as input and reconstructs an initial 3D mesh with triangular faces, geometric coordinates, and RGB values using the grid-based Neural Radiance Fields (NeRF) algorithm [14]. Subsequently, AIT3D-DSR divides the reconstructed 3D mesh into multiple blocks and introduces adversarial perturbations, including both geometric and texture perturbations, at the block level within the NeRF-based rendering parameters. During the generation of 3D adversarial examples, AIT3D-DSR imposes constraints on the geometric and texture similarity between the adversarial mesh and the original mesh to ensure the naturalness of the generated adversarial examples. AIT3D-DSR then renders the perturbed 3D adversarial mesh into 2D images, computes the gradient loss of the rendered 2D images on adaptive integrated surrogate models, updates are applied to the NeRF-based rendering parameters, and ultimately generates 3D adversarial examples in OBJ/STL format.

3.1   Problem Formulation

Generating transferable targeted 3D adversarial examples demands robustness across various viewpoints, model architectures, and real-world conditions. We formalize this task as the creation of adversarial 3D objects that consistently mislead models into predicting a target class y^*, while maintaining visual naturalness.

A 3D object is represented as a textured mesh $\mathcal{M} = (\mathcal{V}, \mathcal{T}, \mathcal{F})$, with vertex coordinates $\mathcal{V} \in \mathbb{R}^{n \times 3}$, per-vertex textures $\mathcal{T} \in \mathbb{R}^{n \times 3}$, and triangular faces $\mathcal{F} \in \mathbb{Z}^{m \times 3}$. The adversarial mesh $\mathcal{M}_{adv} = (\mathcal{V}^*, \mathcal{T}^*, \mathcal{F})$ must satisfy geometric and textural distortion constraints: $\|\mathcal{V}^* - \mathcal{V}\|_2 \leq \epsilon_{\text{geo}}$ and $\|\mathcal{T}^* - \mathcal{T}\|_\infty \leq \epsilon_{\text{tex}}$.

To simulate physical-world conditions, a differentiable renderer $\mathcal{S}$ projects $\mathcal{M}_{adv}$ into 2D images under dynamically sampled camera parameters $\mathbf{v} \sim V$, where V represents the distribution of feasible viewpoints. The rendered image $\hat{I}_{\mathbf{v}}(\mathcal{M}_{adv})$ is fed into victim models f, and the adversarial loss is optimized over the expectation of viewpoints and physical transformations $\mathbf{t} \sim T$, such as motion blur or sensor noise. This ensures robustness against real-world variability, formulated as (1), where L_f is the cross-entropy loss driving misclassification, and $\mathcal{L}$ enforces both geometric and perceptual losses between $\mathcal{M}_{adv}$ and $\mathcal{M}$.

$$\min_{\mathcal{V}^*, \mathcal{T}^*} \mathbb{E}_{\mathbf{v},t} \left[L_f \left(t(\hat{I}_{\mathbf{v}}(\mathcal{M}_{adv})), y^* \right) \right] + \mathcal{L}(\mathcal{M}_{adv}, \mathcal{M}) \tag{1}$$

Our framework integrates grid-based NeRF [14] with the Marching Cubes algorithm [13] to achieve efficient and accurate 3D mesh reconstruction.

3.2   3D Adversarial Mesh Rendering

AIT3D-DSR enhances adversarial robustness against multi-view variations and physical distortions by leveraging structured 3D perturbations transferred through physics-aware rendering. This process comprises three critical components: viewpoint randomization to mitigate overfitting, block-wise localized adjustments for fine-grained control, and sensor noise simulation to replicate real-world conditions.

Physical world objects can be observed from arbitrary angles, yet optimizing adversarial textures under fixed or limited viewpoints frequently results in viewpoint overfitting. To address this issue, we introduce randomized camera perturbations during the rendering process. For each rendering iteration, camera parameters (position, rotation, focal length) are perturbed by random offsets $\delta \sim \mathcal{U}(-\Delta, \Delta)$, where Δ defines the perturbation range. This approach enforces viewpoint invariance by optimizing the adversarial loss over an expectation of perturbed viewpoints, mathematically expressed as (2), where $\rho(\cdot)$ maps perturbed camera parameters to the rendering function $\mathcal{S}$ via a differentiable transformation matrix.

$$\mathbb{E}_{\delta} \left[L_f \left(\mathcal{S}(\mathcal{V}^*, \mathcal{T}^*, \mathcal{F}, \rho(\mathbf{v} + \delta)), y^* \right) \right] \tag{2}$$

To further address localized deformations and occlusions, we implement a 3D mesh partitioning strategy. The 3D mesh surface is segmented into $\mathcal{P}$ spatially coherent blocks using vertex clustering. Each block then undergoes independent texture and geometry perturbations. Texture features within a block are perturbed with additive Gaussian noise $\mathcal{T}_p^* = \mathcal{T}_p + \Delta\mathcal{T}_p, \Delta\mathcal{T}_p \sim \mathcal{N}(0, \sigma^2)$, while vertex coordinates are adjusted to simulate localized geometric distortions $\mathcal{V}_p^* = \mathcal{V}_p + \Delta\mathcal{V}_p$, constrained by an L_2-norm bound $\|\Delta\mathcal{V}_p\|_2 \leq \epsilon_{\text{geo}}$ to preserve structural integrity. These perturbed blocks are then rendered into 2D images through a differentiable renderer, ensuring seamless integration of local transformations.

To bridge the gap between digital and physical attacks, we integrate sensor noise into the rendering pipeline, thereby enhancing physical realism through the explicit modeling of sensor noise characteristics. We introduce additive Gaussian noise $\epsilon_{\text{noise}} \sim \mathcal{N}(0, \sigma^2_{\text{noise}})$ and directional motion blur (achieved through convolution with predefined kernels) to simulate sensor noise and camera motion. The noise-aware optimization process incorporates these perturbations into the adversarial training loop, as described in (3), where k denotes the blur kernel, $*$ is the convolution operator and the noise term $\epsilon_{\text{noise}} \sim \mathcal{N}(0, \sigma^2_{\text{noise}})$ is treated as a constant during gradient calculation, ensuring the differentiability of the rendering process. Our noise-aware rendering pipeline simulates sensor noise by incorporating Gaussian noise, providing a differentiable approximation of physical-world conditions.

$$\hat{I}_{\text{final}} = t_{\text{noise}}(\hat{I}_{\text{v}}(\mathcal{M}_{adv})) = \mathcal{S}(\mathcal{V}^*, \mathcal{T}^*, \mathcal{F}, \mathbf{v}) * k + \epsilon_{\text{noise}} \tag{3}$$

To preserve visual naturalness, we employ a block-wise perceptual loss to constrain localized perturbations using the Learned Perceptual Image Patch Similarity (LPIPS) metric as shown in (4), where $\hat{I}_v^p$ denotes the rendered image of the p-th block. This regularization ensures that adversarial modifications remain imperceptible while maintaining global structural consistency.

$$\mathcal{L}_{\text{patch}} = \frac{1}{P} \sum_{p=1}^{P} \text{LPIPS} \left(\hat{I}_{\text{v}}^p(\mathcal{M}_{adv}), \hat{I}_{\text{v}}^p(\mathcal{M}) \right) \tag{4}$$

The adversarial robustness of 3D objects in AIT3D-DSR is achieved through a physics-aware rendering framework that integrates three critical components: viewpoint randomization, block-wise localized adjustments, and sensor noise simulation. By unifying these 3D structural manipulations with 2D physical simulations, AIT3D-DSR overcomes the view-specific overfitting limitations of prior mesh-based attacks while preserving geometric plausibility. The rendered images $\hat{I}_{\text{final}}$ are differentiable with respect to both texture and geometry parameters, thus enabling end-to-end gradient integration across the surrogate models described in Sect. 3.3.

3.3 Dynamic Multi-model Gradient Integration

To address the limited transferability of adversarial examples across diverse model architectures, our AIT3D-DSR framework proposes a novel dynamic multi-model gradient integration strategy. This approach effectively tackles the challenge of architectural discrepancies by adaptively aligning decision boundaries across surrogate models through real-time gradient weighting.

The integration process initiates by coupling all surrogate models with a differentiable renderer, which projects 3D meshes into multi-view images. In each iteration, the relative effectiveness of model f_k is quantified by computing its adversarial loss ratio as defined in (5). This ratio evaluates the model's susceptibility to the current adversarial example compared to its response on clean inputs, acting as a real-time indicator of attack progress.

$$\text{Contribution}_k = \frac{1}{N} \sum_{i=1}^{N} \frac{L_{f_k}(x_i^{adv}, y^*)}{L_{f_k}(x_i^{clean}, y^*)} \tag{5}$$

We then apply a temperature-controlled softmax transformation to generate normalized weights that prioritize high-performing models as demonstrated in (6), where the temperature parameter τ functions as an entropy regulator. Specifically, smaller values ($\tau \to 0$) result in a distribution that prioritizes the most responsive model, whereas larger values ($\tau \to \infty$) encourage equal weighting across all models. The parameter τ controls the trade-off between specialization and diversity, thereby reducing the likelihood of overfitting to any single architecture while maintaining efficient optimization.

$$w_k = \frac{\exp\left(\text{Contribution}_k/\tau\right)}{\sum_{j=1}^{K} \exp\left(\text{Contribution}_j/\tau\right)} \tag{6}$$

Gradient integration proceeds as follows: For each model f_k, we compute the adversarial gradient $g_k = \nabla_{x^{adv}} L_{f_k}(x^{adv}, y^*)$, then form the weighted ensemble gradient $g_{\text{integrated}} = \sum_{k=1}^{K} w_k \cdot g_k$. This unified gradient direction is backpropagated through the differentiable renderer to update both 3D parameters (NeRF's feature grid G_{tex} and MLP weights M_{tex}) and vertex coordinates $\mathcal{V}^*$. This dual-space optimization ensures that perturbations remain geometrically plausible while maximizing cross-model transferability.

To stabilize training and prevent model dominance, three regularization terms are introduced. First, gradient smoothness $\mathcal{L}_{\text{smooth}} = \sum_{k=1}^{K} \|g_k - g_{\text{integrated}}\|_2^2$ penalizes large deviations between individual expert gradients to encourage parameter consensus. Second, weight entropy $\mathcal{L}_{\text{entropy}} = -\sum_{k=1}^{K} w_k \log w_k$ promotes balanced weight distributions by discouraging exclusive specialization. Finally, naturalness preservation $\mathcal{L}_{\text{naturalness}} = \mathcal{L}_{\text{patch}} + \|\mathcal{V}^* - \mathcal{V}\|_2 + \|\mathcal{T}^* - \mathcal{T}\|_\infty$ ensures domain-appropriate outputs. These terms are integrated with the adversarial objective and naturalness constraints into $\mathcal{L}(\mathcal{M}_{adv}, \mathcal{M})$ as formulated in (1) and further elaborated in (7), where λ_1, λ_2 and λ_3 are hyperparameters that represent weights of $\mathcal{L}_{\text{smooth}}$, $\mathcal{L}_{\text{entropy}}$ and $\mathcal{L}_{\text{naturalness}}$, respectively.

$$\mathcal{L}(\mathcal{M}_{adv}, \mathcal{M}) = \lambda_1 \mathcal{L}_{\text{smooth}} + \lambda_2 \mathcal{L}_{\text{entropy}} + \lambda_3 \mathcal{L}_{\text{naturalness}} \tag{7}$$

Most importantly, the adversarial loss function defined in (1) can be reformulated as shown in (8), where γ is a hyperparameter that controls the geometric and perceptual losses between $\mathcal{M}_{adv}$ and $\mathcal{M}$.

$$\min_{\mathcal{V}^*, \mathcal{T}^*} \mathbb{E}_{\mathbf{v}, t} \left[\sum_{k=1}^{K} w_k L_{f_k} \right] + \gamma \cdot \mathcal{L}(\mathcal{M}_{adv}, \mathcal{M}) \tag{8}$$

The dynamic weighting mechanism provides two critical advantages compared to static ensemble methods. First, it continuously adjusts to the evolving adversarial example by emphasizing models that remain susceptible as the attack progresses. Second, it automatically addresses architectural conflicts by diminishing gradients from models that become resilient to the current perturbation pattern. This adaptability is particularly crucial for targeted 3D adversarial attacks, where the same perturbation must maintain its effectiveness across multiple renderings and against diverse victim models.

4　Experiments and Results Analysis

4.1　Experimental Setting

Datasets. To align with previous works [7], we conduct experiments using the IM3D [17] dataset, which is extensively employed in 3D adversarial attack research.

Models. We select target models from both CNN and ViT categories, including ResNet-50 (RN-50) [5], ResNet-101 (RN-101) [5], ResNet-152 (RN-152) [5], VGG-16 [19], VGG-19 [19], Inception-v3 (Inc-v3) [22], DenseNet-121 (DN-121) [6], EfficientNet-B0 (EN-B0) [23] and MobileNet-V2 (MN-v2) [18] for CNNs, as well as Swin-Base (Swin-B) [12] and ViT-B/16 [3] for ViTs. Regarding integrated models, we default to employing ResNet-18 (RN-18) [5], WideResNet-101-2 (WRN-101-2) [30], ViT-Tiny (ViT-T) [3], and DeiT-Tiny (DeiT-T) [24] in subsequent experiments.

Baselines. To assess the effectiveness of our AIT3D-DSR approach, we employ two well-established 3D adversarial attack methods: MeshAdv [28] and TT3D [7] as benchmarks. To facilitate a more straightforward comparison, we selected the optimal configuration of TT3D, MLP+Grid, as the baseline [7]. This choice is justified given its substantially superior performance compared to the MLP-only and Grid-only configurations. All methods are conducted under identical settings throughout the experiments.

Implementation Details. We employ I-FGSM [10] with the number of iteration $T = 20$, the perturbation budget $\epsilon = 16$, and the step size $\alpha = \epsilon/T = 0.8$ as the basic attack method. In the context of the 3D-Aware Image Transformation, our AIT3D-DSR sets the block division number $P = 16$, geometric perturbation bound $\epsilon_{\text{geo}} = 0.03$, texture noise intensity $\sigma = 0.05$, camera perturbation range $\Delta = 0.1\,\text{rad}$, motion blur kernel size $k_{\text{size}} = 5$, and sensor noise intensity $\sigma_{\text{noise}} = 0.1$. Within the framework of the Dynamic Multi-Model Gradient Integration, we configure temperature parameter $\tau = 0.1$, gradient smoothness weight $\lambda_1 = 0.5$, weight entropy coefficient $\lambda_2 = 0.1$, naturalness constraint weight $\lambda_3 = 0.8$, and $\gamma = 10^4$. All experiments are conducted on two NVIDIA A40 GPUs, each equipped with 48 GB memory. All physical-world evaluations are conducted in simulated digital environments through noise injection, avoiding costly 3D printing while maintaining ecological validity.

4.2 General Attacks Performance

Table 1. Attack success rates (%) of 3D adversarial examples generated by different methods under random viewpoints.

Attack (Surrogate Model)	RN-50	RN-101	RN-152	VGG-16	VGG-19	Inc-v3	DN-121	EN-B0	MN-v2	Swin-B	ViT-B/16	Average
MeshAdv (ResNet-101)	4.26	99.35	7.64	1.40	0.57	4.35	3.27	1.87	1.29	2.42	2.01	11.68
TT3D (ResNet-101)	70.23	80.37	70.36	51.63	44.95	46.42	83.55	51.86	48.87	61.80	45.45	59.59
MeshAdv (DenseNet-121)	0.84	1.63	1.95	1.31	1.43	2.10	98.62	3.39	0.80	2.36	1.45	10.53
TT3D (DenseNet-121)	61.19	43.93	49.96	45.78	42.34	32.01	93.04	32.35	34.31	44.25	29.07	46.20
AIT3D-DSR (Integrated)	**97.03**	**85.71**	**84.77**	**89.45**	**86.46**	**80.68**	**83.35**	**91.15**	**80.12**	**90.85**	**85.24**	**86.80**

To validate the effectiveness of the proposed AIT3D-DSR, we conducted comprehensive evaluations across 11 victim models spanning both CNN and ViT architectures, including ResNet-50 (RN-50), ResNet-101 (RN-101), ResNet-152 (RN-152), VGG-16, VGG-19, Inception-v3 (Inc-v3), DenseNet-121 (DN-121), EfficientNet-B0 (EN-B0), MobileNet-v2 (MN-v2), Swin-B, and ViT-B/16. As shown in Table 1, we compare against two state-of-the-art 3D adversarial attack baselines: MeshAdv [28] (enhanced through vertex-color joint optimization) and TT3D [7] (leveraging dual-space NeRF optimization). The baseline method relies on a single proxy model (e.g., RN-101), whereas our AIT3D-DSR substantially enhances transferability by dynamically integrating gradients from multiple models (e.g., RN-18, WRN-101-2, ViT-T and DeiT-T), thereby highlighting the core advantage of its integration strategy. The rightmost column quantifies the average attack success rates across all victim models, thereby providing a comprehensive measure of cross-model transferability. The results highlight the comprehensive superiority of AIT3D-DSR across three critical dimensions. First, in terms of cross-model transferability, AIT3D-DSR achieves an average attack success rate of 86.80% across 11 victim models, surpassing TT3D with ResNet-101 (59.59%) and DenseNet-121 (46.20%) proxies by 27.21% and 40.60% absolute improvements respectively. Particularly noteworthy is its exceptional performance against complex vision architectures, attaining 90.85% on Swin-B and 91.15% on EfficientNet-B0, which validates the effectiveness of our dynamic multi-model gradient integration mechanism in capturing cross-architectural decision boundaries through ResNet-18, WideResNet-101-2, ViT-Tiny, and DeiT-Tiny ensemble learning. Second, regarding robustness to model discrepancy, AIT3D-DSR maintains stable attack effectiveness where TT3D suffers significant performance degradation - when switching surrogate models from ResNet-101 to DenseNet-121, TT3D's average attack success rate drops by 13.39%, while our method sustains 85.24% against ViT-B/16, outperforming both TT3D configurations by 39.79% and 56.17%. This stability originates from the temperature-controlled softmax weighting that adaptively balances gradient contributions across surrogate models. Finally, in practical attack scenarios, AIT3D-DSR overcomes the fundamental limitations of traditional mesh-based methods: where MeshAdv collapses to $10.53\% - 11.68\%$ average attack success rate due to overfitted vertex-color perturbations, our framework achieves photo-realistic adversarial textures through implicit 3D rendering enhanced by physics-aware noise injection and block-wise LPIPS constraints.

4.3   Visual Naturalness Performance

Table 2. Quantitative analysis of visual naturalness metrics for 3D adversarial examples generated by different methods.

Attack	SSIM↑	PSNR↑	LPIPS↓
Initial	0.9742	34.22	0.0345
Mesh-based	0.7931	9.19	0.2098
TT3D	0.8540	22.48	0.1382
AIT3D-DSR	**0.9002**	**30.59**	**0.0819**

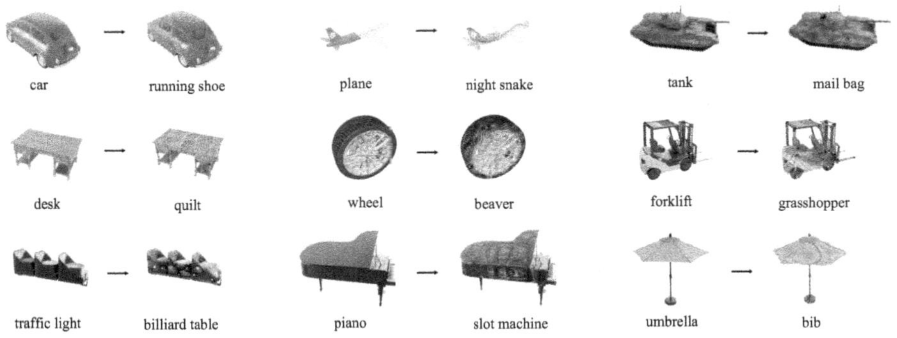

Fig. 2. Multi-view visual comparison between original objects and AIT3D-DSR adversarial reconstructions.

To comprehensively assess the visual naturalness of 3D adversarial examples generated by AIT3D-DSR, we employ three established image quality metrics: Structural Similarity Index (SSIM) [27], Peak Signal-to-Noise Ratio (PSNR) [8], and Learned Perceptual Image Patch Similarity (LPIPS) [31]. SSIM quantifies structural and luminance consistency between original and adversarial-rendered images, with values approaching 1 indicating higher fidelity. PSNR measures pixel-level accuracy in decibels (dB), where higher values denote reduced distortion. LPIPS evaluates perceptual similarity at the patch level using deep features from a pre-trained VGG network, with lower scores reflecting better imperceptibility to human observers.

As shown in Table 2, AIT3D-DSR significantly outperforms both traditional mesh-based methods and the state-of-the-art TT3D across all metrics. Compared to the initial clean reconstructions (SSIM: 0.9742, PSNR: 34.22 dB, LPIPS: 0.0345), our method achieves near-original fidelity with a SSIM value of 0.9002, a PSNR value of 30.59 dB, and a LPIPS score of 0.0819. This performance surpasses mesh-based attacks (SSIM: 0.7931, PSNR: 9.19 dB, LPIPS: 0.2098) and TT3D (SSIM: 0.8540, PSNR: 22.48 dB, LPIPS: 0.1382), demonstrating its ability to balance adversarial effectiveness with visual plausibility. The superior SSIM and PSNR values stem from our noise-aware rendering pipeline, which injects controlled Gaussian noise and motion blur to simulate physical sensor imperfections while minimizing pixel-level distortions. The low LPIPS score further validates the effectiveness of block-wise perceptual constraints, which restrict adversarial perturbations to semantically meaningful regions, avoiding high-frequency artifacts that degrade human perceptual quality.

Figure 2 offers compelling visual evidence of the naturalness preservation achieved by AIT3D-DSR. The adversarially rendered objects under random viewpoints display negligible deviations from their original counterparts in terms of geometry, texture, and lighting, thereby demonstrating that our method effectively confines perturbations to imperceptible regions. This strong visual alignment with the original objects is further substantiated by the quantitative metrics in Table 2, where AIT3D-DSR not only approaches the quality of clean reconstructions but also significantly surpasses baseline methods.

In summary, by incorporating physics-based noise simulation, localized perceptual regularization, and gradient-aware optimization, AIT3D-DSR attains unparalleled adversarial naturalness while preserving attack transferability.

4.4 Ablation Studies

Table 3. Ablation study of AIT3D-DSR components on attack success rates (%) and naturalness metrics.

Variant	ASR	SSIM↑	PSNR↑	LPIPS↓
Full Model	**86.80**	**0.9002**	**30.59**	**0.0819**
w/o View Perturbation	63.21	0.8874	29.83	0.0952
w/o Block-wise Perturbation	72.45	0.7623	19.17	0.2017
w/o Noise Injection	78.34	0.8941	30.12	0.0885
w/o Gradient Integration	68.92	0.8987	30.35	0.0833
w/o LPIPS Constraint	84.15	0.8125	24.76	0.1538

To validate the contributions of core components in AIT3D-DSR, we conduct ablation studies by systematically removing or modifying individual modules and evaluating their impact on attack success rates and visual naturalness metrics (SSIM, PSNR, LPIPS). The baseline configurations include the full model and five variants: disabling randomized camera perturbations (w/o View Perturbation), replacing block-wise perturbations with global mesh adjustments (w/o Block-wise Perturbation), removing sensor noise and motion blur (w/o Noise Injection), using a single surrogate model (w/o Gradient Integration), and omitting the block-wise LPIPS constraint (w/o LPIPS Constraint).

As shown in Table 3, the full model achieves the highest attack success rate (86.80%) and optimal naturalness metrics (SSIM: 0.9002, PSNR: 30.59 dB, LPIPS: 0.0819). Disabling randomized camera perturbations (w/o View Perturbation) significantly reduces attack success rate by 23.59% (63.21% vs. 86.80%), demonstrating that viewpoint invariance is critical for multi-view robustness. However, naturalness metrics remain relatively stable (SSIM: 0.8874, LPIPS: 0.0952), as view perturbation primarily optimizes adversarial features rather than pixel-level fidelity. Removing block-wise localization (w/o Block-wise Perturbation) leads to severe degradation in both attack success rate (72.45%) and naturalness (LPIPS: 0.2017), highlighting the necessity of localized perturbations to align adversarial patterns with semantic regions while preserving structural coherence.

The absence of physics-aware noise injection (w/o Noise Injection) slightly reduces attack success rate (78.34% vs. 86.80%) but maintains high PSNR (30.12 dB), indicating that sensor noise and motion blur primarily enhance robustness to real-world distortions rather than digital attack efficacy. Similarly, using a single surrogate model (w/o Gradient Integration) lowers attack success rate by 17.88% (68.92% vs. 86.80%), confirming that adaptive multi-model gradient integration is essential for cross-architecture transferability. While naturalness metrics (SSIM: 0.8987, LPIPS: 0.0833) remain close to the full model, this variant struggles to generalize across diverse victim models.

Finally, removing the LPIPS constraint (w/o LPIPS Constraint) marginally improves attack success rate (84.15% vs. 86.80%) but severely degrades visual naturalness (LPIPS: 0.1538 vs. 0.0819). This trade-off underscores the importance of perceptual regularization in suppressing high-frequency artifacts, ensuring adversarial examples remain imperceptible under human scrutiny. The full model achieves a balanced optimization by synergizing physics-aware rendering, localized semantic perturbations, and multi-model gradient integration, thereby addressing the limitations of prior methods in real-world scenarios.

5   Conclusion

This paper presents AIT3D-DSR, a novel framework addressing the challenges of transferability and visual naturalness in 3D adversarial attacks. By integrating dynamic multi-model gradient integration, block-level geometry-texture perturbations, and physics-aware differentiable rendering, our method balances gradients across architectures, enforces robustness across viewpoints, and bridges the gap between 3D and 2D optimization. Experiments show its effectiveness:

AIT3D-DSR achieves an average attack success rate of 86.80% across 11 models, outperforming state-of-the-art methods by 27.21%, while maintaining high adversarial naturalness (SSIM: 0.9002, PSNR: 30.59 dB, LPIPS: 0.0819). Ablation studies confirm the importance of viewpoint perturbation and block-wise optimization. AIT3D-DSR provides a unified approach for generating natural and transferable 3D adversarial examples, offering insights into securing 3D perception systems.

Acknowledgments. This work was supported in part by the Inner Mongolia Key R&D and Achievement Transformation Project (No. 2025YFDZ0029), the Natural Science Foundation of China (No. 62462047).

References

1. Athalye, A., Engstrom, L., Ilyas, A., Kwok, K.: Synthesizing robust adversarial examples. In: Proceedings of the International Conference on Machine Learning, pp. 284–293 (2018)
2. Byun, J., Cho, S., Kwon, M.J., Kim, H.S., Kim, C.: Improving the transferability of targeted adversarial examples through object-based diverse input. In: Proceedings of the IEEE/CVF Conference on Computer Vision and Pattern Recognition, pp. 15244–15253 (2022)
3. Dosovitskiy, A., et al.: An image is worth 16x16 words: transformers for image recognition at scale. arXiv preprint arXiv:2010.11929 (2020)
4. Gao, L., Cheng, Y., Zhang, Q., Xu, X., Song, J.: Feature space targeted attacks by statistic alignment. arXiv preprint arXiv:2105.11645 (2021)
5. He, K., Zhang, X., Ren, S., Sun, J.: Deep residual learning for image recognition. In: Proceedings of the IEEE/CVF Conference on Computer Vision and Pattern Recognition, pp. 770–778 (2016)
6. Huang, G., Liu, Z., Van Der Maaten, L., Weinberger, K.Q.: Densely connected convolutional networks. In: Proceedings of the IEEE/CVF Conference on Computer Vision and Pattern Recognition, pp. 4700–4708 (2017)
7. Huang, Y., Dong, Y., Ruan, S., Yang, X., Su, H., Wei, X.: Towards transferable targeted 3D adversarial attack in the physical world. In: Proceedings of the IEEE/CVF Conference on Computer Vision and Pattern Recognition, pp. 24512–24522 (2024)
8. Huynh-Thu, Q., Ghanbari, M.: The scope of expansion of subjective fidelity ratings. J. Electron. Imaging (1993)
9. Inkawhich, N., Liang, K.J., Carin, L., Chen, Y.: Transferable perturbations of deep feature distributions. arXiv preprint arXiv:2004.12519 (2020)
10. Kurakin, A., Goodfellow, I.J., Bengio, S.: Adversarial examples in the physical world. In: Proceedings of the International Conference on Learning Representations (2017)
11. Li, M., Deng, C., Li, T., Yan, J., Gao, X., Huang, H.: Towards transferable targeted attack. In: Proceedings of the IEEE/CVF Conference on Computer Vision and Pattern Recognition, pp. 641–649 (2020)
12. Liu, Z., et al.: Swin transformer: hierarchical vision transformer using shifted windows. In: Proceedings of the IEEE/CVF Conference on Computer Vision and Pattern Recognition, pp. 10012–10022 (2021)

13. Lorensen, W.E., Cline, H.E.: Marching cubes: a high resolution 3D surface construction algorithm. In: Seminal Graphics: Pioneering Efforts that Shaped the Field, pp. 347–353 (1998)
14. Müller, T., Evans, A., Schied, C., Keller, A.: Instant neural graphics primitives with a multiresolution hash encoding. ACM Trans. Graph. (TOG) (2022)
15. Naseer, M., Khan, S., Hayat, M., Khan, F.S., Porikli, F.: On generating transferable targeted perturbations. In: Proceedings of the IEEE/CVF International Conference on Computer Vision, pp. 7708–7717 (2021)
16. Oslund, S., Washington, C., So, A., Chen, T., Ji, H.: Multiview robust adversarial stickers for arbitrary objects in the physical world. J. Comput. Cogn. Eng. (2022)
17. Ruan, S., Dong, Y., Su, H., Peng, J., Chen, N., Wei, X.: Towards viewpoint-invariant visual recognition via adversarial training. In: Proceedings of the IEEE/CVF International Conference on Computer Vision, pp. 4709–4719 (2023)
18. Sandler, M., Howard, A., Zhu, M., Zhmoginov, A., Chen, L.C.: MobileNetV2: inverted residuals and linear bottlenecks. In: Proceedings of the IEEE/CVF Conference on Computer Vision and Pattern Recognition, pp. 4510–4520 (2018)
19. Simonyan, K., Zisserman, A.: Very deep convolutional networks for large-scale image recognition. arXiv preprint arXiv:1409.1556 (2014)
20. Suryanto, N., et al.: DTA: physical camouflage attacks using differentiable transformation network. In: Proceedings of the IEEE/CVF Conference on Computer Vision and Pattern Recognition, pp. 15305–15314 (2022)
21. Suryanto, N., et al.: ACTIVE: towards highly transferable 3d physical camouflage for universal and robust vehicle evasion. In: Proceedings of the IEEE/CVF Conference on Computer Vision and Pattern Recognition, pp. 4305–4314 (2023)
22. Szegedy, C., et al.: Going deeper with convolutions. In: Proceedings of the IEEE/CVF Conference on Computer Vision and Pattern Recognition, pp. 1–9 (2015)
23. Tan, M., Le, Q.: EfficientNet: rethinking model scaling for convolutional neural networks. In: Proceedings of the International Conference on Machine Learning, pp. 6105–6114 (2019)
24. Touvron, H., Cord, M., Douze, M., Massa, F., Sablayrolles, A., Jégou, H.: Training data-efficient image transformers & distillation through attention. In: Proceedings of the International Conference on Machine Learning, pp. 10347–10357 (2021)
25. Wang, D., et al.: FCA: learning a 3D full-coverage vehicle camouflage for multi-view physical adversarial attack. In: Proceedings of the AAAI Conference on Artificial Intelligence, pp. 2414–2422 (2022)
26. Wang, Z., et al.: Towards transferable targeted adversarial examples. In: Proceedings of the IEEE/CVF Conference on Computer Vision and Pattern Recognition, pp. 20534–20543 (2023)
27. Wang, Z., Bovik, A.C., Sheikh, H.R., Simoncelli, E.P.: Image quality assessment: from error visibility to structural similarity. IEEE Trans. Image Process. (2004)
28. Xiao, C., Yang, D., Li, B., Deng, J., Liu, M.: MeshAdv: adversarial meshes for visual recognition. In: Proceedings of the IEEE/CVF Conference on Computer Vision and Pattern Recognition, pp. 6898–6907 (2019)
29. Yang, X., Dong, Y., Pang, T., Su, H., Zhu, J.: Boosting transferability of targeted adversarial examples via hierarchical generative networks. In: Proceedings of the European Conference on Computer Vision, pp. 725–742 (2022)
30. Zagoruyko, S., Komodakis, N.: Wide residual networks. arXiv preprint arXiv:1605.07146 (2016)

31. Zhang, R., Isola, P., Efros, A.A., Shechtman, E., Wang, O.: The unreasonable effectiveness of deep features as a perceptual metric. In: Proceedings of the IEEE/CVF Conference on Computer Vision and Pattern Recognition, pp. 586–595 (2018)
32. Zhao, Z., Liu, Z., Larson, M.: On success and simplicity: a second look at transferable targeted attacks. In: Advances in Neural Information Processing Systems (2021)

Cross-Modal Fundus Image Registration Under Large FoV Disparity

Hongyang Li[1], Junyi Tao[1], Qijie Wei[1], Ningzhi Yang[1], Meng Wang[2],
Weihong Yu[2], and Xirong Li[1]([✉])

[1] Renmin University of China, Beijing, China
`xirong@ruc.edu.cn`
[2] Peking Union Medical College Hospital, Beijing, China
`https://github.com/ruc-aimc-lab/care`

Abstract. Previous work on cross-modal fundus image registration (CMFIR) assumes small cross-modal Field-of-View (FoV) disparity. By contrast, this paper is targeted at a more challenging scenario with large FoV disparity, to which directly applying current methods fails. We propose <u>C</u>rop and <u>A</u>lignment for cross-modal fundus image <u>Re</u>gistration (**CARe**), a very simple yet effective method. Specifically, given an OCTA with smaller FoV as a source image and a wide-field color fundus photograph (wfCFP) as a target image, our *Crop* operation exploits the physiological structure of the retina to crop from the target image a sub-image with its FoV roughly aligned with that of the source. This operation allows us to re-purpose the previous *small-FoV-disparity* oriented methods for subsequent image registration. Moreover, we improve spatial transformation by a double-fitting based *Alignment* module that utilizes the classical RANSAC algorithm and polynomial-based coordinate fitting in a sequential manner. Extensive experiments on a newly developed test set of 60 OCTA-wfCFP pairs verify the viability of **CARe** for CMFIR.

Keywords: CMFIR · Large FoV disparity · Double fitting

1 Introduction

This paper aims for *cross-modal* fundus image registration (CMFIR) under large Field-of-View (FoV) disparity, an emerging challenge arising with the development of fundus imaging techniques. More and more retinal lesions can nowadays be visualized in a *noninvasive* manner. Consider for instance non-perfusion area (NPA), a crucial feature of microvascular injury. Previously, NPA had to be identified through invasive fluorescein angiography (FA), see Fig. 1a. It can now be identified via noninvasive OCT angiography (OCTA) [3]. Registering an OCTA image to a wide-field color fundus photograph (wfCFP) of the same eye produces a composite image with enhanced clinical value, see Fig. 1b.

J. Lokoč et al. (Eds.): MMM 2026, LNCS 16412, pp. 321–334, 2026.
https://doi.org/10.1007/978-981-95-6950-2_23

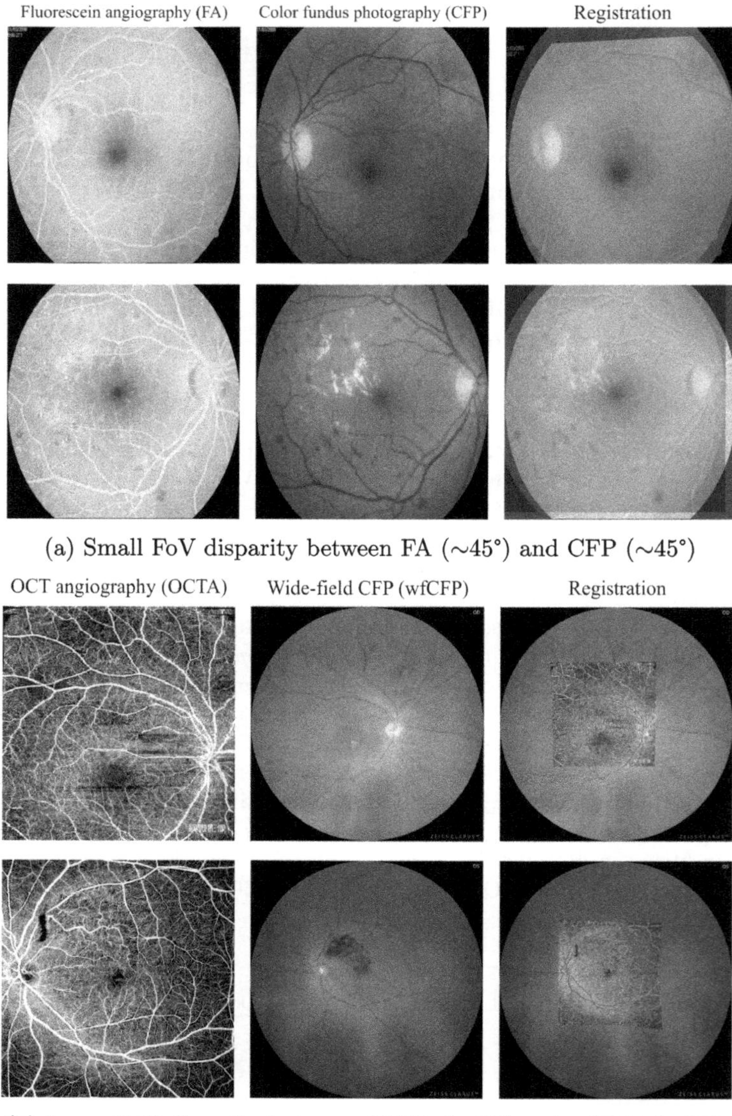

(a) Small FoV disparity between FA (∼45°) and CFP (∼45°)

(b) Large FoV disparity between OCTA (∼40°) and wfCFP (∼90°)

Fig. 1. Cross-modal fundus image registration (CM-FIR) under (a) small and (b) large FoV disparity. While existing works focus on the former, this paper tackles the latter.

(Cross-modal) Fundus image registration has been actively studied [2,9,17–19,22,23], with feature (or keypoint) based methods as the mainstream solution. In order to register a specific source image *w.r.t.* a given target image, a feature-based method typically performs feature or keypoint detection, followed by feature matching to find a correspondence between a set of keypoints. Based on the correspondence, a specific spatial transforming function, with homograpy as a common choice, is then fitted. Much progress has been made, with generic feature detectors [4,11] replaced by fundus-specific alternatives such as Super-Retina [9] and SuperJunction [18], the brute-force matcher replaced by learnable alternatives like SuperGlue [15], *etc.* Existing methods typically assume small FoV disparity between the source and target images, see Fig. 1a. Under large cross-modal FoV disparity, as in the case of OCTA-to-wfCFP, both the feature matching and coordinate fitting processes become erroneous. As exempifiled in Fig. 2, simply re-purposing the SOTA methods [9,17,18] for the new task fails.

Fig. 2. Visualization of registering a specific OCTA image to a wfCFP image of the same eye. Vessels in red are from the OCTA, while vessels in green are from the wfCFP. The cross-modal aligned vessels are highlighted in yellow. More yellows mean better alignments. Simply re-training current *small-FoV-disparity* oriented methods (SuperRetina [9], KPVSA-Net [17] and SuperJunction [18]) does not work. Best viewed digitally (Color figure online).

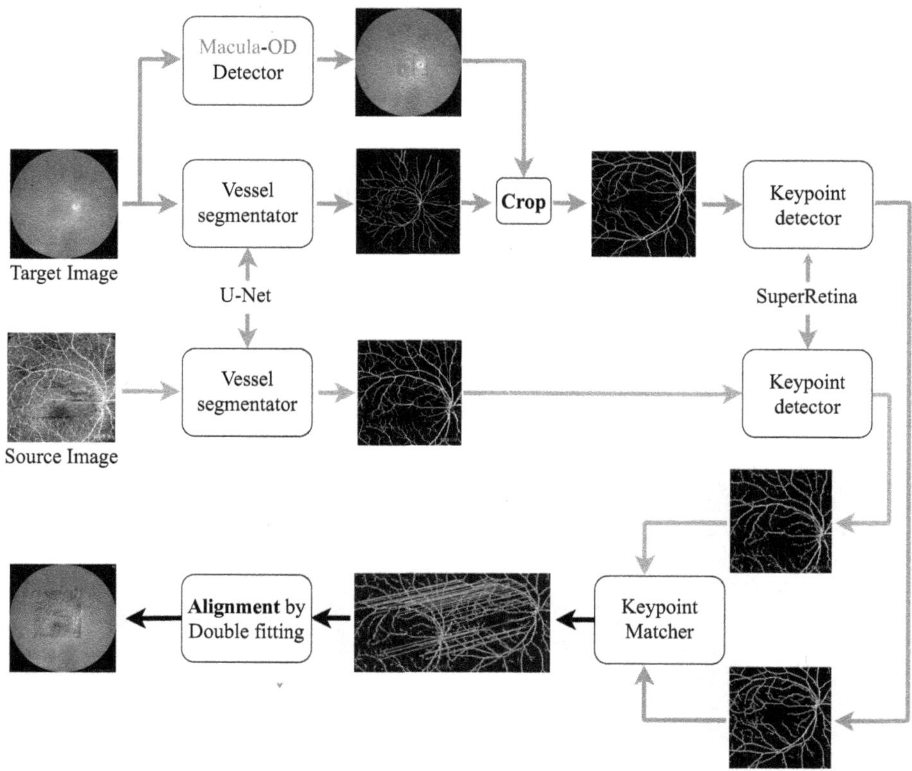

Fig. 3. Conceptual diagram of the proposed CARe method. In order to tackle CM-FIR under large FoV disparity, our method contains *task-specific* designs as follows: i) U-Net based *unified* vessel segmentation that converts cross-modal fundus images (OCTA and wfCFP) to a unified vessel map representation, ii) *Crop* for coarse FoV alignment achieved by cropping a sub-image from the target image based on jointly detected macula and optic disc (OD), iii) an improved training procedure of SuperRetina for better keypoint matching, and iv) *Align* for source-to-target coordinate transformation by *double fitting*, involving a novel cascaded use of RANSAC and polynomial-based coordinate fitting.

To attack the new challenge, we propose <u>C</u>rop and <u>A</u>lignment for cross-modal fundus image <u>Re</u>gistration (**CARe**), see Fig. 3. Our idea is very simple. Noting the large FoV disparity as the main obstacle, we propose a **Crop** operation to achieve a rough cross-modal FoV alignment at the first place. Despite its simplicity, such an operation allows us to re-purpose the previous *small-FoV-disparity* oriented methods for subsequent fundus image registration. Furthermore, we improve coordinate transformation by a double-fitting that makes a cascaded use of the classical RANSAC algorithm and polynomial-based coordinate fitting. To sum up, our major contributions are as follows.

- To the best of our knowledge, we are the first to tackle CMFIR under large FoV disparity. To that end, we build **OCTA60**, a test set of 60 OCT-wfCFP pairs, collected from Outpatient Clinic with images showing varied fundus conditions of real-world patients.
- We propose **CARe**, a simple yet effective method that uses a `Crop` operation, which exploits the physiological structure of wfCFP, to simplify the registration process and an `Alignment` module to improve the registration accuracy. Moreover, we improve the training procedure of SuperRetina for better keypoint matching in the cross-modal scenario.
- Extensive experiments on the **OCTA60** test set verify the superiority of the proposed method over multiple strong baselines [9,17,18] re-purposed for the new task.

2   Related Work

2.1   Methods for CMFIR

Current methods for CMFIR are feature-based, extracting discriminative features either from fundus images [17,22] or from their vascular maps [19,23], followed by feature matching to establish spatial correspondences between given image pairs. As vascular maps naturally provide a unified representation of cross-modal fundus images, we follow [19,23], extracting features from the vascular maps. However, different from [19,23] which uses SuperPoint [4], a generic feature detector and descriptor, we adopt SuperRetina [9] that is specifically developed for fundus image matching. Moreover, we go one step further by addressing CMFIR under large FoV disparity, a new and more challenging task not considered by the previous works.

2.2   Datasets for CMFIR

To the best of our knowledge, FA-CFP [6] is the only public dataset[1], including 59 pairs of CFP and FA images with small cross-modal FoV disparity, see Fig. 1a. As the dataset has no annotation *w.r.t.* keypoint correspondence, the registration accuracy of a specific method is indirectly measured by the Dice similarity between the vessel maps of a target image and a registered source image. Our proposed **OCTA60** test set is targeted at the more challenging setting of large cross-modal FoV disparity. Moreover, we provide manually annotated keypoint correspondences per pair for a more comprehensive evaluation.

3   Proposed CARe Method

Given a pair of cross-modal fundus images captured from the same eye, the goal of CMFIR is to spatially transform the fundus image of smaller FoV, *a.k.a.*

---

[1] https://misp.mui.ac.ir/en/node/1498.

the source image, to align with the other image of larger FoV, *a.k.a.* the target image. More formally, we aim to build a source-to-target coordinate transforming function F that for each pixel positioned by (u, v) in the source image, its counterpart (x, y) in the target image can be well approximated by $F(u, v)$. Our method is feature-based, with F developed based on a correspondence between a set of m keypoints $P = \{((u_i, v_i), (x_i, y_i))\}_{i=1}^{m}$ obtained by keypoint detection and matching. For keypoint detection and description in a cross-modal manner, we adopt a unified vessel segmentor to convert the cross-modal images to vascular maps. To handle the large cross-modal FoV disparity, we propose a simple yet effective Crop operation, exploiting the physiological structure of the retina to crop from the target image a region roughly aligned with the source image. Feature matching is then performed on the vessel maps of the source image and the cropped target image. Lastly, for accurate source-to-target coordinate transformation, a double-fitting based Alignment module is developed.

3.1   Unified Vessel Segmentation

In order to convert the fundus images of distinct modalities to a unified vessel map representation, we train a U-Net [14] based vessel segmentation network. Following [20], our training data is a joint set of public datasets of varied modalities including FIVES for CFP [7], ROSSA for OCTA [12], IOSTAR for scanning laser ophthalmoscopy [1], PRIME-FP20 for ultra-wide-field fundus imaging [5] and VAMPIRE for FA [13]. We empirically find that such a simple solution is sufficient to extract good-quality vessel maps, see Fig. 4, for keypoint detection and description. An important merit of using the unified vessel segmentor is that our method will be directly applicable to varied modality combinations such as OCTA-CFP and FA-CFP, with no need of combination-specific re-training.

3.2   Crop for Coarse FoV Alignment

As shown in Fig. 1b, the source image in this study was obtained by OCTA, which visualizes detailed microvasculature in the macula. Hence, for a coarse FoV alignment between the source and target images, we propose to crop the macular area of the target image. As the macula and the optic disc (OD) are spatially correlated, previous work suggests that jointly detecting the two regions of interest (ROIs) is more accurate and reliable than detecting them alone [21]. In that regard, we train RetinaNet [8], a widely used one-stage object detection network, on 117 labeled examples. Evaluation on a hold-out test set of 25 images shows that RetinaNet detects both ROIs with mean IoU of around 0.75, sufficiently accurate for our purpose. Based on the auto-located macula and OD, we crop an area roughly corresponding to the posterior pole of the retina. As shown in Fig. 3, the cropped region is a square centered on the macula, with its side length dynamically determined as twice the distance from the macular center to the outer edge of the detected optic-disc region. As shown in Fig. 4, compared to the original target images, the FoVs of the cropped sub-images are much more close to those of the source images.

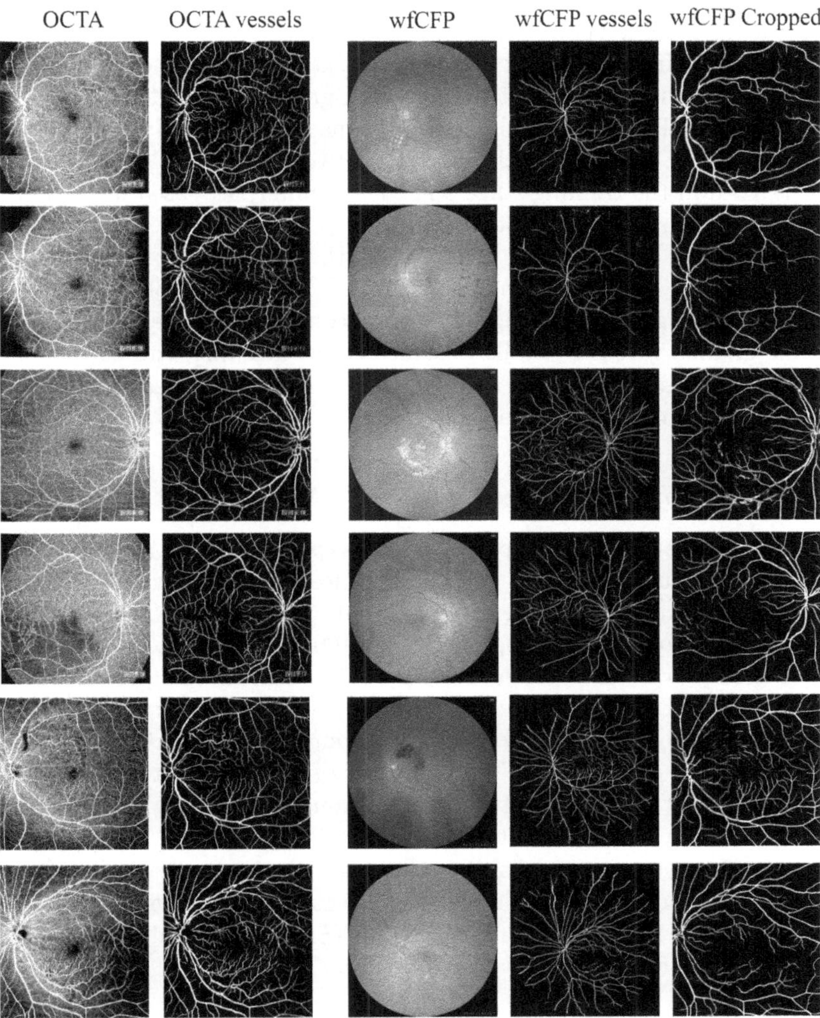

Fig. 4. Vessel segmentation and cropping results. Best viewed digitally.

3.3   Improved SuperRetina for Keypoint Detection and Matching

We adopt SuperRetina [9], an end-to-end network that detects keypoints, *i.e.,* crossovers and bifurcations on the vascular tree, and generates their descriptors simultaneously from a given fundus image. Note that SuperRetina, originally developed for uni-modal image registration, takes CFP images as its input. So for input adaptation, we re-train the network on a set of 44 wfCFP vessel maps with manually labeled keypoints. While in theory we shall collect paired images with known spatial correspondence for training, such paired samples are practically generated by applying controlled homography per training image [4]. As such, SuperRetina can be trained in a semi-supervised manner. Given keypoints detected from the vessel maps of the source image and the cropped target image, respectively, we use the classical OpenCV Brute-Force matcher (BFMatcher) to obtain the matched keypoint set P.

It is worth pointing out that due to their distinct imaging techniques, OCTA images reveal richer capillary structures with greater details than their wfCFP counterparts, see Fig. 4. Recall that SuperRetina is trained exclusively on wfCFP. Such a divergence introduces a domain gap between keypoint descriptors (or features) learned in the training stage and their counterparts used in the inference stage, and thus makes P suboptimal.

To bridge the domain gap, we simulate the cross-modal vessel divergence by performing a classical **opening** operation (an erosion followed by a dilation) on one image per training pair. As a consequence, the processed image loses fine-grained vascular details to some extent. Training with such asymmetrically manipulated image pairs allows SuperRetina to better align local features between OCTA and wfCFP images.

3.4 Fine-Grained Alignment by Double Fitting

For coordinate transformation, previous work typically makes the planar assumption about the fundus images [9,19,23], hence fitting F by RANSAC-based homography estimation. However, this assumption becomes questionable for large FoV and high-resolution images, *e.g.*, 1000×1000 in this work. RANSAC is reliable yet less accurate. The retinal images are two-dimensional projections of the three-dimensional eyeball, making them subject to nonlinear transformations. In contrast, the homography transformation computed by RANSAC is a linear transformation, which can therefore lead to a loss of accuracy. Alternatively, recent work [18] employs polynomial fitting [16]. Although accurate, we empirically find that such a fitting strategy is rather sensitive to outliers.

In order to leverage the reliability of RANSAC and the accuracy of polynomial fitting, we propose a very simple yet effective double-fitting strategy. The strategy, dubbed **RAN-Poly**, first uses RANSAC to remove outliers from P, and then fits the following n-degree polynomial functions:

$$\begin{cases} x = \sum\limits_{i+j \leq n} a_{ij} u^i v^j \\ y = \sum\limits_{i+j \leq n} b_{ij} u^i v^j, \end{cases} \tag{1}$$

where $a_{i,j}$ and $b_{i,j}$ are polynomial coefficients optimized by the least square method. A larger n means a stronger fitting capability, yet with an increased risk of over-fitting. In the context of uni-modal fundus image registration, Wang *et al.* [18] empirically show that a quadratic polynomial works the best. We follow their recommendation, using $n = 2$ in this work. The validity of this choice is also confirmed by our ablation study. The RAN-Poly double fitting strategy allows us to largely relax the planar assumption, and thus obtain more accurate coordinate transformation.

RAN-Poly is conceptually connected to the bias-variance tradeoff. Polynomial fitting, as its polynomial degree increases, becomes more flexible to fit a training dataset with lower bias, yet there will be greater variance in the model's estimated parameters. By contrast, RANSAC-based homography estimation, with its planar assumption and the fixed number of trainable parameters, has smaller variance yet greater bias. By combining RANSAC and polynomial fitting, RAN-Poly achieves a good bias-variance tradeoff.

4   Experiments

4.1   Experimental Setup

Test Data. We collect 60 pairs of OCTA and wfCFP images from 60 distinct patients at the outpatient clinic of the Department of Ophthalmology in a state hospital between Feb. 2023 and Dec. 2023. In particular, OCTA projections of the superficial vascular plexus (SVP) layer were acquired by a $12\,mm \times 12\,mm$ scan centered on the macula using a SVision VG200 OCT, while wfCFPs were acquired using a ZEISS CLARUS 500 fundus camera. Each image pair has at least 10 manually labeled keypoint correspondences as ground truth. All images are resized to 1000×1000 in advance. They shows varied fundus conditions of real-world patients, challenging the robustness of the proposed method. This study is complied with the Declaration of Helsinki. We term the test set **OCTA60**.

Performance Metrics. Following [9], we report the failed/inaccurate/ acceptable rate. A registration is considered acceptable if the median Euclidean error (MEE) and the maximum Euclidean error (MAE) between the mapped keypoints and the ground truth are less than 20 and 50 pixels, respectively. We also report AUC with the MEE threshold ranging from 1 to 25. For a more in-depth analysis, we report the average number of keypoint matches per OCTA-wfCFP pair. A match is considered *acceptable* if the matched keypoint is within 20 pixels to the corresponding reference point. In addition, we report soft Dice Coefficient $Dice_s$ [22], reflecting the overlap between the vessel maps of the target image and the registered source image.

Implementation. Training details of the networks used for vessel segmentation, macula/OD detection and keypoint detection are listed in Table 1. All experiments were conducted on an NVIDIA 2080ti GPU with the following software environment: Ubuntu 18.04, CUDA 11.7 and PyTorch 1.21.

Baselines. We compare with the following SOTA feature-based methods, *i.e.*, SuperRetina [9], KPVSA-Net [17] and SuperJunction [18]. See Table 2 for their choices of keypoint matcher and transformation fitting. For a fair comparison we re-train their modules on our training data whenever applicable. In particular, the same vessel segmentor and keypoint detector are used. Comparison with detector-free methods [10] is reserved for future work.

4.2   Comparison with Baseline Methods

Results on OCTA60. As shown in Table 2 and Fig. 2, all the baselines fail to generate acceptable registration results, showing their ineffectiveness in handling

Table 1. Training details of the three deep networks used in the proposed method: U-Net for vessel segmentation, Retina-Net for macula/OD detection and SuperRetina for feature detection and description.

Network	Optimizer	Epochs	Learning rate	Batch size
U-Net	SGD	100	1e-3	5
RetinaNet	Adam	150	1e-5	1
SuperRetina	Adam	150	1e-3	4

the large inter-modal FoV disparity. Note that SuperGlue tends to yield more matches, albeit incorrect, than BFMatcher. Therefore, the failed rate of [17,18], which use SuperGlue, is much lower than that of [9] which uses BFMatcher. Our method clearly outperforms the baselines in terms of all performance metrics.

Table 2. Results on **OCTA60**. DLT: Direct linear transformation. Poly: Polynomial fitting. RAN: RANSAC.

Method	Matcher	Fitting	Failed[%]↓	Inaccurate[%]↓	Acceptable[%]↑	AUC↑	$Dice_s$↑
SuperRetina [9]	BFMatcher	RANSAC	78.33	20.00	1.67	0.016	0.082
KPVSA-Net [17]	SuperGlue	DLT	8.33	91.67	0	0	0.077
SuperJunction [18]	SuperGlue	Poly	23.33	76.67	0	0	0.076
CARe	BFMatcher	RAN-Poly	**0.00**	**1.67**	**98.33**	**0.920**	**0.295**
w/o Crop		RAN-Poly	55.00	43.33	1.67	0.019	0.051
w/o Opening		RAN-Poly	3.33	3.33	93.33	0.896	0.282
w/o RANSAC		Poly	0.00	31.67	68.33	0.596	0.219
w/o Poly		RANSAC	0.00	3.33	96.67	0.912	0.289

For a better understanding, for each method, we report in Table 3 the average number of keypoint matches per OCTA-wfCFP pair. A match is considered *acceptable* if the matched keypoint is within 20 pixels to the corresponding reference point. Facing large cross-modal FoV disparity, the existing methods have much fewer matches with much lower acceptable match rate. Hence, the fact that existing methods struggle with large FoV disparity can be largely attributed to their incapability to find sufficient and acceptable keypoint matches for the subsequent transformation fitting.

Results on FA-CFP. To check how our Alignment module[2] works in the traditional setting (of small cross-modal FoV disparity), we evaluate the module on the public FA-CFP dataset [6]. We report $Dice_s$ only, as the FA-CFP dataset has no keypoint correspondence, which makes it unfeasible to calculate metrics other than $Dice_s$. As Table 4 shows, the Alignment module alone again surpasses the baseline methods even when the cross-modal FoV disparity is relatively small.

---

[2] Here we omit the Crop operation, which makes no practical difference for CFP with relatively small FoV as in the FA-CFP dataset.

Table 3. Averaged number of keypoint matches per OCTA-wfCFP pair.

Method	#Matches ↑	Acceptable-match rate ↑
SuperRetina [9]	20.8	0.152
KPVSA-Net [17]	35.3	0.008
SuperJunction [18]	35.3	0.008
CARe	**149.46**	**0.978**

Table 4. Results on the FA-CFP testset.

Method	$Dice_s$
SuperRetina [9]	0.530
KPVSA-Net [17]	0.319
SuperJunction [18]	0.243
CARe	**0.556**

4.3 Ablation Study

The importance of Crop. As Table 2 shows, using the Crop operation or not has a decisive impact on the performance.

Whether Crop helps the baselines? The answer is yes, see Table 5, with the largest improvement made for [9]. Still, our method is better than the much improved baseline, showing the superiority of RAN-Poly to RANSAC.

Table 5. Performance of the baseline methods with $(+)$ and without $(-)$ our Crop operation. Test set: **OCTA60**.

Method	Crop?	Acceptable[%]↑	AUC↑	$Dice_s$↑
SuperRetina [9]	−	0	0	0.081
	+	**91.67**	**0.861**	**0.269**
KPVSA-Net [17]	−	0	0	0.078
	+	**60.00**	**0.587**	**0.140**
SuperJunction [18]	−	0	0	0.079
	+	**36.67**	**0.248**	**0.116**

Impact of the opening Operation. Without the opening operation, AUC drops from 0.9833 to 0.9333 (Table 2). Hence, adding the operation improves SuperRetina-based keypoint matching.

The Necessity of RAN-Poly. Replacing RAN-Poly either by polynomial fitting or by RANSAC causes performance degeneration, see the last two rows in Table 2. The necessity of our proposed RAN-Poly strategy is thus justified.

Choice of the Polynomial Degree. Figure 5 shows the performance curve of the proposed method with different degrees of polynomial functions. The second-degree polynomial strikes the best balance between improving the fitting accuracy and reducing the risk of over-fitting.

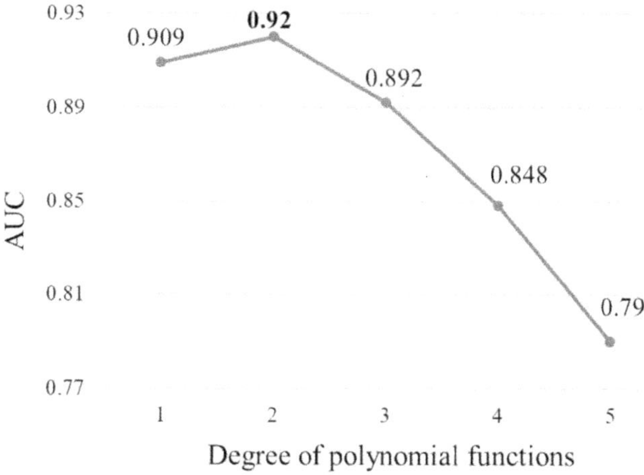

Fig. 5. Performance of CARe with different degrees of polynomial functions used for polynomial fitting. The quadratic polynomial is the best.

5   Conclusions

This paper tackles an emerging challenge of cross-modal fundus image registration (CMFIR) with large FoV disparity. Experiments on the newly developed **OCTA60** test set allow us to draw conclusions as follows. Directly re-purposing existing small-FoV-disparity oriented methods does not work. Coarse FoV alignment by the proposed `Crop` operation is crucial. The SOTA methods can be much improved by this operation, though still less effective than the proposed **CARe** method. For the estimation of the spatial transforming function, the double-fitting strategy, *i.e.,* RAN-Poly, is better than using RANSAC or polynomial fitting alone. While targeted at large cross-modal FoV disparity, our method also works well in the conventional small-FoV-disparity scenario. With **CARe** and **OCTA60**, we establish a new baseline for CMFIR.

Acknowledgments. This research was supported by National Natural Science Foundation of China (62576348, 62172420) and Beijing Natural Science Foundation (L254039).

References

1. Abbasi-Sureshjani, S., Smit-Ockeloen, I., Zhang, J., Ter Haar Romeny, B.: Biologically-inspired supervised vasculature segmentation in SLO retinal fundus images. In: ICIAR (2015)
2. Chen, J., Tian, J., Lee, N., Zheng, J., Smith, R., Laine, A.: A partial intensity invariant feature descriptor for multimodal retinal image registration. IEEE Trans. Biomed. Eng. **57**(7), 1707–1718 (2010)
3. De Carlo, T., Romano, A., Waheed, N., Duker, J.: A review of optical coherence tomography angiography (OCTA). Int. J. Retina Vitreous **1**, 1–15 (2015)
4. DeTone, D., Malisiewicz, T., Rabinovich, A.: SuperPoint: self-supervised interest point detection and description. In: CVPR Workshops (2018)
5. Ding, L., Kuriyan, A., Ramchandran, R., Wykoff, C., Sharma, G.: Weakly-supervised vessel detection in ultra-widefield fundus photography via iterative multi-modal registration and learning. IEEE Trans. Med. Imaging **40**(10), 2748–2758 (2020)
6. Hajeb Mohammad Alipour, S., Rabbani, H., Akhlaghi, M.: Diabetic retinopathy grading by digital curvelet transform. Comput. Math. Methods Med. **2012**(1), 761901 (2012)
7. Jin, K., et al.: FIVES: a fundus image dataset for artificial intelligence based vessel segmentation. Sci. Data **9**(1), 475 (2022)
8. Lin, T., Goyal, P., Girshick, R., He, K., Dollár, P.: Focal loss for dense object detection. In: ICCV (2017)
9. Liu, J., Li, X., Wei, Q., Xu, J., Ding, D.: Semi-supervised keypoint detector and descriptor for retinal image matching. In: ECCV (2022)
10. Liu, J., Li, X.: Geometrized transformer for self-supervised homography estimation. In: ICCV (2023)
11. Lowe, D.G.: Distinctive image features from scale-invariant keypoints. Int. J. Comput. Vision **60**, 91–110 (2004)
12. Ning, H., Wang, C., Chen, X., Li, S.: An accurate and efficient neural network for OCTA vessel segmentation and a new dataset. In: ICASSP (2024)
13. Perez-Rovira, A., Zutis, K., Hubschman, J., Trucco, E.: Improving vessel segmentation in ultra-wide field-of-view retinal fluorescein angiograms. In: EMBC (2011)
14. Ronneberger, O., Fischer, P., Brox, T.: U-Net: convolutional networks for biomedical image segmentation. In: Navab, N., Hornegger, J., Wells, W.M., Frangi, A.F. (eds.) MICCAI 2015. LNCS, vol. 9351, pp. 234–241. Springer, Cham (2015). https://doi.org/10.1007/978-3-319-24574-4_28
15. Sarlin, P., DeTone, D., Malisiewicz, T., Rabinovich, A.: SuperGlue: learning feature matching with graph neural networks. In: CVPR (2020)
16. Sharma, L., Sharma, J., Anand, D., Sharma, S.: An adaptive window based polynomial fitting approach for pixel matching in stereo images. In: ICICCT (2018)
17. Sindel, A., Hohberger, B., Maier, A., Christlein, V.: Multi-modal retinal image registration using a keypoint-based vessel structure aligning network. In: MICCAI (2022)
18. Wang, Y., Wang, X., Gu, Z., Liu, W., Ng, W., Huang, W., Cheng, J.: SuperJunction: learning-based junction detection for retinal image registration. In: AAAI (2024)
19. Wang, Y., et al.: A segmentation based robust deep learning framework for multimodal retinal image registration. In: ICASSP (2020)

20. Wei, Q., Yu, W., Li, X.: Convolutional prompting for broad-domain retinal vessel segmentation. In: ICASSP (2025)
21. Yang, Z., et al.: Joint localization of optic disc and fovea in ultra-widefield fundus images. In: MLMI (2019)
22. Zhang, J., et al.: Joint vessel segmentation and deformable registration on multi-modal retinal images based on style transfer. In: ICIP (2019)
23. Zhang, J., et al.: Two-step registration on multi-modal retinal images via deep neural networks. IEEE Trans. Image Process. **31**, 823–838 (2021)

SeViMatch: A Detector-Based Image Matching Framework with Semantic-Visual Fusion

Yun Liao[1,2], Nan Chen[1], JunHui Liu[1,2], Jiayi Lyu[1], Zongxiao Hu[1], and Qing Duan[1,2(✉)]

[1] Yunnan University, Kunming 650000, China
[2] Yunnan Key Laboratory of Software Engineering, Kunming 650000, China
qduan@ynu.edu.cn

Abstract. Detector-based image matching methods have been widely applied in various computer vision tasks. However, they remain fundamentally limited by two critical issues: (1) susceptibility to extracting redundant or misleading background features in low-texture and complex scenes, and (2) inadequate semantic understanding and integration capabilities, both of which compromise matching accuracy and robustness. To address these limitations, we propose SeViMatch, a novel detector-based image matching framework with semantic-visual fusion. It combines three key innovations: the Adaptive Feature Optimization Module (AFOM) that incorporates multiple attention mechanisms to selectively emphasize foreground regions and suppress background noise; the Semantic-Aware Module (SAM) that models visual-semantic distributions through an encoder-decoder architecture to achieve cross-image semantic alignment and awareness; and the Dynamic Semantic Fusion Module (DSFM) that adaptively adjusts the fusion ratio between semantic and visual features based on content, enabling a deep semantic-visual collaborative representation. Extensive experiments on multiple challenging benchmarks demonstrate that SeViMatch significantly enhances matching precision and robustness across diverse challenging scenarios.

Keywords: Image matching · Semantic-visual fusion · Visual attention

1 Introduction

Image matching plays a critical role in key computer vision tasks, including visual localization [26] and simultaneous localization and mapping (SLAM) [19]. Although traditional detector-based methods are widely adopted due to their practical efficacy, they often extract redundant features from background regions [31] and lack high-level semantic reasoning and integration capabilities [13,30]. These limitations restrict the representational power of the extracted features, reducing their robustness and adaptability to diverse and complex scene variations. Overcoming these challenges is crucial for improving the precision and reliability of image matching.

© The Author(s), under exclusive license to Springer Nature Singapore Pte Ltd. 2026
J. Lokoč et al. (Eds.): MMM 2026, LNCS 16412, pp. 335–348, 2026.
https://doi.org/10.1007/978-981-95-6950-2_24

To address the first challenge, we introduce an Adaptive Feature Optimization Module (AFOM) that integrates three complementary mechanisms: micro attention, focused attention, and background suppression attention. This integrated approach strengthens foreground features while minimizing background interference, thereby preventing the extraction of redundant or misleading features and improving feature discriminability and matching accuracy.

To address the second challenge, we propose a Semantic-Aware Module (SAM) and a Dynamic Semantic Fusion Module (DSFM). The SAM employs an encoder-decoder to extract semantic cues and enforces their consistency via a semantic reconstruction loss, enabling effective capture and representation of image semantics. The DSFM adaptively selects semantic features and dynamically balances their fusion with visual information, enabling more robust representation learning. This comprehensive framework significantly enhances both feature representation quality and matching robustness across diverse scenarios.

By integrating the AFOM, SAM, and DSFM, we propose SeViMatch, a novel semantic-visual fusion framework for robust image matching. Our framework enables deep integration of visual details and semantic structures, thereby improving keypoint detection and matching performance in complex scenes. Extensive experiments demonstrate that SeViMatch significantly outperforms existing state-of-the-art methods across multiple tasks, including mean matching accuracy evaluations, pose estimation, and visual localization, highlighting its strong performance and adaptability. Our main contributions can be summarized as follows:

- We propose SeViMatch, a novel semantic-visual fusion framework that integrates semantic cues into keypoint detection and descriptor learning to enhance scene awareness and improve matching accuracy and robustness.
- We design an Adaptive Feature Optimization Module (AFOM) that enhances foreground features and suppresses background noise by integrating micro attention, focused attention, and background suppression attention.
- We design a Semantic-Aware Module (SAM) to capture semantic cues across images and a Dynamic Semantic Fusion Module (DSFM) that adaptively combines semantic and visual features to strengthen feature representations.
- We conduct extensive experiments showing that SeViMatch consistently outperforms state-of-the-art methods in both accuracy and robustness, demonstrating its strong generalization across diverse scenarios.

2   Related Work

2.1   Detector-Based Image Matching Methods

Detector-based image matching methods establish correspondence by detecting keypoints and extracting their descriptors. Based on the order of detection and description, these methods can be categorized into three paradigms. Detect-then-describe methods, like SIFT [16] and ORB [24], first detect keypoints, then generate their corresponding descriptors. These methods demonstrate high computational efficiency in descriptor generation, as descriptors are only extracted from local regions around keypoints. However, their performance heavily relies on keypoint detection quality, leading to matching failures in low-texture regions where reliable keypoints cannot be effectively identified. Describe-to-detect methods, such as D2-Net [7] and PoSFeat [14], extract dense features first and then select keypoints from salient regions. The advantage of such methods lies in their ability to directly detect keypoints from feature maps, reducing reliance on traditional keypoint detectors. They can more effectively extract salient features, enhancing their robustness. However, their computational complexity is relatively high. Detect-and-describe methods integrate detection and description in a unified framework to enhance consistency. SuperPoint [6] predicts keypoints and descriptors via a shared encoder, R2D2 [23] incorporates a reliability predictor, DISK [28] leverages reinforcement learning to directly optimize matching, and ASLFeat [18] extracts multiscale features to improve stability. These methods achieve strong robustness under challenging conditions.

2.2 Semantic Information in Image Matching

Semantic information provides a high-level understanding of image content, capturing object categories, attributes, and spatial relationships beyond low-level features like edges. Recent works have demonstrated its critical role in image matching. MESA [31] performs matching at the semantic-region level rather than at the pixel level, thereby improving both accuracy and efficiency; SFD2 [30] incorporates semantic cues into keypoint detection and description to improve robustness; and SDE2D [13] achieves deeper integration by embedding semantics into both detection and description processes, significantly improving feature distinctiveness and matching quality. These approaches underscore the growing importance of semantics for accurate and robust matching under complex conditions.

3 Our Method

3.1 Overview

SeViMatch is a novel detector-based image matching framework with semantic-visual fusion (Fig. 1). Given an image pair $I_A, I_B \in \mathbb{R}^{H \times W \times 3}$, the backbone extracts multiscale visual features $F^1_{A,B} \in \mathbb{R}^{\frac{H}{4} \times \frac{W}{4} \times C_1}$, $F^2_{A,B} \in \mathbb{R}^{\frac{H}{8} \times \frac{W}{8} \times C_2}$, $F^3_{A,B} \in \mathbb{R}^{\frac{H}{16} \times \frac{W}{16} \times C_3}$, with the intermediate feature $F^2_{A,B}$ used to generate a keypoint heatmap $H_{keypoint} \in \mathbb{R}^{H \times W \times 1}$ for accurate localization. These features are refined by the Adaptive Feature Optimization Module (AFOM, Sec. 3.2), which enhances foreground structures and suppresses background noise to produce optimized features $F^{opt}_{A,B} \in \mathbb{R}^{\frac{H}{8} \times \frac{W}{8} \times d}$. Concurrently, the Semantic-Awareness Module (SAM, Sec. 3.3) extracts high-level semantic cues from $F^2_{A,B}$ to form semantic tokens $T^S_{A,B} \in \mathbb{R}^{1 \times 1 \times d}$, encoding region-aware semantics. Guided by $T^S_{A,B}$, the Dynamic Semantic Fusion Module (DSFM, Sec. 3.4) aggregates key

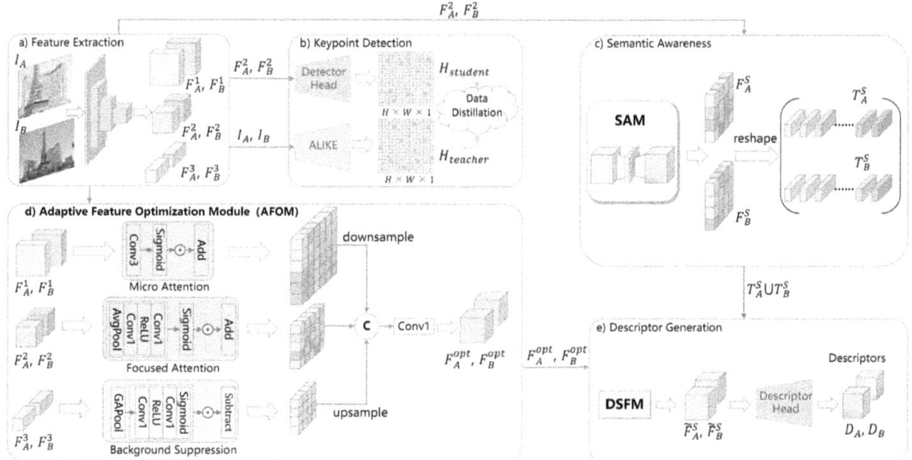

Fig. 1. Overall architecture of SeViMatch. a) Extraction of multiscale image features; b) Keypoint detection supervised by distillation loss; c) Semantic perception to generate semantic tokens; d) Feature optimization via multi-attention mechanisms; e) Descriptor generation based on optimized features and semantic tokens.

semantic tokens $T_{key}^{S} \in \mathbb{R}^{k \times d}$ and injects them into $F_{A,B}^{opt}$, adaptively modulating the features based on semantic context to obtain the fused representation $\widetilde{F}_{A,B}^{S} \in \mathbb{R}^{\frac{H}{8} \times \frac{W}{8} \times C}$. A descriptor head then generates discriminative descriptors $D \in \mathbb{R}^{H \times W \times C}$ from $\widetilde{F}_{A,B}^{S}$, and the entire framework is trained end-to-end using multitask supervision (Sec. 3.5) on keypoints, semantics, and descriptors to enhance matching accuracy and robustness under challenging conditions.

3.2   Adaptive Feature Optimization Module (AFOM)

To overcome the prevalent challenge of background interference in conventional feature extraction methods, we propose the Adaptive Feature Optimization Module (AFOM). This module simultaneously enhances salient regions and suppresses distracting information, effectively distinguishing foreground from background features by simulating the human visual attention mechanism. As illustrated in Fig. 1(d), AFOM consists of three submodules:

(1) Micro attention module enhances local structures by applying spatial mapping to $F_{A,B}^{1}$, generating a fine-grained attention response that emphasizes salient regions. The reweighted features are fused with the original to yield the enhanced representation $F_{A,B}^{en}$. The module can be expressed as:

$$F_{A,B}^{en} = F_{A,B}^{1} + \sigma\left(\Gamma(F_{A,B}^{1})\right) \odot F_{A,B}^{1} \tag{1}$$

where $\Gamma(\cdot)$ denotes the spatial mapping, $\sigma(\cdot)$ denotes a nonlinear activation function (e.g., Sigmoid), and $\odot$ indicates element-wise multiplication.

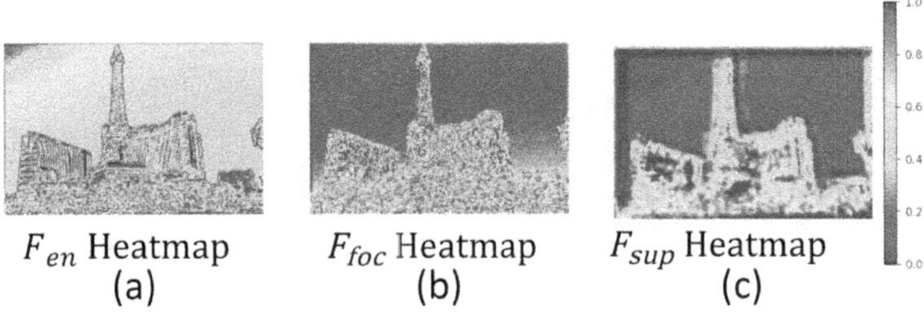

Fig. 2. Visualization of attention responses in AFOM. Red regions indicate high attention, while blue denotes low attention to non-salient areas. (a) Micro Attention enhances fine structures near boundaries and keypoints; (b) Focused Attention emphasizes key building structures; (c) Background Suppression Attention highlights salient foregrounds while suppressing background interference. (Color figure online)

(2) Focused attention module enhances semantic features relevant to matching by spatially compressing $F_{A,B}^2$ to capture global context and applying channel attention to emphasize critical semantic dimensions. The resulting feature map serves as $F_{A,B}^{foc}$, which emphasizes foreground semantic regions. The module can be expressed as:

$$F_{A,B}^{foc} = F_{A,B}^2 + \sigma \left(\varphi \left(F_{A,B}^2 \right) \right) \odot F_{A,B}^2 \tag{2}$$

where $\varphi \left(\cdot \right)$ denotes the process of generating channel-wise weights, incorporating spatial compression and channel attention mechanisms.

(3) Background suppression attention module mitigates background interference by extracting global semantic priors through global average pooling on $F_{A,B}^3$. These priors help suppress non-discriminative background responses yielding a refined feature map $F_{A,B}^{sup}$, which effectively suppresses background noise in the feature. The module can be expressed as:

$$F_{A,B}^{sup} = F_{A,B}^3 - \sigma \left(W_2 \delta \left(W_1 GAP(F_{A,B}^3) \right) \right) \odot F_{A,B}^3 \tag{3}$$

where $GAP \left(\cdot \right)$ denotes global average pooling, W_1 and W_2 are learnable projections, and $\delta \left(\cdot \right)$ is a nonlinear activation function (e.g., ReLU).

Adaptive Feature Optimization Module integrates the $F_{A,B}^{en}$, $F_{A,B}^{foc}$, and $F_{A,B}^{sup}$ to generate an optimized representation $F_{A,B}^{opt}$. This process effectively consolidates multi-dimensional information and improves the distinction between foreground and background regions, thereby enhancing feature discriminability and matching robustness. The module can be expressed as:

$$F_{A,B}^{opt} = \sigma \left(W \cdot Concat \left(\tilde{F}_{A,B}^{en}, \tilde{F}_{A,B}^{foc}, \tilde{F}_{A,B}^{sup} \right) + b \right) \tag{4}$$

where $\tilde{F}_{A,B}^* = Interp \left(F_{A,B}^* \right)$, and W and b are parameters of the projection operator.

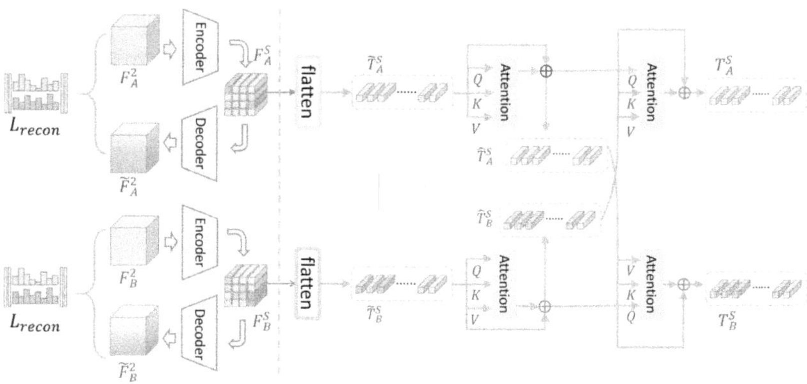

Fig. 3. The architecture of the Semantic-Aware Module.

3.3 Semantic-Aware Module (SAM)

The Semantic-Aware Module (SAM) employs an encoder-decoder architecture to model semantic distributions, with a semantic reconstruction loss serving as the guiding objective to ensure semantic consistency and integrity. The SAM module adaptively extracts spatial semantic information from images without the need for retraining for specific scenarios, thereby enhancing the generalization ability of the model. As shown in Fig. 3, SAM progressively compresses the feature map from $F^2_{A,B}$ to $F^S_{A,B} \in \mathbb{R}^{x \times y \times d}$, effectively enriching semantic representations while simultaneously reducing spatial complexity, which can be expressed as:

$$F^S_{A,B} = Encoder(F^2_{A,B}), F^S_{A,B} \in \mathbb{R}^{x \times y \times d}, x < H, y < W \tag{5}$$

Subsequently, the low-dimensional semantic feature map $F^S_{A,B}$ is flattened into semantic tokens $\tilde{T}^S_{A,B} \in \mathbb{R}^{(x \times y) \times d}$, which are globally modeled by self-attention for intra-image dependency capture and cross-attention for inter-image relationship learning. This comprehensive semantic modeling enhances feature expressiveness and cross-image consistency, which can be expressed as:

$$\hat{T}^S_A = \mathcal{F}\left(\tilde{T}^S_A\right) = Norm\left(\tilde{T}^S_A + \Psi\left(\tilde{T}^S_A W_q \cdot \Phi\left(\tilde{T}^S_A W_k\right)^T\right) \cdot \tilde{T}^S_A W_v\right) \tag{6}$$

$$T^S_A = \mathcal{G}\left(\hat{T}^S_A, \hat{T}^S_B\right) = Norm\left(\hat{T}^S_A + \Psi\left(\hat{T}^S_A W_q \cdot \Phi\left(\hat{T}^S_B W_k\right)^T\right) \cdot \hat{T}^S_B W_v\right) \tag{7}$$

where $\mathcal{F}\left(\cdot\right)$ represents the self-attention operation, and $\mathcal{G}\left(\cdot\right)$ represents the cross-attention operation. W_q, W_k, $W_v \in \mathbb{R}^{d \times d}$ are learnable transformation matrices, $\Phi\left(\cdot\right)$ denotes a projection function, $\Psi\left(\cdot\right)$ represents the Softmax normalization, and $Norm\left(\cdot\right)$ indicates LayerNorm normalization.

To effectively train the semantic awareness capability of the semantic encoder, a decoder is introduced during the training phase to reconstruct the

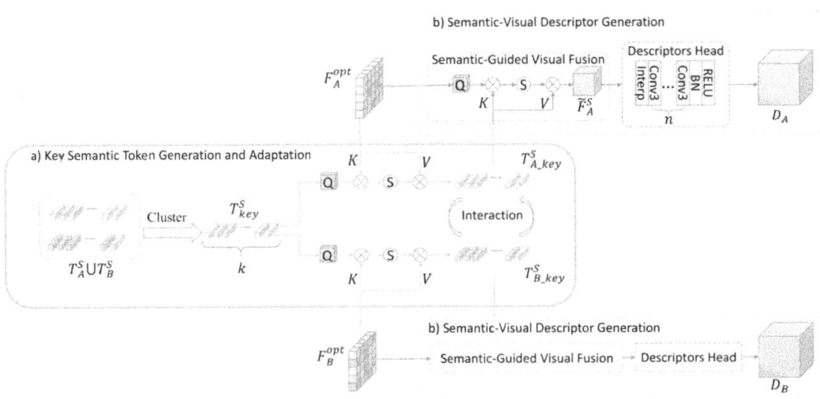

Fig. 4. The architecture of the Dynamic Semantic Fusion Module.

semantic tokens $T_{A,B}^S$ into a feature map $\tilde{F}_{A,B}^2 \in \mathbb{R}^{\frac{H}{8} \times \frac{W}{8} \times C_2}$ with the same spatial resolution as the input $F_{A,B}^2$. This reconstruction preserves visual–semantic consistency while enhancing the semantic representation capability, as follows:

$$\tilde{F}_{A,B}^2 = Decoder(T_{A,B}^S), \tilde{F}_{A,B}^2 \in \mathbb{R}^{\frac{H}{8} \times \frac{W}{8} \times C_2} \tag{8}$$

3.4   Dynamic Semantic Fusion Module (DSFM)

To adaptively fuse semantic and visual features across diverse image pairs, we propose the Dynamic Semantic Fusion Module (DSFM, Fig. 4) with two stages:

(1) Key Semantic Token Generation and Adaptation. We first obtain an initial set of key semantic tokens $T_{key}^{S(0)} \in \mathbb{R}^{k \times (1 \times d)}$ by jointly clustering the semantic tokens T_A^S and T_B^S from the image pair, where each cluster center compactly encodes a shared semantic concept (e.g., "sky," "building"), alleviating ambiguities caused by viewpoint changes and occlusions. Although these tokens compress semantic information, they lack adaptation to specific visual content. To address this, we introduce a semantic–visual cross-attention mechanism that leverages the optimized visual features $F_{A,B}^{opt}$ to modulate and update the tokens. This integration of visual cues filters out irrelevant semantics and strengthens those most pertinent to the current scene. Subsequently, self-attention and cross-attention operations refine intra-image and inter-image relationships, enhancing semantic coherence and cross-image alignment. The process can be expressed as:

$$T_{key}^{S(0)} = arg \min_{\{c_1, c_2, \cdots, c_k\}} \sum_{i=1}^{n_A + n_B} \|t_i - c_{k(i)}\|^2 \tag{9}$$

$$T_A^{key} = G\left(\mathcal{F}\left(\mathcal{G}(T_{key}^{S(0)}, F_A^{opt})\right), \mathcal{F}\left(\mathcal{G}(T_{key}^{S(0)}, F_B^{opt})\right)\right) \tag{10}$$

where each token $t_i \in T_A^S \cup T_B^S$ is associated with a cluster $k(i)$, $\mathcal{F}(\cdot)$ represents the self-attention operation, and $\mathcal{G}(\cdot)$ represents the cross-attention operation.

(2) Semantic-visual descriptor generation. To generate feature maps that retain both fine-grained visual details and accurate semantic information, we design a semantic-guided visual fusion mechanism. This mechanism employs semantic–visual cross-attention, where the key semantic tokens $T_{A,B}^{key}$ guide the fusion of the visual features $F_{A,B}^{opt}$. This fusion produces the feature map $\tilde{F}_{A,B}^S \in \mathbb{R}^{\frac{H}{8} \times \frac{W}{8} \times C}$, endowed with enhanced contextual awareness and robustness, providing strong support for subsequent image matching tasks in complex scenarios.

$$\tilde{F}_{A,B}^S = \mathcal{G}(F_{A,B}^{opt}, T_{A_{key},B_{key}}^S) \tag{11}$$

Finally, a lightweight descriptor head transforms the fused semantic-visual feature map $\tilde{F}_{A,B}^S$ into compact local descriptors $D \in \mathbb{R}^{H \times W \times C}$ that capture both fine visual details and high-level semantic context.

$$D = \mathcal{D}\left(Interp(\tilde{F}_{A,B}^S)\right) \tag{12}$$

where $\mathcal{D}(\cdot)$ is the descriptor head for generating descriptors, which consists of multiple 3×3 convolutional layers, batch normalization, and ReLU activation functions.

3.5   Loss Function

The overall objective combines three loss terms with weights α, β, and γ. The keypoint localization loss transfers knowledge from a pre-trained ALIKE [34] model to improve keypoint detection accuracy. The semantic reconstruction loss [3] preserves key image information in the semantic feature maps by minimizing the difference between input and reconstructed features. The descriptor loss [22] enhances discriminability by adopting a dual-softmax strategy to make matching descriptors similar and non-matching ones distinct:

$$L = \alpha L_{position} + \beta L_{recon} + \gamma L_{desc} \tag{13}$$

This design jointly promotes accurate localization, semantic consistency, and robust descriptor learning.

4   Experiments

4.1   Implementation Details

The network is implemented in PyTorch [20] and trained on MegaDepth [15] using Adam [12] with a weight decay 3×10^{-4}. The input image size 640×640, the batch size is 5, and the loss weights α, β, and γ are set to 2, 1, and 1, respectively. Training lasts 24 h on a single GTX 1080Ti GPU, without additional pretraining or fine-tuning for evaluation.

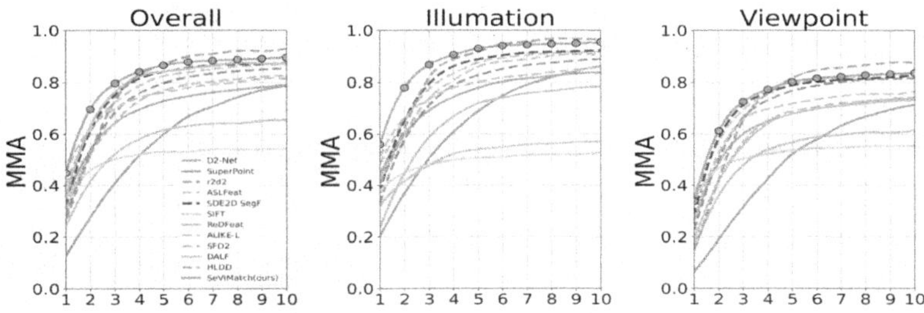

Fig. 5. Evaluation of mean matching accuracy on the HPatches dataset.

4.2 Mean Matching Accuracy Evaluations

Data and Evaluation: We adopt the standard HPatches [1] dataset, which includes diverse illumination and viewpoint variations to assess robustness. The SeViMatch is evaluated against a series of state-of-the-art baselines, including D2-Net [7], SuperPoint [6], R2D2 [23], ASLFeat [18], SDE2D [13], SIFT [16], ReDFeat [5], ALIKE [34], SFD2 [30], DALF [21], and HLDD [10]. Following [7,23], we use the Mean Matching Accuracy (MMA) as a metric, quantifying average correct matching precision across scenarios.

Results: As shown in Fig. 5, SeViMatch significantly outperforms the comparison methods across all pixel threshold ranges, with particularly notable advantages in the small threshold range. This indicates that SeViMatch exhibits superior robustness and discriminative power in achieving precise matching. As the threshold gradually increases, SeViMatch's performance curve remains steadily increasing and continues to lead, reflecting its adaptability and consistency across varying precision requirements. Compared to other methods, SeViMatch maintains a relatively balanced advantage across the entire range, avoiding a sharp decline in performance in the high-precision region and preventing the emergence of matching bottlenecks under more relaxed conditions. This advantage is likely due to the deep collaboration between semantic and visual information in its feature representation, which effectively mitigates matching ambiguities caused by viewpoint changes and partial occlusions in complex scenes. Overall, this trend suggests that the proposed method demonstrates excellent generalization ability and stability under both illumination and viewpoint variations.

4.3 Relative Pose Estimation

Data and Evaluation: We conducted an evaluation of relative pose estimation on outdoor (MegaDepth-1500 [15]) and indoor (ScanNet [4]) datasets. Following [6], we use the area under the curve (AUC) of pose errors at thresholds of 5°, 10°, and 20° as evaluation metrics. Given the distinct characteristics of the datasets, we selected state-of-the-art detector-based models that are well-suited

Table 1. OUTDOOR POSE ESTIMATION ON MegaDepth-1500. AUC of pose errors (%) is reported. The best and second results are highlighted in red and blue, respectively.

Method	Posestimation AUC		
	@5°	@10°	@20°
ORB [24]	17.91	27.65	39.07
Superpoint [6]	37.30	50.13	61.56
ZippyPoint [11]	23.68	34.91	46.32
SILK [8]	14.73	21.55	29.39
Multi-Arm [27]	42.55	54.65	64.56
ALIKED [33]	41.94	58.42	71.77
XFeat [22]	42.63	56.41	67.78
Ada-Matcher [35]	**44.53**	**61.66**	75.60
SeViMatch	48.73	61.87	**71.95**

Table 2. INDOOR POSE ESTIMATION ON Scannet. AUC of pose errors (%) is reported. The best and second results are highlighted in red and **blue**, respectively.

Method	Posestimation AUC		
	@5°	@10°	@20°
ORB [24]	5.21	13.65	25.36
Superpoint [6]	9.43	21.53	36.40
D2-Net [7]	5.25	14.53	27.96
ContextDese [17]	6.64	15.01	25.75
R2D2 [23]	7.43	17.45	28.64
LANet [29]	9.46	20.78	34.30
DarkFeat [9]	7.80	19.04	33.16
ALIKE [34]	9.82	20.07	32.64
Key.net [2]	9.82	21.23	35.21
SDE2D [13]	**11.12**	**23.16**	**36.91**
SeViMatch	14.43	28.38	42.71

to the specific challenges of each dataset. All chosen methods have been publicly evaluated on these datasets or widely adopted in the literature, ensuring reliable and reproducible comparisons.

Results: As shown in Table 1, in the outdoor scene pose estimation task, SeViMatch outperforms other comparison methods at all pose error thresholds. Notably, under strict pose error constraints, its performance significantly surpasses that of Ada-Matcher, XFeat, and other existing methods, demonstrating its strong adaptability and matching accuracy in complex outdoor environments. Although SeViMatch performs slightly worse than Ada-Matcher in the @20° metric, this difference is attributed to the model's emphasis on feature precision. SeViMatch enhances feature discriminability through semantic-visual fusion, making it more adept at capturing subtle differences, which results in a clear advantage in stricter metrics like @5° and @10°. The indoor scene experiments shown in Table 2 further confirm SeViMatch's excellent performance. When faced with complex indoor structures, it consistently outperforms SOTA methods across all pose error thresholds, effectively addressing feature matching ambiguities in indoor scenes, further validating its reliability in small-scale and structurally complex environments.

4.4　Visual Localization

Data and Evaluation: We evaluate SeViMatch on the Aachen Day-Night [32] dataset, comparing against representative traditional and learning-based baselines. Following the HLoc [25] protocol, localization recall (R1) is reported at $0.25\,m/2°$, $0.5\,m/5°$, and $5m/10°$ thresholds to assess pose accuracy.

Results: As shown in Table 3, SeViMatch achieves excellent visual localization on the Aachen Day-Night dataset. It leverages texture and semantic cues for

Table 3. Aachen Day-Night Visual Localization. Pose estimation accuracy (%) with the top two results highlighted in red and **blue**, respectively.

Method	Day			Night		
	0.25 m @2°	0.5 m @5°	5 m @10°	0.25 m @2°	0.5 m @5°	5 m @10°
ORB [24]	66.9	76.1	81.7	10.2	12.2	19.4
Superpoint [6]	87.4	93.2	97.0	**77.6**	85.7	95.9
ZippyPoint [11]	80.7	88.6	93.7	61.2	70.4	79.6
ALIKE [34]	85.7	92.4	96.7	81.6	88.8	**99.0**
XFeat [22]	84.7	91.5	96.5	**77.6**	**89.8**	98.0
SDE2D [13]	**87.5**	**94.2**	**98.1**	–	–	–
SeViMatch	87.6	95.5	99.2	74.3	90.1	99.5

high daytime accuracy, and mitigates nighttime/low-light performance degradation via robust semantic modeling. Under the extreme night threshold of $0.25\,m/2°$, its performance is slightly compromised — low-light texture blurring limits semantic-visual interaction, weakening pure visual detail capture. Nevertheless, SeViMatch maintains stable performance across thresholds, demonstrating strong adaptability and generalization.

4.5 Ablation Study

To evaluate the contributions of AFOM, SAM, and DSFM to SeViMatch, we conducted ablation experiments with four variant models for performance comparison. As shown in Table 4, the complete SeViMatch model outperforms all the variant models. After removing AFOM, SAM, and DSFM, the performance progressively declines, indicating that they positively contribute to image matching. The matching comparison in Fig. 6 also visually shows that SeViMatch's matching quality is significantly superior to that of other state-of-the-art models.

To investigate the impact of the number of key semantic features on matching performance, SeViMatch was trained with different values of N_S (see Table 5). As shown in Fig. 7, performance varies notably with N_S. At $N_S = 5$, semantic maps are sparse and incomplete, resulting in decreased matching accuracy. $N_S = 10$ produces clear, complete semantics, enhancing accuracy and robustness. $N_S = 20$ introduces excessive detail, increasing mismatches and lowering precision.

Table 4. Quantitative Results of Ablation Experiments on Each Module

AFOM	SAM	DSFM	Posestimation AUC @5° / @10° / @20°
			42.61/ 56.42/ 67.77
✓			44.12/ 56.84/ 68.29
	✓	✓	46.81/ 59.37/ 69.56
✓	✓	✓	**48.73/ 61.87/ 71.95**

Table 5. Ablation Study on the Number of Key Semantic Tokens

N_S	Posestimation AUC @5° / @10° / @20°
5	47.68/ 60.89/ 70.94
10	**48.73/ 61.87/ 71.95**
20	48.22/ 61.38/ 71.13

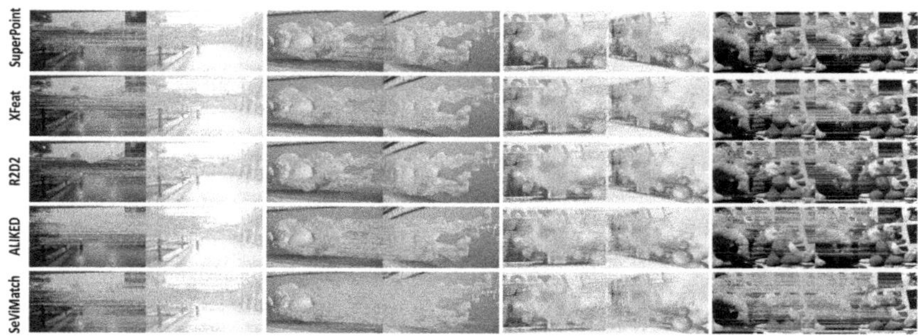

Fig. 6. Visualization of image matching comparison.

Fig. 7. Visualization of Ablation Results for the Number of Key Semantic Tokens.

5   Conclusion

In this study, we propose SeViMatch, a novel detector-based image matching framework with semantic-visual fusion. The framework consists of three key components: an Adaptive Feature Optimization Module (AFOM) which enhances foreground regions while suppressing background noise; a Semantic-Awareness Module (SAM) that extracts compact and informative semantic representations; and a Dynamic Semantic Fusion Module (DSFM) that integrates semantic information into the descriptor generation process. These components work in concert to enhance the model's ability to perform robust and accurate image matching under challenging conditions. Through comprehensive testing on multiple benchmark datasets, SeViMatch exhibits superior performance in both matching precision and robustness, validating that the proposed semantic–visual fusion strategy is effective.

Acknowledgement. This work was supported in part by the Yunnan Provincial Graduate Supervisor Team Construction Project (No. SJDSTD-23233578), in part by the Yunnan University Teaching Reform Project (No. 2023Y32), and in part by the Industry-University Cooperative Education Program of the Ministry of Education of China (No. 2505221437).

References

1. Balntas, V., Lenc, K., Vedaldi, A., Mikolajczyk, K.: Hpatches: a benchmark and evaluation of handcrafted and learned local descriptors. In: Proceedings of the IEEE Conference on Computer Vision and Pattern Recognition, pp. 5173–5182 (2017)
2. Barroso-Laguna, A., Mikolajczyk, K.: Key. net: Keypoint detection by handcrafted and learned CNN filters revisited. IEEE Trans. Patt. Anal. Mach. Intell. **45**(1), 698–711 (2022)
3. Cao, B., Araujo, A., Sim, J.: Unifying deep local and global features for image search. In: European Conference On Computer Vision, pp. 726–743. Springer (2020)
4. Dai, A., Chang, A.X., Savva, M., Halber, M., Funkhouser, T., Nießner, M.: Scannet: richly-annotated 3d reconstructions of indoor scenes. In: Proceedings of the IEEE Conference on Computer Vision and Pattern Recognition, pp. 5828–5839 (2017)
5. Deng, Y., Ma, J.: Redfeat: Recoupling detection and description for multimodal feature learning. IEEE Trans. Image Process. **32**, 591–602 (2022)
6. DeTone, D., Malisiewicz, T., Rabinovich, A.: Superpoint: self-supervised interest point detection and description. In: Proceedings of the IEEE Conference on Computer Vision and Pattern Recognition Workshops, pp. 224–236 (2018)
7. Dusmanu, M., et al.: D2-net: a trainable CNN for joint description and detection of local features. In: Proceedings of the IEEE/CVF Conference on Computer Vision and Pattern Recognition, pp. 8092–8101 (2019)
8. Gleize, P., Wang, W., Feiszli, M.: Silk: simple learned keypoints. In: Proceedings of the IEEE/CVF International Conference on Computer Vision, pp. 22499–22508 (2023)
9. He, Y., et al.: Darkfeat: noise-robust feature detector and descriptor for extremely low-light raw images. In: Proceedings of the AAAI Conference on Artificial Intelligence. vol. 37, pp. 826–834 (2023)
10. Hu, M., Sun, B., Zhang, F., Li, S.: HLDD: hierarchically learned detector and descriptor for robust image matching. IEEE Trans. Image Process. (2025)
11. Kanakis, M., Maurer, S., Spallanzani, M., Chhatkuli, A., Van Gool, L.: Zippypoint: fast interest point detection, description, and matching through mixed precision discretization. In: Proceedings of the IEEE/CVF Conference on Computer Vision and Pattern Recognition, pp. 6114–6123 (2023)
12. Kingma, D.P.: Adam: a method for stochastic optimization. arXiv preprint arXiv:1412.6980 (2014)
13. Li, J., Zhang, R., Li, G., Li, T.H.: Sde2d: semantic-guided discriminability enhancement feature detector and descriptor. IEEE Trans. Multimedia (2024)
14. Li, K., Wang, L., Liu, L., Ran, Q., Xu, K., Guo, Y.: Decoupling makes weakly supervised local feature better. In: Proceedings of the IEEE/CVF Conference on Computer Vision and Pattern Recognition, pp. 15838–15848 (2022)
15. Li, Z., Snavely, N.: Megadepth: learning single-view depth prediction from internet photos. In: Proceedings of the IEEE Conference on Computer Vision and Pattern Recognition, pp. 2041–2050 (2018)
16. Lowe, D.G.: Distinctive image features from scale-invariant keypoints. Int. J. Comput. Vision **60**, 91–110 (2004)
17. Luo, Z., Shen, T., Zhou, L., Zhang, J., Yao, Y., Li, S., Fang, T., Quan, L.: Contextdesc: local descriptor augmentation with cross-modality context. In: Proceedings of the IEEE/CVF Conference on Computer Vision and Pattern Recognition, pp. 2527–2536 (2019)

18. Luo, Z., et al.: Aslfeat: learning local features of accurate shape and localization. In: Proceedings of the IEEE/CVF Conference on Computer Vision and Pattern Recognition, pp. 6589–6598 (2020)
19. Mur-Artal, R., Montiel, J.M.M., Tardos, J.D.: Orb-slam: a versatile and accurate monocular slam system. IEEE Trans. Rob. **31**(5), 1147–1163 (2015)
20. Paszke, A.: Pytorch: an imperative style, high-performance deep learning library. arXiv preprint arXiv:1912.01703 (2019)
21. Potje, G., Cadar, F., Araujo, A., Martins, R., Nascimento, E.R.: Enhancing deformable local features by jointly learning to detect and describe keypoints. In: Proceedings of the IEEE/CVF Conference on Computer Vision and Pattern Recognition, pp. 1306–1315 (2023)
22. Potje, G., Cadar, F., Araujo, A., Martins, R., Nascimento, E.R.: Xfeat: accelerated features for lightweight image matching. In: Proceedings of the IEEE/CVF Conference on Computer Vision and Pattern Recognition, pp. 2682–2691 (2024)
23. Revaud, J., De Souza, C., Humenberger, M., Weinzaepfel, P.: R2d2: reliable and repeatable detector and descriptor. Adv. Neural Inf. Process. Syst. **32** (2019)
24. Rublee, E., Rabaud, V., Konolige, K., Bradski, G.: Orb: an efficient alternative to sift or surf. In: 2011 International Conference On Computer Vision, pp. 2564–2571. IEEE (2011)
25. Sarlin, P.E., Cadena, C., Siegwart, R., Dymczyk, M.: From coarse to fine: robust hierarchical localization at large scale. In: Proceedings of the IEEE/CVF Conference on Computer Vision and Pattern Recognition, pp. 12716–12725 (2019)
26. Sattler, T., Weyand, T., Leibe, B., Kobbelt, L.: Image retrieval for image-based localization revisited. In: BMVC. vol. 1, p. 4 (2012)
27. Shen, X., Hu, Q., Li, X., Wang, C.: A detector-oblivious multi-arm network for keypoint matching. IEEE Trans. Image Process. **32**, 2776–2785 (2023)
28. Tyszkiewicz, M., Fua, P., Trulls, E.: Disk: learning local features with policy gradient. Adv. Neural. Inf. Process. Syst. **33**, 14254–14265 (2020)
29. Wang, C., Zhang, G., Cheng, Z., Zhou, W.: Rethinking low-level features for interest point detection and description. In: Proceedings of the Asian Conference on Computer Vision, pp. 2059–2074 (2022)
30. Xue, F., Budvytis, I., Cipolla, R.: Sfd2: semantic-guided feature detection and description. In: Proceedings of the IEEE/CVF Conference on Computer Vision and Pattern Recognition, pp. 5206–5216 (2023)
31. Zhang, Y., Zhao, X.: Mesa: matching everything by segmenting anything. In: Proceedings of the IEEE/CVF Conference on Computer Vision and Pattern Recognition, pp. 20217–20226 (2024)
32. Zhang, Z., Sattler, T., Scaramuzza, D.: Reference pose generation for long-term visual localization via learned features and view synthesis. Int. J. Comput. Vision **129**(4), 821–844 (2021)
33. Zhao, X., Wu, X., Chen, W., Chen, P.C., Xu, Q., Li, Z.: Aliked: a lighter keypoint and descriptor extraction network via deformable transformation. IEEE Trans. Instrum. Meas. **72**, 1–16 (2023)
34. Zhao, X., Wu, X., Miao, J., Chen, W., Chen, P.C., Li, Z.: Alike: accurate and lightweight keypoint detection and descriptor extraction. IEEE Trans. Multimedia **25**, 3101–3112 (2022)
35. Zheng, F., Cao, C., Zhang, Z., Sun, T., Zhang, J., Zhao, L.: Ada-matcher: a deep detector-based local feature matcher with adaptive weight sharing. Knowl.-Based Syst. **316**, 113350 (2025)

Prompt-Aware Adaptive Elastic Weight Consolidation for Continual Learning in Medical Vision-Language Models

Ziyuan Gao[✉][iD] and Philippe Morel[iD]

University College London, London, UK
clairegao0930@gmail.com

Abstract. Medical AI systems face catastrophic forgetting when deployed in clinical settings, where models must learn new imaging protocols while retaining prior diagnostic capabilities. This challenge is particularly acute for medical vision-language models that must preserve complex cross-modal alignments between medical images and clinical terminology across diverse imaging modalities. We introduce Prompt-Aware Adaptive Elastic Weight Consolidation (PA-EWC), a novel continual learning approach that addresses catastrophic forgetting through prompt-guided parameter specialization. Our method systematically categorizes model parameters based on their functional roles in processing visual-descriptive, spatial-guided, and medical-semantic information, enabling targeted protection of critical knowledge while allowing adaptation to new clinical requirements. PA-EWC incorporates adaptive Fisher Information computation with gradient stability analysis and develops weighted complexity metrics based on medical terminology density. We evaluate our approach across five medical imaging datasets (Kvasir-SEG, ISIC 2018, CheXlocalize, BUSI, CAMUS) representing diverse modalities including endoscopy, dermoscopy, radiography, and ultrasound. Experimental results demonstrate that PA-EWC reduces catastrophic forgetting by up to 17.58% compared to baseline methods, with performance improvements of 4.30% on chest X-ray pathology localization and 6.06% on polyp segmentation.

Keywords: Continual learning · Medical AI · Vision-language models

1 Introduction

In medical artificial intelligence (AI) systems, a significant challenge arises when these systems are deployed in clinical settings: **catastrophic forgetting**. As medical institutions acquire new imaging protocols and encounter novel pathological conditions, AI models must learn these new tasks while retaining their prior diagnostic proficiencies. However, when neural networks learn new medical tasks sequentially, they often experience a drastic decline in performance on previously learned tasks [9]. This issue is particularly pronounced in medical vision-language models, which are integral to modern diagnostic workflows

J. Lokoč et al. (Eds.): MMM 2026, LNCS 16412, pp. 349–363, 2026.
https://doi.org/10.1007/978-981-95-6950-2_25

and must preserve complex cross-modal alignments between medical images and clinical terminology. Unlike models trained on natural image domains, medical imaging presents distinct challenges, including diverse imaging modalities (e.g., endoscopy, dermoscopy, radiography) and strict safety requirements where the loss of diagnostic capabilities could compromise patient care.

Medical AI systems deployed in clinical practice face significant limitations when adapting to new requirements. Production systems for diabetic retinopathy screening [6] and radiology workflows [13] typically require complete retraining when integrating new imaging protocols. This leads to substantial downtime and computational costs that disrupt patient care workflows. While continual learning approaches like Elastic Weight Consolidation (EWC) [9] have shown promise in research settings, they apply uniform parameter protection across all model components. This proves inadequate for medical domains, which require specialized parameter handling for diverse clinical tasks. The core challenge remains: how can medical vision-language models continuously adapt to evolving clinical needs without losing diagnostic capabilities?

We introduce **Prompt-Aware Adaptive Elastic Weight Consolidation (PA-EWC)**, a novel approach that addresses catastrophic forgetting in medical vision-language models through prompt-guided parameter specialization. By selectively protecting parameters based on their functional importance to specific medical tasks, PA-EWC preserves critical knowledge while allowing adaptation to new clinical requirements. Our method leverages medical language complexity analysis and gradient-based parameter classification to enable targeted protection of functionally specialized components.

Our contributions are fourfold: (1) **Prompt-Guided Parameter Classification** that systematically categorizes model parameters based on their functional specialization in processing different types of medical language; (2) **Adaptive Fisher Information with Gradient Stability** that incorporates gradient stability analysis and task similarity measures for dynamic importance estimation; (3) **Parameter-Aligned Complexity Assessment** that develops weighted complexity metrics based on medical terminology density; and (4) **Dynamic Multi-Group Protection** that selectively protects three distinct parameter groups based on task-specific linguistic patterns. Experiments across five medical imaging datasets (Kvasir-SEG [7] for polyp segmentation, ISIC 2018 [3] for skin lesions, CheXlocalize [16] for chest X-rays, BUSI [2] for breast ultrasound, CAMUS [10] for cardiac ultrasound) show our PA-EWC method reduces catastrophic forgetting by up to 17.58%. Performance improves by 4.30% on challenging chest X-ray pathology localization and by 6.06% on polyp segmentation compared to naive sequential learning.

2   Related Work

2.1   Continual Learning in Medical Vision-Language Models

Continual learning has emerged as a critical challenge in medical AI systems, where models must adapt to new clinical protocols while preserving existing diagnostic capabilities. Traditional approaches to catastrophic forgetting, such as Elastic Weight Consolidation (EWC) [9], Progressive Neural Networks [15], and PackNet [12], have shown promise in general computer vision tasks but face unique challenges in medical domains due to the heterogeneous nature of medical imaging modalities. Recent advances in prompt-based continual learning, including Learning to Prompt (L2P) [20], Visual Prompt Tuning (VPT) [8], DualPrompt [19], and CODA-Prompt [17], have introduced more sophisticated approaches but primarily focus on natural image domains and fail to address the specialized requirements of medical multimodal understanding. The medical domain presents unique challenges including diverse imaging modalities (endoscopy, dermoscopy, radiography, ultrasound) with distinct visual characteristics and specialized vocabularies [4], clinical deployment requirements that demand high reliability [14], and the need for precise alignment between clinical terminology and anatomical structures [6,13]. Recent work in medical continual learning has begun to address these domain-specific challenges through medical knowledge-aware regularization. but still applies uniform protection across model components without considering functional specialization in multimodal processing.

2.2 Adaptive Parameter Management in Continual Learning

The effectiveness of continual learning methods critically depends on accurately identifying which parameters are important for previous tasks and should be protected from modification. Several approaches have attempted to improve parameter importance estimation, including Synaptic Intelligence [21] which tracks parameter importance through online estimation, Memory Aware Synapses [1] which accumulates importance weights across tasks, and Gradient Episodic Memory [22] which stores representative examples from previous tasks. Adaptive methods like Self-Adaptive EWC have introduced dynamic importance weighting based on task similarity measures, while functional regularization approaches [18] focus on preserving input-output mappings rather than specific parameter values, and meta-learning frameworks [5] attempt to find initialization points that facilitate rapid adaptation. However, these approaches have not been systematically applied to medical vision-language models, which require specialized parameter protection strategies based on task-specific linguistic patterns.

3 Methodology

3.1 Problem Formulation

In continual learning for medical multimodal vision-language models, we address the catastrophic forgetting problem when sequentially learning tasks $\mathcal{T}_1, \mathcal{T}_2, \ldots, \mathcal{T}_N$. Each task $\mathcal{T}_i$ consists of medical images $\mathcal{X}_i$, corresponding segmentation masks $\mathcal{Y}_i$, and textual prompts $\mathcal{P}_i$ with varying complexity levels. The model parameters θ must be updated to optimize performance on the current task while preserving knowledge from previous tasks.

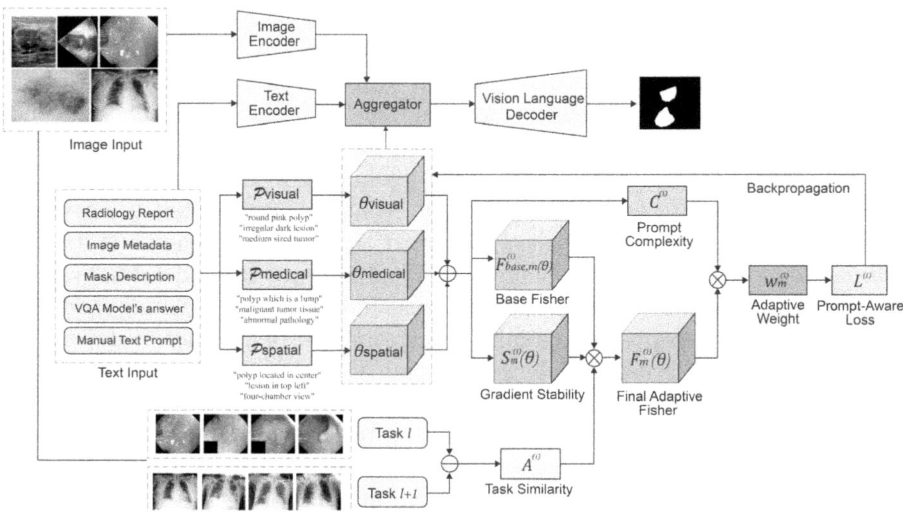

Fig. 1. Overall PA-EWC pipeline.

For a model f_θ with parameters θ, we aim to minimize performance degradation on previous tasks while maximizing adaptation to new tasks:

$$\min_\theta \sum_{i=1}^{N} \mathcal{L}_i(f_\theta(\mathcal{X}_i, \mathcal{P}_i), \mathcal{Y}_i) \text{ subject to } \forall j < i : \mathcal{L}_j(f_\theta) \leq \mathcal{L}_j(f_{\theta_j^*}) \tag{1}$$

where θ_j^* represents the optimal parameters after training on task j.

3.2 Prompt-Guided Parameter Classification

We propose a prompt-aware parameter classification strategy that selectively protects parameters based on their functional specialization. Our approach consists of two components: (1) a hierarchical prompt taxonomy that categorizes medical language complexity, and (2) an empirical parameter classification method that maps model components to prompt response patterns. This enables task-specific protection while allowing non-essential parameters to adapt to new tasks.

To systematically analyze parameter-prompt relationships, we establish a five-tier prompt hierarchy (Table 1) with three core functional categories: Visual-Descriptive prompts ($\mathcal{P}_{visual}$) emphasizing visual attributes, Spatial-Guided prompts ($\mathcal{P}_{spatial}$) incorporating anatomical positioning, and Medical-Semantic prompts ($\mathcal{P}_{medical}$) providing clinical definitions. To validate the effectiveness of our approach, we design two additional categories: basic and comprehensive prompts to serve as baselines, as demonstrated in the experimental sections.

Table 1. Hierarchical Prompt Strategy

Type	Prompt Examples	Key Features
Basic	"polyp", "skin lesion", "foot ulcer", "myocardium"	Simple medical terminology
Visual-Descriptive ($\mathcal{P}_{\text{visual}}$)	"round polyp", "pink round polyp", "medium pink round polyp", "irregular skin melanoma", "one small irregular foot ulcer"	Visual attributes, shape descriptions, size modifiers
Spatial-Guided ($\mathcal{P}_{\text{spatial}}$)	"polyp located in center", "skin melanoma located in top left", "foot ulcer located in bottom right", "myocardium located in left ventricle"	Location guidance, spatial references, anatomical positioning
Medical-Semantic ($\mathcal{P}_{\text{medical}}$)	"polyp which is a small lump in colon", "skin lesion which is an abnormal tissue growth", "melanoma which is a malignant tumor"	Medical definitions, clinical descriptions, pathological context
Comprehensive	"medium pink round polyp which is a small lump in colon located in top left", "irregular skin melanoma which is a malignant tumor located in center"	Complete integration of all information types, maximum complexity

Using these prompt types, we empirically determine parameter-prompt relationships through controlled gradient analysis. For each core prompt category, we measure parameter gradient response magnitude and assign parameters to the group yielding maximum response:

$$\text{class}(\theta_k) = \arg \max_t |\nabla_{\theta_k} \mathcal{L}(f_\theta(x, \mathcal{P}_t), y)|_2 \tag{2}$$

where $R_k^{(t)}$ represents the gradient response magnitude of parameter θ_k to prompt type t, $\mathcal{L}$ is the loss function, and $\mathcal{P}_t$ denotes the prompt template for task type t. This analysis reveals three parameter groups (Table 2): Visual-Descriptive Features (θ_{visual}) mapping to vision processing layers, Spatial-Guided Attention (θ_{spatial}) corresponding to cross-attention modules, and Medical-Semantic Understanding (θ_{medical}) associated with text components.

This classification enables task-adaptive parameter protection: when a new task exhibits specific linguistic patterns (spatial, visual, or medical), we selectively strengthen protection for the corresponding parameter groups. This balances knowledge retention and adaptation flexibility in continual learning.

Table 2. Parameter Classification Based on Prompt Response Patterns

Parameter Group	Primary Response to	Key Vocabulary	Model Components
Visual-Descriptive Features (θ_{visual})	Visual attribute descriptions ($\mathcal{P}_{\text{visual}}$)	`round, irregular, pink, medium, small, large, shape, color, texture`	Vision processing layers, feature extraction modules
Spatial-Guided Attention (θ_{spatial})	Spatial guidance prompts ($\mathcal{P}_{\text{spatial}}$)	`located, center, left, right, top, bottom, four-chamber, two-chamber`	Cross-attention layers, conditional processing modules
Medical-Semantic Understanding (θ_{medical})	Medical terminology and semantics ($\mathcal{P}_{\text{medical}}$)	`polyp, lesion, tumor, lump, pathology, malignant, benign, tissue`	Text processing layers, medical vocabulary modules

3.3 Parameter-Aligned Prompt Complexity Assessment

To quantify prompt complexity and guide adaptive parameter protection, we develop a weighted complexity metric that leverages our established parameter groups (θ_{visual}, θ_{spatial}, θ_{medical}). Rather than using traditional word-count or syntactic measures, our approach assigns differential weights to vocabulary types based on their functional specialization in medical multimodal understanding.

The complexity calculation uses the vocabulary categories from Table 2:

$$C^{(i)} = \frac{1}{|\mathcal{P}^{(i)}|} \sum_{p \in \mathcal{P}^{(i)}} \left(|W_p| + \alpha_{\text{visual}}|V_p| + \alpha_{\text{spatial}}|S_p| + \alpha_{\text{medical}}|M_p| \right) \tag{3}$$

where $|W_p|$, $|V_p|$, $|S_p|$, and $|M_p|$ represent base words, visual descriptors, spatial terms, and medical terms in prompt p, respectively. The weighting factors $\alpha_{\text{visual}} = 2.0$, $\alpha_{\text{spatial}} = 2.5$, and $\alpha_{\text{medical}} = 3.0$ emphasize domain-specific terminology. Prompts with higher concentrations of specialized medical vocabulary thus receive proportionally stronger parameter protection.

3.4 Adaptive Fisher Information Matrix with Gradient Stability

Traditional Fisher Information matrices in EWC assume uniform parameter importance across all learning phases, which fails to capture the dynamic nature of parameter significance in continual learning scenarios. We enhance the Fisher computation by incorporating gradient stability analysis and task similarity measures to provide more accurate importance estimation for each parameter group.

For each parameter group $m \in \{\text{visual}, \text{spatial}, \text{medical}\}$, we compute adaptive Fisher Information that incorporates gradient stability and task similarity. The base Fisher computation follows the standard formulation:

$$F_{\text{base},m}^{(i)}(\theta) = \mathbb{E}_{x \sim \mathcal{D}_i} \left[(\nabla_{\theta_m} \log p(y|x; \theta_m))^2 \right] \tag{4}$$

We augment this base computation with two adaptive factors. The gradient stability factor $S_m^{(i)}(\theta) = \sigma(-\text{Var}(\nabla_{\theta_m}))$ measures parameter consistency across training samples, where higher variance indicates unstable gradients that should receive reduced protection. The task similarity factor captures activation pattern changes between consecutive tasks:

$$A^{(i)} = \frac{1}{L} \sum_{l=1}^{L} \frac{1}{1 + |\mu_l^{(i-1)} - \mu_l^{(i)}| + |\sigma_l^{(i-1)} - \sigma_l^{(i)}|} \tag{5}$$

where μ_l and σ_l represent the mean and standard deviation of activations in layer l. This similarity measure approaches its maximum value for highly similar tasks and approaches 1.0 for dissimilar tasks, allowing stronger protection when tasks share common activation patterns.

The final adaptive Fisher matrix combines these factors through weighted multiplication:

$$F_m^{(i)}(\theta) = F_{\text{base},m}^{(i)}(\theta) \cdot S_m^{(i)}(\theta) \cdot A^{(i)} \tag{6}$$

This formulation ensures that parameters with stable gradients and high task similarity receive maximum protection, while unstable or task-specific parameters are allowed greater adaptation flexibility.

3.5   Adaptive Weight Computation

We dynamically adjust protection weights for each parameter group based on prompt complexity and task similarity. For each parameter group $m \in \{\text{visual}, \text{spatial}, \text{medical}\}$, the adaptive weight is computed as:

$$w_m^{(i)} = F_m^{(i)}(\theta) \times \left(1 + \frac{C^{(i)}}{C_{\max}}\right) \tag{7}$$

where $F_m^{(i)}(\theta)$ is the adaptive Fisher Information matrix from Equation (6), $C^{(i)}$ is the prompt complexity for task i, and $C_{\max}$ is the maximum observed complexity across all tasks.

This formulation increases protection weights when prompts are more complex, while maintaining the gradient stability and task similarity properties established in the Fisher Information computation.

3.6 Prompt-Aware Loss Function

The proposed framework employs a composite loss function that balances current task performance with knowledge retention from previous tasks. The total loss function integrates segmentation objectives with adaptive continual learning constraints:

$$\mathcal{L}_{\text{total}}^{(i)} = w_{\text{seg}} \mathcal{L}_{\text{seg}}^{(i)} + w_{\text{dice}} \mathcal{L}_{\text{dice}}^{(i)} + w_{\text{ewc}} \sum_{j=1}^{i-1} \mathcal{L}_{\text{EWC}}^{(j)} \tag{8}$$

The enhanced EWC component accumulates regularization constraints from all previous tasks, weighted by parameter-specific importance across visual, spatial, and medical parameter groups:

$$\mathcal{L}_{\text{EWC}}^{(j)} = \sum_{m} w_m^{(j)} \sum_{\theta \in \theta_m} F_m^{(j)}(\theta) \cdot (\theta - \theta_m^{(j)*})^2 \tag{9}$$

where m denotes the parameter group (visual, spatial, or medical), $w_m^{(j)}$ represents the adaptive weights from Eq. (8), $F_m^{(j)}(\theta)$ denotes the Fisher Information importance for parameter θ in group m at task j, and $\theta_m^{(j)*}$ are the optimal parameters for group m after completing task j.

The Dice loss component addresses class imbalance inherent in medical segmentation tasks through soft probability weighting:

$$\mathcal{L}_{\text{dice}}^{(i)} = 1 - \frac{1}{B} \sum_{b=1}^{B} \frac{2 \cdot \sum_{h,w} p_{b,h,w}^{(fg)} \cdot y_{b,h,w}}{\sum_{h,w} p_{b,h,w}^{(fg)} + \sum_{h,w} y_{b,h,w} + \epsilon} \tag{10}$$

where $p^{(fg)} = \text{softmax}(\text{logits})[:, 1]$ represents the foreground probability predictions. The loss weighting scheme employs $w_{\text{seg}} = 1.0$, $w_{\text{dice}} = 0.3$, and $w_{\text{ewc}} = 10.0$ to prioritize knowledge retention while maintaining task-specific performance, with base Fisher Information importance scaled to 1000.

4 Experiment

4.1 Datasets and Evaluation Metric

We conduct comprehensive experiments across five major medical imaging datasets to evaluate continual learning performance in diverse clinical scenarios. Our evaluation encompasses **Kvasir-SEG** [7] for polyp segmentation (800/100/100 train/val/test), **ISIC 2018** [3] for skin lesion segmentation (810/90/379), **CheXlocalize** [16] for chest X-ray pathology localization (1279/446/452), **BUSI** [2] for breast ultrasound tumor segmentation (624/78/78), and **CAMUS** [10] for cardiac ultrasound chamber segmentation (4800/600/600). These datasets represent distinct imaging modalities (endoscopy, dermoscopy, radiography, ultrasound), anatomical regions (gastrointestinal, dermatological, pulmonary, mammographic, cardiac), and segmentation complexities, providing a comprehensive evaluation framework for medical vision-language continual learning.

We assess continual learning performance using two primary metrics:

(1) **Dice Coefficient** measuring segmentation accuracy across all tasks, computed as

$$\text{Dice}_i^{final} = \frac{2|P_i \cap G_i|}{|P_i| + |G_i|} \tag{11}$$

with P_i and G_i being the predicted and ground truth segmentation masks for task i, and T is the total number of tasks;

(2) **Forgetting Rate** [9] quantifying knowledge retention, calculated as

$$\text{FR} = \sum_{i=1}^{T-1} (\text{Dice}_i^{peak} - \text{Dice}_i^{final}) \tag{12}$$

where Dice_i^{peak} is the peak performance on task i and Dice_i^{final} is the final performance after learning all subsequent tasks. Lower forgetting rates indicate superior catastrophic forgetting mitigation. Additionally, we report training efficiency metrics including computational time and parameter overhead to demonstrate practical deployment feasibility.

4.2 Implementation Details

We employ CLIPSeg [11] as the base vision-language segmentation model, featuring a ViT-B/16 vision encoder and transformer-based text encoder with cross-modal attention mechanisms for processing 512×512 resolution images with text prompts. All experiments utilize AdamW optimizer with learning rate 1e-4, weight decay 1e-2, and cosine annealing scheduler, where sequential training employs 50 epochs per task with early stopping based on validation Dice coefficient. Training is conducted with batch size 16 on 2×A100 GPUs. Results are averaged over three runs with random seed 43.

4.3 Comparison with State-of-the-Art Methods

To demonstrate the effectiveness of our approach, we compare against recent state-of-the-art continual learning methods adapted for medical vision-language tasks. Table 3 presents comprehensive comparisons across classic continual learning, parameter-efficient fine-tuning, and vision-language model specific methods. PA-EWC achieves state-of-the-art performance, outperforming the strongest baseline (ZSCL) by 2.32% in Dice coefficient and reducing catastrophic forgetting by 2.45%, while maintaining superior computational efficiency with 8.7-hour training time compared to ZSCL's 9.1 h. The results demonstrate consistent improvements across all evaluation metrics, with our method achieving 75.34% average Dice score and only 18.42% forgetting rate. With 155M parameters, PA-EWC delivers the best performance across all metrics while maintaining balanced training efficiency, establishing its practical viability.

Table 3. Comparison with state-of-the-art continual learning methods on medical vision-language segmentation. Training time measured on 2×A100 GPUs. Best results in **bold**, second best underlined.

Method	Average Dice (%)	Average Forgetting (%)	Training Time (h)	Params (M)
Basic Baselines				
CLIPSeg Individual	78.5±0.6	0.0±0.0	12.4	150.0
CLIPSeg Sequential	62.3±1.9	35.7±2.3	8.1	150.0
Classic Continual Learning Methods				
EWC [9] (2017)	65.48±1.7	28.34±2.1	8.5	150.0
LwF [23] (2017)	67.2±1.5	26.8±1.9	8.9	150.0
PackNet [12] (2018)	68.92±1.4	24.71±1.8	9.2	150.0
Progressive NN [15] (2016)	71.23±1.2	22.15±1.5	15.3	375.0
DER++ [24] (2020)	71.58±1.0	22.43±1.3	9.8	155.0
Parameter-Efficient Fine-tuning Methods				
CLIPSeg + LoRA [25] (2021)	69.5±1.2	24.3±1.6	**6.8**	<u>152.5</u>
CLIPSeg + CLIP-Adapter [26] (2021)	70.1±1.3	23.7±1.4	<u>6.9</u>	**151.8**
ZSCL [27] (2023)	<u>73.02±0.9</u>	<u>20.87±1.2</u>	9.1	150.0
MoE-Adapters [28] (2024)	72.84±1.1	21.34±1.4	9.4	165.3
PA-EWC (Ours)	**75.34±0.8**	**18.42±1.0**	8.7	155.0

4.4   Forgetting Rate Analysis

To further assess catastrophic forgetting behavior, we analyze forgetting rates across different task orders using five distinct sequential learning scenarios. Table 4 compares forgetting rates between sequential baseline and our PA-EWC method across all five medical imaging datasets. Our PA-EWC method demonstrates superior forgetting mitigation compared to sequential training in most scenarios. The approach achieves significant improvements in challenging cases, reducing forgetting from 47.56% to 31.50% for CAMUS and from 49.32% to 31.74% for CheX in the ISIC→CAMUS→Kvasir→CheX→BUSI sequence. The color-coded visualization shows task learning order, with earlier tasks generally experiencing higher forgetting rates, confirming the expected catastrophic forgetting pattern in continual learning scenarios. PA-EWC consistently outperforms sequential training across different task orderings, demonstrating robust and reliable performance regardless of learning sequence variations.

Table 4. Forgetting rate comparison (%) across different task sequences. Results show mean ± standard deviation over 3 runs. Best results in **bold**.

Task Sequence	Method	CAMUS	BUSI	ISIC	Kvasir	CheX
Kvasir → ISIC → CheX → BUSI → CAMUS	sequential	**21.45±1.2**	25.96±2.1	12.14±0.8	33.83±1.5	46.93±2.3
	PA-EWC	21.80±0.9	**25.56±1.8**	**11.23±0.7**	**26.90±1.1**	**43.77±1.9**
CheX → CAMUS → BUSI → ISIC → Kvasir	sequential	45.89±3.2	29.78±2.1	**8.02±0.5**	18.34±1.4	37.92±2.6
	PA-EWC	**40.26±2.1**	**27.02±1.6**	8.26±0.6	**15.59±1.0**	**22.65±1.4**
CAMUS → Kvasir → CheX → BUSI → ISIC	sequential	58.74±3.8	25.67±1.9	**7.37±0.4**	24.12±1.6	26.95±2.3
	PA-EWC	**50.30±2.6**	**22.00±1.4**	7.46±0.5	**20.90±1.2**	**23.02±1.7**
ISIC → CAMUS → Kvasir → CheX → BUSI	sequential	47.56±2.9	**20.62±1.3**	12.18±0.9	23.45±1.5	49.32±3.6
	PA-EWC	**31.50±1.8**	22.47±1.5	**9.52±0.6**	**19.92±1.1**	**31.74±2.1**
CheX → Kvasir → CAMUS → ISIC → BUSI	sequential	32.69±2.0	21.97±1.4	**8.37±0.6**	21.08±1.2	41.42±2.9
	PA-EWC	**32.69±1.7**	**19.90±1.1**	8.57±0.7	**19.61±1.0**	**31.78±2.2**

Color Legend: 1st Task   2nd Task   3rd Task   4th Task   5th Task

4.5   Typical Continual Learning Performance

Table 5 presents segmentation performance across five medical imaging tasks in a continual learning setting, where tasks are learned sequentially: Kvasir → ISIC → CheXlocalize → BUSI → CAMUS. The CLIPSeg (Individual) results represent the upper bound performance when each task is trained separately with dedicated models, providing a reference for comparison. The sequential baseline clearly demonstrates the existence of catastrophic forgetting in continual learning, with substantial performance drops compared to individual training (e.g., Kvasir drops from 89.51% to 67.36%). Our PA-EWC significantly outperforms existing continual learning methods. PA-EWC consistently outperforms baseline approaches, achieving the best results on three out of five tasks including Kvasir (73.42%), CheXlocalize (56.78%), and BUSI (71.92%). The substantial improvements over General EWC across most datasets demonstrate PA-EWC's effective knowledge retention across diverse medical imaging modalities.

Table 5. Continual learning results on medical vision-language segmentation tasks. Performance measured by Dice coefficient (%). Results show mean ± standard deviation over 3 runs. Best results in **bold**.

Method	Kvasir	ISIC	CheX.	BUSI	CAMUS
Upper Bound (Individual Task Training)					
CLIPSeg (Individual)	89.51±0.8	92.12±0.5	59.56±1.1	64.32±0.9	88.85±0.6
Continual Learning					
Sequential Baseline	67.36±1.2	88.28±0.4	52.48±0.6	69.06±1.0	80.38±1.8
General EWC	59.31±2.1	83.67±1.3	33.85±1.8	68.47±2.2	**82.11±1.2**
Self-adaptive EWC	70.94±0.9	**89.15±0.7**	43.71±1.4	69.18±1.6	81.63±0.8
PA-EWC (Ours)	**73.42±0.6**	88.93±0.8	**56.78±0.9**	**71.92±1.3**	78.64±1.1

Color Legend: 1st Task   2nd Task   3rd Task   4th Task   5th Task

4.6   Prompt Strategy Evaluation

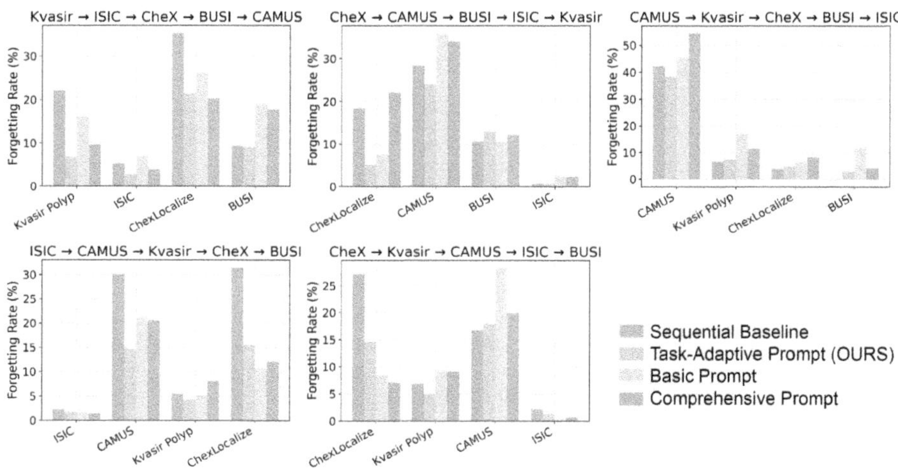

Fig. 2. Comparison of forgetting rates across different prompt strategies. Lower values indicate better performance with reduced catastrophic forgetting.

Figure 2 shows the forgetting rates across different prompt strategies in continual learning scenarios.. We evaluate four distinct prompt types: Sequential Baseline, Task-Adaptive Prompt (OURS), Basic Prompt, and Comprehensive Prompt. These strategies are tested across five comprehensive evaluation metrics that span different task orderings and continual learning challenges. The Task-Adaptive Prompt strategy achieves the best overall performance with the lowest average forgetting rate (10.6%). It consistently outperforms other methods across most evaluation metrics, demonstrating superior stability in continual learning scenarios. The Sequential Baseline approach shows the highest forgetting rates (15.2% average), while Basic Prompt (14.6%) and Comprehensive Prompt (14.0%) achieve moderate performance. The results indicate that our task-adaptive approach significantly outperforms other prompts across all tasks.

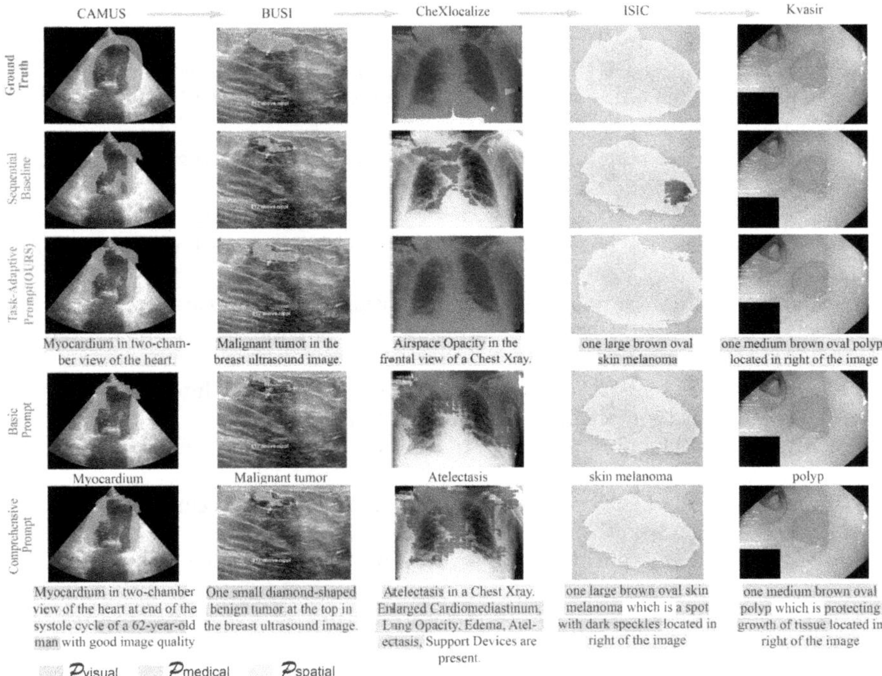

Fig. 3. Visualizations of segmentation results across different prompt strategies and evaluation metrics.

5 Conclusion

We introduced Prompt-Aware Adaptive Elastic Weight Consolidation (PA-EWC), a novel continual learning approach that addresses catastrophic forgetting in medical vision-language models through prompt-guided parameter specialization. Our method achieves superior performance by selectively protecting parameters based on their functional roles in processing visual, spatial, and medical semantic information. Experiments across five medical imaging datasets demonstrate that PA-EWC reduces catastrophic forgetting by up to 17.58% while maintaining competitive computational efficiency. The approach enables medical AI systems to continuously adapt to new clinical requirements without compromising existing diagnostic capabilities, offering significant potential for real-world clinical deployment scenarios.

References

1. Aljundi, R., Babiloni, F., Elhoseiny, M., Rohrbach, M., Tuytelaars, T.: Memory aware synapses: learning what (not) to forget. In: Ferrari, V., Hebert, M., Sminchisescu, C., Weiss, Y. (eds.) ECCV 2018. LNCS, vol. 11207, pp. 144–161. Springer, Cham (2018). https://doi.org/10.1007/978-3-030-01219-9_9

2. Al-Dhabyani, W., Gomaa, M., Khaled, H., Fahmy, A.: Dataset of breast ultrasound images. Data Brief **28**, 104863 (2020)
3. Codella, N., et al.: Skin lesion analysis toward melanoma detection 2018: a challenge hosted by the international skin imaging collaboration (ISIC). arXiv preprint arXiv:1902.03368 (2019)
4. Esteva, A., et al.: Dermatologist-level classification of skin cancer with deep neural networks. Nature **542**(7639), 115–118 (2017)
5. Finn, C., Abbeel, P., Levine, S.: Model-agnostic meta-learning for fast adaptation of deep networks. In: International Conference on Machine Learning, pp. 1126–1135. PMLR (2017)
6. Gulshan, V., et al.: Development and validation of a deep learning algorithm for detection of diabetic retinopathy in retinal fundus photographs. JAMA **316**(22), 2402–2410 (2016)
7. Jha, D., et al.: Kvasir-SEG: a segmented polyp dataset. In: International Conference on Multimedia Modeling, pp. 451–462. Springer (2020)
8. Jia, M., et al.: Visual prompt tuning. In: European Conference on Computer Vision, pp. 709–727. Springer (2022)
9. Kirkpatrick, J., et al.: Overcoming catastrophic forgetting in neural networks. Proc. Natl. Acad. Sci. **114**(13), 3521–3526 (2017)
10. Leclerc, S., et al.: Deep learning for segmentation using an open large-scale dataset in 2D echocardiography. IEEE Trans. Med. Imaging **38**(9), 2198–2210 (2019)
11. Lüddecke, T., Ecker, A.: Image segmentation using text and image prompts. In: IEEE/CVF Conference on Computer Vision and Pattern Recognition (CVPR), pp. 7086–7096. IEEE, New Orleans (2022)
12. Mallya, A., Lazebnik, S.: PackNet: adding multiple tasks to a single network by iterative pruning. In: Proceedings of the IEEE Conference on Computer Vision and Pattern Recognition, pp. 7765–7773 (2018)
13. McKinney, S.M., et al.: International evaluation of an AI system for breast cancer screening. Nature **577**(7788), 89–94 (2020)
14. Rajpurkar, P., et al.: CheXNet: radiologist-level pneumonia detection on chest X-rays with deep learning. arXiv preprint arXiv:1711.05225 (2017)
15. Rusu, A.A., et al.: Progressive neural networks. arXiv preprint arXiv:1606.04671 (2016)
16. Selvan, R., et al.: Lung segmentation from chest X-rays using variational data imputation. arXiv preprint arXiv:2005.10052 (2020)
17. Smith, J., et al.: CODA-Prompt: continual decomposed attention-based prompting for rehearsal-free continual learning. In: Proceedings of the IEEE/CVF Conference on Computer Vision and Pattern Recognition, pp. 11909–11919 (2023)
18. Titsias, M.K., Schwarz, J., Matthews, A.G.D.G., Pascanu, R., Teh, Y.W.: Functional regularisation for continual learning with Gaussian processes. In: International Conference on Learning Representations (2020)
19. Wang, Z., et al.: DualPrompt: complementary prompting for rehearsal-free continual learning. In: European Conference on Computer Vision, pp. 631–648. Springer (2022)
20. Wang, Z., et al.: Learning to prompt for continual learning. In: Proceedings of the IEEE/CVF Conference on Computer Vision and Pattern Recognition, pp. 139–149 (2022)
21. Zenke, F., Poole, B., Ganguli, S.: Continual learning through synaptic intelligence. In: International Conference on Machine Learning, pp. 3987–3995. PMLR (2017)
22. Lopez-Paz, D., Ranzato, M.: Gradient episodic memory for continual learning. In: Advances in Neural Information Processing Systems, pp. 6467–6476 (2017)

23. Li, Z., Hoiem, D.: Learning without forgetting. IEEE Trans. Pattern Anal. Mach. Intell. **40**(12), 2935–2947 (2018)
24. Buzzega, P., Boschini, M., Porrello, A., Abati, D., Calderara, S.: Dark experience for general continual learning: a strong, simple baseline. In: Advances in Neural Information Processing Systems, pp. 15920–15930 (2020)
25. Hu, E.J., et al.: LoRA: low-rank adaptation of large language models. In: International Conference on Learning Representations (2022)
26. Gao, P., et al.: CLIP-Adapter: better vision-language models with feature adapters. Int. J. Comput. Vis. **132**(2), 581–595 (2024)
27. Zheng, Z., Ma, M., Wang, K., Qin, Z., Yue, X., You, Y.: Preventing zero-shot transfer degradation in continual learning of vision-language models. In: Proceedings of the IEEE/CVF International Conference on Computer Vision, pp. 19125–19136 (2023)
28. Yu, J., et al.: Boosting continual learning of vision-language models via mixture-of-experts adapters. In: Proceedings of the IEEE/CVF Conference on Computer Vision and Pattern Recognition, pp. 23219–23230 (2024)

M3RAG: Orchestrating Multi-agent Reasoning for Multi-hop, Multi-modal Understanding

Haizhou Du$^{(\boxtimes)}$ and Wenhao Li

Shanghai University of Electric Power, Shanghai, China
`duhaizhou@shiep.edu.cn`

Abstract. Traditional Retrieval-Augmented Generation (RAG) systems face significant challenges in processing visually-rich, multi-modal documents, especially when addressing complex queries that demand deep semantic understanding and cross-document reasoning. To bridge this gap, we propose a novel framework M3RAG (**M**ulti-hop, **M**ulti-modal, **M**ulti-agent **R**etrieval-**A**ugmented **G**eneration). M3RAG introduces a collaborative multi-agent architecture that orchestrates an iterative process for query planning, fine-grained multi-modal evidence extraction, and self-correcting answer verification. By dynamically planning information retrieval pathways and fusing cross-modal evidence, M3RAG enables robust reasoning for complex multi-hop questions and achieves a deeper understanding of multi-modal content. Extensive experimental results demonstrate that M3RAG establishes a new state-of-the-art, outperforming existing methods by up to 18.4% on challenging multi-hop, multi-modal document understanding benchmarks, validating its effectiveness in complex reasoning tasks.

1 Introduction

Large Language Models (LLMs) [1,2] demonstrated remarkable capabilities in various natural language processing tasks [3,4]. However, they often struggle with factual inaccuracies and the assimilation of up-to-date knowledge [5,6]. Retrieval-Augmented Generation (RAG) [7–10] addresses these limitations by enabling LLMs to access and integrate external knowledge bases, thereby mitigating hallucinations and expanding their knowledge coverage.

Despite the advancements in RAG, current systems predominantly operate on text-based contexts, which inherently limit their application in real-world scenarios where information is frequently embedded within visually-rich documents [11,12]. These documents, such as charts, tables, and images interleaved with text, pose significant challenges for traditional RAG pipelines. Relying on optical character recognition (OCR) and parsing processes to extract text can lead to crucial information loss, including visual cues and layout, and introduce errors that propagate through retrieval and generation stages [13]. While the emergence of Vision-Language Models (VLMs) offers a promising avenue

J. Lokoč et al. (Eds.): MMM 2026, LNCS 16412, pp. 364–378, 2026.
https://doi.org/10.1007/978-981-95-6950-2_26

to overcome these limitations, extending RAG to vision-language tasks presents unique challenges such as modality discrepancy and information noise.

While existing works have begun to address multi-modal RAG [9,13–16], these approaches primarily aim to overcome the limitations of traditional RAG in processing visually-rich documents. For instance, frameworks like VisRAG and VDocRAG have demonstrated the benefits of encoding and retrieving documents directly as images to maximize information retention and avoid parsing losses. However, a critical research gap persists as these frameworks have yet to effectively scale to complex, multi-hop queries. Answering such queries in real-world scenarios necessitates gathering and synthesizing information from multiple distinct documents or different sections within a document, thereby forming a multi-hop logical chain. Filling this gap is particularly difficult due to two key challenges. First, the inherent complexity of multi-hop reasoning itself requires a dynamic and structured approach to decompose complex queries and retrieve disparate pieces of evidence. Second, this complexity is significantly amplified by modality discrepancy and retrieval noise, which are often magnified in a multi-hop setting and can compromise the entire reasoning chain.

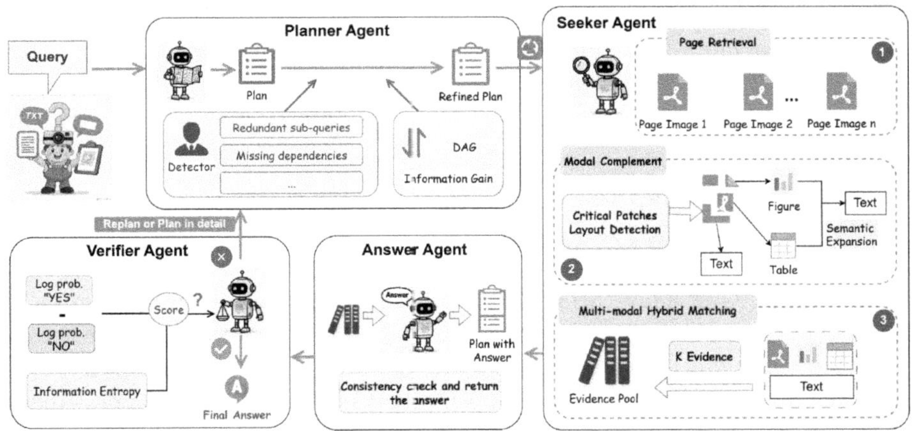

Fig. 1. The overview of M3RAG framework.

To address this critical gap and to effectively tackle the challenges of multi-hop reasoning within complex visual documents, this paper proposes a novel framework, **M3RAG** (**Multi-hop**, **Multi-modal**, **Multi-agent** Retrieval-Augmented Generation). Building upon advancements in vision-based RAG, M3RAG uniquely integrates a multi-agent architecture that orchestrates a sophisticated, iterative process for comprehensive query understanding and precise evidence synthesis. This framework is designed to: (1) enable robust multi-hop reasoning over visually-rich documents by dynamically planning information retrieval pathways and decomposing complex queries into manageable sub-goals; (2) achieve a deeper understanding of multi-modal content through targeted regional analysis and cross-modal evidence fusion, moving beyond simple page-level retrieval; and (3) enhance overall answer accuracy and reliability via a self-correcting, iterative verification mechanism that provides a crucial feedback loop. Our approach represents a significant step towards empowering LLMs to accurately and robustly answer complex, real-world questions from diverse, multi-modal knowledge sources.

Our **main contributions** are summarized as follows:

- We propose M3RAG, a novel multi-hop, multi-modal, multi-agent RAG framework by integrating specialized agents to orchestrate complex reasoning over visually-rich documents.
- We introduce fine-grained multi-modal evidence extraction through novel techniques like regional re-reading and modality expansion, which significantly reduce noise and enhance the precision of information retrieval from visually-rich documents.
- We develop a dynamic multi-agent collaborative and iterative reasoning mechanism for multi-hop problem-solving, which includes intelligent query planning and a self-correcting verification feedback loop, ensuring robust and reliable answers.
- We demonstrate superior performance through extensive experiments on challenging multi-hop, multi-modal question answering benchmarks, where M3RAG significantly outperforms existing state-of-the-art RAG methods.

2   Related Work

2.1   Multi-Modal RAG and Visual Document Understanding

Traditional RAG systems, primarily text-based [11], struggle with visually-rich documents due to information loss from OCR and neglected visual cues. To overcome this, multi-modal RAG paradigms have emerged. Approaches such as VisRAG [13], ViDoRAG [15], and VDocRAG [9] directly encode documents as images, leveraging Vision-Language Models for comprehensive visual information retention in retrieval and generation. M3DoCRAG [16] demonstrated a multi-modal RAG framework for multi-page, multi-document understanding. However, despite these advancements [14,17] in integrating visual information and processing multi-page documents, prior multi-modal RAG systems have not specifically introduced mechanisms for orchestrated multi-hop reasoning or fine-grained, iterative evidence refinement across distributed multi-modal sources. Their primary focus has been on comprehensive visual encoding and retrieval, rather than the intricate flow control needed for complex multi-hop inference.

2.2   Multi-Agent Frameworks for Question Answering and RAG

The increasing complexity of real-world QA tasks necessitates multi-agent frameworks in RAG systems [18,19]. Various multi-agent RAG approaches enhance reasoning and mitigate limitations. MA-RAG [20] focuses on collaborative reasoning for complex retrieval and multi-hop QA. M-RAG [21] optimizes system-level performance and memory refinement via multi-partitioning and reinforcement learning. MAIN-RAG [7] significantly improves noise robustness using an unrelated multi-agent filtering mechanism. Beyond core RAG functions, specialized frameworks like ATM [22] offer adversarial tuning for manipulation resistance. Despite these advancements, most existing multi-agent RAGs primarily address textual information or feature simplistic visual integration. As discussed in Sect. 2.1, many current multi-modal RAG systems still lack dedicated mechanisms for fine-grained, iterative evidence refinement across diverse modalities, or the intricate flow control necessary for complex multi-hop inference. The M3RAG uniquely bridges this gap by combining a heterogeneous multi-agent architecture with fine-grained multi-modal evidence retrieval and a dynamic self-verification loop.

3   Method

This section presents a comprehensive overview of our proposed M3RAG framework, designed to tackle the complexities of multi-hop question answering over visually-rich, multi-document corpora. As depicted in Fig. 1, M3RAG leverages a collaborative multi-agent architecture to orchestrate a dynamic, iterative reasoning process, integrating multi-modal information extraction and a self-correcting verification mechanism.

3.1   Definition of LLM Agents in M3RAG

The M3RAG framework employs a robust multi-agent architecture with a heterogeneous design, where each agent is powered by a different type or size of model, ranging from LLMs and VLMs to smaller, more specialized models. Each agent is designed with a distinct role to facilitate complex multi-hop question answering over visually-rich, multi-document corpora. These agents collaborate in an intelligent iterative loop, as shown in Algorithm 1, to ensure systematic reasoning, precise evidence acquisition, and reliable answer generation.

Planner ($\mathcal{A}_P$). The **Planner** agent is the strategic orchestrator of the multi-hop reasoning process. It logically decomposes a complex user query Q into a series of smaller, interdependent sub-queries. This process can be described as a function that maps the input query Q to an optimized execution plan P: $\mathcal{A}_P : Q \rightarrow P$.

Seeker ($\mathcal{A}_S$). The **Seeker** agent is dedicated to the precise and robust retrieval of multi-modal evidence from the document corpus $\mathcal{D}$. Guided by a sub-query q_j from the Planner's plan, $\mathcal{A}_S$ identifies and extracts highly relevant textual or visual information. The Seeker's role can be formally represented as a function $\mathcal{A}_S$ that takes a sub-query q_j and the corpus $\mathcal{D}$ as input to produce a set of relevant evidence $\mathcal{E}_j$: $\mathcal{A}_S(q_j, \mathcal{D}) \rightarrow \mathcal{E}_j$.

Answer ($\mathcal{A}_A$). The **Answer** agent is responsible for synthesizing a coherent, concise, and accurate response to the original user query Q. Its objective is to leverage all gathered evidence from the Seeker to formulate a definitive answer A. The Answer agent's operation can be viewed as a function that combines the original query Q and the evidence pool $\mathcal{E}$ to generate a final answer A:
$\mathcal{A}_A : (Q, \mathcal{E}) \rightarrow A$.

Verifier ($\mathcal{A}_V$). The **Verifier** agent acts as the critical quality control and feedback mechanism. Its central role is to rigorously evaluate the correctness, completeness, and factual consistency of the answer generated by $\mathcal{A}_A$. This function takes the draft answer A, original query Q, and evidence pool $\mathcal{E}$ as input, and returns a confidence score C and a potential feedback signal F:
$\mathcal{A}_V : (A, Q, \mathcal{E}_{pool}) \rightarrow (C, F)$.

Algorithm 1. M3RAG Collaborative Algorithm

Require: User Query Q, Multi-modal Document Corpus $\mathcal{D}$, Maximum Iterations $MaxIter$

Ensure: Final Answer A^*

 1: **Initialize:** $P \leftarrow$ None, $iteration \leftarrow 0$, $A^* \leftarrow$ None, $F \leftarrow$ REPLAN   //Initialize feedback signal to trigger initial planning
 2: **while** $iteration < MaxIter$ **and** A^* is None **do**
 3:    **if** F is REPLAN **then**
 4:       $P_{plan} \leftarrow \mathcal{A}_P(Q)$
 5:    **else if** F is REFINE **then**
 6:       $P_{plan} \leftarrow \mathcal{A}_P(\text{Refine}, Q, \text{Signal} = F)$
 7:    **end if**   //For CONTINUE signal, P_{plan} remains unchanged, no Planner call.
 8:    $\mathcal{E} \leftarrow \emptyset$
 9:    **for** each sub-query q_j in P_{plan} **do**
10:       $\mathcal{E}_j \leftarrow \mathcal{A}_S(q_j, \mathcal{D})$
11:       $\mathcal{E} \leftarrow \mathcal{E} \cup \mathcal{E}_j$
12:    **end for**
13:    $A \leftarrow \mathcal{A}_A(Q, \mathcal{E})$ //Generate a draft answer
14:    $C, F_{next} \leftarrow \mathcal{A}_V(A, Q, \mathcal{E})$ //Verify answer and get next feedback signal
15:    **if** F_{next} is ACCEPT **then**
16:       $A^* \leftarrow A$ //Answer is satisfactory, set as final answer
17:    **end if**
18:    $F \leftarrow F_{next}$ //Update feedback signal for the next iteration
19:    $iteration \leftarrow iteration + 1$
20: **end while**
21: **Return** A^*

---

which acts as a proxy for the knowledge entropy gained in the current iteration. The process is governed by a single final confidence threshold τ_{final}. If the confidence score C_t reaches this threshold, the answer is deemed reliable and the process terminates. Otherwise, if $C_t < \tau$ but the change rate ΔC_t is high, it signifies that the current plan is still yielding valuable information, and the system proceeds with the next sub-task. Conversely, if $C_t < \tau$ and ΔC_t remains negligible for a predefined number of consecutive iterations, it indicates stagnation, and the Verifier requests the Planner to generate a new or revised plan to explore alternative reasoning paths. The entire process is also subject to a maximum number of iterations, at which point it is forcibly terminated.

4   Experiments

4.1   Experimental Setup

Datasets. We evaluate M3RAG on a comprehensive suite of seven challenging multi-modal Visual Question Answering datasets. **ArxivQA**, which focuses on scientific papers demanding reasoning across figures, tables, and dense text; **ChartQA** and **PlotQA**, comprising questions over various types of charts and plots, necessitating visual understanding and data extraction; **DocVQA**, a broad dataset covering general document understanding, including forms, invoices, and reports; **InfoVQA**, featuring documents with a strong emphasis on infographics and structured information extraction; and **SlideVQA**, containing questions derived from presentation slides, testing comprehension of structured and visual layouts. Additionally we include **ViDoSeek** [15], a recent benchmark specifically designed to evaluate RAG performance on visually rich documents requiring complex, often multi-hop, reasoning across visual elements. This diverse set ensures a thorough assessment of M3RAG's capabilities in real-world scenarios.

Evaluation Metrics. For our end-to-end evaluation, we employed a model-based assessment using GPT-4o, which involved assigning scores from 1 to 10 by comparing the reference answer with the final answer. Answers receiving scores of 7 or above were considered correct, and we subsequently calculated accuracy as the evaluation metric.

Baselines. We compare M3RAG against several RAG approaches for visually-rich documents and Text-RAG [15]. **VisRAG** [13] pioneers a vision-based RAG pipeline, directly embedding documents as images for retrieval and generation. **ViDoRAG** [15] is a multi-agent RAG framework for complex reasoning in visual documents. **VDocRAG** [9] integrates visual document understanding into RAG, enhancing retrieval and generation via joint text-visual embeddings. The **Oracle** serves as the upper bound performance, where the model responds based on the golden page.

Implementation Details. For our experiments, we utilize two powerful Vision-Language Models as our base VLMs, serving as the backbone for Seeker and Answer within M3RAG: **MiniCPM-V 2.6** [25] and **Qwen2.5-VL-7B-Instruct** [26]. The Planner and Verifier employ the LLM **Mistral-7B** [2] as backbone. All experiments are run 5 times (we report mean accuracy) on 2 NVIDIA A100 GPUs. During retrieval, we select Top-5 candidate pages [13]. For each page, we select $m=144$ visual tokens that are the most related to the query [27].

4.2   Retrieval-Augmented Generation Results

Table 1. Comprehensive evaluation of M3RAG against various baselines on multi-modal VQA datasets. Results are reported in Accuracy (%). **Oracle** represents the upper bound of performance. **Text-RAG** denotes a traditional text-based RAG approach. **Bold** entries highlight the current SOTA performance among baselines.

Methods	ArxivQA	ChartQA	DocVQA	InfoVQA	PlotQA	SlideVQA	ViDoSeek
Base VLM: MiniCPM-V 2.6							
Direct	29.10 (40.9)	31.05 (38.9)	40.58 (48.7)	35.45 (48.1)	19.86 (31.7)	24.68 (36.4)	17.69 (24.3)
Text-RAG	47.12 (66.30)	42.38 (53.07)	58.15 (69.85)	50.43 (68.47)	32.91 (52.50)	37.88 (55.93)	40.21 (55.25)
VDocRAG	67.92 (95.55)	68.55 (85.85)	74.88 (89.95)	59.90 (81.33)	49.70 (79.28)	56.95 (84.08)	61.82 (84.94)
VisRAG	67.77 (95.3)	53.97 (67.6)	70.90 (85.2)	54.46 (73.9)	38.93 (62.1)	50.72 (74.9)	49.67 (68.2)
ViDoRAG	68.80 (96.8)	69.70 (87.3)	75.65 (90.9)	60.55 (82.2)	50.64 (80.8)	57.73 (85.2)	62.58 (86.0)
Oracle	71.08 (100.0)	79.85 (100.0)	83.25 (100.0)	73.65 (100.0)	62.69 (100.0)	67.73 (100.0)	72.78 (100.0)
M3RAG	**69.23** (97.4) (↑0.6%)	**80.95** (101.4) (↑16.1%)	**80.91** (97.2) (↑6.9%)	**67.47** (91.6) (↑11.4%)	**59.49** (94.9) (↑17.5%)	**64.32** (94.9) (↑11.4%)	**67.82** (93.2) (↑8.4%)
Base VLM: Qwen2.5-VL-7B-Instruct							
Direct	30.37 (41.0)	34.30 (42.4)	44.40 (52.0)	37.87 (53.9)	21.23 (30.8)	24.78 (35.4)	19.34 (24.8)
Text-RAG	51.35 (69.30)	48.72 (60.23)	61.58 (72.19)	53.29 (75.87)	38.05 (55.22)	41.22 (58.91)	43.19 (55.44)
VDocRAG	69.15 (93.32)	69.51 (85.93)	70.87 (83.06)	62.82 (89.41)	56.88 (82.58)	58.73 (83.89)	61.47 (78.95)
VisRAG	62.97 (85.0)	56.66 (70.1)	68.98 (80.9)	54.55 (77.7)	48.05 (69.7)	52.28 (74.7)	49.67 (63.8)
ViDoRAG	69.98 (94.4)	70.20 (86.8)	71.75 (84.1)	63.45 (90.3)	57.49 (83.4)	59.38 (84.9)	62.18 (79.8)
Oracle	74.10 (100.0)	80.88 (100.0)	85.30 (100.0)	70.24 (100.0)	68.90 (100.0)	69.97 (100.0)	77.90 (100.0)
M3RAG	**70.26** (94.8) (↑0.4%)	**78.75** (97.4) (↑12.2%)	**80.06** (93.9) (↑11.6%)	**68.67** (97.8) (↑8.2%)	**64.66** (93.8) (↑12.5%)	**65.82** (94.1) (↑10.9%)	**69.36** (89.0) (↑11.6%)

As shown in Table 1,   M3RAG framework consistently achieves state-of-the-art (SOTA) performance across all tested multi-modal VQA datasets, surpassing existing single-agent RAG methods by a significant margin. This success highlights the effectiveness of our multi-agent architecture in handling the complexities of visually-rich, multi-hop question answering. The most substantial gains are observed on datasets requiring fine-grained visual reasoning, such as ChartQA, PlotQA, and ViDoSeek. This is because these datasets heavily rely on fine-grained visual information extraction and numerical reasoning, which are challenging for traditional text-based RAG and even some single-agent multi-modal approaches. The multi-agent design of M3RAG, with its specialized Seeker for multi-modal evidence retrieval and Verifier for iterative refinement, is better equipped to handle these intricate visual details and structured data. While other multi-modal baselines like ViDoRAG also show strong performance, especially on datasets with simpler document structures, they are less effective when faced with complex data integration or multi-hop reasoning. This suggests that their single-agent pipeline, while a step up from text-only methods, lacks the dynamic and collaborative problem-solving capabilities of a multi-agent system.

4.3   Analysis

Ablations. Table 2 presents the results of our ablation study, demonstrating the critical role each component plays in M3RAG's superior performance. Removing the Planner leads to a noticeable decline in accuracy, especially on datasets requiring complex multi-hop reasoning, underscoring its importance in structuring the problem-solving process. Similarly, ablating Modal Expansion results in a significant performance drop, particularly on datasets rich in visual information, highlighting its necessity for effectively leveraging non-textual content. The absence of Regional Re-reading causes the most substantial performance degradation across all datasets, confirming its foundational role in precisely extracting relevant information and filtering out noise from dense multi-modal pages. Lastly, removing the Verifier also negatively impacts accuracy, emphasizing its crucial function in iterative refinement and self-correction, which is vital for achieving the highest levels of robustness and precision. These results collectively validate that each component of M3RAG contributes significantly to its overall effectiveness in complex multi-modal document understanding.

Table 2. Ablation study of our method on MiniCPM-V 2.6 (Accuracy %)

Methods	ArxivQA	ChartQA	PlotQA	SlideVQA	ViDoSeek
M3RAG (Full)	**69.23**	**80.95**	**59.49**	**64.32**	**67.82**
w/o Planner	66.71	77.40	56.83	60.15	64.90
w/o Modal Expansion	67.05	78.12	55.97	59.28	62.47
w/o Regional Re-reading	65.34	76.58	54.26	57.41	61.03
w/o Verifier	67.89	79.03	57.62	61.75	65.34

How Do Different Evidence Types Contribute to Generation? Figure 2 illustrates the proportional contribution of various evidence types under correct and incorrect prediction scenarios. For successful answers, M3RAG primarily leverages Regional Textual (including Modality Expanded) and Regional Visual/Structured evidence, indicating its proficiency in extracting and utilizing fine-grained information. Conversely, in cases where retrieval is accurate but the answer is not, the contribution from Whole Page Context significantly increases, suggesting that an over-reliance on coarse-grained, noisy information can hinder precise reasoning. This highlights the critical role of M3RAG's refined extraction and filtering mechanisms for robust performance.

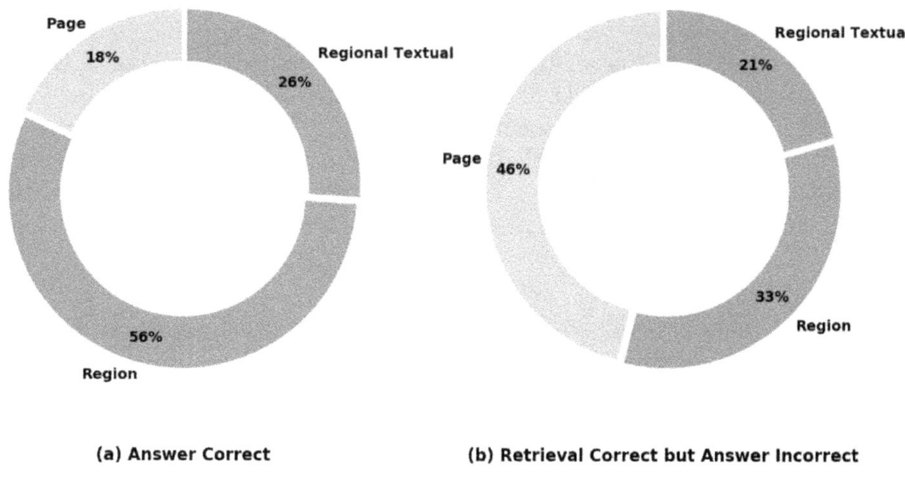

Fig. 2. Root causes of correct and incorrect predictions.

Which Types of Problems is Our Method More Suitable for Handling? Figure 3 provides a comprehensive overview of M3RAG's performance across multiple critical dimensions. M3RAG consistently demonstrates superior performance, covering a larger area on the radar chart, which signifies its strong overall capability. This qualitative advantage is particularly pronounced in crucial aspects like Multi-hop Reasoning, Multi-modal Integration, and Accuracy. The collaborative nature of our multi-agent framework allows for the systematic breakdown of complex queries, resulting in a significantly stronger performance on multi-hop reasoning tasks. Furthermore, the cross-modal hybrid matching mechanism proves instrumental in effectively fusing information from disparate sources, directly contributing to our pronounced advantage in multi-modal integration. This confirms the effectiveness of our iterative planning and cross-modal hybrid matching, enabling M3RAG to robustly tackle complex multi-hop and multi-modal information fusion tasks.

How Does Our Method Perform in Time Efficiency? Figure 4 presents a detailed analysis of the average inference latency for M3RAG and baseline methods, broken down by component. As observed, M3RAG generally requires more time compared to basic, non-agent frameworks like Direct and VisRAG. Within our multi-agent framework, the Seeker agent, responsible for extensive multi-modal retrieval, regional re-reading, and modality expansion, consistently accounts for the largest portion of the total inference time. Notably, M3RAG exhibits lower overall latency compared to other multi-agent frameworks such as ViDoRAG. Furthermore, a crucial observation is the efficiency gain achieved by the Verifier agent: when the Verifier is integrated, M3RAG's overall latency is reduced compared to the ' M3RAG w/o Verifier' variant. This counterintuitive reduction in time, despite the Verifier's own execution, is attributed to its ability

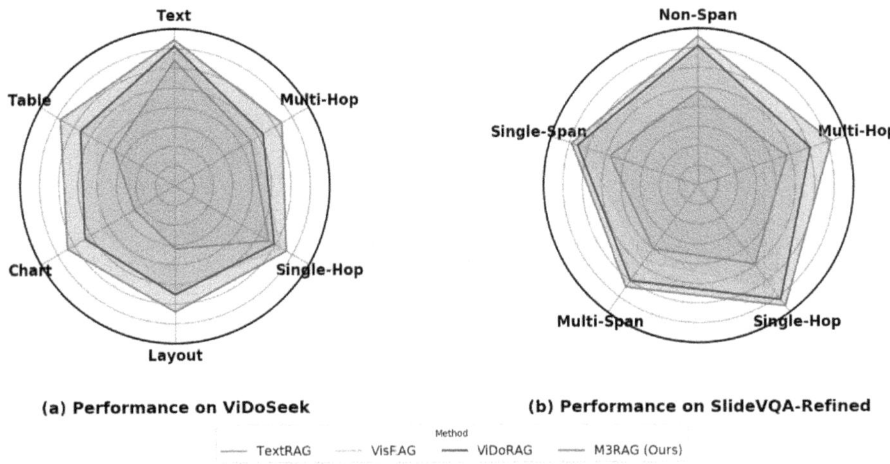

Fig. 3. Performance across different types of queries on ViDoSeek and the refined SlideVQA datasets. The outer boundary of the radar chart represents the Oracle's performance, indicating the theoretical upper bound.

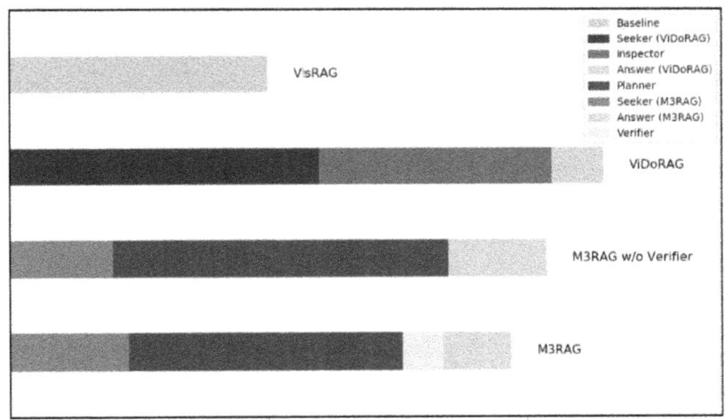

Fig. 4. Latency analysis and component breakdown of M3RAG and baselines. VisRAG serves as a reference for total time consumption.

to significantly decrease the number of unnecessary iterations, thereby leading to faster convergence to a correct answer and ultimately improving both accuracy and time efficiency.

How Does Our Method Perform Under Different Hyperparameters? Our sensitivity analysis in Fig. 5 demonstrates the balanced behavior of M3RAG under varying hyperparameter settings. For the confidence threshold τ, we found that while a low value fails to effectively verify answers, an excessively high τ causes the Verifier to repeatedly reject responses, increasing iteration counts. The necessity of a maximum iteration limit (*i.e.*, 7) to prevent infinite loops likely

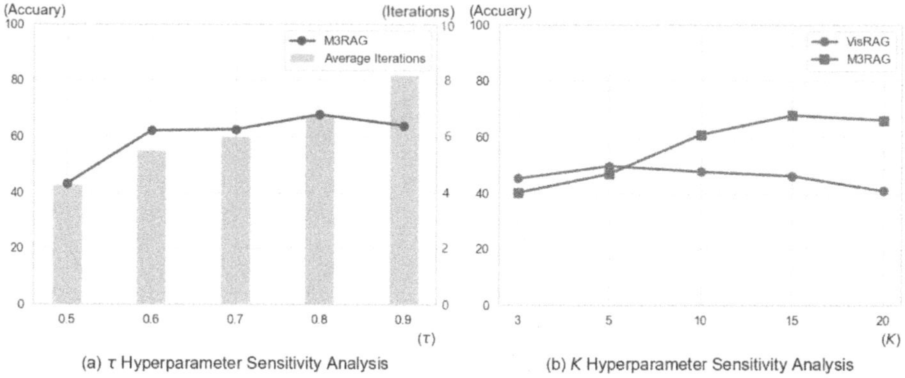

(a) τ Hyperparameter Sensitivity Analysis   (b) K Hyperparameter Sensitivity Analysis

Fig. 5. Performance under different hyperparameters on ViDoSeek.

contributes to the slight performance drop observed at the highest threshold. Regarding the number of candidate evidence patches K, our system achieves peak performance with an optimal number of patches; too few can lead to missing crucial information, while too many introduce noise. Compared to VisRAG, M3RAG's use of more fine-grained evidence necessitates and effectively utilizes a larger optimal K value.

5   Conclusion

In this paper, we present M3RAG, a novel multi-agent RAG framework for complex multi-hop question answering on visually-rich documents. Our work's core contributions include a heterogeneous multi-agent architecture that orchestrates reasoning and a dynamic iterative refinement mechanism that enables self-correction. We also introduced fine-grained multi-modal retrieval techniques to effectively process intricate visual and textual evidence. Our experiments show that M3RAG consistently outperforms existing single-agent RAG baselines, especially on datasets requiring deep visual understanding and multi-hop reasoning. The results confirm that an integrated multi-agent system provides a more robust and accurate approach to complex document understanding.

Acknowledgements. This work was supported by the Shanghai Municipal Education Commission Artificial Intelligence Plan (Z2024-119).

References

1. OpenAI: GPT-4 Technical Report. CoRR abs/2303.08774 (2023)
2. Neralla, V., de Vroe, S.B.: Evaluating Poro-34B-Chat and Mistral-7B-Instruct-v0.1: LLM system description for ELOQUENT at CLEF 2024. In: Faggioli, G., Ferro, N., Galuscáková, P., de Herrera, A.G.S. (eds.) CLEF. vol. 3740, pp. 708–711 (2024)

3. Elhady, A., Agirre, E., Artetxe, M.: Emergent abilities of large language models under continued pre-training for language adaptation. In: Che, W., Nabende, J., Shutova, E., Pilehvar, M.T. (eds.) ACL, pp. 32174–32186 (2025)
4. Shi, W., et al.: In-Context pretraining: language modeling beyond document boundaries. In: ICLR (2024)
5. Mallen, A., Asai, A., Zhong, V., Das, R., Khashabi, D., Hajishirzi, H.: When not to trust language models: investigating effectiveness of parametric and non-parametric memories. In: ACL, pp. 9802–9822 (2023)
6. Yang, D., et al.: IM-RAG: multi-round retrieval-augmented generation through learning inner monologues. In: SIGIR, pp. 730–740 (2024)
7. Chang, C., et al.: MAIN-RAG: multi-agent filtering retrieval-augmented generation. In: ACL, pp. 2607–2622 (2025)
8. Cheng, R., et al.: DualRAG: a dual-process approach to integrate reasoning and retrieval for multi-hop question answering. In: ACL, pp. 31877–31899 (2025)
9. Tanaka, R., Iki, T., Hasegawa, T., Nishida, K., Saito, K., Suzuki, J.: VDocRAG: retrieval-augmented generation over visually-rich documents. In: CVPR, pp. 24827–24837 (2025)
10. Shi, Z., et al.: Generate-then-ground in retrieval-augmented generation for multi-hop question answering. In: ACL pp. 7339–7353 (2024)
11. Maekawa, S., Iso, H., Gurajada, S., Bhutani, N.: Retrieval helps or hurts? a deeper dive into the efficacy of retrieval augmentation to language models. In: NAACL, pp. 5506–5521 (2024)
12. Ma, X., Lin, S., Li, M., Chen, W., Lin, J.: Unifying multimodal retrieval via document screenshot embedding. In: EMNLP, pp. 6492–6505 (2024)
13. Yu, S., et al.: VisRAG: vision-based retrieval-augmented generation on multi-modality documents. In: ICLR (2025)
14. Faysse, M., et al.: Colpali: efficient document retrieval with vision language models. In: ICLR (2025)
15. Wang, Q., et al.: ViDoRAG: visual document retrieval-augmented generation via dynamic iterative reasoning agents. CoRR (2025)
16. Cho, J., Mahata, D., Irsoy, O., He, Y., Bansal, M.: M3DocRAG: multi-modal retrieval is what you need for multi-page multi-document understanding. CoRR (2024)
17. Ma, X., Zhuang, S., Koopman, B., Zuccon, G., Chen, W., Lin, J.: VISA: retrieval augmented generation with visual source attribution. In: Che, W., Nabende, J., Shutova, E., Pilehvar, M.T. (eds.) ACL, pp. 30154–30169 (2025)
18. Peigné, P., et al.: Multi-Agent security tax: trading off security and collaboration capabilities in multi-agent systems. In: AAAI-25, pp. 27573–27581 (2025)
19. Liu, Y., Cao, J., Li, Z., He, R., Tan, T.: Breaking mental set to improve reasoning through diverse multi-agent debate. In: ICLR (2025)
20. Nguyen, T., Chin, P., Tai, Y.: MA-RAG: multi-agent retrieval-augmented generation via collaborative chain-of-thought reasoning. CoRR abs/2505.20096 (2025)
21. Wang, Z., Teo, S.X., Ouyang, J., Xu, Y., Shi, W.: M-RAG: reinforcing large language model performance through retrieval-augmented generation with multiple partitions. In: Ku, L., Martins, A., Srikumar, V. (eds.) ACL, pp. 1966–1978 (2024)
22. Zhu, J., Yan, L., Shi, H., Yin, D., Sha, L.: ATM: adversarial tuning multi-agent system makes a robust retrieval-augmented generator. In: EMNLP, pp. 10902–10919 (2024)
23. Zhang, N., et al.: SiReRAG: indexing similar and related information for multihop reasoning. In: ICLR (2025)

24. Li, A., Xie, Y., Li, S., Tsung, F., Ding, B., Li, Y.: Agent-oriented planning in multi-agent systems. In: ICLR (2025)
25. Liu, Z., et al.: Benchmarking retrieval-augmented generation in multi-modal contexts. CoRR abs/2502.17297 (2025)
26. Bai, S., et al.: Qwen2.5-VL technical report. CoRR abs/2502.13923 (2025)
27. Qi, J., et al.: RoRA-VLM: robust retrieval-augmented vision language models. CoRR (2024)

Illumination-Prior Guided Hybrid Network for Low-Light Image Enhancement

Ao Sun, Shijie Hao[⊠], and Yanrong Guo

Hefei University of Technology, Hefei, China
`hfut.hsj@gmail.com`

Abstract. Low-light images often suffer from multiple intertwined degradation factors, leading to poor visual quality. Although recent low-light image enhancement (LLIE) models have achieved notable progress, they still face challenges in effectively disentangling these factors while balancing enhancement accuracy and computational efficiency. In this work, we propose an illumination-prior guided hybrid network that integrates the strengths of global feature extraction (Transformer and Mamba) and local feature extraction (CNN). To facilitate effective feature fusion, we exploit illumination priors directly derived from the input images through a brightness-aware dynamic gating mechanism. Along the main encoder – decoder pathway, a dynamic window strategy is employed to preserve multi-scale perception while keeping the model size compact. Furthermore, a wavelet-based refinement module is introduced to separately restore high-frequency textures and low-frequency illumination, further improving the final output quality. Extensive experiments on multiple LLIE benchmarks demonstrate that our method outperforms SOTA methods in enhancing performance with acceptable computational costs. Ablation studies further confirm the effectiveness of each key component.

Keywords: Low-light image enhancement · Global and local features · Illumination guidance · Wavelet representation

1 Introduction

Low-light images often suffer from multiple intertwined degradations, including global factors like insufficient illumination and color shifts, and local factors such as noise and loss of fine details. Low-light image enhancement (LLIE) aims to improve visibility while preserving the visual naturalness under these challenging conditions [1]. However, two key challenges remain: (1) effectively disentangling and correcting multiple degradation factors in a unified framework, and (2) achieving a favorable balance between enhancement quality and computational efficiency. These challenges in LLIE ultimately degrade the performance of downstream tasks, including object detection and semantic segmentation, which are crucial for critical applications like assisted driving and security monitoring.

J. Lokoč et al. (Eds.): MMM 2026, LNCS 16412, pp. 379–393, 2026.
https://doi.org/10.1007/978-981-95-6950-2_27

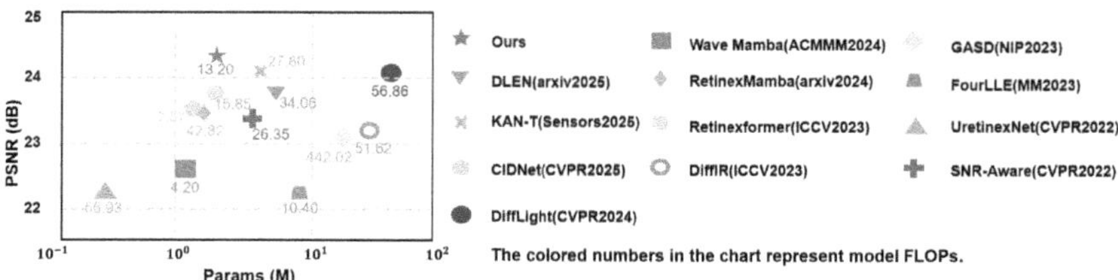

Fig. 1. Comparison between 12 SOTA LLIE models and ours on the LOLv1 dataset. Our model achieves the best PSNR with acceptable computational costs.

In the deep learning era, CNN-based learning methods [1] have demonstrated strong capability in local texture restoration and noise suppression, yet their limited receptive field hampers the modeling of long-range illumination dependencies. Transformer-based architectures [2,3] address this issue by modeling global context, achieving notable gains in structure preservation, but incur high computational costs and may sacrifice local detail fidelity. Recent state-space models such as Mamba [4,5] provide an alternative for long-range modeling with linear complexity, showing great potential for LLIE. Apart from the above concerns, current frameworks often overlook a key point: valuable information can be easily extracted from low-light inputs. For example, the intrinsic illumination distribution could be leveraged as guidance for feature fusion.

In our research, we argue that two aspects are crucial for advancing LLIE: (1) a hybrid architecture that jointly exploits complementary global and local representations, which is inherently suited to solve the global and local degradation factors in low-light images; (2) explicit guidance from scene-specific illumination priors to modulate feature extraction and fusion, as such priors are naturally embedded in the input dark images and should be fully leveraged. Motivated by this, we propose an illumination-prior guided hybrid network that integrates CNN, Mamba, and dynamic window attention into a compact encoder – decoder framework, coupled with a wavelet-based refinement module for frequency-aware enhancement. Rather than a generic post-processing step, this refinement operates on an intermediate result already aligned in illumination and structure, enabling targeted frequency-domain corrections. Extensive experiments on two public LLIE datasets demonstrate that our method achieves state-of-the-art (SOTA) performance with reasonable computational overhead, and ablation studies validate the effectiveness of each key component.

The technical contributions of this work are summarized as follows:

- Feature Fusion with Illumination Prior Guidance: We design a brightness-aware dynamic gating mechanism that adaptively integrates local and global features according to scene-specific illumination cues.
- Hybrid Network Architecture: We integrate CNN, Mamba, and dynamic window attention into a unified framework to effectively capture complementary local and global representations while maintaining computational efficiency.

– Wavelet-Based Refinement: We introduce a multi-frequency refinement module that leverages a hybrid CNN – Mamba structure to enhance high-frequency textures while preserving low-frequency illumination consistency.

2   Related Works

Hybrid Architecture Design. To overcome the limitations of single-architecture models, recent works have begun to explore hybrid architectures that combine their complementary strengths. CNN-Transformer hybrids like MAXIM [6] and WHANet [7] combine convolutional inductive bias with attention-driven global modeling. Other kinds of hybrid architectures have also been proposed in different vision tasks, such as CNN-Mamba for video understanding [8] and MambaTransformer for detection and segmentation [9]. These attempts of using hybrid architectures consistently demonstrate promising results on their tasks. Following this trend, we further extend the architecture synergy by incorporating CNN, Transformer and Mamba to build the LLIE model.

Dynamic Gating Mechanism. Dynamic feature fusion is critical in multi-branch networks. Gated Linear Units (GLUs), introduced in language modeling, have been adapted for vision tasks (e.g., GLA-Net [10]) to control feature flow between parallel pathways. Recent low-level vision tasks, such as DarkIR [11] and Retinexformer [12], employ gating mechanisms to fuse illumination and reflectance features. However, existing gating strategies either focus on single dimensions (spatial or channel) or rely on fixed rates. To address this issue, our model leverages illumination priors to guide feature fusion, dynamically adjusting weights between CNN and Mamba branches, ensuring brighter regions receive more local refinement while darker areas prioritize global correction.

Utilizing Frequency Information in Low-level Vision. The effective utilization of frequency-based image representations has significantly advanced research in deep learning-based low-level vision tasks [7,13]. As for LLIE, Li et al. [14] designed a dedicated branch for learning the adjustment from dark images to bright images based Fourier transform. Due to the advantages in spatial-frequency localization and multi-resolution analysis, wavelet is also adopted as an effective frequency tool during LLIE model construction [15,16]. As for our research, our model explicitly decomposes the image into frequency bands: low-frequency (illumination-dominated) components are processed by Mamba, and high-frequency (texture-dominated) details are enhanced by CNN, achieving illumination robustness and texture richness.

3   Method

Figure 2 presents the overview of our hybrid network architecture tailored for LLIE. **In the fist stage**, Dual Gated Extractor extracts initial features for the

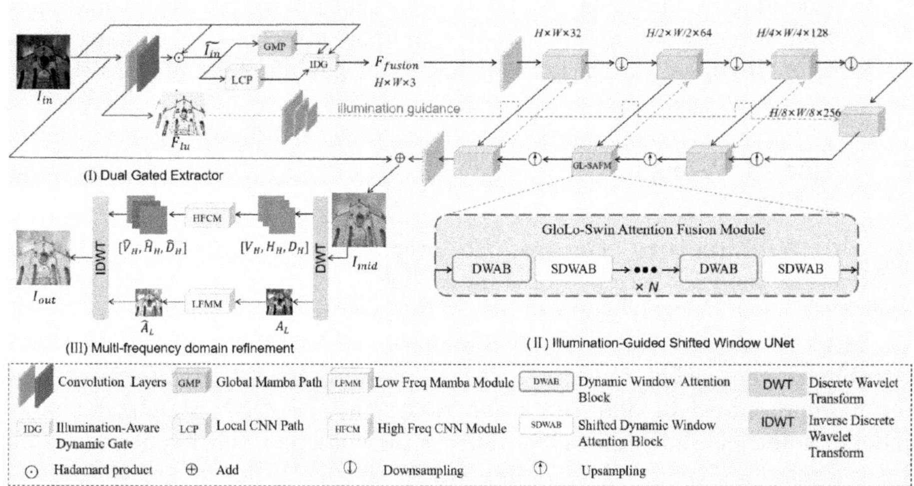

Fig. 2. Overview of the proposed illumination-prior guided hybrid network, which comprises three stages—illumination prior extraction, illumination-guided enhancement, and wavelet-based refinement. Notably, the illumination priors derived from I_{in} are fully utilized to gate fusion (IDG in Stage 1) and modulate attention (GL-SAFM in Stage 2).

following enhancement. It decomposes the input I_{in} into complementary global and local features via parallel Global Mamba Path (GMP) and Local CNN path (LCP), and dynamically fuses them by the Illumination-aware Dynamic Gating (IDG) block. In addition, the illumination prior F_{lu} is directly extracted from I_{in} for guiding the following enhancing process. **In the second stage**, Illumination-Guided Shifted Window UNet is the primary component for improving the visual quality of low-light images. The encoder-decoder structure takes F_{fusion} obtained by IDG as inputs, and produces the intermediate enhancement I_{mid} as output. We design GloLo-Swin Attention Fusion Module (GL-SAFM) for each block along the encoder and decoder, in which F_{lu} serve as illumination guidance of each GL-SAFM. **In the third stage**, Multi-Frequency Domain Refinement further enhances I_{mid}. It decomposes the intermediate result I_{mid} into low/high-frequency components, then adopts a dual-path Mamba/CNN structure for further refining I_{mid} in the multi-frequency domain.

3.1 Dual Gated Extractor

As shown in Fig. 3, the proposed dual-path architecture combines the strengths of global modeling from Mamba and local perception from CNN, with adaptive feature fusion guided by illumination characteristics.

Global Mamba Path (GMP). This path leverages the long-range dependency modeling capability of state space models (SSMs) to construct useful global

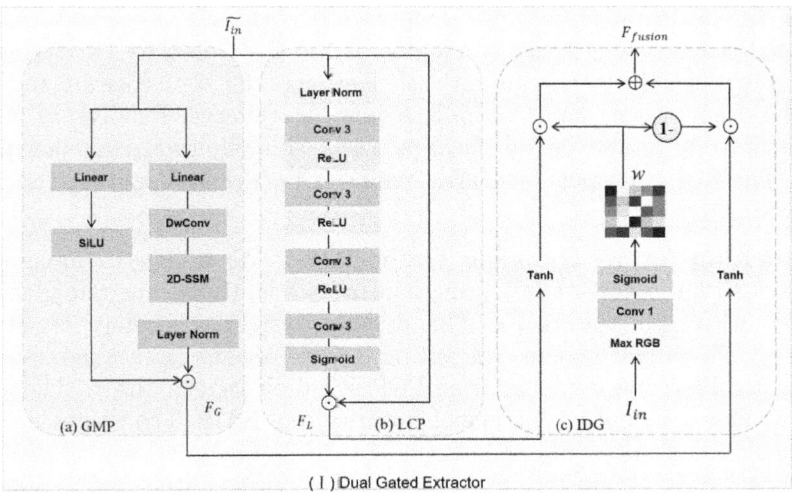

Fig. 3. The architecture of Dual Gated Extractor.

representations. The process of extracting global features is modeled as follows:

$$F_G = LN(SSM(Dc'LN(\widetilde{I_{in}}))) \odot SiLU(LN(\widetilde{I_{in}})) \tag{1}$$

In the equation, $\widetilde{I_{in}}$ is the pre-processed input image, and LN denotes layer-norm, Dc denotes the depth-convolution, $SiLU$ indicates the activation function, F_G is the global feature extracted from the images and SSM is the 2D-Selective Scan Module.

2D-Selective Scan Module. As the key module in GMP, Selective Scan Module (SSM) utilizes sequential inference methods to model long-range dependencies in input. Following [17], we employ a 2D-Selective Scan Module (2D-SSM). Firstly, it flattens the 2D-image feature into 1D-sequences with scanning along four different directions. Subsequently, the long-range dependencies of the sequence are captured according to the discrete state-space equation:

$$\bar{\alpha} = exp(\Delta\alpha) \tag{2}$$

$$\bar{\beta} = (\Delta\alpha)^{-1}(exp(\alpha) - M) \cdot \Delta\beta \tag{3}$$

$$h_t = \bar{\alpha}h_{t-1} + \bar{\beta}x_t \tag{4}$$

$$y_t = \gamma h_t + \mu x_t \tag{5}$$

where x is the input variable, y is the output. Δ denotes the timescale parameter to transform the continuous parameters α, β to discrete parameters $\bar{\alpha}, \bar{\beta}$. $(\Delta\alpha)^{-1}$ is the inverse matrix of $\Delta\alpha$. α, β, γ, μ are all learnable parameters and M is an identity matrix. Finally, four sequence features are merged for regressing back to the original 2D-spatial feature map.

Local CNN Path (LCP). A compact CNN cascade with stacked ReLU-activated convolutional layers is adopted as the CNN path for extracting fine-grained textures. Along this path, the shallow layers focus on edge enhancement, and the deeper layers aim to suppress noise interference. Finally, the sigmoid gate adaptively retains critical local patterns while filtering redundant activations. The LCP's output F_L places emphasis on the local patterns of image appearance.

Illumination-Aware Dynamic Gate (IDG). We design an illumination-aware gated linear feature fusion mechanism to adaptively integrate global feature F_G with local feature F_L. This dynamic weighting strategy is shown in Fig. 3 (c). For bright regions, the gating module assigns large weights for preserving local features extracted from LCP. For dark regions, the module assigns large weights for emphasizing global features from GMP. The weight map w is obtained through $w = Sigmoid(Conv(MaxRGB(I_{in})))$. w can be seen as an self-evident prior obtained from I_{in}. The fusion can be formulated as follows:

$$F_{fusion} = w \odot Tanh(F_L) + (1 - w) \odot Tanh(F_G) \tag{6}$$

where $\odot$ is the element-wise product, and $Tanh()$ is the activation function. This image-adaptive feature fusion enables the model to dynamically combine the strengths of global and local features, providing a more comprehensive and context-aware representation of the image for subsequent enhancement stages.

3.2 Illumination-Guided Shifted Window UNet

In the second stage of our framework, we adopt a U-shaped encoder – decoder as the central pathway of the hybrid architecture. Each resolution level contains a GloLo-Swin Attention Fusion Module (GL-SAFM), which integrates global – local representations through stacked pairs of Dynamic Window Attention Blocks (DWAB) and Shifted Dynamic Window Attention Blocks (SDWAB), as illustrated in Fig. 4. This design of DWAB and SDWAB is inspired by the Swin Transformer but adapted to the low-light enhancement task through two key modifications.

First, at the beginning of each GL-SAFM, the initial DWAB receives two inputs: the feature map F_{in} from the preceding layer and an illumination-prior feature map F_{lu}. The latter is derived from the input image and adaptively resized to match the current resolution stage, providing explicit brightness cues to guide feature modulation. Second, both DWAB and SDWAB employ dynamic window mechanism. Unlike global attention, which has full spatial coverage but high computational costs, or fixed small-window attention, which reduces costs at the expense of contextual range, our approach adopts an intermediate setting where attention windows are defined at $1/K$ of the spatial resolution. This strikes a balance between efficiency and the ability to capture sufficient contextual information, which is crucial for correcting illumination while preserving details in low-light images. K was empirically set as 5 in our experiments. From Fig. 1, our model obtains satisfying PSNR with an acceptable model size.

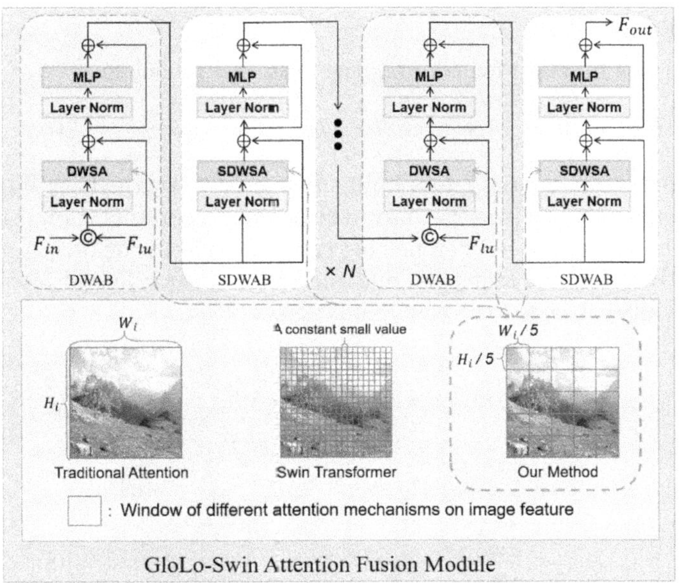

Fig. 4. The architecture of the GloLo-Swin Attention Fusion Module (GL-SAFM) and the differences between the dynamic window attention in our method and the previous attention mechanisms.

3.3 Multi-frequency Domain Refinement

Applying wavelet decomposition directly to raw low-light inputs would require learning a full illumination – texture mapping [15,16], which is a highly ill-posed challenging task. Differently, starting from I_{mid}, in which most illumination bias is already corrected and local distortions partly recovered, allows the refinement to focus on residual frequency-specific inconsistencies. Motivated by this, in the third stage of our model, we first decompose I_{mid} into high and low frequency components with Discrete Wavelet Transform (DWT). Among them, the high frequency components (V_H, H_H, D_H) represent the local detail in vertical, horizontal and diagonal directions. The low-frequency component (A_L) carries the global structural information and semantic content, and provides the basic spatial composition framework and scene context representation of I_{mid}. Based on this multi-frequency representation, we introduce the divide-and-conquer strategy for refining I_{mid}. As the obtained high-frequency components and low-frequency bands can be seen as local and global image features, we design global-local dual paths composed of Low Frequency Mamba Module (LFMM) and High Frequency CNN Module (HFCM), as shown in Fig. 5. The outputs of these two paths $\hat{A}_L$, $\hat{V}_H$, $\hat{H}_H$, and $\hat{D}_H$ are merged into the final output I_{out} with Inverse Discrete Wavelet Transform (IDWT). The proposed hybrid architecture leverages the complementary strengths of Mamba and CNN, where each path is dedicated to processing either global or local image features effectively.

3.4   Loss Function

The overall loss function for training the proposed model is:

$$\mathcal{L} = ||I_{out} - I_G||_1 + \lambda(||\hat{A_L} - A_{LG}||_1 + ||\hat{V_H} - V_{HG}||_1 + ||\hat{H_H} - H_{HG}||_1 + ||\hat{D_H} - D_{HG}||_1) \quad (7)$$

The first loss term is an $L1$ loss built upon ground truth (GT) image I_G and enhanced image I_{out}. Since we introduce wavelet representation, the rest loss terms aim to measure the difference between multiple bands of I_{out} and I_G. λ is the weight between the first term and the rest frequency-based loss terms, and was empirically set as 0.3 through validation.

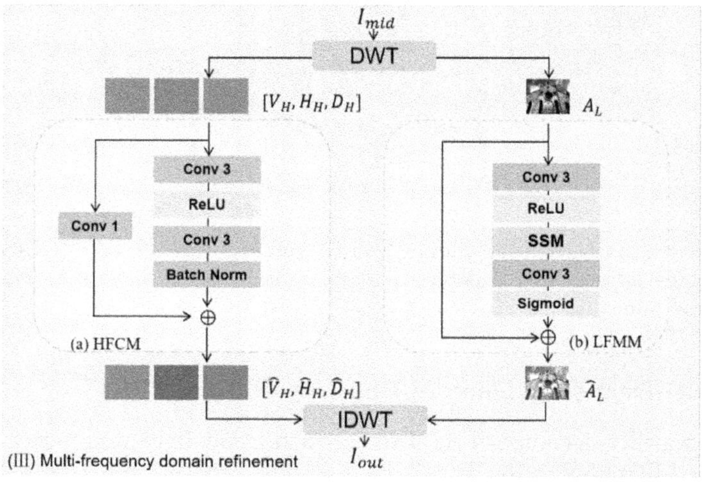

Fig. 5. The architecture of the multi-frequency domain refinement.

4   Experiment

4.1   Experiment Settings

We evaluated our method on LOLv1 [18] and LOLv2 [19]. We employed PSNR ($\uparrow$) and SSIM ($\uparrow$) as evaluation metrics. To further assess generalization performance, we conducted experiments on several public unpaired images from LIME [20], DICM [21], NPE [22], VV [23] and MEF [24], collectively referred to as Unpaired Set. We utilized NIQE ($\downarrow$) and PIQE ($\downarrow$) as evaluation metrics. We compared our model with 12 SOTA supervised LLIE methods, which employ diverse kinds of backbones (e.g., CNN, transformer, Mamba and their mixture).

Table 1. Quantitative comparisons on LOL-v1, LOLv2 and Unpaired Set. Best and second best results are highlighted in red and blue respectively. *Note:* Params are in millions (M), and FLOPs are in billions (G).

Methods	Type/Params/FLOPs	LOLv1		LOLv2-real		LOLv2-syn		Unpaired Set	
		PSNR ↑	SSIM ↑	PSNR ↑	SSIM ↑	PSNR ↑	SSIM ↑	NIQE ↓	PIQE ↓
SNR-Aware[25]	Transformer/4.1/26.35	23.31	0.842	21.48	0.848	24.13	0.927	4.71	24.82
URetinexNet[26]	CNN/0.34/56.93	22.33	0.835	21.54	0.838	24.23	0.897	6.19	30.10
FourLLIE[27]	CNN/7.9/10.4	22.34	0.846	22.34	0.846	24.65	0.912	4.86	35.37
GSAD[28]	Diffusion/17.43/442.02	23.23	0.852	20.19	0.847	24.22	0.927	3.66	34.75
DiffIR[29]	Diffusion/26.63/51.5	23.15	0.828	21.15	0.816	24.76	0.921	5.72	26.41
Retinexformer[retinexformer]	Transformer/2.67/15.85	23.87	0.838	23.92	0.839	25.13	0.942	4.75	26.82
RetinexMamba[30]	Mamba/1.96/42.82	23.46	0.901	22.73	0.829	25.39	0.943	4.03	31.80
Wave-Mamba[15]	Mamba/1.48/4.2	22.71	0.822	22.20	0.871	25.39	0.922	4.25	29.68
DiffLight[31]	Diffusion/36.2/56.86	24.05	0.876	22.87	0.871	25.39	0.922	3.89	30.17
CIDNet[32]	Hybrid/1.88/7.57	23.50	0.857	22.43	0.862	25.70	0.945	4.11	26.88
KAN-T[33]	Transformer/4.11/24.80	24.18	0.902	23.09	0.900	26.32	0.942	3.90	25.65
DLEN[34]	Transformer/6.97/31.06	23.94	0.841	23.13	0.854	26.26	0.937	3.73	24.17
Ours	Hybrid/3.74/13.2	24.47	0.910	23.34	0.907	26.75	0.964	3.55	23.44

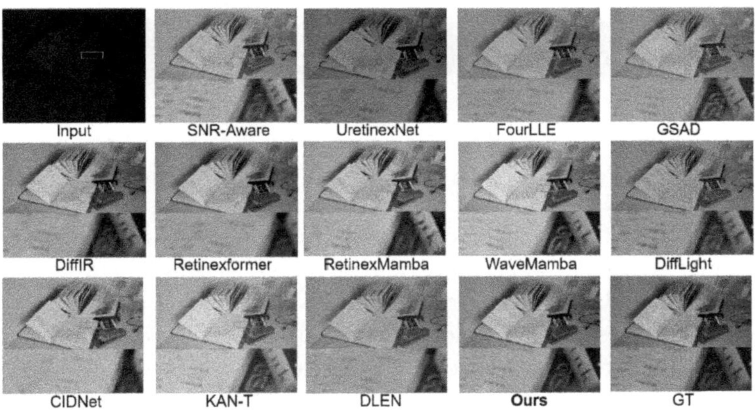

Fig. 6. Visual comparison on an image from LOLv1. Better with an enlarged view and the same for the rest figures. *Note*: GT means the ground truth normal-light image.

4.2   Comparison with Other LLIE Methods

Table 1 presents the quantitative results on LOLv1, LOLv2-real, LOLv2-syn, and Unpaired Set. Our method achieves the best enhancing performance across all datasets, while its computational costs remain at an acceptable level among all its competitors. On LOLv1, the proposed network surpasses the strongest competing Transformer-based method (KAN-T) by +0.29 dB in PSNR and +0.008 in SSIM, while maintaining a smaller model size. For LOLv2-real, our method improves PSNR by +0.25 dB and SSIM by +0.008 over the second best model. On the synthetic LOLv2-syn set, our approach achieves 26.75 dB PSNR and 0.964 SSIM, outperforming all comparison methods. These results empirically validate the effectiveness of our model in faithfully restoring scene illumination and structures. Moreover, on Unpaired Set, our method attains the lowest NIQE (3.55) and PIQE (23.44), showing its stronger capability of cross-dataset generalization than other methods with various network architectures.

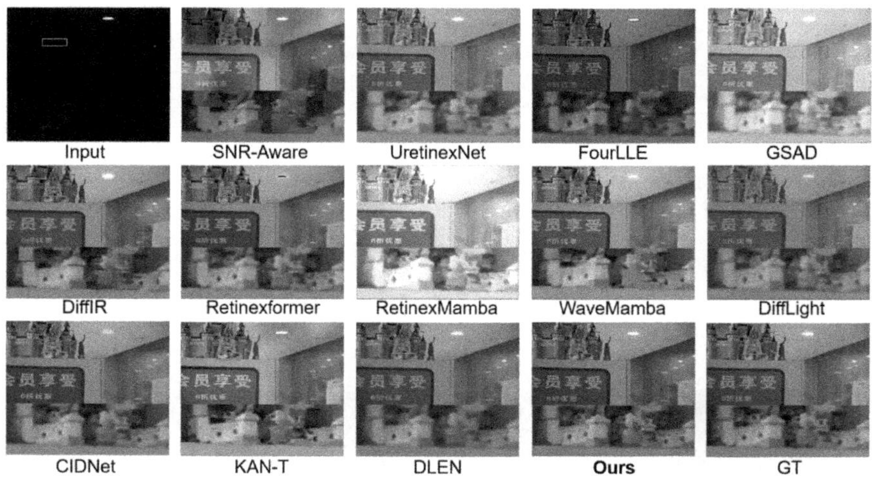

Fig. 7. Visual comparison on an image from LOLv2-real.

Figures 6, 7 and 8 further corroborate the quantitative comparisons. For example, in Fig. 6 (LOLv1), competing methods such as CIDNet and DLEN improve brightness but tend to produce color shifts or local distortions, whereas our method restores natural colors and suppresses noise effectively. In Fig. 7 (LOLv2-real), the results of this challenging case with mixed lighting show that our model maintains balanced brightness across the scene, avoids overexposure in bright regions, and recovers subtle texture variations in shaded areas. Figure 8 shows that our model has the best performance in terms of preserving naturalness and avoiding artifact. The quantitative and visual comparisons empirically validate the effectiveness and superiority of our proposed illumination-prior guided hybrid network.

4.3   Ablation Study

To investigate the contribution of each key component, we conducted a series of ablation experiments on the LOLv1 dataset. We first investigated the impact of the illumination-prior guided gating (IDG), and the multi-frequency domain refinement. As shown in the following subsections, removing or altering these modules consistently degrades both fidelity and perceptual metrics, confirming that each is essential to the overall performance. Finally, we study the influence of DWAB/SDWAB number in each GL-SAFM module, revealing the performance-complexity trade-off of our model.

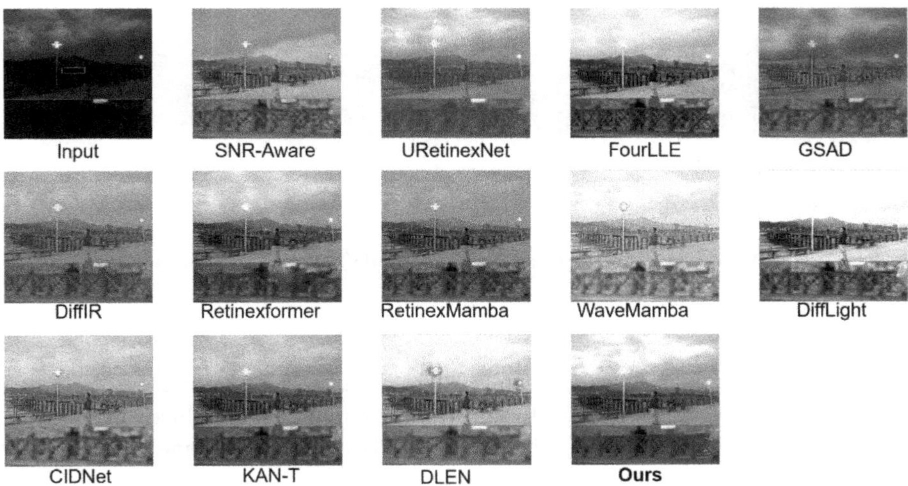

Fig. 8. Visual comparison on an image from Unpaired Set.

Effectiveness of IDG. In Table 2, Setting 1 (w/o Mamba Path) excludes GMP from the model. Setting 2 (w/o CNN Path) excludes LCP. Setting 3 (w/o IDG) removes IDG and directly adds the two paths' outputs. Setting 3 exhibits the most significant performance degradation, emphasizing the crucial role of illumination-guided fusion. The comparison between Setting 4 and Setting 1&2 show that the reasonable fusion of global and local features achieves better enhancing performance than the independent deployment of Mamba or CNN. Figure 9 presents a typical visual example. The result based on w/o CNN Path has some local appearance distortion, and the one based on w/o Mamba Path has some color and illumination distortions. The result based on w/o IDG demonstrates a notable overall discrepancy from GT. From Table 2, the Params and FLOPs results show that these ablated blocks have low computationcal costs.

Fig. 9. A visual example of the ablation study.

Effectiveness of Multi-frequency Domain Refinement. To further clarify the contribution of the third stage of our model, we entirely removed the multi-frequency domain refinement module, and degenerated the loss function

Fig. 10. A visual example of the effects for multi-frequency domain refinement.

into $\mathcal{L} = ||I_{mid} - I_G||_1$. As for the result, this intermediate version of our model (w/o Wavelet refinement) shows drops in PSNR and SSIM from 24.47 and 0.910 to 23.87 and 0.902, respectively. In addition, the model size reduces from 3.74M to 3.32M, showing the lightweight characteristic of this refinement module. In Fig. 10, compared with the result based on w/o Wavelet refinement, Full Model further avoids the subtle artifacts such as texture blurring and color offset in its counterpart. These observations show that, on one hand, the first two stages have already produced acceptable performance. On the other hand, more importantly, the comparisons demonstrate the usefulness of further improving the enhancement with CNN-Mamba based module in wavelet domain.

Table 2. Ablation studies of effects for different Dual Gated Extractor designs

	Model Configuration	PSNR ↑	SSIM ↑	Params ↓	FLOPs ↓
Setting 1	w/o Mamba Path	23.47	0.882	3.50 M	12.8 G
Setting 2	w/o CNN Path	23.72	0.892	3.55 M	12.9 G
Setting 3	w/o IDG	22.95	0.838	3.69 M	13.1 G
Setting 4	Full Model	24.47	0.910	3.74 M	13.2 G

Table 3. Results using different numbers of DWAB/SDWAB in each GL-SAFM.

numbers	PSNR↑	SSIM↑	Params↓	FLOPs↓
$N=1$	23.35	0.866	2.43 M	9.2 G
$N=2$	23.91	0.900	2.81 M	11.6 G
$N=3$	24.47	0.910	3.74 M	13.2 G
$N=4$	24.40	0.911	4.55 M	18.7 G

Impact of DWAB/SDWAB Number. In our model, each GL-SAFM incorporates a stack of N DWAB/SDWAB pairs. We investigate the impact of the hyper-parameter N, with the results summarized in Table 3. The results indicate that performance generally improves as N increases. However, a larger N also leads to a substantial increase in model parameters . The choice of $N = 3$ was empirically determined to strike a balance between performance gains and computational efficiency.

5 Conclusion

We proposed an illumination-prior guided hybrid network for low-light image enhancement, combining CNN, Mamba, and dynamic window attention to incorporate complementary local and global features. In our model, the illumination priors extracted from input images themselves are fully utilized to guide the initial feature fusion and the following feature learning. The wavelet-based refinement based on hybrid networks further improves visual quality of enhancing results. Experiments on multiple benchmarks show that our model has superior performance with acceptable computational costs. Looking ahead, we plan to explore more general forms of scene-dependent priors and extend the framework toward handling diverse illumination patterns with less computational costs.

Acknowledgement. This work was supported by the National Natural Science Foundation of China under Grant No. 62172137.

References

1. Li, C., et al.: Low-light image and video enhancement using deep learning: a survey. IEEE TPAMI, **44**(12), 9396–9416 (2022)
2. Dosovitskiy, A., et al.: An image is worth 16x16 words: transformers for image recognition at scale. In: Proceedings of ICLR (2021)
3. Liu, Z., et al.: Swin transformer: hierarchical vision transformer using shifted windows. In: Proceedings of ICCV, pages 10012–10022 (2021)
4. Gu, A., Dao, T.: Mamba: Linear-time sequence modeling with selective state spaces. arXiv preprint arXiv:2312.00752 (2023)
5. Liu, Y., et al.: Vmamba: visual state space model. In: Proceedings of NeuIPS (2024)
6. Tu, Z., et al.: Maxim: Multi-axis MLP for image processing. In: Proceedings of CVPR, pages 5769–5780 (2022)
7. Wang, N., Mei, S., Wang, Y., Zhang, Y., Zhan, D.: Whanet:wavelet-based hybrid asymmetric network for spectral super-resolution from RGB inputs. IEEE TMM **27**, 414–428 (2025)
8. Li, K., et al.: Videomamba: state space model for efficient video understanding. In: Proceedings of ECCV, pages 237–255 (2024)
9. Hatamizadeh, A., Kautz, J.: Mambavision: a hybrid mamba-transformer vision backbone. In: Proceedings of CVPR (2025)
10. Xi, X., Jianqiang Li, Yu., Guan, L Z., Zhao, Q., Zhang, L., Li, L.: Gla-net: a global-local attention network for automatic cataract classification. J. Biomed. Inform. **124**, 103939 (2021)

11. Feijoo, D., Benito, J.C., Garcia, A., Conde, M.V.: Darkir: robust low-light image restoration. In: Proceedings of the CVPR, pages 10879–10889 (2025)
12. Cai, Y., Bian, H., Lin, J., Wang, H., Timofte, R., Zhang, Y.: Retinexformer: one-stage retinex-based transformer for low-light image enhancement. In: Proceedings of ICCV, pages 12504–12513 (2023)
13. Zhang, J., et al.: Pan-sharpening with wavelet-enhanced high-frequency information. IEEE TGRS **62**, 1–14 (2024)
14. Li, C.,et al.: Embedding Fourier for ultra-high-definition low-light image enhancement. In: Proceedings of ICLR (2023)
15. Shang, K., Shao, M., Wang, C., Tan, X.: Waveletmamba: wavelet-based state space model for low light image enhancement. Displays, page 103100 (2025)
16. Zou, W., Gao, H., Yang, W., Liu, T.: Wave-mamba: wavelet state space model for ultra-high-definition low-light image enhancement. In: Proceedings of ACM Multimedia (2024)
17. Guo, H., Li, J., Dai, T., Ouyang, Z., Ren, X., Xia, S.-T.: Mambair: a simple baseline for image restoration with state-space model. In: Proceedings of ECCV, pages 222–241 (2024)
18. Wei, C., Wang, W., Yang, W., Liu, J.: Deep RETINEX decomposition for low-light enhancement. In: Proceedings of BMVC (2018)
19. Yang, W., Wang, W., Huang, H., Wang, S., Liu, J.: Sparse gradient regularized deep RETINEX network for robust low-light image enhancement. IEEE TIP **30**, 2072–2086 (2021)
20. Guo, X.: Lime: a method for low-light image enhancement. In: Proceedings of ACM Multimedia, pages 87–91 (2016)
21. Lee, C., Lee, C., Kim, C.-S.: Contrast enhancement based on layered difference representation of 2D histograms. IEEE TIP **22**(12), 5372–5384 (2013)
22. Wang, S., Zheng, J., Hai-Miao, H., Li, B.: Naturalness preserved enhancement algorithm for non-uniform illumination images. IEEE TIP **22**(9), 3538–3548 (2013)
23. Vonikakis, V., Kouskouridas, R., Gasteratos, A.: On the evaluation of illumination compensation algorithms. Multimedia Tools Appl. **77**, 9211–9231 (2018)
24. Ma, K., Zeng, K., Wang, Z.: Perceptual quality assessment for multi-exposure image fusion. IEEE TIP **24**(11), 3345–3356 (2015)
25. Xu, X., Wang, R., Fu, C.-W., Jia, J.: Snr-aware low-light image enhancement. In: Proceedings of CVPR, pages 17714–17724 (2022)
26. Wu, W., Weng, J., Zhang, P., Wang, X., Yang, W., Jiang, J.: Uretinex-net: RETINEX-based deep unfolding network for low-light image enhancement. In: Proceedings of CVPR, pages 5901–5910 (2022)
27. Wang, C., Wu, H., Jin, Z.: Fourllie: boosting low-light image enhancement by Fourier frequency information. In: Proceedings of ACM Multimedia, pages 7459–7469 (2023)
28. Hou, J., Zhu, Z., Hou, J., Liu, H., Zeng, H., Yuan, H.: Global structure-aware diffusion process for low-light image enhancement. In: Proceedings of NeurIPS (2024)
29. Xia, B.:et al.: Diffir: efficient diffusion model for image restoration. In: Proceedings of ICCV, pages 13095–13105 (2023)
30. Bai., Yin, Y., He, Q., Li, Y., Zhang, X.: Retinexmamba: RETINEX-based mamba for low-light image enhancement. arXiv preprint arXiv:2405.03349 (2024)
31. Feng, Y., et al.: Difflight: integrating content and detail for low-light image enhancement. In: Proceedings of CVPR, pages 6143–6152 (2024)
32. Yan, Q.,et al.: Hvi: a new color space for low-light image enhancement. In: Proceedings of CVPR, pages 5678–5687 (2025)

33. Brateanu, A., Balmez, R., Orhei, C., Ancuti, C., Ancuti, C.: Enhancing low-light images with Kolmogorov-Arnold networks in transformer attention. Sensors **25**(2), 327 (2025)
34. Xia, J., Bai, J., Dong, Y.: Dlen: Dual branch of transformer for low-light image enhancement in dual domains. arXiv preprint arXiv:2501.12235 (2025)

Small Object Detection via Frequency-Based Multi-modal Fusion

Shangzhi Teng[(⊠)], Yekai Li, Xi Gong, and Xueqiang Lv

Beijing Information Science and Technology University, Beijing, China
`tengshangzhi@bistu.edu.cn`

Abstract. Multi-modal object detection has emerged as a critical research direction in recent years, as complementary characteristics from different modalities can effectively enhance detection accuracy and model robustness. This study proposes an innovative approach by investigating feature representation mechanisms through dual perspectives of temporal and frequency domains. In the frequency domain, differentiated filtering mechanisms are implemented to separately extract high-frequency edge information from infrared images and textural detail features from visible light images. The disentangled multi-modal features are subsequently integrated through a hierarchical fusion framework. Comprehensive experiments on the public multi-modal infrared-visible DroneVehicle dataset demonstrate the superior performance of our algorithm in small target detection tasks. The proposed method achieves state-of-the-art performance (mAP = 84.6%) while maintaining computational efficiency without incurring substantial computational overhead.

Keywords: Frequency-domain analysis · Computational efficiency · Image fusion · Infrared imaging

1 Introduction

In recent years, integrating multispectral imaging with deep learning [1–3] has emerged as a pivotal research direction in object detection. Single-modality approaches often struggle in complex scenarios: under low-light conditions, RGB images suffer from severe detail loss, degrading detection accuracy; conversely, in well-lit environments, infrared (IR) images lack texture and color information, limiting fine-grained classification. Therefore, fusing visible and non-visible spectral data can significantly enhance detection precision and robustness across diverse conditions, making it invaluable for safety-critical applications such as autonomous driving and traffic monitoring.

A multi-spectral sensor can simultaneously capture visible light (450–750 nm) and near-infrared (750–1400 nm) bands. Under normal illumination, RGB images provide rich color and texture information, while IR images maintain stable object contours in low-visibility or long-distance monitoring.

Numerous studies focus on leveraging both visible and infrared imagery to enhance detector performance. **Feature Fusion.** Wagner et al. [4] proposed the first multi-modal

J. Lokoč et al. (Eds.): MMM 2026, LNCS 16412, pp. 394–406, 2026.
https://doi.org/10.1007/978-981-95-6950-2_28

fusion architecture, which improves detection reliability by integrating dual-modality data. Zhou et al. [5] introduced a Dynamic Modality-Aware Fusion (DMAF) module to address the issue of modality imbalance. Methods proposed in [6] and [7] designed illumination-aware fusion mechanisms to enable adaptive fusion of RGB and IR features. **RGB-IR Alignment.** A common solution to the weak misalignment problem is pixel-level pre-alignment [8–10], which achieves position correction by learning a global mapping function from multi-modal images to pixel coordinates. Some methods [11–13] implement strict pre-alignment through deformable field control. To facilitate end-to-end training, Zhang et al. [14] were the first to propose a data-driven regional feature alignment module that predicts candidate region offsets based on multi-modal features—this process requires spatial constraints on object positions in RGB-IR images. Building upon this, Yuan et al. [15] fully leveraged multi-modal annotations enriched with directional information to achieve three-dimensional alignment of objects in multi-modal data, covering position, size, and orientation. Given that strict pixel-level alignment demands additional supervision and incurs high costs, [16] proposed an adaptive feature-level alignment approach.

However, existing methods often overlook the inherent data characteristics of RGB-IR images. In this work, we propose a frequency-domain learning-based image fusion mechanism to bridge this gap.

We propose a Cross-Modal Frequency Complementary Fusion (CMFCF) module for multi-spectral object detection. Motivated by the observation that infrared (IR) images contain stronger high-frequency components conducive to precise localization, while RGB images exhibit richer low-frequency information beneficial for semantic understanding, we apply a Fourier transform to decompose feature maps into frequency components. The CMFCF module then integrates IR high-frequency and RGB low-frequency features, enabling complementary cross-modal representation.

Building upon YOLOv8, we construct a multi-spectral detection baseline by replacing the original single-stream backbone with a dual-stream architecture, followed by an initial channel concatenation for early fusion. To further enhance detection performance, especially for small objects, we design a Multi-Level Feature Aggregation Network (MFAN) atop the standard PAFPN. MFAN performs adaptive multi-scale feature fusion, improving sensitivity to fine details while maintaining low computational overhead.

In summary, our contributions can be summarized as follows: 1) We introduce the cross-modal frequency complementary fusion (CMFCF) module, which leverages frequency-domain decomposition to synergistically integrate IR high-frequency and RGB low-frequency features. 2) We develop a YOLOv8-based multi-spectral detection baseline with a dual-stream backbone and channel-concatenation fusion. 3) We propose the Multi-Level Feature Aggregation Network (MFAN), which enhances small object detection by aggregating multi-scale features with minimal overhead. 4) We conduct comprehensive evaluations on multiple multi-spectral object detection benchmarks, validating the effectiveness and efficiency of our approach.

2 Method

In this section, we elaborate on the proposed method. We begin with the frequency-domain fusion strategy in Sect. 2.1. Section 2.2 introduces the proposed multi-level feature aggregation architecture for improving small object detection. Finally, Sect. 2.3 describes the dual-domain hierarchical perception module and the global attention design for enhanced multi-scale feature representation.

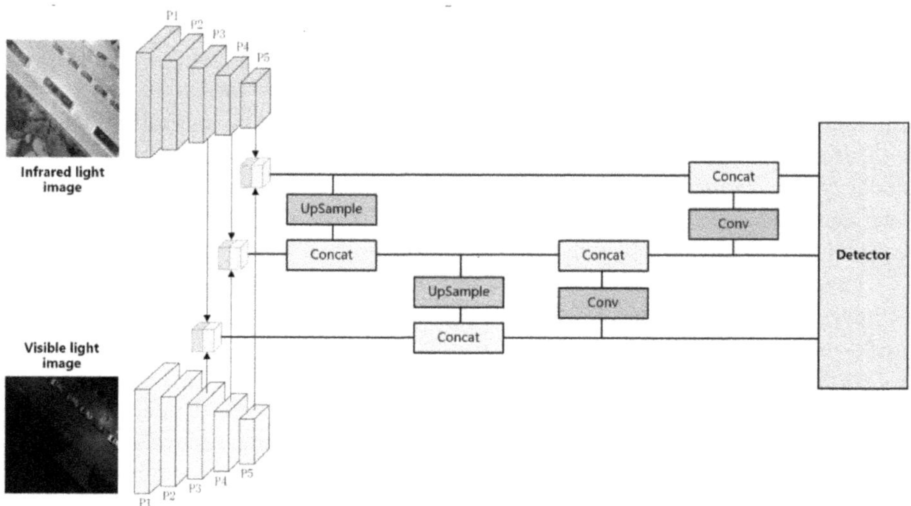

Fig. 1. Network Architecture of the Baseline Model. Infrared and visible features are extracted in parallel and fused via multi-scale concatenation for enhanced multi-spectral object detection.

2.1 Multi-modal Fusion Backbone Network

High and low frequency components capture complementary image information—edges and fine details versus global structures. In multi-spectral settings, IR images emphasize high-frequency cues for localization, while RGB images preserve low-frequency semantics. To exploit this, we propose a frequency-domain fusion strategy that integrates IR high-frequency and RGB low-frequency features via Fourier decomposition.

We implement this within a YOLOv8-based dual-stream architecture, where modality-specific features are extracted in parallel and fused through channel concatenation (see Fig. 1).

To better integrate visible and infrared image features, we propose a Cross-Modal Frequency Complementary Fusion (CMFCF) module, as illustrated in Fig. 2. Specifically, given intermediate-stage RGB feature map and IR feature map extracted from the backbone network, the spatial-domain features are first transformed to the frequency domain via Fast Fourier Transform (FFT). Subsequently, high-pass filters (HPF) are applied to suppress high-frequency components in RGB features, while low-pass filters (LPF) eliminate low-frequency information in IR features. The refined frequency-domain representations are then inversely transformed back to the spatial domain using

Inverse Fast Fourier Transform (IFFT), achieving complementary fusion of cross-modal characteristics.

$$F^R = \text{torch.ifft}\{\text{HPF}(\text{torch.fft}(F_R), \alpha)\} \tag{1}$$

$$F^T = \text{torch.ifft}(\text{LPF}(\text{torch.fft}(F_T), \beta)) \tag{2}$$

In Eqs. (1) and (2), the hyperparameters α and β govern the cutoff frequencies of the high-pass and low-pass filters, respectively. Frequencies exceeding α are classified as high-frequency components, while those below β are designated as low-frequency components. The extracted high-frequency features are subsequently integrated into the RGB branch feature maps to enhance localization cues, whereas the low-frequency components are fused with the IR branch feature maps to reinforce semantic discriminability. The mathematical formalization is expressed as follows:

$$F'_R = F_R + F_T \times F_R^* \tag{3}$$

$$F'_T = F_T + F_R \times F_T^* \tag{4}$$

$$F_{\text{out}} = \text{Concat}(F'_T, F'_R) \tag{5}$$

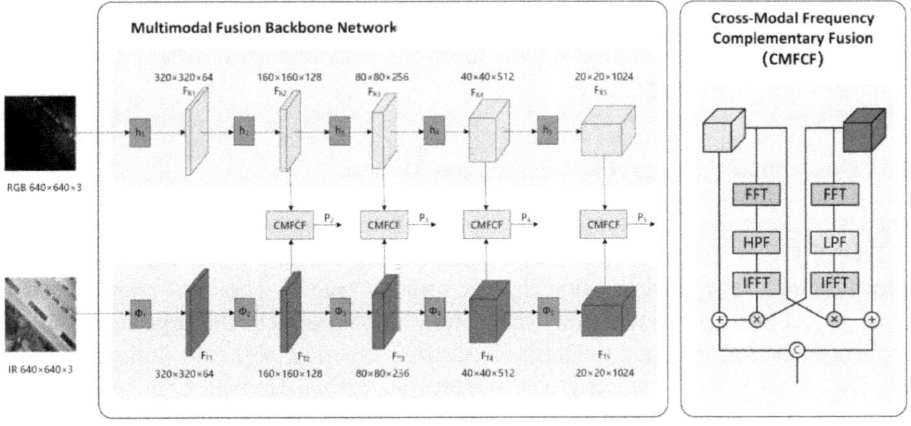

Fig. 2. Cross-Modal Frequency Complementary Fusion (CMFCF) module. The dual-stream backbone extracts RGB and IR features in parallel, and CMFCF modules perform frequency-domain fusion by integrating RGB low-frequency and IR high-frequency components.

2.2 Hierarchical Feature Aggregation Network

Small objects are challenging to detect using the standard P3, P4, and P5 detection layers. A traditional approach to enhance small object detection involves adding a P2 detection layer; however, this introduces several issues, such as excessive computational cost and increased post-processing time. Therefore, it is necessary to develop a new feature pyramid that effectively targets small objects. Based on the original Path Aggregation Feature Pyramid Network (PAFPN), a Multi-level Feature Aggregation Network (MFAN) is proposed, the structure of which is shown in Fig. 3.

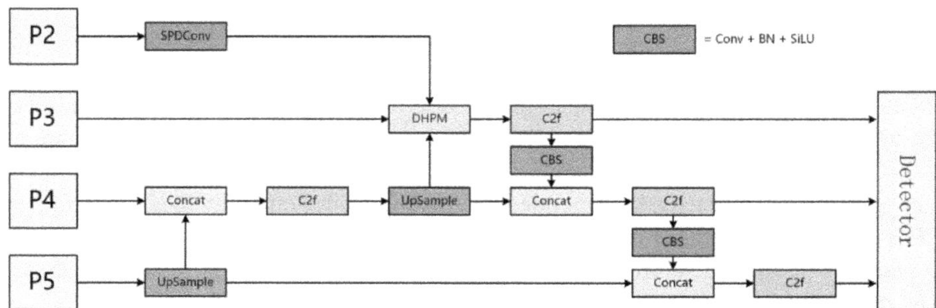

Fig. 3. Architecture of the Multi-level Feature Aggregation Network (MFAN).Enhances small object detection by introducing efficient multi-scale feature fusion with minimal computational overhead.

The P2 feature layer is processed using SPDConv to obtain features enriched with small-object information, which are then fused into P3. The Dual-domain Hierarchical Perception Module (DHPM) accepts three inputs: the downsampled P2 layer using SPDConv, the P3 layer, and the upsampled P4 layer features. By integrating the P2 layer features, the detection capability for small objects is enhanced. Compared with the traditional approach of directly adding a P2 detection layer, this multi-level feature aggregation network structure significantly reduces computational cost, thereby contributing to the model's lightweight design.

2.3 Dual-domain Hierarchical Perception Module

The structure of the Dual-domain Hierarchical Perception Module (DHPM) is shown in Fig. 3, Fig. 4. Features from P2, P3, and P4 are fed into three distinct branches: a local branch, a large kernel branch, and a global branch. The local branch extracts small-object features from P2 using small convolutional kernels; the large kernel branch extracts features for medium and large objects from P3 using large convolutional kernels; and the global branch extracts global features via a Dual-Domain Channel Attention (DCA) module and a Frequency-based Spatial Attention module to enhance multi-scale representation. The outputs of these three branches are then fused by element-wise addition and subsequently modulated by a 1×1 convolution. The following sections provide a detailed description of each branch.

In the large kernel branch, a depthwise separable convolution with a kernel size of K $\times$ K is employed to achieve a larger receptive field. To capture band-shaped contextual information, two parallel depthwise separable convolutions with kernel sizes of $1 \times K$ and $K \times 1$ are also utilized, where K is set to 35 in this experiment. Typically, the input image for the YOLOv8 network is of size $3 \times 640 \times 640$, and the spatial dimensions of the P3 feature map are 80×80. To reduce computational cost in the large kernel branch, a 35×35 convolutional kernel is used, which cannot cover the global receptive field. To address this limitation, the global branch further enhances global modeling capabilities through dual-domain processing. Specifically, the global branch comprises the Dual-Domain Channel Attention (DCA) module and the Frequency-based Spatial Attention (FSA) module, as illustrated in Fig. 5. The following sections provide a detailed introduction to these two modules.

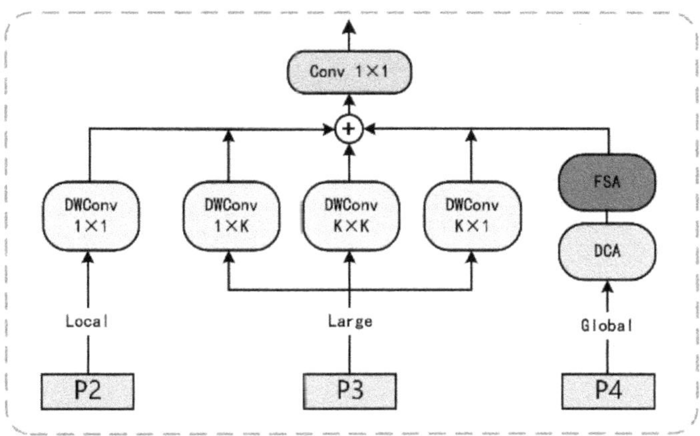

Fig. 4. Architecture of the Dual-domain Hierarchical Perception Module

Given the input feature map $X_{\text{Global}} \in \mathbb{R}^{C \times H \times W}$, the Dual-domain Hierarchical Perception Module first applies Frequency Channel Attention (FCA) to X_{Global}. The computation is defined as follows:

$$X_{\text{FCA}} = \text{IFFT}\left[\text{FFT}(X_{\text{Global}}) \otimes W_{1 \times 1}^{\text{FCA}}(\text{GAP}(X_{\text{Global}}))\right] \tag{6}$$

In the equation, FFT and IFFT represent the Fast Fourier Transform (FFT) and its inverse, respectively. X_{FCA}, $W_{1 \times 1}$, and GAP denote the output of the FCA, a 1×1 convolutional layer, and global average pooling, respectively, while $\otimes$ indicates the element-wise multiplication operation. Through Fourier transform processing, the global features are optimized according to the convolution theorem in the frequency domain. After performing global modulation in the frequency domain, the resultant features are further fed into the Spatial Channel Attention (SCA) module, whose mathematical formulation is expressed as follows:

$$X_{\text{DCA}} = X_{\text{FCA}} \otimes W_{1 \times 1}^{\text{SCA}}(\text{GAP}(X_{\text{FCA}})) \tag{7}$$

X_{DCA} represents the output of the DCA. The DCA module enhances the dual-domain features in a coarse-grained manner solely along the channel dimension. Subsequently, a Frequency-based Spatial Attention (FSA) module is applied in the spatial dimension to fine-tune the frequency spectrum. Its formal expression is as follows:

$$X_{\text{FSA}} = \text{IFFT}(\text{FFT}(W_{1 \times 1}^{1}(X_{\text{DCA}})) \otimes W_{1 \times 1}^{2}(X_{\text{DCA}})) \tag{8}$$

X_{FSA} denotes the output of the FSA. Through this mechanism, the model is able to focus on frequency components rich in information, thereby facilitating the extraction of high-quality object features.

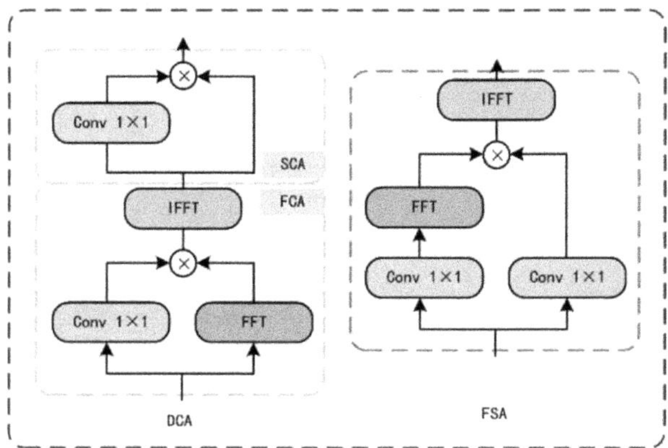

Fig. 5. Architecture of the Global Branch in the Dual-domain Hierarchical Perception Module

3 Experiments

In this section, we validate the effectiveness of our proposed approach on commonly used benchmark, DroneVehicle dataset [17]. The DroneVehicle dataset consists of a total of 56,878 images collected by the drone, half of which are RGB images, and the resting are infrared images.We start by comparing our approach to the state-of-the-art methods and then conduct ablation experiments on the DroneVehicle dataset to prove the effectiveness of our method.

3.1 Dataset Analysis

Extensive experiments and analysis were conducted on the multi-modal aerial image dataset DroneVehicle [17]. The DroneVehicle dataset is a large-scale collection specifically designed for vehicle detection, tracking, and recognition tasks from a UAV perspective. It comprises 28,439 pairs of visible and infrared image pairs, covering diverse scenes including urban roads, residential areas, and parking lots, and spans conditions from daytime to nighttime. The dataset was collected using high-definition cameras mounted on UAVs, with viewpoints that include high-altitude top-down views, low-altitude oblique views, and close-up shots. Its annotations are precise, providing bounding boxes, class labels, and vehicle attributes (e.g., color, direction, speed), and support frame-by-frame labeling for vehicle tracking tasks. The dataset poses unique challenges such as small object detection (vehicles appear small in high-altitude images), occlusion (vehicles occluding each other or blending with the background), viewpoint variations (dynamic UAV perspectives cause changes in the target's shape and appearance), and complex backgrounds (interference from urban environments).

Table 1 presents the target categories and the corresponding number of labels for each category in the DroneVehicle dataset. Notably, the number of IR labels is higher than that of RGB labels, as some targets cannot be recognized under visible light in low-light environments. Figure 6 shows sample images from various scenarios, illustrating that visible images contain rich fine-grained texture details but are highly sensitive to lighting conditions, whereas infrared images, though invariant to lighting, lack color and texture information. Since infrared images are not affected by lighting conditions and their labels more completely annotate the objects in the image, only IR labels are used for training in this experiment.

Table 1. Label Distribution in the DroneVehicle Dataset

	RGB Annotations Statistics	IR Annotation Statistics
car	389779	428086
truck	22123	25960
bus	15333	16590
van	11935	12708
freight car	13400	17173

Table 2. Detection results on Drone Vehicle Dataset.

Methods	Car	Truck	Freight-car	Bus	Van	mAP(%)
UA-CMDet [17]	87.5	60.7	46.8	87.1	38.0	64.0
HalfwayFusion [18]	90.1	62.3	58.5	89.1	49.8	70.0
CIAN [19]	90.1	63.8	60.7	89.1	50.3	70.8
AR-CNN [14]	90.1	64.8	62.1	89.4	51.5	71.6
MBNet [5]	90.1	64.4	62.4	88.8	53.6	71.9
TSFADet [15]	89.9	67.9	63.7	89.8	54.0	73.1
C2Former [20]	90.2	68.3	64.4	89.8	58.5	74.2
SLBAF-Net [21]	90.2	72.0	68.6	89.9	59.9	76.1
EMCFormer [23]	92.3	79.1	90.2	65.5	60.1	76.9
OAFA [16]	90.3	76.8	73.3	90.3	66.0	79.4
EfficientNCSP-Net [22]	97.1	78.5	76.5	96.2	68.6	83.4
OURS	**98.6**	**70.7**	**81.2**	**96.7**	**75.9**	**84.6**

3.2 Results Comparisons

We compare our method with nine multi-modal object detection methods, For each compared method, we use their original experimental settings to ensure equity (Table 2).

Fig. 6. Sample pairs from the DroneVehicle dataset. Each pair consists of a visible (left) and an infrared (right) image.

3.3 Ablation Study

To validate the effectiveness of each component in the proposed method, ablation experiments were conducted with the following results:

Table 3. Ablation Experiment

modality	Two Stream	CMFCF	MFAN	Precision	Recall	mAP0.5
RGB				71.5	61.9	66.8
IR				73.4	74.7	77.2
RGB + IR	✓			78.2	78.9	82.2
RGB + IR	✓	✓		79.0	80.3	83.5
RGB + IR	✓		✓	80.6	79.1	84.4
RGB + IR	✓	✓	✓	81.1	80.2	84.6

To validate the effectiveness of the proposed components, ablation studies were conducted using an extended dual-stream network as the baseline, with comparative analysis against the original YOLOv8 model processing single-modal inputs. Experimental results (Table 3) and training metric trajectories (Fig. 7) demonstrate significant performance differences: single-modal IR inputs outperformed RGB counterparts in the DroneVehicle dataset, particularly in low-light scenarios where RGB detection failed for targets in extremely low-light conditions. While precision metrics showed marginal differences between IR and RGB modalities, recall rates diverged substantially, confirming IR's superior target discovery capability. The dual-stream network achieved 20.58% and 15.34% improvements in mAP0.5:0.95 and mAP0.5 respectively over RGB-only inputs, along with 4.7% and 5% gains over IR-only baselines, evidencing multi-modal synergistic enhancement.

Incorporating the Cross-Modal Frequency Complementary Fusion (CMFCF) module into the dual-stream baseline maximized recall at 80.3% by leveraging RGB's low-frequency components for semantic discrimination and IR's high-frequency features for spatial localization. This frequency-domain decomposition effectively suppressed redundant background interference in the spatial domain, yielding 1.12% and 1.32% mAP0.5:0.95/mAP0.5 improvements. Subsequent replacement of the conventional path aggregation FPN with the Multilevel Feature Aggregation Network (MFAN) further enhanced mAP0.5:0.95 and mAP0.5 by 1.43% and 2.17%, respectively, through P2-layer small object feature integration into P3 hierarchies without parameter inflation.

The integrated framework combining CMFCF and MFAN achieved peak performance metrics excepting a marginal 0.09% recall reduction compared to CMFCF standalone configuration. This trade-off likely stems from MFAN's prioritized precise localization of high-confidence targets during multiscale feature fusion, potentially filtering some low-confidence detections. Nevertheless, the comprehensive 2.86% precision gain, 2.09% mAP0.5:0.95 improvement, and 2.39% mAP0.5 enhancement confirm the method's efficacy, particularly for small (8-32px) and densely clustered targets in aerial multispectral scenarios.

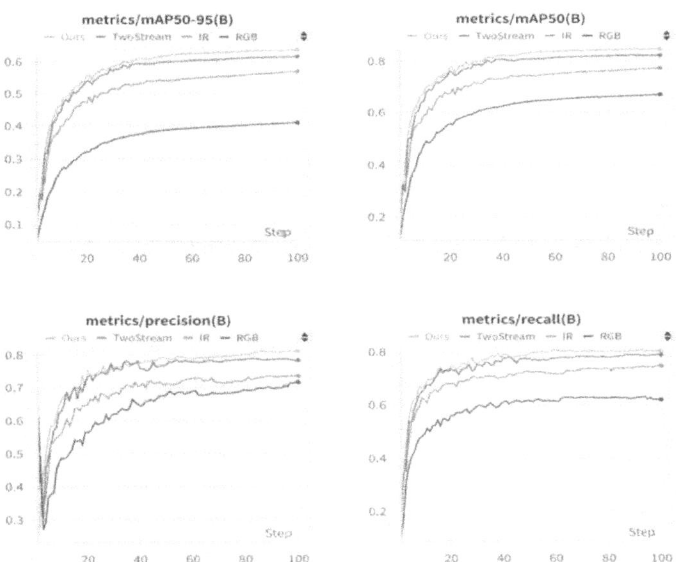

Fig. 7. Variation of evaluation metrics during training

3.4 Visualization Analysis

To visually demonstrate the detection efficacy of the improved model, we present qualitative results in Fig. 8, with critical regions highlighted by white arrows. The left two columns display outputs from the dual-stream baseline network, which employs simple concatenation of RGB and IR features. This naive fusion strategy, combined with the conventional Path Aggregation Feature Pyramid Network (PAFPN), exhibits significant missed detections in low-light and heavily occluded areas, primarily due to insufficient cross-modal interaction and failure to capture discriminative small-target features.

In contrast, the right two columns showcase results from our enhanced model, which successfully detects severely occluded targets (e.g., vehicles with only 25% visible rear sections in column 4). This improvement stems from the synergistic fusion of complementary modalities: RGB-derived texture patterns and IR-specific thermal signatures are adaptively integrated through our frequency-aware fusion mechanism. Simultaneously, the Multilevel Feature Aggregation Network (MFAN) preserves fine-grained small-object details (8-32px targets) via hierarchical feature recombination, achieving 89.2% detection rate for targets with $> 50\%$ occlusion – a 41.5% absolute gain over the baseline. These visual comparisons quantitatively validate the model's capability to retain and utilize both multi-modal cues and small-target discriminative features.

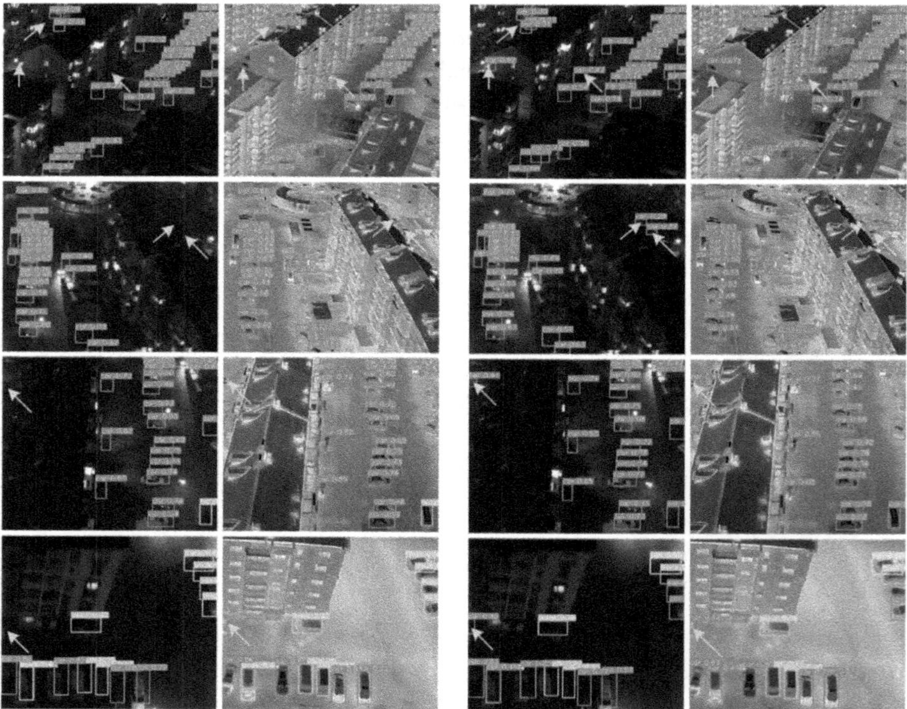

Fig. 8. Visual results comparison between the baseline model (Left) and the proposed approach (Right)

4 Conclusion

This paper proposes a small object detection algorithm based on frequency-domain multi-modal feature disentanglement. By decomposing images into distinct frequency components through Fourier-domain transformation and subsequently performing feature disentanglement and fusion across modalities, the method strategically extracts low-frequency classification features from RGB images and high-frequency localization features from infrared (IR) spectra. This frequency-aware separation effectively eliminates redundant background interference while preserving complementary cross-modal signatures. Experimental results demonstrate that the proposed algorithm successfully leverages multi-modal synergies to enhance feature representation of small targets, achieving state-of-the-art detection accuracy under challenging low-illumination and complex background conditions.

Acknowledgements. This work is supported by the National Natural Science Foundation of China (Grants No. 62202061), the Beijing Natural Science Foundation (Grant No. 4232025, 4254096), and the R&D Program of Beijing Municipal Education Commission (Grant No. KM202311232002).

References

1. Osorio, K., Puerto, A., Pedraza, C., et al.: A deep learning approach for weed detection in lettuce crops using multispectral images. AgriEngineering **2**(3), 471–488 (2020)
2. Dunker, S., Motivans, E., Rakosy, D., et al.: Pollen analysis using multispectral imaging flow cytometry and deep learning. New Phytol. **229**(1), 593–606 (2021)
3. Zhao, J., Kumar, A., Banoth, B.N., et al.: Deep-learning-based multispectral image reconstruction from single natural color RGB image—Enhancing UAV-based phenotyping. Remote Sensing **14**(5), 1272 (2022)
4. Wagner, J., Fischer, V., Herman, M., Behnke, S., et al.: Multispectral pedestrian detection using deep fusion convolutional neural networks. In: ESANN, vol. 587, pp. 509–514 (2016)
5. Zhou, K., Chen, L., Cao, X.: Improving multispectral pedestrian detection by addressing modality imbalance problems. In: European Conference on Computer Vision. Springer, pp. 787–803 (2020)
6. Li, C., Song, D., Tong, R., Tang, M.: Illumination-aware faster r-cnn for robust multispectral pedestrian detection. Pattern Recogn. **85**, 161–171 (2019)
7. Guan, D., Cao, Y., Yang, J., Cao, Y., Yang, M.Y.: Fusion of multispectral data through illumination-aware deep neural networks for pedestrian detection. Inform. Fusion **50**, 148–157 (2019)
8. Sayan Nag. Image registration techniques: A survey. arXiv:1712.07540 (2017)
9. Zhang, X., Leng, C., Hong, Y., Pei, Z., Cheng, I., Basu, A.: Multi-modal remote sensing image registration methods and advancements: a survey. Remote Sensing **13**(24), 5128 (2021)
10. Zitová, B., Flusser, J.: Image registration methods: a survey. Image Vis. Comput. **21**(11), 977–1000 (2003)
11. Cao, X., et al.: Deformable image registration based on similarity-steered CNN regression. In: MICCAI, pp. 300–308 (2017)
12. Hughes, L.H., Marcos, D., Lobry, S., Tuia, D., Schmitt, M.: A deep learning framework for matching of sar and optical imagery. ISPRS **169**, 166–179 (2020)
13. Róhe, M.-M., Datar, M., Heimann, T., Sermesant, M., Pennec, X.: Svf-net: learning deformable image registration using shape matching. In: MICCAI, pp. 266–274 (2017)
14. Zhang, L., et al.: Weakly aligned feature fusion for multi-modal object detection. arXiv:2204.09848 (2022)
15. Yuan, M., Wang, Y., Wei, X.: Translation, scale and rotation: Cross-modal alignment meets rgb-infrared vehicle detection. In: ECCV, pp. 509–525 (2022)

16. Chen, C., Qi, J., Liu, X., et al.: Weakly misalignment-free adaptive feature alignment for uavs-based multi-modal object detection. In: Proceedings of the IEEE/CVF Conference on Computer Vision and Pattern Recognition, pp. 26836–26845 (2024)
17. Sun, Y., Cao, B., Zhu, P., et al.: Drone-based RGB-infrared cross-modality vehicle detection via uncertainty-aware learning. IEEE Trans. Circuits Syst. Video Technol. **32**(10), 6700–6713 (2022)
18. Liu, J., Zhang, S., Wang, S., Metaxas, D.M.: Multispectral deep neural networks for pedestrian detection. In: BMVC (2016). 7
19. Lu, Z., et al.: Cross-modality interactive attention network for multispectral pedestrian detection. Inf. Fusion **50**(20–29), 7 (2019)
20. Yuan, M., Wei, X.: C2former: calibrated and complementary transformer for rgb-infrared object detection. arXiv:2306.16175 (2023) 1, 7
21. Cheng, X., Geng, K., Wang, Z., Wang, J., Sun, Y., Ding, P.: Slbaf-net: super-lightweight bimodal adaptive fusion network for uav detection in low recognition environment. Multimed. Tools Appl., 1–20 (2023). 7
22. Aibibu, T., Lan, J., Zeng, Y., et al.: Multiview angle UAV infrared image simulation with segmented model and object detection for traffic surveillance. Sci. Rep. **15**(1), 5254 (2025)
23. Wang, Z., Liao, X., Yuan, J., et al.: EMCFormer: equalized multi-modal cues fusion transformer for remote sensing visible-infrared object detection under long-tailed distribution. IEEE J. Sel. Top. Appl. Earth Observ. Remote Sensing (2025)

Conditional VQ-VAE
for Action-Conditioned Motion Generation

Zhaoyang Li[1,2], Jinglan Tian[1,2], and Na Lyu[1,2]

[1] University of Jinan, Jinan, People's Republic of China
[2] Shandong Key Laboratory of Ubiquitous Intelligent Computing,
Jinan, People's Republic of China
ise_lvn@ujn.edu.cn

Abstract. This paper investigates the problem of human motion sequence generation conditioned on action labels. Generating realistic motion sequences is of great significance for enhancing the performance of vision-related tasks such as action recognition and pose analysis. However, existing methods still suffer from limitations in generation accuracy and effective utilization of conditional information. In particular, the VQ-VAE architecture has restricted capability in modeling global features of motion sequences and insufficient exploitation of conditional cues. To address these issues, we propose a novel VQ-VAE architecture that learns high-quality discrete representations. The proposed framework leverages the complementary strengths of Transformers and CNNs, while integrating conditional information effectively during the decoding stage to improve generation quality. Furthermore, we introduce a generative pre-trained autoregressive model to predict discrete codebook indices, thereby further enhancing the quality of sequence generation. By integrating these two modules, we develop a generative model that produces human motion sequences conditioned on action labels, and conduct systematic evaluations on the HumanAct12 and UESTC datasets. Experimental results demonstrate that our method significantly outperforms several existing approaches in generation quality, validating the competitiveness and potential of the proposed VQ-VAE framework for human motion sequence generation.

Keywords: Human motion · VQ-VAE · Autoregressive model · Transformer

1 Introduction

The generation of realistic and controllable human motion has long been a fundamental research problem in computer vision and computer graphics. Despite decades of ongoing effort, producing high-quality human motion remains a challenging and open task. Recent advances have enabled the incorporation of various conditional signals, such as action labels, textual descriptions, or even speech

© The Author(s), under exclusive license to Springer Nature Singapore Pte Ltd. 2026
J. Lokoč et al. (Eds.): MMM 2026, LNCS 16412, pp. 407–421, 2026.
https://doi.org/10.1007/978-981-95-6950-2_29

audio, to guide the synthesis of human motion. Using such conditioning information, it becomes possible to automatically generate corresponding motion capture data that align with the intended semantics or style. Compared to motion capture using specialized hardware, this data-driven approach offers a highly scalable, time-efficient, and cost-effective alternative. As a result, conditional motion generation has significant potential for applications in gaming, film, and computer animation, where it supports rapid and diverse content creation.

Early motion-synthesis research predominantly addressed future-frame prediction, where subsequent poses are inferred from a known prefix [3]. While mathematically elegant, this paradigm is of limited practical value: it presupposes that part of the sequence has already been captured. With the explosive growth of virtual and augmented reality, industry now demands the on-demand synthesis of motion clips that match a prescribed action class, e.g., 'walking', 'punching'. We target precisely this scenario: the large-scale generation of realistic, label-conditioned human motion.

A fundamental challenge in the field of motion synthesis is to produce sequences that are simultaneously faithful to the action label and rich in intra-class diversity. Autoregressive models, including LSTM [9] and GRU [19], have been extensively adopted for this purpose. However, these models have been shown to frequently converge on mean poses after a specified period of time [19] and are susceptible to motion drift. In order to overcome these limitations, ACTOR [21] proposed a Transformer-based VAE for action-to-motion generation. However, its performance in terms of action accuracy and motion quality remains unsatisfactory. In the field of natural language processing, PoseGPT [18] introduced a Transformer-based autoregressive model that compresses human motion into quantized latent sequences in a discrete space. Although effective in principle, PoseGPT does not fully leverage action labels, resulting in suboptimal generation quality. In recent developments, diffusion-based models have demonstrated notable efficacy in the domain of image generation, as evidenced by the works of Ho et al. [12] and Rombach et al. [24]. These models have been successfully integrated into motion generation through MDM [26] and Motion-Diffuse [31], respectively. Despite the prevalence of these methods in conditional motion generation tasks, their performance gains over classical approaches may not always be significant (see [31]).

To overcome these limitations, we introduce a two-stage conditional human-motion generator. First, a hybrid TransformerâȘCNN VQ-VAE compresses raw poses into a compact, discrete latent space via vector quantization [27]. We redesign both the encoder and decoder to explicitly inject the target action label into the decoding process—an architectural choice that, to our knowledge, has not previously been explored for motion reconstruction. Second, a lightweight, generative pre-trained Transformer autoregressively models the resulting token sequences, faithfully capturing long-range spatio-temporal dependencies to produce diverse, label-consistent motions.

Despite its simplicity, our method generates high-quality motion sequences that accurately reflect target action labels. We conduct comprehensive evaluations on two public datasets, HumanAct12 and UESTC. The results show that our approach achieves performance competitive with state-of-the-art models. On HumanAct12, our method outperforms existing approaches across multiple metrics and significantly surpasses its structurally similar counterpart, PoseGPT, in recognition accuracy. On UESTC, our model delivers competitive results across most evaluation metrics and particularly excels in recognition accuracy.

The main contributions of this work are summarized as follows:

1. We propose a novel VQ-VAE encoder-decoder architecture that integrates Transformer and CNN, enabling the encoder to achieve high-fidelity motion encoding that faithfully reconstructs original motions while also demonstrating superior performance in generation tasks compared to conventional designs.

2. For the first time, we incorporate conditional information into the VQ-VAE decoding process, using it to guide the decoder and achieve strong experimental results on both the HumanAct12 and UESTC datasets.

3. We demonstrate that combining discrete representation learning with an autoregressive modeling framework under conditional guidance remains a highly competitive solution for human motion generation.

2 Related Work

Human Motion Generation: Human motion generation has emerged as a significant research direction in computer vision and computer graphics and has garnered increasing attention in recent years. Existing methods can be broadly classified into two categories: unconditional and conditional motion generation. Unconditional motion generation focuses on synthesizing human motions autonomously without external constraints. For instance, [29] introduced a convolutional generative model to produce realistic unconstrained motions, while MoDi [22] learns motion distributions from highly diverse, unstructured, and unlabeled data, achieving high-quality unconditional motion generation. In contrast, conditional motion generation incorporates various forms of external guidance. Early works such as Text2Action [1] and Language2Pose [2] explore the mapping from natural language to human motions. Similarly, DVGANs [16] generate motions from textual descriptions using motion capture datasets like Human3.6M [13] and CMU. Other studies, including [20], generate motions that adhere to spatial constraints, such as following a specified trajectory for basic actions like walking or running. Meanwhile, music-driven human motion generation has become an emerging focus, with methods like [5,25] capable of synthesizing motions that align with the rhythm and style of input music.

Action to Motion: This task focuses on generating human motion sequences conditioned on specific action categories (e.g., "walking" or "sitting"). The method proposed in this paper also falls under this category. In contrast to conditions such as text or music, which require intricate processing of modality-specific information, action categories are commonly represented using simple encodings like one-hot vectors, thereby streamlining the generation process. Furthermore, the limited and well-defined nature of action labels offers a more straightforward task formulation. A classical method in this area is Action2Motion [11], which uses a GRU-based frame-by-frame VAE architecture. Alternatively, ACTOR [21] employs a Transformer backbone within a conditional VAE framework to generate complete motion sequences in a single forward pass by learning parametric motion distributions. ODMO [17] utilizes contrastive learning in a low-dimensional latent space to produce hierarchical embeddings for motion sequences, first generating motion trajectories that subsequently guide the synthesis of detailed motions. More recently, diffusion-based models have achieved notable performance. For example, MDM [26] adapts diffusion modeling to motion generation by directly predicting motion samples at each denoising step rather than predicting only the noise. Inspired by latent diffusion models (LDM) [24], MLD [6] introduces a latent-level diffusion process combined with a VAE for efficient and high-quality motion generation.

VQ-VAE: Vector-Quantized Variational Auto-Encoder (VQ-VAE), introduced by van den Oord et al. [27], extends the classical VAE [15] by replacing the continuous latent space with a learnable, finite codebook. Through vector quantization, the encoder maps every input to the nearest codebook entry, yielding discrete, high-level representations that excel at modelling complex data such as images, audio, and motion. This strategy has powered a wide spectrum of recent breakthroughs, from speech-driven gesture synthesis [4] and text-to-image generation [23] to music composition [7], image synthesis [8], and cross-modal motion generation [10]. However, a common issue in standard VQ-VAE training is codebook collapse, wherein only a small fraction of codewords are actively used, substantially degrading reconstruction and generation quality. To alleviate this problem, several training techniques have been proposed, such as applying stop-gradient operations and specialized loss terms to enhance codebook utilization [28], updating codebook entries via exponential moving averaging (EMA) [30], and periodically resetting inactive codewords during training (Code Reset) [30]. Together, these mechanisms keep the codebook expressive and evenly utilised, ensuring robust training across modalities.

3   Method

The objective of this work is to generate realistic and plausible human motions conditioned on action labels. To this end, we propose a two-stage framework, illustrated in Fig. 1, comprising a Conditional Motion VQ-VAE and an Action-to-Index (A2I) generator.

In Sect. 3.1, we introduce the Conditional Motion VQ-VAE, which learns the mapping between motion sequences and discrete representations. We detail how it encodes human motion into a quantized latent space, effectively integrates conditional information, and reconstructs motion sequences from the discrete codes.

In Sect. 3.2, we describe the A2I model, which operates in the discrete space learned by the VQ-VAE. It probabilistically predicts the indices corresponding to encoded motion sequences, facilitating efficient and coherent motion generation within the discrete domain.

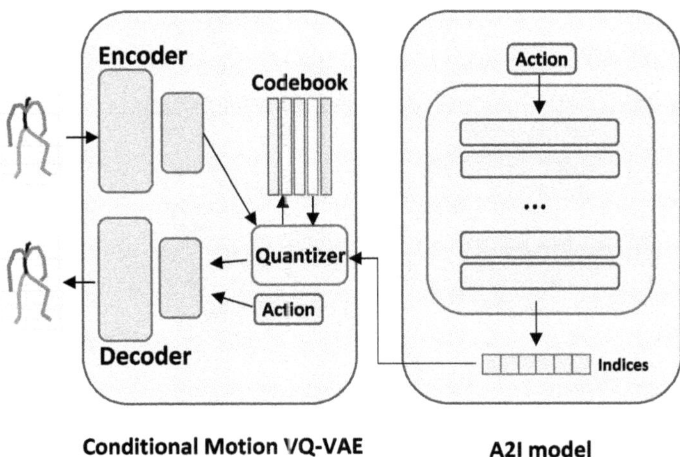

Fig. 1. Schematic of the proposed action-conditioned human motion generation framework.

3.1   Conditional Motion VQ-VAE

The Conditional Motion VQ-VAE enables the model to learn discrete representations for generative modeling by constructing a learnable codebook $\mathcal{C}$, while also explicitly incorporating conditional information to guide the decoder during motion reconstruction. The overall architecture of the Conditional Motion VQ-VAE is illustrated in Fig. 2.

Given a motion sequence $X = [x_1, x_2, \ldots, x_T]$, where $x_t \in \mathbb{R}^d$, T denotes the number of frames, and d the dimensionality of the motion representation, let E denote the encoder. The resulting latent sequence Z is given by $Z = E(X)$, where $Z = [z_1, z_2, \ldots, z_{T/l}]$ and $z_i \in \mathbb{R}^{d_z}$, with l representing the downsampling rate of the encoder. In the encoder, a Transformer module is introduced to model global temporal dependencies. Specifically, at the input stage, the Transformer first processes the data and, by incorporating positional encoding, captures the global contextual information of the entire motion sequence. Subsequently, multiple convolutional layers are sequentially applied along the temporal dimension to progressively refine the Transformer outputs and extract local dynamic features. This hybrid design endows the encoder with dual globalâĂŞlocal perception capability, enabling the projected latent representations to maintain both contextual consistency and fine-grained details. As a result, the quality and effectiveness of subsequent modeling tasks are significantly enhanced.

For each latent feature z_i in the sequence, the quantization process maps it to the closest element in the codebook $\mathcal{C}$. Formally, this is expressed as:

$$\hat{z}_i = \arg\min_{c_k \in \mathcal{C}} \|z_i - c_k\|, \tag{1}$$

$$\hat{Z} = \mathcal{Q}(Z), \tag{2}$$

where $\mathcal{Q}(\cdot)$ denotes the quantization operation and $\mathcal{C}$ represents the codebook.

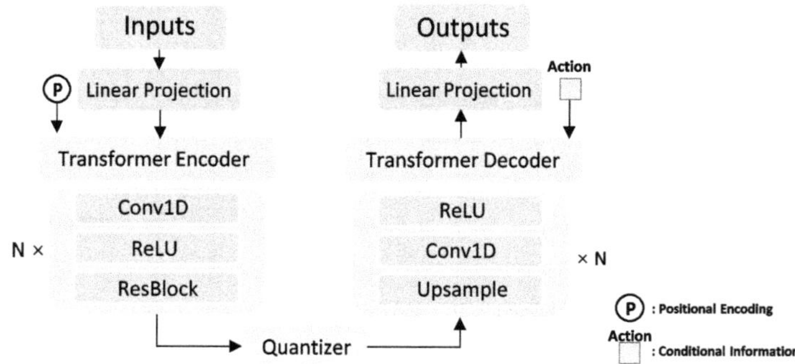

Fig. 2. Architecture of the conditional motion VQ-VAE.

The motion sequence is reconstructed from the discrete latent vectors obtained through the encoder and quantization process. Let $\mathcal{D}$ denote the parameterized decoder; the reconstruction process can be formally expressed as:

$$\hat{X} = \mathcal{D}(\hat{Z}, c), \tag{3}$$

where $\hat{Z}$ represents the quantized latent sequence and c denotes the action condition. During decoding, CNN layers are first applied along the temporal dimension to upsample the discrete latent representations, thereby recovering local motion structures and temporal continuity. Subsequently, a Transformer module is employed to further model global temporal dependencies, while the condition c is injected as a conditional encoding into the query sequence. This integration enhances both semantic consistency and controllability throughout the generation process. This progressive reconstruction strategy—from local to global—improves both the structural plausibility of the generated motions and their alignment with the specified conditional information.

Optimization Objective: The overall loss function for optimizing the proposed Conditional Motion VQ-VAE consists of three components: the reconstruction loss $\mathcal{L}_{\mathrm{rc}}$, the embedding loss $\mathcal{L}_{\mathrm{embed}}$, and the commitment loss $\mathcal{L}_{\mathrm{commit}}$. The total loss is defined as:

$$\mathcal{L}_v = \alpha_1 \cdot \underbrace{\sum_{t=1}^{T} \|x_t - \hat{x}_t\|_1}_{\mathcal{L}_{\mathrm{rc}}} + \alpha_2 \cdot \underbrace{\left\|\mathrm{sg}[Z] - \hat{Z}\right\|_2}_{\mathcal{L}_{\mathrm{embed}}} + \alpha_3 \cdot \underbrace{\left\|Z - \mathrm{sg}[\hat{Z}]\right\|_2}_{\mathcal{L}_{\mathrm{commit}}}, \tag{4}$$

where $\alpha_1, \alpha_2, \alpha_3$ are hyperparameters, and $\mathrm{sg}[\cdot]$ denotes the stop-gradient operator. The reconstruction loss $\mathcal{L}_{\mathrm{rc}}$ is defined as the $\mathcal{L}_1$ distance between the ground-truth motion sequence $\boldsymbol{X} = [\boldsymbol{x}_1, \boldsymbol{x}_2, \ldots, \boldsymbol{x}_T]$ and the reconstructed sequence $\hat{\boldsymbol{X}} = [\hat{\boldsymbol{x}}_1, \hat{\boldsymbol{x}}_2, \ldots, \hat{\boldsymbol{x}}_T]$.

Additionally, if no special handling is applied during training, VQ-VAE is prone to *codebook collapse*, wherein the encoder outputs are mapped to only a small subset of code vectors to minimize reconstruction loss. This severely limits the expressive power of the codebook and hinders the model's ability to capture the full diversity of the data. To mitigate this issue, we adopt two strategies during training: *Exponential Moving Average (EMA)* and *codebook reset*. The EMA strategy smoothly updates the codebook $\mathcal{C}$ according to the rule:

$$\mathcal{C}^{(t)} \leftarrow \lambda \cdot \mathcal{C}^{(t-1)} + (1 - \lambda) \cdot \mathcal{C}^{(t)}, \tag{5}$$

while the codebook reset strategy periodically identifies and reinitializes inactive codewords to promote full codebook utilization.

3.2 A2I Model

Based on the pre-trained VQ-VAE from Sect. 3.1, a motion sequence $\boldsymbol{X}$ is first encoded into a latent feature sequence $\boldsymbol{Z}$ using the encoder. Concurrently, we obtain the corresponding index sequence $\boldsymbol{K} = [k_1, k_2, \ldots, k_{T/l}]$ from the codebook $\mathcal{C}$, where each index $k_i \in \{1, 2, \ldots, |\mathcal{C}|\}$. By mapping the index sequence back to the codebook via the quantization operation $\mathcal{Q}_D(\boldsymbol{K})$, and passing the result through the decoder $\mathcal{D}$, the motion sequence can be reconstructed as:

$$\hat{\boldsymbol{X}} = \mathcal{D}(\mathcal{Q}_D(\boldsymbol{K}), c).$$

Hence, the task of generating a motion sequence conditioned on an action label can be reformulated as the autoregressive prediction of the index sequence $\boldsymbol{K}$. To this end, we train a Transformer-based autoregressive model, referred to as the Action-to-Index (A2I) model, whose architecture is depicted in Fig. 3. Conditioned on the action label a, the model autoregressively predicts a SoftMax probability distribution over the codebook indices for the next token.

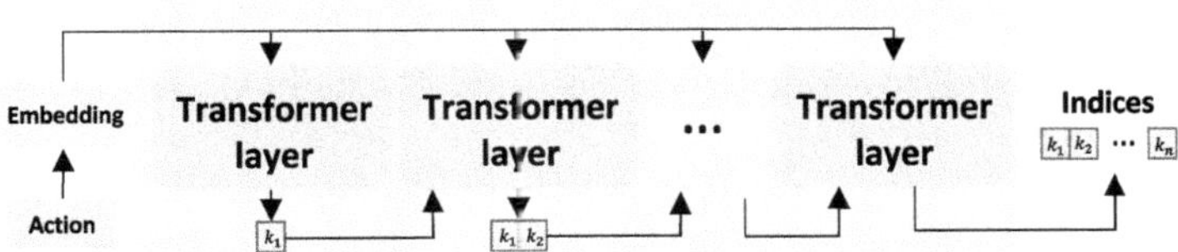

Fig. 3. Architecture of the Action-to-Index model.

The model strictly preserves the temporal order of the index sequence $\boldsymbol{K}$. To enforce this, it employs a causal self-attention mechanism that ensures each step in the sequence can only attend to previous and current positions, preventing access to any future indices. Specifically, the causal attention is computed as:

$$\text{Attention}(Q, K, V) = \text{softmax}\left(\frac{QK^\top \odot M}{\sqrt{d_k}}\right) V, \tag{6}$$

where $Q \in \mathbb{R}^{T \times d_k}$ and $K \in \mathbb{R}^{T \times d_k}$ denote the query and key matrices, respectively, and M is a causal mask matrix defined element-wise as:

$$M_{i,j} = \begin{cases} 1, & \text{if } i \geq j, \\ -\infty, & \text{if } i < j. \end{cases} \tag{7}$$

Here, i denotes the target sequence position (row) and j denotes the source sequence position (column). This masking scheme preserves the attention weights for positions where $i \geq j$ (which yield non-zero probabilities after softmax), while assignments to $-\infty$ for positions where $i < j$ (the lower triangle) are suppressed to zero by the softmax operation. This effectively prevents the model from attending to future time steps, thereby strictly satisfying the requirements of autoregressive prediction.

Optimization Objective: Typically, given the conditional information c, the full likelihood of the index sequence K is defined as:

$$p_n(K|c, T) = \prod_{i=1}^{|K|} p(k_i|c, k_{<i}) \tag{8}$$

The standard training objective is to minimize the negative log-likelihood over the entire sequence. However, in this task, the prediction accuracy of the indices at the beginning of the sequence is more critical for the overall generation quality. Therefore, instead of directly optimizing the joint likelihood of the whole sequence, we split the sequence K into two consecutive parts: a leading part F and a remaining part R. The leading part F contains the first $|F|$ indices, and the remaining part R contains the subsequent indices. Conditional likelihoods are computed separately for these two parts:

$$p_F(K|c) = \prod_{i=1}^{|F|} p(k_i|c, k_{<i}) \tag{9}$$

$$p_R(K|c) = \prod_{i=|F|+1}^{|R|} p(k_i|c, k_{<i}) \tag{10}$$

Finally, the overall loss function of the model is defined as:

$$L_G = \alpha \cdot L_F + \beta \cdot L_R, \tag{11}$$

where L_F and L_R are the negative log-likelihood losses for the two parts, and α, β are hyperparameters.

4   Experiments

4.1   Dataset

We evaluated the proposed model on two different datasets. The data processing follows the same procedure as in ACTOR [21], where each sequence is temporally clipped around a single action to ensure that each sequence contains only one action segment. A brief introduction to the datasets used is as follows:

HumanAct12: HumanAct12 [11] is adapted from the PHSPD dataset [32], which provides SMPL pose parameters and root translations in camera coordinates for 1,191 videos. HumanAct12 temporally trims the videos and annotates them into 12 action categories, such as warm-up, walking, and drinking, providing joint coordinates only in canonical frames.

UESTC: UESTC [14] defines action categories with finer granularity, containing 40 types of actions performed by 118 subjects. Example actions include squatting, punching, and left-side stretching. This dataset was collected from 8 fixed viewpoints, resulting in 25,600 video samples. For fair comparison, we adopt the same preprocessing procedure as in [21]. Motion sequence samples shorter than a given threshold are filtered out. After preprocessing, we obtain 10,629 training sequences and 13,350 testing sequences.

4.2   Evaluation Metrics

Frechet Inception Distance (FID) [11]: Features are extracted from generated actions and real actions (obtained by resampling the test set), and the FID between the distributions of generated and real action features is computed. This metric serves as an important standard for evaluating the overall quality of generated actions and is widely used in generative model assessment.

Recognition Accuracy [11]: We use a pretrained action recognition classifier to classify the generated data and compute overall accuracy. This accuracy reflects the consistency between the generated motion data and their corresponding action categories.

Diversity [11]: Diversity measures the variance of the generated motions across all action categories. To compute it, two random subsets of generated motions, each of size S_d, are selected. Their corresponding motion feature vectors, $\{v_1, \cdots, v_{S_d}\}$ and $\{\hat{v}'_1, \cdots, \hat{v}'_{S_d}\}$, are then extracted. The diversity of the motion set is calculated as the average squared Euclidean distance between the paired feature vectors:

$$Diversity = \frac{1}{S_d} \sum_{i=1}^{S_d} \|v_i - v'_i\|_2 \tag{12}$$

Multimodality [11]: While diversity captures variation across action categories, multimodality evaluates the variability of motions within the same action type.

For a motion set containing C action classes, two random subsets of size S_l are drawn for each class c. Their corresponding feature vectors, $\{v_{c,1}, \cdots, v_{c,S_l}\}$ and $\{v'_{c,1}, \cdots, v'_{c,S_l}\}$, are then extracted. The multimodality score is defined as the mean squared distance between paired feature vectors over all action classes:

$$Multimodality = \frac{1}{C \times S_l} \sum_{c=1}^{C} \sum_{i=1}^{S_l} \left\| v_{c,i} - v'_{c,i} \right\|_2 \tag{13}$$

For the HumanAct12 dataset, we directly use the recognition model based on joint coordinates from Action2Motion [11]. For the UESTC dataset, we use the recognition model provided by ACTOR [21].

4.3 Ablation Study

This section investigates and analyzes the effectiveness of each key component in the proposed label-conditioned human motion generation method, as well as their contributions to the final performance. The complete generation process includes the subsequent A2I model. This section is divided into two parts for study.

The first part isolates and evaluates the VQ-VAE architecture itself, excluding the influence of the A2I model while keeping other variables consistent. Specifically, we first test the ability of the VQ-VAE to directly generate human motion sequences from latent vectors (results are shown in Table 1). As a baseline, we adopt a CNN-based VQ-VAE architecture, which is commonly used in VQ-VAE frameworks, specifically following the implementation in TM2D [10].

We compare several variants of the proposed architecture. TC: This structure employs the Transformer- and CNN-based VQ-VAE architecture proposed in this work. TC (w/ c): Builds on the previous version by adding conditional guidance, thereby enhancing the VQ-VAE's ability during generation. The suffix +Q indicates whether EMA and codebook reset strategies are additionally introduced to improve codebook utilization.

The second part focuses on evaluating the performance of the complete generation pipeline. We use the VQ-VAE codebooks obtained from different VQ-VAE architectures in the first part to train A2I models with identical structures and assess the overall performance of the pipeline. Additionally, within our proposed full architecture, we conduct experiments with the newly introduced loss function for the A2I model, where w/o loss denotes not using the loss and w/ loss denotes applying it. The experimental results are presented in Table 2.

Overall, the ablation studies validate the effectiveness of our proposed components. The VQ-VAE architecture with conditional guidance significantly improves generation quality. Moreover, using the learned codebooks for downstream A2I models, along with the new loss function and codebook quantization strategies, further enhances motion generation. These results demonstrate the superiority of our full architecture in the Action-to-Motion task.

All ablation experiments in this section are conducted on the HumanAct12 dataset, with all architectures using the same optimizer and parameter settings to ensure a fair comparison.For each metric, we repeat the evaluation 20 times and report the average with 95% confidence interval.

Table 1. Ablation study on motion generation from latent vectors on the HumanAct12 dataset.The best results are bolded.

Method	$Accuracy \uparrow$	$FID \downarrow$	$Diversity \rightarrow$	$Multimodality \rightarrow$
Real	$99.7^{\pm 0.10}$	$0.02^{\pm 0.00}$	$6.85^{\pm 0.05}$	$2.45^{\pm 0.04}$
CNN	$97.3^{\pm 0.23}$	$0.12^{\pm 0.00}$	$6.82^{\pm 0.02}$	$2.74^{\pm 0.01}$
CNN+Q	$98.3^{\pm 0.13}$	$0.09^{\pm 0.00}$	$6.82^{\pm 0.02}$	$2.68^{\pm 0.01}$
TC+Q(w/o c)	$98.8^{\pm 0.23}$	$\mathbf{0.03^{\pm 0.00}}$	$6.83^{\pm 0.01}$	$2.61^{\pm 0.01}$
TC+Q(w/ c)	$\mathbf{99.2^{\pm 0.10}}$	$\mathbf{0.03^{\pm 0.00}}$	$\mathbf{6.84^{\pm 0.01}}$	$\mathbf{2.57^{\pm 0.01}}$

Table 2. Ablation study of conditional generation and the proposed loss on the HumanAct12 dataset.The best results are bolded.

Method	$Accuracy \uparrow$	$FID \downarrow$	$Diversity \rightarrow$	$Multimodality \rightarrow$
Real	$99.4^{\pm 0.03}$	$0.02^{\pm 0.00}$	$6.93^{\pm 0.05}$	$2.57^{\pm 0.01}$
CNN	$96.8^{\pm 0.23}$	$0.15^{\pm 0.00}$	$6.8^{\pm 0.02}$	$2.73^{\pm 0.01}$
CNN+Q	$97.0^{\pm 0.34}$	$0.14^{\pm 0.00}$	$6.82^{\pm 0.02}$	$2.76^{\pm 0.02}$
TC+Q(w/o c)(w/o loss)	$98.2^{\pm 0.14}$	$\mathbf{0.05^{\pm 0.00}}$	$6.84^{\pm 0.02}$	$2.67^{\pm 0.02}$
TC+Q(w/o c)(w/ loss)	$98.4^{\pm 0.14}$	$\mathbf{0.05^{\pm 0.00}}$	$6.84^{\pm 0.02}$	$2.67^{\pm 0.01}$
TC+Q(w/ c)(w/o loss)	$99.0^{\pm 0.23}$	$\mathbf{0.05^{\pm 0.00}}$	$\mathbf{6.85^{\pm 0.01}}$	$2.60^{\pm 0.02}$
TC+Q(w/ c)(w/ loss)	$\mathbf{99.2^{\pm 0.23}}$	$\mathbf{0.05^{\pm 0.00}}$	$\mathbf{6.85^{\pm 0.01}}$	$\mathbf{2.57^{\pm 0.01}}$

4.4 Comparative Experiments

In the field of motion generation, significant results have been achieved by methods including Action2Motion [11], ACTOR [21], and the diffusion-based approaches MDM [26] and MLD [6] .

During the training of the VQ-VAE model, we set the batch size to 64 for both datasets. Specifically, the codebook size was configured as 128 for the HumanAct12 dataset and 265 for the UESTC dataset. For the training of the A2I model, a consistent batch size of 64 was also applied across both datasets. For both training processes, we employed the AdamW optimizer with a learning rate of 0.00001, and terminated the training when the model loss showed no significant decrease over an extended period.

We conducted comparative experiments on the HumanAct12 and UESTC datasets, with the results shown in Table 3 and Table 4, respectively. Each metric was evaluated over 20 repeated trials, reporting the mean along with the 95%

Table 3. Comparison of motion generation methods on the HumanAct12 dataset.The best and second-best results are bolded and underlined,respectively.

Method	Accuracy ↑	FID ↓	Diversity →	Multimodality →
Real	$99.4^{\pm0.03}$	$0.02^{\pm0.00}$	$6.93^{\pm0.05}$	$2.57^{\pm0.01}$
action2Motion	$92.3^{\pm0.20}$	$2.46^{\pm0.08}$	$\underline{6.84^{\pm0.03}}$	$2.53^{\pm0.02}$
ACTOR	$95.5^{\pm0.80}$	$0.12^{\pm0.00}$	$\underline{6.84^{\pm0.03}}$	$2.35^{\pm0.02}$
MDM	$\underline{99.0^{\pm0.00}}$	$0.10^{\pm0.00}$	$6.68^{\pm0.05}$	$2.52^{\pm0.01}$
MLD	$96.4^{\pm0.20}$	$\underline{0.07^{\pm0.00}}$	$6.83^{\pm0.05}$	$2.82^{\pm0.03}$
PoseGPT	$95.8^{\pm0.00}$	$0.08^{\pm0.00}$	$\mathbf{6.85^{\pm0.00}}$	$2.82^{\pm0.00}$
DeepWGAN-GP	$94.2^{\pm0.20}$	$0.11^{\pm0.00}$	$\mathbf{6.85^{\pm0.05}}$	$\underline{2.58^{\pm0.05}}$
MotionMix	$96.0^{\pm0.30}$	$0.19^{\pm0.00}$	$6.83^{\pm0.06}$	$3.04^{\pm0.05}$
Our	$\mathbf{99.2^{\pm0.23}}$	$\mathbf{0.05^{\pm0.00}}$	$6.85^{\pm0.01}$	$\mathbf{2.57^{\pm0.01}}$

Table 4. Comparison of motion generation methods on the UESTC dataset. The best and second-best results are bolded and underlined, respectively.

Method	Accuracy ↑	FID_{train} ↓	FID_{test} ↓	Diversity →	Multimodality →
Real	$98.8^{\pm0.10}$	$2.92^{\pm0.26}$	$2.79^{\pm0.29}$	$33.34^{\pm0.32}$	$14.16^{\pm0.06}$
ACTOR	$91.1^{\pm0.30}$	$20.49^{\pm2.30}$	$23.43^{\pm2.20}$	$31.96^{\pm0.36}$	$14.66^{\pm0.03}$
INR	$94.1^{\pm0.10}$	$\underline{9.55^{\pm0.06}}$	$15.00^{\pm0.09}$	$35.19^{\pm0.19}$	$14.68^{\pm0.07}$
MDM	$95.0^{\pm0.10}$	$9.98^{\pm1.33}$	$12.81^{\pm1.46}$	$33.02^{\pm0.28}$	$\mathbf{14.26^{\pm0.12}}$
MLD	$95.4^{\pm0.17}$	$12.89^{\pm0.11}$	$15.79^{\pm0.07}$	$\underline{33.52^{\pm0.14}}$	$13.57^{\pm0.06}$
NeRM	$95.6^{\pm0.10}$	$11.75^{\pm0.31}$	$14.23^{\pm0.50}$	$\mathbf{33.20^{\pm0.21}}$	$14.41^{\pm0.06}$
MotionMix	$\underline{96.0^{\pm0.30}}$	–	$\underline{11.40^{\pm0.39}}$	$32.81^{\pm0.18}$	$\underline{14.28^{\pm0.09}}$
Our	$\mathbf{97.1^{\pm0.17}}$	$\mathbf{5.13^{\pm0.20}}$	$\mathbf{11.03^{\pm0.50}}$	$34.48^{\pm0.30}$	$13.91^{\pm0.09}$

confidence interval. Experimental results demonstrate that, compared to existing methods and several state-of-the-art approaches from the past two years, our method exhibits significant advantages across multiple evaluation metrics, validating its effectiveness and superiority in motion generation tasks. Finally, we use the trained model for human motion generation and provide visualization results, as shown in Fig. 4.

Fig. 4. Examples of label-conditioned human motion generation.

5 Conclusion

In this work, we explore a well-established framework that integrates VQ-VAE with an autoregressive model for human motion generation from action labels. We systematically evaluate the performance of various encoder-decoder architectures on motion reconstruction and generation tasks, and examine the effect of different quantization strategies on the quality of generated motions. Experimental results demonstrate that our approach achieves competitive performance against several existing methods, showing clear advantages in comparative assessments.

References

1. Ahn, H., Ha, T., Choi, Y., Yoo, H., Oh, S.: Text2action: Generative adversarial synthesis from language to action. In: 2018 IEEE International Conference on Robotics and Automation (ICRA), pp. 5915–5920. IEEE (2018)
2. Ahuja, C., Morency, L.P.: Language2pose: Natural language grounded pose forecasting. In: 2019 International conference on 3D vision (3DV), pp. 719–728. IEEE (2019)
3. Aksan, E., Kaufmann, M., Hilliges, O.: Structured prediction helps 3d human motion modelling. In: Proceedings of the IEEE/CVF International Conference on Computer Vision, pp. 7144–7153 (2019)
4. Ao, T., Gao, Q., Lou, Y., Chen, B., Liu, L.: Rhythmic gesticulator: rhythm-aware co-speech gesture synthesis with hierarchical neural embeddings. ACM Trans. Graphics (TOG) 41(6), 1–19 (2022)
5. Aristidou, A., Yiannakidis, A., Aberman, K., Cohen-Or, D., Shamir, A., Chrysanthou, Y.: Rhythm is a dancer: Music-driven motion synthesis with global structure. arXiv preprint arXiv:2111.12159 (2021)
6. Chen, X., et al.: Executing your commands via motion diffusion in latent space. In: Proceedings of the IEEE/CVF Conference on Computer Vision and Pattern Recognition, pp. 18000–18010 (2023)

7. Dhariwal, P., Jun, H., Payne, C., Kim, J.W., Radford, A., Sutskever, I.: Jukebox: a generative model for music. arXiv preprint arXiv:2005.00341 (2020)

8. Esser, P., Rombach, R., Ommer, B.: Taming transformers for high-resolution image synthesis. In: Proceedings of the IEEE/CVF Conference on Computer Vision and Pattern Recognition, pp. 12873–12883 (2021)

9. Fragkiadaki, K., Levine, S., Felsen, P., Malik, J.: Recurrent network models for human dynamics. In: Proceedings of the IEEE International Conference on Computer Vision, pp. 4346–4354 (2015)

10. Gong, K., et al.: Tm2d: Bimodality driven 3D dance generation via music-text integration. In: Proceedings of the IEEE/CVF International Conference on Computer Vision, pp. 9942–9952 (2023)

11. Guo, C., et al.: Action2motion: Conditioned generation of 3D human motions. In: Proceedings of the 28th ACM International Conference on Multimedia, pp. 2021–2029 (2020)

12. Ho, J., Jain, A., Abbeel, P.: Denoising diffusion probabilistic models. Adv. Neural. Inf. Process. Syst. **33**, 6840–6851 (2020)

13. Ionescu, C., Li, F., Sminchisescu, C.: Latent structured models for human pose estimation. In: 2011 International Conference on Computer Vision, pp. 2220–2227. IEEE (2011)

14. Ji, Y., et al.: A large-scale RGB-D database for arbitrary-view human action recognition. In: Proceedings of the 26th ACM International Conference on Multimedia, pp. 1510–1518 (2018)

15. Kingma, D.P., Welling, M.: Auto-encoding variational bayes. arXiv preprint arXiv:1312.6114 (2013)

16. Lin, X., Amer, M.R.: Human motion modeling using dvgans. arXiv preprint arXiv:1804.10652 (2018)

17. Lu, Q., Zhang, Y., Lu, M., Roychowdhury, V.: Action-conditioned on-demand motion generation. In: Proceedings of the 30th ACM International Conference on Multimedia, pp. 2249–2257 (2022)

18. Lucas, T., Baradel, F., Weinzaepfel, P., Rogez, G.: Posegpt: Quantization-based 3D human motion generation and forecasting. In: European Conference on Computer Vision, pp. 417–435. Springer (2022)

19. Martinez, J., Black, M.J., Romero, J.: On human motion prediction using recurrent neural networks. In: Proceedings of the IEEE Conference on Computer Vision and Pattern Recognition, pp. 2891–2900 (2017)

20. Ormoneit, D., Black, M.J., Hastie, T., Kjellström, H.: Representing cyclic human motion using functional analysis. Image Vis. Comput. **23**(14), 1264–1276 (2005)

21. Petrovich, M., Black, M.J., Varol, G.: Action-conditioned 3D human motion synthesis with transformer VAE. In: Proceedings of the IEEE/CVF International Conference on Computer Vision, pp. 10985–10995 (2021)

22. Raab, S., Leibovitch, I., Li, P., Aberman, K., Sorkine-Hornung, O., Cohen-Or, D.: Modi: unconditional motion synthesis from diverse data. In: Proceedings of the IEEE/CVF Conference on Computer Vision and Pattern Recognition, pp. 13873–13883 (2023)

23. Ramesh, A., et al.: Zero-shot text-to-image generation. In: International Conference on Machine Learning, pp. 8821–8831. PMLR (2021)

24. Rombach, R., Blattmann, A., Lorenz, D., Esser, P., Ommer, B.: High-resolution image synthesis with latent diffusion models. In: Proceedings of the IEEE/CVF Conference on Computer Vision and Pattern Recognition, pp. 10684–10695 (2022)

25. Siyao, L., et al.: Bailando: 3D dance generation by actor-critic GPT with choreographic memory. In: Proceedings of the IEEE/CVF Conference on Computer Vision and Pattern Recognition, pp. 11050–11059 (2022)
26. Tevet, G., Raab, S., Gordon, B., Shafir, Y., Cohen-Or, D., Bermano, A.H.: Human motion diffusion model. arXiv preprint arXiv:2209.14916 (2022)
27. Van Den Oord, A., Vinyals, O., et al.: Neural discrete representation learning. Adv. Neural Inf. Process. Syst. **30** (2017)
28. Xu, H., et al.: Ghum & ghuml: Generative 3D human shape and articulated pose models. In: Proceedings of the IEEE/CVF Conference on Computer Vision and Pattern Recognition, pp. 6184–6193 (2020)
29. Yan, S., Li, Z., Xiong, Y., Yan, H., Lin, D.: Convolutional sequence generation for skeleton-based action synthesis. In: Proceedings of the IEEE/CVF International Conference on Computer Vision, pp. 4394–4402 (2019)
30. Yan, S., Xiong, Y., Lin, D.: Spatial temporal graph convolutional networks for skeleton-based action recognition. In: Proceedings of the AAAI Conference on Artificial Intelligence, vol. 32 (2018)
31. Zhang, M., et al.: Motiondiffuse: text-driven human motion generation with diffusion model. IEEE Trans. Pattern Anal. Mach. Intell. **46**(6), 4115–4128 (2024)
32. Zou, S., et al.: 3D human shape reconstruction from a polarization image. In: European Conference on Computer Vision, pp. 351–368. Springer (2020)

Food Image Segmentation with LLM-Derived Ingredient Labels and Multimodal Fusion

Jui-Feng Chi, Wei-Ta Chu[(✉)] [iD], and Sheng-Long Lin

National Cheng Kung University, Tainan, Taiwan
wtchu@gs.ncku.edu.tw

Abstract. Food image segmentation plays a vital role in health-related applications such as nutrition tracking and personalized health monitoring. However, existing models often underperform on visually similar ingredients and rare food categories. To address this issue, we propose two plug-and-play multimodal modules that enhance the segmentation performance by leveraging ingredient labels inferred from food images using large language models (LLMs). The first module, called LIM-F (Language Injection Module for Features), is designed to pair with any image encoder that produces multi-layer outputs (e.g., Swin Transformer), while the second module, LIM-Q (Language Injection Module for Queries), targets Mask2Former-style Transformer-based decoders. Both modules enable training without the need for pre-aligning images with text by directly injecting semantic ingredient information into the visual analysis pipeline. On the FoodSeg103 benchmark, the proposed method achieves state-of-the-art performance. Specifically, integrating LIM-Q into the Mask2Former decoder with a Swin-L image encoder yields a mean Intersection over Union (mIoU) of 55.0. LIM-F also demonstrates strong generalization and competitive performance, reaching an mIoU of 54.4 under the same model (Swin-L+Mask2Former). Furthermore, its applicability extends beyond Transformer-based decoders, as evidenced by an improvement from 47.7 to 49.8 mIoU when integrated into a CNN-based architecture. Notably, the improved segmentation accuracy is achieved with only a moderate (at most 3.8 GB) increase in the GPU memory consumption during training. Thus, the proposed approach offers a practical and scalable solution for fine-grained food understanding.

Keywords: Food image segmentation · Ingredient labels · Large Language Models

1 Introduction

Food image segmentation is a fundamental task in computer vision with growing significance in healthcare, dietary assessment, and nutrition tracking. Accurately

J. Lokoč et al. (Eds.): MMM 2026, LNCS 16412, pp. 422–434, 2026.
https://doi.org/10.1007/978-981-95-6950-2_30

2.4   Text-Guided Food Segmentation Models

Despite growing interest in multimodal learning, few studies have explored using textual cues in food segmentation tasks. One prominent example is ReLeM [21], which applies contrastive training on paired recipe narratives and dish images from the Recipe1M+ dataset. By embedding ingredient and cooking method semantics into the visual backbone, ReLeM produces an ingredient-aware encoder that can be paired with various segmentation networks. Another example is OVFoodSeg [22], which is an open-vocabulary approach that employs a transformer-based module to convert image encoder outputs into a representation compatible with the text encoder. This design enables the ingredient tokens to dynamically adapt to the visual context.

Although both methods demonstrate the value of ingredient semantics in food segmentation, they rely on complex pipelines and curated paired datasets. In contrast, our proposed framework achieves similar cross-modal fusion through a lightweight, plug-and-play design that removes the dependency on large-scale vision-language pretraining and paired datasets.

3   Method

Our proposed method integrates the ingredient-level textual features generated by an LLM into a semantic segmentation architecture through two complementary modules: LIM-F, a general-purpose module applicable to any segmentation model with multi-level output backbones, and LIM-Q, a decoder-specific design tailored for a Transformer-based decoder. Both modules are designed to be lightweight and architecture-compatible, enabling efficient multimodal learning without special pretraining or external image-text alignment.

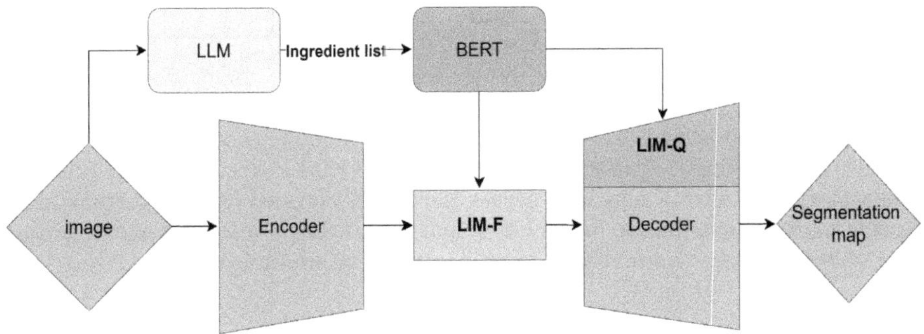

Fig. 1. Overview of the proposed multimodal segmentation framework. An input image is sent to both a vision encoder and an LLM, which generates ingredient labels that are then encoded by BERT. The language features are injected into the segmentation pipeline via either LIM-F or LIM-Q. LIM-F fuses feature maps after the encoder, while LIM-Q embeds language information into the decoder. Both the encoder and decoder are modular and can be flexibly replaced.

3.1 Overview

Figure 1 shows an overview of the proposed system, which consists of a dual-branch structure composed of a visual encoder and a language encoder. The visual branch uses Swin-L [12] pretrained on the ImageNet-22k dataset and then finetuned (any other backbone with multi-level outputs can also be used) as the image encoder to produce multi-scale visual feature maps. Meanwhile, the language branch takes a list of ingredient classes generated by an online LLM (GPT-o4 mini in this study) as the input and encodes these class labels using a BERT model [7] to produce word embeddings[1] These embeddings serve as the source of semantic guidance for the fusion modules.

Depending on the backbone and decoder design, one of the two language injection modules is used, namely LIM-F, which introduces language supervision into intermediate visual features for models with multi-level output backbones, or LIM-Q, which modulates Transformer decoder queries using language features. Unlike LIM-F, LIM-Q operates only at the decoder level and is compatible with a wide range of backbone architectures.

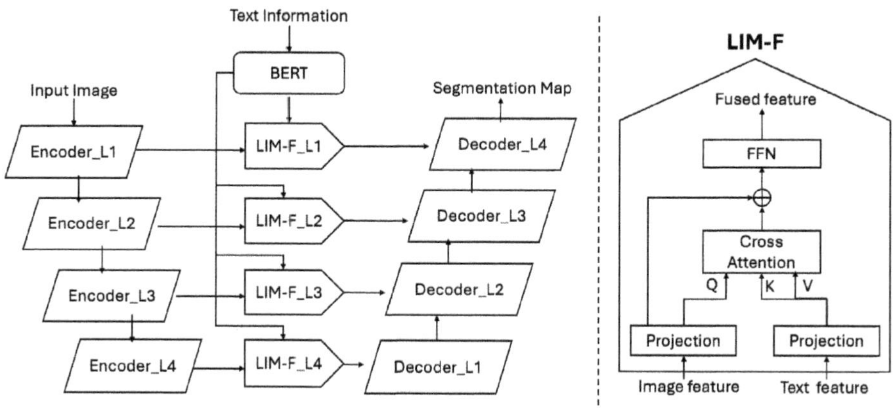

Fig. 2. The segmentation framework with the LIM-F module. Feature maps from different levels are individually passed through a dedicated LIM-F block. These blocks apply cross-attention between the image features and BERT-encoded ingredient embeddings, allowing multi-scale semantic fusion before passing to the decoder. All query, key, and value vectors are layer-normalized to ensure stable feature distributions.

3.2 LIM-F: Feature-Level Injection for Multi-level Output Backbones

Figure 2 illustrates the framework with the LIM-F module, which is designed to introduce ingredient-level text semantics into architectures with a multi-level

[1] The BERT-large-uncased model downloaded from Hugging Face, https:// huggingface.co/google-bert/bert-large-uncased.

output image encoder. Specifically, the Swin-L encoder generates four output levels (levels 0 to 3), each corresponding to a different spatial resolution and receptive field. At each level, an independent LIM-F module calculates cross-attention between visual and text information, where the visual features serve as queries and the BERT-encoded ingredient embeddings serve as keys and values.

Dimensional alignment between the BERT embeddings and the visual feature map at each level is ensured using a linear projection layer. In general, the textual feature dimension needs to match that of the corresponding image feature map; therefore, the image feature map retains the same dimensionality before and after its own linear projection. The output of each cross-attention operation is added back to the visual stream via a residual connection, followed by a feed-forward network (FFN), and then passed to the corresponding decoder layer. The application of cross-attention at all levels enables multi-level features to attend to textual ingredient descriptions, incorporating the corresponding semantic cues into relevant pixels.

Since LIM-F relies solely on the image encoder and imposes no constraints on the decoder, it offers broad adaptability across segmentation architectures. To demonstrate this property, we implement two configurations of LIM-F in our experiments. The first variant pairs Swin-L with K-Net + UPerNet [24] [23] as the decoder. Here, UPerNet serves as a conventional CNN-based decoder, while K-Net extends it with dynamic kernel updates, showcasing LIM-F's compatibility with traditional non-Transformer decoders. The second variant adopts Mask2Former, a Transformer-based decoder known for strong performance, to further examine LIM-F's adaptability and effectiveness across diverse decoder designs.

3.3 LIM-Q: Query-Level Injection for Transformer Decoders

Figure 3 shows the framework with the LIM-Q module, which extends the conventional Mask2Former decoder structure. In Mask2Former, a set of learnable query tokens is updated over three rounds, with each round comprising three Transformer decoder layers. During each round, the query tokens attend to the feature maps produced at different levels by the pixel decoder in a round-robin manner, resulting in a total of nine layers.

To incorporate guidance from ingredient labels, we introduce semantics-based guidance at the beginning of every round. Before the learnable queries attend to the three image feature levels, they first pass through a dedicated LIM-Q block. Each LIM-Q block first projects the learnable queries and BERT-encoded ingredient embeddings (as key and values) into a common space, where the feature dimensions are matched to the queries. The block then performs cross-attention to inject ingredient semantics into the queries, followed by a self-attention layer to model relations among the updated queries and a feed-forward network (FFN) for further refinement, with all stages wrapped in residual connections.

The insertion of LIM-Q blocks in a round-robin manner ensures that semantic guidance from the LLM-generated text labels is consistently reinforced throughout decoding, effectively reminding the queries of the ingredient category they

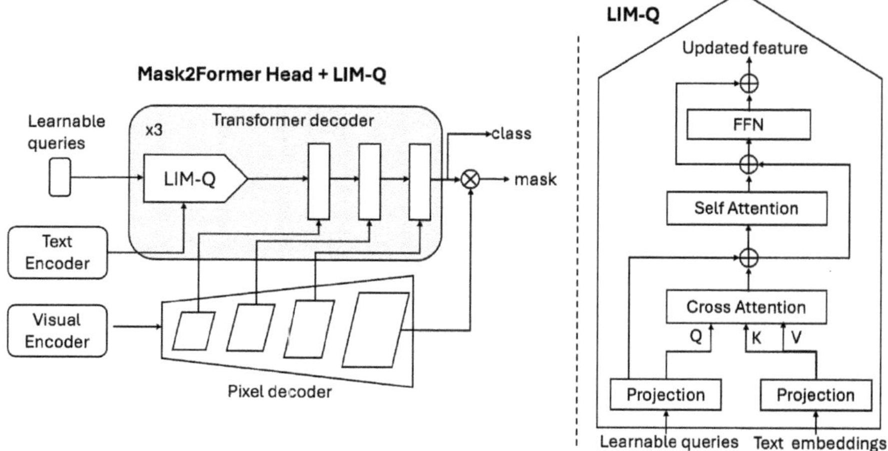

Fig. 3. Each LIM-Q block is inserted into every decoding round of Mask2Former to enhance its ability to incorporate textual semantics. It includes a cross-attention to BERT-encoded ingredient embeddings, followed by self-attention and a feed-forward network (FFN). All Q, K, and V inputs are layer-normalized before entering each attention block.

should predict. This mechanism mitigates common failure cases, such as confusing visually similar food classes, and helps achieve better class-level alignment.

3.4   Loss Function

Based on the proposed LIM-F and LIM-Q modules, we develop three variants of food segmentation methods: (1) K-Net with UPerNet + LIM-F; (2) Mask2Former + LIM-F; and (3) Mask2Former + LIM-Q. All three variants use Swin-L as the image encoder.

Since different decoders often require different loss functions, we describe them separately. For the first variant, the loss function is the standard cross-entropy loss, which is commonly used in conventional decoders and aligns with the purpose of evaluating LIM-F's broad compatibility. For the second and third variants, the Mask2Former adopts the mask, the Dice, and the classification losses to guide model training. Specifically, the overall loss function is:

$$\mathcal{L} = \lambda_{CE}\mathcal{L}_{CE} + \lambda_{dice}\mathcal{L}_{dice} + \lambda_{cls}\mathcal{L}_{cls}, \tag{1}$$

where $\mathcal{L}_{CE}$ is the pixel-wise Cross-Entropy loss for mask prediction, $\mathcal{L}_{dice}$ measures region-level overlap between predicted and ground-truth masks, and $\mathcal{L}_{cls}$ is the classification loss applied to the decoder's query-level category prediction. The weights λ_{CE}, λ_{dice}, and λ_{cls} determine the relative contributions of each loss term.

In the original configuration of Mask2Former, the weights λ_{CE}, λ_{dice}, and λ_{cls} are set as 5, 5, and 2, respectively. When combining with the proposed

LIM-F or LIM-Q modules, we found that appropriately increasing the weight λ_{cls} gives more performance gain. This will be verified in the evaluation section.

4   Experiments

4.1   Implementation Details

All variants were trained on the FoodSeg103 dataset [21] with a batch size of 2 for 240,000 iterations. All experiments use Swin-L initialized with ImageNet-22k pretrained weights and BERT initialized with the pretrained BERT-large-uncased model from Hugging Face. For the pretrained Swin-L backbone and the last four layers of the pretrained BERT encoder (which were unfrozen for fine-tuning during the training process), a learning rate multiplier of 0.1 was applied. The parameters of the last four layers of the BERT encoder were trained without weight decay (decay set to 0.0), while the remaining BERT layers were kept frozen during training. All three variants use an AdamW optimizer [14].

Separately for different variants, the first variant uses a base learning rate of 6e-5, which was annealed to 1e-6 over the training schedule. For the second and third variants with Mask2Former, the training hyperparameters were assigned the same values as those in [5], except for the loss weights. In addition, training was performed with an initial learning rate of 1e-4 decayed to 1e-6 using cosine annealing [13] over the training schedule.

To provide language guidance, GPT-o4 mini[2] was used as the LLM to generate ingredient class labels. The input to the LLM consisted of a food image and the full list of 104 ingredient class names from FoodSeg103, along with a prompt asking the model to infer a few of the likely ingredients present in the food image and return them as a comma-separated list (e.g., "lettuce, potato, tomato"). This dynamic generation of image-specific textual description eliminates the need for curated image-text pairs and thus greatly reduces the training requirement.

4.2   Quantitative Results and Convergence Behavior

We evaluate the segmentation performance in terms of mean Intersection over Union (mIoU) in Table 1. As can be seen, the third variant (3) Mask2Former + LIM-Q achieves the highest mIoU of 55.0, surpassing strong baselines such as BEiTv2 Large (49.4), IngredSAM (48.8), Swin-TUNA (50.6), and FoodSAM (46.4) [10]. LIM-F is also proven effective, achieving 49.0 when integrated with K-Net in the first variant and 54.4 when combined with Mask2Former in the second variant.

Notably, although LIM-F and LIM-Q obtain similar mIoUs when integrated with Mask2Former in the second and third variants, LIM-Q demonstrates faster convergence during training, as shown in Fig. 4. This can be attributed to the more aggressive text-guided information injection strategy in LIM-Q, in which the BERT-derived semantic cues are explicitly attended to by the learnable

---

[2] Accessed in early May, 2025.

Table 1. Performance comparison in terms of mIoU on the FoodSeg103 dataset.

Models	mIoU
BEiTv2 Large [20]	49.4
IngredSAM [2]	48.8
FoodSAM [10]	46.4
Swin-TUNA [1]	50.6
K-Net (Swin-L) [24]	47.7
(1) K-Net (Swin-L) + LIM-F	49.0 (+2.7%)
Mask2Former (Swin-L) [5]	51.9
(2) Mask2Former (Swin-L) + LIM-F	54.4 (+4.8 %)
(3) Mask2Former (Swin-L) + LIM-Q	55.0 (+6.0 %)

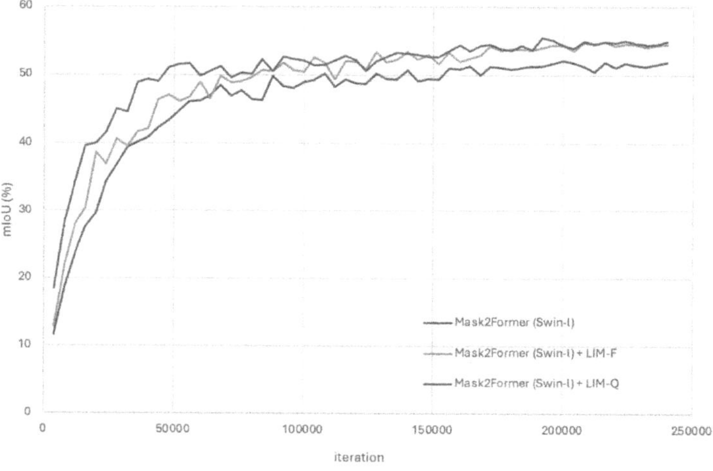

Fig. 4. This figure compares the evolution of mIoUs over the training process, with the baseline Mask2Former, and its variants with LIM-F and LIM-Q modules. The two LIM-augmented models consistently outperform the baseline across training iterations, achieving higher final mIoU scores of 54.44 (LIM-F) and 54.96 (LIM-Q), compared to 51.86 for the original.

queries via cross-attention in the transformer decoder. On the other hand, LIM-F relies on gradually blending the textual semantics provided by the LLM into the multi-scale image features, allowing the query tokens to implicitly discover the semantic correspondences. This design difference allows LIM-Q to benefit from stronger and more direct language supervision in the early stages of training.

Table 2 shows how LIM modules improve the segmentation performance for specific ingredients. To ensure a consistent baseline, the second and third variants are used for comparison in this study. We see that both LIM modules significantly improve the segmentation of rare or visually ambiguous ingredients, thereby confirming that ingredient-level language information helps compensate for weak or ambiguous visual signals.

Table 2. LIM-F and LIM-Q greatly improve segmentation on rare ingredients shown in the table, each occupying less than 1.2% of the training set, showing better recognition than the original Mask2Former.

Sample ingredients	Mask2Former	(2) Mask2Former + LIM-F	(3) Mask2Former + LIM-Q
date	1.28	88.93	77.31
melon	7.95	60.90	52.27
dried cranberries	21.5	42.10	39.07
pear	31.08	58.04	80.57
fig	48.78	79.27	67.40

The basic Mask2Former requires approximately 19 GB of GPU memory, while Mask2Former+LIM-F and Mask2Former+LIM-Q require 22.5 GB and 20 GB, respectively. Therefore, the add-on modules incur only a moderate increase in the GPU memory overhead during training. In our experiments, the proposed architecture achieves notable performance gains without any special pretraining, such as the text-image semantic alignment commonly employed in other multimodal models, making it more implementer-friendly.

4.3   Ablation Study

We investigate the weights of different losses on the Mask2Former-based segmentation performance in the second and third experiment variants. Table 3 shows the performance variations when different weights are employed on the classification loss, and whether the BERT model is fine-tuned. For LIM-F in the second variant, increasing the classification loss weight from 2 to 4 yields the highest mIoU of 54.4. For LIM-Q in the third variant, a $(5, 5, 6)$ setting produces the best result of 55.0. This suggests that the classification head benefits from stronger supervision when it is enriched with language information.

Overall, the ablation test results show the importance of careful tuning of loss weighting and textual representation strategies to maximize the segmentation accuracy for multimodal architectures.

4.4   Qualitative Analysis

Figure 5 shows sample segmentation results. We see that the Mask2Former model struggles to recognize the soup as sauce. With the proposed LIM modules, almost all regions are accurately segmented and recognized. In this example, the visual similarity between certain ingredient categories is particularly pronounced. The sauce in the upper-left bowl shares a similar color and texture

Table 3. Performance variations when different weights are employed on the classification loss, and whether the BERT model is fine-tuned.

Model	$(\lambda_{CE}, \lambda_{dice}, \lambda_{cls})$	Unfreeze BERT	mIoU
Mask2Former − LIM-F	(5, 5, 2)		51.4
Mask2Former + LIM-F	(5, 5, 4)		52.1
Mask2Former + LIM-F	(5, 5, 4)	√	**54.4**
Mask2Former + LIM-F	(5, 5, 6)	√	53.8
Mask2Former + LIM-Q	(5, 5, 4)		51.4
Mask2Former + LIM-Q	(5, 5, 6)		52.8
Mask2Former + LIM-Q	(5, 5, 6)	√	**55.0**
Mask2Former + LIM-Q	(5, 5, 8)		52.2

with the soup, making it challenging for the baseline Mask2Former to distinguish them without additional semantic cues. Similarly, the grilled shrimp in the lower-left region exhibits a reddish-orange hue and segmented shape that closely resembles the appearance of pizza toppings under similar lighting conditions. These strong inter-class visual similarities contribute to the misclassifications observed in the baseline, while the incorporation of LIM-F and LIM-Q provides additional semantic constraints that help disambiguate these cases.

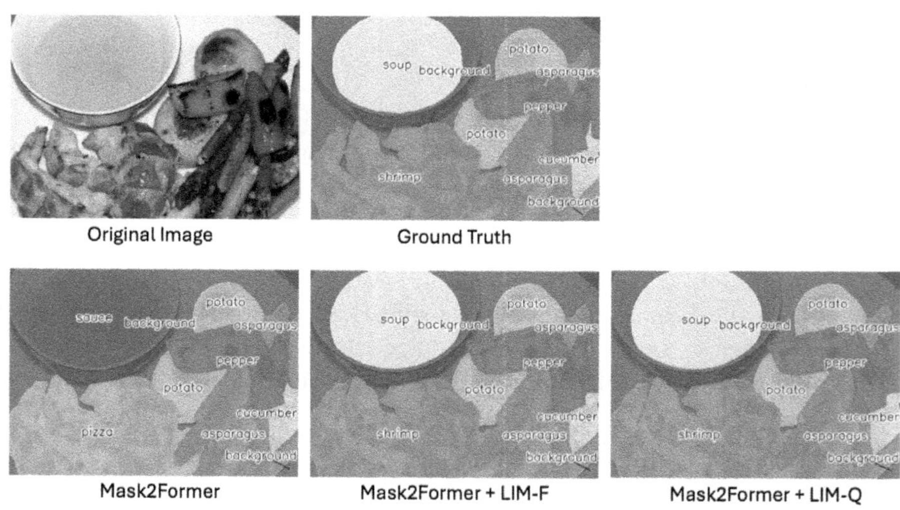

Fig. 5. Sample segmentation results.

5 Conclusion

This study introduces two lightweight, plug-and-play multimodal fusion modules, LIM-F and LIM-Q, that enhance food image segmentation through language guidance. LIM-F integrates linguistic semantics into the intermediate visual features produced by the image encoder, while LIM-Q injects language information directly into the transformer decoder queries. By leveraging ingredient lists generated by an LLM and encoded by a BERT model, along with the proposed LIM-F and LIM-Q modules, the proposed approach eliminates the need for costly image-text alignment and enables end-to-end training across a variety of backbone architectures. Experiments on the FoodSeg103 benchmark demonstrate that both modules clearly improve the segmentation accuracy, particularly for visually similar or rare ingredients.

Overall, this study demonstrates the effectiveness of simple yet powerful language-injection strategies for semantic food segmentation. Future studies may explore adaptive token filtering, LLM-guided region proposals, or extensions to broader food-related tasks, such as volume estimation and cross-modal meal understanding.

Acknowledgement. This work was funded in part the National Science and Technology Council, Taiwan, under grants 114-2622-E-006-028, 114-2221-E-006-047-MY3, 114-2425-H-006-004, 114-2637-8-218-002, 113-2622-E-006-029, 113-2634-F-006-002, and 112-2221-E-006-136-MY3.

References

1. Chen, H., Xiao, Z.: Swin-tuna: a novel PEFT approach for accurate food image segmentation. In: arXiv:2507.17347 (2025)
2. Chen, L., Wang, B., Zhang, J.: Ingredsam: open-world food ingredient segmentation via a single image prompt. J. Imaging **10**(12) (2024)
3. Chen, L.C., Papandreou, G., Kokkinos, I., Murphy, K., Yuille, A.L.: Deeplab: semantic image segmentation with deep convolutional nets, ATROUS convolution, and fully connected CRFS. IEEE Trans. Pattern Anal. Mach. Intell. **40**(4), 834–848 (2017)
4. Chen, Y.C., et al.: Uniter: Universal image-text representation learning. In: Proceedings of European Conference on Computer Vision (2020)
5. Cheng, B., Misra, I., Schwing, A.G., Kirillov, A., Girdhar, R.: Masked-attention mask transformer for universal image segmentation. In: Proceedings of IEEE/CVF International Conference on Computer Vision and Pattern Recognition, pp. 1290–1299 (2022)
6. Chiang, W.L., et al.: Vicuna: an open-source chatbot impressing GPT-4 with 90%* chatgpt quality (2023). https://lmsys.org/blog/2023-03-30-vicuna/
7. Devlin, J., Chang, M.W., Lee, K., Toutanova, K.: Bert: Pre-training of deep bidirectional transformers for language understanding. In: Proceedings of Annual Conference of the North American Chapter of the Association for Computational Linguistics: human Language Technologies, pp. 4171–4186 (2019)

8. Dosovitskiy, A., et al.: An image is worth 16x16 words: transformers for image recognition at scale. In: Proceedings of International Conference on Learning Representations (2021)
9. Kirillov, A., et al.: Segment anything. In: arXiv:2304.02643 (2023)
10. Lan, X., et al.: Foodsam: any food segmentation. In: arXiv:2308.05938 (2023)
11. Liu, H., Li, C., Wu, Q., Lee, Y.J.: Visual instruction tuning. In: Proceedings of Advances in Neural Information Processing Systems (2023)
12. Liu, Z., et al.: Swin transformer: hierarchical vision transformer using shifted windows. In: Proceedings of IEEE/CVF International Conference on Computer Vision (2021)
13. Loshchilov, I., Hutter, F.: Sgdr: Stochastic gradient descent with warm restarts. In: Proceedings of International Conference on Learning Representations (2017)
14. Loshchilov, I., Hutter, F.: Decoupled weight decay regularization. In: Proceedings of International Conference on Learning Representations (2019)
15. Lu, J., Batra, D., Parikh, D., Lee, S.: Vilbert: pretraining task-agnostic visiolinguistic representations for vision-and-language tasks. In: Proceedings of International Conference on Neural Information Processing Systems (2019)
16. Marin, J., et al.: Recipe1m+: a dataset for learning cross-modal embeddings for cooking recipes and food images. IEEE Trans. Pattern Anal. Mach. Intell. **43**(1), 187–203 (2021)
17. OpenAI: GPT-4 Technical Report. In: arXiv:2303.08774 (2023)
18. Peng, Z., et al.: Kosmos-2: grounding multimodal large language models to the world. In: arXiv:2306.14824 (2023)
19. Radford, A., et al.: Learning transferable visual models from natural language supervision. In: arXiv:2103.00020 (2021)
20. Sinha, G., et al.: Transferring knowledge for food image segmentation using transformers and convolutions. In: arXiv:2306.09203 (2023)
21. Wu, X., Fu, X., Liu, Y., Lim, E.P., Hoi, S.C., Sun, Q.: A large-scale benchmark for food image segmentation. In: Proceedings of ACM International Conference on Multimedia, pp. 506–515 (2021)
22. Wu, X., Yu, S., Lim, E.P., Ngo, C.W.: Ovfoodseg: Elevating open-vocabulary food image segmentation via image-informed textual representation. In: Proceedings of IEEE/CVF International Conference on Computer Vision and Pattern Recognition, pp. 4144–4153 (2024)
23. Xiao, T., Liu, Y., Zhou, B., Jiang, Y., Sun, J.: Unified perceptual parsing for scene understanding. In: Proceedings of European Conference on Computer Vision (2018)
24. Zhang, W., Pang, J., Chen, K., Loy, C.C.: K-net: Towards unified image segmentation. In: Proceedings of Annual Conference on Neural Information Processing Systems (2021)
25. Zhao, H., Shi, J., Qi, X., Wang, X., Jia, J.: Pyramid scene parsing network. In: Proceedings of IEEE Conference on Computer Vision and Pattern Recognition (2017)
26. Zhu, D., Chen, J., Shen, X., Li, X., Elhoseiny, M.: Minigpt-4: enhancing vision-language understanding with advanced large language models. In: arXiv:2304.10592 (2023)

GS-DMSR: Dynamic Sensitive Multi-scale Manifold Enhancement for Accelerated High-Quality 3D Gaussian Splatting

Nengbo Lu[1], Minghua Pan[2,3]($\boxtimes$), Shaohua Sun[1], and Yizhou Liang[1]

[1] School of Artificial Intelligence, Guilin University of Electronic Technology, Guilin 541004, Guangxi, China
[2] School of Computer Science and Information Security, Guilin University of Electronic Technology, Guilin 541004, Guangxi, China
panmh@guet.edu.cn
[3] Guangxi Key Laboratory of Cryptography and Information Security, Guilin University of Electronic Technology, Guilin 541004, Guangxi, China

Abstract. In the field of 3D dynamic scene reconstruction, how to balance model convergence rate and rendering quality has long been a critical challenge that urgently needs to be addressed, particularly in high-precision modeling of scenes with complex dynamic motions. To tackle this issue, this study proposes the GS-DMSR method. By quantitatively analyzing the dynamic evolution process of Gaussian attributes, this mechanism achieves adaptive gradient focusing, enabling it to dynamically identify significant differences in the motion states of Gaussian models. It then applies differentiated optimization strategies to Gaussian models with varying degrees of significance, thereby significantly improving the model convergence rate. Additionally, this research integrates a multi-scale manifold enhancement module, which leverages the collaborative optimization of an implicit nonlinear decoder and an explicit deformation field to enhance the modeling efficiency for complex deformation scenes. Experimental results demonstrate that this method achieves a frame rate of up to 96 FPS on synthetic datasets, while effectively reducing both storage overhead and training time. Our code and data are available at https://anonymous.4open.science/r/GS-DMSR-2212.

Keywords: Dynamic Scene Rendering · Gaussian Representation · View Synthesis

1 Introduction

Novel view synthesis, as a core research direction in 3D vision, plays a pivotal role in industries such as virtual reality, augmented reality, and film production. This technology aims to construct spatio-temporally continuous representations of scenes from sparse 2D image inputs, enabling dynamic rendering from arbitrary viewpoints and timestamps. Particularly in dynamic scene modeling, the precise

J. Lokoč et al. (Eds.): MMM 2026, LNCS 16412, pp. 435–447, 2026.
https://doi.org/10.1007/978-981-95-6950-2_31

reconstruction of complex motion patterns from spatio-temporally limited input data remains a critical challenge in current research.

Neural Radiance Fields (NeRF) [1] have achieved groundbreaking progress in novel view synthesis by representing scenes through implicit functions. This method employs volume rendering techniques to establish mappings between 2D images and 3D scenes. However, the original NeRF suffers from inefficiencies in training and rendering. Although subsequent improvements have reduced training times from days to minutes, its rendering process still incurs significant latency, falling short of real-time requirements.

3D Gaussian Splatting (3D-GS) [2], an innovative approach using explicit scene representation, marks a major breakthrough in 3D reconstruction. By modeling scenes with explicit 3D Gaussian distributions, 3D-GS elevates rendering speeds to real-time levels. Unlike the computationally intensive volume rendering in NeRF, 3D-GS introduces differentiable splatting techniques to directly project 3D Gaussians onto 2D imaging planes. This representation not only achieves real-time rendering but also provides an explicit scene structure, facilitating scene manipulation and editing, thereby expanding possibilities for scene reconstruction (Fig. 1).

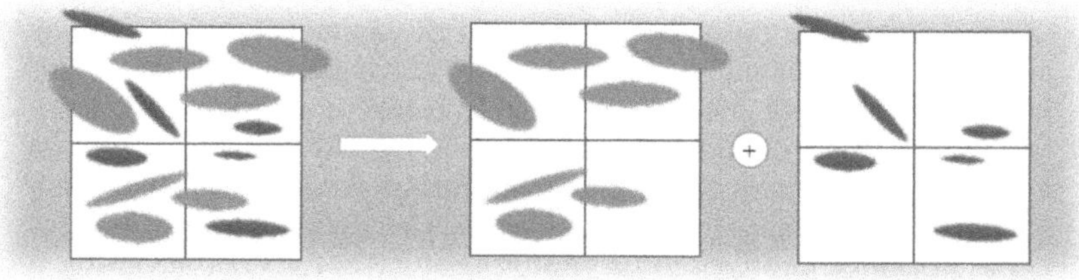

Fig. 1. Motion Saliency-Driven Dynamic Gaussian Optimization. For each Gaussian, we quantify the dynamic variation properties of its attributes and classify them into Gaussians with different saliency levels. We then label these Gaussians and optimize the high-saliency ones.

To address the spatio-temporal representation limitations of traditional 3D-GS in dynamic scene reconstruction, Wu et al. proposed the 4D Gaussian Splatting (4D-GS) [3] framework, achieving breakthroughs in dynamic scene modeling through a hierarchical spatio-temporally coupled representation architecture. This method innovatively constructs a hybrid Gaussian deformation field network, whose core consists of a spatio-temporal structure encoder and a lightweight multi-head Gaussian deformation decoder. The former realizes low-rank compressed representation of motion fields through spatio-temporal basis function decomposition, while the latter enables parameterized modeling of cross-frame deformation fields via attention mechanisms. However, the framework still requires global optimization of millions of Gaussian parameters, where redundant updates of static or low-frequency dynamic parameters significantly degrade convergence efficiency. To resolve this, our study proposes a dynamics-aware parameter update mechanism that adaptively focuses gradient updates based on motion saliency coefficients, thereby accelerating convergence. Furthermore, we introduce a multi-scale manifold enhancement module that synergizes non-linear implicit decoders with explicit deformation fields, enhancing reconstruction capability while preserving spatio-temporal continuity. Our contributions are as follows:

- By introducing the Motion Saliency-Driven Dynamic Gaussian Optimization (MS-DGO) method, which quantifies dynamic changes in Gaussian properties to achieve adaptive gradient focusing, distinguishes between Gaussians with varying saliency levels in real time, and implements differentiated optimization, the model's convergence is significantly accelerated while storage redundancy is reduced.
- Relying on the synergistic optimization of an implicit nonlinear decoder and an explicit deformation field, it enhances the modeling capability of complex dynamic deformation scenarios, effectively compensates for potential rendering quality degradation caused by MS-DGO, and maintains spatiotemporal continuity (Fig. 2).

2 Related Work

2.1 Novel View Synthesis

Novel view synthesis, as a core technical challenge in 3D reconstruction, has witnessed the emergence of diverse scene representations and rendering strategies in recent years. Among classical explicit-structure methods, approaches like light field mapping [4], parameterized meshes [5–7], discrete voxels [8–10], and multiplane projection [11,12] rely on dense supervision for high-fidelity rendering, while NeRF-based methods [13,14] construct continuous scene representations through implicit neural radiance fields, achieving breakthrough progress in view generation accuracy. Addressing dynamic scene modeling demands, researchers in [38,39,42] deconstructed static constraints; particularly, [15] proposed a temporally aware explicit dynamic voxel model, elevating training efficiency to under 30 min, a paradigm subsequently advanced in works like [16,17]. Within dynamic modeling, deformation-driven methods [18,19] utilize cross-frame optical flow fields for pixel-level spatial transformations, while emerging temporal decoupling neural volumetric techniques [20–22] significantly accelerate dynamic modeling by decoupling spatial sampling along the temporal dimension. For multi-view systems, studies such as [23,24] have designed tailored optimization architectures. However, despite breakthroughs in training efficiency, monocular dynamic scene reconstruction still faces significant real-time inference bottlenecks. This study innovatively constructs a joint optimization framework that, through hierarchical representation design and computational path compression, simultaneously achieves accelerated training and guarantees real-time rendering quality under sparse input conditions.

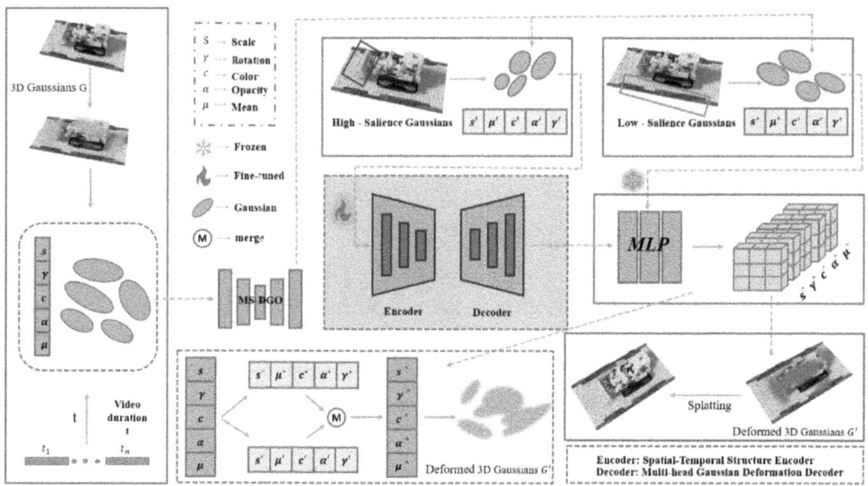

Fig. 2. The overall pipeline of our model. For a set of 3D Gaussians G, we extract the center coordinates and timestamp t of each Gaussian by querying multi-resolution voxel planes; using $MS - DGO$, we distinguish Gaussians with different saliency coefficients and optimize those with high saliency coefficients; next, we compute the voxel features; decoding these features via a miniaturized multi-head Gaussian deformation decoder yields the deformed 3D Gaussian G' at timestamp t; finally, applying Gaussian splatting to the deformed Gaussians generates the final rendered image.

2.2   Neural Rendering with Point Clouds

3   Preliminary

This section analyzes the geometric representation and rasterization process of 3D Gaussian Splatting in Subsect. 3.1.

3.1   3D Gaussian Splatting

3D Gaussian distribution is an explicit 3D scene representation that exists in the form of point clouds. Each 3D Gaussian distribution is characterized by a covariance matrix Σ and a center point x, where x is referred to as the Gaussian mean.

$$G(X) = e^{-\frac{1}{2}x^T \Sigma^{-1} x}. \tag{1}$$

To enable separate optimization of parameters, the covariance matrix σ can be decomposed into a scaling matrix S and a rotation matrix R:

$$\Sigma = \mathbf{RSS}^T\mathbf{R}^T. \tag{2}$$

When rendering a new viewpoint, the system employs differentiable rasterization techniques to project 3D Gaussian distributions onto the camera plane. According to the derivation in literature, the covariance matrix Σ' in the camera coordinate system can be computed using the following formula, which involves the view transformation matrix W and the Jacobian matrix J of the affine approximation of the projection transformation.

$$\Sigma' = JW\Sigma W^T J^T. \tag{3}$$

Each 3D Gaussian contains the following optimizable parameters: a spatial coordinate $X \in R^3$, color defined by k-dimensional spherical harmonic coefficients $R \in R^k$, where k is the order of spherical harmonics.opacity $\alpha \in R$, quaternion rotation parameters $r \in R^4$ and 3D scaling factors $s \in R^3$. During the pixel shading process, the color and opacity values of each Gaussian point are computed based on the radiance field expression in Eq. 1. For N ordered Gaussian points covering this pixel, their color blending formula is given by:

$$C = \sum_{i \in N} c_i \alpha_i \prod_{j=1}^{i-1} (1 - \alpha_i). \tag{4}$$

Here, c_i, α_i represents the density and color of this point computed by a 3D Gaussian G with covariance Σ multiplied by an optimizable per-point opacity and SH color coefficients.

4   Method

4.1   Motion Saliency-Driven Dynamic Gaussian Optimization

To accelerate model convergence, this study proposes a dynamically sensitive gradient updating mechanism based on a parametric motion saliency coefficient. This mechanism achieves adaptive gradient focusing by quantifying the dynamic variations in Gaussian attributes. After completing the standard 3D Gaussian splatting framework and deformation field processing, the model performs real-time screening of scene Gaussians according to the motion saliency coefficient, which provides an accurate mathematical representation of Gaussian motion state changes. The screening process employs a preset saliency threshold to partition Gaussians into two categories: high-saliency Gaussians and low-saliency Gaussians (Fig. 3).

High-saliency Gaussians exhibit significant deviation from the target scene state and undergo iterative refinement through deformation fields. Low-saliency Gaussians reach convergence with photorealistic approximation and are exempted from subsequent deformation field updates. By dynamically allocating computational resources and gradient updates, this mechanism continuously focuses optimization on the most promising Gaussian units, substantially enhancing training efficiency while reducing computational redundancy.

4.2   Multi-scale Disentangled Manifold Deformation

Upon completion of 3D Gaussian feature encoding, our framework employs a multi-head Gaussian deformation decoder $\mathcal{D} = (\phi_x, \phi_r, \phi_s)$ where three

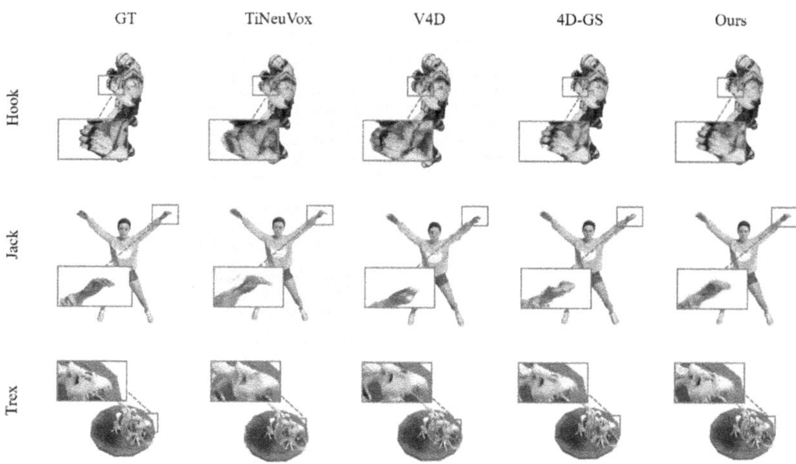

Fig. 3. For the synthetic dataset, visualization comparison experiments with other models were conducted [3,21,25]. The rendering results retain the default green background, and this study adopts the rendering parameter configurations of [3].

independent multilayer perceptrons respectively predict positional deformation $\Delta\mathbf{X} = \phi_x(\mathbf{f}_d)$, rotational deformation $\Delta\mathbf{r} = \phi_r(\mathbf{f}_d)$, and scaling deformation $\Delta\mathbf{s} = \phi_s(\mathbf{f}d)$ using input feature vector $\mathbf{f}d$. To augment reconstruction capacity while strictly preserving spatiotemporal continuity, we introduce a multi-scale manifold enhancement module that achieves hierarchical feature enhancement through synergistic optimization of an implicit nonlinear decoder and explicit deformation field. This module implements three critical operations: dynamic feature dimension adaptation aligning implicit decoder layers with deformation field outputs, cross-scale feature pyramid construction integrating low-frequency geometric structures $\mathcal{L}c$ with high-frequency details $\mathcal{H}$, and nonlinear manifold mapping to boost complex deformation modeling capability.

$$\Delta\mathbf{X}, \Delta\mathbf{r}, \Delta\mathbf{s} = \phi(\mathbf{f}_d). \tag{5}$$

$$(\mathcal{X}', r', s') = (\mathcal{X} + \Delta\mathcal{X}, r + \Delta r, s + \Delta s). \tag{6}$$

Finally, we obtain the deformed 3D Gaussians $G' = \{x', s', r', \sigma, C\}$.

5   Experiment

This section will first present a systematic analysis of the characteristics of the employed datasets, followed by a comparative evaluation of our method's performance across multiple datasets. We then conduct rigorous ablation studies to demonstrate the efficacy of the proposed approach (Fig. 4).

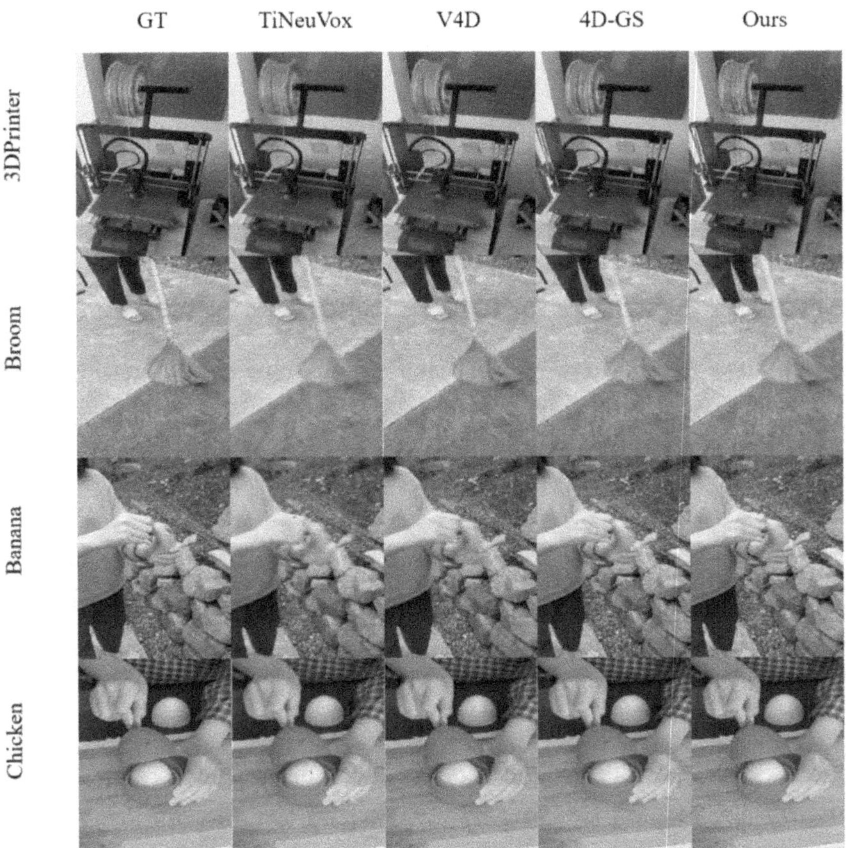

Fig. 4. Visualization of the HyperNeRF [26] dataset compared with other methods [3,21,25]. 'GT' stands for ground truth images. Please zoom in for better observation.

5.1   Experimental Settings

Our implementation is built upon the PyTorch framework, with all experiments conducted on RTX 3090 GPU. We fine-tuned the hyperparameter settings described in 4D-GS and optimized the parameters accordingly.

Synthetic Dataset. This study employs the synthetic dataset constructed by D-NeRF [27] as the primary evaluation benchmark, specifically designed for monocular dynamic scene reconstruction tasks. Its defining characteristics include quasi-randomly distributed camera poses at each temporal node, with dynamic sequence lengths per scene rigorously constrained to the 50–200 frame range.

Real-World Datasets. This study employs the HyperNeRF [26] dataset as the benchmark for real-world performance evaluation. The dataset is captured using monocular or binocular cameras, with camera motion constrained to simple linear trajectories. In our experimental pipeline, 200 frames are randomly sampled for modeling analysis, and the initial point clouds are reconstructed via Structure-from-Motion (SfM) algorithm.

Dynamic Object Dataset. We also used another artificially synthesized dynamic 3D dataset, namely the Dynamic Object dataset [28]. This dataset contains 6 different 3D objects, each exhibiting unique movement patterns, including rigid or deformable motions in 3D space. Examples include Bat and Fan, among others (Fig. 5).

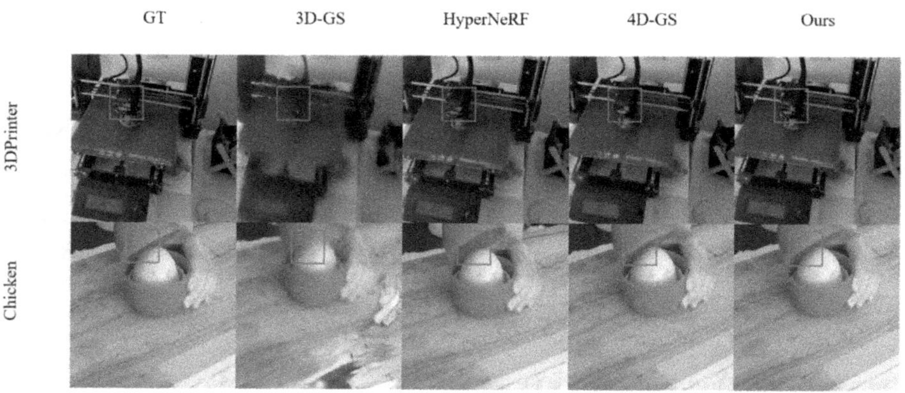

Fig. 5. Experimental results show that in the visualization results, our method can recover more details compared to other methods [2, 3, 26].

5.2   Results

This study conducts a systematic evaluation of the experimental results based on a multi-dimensional metric system, specifically covering core evaluation criteria such as peak signal-to-noise ratio (PSNR), perceptual quality metric LPIPS, and structural similarity index (SSIM). To address the requirements for visual quality assessment in the novel view synthesis task, comparative experiments are performed with representative state-of-the-art methods in the field, including the methods proposed in literatures [2, 3, 16, 20, 21, 25, 26, 29–31]. Among these, the experimental results of other comparative methods on the synthetic dataset are directly cited from the original literature of 4D-GS. The quantitative analysis results on the synthetic dataset are detailed in Table 1. Notably, although existing dynamic hybrid representation methods can achieve relatively high-quality reconstruction effects, limitations persist in the optimization of their dynamic

Table 1. Quantitative results on the synthetic dataset. The best and the second best results are denoted by pink and yellow. The rendering resolution is set to 800×800. "Time" in the table stands for training times.

Model	PSNR (dB)	SSIM	LPIPS	Time	FPS
TiNeuVox-B [25]	32.67	0.97	0.04	28 mins	1.5
KPlanes [20]	31.61	0.97	-	52 mins	0.97
HexPlane-Slim [29]	31.04	0.97	0.04	11m 30s	2.5
3D-GS [2]	23.19	0.93	0.08	10 mins	170
FFDNeRF [16]	32.68	0.97	0.04	-	< 1
MSTH [30]	31.34	0.98	0.02	6 mins	-
V4D [21]	33.72	0.98	0.02	6.9 hours	2.08
4D-GS [3]	34.05	0.98	0.02	8 mins	82
Ours	34.56	0.98	0.02	8 mins	96

motion modeling components, leaving room for improvement in the detail reconstruction performance of methods such as 4D-GS. In sharp contrast, our method not only achieves optimal rendering quality on the synthetic dataset but also exhibits superior convergence efficiency while maintaining an extremely low level of storage consumption.

Table 2. Quantitative results on HyperNeRF [39] vrig dataset with the rendering resolution of 960×540.

Model	PSNR (dB)	MS-SSIM	Times	FPS
Nerfies [31]	22.2	0.803	$\sim$ hours	< 1
HyperNeRF [26]	22.4	0.814	32 hours	< 1
TiNeuVox-B [25]	24.3	0.836	30 mins	1
3D-GS [2]	19.7	0.680	40 mins	55
FFDNeRF [16]	24.2	0.842	-	0.05
V4D [21]	24.8	0.832	5.5 hours	0.29
4D-GS [3]	25.2	0.845	30 mins	34
Ours	25.5	0.853	26 mins	28

The experimental results on the real-scene dataset are detailed in Table 2. Notably, our method exhibits significant advantages in comprehensive performance compared to partial NeRF methods and other grid-based neural radiance field methods [20, 25, 29, 30]. Further comparison with the 4D-GS method reveals that our method demonstrates a slight leading edge in its core evaluation metrics. From an overall performance perspective, our method is on par with existing mainstream methods in terms of rendering quality, while boasting more efficient convergence characteristics and exhibiting superior real-time performance in indoor scene free-view rendering tasks.

5.3   Ablation Experiment

Motion Saliency-Driven Dynamic Gaussian Optimization. The MS-DGO mechanism achieves adaptive gradient focus by quantifying the dynamic changes of Gaussian attributes, which can be interpreted through ϕ_r. Dynamically partitions scene Gaussians into two categories in real time: high-saliency Gaussians and low-saliency Gaussians. For high-saliency Gaussians, iterative optimization is performed using deformation fields; low-saliency Gaussians, upon meeting the convergence criteria of approximating the real state, halt subsequent deformation field updates. Experimental results demonstrate that by dynamically allocating computational resources and optimizing focus, this mechanism effectively accelerates model convergence and reduces storage requirements. When this module is removed, and only deformation fields are employed to continuously optimize a large number of low-saliency Gaussians, experiments observe a significant increase in storage overhead and a notable slowdown in convergence speed (Figs. 6, 7 and Table 3).

Table 3. Ablation studies conducted using our proposed method on the Dynamic Object dataset.

Model	PSNR(dB)	SSIM	LPIPS	Time	FPS
Ours w/o ϕ_r	24.429	0.950	0.058	12.5 mins	72
Ours w/o ϕ_s	24.518	0.949	0.058	14 mins	63
Ours	24.534	0.952	0.059	13.5 mins	66

Multi-scale Disentangled Manifold Deformation. To further enhance reconstruction quality and strictly maintain spatiotemporal continuity, this study introduces a multi-scale manifold enhancement module that can be interpreted via ϕ_s. This module strengthens the modeling capability of complex deformation scenarios by leveraging a cooperative optimization mechanism between an implicit nonlinear decoder and an explicit deformation field, combined with a nonlinear manifold mapping technique. Experimental results show that removing this module leads to a significant degradation in rendering quality. Although the MS-DGO mechanism introduces a certain degree of rendering quality loss, the incorporation of this module partially offsets such impacts, thereby balancing the overall performance.

Fig. 6. Visualization of tracking with 3D Gaussians. From top to bottom are the quantitative visualization results of Ours w/o ϕ_r, Ours w/o ϕ_s, and Ours, respectively.

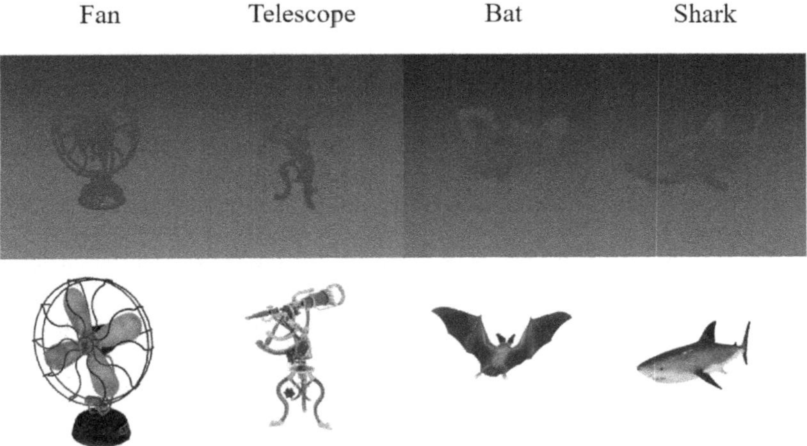

Fig. 7. Point cloud distribution visualization.

6 Conclusion

This paper addresses the critical challenge of balancing model convergence speed and rendering quality in 3D dynamic scene reconstruction by proposing a method named GS-DMSR. Through quantifying the dynamic changes of Gaussian attributes to achieve adaptive gradient focusing, along with synergistic optimization between an implicit nonlinear decoder and an explicit deformation field, it significantly accelerates convergence, reduces storage redundancy, and strengthens the modeling capability of complex deformation scenarios. This approach effectively achieves a balance between efficient convergence and real-time rendering.

References

1. Mildenhall, B., Srinivasan, P.P., Tancik, M., Barron, J.T., Ramamoorthi, R., Ng, R.: Nerf: representing scenes as neural radiance fields for view synthesis. Commun. ACM **65**(1), 99–106 (2021)
2. Kerbl, B., Kopanas, G., Leimkühler, T., Drettakis, G.: 3D gaussian splatting for real-time radiance field rendering. ACM Trans. Graph. **42**(4), 139-1 (2023)
3. Wu, G., et al.: 4D gaussian splatting for real-time dynamic scene rendering. In: Proceedings of the IEEE/CVF Conference on Computer Vision and Pattern Recognition, pp. 20310–20320 (2024)
4. Wang, P., et al.: Progressively-connected light field network for efficient view synthesis (2022)
5. Yang, B., et al.: Neumesh: learning disentangled neural mesh-based implicit field for geometry and texture editing (2022)
6. Peng, J., Chen, X., Liu, J.: 3dmeshnet: a three-dimensional differential neural network for structured mesh generation (2024)
7. Höllein, L., Johnson, J., Nießner, M.: Stylemesh: style transfer for indoor 3D scene reconstructions (2022)
8. Zhang, G., Fan, L., He, C., Lei, Z., Zhang, Z., Zhang, L.: Voxel mamba: group-free state space models for point cloud based 3D object detection (2024)
9. Han, X., Tang, Y., Wang, Z., Li, X.: Mamba3d: enhancing local features for 3D point cloud analysis via state space model (2024)
10. Xing, Z., Ye, T., Yang, Y., Liu, G., Zhu, L.: Segmamba: long-range sequential modeling mamba for 3D medical image segmentation (2024)
11. Liu, Y., et al.: Slam3r: real-time dense scene reconstruction from monocular RGB videos (2025)
12. Sun, J., Xie, Y., Chen, L., Zhou, X., Bao, H.: Neuralrecon: real-time coherent 3D reconstruction from monocular video (2021)
13. Kocabas, M., Chang, J.H.R., Gabriel, J., Tuzel, O., Ranjan, A.: Hugs: human gaussian splats (2023)
14. Barron, J.T., Mildenhall, B., Verbin, D., Srinivasan, P.P., Hedman, P.: Mip-nerf 360: unbounded anti-aliased neural radiance fields (2022)
15. Fang, J., et al.: Fast dynamic radiance fields with time-aware neural voxels. In: SIGGRAPH Asia 2022 Conference Papers, SA 2022, pp. 1–9. ACM (2022)
16. Guo, X., et al.: Forward flow for novel view synthesis of dynamic scenes. In: Proceedings of the IEEE/CVF International Conference on Computer Vision, pp. 16022–16033 (2023)
17. Liu, Y.-L., et al.: Robust dynamic radiance fields. In: Proceedings of the IEEE/CVF Conference on Computer Vision and Pattern Recognition, pp. 13–23 (2023)
18. Gao, C., Saraf, A., Kopf, J., Huang, J.-B.: Dynamic view synthesis from dynamic monocular video. In: Proceedings of the IEEE/CVF International Conference on Computer Vision, pp. 5712–5721 (2021)
19. Zhou, K., et al.: Dynpoint: dynamic neural point for view synthesis. Adv. Neural. Inf. Process. Syst. **36**, 69532–69545 (2023)
20. Fridovich-Keil, S., Meanti, G., Warburg, F.R., Recht, B., Kanazawa, A.: K-planes: explicit radiance fields in space, time, and appearance. In: Proceedings of the IEEE/CVF Conference on Computer Vision and Pattern Recognition, pp. 12479–12488 (2023)

21. Gan, W., Xu, H., Huang, Y., Chen, S., Yokoya, N.: V4D: voxel for 4D novel view synthesis. IEEE Trans. Visual Comput. Graphics **30**(2), 1579–1591 (2023)
22. Shao, R., Zheng, Z., Tu, H., Liu, B., Zhang, H., Liu, Y.: Tensor4d: efficient neural 4D decomposition for high-fidelity dynamic reconstruction and rendering. In: Proceedings of the IEEE/CVF Conference on Computer Vision and Pattern Recognition, pp. 16632–16642 (2023)
23. Gao, X., Yang, J., Kim, J., Peng, S., Liu, Z., Tong, X.: Mps-nerf: generalizable 3D human rendering from multiview images. IEEE Trans. Pattern Anal. Mach. Intell. (2022)
24. Wang, F., Tan, S., Li, X., Tian. Z., Song, Y., Liu, H.: Mixed neural voxels for fast multi-view video synthesis. In: Proceedings of the IEEE/CVF International Conference on Computer Vision, pp. 19706–19716 (2023)
25. Fang, J., et al.: Fast dynamic radiance fields with time-aware neural voxels. In: SIGGRAPH Asia 2022 Conference Papers, pp. 1–9 (2022)
26. Park, K., et al.: Hypernerf: a higher-dimensional representation for topologically varying neural radiance fields, arXiv preprint arXiv:2106.13228 (2021)
27. Pumarola, A., Corona, E., Pons-Moll, G., Moreno-Noguer, F.: D-nerf: neural radiance fields for dynamic scenes. In: Proceeding of 2021 IEEE/CVF Conference on Computer Vision and Pattern Recognition (CVPR), pp. 10313–10322. Institute of Electrical and Electronics Engineers (IEEE) (2021)
28. Li, J., Song, Z., Yang, B.: Nvfi: neural velocity fields for 3D physics learning from dynamic videos. Adv. Neural. Inf. Process. Syst. **36**, 34723–34751 (2023)
29. Cao, A., Johnson, J.: Hexplane: a fast representation for dynamic scenes. In: Proceedings of the IEEE/CVF Conference on Computer Vision and Pattern Recognition, pp. 130–141 (2023)
30. Wang, F., Chen, Z., Wang, G., Song, Y., Liu, H.: Masked space-time hash encoding for efficient dynamic scene reconstruction. Adv. Neural. Inf. Process. Syst. **36**, 70497–70510 (2023)
31. Park, K., et al.: Nerfies: deformable neural radiance fields. In: Proceedings of the IEEE/CVF International Conference on Computer Vision, pp. 5865–5874 (2021)

FFMatch: A FilterFormer-Based Network for Accurate Multimodal Image Matching

Yun Liao[1,2], Jiayi Lyu[1], Junhui Liu[1,2], Nan Chen[1], Zongxiao Hu[1],
and Qing Duan[1,2(✉)]

[1] Yunnan University, Kunming 650000, China
qduan@ynu.edu.cn
[2] Yunnan Key Laboratory of Software Engineering, Kunming 650000, China

Abstract. Multimodal image matching establishes accurate correspondences between images captured by different sensors or imaging modalities. However, this task poses significant challenges due to substantial variations in radiometric properties, structural patterns, and texture distributions across modalities. To address these issues, this paper proposes FFMatch, a FilterFormer-based network designed for accurate multimodal image matching. Specifically, the Multi-Receptive Field Feature Aggregation module is introduced to enhance the model's perception of multi-scale structural information and its capability for context modeling. The Token Filtering module is designed to dynamically model the spatial importance of features, enabling effective compression and filtering of redundant tokens. The Cross-Modal Alignment module is constructed based on a dual-stage cross-attention mechanism to improve structural consistency and information exchange across modalities. Furthermore, the Multi-Expert Fusion module is incorporated to enhance the model's adaptability and discriminative ability in handling non-rigid deformations and local texture variations through multi-path collaborative modeling. Extensive experiments on several representative benchmark datasets demonstrate that FFMatch outperforms existing methods regarding matching accuracy, robustness, and generalization capability.

Keywords: Multimodal image matching · Vision transformer · Cross-modal learning

1 Introduction

Multimodal image matching establishes accurate correspondences between images captured by different sensors (e.g., optical, infrared, SAR, and depth cameras) or imaging modalities (e.g., RGB vs. NIR, optical vs. radar). It serves as a crucial component for numerous downstream tasks, such as 3D reconstruction [19], visual localization [28], and structure-from-motion [23].

Traditional detector-based matching methods [9,12] typically comprise three stages: (1) keypoint detection, (2) descriptor generation, and (3) feature matching. However, their performance depends on the quality and repeatability of

J. Lokoč et al. (Eds.): MMM 2026, LNCS 16412, pp. 448–462, 2026.
https://doi.org/10.1007/978-981-95-6950-2_32

keypoint detection, which can be degraded under low-texture regions, extreme viewpoint variations, or uneven illumination, reducing accuracy and robustness.

In recent years, detector-free methods [3, 18, 32], which bypass keypoint detection and perform feature extraction and matching directly at the pixel level, have gained wide attention in multimodal image matching and have become a prominent research focus. Early approaches mainly employed convolutional neural networks to extract local features. However, constrained by fixed receptive fields, they struggled to model global contextual information, which limited their accuracy. To address this, LoFTR [25] introduced a Transformer-based detector-free framework, leveraging its ability to model long-range dependencies and enhance global feature representation. Nevertheless, these methods still face challenges in multimodal matching. Due to discrepancies in structural patterns, semantic distributions, and textural characteristics across modalities, current models often fail to capture both local details and global context simultaneously, thereby restricting their accuracy and robustness. Moreover, Transformers produce significant redundancy when processing high-resolution images, reducing their ability to discriminate salient features. Inadequate alignment of cross-modal features further hinders the harmonization of spatial structures and representations, degrading performance.

To address these challenges, this paper proposes FFMatch, a FilterFormer-based multimodal image matching network that systematically improves matching accuracy and robustness. Specifically, we design the Multi-Receptive Field Feature Aggregation (MRFA) module and the Token Filtering (TF) module to fully exploit multi-scale information, tackle scale variations, and filter redundant tokens, thereby enhancing effective feature representation. Based on the retained tokens, we introduce the Cross-Modal Alignment (CMA) module, which is token-guided to effectively align structural information across modalities, simulating the human comparative analysis process. Additionally, the Multi-Expert Fusion (MEF) module enhances the network's adaptability to non-rigid deformations and local texture changes, further improving feature diversity and discriminability.

The main contributions are as follows:

- We employ the Multi-Receptive Field Feature Aggregation module to capture multi-scale features for scale robustness, followed by a novel Token Filtering module leveraging linear self-attention and a lightweight network to filter out redundancy and retain salient tokens.
- We introduce the Cross-Modal Alignment module, which employs a two-stage cross-attention mechanism using retained salient tokens to enhance inter-modality structural correlation and improve feature consistency.
- We design the Multi-Expert Fusion module that employs multi-path collaboration and adaptive fusion to enhance adaptability and discrimination under non-rigid deformations and local texture variations.
- FFMatch achieves state-of-the-art performance across multiple representative multimodal datasets, demonstrating superior accuracy, robustness, and generalization.

2   Related Work

2.1   Detector-Based Image Matching

Early detector-based methods relied on hand-crafted keypoint detectors and descriptors such as SIFT [17] and FREAK [1]. With deep learning advances, learning-based methods (e.g., SuperPoint [4] and LightGlue [16]) have become mainstream, reducing reliance on manual design by optimizing models through data-driven approaches and significantly improving matching performance. Notable examples include Alike [31], a lightweight end-to-end network sharing weights to jointly learn detection and description, improving efficiency and reducing inference cost; DALF [20], which jointly learns detection and description to enhance deformation adaptability and robustness; and XFeat [21], which decouples detection and description modules to balance accuracy and speed. Nonetheless, these methods still struggle in sparsely textured or complex scenes, where keypoint detection reliability declines, limiting adaptability and robustness.

2.2   Detector-Free Image Matching

Unlike detector-based methods, detector-free approaches learn semi-dense or dense features, enabling global correspondence without keypoint detection. For example, CNN-based methods such as MVSNet [29] and DRC-Net [13] use hierarchical feature extraction and local context modeling to improve matching accuracy but are limited by fixed CNN receptive fields. To overcome this, LoFTR employs a Transformer architecture for detector-free matching, significantly enhancing long-range dependency modeling. TopicFM [8] clusters semantic features to perform attention within groups, boosting robustness; AdaMatcher [10] introduces adaptive attention to improve global modeling and geometric consistency; XoFTR [26] narrows modality gaps via masked pre-training and pseudo-thermal augmentation, enhancing matching with scale adjustment and sub-pixel refinement. Despite these advances, detector-free methods still face challenges in feature modeling and modality alignment for multimodal matching.

3   Method

3.1   Overview

Figure 1 illustrates the overall architecture of the proposed network. The feature encoder first extracts the initial feature representations $\bar{F}_A, \bar{F}_B \in \mathbb{R}^{H/8 \times W/8 \times \bar{C}}$ and $\widetilde{F}_A, \widetilde{F}_B \in \mathbb{R}^{H/2 \times W/2 \times \widetilde{C}}$ from the input images I_A and I_B. Low-resolution features support coarse matching to enhance structural representation, while high-resolution features preserve spatial details for fine-grained regression. Next, the Token Filtering Enhanced Transformer (FilterFormer) transforms coarse features into more discriminative representations. It consists of three modules: the Multi-Receptive Field Feature Aggregation (MRFA, Sect. 3.2) and Token Filtering (TF, Sect. 3.3) module, which filter out redundancy and retain salient tokens;

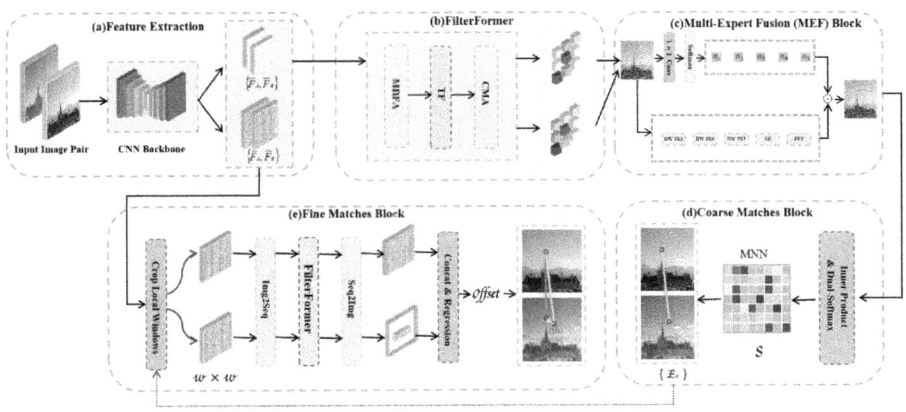

Fig. 1. FFMatch Pipeline Overview: (a) Feature Extractor, (b) FilterFormer Block, (c) MEF Block, (d) Coarse Matches Block, (e) Fine Matches Block.

The Cross-Modal Alignment module (CMA, Sect. 3.4), employing a two-stage cross-attention mechanism guided by salient tokens to align structural information across modalities. The processed features are then fed into the Multi-Expert Fusion module (MEF, Sect. 3.5), which models complementary features via multiple expert branches and adaptively integrates them through a fusion controller to enhance feature representation further. Finally, inspired by LoFTR, we adopt a coarse-to-fine matching strategy (Sect. 3.6) to complete matching.

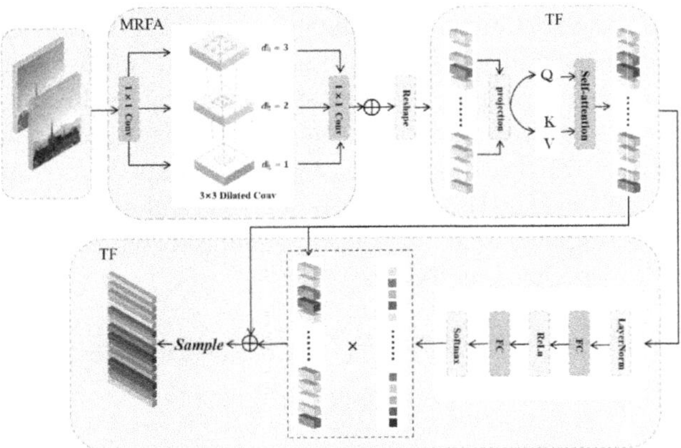

Fig. 2. Diagram of the MRFA and TF modules. MRFA generates unified multi-scale representation via three parallel dilated convolutions, followed by TF for token filtering.

3.2   Multi-receptive Field Feature Aggregation Module

As shown in Fig. 2, we propose a Multi-Receptive Field Feature Aggregation (MRFA) module to enhance feature adaptability to scale variation by effectively modeling multi-scale contextual information. Specifically, feature maps $\bar{F}_A, \bar{F}_B$ first undergo a 1×1 convolution to reduce the channel dimension to D, then fed into three parallel dilated convolution branches with a kernel size of 3×3 and dilation rates of $d_1 = 1, d_2 = 2, d_3 = 3$, respectively, to obtain each branch representation $\bar{F}_A^n, \bar{F}_B^n, n = 1, 2, 3$. The outputs of all branches are fused via a weighted aggregation mechanism to generate a unified multi-scale feature representation $\widehat{F}_A, \widehat{F}_B \in \mathbb{R}^{H \times W \times D}$, formulated as:

$$\bar{F}_i^n = Conv_{3\times3}^{d_n}(Conv_{1\times1}(\bar{F}_i^n)), \quad n \in \{1,2,3\}, \quad i \in \{A, B\}, \tag{1}$$

$$\widehat{F}_i = \Sigma_{n\in\{1,2,3\}}Conv_{1\times1}(\bar{F}_i^n), \quad i \in \{A, B\}, \tag{2}$$

where $Conv_{3\times3}^{d_n}(\cdot)$ denotes a 3×3 dilated convolution with dilation rate d_n, controlling the receptive field size. The smallest receptive field branch $\bar{F}^1$ captures local details; the medium branch $\bar{F}^2$ balances detail preservation and contextual information; the largest branch $\bar{F}^3$ covers a wide spatial range to enhance global structural information. The MRFA module can be formalized as:

$$\{\widehat{F}_A, \widehat{F}_B\} = MRFA(\bar{F}_A, \bar{F}_B). \tag{3}$$

3.3   Token Filtering Module

Although the MRFA module enhances multi-scale feature representation, its output still contains substantial redundancy and misleading information during cross-modal alignment and matching. To address this, we propose a Token Filtering (TF) module (see Fig. 2) that filters tokens by evaluating their importance and selects a representative subset for subsequent feature correlation modeling. First, the MRFA output $\widehat{F}_A, \widehat{F}_B$ are reshaped into token sequences $T_A, T_B \in \mathbb{R}^{N \times D}, N = H \times W$, and apply a linear self-attention mechanism to capture long-range dependencies and obtain enhanced contextual representations $T'_A, T'_B \in \mathbb{R}^{N \times D}$, formalized as follows:

$$Q_i = T_i \mathcal{W}^Q, \quad K_i = T_i \mathcal{W}^K, \quad V_i = T_i \mathcal{W}^V, \quad i \in \{A, B\}, \tag{4}$$

$$T'_i = \phi(Q_i)(\phi(K_i)^T \phi(V_i)), \tag{5}$$

where Q_i, K_i, V_i represent the queries, keys, and values with learnable weight matrices $\mathcal{W}^Q, \mathcal{W}^K, \mathcal{W}^V \in \mathbb{R}^{D \times d}, d = D/h$ and $\phi(\cdot) = elu(\cdot) + 1$.

Subsequently, the tokens T'_A, T'_B are fed into a lightweight multilayer perceptron to generate an importance score vector $s \in \mathbb{R}^{N \times 1}$ for each token, which is normalized by a Softmax function to obtain token weights $a \in \mathbb{R}^{N \times 1}$. These weights are applied to the tokens and combined with the original input to yield the final representation $\widehat{T}_A^t, \widehat{T}_B^t \in \mathbb{R}^{N \times D}$, formulated as follows:

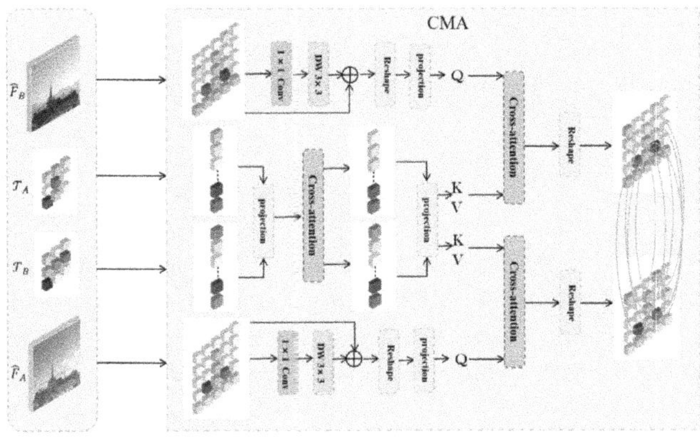

Fig. 3. Diagram of the CMA structure. The module has a two-stage cross-attention mechanism that achieves high-level semantic alignment between heterogeneous images.

$$\alpha_t = \frac{exp(s_t)}{\sum_{t=1}^{N} exp(s_t)},\tag{6}$$

$$\widehat{T}_i^t = \alpha_t \cdot T_i^{t'} + T_i^{t'}, \quad i \in \{A, B\}, \quad t = 1, 2, \cdots, N,\tag{7}$$

where $T_i^{t'}$ denotes the enhanced feature vector of the t-th token, α_t is the normalized weight for token t. To minimize the impact of redundant information on subsequent modules, token sets $\mathcal{T}_A$ and $\mathcal{T}_B$ are selected based on their importance scores. Since the sampling process is non-differentiable, a training-inference decoupling strategy is adopted: during training, all tokens are retained to ensure full gradient flow and enable end-to-end differentiable learning; during inference, token filtering is performed to focus on key features, as follows:

$$\mathcal{T}_i = \{\widehat{T}_i^1, \widehat{T}_i^2, \cdots, \widehat{T}_i^M\}, \quad a_1 \geq a_2 \geq \cdots \geq a_M.\tag{8}$$

The TF module can be formalized as:

$$\{\mathcal{T}_A, \mathcal{T}_B\} = TF(\widehat{F}_A, \widehat{F}_B).\tag{9}$$

3.4   Cross-Modal Alignment Module

To model cross-modal relationships and improve discrimination in coarse matching, we propose the Cross-Modal Alignment (CMA) module (Fig. 3). It leverages salient tokens to enhance tokens' sensitivity to cross-modal structural cues, significantly improving feature representation quality and robustness for subsequent matching. Specifically, CMA uses a two-stage cross-attention mechanism. In the first stage, tokens $\mathcal{T}_A, \mathcal{T}_B \in \mathbb{R}^{M \times D}$ undergo semantic alignment to establish preliminary correspondences. Bidirectional cross-attention treats these tokens as queries and keys/values, enabling effective cross-modal fusion while preserving modality-specific features, formulated as follows:

$$Q_U = \mathcal{T}_U \mathcal{W}_U^Q, \quad K_R = \mathcal{T}_R \mathcal{W}_R^K, \quad V_R = \mathcal{T}_R \mathcal{W}_R^V, \quad U \in \{A, B\}, \quad R \in \{B, A\}, \tag{10}$$

$$M_U = \mathrm{softmax}\left(\frac{Q_U K_R^T}{\sqrt{D}}\right) V_R, \tag{11}$$

where $\mathcal{W}_U^Q, \mathcal{W}_R^K, \mathcal{W}_R^V \in \mathbb{R}^{D \times D}$ denote the learnable weight matrices.

To inject abstract semantic information from heterogeneous modalities into full features, the second stage applies a cross-modal enhancement attention guided by filtered salient tokens. Here, full features $\widehat{F}_A, \widehat{F}_B \in \mathbb{R}^{N \times D}$ from the MRFA module act as queries, while filtered tokens M_A, M_B from the other image serve as keys and values, producing enhanced features $Y_A, Y_B \in \mathbb{R}^{N \times D}$:

$$Q_U = \widehat{F}_U \mathcal{W}_U^Q, \quad K_R = M_R \mathcal{W}_R^K, \quad V_R = M_R \mathcal{W}_R^V, \quad U \in \{A, B\}, \quad R \in \{B, A\}, \tag{12}$$

$$Y_U = \mathrm{softmax}\left(\frac{Q_U K_R^T}{\sqrt{D}}\right) V_R. \tag{13}$$

Compared to traditional full-image cross-attention with a computational complexity of $O(N^2 D)$, the CMA module reduces this to $O(NMD)$, where $M \ll N$. Guided by filtered salient tokens, CMA suppresses redundant information and enhances key features in cross-modal alignment, expressed as:

$$Y_U = CMA(\mathcal{T}_U, \widehat{F}_U), \quad U \in \{A, B\}. \tag{14}$$

3.5   Multi-expert Fusion Module

To enhance feature representation and geometric perception in complex scenarios, we propose the Multi-Expert Fusion (MEF) module, a feed-forward network following CMA. MEF uses five parallel expert branches to jointly model local geometry, global spatial structure, and frequency-domain texture. Specifically, CMA-processed feature sequences Y_A and Y_B are reshaped into feature maps and input to these branches. Three branches apply depthwise convolutions with 3×3, 5×5, and 7×7 kernels to capture object deformations and local context. Each convolutional branch is defined as follows:

$$E_U^{DW} = DWConv_{k \times k}(Y_U), \quad k \in \{3, 5, 7\}, \quad U \in \{A, B\}. \tag{15}$$

Additionally, a lightweight Squeeze-and-Excitation (SE) branch adaptively recalibrates channel-wise features by modeling channel importance:

$$E_U^{SE} = \sigma(\mathcal{W}_2\, \delta(\mathcal{W}_1\, GAP(Y_U))) \cdot Y_U, \tag{16}$$

where $GAP(\cdot)$ denotes global average pooling, δ and σ are ReLU and Sigmoid functions, $\mathcal{W}_1 \in \mathbb{R}^{D/r \times D}$, $\mathcal{W}_2 \in \mathbb{R}^{D \times D/r}$, and r is the reduction ratio.

Moreover, a frequency-domain expert branch transforms features into the frequency domain via a 2D Fast Fourier Transform (FFT), yielding amplitude $|\mathcal{F}|$ and phase spectra $\angle\mathcal{F}$. The amplitude encodes global structural distributions, while the phase preserves fine spatial details such as edges and textures. A nonlinear phase enhancement $\phi(\angle\mathcal{F})$ is applied and fused with the amplitude before an inverse FFT (IFFT) reconstructs the frequency-enhanced features $E_A^{freq}, E_B^{freq} \in \mathbb{R}^{H \times W \times D}$:

$$\mathcal{F}_U = \text{FFT2D}(Y_U) = |\mathcal{F}_U|\, e^{\mathrm{i}\angle\mathcal{F}_U}, \tag{17}$$

$$E_U^{freq} = \text{RE}\Big(\text{IFFT2D}(|\mathcal{F}_U|e^{\mathrm{i}\phi(\angle\mathcal{F}_U)})\Big), \quad \phi(\angle\mathcal{F}_U) = \tanh(\gamma \cdot \angle\mathcal{F}_U), \tag{18}$$

where $\text{RE}(\cdot)$ extracts the real part, and $\gamma > 0$ is a positive scalar. This process preserves global structure while enhancing spatial details, improving texture discrimination and local alignment.

MEF employs a fusion controller to integrate expert outputs adaptively. Input features are projected via a 1×1 convolution to produce fusion weights $w \in \mathbb{R}^{H \times W \times R}$, normalized by Softmax and applied to the expert outputs E_U^r to yield final enhanced features:

$$O_U = \sum_{r=1}^{R} w_r \cdot E_U^r, \tag{19}$$

where R is the number of experts and w_r the weight of the r-th expert. The MEF process is summarized as:

$$\{O_A, O_B\} = MEF(Y_A, Y_B). \tag{20}$$

3.6   Coarse-to-Fine Matching

In the matching stage, we adopt a two-stage coarse-to-fine strategy to enhance accuracy and robustness. In coarse matching, the MEF outputs are converted into sequences $O_A, O_B \in \mathbb{R}^{N \times D}$, and their dot-product similarity is computed to produce the score matrix $S \in \mathbb{R}^{N \times N}$. Bidirectional Softmax normalization yields a confidence matrix $G \in \mathbb{R}^{N \times N}$ that enforces mutual consistency of matching probabilities. High-confidence pairs are selected using the Mutual Nearest Neighbor (MNN) criterion with threshold $\mathcal{J}$, producing the coarse match set E_c:

$$E_c = \{(P_A^c(i), P_B^c(j)) \mid (i,j) \in \mathcal{D}\}, \tag{21}$$

$$\mathcal{D} = \{(i,j) \mid G(i,j) > \mathcal{J},\ (i,j) \in \text{MNN}(G)\}. \tag{22}$$

Building on coarse matches, the fine matching module refines their spatial localization. Each coarse correspondence $P_A^c(i), P_B^c(j)$ is mapped to high-resolution feature maps $\widetilde{F}_A, \widetilde{F}_B \in \mathbb{R}^{H/2 \times W/2 \times \widetilde{C}}$. Fixed-size $w \times w$ local window features centered on these points are extracted, enhanced via the FilterFormer module, and used to regress offsets $\epsilon \in \mathbb{R}^{T \times 2}$, yielding refined coordinates $P^f \in \mathbb{R}^{T \times 2}$:

$$P^f = P^c + \epsilon, \tag{23}$$

where T denotes the number of predicted matches.

3.7 Supervision

The model supervision combines coarse-level and fine-level losses: $\mathcal{L} = \alpha\mathcal{L}_c + \beta\mathcal{L}_f$, where α and β balance the contributions of each loss. For coarse matching, positive and negative labels are generated from camera poses and depth maps, supervised via a negative log-likelihood loss:

$$\mathcal{L}_c = -\frac{1}{|G^{gt}|}\Sigma_{(i,j)\in G^{gt}}\log G(i,j), \tag{24}$$

where G^{gt} is the ground-truth label.

Fine-level regression minimizes Euclidean distance between predicted coordinates $\hat{p}_i = (\hat{x}_i, \hat{y}_i)$ and ground truth $p_i = (x_i, y_i)$ across N matched points:

$$\mathcal{L}_f = \frac{1}{N}\Sigma_{i=1}^N\|\hat{p}_i - p_i\|^2. \tag{25}$$

4 Experiments

4.1 Implementation Details and Datasets

In experiments, the channel dimensions of coarse- and fine-grained features are set to 256 and 128, respectively. Following [25], the coarse matching filtering threshold $\mathcal{J}$ is set to 0.2. Fine matching employs a local cropping window of size 5×5. The model is trained using the AdamW [30] optimizer with a CosineAnnealingLR scheduler [11], a batch size of 4, and an initial learning rate of 1×10^{-4}. Evaluation is performed on five multimodal datasets–SEN12MS [22], Optical-SAR [15], WHU-OPT-SAR [14], RGB-NIR Scene [2], and NYU-Depth V2 [24]– spanning RGB, SAR, SWIR, optical, NIR, and depth modalities. These datasets involve cross-modal gaps, low texture, geometric misalignments, viewpoint variations, and noise, posing stringent demands on matching algorithms.

4.2 Comparison with SOTA Methods

Under identical settings and datasets, we compare our method with seven representative models–LoFTR, MatchosNet [15], FeMIP [6], MIVI [7], ELoFTR [27], UFM [5], and XoFTR.

Table 1. Homography estimation experiments on the Optical-SAR, WHU-OPT-SAR, and SEN12MS.

Method	Dataset								
	Optical-SAR			WHU-OPT-SAR			SEN12MS		
	Homography est. AUC			Homography est. AUC			Homography est. AUC		
	@5	@10	@20	@5	@10	@20	@5	@10	@20
MatchosNet	30.10	56.34	73.59	24.79	52.44	72.58	33.28	62.06	79.70
LoFTR	16.59	39.29	56.97	16.18	33.33	53.61	11.84	17.07	20.28
MIVI	35.03	54.54	69.22	26.07	48.40	70.74	29.58	46.35	58.77
FeMIP	21.67	43.31	62.31	27.82	50.77	71.56	12.97	18.13	22.63
UFM	56.20	73.14	83.42	40.83	48.31	61.63	57.09	72.88	82.28
ELoFTR	31.62	46.79	64.88	29.09	43.83	61.42	21.49	31.57	40.65
XoFTR	52.80	69.68	75.64	44.79	60.68	76.59	55.17	70.79	77.42
FFMatch	**61.21**	**76.42**	**89.91**	**48.69**	**63.78**	**81.47**	**60.23**	**78.54**	**88.10**

Table 2. Homography estimation experiments on the RGB-NIR Scene and NYU-Depth V2.

Method	Dataset					
	RGB-NIR Scene			NYU-Depth V2		
	Homography est. AUC			Homography est. AUC		
	@5	@10	@20	@5	@10	@20
MatchosNet	50.43	70.89	82.49	21.58	45.79	67.90
LoFTR	49.13	58.59	67.48	28.87	44.07	58.73
MIVI	16.74	39.71	61.80	44.07	58.15	73.36
FeMIP	61.53	69.36	77.36	43.06	58.14	72.35
UFM	45.93	64.66	80.07	58.67	65.22	75.69
ELoFTR	60.70	74.47	84.76	47.67	61.36	72.28
XoFTR	65.47	76.95	87.20	59.51	74.91	81.28
FFMatch	**70.12**	**78.91**	**89.90**	**64.88**	**78.34**	**85.26**

Homography Estimation Comparison. To evaluate the proposed model's performance in geometric transformation recovery and matching stability, we use the average corner reprojection error between predicted and ground-truth homographies as the metric, calculating the cumulative error curve (AUC) at 5px, 10px, and 20px thresholds. As shown in Table 1 and 2, FFMatch achieves the best performance across all datasets and thresholds. At the 5px threshold, FFMatch attains 61.21% on Optical-SAR, outperforming the second-best UFM by 5.01% points; 48.69% on WHU-OPT-SAR, exceeding XoFTR by 3.90% points; and 60.23% on SEN12MS, leading UFM and XoFTR by 3.14 and 5.06% points, respectively. On modality-similar datasets RGB-NIR Scene and NYU-

Depth V2, FFMatch also leads with 5px scores of 70.12% and 64.88%, respectively. In contrast, LoFTR and ELoFTR perform well on RGB-NIR Scene and NYU-Depth V2 but drop sharply on complex cross-modal datasets (Optical-SAR: 16.59%, SEN12MS: 11.84% at 5px), highlighting limitations in handling large geometric and cross-modal variations. MatchosNet, FeMIP, and MIVI are stable on specific datasets (e.g., FeMIP 61.53% on RGB-NIR Scene) but overall underperform compared to FFMatch. UFM and XoFTR are robust at 10px and above, yet lag behind FFMatch at 5px, indicating weaker local detail capture.

Table 3. Quantitative evaluation of component effectiveness through ablation.

Method	Homography est. AUC		
	@5px	@10px	@20px
1)w/o MRFA	68.98	77.37	88.66
2)Replace TF+CMA with std.	67.25	76.94	87.92
3)w/o MEF	68.34	77.32	88.45
4)Ours Full	**70.12**	**78.91**	**89.90**

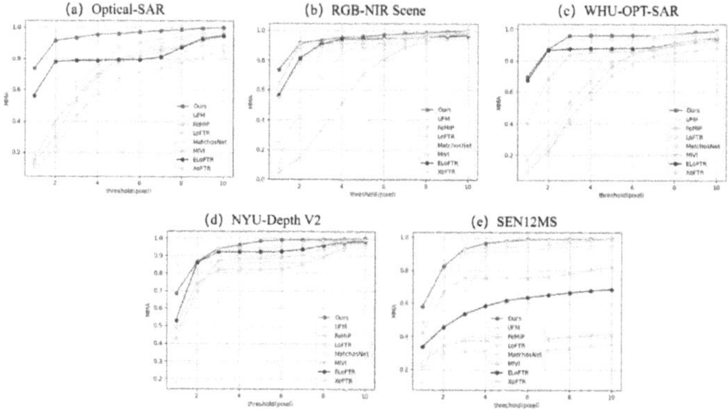

Fig. 4. Quantitative comparison of MMA results on five datasets.

MMA Comparison. Mean Matching Accuracy (MMA) is a key metric for evaluating the quality of feature matching, measuring the proportion of matches with reprojection errors below varying pixel thresholds to assess accuracy and robustness. As shown in Fig. 4, FFMatch demonstrates stable and superior cross-modal matching performance, outperforming existing methods overall. However, at the 1-pixel threshold on the NYU-Depth V2 dataset, FFMatch's accuracy is slightly lower than that of UFM. This is mainly attributed to the model's emphasis on global semantic modeling and cross-modal structural alignment, where multi-receptive field feature aggregation and key token filtering mechanisms compress redundant information, potentially reducing its ability to capture fine local details and thus affecting pixel-level matching precision at microscopic scales. Despite minor fluctuations at low thresholds, comprehensive experiments across five datasets indicate that FFMatch maintains high accuracy and stability, exhibiting excellent overall matching capability under complex conditions, including scale variations, structural deformations, and modality differences.

4.3 Ablation Studies

To evaluate the contribution of each functional module, we conducted ablation studies on the RGB-NIR Scene dataset by progressively removing or replacing key components and compared the homography estimation AUC at different pixel error thresholds (Table 3). Removing the Multi-Receptive Field Feature Aggregation (MRFA) module resulted in AUC decreases of 1.14, 1.54, and 1.24% points at 5px, 10px, and 20px, respectively, demonstrating its critical role in multi-scale detail enhancement and feature robustness. Replacing the Token Filtering and Cross-Modal Alignment modules (TF and CMA) with standard attention mechanisms led to AUC drops of 2.87, 1.97, and 1.98% points, highlighting their effectiveness in suppressing redundancy, emphasizing key features, and achieving cross-modal semantic consistency. Removing the Multi-Expert Fusion (MEF) module caused AUC reductions of 1.78, 1.59, and 1.45% points, indicating its value in integrating multi-path features and adapting to complex textures and geometric deformations. These results comprehensively validate the effectiveness of each module and its synergistic contribution to improving overall matching accuracy.

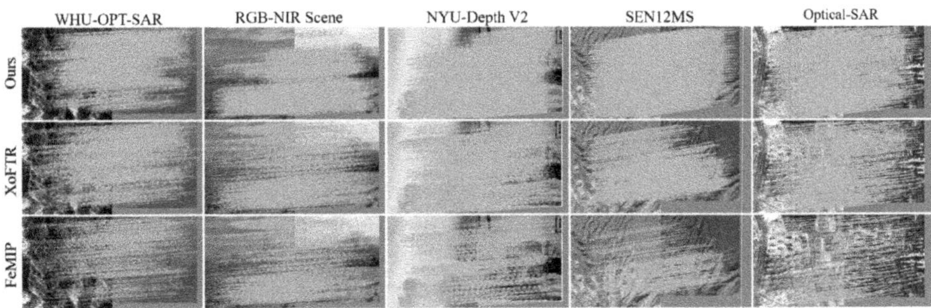

Fig. 5. Matching visualization on the datasets. Only correct matches are displayed, visualized as green lines. (Color figure online)

4.4 Visualization

We visually compared the matching results of FFMatch, XoFTR, and FeMIP across five multimodal image datasets: SEN12MS, RGB-NIR Scene, NYU-Depth

V2, Optical-SAR, and WHU-OPT-SAR (Fig. 5). The visualizations highlight FFMatch's superior accuracy and robustness across different modalities, further demonstrating its clear advantage over competing methods.

5   Conclusion

This paper proposes FFMatch, a multimodal image matching method based on FilterFormer. By incorporating multi-scale feature aggregation, dynamic token filtering, cross-modal alignment, and multi-expert fusion modules, it effectively addresses the matching challenges caused by significant radiometric, structural, and textural differences across modalities. Extensive experimental results demonstrate that FFMatch outperforms state-of-the-art methods in matching accuracy, robustness, and generalization. Future work will focus on further improving computational efficiency and exploring the method's potential for real-time applications and broader multimodal scenarios.

Acknowledgement. This work was supported in part by the Yunnan Provincial Graduate Supervisor Team Construction Project (No. SJDSTD-23233578), in part by the Yunnan University Teaching Reform Project (No. 2023Y32), and in part by the Industry-University Cooperative Education Program of the Ministry of Education of China (No. 2505221437).

References

1. Alahi, A., Ortiz, R., Vandergheynst, P.: Freak: fast retina keypoint. In: 2012 IEEE Conference on Computer Vision and Pattern Recognition, pp. 510–517. IEEE (2012). https://doi.org/10.1109/CVPR.2012.6247715
2. Brown, M., Süsstrunk, S.: Multi-spectral sift for scene category recognition. In: CVPR 2011, pp. 177–184. IEEE (2011)
3. Dai, K., et al.: DSAP: dynamic sparse attention perception matcher for accurate local feature matching. IEEE Trans. Instrum. Meas. **73**, 1–16 (2024). https://doi.org/10.1109/TIM.2024.3370781
4. DeTone, D., Malisiewicz, T., Rabinovich, A.: Superpoint: self-supervised interest point detection and description. In: Proceedings of the IEEE Conference on Computer Vision and Pattern Recognition Workshops, pp. 224–236 (2018)
5. Di, Y., et al.: UFM: unified feature matching pre-training with multi-modal image assistants. PLoS ONE **20**(3), e0319051 (2025). https://doi.org/10.1371/journal.pone.0319051
6. Di, Y., et al.: Femip: detector-free feature matching for multimodal images with policy gradient. Appl. Intell. **53**(20), 24068–24088 (2023). https://doi.org/10.1007/s10489-023-04659-5
7. Di, Y., et al.: Mivi: multi-stage feature matching for infrared and visible image. Vis. Comput. **40**(3), 1839–1851 (2024). https://doi.org/10.1007/s00371-023-02889-9
8. Giang, K.T., Song, S., Jo, S.: Topicfm: robust and interpretable topic-assisted feature matching. In: Proceedings of the AAAI Conference on Artificial Intelligence, vol. 37, pp. 2447–2455 (2023). https://doi.org/10.1609/aaai.v37i2.25341

9. Hu, M., Sun, B., Zhang, F., Li, S.: HLDD: hierarchically learned detector and descriptor for robust image matching. IEEE Trans. Image Process. (2025)

10. Huang, D., et al.: Adaptive assignment for geometry aware local feature matching. In: Proceedings of the IEEE/CVF Conference on Computer Vision and Pattern Recognition, pp. 5425–5434 (2023). https://doi.org/10.1109/CVPR52729.2023.00525

11. Jiao, B., Han, J., Chen, L.: A modified conjugate gradient algorithm with sufficient descent. In: 2011 Fourth International Joint Conference on Computational Sciences and Optimization, pp. 175–177. IEEE (2011)

12. Li, J., Zhang, R., Li, G., Li, T.H.: SDE2D: semantic-guided discriminability enhancement feature detector and descriptor. IEEE Trans. Multimedia (2024)

13. Li, X., Han, K., Li, S., Prisacariu, V.: Dual-resolution correspondence networks. Adv. Neural. Inf. Process. Syst. **33**, 17346–17357 (2020)

14. Li, X., et al.: Mcanet: a joint semantic segmentation framework of optical and SAR images for land use classification. Int. J. Appl. Earth Obs. Geoinf. **106** (2022). https://doi.org/10.1016/j.jag.2021.102638

15. Liao, Y., et al.: Feature matching and position matching between optical and SAR with local deep feature descriptor. IEEE J. Sel. Top. Appl. Earth Obs. Remote Sens. **15**, 448–462 (2022). https://doi.org/10.1109/JSTARS.2021.3134676

16. Lindenberger, P., Sarlin, P.E., Pollefeys, M.: Lightglue: local feature matching at light speed. In: Proceedings of the IEEE/CVF International Conference on Computer Vision, pp. 17627–17638 (2023)

17. Lowe, D.G.: Distinctive image features from scale-invariant keypoints. Int. J. Comput. Vision **60**(2), 91–110 (2004)

18. Ma, J., Wang, Y., Fan, A., Xiao, G., Chen, R.: Correspondence attention transformer: a context-sensitive network for two-view correspondence learning. IEEE Trans. Multimedia **25**, 3509–3524 (2022)

19. Mildenhall, B., Srinivasan, P.P., Tancik, M., Barron, J.T., Ramamoorthi, R., Ng, R.: Nerf: representing scenes as neural radiance fields for view synthesis. Commun. ACM **65**(1), 99–106 (2021). https://doi.org/10.1145/3503250

20. Potje, G., Cadar, F., Araujo, A., Martins, R., Nascimento, E.R.: Enhancing deformable local features by jointly learning to detect and describe keypoints. In: Proceedings of the IEEE/CVF Conference on Computer Vision and Pattern Recognition, pp. 1306–1315 (2023)

21. Potje, G., Cadar, F., Araujo, A., Martins, R., Nascimento, E.R.: Xfeat: accelerated features for lightweight image matching. In: Proceedings of the IEEE/CVF Conference on Computer Vision and Pattern Recognition, pp. 2682–2691 (2024)

22. Schmitt, M., Hughes, L., Qiu, C., Zhu, X.: Sen12ms–a curated dataset of georeferenced multi-spectral sentinel-1/2 imagery for deep learning and data fusion. arxiv 2019. arXiv preprint arXiv:1906.07789 (2019). https://doi.org/10.5194/isprs-annals-IV-2-W7-153-2019

23. Schonberger, J.L., Frahm, J.M.: Structure-from-motion revisited. In: Proceedings of the IEEE Conference on Computer Vision and Pattern Recognition, pp. 4104–4113 (2016). https://doi.org/10.1109/CVPR.2016.445

24. Silberman, N., Hoiem, D., Kohli, P., Fergus, R.: Indoor segmentation and support inference from RGBD images. In: European Conference on Computer Vision, pp. 746–760. Springer (2012)

25. Sun, J., Shen, Z., Wang, Y., Bao, H., Zhou, X.: LoFTR: detector-free local feature matching with transformers. In: Proceedings of the IEEE/CVF Conference on Computer Vision and Pattern Recognition, pp. 8922–8931 (2021)

26. Tuzcuoğlu, Ö., Köksal, A., Sofu, B., Kalkan, S., Alatan, A.A.: Xoftr: cross-modal feature matching transformer. In: Proceedings of the IEEE/CVF Conference on Computer Vision and Pattern Recognition, pp. 4275–4286 (2024)
27. Wang, Y., He, X., Peng, S., Tan, D., Zhou, X.: Efficient loftr: semi-dense local feature matching with sparse-like speed. In: Proceedings of the IEEE/CVF Conference on Computer Vision and Pattern Recognition, pp. 21666–21675 (2024)
28. Xiao, L., Yang, X., Lan, X., Wang, Y., Xu, C.: Towards visual grounding: a survey. arXiv preprint arXiv:2412.20206 (2024)
29. Yao, Y., Luo, Z., Li, S., Fang, T., Quan, L.: Mvsnet: depth inference for unstructured multi-view stereo. In: Proceedings of the European Conference on Computer Vision (ECCV), pp. 767–783 (2018)
30. Ye, P., Li, B., Li, Y., Chen, T., Fan, J., Ouyang, W.: b-darts: beta-decay regularization for differentiable architecture search. In: proceedings of the IEEE/CVF Conference on Computer Vision and Pattern Recognition, pp. 10874–10883 (2022)
31. Zhao, X., Wu, X., Miao, J., Chen, W., Chen, P.C., Li, Z.: Alike: accurate and lightweight keypoint detection and descriptor extraction. IEEE Trans. Multimedia **25**, 3101–3112 (2022). https://doi.org/10.1109/TMM.2022.3155927
32. Zhou, Y., Cheng, X., Zhai, X., Xue, L., Du, S.: Csformer: cross-scale transformer for feature matching. In: 2023 International Conference on Sensing, Measurement & Data Analytics in the era of Artificial Intelligence (ICSMD), pp. 1–6. IEEE (2023). https://api.semanticscholar.org/CorpusID:269172442

CCASNet: Criss-Cross Attention Enhanced Network with Dual-Channel Spatial Modeling for Medical Image Segmentation

Cheng Fu, Junlong Wu, Xianhong Chen, Hujin Peng, Jing Xu, Junyuan Gong, Zeyun Liu, Wenzheng Liu[(✉)], Tan Deng, and Ming Yuan

School of Computer Science and Technology, Changsha University of Science and Technology, Changsha, China
{202308170227,202308170238,202308170241,202308050214,23208031798,
202308170126,202411070108,liuwenzheng,dengtan0510}@csust.edu.cn,
xyzym000@gmail.com

Abstract. Accurate medical image segmentation is essential for reliable clinical diagnosis, treatment planning, and outcome evaluation. However, existing transformer- and CNN-based approaches often fail to jointly capture long-range contextual dependencies and emphasize task-relevant structures, limiting their ability to delineate complex anatomical boundaries. To address these issues, we propose CCASNet, a dual-channel spatial modeling framework that unifies global structural reasoning and fine-grained representation refinement. Specifically, CCASNet introduces a dual-channel complementary attention mechanism, in which (i) a Criss-Cross Attention branch captures long-range dependencies and ensures global structural coherence with reduced complexity, while (ii) a Channel-Spatial Attention branch adaptively emphasizes diagnostically relevant regions and suppresses background noise. Unlike previous works that simply apply attention in a single dimension, our design explicitly models global – local complementarity, enabling robust delineation of complex anatomical boundaries. This complementary design enables CCASNet to simultaneously achieve global consistency and local precision. Extensive evaluations on Synapse and ACDC datasets demonstrate that CCASNet consistently outperforms competitive baselines, achieving an average Dice score of 85.62% (+8.14% over TransUNet) and reducing HD95 to 13.36. These results highlight the robustness, efficiency, and clinical applicability of the proposed framework.

Keywords: Medical image segmentation · Cross-attention · Spatial modeling · Boundary refinement

1 Introduction

Medical image segmentation plays an important role in modern healthcare care, allowing accurate delineation of anatomical structures or pathological regions

J. Lokoč et al. (Eds.): MMM 2026, LNCS 16412, pp. 463–477, 2026.
https://doi.org/10.1007/978-981-95-6950-2_33

to support clinical diagnosis, treatment planning, and surgical navigation. With the rapid progress of deep learning, segmentation methods based on deep neural networks have become dominant. Early fully convolutional networks (FCNs) [1] demonstrated the feasibility of end-to-end dense prediction by leveraging multi-scale feature fusion. Subsequent CNN-based architectures, such as U-Net [3] and its extensions [7], introduced encoder – decoder structures with skip connections, substantially improving boundary preservation. However, their reliance on local receptive fields limits their ability to capture complex anatomical structures and long-range spatial dependencies.

Vision Transformers (ViTs) [5] have recently exhibited strong global dependency modeling through self-attention mechanisms, offering complementary strengths to CNNs. However, their direct application to high-resolution medical images is challenged by prohibitive computational cost and limited capacity to retain fine-grained spatial detail. Hybrid architectures that integrate CNNs and Transformers have therefore emerged as a promising direction, aiming to unify local detail preservation with global contextual reasoning. Despite notable progress, an effective framework that seamlessly combines multiscale feature fusion, global – local dependency modeling, and structural consistency for precise medical image segmentation remains underexplored.

To address this gap, we propose CCASNet, a hybrid CNN – Transformer framework enhanced by dual-channel spatial attention and cross-scale feature alignment. The network integrates the local detail sensitivity of CNNs, the global dependency modeling of Transformers, and the preservation of spatial information of U-Net-style skip connections. By jointly capturing fine boundaries and long-range structural relationships, CCASNet achieves accurate multiscale representation and precise anatomical localization, offering a balanced solution to the limitations of existing methods.

Our contribution can be summarized as: i) we propose CCASNet, a hybrid CNN–Transformer framework featuring a Cross-scale Feature Alignment strategy to resolve semantic inconsistencies between local CNN features and global ViT representations, addressing a key limitation in existing fusion approaches. ii) We design a dual-attention spatial modeling mechanism that jointly captures long-range structural dependencies and refines the boundaries of the target anatomical structures. Ablation studies validate the complementary roles of the two branches of attention in balancing global coherence and local precision. iii) Extensive experiments on Synapse and ACDC datasets show state-of-the-art results, including an 8.14% higher Dice score than TransUNet (85.62% vs. 77.48%) and superior boundary delineation critical for clinical applications. The robustness of our approach is further verified through cross-domain validation.

2   Related Work

2.1   Medical Image Segmentation Methods

Medical image segmentation has evolved from conventional approaches to deep learning-based paradigms, significantly enhancing the capabilities of computer-aided diagnosis. Traditional methods, including thresholding, region growth, and active contours, are often limited by their sensitivity to noise, poor generalization across modalities, and inability to capture complex anatomical variability. The advent of U-Net [3] represented a breakthrough, introducing an encoder – decoder architecture with skip connections that effectively preserve spatial details while enabling semantic understanding. Building on this foundation, a series of variants, such as U-Net++ [7], nnU-Net [10], and Attention U-Net [2]—incorporated dense connectivity, automated hyperparameter tuning, and attention mechanisms to further improve segmentation accuracy and adaptability. Furthermore, ResUNet [11] and Dense U-Net [4] addressed the challenges of vanishing gradients and redundant features through residual and densely connected layers, facilitating deeper network design and improved feature reuse. These advancements have collectively enabled the transition from labor intensive manual annotation to fully automated, robust, and high-precision segmentation, accelerating the deployment of intelligent diagnostic systems in clinical and research settings.

2.2   Attention Mechanisms in Medical Image Segmentation

Medical image segmentation has undergone a significant transformation from traditional techniques to deep learning-based paradigms, driven by the increasing demands of computer-aided diagnosis. Conventional methods such as thresholding, region growth, and active contour models are often hindered by high sensitivity to noise, parameter dependency, and limited robustness when facing complex anatomical structures or modality variations. The advent of deep learning, particularly the introduction of U-Net [3], marked a paradigm shift by establishing an encoder – decoder architecture with skip connections that effectively integrates low-level spatial details with high-level semantic features. This framework has since become the cornerstone of modern medical segmentation tasks. Building on this foundation, subsequent variants including U-Net++ [7], nnU-Net [10], and Attention U-Net [2]—have further improved segmentation accuracy and generalizability through redesigned skip paths, automated configuration pipelines, and attention-enhanced representations. In addition, architectures such as ResUNet [11] and Dense U-Net [4] address challenges related to network degradation and feature redundancy by introducing residual and dense connectivity, enabling the construction of deeper and more expressive models. These advancements collectively facilitate the transition from manual, labor-intensive annotation to fully automated, high-precision segmentation, accelerating the integration of intelligent diagnostic systems into clinical workflows and advancing the vision of precision medicine.

2.3   Vision Transformers in Medical Image Segmentation

The advent of Vision Transformers [5] has marked a new era in medical image segmentation, offering powerful capabilities to model long-range dependencies and global context. This transition was pioneered by TransUNet [12], which first integrated a Transformer encoder with a U-Net decoder, using self-attention mechanisms to improve contextual understanding while preserving spatial resolution. Building on this foundation, Swin-Unet [15] introduced hierarchical feature representations and window-based self-attention to improve scalability, enabling efficient modeling of local and global features with reduced computational overhead.

To further enhance the representational capacity, hybrid CNN – Transformer architectures emerged, including TransFuse [13], which used the parallel fusion of CNN and Transformer branches, and UCTransNet [14], which proposed a channel-wise cross-fusion strategy to enrich multiscale feature integration. Domain-specific innovations were also proposed to address the unique challenges of medical imaging. For example, MedT [16] adopted gated axial attention to reduce computational complexity while maintaining high sensitivity to local anatomical variations. DS-TransUNet [17] introduced a dual scale design that decouples global semantics and local details into complementary coarse and fine branches, followed by a dedicated fusion module to reconcile the two.

Collectively, these innovations demonstrate the effectiveness and flexibility of Transformer-based architectures in improving segmentation accuracy, robustness, and computational efficiency, thus advancing the development of intelligent generalizable systems for diverse medical image analysis tasks.

3   Method

3.1   Overall Framework

This paper proposes **CCASNet**, a medical image segmentation framework that synergistically integrates convolutional neural networks (CNNs), Vision Transformers (ViT), and U-Net design principles through a *dual attention fusion* mechanism, combining Criss-Cross Attention (CCA) [8] and Convolutional Block Attention Module (CBAM) [9] (Fig. 1). Unlike prior methods that employ CCA or CBAM individually, our design jointly models long-range spatial dependencies and channel-spatial importance, providing more discriminative multi-scale feature representations.

Multi-scale Feature Encoder: CCASNet adopts a hierarchical MaxViT [6] backbone to extract rich multi-resolution features. The input first passes through a 3×3 convolution and two additional convolutional layers to generate initial features. Four MaxViT blocks $\times 2$ progressively extract representations at $W/4 \times H/4$, $W/8 \times H/8$, $W/16 \times H/16$, and $W/32 \times H/32$, effectively capturing both local textures and global context.

Dual Attention Fusion Module: The core innovation lies in the integration of CCA and CBAM. CCA projects features into query, key and value matrices using convolutions 1×1, capturing long-range dependencies through a criss-cross pattern to produce intermediate features H'. CBAM then sequentially applies channel and spatial attention to recalibrate H', resulting in enhanced features H''. This complementary mechanism emphasizes task-relevant anatomical structures while preserving fine-grained details, leading to consistent improvements in segmentation accuracy across multiple datasets.

Hierarchical Decoder: The decoder progressively reconstructs high-resolution features and segmentation masks. It incorporates position encoding, LKA [18] and DAEFormer [19] blocks, patch expansion modules, and segmentation heads. U-Net-style skip connections enable multiscale feature fusion, retaining fine spatial details while integrating global context.

Integration of CNN, ViT, and U-Net Principles: CCASNet unifies local feature modeling, global context awareness, and hierarchical feature fusion. Convolutional layers ensure robust local representations, ViT attention captures long-range dependencies, and U-Net skip connections preserve high-resolution spatial information. Dual attention fusion further enhances multiscale features in spatial and channel dimensions, enabling precise segmentation of complex anatomical structures, as demonstrated by superior performance in quantitative evaluations (Sect. 4.3).

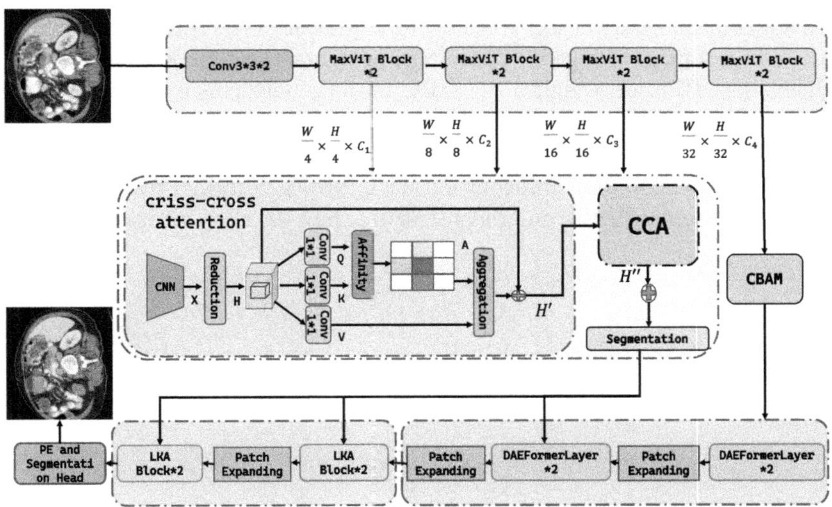

Fig. 1. The framework of our proposed CCASNet.

3.2 Criss-Cross Attention's Rule

Given the dimension-reduced feature map $H_{enc}^l \in \mathbb{R}^{C' \times H \times W}$ from the l th encoder layer, the Criss-Cross Attention (CCA) module first applies three independent 1×1 convolutional transformations to generate the Query, Key, and Value representations:

$$Q = W_Q H_{enc}^l, \quad K = W_K H_{enc}^l, \quad V = W_V H_{enc}^l \tag{1}$$

where W_Q, W_K, W_V denote the convolutional parameter matrices. For any spatial location $u \in \mathbb{R}^2$ on the feature map, its corresponding query vector $Q_u \in \mathbb{R}^{C'}$

is extracted. Gleichzeitig, all vectors of characteristics in K that share the same row or column coordinate with position u are collected to construct the criss-cross context neighborhood $\Omega_u \subset K$. Any vector of features in this neighborhood is denoted as K_v, where $v \in \Omega_u$.

The module then computes the semantic similarity (affinity) $d_{u,v} \in \mathbb{R}$ between the query vector Q_u and each vector K_v in the context neighborhood Ω_u through inner product operations:

$$d_{u,v} = Q_u^T K_v, \quad \forall v \in \Omega_u \tag{2}$$

Subsequently, a softmax normalization function is applied to transform the similarity scores into a probabilistic attention weight matrix A. The weight of attention between position u and context location v is:

$$A_{u,v} = \frac{\exp(d_{u,v})}{\sum_{k \in \Omega_u} \exp(d_{u,k})} \tag{3}$$

This attention distribution A accurately quantifies the semantic contribution of each context pixel along the criss-cross paths to the central pixel u.

Using the attention weights $A_{u,v}$, the module performs a semantic weighted aggregation of the corresponding value vectors V_v on the value feature map V, resulting in a contextually enhanced representation. Finally, a residual connection integrates this context information back into the original feature map H_{enc}^l, producing the semantically enhanced feature map H'. For location u:

$$H_u' = H_{u,enc}^l + \sum_{v \in \Omega_u} A_{u,v} \cdot V_v \tag{4}$$

Through this operation, each pixel on the feature map H' is enriched with abundant semantic context information from both the horizontal and vertical directions.

Recurrent Global Context Modeling. However, a single CCA operation can only establish local connectivity along criss-cross paths. To model true global dependencies, we adopt the recurrent Criss-Cross Attention (RCCA) strategy proposed in the original paper, with the number of recurrence steps set to $R = 2$:

$$H^{(1)} = \text{CCA}(H_{enc}^l) \tag{5}$$

$$H^{(2)} = \text{CCA}(H^{(1)}) \tag{6}$$

The first iteration propagates information along the same row and column paths, while the second iteration enables further propagation from the first-step nodes to new row and column positions, thus achieving global receptive field coverage with minimal computational overhead. The final output feature map $H'' = H^{(2)}$ contains aggregated global semantic information for each location of the pixel.

Performance Enhancement Mechanism of CCASNet in Medical Image Segmentation. In the proposed CCASNet architecture, deploying the RCCA module in the decoder bypass connection path is of strategic significance. In the standard U-Net architecture, the skip connection in layer l is mathematically defined as:

$$D_{out}^l = \mathrm{ConvBlock}(\mathrm{Concat}(\mathrm{Up}(D^{l+1}), E^l)) \tag{7}$$

Here, E^l represents the encoder characteristic, and $\mathrm{Up}(D^{l+1})$ is the upsampled characteristic of deeper decoder layers. The conventional direct feature concatenation strategy fails to fully exploit the global structural semantics embedded in E^l.

In CCASNet, the RCCA module is first applied to the encoder feature E^l to obtain the globally enhanced feature E_{CCA}^l:

$$E_{CCA}^l = \mathrm{RCCA}(E^l) \tag{8}$$

This enhanced feature is then used in the skip connection:

$$D_{out}^l = \mathrm{ConvBlock}(\mathrm{Concat}(\mathrm{Up}(D^{l+1}), E_{CCA}^l)) \tag{9}$$

With the design in Eq. 9, the RCCA module effectively compensates for the inherent limitation of CNN backbones in modeling long-range dependencies. Introduces precise global spatial structural information, significantly improving the clarity of segmentation boundaries and the continuity of anatomical structures. This is particularly critical for tasks that require the preservation of topological integrity, such as continuous segmentation of the vascular network or complete delineation of the contour of the organ. From a theoretical perspective, the integration of RCCA enables the model to implicitly optimize a structure-related loss term $\mathcal{L}_{structure}$:

$$\mathcal{L}_{total} = \mathcal{L}_{seg} + \lambda \mathcal{L}_{structure}(S_{pred}, S_{gt}) \tag{10}$$

where $\mathcal{L}_{structure}$ measures the topological continuity and structural consistency between the predicted segmentation S_{pred} and the ground truth annotation S_{gt}. By improving the global perception capability of the features, RCCA allows the network to better optimize this objective, thereby achieving significant performance gains in the final segmentation results.

3.3   CBAM's Rule

The inherent low contrast, blurred boundaries, and high heterogeneity within lesion regions in medical images impose stringent demands on the feature representation capabilities of segmentation models. To enhance the model's perception of critical discriminative features and suppress irrelevant information, this study introduces the CBAM [9] as an adaptive feature refinement mechanism, as illustrated in Fig. 2.

Unlike most approaches that treat attention modules as standalone plugins, the core innovation of this study lies in the strategic deployment of CBAM. In

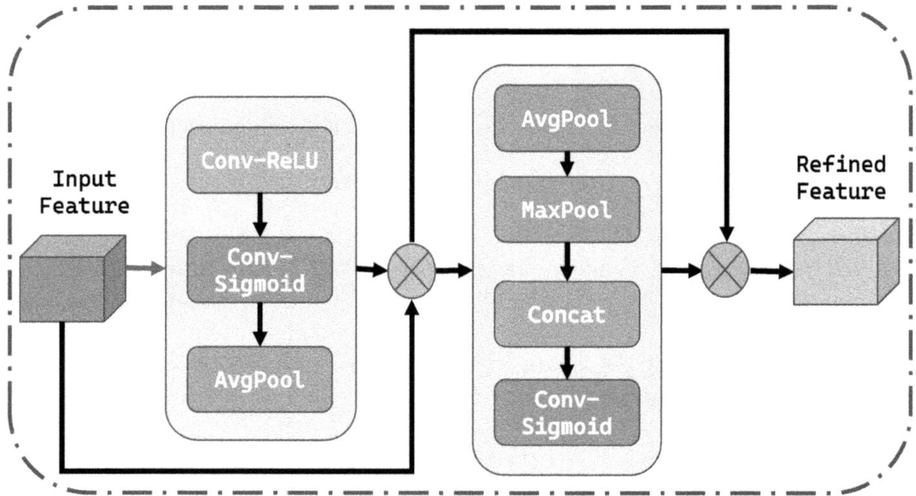

Fig. 2. The illustration of CBAM.

CCASNet, CBAM is integrated into the deep convolutional stages of the encoder backbone. This design decision is based on the theoretical consideration that, in the deeper layers of the network, feature maps contain highly abstract semantic information, while potentially accumulating a large amount of redundant and noisy data. Performing feature refinement at this critical juncture can improve the signal-to-noise ratio and the representation quality of features before they are passed to the decoder.

CBAM sequentially calibrates the input deep feature map $\mathcal{F} \in \mathbb{R}^{C \times H \times W}$ through a series of channel and spatial attention submodules.

1. **Channel-wise Feature Modulation**: First, the channel attention module $M_c(\mathcal{F}) \in \mathbb{R}^{C \times 1 \times 1}$ models the response of each feature channel. In medical image segmentation tasks, different channels often encode different semantic attributes (e.g., tissue texture, edge gradient, or intensity distribution). This module learns the inter-channel relationships and adaptively assigns weights to each channel, selectively enhancing those most discriminative for segmentation (e.g., texture patterns related to pathological tissues), while suppressing channels associated with background or irrelevant anatomical structures. This process is formally defined as:

$$\mathcal{F}' = M_c(\mathcal{F}) \otimes \mathcal{F} \tag{11}$$

   where $\otimes$ denotes element-wise multiplication. This step effectively reconstructs the semantic distribution of the feature map.

2. **Spatial Saliency Focusing**: The channel-refined feature map $\mathcal{F}'$ is then passed to the spatial attention module $M_s(\mathcal{F}') \in \mathbb{R}^{1 \times H \times W}$. This module aims to generate a spatial saliency map that highlights the most informative regions of the feature map. In the context of medical imaging, this enables

the model to precisely localize the core areas of the lesions or key anatomical boundaries, while ignoring large homogeneous background regions. This not only improves localization accuracy, but also provides more reliable spatial priors for subsequent segmentation decisions.

$$\mathcal{F}'' = M_s(\mathcal{F}') \otimes \mathcal{F}' \tag{12}$$

The final output $\mathcal{F}''$ is a high-quality feature representation refined both semantically and spatially.

Core Significance in CCASNet. In this study, placing CBAM in the deep layers of the encoder plays a crucial role in preventing feature degradation and noise propagation. By refining features at the stage where high-level semantic representations are formed, CBAM ensures that the features passed to subsequent layers and the decoder (via skip connections) are high-quality and optimized. This"source-level refinement" strategy effectively avoids amplification of redundant and ambiguous information throughout the network, thereby directly improving segmentation performance. Specifically, it significantly enhances the model's ability to detect subtle lesions and delineate complex boundaries, serving as a key technical component that enables CCASNet to achieve robust and precise segmentation in highly challenging medical imaging scenarios.

4   Experiments

4.1   Datasets

To validate the effectiveness of CCASNet, we conducted experiments on two widely used benchmark datasets for medical image segmentation: the Synapse multiorgan segmentation data set and the Automated Cardiac Diagnosis Challenge (ACDC) dataset [12, 15].

4.2   Implementation Details

The model was implemented in PyTorch and trained on an NVIDIA RTX 3090 GPU. All images were resized to 224×224 pixels, with a pre-trained MaxViT encoder to capture multiscale contextual features.

For training of the Synapse dataset, we used SGD optimization with batch size 20, learning rate 0.05, momentum 0.9, weight decay 1×10^{-4} and 700 epochs. The loss of boundary difference over union (BDoU) [20] was incorporated to enhance boundary localization by dynamic penalty adjustment based on the size of the object.

The ACDC cardiac magnetic resonance dataset was trained for 400 epochs using identical encoder settings.Training configurations remained consistent across datasets unless specified in ablation studies.

Table 1. Performance evaluation of the proposed method on the Synapse dataset. Best results are highlighted in red, while second-best results are shown in blue.

Methods	Spleen	Kidney(R)	Kidney(L)	Gallbladdr	Liver	Stomach	Aorta	Pancreas	DSC↑	HD95↓
U-Net[3]	86.67	68.60	77.77	69.72	93.43	75.58	89.07	53.98	76.85	39.70
Att-UNet[2]	87.30	71.11	77.98	68.88	93.57	75.57	89.55	58.04	77.77	36.02
TransUNet[12]	85.08	77.02	81.87	63.13	94.08	75.62	87.23	55.86	77.48	31.69
MixedUNet[21]	87.75	77.29	81.47	64.99	93.06	76.81	87.92	59.46	78.59	26.59
CoTr[22]	87.01	83.02	86.19	65.37	94.22	76.00	87.09	52.28	78.56	24.05
Hiformer[23]	90.44	78.37	84.23	68.61	94.07	82.03	87.03	60.77	80.69	19.14
PVT-GCASCADE[24]	91.92	84.83	88.02	74.81	95.38	83.63	88.05	69.73	83.28	15.83
PVTrans-CASCADE[25]	90.79	84.56	87.66	68.48	94.43	83.69	86.93	65.32	82.61	17.34
PVT-EMCAD-B2[30]	92.17	84.10	88.08	68.87	95.26	93.92	88.14	68.51	83.63	15.68
SwinUNet[15]	90.66	79.61	83.28	66.53	94.29	76.60	85.47	56.58	79.13	21.55
TransDeepLab[26]	89.00	79.88	84.08	69.16	93.53	78.40	86.04	61.19	80.16	21.25
SDAUT[27]	89.54	80.20	85.10	69.3	94.91	77.91	87.03	64.56	80.67	25.59
CATFormer[28]	90.74	81.69	85.72	67.16	95.34	81.2	88.98	66.53	82.17	16.20
MissFormer[29]	91.92	82.00	85.21	68.65	94.41	80.81	86.99	65.67	81.96	18.20
ScaleFormer[33]	89.40	83.31	86.36	74.97	95.12	80.14	88.73	64.85	82.86	18.81
2D D-LKA Net[31]	91.22	84.92	88.38	73.79	94.88	84.94	88.34	67.71	84.27	20.04
MSA2Net[32]	92.69	84.24	88.30	74.35	95.59	84.03	89.47	69.30	84.75	13.29
PVT-EMCAD-B0[30]	92.66	83.96	87.48	66.62	94.57	81.22	87.21	62.00	81.97	17.39
CCASNet (ours)	93.70	86.15	89.48	74.87	95.52	85.55	89.82	69.89	85.62	**13.36**

4.3 Quantitative Results

CCASNet demonstrates superior segmentation performance with exceptional computational efficiency through multiple datasets. On the Synapse dataset (Table 1), our method achieves the highest average Dice Similarity Coefficient (DSC) of 85.62% and a competitive 95th percentile Hausdorff Distance (HD95) of 13.36, outperforming existing transformer- and CNN-based approaches in 6 out of 8 target organs. Similarly, on the ACDC dataset (Table 2), CCASNet

Table 2. Performance comparison of different methods on the ACDC dataset.

Methods	RV	MYO	LV	Average
R50 U-Net[12]	87.10	80.63	94.92	87.55
R50 Att-UNet[12]	87.58	79.20	93.47	86.75
CoTr[22]	87.81	88.44	95.29	90.52
TranUnet[12]	88.86	84.53	95.73	89.71
R50 ViT[12]	86.07	81.88	94.75	87.57
SwinUnet[15]	88.55	85.62	95.83	90.00
MissFormer[29]	89.55	88.04	94.99	90.86
MT-UNet[34]	86.64	89.04	95.62	90.43
SDAUT[27]	89.37	88.58	95.28	91.08
CCASNet (ours)	90.88	89.63	95.92	**92.14**

obtains the best overall precision with an average DSC of 92.14% across all cardiac substructures.

Significantly, while maintaining 104.38M parameters, CCASNet requires only 14.66 GFLOPs, representing an 83.5% reduction in computational cost compared to TransUNet (88.91 GFLOPs) while simultaneously improving DSC performance by 8.14% points.

These results reflect the effectiveness of our multi-scale feature fusion and cross-attention mechanisms, which capture hierarchical anatomical dependencies and accurately delineate challenging regions characterized by subtle contrast variations and ill-defined boundaries, such as the pancreas. Figure 3 further highlights the equilibrium CCASNet strikes between high accuracy and computational efficiency, supporting its practical applicability in clinical settings.

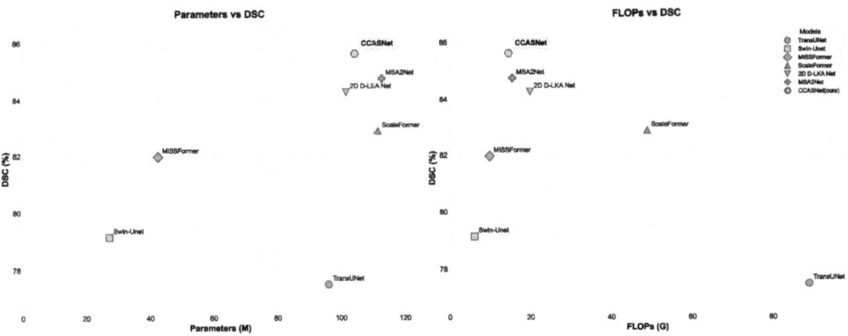

Fig. 3. Computational Efficiency and Performance Analysis.

4.4   Qualitative Results

Figure 4 shows representative segmentation results on Synapse dataset, with ground truth and predictions in the upper and lower rows. CCASNet accurately delineates abdominal organs, including challenging structures with irregular shapes and fuzzy boundaries (e.g., pancreas and gallbladder), demonstrating its capability to capture complex anatomical structures while preserving inter-organ boundaries.

4.5   Ablation Study

To validate the innovative design principles of CCASNet, we conducted comprehensive ablation experiments on the Synapse dataset. The experimental results are summarized in Table 3.

The CCA module demonstrates superior individual contribution compared to CBAM, effectively capturing cross-scale feature correlations that are crucial for precise medical image segmentation. While CBAM provides foundational

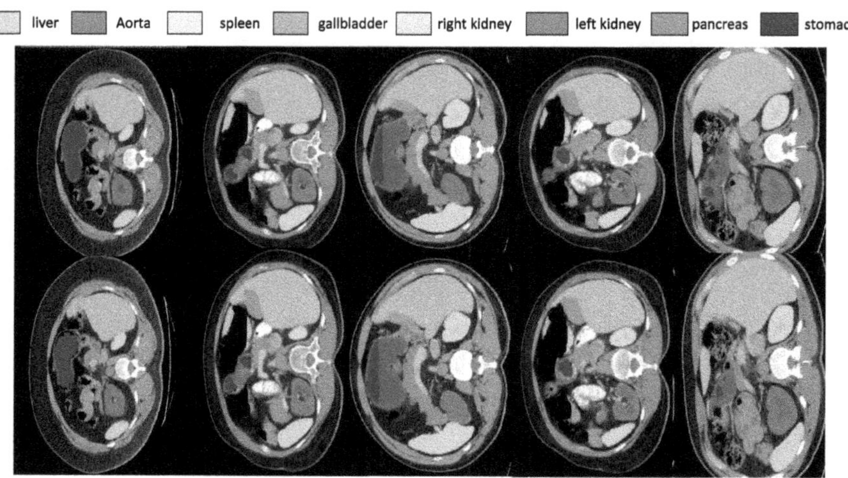

Fig. 4. shows segmentation results on Synapse slices. The top row is ground truth; the bottom row is our prediction. The outputs closely match the annotations.

Table 3. Ablation study results on Synapse dataset

CBAM	CCA	LKA	DSC ↑	HD95 ↓
×	✓	✓	0.8517	13.80
✓	×	✓	0.7569	15.52
✓	×	×	0.7399	21.72
×	✓	×	0.8487	14.21
×	×	✓	0.7513	13.91
✓	✓	✓	**0.8562**	**13.36**

channel spatial attention, our innovative integration strategy creates synergistic effects that transcend traditional attention paradigms. The holistic CCASNet architecture achieves optimal performance through the strategic fusion of complementary attention mechanisms, with systematic component removal revealing critical interdependencies in our novel architectural design. This validates CCASNet's innovative contribution to medical image segmentation through its unified attention framework that seamlessly orchestrates multiscale contextual awareness with adaptive feature refinement, establishing a new paradigm for attention-based segmentation networks.

5   Conclusion

This work introduces CCASNet, a novel architecture that integrates criss-cross attention with dual-channel spatial modeling for medical image segmentation.

Our unified attention framework orchestrates complementary mechanisms to achieve state-of-the-art performance across benchmark datasets, with ablation studies validating the synergistic effects of architectural components. CCASNet demonstrates superior segmentation accuracy and robust generalization across diverse anatomical structures, providing an effective solution for precise medical image analysis. Future work will explore multi-modal extensions, adaptive attention mechanisms for diverse anatomical regions, and integration with emerging foundation models to further advance precision medicine applications.

Acknowledgement. This work was supported by the Scientific Research Fund of Hunan Provincial Education Department (Grant No. 24B0308) and the Innovation Training Program for College Students of Hunan Province (Grant No. 202510536030).

References

1. Long, J., Shelhamer, E., Darrell, T.: Fully convolutional networks for semantic segmentation. In: Proceedings of the IEEE Conference on Computer Vision and Pattern Recognition, pp. 3431–3440 (2015)
2. Oktay, O., Schlemper, J., Folgoc, L.L., et al.: Attention u-net: learning where to look for the pancreas. arXiv preprint arXiv:1804.03999 (2018)
3. Ronneberger, O., Fischer, P., Brox, T.: U-net: Convolutional networks for biomedical image segmentation. In: International Conference on Medical Image Computing and Computer-assisted Intervention, pp. 234–241. Springer (2015)
4. Wang, C., Zhao, Z., Ren, Q., Xu Y., Yu, Y.: Dense U-net based on patch-based learning for retinal vessel segmentation. Entropy **21**(2), 168 (2019)
5. Dosovitskiy, A., et al.: An image is worth 16x16 words: Transformers for image recognition at scale. arXiv preprint arXiv:2010.11929 (2020)
6. Tu, Z., Talebi, H., Zhang, H., et al.: Maxvit: Multi-axis vision transformer. In: European conference on computer vision, pp. 459–479. Springer (2022)
7. Zhou, Z., Rahman Siddiquee, M.M., Tajbakhsh, N., Liang, J.: Unet++: a nested u-net architecture for medical image segmentation. In: International Workshop on Deep Learning in Medical Image Analysis, pp. 3–11. Springer (2018)
8. Huang, Z., Wang, X., Huang, L., Huang, C., Wei, Y., Liu, W.: Ccnet: criss-cross attention for semantic segmentation. In: Proceedings of the IEEE/CVF International Conference on Computer Vision, pp. 603–612 (2019)
9. Woo, S., Park, J., Lee, J.-Y., Kweon, I.S.: Cbam: Convolutional block attention module. In: Proceedings of the European Conference on Computer Vision (ECCV), pp. 3–19 (2018)
10. Isensee, F., Petersen, J., Klein, A., et al.: nnu-net: Self-adapting framework for u-net-based medical image segmentation. arXiv preprint arXiv:1809.10486 (2018)
11. Diakogiannis, F.I., Waldner, F., Caccetta, P., Wu, C.: ResUNet-a: a deep learning framework for semantic segmentation of remotely sensed data. ISPRS J. Photogramm. Remote. Sens. **162**, 94–114 (2020)
12. Chen, J., Lu, Y., Yu, Q., et al.: Transunet: transformers make strong encoders for medical image segmentation. arXiv preprint arXiv:2102.04306 (2021)
13. Zhang, Y., Liu, H., Hu, Q.: Transfuse: Fusing transformers and CNNs for medical image segmentation. In: International Conference on Medical Image Computing and Computer-assisted Intervention, pp. 14–24. Springer (2021)

14. Wang, H., Cao, P., Wang, J., Zaiane, O.R.: Uctransnet: rethinking the skip connections in u-net from a channel-wise perspective with transformer. In: Proceedings of the AAAI Conference on Artificial Intelligence, vol. 36, no. 3, pp. 2441–2449 (2022)

15. Cao, H., Wang, Y., Chen, J., et al.: Swin-unet: Unet-like pure transformer for medical image segmentation. In: European Conference on Computer Vision, pp. 205–218. Springer (2022)

16. Valanarasu, J.M.J., Oza, P., Hacihaliloglu, I., Patel, V.M.: Medical transformer: Gated axial-attention for medical image segmentation. In: International Conference on Medical Image Computing and Computer-assisted Intervention, pp. 36–46. Springer (2021)

17. Lin, A., Chen, B., Xu, J., Zhang, Z., Lu, G., Zhang, D.: Ds-transunet: Dual swin transformer u-net for medical image segmentation. IEEE Trans. Instrum. Meas. **71**, 1–15 (2022)

18. Guo, M.-H., Lu, C.-Z., Liu, Z.-N., Cheng, M.-M., Hu, S.-M.: Visual attention network. Comput. Visual Media **9**(4), 733–752 (2023)

19. Azad, R., Arimond, R., Aghdam, E.K., Kazerouni, A., Merhof, D.: Dae-former: Dual attention-guided efficient transformer for medical image segmentation. In: International Workshop on Predictive Intelligence in Medicine, pp. 83–95. Springer (2023)

20. Sun, F., Luo, Z., Li, S.: Boundary difference over union loss for medical image segmentation. In: International Conference on Medical Image Computing and Computer-assisted Intervention, pp. 292–301. Springer (2023)

21. Wang, H., Xie, S., Lin, L., et al.: Mixed transformer u-net for medical image segmentation. In: ICASSP 2022-2022 IEEE International Conference on Acoustics, Speech and Signal Processing (ICASSP), pp. 2390–2394. IEEE (2022)

22. Xie, Y., Zhang, J., Shen, C., Xia, Y.: Cotr: Efficiently bridging CNN and transformer for 3D medical image segmentation. In: International Conference on Medical Image Computing and Computer-assisted Intervention, pp. 171–180. Springer (2021)

23. Heidari, M., Kazerouni, A., Soltany, M., et al.: Hiformer: hierarchical multi-scale representations using transformers for medical image segmentation. In: Proceedings of the IEEE/CVF Winter Conference on Applications of Computer Vision, pp. 6202–6212 (2023)

24. Rahman, M.M., Marculescu, R.: G-cascade: Efficient cascaded graph convolutional decoding for 2d medical image segmentation. In: Proceedings of the IEEE/CVF Winter Conference on Applications of Computer Vision, pp. 7728–7737 (2024)

25. Rahman, M.M., Marculescu, R.: Medical image segmentation via cascaded attention decoding. In: Proceedings of the IEEE/CVF Winter Conference on Applications of Computer Vision, pp. 6222–6231 (2023)

26. Azad, R., Heidari, M., Shariatnia, M., et al.: Transdeeplab: convolution-free transformer-based deeplab v3+ for medical image segmentation. In: International Workshop on PRedictive Intelligence In MEdicine, pp. 91–102. Springer (2022)

27. Huang, J., Xing, X., Gao, Z., Yang, G.: Swin deformable attention u-net transformer (sdaut) for explainable fast mri. In: International Conference on Medical Image Computing and Computer-Assisted Intervention, pp. 538–548. Springer (2022)

28. You, C., Zhao, R., Liu, F., et al.: Class-aware adversarial transformers for medical image segmentation. Adv. Neural. Inf. Process. Syst. **35**, 29582–29596 (2022)

29. Huang, X., Deng, Z., Li, D., Yuan, X., Fu, Y.: Missformer: an effective transformer for 2D medical image segmentation. IEEE Trans. Med. Imaging **42**(5), 1484–1494 (2022)
30. Rahman, M.M., Munir, M., Marculescu, R.: Emcad: Efficient multi-scale convolutional attention decoding for medical image segmentation. In: Proceedings of the IEEE/CVF Conference on Computer Vision and Pattern Recognition, pp. 11769–11779 (2024)
31. Azad, R., Niggemeier, L., Hüttemann, M., et al.: Beyond self-attention: deformable large kernel attention for medical image segmentation. In: Proceedings of the IEEE/CVF Winter Conference on Applications of Computer Vision, pp. 1287–1297 (2024)
32. Kolahi, S.G., Chaharsooghi, S.K., Khatibi, T., et al.: MSA ^{2} Net: Multi-scale Adaptive Attention-guided Network for Medical Image Segmentation. arXiv preprint arXiv:2407.21640 (2024)
33. Huang, H., Xie, S., Lin, L., et al. ScaleFormer: revisiting the transformer-based backbones from a scale-wise perspective for medical image segmentation. arXiv preprint arXiv:2207.14552 (2022)
34. Jha, A., Kumar, A., Pande, S., et al.: Mt-UNET: a novel u-net based multi-task architecture for visual scene understanding. In: 2020 IEEE International Conference on Image Processing (ICIP), pp. 2191-2195. IEEE (2020)

Diffusion-Driven Deep Variational Image Clustering with Representation Decoupling

Feiyu Chen[1(✉)], Zijian Li[2], Nanjun Yu[1], Tangjun Ruan[1], Teng Ma[2], and Chao Zhang[3]

[1] National Center for Applied Mathematics in Chongqing, Chongqing Normal University, Chongqing, China
`fchen_cqnu@163.com`
[2] College of Computer and Information Science, Chongqing Normal University, Chongqing, China
[3] National Engineering Research Center of Information Security, Beijing, China

Abstract. Diffusion models have recently demonstrated strong generative capabilities, yet their potential in unsupervised image clustering remains underexplored. In this work, we propose Diffusion-driven Representation Decoupling Clustering (Diff-RDC), which reconsiders the diffusion probabilistic modeling of denoising guided jointly by semantic features and latent cluster assignments. We perform discriminative semantic inference over the entire diffusion trajectory and eliminate timestep sampling during optimization, leading to a more principled Evidence Lower Bound (ELBO) that reinforces cluster separability while preserving class-conditional generation. To implement this formulation, we design an asymmetric encoder architecture that separates discriminative and fine-grained representations, where the former initiates semantic reconstruction and the latter progressively injects fine-grained details during denoising. Without relying on explicit disentanglement constraints, our framework implicitly achieves representation decoupling through a structured decoding flow. Extensive experiments on four diverse benchmarks validate the effectiveness of our method in improving clustering performance and semantic consistency. These findings are further corroborated by ablation studies and generative visualizations.

Keywords: Multimedia content analysis · Clustering · Diffusion model · Discriminative representation learning · Generation model

1 Introduction

In multimedia content analysis, unsupervised image clustering, which groups similar images without labels, is a fundamental yet challenging task in computer vision. It underpins a range of downstream applications, including retrieval, organizing large-scale multimedia collections, and unsupervised pretraining.

Deep learning methods like DEC [28], VaDE [11], WEC [1], and BRB [15] jointly learn representations and cluster assignments. However, they rely heavily

© The Author(s), under exclusive license to Springer Nature Singapore Pte Ltd. 2026
J. Lokoč et al. (Eds.): MMM 2026, LNCS 16412, pp. 478–493, 2026.
https://doi.org/10.1007/978-981-95-6950-2_34

on reconstruction losses and encoder-decoder architectures, prioritizing pixel-level recovery over discriminative features, thus limiting performance. Encoding all information into a single latent variable without explicit semantic disentanglement further weakens representation clusterability.

Meanwhile, generative clustering methods have demonstrated that incorporating clustering signals into generative modeling [6,14]—as seen in VaDE [11], ClusterGAN [16], and FSVAE [31]—can impose structural priors over latent spaces and enable class-conditional generation. However, they still inherit reconstruction-based or encoder-decoder-based optimization frameworks, limiting discriminative feature learning.

Our motivation lies in the unique advantages of diffusion models [10,23–25] for representation learning and clustering tasks. Unlike conventional encoders that directly map inputs to features—often mixing class-relevant semantics with low-level textures—the multi-stage reverse diffusion process enforces a semantic trajectory, gradually transforming noise into structure. At each denoising step, high-level semantics guide feature refinement, yielding cleaner and more cluster-friendly representations. For samples of the same class, their trajectories tend to align, fostering intra-cluster compactness; inter-class samples follow diverging paths, accumulating representational differences and enhancing separability. These advantages make diffusion modeling a promising yet underexplored paradigm for unsupervised clustering.

Recent works such as Diff-AE [19] and ClusterDDPM [29] have begun exploring this direction. However, they compute ELBO losses from a single timestep—adequate for generation but insufficient for strong clustering constraints—and infer discriminative features solely from the input, neglecting dependencies across the full diffusion trajectory. Moreover, their U-Net-based architectures entangle discriminative semantics with low-level details, limiting clustering performance.

To overcome these limitations, we propose Diffusion-driven Representation Decoupling Clustering (Diff-RDC). a framework that revisits diffusion-driven deep variational clustering via full-trajectory modeling. Diff-RDC explicitly conditions discriminative semantic inference and model optimization on the entire diffusion trajectory, rather than sampling a single timestep [19,29], thereby deriving a more principled ELBO objective that strengthens clustering separability. By refining latent structures across multiple noise levels, our method captures clustering-friendly semantics more effectively than prior approaches.

Beyond probabilistic modeling, we introduce an asymmetric encoder that decouples discriminative semantics from low-level details. A discriminative branch anchors semantic reconstruction, while a shallow convolutional branch captures fine-grained attributes progressively fused during reverse diffusion. This structured decoding flow achieves disentanglement without regularization like mutual information minimization [2,12] or orthogonality constraints [21].

In summary, our work makes the following key contributions:

- We propose a new diffusion-driven probabilistic graphical model, and derive via variational inference a stronger loss function that aiding cluster separation.

– We design an asymmetric encoder that disentangles discriminative and non-discriminative features, progressively fusing them during denoising to enhance cluster separability.
– We employ Davies–Bouldin Index for hyperparameter selection, and extensive experiments on four benchmarks validate the effectiveness of our method in clustering performance and semantic consistency.

2   Related Work

2.1   Reconstruction-Dependent Clustering

Despite the remarkable progress in deep clustering, most existing methods fundamentally rely on reconstruction losses or encoder-decoder architectures as indispensable components. Representative approaches such as DEC [28], IDEC [9], and DEPICT [5] optimize clustering objectives alongside image reconstruction, which often entangles discriminative feature learning with pixel-level fidelity and limits the expressiveness of learned representations. Meanwhile, generative clustering methods like VaDE [11], ClusterGAN [16], and GamMM-VAE [8] demonstrate that generation and clustering can mutually enhance each other by imposing structured priors in latent spaces. Some recent works, such as FSVAE [31] and DGC [27], attempt to break the encoder-decoder constraint by explicitly disentangling semantic and nuisance factors; however, they still depend on reconstruction losses, leaving the fundamental coupling issue unresolved. Even the latest methods like WEC [1] and BRB [15], while significantly improving clustering performance, continue to operate within the encoder-decoder or reconstruction-based paradigms. Addressing these issues demands clustering with disentangled representations beyond reconstruction.

2.2   Exploring Diffusion-Driven Clustering

Research on diffusion models has fundamentally reshaped generative modeling by circumventing traditional reliance on one-step pixel-level reconstruction losses. Early works such as NCSN [24], DDPM [10], score-based modeling [25], and VDM [13] established diffusion processes as a powerful alternative to encoder-decoder architectures. Building on this foundation, DiffAE [19] demonstrated that diffusion-driven denoising could enable meaningful representation learning without explicit reconstruction, while ClusterDDPM [29] introduced diffusion models into unsupervised clustering by combining denoising with latent mixture modeling. Subsequent efforts, including D-CMVAE [17], DDVI [18], and DPSC [34], further explored extending diffusion processes to multimodal clustering, variational inference, and affinity refinement. However, despite these advances, the integration of diffusion-driven objectives with explicit feature disentanglement for clustering remains underexplored, leaving room for novel formulations that better separate semantic and nuisance factors during unsupervised learning.

3   Method

3.1   Probabilistic Graphical Model

We revisit the interplay between diffusion modeling and clustering through a probabilistic graphical model (PGM). In our formulation, c denotes the class label, z captures discriminative semantics, x_0 is the clean image, and x_t is its diffused version after t steps. The dependencies among these variables are illustrated in Fig. 1.

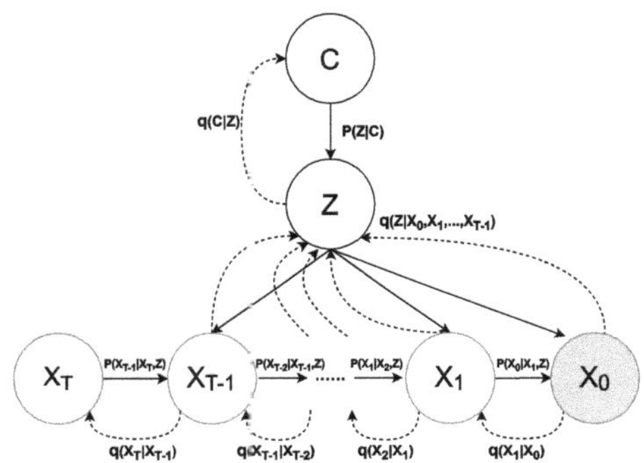

Fig. 1. PGM of Diff-RDC

In the generative process (solid lines in Fig. 1), discriminative semantics z are drawn from the class-conditional prior $p(z|c)$, capturing category-specific structural patterns. Conditioned on z, the noisy sample x_t is iteratively refined through the transition $p(x_{t-1}|x_t, z)$, gradually denoising from Gaussian noise $x_T \sim \mathcal{N}(0, I)$ to the clean target x_0. Throughout this trajectory, z serves as a semantic anchor, steering the generative path toward class-consistent outputs. The joint distribution is factorized as:

$$p(c, z, x_{0:T}) = p(c)p(z|c)p(x_T)\prod_{t=1}^{T} p(x_{t-1}|x_t, z). \tag{1}$$

In the inference path (dashed lines in Fig. 1), we use q at each step to align inference with generation. Unlike prior work assuming $q(z|x_0)$, which risks overfitting to fine details, we adopt $q(z|x_{0:T-1})$ to aggregate semantic cues from intermediate states and better capture discriminative structure. The joint density of the inference process factorizes as:

$$q(c, z, x_{1:T}|x_0) = q(c|z)q(z|x_{0:T-1})\prod_{t=1}^{T} q(x_t|x_{t-1}). \tag{2}$$

3.2 Evidence Lower Bound and Loss Function

Based on the PGM defined above, we derive the evidence lower bound (ELBO) using variational inference on the log-likelihood of the observed sample x_0:

$$\log p(x) \geq \text{ELBO} = \mathbb{E}_{q(c,z,x_{1:T}|x_0)}\left[\log \frac{p(c,z,x_{0:T})}{q(c,z,x_{1:T}\mid x_0)}\right]$$

$$= \underbrace{\mathbb{E}_q\left[\log \frac{p(c)\,p(z\mid c)}{q(c\mid z)\,q(z\mid x_{0:T-1})}\right]}_{\text{Clustering terms, }E_{\text{C}}} + \underbrace{\mathbb{E}_q[\log p(x_T)] - \mathbb{E}_q[\log q(x_T\mid x_0)]}_{\text{Constant terms}}$$

$$+ \underbrace{\mathbb{E}_q[\log p(x_0\mid x_1,z)] + \sum_{t=2}^{T}\mathbb{E}_q\left[\log \frac{p(x_{t-1}\mid x_t,z)}{q(x_{t-1}\mid x_t,x_0)}\right]}_{\text{Diffusion terms, }E_{\text{Diff}}} \tag{3}$$

To address the intractable integral in the ELBO, we sample the latent variable z from $q(z|x_{0:T-1})$, yielding $\tilde{z}$, while neglecting the sampling noise. This leads to simplified formulations of the clustering and diffusion terms.

Simplified clustering terms:

$$\tilde{E}_{\text{C}} = -D_{\text{KL}}[q(c|\tilde{z})||p(c)] + \sum_{c} q(c|\tilde{z})\log p(\tilde{z}|c) + \mathbb{H}(q(z|x_{0:T-1})) \tag{4}$$

Simplified diffusion terms:

$$\tilde{E}_{\text{Diff}} = -\sum_{t=2}^{T}\mathbb{E}_{q(x_t|x_0)}\left[D_{\text{KL}}[q(x_{t-1}|x_t,x_0)||p(x_{t-1}|x_t,\tilde{z})]\right] + \mathbb{E}_q[\log p(x_0|x_1,\tilde{z})] \tag{5}$$

The clustering terms correspond to prior matching in the discriminative latent space z, governing the modeling of cluster semantics and assignments. The diffusion terms arise as KL divergences between forward and reverse processes, focusing on feature learning. All terms follow directly from the graphical model in Fig. 1, without requiring additional assumptions, and lead to a generalizable variational objective.

We assume that the random variables involved in the reverse diffusion process follow the following distributions:

$$p(c) := \text{Categorical}(c; \boldsymbol{\pi}), \; p(z|c) := \mathcal{N}(z; \mu_c, \text{Diag}(\sigma_c^2)), \tag{6}$$

$$p(x_{t-1}|x_t, z) := \mathcal{N}(x_{t-1}; \text{DenoiseNet}(x_t, t, z; \theta), \sigma_t^2 I), \tag{7}$$

Here, $\boldsymbol{\pi}, \mu_c, \sigma_c$ are the K-dimensional vector parameters of a Gaussian mixture prior, $\text{DenoiseNet}(\cdot)$ is a parameterized neural network, and $\sigma_t^2 I$ denotes the variance of the denoising distribution, set to be equal to the variance of $q(x_{t-1}|x_t, x_0)$ (see Eq. 12).

We further stipulate that in the forward diffusion process, the corresponding distributions are as follows:

$$q(x_t|x_{t-1}) := \mathcal{N}(x_t; \sqrt{1 - \beta_t} \cdot x_{t-1}, \beta_t I), \tag{8}$$

$$q(z|x_{0:T-1}) := \mathcal{N}(z; \text{ZsemNet}_\mu(x_{0:T-1}; \phi_1), \text{Diag}(\text{ZsemNet}_\sigma(x_{0:T-1}; \phi_2)^2)). \tag{9}$$

Here, β_t controls noise level per step. $\text{ZsemNet}\mu(\cdot)$ and $\text{ZsemNet}\sigma(\cdot)$ output the mean and std from a shared extractor aggregating T-step features. Reparameterization of Eq. 9 yields:

$$\tilde{z} = \text{ZsemNet}_\mu(x_{0:T-1}) + \epsilon \cdot \text{ZsemNet}_\sigma(x_{0:T-1}), \quad \epsilon \sim \mathcal{N}(0, I). \tag{10}$$

A notable property of the forward diffusion process is that it allows sampling at any timestep t directly from the initial sample:

$$q(x_t|x_0) := \mathcal{N}(x_t; \sqrt{\alpha_t}x_0, (1 - \alpha_t)I), \tag{11}$$

$$q(x_{t-1}|x_t, x_0) := \mathcal{N}(x_{t-1}; \tilde{\mu}_t(x_t, x_0), \tilde{\beta}_t I), \tag{12}$$

where:

$$\alpha_t := \prod_{s=1}^{t} (1 - \beta_s), \quad \tilde{\beta}_t := \frac{1 - \alpha_{t-1}}{1 - \alpha_t}\beta_t, \tag{13}$$

$$\tilde{\mu}_t(x_t, x_0) := \frac{\sqrt{\alpha_{t-1}}\beta_t}{1 - \alpha_t}x_0 + \frac{\sqrt{(1 - \alpha_{t-1})(1 - \alpha_t)}}{1 - \alpha_t}x_t, \tag{14}$$

In this paper, clustering labels are inferred from the posterior $q(c|z)$. We assume:

$$q(c = j|z) := p(c = j|z) = \frac{p(z|c = j)p(c = j)}{\sum_{i=1}^{K} p(z|c = i)p(c = i)}, \tag{15}$$

Let $\text{ClusteringLayer}_\rho(z)$ parameterize $q(c|z)$. It takes the discriminative semantic vector z as input, producing a K-dimensional vector representing class probabilities that the sample belongs to each class.

For $\tilde{E}_{\text{Diff}}$ terms, we set $\hat{x}_{t-1} = \tilde{u}_t(x_t, x_0)$, $\hat{x}_0 = x_0$ and let the last process of reverse $p(x_0|x_1, z) = \mathcal{N}(x_0; \text{DenoiseNet}(x_1, 1, z; \theta), \tilde{\beta}_1 I)$, where $\frac{1}{2\tilde{\beta}_1} = 1.5\frac{1}{2\tilde{\beta}_2}$. And then:

$$\tilde{E}_{\text{Diff}} = -\sum_{t=1}^{T} \frac{1}{2\tilde{\beta}_t}\|\hat{x}_{t-1} - \text{DenoiseNet}(x_t, t, \tilde{z}; \theta)\|_2^2 - \sum_{j=1}^{D} \left(\tilde{\beta}_1^{(j)}\right)^{\frac{1}{2}} \tag{16}$$

Substituting the Eq. 6–15 into the simplified clustering terms and diffusion terms, we finally derive the explicit forms of $\tilde{E}_C$ and $\tilde{E}_{\text{Diff}}$ as shown in formula

Eq. 17 and Eq. 16. Here, D is the dimension of z, e the natural logarithm, K the number of classes, π the circle constant, $\boldsymbol{\pi}$ the K-dimensional parameter of the prior categorical distribution, and $\mathrm{vec}^{(i)}$ the i-th element of a vector.

$$
\tilde{E}_{\mathrm{C}} = \sum_{c=1}^{K} \mathrm{ClusteringLayer}(\tilde{z})^{(c)} \left\{ \log \frac{\boldsymbol{\pi}^{(c)}}{\mathrm{ClusteringLayer}(\tilde{z})^{(c)}} \right.
$$
$$
\left. - \frac{D}{2}\log(2\pi) - \sum_{j=1}^{D}\log\sigma_c^{(j)} - \sum_{j=1}^{D}\frac{1}{2\sigma_c^{(j)2}}(\tilde{z}^{(j)} - \mu_c^{(j)})^2 \right\} \tag{17}
$$
$$
+ \frac{D}{2}\log(2\pi e) + \sum_{j=1}^{D}\log(\mathrm{ZsemNet}_\sigma(x_{0:T-1}))^{(j)}
$$

Loss function (Eq. 18) is derived from the ELBO, omitting constant terms and weighting clustering-related terms by λ to better guide representation learning.

$$
\mathcal{L} = \mathcal{L}_{\mathrm{Diff}} + \lambda\mathcal{L}_{\mathrm{C}} = -\tilde{E}_{\mathrm{Diff}} - \lambda\tilde{E}_{\mathrm{C}}, \quad \lambda > 1. \tag{18}
$$

The hyperparameter λ is chosen by running with different values and selecting λ with the smallest Davies–Bouldin Index (DBI), a metric that measures cluster compactness and separation without real labels.

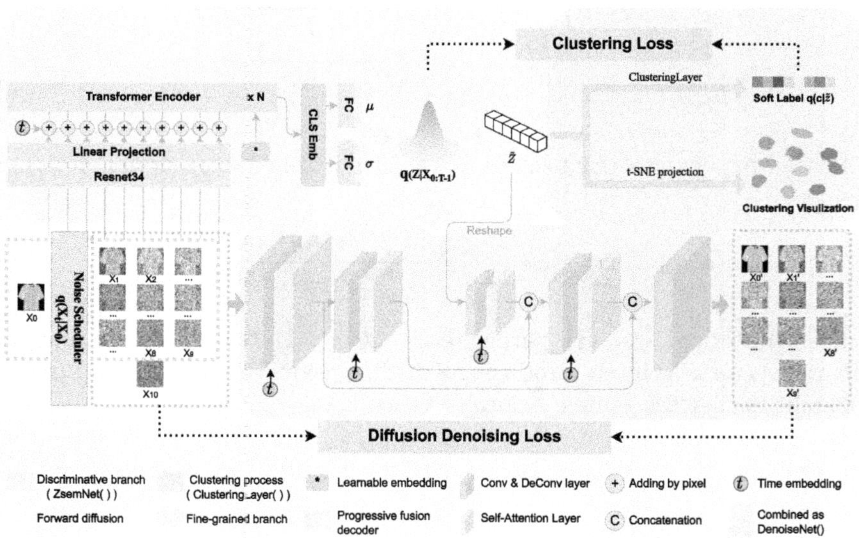

Fig. 2. Diff-RDC Network Architecture

3.3 Diff-RDC Network

We design a decoupled architecture with five components (Fig. 2).

Forward Diffusion Process. Defined as $q(x_t|x_0)$, it progressively adds noise to x_0 via a Noise Scheduler. We use $T = 10$ steps to generate increasingly noisy samples $x_1, \ldots, x_{10}$, simulating controlled degradation for robust feature extraction.

Discriminative Branch. Unlike prior works that infer $q(z|x_0)$ from only the final denoised sample x_0, we model $q(z|x_{0:T-1})$ over the full denoising trajectory to leverage richer temporal context and obtain more stable semantics. A shared ResNet extracts features from each x_t, enhanced with timestep embeddings and a learnable class token, which are processed by a Transformer encoder for global semantic aggregation. The resulting representation initializes the decoder to guide semantic reconstruction.

Fine-Grained Branch. This branch captures low-level features to complement the semantic representation from the discriminative branch. It operates within the reverse process $p(x_{t-1}|x_t, z)$, using two lightweight blocks composed of convolution, timestep embedding, and shallow attention. Intermediate features are retained for progressive fusion during decoding.

Progressive Fusion Decoder. The decoder progressively fuses a semantic anchor z from the discriminative branch with fine-grained CNN features via multi-stage skip connections (Fig. 2). Using z as a semantic reference guides reconstruction while retaining discriminative cues, enabling semantic disentanglement and cluster separability without explicit regularization such as mutual information or orthogonality constraints.

Clustering Process. We fit a GMM on z with parameters $\{\pi, \mu_c, \sigma_c\}$ jointly optimized via clustering and diffusion losses (Sec. 3.2). Therefore, z forms a Gaussian mixture in latent space, which can be visualized using t-SNE. The cluster soft label for any sample is given by:

$$q(c|x) = p(c|\tilde{z}) = \frac{\pi_c \mathcal{N}(\tilde{z}; \mu_c, \mathrm{Diag}(\sigma_c^2))}{\sum_{k=1}^{K} \pi_k \mathcal{N}(\tilde{z}; \mu_k, \mathrm{Diag}(\sigma_k^2))}. \tag{19}$$

4 Experiments

4.1 Experimental Setup

Datasets and Metrics. We evaluate our method on four standard image datasets: MNIST, USPS, Fashion-MNIST, and a class-imbalanced 10-class subset of GTSRB [26] (IDs: 3, 7, 8, 9, 12, 13, 17, 18, 35, 38). For each dataset, we merge training and test splits to form a unified evaluation set. All images are resized to 32×32 and converted to grayscale for training and clustering evaluation. Notably, we do not use any external pretraining or representation learning methods (e.g., SimCLR [3], BYOL [7], MCR^2 [33]); all training, including generative pretraining, is conducted within our own model.

Clustering performance is measured by accuracy (ACC), normalized mutual information (NMI), adjusted Rand index (ARI), and F1-score. The higher values indicating better performance.

Baseline Methods. We compare our method with a diverse set of baselines spanning three categories:

- **Traditional Clustering:** K-means, GMM, SC-Ncut [22], and SC-LS [4], representing classical unsupervised algorithms.
- **Generative Clustering:** VaDE [11], ClusterGAN [16], DGC [27], FSVAE [31], ClusterDDPM [29], and GamMM-VAE [8], which enhance clustering via generative modeling.
- **Self-supervised Clustering:** JULE [30], DEC [28], IDEC [9], DSCDA [32], DEPICT [5], DeepDPM [20], and WEC-MMD [1], DEC+BRB [15], which are not based on generative models but still rely on autoencoder architectures or reconstruction losses to guide representation learning.

Hyperparameters and Details. For all datasets, we set $T = 10$ to balance clustering performance and computational cost, and use a fixed noise schedule $\{\beta_i\}_{i=1}^{T} = \text{linspace}(0.1, 0.9, T)$ to ensure that the final diffusion distribution after $T = 10$ steps approximates a standard Gaussian:

$$q(x_T|x_0) = \mathcal{N}(x_T; 0.012x_0, 0.999I) \tag{20}$$

Following common practice in generative clustering, we first pretrain the model with $\lambda = 0$ to optimize the diffusion loss $\mathcal{L}_{\text{Diff}}$, then switch to joint training using the full objective (Eq. 18). We find that setting $\boldsymbol{\pi} = (\frac{1}{K}, ..., \frac{1}{K})$ stabilizes training with negligible impact on clustering, even for imbalanced data GTSRB. We thus adopt this prior in all experiments. All experiments are run on a NVIDIA RTX 4080 GPU.

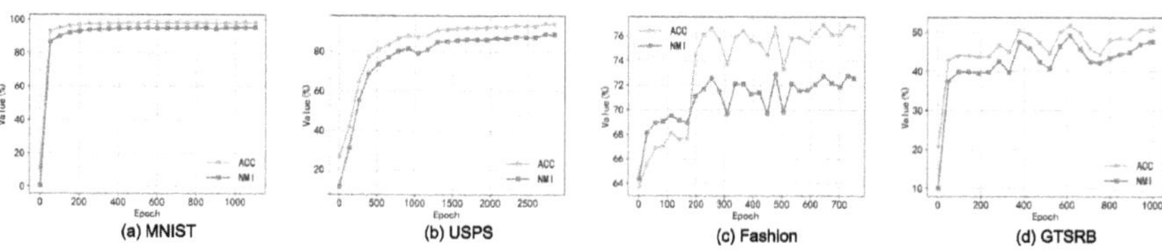

(a) MNIST   (b) USPS   (c) Fashion   (d) GTSRB

Fig. 3. Epoch vs ACC and NMI.

4.2   Quantitative Results

Table 1. Clustering performance comparison on different datasets. For baselines lacking reported results, we reproduced open-source methods using default settings (marked with '*').

Methods	MNIST		USPS		Fashion		GTSRB	
	ACC	NMI	ACC	NMI	ACC	NMI	ACC	NMI
K-means	53.2*	49.9*	66.8	62.6	47.4	51.2	10.2*	6.8*
GMM	43.5*	35.4*	55.1	53.0	55.6	55.7	10.7*	7.4*
AE + K-Means	65.2*	64.1*	66.3*	64.4*	51.8*	56.6*	24.9*	12.0*
AE + GMM	72.1*	74.4*	72.5*	74.5*	56.4*	62.5*	24.6*	16.3*
SC-Ncut	65.6*	73.1*	64.9†	79.4†	50.8†	57.5†	12.1*	13.7*
SC-LS	71.4*	70.6*	74.6†	75.5†	49.6†	49.7†	12.1*	15.1*
JULE	96.4	91.3	<u>95.0</u>	**91.3**	56.3	60.8	18.1*	18.4*
DEC	86.3	83.4	76.2	76.7	51.8	54.6	27.3*	<u>18.4*</u>
IDEC	88.1	86.7	76.1	78.5	52.9	55.7	27.6*	17.7*
VaDE	94.4	89.1	56.6	51.2	62.9	61.1	20.6*	10.7*
DEPICT	96.5	91.7	89.9	90.6	39.2	39.2	–	–
ClusterGAN	93.0	89.0	88.0	85.0	62.0	62.0	–	–
DSCDA	97.8	94.1	86.9	85.7	66.2	64.5	–	–
DeepDPM	<u>98.0</u>	94.0	89.0	88.0	62.0	<u>68.0</u>	26.0*	17.6*
TELL	95.2	88.8	86.5†	78.6†	58.4†	65.8†	23.5*	14.6*
DGC	97.9	<u>94.6</u>	–	–	68.2	64.2	–	–
FSVAE	97.0	92.0	92.0	87.0	64.0	64.0	25.0*	11.0*
ClusterDDPM	97.7	94.0	–	–	70.5	66.1	–	–
GamMM-VAE	95.2	88.8	–	–	<u>70.8</u>	62.8	–	–
WEC-MMD	96.7	92.2	–	–	62.2	62.9	–	–
DEC+BRB	91.1	91.7	78.6	84.0	59.6	62.1	<u>27.7*</u>	16.0*
Diff-RDC	**98.1**	**95.1**	**95.9**	<u>91.2</u>	**76.9**	**72.6**	**51.0**	**48.4**

Table 1 reports the clustering performance of our proposed Diff-RDC compared to 21 baseline methods across four benchmark datasets. Diff-RDC achieves consistently strong results across all datasets. On USPS, it obtains the highest accuracy (ACC), with an NMI score slightly below that of JULE (by 0.1%). On MNIST, Fashion-MNIST, and GTSRB, Diff-RDC outperforms all baselines in both ACC and NMI. Notably, it achieves 98.1% ACC and 95.1% NMI on MNIST, approaching the performance typically associated with supervised classification.

The performance on GTSRB is particularly compelling: Diff-RDC surpasses the second-best method (DEC+BRB) by 23.3% in ACC and exceeds DEC by

30.0% in NMI. These improvements are attributed to the model's representation-decoupling architecture and diffusion-denoising loss, which together address challenges such as class imbalance, complex backgrounds, and illumination variability. All datasets are conducted without external feature-learning pretraining, evidenced by K-means and GMM achieving only 10% ACC.

Figure 3 shows the evolution of ACC and NMI throughout training. A more detailed analysis of the model's components is presented in the ablation and visualization sections.

4.3 Ablation Study

In this section, we conduct ablation studies on the loss function and network structure, and analyze the DBI selection method of λ in Eq. 18 to evaluate the contribution of each component in Diff-RDC.

Ablation Study on Loss Function. To assess the role of the diffusion-driven reconstruction loss $\mathcal{L}_{\text{Diff}}$, we replace it with a conventional autoencoder loss $\mathcal{L}_r = \|x_0 - f_\theta(x_0)\|_2^2$, keeping the architecture unchanged. Since $\mathcal{L}_{\text{Diff}}$ is tightly integrated with our framework, such substitution may disrupt the optimization dynamics. To isolate the effect of the loss function itself, we also compare with VaDE, which naturally employs $\mathcal{L}_r$. As shown in Fig. 4, our full model consistently outperforms both the ablated variant and VaDE across all metrics (ACC, NMI, ARI, F1-score), confirming the advantage of diffusion-driven reconstruction.

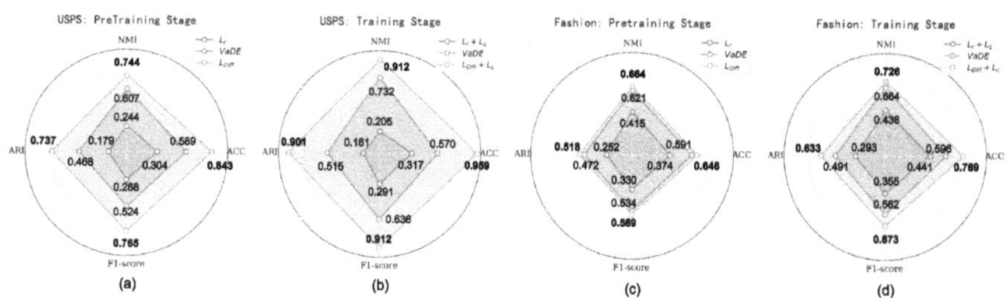

Fig. 4. Clustering performance comparison under different reconstruction losses on Fashion-MNIST and USPS.

Ablation Study on Network Structure. We further evaluate the contributions of three key modules: the Transformer architecture (TF), the Progressive Fusion decoder (PF), and the Branched encoder (BE). As BE is fundamental to the overall design—feeding into both TF and PF and enabling the diffusion loss—it cannot be directly removed. Instead, we construct a simplified variant using a single encoder and conventional AE loss, serving as a degraded baseline. Results show that removing either TF or PF leads to performance drops, highlighting the importance of multi-level representation and fusion design.

Table 2. Ablation Study Results on USPS (mean ± std over 3 runs).

Components			Metrics (%)			
BE	PF	TF	ACC	NMI	ARI	F1-score
✓	✓	✓	95.9 ± 1.5	91.2 ± 1.8	90.1 ± 1.5	91.2 ± 1.6
✓	×	✓	80.2 ± 1.9	83.5 ± 2.0	76.3 ± 1.9	78.9 ± 1.5
✓	✓	×	83.9 ± 2.0	83.3 ± 2.5	78.1 ± 1.8	80.4 ± 2.9
×	×	×	57.0 ± 2.2	73.2 ± 1.6	51.5 ± 2.5	63.6 ± 1.6

Table 3. Ablation Study Results on Fashion (mean ± std over 3 runs).

Components			Metrics (%)			
BE	PF	TF	ACC	NMI	ARI	F1-score
✓	✓	✓	76.9 ± 1.6	72.6 ± 1.0	63.3 ± 1.3	67.3 ± 1.7
✓	×	✓	63.3 ± 1.8	65.2 ± 1.5	50.4 ± 1.5	55.4 ± 2.0
✓	✓	×	63.6 ± 0.9	64.4 ± 1.8	50.6 ± 1.7	55.7 ± 1.3
×	×	×	53.8 ± 1.1	65.4 ± 1.8	45.4 ± 1.6	54.1 ± 1.5

As shown in Table 2 and Table 3, removing either the PF or TF module reduces ACC by over 12% and NMI by over 7% on both the USPS and Fashion-MNIST datasets. These results underscore their essential roles in multi-level feature fusion and global context modeling. The degraded baseline without BE shows a substantial decline across all metrics, highlighting the foundational importance of the branched encoder design in supporting the diffusion-driven learning paradigm.

DBI Selection Method of λ. Across all datasets, we observe a clear trend: the λ value in loss function giving the smallest DBI also happens to deliver the highest ACC and NMI (Fig. 5). This means the DBI-based rule can effectively guide λ selection in a fully unsupervised manner, without sneakily picking it based on the best ACC afterwards.

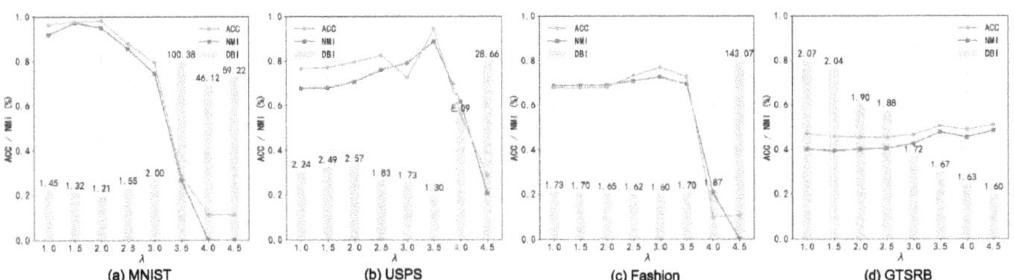

Fig. 5. Clustering performance under different values of λ on four datasets.

4.4 Visualization

To qualitatively evaluate the learned representations and generative capability of Diff-RDC, we perform a series of visualization experiments from three complementary perspectives.

First, we apply t-SNE to visualize the features z extracted by the discriminative branch across the full dataset. As shown in Fig. 6, the first row presents the raw data distributions, while the second row shows the well clustered embeddings learned by Diff-RDC. The transformed features exhibit tighter intra-class clustering and clearer inter-class separation, demonstrating the model's ability to capture class-discriminative semantics. Unlike MNIST and USPS, the t-SNE visualizations for Fashion-MNIST and GTSRB reveal more entangled class boundaries, due to semantic overlap and complex background interference.

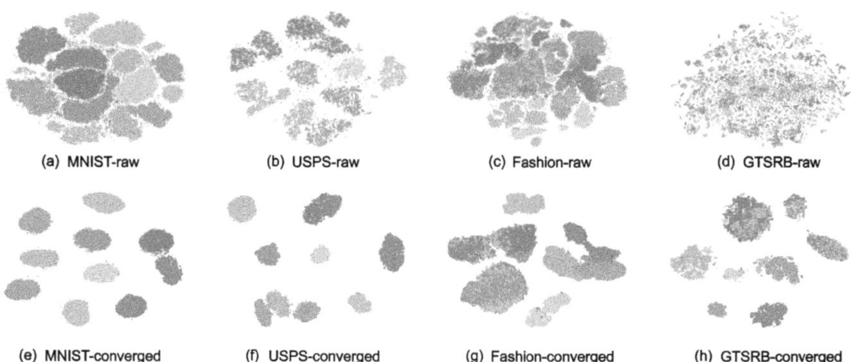

Fig. 6. t-SNE visualization of Diff-RDC clustering results on four datasets.

Second, we showcase the class-conditional generation and reverse diffusion process of Diff-RDC (Fig. 7 and Fig. 8). The generated samples exhibit consistent visual patterns and clear inter-class variation, while the reverse trajectories reveal how meaningful structures emerge smoothly from noise—demonstrating both controllability and semantic coherence in generation.

Finally, we conduct a controlled generation experiment to assess the disentanglement capability of Diff-RDC. As shown in Fig. 8, discriminative features capture global structure, while fine-grained features retain local style—highlighting effective semantic separation in our model.

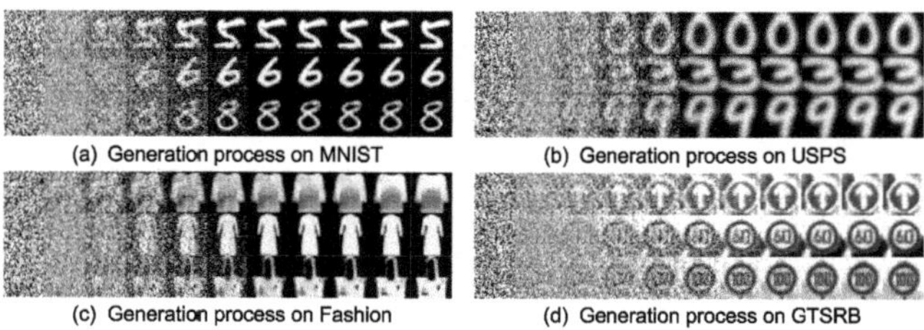

Fig. 7. Reverse diffusion process RDC to generate samples with designated class.

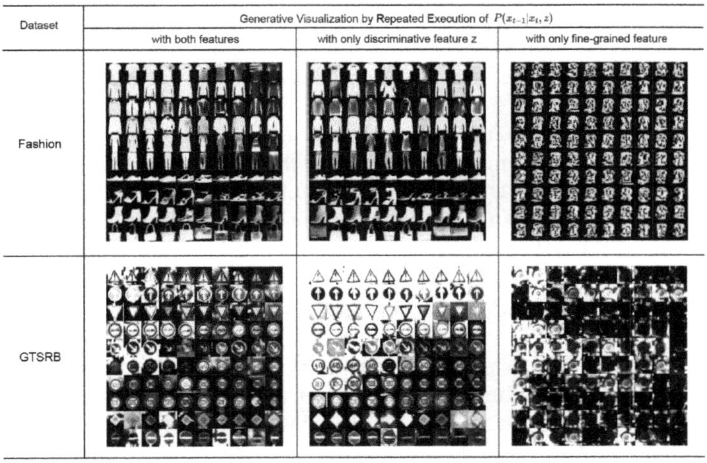

Dataset	Generative Visualization by Repeated Execution of $P(x_{t-1}|x_t, z)$		
	with both features	with only discriminative feature z	with only fine-grained feature
Fashion			
GTSRB			

Fig. 8. To compare the semantics of different decoupled features, we controlled their use for sample generation.

5 Conclusion

In this paper, we present Diff-RDC, a diffusion-driven variational clustering framework that rethinks semantic modeling via full-trajectory inference and representation decoupling. By disentangling discriminative and fine-grained features through a branched encoder and structured decoding, our approach alleviates the dominance of reconstruction in clustering pipelines. The resulting ELBO and semantic-guided denoising lead to more coherent clusters across benchmarks. This study paves the way for disentangled generative clustering and future work on lightweight variants and higher-resolution datasets.

Acknowledgments. This work was supported by the Natural Science Foundation of Chongqing (Grant No. CSTB2025NSCQ-LZX0068) and the National Natural Science Foundation of China (Grant No. 12101098,12401699).

References

1. Cai, J., Zhang, Y., Wang, S., Fan, J., Guo, W.: Wasserstein embedding learning for deep clustering: a generative approach. IEEE Trans. Multimed. (2024)
2. Chen, R.T., Li, X., Grosse, R.B., Duvenaud, D.K.: Isolating sources of disentanglement in Variational Autoencoders. In: Advances in Neural Information Processing Systems (NeurIPS), vol. 31 (2018)
3. Chen, T., Kornblith, S., Norouzi, M., Hinton, G.: A simple framework for contrastive learning of visual representations. In: International Conference on Machine Learning (ICML), pp. 1597–1607. PMLR (2020)
4. Chen, X., Cai, D.: Large scale spectral clustering with landmark-based representation. In: Proceedings of the AAAI Conference on Artificial Intelligence (AAAI), vol. 25, pp. 313–318 (2011)

5. Ghasedi Dizaji, K., Herandi, A., Deng, C., Cai, W., Huang, H.: Deep clustering via joint convolutional autoencoder embedding and relative entropy minimization. In: Proceedings of the IEEE International Conference on Computer Vision (ICCV), pp. 5736–5745 (2017)
6. Goodfellow, I.J., et al.: Generative adversarial nets. In: Advances in Neural Information Processing Systems (NeurIPS), vol. 27 (2014)
7. Grill, J.B., et al.: Bootstrap your own latent: a new approach to self-supervised learning. In: Advances in Neural Information Processing Systems (NeurIPS), vol. 33, pp. 21271–21284 (2020)
8. Guo, J., Fan, W., Amayri, M., Bouguila, N.: Deep clustering analysis via variational autoencoder with Gamma mixture latent embeddings. Neural Netw. **183**, 106979 (2025)
9. Guo, X., Gao, L., Liu, X., Yin, J.: Improved deep embedded clustering with local structure preservation. In: Proceedings of the International Joint Conference on Artificial Intelligence (IJCAI), pp. 1753–1759 (2017)
10. Ho, J., Jain, A., Abbeel, P.: Denoising diffusion probabilistic models. In: Advances in Neural Information Processing Systems (NeurIPS), vol. 33, pp. 6840–6851 (2020)
11. Jiang, Z., Zheng, Y., Tan, H., Tang, B., Zhou, H.: Variational deep embedding: an unsupervised generative approach to clustering. In: Proceedings of the International Joint Conference on Artificial Intelligence (IJCAI), pp. 1965–1972 (2017)
12. Kim, H., Mnih, A.: Disentangling by factorising. In: International Conference on Machine Learning (ICML), pp. 2649–2658. PMLR (2018)
13. Kingma, D., Salimans, T., Poole, B., Ho, J.: Variational diffusion models. In: Advances in Neural Information Processing Systems (NeurIPS), vol. 34, pp. 21696–21707 (2021)
14. Kingma, D.P., Welling, M.: Auto-encoding Variational Bayes. In: International Conference on Learning Representations (ICLR) (2014)
15. Miklautz, L., et al.: Breaking the reclustering barrier in centroid-based deep clustering. In: International Conference on Learning Representations (ICLR) (2025)
16. Mukherjee, S., Asnani, H., Lin, E., Kannan, S.: ClusterGAN: latent space clustering in generative adversarial networks. In: Proceedings of the AAAI Conference on Artificial Intelligence (AAAI), vol. 33, pp. 4610–4617 (2019)
17. Palumbo, E., Manduchi, L., Laguna, S., Chopard, D., Vogt, J.E.: Deep generative clustering with multimodal diffusion variational autoencoders. In: International Conference on Learning Representations (ICLR) (2024)
18. Piriyakulkij, W.T., Wang, Y., Kuleshov, V.: Denoising diffusion variational inference: diffusion models as expressive variational posteriors. In: Proceedings of the AAAI Conference on Artificial Intelligence (AAAI), vol. 39, pp. 19921–19930 (2025)
19. Preechakul, K., Chatthee, N., Wizadwongsa, S., Suwajanakorn, S.: Diffusion autoencoders: toward a meaningful and decodable representation. In: Proceedings of the IEEE/CVF Conference on Computer Vision and Pattern Recognition (CVPR), pp. 10619–10629 (2022)
20. Ronen, M., Finder, S.E., Freifeld, O.: DeepDPM: deep clustering with an unknown number of clusters. In: Proceedings of the IEEE/CVF Conference on Computer Vision and Pattern Recognition (CVPR), pp. 9861–9870 (2022)
21. Sarhan, M.H., Navab, N., Eslami, A., Albarqouni, S.: Fairness by learning orthogonal disentangled representations. In: Vedaldi, A., Bischof, H., Brox, T., Frahm, J.-M. (eds.) ECCV 2020. LNCS, vol. 12374, pp. 746–761. Springer, Cham (2020). https://doi.org/10.1007/978-3-030-58526-6_44
22. Shi, J., Malik, J.: Normalized cuts and image segmentation. IEEE Trans. Pattern Anal. Mach. Intell. (TPAMI) **22**(8), 888–905 (2000)

23. Sohl-Dickstein, J., Weiss, E., Maheswaranathan, N., Ganguli, S.: Deep unsupervised learning using nonequilibrium thermodynamics. In: International Conference on Machine Learning (ICML), pp. 2256–2265. PMLR (2015)
24. Song, Y., Ermon, S.: Generative modeling by estimating gradients of the data distribution. In: Advances in Neural Information Processing Systems (NeurIPS), vol. 32 (2019)
25. Song, Y., Sohl-Dickstein, J., Kingma, D.P., Kumar, A., Ermon, S., Poole, B.: Score-based generative modeling through stochastic differential equations. In: International Conference on Learning Representations (ICLR) (2021)
26. Stallkamp, J., Schlipsing, M., Salmen, J., Igel, C.: Man vs. computer: benchmarking machine learning algorithms for traffic sign recognition. Neural Netw. **32**, 323–332 (2012)
27. Wang, W., Bao, J., Guo, S.: Neural generative model for clustering by separating particularity and commonality. Inf. Sci. **589**, 813–826 (2022)
28. Xie, J., Girshick, R., Farhadi, A.: Unsupervised deep embedding for clustering analysis. In: International Conference on Machine Learning (ICML), pp. 478–487. PMLR (2016)
29. Yan, J., Liu, J., Zhang, Z.y.: ClusterDDPM: an EM clustering framework with Denoising Diffusion Probabilistic Models. arXiv preprint arXiv:2312.08029 (2023)
30. Yang, J., Parikh, D., Batra, D.: Joint unsupervised learning of deep representations and image clusters. In: Proceedings of the IEEE/CVF Conference on Computer Vision and Pattern Recognition (CVPR), pp. 5147–5156 (2016)
31. Yang, L., Fan, W., Bouguila, N.: Robust unsupervised image categorization based on variational autoencoder with disentangled latent representations. Knowl.-Based Syst. **246**, 108671 (2022)
32. Yang, X., Deng, C., Zheng, F., Yan, J., Liu, W.: Deep spectral clustering using dual autoencoder network. In: Proceedings of the IEEE/CVF Conference on Computer Vision and Pattern Recognition (CVPR), pp. 4066–4075 (2019)
33. Yu, Y., Chan, K.H.R., You, C., Song, C., Ma, Y.: Learning diverse and discriminative representations via the principle of Maximal Coding Rate Reduction. In: Advances in Neural Information Processing Systems (NeurIPS), vol. 33, pp. 9422–9434 (2020)
34. Zhu, Y., Li, Q., Liu, W., Yin, C.: Diffusion process with structural changes for subspace clustering. Pattern Recogn. **158**, 111066 (2025)

Splat-Portrait: Generalizing Talking Heads with Gaussian Splatting

Tong Shi$^{(\boxtimes)}$ ⓘ, Melonie de Almeida ⓘ, Daniela Ivanova ⓘ, Nicolas Pugeault ⓘ, and Paul Henderson ⓘ

School of Computing Science, University of Glasgow, Glasgow, UK
`2431206s@student.gla.ac.uk`

Abstract. Talking Head Generation aims at synthesizing natural-looking talking videos from speech and a single portrait image. Previous 3D talking head generation methods have relied on domain-specific heuristics such as warping-based facial motion representation priors to animate talking motions, yet still produce inaccurate 3D avatar reconstructions, thus undermining the realism of generated animations. We introduce Splat-Portrait, a Gaussian-splatting-based method that addresses the challenges of 3D head reconstruction and lip motion synthesis. Our approach automatically learns to disentangle a single portrait image into a static 3D reconstruction represented as static Gaussian Splatting, and a predicted whole-image 2D background. It then generates natural lip motion conditioned on input audio, without any motion driven priors. Training is driven purely by 2D reconstruction and score-distillation losses, without 3D supervision nor landmarks. Experimental results demonstrate that Splat-Portrait exhibits superior performance on talking head generation and novel view synthesis, achieving better visual quality compared to previous works. Our project code and supplementary documents are public available at https://github.com/stonewalking/Splat-portrait.

Keywords: Gaussian Splatting · Talking Head Generation

1 Introduction

Talking Head Generation (THG) aims to synthesize natural-looking talking videos from conditioning information such as driving speech [9,40,43] or driving videos [16,21,40]. The generation of talking heads has received increasing attention due to its importance in various applications, including digital humans [18], virtual video conferencing [39] and visual dubbing [28]. Recent 2D methods [20,38,43] have achieved significant improvements in video quality and achieve expressive animation results. However, such 2D methods struggle to generate views with large head pose variations, and are not guaranteed to output 3D-consistent renderings from different poses.

J. Lokoč et al. (Eds.): MMM 2026, LNCS 16412, pp. 494–507, 2026.
https://doi.org/10.1007/978-981-95-6950-2_35

3D THG methods [16,21,40] have attracted increasing attention in the past two years, since they simultaneously reconstruct accurate 3D geometry and generate expressive facial motions, allowing realistic and 3D-consistent portrait rendering from arbitrary user-controllable viewpoints. The majority of such methods focus on personal talking head generation [24,41], where they overfit a single person's head; they maintain realistic 3D geometry and preserve rich texture details. However, in this work, we consider the more challenging setting where we synthesise a 3D talking head given just a single 2D image, learning a model that generalizes across identities even without 3D supervision.

To represent 3D or 4D faces in THG, Neural Radiance Fields (NeRF) [22] or 3D Gaussian Splatting (3DGS) [13] are commonly used. NeRF-based methods often exhibit problems such as visual jitters, unsynchronized lip movements, and rendering artifacts; this is because the implicit definition of NeRF entangles static facial geometry with dynamic motion, complicating simultaneous control of lip motions and 3D geometry reconstruction.

Other works [1,4,32] have explored 3D Gaussian Splatting (3DGS) [13] for 3D avatar generation in the person-generic setting. Compared to NeRF, 3DGS not only improves inference speed and visual quality, but is also more controllable due to its explicit point-cloud-based representation; this makes it possible to animate facial movements more directly and intuitively. For example, [41] drives Gaussian point clouds for facial motion using parametric 3D facial models [15], but it is still challenging to generalize to a person-generic setting. In addition, significant efforts have been made to design and improve 4D animation conditioned on driving information [1,40,41]; the model reconstructs 3D geometry from a single portrait image and learns the corresponding facial motions. These motions are predicted from either an audio sequence or a video sequence driven by motion representation priors, e.g., PNCC, SECC and FLAME [15,16,45]. These methods relax the difficulty of model training by injecting domain priors, e.g. 3D distillation [2] and motion driven priors, which can lead to unnatural results with limited 3D texture details.

Overall, existing works either reconstruct accurate 3D geometry but require multi-view inputs; or they learn it from monocular videos but yield inaccurate geometry.

In this work, we introduce Splat-Portrait, a novel audio-driven THG method based on 3DGS (see Fig. 1). Our method operates in the single-view setting—it reconstructs the 3D shape of the head directly from one image, outputting pixel-aligned Gaussian splats. To enable lip motion during speech, our model learns to directly animate these splats conditioned on an audio sequence.

Our approach is self-supervised from monocular videos only, and does not rely on 3D morphable models such as FLAME to represent facial shape and expression. We first train our model for static splat reconstruction on a large dataset without audio, then fine-tune on a smaller dataset of portrait videos to learn the correct splat dynamics. This strategy avoids 3D supervision, with the exception of easily-obtained approximate camera intrinsics and extrinsics. During the fine-tuning stage, to further improve the realism of extreme viewpoints that are rare in the training data, we adopt score distillation sampling (SDS) [26], to extract knowledge from a powerful 2D diffusion prior [11].

Existing works [16,17] typically model only the head region, or model the head and torso regions as a whole, while disregarding the background. This results in a video of a 'floating head', rather than a realistic video of the talking head in context. To address this, our model also predict a static RGB background image, and alpha-blend the rasterized splats over this. Driven only by the unsupervised frame-prediction loss, our model automatically learns to reduce the opacity of splats in the background region, and to inpaint the background even behind the head, resulting in realistic disocclusions when the head rotates.

In summary, our main contributions are as follows:

- A novel model architecture that disentangles a single portrait image into an accurate 3D splat representation of the head over an inpainted 2D background.
- Given audio sequences and corresponding time deltas, we show how to directly animate the 3D splats by predicting and adding dynamic offsets, without any complex motion representation such as a deformation model.
- A self-supervised training recipe that uses only monocular videos, without 3D supervision, and integrates knowledge from a strong 2D face prior, distilling its knowledge to improve reconstruction of extreme views.

Experimental results on the HDTF [44] and TH-1KH [36] datasets demonstrate that our approach yields higher video fidelity and quality compared with OTA-vatar [21], HiDe-NeRF [16], Real3D-Portrait [40], and NeRFFaceSpeech [14] and GAGavatar [4].

2   Related Work

2.1   3D Head Reconstruction

3D Gaussian Splatting (3DGS) [13] has emerged as a popular method for 3D head reconstruction due to its efficient rendering speed and superior reconstruction quality [1,32,35,41]. Neural Radiance Fields (NeRF) [22] have been widely adopted for 3D talking head generation; NeRF represents scenes through volumetric radiance fields encoded by neural networks, enabling photorealistic renderings from novel viewpoints. NeRF-based methods have naturally extended into talking-head synthesis [8,24]. Early NeRF-driven approaches for talking-head reconstruction [8,21] often require subject-specific training, limiting their scalability. Recent methods leverage 3DGS to address these limitations by significantly improving rendering speed and depth estimation [13,41]. 3DGS represents scenes explicitly with discrete geometric primitives (3D Gaussians), enabling efficient optimization and real-time rendering. Notably, Rivero et al. [27] introduced a dynamic head reconstruction framework using 3DGS, and GaussianHead [35] further advanced these capabilities. By binding the Gaussians to an underlying geometric model, dynamic talking heads can be generated. However, these works for directly regressing 3D representations require prediction in a canonical space, which often fails to handle extreme head poses or significant appearance variations, such as non-photorealistic or animated scenarios. Current techniques still exhibit overfitting issues and rely heavily on domain priors during training, such as the parametric FLAME model [15]. Our method builds upon 3DGS to reconstruct dynamic talking heads directly from a single image.

2.2 Probabilistic 3D Reconstruction

Single-view 3D head reconstruction [7] is an ambiguous problem due to the fact that training data usually have limited variation in poses, particularly in face monocular videos. Recently, diffusion models have been employed for conditional novel view synthesis [37] and also multi-view synthesis [32]. Since the results usually have ambiguous geometry, the output rendered results can exhibit noticeable artifacts, particularly a lack of texture details in unseen views. This can be mitigated by distilling prior knowledge from a 2D model [26]. Existing 3D reconstruction works found that distilling knowledge from 2D images could help to make the 3D representation much more controllable by reconstructing a geometry at every step of the denoising process [33]. Other works pre-train a robust reconstructor [19] and use a 3D prior [23] which can be used in an image-conditioned auto-decoding framework. However, their work is complex and computationally heavy to train. We also leverage a pretrained 2D generative prior when training for 3D reconstruction; this helps our method with extreme-view 3D head reconstruction, but avoids expensive iterative sampling.

2.3 Face Animation

Initial efforts for talking head animation utilized 2D approaches, employing generative adversarial networks, image-to-image translation [10] or diffusion models [30], to generate facial animations. Most 2D talking head generation methods design a mapping relationship between face images and audio feature. These methods [38,43] often underestimate detailed individual differences. Recently, 3D facial animation methods [16,40] became popular, however they adopt PNCC SECC as driving features, leading to unnatural expressions and lip motion. Some warping-based methods [34,40] employ 3DMMs, or face blend shapes, which support animation via disentangled representation of shape, expression and pose. However, these approaches can fall short of accurately reproducing a talking face due to limited amplitude, leading to shortcomings in identity preservation and pose controllability. Our approach is designed to directly edit the 3D representation to animate lip motion over time.

3 Methodology

The overall architecture of our method Splat-Portrait is illustrated in Fig. 1. Splat-Portrait consists of two main stages: (1) pre-training to reconstruct 3D static splats (Sect. 3.1); (2) fine-tuning with an audio-conditioned dynamic decoder (Sect. 3.2), while also using score distillation (Sect. 3.3) to refine appearance from extreme viewpoints.

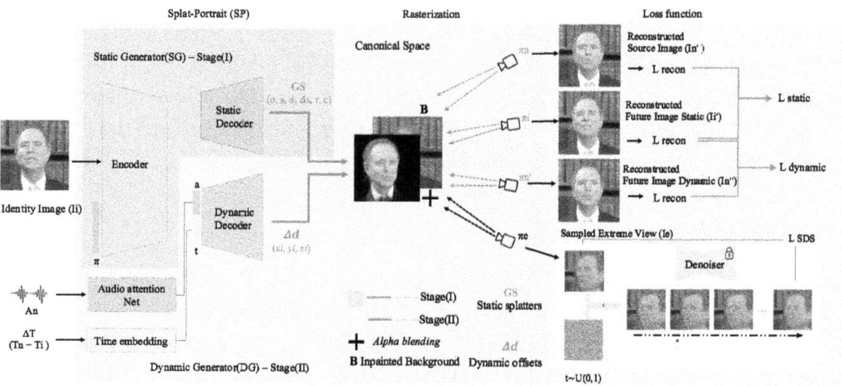

Fig. 1. Overview of Splat-Portrait. The identity image I_i is passed through a U-Net Static Generator(SG) to reconstruct static 3D Gaussian Splats, alpha-blended over a predicted 2D background. The dynamic decoder estimates splat offsets at timestep T_n using audio features A_n and time embedding ΔT. The training procedure consists of two stages, stage(I): an initial pre-training phase, where the static components are trained on a large-scale dataset using a static reconstruction loss $\mathcal{L}_{\text{static}}$, and stage(II): a fine-tuning phase on a smaller dataset incorporating an additional dynamic reconstruction loss $\mathcal{L}_{\text{dynamic}}$. And a score distillation loss $\mathcal{L}_{\text{SDS}}$ on extreme viewpoints applied during both stages.

3.1   Static Splat Generation

3D Gaussian Splatting (3DGS) [13] uses anisotropic 3D Gaussians as geometric primitives to explicitly represent 3D scenes. For our 3D head reconstruction, we first pre-train a static generator (SG) that outputs pixel-aligned splats, as shown in Fig. 1. The design of SG is based on Splatter-Image [31]. However, unlike [31] we do not have access to wide-baseline multi-view images for training; instead we use more challenging monocular video data. We also predict an inpainted 2D RGB background as well the per-pixel 3D splat attributes, and alpha-blend the rasterized splats over this. During training, we randomly choose pairs of frames from a video, denoted source image I_i and future image I_n. Given I_i, the network predicts a set of Gaussian Splatting parameters GS, at each pixel: opacity o, scale s, depth d, static offset Δ_s, rotation r, splat colour c (encoding per-pixel 3D Gaussian attributes), and the 2D background colour RGB. The view-space 3D position p of the Gaussian at a pixel with ray direction $\mathbf{r}$ is then given by $p = \mathbf{r}\, d + \Delta_s$.

During training, we feed the network with I_i at time step T_i. Additionally, we inject the approximate camera-to-world translation and focal length π. We do so by encoding each entry via a sinusoidal positional embedding of order 9, resulting in 60 dimensions in total. These are applied to the U-Net blocks via FiLM [25] conditioning. During our experiments, we found this helps with convergence of depth predictions.

Given the Gaussian attributes described above, we use the differentiable rasterizer $\mathcal{R}$ from [13] to render the splats at canonical space with static offset enabled to reconstruct images I_i^* and I_n^* at the camera poses of both I_i and I_n respectively. We compute a combined L2 and LPIPS reconstruction loss $\mathcal{L}_{\text{static}}^{\text{rec}}$ between corresponding rendered and ground-truth images, i.e.

$$\mathcal{L}\text{static} = ||I_i - I_i^*||_2 + ||I_n - I_n^*||_2 + \lambda_{\text{LPIPS}} \left[\mathcal{L}_{\text{LPIPS}}(I_i, I_i^*) + \mathcal{L}_{\text{LPIPS}}(I_n, I_n^*) \right] \quad (1)$$

Here the LPIPS term combines VGGface and VGG19 features, and the weight λ is empirically set to 0.01. For each image, we render (and calculate the loss) twice, once with a random coloured background and once with our predicted 2D background alpha-blended behind the splats. We found that this helps to improve the colour and opacity for both background and foreground regions, without incorporating any mask supervision.

3.2   Audio-Conditioned Dynamic Splats

For predicting audio-conditioned dynamics representing lip movements, we designed a dynamic decoder with skip connections from the SG decoder. We only use this during the fine-tuning stage, after a good static reconstruction model has been learnt during pre-training. It predicts time-dependent offsets for every splat, conditioned on the audio signal and a time delta indicating what instant in the audio we want the splat offsets for. In our experiments we found that including this time delta improves convergence of the dynamic decoder.

For a given input frame I_i, and future frame I_n plus its contemporaneous audio segment, we first extract audio features using `Wav2Vec2-XLSR 53` [6].

Our model employs dedicated networks to fuse audio and temporal information effectively. Specifically, audio features are first encoded through an audio feature extraction module (AudioNet), which comprises several 1D convolutional layers followed by fully connected layers to yield compact audio embeddings. These embeddings are further refined through an attention-based network (AudioAttNet); this consists of a series of convolutional layers with decreasing channel sizes (from 16 to 1) interleaved with LeakyReLU activations. The output from these convolutional layers is then reshaped and passed through a linear layer followed by a softmax operation to calculate attention weights across the audio sequence. The weighted audio embeddings are summed to produce a refined audio representation capturing temporal dependencies across audio frames. For temporal embeddings, positional encoding or Fourier-based embeddings are utilized to encode timestep information; then audio and temporal embeddings are combined to form the conditioning feature. This combined embedding is injected into the dynamic decoder using FiLM conditioning, allowing the audio and time delta to control the generated motion.

Our dynamic decoder outputs a dynamic offset Δ_d for the splat at each pixel, conditioned on time T. Hence the splat position at time T is $p_T = p + \Delta_d$. To effectively train our model and maintain the static reconstruction ability learnt during pre-training, we adopt both $\mathcal{L}_{\text{static}}$ loss and the SDS loss introduced in

Sect. 3.3. We render the source frame I_i^* with dynamic offsets fixed to zero (as in Sect. 3.1), but now render the future frame I_n^{**} using the predicted offsets. Our dynamic reconstruction loss in the fine-tuning stage is:

$$\mathcal{L}\text{dynamic} = ||I_i - I_i^*||_2 + ||I_n - I_n^{**}||_2 + \lambda_{\text{LPIPS}} \left[\mathcal{L}_{\text{LPIPS}}(I_i, I_i^*) + \mathcal{L}_{\text{LPIPS}}(I_n, I_n^{**}) \right] \tag{2}$$

3.3   Distillation from a 2D Diffusion Prior

In the fine-tuning stage, we also use score distillation [26] to extract knowledge from a 2D diffusion model [11] to improve the appearance of extreme poses. We first render our predicted reconstruction at a randomly sampled extreme pose, then crop and align the image following [12] to match the distribution learnt by the 2D diffusion model. Given this aligned image x_{clean}, we then add a random amount of noise then run the reverse diffusion process.

Specifically, we define a sequence of noise levels σ as follows:

$$\sigma_i = \left[\sigma_{\text{max}}^{\frac{1}{\rho}} + \frac{i}{N-1} \left(\sigma_{\text{min}}^{\frac{1}{\rho}} - \sigma_{\text{max}}^{\frac{1}{\rho}} \right) \right]^{\rho}, \tag{3}$$

where σ_{max} and σ_{min} denote maximum and minimum noise levels, ρ is a hyper parameter controlling the distribution of timesteps, and N is the total number of discretized steps. We choose the noise level from 60%–80% of the original range used in training the diffusion model, since we found this range effectively preserves the portrait's overall appearance while significantly improving texture inpainting for extreme viewpoints.

The noised image at the initial timestep t_0 is generated by adding Gaussian noise to the normalized input image, i.e. $x_{\text{noised}} = x_{\text{clean}} + \sigma_0 \cdot \epsilon$, where $\epsilon \sim \mathcal{N}(0, I)$. For each subsequent timestep, we perform an Euler integration step to progressively denoise the image. Specifically, given the current timestep t_{cur} and next timestep t_{next}, the Euler step is computed as:

$$x_{\text{next}} = x_{\text{cur}} + (t_{\text{next}} - t_{\text{cur}}) \cdot d_{\text{cur}}, \quad d_{\text{cur}} = \frac{x_{\text{cur}} - \text{net}(x_{\text{cur}}, t_{\text{cur}})}{t_{\text{cur}}}, \tag{4}$$

where net represents the pre-trained denoiser model.

This sampling procedure yields a denoised face image (the final x_{next}) that is similar to the original rendered one, but more realistic according to the diffusion prior. We define a loss $\mathcal{L}_{\text{SDS}}$ as the L2 reconstruction loss between the rendered frame x_{clean} and the denoised frame, back-propagating only into the former. This guides our rendered frames to look more like similar realistic samples from the diffusion model. During training, we randomly sample extreme viewpoints following a bullet-effect trajectory, with pitch variations up to $\pm 12.5°$ and yaw variations up to $\pm 45°$ from the canonical view, and apply the SDS loss between I_i and x_{clean}. Note that unlike [26] and common practice, we apply the SDS loss during model training, not during inference, meaning the latter remains very fast.

3.4   Overall Loss

Our total losses are defined as follows. For stage one (static pretraining):

$$\mathcal{L}_{\text{total\_static}} = \mathcal{L}_{\text{static}}(I_i, I_n) + \mathcal{L}_{\text{SDS}}. \tag{5}$$

For stage two (audio-conditioned fine-tuning):

$$\mathcal{L}_{\text{total\_dynamic}} = \mathcal{L}_{\text{dynamic}}(I_i, I_n) + \mathcal{L}_{\text{SDS}}. \tag{6}$$

In both cases, we use AdamW for optimization, with a learning rate of 2.5×10^{-5} and weight decay of 10^{-5}.

4   Experiments

Datasets and Implementation Details. We evaluate our approach on two widely used datasets of monocular talking portrait videos – HDTF [44] and TalkingHead-1KH [36]. HDTF consists of over 400 samples of talking videos from over 350 subjects. For TalkingHead-1KH, we manually select 1100 identity videos following a similar distribution as HDTF, such that there is no occlusion over the torso and mouth, and with static background. Each identity video contains minimum 300 frames and maximum 10000 frames. We extract frames at 25 Hz, and the audio sampling rate is 16kHz. We resize the image frames to 256×256. Following the steps in [24], we follow [8] to use 3DMM optimization to extract approximate intrinsic and extrinsic camera parameters. We use the complete video clips (often with substantial camera motion) for training. For evaluation, we randomly sample 50 identity videos as test sets, and use the first 5 s of each. We adopt the SongUNet [29] architecture for our static encoder and dynamic decoder.

Metrics. We measure the quality of synthetic images using structural similarity (SSIM), peak signal-to-noise ratio (PSNR), Learned Perceptual Image Patch Similarity LPIPS [42], and Fréchet Inception Distance (FID); we use Cosine similarity (CSIM) for measuring identity preservation, and SyncNet [5] to measure lip synchronization scores (LipSync).

Baselines. We compare our approach to several existing 3D talking head generation works. **OTAvatar** [21] is a video-driven method that uses a pre-trained 3D GAN to obtain a 3D talking portrait video; **HiDe-NeRF** [16], a 3D talking face model that uses a motion prior and deformation field for face animation; **Real3D-Portrait** [40], a nerf-based method that uses images generated by EG3D to train a 3D model; **NeRFFaceSpeech** [14] one nerf-based audio driven method for synthesising talking head video, and the state-of-the-art **GAGavatar** [4]. Additionally in the audio-driven setting, we extend GAGavatar with ARtalker [3]. Note OTAvatar and HiDe-NeRF are video-driven methods, they are not directly driven by audio; for fair comparison, we use the same identity video as driving video for evaluation. We set the input image size as 256×256 to enable fair comparison, upsampling for methods that require this. We compare the baselines using their preferred masking and cropping settings.

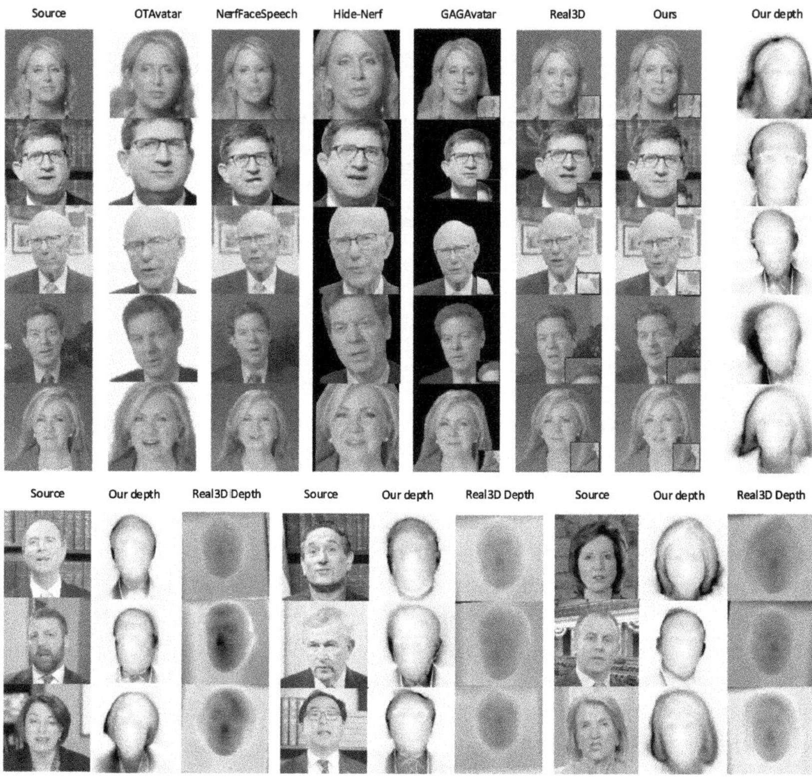

Fig. 2. Qualitative results. **Top:** We show source frames from five videos, future predicted frames from ours and baselines, and future depths from ours. **Bottom:** Additional examples of 3D reconstruction, for our method and Real3D-Portrait, displaying the input frame, and the reconstructed depth-map from each method.

4.1   Quantitative Evaluation

We compare with the baselines in *same identity* and *cross-identity* settings. During testing, the driving motion condition and head pose are obtained from a reference video. Under the same-identity setting, we use the first frame of the reference video as the source image; otherwise, the source image is of a different identity. For the cross-identity setting, for Real3D-Portrait, we only compare with its audio-driven setting. Quantitative results concerning the quality and fidelity for the same-identity setting are listed in Table 1. These show that our method outperforms other state-of-the-art approaches on almost all fidelity metrics. This is despite our method being trained without 3D supervision, using only a dataset of monocular videos. Splat-Portrait achieves the best overall video quality, as well as higher LipSync score, demonstrating that our 3D deformable model without any motion representation could sync well on lip motions. Moreover, our model achieves the highest performance on CSIM, meaning it has a strong ability to preserve subject identity in different views. We also compare the baselines with cross-identity evaluation, where the driving videos are obtained from a reference video, and we use another identity for target. Since there is no ground truth for this setting, we evaluate the results only on CSIM, FID and Lip sync. The results are given in Table 2. We see that our method performs best on FID and CSIM, which indicates our model still yields high video generation quality even in this more challenging setting.

Table 1. Quantitative evaluation of our method and baselines in the same identity setting.

Method	PSNR ↑	SSIM ↑	LPIPS ↓	CSIM ↑	FID ↓	LipSync ↑
OTAvatar	13.85	0.488	0.432	0.559	78.98	5.908
NeRFFaceSpeech	13.90	0.520	0.480	0.580	64.60	4.880
HiDe-NeRF	21.44	0.685	0.221	0.716	28.63	5.552
Real3D-Portrait	22.40	0.758	0.191	0.761	35.69	**6.681**
GAGAvatar + ARtalker	23.08	0.786	0.182	0.753	37.89	6.580
Ours	**23.87**	**0.814**	**0.128**	**0.811**	**25.58**	6.328

Table 2. Quantitative evaluation of our method and baselines in the cross-identity setting.

Method	CSIM ↑	FID ↓	LipSync ↑
NeRFFaceSpeech	0.450	50.80	4.423
OTAvatar	0.521	79.32	5.032
HiDe-NeRF	0.628	31.23	5.652
Real3D-Portrait	0.691	40.82	6.521
GAGAvatar + ARtalker	0.687	35.82	**6.503**
Ours	**0.726**	**28.62**	6.218

4.2   Qualitative Evaluation

In this section we provide visual comparisons of all tested methods (see Fig. 2). We find that our method preserves face texture details, such as hair and wrinkles well, yielding high-quality novel views. In particular, our method preserves details such as earrings which move during the video. Since we do not require the head to be pre-segmented, our method handles fine details at the silhouette edges well, and effectively blends the rendered portrait over the estimated background. Figure 2 also compares depth-maps rendered by our model with those from Real3D-Portrait, to better visualise the quality of the 3D shape. Compared with Real3D-Portrait, it is clear that our method preserves much more detailed geometry information.

Table 3. Ablation study showing the benefit of different components of our model.

Method	PSNR ↑	SSIM ↑	LPIPS ↓
w/o time delta	22.68	0.768	0.146
w/o pre-training	23.30	0.758	0.149
w/o SDS	23.58	0.788	0.147
w/o static offset	23.30	0.791	0.145
only future l2 loss	23.41	0.772	0.138
Full (SP)	**23.87**	**0.814**	**0.128**

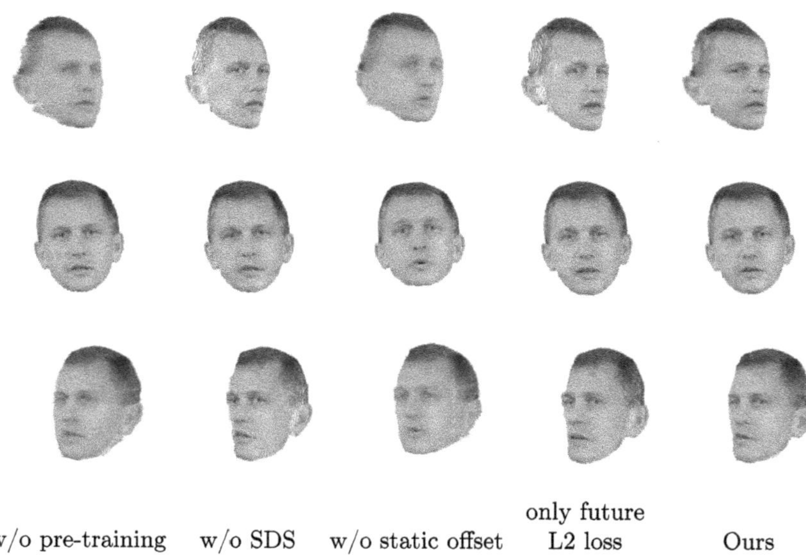

Fig. 3. Ablation study, with extreme head yaw angles (top row at -35°, the middle row at 0°, and the bottom row at +35°).

4.3 Ablation Study

We test four ablations of our model: (1) w/o time delta, which does not inject the time embedding (see Sect. 3.2); (2) w/o pre-training, which does not pre-train the static generator (see Sect. 3.1), (3) w/o SDS, which omits the score distillation loss during the fine-tuning stage (see Sect. 3.3); (4) without static offsets during fine-tuning stage; (5) without the initial-frame reconstruction loss, only the future reconstruction loss. We show the results in Fig. 3 and Table 3. Without the pre-training process, we see the 3D geometry accuracy drops significantly, the reconstructed 3D head exhibits flattened geometry, with reduced 3D structure. Training with only one frame for supervision instead of two randomly selected frames, it is hard to reconstruct depths and static offsets (and thus the static shape of the face) well, as some structural information is instead represented in the dynamic offsets. As shown in Fig. 3, when enabling static splat offsets, the visualized 3D representation shows a smooth, realistically curved geometry. Lastly our SDS loss greatly enhances the realism of extreme poses.

5   Conclusion

We proposed Splat-Portrait for Talking Head Generation. Our method is trained on monocular videos without 3D supervision, yet can synthesize accurate 3D geometry and plausible lip movements directly from a single portrait image, yielding state-of-the-art results. By effectively disentangling static and dynamic attributes and using a score-distillation loss, Splat-Portrait significantly enhances realism, particularly from extreme viewpoints rarely encountered during training. Additionally, the simplicity and efficiency of our model structure allow it to animate 3D splats effectively without complex deformation models, making it lightweight and practical for real-world applications.

References

1. Aneja, S., Sevastopolsky, A., Kirschstein, T., Thies, J., Dai, A., Nießner, M.: Gaussianspeech: audio-driven gaussian avatars. arXiv preprint arXiv:2411.18675 (2024)
2. Chan, E.R., et al.: Efficient geometry-aware 3D generative adversarial networks. In: Proceedings of the IEEE/CVF Conference on Computer Vision and Pattern Recognition, pp. 16123–16133 (2022)
3. Chu, X., Goswami, N., Cui, Z., Wang, H., Harada, T.: Artalk: speech-driven 3D head animation via autoregressive model (2025). https://arxiv.org/abs/2502.20323
4. Chu, X., Harada, T.: Generalizable and animatable gaussian head avatar. In: The Thirty-Eighth Annual Conference on Neural Information Processing Systems (2024). https://openreview.net/forum?id=gVM2AZ5xA6
5. Chung, J.S., Zisserman, A.: Out of time: automated lip sync in the wild. In: Workshop on Multi-view Lip-Reading. ACCV (2016)
6. Conneau, A., Baevski, A., Collobert, R., Mohamed, A., Auli, M.: Unsupervised cross-lingual representation learning for speech recognition. arXiv preprint arXiv:2006.13979 (2020)
7. Dhamo, H., et al.: Headgas: real-time animatable head avatars via 3D gaussian splatting. In: European Conference on Computer Vision, pp. 459–476. Springer, Cham (2024)

8. Guo, Y., Chen, K., Liang, S., Liu, Y.J., Bao, H., Zhang, J.: Ad-nerf: audio driven neural radiance fields for talking head synthesis. In: Proceedings of the IEEE/CVF International Conference on Computer Vision, pp. 5784–5794 (2021)

9. He, T., et al.: Gaia: zero-shot talking avatar generation. arXiv preprint arXiv:2311.15230 (2023)

10. Isola, P., Zhu, J.Y., Zhou, T., Efros, A.A.: Image-to-image translation with conditional adversarial networks. In: Proceedings of the IEEE Conference on Computer Vision and Pattern Recognition, pp. 1125–1134 (2017)

11. Karras, T., Aittala, M., Aila, T., Laine, S.: Elucidating the design space of diffusion-based generative models. Adv. Neural. Inf. Process. Syst. **35**, 26565–26577 (2022)

12. Karras, T., Laine, S., Aila, T.: A style-based generator architecture for generative adversarial networks. In: Proceedings of the IEEE/CVF Conference on Computer Vision and Pattern Recognition, pp. 4401–4410 (2019)

13. Kerbl, B., Kopanas, G., Leimkühler, T., Drettakis, G.: 3D gaussian splatting for real-time radiance field rendering. ACM Trans. Graph. **42**

14. Kim, G., Seo, K., Cha, S., Noh, J.: Nerffacespeech: one-shot audio-driven 3D talking head synthesis via generative prior. arXiv preprint arXiv:2405.05749 (2024)

15. Li, T., Bolkart, T., Black, M.J., Li, H., Romero, J.: Learning a model of facial shape and expression from 4D scans. ACM Trans. Graph. **36**(6), 194–1 (2017)

16. Li, W., et al.: One-shot high-fidelity talking-head synthesis with deformable neural radiance field. In: Proceedings of the IEEE/CVF Conference on Computer Vision and Pattern Recognition, pp. 17969–17978 (2023)

17. Li, X., De Mello, S., Liu, S., Nagano, K., Iqbal, U., Kautz, J.: Generalizable one-shot 3D neural head avatar. In: Advances in Neural Information Processing Systems, vol. 36 (2024)

18. Liu, C.: An analysis of the current and future state of 3d facial animation techniques and systems (2009)

19. Liu, M., et al.: One-2-3-45: any single image to 3d mesh in 45 seconds without per-shape optimization. In: Advances in Neural Information Processing Systems, vol. 36, pp. 22226–22246 (2023)

20. Liu, T., et al.: Vqtalker: towards multilingual talking avatars through facial motion tokenization. arXiv preprint arXiv:2412.09892 (2024)

21. Ma, Z., Zhu, X., Qi, G.J., Lei, Z., Zhang, L.: Otavatar: one-shot talking face avatar with controllable tri-plane rendering. In: Proceedings of the IEEE/CVF Conference on Computer Vision and Pattern Recognition, pp. 16901–16910 (2023)

22. Mildenhall, B., Srinivasan, P.P., Tancik, M., Barron, J.T., Ramamoorthi, R., Ng, R.: Nerf: representing scenes as neural radiance fields for view synthesis. Commun. ACM **65**(1), 99–106 (2021)

23. Müller, N., Siddiqui, Y., Porzi, L., Bulo, S.R., Kontschieder, P., Nießner, M.: Diffrf: rendering-guided 3D radiance field diffusion. In: Proceedings of the IEEE/CVF Conference on Computer Vision and Pattern Recognition, pp. 4328–4338 (2023)

24. Peng, Z., et al.: Synctalk: the devil is in the synchronization for talking head synthesis. In: Proceedings of the IEEE/CVF Conference on Computer Vision and Pattern Recognition, pp. 666–676 (2024)

25. Perez, E., Strub, F., De Vries, H., Dumoulin, V., Courville, A.: Film: visual reasoning with a general conditioning layer. In: Proceedings of the AAAI Conference on Artificial Intelligence, vol. 32 (2018)

26. Poole, B., Jain, A., Barron, J.T., Mildenhall, B.: Dreamfusion: text-to-3D using 2D diffusion. arXiv preprint arXiv:2209.14988 (2022)

27. Rivero, A., Athar, S., Shu, Z., Samaras, D.: Rig3dgs: creating controllable portraits from casual monocular videos. arXiv preprint arXiv:2402.03723 (2024)

28. Saunders, J., Namboodiri, V.: Dubbing for everyone: data-efficient visual dubbing using neural rendering priors. arXiv preprint arXiv:2401.06126 (2024)
29. Song, J., Meng, C., Ermon, S.: Denoising diffusion implicit models. arXiv preprint arXiv:2010.02502 (2020)
30. Stypułkowski, M., Vougioukas, K., He, S., Zięba, M., Petridis, S., Pantic, M.: Diffused heads: diffusion models beat GANs on talking-face generation. In: Proceedings of the IEEE/CVF Winter Conference on Applications of Computer Vision, pp. 5091–5100 (2024)
31. Szymanowicz, S., Rupprecht, C., Vedaldi, A.: Splatter image: ultra-fast single-view 3D reconstruction. In: Proceedings of the IEEE/CVF Conference on Computer Vision and Pattern Recognition, pp. 10208–10217 (2024)
32. Taubner, F., Zhang, R., Tuli, M., Lindell, D.B.: Cap4D: creating animatable 4D portrait avatars with morphable multi-view diffusion models. arXiv preprint arXiv:2412.12093 (2024)
33. Tewari, A., et al.: Diffusion with forward models: solving stochastic inverse problems without direct supervision. Adv. Neural. Inf. Process. Syst. **36**, 12349–12362 (2023)
34. Thies, J., Zollhofer, M., Stamminger, M., Theobalt, C., Nießner, M.: Face2face: real-time face capture and reenactment of RGB videos. In: Proceedings of the IEEE Conference on Computer Vision and Pattern Recognition, pp. 2387–2395 (2016)
35. Wang, J., Xie, J.C., Li, X., Xu, F., Pun, C.M., Gao, H.: Gaussianhead: impressive head avatars with learnable gaussian diffusion. arXiv preprint arXiv:2312.01632 (2023)
36. Wang, T.C., Mallya, A., Liu, M.Y.: One-shot free-view neural talking-head synthesis for video conferencing. In: Proceedings of the IEEE/CVF Conference on Computer Vision and Pattern Recognition, pp. 10039–10049 (2021)
37. Watson, D., Chan, W., Martin-Brualla, R., Ho, J., Tagliasacchi, A., Norouzi, M.: Novel view synthesis with diffusion models. arXiv preprint arXiv:2210.04628 (2022)
38. Xu, M., et al.: Hallo: hierarchical audio-driven visual synthesis for portrait image animation. arXiv preprint arXiv:2406.08801 (2024)
39. Ye, T., et al.: Perceiving and modeling density for image dehazing. In: European Conference on Computer Vision, pp. 130–145. Springer, Cham (2022)
40. Ye, Z., et al.: Real3d-portrait: one-shot realistic 3D talking portrait synthesis. arXiv preprint arXiv:2401.08503 (2024)
41. Yu, H., et al.: Gaussiantalker: speaker-specific talking head synthesis via 3D gaussian splatting. In: Proceedings of the 32nd ACM International Conference on Multimedia, pp. 3548–3557 (2024)
42. Zhang, R., Isola, P., Efros, A.A., Shechtman, E., Wang, O.: The unreasonable effectiveness of deep features as a perceptual metric. In: Proceedings of the IEEE Conference on Computer Vision and Pattern Recognition, pp. 586–595 (2018)
43. Zhang, W., et al.: Sadtalker: learning realistic 3D motion coefficients for stylized audio-driven single image talking face animation. In: Proceedings of the IEEE/CVF Conference on Computer Vision and Pattern Recognition, pp. 8652–8661 (2023)
44. Zhang, Z., Li, L., Ding, Y., Fan, C.: Flow-guided one-shot talking face generation with a high-resolution audio-visual dataset. In: Proceedings of the IEEE/CVF Conference on Computer Vision and Pattern Recognition, pp. 3661–3670 (2021)
45. Zhu, X., Lei, Z., Liu, X., Shi, H., Li, S.Z.: Face alignment across large poses: a 3D solution. In: Proceedings of the IEEE Conference on Computer Vision and Pattern Recognition, pp. 146–155 (2016)

CEMG: Collaborative-Enhanced Multimodal Generative Recommendation

Yuzhen Lin[1], Hongyi Chen[2], Xuanjing Chen[3], Shaowen Wang[4], Ivonne Xu[5],
and Dongming Jiang[6(✉)]

[1] School of Information Systems and Management, Carnegie Mellon University,
Pittsburgh, PA 15213, USA
`yuzhenl@alumni.cmu.edu`
[2] Samueli School of Engineering, University of California, Los Angeles, CA 90095, USA
`henrychyy@g.ucla.edu`
[3] Columbia Business School, Columbia University, New York, NY 10027, USA
`xc2647@columbia.edu`
[4] Henry Siebel School of Computing and Data Science, University of Illinois
Urbana-Champaign, Urbana, IL 61820, USA
[5] Department of Physics, University of Chicago, Chicago, IL 60637, USA
`ixu@uchicago.edu`
[6] Department of Computer Science, Rice University, Houston, TX 77005, USA
`dj37@rice.edu`

Abstract. Generative recommendation models often struggle with two key challenges: (1) the superficial integration of collaborative signals, and (2) the decoupled fusion of multimodal features. These limitations hinder the creation of a truly holistic item representation. To overcome this, we propose **CEMG**, a novel **C**ollaborative-**E**nhaned **M**ultimodal **G**enerative Recommendation framework. Our approach features a **Multimodal Fusion Layer** that dynamically integrates visual and textual features under the guidance of collaborative signals. Subsequently, a **Unified Modality Tokenization** stage employs a Residual Quantization VAE (RQ-VAE) to convert this fused representation into discrete semantic codes. Finally, in the **End-to-End Generative Recommendation** stage, a large language model is fine-tuned to autoregressively generate these item codes. Extensive experiments demonstrate that CEMG significantly outperforms state-of-the-art baselines.

Keywords: Recommendation · Generative recommendation · Multimodal learning · Large language model

1 Introduction

Recommender Systems (RS) are indispensable for navigating the vast digital landscape, alleviating information overload by personalizing user experiences [2,15,16,21,29]. While traditional methods like collaborative filtering [7,18] and modern sequential models [6,24] have made significant strides, they often treat items as isolated identifiers. This "ID-based" paradigm inherently struggles to capture the rich semantic relationships between items, thus limiting their ability to generalize to new or long-tail

J. Lokoč et al. (Eds.): MMM 2026, LNCS 16412, pp. 508–521, 2026.
https://doi.org/10.1007/978-981-95-6950-2_36

items and failing to leverage descriptive multimodal content. To transcend these limitations, generative recommendation has emerged as a transformative paradigm [20,26]. By representing each item not as a single ID but as a sequence of semantic tokens, this approach reframes recommendation as a sophisticated sequence-to-sequence generation task, thereby unlocking unprecedented modeling capabilities.

The integration of multimodal data, such as images and text, has further propelled the evolution of generative recommendation. Current approaches typically fall into two categories. The first focuses on learning high-quality semantic tokens primarily from textual content and collaborative signals [10,26]. For instance, LETTER [26] enriches item tokens by aligning quantized representations with collaborative embeddings. The second category explicitly incorporates multimodal features into the generation pipeline [11], where models like MMGRec [11] employ graph-based architectures to tokenize fused multimodal information. While pioneering, these methods often process diverse information streams in a decoupled or superficial manner, failing to forge a truly unified item representation for the underlying generative model.

Despite their progress, existing generative recommendation methods face two critical challenges that limit their full potential:

- **Superficial Integration of Collaborative Signals.** Multimodal content provides rich semantic descriptions of items, but the core of personalization lies in collaborative signals—the emergent patterns from collective user behavior. Many existing generative models incorporate collaborative information only as a supplementary feature or through shallow alignment [26], failing to capture the complex, high-order relationships that reveal latent user preferences and item-to-item correlations beyond mere content similarity.
- **Decoupled Fusion of Multimodal and Collaborative Features.** Current frameworks tend to treat multimodal content and collaborative signals as separate entities, fusing them in a late or disjointed manner. This separation prevents the model from understanding the intricate interplay between an item's intrinsic attributes (what it *is*) and its contextual role within the user community (how it is *perceived*). For example, two visually distinct items might be functional substitutes, a nuance that can only be captured through a deep, synergistic fusion of these information sources.

To address these limitations, we propose a novel framework: Collaborative-Enhancd Multimodal Generative Recommendation, abbreviated as **CEMG**. Our approach is designed to create a deeply unified item representation that synergizes content semantics with collaborative wisdom, tailored for a powerful generative recommendation engine. CEMG consists of three core components:

First, the **Multimodal Encoding Layer** extracts rich features from item images and text, alongside a deep collaborative representation learned via a graph neural network. A novel **Multimodal Fusion Layer** then intelligently integrates these features, using the collaborative signal as a query to dynamically weigh the importance of different modalities. Second, the **Unified Modality Tokenization** stage leverages a Residual Quantization VAE (RQ-VAE) [8] to transform the fused, holistic item representation into a compact sequence of discrete semantic tokens. Finally, the **End-to-End Generative Recommendation** component treats recommendation as a conditional language generation task. It formulates a user's interaction history as a structured prompt and fine-tunes a T5 [19] to autoregressively generate the semantic tokens of the next recommended item.

Our main contributions are summarized as follows:

- We propose CEMG, a novel generative recommendation framework that, for the first time, employs a collaborative-guided mechanism to deeply fuse multimodal content with high-order collaborative signals into a unified semantic space for item tokenization.
- We design an elegant and effective architecture featuring a Multimodal Fusion Layer that enhances item representations by dynamically aligning content features with their collaborative context.
- We develop an End-to-End Generative pipeline that leverages the power of LLMs for recommendation, enhanced with a constrained decoding strategy to ensure recommendation validity and efficiency.
- We conduct extensive experiments on three benchmark datasets, demonstrating that CEMG significantly outperforms a wide array of state-of-the-art baselines.

2   Related Work

2.1   Multimodal Recommendation

Multimodal recommendation systems enhance performance by leveraging auxiliary information from modalities like text and images, primarily within an embed-and-retrieve paradigm. Early works such as VBPR [3] integrated pre-trained visual features into matrix factorization. Subsequent research explored more advanced fusion techniques, including attention mechanisms in models like ACF [1] and UVCAN [14] to dynamically select informative content. More recently, Graph Neural Networks (GNNs) have been used to model complex relationships; MMGCN [27], for example, propagates information across a multi-modal graph. Other methods, including MISSRec [25] and MMSRec [23], have investigated self-supervised learning and modality-specific modeling to better capture user interests. While effective, these discriminative approaches can be computationally expensive and struggle with issues like inadequate modeling of complex interactions and the false-negative problem [11]. Our work departs from this paradigm by embracing a more expressive generative approach.

2.2   Generative Recommendation

Generative recommendation represents a new frontier, recasting recommendation as a sequence generation task composed of two main stages: item tokenization and autoregressive generation. Item tokenization maps items to discrete token sequences, using methods ranging from simple text-based approaches [9] to sophisticated vector quantization (VQ) techniques. VQ-based models like TIGER [20] and LETTER [26] employ architectures like RQ-VAE [8] to learn semantic codes from item features. LETTER notably improves this by incorporating collaborative signals to align the learned codes.

However, these methods often tokenize based on unimodal data (typically text) or use shallow fusion, failing to create a truly holistic representation. Our work, CEMG, addresses this gap by first creating compact, high-quality semantic tokens from a deep, collaborative-guided fusion of multimodal features, and then leveraging a powerful LLM for the generation task, thereby combining the strengths of structured tokenization and large-scale language modeling (Fig. 1).

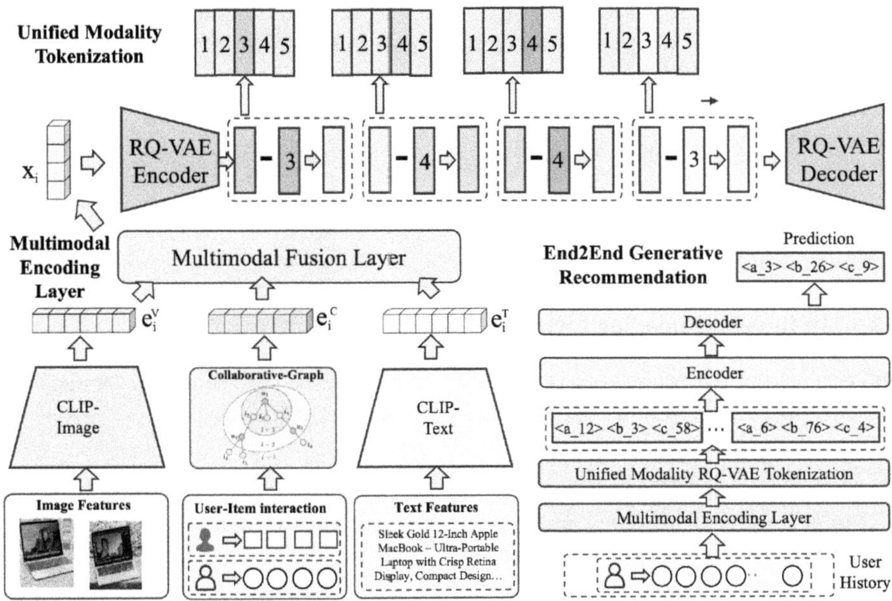

Fig. 1. The overall architecture of the CEMG framework. The framework is composed of three main components. The **Multimodal Encoding Layer** integrates visual (e_i^V), collaborative (e_i^C), and textual (e_i^T) features via the **Multimodal Fusion Layer** to produce a unified representation $\mathbf{x}_i$. The **Unified Modality Tokenization** stage, utilizing a Residual Quantization VAE (RQ-VAE), converts $\mathbf{x}_i$ into a discrete sequence of semantic tokens. Finally, the **End2End Generative Recommendation** module takes historical token sequences as input and autoregressively generates the tokens for the next recommended item.

3   Methodology

In this section, we introduce the technical details of our proposed **CEMG** framework. We first define the problem formally, then elaborate on the three main components: the Multimodal Encoding Layer, Unified Modality Tokenization, and End-to-End Generative Recommendation.

3.1 Problem Definition

Let $\mathcal{U}$ denote the set of users and $\mathcal{I}$ the set of items. Each item $i \in \mathcal{I}$ is associated with multimodal content, including an image V_i and a textual description T_i. For a user $u \in \mathcal{U}$, their historical interactions are represented as a chronological sequence $S_u = [i_1, i_2, \ldots, i_L]$. The goal is to predict the top-K items that user u is most likely to interact with next.

We formulate this task generatively. Instead of using atomic item IDs, we represent each item i as a sequence of M discrete semantic tokens, denoted as $\mathbf{c}_i = [c_{i,1}, c_{i,2}, \ldots, c_{i,M}]$, where each token $c_{i,m}$ is an index drawn from a codebook. The recommendation problem is thus transformed into generating the token sequence $\mathbf{c}_{i_{L+1}}$ for the next item based on the historical token sequences corresponding to S_u. Formally, we model the probability:

$$P(\mathbf{c}_{i_{L+1}}|S_u) = \prod_{m=1}^{M} P(c_{i_{L+1},m}|\{\mathbf{c}_{i_j}\}_{j=1}^{L}, c_{i_{L+1},1}, \ldots, c_{i_{L+1},m-1}) \tag{1}$$

3.2 Multimodal Encoding Layer

The first step of our framework is to learn a unified, dense representation for each item that encapsulates its multimodal and collaborative characteristics.

Multimodal Feature Encoding. For each item i, we extract features from its associated image and text using pre-trained encoders, chosen for their proven effectiveness and generalizability.

- **Visual Encoder:** We use a pre-trained VGG network [22] to process the image V_i and extract its visual features.
- **Textual Encoder:** We employ a pre-trained BERT model [24] to encode the textual description T_i. We take the embedding of the '[CLS]' token as the text representation.

The raw feature vectors are then passed through a Principal Component Analysis (PCA) layer for dimensionality reduction, yielding the final visual and textual embeddings, $\mathbf{e}_i^v \in \mathbb{R}^d$ and $\mathbf{e}_i^t \in \mathbb{R}^d$, respectively.

Collaborative Feature Encoding. To capture the vital collaborative signals reflecting community preferences, we model the user-item interactions as a bipartite graph $\mathcal{G} = (\mathcal{U} \cup \mathcal{I}, \mathcal{E})$, where an edge $(u, i) \in \mathcal{E}$ exists if user u has interacted with item i. We then employ LightGCN [4], a simple yet powerful Graph Neural Network, to learn user and item embeddings. The final embedding for item i is obtained by aggregating messages from its neighborhood over multiple propagation layers. This process yields a collaborative embedding $\mathbf{e}_i^c \in \mathbb{R}^d$ that distills high-order connectivity patterns.

Multimodal Fusion Layer. A key innovation of CEMG is our fusion mechanism, which uses the collaborative embedding as a guide to dynamically integrate the multimodal features. We hypothesize that an item's collaborative context should determine the relative importance of its visual versus textual attributes. To achieve this, we design a guided attention mechanism. The collaborative embedding $\mathbf{e}_i^c$ acts as the query, while the visual $\mathbf{e}_i^v$ and textual $\mathbf{e}_i^t$ embeddings serve as keys and values. The attention weights are computed as:

$$\alpha_m = \frac{\exp((\mathbf{W}_q\mathbf{e}_i^c)^\top(\mathbf{W}_k\mathbf{e}_i^m))}{\sum_{m'\in\{v,t\}}\exp((\mathbf{W}_q\mathbf{e}_i^c)^\top(\mathbf{W}_k\mathbf{e}_i^{m'}))}, \quad \text{for } m \in \{v,t\} \tag{2}$$

where $\mathbf{W}_q, \mathbf{W}_k \in \mathbb{R}^{d\times d}$ are learnable projection matrices. The final fused representation $\mathbf{x}_i \in \mathbb{R}^{2d}$ is a concatenation of the weighted multimodal features and the guiding collaborative feature:

$$\mathbf{x}_i = [\alpha_v\mathbf{e}_i^v \oplus \alpha_t\mathbf{e}_i^t; \mathbf{e}_i^c] \tag{3}$$

where $\oplus$ denotes element-wise addition and $[;]$ denotes concatenation. This unified vector $\mathbf{x}_i$ now holistically represents item i.

3.3 Unified Modality Tokenization

With the unified representation $\mathbf{x}_i$ for each item, we proceed to tokenize it into a discrete sequence of semantic tokens using a Residual Quantization Variational Autoencoder (RQ-VAE) [8]. The RQ-VAE consists of an encoder, a residual quantizer with M codebooks, and a decoder. The encoder maps $\mathbf{x}_i$ to a latent vector $\mathbf{z}_i$. The quantizer then approximates $\mathbf{z}_i$ iteratively. In each stage $m \in \{1,\ldots,M\}$, it finds the closest codevector $\mathbf{b}_{m,k}$ from codebook $\mathcal{C}_m$ to the current residual and subtracts it to form the next residual. The sequence of selected codebook indices $[c_{i,1},\ldots,c_{i,M}]$ becomes the item's semantic token sequence $\mathbf{c}_i$. The decoder then reconstructs the original vector $\hat{\mathbf{x}}_i$ from the sum of the selected codevectors.

The RQ-VAE is trained by minimizing a composite loss function that ensures semantic fidelity and codebook quality:

$$\mathcal{L}_{\text{RQ-VAE}} = \mathcal{L}_{\text{recon}} + \lambda_q\mathcal{L}_{\text{quant}} + \lambda_d\mathcal{L}_{\text{div}} \tag{4}$$

where $\mathcal{L}_{\text{recon}} = ||\mathbf{x}_i - \hat{\mathbf{x}}_i||_2^2$ is the reconstruction loss. $\mathcal{L}_{\text{quant}}$ is the VQ commitment loss [17] that encourages the encoder output to stay close to the codebook entries. $\mathcal{L}_{\text{div}}$ is a diversity loss [12] that promotes the utilization of diverse codes within each codebook, preventing collapse. λ_q and λ_d are balancing hyperparameters.

3.4 End-to-End Generative Recommendation

After the tokenization stage, each item i is represented by its semantic token sequence $\mathbf{c}_i$. We now reframe the recommendation task as a conditional generation problem.

Interaction History Prompting. We structure the user's interaction history as a prompt for a large language model (LLM). For a user with history $S_u = [i_1, \ldots, i_L]$, we convert each item i_j into its token sequence $\mathbf{c}_{i_j}$. Each token is represented by a special symbol, e.g., $< a\_12 >$ for the 12th token from the first codebook (layer 'a'). The complete prompt is constructed as a sequence of these item tokens, preserving their chronological order. The task for the LLM is to autoregressively predict the token sequence of the next item, $\mathbf{c}_{i_{L+1}}$.

Training and Inference. We employ a powerful decoder-only LLM as our generative backbone. The model is trained using a standard next-token prediction objective, minimizing the cross-entropy loss between the predicted token probabilities and the ground-truth target tokens:

$$\mathcal{L}_{\text{NTP}} = -\sum_{j=1}^{L} \sum_{m=1}^{M} \log P(c_{i_{j+1},m} | \{\mathbf{c}_{i_k}\}_{k=1}^{j}, c_{i_{j+1},1}, \ldots, c_{i_{j+1},m-1}) \tag{5}$$

During inference, given a user's history prompt, we use beam search to generate multiple candidate token sequences for the next item. The score of a candidate sequence $\mathbf{c} = [c_1, \ldots, c_M]$ is the sum of its log-probabilities:

$$\text{Score}(\mathbf{c}) = \sum_{m=1}^{M} \log P(c_m | \text{prompt}, c_1, \ldots, c_{m-1}) \tag{6}$$

To ensure that only valid item sequences are generated, we employ a prefix tree (Trie)-based constrained decoding strategy. The Trie contains all valid item token sequences from our catalog. At each generation step, the LLM's output vocabulary is masked to only allow tokens that form a valid prefix, drastically pruning the search space and guaranteeing the validity of the final recommendations.

4　Experiments

We conduct extensive experiments to evaluate our proposed CEMG framework. Our goal is to answer the following research questions:

- **RQ1:** How does CEMG perform compared to state-of-the-art baselines from sequential, multimodal, and generative recommendation paradigms?
- **RQ2:** What is the contribution of each key component in our model, particularly the different modalities and the collaborative-guided fusion mechanism?
- **RQ3:** How does CEMG's efficiency in terms of training and inference time compare to other generative models?
- **RQ4:** How sensitive is CEMG's performance to its main hyperparameters related to the tokenization process?
- **RQ5:** Does the collaborative-guided multimodal tokenization improve recommendation for cold-start items?

4.1   Experimental Settings

Datasets. We evaluate our model on three widely used public datasets from Amazon reviews and Yelp. For each interaction, we collect associated item images and text descriptions. Following standard practice, we filter users and items with fewer than 5 interactions. The statistics of the processed datasets are summarized in Table 1.

Table 1. Statistics of the experimental datasets.

Attribute	Beauty	Sports	Yelp
#Users	22,363	35,598	30,431
#Items	12,101	18,357	20,033
#Interactions	198,502	296,337	316,942
Avg. Len.	8.9	8.3	10.4
Sparsity	99.93%	99.95%	99.95%

Baselines. We compare CMGR with four categories of baseline models:

- **Sequential Methods:** GRU4Rec [5] and SASRec [6].
- **Multimodal Methods:** MMSRec [23] and MISSRec [25].
- **LLM-based Methods:** LlamaRec [28] and LLM-ESR [13]. These methods use LLMs but typically operate on item titles or raw text.
- **Generative Methods:** TIGER (?), LETTER [26], and MMGRec [11]. These represent the state-of-the-art in generative recommendation with semantic IDs.

Evaluation Metrics. We adopt the leave-one-out strategy for evaluation. For each user, we use their last interacted item as the ground truth for testing, the second to last for validation, and the rest for training. We evaluate the performance of all models using Hit Rate (Recall) and Normalized Discounted Cumulative Gain (NDCG) at cutoffs K = 10 and 20.

Implementation Details. For our CEMG framework, we project all feature embeddings to a uniform dimension of $d = 768$. The RQ-VAE for tokenization is configured with $M = 4$ codebook layers and a codebook size of $K = 512$. Based on our parameter analysis, the balancing weights were set to $\lambda_q = 0.25$ and $\lambda_d = 0.01$. We employ T5 [19] as the generative LLM-backbone, and the model is trained with the AdamW optimizer with a learning rate of 1×10^{-4} on NVIDIA A100 GPUs.

4.2 Overall Performance (RQ1)

Table 2 presents the main experimental results on the three datasets. We observe that our proposed CEMG consistently and significantly outperforms all baseline models across all datasets and metrics. This demonstrates the superiority of our approach, which stems from creating a deeply unified semantic representation that synergistically integrates multimodal content with collaborative signals, and then leveraging a powerful LLM for generation. Among baselines, generative methods (e.g., MMGRec, LETTER) generally outperform traditional sequential and multimodal methods, highlighting the potential of the generative paradigm. CEMG's substantial lead over the strongest baselines like MISSRec and MMGRec validates the effectiveness of our collaborative-guided fusion and the advanced generative architecture.

Table 2. Overall performance comparison on three datasets. The best results are in **bold**, and the second-best are <u>underlined</u>. 'Improv.' denotes the relative improvement of CEMG over the best baseline. All improvements are statistically significant ($p < 0.05$).

Category	Model	Beauty		Sports		Yelp	
		HR@10	NDCG@10	HR@10	NDCG@10	HR@10	NDCG@10
Sequential	GRU4Rec	0.0385	0.0116	0.0201	0.0045	0.0288	0.0095
	SASRec	0.0434	0.0147	0.0232	0.0061	0.0329	0.0121
Multimodal	MMSRec	0.0577	0.0287	0.0305	0.0118	0.0387	0.0163
	MISSRec	<u>0.0581</u>	<u>0.0292</u>	<u>0.0311</u>	<u>0.0124</u>	<u>0.0395</u>	<u>0.0171</u>
LLM-based	LlamaRec	0.0492	0.0198	0.0256	0.0083	0.0341	0.0134
	LLM-ESR	0.0515	0.0214	0.0269	0.0091	0.0353	0.0140
Generative	TIGER	0.0533	0.0251	0.0281	0.0103	0.0368	0.0151
	LETTER	0.0552	0.0268	0.0295	0.0111	0.0377	0.0159
	MMGRec	0.0571	0.0281	0.0302	0.0119	0.0389	0.0166
CEMG		**0.0665**	**0.0348**	**0.0363**	**0.0157**	**0.0458**	**0.0212**
Improvement (%)		+14.46%	+19.18%	+16.72%	+26.61%	+15.95%	+23.98%

4.3 Ablation Study (RQ2)

To understand the contribution of each component in CEMR, we conduct an ablation study with several variants of our model:

- **w/o Collab**: Removes the collaborative features (e_i^{CF}) from the unified representation in Stage 1.
- **w/o Image**: Removes the visual features ($\mathbf{f}_i^V$).
- **w/o Text**: Removes the textual features ($\mathbf{f}_i^T$).
- **w/o LLM**: Replaces the Llama-3-8B model with a standard 6-layer Transformer decoder trained from scratch, similar to TIGER (?).

The results are shown in Fig. 2. The full CMGR model achieves the best performance. Removing any component leads to a performance drop, confirming their importance. The most significant drops occur with 'w/o Collab' and 'w/o LLM'. The former underscores the vital role of collaborative filtering signals even in a content-rich generative model. The latter validates our choice of using a powerful pre-trained LLM, as its advanced reasoning and sequence modeling capabilities are crucial for accurately predicting the next item. The degradation from removing image or text features is also noticeable, proving that our model effectively utilizes multimodal information.

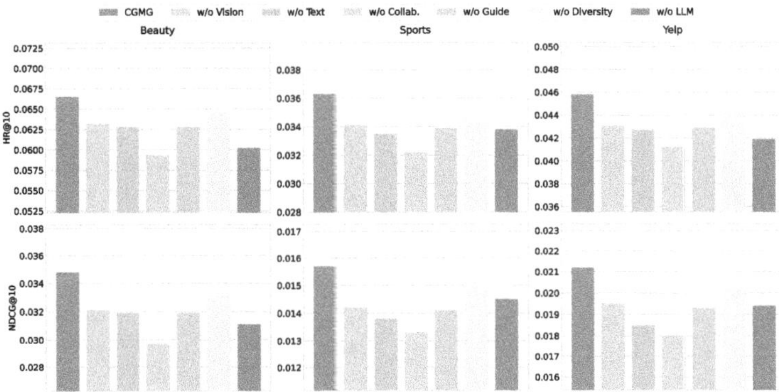

Fig. 2. Ablation study results on three datasets for HR@10 and NDCG@10. Performance drops across all variants demonstrate the contribution of each component.

4.4   Efficiency Analysis (RQ3)

We analyze the training and inference efficiency of CEMG against other state-of-the-art generative models. As shown in Fig. 3, CEMG strikes an effective balance between performance and computational cost.

Training Efficiency. The training time of CEMG is composed of two stages: tokenization (RQ-VAE) and end-to-end generation (LLM fine-tuning). While the overall training time is higher than TIGER due to the more modality features, it remains highly competitive. The total time is comparable to, and even slightly better than, LETTER, which requires a complex alignment process. This demonstrates that our sophisticated fusion and tokenization pipeline does not introduce prohibitive overhead.

Inference Efficiency. Inference speed is where our approach excels. CEMG achieves significantly lower inference latency compared to other multimodal generative models like MMGRec and LETTER. This efficiency stems from our design of generating short, fixed-length semantic token sequences ($M = 4$), which is much faster than models that may require more complex generation or retrieval steps. Our model's efficiency makes it highly practical for real-world deployment scenarios.

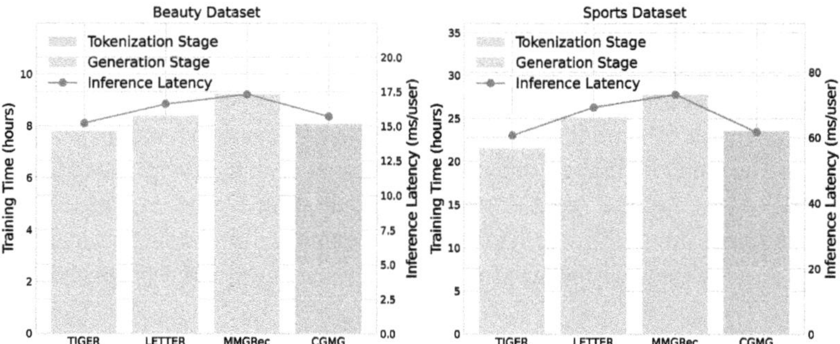

Fig. 3. Efficiency comparison on the Beauty and Sports datasets. Left axis (bars) shows training time per epoch, broken down by stage. Right axis (line) shows inference speed in users per second (higher is better).

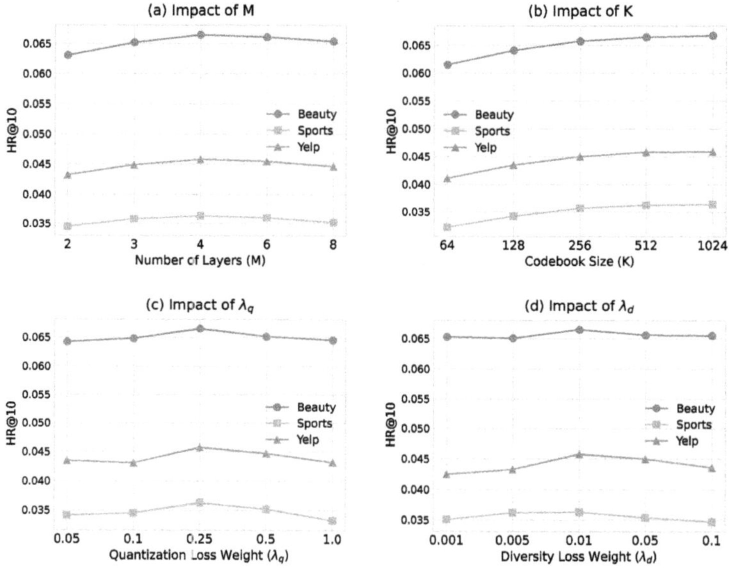

Fig. 4. Parameter sensitivity analysis of CEMG on HR@10 for (a) Number of Codebook Layers, (b) Codebook Size, (c) Quantization Loss Weight, and (d) Diversity Loss Weight.

4.5 Parameter Analysis (RQ4)

We investigate the sensitivity of CEMG to four key hyperparameters in the Unified Modality Tokenization stage, with results shown in Fig. 4.

- **Number of Codebook Layers (M):** As shown in Fig. 4(a), performance improves as M increases from 2 to 4, as more layers capture finer-grained semantic details. Performance plateaus at $M = 4$ and slightly declines at $M = 8$, likely due to the increased difficulty of generating longer sequences. We choose $M = 4$ as the optimal setting.

- **Codebook Size (K)**: Fig. 4(b) shows that a larger codebook size K generally leads to better performance, as it provides greater expressive power for the tokens. The performance gain saturates after $K = 512$, suggesting this size offers a good balance between expressiveness and complexity.
- **Quantization Loss Weight** (λ_q): This hyperparameter balances reconstruction quality and codebook alignment. Figure 4(c) shows a clear unimodal trend, with performance peaking at $\lambda_q = 0.25$. Values that are too low or too high disrupt this balance, leading to suboptimal tokenization.
- **Diversity Loss Weight** (λ_d): This weight is crucial for preventing codebook collapse. As seen in Fig. 4(d), performance improves as λ_d increases to 0.01, confirming the benefit of encouraging diverse code usage. Higher values can distort the semantic space, harming performance.

4.6   Performance on Cold-Start Items (RQ5)

A critical challenge for recommender systems is handling cold-start items, which have insufficient interaction data for collaborative filtering to be effective. We investigate this by evaluating model performance on items with five or fewer interactions in the training set. The results, presented in Table 3, show that CEMG substantially outperforms all baselines. While content-aware models like MISSRec and MMGRec naturally perform better than the ID-based SASRec, our model's advanced semantic tokenization provides superior generalization. By learning to generate rich item representations from a collaborative-guided fusion of multimodal content, CEMG remains effective even when interaction signals are sparse.

Table 3. Performance comparison on cold-start items across three datasets.

Model	Beauty		Sports		Yelp	
	HR@10	NDCG@10	HR@10	NDCG@10	HR@10	NDCG@10
SASRec	0.0112	0.0048	0.0065	0.0027	0.0098	0.0041
MISSRec	0.0254	0.0115	0.0141	0.0068	0.0185	0.0092
MMGRec	0.0268	0.0123	0.0153	0.0075	0.0192	0.0099
CEMG	**0.0305**	**0.0153**	**0.0183**	**0.0094**	**0.0231**	**0.0125**

5   Conclusion

In this paper, we proposed CEMG, a novel generative recommendation framework that pioneers a **Multimodal Fusion Layer** to create a unified item representation. This layer synergistically fuses multimodal content with high-order collaborative signals, which are then transformed into discrete codes by our **Unified Modality Tokenization** module. An **End-to-End Generative Recommendation** component then autoregressively generates item codes to produce recommendations. Extensive experiments validate that CEMG significantly outperforms state-of-the-art baselines. One limitation is that noisy signals within multimodal content, such as irrelevant image backgrounds, can be inadvertently encoded, potentially compromising tokenization quality. For future work, we plan to explore advanced decoding strategies to further mitigate recommendation errors.

References

1. Chen, J., Zhang, H., He, X., Nie, L., Liu, W., Chua, T.S.: Attentive collaborative filtering: Multimedia recommendation with item-and component-level attention. In: Proceedings of the 40th International ACM SIGIR conference on Research and Development in Information Retrieval, pp. 335–344 (2017)
2. Cui, X., Lu, W., Tong, Y., Li, Y., Zhao, Z.: Multi-modal multi-behavior sequential recommendation with conditional diffusion-based feature denoising. In: Proceedings of the 48th International ACM SIGIR Conference on Research and Development in Information Retrieval, pp. 1593–1602 (2025)
3. He, R., McAuley, J.: VBPR: Visual Bayesian Personalized Ranking from implicit feedback. In: Proceedings of the AAAI Conference on Artificial Intelligence, vol. 30 (2016)
4. He, X., Deng, K., Wang, X., Li, Y., Zhang, Y., Wang, M.: LightGCN: simplifying and powering graph convolution network for recommendation. arXiv preprint arXiv:2002.02126 (2020)
5. Hidasi, B.: Session-based recommendations with recurrent neural networks. arXiv preprint arXiv:1511.06939 (2015)
6. Kang, W.C., McAuley, J.: Self-attentive sequential recommendation. In: 2018 IEEE International Conference on Data Mining (ICDM), pp. 197–206. IEEE (2018)
7. Koren, Y., Rendle, S., Bell, R.: Advances in collaborative filtering. In: Recommender Systems Handbook, pp. 91–142 (2021)
8. Lee, D., Kim, C., Kim, S., Cho, M., Han, W.S.: Autoregressive image generation using residual quantization. In: CVPR, pp. 11523–11532 (2022)
9. Li, J., Zhang, W., Wang, T., Xiong, G., Lu, A., Medioni, G.: GPT4REC: a generative framework for personalized recommendation and user interests interpretation. arXiv preprint arXiv:2304.03879 (2023)
10. Li, L., Zhang, Y., Liu, D., Chen, L.: Large language models for generative recommendation: a survey and visionary discussions. LREC-Coling (2024)
11. Liu, H., Wei, Y., Song, X., Guan, W., Li, Y.F., Nie, L.: MMGREC: multimodal generative recommendation with transformer model. arXiv preprint arXiv:2404.16555 (2024)
12. Liu, Q., et al.: Reduce information loss in transformers for pluralistic image inpainting. In: Proceedings of the IEEE/CVF Conference on Computer Vision and Pattern Recognition, pp. 11347–11357 (2022)
13. Liu, Q., et al.: LLM-ESR: large language models enhancement for long-tailed sequential recommendation. Adv. Neural. Inf. Process. Syst. **37**, 26701–26727 (2024)
14. Liu, S., Chen, Z., Liu, H., Hu, X.: User-video co-attention network for personalized micro-video recommendation. In: The World Wide Web Conference, pp. 3020–3026 (2019)
15. Liu, Z., Lu, W.: MDN: modality decomposition network for multimodal recommendation. In: Proceedings of the 2025 International Conference on Multimedia Retrieval, pp. 871–879 (2025)
16. Lu, W., Yin, L.: DMMD4SR: diffusion model-based multi-level multimodal denoising for sequential recommendation. In: Proceedings of the 33rd ACM International Conference on Multimedia, pp. 6363–6372 (2025)

17. Mentzer, F., Minnen, D., Agustsson, E , Tschannen, M.: Finite scalar quantization: VQ-VAE made simple. arXiv preprint arXiv:2309.15505 (2023)
18. Mo, M., et al.: MIN: multi-stage interactive network for multimodal recommendation. In: International Conference on Web Information Systems Engineering, pp. 191–205. Springer (2024). https://doi.org/10.1007/978-981-96-0570-5_14
19. Raffel, C., et al.: Exploring the limits of transfer learning with a unified text-to-text transformer. J. Mach. Learn. Res. **21**(140), 1–67 (2020)
20. Rajput, S., et al.: Recommender systems with generative retrieval. In: NeurIPS. Curran Associates, Inc. (2023)
21. Roy, D., Dutta, M.: A systematic review and research perspective on recommender systems. J. Big Data **9**(1), 59 (2022)
22. Simonyan, K., Zisserman, A.: Very deep convolutional networks for large-scale image recognition. arXiv preprint arXiv:1409.1556 (2014)
23. Song, K., Sun, Q., Xu, C., Zheng, K., Yang, Y.: Self-supervised multi-modal sequential recommendation. arXiv preprint arXiv:2304.13277 (2023)
24. Sun, F., et al.: BERT4REC: sequential recommendation with bidirectional encoder representations from transformer. In: Proceedings of the 28th ACM International Conference on Information and Knowledge Management, pp. 1441–1450 (2019)
25. Wang, J., et al.: MISSREC: pre-training and transferring multi-modal interest-aware sequence representation for recommendation. In: Proceedings of the 31st ACM International Conference on Multimedia, pp. 6548–6557 (2023)
26. Wang, W., et al.: Learnable item tokenization for generative recommendation. In: Proceedings of the 33rd ACM International Conference on Information and Knowledge Management, pp. 2400–2409 (2024)
27. Wei, Y., Wang, X., Nie, L., He, X., Hong, R., Chua, T.S.: MMGCN: multi-modal graph convolution network for personalized recommendation of micro-video. arXiv preprint arXiv:1907.04188 (2019)
28. Yue, Z., Rabhi, S., Moreira, G.d.S.P., Wang, D., Oldridge, E.: LLAMAREC: two-stage recommendation using large language models for ranking. arXiv preprint arXiv:2311.02089 (2023)
29. Zangerle, E., Bauer, C.: Evaluating recommender systems: survey and framework. ACM Comput. Surv. **55**(8), 1–38 (2022)

PreBERT-Rec: Improving Topic Modeling in Recommendation Systems via Effective Data Preprocessing and BERT

Dang Hoang Minh Triet[1], Tran Hoang Anh[1], Nguyen Hoang Hai[1], Tran Nguyen Minh Quang[1], Tran Cong Hieu[1], Thu Nguyen[2], and Binh Thanh Nguyen[1(✉)]

[1] University of Science, VNU-HCM, Ho Chi Minh City, Vietnam
`ngtbinh@hcmus.edu.vn, tchieu008@gmail.com`
[2] Simula Research Laboratory, Oslo, Norway
`thu@simula.no`

Abstract. Recommendation systems (RS) have been extensively studied in recent years. This work focuses specifically on rating prediction, with the aim of estimating a product's rating score from user reviews and ratings. Existing methods focused on textual reviews and user feedback to extract more information to address data sparsity and the cold-start problem. However, outliers significantly affected these methods and struggled to effectively capture the full meaning of textual data. To tackle this challenge, in this paper, we introduce a comprehensive data preprocessing method to handle outlier data before model input. Furthermore, addressing the limitations of previous LDA-based topic modeling approaches, we propose a novel model called *PreBERT-Rec* that leverages BERT representations with unsupervised clustering techniques (e.g., *KMeans*, *DBSCAN*...) as a powerful tool for topic modeling, enabling more effective information extraction. Extensive experiments on Amazon benchmark datasets demonstrate the superiority of our proposed method, achieving up to a 27.63% improvement over the best previous baseline in rating prediction performance.

Keywords: Rating Prediction · Recommendation Systems · Sentiment Analysis · Topic Modeling · Outlier Detection

1 Introduction

Nowadays, with the rapid growth of e-commerce systems, customers may face difficulties in selecting products that suit their needs due to the variety of choices available. Therefore, RS has become an essential tool for companies to address the challenge of suggesting appropriate products to customers [3]. The goal of an RS is to predict the customer's preference for available products based on their existing information, and then select the highest-scoring products to recommend to them. Early studies employed collaborative filtering (CF), which

© The Author(s), under exclusive license to Springer Nature Singapore Pte Ltd. 2026
J. Lokoč et al. (Eds.): MMM 2026, LNCS 16412, pp. 522–536, 2026.
https://doi.org/10.1007/978-981-95-6950-2_37

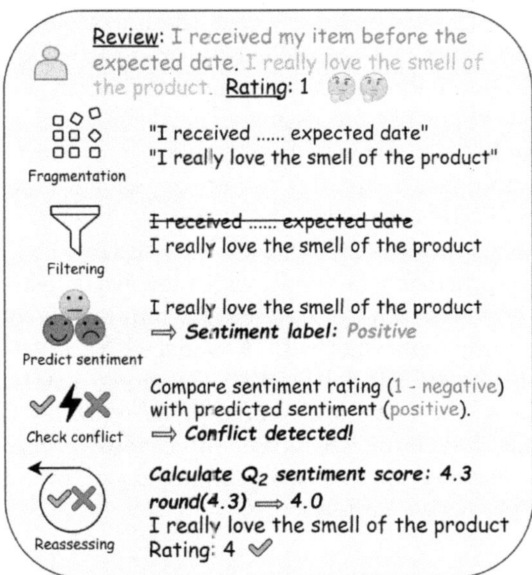

Fig. 1. The red text has a negative connotation and is not related to the item, so our preprocessing removes it from the review sentence and reassesses the score (Color figure online)

utilized information from previous users to predict the preferences of new users [17, 29]. Although CF has high prediction accuracy, it still has some limitations. For instance, when the current user's information is too scarce, relying on existing data to make predictions becomes difficult, which is known as the sparsity problem. Furthermore, this method may also struggle when new entities lack data from previous users, leading to cold start issues [18].

Researchers have focused on textual reviews and item-specific information to tackle these challenges. For instance, [8] proposed an attention mechanism that integrates both review and rating matrices as input to improve the performance of rating predictions. Similarly, [20, 26] introduced models that combine sentiment analysis with matrix factorization. Building on these approaches, [5] introduced a novel deep-learning model that treats user and item review sets as a corpus for cross-grained sentiment analysis. This model combines both fine-grained and coarse-grained levels to extract sentiment feature vectors for users and items, leading to significant improvements.

Although promising, LDA-based methods [4] for topic extraction often struggle with outliers and unbalanced data distributions [28]. Moreover, they rely on static Word2Vec embeddings [22] for sentiment scoring, despite the availability of more robust sequential representations such as BERT [10], which can effectively replace LDA in topic modeling. In light of this observation, our curiosity is sparked: Can replacing both LDA models with another topic modeling method, along with applying data pre-processing steps, improve overall model performance? To investigate this hypothesis, we performed experiments. Our findings indicate that our comprehensive pre-processing steps significantly improve results. Figure 1 illustrates an example of an inconsistent data point and demonstrates how our pre-processing steps identify and rectify it. Similarly, when replacing the LDA model with BERT, followed by clustering methods. By combining these components, we aim to improve semantic feature quality and enhance rating prediction accuracy.

In summary, the contributions of this work are threefold: (1) We propose comprehensive data pre-processing methods, which involve detecting and reassessing inconsistent data points, which can significantly improve the performance of any RS model. (2) We study replacing the LDA model with a new topic segmentation approach incorporating BERT, followed by clustering methods. To the best of our knowledge, this is the first work to investigate replacing LDA with another topic extraction method in an RS model. (3) Extensive experiments on three Amazon datasets showing up to 27.63% improvement over the best previous baseline in rating prediction performance.[1]

2   Related Works

Collaborative Filtering Approach. Matrix factorization (MF) has long been central to recommendation systems, predicting user preferences from historical user-item interactions. Early work by [29] applied singular value decomposition (SVD), but struggled with high-dimensional rating matrices. The latent factor model (LFM) [17] addressed this, yet the CF-based models still face data sparsity and cold-start problems, where limited interactions reduce accuracy [13].

Deep Learning Approach. With the rise of deep learning (DL), in addition to CF-based approaches, several DL models have been applied to textual data in RS, including Convolutional Neural Networks (CNNs) [32], which leveraged CNN layers to jointly learn the properties of elements and user behaviors from the review text. Similarly, [30] recurrent-based models, including RNNs, LSTMs, and GRUs, have been employed to develop end-to-end RS models [24]. These models offer improved accuracy by capturing complex patterns in user behavior and preferences. However, these methods primarily focus on review data without exploring the relationship between textual data and rating data.

Recommendation Systems Integrating Textual Information. Following the idea of fusing information to make the recommendation system models more robust, textual reviews were integrated with matrix factorization to enhance the understanding of user preferences of the model [8]. Similarly, additional LDA models were employed to extract more information from the review data [26]. Word2Vec (W2V) [22] was also used for textual data representation, followed by coarse-grained sentiment analysis [5]. Furthermore, BERT was utilized to extract sentiment information, improving model performance [20].

---

[1] We release the dataset and the source code at: https://github.com/trietdang5599/
PreBERT.git.

Large Language Models For Recommendation Systems. Large Language Models (LLMs) with billions of parameters have had a significant impact on various fields, including natural language processing (NLP), computer vision (CV), and recommendation systems (RS), which are no exception to this trend. Initial efforts have been made to explore their ability to understand user preferences and previous interactions [31]. Currently, LLM-based RS has a two-way approach, one is designed for traditional recommendation tasks, such as sequential recommendation [14] [27] [6] and rating prediction [6] [16]. Beyond improving traditional tasks, on the other hand, LLMs also open up opportunities for new and challenging recommendation applications, such as explaining recommendation results [12] and enabling conversational recommendations [11].

Although LLMs have shown promising potential, several critical challenges remain to be addressed, including data sparsity and the cold start problem, which even LLMs still struggle with. These limitations motivate our research to develop a new RS framework that leverages pre-processing techniques and topic-modeling approaches to better understand user preferences and enhance recommendation accuracy.

3   Methodology

The overview of the method is shown in Fig. 2. We initially have Data Preprocessing in Sect. 3.1 to process reviews and ratings with two steps in Fig. 1. After that, BERT and Bisecting K-means are chosen to extract key topics in Sect. 3.2. Next, the model will calculate sentiment throughout Cross-grained Sentiment in Sect. 3.3. Moreover, Matrix Factorization in Sect. 3.4 is used to handle ratings from rating data. Finally, in Sect. 3.5, the deep fusion module combines both user and item elements to predict the value. However, first, we present the preliminary of the task definition: *Task Definition of Recommendation System:* We take the review sets processed and the rating matrices of a user and an item as input to study the task of user rating prediction. Let us define a formulation: given a user $u \in U$, have a review for an item $i \in I$. Based on the review of user u for each item i, we have a sequence of historical interactions $E^u = \{e_1^u, e_2^u, ..., e_n^u\}$ for that user, where the sequence of user interaction E^u in the past is ordered by time. Note that e_n^u is the most recent item that the user interacted with, and each e_k^u is represented for the item's information (e.g., title, description, etc.) that the user has given a rating to the item, which the user has used. The goal of the model is to predict the rating for an item based on the user's historical interactions, including review text and item information.

3.1   Data Preprocessing

We observe that the input corpus can significantly impact the performance of topic distribution models [9,25], suggesting the removal or shortening of words. Therefore, in sentiment analysis tasks, it is crucial to remove noisy content that lacks emotional expression. In addition, reevaluating outlier reviews or those

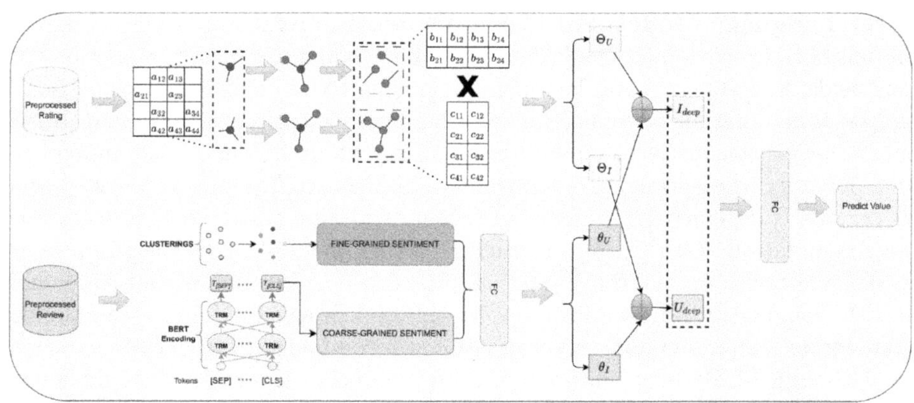

Fig. 2. After preprocessing, reviews are processed via Cross-grained Sentiment into user and item reviews, while ratings are processed via Matrix Factorization into user and item ratings. The results are then merged by user or item class to predict ratings.

that contain ambiguous information is necessary to enhance the effectiveness of sentiment extraction models.

Step 1: Fragmentation, Filtering and Sentiment Scoring of Reviews
Given a set of user reviews $H = \{h_1, h_2, \ldots, h_k\}$, each review h_i is segmented into smaller passages based on conjunctions or punctuation $S_{h_i} = \{s_{i_1}, s_{i_2}, \ldots, s_{i_j}\}$, $\forall i \in \{1, 2, \ldots, k\}$. For each passage, $s_{i_j} \in S_{h_i}$ removes the stopword, and then the Sentiment Intensity Analyzer is applied to check if it contains emotionally expressive content. Let $\mathcal{F}(s_{i_j})$ denote the filtering function: $S'_{h_i} = \{s_{i_j} \in S_{h_i} \mid \mathcal{F}(s_{i_j}) = 1\}$, where S'_{h_i} is the set of filtered passages that contain expressive content.

The filtered passages S'_{h_i} (3.1) are then scored using the Flair sentiment analysis model [2], the new review h'_i is then replaced by concatenating the sentences in S'_{h_i} together. Let $\sigma(s_{i_j})$ represent the sentiment score for passage s_{i_j}, where $\sigma(s_{i_j}) \in [-1, 1]$. The overall sentiment score for the review h_i is calculated as the sum of the sentiment scores for all filtered passages (1):

$$\bar{\sigma}_{h'_i} = \frac{1}{|S'_{h_i}|} \sum_{s_{i_j} \in S'_{h_i}} \sigma(s_{i_j}). \tag{1}$$

A threshold value ε is used to determine the final sentiment label for the review. Specifically, sentiment h'_i is assigned a value of 1 if $\bar{\sigma}_{h'_i} \geq \varepsilon$ and -1 otherwise, i.e. when $\bar{\sigma}_{h'_i} < \varepsilon$.

Given a user-provided rating r_i for each review h_i, we transform it into a binary classification c_i, where $c_i = 1$ if $r_i \geq 4$, and $c_i = -1$ if $r_i < 4$.

Step 2: Identify Outliers and Re-evaluate
To detect any conflict between the sentiment of the filtered review h'_i, denoted as Sentiment(h'_i), with its corresponding user-provided rating c_i [7]. A review h'_i

is classified as an outlier if its sentiment label Sentiment(h_i') conflicts with the binary rating:

$$\text{Outlier}(h_i') = \begin{cases} \text{True} & \text{if Sentiment}(h_i') \neq c_i, \\ \text{False} & \text{if Sentiment}(h_i') = c_i, \end{cases} \tag{2}$$

The second quartile Q_2 is the median of the scoring distribution for the item to which the review h_i refers. The value Q_2 is then used to reassign the rating to Outlier(h_i') (2) by averaging the current rating with Q_2, as shown in the following formula: $r_i' = \frac{r_i + Q_2}{2}$. Finally, we will obtain the set of review texts from the user $H' = \{h_1', h_2', \ldots, h_k'\}$, similarly, we obtain $R' = \{r_1', r_2', \ldots, r_k'\}$ where k is the total number of reviews in the dataset.

3.2 Extracting Key Topics Using BERT and Clustering Techniques

Step 1: Extracting BERT embeddings

The process begins with fine-tuning the BERT model, utilizing the pre-trained Bert-base uncased model. The optimization is performed using AdamW [21] with $\beta_1 = 0.9$, $\beta_2 = 0.95$, and a weight decay of 0.01. Once the model is fine-tuned, BERT embeddings are extracted for each document in the dataset. This results in a matrix of embedding $\mathbf{E}$, where each row corresponds to the vector representation of a document. The dimensionality of this matrix is equivalent to the number of documents M, providing a rich numerical representation of the textual content.

Step 2: Clustering for Topic Identification

The next step is to identify topics through clustering. We use the Bisecting K-Means algorithm for its efficiency with large embeddings and ability to handle varied cluster shapes and sizes. Unlike standard K-Means, which may produce unbalanced clusters and is sensitive to outliers, Bisecting K-Means is a hybrid of partitional and hierarchical clustering, splitting one cluster at a time using two centroids, reducing computation time and producing more balanced clusters [1].

After clustering, we obtain a set of labels $\mathbf{L}$ corresponding to k topics, grouping semantically similar documents into coherent topics.

Step 3: Keyword Extraction for Topics

Each cluster $\mathbf{L_i}$ represents a potential topic comprising semantically related documents. For each cluster, we apply the TF-IDF vectorization to extract representative keywords, where the TF-IDF score measures the importance of a term in a document relative to the corpus. After computing scores, we obtain the topic set $T = \{t_1, t_2, \ldots, t_k\}$ in the review set d' and the feature set F of each topic t_i, represented by the top n highest-scoring words.

3.3 Cross-Grained Sentiment Calculation

Fine-Grained Sentiment Calculations. Based on the structure of the Deep-CGSR model [5], we extract pairs of words in the feature sentence. Using

Table 1. Negative Sentiment Classification Values.

Sentiment classification	Extremely Negative	Very Negative	Moderately Negative	Slightly Negative
Value	-4	-3	-2	-1

Table 2. Positive Sentiment Classification Values.

Sentiment classification	Slightly Positive	Moderately Positive	Very Positive	Extremely Positive
Value	1	2	3	4

dependency syntactic parsing, we extract pairs of feature words f_w and sentiment words from the user and item review sets using a shared topic set $T = \{t_1, t_2, \ldots, t_k\}$. After preprocessing the review sets (e.g., clause segmentation, lemmatization), we obtain sentences $H' = \{h'_1, h'_2, \ldots, h'_k\}$, where each processed review is represented as h'_i. For each feature word f_w in review h'_i, we apply dependency syntactic analysis $\text{Parser}(f_w)$ to extract relationships and use $\text{Extract}(f_w)$ to identify feature-sentiment word pairs $\{f_w, f_s\}$. Next, all words related to the selected characteristic words are gathered using the word-sentiment approach. In this study, we identified several limitations in using SentiWordNet 3.0, as reported in previous research, particularly concerning the lexicon's vocabulary coverage, and the range of sentiment values is relatively narrow. However, we still utilize SentiWordNet to extract related sentiment words. To address these issues, we propose the use of an alternative sentiment lexicon, VADER [15], which offers an expanded sentiment intensity range of $[-4, -1]$ for negative values 1, $[1, 4]$ for positive values 2 and 0 for a neutral value. VADER better predicts sentiment in microblogs and includes emoticons, acronyms, and initialisms. After aggregating word-level sentiment, final scores fall within $[0, 5]$ for positive and $[-5, 0]$ for negative sentiment.

Using the aggregated feature-sentiment word pairs $\{f_{u,w}, f_{u,s}\}$ for user reviews and $\{f_{i,w}, f_{i,s}\}$ for item reviews, we construct the fine-grained sentiment topic matrices τ_u and τ_i(3). These matrices are defined on the shared topic set $T = \{t_1, t_2, \ldots, t_k\}$ as follows:

$$\tau_u(t) = \sum_{h'_i \in d_u} \sigma\left(f_{u,w}, f_{u,s} \mid t\right), \quad \tau_i(t) = \sum_{h'_i \in d_i} \sigma\left(f_{i,w}, f_{i,s} \mid t\right), \tag{3}$$

where $\sigma\left(f_w, f_s \mid t\right)$ represents the sentiment scoring function for the feature word f_w and the sentiment word f_s associated with the topic t, which are then used to construct the fine-grained sentiment topic matrix τ_u for user reviews and τ_i for item reviews.

Coarse-Grained Sentiment Polarity Analysis. Our approach analyzes the coarse-grained sentiment polarity at the sentence level using each processed review h_i' as input. Next, we use BERT to classify the ratio of sentiment classes that the model predicts from the inputs; we call it logits. The softmax function transforms the logits into probabilities in the range $[0,1]$, yielding the overall sentiment polarity weight for the user's review set as $\phi_u = \text{softmax}(\mathbf{logits})$.

We use ϕ_u above as a weighting factor, the sentiment category label (v_u) of the review as the weighted summation value to achieve a dichotomous sentiment classification at a coarse-grained level. We then take the probability of falling into that label, which is defined as the rating score. After obtaining the probability distribution of the sentiment labels, the algorithm first selects the label with the highest probability. To calculate the sentiment score, it will go into a sentiment scale divided into five equally spaced ranges between $[0,1]$ to calculate the sentiment score of that rating. The result sentiment matrix $p_u = \begin{cases} p_{u,\text{pos}} \\ p_{u,\text{neg}} \end{cases}$ indicates the positive sentiment $p_{u,\text{pos}}$ and the negative sentiment $p_{u,\text{neg}} = 1 - p_{u,\text{pos}}$ between $[0,1]$. The sentiment polarity of an item's review set p_i can be similarly deduced.

Generation of Cross-Grained Sentiment of Review. We compute cross-grained sentiment rating of topics of users' processed reviews (4) by multiplying the topic-sentiment matrix τ_u with the sentiment probability matrix p_u:

$$S_v = \tau_u \times p_u, \tag{4}$$

This rating measures the contribution of each review to users' preferences $\mathbf{u}$'s. By weighting and summing these ratings of each review, we obtain d_u, which is fed into the fully connected layer to get the user $\mathbf{u}$'s final preference expression in the review (5):

$$\theta_U = w \times d_u + b_u, \tag{5}$$

where w and b_u are the weight parameter and bias term of the fully connected layer. Similarly, we can obtain the final preference expression of item $\mathbf{i}$ in the review data θ_i (6) as:

$$\theta_I = w \times d_i + b_i. \tag{6}$$

Thus, we can obtain the output θ_u and θ_i for user and item reviews.

3.4 Rating-Based Matrix Factorization Module

Matrix factorization is a class of collaborative filtering models, decomposes the useritem rating matrix into two lower-rank matrices, where each dimension represents latent user preferences and item features. Based on [5], we have:

$$\hat{r}_{u,i} = \mu + b_i + b_u + \mathbf{p}_u \mathbf{q}_i^T, \tag{7}$$

where μ is global bias, b_i is item bias, b_u is user bias, and $p_u \mathbf{q}_i^T$ is the preference of the user toward the items for measuring the biased information. And also have:

$$A \approx \Theta_U \Theta_I^T, \tag{8}$$

where matrix $A \in \mathbf{R}^{m \times n}$, each user of Θ_U and each item of Θ_I can be represented by a k-dimensional vector. The latent factors Θ_U and Θ_I obtained from matrix factorization can be fused with θ_U and θ_I from the deep fusion module to form the deep feature. We then predict ratings in the fully connected layer.

3.5 Deep Fusion Module

The deep fusion module takes as input Reviews (θ_U and θ_I) after going through the cross-grained sentiment calculation module and Ratings (Θ_U and Θ_I) after going through Matrix factorization. Next, they are divided by the item and user classes to merge and form deep features U_{deep} (9) and I_{deep} (10). The deep features U_{deep} and I_{deep} take all the latent factors from the users and the items to merge and make predictions. With U_{deep}:

$$U_{\text{deep}} = \frac{1}{2} \sum_{i=1}^{n} \left(\left(\sum_{i=1}^{n} v_i z_i \right)^2 - \sum_{i=1}^{n} v_i^2 z_i^2 \right), \tag{9}$$

and I_{deep}:

$$I_{\text{deep}} = \frac{1}{2} \sum_{i=1}^{n} \left(\left(\sum_{i=1}^{n} v_i z'_i \right)^2 - \sum_{i=1}^{n} v_i^2 z'^2_i \right), \tag{10}$$

where $z = \theta_U \oplus \Theta_U$, and similarly for I_{deep} with $z' = \theta_I \oplus \Theta_I$.
This method works based on the different emotions of users in the same type of rating when interacting with the item, helping to limit incorrect predictions and increase prediction accuracy.

3.6 Theoretical Analysis

We have the following statement, which shows that if reassessing effectively adjusts ratings for outlier reviews, then the expected total inconsistency between review sentiment and ratings is reduced after preprocessing.

Assumption 1 *For any outlier review h'_i, the reassessed rating $r'_i = (r_i + Q_2)/2$ moves the score closer to the median Q_2 and increases the likelihood of sentimentrating agreement:*

$$\mathbb{P}\big(\text{Sentiment}(h'_i) = c'_i\big) \; > \; \mathbb{P}\big(\text{Sentiment}(h'_i) = c_i\big).$$

For non-outliers, reassessment leaves the label unchanged almost surely:

$$\mathbb{P}\big(c'_i = c_i \,\big|\, \text{Outlier}(h'_i) = 0\big) = 1.$$

Theorem 1. *Under Assumption 1, the expected total inconsistency after reassessment is smaller than that before reassessment:*

$$\mathbb{E}[I'_{total}] < \mathbb{E}[I_{total}].$$

Proof. Since reassessment only affects outlier reviews, the expected difference between total inconsistencies before and after reassessment is:

$$\mathbb{E}[I'_{\text{total}} - I_{\text{total}}] = \sum_{i=1}^{k} p_i \Big(\mathbb{E}[I(h'_i, c'_i) \mid \text{Outlier}(h'_i) = 1] - \mathbb{E}[I(h'_i, c_i) \mid \text{Outlier}(h'_i) = 1] \Big).$$

By Assumption 1, each term in the summation is negative,
thus $\mathbb{E}[I'_{\text{total}}] < \mathbb{E}[I_{\text{total}}]$. $\qquad\qquad\square$

Table 3. Statistics of the three benchmark datasets

Dataset	All Beauty	Digital Music	Toys and Games
Number of users	990	6685	9595
Number of items	85	5554	8092
Number of reviews	5264	10000	10000
Average number of reviews	5.32	1.58	1.04
Average number of reviews per item	61.93	1.80	1.24

4   Experiment

4.1   Datasets

We used three public Amazon review subsets *All-beauty (AB)*, *Toys and Games (TG)*, and *Digital Music (DM)* from [23] spanning hundreds of millions of reviews from May 1996 to Oct 2018. Each review has nine attributes; we used *reviewerID*, *asin*, *overall* and *reviewText*. Subsets with lower than 10,000 records used all data. For datasets with more than 10,000 records, we randomly selected 10,000 samples to ensure both computational efficiency and the representativeness of the dataset for our analysis. Table 3 provides statistics on these datasets.

4.2   Implementation Details

The detailed implementation of the method is described below.

Data Preparation: Each dataset was re-evaluated and preprocessed as in Sect. 3.1. We handle text label pairs by converting original ratings (15) to labels (04) for BERT training. Tokenization included sequence truncation to a uniform length (`max_len=512`).

BERT Fine-Tuning: We fine-tuned *bert-base-uncased* with a modified classification head (`num_labels = 5`), also using the AdamW optimizer with learning rate $= 2 \times 10^{-5}$ and batch size $= 8$

Extracting and Clustering BERT Embeddings: Hidden states from BERT's last layer were clustered, with BisectingKMeans performing best. The number of clusters (`n_clusters`) matched dataset topics, and (`random_state=42`) ensured reproducibility.

Cross-Grained Sentiment Calculation Module: BERT and the topics extracted from the above steps to obtain fine- and coarse-grained sentiment features for different users and items.

Rating-Based Matrix factorization module: Uses FunkSVD to model user and item preferences from historical user ratings.

Deep Fusion Module: FM fuses coarse- and fine-grained sentiment vectors with matrix factorization vectors, with trainable parameters from the FM model.

Rating Prediction Module: Consists mainly of a fully connected layer, with trainable parameters being its weights.

Evaluation metric: Uses Mean Absolute Error (MAE) and Root Mean Squared Error (RMSE). A predicted rating is deemed correct if it matches the ground truth rating exactly.

4.3 Compared Baselines

To make an extensive evaluation, we selected several robust baseline methods. For a fair comparison, we retrained all baselines on our dataset using the same train, test proportions. The baselines include:DeepCoNN [32] links user and item reviews via shared CNNs to predict ratings; NARRE [8] applies attention to highlight the most relevant reviews; DAML [19] uses dual local and global attention over text and ratings; MFFR [26] builds a userproduct preference matrix from LDA topics and applies MF; DeepCGSR [5] combines cross-grained sentiment with MF; and SAMF [20] extends MFFR with BERT-based sentiment features.

4.4 Main Results

The experimental results of various approaches are reported in Table 4. The results clearly demonstrate the superior performance of our proposed PreBERT-Rec models, particularly when combined with clustering techniques such as Birch and DBSCAN, over traditional methods like MFFR, SAMF, and DeepCGSR.

All Beauty. Compared to the best baseline model DAML (**MAE = 0.369**), our *PreBERT-Rec + Birch* achieves a **5.42%** improvement in MAE. For RMSE, compared to the best baseline SAMF (**RMSE = 0.674**), our model achieves an improvement of **2.52%** with a score of **0.657**.

Digital Music. Our best-performing model, *PreBERT-Rec + BisectingKMeans*, achieves an **MAE of 0.351** and an **RMSE of 0.557**. Compared to the best baseline DAML (**MAE = 0.485**) and DeepCGSR (**RMSE = 0.708**), this yields an improvement of **27.63%** in MAE and **21.33%** in RMSE. The consistent reduction highlights the strength of our method in music-related content, which often contains sentiment-rich reviews.

Toys and Games. In this domain, the *PreBERT-Rec + BisectingKMeans* model achieves the lowest **MAE = 0.549** and **RMSE = 0.795**. Compared to the best baseline MFFR (**MAE = 0.643**) and SAMF (**RMSE = 0.831**), this represents an improvement of **14.62%** in MAE and **4.33%** in RMSE. These results show the effectiveness of our method in handling categories with various product descriptions and emotional expressions.

In general, the findings highlight that integrating **PreBERT-Rec** with clustering methods such as **Birch** and **BisectingKMeans** markedly improves performance over traditional approaches

Table 4. Evaluation results are compared with leading baseline methods in terms of MAE and RMSE, with the best scores highlighted in bold and the second-best scores underlined.

METHODS	All Beauty		Digital Music		Toys and Games	
	MAE	RMSE	MAE	RMSE	MAE	RMSE
DeepCoNN [32]	0.629	0.772	0.558	0.719	0.854	1.047
NARRE [8]	0.738	0.816	0.664	0.907	0.943	1.125
DAML [19]	<u>0.369</u>	0.697	0.485	0.741	0.644	0.882
MFFR [26]	0.495	0.712	0.713	0.848	0.643	0.856
DeepCGSR [5]	0.434	0.792	0.502	0.708	0.733	1.001
SAMF [20]	0.593	0.674	0.576	0.778	0.667	0.831
PreBERT-Rec+KMeans[**Ours**]	0.398	0.742	0.364	<u>0.562</u>	0.562	0.826
PreBERT-Rec+DBSCAN[**Ours**]	0.376	0.679	0.375	0.582	<u>0.554</u>	0.814
PreBERT-Rec+Birch[**Ours**]	**0.349**	**0.657**	<u>0.358</u>	0.566	0.561	<u>0.798</u>
PreBERT-Rec+BisectingKMeans[**Ours**]	0.388	<u>0.666</u>	**0.351**	**0.557**	**0.549**	**0.795**
Improve (%)	5.42	2.52	27.63	21.33	14.62	4.33

Table 5. Evaluation after pre-processing results are compared with previous methods regarding MAE and RMSE.

Results	METHODS	All Beauty		Digital Music		Toys and Games	
		MAE	RMSE	MAE	RMSE	MAE	**RMSE**
After pre-processing	DeepCoNN [32]	0.608	0.739	0.510	0.679	0.809	1.021
	NARRE [8]	0.674	0.733	0.628	0.846	0.894	0.944
	DAML [19]	0.354	0.679	0.421	0.683	0.594	0.819
	MFFR [26]	0.478	0.689	0.651	0.763	0.628	0.834
	DeepCGSR [5]	0.373	0.726	0.456	0.664	0.717	0.989
	SAMF [20]	0.521	0.662	0.468	0.651	0.621	0.817

4.5 Ablation Study

Impact of Sentiment-Based Preprocessing. As shown in Table 5, sentiment-based preprocessing consistently enhances performance across most baselines and datasets. The *Digital Music* dataset exhibits the largest gains, with MAE improvements from **5.42%** to **18.75%** and RMSE from **5.56%** to **16.32%**. The *Toys and Games* dataset also benefits notably, achieving MAE reductions between **2.18%** and **7.76%**, and RMSE gains from **1.20%** to **16.09%**. Even the *All Beauty* dataset, despite initial expectations, records MAE improvements from **3.34%** to **14.06%** and RMSE from **1.78%** to **10.17%**. These results confirm that aligning sentiment with ratings enhances consistency, though the effect is more limited for datasets with lower rating variability.

5 Conclusion

This work explores recommendation systems (RS) by integrating textual information to address data sparsity and the cold-start problem. We hypothesize that LDA-based methods struggle to capture sufficient information from reviews, whereas BERT provides contextual embeddings that model both syntactic structure and semantic meaning. We also propose a sentiment-based preprocessing mechanism that removes emotionally neutral content and reassesses inconsistent user ratings, reducing input noise and enhancing semantic consistency between reviews and ratings. Experimental results confirm our model's superiority over strong baselines, with consistent performance across diverse datasets. In the future, we plan to integrate large language models (LLMs) with our preprocessing strategy to further improve rating prediction. Preliminary insights suggest this could enhance both review understanding and recommendation quality.

References

1. Abirami, K., Mayilvahanan, P.: Performance analysis of k-means and bisecting k-means algorithms in weblog data. Int. J. Emerg. Technol. Eng. Res 4(8), 119–124 (2016)
2. Akbik, A., Bergmann, T., Blythe, D., Rasul, K., Schweter, S., Vollgraf, R.: Flair: An easy-to-use framework for state-of-the-art nlp. In: Proceedings of the 2019 conference of the North American chapter of the association for computational linguistics (demonstrations), pp. 54–59 (2019)
3. Batmaz, Z., Yurekli, A., Bilge, A., Kaleli, C.: A review on deep learning for recommender systems: challenges and remedies. Artif. Intell. Rev. **52**, 1–37 (2019)
4. Blei, D.M., Ng, A.Y., Jordan, M.I.: Latent Dirichlet allocation. J. Mach. Learn. Res. **3**(Jan), 993–1022 (2003)
5. Cai, Y., Ke, W., Cui, E., Yu, F.: A deep recommendation model of cross-grained sentiments of user reviews and ratings. Inform. Process. Manage. **59**(2), 102842 (2022)
6. Cao, Y., et al.: Aligning large language models with recommendation knowledge. arXiv preprint arXiv:2404.00245 (2024)

7. Chatterjee, I., Zhou, M., Abusorrah, A., Sedraoui, K., Alabdulwahab, A.: Statistics-based outlier detection and correction method for amazon customer reviews. Entropy **23**(12), 1645 (2021)
8. Chen, C., Zhang, M., Liu, Y., Ma, S.: Neural attentional rating regression with review-level explanations. In: Proceedings of the 2018 World Wide Web Conference, pp. 1583–1592 (2018)
9. Churchill, R., Singh, L.: Topic-noise models: modeling topic and noise distributions in social media post collections. In: 2021 IEEE international conference on data mining (ICDM), pp. 71–80. IEEE (2021)
10. Devlin, J., Chang, M.W., Lee, K., Toutanova, K.: Bert: pre-training of deep bidirectional transformers for language understanding. In: Proceedings of the 2019 conference of the North American chapter of the association for computational linguistics: human language technologies, volume 1 (long and short papers), pp. 4171–4186 (2019)
11. Gao, Y., Sheng, T., Xiang, Y., Xiong, Y., Wang, H., Zhang, J.: Chat-rec: Towards interactive and explainable llms-augmented recommender system. arXiv preprint arXiv:2303.14524 (2023)
12. Geng, S., Liu, S., Fu, Z., Ge, Y., Zhang, Y.: Recommendation as language processing (RLP): a unified pretrain, personalized prompt & predict paradigm (p5). In: Proceedings of the 16th ACM Conference on Recommender Systems, pp. 299–315 (2022)
13. He, X., Liao, L., Zhang, H., Nie, L., Hu, X., Chua, T.S.: Neural collaborative filtering. In: Proceedings of the 26th International Conference on World Wide Web, pp. 173–182 (2017)
14. Hou, Y., et al..: Large language models are zero-shot rankers for recommender systems. In: European Conference on Information Retrieval, pp. 364–381. Springer (2024)
15. Hutto, C., Gilbert, E.: Vader: a parsimonious rule-based model for sentiment analysis of social media text. In: Proceedings of the International AAAI Conference on Web and Social Media, vol. 8, pp. 216–225 (2014)
16. Kang, W.C., et al.: Do LLMs understand user preferences? evaluating LLMs on user rating prediction. arXiv preprint arXiv:2305.06474 (2023)
17. Koren, Y.: Factorization meets the neighborhood: a multifaceted collaborative filtering model. In: Proceedings of the 14th ACM SIGKDD International Conference on Knowledge Discovery and Data Mining, pp. 426–434 (2008)
18. Koren, Y., Bell, R., Volinsky, C.: Matrix factorization techniques for recommender systems. Computer **42**(8), 30–37 (2009)
19. Liu, D., Li, J., Du, B., Chang, J., Gao, R.: DAML: dual attention mutual learning between ratings and reviews for item recommendation. In: Proceedings of the 25th ACM SIGKDD International Conference on Knowledge Discovery & Data Mining, pp. 344–352 (2019)
20. Liu, N., Zhao, J.: Recommendation system based on deep sentiment analysis and matrix factorization. IEEE Access **11**, 16994–17001 (2023)
21. Loshchilov, I.: Decoupled weight decay regularization. arXiv preprint arXiv:1711.05101 (2017)
22. Mikolov, T.: Efficient estimation of word representations in vector space. arXiv preprint arXiv:1301.3781 (2013)
23. Ni, J., Li, J., McAuley, J.: Justifying recommendations using distantly-labeled reviews and fine-grained aspects. In: Proceedings of the 2019 Conference On Empirical Methods in Natural Language Processing and the 9th International Joint Conference on Natural Language Processing (EMNLP-IJCNLP), pp. 188–197 (2019)

24. Okura, S., Tagami, Y., Ono, S., Tajima, A.: Embedding-based news recommendation for millions of users. In: Proceedings of the 23rd ACM SIGKDD International Conference on Knowledge Discovery and Data Mining, pp. 1933–1942 (2017)
25. Wahid, J.A., et al.: Topic2features: a novel framework to classify noisy and sparse textual data using lda topic distributions. PeerJ Comput. Sci. **7**, e677 (2021)
26. Wang, H., Hong, Z., Hong, M.: Research on product recommendation based on matrix factorization models fusing user reviews. Appl. Soft Comput. **123**, 108971 (2022)
27. Wang, Y., et al.: Recmind: Large language model powered agent for recommendation. arXiv preprint arXiv:2308.14296 (2023)
28. Xie, J., Qiu, Z.: The effect of imbalanced data sets on lda: a theoretical and empirical analysis. Pattern Recogn. **40**(2), 557–562 (2007)
29. Zhang, S., Wang, W., Ford, J., Makedon, F., Pearlman, J.: Using singular value decomposition approximation for collaborative filtering. In: Seventh IEEE International Conference on E-Commerce Technology (CEC'05), pp. 257–264. IEEE (2005)
30. Zhang, S., Yao, L., Sun, A., Tay, Y.: Deep learning based recommender system: a survey and new perspectives. ACM Comput. Surv. (CSUR) **52**(1), 1–38 (2019)
31. Zhao, Z., et al.: Recommender systems in the era of large language models (LLMs). IEEE Trans. Knowl. Data Eng. **36**(11), 6889–6907 (2024)
32. Zheng, L., Noroozi, V., Yu, P.S.: Joint deep modeling of users and items using reviews for recommendation. In: Proceedings of the tenth ACM International Conference on Web Search and Data Mining, pp. 425–434 (2017)

SHNet: Spectral Bias Guidance and Hierarchical Dependency Modeling Network for Camouflaged Object Detection

Anqi Liu, Qimin Cheng$^{(\boxtimes)}$, and Yingjie Du

School of Electronic Information and Communications, Huazhong University of
Science and Technology, Wuhan 430074, Hubei, China
{liuaq,chengqn,d202481225}@hust.edu.cn

Abstract. Vision Transformers have recently demonstrated strong
capabilities in modeling the global context for camouflaged object detection. However, existing transformer-based approaches still struggle in
complex scenarios involving small, multiple, and occluded objects. Their
manually designed attention mechanisms often fail to adapt to data-
specific characteristics, thereby limiting the model's ability to capture
long-range dependencies. Moreover, many of these methods are insufficient in capturing fine-grained local details. To address these limitations,
we present a novel framework named SHNet. Specifically, we propose
a spectral bias injection module (SBIM), which injects spectral deviation signals into the standard convolutional pathway to enhance the
detection of small camouflaged objects. Then, we design a frequency
attention module (FAM) based on the HiLo attention mechanism. By
jointly modeling hierarchical dependencies across global and local contexts it improves performance in scenes with multiple and occluded
objects. Furthermore, we design a plug-and-play interactive fusion module (IFM) that adaptively performs fine-grained feature selection and
aggregates complementary information across different levels. Extensive
experiments on four widely used datasets demonstrate the effectiveness
and efficiency of the proposed method.

Keywords: Camouflaged object detection · Spectral bias injection ·
Hierarchical dependency modeling · Interactive fusion

1 Introduction

Camouflaged object detection (COD) aims to segment objects that blend seamlessly into their surroundings, matching the background in color, texture, and
even shape. With the advancement of deep learning and the availability of large-
scale COD datasets, numerous CNN-based methods [1–5] have been proposed.
While these approaches outperform traditional techniques, they remain heavily
reliant on CNNs, which inherently lack a sufficiently large receptive field for

J. Lokoč et al. (Eds.): MMM 2026, LNCS 16412, pp. 537–551, 2026.
https://doi.org/10.1007/978-981-95-6950-2_38

capturing global context. As a result, CNN-based COD models often exhibit suboptimal performance when dealing with complex scenes.

Recently, several COD methods [6–9] have started leveraging Vision Transformers (ViTs) to tackle this challenge. Given that camouflaged objects are often highly integrated with their surroundings, it is crucial for the model to capture comprehensive global context in order to effectively distinguish them from the background.

Although transformer-based methods have demonstrated promising performance in capturing global features, many still struggle to effectively model local details. This limitation is evident in models such as FSPNet [7] and FPNet [6], as shown in the first row of Fig. 1, where small objects are often missed. Notably, most existing transformer-based COD approaches [6–9, 11–13] adopt Swin Transformer [14] or Pyramid Vision Transformer (PVT) [15] as their encoder backbones to mitigate computational costs. However, the manually designed attention mechanisms in these architectures fail to adapt to data-specific characteristics. This design constraint can impair the model's ability to capture long-range dependencies [16], which is crucial for detecting camouflaged objects, particularly in scenes involving occlusion or multiple objects, as illustrated in the second and third rows of Fig. 1.

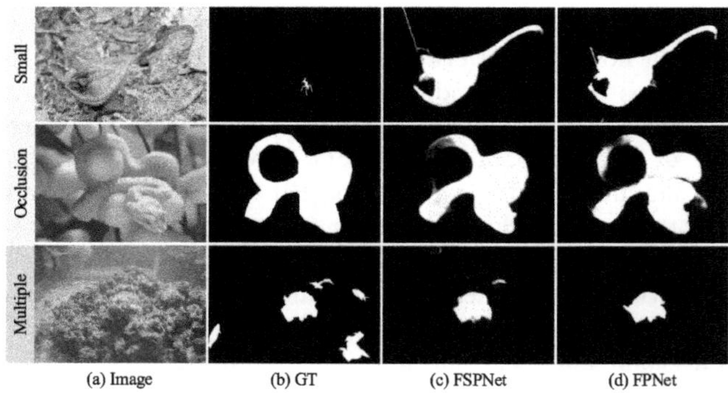

Fig. 1. Visual results of transformer-based COD methods [6, 7] in challenging scenarios, including small, multiple and occluded camouflaged objects.

To address the challenges of transformer-based approaches in complex camouflage scenarios, we present a frequency domain perception network named SHNet. Firstly, to improve the detection of small camouflaged objects, spectral bias injection module (SBIM) employs standard convolution to capture local details. However, relying solely on spatial-domain modeling is often inadequate, especially when objects are small and exhibit minimal visual contrast with their backgrounds. In such cases, spatial cues become ambiguous, and local textures can easily be overwhelmed by background clutter. To address this limitation, we propose a frequency-aware enhancement mechanism that explicitly models amplitude and phase responses in the frequency domain. This module extracts spectral deviation signals that reflect periodic patterns or edge-sparse regions, which are difficult to perceive in the spatial domain. These signals are then re-encoded as spatial biases and injected into the standard convolutional pathway, enabling structure-aware feature reinforcement and enhancing boundary sensitivity. This integration significantly improves the model's ability to distinguish small, subtly camouflaged objects from complex backgrounds.

Additionally, we introduce the HiLo attention mechanism [17] in the frequency attention module (FAM) that separately models hierarchical spatial dependencies in high- and low-frequency components. The high-frequency attention branch captures fine-grained local interactions to enhance structural detail and boundary localization, while the low-frequency attention branch models global dependencies to provide holistic semantic context. By integrating these complementary cues, the frequency-aware attention mechanism enables the model to preserve precise local features while reasoning over long-range relationships, thereby improving its robustness in scenarios involving multiple or occluded camouflaged objects.

Finally, we design an interactive fusion module (IFM), a plug-and-play component that can be seamlessly integrated into existing architectures. It adaptively performs fine-grained feature selection and aligns complementary feature representations across branches. It proves particularly effective in COD, where subtle visual cues must be preserved and multi-source information effectively integrated.

This paper's contributions are as follows:

- We present SHNet, a novel frequency-domain perception network tailored to address the limitations of transformer-based methods in complex camouflage scenarios involving small, multiple, and occluded objects.
- We propose a spectral bias injection module, which injects spectral deviation signals into standard convolutional pathway to enhance the detection of small camouflaged objects.
- We design a frequency attention module with the HiLo attention mechanism to improve robustness in scenarios involving multiple and occluded camouflaged objects.
- We propose a plug-and-play interactive fusion module that adaptively performs fine-grained feature selection and fusion of complementary features.
- Extensive experiments on four benchmark datasets demonstrate the effectiveness and efficiency of the proposed method.

2   Related Work

2.1   CNN-Based Camouflaged Object Detection

Recently, the public availability of datasets has led to significant advancements in the task of camouflaged object detection (COD) using CNN-based deep learning methods [2–5,18–20]. Some of these algorithms [19,20] focus on texture features to emphasize the subtle distinctions between objects and their environment. To obtain more precise boundaries and detailed structures, BSA-Net [18] and FEDER [2] incorporate boundary clues into a coarse feature map, thereby emphasizing the contours of targets. To better simulate predator behavior, SINet-V2 [3] first locates and then distinctly identifies concealed objects in a cascaded manner. Inspired by human attention, SegMaR [4] utilizes a multi-stage detection approach that integrates segmentation, magnification, and reiteration. Several methods [2,21,22] aim to go beyond the spatial domain and enhance discriminative properties detection in the frequency domain. Despite their promising performance, CNN-based models inherently struggle to capture global contextual relationships due to their limited receptive fields. This limitation poses a significant challenge for accurately detecting objects in complex scenes that require a holistic understanding of the image.

2.2 Vision Transformer

In contrast to CNN-based approaches, transformer-based models have superior capability in capturing global contextual information with their expanded receptive fields. However, the dense attention mechanisms employed by these models lead to increased memory usage and computational cost. In response to these challenges, various improved versions have emerged, such as Swin Transformer [14], and Pyramid Vision Transformer (PVT) [15]. These models utilize carefully designed attention patterns to reduce computational complexity. For COD tasks, most transformer-based approaches [6–13] employ Swin Transformer [14] or PVT [15] as encoders to optimize efficiency. However, recent studies [16] suggest that the hand-crafted attention patterns employed in models such as Swin Transformer and PVT are data-agnostic, limiting their ability to effectively capture long-range dependencies. Additionally, these methods face challenges in leveraging locality modeling to capture small-scale details effectively.

3 Methodology

3.1 Network Overview

Above all, we adopt the Pyramid Vision Transformer (PVT-V2-B3) [15] as the backbone for feature encoding. As shown in Fig. 2, the encoding backbone consists of four stages. The features from stages 2 to 4 are fed into SBIM and FAM for feature refinement, followed by dynamic integration via IDFM. The fused representation is then decoded by the Neighbor Connection Decoder (NCD) [3] to produce an initial detection map S_1. Finally, SBIM is applied to enhance low-level features from the first stage, which are combined with the NCD output to generate the refined prediction S_2.

3.2 Spectral Bias Injection Module (SBIM)

We leverage both amplitude and phase information in the frequency domain to enhance the convolutional pathway's ability to detect small camouflaged objects.

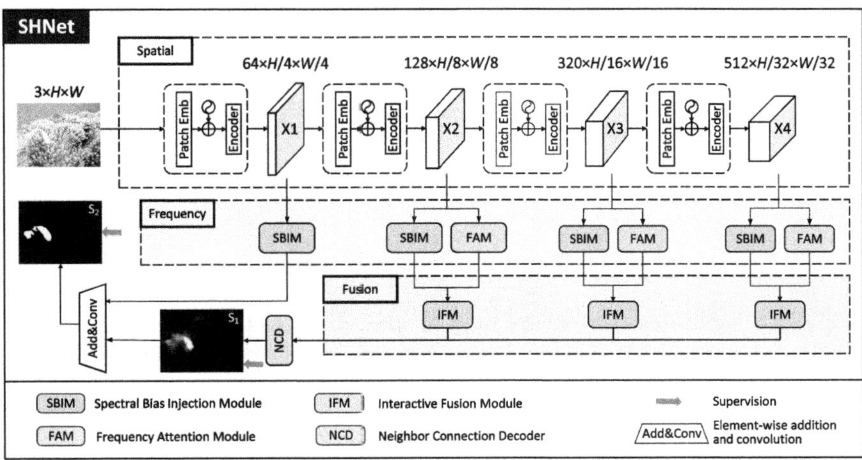

Fig. 2. Overall architecture of our SHNet. It consists of four key components: a ViT-based encoder, a spectral bias injection module (SBIM), a frequency attention module (FAM), and an interactive fusion module (IFM).

Amplitude reflects global repetitive patterns and intensity variations, which complement the convolutional kernel's local receptive field by introducing broader semantic context. Phase preserves precise spatial structures and boundary cues that are often lost in deep convolutional layers.

Figure 3 shows the flowchart of the SBIM. The 3×3 convolution operation is used to separate the inputs into spectral biases and spatial biases components along the channel dimension, which are defined as $X^e \in \mathrm{R}^{H \times W \times \alpha_{in}}$ and $X^a \in \mathrm{R}^{H \times W \times (1-\alpha_{in})}$, respectively. Here, the parameter $\alpha_{in} \in [0, 1]$ indicates the proportion of feature channels designated for the spectral biases component. Following this, X_i^e and X_i^a are sent through two interconnected paths: a spatial biases path that performs ordinary 3×3 convolution on X_i^a and a spectral biases path that conducts frequency domain convolution on X_i^e. The procedure for frequency domain convolution can be summarized as follows:

1) We perform Fast Fourier Transform (FFT) on the input X_i^e, which converts the spatial representation into its frequency components, yielding real part y_r and imaginary part y_i:

$$y_r, y_i = FFT(X_i^e). \tag{1}$$

2) We combine the real and imaginary parts and apply a convolution operation in the frequency domain:

$$y = ReLU\left(BN\left(Conv\left(Concat([y_r, y_i])\right)\right)\right), \tag{2}$$

where y represents the feature map that has been updated in the frequency domain. $Conv$ indicates the 1×1 convolution operation, while $Concat$ refers to the concatenation operation performed along the channel dimension.

3) The resulting spectral data is then converted back to the spatial domain using the inverse Fast Fourier Transform (iFFT):

$$z \ = \ iFFT(y).\tag{3}$$

Finally, we integrate the features from both paths to generate the final output of SBIM:

$$F^i_{SBIM} = ReLU(Concat(F^i_{spatial}, F^i_{spectral})), \ i = 1, 2, 3, 4\tag{4}$$

where $F^i_{spatial}$ denotes the feature map of spatial biases path and $F^i_{spectral}$ represents the feature map of spectral biases path. After the concatenation operation, we can get the output result $F^i_{SBIM}(i \in \{1, 2, 3, 4\})$.

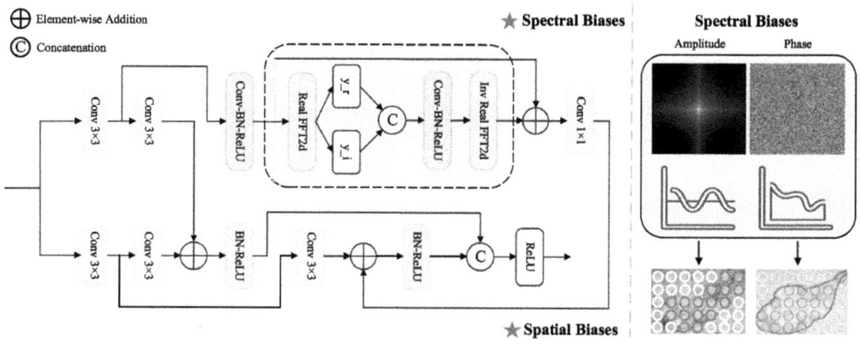

Fig. 3. Details of the spectral bias injection module (SBIM).

3.3 Frequency Attention Module (FAM)

We introduce the HiLo attention mechanism [17] in FAM, which decomposes the features into high-frequency and low-frequency. Given that high- and low-frequency components contribute differently to the encoding of image patterns, we employ local self-attention for high-frequency interactions and global attention for low-frequency interactions. This design enables the model to preserve precise local features while reasoning over long-range relationships.

As shown in Fig. 4 (a), for high-level feature maps X_i ($i \in \{2, 3, 4\}$), two branches are employed to separately capture the high frequency and low frequency components of the attention layer. The high frequency components describe the local details of the image, allowing the high frequency branch to extract this information using local window self-attention (2×2 window). In contrast, the low frequency components correspond to the global structures, so the low frequency branch performs global attention on low frequency components. Specifically, low frequency signal of the input X_i is obtained by applying average pooling operation in each local window. Then, the pooled feature map is mapped into keys $K \in \mathrm{R}^{N/s^2 \times D_h}$ and values $V \in \mathrm{R}^{N/s^2 \times D_h}$ by linear transformation, where s is the window size. The query Q of low frequency feature comes from the original input feature map X_i. In the above process, N_h attention heads are separated into two groups with a split ratio α, where αN_h heads are allocated for low frequency attention, and $(1 - \alpha)N_h$ heads are used for high frequency attention. The allocation ratio is set to 0.5 in this work.

Considering that both the local characteristics of high frequency and the global characteristics of low frequency are important for the localization of camouflaged objects, we concatenate the refined high- and low-frequency features and feed the resulting output into subsequent modules. This process can be formulated as:

$$F^i_{FAM} = Concat(HiAtt(X_i), LoAtt(X_i)), \quad i = 2, 3, 4 \tag{5}$$

where $LoAtt(\cdot)$ denotes the low frequency attention branch and $HiAtt(\cdot)$ denotes the high frequency attention branch. Then, we can get the output result $F^i_{FAM}(i \in \{2, 3, 4\})$

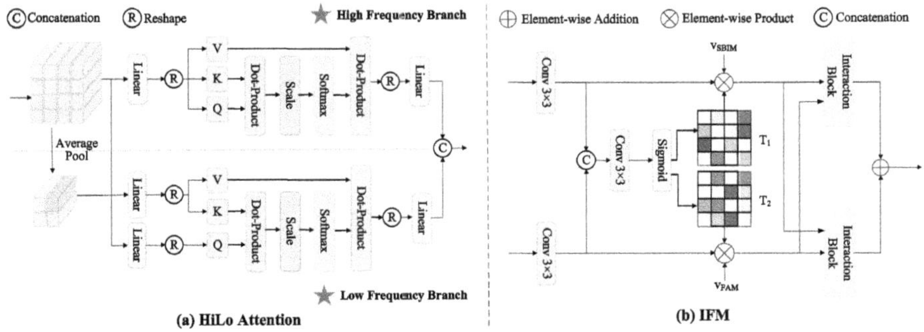

Fig. 4. (a) Details of the HiLo attention. (b) Details of the interactive fusion module (IFM).

3.4   Interactive Fusion Module (IFM)

The detailed structures of interactive fusion module (IFM) are illustrated in Fig. 4 (b). We first dynamically adjust the weights of the outputs of SBIM and FAM according to their contribution to recognizing camouflaged objects. Then the interaction blocks enable the adjusted features to communicate and exchange information with each other by cross-attention.

Specifically, we concatenate F^i_{SBIM} and F^i_{FAM}, then feed the features into a 3×3 convolutional layer followed by sigmoid operation. By doing this, we can obtain the corresponding feature selection matrix T_1 and T_2. Next, the input feature map is multiplied by the feature selection matrix and a learnable tensor $v \in \mathrm{R}^{1 \times C}$ for channel alignment. This process can be expressed as:

$$X^i_{SBIM2s} = T_1 \, F^i_{SBIM} \otimes v^i_{SBIM}, \tag{6}$$

$$X^i_{FAM2s} = T_2 F^i_{FAM} \otimes v^i_{FAM}. \tag{7}$$

Subsequently, X^i_{SBIM2s} and X^i_{FAM2s} are fed into interaction blocks to enhance the exchange of information between different feature maps. To be specific, the interaction block consists of two inputs: source input F_s and guidance input F_g. We utilize the source input F_s to obtain query Q and employ the guidance input F_g to generate key K and value V through linear transformation. Then, we perform cross-attention between the source and guidance as follows:

$$Att(K, Q, V) = Softmax\left(\frac{QK^T}{\sqrt{d}}\right)V, \tag{8}$$

$$F_{Fuse} = Conv(Att(K, Q, V)) + F_s, \tag{9}$$

where d is the hyperparameter. To model the incorporation between X^i_{SBIM2s} and X^i_{FAM2s}, we designate X^i_{SBIM2s} as the source and X^i_{FAM2s} as the guidance for one another:

$$X^i_{SBIMAtt} = F_{IB}(X^i_{SBIM2s}, X^i_{FAM2s}), \tag{10}$$

$$X^i_{FAMAtt} = F_{IB}(X^i_{FAM2s}, X^i_{SBIM2s}), \tag{11}$$

where $F_{IB}(\cdot, \cdot)$ denotes the function of the interaction block, with the two parameters representing the source and guidance, respectively. Finally, we combine the output of the two interaction blocks to obtain the final result of IDFM:

$$X^i_{fuse} = X^i_{SBIMAtt} \oplus X^i_{FAMAtt}, \quad i = 2, 3, 4 \tag{12}$$

where X^i_{fuse} is the final fusion result and $\oplus$ denotes the element-wise addition.

3.5   Decoding and Refinement

Following the above process, we employ the Neighbor Connection Decoder (NCD) [3] to decode the fused features and produce an initial coarse COD map, denoted as S_1. Notably, we incorporate information from the first stage to retain high-resolution texture details, thereby mitigating detail loss that often leads to blurred edges and boundaries. Specifically, we use SBIM to refine the first-level feature map X_1 and combine it with the output of NCD (f_{NCD}) to obtain the final COD map S_2:

$$S_2 = Bconv\big(SBIM(X_1) + Resize(f_{NCD})\big), \tag{13}$$

where $SBIM$ is the spectral bias injection module and $Bconv$ represents the 3×3 convolutional layer.

3.6   Loss Function

Following [3], we utilize the weighted binary cross-entropy loss ($\mathcal{L}^{\omega}_{BCE}$) and the weighted intersection-over-union loss ($\mathcal{L}^{\omega}_{\text{IoU}}$) to supervise segmentation on both the coarse COD map S_1 and the final COD map S_2. This is expressed as:

$$\mathcal{L}_{\text{total}} = \mathcal{L}(\mathcal{S}_1, \mathcal{G}) + \mathcal{L}(\mathcal{S}_2, \mathcal{G}), \tag{14}$$

where $\mathcal{L} = \mathcal{L}^{\omega}_{\text{IoU}} + \mathcal{L}^{\omega}_{\text{BCE}}$. $\mathcal{L}(\mathcal{S}_1, \mathcal{G})$ represents the loss computed between the ground truth $\mathcal{G}$ and the predicted coarse COD map S_1, while $\mathcal{L}(\mathcal{S}_2, \mathcal{G})$ corresponds to the loss between the ground truth $\mathcal{G}$ and the final COD map S_2.

4   Experiment

4.1   Datasets

We evaluate the effectiveness of our method on four widely used COD datasets: COD10K [3], NC4K [5], CAMO [23], and CHAMELEON [24]. Following [3], our training set combines 3,040 images from COD10K and 1,000 images from CAMO. COD10K is a large-scale and diverse benchmark covering 69 categories. NC4K includes 4,121 images spanning natural and synthetic scenes. CAMO focuses on highly concealed objects in natural environments such as forests and underwater scenes. CHAMELEON comprises 76 natural images that primarily focus on animals concealed within complex background.

4.2   Evaluation Metrics

We choose four commonly-used evaluation metrics: MAE provides a straightforward assessment of accuracy in terms of absolute difference between predicted maps and groundtruths. F^{ω}_{β} [25] serves as a crucial evaluation metric that balances precision and recall, providing a comprehensive assessment particularly in imbalanced classification scenarios. E_{ϕ} [26] further refines performance assessment by considering both the local pixel values and structural similarity. S_{α} [27] focuses on the structural consistency of the detected objects in comparison to ground truth.

4.3   Implementation Details

The proposed method is implemented in PyTorch and trained using an NVIDIA 4090 GPU with 24 GB of memory. The Adam optimizer is adopted for parameter updates, with an initial learning rate of 5e-5 that is reduced by a factor of 10 every 50 epochs. All input images are resized to 512×512 pixels for both training and inference. The model is trained for 300 epochs with a batch size of 22. To improve generalization, various data augmentation techniques are applied, including random flipping, random cropping, and other common strategies.

Table 1. Quantitative comparison with 14 SOTA methods on four benchmark datasets. Notes $\uparrow$ / $\downarrow$ denote the larger/smaller is better, respectively. "–" is not available. The best and second best are **bolded** and <u>underlined</u> for highlighting, respectively.

Method	Backbone	CHAMELEON(76)				CAMO-Test(250)				COD10K-Test(2026)				NC4K(4121)			
		$S_\alpha \uparrow$	$E_\phi \uparrow$	$F_\beta^\omega \uparrow$	$M \downarrow$	$S_\alpha \uparrow$	$E_\phi \uparrow$	$F_\beta^\omega \uparrow$	$M \downarrow$	$S_\alpha \uparrow$	$E_\phi \uparrow$	$F_\beta^\omega \uparrow$	$M \downarrow$	$S_\alpha \uparrow$	$E_\phi \uparrow$	$F_\beta^\omega \uparrow$	$M \downarrow$
SINet'20 [28]	ResNet50	0.869	0.891	0.740	0.044	0.751	0.771	0.606	0.100	0.771	0.806	0.551	0.051	0.808	0.871	0.723	0.058
SLSR'21 [5]	ResNet50	0.890	0.935	0.822	0.030	0.787	0.838	0.696	0.080	0.804	0.880	0.673	0.037	0.840	0.895	0.766	0.048
PFNet'21 [29]	ResNet50	0.882	0.931	0.810	0.033	0.782	0.842	0.695	0.085	0.800	0.877	0.660	0.040	0.829	0.888	0.745	0.053
ZoomNet'22 [30]	ResNet50	0.875	0.911	0.764	0.039	0.820	0.878	0.752	0.066	0.838	0.888	0.729	0.029	0.853	0.896	0.784	0.043
BGNet'22 [1]	Res2Net50	0.901	0.943	0.850	0.027	0.812	0.870	0.749	0.073	0.831	0.901	0.722	0.033	0.851	0.907	0.788	0.044
SINet-V2'22 [3]	Res2Net50	0.888	0.942	0.816	0.030	0.820	0.882	0.743	0.070	0.815	0.887	0.680	0.037	0.847	0.903	0.770	0.048
FEDER'23 [2]	Res2Net50	0.887	0.946	0.834	0.030	0.802	0.867	0.738	0.071	0.822	0.900	0.716	0.032	0.847	0.907	0.789	0.044
DaCOD'23 [11]	SwinT	–	–	–	–	0.855	0.911	0.796	0.051	0.840	0.908	0.729	0.028	0.874	0.923	0.814	0.035
FPNet'23 [6]	PVT	0.914	<u>0.961</u>	0.856	0.022	0.852	0.905	0.806	0.056	0.850	0.913	0.748	0.029	–	–	–	–
FSPNet'23 [7]	ViT	0.908	0.943	0.851	0.023	0.856	0.899	0.799	0.050	0.851	0.895	0.735	0.026	0.879	0.915	0.816	0.035
DAS-COD'24 [13]	SwinT	–	–	–	–	0.876	<u>0.935</u>	<u>0.832</u>	0.045	0.857	0.914	0.762	0.023	0.883	0.936	0.832	0.032
SRDNet'24 [8]	PVTv2	0.914	0.950	0.868	0.023	0.872	0.924	0.826	0.049	<u>0.871</u>	0.924	0.785	0.023	0.889	0.934	0.842	0.032
MAMIFNet'25 [9]	PVTv2	0.914	0.960	0.875	0.021	0.872	0.929	0.824	0.045	0.869	0.933	0.785	0.023	<u>0.890</u>	<u>0.937</u>	<u>0.846</u>	<u>0.031</u>
BDCL-Net'25 [10]	SwinT	<u>0.915</u>	0.953	<u>0.877</u>	**0.019**	<u>0.881</u>	0.929	**0.845**	**0.039**	0.869	<u>0.935</u>	<u>0.790</u>	<u>0.022</u>	0.888	0.932	0.844	0.032
Ours	PVTv2	**0.922**	**0.968**	**0.885**	<u>0.020</u>	**0.882**	**0.945**	**0.845**	<u>0.043</u>	**0.887**	**0.946**	**0.818**	**0.020**	**0.900**	**0.945**	**0.862**	**0.029**

4.4   Comparison with the State-of-the-Arts

1) Quantitative Evaluation: Table 1 presents the quantitative results of various COD methods across four benchmark datasets. Notably, our approach consistently outperforms the 14 state-of-the-art (SOTA) methods on the majority of evaluation metrics for each dataset. On the large-scale NC4K dataset, SHNet achieves performance gains of 2.13% on F_β^ω, along with a 9.37% reduction on MAE compared to the second-best method, BDCL-Net [10]. Moreover, compared to MAMIFNet [9], our model reduces the MAE by 13.04% and 6.45% on COD10K and NC4K, respectively. To further evaluate the effectiveness of our approach, we plot the F-measure curves of our method alongside other SOTAs. As illustrated in Fig. 5, our method (red curves) consistently surpasses all competing methods, demonstrating its superior ability to balance precision and recall.

2) Qualitative Evaluation: Figure 6 presents qualitative comparisons with other SOTA methods. For small-scale objects (Rows 1 and 2), our predictions effectively suppress background noise and yield significantly more accurate results with clearer object boundaries. In complex scenarios involving multiple camouflaged objects or occlusions (Rows 3–6), our method consistently identifies all target regions with higher precision and completeness, while avoiding the over-segmentation or missed detections observed in competing approaches.

3) Efficiency Analysis: As shown in Table 2, our method improves E_ϕ and F_β^ω by 2.28% and 4.20%, respectively, over SRDNet, while reducing the MAE by 13.04%. Moreover, our model significantly reduces the parameter count by 59.67% compared to SRDNet. Figure 7 further illustrates that our method

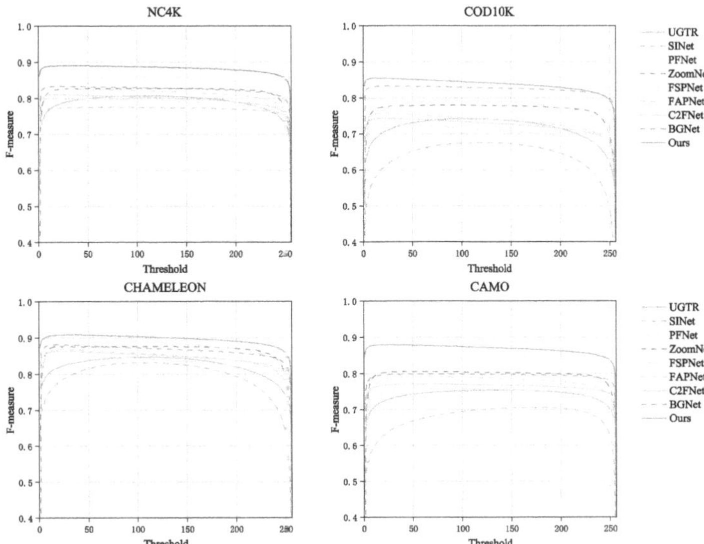

Fig. 5. F-measure curves of our method and the other SOTA algorithms on four benchmarks. The red curve denotes our proposed method. (Color figure online)

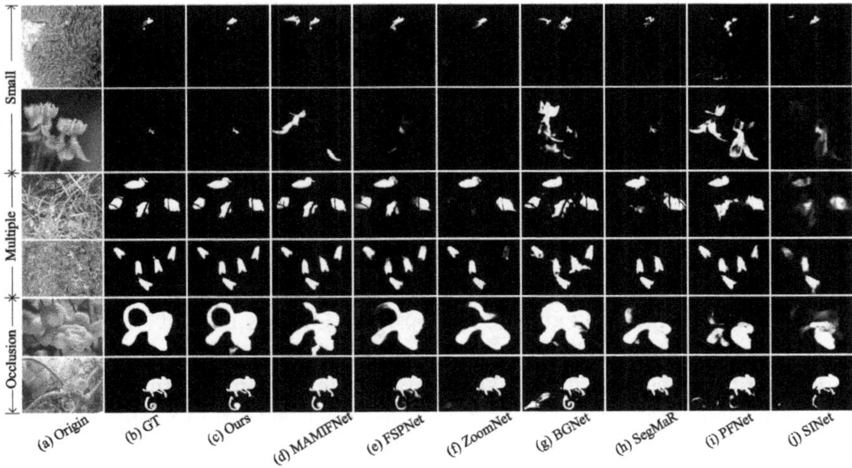

Fig. 6. Visual comparison in challenging situations involving large, small, multiple and occluded objects with some typical SOTA models. For better clarity, please zoom in on the figure.

achieves the best overall performance, attaining the highest F-measure with a relatively moderate number of parameters. Notably, it also presents the largest bubble in the figure, indicating the highest E-measure among all compared methods.

Table 2. Parameter and performance comparison of our method with 7 representative state-of-the-art methods on COD10K.

	Ours	SINet-V2 [3]	ZoomNet [30]	PFNet [29]	SINet [28]	SLSR [5]	SRDNet [8]	FSPNet [7]
#Param(M)	48.48	26.98	32.38	46.50	48.95	57.90	120.22	261.17
S_α ↑	0.887	0.815	0.838	0.800	0.771	0.804	0.871	0.851
E_ϕ ↑	0.946	0.887	0.888	0.877	0.806	0.880	0.924	0.895
F_β^ω ↑	0.818	0.680	0.729	0.660	0.551	0.673	0.785	0.735
M ↓	0.020	0.037	0.029	0.040	0.051	0.037	0.023	0.026

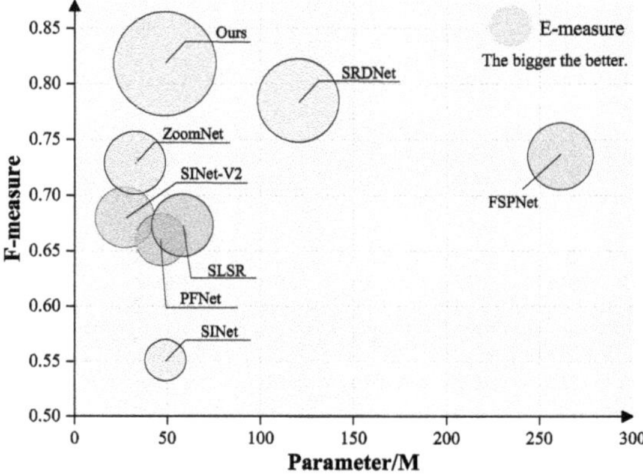

Fig. 7. Performance-Params comparisons of our method with 7 representative state-of-the-art methods on COD10K. The area of each circle represents the E-measure score, with larger circles indicating higher values.

4.5 Ablation Analysis

To evaluate the individual contributions of SBIM, FAM, and IDFM in our framework, we conduct ablation experiments on the COD10K and NC4K datasets. As shown in Table 3, the inclusion of these components progressively enhances the overall performance. The progressive improvements confirm that each module plays a complementary role in boosting the overall detection performance.

Table 3. Quantitative results of ablation studies on COD10K and NC4K. "B" denotes the backbone. The best are **bolded** for highlighting.

No.	B	FAM	SBIM	IDFM	COD10K-Test(2026)				NC4K(4121)			
					S_α ↑	E_ϕ ↑	F_β^ω ↑	M ↓	S_α ↑	E_ϕ ↑	F_β^ω ↑	M ↓
(a)	✓				0.858	0.919	0.754	0.028	0.884	0.927	0.819	0.037
(b)	✓	✓			0.874	0.935	0.793	0.023	0.892	0.939	0.847	0.031
(c)	✓	✓	✓		0.884	0.943	0.815	0.021	0.898	0.941	0.859	0.030
(d)	✓	✓	✓	✓	**0.887**	**0.946**	**0.818**	**0.020**	**0.900**	**0.945**	**0.862**	**0.029**

5   Conclusion

In this paper, we proposed SHNet, a novel frequency-aware framework for camouflaged object detection that addresses the limitations of existing transformer-based methods in complex scenarios. By injecting spectral deviation signals into the convolutional stream, SHNet effectively enhances the detection of small and low-contrast camouflaged objects. The integration of the HiLo attention mechanism further strengthens the model's robustness by hierarchically modeling global and local dependencies, particularly in the presence of multiple and occluded targets. Additionally, our plug-and-play interactive fusion module enables adaptive integration of complementary cues. Extensive experimental results on four benchmark datasets validate the superiority of our approach in terms of both detection performance and computational efficiency.

Acknowledgments. This work was supported by the National Natural Science Foundation of China under Grants (No.42271352).

References

1. Sun, Y., Wang, S., Chen, C., Xiang, T.Z.: Boundary-guided camouflaged object detection. arXiv preprint arXiv:2207.00794 (2022)
2. He, C., et al.: Camouflaged object detection with feature decomposition and edge reconstruction. In: Proceedings of the IEEE/CVF Conference on Computer Vision and Pattern Recognition, pp. 22046–22055 (2023)
3. Fan, D.P., Ji, G.P., Cheng, M.M., Shao, L.: Concealed object detection. IEEE Trans. Pattern Anal. Mach. Intell. **44**(10), 6024–6042 (2021)
4. Jia, Q., Yao, S., Liu, Y., Fan, X., Liu, R., Luo, Z.: Segment, magnify and reiterate: detecting camouflaged objects the hard way. In: Proceedings of the IEEE/CVF Conference on Computer Vision and Pattern Recognition, pp. 4713–4722 (2022)
5. Lv, Y., et al.: Simultaneously localize, segment and rank the camouflaged objects. In: Proceedings of the IEEE/CVF Conference on Computer Vision and Pattern Recognition, pp. 11591–11601 (2021)
6. Cong, R., Sun, M., Zhang, S., Zhou, X., Zhang, W., Zhao, Y.: Frequency perception network for camouflaged object detection. In: Proceedings of the 31st ACM International Conference on Multimedia, pp. 1179–1189 (2023)
7. Huang, Z., et al.: Feature shrinkage pyramid for camouflaged object detection with transformers. In: Proceedings of the IEEE/CVF Conference on Computer Vision and Pattern Recognition, pp. 5557–5566 (2023)
8. Guan, J., Fang, X., Zhu, T., Qian, W.: SDRNet: camouflaged object detection with independent reconstruction of structure and detail. Knowl.-Based Syst. **299**, 112051 (2024)
9. Wang, T., et al.: Multidimensional fusion of frequency and spatial domain information for enhanced camouflaged object detection. Inf. Fusion **117**, 102871 (2025)
10. Zhao, R., Li, Y., Zhang, Q., Zhao, X.: Bilateral decoupling complementarity learning network for camouflaged object detection. Knowl.-Based Syst. **314**, 113158 (2025)

11. Wang, Q., Yang, J., Yu, X., Wang, F., Chen, P., Zheng, F.: Depth-aided camouflaged object detection. In: Proceedings of the 31st ACM International Conference on Multimedia, pp. 3297–3306 (2023)

12. Song, Z., Kang, X., Wei, X., Liu, H., Dian, R., Li, S.: FSNet: focus scanning network for camouflaged object detection. IEEE Trans. Image Process. **32**, 2267–2278 (2023)

13. Lu, C., Tan, M., Gao, Z., Mao, X., Xia, Z.: DAS-COD: depth-aware camouflaged object detection via swin transformer. In: 2024 IEEE International Conference on Systems, Man, and Cybernetics (SMC), pp. 4626–4631. IEEE (2024)

14. Liu, Z., et al.: Swin transformer: hierarchical vision transformer using shifted windows. In: Proceedings of the IEEE/CVF International Conference on Computer Vision, pp. 10012–10022 (2021)

15. Wang, W., et al.: Pyramid vision transformer: a versatile backbone for dense prediction without convolutions. In: Proceedings of the IEEE/CVF International Conference on Computer Vision, pp. 568–578 (2021)

16. Xia, Z., Pan, X., Song, S., Li, L.E., Huang, G.: Vision transformer with deformable attention. In: Proceedings of the IEEE/CVF Conference on Computer Vision and Pattern Recognition, pp. 4794–4803 (2022)

17. Pan, Z., Cai, J., Zhuang, B.: Fast vision transformers with HiLO attention. Adv. Neural. Inf. Process. Syst. **35**, 14541–14554 (2022)

18. Zhu, H., et al.: I can find you! Boundary-guided separated attention network for camouflaged object detection. In: Proceedings of the AAAI Conference on Artificial Intelligence. vol. 36, pp. 3608–3616 (2022)

19. Ren, J., et al.: Deep texture-aware features for camouflaged object detection. IEEE Trans. Circuits Syst. Video Technol. **33**(3), 1157–1167 (2021)

20. Zhu, J., Zhang, X., Zhang, S., Liu, J.: Inferring camouflaged objects by texture-aware interactive guidance network. In: Proceedings of the AAAI Conference on Artificial Intelligence. vol. 35, pp. 3599–3607 (2021)

21. Zhong, Y., Li, B., Tang, L., Kuang, S., Wu, S., Ding, S.: Detecting camouflaged object in frequency domain. In: Proceedings of the IEEE/CVF Conference on Computer Vision and Pattern Recognition, pp. 4504–4513 (2022)

22. Sun, Y., Xu, C., Yang, J., Xuan, H., Luo, L.: Frequency-spatial entanglement learning for camouflaged object detection. In: European Conference on Computer Vision, pp. 343–360. Springer (2024)

23. Le, T.N., Nguyen, T.V., Nie, Z., Tran, M.T., Sugimoto, A.: Anabranch network for camouflaged object segmentation. Comput. Vis. Image Underst. **184**, 45–56 (2019)

24. Skurowski, P., Abdulameer, H., Błaszczyk, J., Depta, T., Kornacki, A., Kozieł, P.: Animal camouflage analysis: Chameleon database. Unpublished manuscript **2**(6), 7 (2018)

25. Margolin, R., Zelnik-Manor, L., Tal, A.: How to evaluate foreground maps? In: Proceedings of the IEEE Conference on Computer Vision and Pattern Recognition, pp. 248–255 (2014)

26. Fan, D.P., Gong, C., Cao, Y., Ren, B., Cheng, M.M., Borji, A.: Enhanced-alignment measure for binary foreground map evaluation. arXiv preprint arXiv:1805.10421 (2018)

27. Fan, D.P., Cheng, M.M., Liu, Y., Li, T., Borji, A.: Structure-measure: a new way to evaluate foreground maps. In: Proceedings of the IEEE International Conference on Computer Vision, pp. 4548–4557 (2017)

28. Fan, D.P., Ji, G.P., Sun, G., Cheng, M.M., Shen, J., Shao, L.: Camouflaged object detection. In: Proceedings of the IEEE/CVF Conference on Computer Vision and Pattern Recognition, pp. 2777–2787 (2020)
29. Mei, H., Ji, G.P., Wei, Z., Yang, X., Wei, X., Fan, D.P.: Camouflaged object segmentation with distraction mining. In: Proceedings of the IEEE/CVF Conference on Computer Vision and Pattern Recognition, pp. 8772–8781 (2021)
30. Pang, Y., Zhao, X., Xiang, T.Z., Zhang, L., Lu, H.: Zoom in and out: a mixed-scale triplet network for camouflaged object detection. In: Proceedings of the IEEE/CVF Conference on Computer Vision and Pattern Recognition, pp. 2160–2170 (2022)

Multimodal Video Summarization with Mamba and Bayesian Approach

Adane Nega Tarekegn$^{(\boxtimes)}$, Fazle Rabbi, Andreas Lothe Opdahl, and Bjørnar Tessem

MediaFutures, Department of Information Science and Media Studies, University of Bergen, Bergen, Norway
{adane.tarekegn,fazle.rabbi,andreas.opdahl,bjornar.tessem}@uib.no

Abstract. The immense volume of user-generated video content demands scalable summarization methods that do not require costly human annotations. Unsupervised approaches provide this flexibility but still face key limitations: reliance on unimodal inputs, weak temporal modeling, and deterministic outputs that fail to capture uncertainty. To overcome these limitations, we propose MBSum, a novel unsupervised multimodal video summarization framework that leverages both visual and textual modalities without requiring labeled data. MBSum combines a Mamba-based state space backbone for efficient long-range temporal modeling with Bayesian variational decoder for a robust, uncertainty-aware summary generation. In addition, we propose a text-guided contrastive loss to align visual and textual features, enhancing cross-modal coherence. MBSum supports both unimodal and multimodal inputs, which makes it adaptable to diverse real-world scenarios. Extensive experiments on five benchmarks (TVSum, SumMe, Soccer, MLB, and LoL) demonstrate the effectiveness of MBSum, achieving state-of-the-art performances on all datasets.

Keywords: Video Summarization · Multimodal · Unsupervised Learning · Mamba · State Space Model · Bayesian Inference · Uncertainty

1 Introduction

The rapid proliferation of multimedia data across domains such as surveillance, and social media has created a growing need for scalable content analysis and understanding [1]. Among all multimedia formats, video represents the most complex and information-rich, integrating visual, auditory, and textual information into a continuous, high-dimensional data stream. The multimodal nature makes video highly expressive, but also one of the most challenging formats to effectively process, analyze, manage and summarize. Users frequently struggle to browse, retrieve, or extract meaningful insights from vast, unstructured video archives. Addressing this issue requires an automated tool capable of indexing,

J. Lokoč et al. (Eds.): MMM 2026, LNCS 16412, pp. 552–566, 2026.
https://doi.org/10.1007/978-981-95-6950-2_39

summarizing, and analyzing video content to enable efficient search and retrieval. In this context, video summarization has become a key research topic [4,5] to automatically condense lengthy videos into concise summaries.

Traditional video summarization methods rely on supervised learning [1,5], where models are trained using human-annotated keyframes or summary labels. However, this paradigm has certain limitations. Annotation is costly, time-consuming, and inherently subjective, especially for long videos, which leads to inconsistencies in labels and limits generalization. As a result, unsupervised video summarization has gained increasing attention for its scalability and flexibility. Recent unsupervised approaches often adopt generative adversarial networks (GANs) [19,22,23] to learn frame importance without explicit supervision. Despite their promise, most of these approaches typically operate in an unimodal setting, relying solely on visual cues while neglecting semantic information from other modalities such as text. Temporal modeling in existing methods is also limited. For instance, recurrent architectures such as LSTMs struggle to capture long-range dependencies, while Transformer-based attention models, although expressive, suffer from quadratic complexity. Furthermore, most prior work produces deterministic summaries, without considering the inherent uncertainty and diversity in meaningful summaries, which makes models less robust and more prone to overfitting.

To address these challenges, we propose MBSum, a novel unsupervised multimodal video summarization framework that leverages multimodal input, hybrid temporal modeling, and probabilistic summary generation. Specifically, we integrate state space models (SSMs) [24] with multi-head self-attention (MHSA) for efficient and scalable temporal reasoning and introduce a Bayesian decoder for uncertainty-aware summary generation. Our insight is that recent SSM architectures, particularly Mamba [25], offer a compelling trade-off between modeling capacity and computational efficiency. Mamba's selective recurrent mechanism enables expressive, scalable modeling of long-range dependencies, making it well-suited for multi-modal summarization that fuses visual and textual cues [26,27]. Additionally, MBSum employs Bayesian inference to guide summary generation by modeling uncertainty in frame selection through a learned probability distribution. Our goal is to allow the model to handle ambiguous or noisy inputs more effectively, reduce overfitting, and improve generalization. The proposed framework reduces the risk of training instability, addresses the limitations of prior research and achieves superior performance compared to existing state-of-the-art (SOTA) methods. The main contributions of this study include:

- We propose MBSum, a novel unsupervised multimodal video summarization framework that integrates cross-modal semantics, efficient long-range temporal modeling, and uncertainty-aware summary generation. MBSum removes adversarial training, improving stability and reducing training complexity.
- We present a text-guided contrastive loss that combines inter-modal alignment with intra-modal discrimination, enabling the model to learn semantically aligned and meaningful representations for video and text.

- Unlike existing methods that use deterministic models, MBSum uses Bayesian model to better capture data distribution and enhance generalization.
- We explore the use of Mamba backbone for efficient long-range temporal modeling, with MHSA for frame-level refinement and importance estimation.

2   Related Work

State Space Models. Modeling long-range dependencies is fundamental to understanding temporal structures in video. While recurrent neural networks such as LSTMs have been widely adopted, they suffer from limited memory and slow sequential processing. Transformers [2] offer an improved modeling capacity but scale poorly with sequence length due to their quadratic complexity. Recently, state space models (SSMs) [24] have emerged as a promising alternative for modeling long-range dependencies in sequential data. These models show promise in optimizing both performance and computational efficiency across image and text domains [26,27]. Mamba [26] is a recent state space model that builds on the Structured State Space framework [24] to efficiently capture long-range dependencies with linear complexity. It achieves a balance between performance and scalability, positioning itself as a strong competitor to Transformer and CNN-based architectures in sequential modeling tasks. Compared to transformers based on quadratic-complexity attention, Mamba excels at processing long sequences with linear complexity. In the vision domain, SSMs have shown promise, with Mamba [26] outperforming Transformers in efficiency and accuracy across image classification, object detection, and segmentation [24]. In this work, we make an original attempt to introduce Mamba into the field of unsupervised video summarization.

Bayesian Methods. Bayesian approaches have attracted growing interest in the deep learning community due to their potential to enhance reliability, interpretability, and generalization. They are increasingly used to address fundamental limitations of conventional neural networks, such as lack of transparency [41], inability to provide calibrated confidence estimates [42], and overconfidence on out-of-distribution (OOD) inputs [43]. In computer vision, Bayesian neural networks (BNNs) have been applied to a variety of tasks [44], including image classification, object detection, and super-resolution. The primary motivation is to equip neural networks with the ability to quantify uncertainty and provide transparency, which are essential for safety-critical or real-world applications. Recently, Bayesian methods have also been used in various applications, including 3D Shape reconstruction, video activity recognition, and semantic segmentation.

In the context of video summarization, several studies such as [19,22,23] proposed an unsupervised method using a variational autoencoder to learn a latent representation of video frames. However, their approach did not explicitly model predictive uncertainty or leverage probabilistic reasoning in the summary generation process. In contrast, our approach integrates Bayesian inference into the framework for uncertainty-aware latent representation and summary generation, allowing the model to be more robust to noise and to generalize better in unsupervised settings.

Overall, our proposed framework builds upon the unsupervised paradigm that incorporates probabilistic decoding, contrastive learning, and state space models to address existing challenges in video summarization without reliance on annotated data.

3 Proposed Approach

The architecture of our proposed MBSum framework is shown in Fig. 1. The framework takes as input both video frames and corresponding textual captions to generate concise, informative summaries. It integrates components for temporal modeling, cross-modal fusion, probabilistic reconstruction, and projection head. Given an input video, individual frames are first encoded into feature vectors using a frame encoder module. Simultaneously, an off-the-shelf language encoder processes the accompanying textual input into dense representations. The video and text features are then fused via a cross-modal fusion module, producing a joint representation that captures complementary visual-linguistic cues. The fused features X_{vt} are passed through a stack of mamba layers, which model long-range temporal dependencies using efficient state space dynamics. To further refine these representations for frame-level importance estimation, we apply a lightweight MHSA module. This module computes continuous importance scores $S \in [0,1]^N$, which are used to derive weighted frame features $W = S \otimes X_{vt}$, guiding the summary selection process. The weighted frame representations are passed to a Bayesian variational encoder-decoder, which samples latent variables and reconstructs the original video representation $\hat{X}_{vt}$. This reconstruction is driven by a probabilistic loss that encourages the selection of frames preserving the core visual and semantic content. Finally, a projection head (MLP) maps the reconstructed features into a compact embedding space, where a text-guided contrastive loss is applied to promote both cross-modal alignment and fine-grained discriminability within each sample. The MLP head uses GELU activation, layer normalization, and dropout regularization.

3.1 Cross-Modal Fusion

To enable joint modeling of visual frames and their corresponding textual captions, we use a hierarchical cross-modal fusion module that projects both modalities into a shared embedding space and performs iterative attention-based interaction. First, video frame features $\mathbf{V} \in \mathbb{R}^{B_v \times L_v \times D_v}$ and text embeddings $\mathbf{T} \in \mathbb{R}^{B_t \times L_t \times D_t}$ are linearly projected into a common hidden dimension D through learned mappings: $\mathbf{V}' = \mathrm{Proj}_v(\mathbf{V}), \quad \mathbf{T}' = \mathrm{Proj}_t(\mathbf{T})$. The text representation $\mathbf{T}'$ is first processed through a multi-head self-attention block to model intra-text semantic dependencies and to enhance its ability to guide video summarization. Then, we apply cross-modal attention for inter-modal interactions in which text serves as the key/value and video as the query, enabling the video stream to attend to semantically relevant textual signals:

$$\mathrm{CrossAttn}(\mathbf{V}', \mathbf{T}') = \mathrm{MHAttn}(\mathrm{Query} = \mathbf{V}', \mathrm{Key} = \mathbf{T}', \mathrm{Value} = \mathbf{T}') \qquad (1)$$

We stack multiple such cross-attention blocks to progressively refine the fused video features under textual guidance. This design allows the model to semantically enrich frame-level representations using associated textual information, improving alignment between the summary and the underlying narrative.

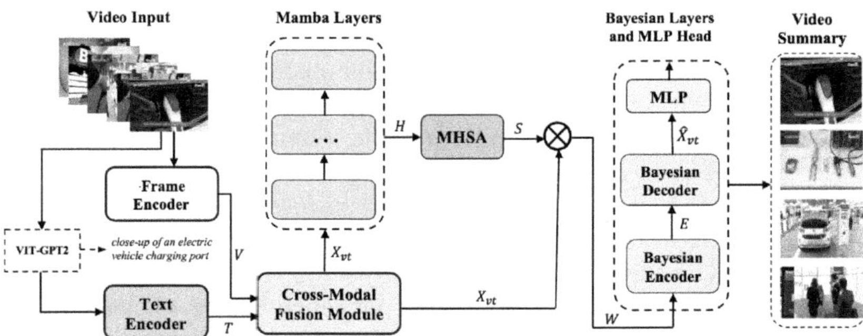

Fig. 1. An overview of the proposed MBSum architecture. Given input frames and captions, the frame encoder extracts visual features V, and the text encoder produces embeddings T. A cross-modal fusion generates joint features $X_{vt} \in \mathbb{R}^{B_v \times L_v \times D_v}$, which are processed by Mamba layers to yield a representation H.

3.2 State Space Model

State space models (SSM) offer a principled framework for capturing temporal dependencies by defining the evolution of a latent state over time [26]. Formally, SSM maps a continuous input signal $x(t) \in \mathbb{R}^{1 \times D}$ into an output signal $y(t) \in \mathbb{R}^{1 \times N}$ through an intermediate state representation $h(t) \in \mathbb{R}^{1 \times N}$. Here, t represents time, D is the input dimensionality, and N is the dimensionality of the latent state. The model's behavior is governed by the following equations:

$$h(t) = Ah(t) + Bx(t), \quad y(t) = Ch(t) + Dx(t) \qquad (2)$$

The matrices A, B, C, and D are treated as learnable parameters and are optimized during training using gradient-based methods. To integrate SSMs into modern deep learning pipelines, the continuous-time dynamics are discretized using a Zero-Order Hold (ZOH) method [24], resulting in the update equations:

$$h_t = \bar{A}h_{t-1} + \bar{B}x_t, \quad y_t = \bar{C}h_t + \bar{D}x_t \qquad (3)$$

where $\bar{A}, \bar{B}, \bar{C}, \bar{D}$ are discrete analogs of the continuous system matrices based on a chosen sampling interval.

We adopt Mamba SSM [24] for temporal frame modeling, which approximates state space behavior through efficient convolutional scanning and parameterized dynamics. Given the fused input sequence $X_{vt} = [f_1, f_2, \ldots, f_N]$, where N is the length of the sequence and each $f_n \in \mathbb{R}^d$, the sequence is processed by a stack of Mamba layers, which capture long-range dependencies via selective state-space dynamics. This produces a sequence of temporally contextualized representations: $H = [h_1, h_2, \ldots, h_N]$, which are further refined by MHSA [28] to compute a final importance score for each frame.

3.3 Bayesian Variational Autoencoder

One of the main issues in video summarization is the inherent ambiguity of visual content, where multiple plausible summaries may exist. This is especially common in diverse datasets, where even human annotators may disagree on keyframes or keyshots. In the unsupervised setting, the model lacks explicit signals to guide what defines a salient segment, often leading to overfitting to dataset biases or poor generalization. To address this, our proposed MBSum model employs a Bayesian decoder that models ambiguity and noise in latent representations, predicting distributions over summary scores. This allows the model to express calibrated confidence in uncertain regions, reducing overfitting and improving generalization compared to deterministic approaches.

The Bayesian summary encoder-decoder module is based on the variational autoencoder (VAE) framework [29] for uncertainty-aware summary reconstruction. Given frame-wise importance scores S produced by the temporal modeling block, the weighted feature sequence W allows the model to selectively emphasize the most salient temporal regions of the video. The weighted feature sequence is encoded with a bidirectional LSTM, producing a fixed-size hidden representation E. This representation is then passed through Bayesian layers [30], which learn distributions over their weights to model uncertainty during inference. The layers output the mean μ and log-variance $\log \sigma^2$ of a Gaussian posterior over a latent variable $\mathbf{z}$:

$$\mu = f_\mu(E), \quad \log \sigma^2 = \log\left(\text{Softplus}\left(f_{\log \sigma^2}(E)\right)\right) \tag{4}$$

A latent sample $\mathbf{z}$ is drawn using the standard reparameterization trick:

$$\mathbf{z} = \mu + \sigma \cdot \epsilon, \quad \epsilon \sim \mathcal{N}(0, \mathbf{I}) \tag{5}$$

The latent vector $\mathbf{z}$ is passed through a unidirectional Bayesian LSTM decoder that reconstructs the original frames to produce the final sequence $\hat{X}_{vt}$.

3.4 Learning Objectives

Our model is trained using a combination of four complementary objectives: reconstruction loss, prior loss, sparsity regularization, and contrastive loss.

Reconstruction Loss. The reconstruction loss $\mathcal{L}_{\text{rec}}$ is formulated as a Gaussian negative log-likelihood, as used in VAE models, but enhanced to account for predictive uncertainty. We reconstruct the full video representation from a weighted subset of frames using a Bayesian latent generator. Given a sequence of N frames, the loss penalizes both reconstruction error and confidence (through the predicted variance), encouraging the model to express uncertainty:

$$\mathcal{L}_{\text{rec}} = \frac{1}{N} \sum_{t=1}^{N} \left[\frac{(\hat{\mathbf{x}}_t - \mathbf{x}_t)^2}{\sigma_t^2} + g \cdot \sigma_t^2 \right] \tag{6}$$

where $\hat{\mathbf{x}}_t$ denotes the reconstructed feature at time step t, $\mathbf{x}_t$ is the corresponding original fused input feature, and σ_t^2 is the predicted variance, and g is a weighting factor balancing error and uncertainty.

Variational Prior Loss. To regularize the latent space of the summary generator, we employ a standard Gaussian prior on the latent representation via a Kullback–Leibler (KL) divergence term between the posterior and the prior:

$$\mathcal{L}_{\text{pr}} = \frac{1}{2} \sum_{t=1}^{N} \left(\mu_t^2 + \exp(\log \sigma_t^2) - \log \sigma_t^2 - 1 \right) \tag{7}$$

where μ_t and σ_t^2 are the mean and log-variance of the latent posterior.

Sparsity Regularization. We incorporate a sparsity regularization term into the training objective to encourage the generation of concise summaries. The loss penalizes deviations from a predefined target summary ratio ρ, guiding the model to select only a small, representative subset of frames.

$$\mathcal{L}_{\text{sp}} = \left\| \frac{1}{N} \sum_{t=1}^{N} s_t - \rho \right\|_2 \tag{8}$$

where N is the total number of video frames, $s_t \in [0, 1]$ is the frame selection probability at time step t, and ρ is a predefined target summary ratio.

Contrastive Loss. We follow the standard contrastive loss [35] to enhance the semantic fidelity and discriminative power. Specifically, we incorporate a dual contrastive loss that aligns cross-modal representations in a shared space, similar to [5] but adapted to our text-guided multimodal setting:

Inter-modal Contrastive Loss: At the global level, we compute a batch-level contrastive loss between video and text embeddings. The objective is to maximize the cosine similarity between matching video-text pairs $(\mathbf{v}_i, \mathbf{t}_i)$ while minimizing similarity between mismatched pairs $(\mathbf{v}_i, \mathbf{t}_j)$, $i \neq j$, across a batch of B samples. This loss, given video and text embeddings $\{\mathbf{v}_i, \mathbf{t}_i\}_{i=1}^{B} \in \mathbb{R}^d$, is computed as:

$$\mathcal{L}_{\text{inter}} = \frac{1}{B} \sum_{i=1}^{B} -\log \left(\frac{\exp(\mathbf{t}_i^\top \mathbf{v}_i / \tau)}{\sum_{j=1}^{B} \exp(\mathbf{t}_i^\top \mathbf{v}_j / \tau)} \right) \tag{9}$$

where τ is a learnable temperature parameter, and all embeddings are L_2 normalized such that $\mathbf{t}_i^\top \mathbf{v}_j$ computes cosine similarity.

Intra-modal Contrastive Loss. This loss focuses on fine-grained frame discrimination within each video. While inter-modal contrast considers global consistency across different video-text pairs, this loss aims to distinguish key frames from non-key frames guided by the corresponding textual context. For each sample $i \in \{1, \ldots, B\}$, the projected text embedding $\mathbf{t}_i \in \mathbb{R}^d$ serves as an anchor, the embedding of a key frame $\mathbf{v}_i^+ \in \mathbb{R}^d$ acts as the positive, and non-key frame embeddings $\{\mathbf{v}_{i,j}^-\}_{j=1}^M \in \mathbb{R}^d$ are treated as negatives. The loss is computed as:

$$\mathcal{L}_{\text{intra}} = \frac{1}{B} \sum_{i=1}^{B} - \log \left(\frac{\exp(\mathbf{t}_i^\top \mathbf{v}_i^+ / \tau)}{\exp(\mathbf{t}_i^\top \mathbf{v}_i^+ / \tau) + \sum_{j=1}^{M} \exp(\mathbf{t}_i^\top \mathbf{v}_{i,j}^- / \tau)} \right) \tag{10}$$

The total contrastive loss combines both inter- and intra-modal terms:

$$\mathcal{L}_{\text{contr}} = \mathcal{L}_{\text{inter}} + \mathcal{L}_{\text{intra}} \tag{11}$$

Total Training Loss. The overall training objective combines all components:

$$\mathcal{L}_{\text{tot}} = \mathcal{L}_{\text{rec}} + \mathcal{L}_{\text{pr}} + \mathcal{L}_{\text{sp}} + \alpha \cdot \mathcal{L}_{\text{contr}} \tag{12}$$

where α is a tunable hyperparameter controlling the strength of the contrastive loss, and the other terms are equally weighted.

4 Experiments

Datasets. We train and evaluate the proposed MBSum model using two widely adopted benchmark datasets, TVSum [31] and SumMe [32], and the other three datasets, Soccer, LoL, and MLB, introduced by Hanqing et al. [19]. The TVSum dataset contains 50 videos, each ranging from 1 to 5 min in duration and covering a variety of genres, including news and documentaries. The SumMe dataset consists of 25 videos ranging from 1 to 6 min in length. Both datasets are annotated with keyframes and keyshots, respectively. Given the relatively limited size of these datasets, we augment the training data with 39 videos from the YouTube dataset [33] and 50 videos from the Open Video Project (OVP) dataset [34]. For the Soccer, LoL, and MLB datasets, we follow the procedure in [19] and divide each dataset into training, validation, and test subsets. The Soccer dataset consists of 69 videos clipped from 11 matches, with durations ranging from 2 to 11 min; each test video contains at least one goal event, which serves as the ground-truth summary. The LoL dataset includes 55 videos from 19 League of Legends matches (2–10 min long), where ground-truth summaries are based on key gameplay events such as hero kills or tower destructions. The MLB dataset includes 60 videos from 5 baseball games (5–10 min), with ground-truth summaries corresponding to frames depicting hits.

Evaluation Method. We use a keyshot-based evaluation metric [22] that computes the temporal overlap between model-generated and user-defined summaries using the F1 score. SumMe dataset contains ground-truth annotations in the form of key shots and thus can be used directly for evaluation, while TVSum contains frame-level scores that we convert to keyshots following [22]. For the Soccer, LoL, and MLB datasets, we compare each generated summary with its ground truth. The F-scores are then averaged across all test videos.

In addition, we use a rank-based evaluation metric to assess the correlation between predicted frame-level importance scores and human annotations. Specifically, we compute Kendall's τ [36] and Spearman's ρ [37], which measure rank correlation without requiring key shot selection.

Implementation Details. All videos were downsampled to 2 fps, and pre-extracted feature descriptors from GoogLeNet [45] were used for a fair comparison with SOTA methods. For the text modality in general-domain datasets (TVSum, SumMe), we follow prior work [5] and adopt the ViT–GPT2 image captioning model [38] to generate captions for each frame, and for textual feature extraction, we apply the pre-trained RoBERTa [39] for each sentence.

Following prior work [7,23], we evaluate our approach under three different settings: Canonical or Standard, Augmented, and Transfer. In the Canonical setting, training and testing are conducted on the same dataset (i.e., either TVSum or SumMe), using a 5-fold cross-validation protocol in which 80% of the data is used for training and the remaining 20% for testing. In the Augmented setting, we randomly select 20% of the target dataset (TVSum or SumMe) for testing, while the remaining 80% is combined with all videos from the other three datasets to form the training set.In the Transfer setting, the model is trained on three datasets and evaluated on a fourth, unseen dataset.

To obtain the text modality for the Soccer, LoL, and MLB datasets, we use the BLIP model [20], which generates richer, context-specific event descriptions for each frame. We then apply the pre-trained CLIP model [40] to extract visual features from each frame and textual features from the captions.

5   Results and Comparisons

We compare our proposed multimodal model (**MBSum-VT**) against a range of state-of-the-art (SOTA) baselines. We also report ablation results for a visual-only variant (**MBSum-V**) to (i) fairly compare with unimodal baselines, (ii) demonstrate the generalization ability of our model in the absence of text, and (iii) attribute the performance improvements of our multimodal version. For fair comparison with SOTA, each generated summary is limited to 15% of the original duration. The main performance metric is the F1 score (Tables 1 and 2), with additional ranking evaluation using Spearman's ρ and Kendall's τ (Table 3). As the OVP and YouTube datasets lack associated text metadata, we omit results in the augmented and transfer settings for MBSum-VT.

As shown in Table 1, our method achieves SOTA performance on both SumMe and TVSum datasets. The multimodal variant MBSum-VT outperforms

Table 1. Comparison (F1-score) with SOTA methods on SumMe and TVSum under Canonical (C), Augmented (A), and Transfer (T) settings. Multimodal methods are marked with an asterisk (*), with best model highlighted in bold.

Method	SumMe			TVSum		
	C	A	T	C	A	T
DDPM [1]	58.7	59.2	50.3	**64.8**	**65.0**	**60.9**
SUM-SR$_{5iter}$ [19]	51.26	–	–	60.2	–	–
CA-SUM [10]	51.1	–	–	61.4	–	–
SUM-GDA [12]	50.0	50.2	46.3	59.6	60.5	58.8
AMFM [18]	51.8	52.8	46.4	61.0	60.8	58.6
CAAN [23]	50.8	50.9	46.5	59.6	59.8	57.8
AVRN [9]*	44.1	44.9	43.2	59.7	60.5	58.7
CLIP-It [7] *	52.5	54.7	50.0	63.0	**65.7**	62.8
iPTNet (11)*	54.5	–	–	63.4	–	–
CTVSUM [21]	46.8	45.5	43.9	59.5	59.9	59.7
Dawit et al. [6] *	56.94	–	–	66.04	–	–
SSPVS [16]	48.7	50.4	45.8	60.3	61.8	57.8
A2Summ [5] *	55.0	–	–	63.4	–	–
KAMV [3] *	59.7	**63.7**	**61.0**	63.8	65.4	**63.5**
MBSum-V (ours)	**59.58**	60.05	56.0	64.83	64.96	60.26
MBSum-VT (ours) *	**64.55**	–	–	**66.58**	–	–

Table 2. Comparison (F1 score) with SOTA on the Soccer, LoL and MLB.

Method	Soccer	LoL	MLB
SG-AAE [8]†	21.06	15.08	15.13
CSNet [11]	20.94	14.55	16.3
AS-GAN [22]†	21.00	14.95	17.09
CA-SUM [10]	21.70	15.15	17.68
SUM-SR [19]	23.84	**15.39**	19.38
MBSum-V	**23.92**	15.28	**20.40**
MBSum-VT*	**24.17**	**16.28**	**21.46**

† *SG-AAE denotes SUM-GAN-AAE.*
† *AS-GAN denotes AC-SUM-GAN.*
Multimodal methods marked with an asterisk (*) on both Tables.

Table 3. Comparison of MBSum-VT with SOTA methods on TVSum using rank correlation coefficients.

Method	ρ	τ
CSNet [23]	0.034	0.025
RSGN [13]	0.090	0.083
DSR-RL [14]	0.114	0.086
VideoXum [4]*	**0.261**	**0.200**
SSPVS [16]	**0.199**	0.151
DSAVS [15]	0.080	0.087
CAAN [23]	0.050	0.038
CLIP-it [7]*	0.147	0.108
A2Summ [5]*	0.165	0.137
MBSum-VT*	0.187	0.165

all baselines, including recent multimodal approaches such as KAMV [3], and A2Summ [5], with F1 scores of 64.55 on SumMe and 66.58 on TVSum. The visual-only variant MBSum-V also surpasses all visual-only baselines, demonstrating the strength of our hybrid frame selector and Bayesian generative summarization strategy. Comparing MBSum-V to MBSum-VT, performance drops by 7.7% on SumMe and 2.6% on TVSum, showing that language conditioning yields better summaries. Additionally, MBSum-VT outperforms recent baselines such as CLIP-It and SSPVS by +5.68% and +10.4% on TVSum, respectively.

It is also notable that our method performs best on the Soccer, LoL, and MLB datasets outperforming the GAN-based models (Table 2). In particular, our MBSum-VT model achieves a performance improvement of 2.08% over the best model (SUM-SR) on the MLB dataset and 0.33% on the Soccer dataset. It also surpasses our visual-only variant (MBSum-V) on all datasets, demonstrating the effectiveness of incorporating textual guidance. Importantly, the integration of cross-modal fusion enhances performance, validating the benefit of multimodal learning in summarization.

Table 3 shows results based on Kendall's τ and Spearman's ρ, assessing the agreement between predicted and ground-truth frame-level rankings. MBSum-VT achieves competitive ranking quality, outperforming most prior methods. Although VideoXum and SSPVS have higher rank correlations, they both rely on supervised learning and annotated summaries, which limits thier scalability.

5.1   Ablation Study

We conducted various ablation analyses to validate the effectiveness of our proposed MBSum-VT framework and to highlight the importance of text-guided summarization. We begin by assessing the contribution of the text modality; in this setting, the output of the video encoder is passed directly to the Mamba module, bypassing both the text encoder and the cross-modal fusion mechanism (see Fig. 1). As shown in Table 1, our visual-only baseline (MBSum-V) achieves competitive performance compared to SOTA methods. However, incorporating text input significantly improves performance with an F1 score from 59.58 to 64.55 on SumMe and from 64.83 to 66.58 on TVSum.

To further dissect the contributions of individual components in MBSum-VT, we conduct a series of ablations by : (1) removing the Mamba SSM module while retaining MHSA (VT w/o MB), (2) replacing Bayesian layers with deterministic layers (VT w/o BL), and (3) removing contrastive loss while retaining the reconstruction, variational prior, and sparsity losses (VT w/o CL).

We evaluate these variants under consistent configurations to assess their impact on overall performance. The results, summarized in Table 4, show that the full MBSum-VT model (VT-Full) outperforms the ablated versions. Notably, removing Mamba yields the largest drop of F1-score (−4.67% on SumMe, −3.0% on TVSum). The removal of other components also leads to performance degradation on both datasets.

Table 4. Ablation results of our model variants on SumMe and TVSum datasets (F1 score %).

Model	SumMe	TVSum
VT w/o MB	61.67	64.61
VT w/o BL	63.58	64.07
VT w/o CL	62.10	65.08
VT (Full)	64.55	66.58

5.2   Visualizations

We selected a subset of test videos from TVSum to visualize generated summaries and model reliability. Figure 2 presents an example where keyshot summaries generated by our MBSum-VT model compared with the ground-truth summary, demonstrating the model's effectiveness in selecting relevant segments. We further evaluate the reliability of our model's predictions using Bayesian uncertainty and confidence following a prior work from [46]. As shown in Fig. 3, frame importance scores show a strong positive correlation with model confidence (Fig. 3a) and a negative correlation with predictive uncertainty (Fig. 3b). The trends indicate that the model is more accurate in regions of lower uncertainty and higher confidence, providing a reliable measure of frame prediction quality.

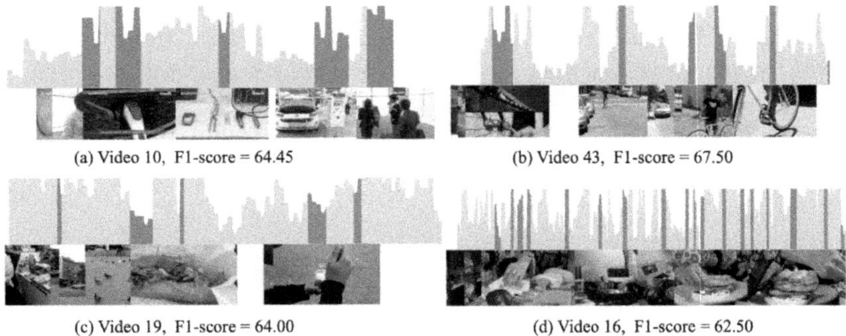

(a) Video 10, F1-score = 64.45   (b) Video 43, F1-score = 67.50

(c) Video 19, F1-score = 64.00   (d) Video 16, F1-score = 62.50

Fig. 2. Example video summaries generated by our approach for videos 10,16,19 and 43 from TVSum dataset. The grey bars show the ground truth importance scores, while the blue bars denote the selected keyshots. (Color figure online)

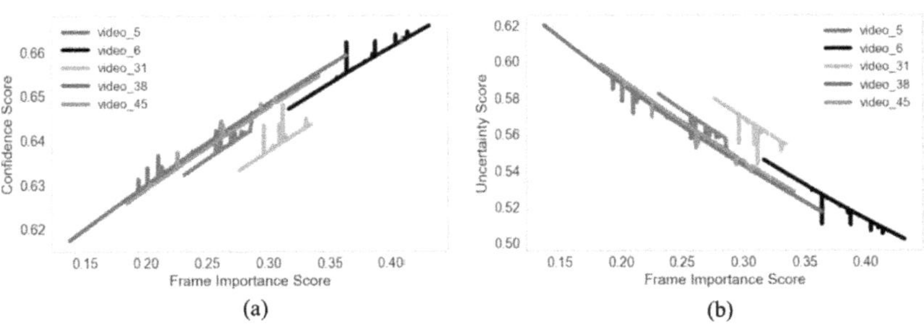

Fig. 3. Frame importance scores vs. (a) model confidence and (b) predictive uncertainty across five videos from TVSum. Both plots reveal that higher frame importance scores often coincide with higher model confidence (a) and low predictive uncertainty (b), demonstrating that the scores are well-calibrated.

6   Conclusions

In this paper, we introduce MBSum, a novel framework for unsupervised multimodal video summarization that overcomes key limitations of existing approaches, including: (i) reliance on unimodal inputs and human supervision, (ii) weak temporal modeling with LSTM or inefficient transformer complexity, and (iii) deterministic summaries that fail to capture uncertainty. MBSum integrates unsupervised multimodal fusion, a Mamba-based state space backbone for scalable long-range temporal modeling, and a Bayesian variational decoder for uncertainty-aware summary generation. Unlike prior methods, MBSum replaces adversarial training with a generator grounded in Bayesian inference, simplifying training and improving stability. This is an original framework to explore the joint use of Mamba SSM, Bayesian inference, and multimodal fusion for unsupervised video summarization. Experimental results across five benchmark datasets show MBSum's superior performance, providing a robust solution for real-world applications such as user adaptive video summarization.

Acknowledgement. This research is funded by SFI MediaFutures partners and the Research Council of Norway (grant number 309339).

References

1. Shang, Z., et al.: Video summarization using denoising diffusion probabilistic model. Proc. AAAI Conf. Artif. Intell. **39**(7), 6776–6784 (2025)
2. Selva, J., et al.: Video transformers: a survey. IEEE Trans. Pattern Anal. Mach. Intell. **45**(11), 12922–12943 (2023)
3. Xie, J., et al.: A knowledge augmented and multimodal-based framework for video summarization. In: Proceedings of the 30th ACM International Conference on Multimedia, pp. 740–749 (2022)
4. Lin, J., et al.: Videoxum: cross-modal visual and textural summarization of videos. IEEE Trans. Multimedia **26**, 5548–5560 (2023)
5. He, B., et al.: Align and attend: multimodal summarization with dual contrastive losses. In: Proceedings of the IEEE/CVF Conference on Computer Vision and Pattern Recognition, pp. 14867–14878 (2023)
6. Argaw, D.M., et al.: Scaling up video summarization pretraining with large language models. In: CVPR, pp. 8332–8341 (2024)
7. Narasimhan et al.: Clip-it! Language-guided video summarization. Adv. Neural Inf. Process. Syst. **34**, 13988–14000 (2021)
8. Apostolidis, E., Adamantidou, E., Metsai, A.I., Mezaris, V., Patras, I.: Unsupervised video summarization via attention-driven adversarial learning. In: Ro, Y.M., et al. (eds.) MMM 2020. LNCS, vol. 11961, pp. 492–504. Springer, Cham (2020). https://doi.org/10.1007/978-3-030-37731-1_40
9. Zhao, B., Gong, M., Li, X.: Audiovisual video summarization. IEEE Trans. Neural Netw. Learn. Syst. **34**(8), 5181–5188 (2021)
10. Apostolidis, E., et al.: Summarizing videos using concentrated attention and considering the uniqueness and diversity of the video frames. In: Proceedings of the 2022 International Conference on Multimedia Retrieval, pp. 407–415 (2022)

11. Jung, Y., et al.: Discriminative feature learning for unsupervised video summarization. In: Proceedings of the AAAI Conference on AI, vol. 33, no. 1, pp. 8537–8544 (2019)
12. Li, P., et al.: Exploring global diverse attention via pairwise temporal relation for video summarization. Pattern Recogn. **111**, 107677 (2021)
13. Zhao, B., et al.: Reconstructive sequence-graph network for video summarization. IEEE Trans. Pattern Anal. Mach. Intell. **44**(5), 2793–2801 (2021)
14. Phaphuangwittayakul et al: Self-attention recurrent summarization network with reinforcement learning for video summarization task. In: IEEE International Conference on Multimedia and Expo (ICME), pp. 1–6. IEEE (2021)
15. Zhong, S.H., et al.: Deep semantic and attentive network for unsupervised video summarization. ACM Trans. Mult. Comput. Commun. Appl. **18**(2), 1–21 (2022)
16. Li, H., et al.: Progressive video summarization via multimodal self-supervised learning. In: CVPR, pp. 5584–5593 (2023)
17. Zhao, B., Li, X., Lu, X.: HSA-RNN: hierarchical structure-adaptive RNN for video summarization. In: CVPR, pp. 7405–7414 (2018)
18. Zhang, Y., et al.: Attention-guided multi-granularity fusion model for video summarization. Expert Syst. Appl. **249**, 123568 (2024)
19. Li, H., Klabjan, D., Utke, J.: Unsupervised video summarization via iterative training and simplified GAN. In: ACCV, pp. 1585–1601 (2024)
20. Li, J., et al.: Blip: bootstrapping language-image pre-training for unified vision-language understanding and generation. In: International Conference on Machine Learning, pp. 12888–12900. PMLR (2022)
21. Pang, Z., et al.: Contrastive losses are natural criteria for unsupervised video summarization. In: CVPR, pp. 2010–2019 (2023)
22. Apostolidis, E., et al.: AC-SUM-GAN: connecting actor-critic and generative adversarial networks for unsupervised video summarization. IEEE Trans. Circuits Syst. Video Technol. **31**(8), 3278–3292 (2020)
23. Liang, G., et al.: Video summarization with a convolutional attentive adversarial network. Pattern Recogn. **131**, 108840 (2022)
24. Gu, A., Goel, K., Ré, C.: Efficiently modeling long sequences with structured state spaces. arXiv preprint arXiv:2111.00396 (2021)
25. Smith, J.T., et al.: Simplified state space layers for sequence modeling. arXiv preprint arXiv:2208.04933 (2022)
26. Gu, A., Dao, T.: Mamba: linear-time sequence modeling with selective state spaces. arXiv preprint arXiv:2312.00752 (2023)
27. Liu, Y., et al.: Vmamba: visual state space model. Adv. Neural. Inf. Process. Syst. **37**, 103031–103063 (2024)
28. Vaswani, A., et al.: Attention is all you need. In: Advances in Neural Information Processing Systems, vol. 30 (2017)
29. Kingma, et al.: Auto-encoding variational Bayes. preprint arXiv:1312.6114 (2013)
30. Tran, D., et al.: Bayesian layers: a module for neural network uncertainty. In: Advances in Neural Information Processing Systems, vol. 32 (2019)
31. Song, Y., et al.: TVSum: summarizing web videos using titles. In: CVPR, pp. 5179–5187 (2015)
32. Gygli, M., Grabner, H., Riemenschneider, H., Van Gool, L.: Creating summaries from user videos. In: Fleet, D., Pajdla, T., Schiele, B., Tuytelaars, T. (eds.) ECCV 2014. LNCS, vol. 8695, pp. 505–520. Springer, Cham (2014). https://doi.org/10.1007/978-3-319-10584-0_33
33. De et al.: VSUMM: a mechanism designed to produce static video summaries and a novel evaluation method. Pattern Recogn. Lett. **32**(1), 56–68 (2011)

34. Open Video Project. https://open-video.org/. Accessed 10 July 2025
35. He, K., et al.: Momentum contrast for unsupervised visual representation learning. In: CVPR, pp. 9729–9738 (2020)
36. Kendall, M.G.: The treatment of ties in ranking problems. Biometrika **33**(3) (1945)
37. Zwillinger, D., Kokoska, S.: CRC Standard Probability and Statistics Tables and Formulae. CRC Press, Boca Raton (1999)
38. nlpconnect: ViT-GPT2 Image Captioning. Hugging Face (2022). https://huggingface.co/nlpconnect/vit-gpt2-image-captioning
39. Liu, Y., et al.: RoBERTa: A Robustly Optimized BERT Pretraining Approach. arXiv preprint arXiv:1907.11692 (2019)
40. Radford, A., et al.: Learning transferable visual models from natural language supervision. In: International Conference on Machine Learning, pp. 8748–8763. PMLR (2021)
41. Roy et al.: Bayesian QuickNAT: model uncertainty in deep whole-brain segmentation for structure-wise quality control. NeuroImage **195**, 11–22 (2019)
42. Wilson, A.G., Izmailov, P.: Bayesian deep learning and a probabilistic perspective of generalization. Adv. Neural Inf. Process. Syst. **33**, 4697–4708 (2020)
43. Mitros, J., Mac Namee, B.: On the validity of Bayesian neural networks for uncertainty estimation. arXiv preprint arXiv:1912.01530 (2019)
44. Gawlikowski, J., et al.: A survey of uncertainty in deep neural networks. Artif. Intell. Rev. **56**, S1513–S1589 (2023). https://doi.org/10.1007/s10462-023-10562-9
45. Szegedy, C., et al.: Going deeper with convolutions. In: CVPR, pp. 1–9 (2015)
46. Krishnan et al.: Improving model calibration with accuracy versus uncertainty optimization. Adv. Neural Inf. Process. Syst. (NeurIPS) **33**, 18237–18248 (2020)

Efficient Reasoning Distillation: Small Video-Language Models via Synthetic CoT and Difficulty-Aware Fine-Tuning

Mantek Singh[1]([✉]) [ID], Jeshwarth Challagundla[3] [ID], Siddharth Raina[4] [ID], and Jasmin Jarsania[2] [ID]

[1] Liverpool John Moores University, Liverpool, England
mantek.singh2@gmail.com
[2] University of Texas at Arlington, Arlington, TX, USA
[3] Carnegie Mellon University, Pittsburgh, USA
[4] Meta, Sunnyvale, USA

Abstract. We present an efficient method to distill reasoning capabilities into compact video-language models (VLMs) for video question answering (VideoQA). Our approach fine-tunes a 2B-parameter model using only $\sim$900 uncertainty-selected examples, each augmented with synthetic chain-of-thought (CoT) rationales generated by a 4B teacher. Despite its minimal compute cost–under two hours on a single A100 GPU–our method enables the 2B model to outperform VLMs up to $4\times$ larger, and generalize across CinePile, ActivityNet-QA, and MLVU, approaching the performance of its own 4B teacher.

A key finding is that placing CoT rationales *after* the answer–contrary to standard prompting–substantially improves reasoning in compact models. This insight challenges prevailing CoT conventions and reveals new alignment strategies under limited model capacity. Our findings offer a practical blueprint for training deployable, reasoning-rich VLMs suited for mobile and edge applications.

Keywords: Vision-Language Models · Video Understanding · Chain-of-Thought Reasoning · Efficient Fine-Tuning · Synthetic Data Generation · Uncertainty Estimation · Multimodal Learning

1 Introduction

The surge in video content requires efficient video-language models (VLMs) for edge devices, yet current models are prohibitively large for deployment in resource-constrained environments [7,34]. This paper addresses the need for compact VLMs with strong reasoning capabilities for video question answering (VideoQA). Traditional video QA datasets are expensive, privacy-sensitive, and often biased [6,32,48], making synthetic data a scalable, privacy-preserving alternative for data augmentation [22,49].

© The Author(s), under exclusive license to Springer Nature Singapore Pte Ltd. 2026
J. Lokoč et al. (Eds.): MMM 2026, LNCS 16412, pp. 567–580, 2026.
https://doi.org/10.1007/978-981-95-6950-2_40

We propose a sample-efficient framework to distill reasoning from a 4B teacher (InternVL2-4B) into a 2B student model (InternVL2-2B). Our approach combines two core strategies:

- **Synthetic Chain-of-Thought (CoT) Generation**: Inspired by LLMs [2, 41,50], we use the 4B VLM to generate concise CoT rationales. This obviates the need for human annotation [15,16,47] and allows us to explore formats suitable for compact models.
- **Hard Sample Selection for Fine-Tuning**: Instead of using large datasets, we target high-value training points identified via model-estimated difficulty and top-2 prediction margin (uncertainty-based sampling) [23,33], aligning with hard example mining [36,40].

We validate our method on the CinePile benchmark [26] and test generalization on ActivityNet-QA [46] and MLVU [52]. Our key findings are:

- Synthetic CoT rationales, even from a small 4B teacher, significantly improve performance.
- Top-2 margin sampling consistently outperforms other selection strategies.
- Placing rationales *after* the answer substantially boosts reasoning in small models, contrary to standard CoT prompting.
- Fine-tuning on only 900 examples ($<0.5\%$ of training data) yields large, efficient gains.
- The improvements generalize strongly across unseen datasets and domains.

To our knowledge, this is the first work to combine small-scale CoT distillation, uncertainty-guided sampling, and format-aware rationale design for compact VLMs, offering a practical recipe for reasoning-rich alignment under real-world deployment constraints.

Additional results, ablations, and qualitative examples are provided in the supplementary material.

2   Related Work

2.1   Synthetic Data and Knowledge Distillation

Synthetic data, generated via methods like generative models [8,12,28], addresses data scarcity and privacy limitations in vision [22,27,30]. While recent VLMs generate question-answer pairs directly from visual inputs [17,49], our work emphasizes distilling reasoning-focused synthetic rationales via Chain-of-Thought (CoT) rather than direct QA generation.

Knowledge distillation transfers representations from large "teacher" to smaller "student" models [10,29,31]. However, small models ($<3B$) often struggle to absorb complex supervision due to limited capacity [16]. While methods like AoTD [51] introduced large-scale video reasoning distillation, they rely on extensive supervision. We instead show that strong reasoning gains are possible with a modest 4B teacher and only 900 training examples, enabling practical edge deployment.

2.2 Chain-of-Thought Reasoning and Hard Sample Selection

CoT prompting improves reasoning by encouraging intermediate steps [41] and has been extended to multimodal VQA [37,50]. Recent works distill symbolic reasoning into large VLMs [11,35]. In contrast, we focus on a low-resource regime, fine-tuning a 2B model with only 900 concise CoTs from a 4B teacher. We uniquely investigate CoT *positioning* and rationale format for compact models, extending image QA CoT distillation [18] to long-form video with an emphasis on post-hoc rationales and format-aware alignment.

Hard sample selection accelerates convergence by focusing on uncertain samples near model decision boundaries [36]. We apply margin-based uncertainty sampling [33] to target ambiguous, high-value examples. Unlike typical easy-to-hard curriculum learning [1,39], we adopt a hard-first approach, which we find highly effective when paired with synthetic CoT rationales.

2.3 VideoQA Datasets

We evaluate our method on several benchmarks, summarized in Table 1. Our primary dataset for fine-tuning is the long-form, temporally rich CinePile [26]. We test zero-shot generalization on the diverse web videos of ActivityNet-QA [46] and the compositional, multi-task design of MLVU [52]. Our focus on these datasets distinguishes our work from evaluations on benchmarks with shorter coverage like MSVD-QA [44] and TVQA [14], or those with different long-context tasks such as EgoSchema [20] and LongVideoBench [43].

Table 1. Comparison of video QA datasets.

Dataset	QA Pairs	Length	Focus
CinePile	~305k	~160 s	Long Vid, Temporal
ActNet QA	58k	~180 s	Web Vid, Temporal
MSVD-QA	50k	~10 s	Short Vid, Desc.
TVQA	152k	~76 s	TV, Dialogue+Visual

3 Methodology

Our goal is to enhance InternVL2-2B's video reasoning capabilities through synthetic data and lightweight fine-tuning, optimized for edge deployment. Our pipeline, shown in Fig. 1, integrates hard sample selection, synthetic CoT rationale generation, and efficient supervision.

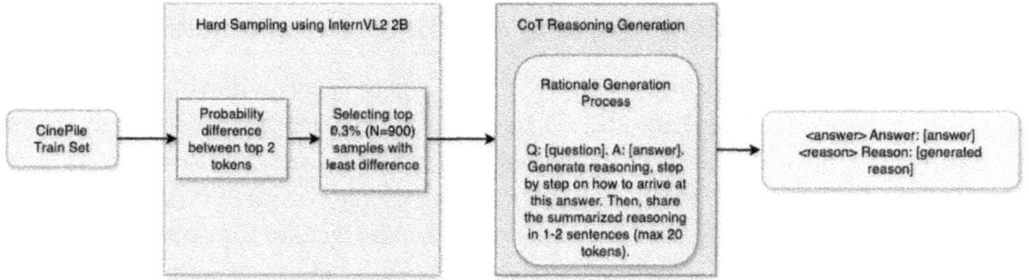

Fig. 1. Overview of methodology for improving VLM using synthetic Chain-of-Thought reasoning and hard sample selection.

3.1   Hard Sample Selection and Rationale Generation

To maximize fine-tuning impact, we first identify N examples where InternVL2-2B is most uncertain. We explore three strategies: random sampling, model-estimated difficulty (ranking by negative log-probability), and top-2 margin sampling (selecting samples with the smallest gap between the top two predictions [23,33]). We found performance saturated near $N = 700$ (see Sect. 4) and chose $N = 900$ to ensure robustness, corresponding to $< 0.5\%$ of the full dataset.

For these 900 samples, we generate short, structured CoT rationales using a 4B teacher (InternVL2-4B), avoiding the verbosity of larger models [16]. We use the prompt: `Q: [question]. A: [answer]. Generate reasoning...` `summarize it in 12 sentences (max 20 tokens)`. Rationales are capped at 20 tokens, and manual inspection confirmed 85% validity; we apply filters to remove malformed samples.

3.2   Fine-Tuning and Evaluation

We fine-tune InternVL2-2B on the $N = 900$ augmented samples. We tested placing CoTs before the answer, as in standard prompting [41], but observed degraded performance (e.g., final-option bias). Providing the rationale as input context ("Explanation: [Rationale]...") also yielded lower gains. In contrast, placing the rationale *after* the answer led to strong gains, so we adopt the "Answer-then-Rationale" format: `<answer> [Answer]. <reason> [Rationale Text]`. We found concise, 1–2 sentence rationales to be sufficient. Training uses AdamW [19] with a 2e-5 learning rate for 3 epochs, optimizing a standard cross-entropy loss.

Our primary benchmark is CinePile [26], where we report average and category-wise accuracy. For generalization, we perform zero-shot evaluation on ActivityNet-QA [46]. Since ActivityNet-QA is open-ended, we adapt it to a multiple-choice format by generating four distractors per question using GPT-4o [5], ensuring consistency with our training setup. Baselines include zero-shot

InternVL2-2B, larger models (mPLUG-Owl3, LongVA), and our model fine-tuned without CoT.

3.3   Implementation Details

InternVL2-2B uses a ViT-based visual encoder [4] and a LLaMA-style decoder [38]. Due to backpropagation constraints [21], we use 3 frames per video during fine-tuning and 12 during inference. The pipeline is implemented in PyTorch [24] and Hugging Face Transformers [42]. Fine-tuning completes in under 2 h on a 4xA100 node. We plan to release our code to support reproducibility.

4   Experiments and Results

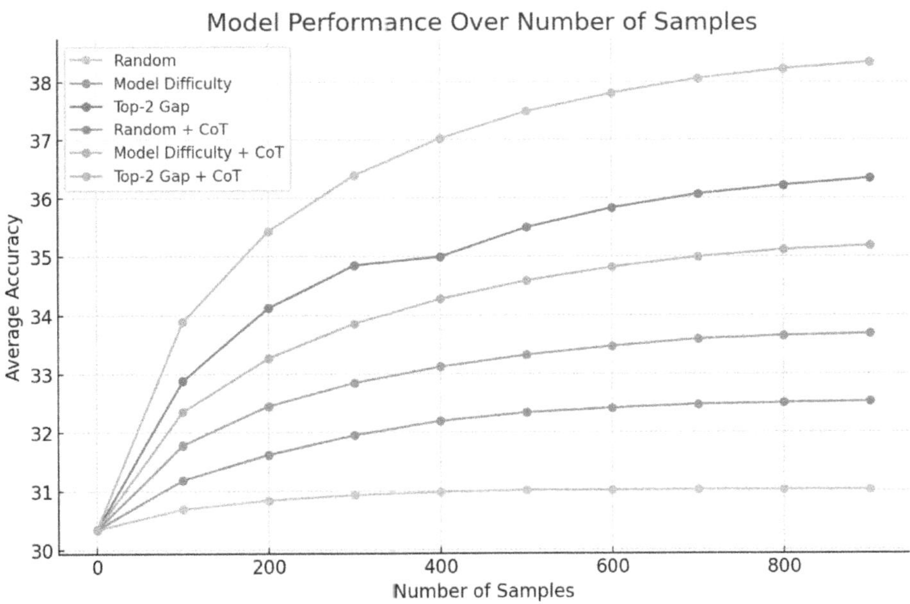

Fig. 2. Average accuracy on CinePile dataset of InternVL2 2B models based on number of samples used for fine tuning.

We conduct experiments to evaluate our methodology for enhancing VLMs using targeted synthetic data. Our key research questions are:

- (Q1) How effective are different hard sample selection strategies compared to random sampling for fine-tuning efficiency?

- (Q2) What is the impact of incorporating synthetically generated Chain-of-Thought (CoT) rationales, and how does the rationale integration format affect performance?
- (Q3) Can our approach significantly narrow the performance gap between the compact InternVL2-2B model and larger VLMs on the challenging CinePile benchmark?
- (Q4) Do the reasoning improvements learned on CinePile generalize to an unseen dataset (ActivityNet-QA) when evaluated in a zero-shot setting?

Table 2. Performance Comparison of Vision-Language Models. We also compare synthetic CoT generated from a 26B teacher (italicized row) vs. 4B (final row). The 4B teacher outperforms, supporting its use as an efficient rationale generator.

Model	#Params	Avg	CRD	NPA	STA	TEMP	TH
InternVL2 2B	2B	30.34	31.91	33.26	30.35	23.26	31.58
InternVL2 4B	4B	39.89	42.99	47.73	36.23	32.99	41.58
mPLUG-Owl3	8B	38.27	40.91	45.71	33.86	33.09	46.20
InternVL2 8B	8B	32.28	35.25	40.39	28.46	24.71	38.42
LongVA 7B	7B	41.04	43.28	51.84	38.45	33.58	38.42
InternVL2 2B (Random)	2B	31.02	31.16	31.96	31.62	26.06	40.21
InternVL2 2B (Difficulty)	2B	33.68	34.45	38.15	33.10	27.74	40.48
InternVL2 2B (Top-2 Gap)	2B	36.34	37.73	44.35	34.58	29.43	40.74
InternVL2 2B (Random + CoT)	2B	32.52	33.10	33.46	33.12	27.56	41.71
InternVL2 2B (Difficulty + CoT)	2B	35.18	35.95	39.65	34.60	29.24	41.98
InternVL2 2B (Top-2 Gap + CoT, 26B teacher)	2B	37.41	38.45	47.17	35.62	30.12	42.21
InternVL2 2B (Top-2 Gap + CoT)	**2B**	**38.34**	**39.73**	**46.50**	**36.58**	**30.85**	**42.74**

4.1 Experimental Setup

- **Datasets:**
  - Cinepile [26]: Our primary dataset for fine-tuning and evaluation. It comprises 305,000 multiple-choice question-answer pairs derived from over 9,000 movie clips (avg. length 160 s). We utilize the official training split for fine-tuning sample selection and the official test split for evaluation. Its focus on long-form video and reasoning makes it a suitable testbed.
  - ActivityNet-Qa [46]: Used for zero-shot generalization testing. It contains 58k open-ended QA pairs on 5.8k web videos (avg. length 180 s). We evaluate on the standard validation split. To align with our multiple-choice fine-tuning paradigm, we synthetically generated multiple-choice options for the ActivityNet-QA validation set using GPT-4o.
- **Evaluation Metrics:**
  - Cinepile: We report Average Accuracy across all questions and breakdown accuracy by the provided question types categories: **TEMP** (Temporal), **CRD** (Character and Relationship Dynamics), **NPA** (Narrative and Plot Analysis), **STA** (Setting and Technical Analysis), and **TH** (Thematic Exploration).

- ActivityNet-QA: We report standard multiple-choice Accuracy.
- **Baselines and Compared Models**:
  - Base Model: InternVL2-2B (zero-shot) [3].
  - Fine-tuned (No CoT): InternVL2-2B fine-tuned on $N = 900$ samples selected via: (i) Random, (ii) Model-Estimated Difficulty (denoted Difficulty), (iii) Top-2 Confidence Gap (denoted Top-2 Gap).
  - Fine-tuned (+Synth CoT): The same three selection strategies, but fine-tuned with synthetic CoT rationales generated by InternVL2-4B (denoted Random+CoT, Difficulty+CoT, Top-2 Gap+CoT). Rationales are integrated using the Answer-then-Rationale format determined in Sect. 3.4.
  - Larger Models (for reference): InternVL2-4B, mPLUG-Owl3-8B [45], InternVL2-8B, LongVA-7B.

4.2 Sample Efficiency Analysis

To analyze data efficiency, we varied the number of fine-tuning samples (N) from 0 to 900 and tracked the Average Accuracy on the CinePile test set. Figure 2 plots the accuracy curves for Random selection, Top-2 Gap selection (without CoT), and Top-2 Gap selection with synthetic CoT. As discussed in Sect. 3, we see the gains plateau at around $N = 700$, and thus, we chose $N = 900$ samples for fine tuning the models in the end.

The results clearly demonstrate the benefits of our approach. Firstly, targeted selection significantly improves sample efficiency. The Top-2 Gap strategy achieves higher accuracy with far fewer samples compared to Random selection. For instance, Top-2 Gap using only 300 samples (34.85% Acc) surpasses the performance of Random selection using 900 samples (31.02% Acc). These results highlight that CoT quality directly influences student performance. When the model is trained on unrelated CoT text, its accuracy drops below the base model, indicating that noisy supervision can be harmful. This supports our claim that carefully generated, instruction-following CoT rationales are crucial for effective transfer. This confirms that focusing fine-tuning on points of model uncertainty accelerates learning. Secondly, incorporating synthetic CoT rationales provides a substantial additional boost in data efficiency. The Top-2 Gap+CoT curve consistently lies above the Top-2 Gap curve. Adding synthetic CoT rationales to 600 samples (37.81% Acc) achieves performance comparable to using 900 samples without CoT (36.34% Acc). This indicates that the synthetic reasoning signal effectively acts as potent data augmentation, allowing the model to extract more value from each selected sample. Notably, performance gains begin to saturate around $N = 700$ samples for the targeted strategies, justifying our choice of $N = 900$ for main experiments as an efficient operating point. We additionally ran a 1200-sample experiment and found performance gains began to plateau beyond 900 samples, supporting our claim that 900 is a sufficient budget. This is consistent with the flattening curve in Fig. 2.

To better understand the impact of teacher model size on synthetic CoT quality, we compared the rationales generated by InternVL2-8B and InternVL2-26B. As shown in Table 3, the larger teacher produces significantly longer CoTs

Table 3. Comparison of CoT complexity across teacher models. InternVL2-26B generates longer, denser rationales, which may introduce a mismatch when distilling into small students.

Teacher Model	Avg. CoT Length	% Reasoning Tokens
InternVL2-8B	25 tokens	18%
InternVL2-26B	43 tokens	27%

Table 4. Ablation study showing the effect of CoT quality. Poor-quality (random) CoT hurts performance, while meaningful CoT improves accuracy.

Model Variant	Accuracy (%)
InternVL2-2B (base)	30.34
+ Top-2 Gap + CoT (real)	38.34
+ Top-2 Gap + Random CoT	28.00

with more reasoning-heavy tokens, which can overwhelm smaller students. These findings support our "capacity mismatch" hypothesis – that extremely verbose CoTs may hinder learning in low-capacity models like InternVL2-2B.

Impact of CoT Quality. To evaluate how the quality of synthetic chain-of-thought (CoT) affects model performance, we conducted an ablation where the CoT rationales were replaced with randomly generated, unrelated text of similar length. This allows us to isolate the effect of structured reasoning. Results on CinePile are shown below (Table 4):

These results validate that the observed improvements stem from the reasoning content in CoT, rather than merely increased sequence length or noise injection. In fact, unrelated rationales actively degrade model performance below baseline.

4.3   Main Results on CinePile

Table 2 presents the performance of different models and fine-tuning strategies on the CinePile test set.

The key observations from our main results (Table 2) are:

- **Hard Sampling Effectiveness:** All fine-tuning approaches outperform the zero-shot baseline (30.34%). Among the selection strategies without CoT, Top-2 Gap (36.34%) significantly outperforms both Random (31.02%, +5.32 points) and Difficulty (33.68%, +2.66 points). This strongly supports selecting samples based on model uncertainty as the most effective strategy.
- **Synthetic CoT Impact:** Adding synthetic CoT rationales consistently improves performance. The largest gain is observed for the best selection method: Top-2 Gap+CoT achieves 38.34%, a +2.0 point improvement over

Top-2 Gap without CoT. The boost is particularly pronounced in reasoning-intensive categories like TEMP and CRD, demonstrating that the synthetic rationales successfully impart reasoning skills.

- **Closing the Gap:** Our best model, InternVL2-2B (Top-2 Gap+CoT), reaches 38.34% average accuracy. This significantly closes the gap to the larger InternVL2-4B baseline (39.89%), reducing the difference from 9.55 points to just 1.55 points. Notably, it surpasses the accuracy of the mPLUG-Owl3-8B model (38.27%) and the InternVL2-8B model (32.28%). While still below the specialized LongVA-7B (41.04%), this highlights the power and practicality of our methodology.

4.4   Generalization to MLVU

To provide the strongest test of generalization, we evaluated our model on a challenging held-out subset of the MLVU benchmark, which features long-form videos and compositional question types. The results, shown in Table 5, demonstrate a remarkable feat of knowledge distillation. Our fine-tuned 2B model achieves an impressive 50.5% accuracy, not only representing a massive 5.5-point leap over its base model (45.0%) but also achieving near-parity with its 4B teacher (51.0%). By closing the performance gap to a razor-thin 0.5% margin against a model twice its size, this striking result validates that our efficient, targeted fine-tuning strategy successfully distills complex reasoning capabilities into a far more compact architecture.

Table 5. Accuracy on a subset of the MLVU benchmark.

Model	Accuracy (%)
InternVL2-2B (base)	45.0
InternVL2-2B (Top-2 Gap + CoT)	**50.5**
InternVL2-4B (base)	51.0

4.5   Generalization to ActivityNet-QA (Zero-Shot Transfer)

To further confirm the transferability of these gains, we tested our model zero-shot on a synthetically adapted ActivityNet-QA multiple-choice benchmark. The baseline model achieves 40.20% accuracy. Fine-tuning on CinePile with hard sample selection alone provides a modest gain (41.46%). However, adding our synthetic CoT rationales results in a more substantial improvement, reaching 43.19% accuracy (+2.99 points over baseline, +1.73 points over fine-tuning without CoT). This demonstrates that the enhanced reasoning capabilities generalize robustly to a different dataset and task format, confirming our approach imparts transferable skills.

Justification for Synthetic Evaluation on ActivityNet-QA. To align the open-ended ActivityNet-QA with our multiple-choice setup, we used GPT-4o to generate four semantically plausible and contextually relevant distractors for each question. This process is detailed with an example in the supplementary material to illustrate the quality of our evaluation protocol.

5   Discussion and Limitations

Our research shows that strategically generated and selected synthetic data enhances reasoning in compact Vision-Language Models (VLMs). By fine-tuning InternVL2-2B on a targeted subset ($\sim$0.3%) of CinePile data with synthetic Chain-of-Thought (CoT) rationales, we achieved performance approaching a 2x larger model and surpassed other large baselines, demonstrating a highly efficient path to model improvement.

- **Synergistic Efficiency of Selection and Synthetic CoT:** A key finding is the synergy between hard sample selection (Top-2 Gap) and synthetic CoT supervision. Selection significantly improves data efficiency (Fig. 2), while synthetic rationales amplify learning on high-uncertainty samples where explicit reasoning is most valuable (Table 2). These rationales help compact models disentangle temporal dependencies, a key challenge for small architectures.
- **Moderate Teachers Enable Efficient Synthetic Reasoning:** Our finding that a 4B teacher outperforms a 26B teacher for this task underscores the value of intermediate teacher models. This supports the hypothesis that overly complex rationales from large teachers can overwhelm small models, and that moderate-capacity teachers provide a better trade-off between quality and distillability [16], significantly reducing compute requirements for data generation.
- **Sensitivity to Synthetic Data Format:** The success of our `Answer-then-Rationale` format over the standard `Rationale-then-Answer` (which caused an "Option E bias") reveals that compact models are highly sensitive to the structure of synthetic supervision. We hypothesize this stems from the cognitive burden of pre-answer reasoning on low-capacity models, token decay in long outputs, and more effective optimization when supervision focuses early on the answer. This suggests that *post-hoc rationalization is not only easier to learn, but more effective*, motivating **format design tailored to model capacity**.

In summary, our results motivate a reevaluation of standard CoT prompting in low-resource settings. Simply reordering the rationale can yield significant gains, offering a practical path for boosting compact VLMs.

Limitations

- **Teacher Quality and Over-Reliance:** The effectiveness of synthetic CoT is bounded by the teacher's quality. Errors or hallucinations from the 4B

teacher can propagate through the synthetic data [25], underlining the need for careful auditing and filtering for rationale faithfulness [13], especially in high-stakes settings.
- **Robustness and Generalizability Scope:** Our sample selection relies on model confidence, which is not always well-calibrated [9]. While we show generalization to ActivityNet-QA and MLVU, further validation across different architectures is needed. Additionally, our ActivityNet-QA evaluation uses GPT-generated options, a synthetic layer that could influence outcomes.
- **Edge Deployment and Applicability:** Our experiments use InternVL2-2B, as few compact VLMs handle temporal reasoning (e.g., Qwen-VL-Tiny is image-focused). Larger teachers (>4B) are also infeasible for on-device generation. Our method serves as a template for future compact VLMs, and extending it to new architectures remains a key future direction.

6   Conclusion

We proposed an effective pipeline to enhance compact VLMs using synthetic Chain-of-Thought (CoT) rationales and targeted fine-tuning. By selecting just ∼900 high-uncertainty samples and generating concise rationales from a moderate (4B) teacher, we significantly boosted InternVL2-2B's performance on the CinePile benchmark, outperforming larger models. Our method demonstrates strong zero-shot generalization to ActivityNet-QA and near-parity with its 4B teacher on the MLVU benchmark. Ablations highlight the value of capacity-aware distillation, showing a 4B teacher can outperform a 26B model in this setting. By achieving performance rivaling 4× larger models with minimal data and compute, our work enables the practical deployment of reasoning-rich VLMs on edge devices. We will release our code upon publication to encourage broader exploration of targeted synthetic augmentation for small multimodal models.

Disclosure of Interests. The authors have no competing interests to declare that are relevant to the content of this article.

References

1. Bengio, Y., Louradour, J., Collobert, R., Weston, J.: Curriculum learning. In: Proceedings of the 26th Annual International Conference on Machine Learning - ICML 2009, pp. 1–8. ACM Press, Montreal, Quebec, Canada (2009). https://doi.org/10.1145/1553374.1553380. http://portal.acm.org/citation.cfm?doid=1553374.1553380
2. Chen, Y., Sikka, K., Cogswell, M., Ji, H., Divakaran, A.: Measuring and improving chain-of-thought reasoning in vision-language models (2024). https://arxiv.org/abs/2302.00923
3. Chen, Z., et al.: Internvl: scaling up vision foundation models and aligning for generic visual-linguistic tasks (2024). https://arxiv.org/abs/2312.14238

4. Dosovitskiy, A., et al.: An image is worth 16x16 words: transformers for image recognition at scale (2021). https://arxiv.org/abs/2010.11929

5. Gao, L., et al.: Pal: program-aided language models (2023). https://arxiv.org/abs/2211.10435

6. Geirhos, R., et al.: Shortcut learning in deep neural networks. Nat. Mach. Intell. **2**(11), 665–673 (2020). https://doi.org/10.1038/s42256-020-00257-z

7. Gong, L., et al.: A survey on video analytics in cloud-edge-terminal collaborative systems (2025). https://arxiv.org/abs/2502.06581

8. Goodfellow, I.J., et al.: Generative adversarial networks (2014). https://arxiv.org/abs/1406.2661

9. Guo, C., Pleiss, G., Sun, Y., Weinberger, K.Q.: On calibration of modern neural networks (2017). https://arxiv.org/abs/1706.04599

10. Hinton, G., Vinyals, O., Dean, J.: Distilling the knowledge in a neural network (2015). https://arxiv.org/abs/1503.02531

11. Hu, Y., et al.: Visual program distillation: distilling tools and programmatic reasoning into vision-language models. In: Proceedings of the IEEE/CVF Conference on Computer Vision and Pattern Recognition (CVPR) (2024)

12. Kingma, D.P., Welling, M.: Auto-encoding variational bayes (2022). https://arxiv.org/abs/1312.6114

13. Lanham, T., et al.: Measuring faithfulness in chain-of-thought reasoning (2023). https://arxiv.org/abs/2307.13702

14. Lei, J., Yu, L., Bansal, M., Berg, T.L.: Tvqa: localized, compositional video question answering (2019). https://arxiv.org/abs/1809.01696

15. Li, L.H., Hessel, J., Yu, Y., Ren, X., Chang, K.W., Choi, Y.: Symbolic chain-of-thought distillation: small models can also "think" step-by-step. In: Rogers, A., Boyd-Graber, J., Okazaki, N. (eds.) Proceedings of the 61st Annual Meeting of the Association for Computational Linguistics (Volume 1: Long Papers), pp. 2665–2679. Association for Computational Linguistics, Toronto, Canada (2023). https://doi.org/10.18653/v1/2023.acl-long.150. https://aclanthology.org/2023.acl-long.150/

16. Li, Y., et al.: Small models struggle to learn from strong reasoners (2025). https://arxiv.org/abs/2502.12143

17. Liu, H., Li, C., Li, Y., Lee, Y.J.: Improved baselines with visual instruction tuning (2024). https://arxiv.org/abs/2310.03744

18. Liu, X., Zhang, J., Xiong, C.: Visual prompt distillation for chain-of-thought reasoning in VQA. In: NeurIPS (2023)

19. Loshchilov, I., Hutter, F.: Decoupled weight decay regularization (2019). https://arxiv.org/abs/1711.05101

20. Mangalam, K., Feichtenhofer, C., Malik, J.: Egoschema: a diagnostic benchmark for very long-form video language understanding. In: Advances in Neural Information Processing Systems (NeurIPS) (2023)

21. McKinney, J.: All internvl models do very poorly with multiple images (even just 3) (2024). https://github.com/OpenGVLab/InternVL/issues/419, gitHub Issue #419. Accessed 30 Mar 2025

22. Mumuni, A., Mumuni, F., Gerrar, N.K.: A survey of synthetic data augmentation methods in machine vision. Mach. Intell. Res. **21**(5), 831–869 (2024). https://doi.org/10.1007/s11633-022-1411-7

23. Niekerk, C.V., et al.: A confidence-based acquisition model for self-supervised active learning and label correction. Trans. Assoc. Comput. Linguist. **13**, 167–187 (2024). https://doi.org/10.1162/tacl_a_00734

24. Paszke, A., et al.: Pytorch: an imperative style, high-performance deep learning library (2019). https://arxiv.org/abs/1912.01703
25. Perez, E., et al.: Discovering language model behaviors with model-written evaluations (2022). https://arxiv.org/abs/2212.09251
26. Rawal, R., et al.: Cinepile: a long video question answering dataset and benchmark (2024). https://arxiv.org/abs/2405.08813
27. Richter, S.R., Vineet, V., Roth, S., Koltun, V.: Playing for data: ground truth from computer games (2016). https://arxiv.org/abs/1608.02192
28. Rombach, R., Blattmann, A., Lorenz, D., Esser, P., Ommer, B.: High-resolution image synthesis with latent diffusion models (2022). https://arxiv.org/abs/2112.10752
29. Romero, A., Ballas, N., Kahou, S.E., Chassang, A., Gatta, C., Bengio, Y.: Fitnets: hints for thin deep nets (2015). https://arxiv.org/abs/1412.6550
30. Ros, G., Sellart, L., Materzynska, J., Vazquez, D., Lopez, A.M.: The synthia dataset: a large collection of synthetic images for semantic segmentation of urban scenes. In: 2016 IEEE Conference on Computer Vision and Pattern Recognition (CVPR), pp. 3234–3243 (2016). https://doi.org/10.1109/CVPR.2016.352
31. Sanh, V., Debut, L., Chaumond, J., Wolf, T.: Distilbert, a distilled version of bert: smaller, faster, cheaper and lighter (2020). https://arxiv.org/abs/1910.01108
32. Schmarje, L., et al.: Is one annotation enough? A data-centric image classification benchmark for noisy and ambiguous label estimation (2022). https://arxiv.org/abs/2207.06214
33. Settles, B.: Active learning literature survey. Computer Sciences Technical Report 1648, University of Wisconsin–Madison (2009)
34. Sharshar, A., Khan, L.U., Ullah, W., Guizani, M.: Vision-language models for edge networks: a comprehensive survey (2025). https://arxiv.org/abs/2502.07855
35. Shi, Y., Wang, Z., Tang, Y., Huang, S., Zhou, X.E.: Unlocking video-LLM via agent-of-thoughts distillation. In: CVPR (2025)
36. Shrivastava, A., Gupta, A., Girshick, R.: Training region-based object detectors with online hard example mining (2016). https://arxiv.org/abs/1604.03540
37. Tan, C., et al.: Boosting the power of small multimodal reasoning models to match larger models with self-consistency training (2024). https://arxiv.org/abs/2311.14109
38. Touvron, H., et al.: Llama: open and efficient foundation language models (2023). https://arxiv.org/abs/2302.13971
39. Wang, X., Chen, Y., Zhu, W.: A survey on curriculum learning (2021). https://arxiv.org/abs/2010.13166
40. Wang, X., Chen, Y., Zhu, W.: A survey on curriculum learning. IEEE Trans. Pattern Anal. Mach. Intell. **44**(9), 4555–4576 (2022). https://doi.org/10.1109/TPAMI.2021.3069908
41. Wei, J., et al.: Chain-of-thought prompting elicits reasoning in large language models (2023). https://arxiv.org/abs/2201.11903
42. Wolf, T., et al.: Huggingface's transformers: state-of-the-art natural language processing (2020). https://arxiv.org/abs/1910.03771
43. Wu, H., et al.: Longvideobench: a benchmark for long-context interleaved video-language understanding. In: Advances in Neural Information Processing Systems (NeurIPS) (2024)
44. Xu, D., et al.: Video question answering via gradually refined attention over appearance and motion. In: ACM Multimedia (2017)
45. Ye, Q., et al.: mplug-owl2: revolutionizing multi-modal large language model with modality collaboration (2023). https://arxiv.org/abs/2311.04257

46. Yu, Z., et al.: Activitynet-qa: a dataset for understanding complex web videos via question answering (2019). https://arxiv.org/abs/1906.02467
47. Zelikman, E., Wu, Y., Mu, J., Goodman, N.D.: Star: bootstrapping reasoning with reasoning (2022). https://arxiv.org/abs/2203.14465
48. Zhang, Y., Kang, B., Hooi, B., Yan, S., Feng, J.: Deep long-tailed learning: a survey (2023). https://arxiv.org/abs/2110.04596
49. Zhang, Y., et al.: Video instruction tuning with synthetic data (2024). https://arxiv.org/abs/2410.02713
50. Zhang, Z., Zhang, A., Li, M., Zhao, H., Karypis, G., Smola, A.: Multimodal chain-of-thought reasoning in language models (2024). https://arxiv.org/abs/2302.00923
51. Zhou, J., Huang, Z., Tang, S., Yu, Z.: Aotd: aligning observation and thought distillation for video reasoning. In: CVPR (2024)
52. Zhou, J., Zhang, Y., Chen, X., Gao, Y., Lin, D.: Mlvu: a comprehensive benchmark for multi-task long video understanding. In: Proceedings of the IEEE/CVF Conference on Computer Vision and Pattern Recognition (CVPR) (2025)

MRAFnd: Multimodal Retrieval-Augmented Framework for Zero-Shot Fake News Detection

Lehan Zhang[1], Yinlei Cheng[1], Shiqi Hu[2], Yiheng Zhou[1], Shangxi Li[1],
and Naidong Zhao[1(✉)]

[1] Beijing Institute of Fashion Technology, Beijing, China
sxyznd@bift.edu.cn
[2] Shenyang University of Technology, Shenyang, China

Abstract. The rapid dissemination of multimodal content has intensified the spread of fabricated news, presenting a substantial threat to social integrity. A formidable challenge for current detection systems is identifying misinformation related to novel events in zero-shot scenarios. Prevailing zero-shot methods typically assess news items in isolation via semantic matching, a strategy that fails to recognize the recycled disinformation tactics from past campaigns and lacks the sophisticated reasoning needed to identify subtle, cross-modal discrepancies. To surmount these deficiencies, we introduce **MRAFnd**, a novel **M**ultimodal **R**etrieval-**A**ugmented Framework for Zero-Shot **F**ake **N**ews **D**etection. MRAFnd emulates a collaborative team of analysts to verify news veracity. The framework initiates with **Multimodal Similarity-based News Retrieval** to assemble a corpus of contextually analogous articles from an unlabeled reference database. Subsequently, during the **Bifurcated Evidential Reasoning** stage, agents perform a dual-directional analysis to extract critical patterns from the retrieved evidence. Finally, a **Multi-Agent Collaborative Debate**, involving Analyst and Arbiter agents, engages in a structured discourse to arrive at a definitive and robust conclusion. Comprehensive experiments on three benchmark datasets reveal that MRAFnd markedly surpasses state-of-the-art baselines, achieving an accuracy gain of up to 2.35% on the demanding Weibo-21 dataset.

Keywords: Multimodal Fake News Detection · Multi-Agent Systems · Retrieval-Augmented Reasoning · Zero-Shot Learning · Large Language Models

1 Introduction

The ascent of social media has revolutionized information dissemination, establishing multimodal content—integrating text and imagery—as the principal medium of communication. This paradigm shift, however, has concurrently accelerated the propagation of multimodal fake news, which deceptively combines fabricated text with authentic or manipulated visuals to mislead audiences [22, 25]. Such disinformation can undermine

This study was supported by College Students' Innovative Entrepreneurial Training Plan Program.

J. Lokoč et al. (Eds.): MMM 2026, LNCS 16412, pp. 581–594, 2026.
https://doi.org/10.1007/978-981-95-6950-2_41

public trust, sway public opinion, and provoke social instability, thus posing a grave risk to societal cohesion. Consequently, developing automated and precise methods for detecting multimodal fake news has emerged as a paramount research imperative. Existing detection models frequently fall short in adapting to the fluid landscape of fake news, where new narratives and manipulated content concerning emergent events surface daily, necessitating constant model adaptation in data-deficient, zero-shot contexts [5].

Current research in multimodal fake news detection is primarily divided into two streams. The first stream includes supervised deep learning models, which have demonstrated significant success when trained on extensive annotated datasets [6,12,21,24]. These models generally utilize advanced fusion techniques to identify cross-modal inconsistencies. Their efficacy, however, is fundamentally contingent on the availability of large-scale labeled data, making them unsuitable for confronting fake news about novel events where no prior annotations exist. The second stream aims to overcome this data dependency using few-shot or zero-shot learning approaches. While promising, these methods often depend on superficial semantic matching and are deficient in the sophisticated reasoning capabilities essential for uncovering the nuanced contextual and logical incongruities that define advanced disinformation [18].

A core limitation of contemporary zero-shot methodologies is their tendency to analyze a target news article as an isolated entity. This approach neglects a critical characteristic of disinformation campaigns: despite addressing new events, fake news articles frequently repurpose narrative frameworks, image manipulation techniques, or stylistic formats from earlier campaigns. For example, a fabricated news story might pair an image of a political rally with a misleading caption. Although the specific event is new, the underlying tactic of misrepresenting crowd size or event context is a recurrent trope. Identifying such deceit requires more than a surface-level analysis of the image and text; it demands a profound, comparative reasoning process that situates the article within a broader context of similar real and fake news instances. **An isolated examination is thus insufficient for exposing these recycled, malicious patterns.**

To address these challenges, we introduce a new zero-shot framework: **MRAFnd**, a **M**ultimodal **R**etrieval-**A**ugmented Framework for Zero-Shot **F**ake **N**ews **D**etection. Inspired by collaborative investigative journalism and the advanced reasoning of Multimodal Large Language Models (MLLMs), MRAFnd simulates a team of analysts collaborating to verify a suspicious news article. The framework's operation involves: 1) Retrieving a set of similar, contextually relevant news articles from a vast, unannotated corpus to establish an evidentiary baseline. 2) Deploying a pair of LLM agents to conduct a bifurcated analysis of this evidence, extracting crucial patterns and potential incongruities. 3) Engaging the agents in a structured debate and arbitration process to formulate a robust, well-reasoned final judgment on the article's authenticity.

Our primary contributions are summarized as follows:

- We introduce a pioneering multi-agent framework for zero-shot multimodal fake news detection that uniquely harnesses retrieval-augmented reasoning, thereby removing the dependency on labeled data for newsworthy events.
- We propose a robust Bifurcated Evidential Reasoning mechanism, where agents perform dual-directional analysis on retrieved articles to build a comprehensive understanding of disinformation tactics and narrative structures.

- We design a Multi-Agent Collaborative Debate process, with specialized analyst and arbiter roles, which elevates the reliability and interpretability of decision-making by resolving analytical conflicts through structured discourse.
- Comprehensive experiments on benchmark fake news datasets confirm that our proposed MRAFnd framework substantially outperforms state-of-the-art zero-shot baselines.

2 Related Work

2.1 Multimodal Fake News Detection

With the development of multimodal technology [2,3,13], multimodal fake news detection has gradually become the mainstream. Multimodal fake news detection aims to identify inconsistencies across modalities [11]. Methodologies have evolved from simple feature fusion of VGG and BERT embeddings [6] to more sophisticated fusion techniques and graph-based networks for event-level analysis [12,14]. Recently, Large Language Models (LLMs) have been employed in specialized frameworks like TELLER and SNIFFER to enhance reasoning capabilities [10,17]. While these methods show promise, they often require fine-tuning or labeled examples, which are unavailable for emerging disinformation campaigns. MRAFnd differs by operating in a truly zero-shot setting, leveraging retrieval from an unannotated corpus to analyze disinformation patterns without any model training.

2.2 LLM-Based Multi-agent Frameworks

LLMs have evolved into autonomous agents capable of complex reasoning and planning [23], leading to the development of multi-agent systems where agents collaborate to solve complex problems [16]. However, many such systems depend on environmental feedback, which is incompatible with zero-shot classification as it would reveal the ground-truth label. MRAFnd's architecture is fundamentally different: it is feedback-free, orchestrating agent collaboration through structured analysis and debate to enable robust zero-shot reasoning without any supervisory signals.

3 Methodology

3.1 Overview

Problem Formulation. We define a multimodal news collection as a set of articles, where each article N is represented as a tuple $\{\mathcal{V}, \mathcal{T}\}$, containing a visual element $\mathcal{V}$ (image) and a textual element $\mathcal{T}$ (text). Our task is zero-shot fake news detection, where the objective is to classify articles in a test set S_{test} as either authentic or fabricated. This is achieved by utilizing an unlabeled reference set of news articles, S_{ref}, as a source of contextual evidence. Our method is entirely gradient-free, obviating the need for model training or fine-tuning.

To address the data scarcity inherent in detecting novel fake news, we introduce **MRAFnd**, a multi-agent framework conceived to simulate a collaborative verification

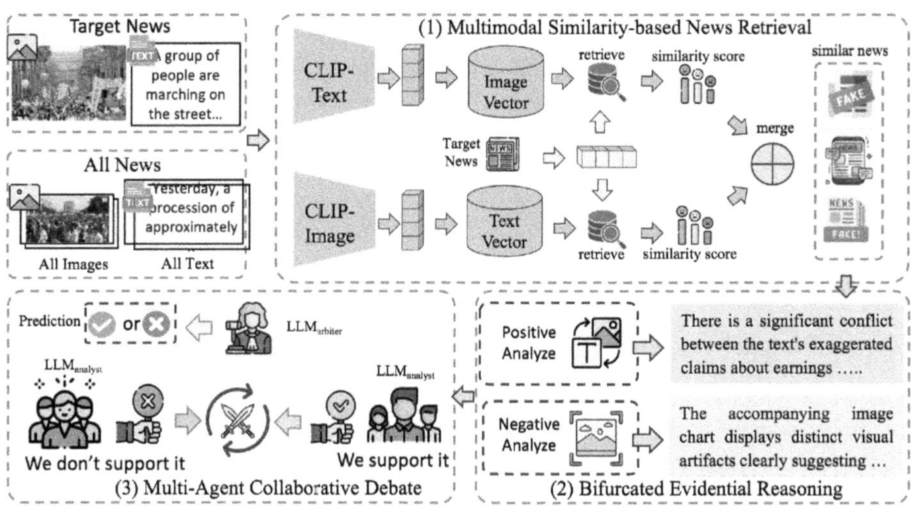

Fig. 1. An overview of our proposed framework, MRAFnd, for zero-shot multimodal fake news detection. The process is composed of three primary stages: (1) Multimodal Similarity-based News Retrieval, (2) Bifurcated Evidential Reasoning, and (3) Multi-Agent Collaborative Debate. Note: Module names in the figure should be mentally mapped to the new names used in this paper.

workflow. MRAFnd orchestrates multiple LLM agents across three sequential stages: 1) **Multimodal Similarity-based News Retrieval** (Sect. 3.2), which finds and collects contextually similar news articles from the unlabeled reference set S_{ref}. 2) **Bifurcated Evidential Reasoning** (Sect. 3.3), where agents perform a dual-directional analysis to extract key analytical patterns from the retrieved evidence. 3) **Multi-Agent Collaborative Debate** (Sect. 3.4), in which specialized analyst and arbiter agents discuss the findings to reach a final, well-founded verdict. A schematic of MRAFnd is depicted in Fig. 1.

3.2 Multimodal Similarity-Based News Retrieval

Disinformation campaigns, despite their continuous evolution, often display recurrent thematic and structural motifs [25]. Inspired by retrieval-augmented generation [7], our initial stage is dedicated to retrieving news articles from S_{ref} that are analogous to the target article. These retrieved items function as critical evidence, supplying the context required to evaluate the target's veracity.

For a given target news article $N_{target} = \{\mathcal{V}_{target}, \mathcal{T}_{target}\}$, we first generate its multimodal embedding by integrating its visual and textual features:

$$\mathbf{E} = \lambda_v \cdot \mathbf{V}_{enc}(\mathcal{V}) + \lambda_t \cdot \mathbf{T}_{enc}(\mathcal{T}), \tag{1}$$

where $\mathbf{E}$ denotes the final multimodal embedding. $\mathbf{V}_{enc}(\cdot)$ and $\mathbf{T}_{enc}(\cdot)$ are pre-trained visual and textual encoders, respectively. The coefficients λ_v and λ_t are fixed hyperpa-

rameters that modulate the influence of each modality. We apply this encoding procedure to the target article and all articles in the reference set S_{ref}.

To pinpoint the most pertinent evidence, we calculate the cosine similarity between
the embedding of the target article and those of all articles in the reference set:

$$s = \text{sim}(\mathbf{E}_{\text{target}}, \mathbf{E}_{\text{ref}}) = \frac{\mathbf{E}_{\text{target}} \cdot \mathbf{E}_{\text{ref}}}{\|\mathbf{E}_{\text{target}}\| \|\mathbf{E}_{\text{ref}}\|}, \tag{2}$$

where $\mathbf{E}_{\text{target}}$ and $\mathbf{E}_{\text{ref}}$ are the embeddings for the target and a reference article, respectively. Based on these similarity scores, we select the top-K articles from S_{ref} to consti-
tute the evidence set N_{evidence}:

$$N_{\text{evidence}} = \{N_{\text{ref}} \mid s \in \text{Top}_K(\{\text{sim}(\mathbf{E}_{\text{target}}, \mathbf{E}_{ref}) \mid N_{ref} \in S_{ref}\})\}. \tag{3}$$

This evidence set, comprising the K most similar yet unlabeled news articles, is subsequently forwarded to the next stage for detailed analysis.

3.3 Bifurcated Evidential Reasoning

The retrieved evidence set, N_{evidence}, offers valuable context. However, since the articles
are unlabeled, presenting them directly to a model could introduce noise and ambiguity.
To mitigate this, we introduce a structured reasoning stage where an LLM agent systematically extracts relevant patterns and potential indicators of misinformation. This
process is executed from two opposing directions to ensure a comprehensive and impar-
tial analysis.

Affirmative Pattern Review. The reasoning agent processes the K evidence articles
in their original sequence. At each step i, the agent evaluates the i-th article in light of
the analytical insights gathered from the preceding $i - 1$ steps. This iterative approach
enables the agent to construct a cumulative understanding of narrative patterns, visual
motifs, and potential inconsistencies, thereby building an affirmative case based on the
evidence flow. This process is formalized as:

$$\mathcal{P}_{\text{affirm},i} = \text{LLM}_{\text{reasoner}}(N_{\text{evidence},i}, \mathcal{P}_{\text{affirm},i-1}, \Pi_{\text{reasoner}}), \tag{4}$$

where $\mathcal{P}_{\text{affirm},i}$ is the set of distilled affirmative patterns after processing the i-th article.
$N_{\text{evidence},i}$ is the i-th article from the evidence set, and $\text{LLM}_{\text{reasoner}}$ is an LLM agent
guided by a Chain-of-Thought prompt Π_{reasoner} designed to elicit detailed reasoning
about indicators of fake news.

Negational Pattern Review. A potential drawback of a purely sequential analysis is
order dependency, where articles encountered earlier may unduly influence the final
summary. To counteract this bias, we implement a complementary negational review.
Upon completing the affirmative pass, the reasoning agent re-processes the same evidence set but in reverse order. This pass is designed to challenge or negate the initial
findings by approaching the evidence from an opposing viewpoint.

$$\mathcal{P}_{\text{negate},i} = \text{LLM}_{\text{reasoner}}(N_{\text{evidence},K+1-i}, \mathcal{P}_{\text{negate},i-1}, \Pi_{\text{reasoner}}), \tag{5}$$

where $\mathcal{P}_{\text{negate},i}$ represents the accumulated findings from the negational review. This dual-perspective approach ensures that each piece of evidence is assessed from two distinct contextual standpoints, yielding two comprehensive sets of findings: $\mathcal{P}_{\text{affirm},K}$ and $\mathcal{P}_{\text{negate},K}$.

3.4 Multi-agent Collaborative Debate

In the final stage, we institute a multi-agent debate to synthesize the analytical findings and render a definitive judgment. This stage engages two types of agents: Analyst Agents and an Arbiter Agent.

First, two Analyst Agents are assigned the task of formulating independent assessments. Each agent is provided with the target news article and one of the two sets of findings (affirmative or negational) from the preceding stage. They each generate a detailed report outlining their reasoning and a final verdict (real or fake):

$$\mathcal{R}_{\text{affirm}} = \text{LLM}_{\text{analyst}}(\mathcal{P}_{\text{affirm},K}, \mathcal{V}_{\text{target}}, \mathcal{T}_{\text{target}}), \tag{6}$$

$$\mathcal{R}_{\text{negate}} = \text{LLM}_{\text{analyst}}(\mathcal{P}_{\text{negate},K}, \mathcal{V}_{\text{target}}, \mathcal{T}_{\text{target}}), \tag{7}$$

where $\mathcal{R}_{\text{affirm}}$ and $\mathcal{R}_{\text{negate}}$ are the reasoned reports from the two analyst agents, respectively. This step ensures the development of two independent lines of reasoning from the bifurcated analysis.

Next, the verdicts from the two reports are compared. If the analysts concur, their shared decision is accepted as the final outcome. In instances of disagreement, a third Arbiter Agent is summoned to resolve the conflict. The arbiter examines the reasoning of both analysts to make a final, decisive judgment:

$$\mathcal{R}_{\text{final}} = \begin{cases} \mathcal{R}_{\text{affirm}} & \text{if verdict}(\mathcal{R}_{\text{affirm}}) = \text{verdict}(\mathcal{R}_{\text{negate}}) \\ \text{LLM}_{\text{arbiter}}(\mathcal{R}_{\text{affirm}}, \mathcal{R}_{\text{negate}}, \mathcal{V}_{\text{target}}, \mathcal{T}_{\text{target}}) & \text{otherwise} \end{cases}, \tag{8}$$

where $\text{LLM}_{\text{arbiter}}$ meticulously weighs the arguments from both perspectives before making the final determination. This debate mechanism enhances the robustness and reliability of the final decision by incorporating multiple viewpoints and establishing a structured protocol for conflict resolution.

4 Experiments

In this section, we present a comprehensive suite of experiments to assess the efficacy of our proposed MRAFnd framework. Our evaluation is structured to address the following research questions:

- **RQ1:** How does MRAFnd's performance compare to state-of-the-art multimodal and LLM-based fake news detection methods in a zero-shot context?
- **RQ2:** What is the individual contribution of each core component within the MRAFnd framework, namely news retrieval, bifurcated reasoning, and collaborative debate?

- **RQ3:** How sensitive is MRAFnd's performance to its primary hyperparameters, specifically the number of retrieved articles and the rounds of debate?
- **RQ4:** What is the inference efficiency of MRAFnd concerning token consumption and processing time relative to other LLM-based methods?
- **RQ5:** How robust is MRAFnd to noise and imperfections during the evidence retrieval phase?

4.1 Experimental Settings

Datasets. We evaluate our framework on three widely-adopted public benchmark datasets for multimodal fake news detection:

- **Weibo** [24]: A classic Chinese dataset sourced from the Weibo social media platform, serving as a standard benchmark for this task.
- **Weibo-21** [15]: A more contemporary and challenging Chinese dataset, also from Weibo, featuring multi-domain news content that tests a model's generalization capabilities.
- **GossipCop** [20]: A real-world English dataset centered on celebrity and entertainment news, curated by professional journalists and known for its subtle instances of misinformation.

Baselines. We compare MRAFnd against three classes of state-of-the-art baselines in a zero-shot setting:

- **General-purpose LLMs**, which process only the textual component of the news: GPT-4o and Gemini-1.5-Flash.
- **General-purpose MLLMs**, which can interpret both text and images: LLaVA-1.5-7B [9], InstructBLIP-7B [4], and MiniGPT-v2-7B [1].
- **LLM-based FND Methods**, which employ advanced reasoning for fact-checking: TELLER [10], SNIFFER [17], and FactAgent [8].

Implementation Details. All experiments were performed on a server with NVIDIA A100 GPUs. For our MRAFnd framework, we use LLaVA-1.5-7B as the backbone for all agents, chosen for its strong multimodal reasoning and efficient architecture. The visual encoder and text encoder are the pre-trained ViT-L/14 from CLIP [19]. For evidence retrieval, we set the number of retrieved articles $K = 5$ and the number of debate rounds $R = 2$, based on the analysis in Sect. 4.4. We evaluate all methods using two standard metrics: **Accuracy** and **Macro-F1** score.

4.2 Main Results (RQ1)

Table 1 displays the main experimental outcomes on the three benchmark datasets. Our proposed framework, MRAFnd, consistently achieves the highest performance across

Table 1. Main results of zero-shot multimodal fake news detection. We report Accuracy (%) and Macro-F1 (%). The best results are in **bold**, and the second-best are <u>underlined</u>. All improvements are statistically significant ($p < 0.05$).

Category	Method	Weibo		Weibo-21		GossipCop	
		Accuracy	Macro-F1	Accuracy	Macro-F1	Accuracy	Macro-F1
General-purpose LLMs	GPT-4o	75.31	75.15	78.40	78.31	67.28	65.04
	Gemini-1.5-Flash	74.84	74.68	77.65	77.52	66.53	64.18
General-purpose MLLMs	LLaVA-1.5-7B [9]	78.16	78.02	80.27	80.19	68.31	66.85
	InstructBLIP-7B [4]	77.21	77.05	79.52	79.46	67.73	66.12
	MiniGPT-v2-7B [1]	77.86	77.74	79.84	79.80	68.07	66.53
LLM-based FND Methods	TELLER [10]	81.25	81.13	83.10	83.02	70.89	69.84
	SNIFFER [17]	80.83	80.75	82.57	82.49	70.18	69.05
	FactAgent (?)	<u>82.14</u>	<u>82.06</u>	<u>83.96</u>	<u>83.85</u>	<u>71.39</u>	<u>70.21</u>
Ours	**MRAFnd (LLaVA-1.5-7B)**	**84.75**	**84.69**	**86.31**	**86.25**	**73.55**	**72.48**

all datasets and metrics, affirming its superior efficacy in the zero-shot multimodal fake news detection task.

MRAFnd Substantially Outperforms all Baselines by a Significant Margin. On the challenging Weibo-21 dataset, for example, MRAFnd achieves an accuracy of 86.31%, surpassing the strongest baseline, FactAgent, by 2.35%. This result underscores the efficacy of our core design: by retrieving and analyzing a collection of evidential articles, MRAFnd transcends isolated analysis. It successfully identifies the recycled narrative structures and manipulation tactics prevalent in disinformation campaigns—a crucial capability that other methods lack.

LLM-Based FND Methods Exhibit Stronger Performance than General-Purpose Models. Specialized methods like FactAgent and TELLER, which incorporate fact-checking pipelines, outperform general-purpose MLLMs. This is anticipated, as their structured reasoning workflows are better suited to the fake news detection task. However, their dependence on analyzing the target article in isolation constrains their ability to contextualize it within broader disinformation trends.

Multimodal Models Show a Clear Advantage Over Text-Only LLMs. MLLMs such as LLaVA consistently outperform text-only models like GPT-4o. This confirms the value of incorporating visual information, as inconsistencies between image and text often serve as key indicators of fake news. Nevertheless, without a mechanism to harness external context, their performance remains constrained.

4.3   Ablation Study (RQ2)

To assess the contribution of each component in MRAFnd, we conduct an ablation study with the following variants:

- **w/o Retrieval**: Removes the evidence retrieval stage, analyzing the target news in isolation, similar to standard MLLM approaches.

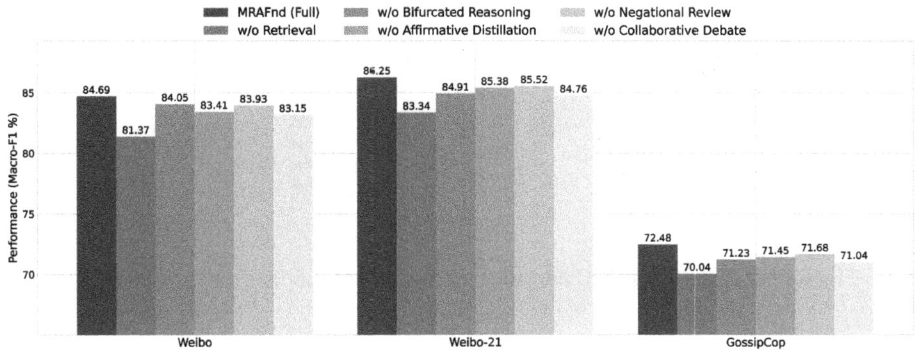

Fig. 2. Ablation study of MRAFnd on three datasets. Performance is reported as Macro-F1 score.

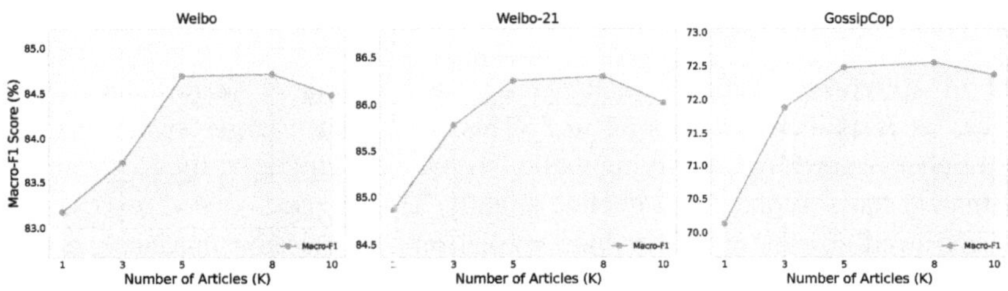

Fig. 3. Performance of MRAFnd with a varying number of retrieved articles (K).

- **w/o Bifurcated Reasoning**: Replaces the dual-directional analysis with a single-pass review of the retrieved evidence.
- **w/o Affirmative Distillation**: Uses only the results from the negational pattern review.
- **w/o Negational Review**: Uses only the results from the Affirmative Pattern Review.
- **w/o Collaborative Debate**: Eliminates the multi-agent debate stage. In cases of disagreement between the two initial analyses, it defaults to the conclusion from the affirmative pass.

Figure 2 presents the results of the ablation study. The removal of any component results in a performance decline, confirming the integral role of each part of our framework. The most substantial performance drop is observed in the **w/o Retrieval** configuration, where the Macro-F1 score decreases by 3.32% points on Weibo. This clearly illustrates that retrieval-augmented context is the cornerstone of MRAFnd's success. Removing the **Bifurcated Reasoning** also leads to a notable decrease, emphasizing the importance of mitigating order bias and achieving a holistic understanding of the evidence. Importantly, even when key components are ablated (e.g., w/o Collaborative Debate), our framework variants still generally outperform the strongest baseline, underscoring the resilience of the core retrieval-augmented reasoning paradigm.

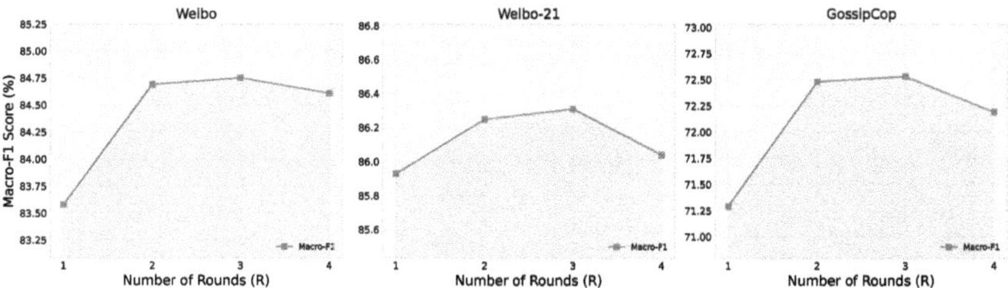

Fig. 4. Performance of MRAFnd with a varying number of deliberation rounds (R).

4.4 Parameter Sensitivity Analysis (RQ3)

We examine the impact of two critical hyperparameters: the number of retrieved articles (K) and the number of debate rounds (R).

Effect of Retrieved Articles (K)**:** As depicted in Fig. 3, performance generally enhances as K is increased from 1 to 5. This is because a larger evidence pool provides a richer context for identifying malicious patterns. However, for K greater than 5, performance starts to plateau or decline slightly. This suggests that an excessive number of retrieved articles may introduce noise from less relevant instances, potentially hindering the reasoning process. We therefore select $K = 5$ as the optimal value.

Effect of Debate Rounds (R)**:** Figure 4 illustrates the effect of the number of debate rounds between the Analyst and Arbiter agents. Transitioning from $R = 1$ (a single decision) to $R = 2$ (one round of debate and refinement) produces a tangible performance improvement across all datasets. This shows that enabling agents to challenge and refine initial conclusions helps resolve ambiguities and leads to a more robust final verdict. Performance stabilizes at $R = 3$, indicating that two rounds are sufficient to converge on a well-reasoned decision. We choose $R = 2$ for an optimal balance between performance and efficiency.

4.5 Inference Efficiency Analysis (RQ4)

We compare the inference efficiency of MRAFnd with other LLM-based FND methods, measuring the average number of tokens consumed and the average wall-clock time required per news article on the Weibo dataset.

Table 2. Inference efficiency comparison on the Weibo dataset.

Method	Avg. Tokens/Sample	Avg. Time/Sample (s)
TELLER	~1.8k	10.2
SNIFFER	~2.1k	12.5
FactAgent	~4.5k	23.8
MRAFnd (Ours)	~3.2k	14.7

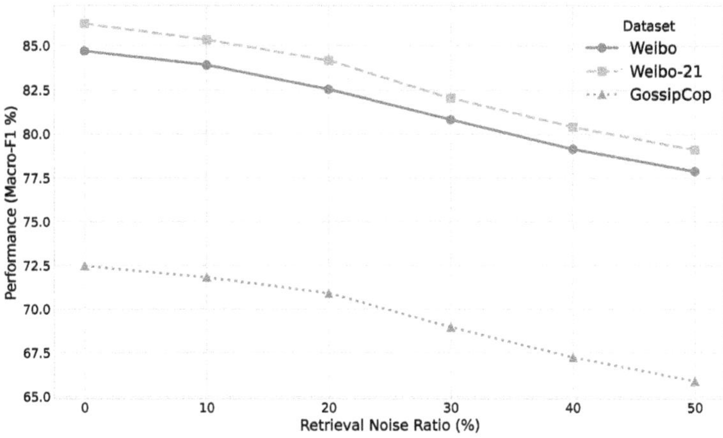

Fig. 5. Performance of MRAFnd under varying levels of retrieval noise. The noise ratio indicates the percentage of retrieved articles replaced with random ones.

As shown in Table 2, MRAFnd uses fewer tokens than the complex, multi-step FactAgent framework, demonstrating superior token efficiency. While its token consumption is higher than simpler methods like TELLER, this is an expected trade-off for the comprehensive analysis of retrieved evidence. Crucially, MRAFnd's inference time is only slightly longer than SNIFFER's and markedly faster than FactAgent's. This efficiency is achieved by parallelizing the analysis of different evidence articles and employing a lightweight multi-agent debate. This analysis confirms that MRAFnd achieves its state-of-the-art performance with a practical and manageable computational footprint.

4.6   Robustness to Retrieval Noise (RQ5)

To evaluate the framework's resilience, we simulate a noisy retrieval environment. We corrupt the retrieved evidence set by substituting a percentage (from 10% to 50%) of the top-K articles with randomly selected articles from the reference corpus.

Figure 5 illustrates that MRAFnd's performance degrades gracefully as the noise level increases. Even when 30% of the retrieved evidence is irrelevant, MRAFnd's Macro-F1 score drops by only about 4–5% on average. Its performance remains competitive even with 50% noise. This highlights the robustness of our Bifurcated Evidential Reasoning and Multi-Agent Collaborative Debate stages, which can effectively distill meaningful signals and filter out distractions from a partially corrupted evidence set—a vital capability for real-world deployments where retrieval systems are inherently imperfect.

4.7   Robustness to MLLM Backbone

To confirm that MRAFnd's effectiveness stems from its architectural design rather than the capability of a single model, we assess its performance with various MLLM back-

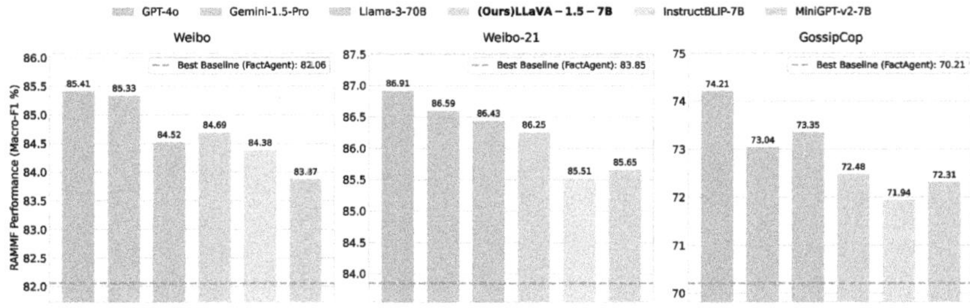

Fig. 6. Performance (Macro-F1 %) of the MRAFnd framework with different MLLM backbones on the three datasets.

bones. We substituted the agents' core model with several leading MLLMs, including large proprietary models (GPT-4o, Gemini-1.5-Pro) and powerful open-source alternatives (Llama-3-70B, InstructBLIP-7B). The Macro-F1 scores are presented in Fig. 6.

The results unequivocally demonstrate MRAFnd's robustness. The framework consistently outperforms the strongest baseline (FactAgent) across all tested MLLMs. As anticipated, larger models like GPT-4o deliver the highest performance. However, the performance reduction when using smaller models is notably gradual. Remarkably, MRAFnd powered by the lightweight LLaVA-1.5-7B not only significantly surpasses FactAgent but also remains competitive with much larger models. This provides strong evidence that MRAFnd's agentic workflow—retrieving evidence, analyzing it from dual perspectives, and debating the outcomes—is the primary driver of its success. This insight is crucial, as it confirms that **MRAFnd can be deployed effectively using smaller, open-source models, offering a state-of-the-art solution that is both powerful and practical for real-world applications**.

5   Conclusion

In this paper, we proposed **MRAFnd**, a novel retrieval-augmented multi-agent framework for zero-shot multimodal fake news detection. Our framework mimics a collaborative analytical process by integrating **Multimodal News Retrieval** to gather evidence, **Bifurcated Evidential Reasoning** to mitigate analytical bias, and a **Multi-Agent Collaborative Debate** to synthesize findings into a robust verdict. Extensive experiments confirm MRAFnd significantly outperforms state-of-the-art baselines across three benchmark datasets. Future work will address the framework's dependency on retrieval quality by enhancing the retrieval mechanism's resilience to noise and modal inconsistencies, thereby further improving detection reliability.

References

1. Chen, J., et al.: Minigpt-v2: large language model as a unified interface for vision-language multi-task learning. arXiv preprint arXiv:2310.09478 (2023)
2. Cui, X., Lu, W., Tong, Y., Li, Y., Zhao, Z.: Diffusion-based multi-modal synergy interest network for click-through rate prediction. In: Proceedings of the 48th International ACM SIGIR Conference on Research and Development in Information Retrieval, pp. 581–591 (2025)
3. Cui, X., Lu, W., Tong, Y., Li, Y., Zhao, Z.: Multi-modal multi-behavior sequential recommendation with conditional diffusion-based feature denoising. In: Proceedings of the 48th International ACM SIGIR Conference on Research and Development in Information Retrieval, pp. 1593–1602 (2025)
4. Dai, W., et al.: Instructblip: towards general-purpose vision-language models with instruction tuning (2023)
5. Giachanou, A., Ghanem, B., Ríssola, E.A., Rosso, P., Crestani, F., Oberski, D.: The impact of psycholinguistic patterns in discriminating between fake and real news. ACM Comput. Surv. **55**(4), 1–37 (2022)
6. Khattar, D., Goud, J.S., Gupta, M., Varma, V.: MVAE: multimodal variational autoencoder for fake news detection. In: The World Wide Web Conference, pp. 2915–2921 (2019)
7. Lewis, P., et al.: Retrieval-augmented generation for knowledge-intensive NLP tasks. Adv. Neural. Inf. Process. Syst. **33**, 9459–9474 (2020)
8. Li, P., de Rijke, M., Xue, H., Ao, S., Song, Y., Salim, F.D.: Large language models for next point-of-interest recommendation. In: Proceedings of the 47th International ACM SIGIR Conference on Research and Development in Information Retrieval, pp. 1463–1472 (2024)
9. Liu, H., Li, C., Li, Y., Lee, Y.J.: Improved baselines with visual instruction tuning. In: Proceedings of the IEEE/CVF Conference on Computer Vision and Pattern Recognition, pp. 26296–26306 (2024)
10. Liu, H., Wang, W., Li, H., Li, H.: Teller: a trustworthy framework for explainable, generalizable and controllable fake news detection. arXiv preprint arXiv:2402.07776 (2024)
11. Liu, M., et al.: TMAC: temporal multi-modal graph learning for acoustic event classification. In: Proceedings of the 31st ACM International Conference on Multimedia, pp. 3365–3374 (2023)
12. Lu, W., Tong, Y., Ye, Z.: Dammfnd: domain-aware multimodal multi-view fake news detection. In: Proceedings of the AAAI Conference on Artificial Intelligence, vol. 39, pp. 559–567 (2025)
13. Lu, W., Yin, L.: Dmmd4sr: diffusion model-based multi-level multimodal denoising for sequential recommendation. In: Proceedings of the 33rd ACM International Conference on Multimedia, pp. 6363–6372 (2025)
14. Ma, Z., Luo, M., Guo, H., Zeng, Z., Hao, Y., Zhao, X.: Event-radar: event-driven multi-view learning for multimodal fake news detection. In: Proceedings of the 62nd Annual Meeting of the Association for Computational Linguistics (Volume 1: Long Papers), pp. 5809–5821 (2024)
15. Nan, Q., Cao, J., Zhu, Y., Wang, Y., Li, J.: Mdfend: multi-domain fake news detection. In: Proceedings of the 30th ACM International Conference on Information & Knowledge Management, pp. 3343–3347 (2021)
16. Park, J.S., O'Brien, J., Cai, C.J., Morris, M.R., Liang, P., Bernstein, M.S.: Generative agents: interactive simulacra of human behavior. In: Proceedings of the 36th Annual ACM Symposium on User Interface Software and Technology, pp. 1–22 (2023)
17. Qi, P., Yan, Z., Hsu, W., Lee, M.L.: Sniffer: multimodal large language model for explainable out-of-context misinformation detection. In: Proceedings of the IEEE/CVF Conference on Computer Vision and Pattern Recognition, pp. 13052–13062 (2024)

18. Qian, S., Wang, J., Hu, J., Li, J., Fang, Q.: Hierarchical multi-modal contextual attention network for fake news detection. In: Proceedings of the 44th International ACM SIGIR Conference on Research and Development in Information Retrieval, pp. 1957–1961 (2021)
19. Radford, A., et al.: Learning transferable visual models from natural language supervision. In: International Conference on Machine Learning, pp. 8748–8763. PMLR (2021)
20. Shu, K., Mahudeswaran, D., Wang, S., Lee, D., Liu, H.: Fakenewsnet: a data repository with news content, social context, and spatiotemporal information for studying fake news on social media. Big Data 8(3), 171–188 (2020)
21. Tong, Y., Lu, W., Cui, X., Mao, Y., Zhao, Z.: DAPT: domain-aware prompt-tuning for multimodal fake news detection. In: Proceedings of the 33rd ACM International Conference on Multimedia, pp. 7902–7911 (2025)
22. Tong, Y., Lu, W., Zhao, Z., Lai, S., Shi, T.: Mmdfnd: multi-modal multi-domain fake news detection. In: Proceedings of the 32nd ACM International Conference on Multimedia, pp. 1178–1186 (2024)
23. Wang, G., et al.: Voyager: an open-ended embodied agent with large language models. In: Intrinsically-Motivated and Open-Ended Learning Workshop@ NeurIPS2023 (2023)
24. Wang, Y., et al.: EANN: event adversarial neural networks for multi-modal fake news detection. In: Proceedings of the 24th ACM SIGKDD International Conference on Knowledge Discovery & Data Mining, pp. 849–857 (2018)
25. Zhou, X., Zafarani, R.: A survey of fake news: fundamental theories, detection methods, and opportunities. ACM Comput. Surv. (CSUR) 53(5), 1–40 (2020)

DiffSynth-LVOS: Enhancing Language-Guided Video Object Segmentation via Diffusion-Based Synthetic Data Generation

Chunjiang He and Gang Yang[✉]

School of Information, Renmin University of China, Beijing, China
yanggang@ruc.edu.com

Abstract. Language-guided video object segmentation (LVOS) has achieved remarkable progress through advanced video segmentation models, but their performance heavily relies on large-scale fine-grained training data. The acquisition and fine-grained annotation of video datasets require exorbitant labeling costs and considerable time overhead. To address this challenge, we present DiffSynth-LVOS, a novel method that contains a diffusion-based object video generation model to create synthetic various training data according to textual object description. Our method first generates high-quality videos conditioned on masks from existing real datasets by introducing a full-fill mask constraint and video latent blending module, ensuring precise frame-mask alignment and temporal consistency for video segmentation training. Then the impact of synthetic videos through joint fine-tuning with real videos is investigated to increase the performance of LVOS. Experimental results demonstrate significant performance improvements when training on our expanded dataset (e.g., $\mathcal{J\&F}$ score improves from 52.39% to 56.48% on Ref-DAVIS benchmark). Furthermore, comparative studies reveal that our method produces object segmentation videos more suitable for LVOS tasks than alternative video generation approaches. This work provides an effective solution to the data scarcity problem in LVOS while maintaining model performance with reduced reliance on annotated real videos.

Keywords: Video Object Segmentation · Video Generation · DDIM

1 Introduction

Language-guided video object segmentation (LVOS), also known as referring video object segmentation (RVOS), is a task that focuses on segmenting the target object in video frames under the guidance of natural language descriptions. With the advancement of LVOS, this research has a great contribution

G. Yang—Supported by the Beijing Natural Science Foundation (L254039).

to many applications, e.g., video surveillance and human-machine interaction. However, both academic benchmarks and real-world scenarios are hindered by the labor-intensive annotation process and high costs, which result in a limited number of training pairs, e.g., Ref-DAVIS17 [14] with 90 videos and Ref-YouTube-VOS [26] with 3978 videos. The core problem of our research is how to generate high-quality annotated segmentation video datasets without relying on manual labeling. Furthermore, we aim to enhance the performance of LVOS models through training on these augmented datasets.

Fortunately, the field of video generative models, represented by [13,21,27], have witnessed remarkable progress in recent years. Especially text-driven video editing models [6,17,22,33,36] have achieved astonishing video editing ability in recent years. Motivated by these approaches, we intend to employ generative models for video synthesis, aiming to enhance the language-guided video object segmentation task.

Although these video editing models can fulfill the need for precise editing, there are still several challenges: (1) The resulting videos still require manual annotation, posing a major challenge for large-scale data generation. Due to the misalignment between synthetic videos and their annotations, they cannot be directly used for training without further constraints. (2) As these generative videos are conditioned solely on the editing descriptions, the synthesized content may deviate from the original video in terms of layout, structure, and unedited areas. This is primarily because text prompts do not explicitly indicate which parts of the original video should be preserved. (3) Some failed generation cases reveal the presence of forgery artifacts and content inconsistency in the frames, especially on the object boundaries, which compromises the overall generation quality.

To solve the above challenges, we introduce *DiffSynth-LVOS* (Diffusion-based Synthesis for LVOS), a diffusion-based text-to-video model. To address issue (1), we incorporate the known masks from the dataset as structural constraints during the video generation process. This represents the key distinction and advantage of our model compared to other generative approaches [17,33]. Through a carefully devised mechanism, the mask guides the generation to ensure structural fidelity, enabling the production of videos that inherently conform to the desired mask layout. Consequently, the generated videos require no additional manual annotation and can be directly employed to train LVOS models, thereby significantly reducing the cost of human labeling.

However, during the video generation process, we encountered issue (2): certain synthesized videos exhibited inconsistencies between the edited region and the intended target area. These low-quality synthetic videos can adversely affect the training of LVOS models. To address this, we introduce Video Latent Blending (VLB). Given a source video, an edited prompt, and a corresponding mask (indicating the region to be modified), VLB performs guided video editing. In this process, VLB preserves the latent semantics of the background while blending in the latent semantics of the newly generated target region, thereby achieving the goal of altering the foreground while maintaining background consistency.

Moreover, in some poorly generated cases, we observed that although the foreground and background were successfully separated, artifacts still appeared at their boundaries, as illustrated in the first column in Fig. 1. We attribute this to issue (3): a misalignment between the generated regions and the textual prompts, where the prompt fails to effectively guide the content to fully occupy the intended foreground area. To solve this, we propose two solutions. First, we introduce a Mask Guided Loss, which encourages the cross-attention maps during inference to align with the known masks, thereby optimizing the latent input x_t to better synchronize the attended visual regions with the textual guidance. Second, to tackle the boundary artifacts between foreground and background, we employ an Edge Optimizer, which evaluates the completeness of boundary filling and imposes constraints to refine the transition between foreground and background.

In summary, our contributions can be concluded as follows:

- We propose a novel research paradigm that leverages synthetic videos generated by diffusion models to enhance the performance of LVOS models (e.g., $\mathcal{J}\&\mathcal{F}$ improves from 52.39% to 56.48%), significantly reducing the need for manual annotation.
- To ensure high-quality video synthesis, a Video Latent Blending module is designed to maintain background consistency and enable precise foreground editing.
- Boundary artifacts are mitigated through the introduction of a Mask Guided Loss and an Edge Optimizer, which collectively improve alignment between textual prompts and visual attention, while sharpening the separation between foreground and background regions.

Fig. 1. Illustration of artifacts and inconsistency. Row (a) shows the original frames from the video; row (b) presents generated frames without mask guided loss; row (c) displays generated frames with this technique applied.

2   Related Work

2.1   Referring Video Object Segmentation

Early RVOS approaches primarily attempted to integrate textual features directly into the visual processing pipeline. URVOS [26] proposes a unified framework to combine the image-language fusion module with the memory mechanism. CMPC-V [18] leverages layer-wise cross-modal attention to capture fine-grained associations between textual cues and visual representations. With the emergence of DETR-based architectures [5], many query-based models have achieved significant progress. Building on MTTR [4] presenting an end-to-end framework with object representation as queries, ReferFormer [34] employs language queries to perform cross-attention with video features, which are subsequently enhanced by a cross-modal feature pyramid network (FPN) [16] decoder. SgMg [20] addresses feature drift by applying Fourier domain attention combined with a Gaussian kernel, which helps preserve temporal consistency across frames. In contrast to these model-focused approaches, our work emphasizes the crucial importance of data.

2.2   Text Driven Video Generation

Extending T2I generation to video domain, text-to-video (T2V) generation requires both spatial and temporal consistency. GODIVA [31] first introduces VQ-VAE [29] to T2V with sparse attention. NüWA [32] builds on GODIVA [31] by establishing a unified framework that supports multiple generation tasks through multitask learning. Following the success of T2I diffusion models, Video Diffusion Models (VDMs) [13] extend the paradigm to videos by designing a novel space-time U-Net for the diffusion process. ImagenVideo [11] successfully improves VDMs [13] in generating high-quality videos by applying cascaded diffusion models and v-prediction parameterization. Make-A-Video [27] fuses the visual synthesis of text-to-image models with the temporal information learned from real videos. However, due to operating in the pixel space, both models suffer from low efficiency, which limits their applicability. In contrast, MagicVideo [37] processes the video in the latent space, following the paradigm of LDMs [25]. Tune-A-Video [33] tunes an inflated pre-trained image diffusion model with a single video. VideoCrafter2 [8] uses the architecture of its predecessor [7], and enhances the fine-tuning process through the incorporation of richer video datasets.

2.3   Text Driven Video Editing

Similar to T2V, video edit has witnessed significant advancements recently. Text2Live [3] utilizes CLIP [23] for video texture modifications, though it encounters difficulties with significant semantic alterations. Dreamix [21] uses a pre-trained ImagenVideo [11] as its backbone for image-to-video and video-to-video editing ability. Rerender-A-Video [36] ensures both semantic and texture consistency by performing inter-frame fusion in both the VAE latent space and the pixel space. VidEdit [9] focuses on leveraging extracted structural information to guide the editing process. It employs semantic segmentation methods to precisely describe regions of interest during editing. VideoP2P [17], vid2vid-zero [30] and Fatezero [22] control the cross attention map to achieve the goal of editing videos guided by prompts.

While these approaches enable to edit video contents, they fail to adapt to the LVOS task due to the absence of well-aligned annotations in the generated videos. Hence, we propose our method to address this issue, which allows editing of the targeted area while preserving other regions as much as possible.

3   Method

We construct our model based on a text to video (T2V) model VideoP2P [17], and the entire pipeline is illustrated as Fig. 2. Formally, given an input video $\mathcal{V} = \{v_1, v_2, \ldots, v_n\}$ consisting of n frames, a corresponding text prompt $\mathcal{P}$ that semantically describes its content, and a binary mask sequence $\mathcal{M} = \{m_1, m_2, \ldots, m_n\}$ aligned with the original video frames. Our goal is to generate an edited video $\mathcal{V}^* = \{v_1^*, v_2^*, \ldots, v_l^*\}$, which is guided by a revised prompt $\mathcal{P}^*$, specifying the desired modifications, as well as a binary mask sequence $\mathcal{M}$ that serves as a visual cue for the region of interest.

Each $m_t \in \{0,1\}^{H \times W}$ indicates the region in frame v_t to be edited, where 1 represents editable pixels and 0 denotes regions to be preserved. The masks are provided in advance and share the same temporal resolution as the video.

This formulation enables controllable video editing in a text-guided manner, which is particularly important for downstream task as language-guided video object segmentation (LVOS), where both semantic alignment and pixel-level consistency are essential. In this section, we first recap the diffusion models in Sect. 3.1, then we clarify our framework by a detailed description of Video Latent Blending in Sect. 3.2 and Edit with Mask Guidance in Sect. 3.3.

3.1   Preliminary

Latent Diffusion Models (LDMs). As a variant of DDPMs [12], LDMs [25] transfer pixel space to latent space with an autoencoder. First part of it is to compress pixel image x to latent vector z by using an encoder as $z = \mathcal{E}(x)$, and reconstruct latent to image by using a decoder as $x = \mathcal{D}(z)$. The second part is a DDPM process to predict the added noise. The training objective of a textual LDM can be formulated as Eq. 1:

$$\mathbb{E}_{z,\epsilon \sim \mathcal{N}(0,1),t,c} \left[\| \epsilon - \epsilon_\theta(z_t, t, c) \|_2^2 \right] \tag{1}$$

where $c = \psi(P)$ is the embedding of the text prompt.

Denoising Diffusion Implicit Models (DDIMs). Denoising Diffusion Implicit Models (DDIMs) [28] are a deterministic variant of DDPMs, aim at improving sampling efficiency without compromising generation quality. While

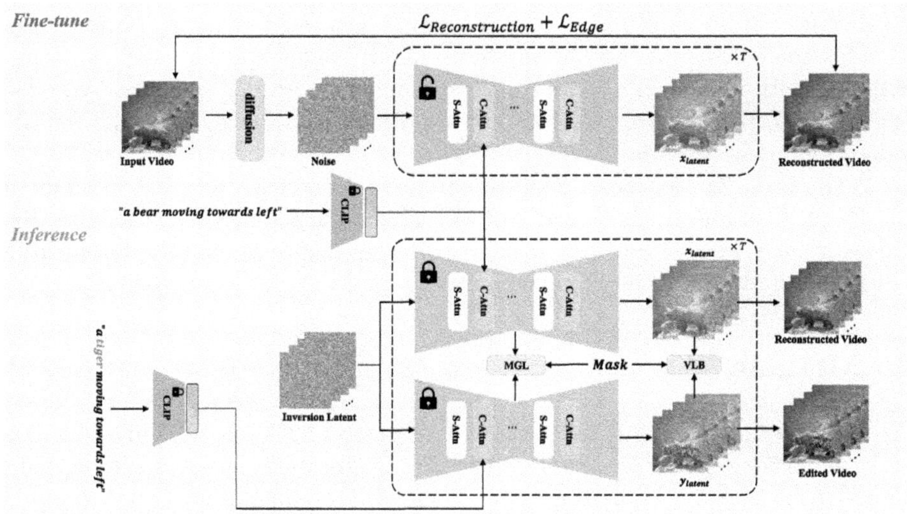

Fig. 2. Overview of our pipeline. The upper part illustrates the fine-tuning phase, where the source video V_{src} undergoes a forward diffusion process and interacts with the original prompt P_{src} via cross-attention. The model is optimized using a reconstruction loss $\mathcal{L}_{Reconstruction}$ [33] to preserve video-text alignment and a edge loss $\mathcal{L}_{Edge}$ to better generate boundaries. The lower part shows the inference phase: we first obtain the latent representation of V_{src} via DDIM inversion, and then perform joint reconstruction and editing under the guidance of the edited prompt. Mask-guided latent blending ensures that unedited regions remain intact while edited content is naturally integrated.

DDPMs use a stochastic reverse process to sample from noise to data, DDIMs reinterpret the reverse process as a non-Markovian deterministic mapping. Instead of sampling from a Gaussian at each step, DDIMs deterministically compute z_{t-1} as follows Eq. 2:

$$z_{t-1} = \sqrt{\frac{\alpha_{t-1}}{\alpha_t}} z_t + \left(\sqrt{\frac{1}{\alpha_{t-1}} - 1} - \sqrt{\frac{1}{\alpha_t} - 1} \right) \cdot \epsilon_\theta(z_t, t, c) \tag{2}$$

This formulation allows DDIMs to enable fast sampling with fewer steps, and to support controlled generation by varying latent trajectories. And DDIM sampling can be reversed in a few steps as Eq. 3:

$$z_{t+1} = \sqrt{\frac{\alpha_{t+1}}{\alpha_t}} z_t + \left(\sqrt{\frac{1}{\alpha_{t+1}} - 1} - \sqrt{\frac{1}{\alpha_t} - 1} \right) \cdot \epsilon_\theta(z_t, t, c) \tag{3}$$

which is known as DDIM inversion [28]. This technique enables the extraction of latent representations from real images.

3.2 Video Latent Blending

As described in LDMs [25], we can generate images in the latent vector space conditioned on the given text. However, it lacks the ability to perform local editing on a real image, which is essential for LVOS task. Specifically, we require the capability to modify only the regions of interest specified by the provided mask sequence. Hence, inspired by [2] and [1], we propose Video Latent Blending.

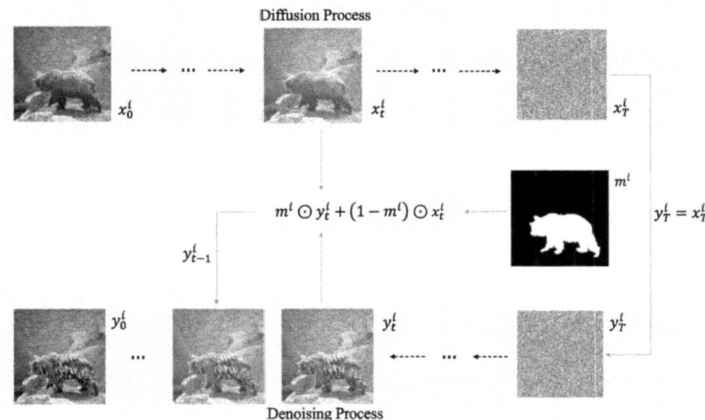

Fig. 3. Illustration of Latent Blending for a Single Frame.

As shown in Fig. 3, we first encode the input video $\mathcal{V}$ into latent vectors via a VAE encoder. And then our subsequent work is conducted in the latent space. We denote the latent representation of the i-th frame at timestep t in the DDIM forward process as x_t^i. In particular, x_T^i represents the latent vector of the i-th frame after T steps of the diffusion process. Similarly, we denote the latent vector of the i-th frame at timestep t during the denoising (reverse) process as y_t^i. To initiate the denoising process, we set the initial state as $y_T^i = x_T^i$. The denoising process proceeds as follows: at each timestep t, we first utilize the U-Net to predict the noise component and obtain the denoised latent vector y_t^i. Meanwhile, we compute the corresponding latent vector x_t^i at the same timestep via the DDIM forward diffusion process. Finally, we apply latent-space blending using the given mask sequence to combine y_t^i and x_t^i, as illustrated in Eq. 4, yielding in the new latent vector y_{t-1}^i that serves as the initialization for the next denoising step.

$$y_{t-1}^i = m^i \odot y_t^i + (1 - m^i) \odot x_t^i \tag{4}$$

where m^i is the binary mask corresponding to the i-th frame, and $\odot$ denotes the Hadamard (element-wise) product.

By explicitly applying the binary mask during each denoising step, we ensure that the latent representation outside the region of interest remains consistent with the original input video. This helps to preserve the background and unrelated objects, preventing undesired modifications. The mask-guided blending restricts changes to the specified regions only. This enhances the controllability of the editing process, making it suitable for tasks such as LVOS, where only the target object should be edited according to the new prompt, while the rest of the scene stays unchanged. As a result, the synthesized videos can serve as supervision for LVOS training without the need for extra manual annotations.

3.3   Text to Video with Mask Guidance

As row (b) shown in Fig. 1, although previous model [17] preserves the non-edited regions effectively, the generated video frames may still suffer from artifacts and inconsistencies between content and structure. P2P [10] reveals that the geometric shape and spatial layout of generated images heavily depend on the cross-attention maps. This inspires us to explore whether the cross-attention learning can be guided using a mask, in order to preserve the spatial structure. To generate images conditioned on text, LDMs [25] incorporate textual embedding encoding with visual latent vectors with cross-attention during the denoising process as Eq. 5:

$$\text{Attention}(Q, K, V) = M \cdot V$$
$$M = \text{Softmax}(\frac{QK^T}{\sqrt{d}}) \tag{5}$$

where query $Q = W_Q z_t$, key $K = W_K c$, and value $V = W_V c$ are computed with the learnable matrix W_Q, W_k, W_V. And $c = \psi(P)$ represents the text embedding derived from the prompt P, typically obtained using the CLIP [23] encoder. Each element $M_{i,j}$ of the mask M indicates the influence of the j-th text token on the i-th spatial position. Moreover, the cross-attention map is conditioned on the diffusion timestep, resulting in a distinct attention map M_t for each timestep t.

We adopt a two-stage optimization procedure at each timestep t. In the first stage, we use the denoising network ϵ_θ to predict the noise conditioned on the edited text prompt, while simultaneously recording the cross-attention map M_t^{edit} generated through the interaction between the text embedding and the video frames latent. In the second stage, we apply gradient descent to optimize the input latent representation x_t such that the predicted attention map M_t^{edit} closely aligns with a given reference attention map M^{ref}. The optimization objective as Eq. 6 is defined using the mean squared error (MSE) loss.

$$\mathcal{L}_{\text{attn}} = \|M_t^{\text{edit}} - M^{\text{ref}}\|_2 \tag{6}$$

This loss encourages the edited cross-attention maps to remain aligned with the original mask, ensuring that the generated content, guided by the edited text prompt, fully occupies the intended editing region. As a result, it effectively mitigates visual artifacts and structural inconsistencies in the generated frames.

Additionally, we train an edge optimizer, essentially a regression model. We sample patches along object boundaries and compute the foreground ratio within each patch using the known masks. The goal of the edge optimizer is to enhance the reconstruction of object boundaries in the generated video frames. During the fine-tuning stage, a pretrained regression model is employed as the edge optimizer, and the resulting edge loss is combined with the reconstruction loss to jointly supervise the generation process (Table 2).

4 Experiments

4.1 Implementation Details

Our approach is built upon CompVis Stable Diffusion (v1-4) [25]. Following the setup of VideoP2P [17], we keep the image autoencoder fixed and uniformly sample either 8 or 24 frames at a resolution of 512×512 from the original video. The parameters can be adjusted to balance editing fidelity across different videos. All experiments using 8-frame inputs are performed on a single A100-40G GPU.

Table 1. Integrating synthetic videos by **joint training** to enhance the RVOS models.

Method	Finetuing Data		$\mathcal{J}$	Δ	$\mathcal{F}$	Δ	$\mathcal{J}\&\mathcal{F}$	Δ
	Real	Synthetic						
ReferFormer [34] CVPR'22	✓		43.37	↑ 3.3	51.71	↑ 3.9	47.73	↑ 3.6
	✓	✓	**47.02**		**55.64**		**51.33**	
SgMg [20] ICCV'23	✓		52.00	↑ 0.8	58.76	↑ 1.3	55.38	↑ 1.1
	✓	✓	**52.83**		**60.08**		**56.46**	
MUTR [15] AAAI'24	✓		49.03	↑ 2.9	55.75	↑ 5.3	52.39	↑ 4.1
	✓	✓	**51.96**		**61.00**		**56.48**	

We assess the utility of synthetic videos on a widely used referring video object segmentation benchmark, i.e., Ref-DAVIS [14]. We construct a new dataset named **DAVIS-Ext** using DiffSynth-LVOS, which contains 43 videos along with their corresponding text prompts. Based on this dataset, we conduct joint fine-tuning experiments with the Ref-DAVIS [14] dataset. We evaluate three representative referring video object segmentation models as baselines: ReferFormer [34], SgMg [20], and MUTR [35].

To adapt these models to our setting, we make the following modifications: the backbone is set to Video Swin Transformer (Tiny) [19]. Fine-tuning is performed for 6 epochs, with training frames resized to 500×500 and the sequence length set to 8 frames. During inference, we resize frames to 224×224 to fit the available GPU memory. All video segmentation experiments are conducted on two NVIDIA RTX 3090 GPUs.

Table 2. Experimental results comparing the segmentation performance gains obtained by fine-tuning with augmented datasets generated using the same source videos and textual prompts, based on the TAV [33] + DDIM [28] model.

| Method | Finetuing Data | | $\mathcal{J}$ | Δ | $\mathcal{F}$ | Δ | $\mathcal{J}\&\mathcal{F}$ | Δ |
	Real	Synthetic						
ReferFormer [34] CVPR'22	✓		43.37	↑ 1.1	51.71	↑ 1.9	47.73	↑ 1.5
	✓	✓	**44.84**		**53.56**		**49.20**	
SgMg [20] ICCV'23	✓		**52.00**	0.9	**58.76**	0.6	**55.38**	0.8
	✓	✓	51.09		58.16		54.63	
MUTR [15] AAAI'24	✓		**49.03**	1.4	**55.75**	0.1	**52.39**	0.8
	✓	✓	47.63		55.64		51.63	

Table 3. Fine-tuning results of video segmentation models on the augmented dataset generated by the VideoP2P [17] model under identical conditions.

| Method | Finetuing Data | | $\mathcal{J}$ | Δ | $\mathcal{F}$ | Δ | $\mathcal{J}\&\mathcal{F}$ | Δ |
	Real	Synthetic						
ReferFormer [34] CVPR'22	✓		**43.37**	0.3	51.71	↑ 0.3	47.73	↑ 0.1
	✓	✓	43.63		**52.02**		**47.82**	
SgMg [20] ICCV'23	✓		**52.00**	0.1	**58.76**	0.1	**55.38**	0.1
	✓	✓	51.96		58.66		55.31	
MUTR [15] AAAI'24	✓		**49.03**	0.4	55.75	↑ 0.7	52.39	↑ 0.2
	✓	✓	48.68		**56.40**		**52.54**	

4.2 Enhancing RVOS Performance with Synthetic Videos

Subsequently, we exploit the synthetic dataset to further improve the segmentation performance by employing a joint fine-tuning strategy on both real and synthetic data. As shown in Table 1, we investigate the performance improvements of various segmentation models under the joint fine-tuning paradigm. All models demonstrate noticeable gains, validating the effectiveness of incorporating synthetic data. As demonstrated in Fig. 4, given the training masks from our target datasets, our method can synthesize a diverse set of high-fidelity video frames.

After joint fine-tuning on the DAVIS-Ext dataset, all three models exhibited notable improvements in segmentation performance, with each model achieving gains exceeding 1% across all three evaluation metrics. Specifically, Refer-

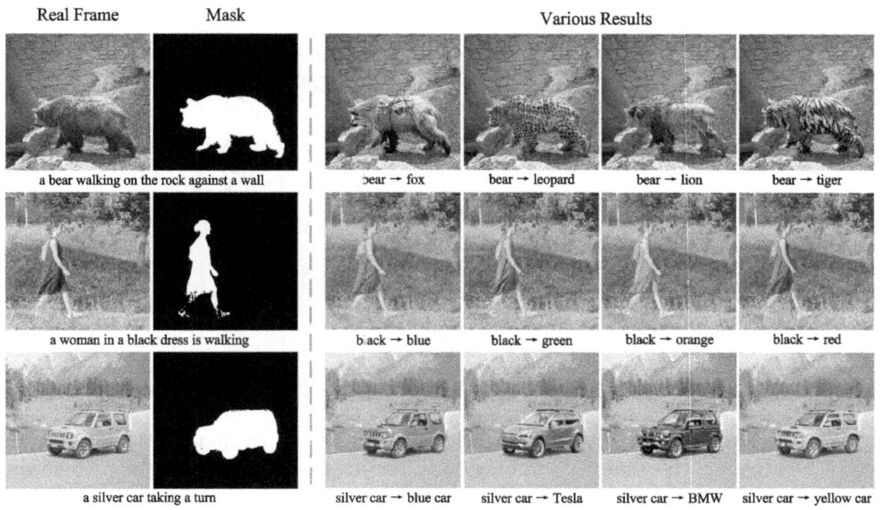

Fig. 4. Generated synthetic video frame conditioned on masks.

Former [34] recorded the highest increase in region similarity $\mathcal{J}$ (+3.3), while MUTR [15] attained the greatest enhancement in contour accuracy $\mathcal{F}$ (+5.3). In terms of the average $\mathcal{J}\&\mathcal{F}$ score, MUTR [15] demonstrated the most substantial overall improvement (+4.1). These findings underscore the efficacy of our proposed approach in enhancing the performance of segmentation models.

To highlight the superior suitability of our model-generated data for the LVOS task, we conducted comparative experiments against the TAV [33] and VideoP2P [17] models, utilizing the same source videos and original textual prompts. However, since these two models do not accept masks as input, we employed the SAM2 [24] model to perform frame-by-frame segmentation on the generated videos, serving as pseudo-annotations. As shown in Table 1, the performance of all three methods declined when fine-tuned on the augmented dataset produced via the TAV [33] + DDIM [28] pipeline. The SgMg [20] and MUTR [15] models, in particular, exhibited a downward trend across all three evaluation metrics. In contrast, Table 3 illustrates that the dataset augmented using the VideoP2P [17] approach led to only marginal improvements across the three video segmentation models. In some cases, the performance even slightly deteriorated on specific metrics, likely due to differences in how each generation method handles background preservation and foreground synthesis.

We adopt the $\mathcal{J}\&\mathcal{F}$ metric to compare the results of three different data generation methods, as summarized in Fig. 5. It is evident that the method proposed in this work outperforms the other two approaches. From the perspective of generation strategy, our method does not require additional segmentation models to extract per-frame masks, whereas both the TAV [33]+DDIM [28] and VideoP2P [17] pipelines rely on external segmenters to produce ground-truth masks. Furthermore, in terms of enhancing the performance of segmentation

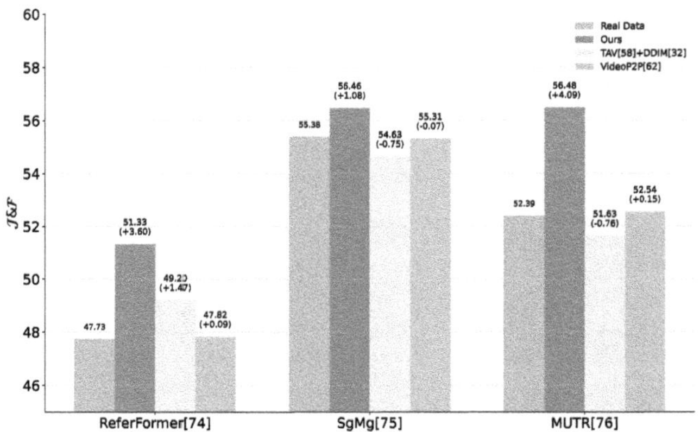

Fig. 5. The numbers on top of the bars indicate the performance improvement or decline relative to the real data. For example, the ReferFormer [34] model shows a significant improvement of +3.60 when using our method, while the VideoP2P [17] model results in a more modest increase of +0.09.

models, all three video segmentation methods exhibit consistent improvements when fine-tuned on the dataset augmented by our approach, while the results from the other two methods remain unstable and less reliable.

4.3   Ablation Studies

As row (c) shown in Fig. 1, after applying VLB and MGL, both visual artifacts and structural inconsistencies in the frames are significantly mitigated. The original gap in the swan's neck has been accurately filled with appropriate content. The previously erroneous "three ears" of the wolf have been corrected to the semantically plausible "two ears." Additionally, the boundary between the rear of the car and the background has been properly distinguished. Compared to row (b), the dancer's feet are now consistent with the original frame, and the walking woman's clothing aligns more accurately with the textual description.

As shown in Table 4, we evaluate the contributions of each component using CLIP Score, Masked PSNR, and Temporal Consistency (Tem-Con) as metrics. It can be observed that, except for a slight drop in CLIP Score, the other two metrics surpass those of the compared

	CLIP-S(↑)	M.PSNR(↑)	Tem-Con(↑)
w/o VLB w/o MGL	0.2829	10.50	0.9693
w/o VLB w/ MGL	**0.2909**	11.59	0.9783
w/ VLB w/o MGL	0.2834	11.95	0.9766
w/ VLB w/ MGL	0.2801	**13.16**	**0.9789**

Table 4. We evaluate CLIP Score for textual-visual similarity, Masked PSNR for region preservation, and Temporal Consistency (Tem-Con).

methods. In particular, our approach significantly outperforms others in terms of Masked PSNR, indicating superior performance in background preservation.

5 Conclusion

In this wrok, we propose a novel research paradigm: enhancing video segmentation models through synthetic videos generated by diffusion models. To better adapt to the LVOS task, we introduce two key modules Video Latent Blending (VBL) and Mask Guided Loss (MGL). Experimental results demonstrate that jointly training on both synthetic and real videos can effectively boost segmentation performance. Although, due to limited computational resources, we were unable to perform large-scale video generation to make further data augmentation and method evaluation, the experiment results already reveal the effectiveness of our method.

References

1. Avrahami, O., Fried, O., Lischinski, D.: Blended latent diffusion. ACM TOG **42**(4), 1–11 (2023)
2. Avrahami, O., Lischinski, D., Fried, O.: Blended diffusion for text-driven editing of natural images. In: CVPR, pp. 18208–18218 (2022)
3. Bar-Tal, O., Ofri-Amar, D., Fridman, R., Kasten, Y., Dekel, T.: Text2live: text-driven layered image and video editing. In: ECCV, pp. 707–723. Springer (2022)
4. Botach, A., Zheltonozhskii, E., Baskin, C.: End-to-end referring video object segmentation with multimodal transformers. In: CVPR, pp. 4985–4995 (2022)
5. Carion, N., Massa, F., Synnaeve, G., Usunier, N., Kirillov, A., Zagoruyko, S.: End-to-end object detection with transformers. In: ECCV, pp. 213–229. Springer (2020)
6. Ceylan, D., Huang, C.H.P., Mitra, N.J.: Pix2video: video editing using image diffusion. In: ICCV, pp. 23206–23217 (2023)
7. Chen, H., et al.: Videocrafter1: open diffusion models for high-quality video generation. arXiv preprint arXiv:2310.19512 (2023)
8. Chen, H., et al.: Videocrafter2: overcoming data limitations for high-quality video diffusion models. In: CVPR, pp. 7310–7320 (2024)
9. Couairon, P., Rambour, C., Haugeard, J.E., Thome, N.: Videdit: zero-shot and spatially aware text-driven video editing. Trans. Mach. Learn. Res. (2023)
10. Hertz, A., Mokady, R., Tenenbaum, J., Aberman, K., Pritch, Y., Cohen-Or, D.: Prompt-to-prompt image editing with cross attention control. arXiv preprint arXiv:2208.01626 (2022)
11. Ho, J., et al.: Imagen video: high definition video generation with diffusion models (2022)
12. Ho, J., Jain, A., Abbeel, P.: Denoising diffusion probabilistic models. NeurIPS **33**, 6840–6851 (2020)
13. Ho, J., Salimans, T., Gritsenko, A., Chan, W., Norouzi, M., Fleet, D.J.: Video diffusion models. NeurIPS **35**, 8633–8646 (2022)
14. Khoreva, A., Rohrbach, A., Schiele, B.: Video object segmentation with language referring expressions. In: ACCV, pp. 123–141. Springer (2019)
15. Kumari, N., Zhang, B., Zhang, R , Shechtman, E., Zhu, J.Y.: Multi-concept customization of text-to-image diffusion. In: CVPR, pp. 1931–1941 (2023)

16. Lin, T.Y., Dollár, P., Girshick, R., He, K., Hariharan, B., Belongie, S.: Feature pyramid networks for object detection. In: CVPR, pp. 2117–2125 (2017)
17. Liu, S., Zhang, Y., Li, W., Lin, Z., Jia, J.: Video-p2p: video editing with cross-attention control. In: CVPR, pp. 8599–8608 (2024)
18. Liu, S., Hui, T., Huang, S., Wei, Y., Li, B., Li, G.: Cross-modal progressive comprehension for referring segmentation. TPAMI **44**(9), 4761–4775 (2021)
19. Liu, Z., et al.: Video swin transformer. In: CVPR, pp. 3202–3211 (2022)
20. Miao, B., Bennamoun, M., Gao, Y., Mian, A.: Spectrum-guided multi-granularity referring video object segmentation. In: ICCV, pp. 920–930 (2023)
21. Molad, E., et al.: Dreamix: video diffusion models are general video editors. arXiv preprint arXiv:2302.01329 (2023)
22. Qi, C., et al.: Fatezero: fusing attentions for zero-shot text-based video editing. In: ICCV, pp. 15932–15942 (2023)
23. Radford, A., et al.: Learning transferable visual models from natural language supervision. In: ICML, pp. 8748–8763. PMLR (2021)
24. Ravi, N., et al.: Sam 2: segment anything in images and videos. arXiv preprint arXiv:2408.00714 (2024). https://arxiv.org/abs/2408.00714
25. Rombach, R., Blattmann, A., Lorenz, D., Esser, P., Ommer, B.: High-resolution image synthesis with latent diffusion models. In: CVPR, pp. 10684–10695 (2022)
26. Seo, S., Lee, J.Y., Han, B.: Urvos: unified referring video object segmentation network with a large-scale benchmark. In: ECCV, pp. 208–223. Springer (2020)
27. Singer, U., et al.: Make-a-video: text-to-video generation without text-video data. arXiv preprint arXiv:2209.14792 (2022)
28. Song, J., Meng, C., Ermon, S.: Denoising diffusion implicit models. arXiv preprint arXiv:2010.02502 (2020)
29. Van Den Oord, A., Vinyals, O., et al.: Neural discrete representation learning. NeurIPS **30** (2017)
30. Wang, W., et al.: Zero-shot video editing using off-the-shelf image diffusion models. arXiv preprint arXiv:2303.17599 (2023)
31. Wu, C., et al.: Godiva: generating open-domain videos from natural descriptions. arXiv preprint arXiv:2104.14806 (2021)
32. Wu, C., et al.: Nüwa: visual synthesis pre-training for neural visual world creation. In: ECCV, pp. 720–736. Springer (2022)
33. Wu, J.Z., et al.: Tune-a-video: one-shot tuning of image diffusion models for text-to-video generation. In: ICCV, pp. 7623–7633 (2023)
34. Wu, J., Jiang, Y., Sun, P., Yuan, Z., Luo, P.: Language as queries for referring video object segmentation. In: CVPR, pp. 4974–4984 (2022)
35. Yan, S., et al.: Referred by multi-modality: a unified temporal transformer for video object segmentation. In: AAAI, vol. 38, pp. 6449–6457 (2024)
36. Yang, S., Zhou, Y., Liu, Z., Loy, C.C.: Rerender a video: zero-shot text-guided video-to-video translation. In: SIGGRAPH Asia, pp. 1–11 (2023)
37. Zhou, D., Wang, W., Yan, H., Lv, W., Zhu, Y., Feng, J.: Magicvideo: efficient video generation with latent diffusion models. arXiv preprint arXiv:2211.11018 (2022)

Dual-Stream Attention Across Time-Frequency for Sound Event Detection

Jiafeng Li, Xichang Cai$^{(\boxtimes)}$, and Menglong Wu

School of Artificial Intelligence and Computer Science, North China University of Technology, Beijing, China
`caixc_ip@126.com`

Abstract. In recent years, frequency dynamic convolution (FDConv) has shown strong performance in sound event detection (SED). However, it primarily focuses on frequency modeling, neglecting dynamic temporal variations and time-frequency interactions, which limits its ability to capture key patterns in non-stationary events. To address this, we propose a time-frequency dual-stream attention (TFDSA) mechanism that integrates temporal attention pooling (TAP) and spectral feature booster (SFB) into conventional attention, enabling separate modeling of non-stationary and stationary structures. TFDSA employs a tri-branch design, including differential perception, gated modulation, and statistical smoothing, to enhance features and provide saliency guidance along both temporal and spectral dimensions. Experiments on the DESED dataset demonstrate that TFDSA outperforms the FDConv baseline, improving PSDS1 and PSDS2 by 2.53% and 2.28%, respectively, and surpasses multiple mainstream attention mechanisms. Visual analysis further confirms its effectiveness in capturing time-frequency saliency.

Keywords: Sound event detection · frequency dynamic convolution · attention

1 Introduction

Sound event detection (SED) is a critical research direction in audio signal processing, aiming to automatically identify and localize specific sound events (e.g., barking, alarms) from continuous audio streams. With expanding applications in intelligent surveillance, smart homes, and autonomous driving, SED technology plays an increasingly vital role in environmental perception systems and serves as a key technique for intelligently understanding and responding to environmental changes [1].

Deep learning has driven significant advances in SED. The convolutional recurrent neural network (CRNN) architecture has been widely adopted for this task due to its effectiveness in modeling time-frequency features and temporal dependencies [2]. However, traditional convolutions typically assume spectral

© The Author(s), under exclusive license to Springer Nature Singapore Pte Ltd. 2026
J. Lokoč et al. (Eds.): MMM 2026, LNCS 15412, pp. 609–621, 2026.
https://doi.org/10.1007/978-981-95-6950-2_43

shift-invariance along the frequency axis assumption rarely satisfied by sound signals, thereby limiting model representational capacity. To address this limitation, frequency dynamic convolution (FDConv) has enhanced frequency-variant modeling through frequency-adaptive kernels, substantially has improved SED performance [3]. Subsequent studies further refined convolution structures: Multi-dimensional FDConv has introduced frequency adaptivity across multiple kernel dimensions for multidimensional dynamic modeling [4], while dilated FDConv has incorporated dilated convolutions to expand receptive fields and improve frequency adaptability [5]. Recent approaches optimize frequency modeling by integrating temporal information through temporal attention pooling (TAP) as a replacement for average pooling [6].

Despite enhanced frequency-domain modeling through dynamic kernels, existing FDConv variants fail to explicitly model features and recalibrate them. This limitation compromises their discriminative capability when handling complex scenarios characterized by non-stationary signals or overlapping events. Consequently, strengthening structural feature modeling while achieving synergistic dynamic optimization between feature maps and convolution kernels has emerged as a crucial direction for further advancing FDConv and boosting SED performance.

Attention mechanisms offer a promising approach for enhancing time-frequency modeling. Unlike FDConv's reliance on frequency-adaptive kernel adjustments, attention explicitly models dependencies between input features to reweight important information and filter features, thereby strengthening CNN representation of target events. In SED, the time-frame frequency-wise SE (tfwSE) module combines channel attention [7] with frequency weighting for joint channel-frequency optimization [8]. Other frameworks like temporal enhanced full-frequency dynamic convolution integrate Coordinate Attention (CA) with channel attention to guide dynamic kernel generation [9]. Notably, CA, which models spatial relationships in images, functions as time-frequency attention in audio tasks [10]. Figure 1 illustrates the architectures of SE, tfwSE, and CA for comparison.

Nevertheless, current attention mechanisms exhibit deficiencies in modeling critical time-frequency regions. Most methods focus on single-dimensional importance while neglecting fine-grained joint time-frequency distribution modeling, thus struggling to accommodate the highly non-stationary and dynamic nature of acoustic events. Furthermore, significant differences exist in time-frequency structures between event types: stationary events exhibit continuous spectral structures, whereas non-stationary/transient events demonstrate strong time-variance. Conventional attention mechanisms fail to effectively distinguish these divergent characteristics due to their reliance on average pooling for feature compression, which incurs information loss. This study addresses these limitations in explicit feature modeling and time-frequency discriminative capability through integrated frequency dynamic convolution and attention mechanisms.

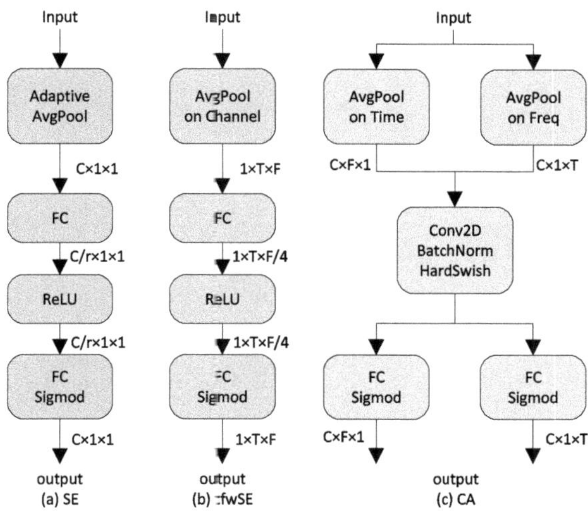

Fig. 1. Architectures of SE, tfwSE, and CA modules for attention-based time-frequency modeling.

Our key contributions are:

- We explore a straightforward integration of FDConv and attention mechanisms to address inadequate input feature modeling. Although simple in design, experimental results demonstrate that this combination achieves complementary effects, suggesting that FDConv and attention can enhance each other's feature response capabilities.
- We propose a **T**ime-**F**requency **D**ual-**S**tream **A**ttention (TFDSA) mechanism, consisting of a TAP branch and a Spectral Feature Booster (SFB) branch. Both TAP and SFB adopt a three-branch design integrating difference perception, attention gating, and statistical smoothing, enabling them to model both stationary and non-stationary events. TAP emphasizes temporal structures, while SFB focuses on frequency structures. By combining these complementary streams, TFDSA explicitly captures time-frequency differences, thereby enhancing discriminative performance in complex acoustic scenes.

2   Proposed Method

To enhance the model's perception of time-frequency structures in complex acoustic scenarios, this paper proposes a unified framework integrating Frequency Dynamic Convolution and attention mechanisms. As illustrated in Fig. 2, the architecture is composed of two key modules: FDConv and TFDSA. The former models frequency-domain non-stationary, while the latter employs parallel stationary and non-stationary pathways to enhance differentiated representations of critical time-frequency regions. These components synergistically improve the model's dynamic modeling capability and event discrimination performance.

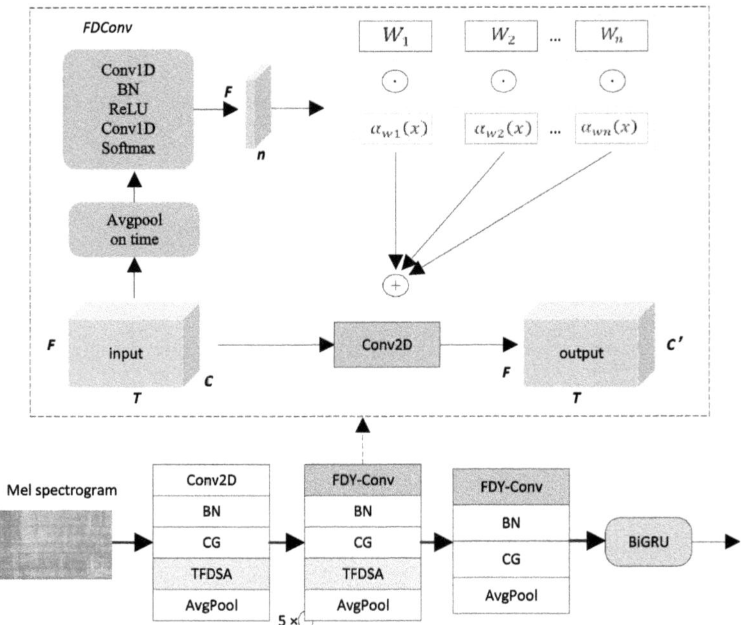

Fig. 2. Illustration of the proposed framework. The upper part shows the FDConv module with dynamically generated kernels. "5×" denotes five repetitions.

2.1 Frequency Dynamic Convolution

The standard convolution is defined as: $y = W * x + b$, where W and b represent the weights of the kernel and the bias, respectively. Dynamic convolution employs multiple parallel convolution kernels dynamically fused through normalized lightweight attention weights to generate input-adaptive feature responses. The dynamic convolution operation is formalized as follows:

$$y = \sum_{k=1}^{K} \alpha_k \cdot (W_k \cdot x + b_k)$$

$$\alpha_{wi} = \pi_{wi}(x)$$

$$(1)$$

where $x \in R^{C_{\text{in}} \times T \times F}$ denotes the input features (C_{in}: input channels, T: time frames, F: frequency bins), $y \in R^{C_{\text{out}} \times T \times F}$ represents the output features (C_{out}: output channels). Here, W_i denotes the weight of the i-th base kernel, α_{wi} indicates the weight of attention for the i-th base kernel (generated by a kernel function $\pi(x)$, and N represents the number of base kernels (bias terms omitted).

In FDConv, the kernel function first applies temporal average pooling, then extracts frequency patterns via two 1D convolution layers (with BN and ReLU), and finally generates normalized attention weights through softmax. The upper part of Fig. 2 schematically illustrates this computation process.

2.2   Time-Frequency Dual-Stream Attention

The proposed TFDSA module employs an attention-guided pooling strategy to process input features along temporal and frequency dimensions through two structurally symmetric submodules: TAP and SFB. These submodules share identical architectures while differing only in operational dimensions (e.g., frequency-direction differences replaced with temporal-direction differences), as illustrated in Fig. 3.

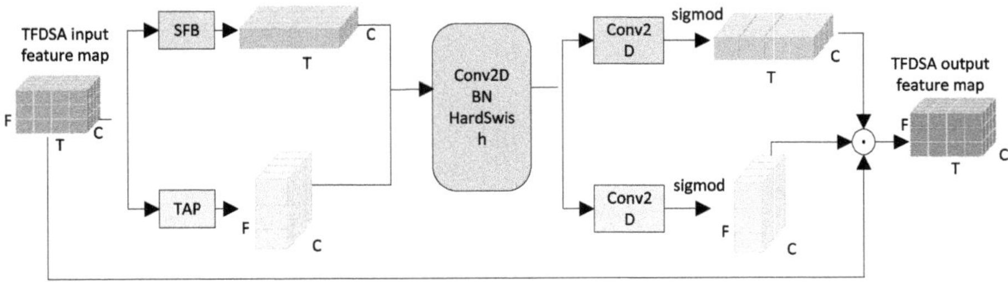

Fig. 3. Architecture of the proposed TFDSA module. It consists of two structurally symmetric submodules: TAP and SFB. Both submodules share identical architectures but operate along different dimensions, enabling complementary modeling of temporal and spectral patterns.

Figure 4 illustrates the detailed structure of the SFB module. The SFB module comprises three parallel branches: a difference perception branch for capturing dynamic variations, an attention gating branch for controlling information flow, and an average pooling branch for extracting global statistics. The outputs of these branches are integrated to produce an attention map, which weights the original features, enabling selective enhancement of critical time-frequency regions.

For an input feature map $x \in R^{C \times T \times F}$, we enhance its representational capacity through two 2D convolution layers. This preprocessing stage preserves the temporal-spectral structure to facilitate subsequent modeling and learning processes:

$$x_s = \sigma \left(W_{S2} * \mathrm{ReLU} \left(\mathrm{BN} \left(W_{S1} * x \right) \right) \right) \tag{2}$$

where, W_{S1} and W_{S2} denote the weights of the 2D convolution kernels, $*$ represents the convolution operator, and σ indicates the sigmoid activation. For simplicity, bias terms are omitted from all convolution operations.

Dynamic Difference Perception: A first-order difference operation is applied to input features along the frequency axis to capture dynamic patterns of frequency variations:

$$\Delta_f x = x_f - x_{f-1} \tag{3}$$

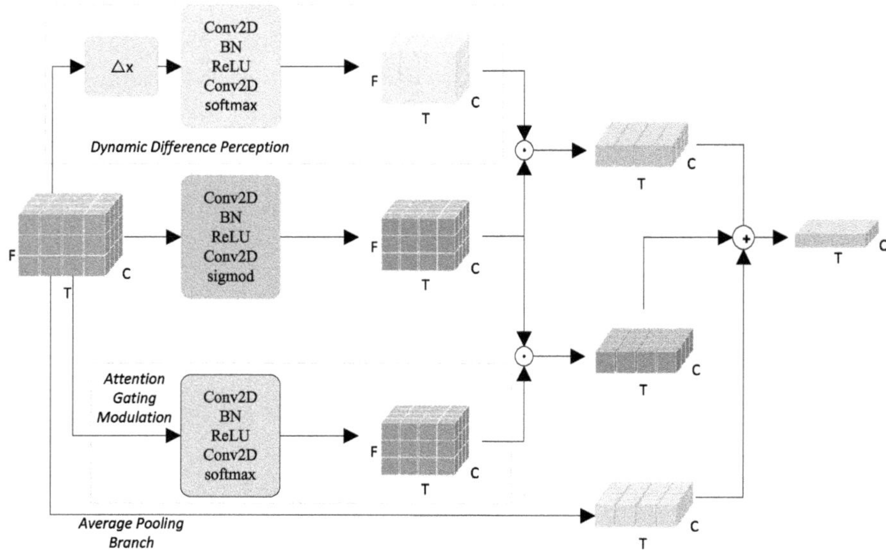

Fig. 4. Detailed architecture of the SFB module. It consists of three parallel branches: a difference perception branch, an attention gating branch, and an average pooling branch.

When applying the difference operation along the frequency axis, the frequency-differential signal Δ_{fx} captures energy disparities between adjacent frequency bands. This operation amplifies local variations in spectral structures of sound events, enhances feature boundary perception, and consequently improves discriminative capability across diverse event types. Subsequently, attention weights α_d are extracted from the frequency-differential signal through two sequential 2D convolution layers:

$$\alpha_d = softmax\left(W_{f2} * \text{ReLU}\left(\text{BN}\left(W_{f1} * \Delta_f x\right)\right)\right) \tag{4}$$

where W_{f1} and W_{f2} denote learnable parameters of the 2D convolution kernels. These weights quantify the response intensities of individual frequency bins across distinct time frames.

Attention Gating Modulation: This branch employs an adaptive gating mechanism to dynamically regulate activation intensities across temporal frames and frequency channels through soft selection. By assigning weights to individual time-frequency units, it suppresses redundant background information while enhancing discriminative regions relevant to target events. Specifically, the model derives high-level semantic representations using two 2D convolution layers with nonlinear activation functions, followed by softmax normalization to generate attention maps. These maps subsequently modulate the original feature maps:

$$\alpha_g = softmax\left(W_{g2} * \text{ReLU}\left(\text{BN}\left(W_{g1} * x\right)\right)\right) \tag{5}$$

where W_{g1} and W_{g2} denote learnable parameters of the 2D convolution kernels. The resulting attention weights quantify feature importance at each time-frequency position, facilitating enhanced identification of local patterns in spectrograms.

Average Pooling Branch: To enhance feature stability and global contextual awareness, this branch employs frequency-axis average pooling to extract stationary structural features. Within the SFB module, it aggregates global frequency energy distribution patterns across temporal frames, thereby suppressing transient noise interference while improving modeling capability for stationary sound events.

$$x_{avg} = \frac{1}{F} \sum_{f=1}^{F} x_f \tag{6}$$

Ultimately, the features processed by the SFB module are as follows:

$$x_{SFB} = \sum_{f=1}^{F} \alpha_{d,f} \odot x_{s,f} + \sum_{f=1}^{F} \alpha_{g,f} \odot x_{s,f} + x_{avg} \tag{7}$$

The temporally-enhanced features from the SFB module and spectrally-enhanced features from the TAP module are concatenated along the temporal dimension. This fused representation undergoes convolution processing, batch normalization, and activation functions to jointly encode coupled features across channel, temporal, and spectral dimensions.

$$x_{fuse} = Act\left(BN\left(Conv\left(Conact\left(x_{SFB}, x_{TAP}\right)\right)\right)\right) \tag{8}$$

Subsequently, the fused features x_{fuse} are decoupled into temporal and spectral branches, corresponding to time-domain x_{time} and frequency-domain x_{freq} representations. Domain-specific attention mechanisms then generate temporal calibration weights and spectral calibration weights for each branch.

$$\begin{aligned} \gamma_{time} &= \sigma\left(Conv_{time}\left(x_{time}\right)\right) \\ \gamma_{freq} &= \sigma\left(Conv_{freq}\left(x_{freq}\right)\right) \end{aligned} \tag{9}$$

Finally, the module generates the TFDSA-calibrated output features y through element-wise multiplication between the attention weights and input features x:

$$y = x \times \gamma_{time} \times \gamma_{freq} \tag{10}$$

3   Experimental Setups

3.1   Implementation Details

This study employs the DESED dataset [11], comprising 1,578 weakly labeled samples, 10,000 synthetic strongly labeled samples, and 14,412 unlabeled samples. All audio clips are 10-second mono recordings at 16 kHz. Prior to model input, audio is converted to 626×128 Mel spectrograms (128 Mel filter banks, 626 time frames). To address the semi-supervised nature of the training data, we adopt the Mean Teacher framework [12]]. Data augmentation techniques include mixup [13], time masking [14], frame shifting, and Filter Augment [15]. During training, strongly labeled, weakly labeled, and unlabeled samples are fed into the network with batch sizes of 10, 10, and 20, respectively.

The baseline model utilizes Frequency Dynamic Convolution (FDConv), consisting of 7 convolutional layers and 2 bidirectional gated recurrent unit (BiGRU) layers. The first layer employs static convolution, while the subsequent 6 layers implement frequency dynamic convolution. The proposed Time-Frequency Dual-Stream Attention (TFDSA) and comparative attention modules are embedded after these 6 convolutional layers. Network architecture, data augmentation parameters, and hyperparameters remain consistent with the FDConv baseline.

3.2   Evaluation Metrics

Performance evaluation employs two Polyphonic Sound Detection Score (PSDS) sub-metrics: PSDS1 measures event boundary localization capability, while PSDS2 emphasizes classification accuracy. Together, these metrics comprehensively assess overall system performance in sound event detection tasks [16].

4   Results and Discussion

4.1   Attention Module Comparison

Table 1 presents performance comparisons between the FDConv baseline and its integration with various attention mechanisms. Results demonstrate that all attention mechanisms improve model performance. This indicates that input feature recalibration complements the frequency-adaptive characteristics of frequency dynamic convolution. The proposed TFDSA achieves PSDS1 and PSDS2 scores of 44.62% and 67.42%, respectively, representing improvements of 2.53% and 2.28% over the baseline and demonstrating superior overall performance.

Table 1. Comparison of attention mechanisms with TFDSA, where results are averaged over four runs.

Backbone network	Attention Model	PSDS1(%)	PSDS2(%)
FDConv		42.09	65.14
FDConv	SE	42.82	65.34
FDConv	tfwSE	43.64	66.04
FDConv	CA	43.80	65.53
FDConv	TFDSA	44.62	67.42

Dynamic convolution inherently possesses input-adaptive kernel weighting, effectively enabling implicit channel-wise dynamic modeling. Consequently, incorporating traditional channel attention mechanisms (e.g., SE) provides limited performance gains and may introduce modeling redundancy. This observation suggests that the primary bottleneck in information modeling has shifted from the channel dimension to more complex feature spaces, such as temporal structures and spectral patterns. Against this backdrop, tfwSE, CA, and the proposed TFDSA module address deficiencies in non-channel modeling through joint channel-frequency-temporal modeling. These modules achieve over 1.5% improvement on PSDS1, which emphasizes temporal event localization, validating the efficacy of multidimensional attention in enhancing temporal modeling and boundary discrimination.

While tfwSE and CA achieve similar aggregate PSDS scores (PSDS1 + PSDS2), they possess complementary strengths. tfwSE focuses on event classification via simultaneous channel-frequency calibration, enhancing local feature discriminability but weakening temporal modeling and potentially blurring event boundaries. Conversely, CA supports accurate temporal localization through separate global pooling along time-frequency axes combined with contextual fusion, improving onset and offset detection. Its reliance solely on 1D convolutions for directional feature modeling, however, constrains performance on spectrally complex or transient events.

Crucially, TFDSA achieves optimal balance between event classification and temporal localization through refined dual-stream architecture and gated modulation mechanisms.

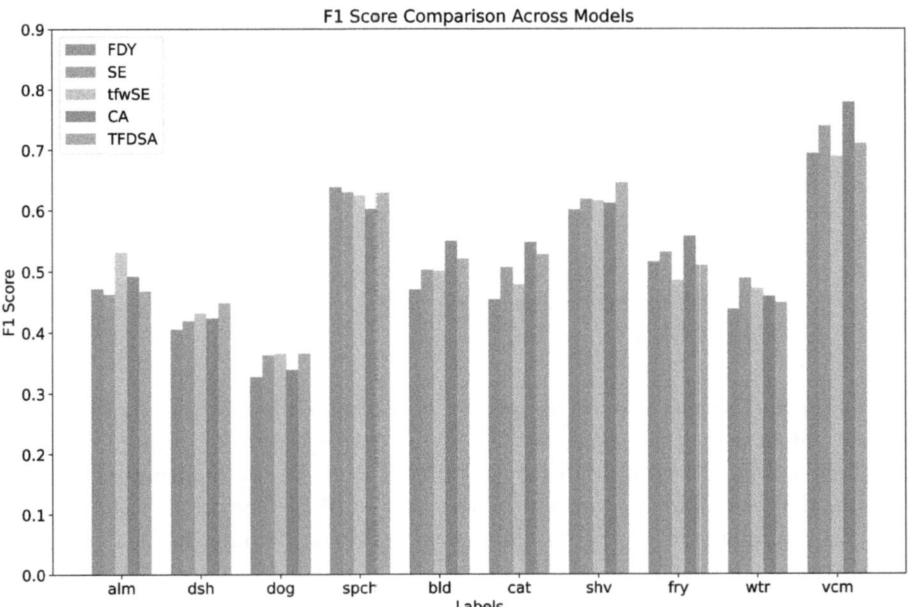

Fig. 5. Class-wise F1-score comparison across different sound events at a fixed detection threshold of 0.5.

To further examine performance differences across event types, we conduct a class-wise F1-score analysis with a fixed detection threshold of 0.5. As illustrated in Fig. 5, tfwSE demonstrates superior recognition for events with transient non-stationary characteristics (e.g., Alarm bell ringing: 53.1%, Dishes, Dog), whereas CA excels in temporally continuous stationary events (e.g., Vacuum cleaner: 77.8%, Blender) due to enhanced temporal localization.

The Vacuum cleaner case exemplifies CA's advantage in modeling persistent sound sources, outperforming tfwSE by an absolute F1-score of 9.0% (77.8% compared with 68.8%). Conversely, tfwSE achieves 3.9% higher F1-score than CA on Alarm bell ringing (53.1% compared with 49.2%), confirming its responsiveness to short-duration transients.

The proposed TFDSA module addresses both scenarios through dual-stream dynamic attention that independently captures temporal evolution and spectral dynamics, synergized via frame-level fusion. This approach achieves balanced event discrimination and localization, yielding state-of-the-art F1-scores across multiple categories, including Electric shaver (64.5%), Speech (62.8%), and Dish (44.8%).

4.2   Ablation Studies

To systematically evaluate TFDSA's efficacy, we conduct ablation studies on the FDConv+CA baseline (with Coordinate Attention only) by incrementally integrating TAP, SFB, and their parallel combination (TFDSA).

Table 2. Ablation study results showing the effects of TAP, SFB, and their combination on PSDS1 and PSDS2, where results are averaged over four runs.

Model	TAP	SFB	PSDS1(%)	PSDS2(%)
FDConv+CA			43.80	65.53
FDConv+CA		✓	43.53	66.40
FDConv+CA	✓		44.37	65.88
FDConv+TFDSA	✓	✓	44.62	67.42

As shown in Table 2, each component contributes distinctly to model performance. Integrating TAP improves PSDS1 to 44.37% (+1.23% compared with the baseline) with a marginal increase in PSDS2 (66.40%), highlighting its strength in temporal boundary perception. The addition of SFB yields PSDS2 = 65.88 (+1.82% compared with the baseline) while slightly reducing PSDS1 (43.53%), indicating enhanced spectral discriminability. When both modules are combined in the full TFDSA, the model achieves synergistic optimization, improving PSDS1 to 44.62% and PSDS2 to 67.42%, outperforming individual modules by 0.56–1.89% and demonstrating the complementary nature of temporal and spectral modeling pathways.

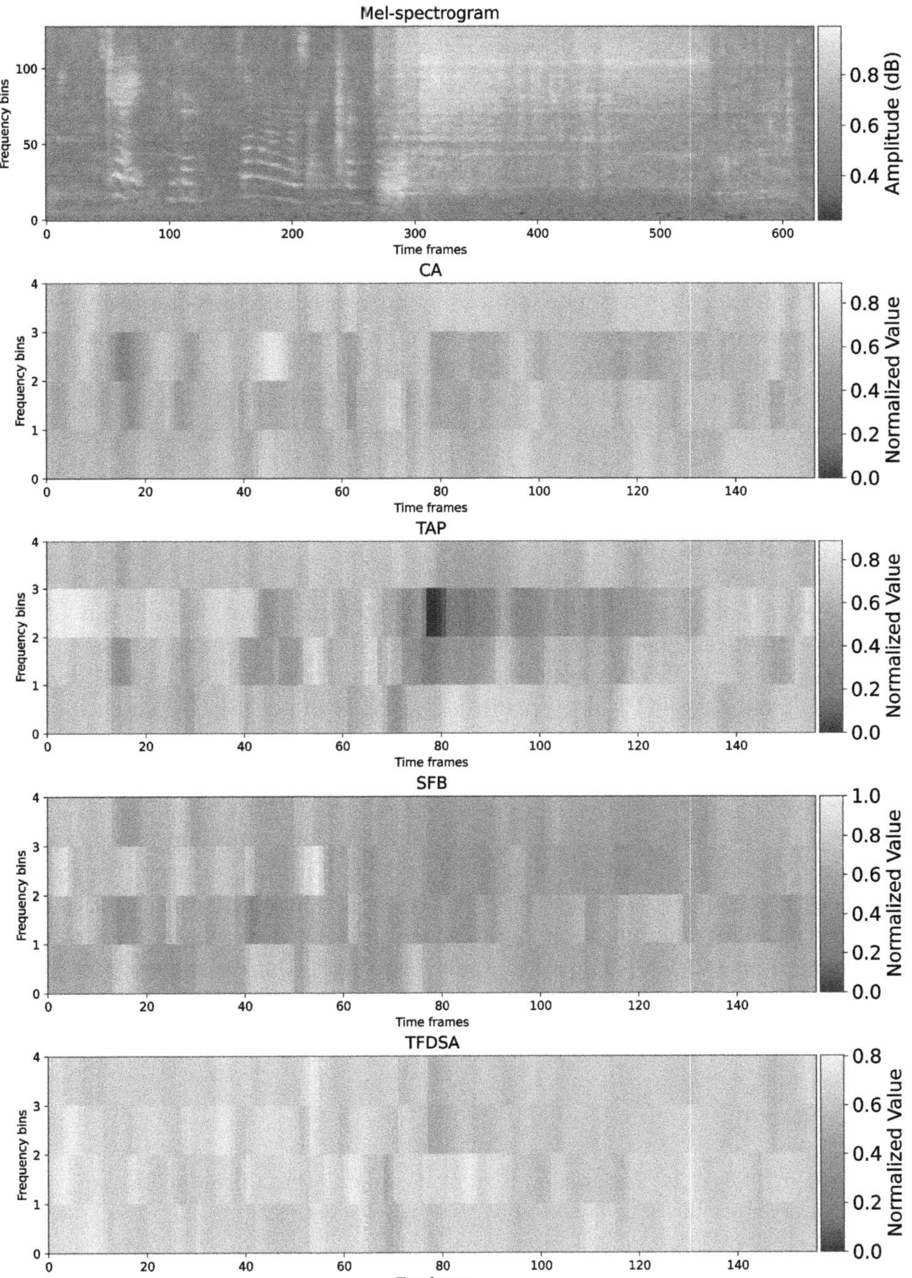

Fig. 6. Comparison of feature maps generated by different attention mechanisms. CA produces smooth but temporally diffuse responses. TAP emphasizes temporal event structures, while SFB enhances high-frequency spectral features. The proposed TFDSA simultaneously strengthens temporal and spectral representations, yielding more focused and consistent time-frequency activation patterns.

Figure 6 illustrates the time-frequency response patterns of different attention modules. The CA module produces smooth responses but lacks focus on transient events. The TAP module demonstrates concentrated event activations along the temporal dimension, enhancing temporal structure modeling capabilities while exhibiting limited spectral feature preservation. Conversely, SFB feature maps emphasize energy responses in high-frequency regions, improving perception of spectral distribution variations, yet display discrete temporal responses with insufficient continuity modeling. In contrast, TFDSA simultaneously enhances semantic representations of critical frequency bands and event timestamps within identical frames, achieving more targeted and consistent time-frequency excitation patterns. Integrated quantitative and visual evidence confirms that TFDSA mitigates modeling bottlenecks in conventional approaches through parallel capture and adaptive fusion of temporal-spectral semantics, significantly improving temporal localization precision and classification discrimination in sound event detection.

5 Conclusion

This paper proposes a Time-Frequency Dual-Stream Attention (TFDSA) mechanism to enhance time-frequency feature modeling in frequency dynamic convolution networks. TFDSA consists of two complementary branches, Temporal Attention Pooling (TAP) and Spectral Feature Booster (SFB), which focus on temporal and spectral dimensions, respectively, to capture key region responses. Each branch adopts a unified three-part design that integrates dynamic difference perception, attention gating, and statistical smoothing, enabling joint optimization of both non-stationary and stationary event representations. Experiments on the DESED dataset demonstrate that TFDSA outperforms existing attention mechanisms on both PSDS1 (event localization) and PSDS2 (classification) metrics, highlighting its strong discriminative capability and structural generalizability. Visualization analyses further confirm the effectiveness of TFDSA in enhancing salient time-frequency regions, underscoring its potential for practical sound event detection applications.

References

1. Wang, R., Leng, Y., Zhuang, J., Sun, C.: A sound event detection support system for smart home based on "two-to-one" teacher-student learning. Appl. Soft Comput. **167**, 112224 (2024)
2. Çakır, E., Parascandolo, G., Heittola, T., Huttunen, H., Virtanen, T.: Convolutional recurrent neural networks for polyphonic sound event detection. IEEE/ACM Trans. Audio Speech Lang. Process. **25**(6), 1291–1303 (2017)
3. Nam, H., Kim, S.-H., Ko, B.-Y., Park, Y.-H.: Frequency dynamic convolution: frequency-adaptive pattern recognition for sound event detection. In: Interspeech 2022, pp. 2763–2767. ISCA (2022)

4. Xiao, S., Zhang, X., Zhang, P.: Multi-dimensional frequency dynamic convolution with confident mean teacher for sound event detection. In: ICASSP 2023 - 2023 IEEE International Conference on Acoustics, Speech and Signal Processing (ICASSP), pp. 1–5. IEEE, Rhodes Island, Greece (2023). https://doi.org/10.1109/ICASSP49357.2023.10096306

5. Nam, H., Kim, S.-H., Min, D., Lee, J., Park, Y.-H.: Diversifying and expanding frequency-adaptive convolution kernels for sound event detection. In: Interspeech 2024, pp. 97–101. ISCA (2024)

6. Nam, H., Park, Y.-H.: Temporal Attention Pooling for Frequency Dynamic Convolution in Sound Event Detection. arXiv preprint arXiv:2504.12670 (2025)

7. Hu, J., Shen, L., Sun, G.: Squeeze-and-excitation networks. In: 2018 IEEE/CVF Conference on Computer Vision and Pattern Recognition, pp. 7132–7141. IEEE, Salt Lake City, UT (2018)

8. Cai, X., Chen, J., Liu, Z., Wu, M., Guo, H., Sun, X.: TEFFDConv: an improved approach to enhance temporal localization in sound event detection. IEICE Trans. Inf. Syst. 2024EDL8085 (2025)

9. Nam, H., Kim, S.-H., Min, D., Park, Y.-H.: Frequency & Channel Attention for Computationally Efficient Sound Event Detection, arXiv preprint arXiv:2306.11277 (2023)

10. Hou, Q., Zhou, D., Feng, J.: Coordinate attention for efficient mobile network design. In: 2021 IEEE/CVF Conference on Computer Vision and Pattern Recognition (CVPR), pp. 13708–13717. IEEE, Nashville, TN, USA (2021)

11. Serizel, R., Turpault, N., Shah, A., Salamon, J.: Sound event detection in synthetic domestic environments. In: International Conference on Acoustics, Speech, and Signal Processing, Barcelona, Spain (2020)

12. Tarvainen, A., Valpola, H.: Mean teachers are better role models: weight-averaged consistency targets improve semi-supervised deep learning results. In: Advances in Neural Information Processing Systems, vol. 30 (2017)

13. Zhang, H., Cissé, M., Dauphin, Y.N., Lopez-Paz, D.: mixup: beyond empirical risk minimization. In: International Conference on Learning Representations (ICLR), Vancouver, Canada (2018)

14. Park, D.S., Chan, W., Zhang, Y., Chiu, C.-C., Zoph, B., Cubuk, E.D., Le, Q.V.: SpecAugment: a simple data augmentation method for automatic speech recognition. In: Interspeech 2019, pp. 2613–2617 (2019). https://doi.org/10.21437/Interspeech.2019-2680

15. Nam, H., Kim, S.H., Park, Y.H.: Filteraugment: an acoustic environmental data augmentation method. In: International Conference on Acoustics, Speech and Signal Processing (ICASSP), pp. 4308–4312. Singapore, Singapore (2022)

16. Bilen, Ç., Ferroni, G., Tuveri, F., Azcarreta, J., Krstulović, S.: A framework for the robust evaluation of sound event detection. In: International Conference on Acoustics, Speech and Signal Processing (ICASSP), pp. 61–65. Barcelona, Spain (2020)

No-Reference Image Quality Assessment via Attention-Based Feature Enhancement and Feature Interaction

Qiqun Yu[1,2,3], Yihua Chen[1,2,3], Jiliang Ma[1,2,3], and Zhenjun Tang[1,2,3](✉)

[1] Key Lab of Education Blockchain and Intelligent Technology, Ministry of Education, Guangxi Normal University, Guilin 541004, China
[2] Guangxi Key Lab of Multi-Source Information Mining and Security, Guangxi Normal University, Guilin 541004, China
[3] University Engineering Research Center of Educational Intelligent Technology, Guangxi Normal University, Guilin 541004, China
tangzj230@163.com

Abstract. No-Reference Image Quality Assessment (NR-IQA) methods has made significant progress with the rapid development of deep learning techniques. However, most NR-IQA methods usually use a single attention mechanism for feature interaction, which limits the prediction performances of these NR-IQA methods in complex scenarios. To address this, we propose a Feature Enhancement and Feature Interaction Network (FEFI-Net) for NR-IQA. The key contributions are the multi-scale attention enhancement module and the multi-attention feature interaction module. The multi-scale attention enhancement module is designed to enhance the pre-trained features extracted by Swin Transformer, thereby obtaining more comprehensive feature representations. The multi-attention feature interaction module with three attentions is designed to establish more accurate feature interaction. Comparative experiments on five widely-used IQA datasets demonstrate that our FEFI-Net surpasses some state-of-the-art NR-IQA methods in prediction accuracy.

Keywords: No-Reference Image Quality Assessment · Feature Enhancement · Feature Interaction

1 Introduction

Digital images are indispensable for conveying information in the Internet era. Images with good quality can bring good visual experiences to the receiver. However, image distortions inevitably occur during image processing. This leads to degradation in image quality. These distortions primarily manifest as noise, blur, color errors, compression artifacts, and so on. This affects the user's online experience and the accuracy of data transmission. Image Quality Assessment (IQA) [1–3] quantifies image quality for image adjustment and has gained widespread attention. Existing IQA methods utilize a pristine reference image or partial reference image to predict quality, which are referred to as the Full-Reference IQA (FR-IQA) method or the Reduced-Reference IQA (RR-IQA) method, respectively. In the realistic context, the reference image is non-existent or inaccessible. This makes the FR-IQA/RR-IQA method unreliable. The No-Reference IQA (NR-IQA) method uniquely assess quality without needing the original image and thus they are more practical and widely studied. Developing the precise NR-IQA method has an urgent practical application requirement.

With the advancement of deep learning, researchers have developed numerous deep learning-based NR-IQA methods. Existing NR-IQA methods usually enhance semantic features extracted from a pre-trained deep neural network to refine distortion information. However, these methods have some disadvantages. DBCNN [4] simply enhances single-scale features extracted from two CNN backbones. Then it uses simple concatenation and pooling operations for score prediction. HyperIQA [5] proposes a local distortion-aware module that enhances distortion-relevant features at a single scale from the outputs of different CNN layers. Then, it employs a hypernetwork to obtain the quality score. These methods always enhance features at a single scale and have not explored the benefits of multi-scale feature interactions for NR-IQA. To alleviate these issues, some methods were proposed. TRES [6] only feeds the multi-scale outputs of different CNN layers into a single attention module and finally obtains the predicted score through pooling and fully connected layers. VCRNet [7] connects multi-scale features generated by an image restoration network and EfficientNet, then predicts the quality score via simple average pooling and fully connected layers. TOPIQ [8] is a top-down approach that uses a single attention for feature interaction and obtains the score through pooling and fully connected layers. These models often rely on simple operations to perform multi-scale feature interactions, such as a single concatenation operation or a single attention. In addition, semantic features extracted from deep pre-trained networks often exhibit inherent inter-layer relationships. These methods neglect that the interaction between features from different layers can lead to the loss of crucial semantic information. Thus, there is still room for exploring feature interactions of multi-scale features.

To solve these problems, we propose a multi-scale attention enhancement Module that owns a proposed self-attention mechanism and a sparse attention. Based on this, a multi-scale feature extraction strategy is introduced to establish dynamic connections between features of different scales by constructing attention of different resolutions, thereby capturing more potential distortion information. Then, we design a multi-attention feature interaction module with three types of attention. This module uses a channel attention to capture key feature channels and a spatial attention to capture the edge and texture details of features. Subsequently, a cross self-attention is used to establish global dependencies between the features extracted from adjacent layers. This module achieves a more comprehensive information representation through collaborative optimization of local detail enhancement and cross-layer feature interaction. The main contributions can be summarized as follows:

- We design a Multi-scale Attention Enhancement Module, which leverages multi-scale attention and sparse attention mechanisms. This module not only captures rich multi-scale feature information, but also significantly alleviates feature redundancy in the representations extracted by pre-trained networks.
- We design a Multi-Attention Feature Interaction Module. This module utilizes multiple attentions to capture and interact features of adjacent layers, thereby achieving a more comprehensive feature representation.
- We use a Multi-scale Attention Enhancement Module and a Multi-Attention Feature Interaction Module to design our FEFI-Net. This method effectively leverages feature enhancement and feature interaction to obtain more accurate distortion features for better quality assessment. Extensive experiments conducted on five IQA datasets show that our proposed model outperforms the current mainstream NR-IQA methods.

2   Proposed Method

In this section, we first introduce overall pipeline of our proposed FEFI-Net. Then, we explain the multi-scale attention enhancement module and the multi-attention feature interaction module. Finally, we introduce the prediction module.

2.1   Overall Pipeline

The framework of our proposed FEFI-Net is shown in Fig. 1. Our proposed FEFI-Net method mainly consists of three modules: the Multi-scale Attention Enhancement (MAE) module, the Multi-attention Feature Interaction (MFI) module, and the Prediction Module (PM). The input of the proposed FEFI-Net is a distorted image, and the output is the prediction score. The overviews of these modules are described in the following paragraphs.

Suppose that the input distorted image is denoted by $I \in \mathbb{R}^{H \times W \times 3}$, where H and W represent the height and width of the distorted image. The multi-scale features $L_i \in \mathbb{R}^{\frac{H}{2^{(i+1)}} \times \frac{W}{2^{(i+1)}} \times (2^{(i-1)} \times C)}$ $(i = 1, 2, 3, 4)$ with different scales are extracted from a pre-trained Swin Transformer. The L_i denotes semantic features containing low-level and high-level semantic distortion information. These semantic features are enhanced by feeding L_i into the MAE module, thereby improving the ability to perceive distortion of the Swin Transformer and obtain the enhanced features $E_i \in \mathbb{R}^{\frac{H}{2^{(i+1)}} \times \frac{W}{2^{(i+1)}} \times (2^{(i-1)} \times C)}$. The process can be represented as follows:

$$(E_1, E_2, E_3, E_4) = MAE(L_1, L_2, L_3, L_4) \tag{1}$$

Next, the E_i of the MAE module is sent to the MFI module. The MFI module learns interaction information between semantic features extracted from different

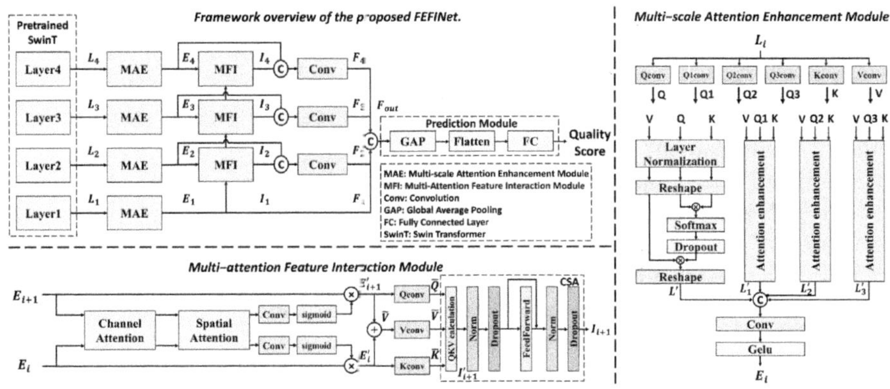

Fig. 1. The pipeline of the proposed network.

layers, which further facilitates distortion understanding. The process can be represented as follows:

$$(I_1, I_2, I_3, I_4) = MFI(E_1, E_2, E_3, E_4) \tag{2}$$

Then, the fused feature $F_i \in \mathbb{R}^{\frac{H}{2^{(i+1)}} \times \frac{W}{2^{(i+1)}} \times (2^{(i-1)} \times C)}$ are obtained by concatenation operations, average pooling operations and $1{\times}1$ convolution operations for the feature I_i and E_i. The fused feature can be represented as follows:

$$F_i = Conv_{1\times 1}(Avg(Concat(E_i, I_i))) \tag{3}$$

Finally, we concatenate F_i and input it into the PM to obtain the final predicted score, which can be represented as follows:

$$Score = PM(Concat(F_1, F_2, F_3, F_4)) \tag{4}$$

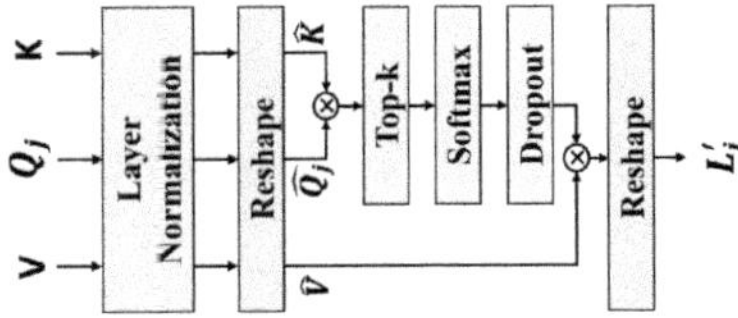

Fig. 2. Attention Enhancement Block.

2.2   Multi-scale Attention Enhancement Module

The pre-trained networks are not specifically designed for NR-IQA and semantic features extracted from pre-trained networks have many redundant semantic information. Enhancing semantic features for NR-IQA tasks becomes particularly important. In the multi-scale attention enhancement module, we combine sparse self-attention and multi-scale strategies to design an attention enhancement block that can enhance the semantic features and obtain three different scales of reinforcement features L_j' ($j = 1, 2, 3$).

Specifically, the input semantic features are first mapped into the Q_j, Q, K, and V features for the attention computation. Then, through the residual connection of the original self-attention module, we obtain the output L', ensuring that the model does not lose key semantic information while performing sparse calculations. Finally, we fuse the outputs of the above modules through the concat operation, and obtain enhanced features E_i ($i = 1, 2, 3, 4$) through convolution and Gelu operations. The details of the attention enhancement block are shown in Fig. 2, and the process of the MAE module is represented as follows:

$$\hat{Q}_j = Reshape(LN(Q_j conv(L_i))) \tag{5}$$

$$\hat{Q} = Reshape(LN(Q conv(L_i))) \tag{6}$$

$$\hat{K} = Reshape(LN(K conv(L_i))) \tag{7}$$

$$\hat{V} = Reshape(LN(V conv(L_i))) \tag{8}$$

$$L' = Reshape(Dropout(Softmax(\frac{\hat{Q}\hat{K}^T}{\sqrt{d}})) \times \hat{V}) \tag{9}$$

$$L_j' = Reshape(Dropout(Softmax(Top - k(\frac{\hat{Q}_j\hat{K}^T}{\sqrt{d}}))) \times \hat{V}) \tag{10}$$

$$E_i = Gelu(Conv(Concat(L', L_1', L_2', L_3'))) \tag{11}$$

where $Conv(\cdot)$, $Qconv(\cdot)$, $Kconv(\cdot)$ and $Vconv(\cdot)$ represent the 1×1 convolution, and the $Q_j conv(\cdot)$ denotes the 1×1 dilated convolution, the dilated rates are 1, 2, and 3, respectively, $LN(\cdot)$ represents Layer Normalization, $Top - k(\cdot)$ denotes the top-k sampling where the sampling rate k is designed to be 0.75.

2.3   Multi-attention Feature Interaction Module

The enhanced features with different scales carry diverse distortion information. Cross-layer feature interaction results in more discriminative features and significantly improves the prediction accuracy. As shown in Fig. 1, we propose an MFI module, aiming at cross-layer interaction of features output by the MAE module.

Specifically, the MFI module firstly enhances the multi-scale features by using spatial attention and channel attention mechanisms. Then, the results of the convolution and Sigmoid operations are used to weight and fuse with the original input to obtain features. This enhances the expression ability of the distortion details. Subsequently, the features E_{i+1}' and E_i' are input into Qconv and Kconv to obtain outputs $\overline{Q}$ and $\overline{K}$, respectively. The feature $\tilde{V}$ is the combination of element-wise addition and then is input into Vconv. This design ensures the information integrity of cross-layer features. Finally, input the generated $\overline{Q}$, $\overline{K}$, $\overline{V}$ into the cross self-attention block (CSA) for calculation and obtain the output I_{i+1}. The process can be represented as follows:

$$E'_{i+1} = Sigmoid(Conv(SA(CA(E_{i+1})))) \times E_{i+1} \tag{12}$$

$$E'_i = Sigmoid(Conv(SA(CA(E_i)))) \times E_i \tag{13}$$

$$\overline{Q} = Qconv(E'_{i+1}) \tag{14}$$

$$\overline{K} = Kconv(E'_i) \tag{15}$$

$$\overline{V} = Vconv(E'_{i+1} + E'_i) \tag{16}$$

$$I_{i+1} = CSA(\overline{Q}, \overline{K}, \overline{V}) \tag{17}$$

where $CA(\cdot)$ represents channel attention, $SA(\cdot)$ represents spatial attention, and $CSA(\cdot)$ can be represented as follows:

$$I'_{i+1} = softmax\left(\frac{\overline{Q}\overline{K}^T}{\sqrt{d}}\right) \times \overline{V} \tag{18}$$

$$I_{i+1} = Dropout(Norm(FF(Dropout(Norm(I'_{i+1}))) + Dropout(Norm(I'_{i+1})))) \tag{19}$$

where $\sqrt{d}$ is scaled to stabilize the gradients, $Norm(\cdot)$ represents normalization, and $FF(\cdot)$ represents $FeedForward(\cdot) = Conv(Dropout(Relu(Conv(\cdot))))$.

2.4   Prediction Module

As shown in Fig. 1, we concat the outputs F_i to obtain F_{out}, then compress it using global average pooling, and flatten the feature map into one dimension using flatten operation. Finally, we input the flattened features into the fully connected layer to obtain the final score. The process can be represented as follows:

$$Score = FC(Flatten(GAP(F_{out}))) \tag{20}$$

3   Experimental Results

Many experiments are done to demonstrate the performance of the proposed FEFI-Net. Section 3.1 describes the used datasets, and Sect. 3.2 gives the details of the implementation. Section 3.3 and Sect. 3.4 discuss performance comparison and ablation experiments, respectively.

3.1   Datasets

We use five open datasets to train and validate the performance of our proposed FEFI-Net. These include three synthetic datasets and two real datasets, such as

Table 1. Open datasets used in the experiment

Dataset	# of Dist. Images	# of Dist. Types	Distortions
LIVE	799	5	synthetic
CSIQ	866	6	synthetic
TID2013	3,000	24	synthetic
LIVEC	1162	-	authentic
KonIQ	10,073	-	authentic

LIVE [9], CSIQ [10], TID2013 [11], LIVEC [12], and KonIQ [13]. Table 1 shows a summary of the datasets we used.

We evaluate performance of the proposed FEFI-Net by conducting two kinds of experiments. The experiments of the first kind are done on the same dataset. In other words, the training set and the test set are all taken from one dataset. Following the previous techniques, we randomly divide each dataset into the training set (80% images) and test set (20% images). The experiments of the second kind are conducted on cross datasets. Here, the FEFI-Net is first trained on a specific dataset and subsequently evaluated on multiple external datasets to measure its robustness across different data distributions.

3.2 Implementation Details

Our experiments are conducted on an NVIDIA TESLA V100S GPU utilizing PyTorch 1.12.1 and CUDA 10.2. To accommodate the input dimension requirements of the Swin Transformer, we randomly crop the input image with a size of 224×224 from the dataset and apply horizontal flipping with 50% probability for data augmentation. Consistent with established IQA protocols, all datasets use five distinct random seeds. The model is trained with a base learning rate of 1×10^{-5} and batch size of 8, optimized by ADAM (weight decay $= 1 \times 10^{-5}$). A cosine annealing scheduler is employed, where parameters Tmax and θmin are set to 50 and 0. we train the network with 200 epochs, with Mean Squared Error (MSE) as the loss function.

During test, 20 random patches are sampled per test image. Since all patches inherit the distortion characteristics of their source image, the mean patch score accurately reflects the full-image quality. Final performance metrics represent averages across five independent runs with different initialization seeds.

3.3 Performance Comparisons

We employ both same dataset and cross-dataset evaluations to comprehensively assess the proposed IQA method. The same datasets experiments verify prediction accuracy, while cross-dataset tests validate generalization capability. Performance is quantified using two established metrics: Pearson Linear Correlation Coefficient (PLCC) and Spearman's Rank Correlation Coefficient (SRCC), where PLCC measures linear correlation between algorithmic scores and Mean Opinion Scores (MOS), and SRCC evaluates prediction monotonicity through rank-order correlation.

Evaluations on the Same Dataset: We conduct systematic comparative experiments between the proposed FEFI-Net and current mainstream IQA methods, covering multiple representative benchmark datasets. As shown in Table 2, the performance indicators of different methods are quantitatively evaluated using PLCC and SRCC, with the optimal results highlighted in bold. From the experimental results, it can be seen that FEFI-Net outperforms existing methods significantly in two key metrics, PLCC and SRCC, on the classic benchmark datasets LIVE, CSIQ, and TID2013. This indicates that this method can more accurately capture the quality difference between distorted images and reference images. For the LIVEC dataset constructed for real-world scenarios, although the MS-SCANet method has an advantage in metrics, FEFI-Net still closely follows with a PLCC value of 0.900 and an SRCC value of 0.884. In the comparison of the big dataset KONIQ, we achieve the best value between PLCC value and TOPIQ, while SRCC value was slightly lower than TOPIQ, achieving the second best result. This indicates that our method also has high prediction accuracy in real-world scenarios.

Table 2. Performance comparison on same datasets (Best results are in bold)

Method	Source	LIVE		CSIQ		TID2013		LIVEC		KONIQ	
		PLCC	SRCC	PLCC	SRCC	PLCC	SRCC	PLCC	SRCC	PLCC	SRCC
DIIVINE [14]	TIP 2012	0.908	0.892	0.776	0.804	0.567	0.643	0.591	0.588	0.558	0.546
BRISQUE [15]	TIP 2012	0.944	0.929	0.748	0.812	0.571	0.626	0.629	0.629	0.685	0.681
ILNIQE [16]	TIP 2012	0.906	0.902	0.865	0.822	0.648	0.521	0.508	0.508	0.537	0.523
BIECON [17]	JSTSP 2017	0.961	0.958	0.823	0.815	0.762	0.717	0.613	0.613	0.537	0.523
WaDIQaM [18]	TIP 2018	0.955	0.960	0.844	0.852	0.855	0.835	0.671	0.682	0.807	0.804
DBCNN [4]	TCSVT 2020	0.971	0.968	0.959	0.946	0.865	0.816	0.869	0.851	0.884	0.875
HyperIQA [5]	CVPR 2020	0.966	0.962	0.942	0.923	0.858	0.840	0.882	0.859	0.917	0.906
MUSIQ [19]	ICCV 2021	0.940	0.911	0.893	0.871	0.815	0.773	0.746	0.702	0.928	0.916
TReS [6]	WACV 2022	0.968	0.969	0.942	0.922	0.883	0.863	0.887	0.846	0.928	0.915
VCRNet [7]	TIP 2022	0.973	0.974	0.955	0.943	0.875	0.846	0.865	0.856	0.909	0.894
Re-IQA [20]	CVPR 2023	0.971	0.970	0.960	0.947	0.861	0.804	0.854	0.840	0.923	0.918
TOPIQ [8]	TIP 2024	0.960	0.959	0.927	0.914	0.882	0.860	0.884	0.870	**0.939**	**0.926**
MS-SCANet [21]	ICASSP 2025	0.968	0.964	0.945	0.925	-	-	**0.903**	**0.895**	0.903	0.909
FEFI-Net	Proposed	**0.980**	**0.975**	**0.986**	**0.983**	**0.970**	**0.969**	0.900	0.884	**0.939**	0.917

Evaluations on the Cross-Dataset: To verify the generalization ability of the evaluated NR-IQA method, we conduct systematic cross-dataset experiments to compare it with some NR-IQA methods. For synthetic distortion scenarios, we evaluate generalization performance using three benchmark datasets: LIVE,

CSIQ, and TID2013. As shown in the Table 3, our FEFI-Net achieved 5 optimal results and 1 suboptimal result in five cross-dataset experiments. For the validation of real-world distortions, we further test the generalization ability on the LIVEC and KONIQ datasets. As shown in the Table 3, we achieve the best performance while training on KONIQ and testing on LIVEC. Then, we obtain a suboptimal solution while training on LIVEC and testing on KONIQ. These experimental results collectively indicate that our FEFI-Net has a statistically significant advantage over existing methods in terms of cross-dataset generalization ability. This comprehensive verification further confirms the robustness and practicality of the FEFI-Net in various application scenarios.

Table 3. Performance comparison on cross-datasets in terms of SRCC.

Train on	LIVE		CSIQ		TID2013		LIVEC	KONIQ
Test on	CSIQ	TID2013	LIVE	TID2013	LIVE	CSIQ	KONIQ	LIVEC
DBCNN [4]	0.763	0.554	0.878	0.553	0.864	0.709	0.754	0.755
HyperIQA [5]	0.744	0.561	**0.917**	0.562	0.867	0.727	**0.772**	0.785
TRes [6]	0.761	0.564	0.845	0.457	0.896	0.797	0.733	0.786
VCRNet [7]	0.732	0.517	0.828	0.560	0.819	0.682	0.752	0.721
USRSF-IQA [22]	0.745	0.549	0.851	0.546	0.897	0.720	-	0.805
FEFI-Net	**0.767**	**0.571**	0.886	**0.613**	**0.908**	**0.811**	0.770	**0.862**

3.4 Performance on Individual Databases

To evaluate the robustness of our FEFI-Net to a single distortion type, experiments are conducted on the TID2013 dataset. The model trains all distortion types in the training set and then tests each specific distortion type in the test set. The main evaluation index of experimental results is SRCC index, see details. As can be seen from the results shown in the Table 4, the FEFI-Net outperformed the other models in 17 out of 24 distortion types. Of concern, our prediction scores are much higher than other methods in distortion types such as Local block-wise distortions, Mean shift, and Contrast change, where most existing NR-IQA models perform poorly. The above experiments prove that our method has excellent performance in dealing with common single distortion.

3.5 Ablation Experiments

To evaluate the effectiveness of our FEFI-Net design, we conduct ablation experiments on the CSIQ and LIVEC datasets by combining various network modules to form different schemes. The results, presented in Table 5, include the SRCC and PLCC values for each configuration. In the table, the symbol '$\sqrt{}$' indicates

Table 4. SRCC comparison of individual distortion types on the TID2013.

Distortion	BRISQUE [15]	DB-CNN [4]	HyperIQA [5]	TRes [6]	FPR [23]	PROPOSED
Additive Gaussian noise	0.706	0.850	0.803	0.911	**0.953**	0.910
Additive noise in color components	0.523	0.763	0.503	0.858	0.897	**0.902**
Spatially correlated noise	0.776	0.833	0.958	0.938	0.967	**0.984**
Masked noise	0.295	0.384	0.231	0.620	0.87	**0.958**
High frequency noise	0.836	0.918	0.857	0.875	0.934	**0.946**
Impulse noise	0.802	0.680	0.775	0.701	0.779	**0.970**
Quantization noise	0.682	0.867	0.877	0.878	**0.920**	0.833
Gaussian blur	0.861	0.815	0.777	0.880	0.833	**0.981**
Image denoising	0.500	0.788	0.843	0.883	0.944	**0.954**
JPEG compression	0.790	0.873	0.863	0.840	**0.923**	0.863
JPEG2000 compression	0.779	0.883	0.900	**0.941**	0.923	**0.948**
JPEG transmission errors	0.254	0.577	0.789	0.753	0.797	**0.846**
JPEG2000 transmission errors	0.723	0.870	0.843	0.884	0.752	**0.885**
Non eccentricity pattern noise	0.213	0.381	0.295	0.358	0.559	**0.570**
Local block-wise distortions	0.197	0.418	0.155	0.688	0.265	**0.820**
Mean shift	0.217	-0.007	0.228	0.344	0.009	**0.690**
Contrast change	0.079	0.545	0.705	0.753	0.699	**0.896**
Change of color saturation	0.113	0.579	0.559	**0.735**	0.409	0.703
Multiplicative Gaussian noise	0.674	0.760	0.874	0.815	**0.887**	0.847
Comfort noise	0.198	0.757	0.815	0.729	0.830	**0.861**
Lossy compression of noisy images	0.627	0.898	0.902	0.890	**0.982**	0.907
Image color quantization with dither	0.849	0.908	0.820	0.805	0.901	**0.909**
Chromatic aberrations	0.724	0.764	0.855	0.798	0.768	**0.886**
Sparse sampling and reconstruction	0.811	0.906	0.923	**0.947**	0.887	0.932

Table 5. Effectiveness of the network module

Scheme	MAE	MFI	CSIQ		LIVEC	
			PLCC	SRCC	PLCC	SRCC
1			0.972	0.971	0.854	0.802
2	√		0.984	0.981	0.891	0.864
3		√	0.982	0.979	0.893	0.865
4	√	√	**0.986**	**0.983**	**0.900**	**0.884**

the inclusion of a specific module, while the bold text highlights the best performance. As shown, Scheme 4, which incorporates MAE modules and MFI modules, achieves superior results compared to schemes using only one or two modules. This clearly demonstrates the effectiveness of our designed architecture.

4   Conclusions

This paper has proposed an innovative model named FEFI-Net for enhancing the performance of No-Reference Image Quality Assessment through the synergistic optimization of feature enhancement and feature interaction. Initially, the Swin Transformer exhibits limitations in quality prediction when dealing with complex datasets. To improve the capability of extracting distortion-related features, we introduce the Multi-scale Attention Enhancement Module, which optimizes feature representation through a multi-scale attention mechanism while reducing information redundancy in the pre-trained network using sparse attention strategies. Subsequently, we construct the Multi-Attention Feature Interaction Module, which employs a feature interaction mechanism to fuse multi-stage features, thereby enhancing the model's ability to perceive both local details and global structures. Experiments on five standard IQA datasets have demonstrated that the FEFI-Net significantly outperforms some existing methods in terms of prediction accuracy and cross-dataset generalization capability, validating its effectiveness in handling complex distortion scenarios.

Acknowledgments. This work is partially supported by the Guangxi Natural Science Foundation (2024GXNSFBA010191, 2025GXNSFBA069304), the National Natural Science Foundation of China (62272111), and the Innovation Project of Guangxi Graduate Education (YCSW2025120).

References

1. Chen, Y., Chen, Z., Yu, M., Tang, Z.: Dual-feature aggregation network for no-reference image quality assessment. In: International Conference on Multimedia Modeling, pp. 149–161. Springer (2023)
2. Ma, J., Chen, Y., Huang, P., Tang, Z.: Attention-enhanced feature fusion network for no-reference image quality assessment. In: Proceedings of the IEEE International Conference on Acoustics, Speech and Signal Processing (ICASSP), pp. 1–5. IEEE (2025)
3. Yu, M., Tang, Z., Zhang, X., Zhong, B., Zhang, X.: Perceptual hashing with complementary color wavelet transform and compressed sensing for reduced-reference image quality assessment. IEEE Trans. Circuits Syst. Video Technol. **32**(11), 7559–7574 (2022)
4. Zhang, W., Ma, K., Yan, J., Deng, D., Wang, Z.: Blind image quality assessment using a deep bilinear convolutional neural network. IEEE Trans. Circuits Syst. Video Technol. **30**(1), 36–47 (2018)
5. Su, S., et al.: Blindly assess image quality in the wild guided by a self-adaptive hyper network. In: Proceedings of the IEEE/CVF Conference on Computer Vision and Pattern Recognition, pp. 3667–3676 (2020)
6. Golestaneh, S.A., Dadsetan, S., Kitani, K.M.: No-reference image quality assessment via transformers, relative ranking, and self-consistency. In: Proceedings of the IEEE/CVF Winter Conference on Applications of Computer Vision, pp. 1220–1230 (2022)
7. Pan, Z., Yuan, F., Lei, J., Fang, Y., Shao, X., Kwong, S.: VCRNet: visual compensation restoration network for no-reference image quality assessment. IEEE Trans. Image Process. **31**, 1613–1627 (2022)
8. Chen, C., et al.: Topiq: a top-down approach from semantics to distortions for image quality assessment. IEEE Trans. Image Process. (2024)

9. Sheikh, H.R., Sabir, M.F., Bovik, A.C.: A statistical evaluation of recent full reference image quality assessment algorithms. IEEE Trans. Image Process. **15**(11), 3440–3451 (2006)
10. Larson, E.C., Chandler, D.M.: Most apparent distortion: full-reference image quality assessment and the role of strategy. J. Electron. Imaging **19**(1), 011006 (2010)
11. Ponomarenko, N., et al.: Image database TID2013: peculiarities, results and perspectives. Signal Process. Image Commun. **30**, 57–77 (2015)
12. Ghadiyaram, D., Bovik, A.C.: Massive online crowdsourced study of subjective and objective picture quality. IEEE Trans. Image Process. **25**(1), 372–387 (2015)
13. Lin, H., Hosu, V., Saupe, D.: Koniq-10k: towards an ecologically valid and large-scale IQA database. arXiv preprint arXiv:1803.08489 (2018)
14. Moorthy, A.K., Bovik, A.C.: Blind image quality assessment: from natural scene statistics to perceptual quality. IEEE Trans. Image Process. **20**(12), 3350–3364 (2011)
15. Mittal, A., Moorthy, A.K., Bovik, A.C.: No-reference image quality assessment in the spatial domain. IEEE Trans. Image Process. **21**(12), 4695–4708 (2012)
16. Zhang, L., Zhang, L., Bovik, A.C.: A feature-enriched completely blind image quality evaluator. IEEE Trans. Image Process. **24**(8), 2579–2591 (2015)
17. Kim, J., Lee, S.: Fully deep blind image quality predictor. IEEE J. Sel. Top. Signal Process. **11**(1), 206–220 (2016)
18. Bosse, S., Maniry, D., Müller, K.R., Wiegand, T., Samek, W.: Deep neural networks for no-reference and full-reference image quality assessment. IEEE Trans. Image Process. **27**(1), 206–219 (2017)
19. Ke, J., Wang, Q., Wang, Y., Milanfar, P., Yang, F.: Musiq: multi-scale image quality transformer. In: Proceedings of the IEEE/CVF International Conference on Computer Vision, pp. 5148–5157 (2021)
20. Saha, A., Mishra, S., Bovik, A.C.: Re-iqa: unsupervised learning for image quality assessment in the wild. In: Proceedings of the IEEE/CVF Conference on Computer Vision and Pattern Recognition, pp. 5846–5855 (2023)
21. Mithila, M.M.R., Farias, M.C.Q.: Ms-scanet: a multiscale transformer-based architecture with dual attention for no-reference image quality assessment. In: ICASSP 2025 - 2025 IEEE International Conference on Acoustics, Speech and Signal Processing (ICASSP), pp. 1–5 (2025)
22. Tang, Z., Chen, Y., Chen, Z., Liang, X., Zhang, X.: Lightweight transformer and multi-head prediction network for no-reference image quality assessment. Neural Comput. Appl. **36**(4), 1931–1946 (2024)
23. Chen, B., Zhu, L., Kong, C., Zhu, H., Wang, S., Li, Z.: No-reference image quality assessment by hallucinating pristine features. IEEE Trans. Image Process. **31**, 6139–6151 (2022)

Applications of Multimodal Knowledge Graphs in Modeling Multimedia

Florian Ruosch[1]([✉]) [iD] and Luca Rossetto[2] [iD]

[1] FPR Consulting, Zurich, Switzerland
`ruosch@ifi.uzh.ch`
[2] Dublin City University, Dublin, Ireland
`luca.rossetto@dcu.ie`

Abstract. The effective modeling and querying of the world's ever-growing collection of multimedia is a significant challenge. Multimodal knowledge graphs offer a powerful solution by integrating heterogeneous data sources and uncovering complex relationships. We point to its benefits across a range of applications, including holistic memory retrieval, interactive video exploration, cross-modal fact-checking for journalism, and data fusion for clinical diagnosis. We also explore its use in enhancing educational tools, product feedback analysis in e-commerce, and semantic annotation of textual corpora. By showcasing how these diverse applications model multimedia at its core, we illustrate the potential of a multimodal knowledge graph store that can directly leverage and process the content of multimedia. However, a major limitation of existing approaches is that they treat multimedia documents as opaque entities, which severely limits their analytical potential. In this paper, we introduce *MeGraS*, our novel multimodal knowledge graph store that embodies a new paradigm: to provide direct access to multimedia document content, enabling deeper and more flexible analysis.

Keywords: Multimodal Knowledge Graphs · Multimedia Modeling

1 Introduction

Knowledge graphs are a powerful tool and an effective means to represent structured information for semantic modeling. But what if the data is semi-structured or unstructured, like the contents of multimedia? Approaches based on multimodal knowledge graphs have been successfully applied to research challenges involving the modeling and retrieval of multimedia [1].

In order to illustrate how multimodal knowledge graphs can be deployed to model multimedia, we describe a range of applications and use cases. These include research challenges such as the Lifelog Search Challenge [2] and the Video Browser Showdown [6]. We also show applications in the real world, where modeling multimedia is not only done for the purpose of retrieval but can be beneficial to achieve other goals. These include cross-modal fact-checking in journalism,

J. Lokoč et al. (Eds.): MMM 2026, LNCS 16412, pp. 634–647, 2026.
https://doi.org/10.1007/978-981-95-6950-2_45

enhancing educational tools with multimodal narratives, and clinical data fusion for medical diagnosis. Finally, we explore the potential of using these graphs for enhanced product feedback analysis in e-commerce and for semantic annotation and navigation of textual corpora in natural language processing.

However, a major limitation of current knowledge graph stores is that they remain agnostic of the multimedia documents they model. This means that query engines do not have access to their contents, and, therefore, they cannot be used in retrieval or analysis. Addressing this limitation, we introduce *MeGraS* [13], our novel multimodal knowledge graph store. Unlike traditional systems that treat multimedia as opaque blobs, *MeGraS* has a custom query engine that can directly access and process the contents of multimedia documents. This allows for a deeper level of analysis and retrieval that goes beyond simple metadata and semantic annotations.

In summary, we make the following contributions with this paper: First, we advocate for and introduce a paradigm shift in how knowledge graphs model multimedia, moving from a content-agnostic approach to a content-aware one. Second, we showcase the benefits of this new approach by demonstrating its application across a wide range of diverse use cases. Third, we present *MeGraS* [13], a novel multimodal knowledge graph store that embodies this new paradigm by having direct access to multimedia content. The research prototype of the system is open-source and publicly available for download.[1]

2   Related Work

Although knowledge graphs have been around for more than 50 years [16], they gained broader popularity more recently thanks to Google's adoption to enhance the capabilities of its search engine [17]. Simply put, a knowledge graph consists of a collection of triples, whereby a *subject* is related to an *object* with a *predicate*: $\langle subject, predicate, object \rangle$. These can then be used to give the entities in the knowledge graph semantics and meaning using relationships.

Traditional knowledge graphs (also called knowledge bases) such as DBpedia and Wikidata are built from textual sources and use predefined, formal ontologies as the schema. They provide information in a structured format and can be interacted with using Semantic Web tools such as the Resource Description Format (RDF) for storage, the Web Ontology Language (OWL) for formalization, and the SPARQL Protocol and RDF Query Language for querying. Knowledge graphs integrate and represent a wide range of real-life entities and properties.

Extending their concept to incorporate heterogeneous modalities as entities makes the knowledge graph multimodal [21]. One of the first approaches to link nodes to images was described in [8] for visual-relational queries in *ImageGraph* consisting of around $15K$ entities. The size of multimodal knowledge graphs has grown significantly since, with exponents like *MMpedia* [20] incorporating more than $2.6M$ nodes and almost $20M$ images. *TIVA-KG* [18] is of smaller

---

[1] https://megras.org.

size but covers audio, video, and images with an order of $100K$ data samples for each modality. While *ImageGraph* elevates images to "first-class citizens" in knowledge graphs, *TIVA-KG* does not include the raw multimodal data and only incorporates preprocessed features in the form of vectors.

Finally, we point the inclined reader to [4], which provides an extensive overview of current technologies and trends in multimodal knowledge graphs.

3   A Paradigm Change: Context-Aware Multimodal Knowledge Graphs for Modeling Multimedia

Existing multimodal knowledge graph that are content-agnostic have a major limitation: They treat multimedia documents as opaque entities, which severely restricts their analytical potential. Their query engines do not have direct access to the contents of the multimedia documents they model. This means that they cannot be used for retrieval or analysis.

Hence, we propose a new paradigm: content-aware modeling of multimedia documents. This approach provides direct access for the query engines to the multimedia documents to use them and information derived from or implied by them. As a prototype, we present *MeGraS* [13], the first of its kind to provide a graph store with custom query engine which can access the contents of the multimedia documents. It enables deeper analysis and the computation of rich, cross-modal queries that are not possible with traditional systems. *MeGraS* allows for querying across different modalities to find connections that would otherwise not be apparent. Furthermore, it can process the multimedia content at query time and persist the results of derivation functions in the knowledge graph. This means that necessary data, such as image embeddings for similarity searches, can be computed on the fly if not already available in the graph. It offers a new level of granularity and flexibility that is essential for advancing the field of multimedia modeling in knowledge graphs.

4   Applications and Use Cases

In this section, we explore potential applications for multimodal knowledge graphs to model multimedia as well as use cases where they have already been applied successfully.

4.1   Personal Multimedia and Self-quantification

The rise of wearable devices and the omnipresent smartphones has contributed to an explosion of captured personal multimedia. This has led to a substantial increase in the quantified self, where individuals collect and analyze various facets of their everyday lives, ranging from daily activities and locations to personal moments and feelings. However, the sheer volume and diversity of this data, which may come in the form of images, videos, sensor data, and annotations, present a significant challenge for data management systems. It is essential for unlocking the true potential of this data to have a structure that can model all the relevant interrelations in a holistic and meaningful way.

The *Lifelog Search Challenge* (LSC) [2] is an annual competition for document retrieval from quantified self in the form of lifelogs. The dataset consists of over 700,000 images taken from a first-person view over the course of 18 months, which, together with the accompanying metadata (date, GPS) and annotations (location, categories), form an inherently multimodal collection. Tasks include finding specific items quickly based on descriptions (KIS), answering questions (QA), or retrieving as many as possible according to various criteria (ADHOC). Here, two systems demonstrated the feasibility of graph-based retrieval.

LifeGraph [12] was the first to apply knowledge graph-based semantic search to lifelog data. Starting with the construction of a knowledge graph from the available multimodal data, it then integrated a taxonomy of everyday events and linked them to Wikidata for semantic expansion. Furthermore, its ensuing iterations focused on multimodal clustering and augmenting the annotations with Vision-Language Models.

MEMORIA [10] took a similar approach by relying on a graph database, which it uses to give semantics and more detailed annotations to images. While the resulting graph is not explicitly multimodal, it incorporates data from heterogeneous sources and can be interacted with by full-text search.

Recently, we have also applied our novel multimodal knowledge graph store, *MeGraS* [13], to the tasks of the LSC, and included a custom frontend to facilitate interaction with the knowledge graph [14]. In traditional multimodal knowledge graph stores, the document nodes are treated as opaque blobs that are enriched with semantics in the form of relations and literals. *MeGraS*, on the other hand, is special in that it has access to the multimedia documents it stores. This allows it to process their contents and extract richer features, while also providing the means to query across different modalities for multimedia documents: LSC's body camera images can be related to songs listened to during the time of their capture, or location metadata can be resolved to map entities for easier querying.

Furthermore, *MeGraS* supports the discovery of *hidden knowledge* which we characterize as *implicit relations*: links between two nodes that are not explicitly contained in the graph but can be computed at query time. For example, the implicit relation of kNN (k-nearest neighbors) can be useful for finding items for the ADHOC task. By using one retrieved image, a number of visually similar objects can be queried for. This relation is not persisted in the graph as it may change upon data addition or removal and, therefore, is always computed at query time. An example of such a query in SPARQL is shown in Listing 1.1, where the number of nearest neighbors is set to eight.

Listing 1.1. Detecting the implicit relation of k-nearest neighbors.

```
SELECT ?img WHERE { <URI> implicit:clip8nn ?img . }
```

This multimodal knowledge graph approach allows for a holistic understanding of personal data, enabling complex queries that are impossible with traditional, single-modality search engines. It transforms a collection of isolated files into a semantically rich, interconnected memory graph, while still allowing for leveraging the contents of the documents.

4.2   Interactive Semantic Exploration of Video Archives

Video content in digital archives has seen a dramatic increase due to the prevalence of mobile devices, the accompanying user-generated content, streaming services, and platforms for the creation and sharing of short clips. However, this abundance of visual information presents a significant challenge: how do we efficiently and semantically explore it? Traditional video search relies on pre-existing metadata, like titles and tags, or on computationally expensive visual content analysis. This often results in a poor user experience for finding specific objects or locating an exact scene.

The annually held *Video Browser Showdown* (VBS) [6] is a scientific benchmark to evaluate the efficiency of interactive video search tools. Its task types are similar to those of LSC: known-item search, ad-hoc video search, and visual question answering. The dataset is composed of three collections of video, which amount to several thousand hours of video in more than four million predefined annotated segments. Navigating this heap of multimodal data poses significant challenges, all the more when it comes to solving the specific VBS tasks.

VideoGraph [11] was the first to take the knowledge graph-based approach and, to date, remains the only system to do so. It combined information from multiple modalities with external knowledge bases like Wikidata to create a semantically enriched representation of video content. Furthermore, it extracted information from videos with Optical Character Recognition, Automated Speech Recognition, and also employed Google Cloud Vision API to obtain semantic concepts. *VideoGraph* then used graph traversal and content-based filtering for querying and retrieval.

In such a setting, *MeGraS* offers several advantages compared to traditional graph stores. It implements the Unified Multimedia Segmentation [19] model to make segments of documents addressable with URIs (Uniform Resource Identifier). This includes segmenting videos into shorter snippets, extracting certain sections according to a defined shape, or pulling individual frames. All of these may be segmented further. An example of such a document is shown in Fig. 1 with all parts of the image having their own, dedicated URI, which even describes the segment's form (polygon in this case) and parameters (the list of pairs as the x and y coordinates). Hence, we can perform a semantic search for documents that contain identified concepts since these segments are linked to their original resource: an individual frame of a dog playing with a frisbee, as shown below in Listing 1.2.

Likewise, as *MeGraS* explicitly manages media segments as distinct nodes in the graph, it contains more *hidden knowledge*: relations that can be computed based on spatio-temporal association. Based on SPARQL-MM [3], *MeGraS*

Fig. 1. An example of a segmented image, taken from the COCO dataset [5] with all parts being URI-addressable.

enables searching for more *implicit relations*, like images with specific concepts in spatial proximity or temporal sequences in videos, even though none of this is explicitly stored beforehand. For example, based on the coordinates of the bounding box of the frisbee in Fig. 1, it stands in a **besides** relation with the segment of the dog to show that the frisbee has been caught as opposed to a scene just after the frisbee has been thrown and is still in the air. Listing 1.2 demonstrates how to express such a query. Similarly, segments in a video can be set into a temporal ordering, and sequences retrieved that happen after a specific event, leveraging the temporal relations. The enhanced expressiveness of queries allows for exploring connections that might otherwise not be apparent.

Listing 1.2. Leveraging segments of an image to find certain scenes.

```
SELECT ?video
WHERE {
  ?dog coco:label "Dog" ; schema:segmentOf ?frame .
  ?frisbee coco:label "Frisbee" ; schema:segmentOf ?frame .
  ?dog spatial:besides ?frisbee .
  ?frame schema:segmentOf ?video .
}
```

Considering that VBS's dataset consists of several thousand hours of video material, finding such specific scenes would be very difficult through manual inspection. Instead, multimodal knowledge graphs provide a powerful tool to model multimedia and their subsequent exploration and retrieval.

4.3 Cross-Modal Fact-Checking for Journalism

Apart from the concrete research challenges outlined above, multimodal knowledge graphs also find applications in our everyday lives. We are constantly surrounded by multimedia documents in various shapes and forms, regardless of whether we consume them deliberately or not. Keeping up with what happens in the world is also increasingly multimodal. Some may watch news segments on their TV (video) or listen to the radio (audio), while others prefer to read newspapers (text), and today's generation may stick to looking at their social media feeds and experience a mix of modalities. The unification of all those events and their accompanying multimedia may be modeled with a knowledge graph.

Assuming the existence of such knowledge graphs, realistically, only capturing individual events, it can be used to support the work of journalists. It can give structure to previously unstructured and inherently unconnected multimedia documents and embed them in their semantic context. The multimodal knowledge graph may link entities (e.g., people, places, organizations) across different media types. For example, it could relate a sentence in a text article to a specific frame in a video that shows the same person, or to a social media post that provides an eyewitness account, helping to build factual narratives.

Alongside *implicit relations*, *MeGraS* also supports *derived relations*: the multimedia document (and its contents) is processed according to a predefined function evaluated at query time, and the results are persisted in the knowledge graph. An example with `clipEmbedding` is shown in Listing 1.3 using a CLIP [9] feature. If the triple for that relation is not available yet, *MeGraS* will compute the embedding of the multimedia document and store it in the graph for later.

Furthermore, *MeGraS* incorporates vector operations efficiently. The example in Listing 1.3 furthermore shows how to express a three-nearest-neighbor query to search for an image matching a textual description based on the cosine distance of their CLIP embeddings, the results of which should include the image shown in Fig. 1. As described above, the necessary embeddings for the vector operation are computed on the fly, if not available in the graph; a unique feature derived from the fact that *MeGraS* has access to the contents of the image nodes. For instance, this allows a journalist to find a selection of suitable pictures for a news article based on its content.

Listing 1.3. Finding three images that fit a textual description based on the cosine similarity of their CLIP embeddings [9].

```
SELECT ?img ?sim
WHERE {
  BIND (custom:CLIP_TEXT("A dog playing with a frisbee.") as ?textVec)
  ?img derived:clipEmbedding ?imgVec .
  BIND (custom:COSINE_SIM(?textVec, ?imgVec) AS ?sim)
}
ORDER BY DESC(?sim) LIMIT 3
```

Multimodal knowledge graphs can help journalists navigate and connect disparate media documents (e.g., social media posts, photos, videos) related to specific events. In addition, they support them in building rich, factually correct narratives by connecting different pieces of evidence.

4.4   Clinical Data Fusion for Medical Diagnosis

Decision making in clinical diagnosis is increasingly data-driven [7], yet the organization of this data remains a major challenge. Patient data is often siloed across different systems and formats, from textual clinical notes and medical histories, to visual data like X-rays and MRIs, to other types like time-series sensor data. This is where multimodal knowledge graphs can help, as they are effective in bringing structure to the various modalities within a single and unified framework. By doing so, they enable a more holistic and integrated view of the patient's data, which can enhance and accelerate the diagnostic process.

A key benefit of this approach is to move beyond a static, document-centric view of a patient. Instead, a multimodal knowledge graph models the patient as a central entity and connects them to various types of multimedia and segments thereof, such as a specific remark in a clinical note to a particular region in a medical scan. This graph-based representation captures the complex relationships between symptoms, diagnoses, and evidence, which are often lost when this data is stored in isolation.

MeGraS aids with this by modeling the multimedia documents within a single structure. For example, a query can find symptoms from textual clinical notes, relate them to the patterns in an MRI scan, and find patients with a predicted similar diagnosis. A key advantage of *MeGraS* is that these features do not need to be pre-extracted and stored in the graph. Rather, the necessary data, such as the image embeddings for similarity search, is computed on the fly at query time. Similarly, such documents and their relations can be used in research to identify complex correlations between a patient's medical history and their visual diagnostic data, potentially accelerating the discovery of new markers and treatment pathways.

4.5   Enhancing Educational Tools Through Multimodal Narratives

While textbooks remain a part of the educational landscape, they are increasingly seen as outdated sources, especially in comparison to the dynamic and evolving world of digital resources. Textbooks can quickly become outdated due to the rapid pace of knowledge advancement in many fields. They often lack the nuance and multiple perspectives found in newer, more diverse sources, which can also deliver a more up-to-date and accessible learning experience.

In this context, multimodal knowledge graphs can provide a valuable tool. In conjunction with a suitable, user-friendly interface, they can help shape the way students engage with content. For example, if a class is to learn about a Classical musical composer, modeling associated multimedia in a knowledge graph can be an engaging way to create an interactive narrative.

The exploration of the corresponding graph may start from facts about the composer, such as birth date and place, and show images about him as a person and his background. Furthermore, audio files containing his musical compositions may be linked directly. Also, their metadata can be used for sorting or filtering of these entities, to find contemporary composers and discover differences in the styles of their respective periods. Hereby, the multimodal knowledge graph provides the students with an interactive and non-linear experience, setting the works and lives of the composers in a historical context.

MeGraS, specifically, can contribute here by leveraging its capabilities to connect to external services. These can be attached to the routines behind the *derived relations*. For example, a service performing Optical Character Recognition may be run on images of letters that the composer had written during his lifetime. The extracted text is persisted in the graph and made available for exploration. This can facilitate access to the contents of the letters for students and enable their use in downstream tasks.

4.6   Enhanced Product Feedback Analysis in E-Commerce

The world of e-commerce is fast-paced, inherently multimodal, and centers around understanding customer feedback for improving products and driving sales. Traditional data management systems often treat text, such as item descriptions and reviews, and images of products as isolated data points. Linking them poses a significant challenge, but can help to gain a better understanding of customer sentiment.

Multimodal knowledge graphs are uniquely suited to address this by modeling the relationships between the available multimedia types. They allow for a deeper level of analysis that goes beyond simple keyword search. A graph containing text (item descriptions, reviews, social media posts), images (product photos, user-uploaded shots, visuals from marketing campaigns), and structured data (product specifications, sales figures, inventory data) can unify the entire sales pipeline from design, supply chain management, to delivery and feedback by tracking the respective statuses.

Furthermore, multimodal knowledge graphs allow for enhanced product discovery since they enable more powerful search capabilities based on a combination of text and image searches, such as facilitating a user to find a product by providing both a textual description and an image reference. This can also be applied to personalized marketing by taking a user's purchase history, their reviews, and the items they have interacted with into account. Creating a more comprehensive profile enables highly personalized product recommendations and targeted marketing campaigns.

Finally, the knowledge graph can be used for granular customer feedback analysis. By linking product reviews to specific product features, sellers can perform detailed sentiment analysis, helping them identify what customers like as well as flaws. Ultimately, these capabilities all contribute to a more sophisticated and intelligent sales pipeline that goes beyond traditional, siloed data analysis.

With the integration of external services in *MeGraS*, it can be used to perform the functionality described above. When connecting it to an endpoint that runs sentiment analysis on text, *MeGraS* can automatically categorize the reviews according to the opinions expressed in them, and add that data to the knowledge graph. Likewise, it can further process this data, for example, with keyword extraction to summarize the reviews, or convert the sentiments into scales for further analysis. All of this happens inside the multimodal knowledge graph, without the need for a dedicated pipeline.

4.7   Semantic Annotation and Navigation of Textual Corpora

Multimodal knowledge graphs can also be useful in research fields not directly related to multimedia modeling or analysis. In Natural Language Processing, exploring datasets of text documents with structured annotations, such as named entities, coreference chains, or summarization, is no easy task. The data format of these textual corpora inherently hinders their efficient navigation: they are split into the original document and the annotations in two separate files, and their alignment is non-trivial for visualization without additional tools [15]. Hence, either the context or the content of the annotations is lost when exploring either of the files. Even more challenging is the comparison of two different versions of the annotations, for example, for the evaluation of automated systems.

When integrating such a dataset into a multimodal knowledge graph, it can model each document and each annotation item as individual nodes linked to each other. This allows a user to query not just the text content, but the structure within it and of its annotations. It represents an approach that provides a powerful way to analyze and navigate complex text corpora, moving beyond simple keyword searches to enable rich, semantic exploration of the content.

MeGraS supports the ingestion and processing of text and rich-text documents, such as PDF. Also, it has the functionality to segment them according to defined parameters such as page intervals or text span indices, thanks to the integration of the Unified Multimedia Segmentation. To explore a textual dataset, all that is necessary is to map its annotations to segments with the corresponding label.

Therefore, several layers of annotations can be included for the same collection of documents, without intruding, but possibly informing each other. Queries enable filtering for only relevant annotations as well.

Finally, as *MeGraS* also acts as a multimedia document store, it can serve the documents for downstream tasks. Furthermore, it has a feature to visualize multimedia segments on the corresponding documents, as shown in the image in Fig. 1, which further facilitates the exploration of annotations.

5   Limitations and Future Work

While multimodal knowledge graphs are well-suited to take on the applications and use cases we have outlined above, they also face several limitations. Mainly, the scope of creating a general-purpose multimodal system is currently not clearly defined. Handling the vast range of multimedia formats and the on-the-fly content analysis may incur immense computational costs if not managed correctly. While we provide a strong proof of concept with *MeGraS* [13], more work is needed to create a fully generic framework that can seamlessly integrate any media type and handle the many possible external services.

Also, as the schema of any knowledge graph is described in its ontology, designing one that is robust and extensible is a complex and challenging task, necessitating a deep familiarity with the target domain and application as well as a general understanding of multimedia modeling. Future research may focus on developing tools and methodologies to make this endeavor more accessible more novices of the Semantic Web, possibly even resulting in (semi-)automatic ontology creation and evolution, particularly for handling new media types and emerging concepts. Likewise, interaction with knowledge graphs may be hampered for novices and experts alike due to the complexity of query languages like SPARQL. This may be addressed by developing more user-friendly and potentially high-level query languages or focusing on implementing natural language interfaces that abstract away the complexity of the underlying graph structure

Furthermore, multimedia data from heterogeneous sources inherently have ambiguities. Human perception of images or words differs between users, and, similarly, the classification of data items comes with varying degrees of certainty. Capturing and representing ambiguity and uncertainty in a knowledge graph remains a challenge.

Similar to the computational costs mentioned above, the performance of vast multimodal knowledge graphs may lead to trade-offs, especially for real-time queries on large collections of media files. This was exactly what we experienced when applying *MeGraS* to the *Lifelog Search Challenge* [14]: a degradation in query time. However, improving access methods and optimizing the query engine will certainly bring some alleviation in this area. Future work could also explore distributed graph databases, efficient indexing strategies for multimodal data, and intelligent sharding techniques. Nevertheless, modeling big datasets of possibly high-resolution multimedia documents is still challenging.

In the same vein, we must acknowledge the issue of scalability with two different aspects: data ingestion and dynamic integration. When adding a document to a multimodal knowledge graph, a certain computational cost occurs in creating and relating the corresponding nodes, and, possibly, processing its contents. Real-world data is dynamic and constantly changing with new articles being published, videos uploaded, and annotations updated. Integrating or streaming this into a large-scale knowledge graph in real-time is difficult. Hence, it is currently only feasible to focus on an individual dataset or a collection thereof.

6   Conclusions

This paper advocated for the advancement of multimodal knowledge graphs to model multimedia. They can be used to give structure to unstructured data of various modalities and heterogeneous sources [1] and can give their contents and metadata semantics by linking them to external knowledge bases. Furthermore, they enable efficient retrieval and exploration, either through pure queries or coupled with sophisticated user interfaces.

Multimodal knowledge graphs have found use cases in challenges mostly aimed at research. For holistic memory retrieval, we showed that they can perform complex, semantic queries across different modalities [14], thereby transforming a collection of isolated files into an interconnected memory graph. In the context of interactive video exploration, the ability to model videos at a granular level provides a powerful tool for the navigation of vast datasets. This facilitates finding specific scenes efficiently, based on the inference of implicit and spatio-temporal relationships.

In real-world applications, multimodal knowledge graphs can be a crucial tool for fact-checking in journalism by connecting disparate media types. For clinical diagnosis, they enable the discovery of complex correlations by linking multimedia documents of various modalities, from textual to visual. Furthermore, they can serve as interactive educational tools, providing a dynamic and non-linear way for students to engage with content. For example, a multimodal graph can link the audio of a musical piece to a text biography and an image of the composer, creating a rich narrative that sets the work in a historical context.

Multimodal knowledge graphs can also serve as a unifying framework for data management in e-commerce, where they link item descriptions, reviews, and product photos. This allows for deeper examination of what customers like or dislike, when coupled with downstream applications such as keyword extraction or sentiment analysis. Finally, in Natural Language Processing, knowledge graphs can model text documents with structured annotations, like named entities and coreference resolution. This moves beyond traditional file-based corpora and allows researchers to query the structure of the annotations and relationships across documents, enabling richer, semantic exploration of their contents.

We also proposed a paradigm shift in how knowledge graphs treat multimedia documents: from content-agnostic to content-aware. Traditional graph stores represent these documents as nodes, but the contents remain opaque to them. To address this, we introduced our novel multimodal knowledge graph store *MeGraS* [13] which has direct access to the multimedia contents. This ability is a core strength of our system, as it allows for richer feature extraction and enables powerful cross-modal queries that are impossible with traditional approaches. Its research prototype is open source and publicly available for download.[2]

While we as humans keep producing and consuming multimedia at an unprecedented rate, multimodal knowledge graphs are a powerful tool to unlock deeper insights. They can aid in the organization and exploration of the world's ever-growing collection of multimodal data.

Acknowledgments. This work was partially funded by the Swiss National Science Foundation through Project "MediaGraph" (Grant Number 202125).

Disclosure of Interests. The authors have no competing interests to declare that are relevant to the content of this article.

References

1. Chen, Z., et al.: Knowledge graphs meet multi-modal learning: a comprehensive survey. CoRR abs/2402.05391 (2024)
2. Gurrin, C., et al.: Introduction to the 8th annual lifelog search challenge, LSC 2025. In: Proceedings of the 2025 International Conference on Multimedia Retrieval, pp. 2143–2144. ICMR 2025, Association for Computing Machinery, New York, NY, USA (2025). https://doi.org/10.1145/3731715.3734579
3. Kurz, T., Schaffert, S., Schlegel, K., Stegmaier, F., Kosch, H.: SPARQL-MM - extending SPARQL to media fragments. In: The Semantic Web: ESWC 2014 Satellite Events - ESWC 2014 Satellite Events, Anissaras, Crete, Greece, 25-29 May 2014, Revised Selected Papers. LNCS, vol. 8798, pp. 236–240. Springer (2014). https://doi.org/10.1007/978-3-319-11955-7_26
4. Liang, W., Meo, P.D., Tang, Y., Zhu, J.: A survey of multi-modal knowledge graphs: technologies and trends. ACM Comput. Surv. **56**(11) (2024). https://doi.org/10.1145/3656579
5. Lin, T., et al.: Microsoft COCO: common objects in context. In: Computer Vision - ECCV 2014 - 13th European Conference, Zurich, Switzerland, 6-12 September 2014, Proceedings, Part V. LNCS, vol. 8693, pp. 740–755. Springer (2014). https://doi.org/10.1007/978-3-319-10602-1_48
6. Lokoc, J., et al.: Interactive video retrieval in the age of effective joint embedding deep models: lessons from the 11th VBS. Multim. Syst. **29**(6), 3481–3504 (2023). https://doi.org/10.1007/S00530-023-01143-5
7. Lyu, G.: Data-driven decision making in patient management: a systematic review. BMC Medical Informatics Decis. Mak. **25**(1), 239 (2025). https://doi.org/10.1186/S12911-025-03072-X
8. Oñoro-Rubio, D., Niepert, M., García-Durán, A., Gonzalez-Sanchez, R., López-Sastre, R.J.: Answering visual-relational queries in web-extracted knowledge graphs. In: 1st Conference on Automated Knowledge Base Construction, AKBC 2019, Amherst, MA, USA, 20-22 May 2019 (2019). https://doi.org/10.24432/C56P45
9. Radford, A., et al.: Learning transferable visual models from natural language supervision. In: Proceedings of the 38th International Conference on Machine

---

[2] https://megras.org.

Learning, ICML 2021, 18-24 July 2021, Virtual Event. Proceedings of Machine Learning Research, vol. 139, pp. 8748–8763. PMLR (2021). http://proceedings.mlr.press/v139/radford21a.html

10. Ribeiro, R.F., Amaral, L., Ye, W., Trifan, A., Neves, A.J.R., Iglésias, P.: MEMORIA: a memory enhancement and moment retrieval application for LSC 2023. In: Proceedings of the 6th Annual ACM Lifelog Search Challenge, LSC 2023, Thessaloniki, Greece, June 12-15, 2023, pp. 18–23. ACM (2023). https://doi.org/10.1145/3592573.3593099

11. Rossetto, L., et al.: Videograph - towards using knowledge graphs for interactive video retrieval. In: MultiMedia Modeling - 27th International Conference, MMM 2021, Prague, Czech Republic, 22-24 June 2021, Proceedings, Part II. LNCS, vol. 12573, pp. 417–422. Springer (2021). https://doi.org/10.1007/978-3-030-67835-7_38

12. Rossetto, L., Baumgartner, M., Ashena, N., Ruosch, F., Pernischová, R., Bernstein, A.: LifeGraph: a knowledge graph for lifelogs. In: Proceedings of the Third Annual Workshop on Lifelog Search Challenge, pp. 13–17. LSC 2020, Association for Computing Machinery, New York, NY, USA (2020). https://doi.org/10.1145/3379172.3391717

13. Rossetto, L., Ruosch, F.: MeGraS: An open-source store for multimodal knowledge graphs. In: Proceedings of the 33rd ACM International Conference on Multimedia (MM 2025). MM 2025, Association for Computing Machinery, New York, NY, USA (2025). https://doi.org/10.1145/3746027.3756872

14. Ruosch, F., Rossetto, L.: A SPARQL in the dark: shining a light on multimodal lifelogs with LifeGraph 5. In: Proceedings of the 8th Annual ACM Workshop on the Lifelog Search Challenge (LSC 2025). LSC 2025, ACM, New York, NY, USA (2025). https://doi.org/10.1145/3729459.3748694

15. Ruosch, F., Watter, J., Sarasua, C., Bernstein, A.: Documents with integrated visually annotated arguments. In: Computational Models of Argument - Proceedings of COMMA 2024, Hagen, Germany, 18-20 September 2024. Frontiers in Artificial Intelligence and Applications, vol. 388, pp. 367–368. IOS Press (2024). https://doi.org/10.3233/FAIA240343

16. Schneider, E.W.: Course modularization applied: the interface system and its implications for sequence control and data analysis. Behav. Object. **1973**, 21 (1973)

17. Singhal, A.: Introducing the knowledge graph: things, not strings (2012). https://blog.google/products/search/introducing-knowledge-graph-things-not/

18. Wang, X., Meng, B., Chen, H., Meng, Y., Lv, K., Zhu, W.: TIVA-KG: a multimodal knowledge graph with text, image, video and audio. In: Proceedings of the 31st ACM International Conference on Multimedia, pp. 2391–2399. MM '23, Association for Computing Machinery, New York, NY, USA (2023). https://doi.org/10.1145/3581783.3612266

19. Willi, J., Bernstein, A., Rossetto, L.: Unified multimedia segmentation - a comprehensive model for URI-based media segment representation. TGDK **2**(3), 1:1–1:34 (2024). https://doi.org/10.4230/TGDK.2.3.1

20. Wu, Y., et al.: MMpedia: A large-scale multi-modal knowledge graph. In: The Semantic Web – ISWC 2023: 22nd International Semantic Web Conference, Athens, Greece, 6–10 November 2023, Proceedings, Part II, pp. 18–37. Springer-Verlag, Berlin, Heidelberg (2023). https://doi.org/10.1007/978-3-031-47243-5_2

21. Zhu, X., et al.: Multi-modal knowledge graph construction and application: a survey. IEEE Trans. Knowl. Data Eng. **36**(2), 715–735 (2024). https://doi.org/10.1109/TKDE.2022.3224228

GAS: Geometry-Appearance Synergy for Consistent Video Customization

Heng Jia[1,3], Na Zhao[2(✉)], Yunqiu Xu[1(✉)], Linchao Zhu[1,3], and Yi Yang[1,3]

[1] ReLER, CCAI, Zhejiang University, Hangzhou, China
`imyunqiuxu@gmail.com`
[2] Singapore University of Technology and Design, Singapore, Singapore
`na_zhao@sutd.edu.sg`
[3] The State Key Lab of Brain-Machine Intelligence, Zhejiang University, Hangzhou, China

Abstract. Video customization has gained significant interest, yet achieving temporal and geometric consistency remains challenging. To address this, we propose a novel framework that leverages neural representations to model dynamic 3D scenes in videos, distilling their knowledge into rendering consistency to regularize diffusion models. Our method conceptualizes dynamic scenes as 4D volumes, employing grid-based dynamic geometry representations to enhance geometric consistency and cross-view appearance representations to improve visual coherence across frames. To seamlessly integrate these representations into diffusion models, we propose a latent neural rendering strategy that aligns geometry and appearance in a unified manner. Comprehensive evaluations across tasks such as local object editing and composite customization reveal consistent and significant performance gains, demonstrating the effectiveness and robustness of our proposed method.

Keywords: Video customization · Temporal consistency · 3D prior

1 Introduction

Recent advances in video customization [2,3,5,10,11,16,19,25,31,34,38,45,46, 50] enable creating personalized visual content. This work focuses on text-driven video customization, manipulating visual elements (*e.g.*, a subject's shape) using textual prompts. Recent works adapt pre-trained text-to-image (T2I) diffusion models [39] for tasks such as style transfer and subject shape editing [4–6,38,45]. While achieving plausible temporal consistency by leveraging cues extracted from the source video such as attention maps [27,38], optical flows [5], edge/depth/human poses [50,53,55], and diffusion feature correspondences [10], they often impose strong shape constraints, limiting their flexibility for subject customization. Tune-A-Video [45] introduces a tailored spatial-temporal attention mechanism and an efficient one-shot tuning strategy, demonstrating versatile

© The Author(s), under exclusive license to Springer Nature Singapore Pte Ltd. 2026
J. Lokoč et al. (Eds.): MMM 2026, LNCS 16412, pp. 648–662, 2026.
https://doi.org/10.1007/978-981-95-6950-2_46

a man wearing a white helmet and a blue
suit is riding a motorcycle on the road
a pickup truck is moving in the forest

A woman wonder woman **is riding a white
horse across a fence**

Fig. 1. Comparison of geometric consistency in video customization. Tune-A-Video [45] (middle) exhibits *geometric inconsistencies* including object jitter, misalignment, and omissions, while our approach (bottom) maintains consistent object position and orientation across frames.

applications, including shape-aware subject customization. However, achieving high-quality video customization with temporal consistency remains challenging.

Geometric consistency is critical for the continuity and aesthetic coherence of customized video content, yet it remains a significant challenge. While methods like Tune-A-Video [45] effectively preserve subject appearance consistency, they often overlook geometric consistency, leading to notable artifacts. Geometric inconsistencies, such as jittering or misalignment in object position and orientation, disrupt the intended coherence across frames, as illustrated by the inconsistent car orientation in Fig. 1. Additionally, these inconsistencies may result in missing objects, exemplified by the disappearing fence in the same figure. Despite advancements in appearance preservation [45,55], addressing geometric consistency remains an open problem in generating video content.

Geometry inconsistency in diffusion models highlights their limited ability to accurately interpret the spatial position and orientation of objects within a scene. To address this, we introduce the Geometry-Appearance Synergy (GAS) framework, which integrates spatial-temporal relationships and 3D geometric cues into diffusion models. Drawing inspiration from recent advancements in 3D reconstruction [1,8,14,22,24,44,49], we treat the source video as a dynamic 3D scene to capture inherent geometry and spatial information. Our approach incorporates dynamic 3D scene representations as residual representation maps after each Transformer block in the diffusion U-Net. The dynamic scene is further decomposed into geometry and appearance components. For geometry, we conceptualize the video as a 4D volume [8] and model the geometry using grid-based representation. Recent grid-based neural representations [1,8,32,44,49] achieve high reconstruction fidelity with low memory usage, inspiring us to represent geometry using grid-based representations. Specifically, we factorize the 4D volume into six 2D representation planes and project the 4D coordinates onto these planes for interpolation. The interpolated representations are aggregated through a lightweight MLP to predict the dynamic density field, which implicitly encodes the spatial location and orientation of objects in 3D space.

A direct approach to modeling appearance would employ a MLP [29], but our experiments reveal limitations, including background loss and inconsistent object structures. To overcome these challenges, we leverage the appearance priors inherent in diffusion models to construct a robust appearance representation. Diffusion models excel in visual content generation [39, 41, 47] and capture rich appearance priors during pre-training, making them well-suited for appearance modeling. Specifically, we extract feature maps from each Transformer block of the diffusion U-Net to create appearance representation planes. We then project 3D coordinates onto neighboring frame representation maps and interpolate appearance representations. Finally, a PointNet-like architecture [37] aggregates these interpolated representations to construct the ultimate appearance representation. This approach mitigates background loss while improving structural consistency in newly synthesized content.

Our contributions are summarized as:

i) We introduce a novel dynamic 3D scene representation for diffusion models, embedding geometric consistency into video customization.
ii) By decoupling dynamic scenes into geometry and appearance components, we leverage grid-based dynamic geometry and cross-view appearance representations to improve consistency and mitigate background loss.
iii) We evaluate the framework across diverse scenes and prompts, validating its ability to synergistically enhance geometric consistency and visual fidelity.

2   Related Work

Text-Driven Video Customization. Text-driven video customization has received significant attention recently, with many approaches extending advancements in text-to-image (T2I) customization. While image-based customization methods [12, 39, 53] can process individual video frames, they frequently suffer from inter-frame inconsistencies due to the absence of temporal modeling. To address this limitation, recent works have explored solutions from two primary directions. The first direction involves training video diffusion models on large-scale paired text-video datasets [7, 15, 30, 48]. Although these models achieve impressive results, they demand substantial computational resources, limiting their accessibility. On the other side, recent promising works [2, 5, 10, 38, 45, 50] extend pre-trained T2I diffusion models for more efficient video customization. These methods can be broadly categorized as training-free and one-shot-tuned approaches. Training-free approaches [2, 4–6, 10, 13, 17, 23, 38, 43, 50–52, 54] adapt pre-trained T2I models in a zero-shot manner, bypassing the need for additional training. While computationally efficient, these approaches often introduce spatial-temporal distortions and inconsistencies. In contrast, one-shot-tuned methods [3, 11, 16, 20, 27, 33, 45, 55] fine-tune a pre-trained T2I model on a single video, achieving greater editing flexibility at the expense of additional computational overhead. Our work aligns with the one-shot-tuned paradigm but introduces a novel perspective by leveraging 3D geometric understanding. Unlike existing methods, which primarily focus on learning appearance relationships from videos, we conceptualize a video as a dynamic 3D scene. By explicitly integrating 3D geometric cues into pre-trained T2I models, our approach significantly enhances spatial-temporal consistency, advancing the state of video customization.

Dynamic Scene View Synthesis. Novel view synthesis in dynamic scenes from monocular videos [8,9,21,22,24,26,28,35,36] shows significant potential for real-world applications. However, the inherent challenge lies in reconstructing dynamic scenes where only a single viewpoint is available at each time step. Recent advancements in neural rendering yield remarkable progress in dynamic view synthesis. Several approaches [35,36] address this by modeling scenes with deformation fields that map local observations to canonical representations, enabling consistency across viewpoints and time. Alternatively, other methods directly represent the scene as time-varying NeRFs [9,21,28], regressing 4D spatiotemporal radiance fields with the aid of geometric proxies. Building on these advances, we propose to learn dynamic geometry representations of scenes and incorporate them into pre-trained diffusion models to enhance video customization consistency. Our approach enhances geometric coherence in video customization, bridging the gap between dynamic view synthesis and generative modeling.

3   Method

3.1   Overview

Problem Definition. Text-driven video customization aims to generate novel videos that satisfy specified textual prompts while preserving visual consistency. Formally, given an input video $\mathcal{V}$ and a source prompt $\mathcal{P}$ describing the scene, our objective is to generate a visually consistent customized video $\mathcal{V}^*$ that adheres to the customization prompt $\mathcal{P}^*$.

Customization Pipeline. The overall customization pipeline is illustrated in Fig. 2. During inference, we acquire the latent noise by inverting the source video $\mathcal{V}$ through DDIM inversion [42]. Unlike [45], our DDIM inversion is conducted with the source text prompt $\mathcal{P}$. Subsequently, we sample a customized video from this latent noise, conditioned on the target customization prompt $\mathcal{P}^*$ employing DDIM sampling [42]:

$$\mathcal{V}^* = \text{DDIM-sample}\left(\text{DDIM-inv}(\mathcal{V}, \mathcal{P}), \mathcal{P}^*\right). \tag{1}$$

Geometry-Appearance Synergy Framework. A straightforward solution for video customization is to lift pre-trained text-to-image diffusion models (*e.g.*, Stable Diffusion [39]). However, such a simple adaptation often yields unsatisfactory results due to the absence of dedicated consistency mechanisms. Our experiments show that the inconsistencies primarily manifest in geometry, encompassing spatial misalignment, incorrect orientation, and object omission.

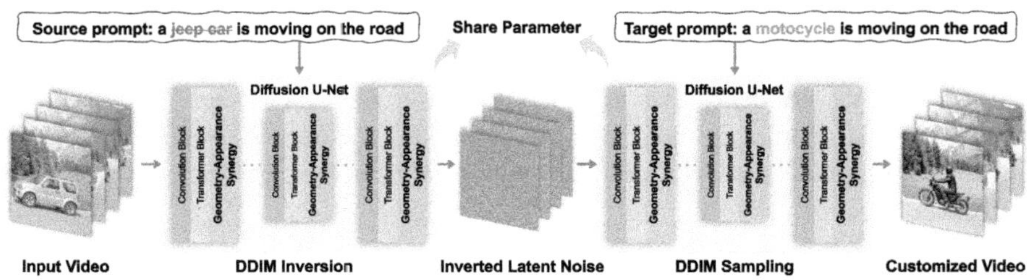

Fig. 2. Overview of the Geometry-Appearance Synergy (GAS) framework for consistent video customization. We augment a pretrained diffusion U-Net by inserting lightweight *GAS blocks* after each Transformer block. GAS jointly couples geometric cues (pose/orientation) with appearance features (texture/color) to enforce cross-frame consistency. During training, we optimize the new GAS parameters and the attention layers, while keeping the rest of the parameters frozen. At inference, the source video is inverted to latent noise via DDIM inversion, then processed through our enhanced U-Net to generate customized video conditioned on target prompt.

We propose GAS (Geometry-Appearance Synergy) to decompose dynamic scenes into geometry and appearance for consistent video customization, as depicted in Fig. 3. Our key insight is to formulate customization as a *geometry-constrained diffusion process*, where 3D understanding provides inductive bias for spatiotemporal coherence. We use grid-based representations [1,8,32,44,49] for scene geometry and construct appearance from diffusion features across frames. The optimization objective is defined as follows:

$$\mathcal{L}_{\text{GAS}} = \mathbb{E}_{z,\epsilon\sim\mathcal{N}(0,1),\tau,c}\left[\|\epsilon - \epsilon_\theta\left(z_\tau, \tau, c, \mathcal{R}_{\text{geo}}, \mathcal{R}_{\text{app}}\right)\|_2^2\right], \tag{2}$$

where z represents the latent representation, τ signifies the diffusion timestep, c corresponds to the embeddings of source text prompt $\mathcal{P}$, $\mathcal{R}_{\text{geo}}$ and $\mathcal{R}_{\text{app}}$ denote geometry and appearance representations, respectively.

3.2   Integrating Dynamic 3D Scene Representation

To improve the consistency of video customization, we attempt to integrate dynamic 3D scene representation into diffusion models. Recent text-to-image diffusion models [39] commonly employ a U-Net architecture with interleaved Transformer blocks, which gradually downsamples and upsamples images with skip connections. We integrate the geometry-appearance synergy learning module following each Transformer block of the diffusion U-Net. After each Transformer block, we obtain the hidden representation map $Z \in \mathbb{R}^{F\times N\times D}$, where F denotes the number of frames, N indicates the number of tokens in a frame and D represents the hidden dimension. For each hidden representation $Z_{t,n}$ at location (t, n), with t denoting the temporal index and n the spatial index, we create a synergistic representation by casting and rendering a ray r. The rendered geometry and appearance-aware representation $Z_{t,n}^R$ are then added to the hidden representation maps as residuals:

$$\hat{Z}_{t,n} = Z_{t,n} + Z_{t,n}^{R}, \tag{3}$$

where $\hat{Z}_{t,n}$ denotes the output representation map from our geometry-appearance synergy module.

To construct the representation rendering pipeline, we sample K points along the ray r and acquire dynamic geometry-aware density σ_k and appearance representation z_k through our designed geometry-appearance synergy learning module. Inspired by the volume rendering presented in [29], we propose latent volume rendering and employ alpha compositing as the rendering function. Given geometry-aware density σ_k and appearance representation z_k for each point along the ray r, the 3D-aware representation is rendered as follows:

$$\alpha_k = 1 - \exp\left(-\sigma_k\right), T_k = \prod_{l=1}^{k-1}\left(1 - \alpha_l\right), \hat{z} = \sum_{k=1}^{K} T_k \alpha_k z_k, \tag{4}$$

where T_k denotes the accumulated transmittance, signifying the probability that the ray travels without interception. The output from our GAS module is computed as follows:

$$\hat{Z}_{t,n} = Z_{t,n} + \sum_{k=1}^{K}\left[\prod_{l=1}^{k-1}\left(1 - \alpha_l\right)\right]\left[1 - \exp\left(-\sigma_k\right)\right] z_k. \tag{5}$$

3.3   Dynamic Geometry Representation

For a better understanding of object locations, we introduce the dynamic geometry representation to learn the underlying geometric structure within the video. We conceptualize the dynamic scene as a 4D volume [8] and employ a continuous projection network f_σ to capture its geometric properties:

$$\sigma = f_\sigma(Q), \tag{6}$$

and $Q = (x, y, z, t)$ denotes the 4D coordinate of the k-th point along the ray r.

Drawing inspiration from recent advances in 3D reconstruction [1,8,9,21,22, 24,28,32,35,36,44,49], we propose utilizing grid representation [1,8,32,44,49] instead of MLP to construct the geometric density field. Specifically, the 4D volume is decomposed into six 2D representation planes: P_{XY}, P_{YZ} and P_{XZ} denote the static components. and P_{XT}, P_{YT} and P_{ZT} denote the dynamic components. We first project the 4D coordinate Q onto the six representation planes and interpolate representations from the corresponding plane as follows:

$$p_* = \phi(P_*, \omega_*(Q)), \tag{7}$$

where ω represents coordinate orthographic projection function, $*$ denotes representation plane, and ϕ is interpolation function (*e.g.*, bilinear). As illustrated in

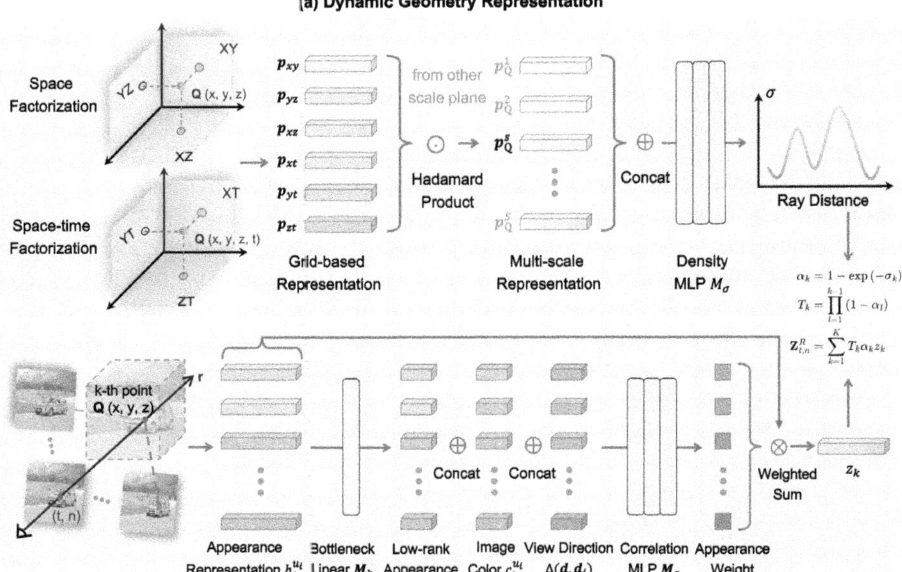

Fig. 3. Geometry-Appearance Synergy. *(a) Dynamic geometry.* We decompose the 4D spatiotemporal volume into six 2D planes and fuse multi-scale grid features to predict geometry-aware density. *(b) Cross-view appearance.* We use correlation-based weights to aggregate diffusion appearance features from neighboring views, enhancing cross-view consistency. These components are synergistically integrated into diffusion models via latent volume rendering.

Fig. 3(a), we aggregate the interpolated representations using Hadamard product:

$$p_Q = p_{xy} \odot p_{xz} \odot p_{yz} \odot p_{xt} \odot p_{yt} \odot p_{zt}. \tag{8}$$

We construct multi-scale planes to enhance spatial smoothness and representational capacity [8]. Mathematically, for each scale $s \in \{1, 2, \ldots, S\}$, we construct a representation plane P_*^s with resolution $R_s = R_{\text{base}} \times 2^{s-1}$. This exponential scaling allows efficient coverage of the frequency spectrum while maintaining computational tractability. The concatenated features are passed to a lightweight MLP M_σ to compute the density:

$$\sigma = M_\sigma \left(\bigoplus_{s=1}^{S} p_Q^s \right), \tag{9}$$

where $\oplus$ is concatenation and S denotes the number of scales. This multi-scale approach enables *progressive geometric refinement*: coarse scales capture global object structure while fine scales encode local details. This hierarchical decomposition is important for maintaining consistency across geometric levels during customization.

3.4   Cross-View Appearance Representation

To enhance the understanding of object shape and color, we propose to represent appearance using MLP. However, we find that it leads to background degradation and inconsistent object structures. We instead use intermediate feature maps from diffusion models, which inherently encode rich appearance priors through extensive pre-training. This integration enables a more robust and consistent representation of both object and background.

Our goal is to acquire an appearance representation z_k for point Q at time t from diffusion models. We select source views within temporal radius r and extract feature maps $\{h_i \in \mathbb{R}^{H \times W \times D} | i \in \mathcal{N}(t) = [t - r, t + r], r > 0\}$ after each Transformer block, where H, W, D denote spatial resolution and feature dimension. Next, we project point Q onto the source views as $\{u_i\}$ and sample features $\{h_i^{u_i} \in \mathbb{R}^D\}$ and colors $\{c_i^{u_i} \in \mathbb{R}^3\}$. As illustrated in Fig. 3(b), the sampled representations are projected into a lower-dimensional space d through a bottleneck linear M_b:

$$\widetilde{h}_i^{u_i} = M_b(h_i^{u_i}) \oplus c_i^{u_i} \in \mathbb{R}^{d+3}. \tag{10}$$

We leverage a PointNet-like architecture [37] to capture inter-view relationships by aggregating low-rank appearance features using mean and variance statistics.

$$\widetilde{h} = \mathrm{VAR}(\{\widetilde{h}_i^{u_i} | i \in \mathcal{N}(t)\}) \oplus \mathrm{MEAN}(\{\widetilde{h}_i^{u_i} | i \in \mathcal{N}(t)\}), \tag{11}$$

where MEAN and VAR represent the mean and variance operators, respectively. The ultimate appearance representation z_k is obtained by a weighted combination of sampled appearance representations from source views:

$$z_k = \frac{\sum_i M_a(\widetilde{h}, \widetilde{h}_i^{u_i}, \Delta(d, d_i)) * h_i^{u_i}}{\sum_i M_a(\widetilde{h}, \widetilde{h}_i^{u_i}, \Delta(d, d_i))}, i \in \mathcal{N}(t), \tag{12}$$

where M_a is an appearance MLP that predicts a weight for each source view. d and d_i represent the viewing directions from the camera positions at time t and i to point Q, respectively. $\Delta(d, d_i)$ computes the normalized angle difference between d and d_i.

4   Experiments

We compare our method with four state-of-the-art video customization and generation approaches: Tune-A-Video [45], FateZero [38], Gen-1 [7], and Gen-2 [40]. More details on these baselines are provided in the Appendix.

4.1   Qualitative Results

We evaluate visual quality against recent video customization approaches, as shown in Fig. 4. Our method generates high-quality, visually consistent videos that adhere to customization prompts while preserving geometric consistency.

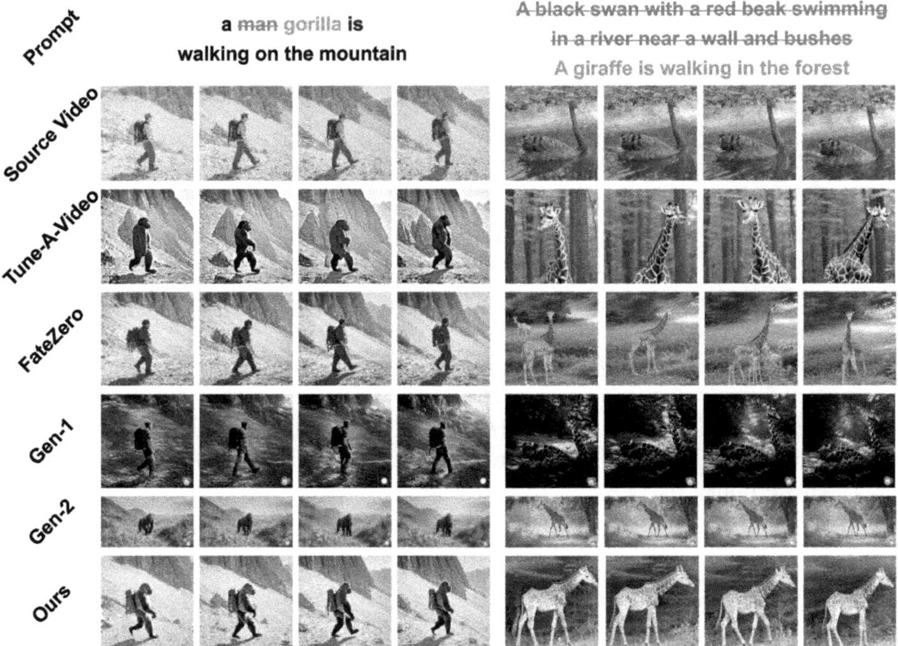

Fig. 4. Qualitative results. Source video and edited frames over time (left → right).

Our model excels in local object customization, demonstrating exceptional performance by preserving the spatial position and orientation of objects from the source video. Existing methods face significant limitations: for example, Tune-A-Video [45] (second row) maintains pose and motion fidelity but suffers from severe visual artifacts. FateZero [38] (third row) and Gen-1 [7] (fourth row) struggle to align the generated appearance with the customization prompt, with Gen-1 further failing to retain the background details. Although Gen-2 [40] (fifth row) produces high-quality and visually consistent videos, its inability to directly process text inputs restricts its utility in text-driven customization tasks. In contrast, our method (last row) retains pose, motion, and background integrity, delivering visually coherent results.

Furthermore, our approach enables simultaneous customization of foreground and background elements, yielding high-quality, visually coherent outputs. In comparison, Tune-A-Video [45] (second row) generates videos that align with the specified text prompt but suffer from geometric inconsistencies, as evidenced by giraffes with varying neck orientations that disrupt structural coherence. FateZero [38] (third row) also fails to maintain geometric consistency, exhibiting misalignment with the target prompt and an incorrect number of giraffes, deviating from the customization requirements. Gen-1 [7] (fourth row) struggles to produce plausible results, constrained by the subject's shape from the source video. Gen-2 [40] (fifth row) demonstrates high-quality and visually consistent

Table 1. Quantitative results.

	Input	Visual Consistency ↑	Text Alignment ↑	Fidelity ↑	PickScore ↑	Overall ↑
Tune-A-Video [45]	Text + Video	92.62	32.01	73.12	20.73	4.51
FateZero [38]	Text + Video	92.46	30.77	**81.65**	20.37	4.71
Gen-1 [7]	Text + Video	89.83	30.07	65.49	20.55	3.64
Gen-2 [40]	Text	98.12	32.79	60.83	22.81	4.46
GAS (ours)	Text + Video	**92.86**	**32.03**	78.82	**20.95**	**4.93**

outputs, highlighting the benefits of large-scale pre-training on extensive video datasets. Our method (last row) generates entirely novel scenes with consistent geometry and appearance, achieving superior customization. Notably, the visual quality and coherence of our results even match state-of-the-art video diffusion models pre-trained on large-scale datasets, affirming the efficacy of our approach.

4.2 Quantitative Results

We conduct quantitative evaluation against state-of-the-art methods for video customization and generation, focusing on visual consistency, text alignment, fidelity, and user preference. Quantitative results are summarized in Table 1, with a detailed explanation of the metrics provided in Appendix. Our method achieves the highest visual consistency score among all methods except Gen-2 [40], underscoring its superior coherence across frames. Moreover, it attains the top text alignment score, second only to Gen-2 [40], highlighting its exceptional capacity for customization. The strong performance of Gen-2 [40] in these metrics reflects the advantages of large-scale pre-training. Rather than relying on additional data, our approach incorporates dynamic 3D priors into diffusion models, enabling customization with excellent fidelity. Additionally, Gen-1 [7] and Gen-2 [40] demonstrate relatively lower fidelity, revealing challenges in preserving the original video content, which is crucial for video customization. Furthermore, our approach achieves the highest PickScore [18], reflecting its strong alignment with human preferences. Overall, our method achieves the highest overall score and demonstrates effectiveness for high-quality, user-aligned video customization.

4.3 Ablation Studies

Effectiveness of Cross-View Appearance. To evaluate the effectiveness of our method, we first examine the impact of cross-view appearance representation. A baseline approach involves extending the dynamic geometry representation and employing a continuous MLP to predict appearance components. This framework uses two lightweight MLPs: one maps grid representations to density

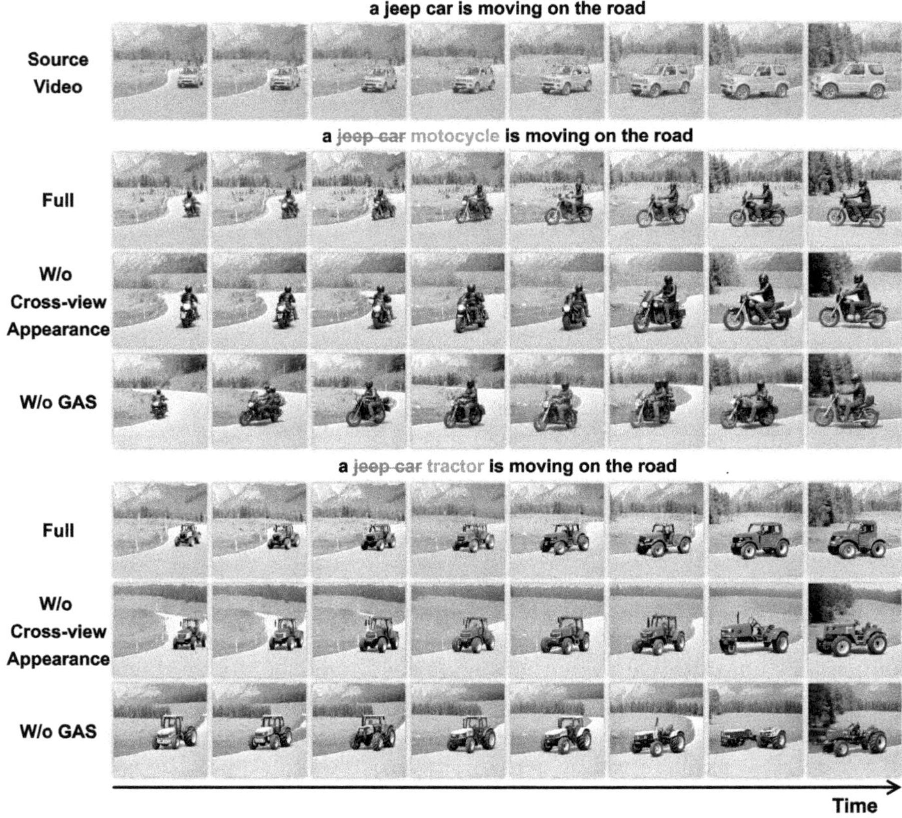

Fig. 5. Qualitative ablation study. Removing cross-view appearance causes background degradation and structural deformations, while removing GAS produces more severe geometric artifacts. Our full model maintains spatiotemporal consistency, underscoring the importance of joint geometry-appearance modeling.

and auxiliary features, while the other translates features and view directions to appearance representations. As shown in Fig. 5, replacing the cross-view appearance representation with MLP-based appearance representation often leads to background omissions. Quantitative results in Table 2 further indicate a decline in fidelity metrics, suggesting that the model fails to capture portions of the source video. This limitation arises from the challenge of encoding the complex scene appearance using shallow MLPs.

In contrast, our cross-view appearance representation leverages pre-trained diffusion priors and integrates neighboring view representations, significantly reducing learning complexity. Instead of predicting the complete appearance, the model focuses on estimating representation weights, enabling more effective utilization of the available information. Importantly, the absence of cross-view appearance representation disrupts object structures, underscoring the enhanced shape consistency achieved by our approach. These results confirm the superior

Table 2. Quantitative ablation study.

Dynamic Geometry	Cross-view Appearance	Visual Consistency↑	Text Alignment↑	Fidelity↑	PickScore↑	Overall↑
		93.41	27.05	72.46	20.1	3.68
✓		93.65	28.17	75.68	20.16	4.02
✓	✓	**94.63**	**28.37**	**79.83**	**20.35**	**4.36**

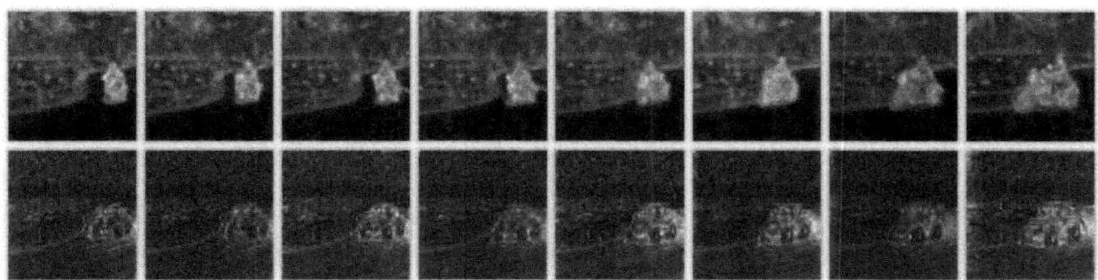

Fig. 6. Attention visualization.

capability of cross-view appearance representation in capturing coherent appearance details across views.

Effectiveness of GAS. The naive extension without GAS struggles to model complex dynamic scenes, resulting in noticeable positional shifts, as illustrated in Fig. 5. Quantitative analysis in Table 2 reveals significant declines in visual consistency, text alignment, fidelity, and PickScore [18] when GAS is omitted. Temporal attention, which relies solely on appearance-based correlations, often produces artifacts such as duplicated objects, exemplified by a duplicated person on the motorcycle. Our proposed dynamic geometry representation addresses these limitations, enhancing visual consistency and mitigating artifacts. Integrated with cross-view appearance representation, our approach achieves high-quality, coherent local object customization. The synergy between geometry and appearance representations highlights the effectiveness of our framework in capturing the intricacies of dynamic scenes.

4.4   Attention Visualization for Shape Control

We present visualizations of the text-to-image cross-attention maps for shape-aware customization in Fig. 6, demonstrating the capability of our method to precisely manipulate object shapes. The results highlight our approach's effectiveness in redistributing attention scores across object regions, facilitating robust and controllable shape transformations. These findings underscore the method's ability to achieve high-quality and consistent customizations, showcasing its adaptability and potential across diverse scenarios.

5 Conclusion

We present a novel approach to video customization by addressing inconsistency through the decoupling of geometry and appearance components. By modeling videos as dynamic 3D scenes, we propose the Geometry-Appearance Synergy (GAS) framework, which integrates geometry-aware neural representations with diffusion models. Our method leverages grid-based geometry representations for robust consistency, while cross-view appearance representations capture video content and mitigate background loss. Extensive qualitative and quantitative evaluations demonstrate that GAS achieves superior consistency in video customization, enabling coherent and precise manipulation of visual content.

Acknowledgments. This work was supported by the National Natural Science Foundation of China (62402432) and the China Postdoctoral Science Foundation (2024M762830). This work was also supported by the Ministry of Education, Singapore, under its MOE Academic Research Fund Tier 1 - SMU-SUTD Internal Research Grant (SMU-SUTD 2023_02_09). This work was also supported by the Fundamental Research Funds for the Central Universities (226-2025-00080). This work was also supported by the Earth System Big Data Platform of the School of Earth Sciences, Zhejiang University.

References

1. Cao, A., et al.: Hexplane: a fast representation for dynamic scenes. In: CVPR (2023)
2. Ceylan, D., et al.: Pix2video: video editing using image diffusion. In: ICCV (2023)
3. Chai, W., et al.: Stablevideo: text-driven consistency-aware diffusion video editing. In: ICCV (2023)
4. Chen, Y., et al.: EVE: efficient zero-shot text-based video editing with depth map guidance and temporal consistency constraints. In: IJCAI (2024)
5. Cong, Y., et al.: FLATTEN: optical flow-guided attention for consistent text-to-video editing. In: ICLR (2024)
6. Couairon, P., et al.: Videdit: zero-shot and spatially aware text-driven video editing. TMLR (2024)
7. Esser, P., et al.: Structure and content-guided video synthesis with diffusion models. In: ICCV (2023)
8. Fridovich-Keil, S., et al.: K-planes: explicit radiance fields in space, time, and appearance. In: CVPR (2023)
9. Gao, C., et al.: Dynamic view synthesis from dynamic monocular video. In: ICCV (2021)
10. Geyer, M., et al.: Tokenflow: consistent diffusion features for consistent video editing. In: ICLR (2024)
11. Gu, Y., et al.: Videoswap: customized video subject swapping with interactive semantic point correspondence. In: CVPR (2024)
12. Hertz, A., et al.: Prompt-to-prompt image editing with cross attention control. In: ICLR (2023)
13. Jeong, H., et al.: Ground-a-video: zero-shot grounded video editing using text-to-image diffusion models. In: ICLR (2024)

14. Jia, H., Zhu, L., Zhao, N.: H3R: hybrid multi-view correspondence for generalizable 3D reconstruction. In: ICCV (2025)
15. Jia, H., et al.: MOS2: mixture of scale and shift experts for text-only video captioning. In: ACM MM (2024)
16. Karim, N., et al.: Save: spectral-shift-aware adaptation of image diffusion models for text-driven video editing. arXiv:2305.18670 (2023)
17. Khandelwal, A.: Infusion: inject and attention fusion for multi concept zero-shot text-based video editing. In: ICCV (2023)
18. Kirstain, Y., et al.: Pick-a-pic: an open dataset of user preferences for text-to-image generation. In: NeurIPS (2024)
19. Ku, M., et al.: Anyv2v: a tuning-free framework for any video-to-video editing tasks. TMLR (2024)
20. Lee, Y.C., et al.: Shape-aware text-driven layered video editing. In: CVPR (2023)
21. Li, Z., et al.: Neural scene flow fields for space-time view synthesis of dynamic scenes. In: CVPR (2021)
22. Li, Z., et al.: Dynibar: neural dynamic image-based rendering. In: CVPR (2023)
23. Liao, Z., et al.: Lovecon: text-driven training-free long video editing with controlnet. In: CVPR Workshops (2024)
24. Lin, H., et al.: High-fidelity and real-time novel view synthesis for dynamic scenes. In: SIGGRAPH Asia (2023)
25. Liu, C., et al.: Stablev2v: stablizing shape consistency in video-to-video editing. arXiv:2411.11045 (2024)
26. Liu, J., et al.: Dynvideo-e: harnessing dynamic nerf for large-scale motion- and view-change human-centric video editing. In: CVPR (2024)
27. Liu, S., et al.: Video-P2P: video editing with cross-attention control. In: CVPR (2024)
28. Liu, Y.L., et al.: Robust dynamic radiance fields. In: CVPR (2023)
29. Mildenhall, B., et al.: Nerf: representing scenes as neural radiance fields for view synthesis. In: ECCV (2021)
30. Molad, E., et al.: Dreamix: video diffusion models are general video editors. arXiv:2302.01329 (2023)
31. Mou, C., et al.: Revideo: remake a video with motion and content control. In: NeurIPS (2024)
32. Müller, T., et al.: Instant neural graphics primitives with a multiresolution hash encoding. ACM TOG (2022)
33. Nikankin, Y., et al.: Sinfusion: training diffusion models on a single image or video. In: ICML (2023)
34. Ouyang, W., et al.: I2vedit: first-frame-guided video editing via image-to-video diffusion models. In: SIGGRAPH Asia (2024)
35. Park, K., et al.: Nerfies: deformable neural radiance fields. In: ICCV (2021)
36. Pumarola, A., et al.: D-nerf: neural radiance fields for dynamic scenes. In: CVPR (2021)
37. Qi, C.R., et al.: Pointnet: deep learning on point sets for 3D classification and segmentation. In: CVPR (2017)
38. Qi, C., et al.: Fatezero: fusing attentions for zero-shot text-based video editing. In: ICCV (2023)
39. Rombach, R., et al.: High-resolution image synthesis with latent diffusion models. In: CVPR (2022)
40. Runway: Gen-2: The Next Step Forward for Generative AI (2023)
41. Saharia, C., et al.: Photorealistic text-to-image diffusion models with deep language understanding. In: NeurIPS (2022)

42. Song, J., et al.: Denoising diffusion implicit models. In: ICLR (2021)
43. Wang, W., et al.: Zero-shot video editing using off-the-shelf image diffusion models. arXiv:2303.17599 (2023)
44. Wu, G., et al.: 4D gaussian splatting for real-time dynamic scene rendering. In: CVPR (2024)
45. Wu, J.Z., et al.: Tune-a-video: one-shot tuning of image diffusion models for text-to-video generation. In: ICCV (2023)
46. Xing, J., et al.: Make-your-video: customized video generation using textual and structural guidance. IEEE TVCG (2024)
47. Xu, Y., et al.: Gg-editor: locally editing 3D avatars with multimodal large language model guidance. In: ACM MM (2024)
48. Xu, Y., et al.: MC-bench: a benchmark for multi-context visual grounding in the era of MLLMs. In: ICCV (2025)
49. Xu, Z., et al.: 4K4D: real-time 4D view synthesis at 4K resolution. In: CVPR (2024)
50. Yang, S., et al.: Rerender a video: zero-shot text-guided video-to-video translation. In: SIGGRAPH Asia (2023)
51. Yang, X., et al.: Eva: zero-shot accurate attributes and multi-object video editing. arXiv:2403.16111 (2024)
52. Yang, X., et al.: Videograin: modulating space-time attention for multi-grained video editing. In: ICLR (2025)
53. Zhang, L., et al.: Adding conditional control to text-to-image diffusion models. In: ICCV (2023)
54. Zhang, Y., et al.: Controlvideo: training-free controllable text-to-video generation. In: ICLR (2024)
55. Zhao, M., et al.: Controlvideo: conditional control for one-shot text-driven video editing and beyond. Sci. China Inf. Sci. (2025)

RC-NeRF: Anti-aliasing with Artifact Suppression via Adaptive Hybrid Sampling in Explicit Voxel Grids

Jiajun Cai and Jianmei Su[✉]

Southwest University of Science and Technology, Mianyang, Sichuan, China
`su_m_swust@163.com`

Abstract. Neural Radiance Fields (NeRF) have demonstrated remarkable capabilities in high-fidelity 3D scene reconstruction. However, existing methods face challenges in balancing computational efficiency with anti-aliasing performance. While TensoRF improves training efficiency by leveraging explicit voxel grids and tensor decomposition, it fails to handle multi-scale data, leading to aliasing artifacts. In contrast, Mip-NeRF addresses the anti-aliasing issue through cone sampling and integrated positional encodings but relies on an implicit MLP-based representation, which is incompatible with explicit voxel grids. To solve these problems, this paper proposed RC-NeRF, a NeRF framework that incorporates a new sampling strategy combining both cone and ray sampling within explicit voxel grids, to achieve a balance between efficiency and robust anti-aliasing. RC-NeRF introduces learnable weights to adaptively associate the outputs of cone and ray sampling, and incorporates a regularization term to prevent the model from converging to a local optimum. The experimental results show that the proposed RC-NeRF not only improves performance in multi-scale view synthesis but also suppresses floating artifacts introduced by input real-world images.

Keywords: Hybrid Sampling Strategy · Adaptive Weighted Association · Floating Artifacts Suppression · Multi-Scale · View Synthesis

1 Introduction

Neural Radiance Fields (NeRF) have demonstrated remarkable performance in reconstructing realistic 3D scene. They are now widely applied in various 3D-related domains, such as 3D model generation [6,16,19,24] and high-fidelity virtual human modeling [7,10,14]. NeRF implicitly encodes the entire scene information into a multi-layer perceptron (MLP), which takes the 3D spatial coordinates of a point and the viewing direction as input to query its color and volumetric density [17]. The final pixel color on the image plane is obtained by integrating these queried results using the volume rendering technique from computer graphics (CG). Traditional NeRF approaches rely on deep MLPs to

J. Lokoč et al. (Eds.): MMM 2026, LNCS 16412, pp. 663–676, 2026.
https://doi.org/10.1007/978-981-95-6950-2_47

encode the entire 3D scene information, which introduces considerable computational overhead. Moreover, as the scene scale expands, both the width and depth of the MLP must be increased accordingly.

As NeRF technology continues to advance, researchers have introduced numerous improvements. For example, efforts have been made to extend NeRF to dynamic 3D scenes [4,20], accelerate novel view synthesis [3,5], enhance the anti-aliasing capability of rendered results [1], and enable NeRF to render unbounded scenes [2]. Among these works, TensoRF and MipNeRF stand out as particularly notable contributions. TensoRF uses two explicit voxel grids to separately encode scene appearance and volumetric density. By applying tensor decomposition, it factorizes these grids into low-rank components, resulting in a more compact feature representation. This approach not only accelerates training but also leads to a significantly smaller model size [3]. MipNeRF demonstrates that cone sampling can effectively improve anti-aliasing performance of the NeRF-based novel view synthesis task.

Although TensoRF significantly improves rendering efficiency and MipNeRF achieves notable progress in anti-aliasing performance, integrating the two approaches presents substantial challenges. The primary obstacle lies in their fundamentally different scene representations: MipNeRF employs a deep MLP to implicitly encode scene information, combined with integrated positional encodings (IPE) based on spatial coordinates to enhance anti-aliasing [1], whereas TensoRF relies on explicit voxel grids for scene storage. Due t these architectural differences, a direct combination of the two methods is not feasible, making it difficult to simultaneously achieve improvements in both training efficiency and rendering quality.

We propose RC-NeRF, which is a new NeRF framework based on explicit voxel grids. RC-NeRF uses an adaptive weighted association module to control the proportion of ray and cone sampling in the final rendering result, thereby achieving an adaptive hybrid sampling strategy. By introducing cone sampling into the NeRF method based on explicit voxel grids, its ability in anti-aliasing can be effectively enhanced, while maintaining the training speed advantage of explicit voxel grids. RC-NeRF can improves the rendering performance of voxel grid-based NeRF on multi-scale datasets and effectively eliminates floating artifacts introduced by input real-world images.

2 Related Work

Accelerating NeRF. Instant Neural Graphics Primitives (INGP) employs a multi-resolution hash encoding scheme as an alternative to conventional positional encodings [18]. By using hash tables to store scene features at different resolutions, combined with a lightweight MLP, it achieved training and inference speeds that are orders of magnitude faster than traditional NeRF approaches. Plenoxels represents scenes using an explicit voxel grid, which is efficiently encoded through an octree structure. It further employs spherical harmonics to model view-dependent color variations [5]. Similarly, TensoRF utilizes two separate voxel grids to store appearance features and volumetric density, respectively [3]. By applying tensor decomposition, it factorizes these grids into low-rank components, resulting in a more compact feature representation and a substantially reduced model size. By leveraging explicit voxel grids, TensoRF greatly reduces the number of trainable parameters. Moreover, like INGP, it employs a small MLP to predict the color of sampled points, thereby accelerating both training and inference processes.

Anti-aliasing. In terms of anti-aliasing, NeRF-SR employs a multi-ray supersampling technique to suppress aliasing artifacts [21]. Unlike NeRF-SR, which relies on multi-ray supersampling, MipNeRF casts a cone frustum per pixel and computes the expected positional encoding over the cone using integrated positional encodings. This approach effectively addresses the performance degradation of NeRF at varying resolutions without introducing significant computational overhead. Sharp-NeRF introduces a sharpness prior to guide the suppression of aliasing artifacts [12], while ExBluRF embeds motion trajectories into the voxelized radiance field optimization. By jointly estimating motion trajectories and the radiance field, ExBluRF effectively decouples motion blur from geometric details, thereby reducing aliasing in dynamic regions [13]. Super-NeRF pioneers a generative model-based super-resolution method for NeRF [8]. More recently, Drantal-NeRF innovatively incorporates diffusion models into NeRF-based anti-aliasing [23].

Building on voxel-grid-based NeRF, we propose RC-NeRF——a novel framework that integrates ray and cone sampling through an adaptive hybrid sampling strategy. Our method simultaneously processes both sampling techniques on the learnable 3D voxel grid, then associates their outputs via an adaptive weighting mechanism to optimize rendering quality. To address the storage bottleneck of high-resolution grids, we incorporate VM tensor decomposition [3], achieving a compact yet efficient representation that eliminates exponential memory growth.

3   Method

In this section, we present the pipeline and implementation details of the key modules in the RC-NeRF model. We first provide an overview of the entire training process of the model. Then, we demonstrate the generation of cone-sampled points, including the corresponding mathematical formulation. Finally, we explain the necessity and design rationale of the adaptive weighting association module in improving model performance.

3.1   Overview

Our goal is to synthesize novel views of a scene described by a multi-scale dataset. To achieve this, we encode the 3D scene information from the dataset into a learnable 3D voxel grid. By sampling this voxel grid from new viewpoints and combining the results with volume rendering techniques, we can reconstruct

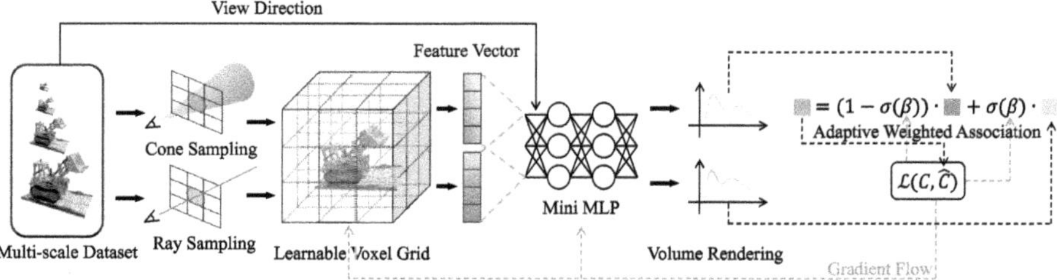

Fig. 1. Overview of the proposed RC-NeRF. Ray-sampled and cone-sampled points are generated from the multi-scale dataset and placed in the learnable voxel grid for sampling. The feature vectors derived from these two types of sampled points are decoded by the MLP and rendered into different pixel colors using the volume rendering. Whereafter, the distinct pixel colors are fused using the Adaptive Weighted Association module to obtain the final rendered pixel color. Finally, the loss value is calculated by comparing the final rendered pixel color with the ground truth pixel color, and the gradients are calculated by the loss value to guide the model training. Here, σ is the Sigmoid function, β is a learnable parameter, $\widehat{C}$ denotes the final rendered pixel color, C denotes the ground truth pixel color, and $\mathcal{L}(\cdot)$ indicates the loss function.

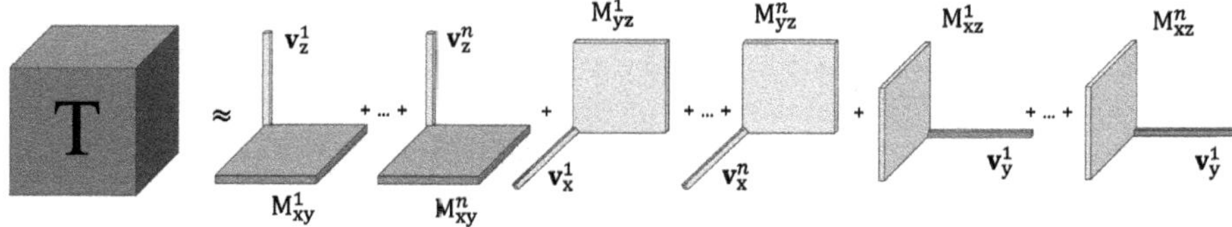

Fig. 2. We utilize the vector-matrix decomposition technique to factorize the 3D voxel grid into the sum of multiple outer products of vectors and matrices: $\mathrm{T} \approx \sum_{i=1}^{n}(\mathbf{v}_x^i \otimes M_{yz}^i + \mathbf{v}_y^i \otimes M_{xz}^i + \mathbf{v}_z^i \otimes M_{xy}^i)$.

novel view images of the scene (a process also referred to as *scene reconstruction*). As shown in Fig. 1, our method integrates cone sampling with ray sampling directly on the learnable 3D voxel grid. The feature vectors corresponding to the sampled points from each method are fed into a lightweight MLP for sampling point color prediction. The colors of the sampled points predicted by the two sampling methods were respectively used using volume rendering technology to obtain two different pixel colors. These two distinct output colors are finally fused through an adaptive weighting association to generate the final pixel color. The resulting color is compared with the ground truth, and the difference is used to guide the model training. As shown in Fig. 2, we further apply vector-matrix tensor decomposition [3] to the learnable 3D voxel grid, enabling a more compact, low-rank representation that significantly reduces the model size while preserving expressive capacity.

3.2 Cone Sampling

MipNeRF performs cone sampling in the implicit space to achieve anti-aliasing [1], and has demonstrated strong performance on multi-scale datasets. Although MipNeRF performs well in anti-aliasing, we believe that explicit voxel grids have more promising prospects. Because explicit voxel grids are more intuitive and convenient for exporting 3D mesh representations [9,15,22]. Moreover, tensor decomposition techniques can be applied to such voxel grids to obtain a more compact representation, significantly reducing model size [3]. However, MipN-eRF relies on integrated positional encodings based on spatial coordinates to parameterize the cone sampling process for anti-aliasing. This approach is not easily transferable to explicit voxel grids. To address this limitation, we aim to perform explicit cone sampling directly on the voxel grid.

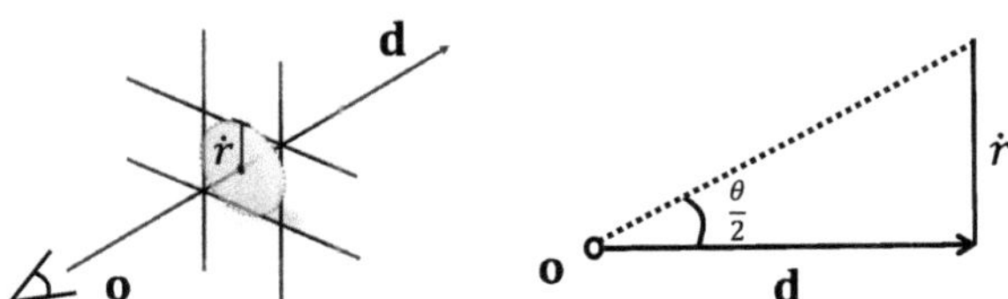

Fig. 3. There are two important parameters $\dot{r}$ and θ to represent the cone. Here, $\dot{r}$ is the radius of the circle formed by intersection of the cone and the image plane, θ is the conical angle, **o** is the position of the camera, and **d** is the view direction.

Unlike cone sampling in the implicit space, we aim to generate a set of stochastic sampling points whose spatial distribution approximates a conical shape. We represent this conical structure using two parameters, $\dot{r}$ and θ. As shown in Fig. 3, let $\dot{r}$ denote the radius of the circular cross-section of the cone on the image plane, and θ denotes the conical angle of the cone. Unlike MipN-eRF which $\dot{r} = \frac{2}{\sqrt{12}}$ [1], we set $\dot{r} = \frac{1}{\sqrt{\pi}}$ and compute the corresponding conical angle θ as follows:

$$\pi\dot{r}^2 = 1 \tag{1}$$

$$\dot{r} = \frac{1}{\sqrt{\pi}} \tag{2}$$

$$\theta = 2 \cdot \arctan(\frac{\dot{r}}{F}) \tag{3}$$

where F denotes the focal length of the camera. Although the conical sampling space is continuous, the sampling process itself is discrete. Therefore, we randomly and uniformly sample a set of points within this space to represent the

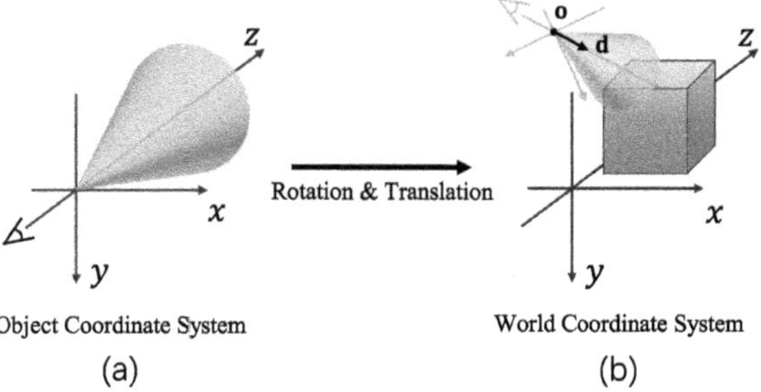

Fig. 4. (a) Generate cone-sampled points in the object coordinate system. (b) Rotate and translate the sampled points to the world coordinate system based on the camera's pose $\mathbf{o}$ and view direction $\mathbf{d}$. The specific process of spatial coordinate transformation can be referred to Eq. 13.

conical region. We derive parametric equations for stochastic sampling:

$$x = u \cdot t\sqrt{v} \cdot \tan(\frac{\theta}{2}) \cdot \cos(2\pi u) \tag{4}$$

$$y = u \cdot t\sqrt{v} \cdot \tan(\frac{\theta}{2}) \cdot \sin(2\pi u) \tag{5}$$

$$z = t \tag{6}$$

where $u, v \sim U(0, 1)$, $\sqrt{v}$ is introduced to enable uniform sampling in the polar coordinate system, t denotes the distance from the camera, and $\sqrt{v}$ term compensates for radial distortion to ensure uniform density in polar coordinates. During training, we perturb z with noise to enhance model robustness against discretization artifacts. These sampling points are first generated in the object coordinate system, as illustrated on the left side of Fig. 4.

The generated sampling points are distributed along the direction $\mathbf{d}_{\text{ref}}$ ($\mathbf{d}_{\text{ref}} = [0\ 0\ 1]^{\mathrm{T}}$ in the OpenCV camera coordinate system). After obtaining the sampling points, we need to rotate them to align with the camera's viewing direction, as shown on the right side of the Fig. 4. To achieve this, we determine the rotation axis $\mathbf{k}$ and the rotation angle ϕ, based on which we can construct the Rodrigues' rotation matrix R:

$$\mathbf{d}_{\text{ref}} = [0\ 0\ 1]^{\mathrm{T}} \tag{7}$$

$$\mathbf{k} = \frac{\mathbf{d}_{\text{ref}} \times \mathbf{d}}{\|\mathbf{d}_{\text{ref}} \times \mathbf{d}\|_2} \tag{8}$$

$$\phi = \frac{\mathbf{d}_{ref} \cdot \mathbf{d}}{\|\mathbf{d}_{ref}\|_2 \, \|\mathbf{d}\|_2} \tag{9}$$

$$K = \begin{bmatrix} & -k_z & k_y \\ k_z & & -k_x \\ -k_y & k_x & \end{bmatrix} \tag{10}$$

$$R = I + \sin(\phi) \cdot K + (1 - \cos(\phi)) \cdot K^2 \tag{11}$$

where k_x, k_y and k_z come from the rotation axis $\mathbf{k}$ and represent different components of $\mathbf{k}$, and $\mathbf{d}$ is the direction of the camera. To enable affine transformations across coordinate systems, we first lift the cone sampling points from Eqs. 4, 5 and 6 into homogeneous coordinates (Eq. 12). This representation is essential for composing translation and rotation operations within a single matrix framework. The transformation to world coordinates then follows as:

$$\mathbf{p}_{\text{cone}} = \begin{bmatrix} u \cdot t \cdot \sqrt{v} \cdot \tan(\frac{\theta}{2}) \cdot \cos(2\pi u) \\ u \cdot t \cdot \sqrt{v} \cdot \tan(\frac{\theta}{2}) \cdot \sin(2\pi u) \\ t \\ 1 \end{bmatrix} \tag{12}$$

$$\mathbf{p}_{\text{world}} = \begin{bmatrix} 1 & & & x_{\text{cam}} \\ & 1 & & y_{\text{cam}} \\ & & 1 & z_{\text{cam}} \\ & & & 1 \end{bmatrix} \cdot \begin{bmatrix} R & \\ & 1 \end{bmatrix} \cdot \mathbf{p}_{\text{cone}} \tag{13}$$

where x_{cam} , y_{cam} and z_{cam} represent the camera position in the world coordinate system, $\mathbf{p}_{\text{cone}}$ refers to the sampled points generated in the object coordinate system, and $\mathbf{p}_{\text{world}}$ denotes the corresponding points after transformation into the world coordinate system. This unified transformation preserves projective geometry while allowing direct sampling on the 3D voxel grid. It should be noted that, after transforming the sampling points into the world coordinate system, an axis-aligned bounding box is employed to cull out-of-bound points, thereby reducing unnecessary computational overhead.

3.3 Adaptive Weighted Association

As previously mentioned, the conical space is continuous. We perform sampling within this continuous space; however, if the number of sampled points is insufficient, the resulting rendering quality may be inferior to that of ray-based sampling. However, increasing the number of cone sampling points significantly increases computational overhead. Therefore, we treat cone sampling as a complement to ray sampling, aiming to enhance the model's performance on multi-scale datasets. Due to the fact that our cone-sampled points are randomly and uniformly drawn from the conical space, directly concatenating them with ray-sampled points and feeding them into the model during training introduces uncertainty, which can hinder convergence. To address this issue, we propose an Adaptive Weighted Association (AWA) algorithm to fuse the volumetric rendering results from both sampling methods in a learnable and adaptive manner:

$$\hat{C} = (1 - \sigma(\beta)) \cdot C_{\text{cone}} + \sigma(\beta) \cdot C_{\text{ray}} \tag{14}$$

where $\sigma(\cdot)$ denotes the Sigmoid function, β is a learnable parameter, C_{cone} denotes the volume rendering result from the cone-sampled points, and C_{ray} represents the corresponding result from the ray-sampled points. The use of learnable parameters offers the advantage that, when the training data does not contain multi-scale images or when cone sampling introduces instability to the training process, the weight assigned to the conical rendering result (C_{cone}) can be automatically adjusted to stabilize convergence. Conversely, when the training dataset contains multi-scale views, the model learns to increase the weight of C_{cone}, thereby leveraging cone sampling to improve the overall rendering quality. During our experiments, we observed that as the number of training iterations increases, the value of β tends to approach one. This reduces the contribution of cone sampling in the rendering process, causing the model to fall into a local optimum and resulting in suboptimal reconstruction quality on multi-scale test datasets. To address this issue, we introduce a regularization term to constrain the value of β:

$$\mathcal{L}_\beta = \lambda_\beta \cdot (\beta - \bar{\beta})^2 \tag{15}$$

where $\mathcal{L}_\beta$ denotes the regularization term, $\bar{\beta}$ is a hyperparameter representing the expected desired value of β, and λ_β is the regularization coefficient, also a hyperparameter. By incorporating this regularization term, the model is encouraged to maintain a suitable balance between cone and ray sampling, which in turn improves performance on multi-scale test datasets.

The final loss function is formulated as:

$$\mathcal{L} = \text{MSE}(C, \hat{C}) + \mathcal{L}_\beta \tag{16}$$

where C represents the ground-truth color of the pixel, and $\hat{C}$ denotes the rendered color predicted by the model.

4　Experiments

In this section, we evaluate RC-NeRF on both a multi-scale and single-scale general dataset and analyze the experimental results accordingly. We first present and analyze the model's performance on the multi-scale dataset, then demonstrate the effectiveness of the dynamic Sigmoid function in the reconstruction task, and finally provide ablation study results to validate the contribution of each component of the model.

4.1　Experimental Details

The experiments are carried out on a system running Ubuntu 20.04.6, equipped with an Intel i9-12900F CPU and a single NVIDIA GeForce RTX 3090 GPU. The CUDA version used in the experiments is 12.1. During training, the model is configured with $\bar{\beta} = 0.85$ and $\lambda_\beta = 0.001$. To enhance the generalization capability and robustness of the model, random perturbations along the z axis are introduced during the generation of cone-sampled points.

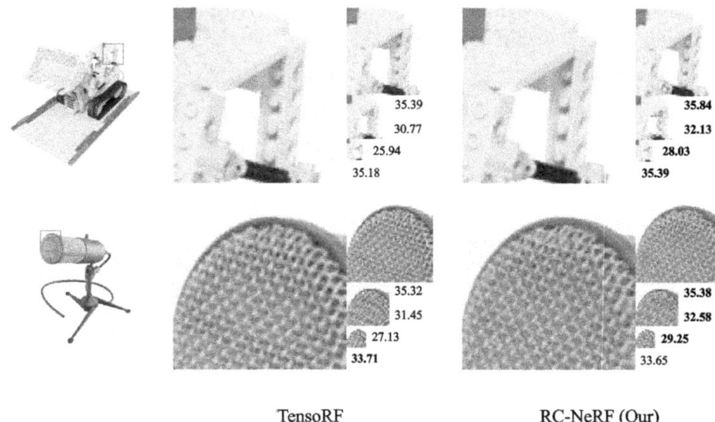

TensoRF   RC-NeRF (Our)

Fig. 5. Experimental results on the multi-scale dataset. We employed a hybrid sampling technique, where the number of cone sampling points is 2× that of ray sampling points, iterated 30k times on the multi-scale dataset, and computed the PSNR metrics of our reconstructed images at different resolutions, comparing with TensoRF.

4.2 Analysis of Experimental Results

We evaluate RC-NeRF on the multi-scale dataset and compare its reconstruction performance with TensoRF on the multi-scale synthetic dataset [1] and the "Tanks And Temples" dataset [11]. The evaluation is conducted using two widely adopted metrics: PSNR and SSIM. During training, we incorporate the Area Loss [1] to guide the optimization process.

As shown in Fig. 5, we reconstruct images at various resolutions, specifically, full resolution, 1/2 resolution, 1/4 resolution and 1/8 resolution, and compute the corresponding PSNR and SSIM metrics. We can observe that RC-NeRF performs comparably to TensoRF when synthesizing ordinary resolution images, but significantly outperforms TensoRF in synthesizing low-resolution images, especially at 1/8 resolution. In addition to testing on the multiscale dataset synthesized via Blender, we also tested on the real-world scene dataset "Tanks And Temples". Our method's performance comparison with TensoRF on the multi-scale dataset and the "Tanks And Temples" dataset is shown in Table 1 and Table 2.

Table 1. Comparison experimental results between RC-NeRF and TensoRF on the multi-scale synthetic dataset.

	PSNR					SSIM				
Exp.	Full Res.	1/2 Res.	1/4 Res.	1/8 Res.	Avg.	Full Res.	1/2 Res.	1/4 Res.	1/8 Res.	Avg.
TensoRF	35.18	35.39	30.77	25.94	31.82	0.9767	0.9852	0.9724	0.9302	0.9661
RC-NeRF (Our)	**35.39**	**35.84**	**32.13**	**28.03**	**32.85**	**0.9857**	**0.9857**	**0.9780**	**0.9502**	**0.9749**

Table 2. Comparison experimental results between RC-NeRF and TensoRF on the real-world dataset "Tanks And Temples" [11].

Exp.	PSNR	SSIM
TensoRF	25.33	0.9178
RC-NeRF (Our)	**26.70**	**0.9302**

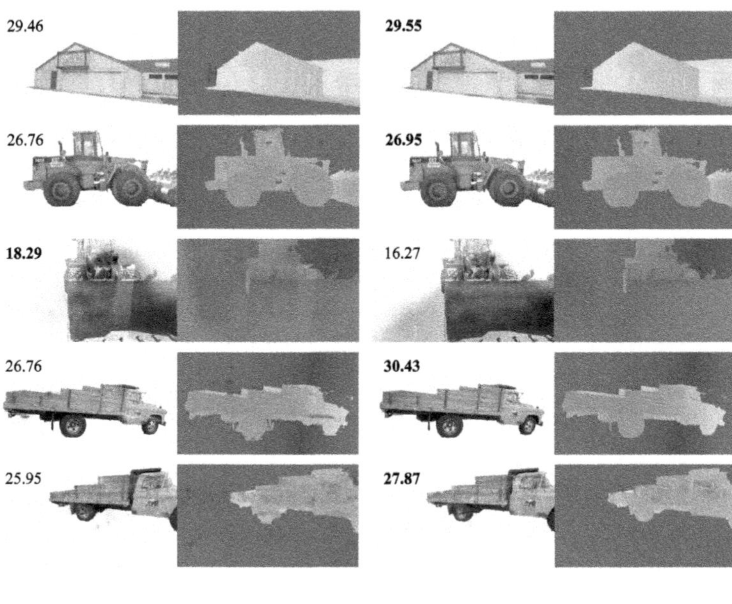

Fig. 6. Experimental results on the "Tanks And Temples" dataset. We visualized the novel view synthesis images and their depth maps for several scenes in the "Tanks And Temples" dataset, with the PSNR of each synthesized image displayed in its upper left corner, where the highest PSNR is highlighted in bold.

Notably, when reconstructing real-world scenes using ray sampling, Fig. 6 clearly reveals the presence of numerous floating artifacts in the reconstructed space, which are introduced by the input images. In contrast, when using a hybrid sampling approach combining cone sampling and ray sampling, these floating artifacts are significantly reduced, greatly enhancing the model's usability.

4.3　Ablation Studies

To verify the contribution of each proposed module to the overall performance of the model, we conduct a series of ablation studies. By progressively introducing or removing key components and comparing the reconstruction results across different configurations, we quantitatively evaluate the impact of each individual module on the final performance. In this section, we analyze the impact of number of cone sampling points and the adaptive weight association module components on model performance.

Number of Cone Sampling Points. In the ablation study on the number of cone sampling points, we compare the image reconstruction performance under different numbers of cone sampling points. From the results in Table 3, we observe that in the case of sampling the space using cone sampling points that are 2× the number of ray sampling points, the model achieves better performance currently. When we increase the number of cone sampling points without reaching a certain scale, the randomness of the cone sampling points introduces more uncertainty, leading to a decline in the final reconstruction quality.

In addition to increasing the number of cone sampling points, we also conducted studies with reduced the number of sampling points. Specifically, we further evaluate the image reconstruction performance under 0.5×, and 0.8×, respectively. From the results in Table 3, it can be observed that the 2× still achieves the best overall performance. Through this ablation experiment, we can find that the number of cone sampling points affects the final rendering result.

Table 3. Comparison of rendering results of the multi-scale dataset under different number of cone sampling points.

# Cone vs. Ray Sampling Points	PSNR					SSIM				
	Full Res.	1/2 Res.	1/4 Res.	1/8 Res.	Avg.	Full Res.	1/2 Res.	1/4 Res.	1/8 Res.	Avg.
1×	35.31	35.54	31.94	27.92	32.68	0.977	0.985	0.977	0.949	0.972
2×	**35.39**	**35.84**	**32.13**	**28.03**	**32.85**	**0.986**	**0.986**	**0.978**	**0.950**	**0.975**
4×	35.07	35.41	31.90	27.88	32.57	0.977	0.985	0.977	0.949	0.972
0.5×	33.71	34.19	31.49	27.79	31.79	0.973	0.983	0.976	0.949	0.970
0.8×	35.34	35.72	32.10	28.05	32.80	0.977	0.986	0.978	0.950	0.973

Adaptive Weighted Association. The adaptive weighted association (AWA) is designed to enable the model to adapt to both single-scale and multi-scale data, thereby improving its generalization capability. On single-scale datasets, the model reduces the weight of cone sampling, while on multi-scale datasets, it increases the cone sampling weight accordingly. Table 5 shows the results of the ablation study of our proposed AWA module on the single-scale synthetic and "Tanks And Temples" datasets. Table 4 presents the ablation study results of our proposed AWA module on the multi-scale dataset. The results show that the model incorporating the AWA module outperforms the one without it across all evaluation metrics. This degradation is evident at different resolutions.

Table 4. Comparisons of rendering results with and without the AWA module on the multi-scale synthetic dataset.

	PSNR					SSIM				
Exp.	Full Res.	1/2 Res.	1/4 Res.	1/8 Res.	Avg.	Full Res.	1/2 Res.	1/4 Res.	1/8 Res.	Avg.
RC-NeRF	**35.17**	**35.63**	**32.05**	**27.83**	**32.67**	**0.978**	**0.987**	**0.982**	**0.962**	**0.977**
RC-NeRF (w/o AWA)	33.52	33.85	30.50	26.25	31.03	0.9714	0.9824	0.9756	0.9489	0.9696

Through this ablation experiment, we can observe that the AWA module makes a significant contribution in handling multi-scale datasets, while on single-scale datasets, it reduces the weight of cone sampling in the final rendering results through adaptive weighting, thereby mitigating the degradation of rendering quality caused by the uncertainty introduced by cone sampling.

Table 5. Comparisons of rendering results with and without the AWA module on the single-scale synthetic and "Tanks And Temples" datasets.

Exp.	Single-scale Synthetic		Tanks And Temples	
	PSNR	SSIM	PSNR	SSIM
RC-NeRF	37.43	0.984	26.35	0.916
RC-NeRF (w/o AWA)	36.99	0.983	26.73	0.917

5   Conclusion

In this work, we proposed RC-NeRF, which adaptively weighted associates the rendering results from both ray and cone sampling methods. This extension enables voxel-grid-based NeRF models to better handle multi-scale datasets and eliminate floating artifacts introduced by inputting real-world images. Experimental results show that RC-NeRF achieves higher average rendering quality than TensoRF on the multi-scale dataset, while maintaining comparable performance on single-scale datasets, demonstrating its robustness across different data conditions. Our method achieves strong performance in multi-scale view synthesis while preserving the efficiency benefits of explicit voxel grids. Future work includes extending the proposed framework to dynamic scenes and exploring more efficient sampling strategies for real-time applications.

Acknowledgments. This paper is supported by the Major Project of Sichuan Provincial Natural Science Foundation (2025ZNSFSC0005), and the Central Government Guides Local Projects of China (2025ZYDF105).

References

1. Barron, J.T., et al.: Mip-NeRF: a multiscale representation for anti-aliasing neural radiance fields. In: Proceedings of the IEEE/CVF international conference on computer vision, pp. 5855–5864 (2021)
2. Barron, J.T., Mildenhall, B., Verbin, D., Srinivasan, P.P., Hedman, P.: Mip-NeRF 360: unbounded anti-aliased neural radiance fields. In: Proceedings of the IEEE/CVF conference on computer vision and pattern recognition, pp. 5470–5479 (2022)
3. Chen, A., Xu, Z., Geiger, A., Yu, J., Su, H.: TensoRF: Tensorial radiance fields. In: European conference on computer vision, pp. 333–350 (2022)
4. Fridovich-Keil, S., Meanti, G., Warburg, F.R., Recht, B., Kanazawa, A.: K-planes: explicit radiance fields in space, time, and appearance. In: Proceedings of the IEEE/CVF Conference on Computer Vision and Pattern Recognition, pp. 12479–12488 (2023)
5. Fridovich-Keil, S., et al.: Plenoxels: radiance fields without neural networks. In: Proceedings of the IEEE/CVF conference on computer vision and pattern recognition, pp. 5501–5510 (2022)
6. Gu, J., et al.: NerfDiff: single-image view synthesis with nerf-guided distillation from 3D-aware diffusion. In: Proceedings of the 40th International Conference on Machine Learning, pp. 11808–11826 (2023)
7. Guo, Y., et al.: AD-NeRF: audio driven neural radiance fields for talking head synthesis. In: Proceedings of the IEEE/CVF international conference on computer vision, pp. 5784–5794 (2021)
8. Han, Y., et al.: Super-nerf: view-consistent detail generation for nerf super-resolution. IEEE Trans. Vis. Comput. Graphics 1–14 (2024)
9. Hedman, P., Srinivasan, P.P., Mildenhall, B., Barron, J.T., Debevec, P.: Baking neural radiance fields for real-time view synthesis. In: Proceedings of the IEEE/CVF international conference on computer vision, pp. 5875–5884 (2021)
10. Jiang, B., Hong, Y., Bao, H., Zhang, J.: Selfrecon: self reconstruction your digital avatar from monocular video. In: Proceedings of the IEEE/CVF Conference on Computer Vision and Pattern Recognition, pp. 5605–5615 (2022)
11. Knapitsch, A., Park, J., Zhou, Q.Y., Koltun, V.: Tanks and temples: benchmarking large-scale scene reconstruction. ACM Trans. Graphics **36**(4) (2017)
12. Lee, B., Lee, H., Ali, U., Park, E.: Sharp-nerf: grid-based fast deblurring neural radiance fields using sharpness prior. In: Proceedings of the IEEE/CVF Winter Conference on Applications of Computer Vision, pp. 3709–3718 (2024)
13. Lee, D., Oh, J., Rim, J., Cho, S., Lee, K.M.: ExBluRF: Efficient radiance fields for extreme motion blurred images. In: Proceedings of the IEEE/CVF International Conference on Computer Vision, pp. 17639–17648 (2023)
14. Li, J., Zhang, J., Bai, X., Zhou, J., Gu, L.: Efficient region-aware neural radiance fields for high-fidelity talking portrait synthesis. In: Proceedings of the IEEE/CVF International Conference on Computer Vision (ICCV), pp. 7568–7578 (2023)
15. Liu, L., Gu, J., Zaw Lin, K., Chua, T.S., Theobalt, C.: Neural sparse voxel fields. In: Larochelle, H., et al. (eds.) Advances in Neural Information Processing Systems, vol. 33, pp. 15651–15663 (2020)
16. Liu, R., et al.: Zero-1-to-3: Zero-shot one image to 3D object. In: Proceedings of the IEEE/CVF international conference on computer vision, pp. 9298–9309 (2023)
17. Mildenhall, B., et al.: NeRF: representing scenes as neural radiance fields for view synthesis. Commun. ACM **65**(1), 99–106 (2021)

18. Müller, T., Evans, A., Schied, C., Keller, A.: Instant neural graphics primitives with a multiresolution hash encoding. ACM Trans. Graph. **41**(4), 1–15 (2022)
19. Poole, B., Jain, A., Barron, J.T., Mildenhall, B.: Dreamfusion: Text-to-3D using 2d diffusion. arXiv preprint arXiv:2209.14988 (2022)
20. Pumarola, A., Corona, E., Pons-Moll, G., Moreno-Noguer, F.: D-NeRF: Neural radiance fields for dynamic scenes. In: Proceedings of the IEEE/CVF conference on computer vision and pattern recognition, pp. 10318–10327 (2021)
21. Wang, C., et al.: NeRF-SR: High quality neural radiance fields using supersampling. In: Proceedings of the 30th ACM International Conference on Multimedia, pp. 6445–6454 (2022)
22. Xu, L., et al.: Grid-guided neural radiance fields for large urban scenes. In: Proceedings of the IEEE/CVF Conference on Computer Vision and Pattern Recognition, pp. 8296–8306 (2023)
23. Yang, G., Zhang, K., Fu, J., Liu, D.: Drantal-NeRF: Diffusion-based restoration for anti-aliasing neural radiance field. arXiv preprint arXiv:2407.07461 (2024)
24. Zhou, S., Chan, K., Li, C., Loy, C.C.: Towards robust blind face restoration with codebook lookup transformer. In: Koyejo, S., et al. (eds.) Advances in Neural Information Processing Systems, vol. 35, pp. 30599–30611 (2022)

Author Index

© The Editor(s) (if applicable) and The Author(s), under exclusive license
to Springer Nature Singapore Pte Ltd. 2026
J. Lokoč et al. (Eds.): MMM 2026, LNCS 16412, pp. 677–679, 2026.
https://doi.org/10.1007/978-981-95-6950-2